THE NEW CAMBRIDGE HISTORY OF

ISLAM

★

VOLUME 3

The Eastern Islamic World Eleventh to Eighteenth Centuries

Volume 3 of *The New Cambridge History of Islam* traces the second great expansion of the Islamic world eastwards from the eleventh century to the eighteenth. As the faith crossed new cultural boundaries, the trader and the mystic assumed as great an importance as the soldier and the administrator. Distinctive Islamic idioms began to emerge from other great linguistic traditions apart from Arabic, especially in Turkish, Persian, Urdu, Swahili, Malay and Chinese. The Islamic world transformed and absorbed new, vital influences. As the essays in this collection demonstrate, three major features distinguish the time and place both from the earlier experience of Islam and from the universal modernity of the nineteenth and twentieth centuries. First, the steppe tribal peoples of Central Asia, many Turkic, had a decisive impact on the Islamic lands. Second, Islam expanded along the trade routes of the Indian Ocean and the South China Sea, in a quite different manner from the conquests of the heroic age. And, third, Islam interacted with Asian spirituality, including forms we today label Hinduism, Jainism, Sikhism, Buddhism, Taoism and Shamanism. It was during this period, and through exploration across land and sea, that Islam became a truly world religion.

DAVID O. MORGAN is Professor Emeritus of History and Religious Studies in the Department of History, University of Wisconsin-Madison. He is the author of *The Mongols* (2nd edition, 2007) and *Medieval Persia 1040–1797* (1988), and is General Editor of Cambridge Studies in Islamic Civilization.

ANTHONY REID, formerly Director, Asia Research Institute and Professor in the Department of History at the National University of Singapore, is currently Professor Emeritus at the Australian National University, Canberra. His recent books include *Southeast Asia in the Age of Commerce* (2 vols., 1988–93), *Charting the Shape of Early Modern Southeast Asia* (1999), *An Indonesian Frontier: Acehnese and Other Histories of Sumatra* (2004) and *Imperial Alchemy: Nationalism and Political Identity in Southeast Asia* (2010).

THE NEW CAMBRIDGE HISTORY OF

ISLAM

The New Cambridge History of Islam offers a comprehensive history of Islamic civilisation, tracing its development from its beginnings in seventh-century Arabia to its wide and varied presence in the globalised world of today. Under the leadership of the Prophet Muḥammad, the Muslim community coalesced from a scattered, desert population and, following his death, emerged from Arabia to conquer an empire which, by the early eighth century, stretched from India in the east to Spain in the west. By the eighteenth century, despite political fragmentation, the Muslim world extended from West Africa to South-East Asia. Today, Muslims are also found in significant numbers in Europe and the Americas, and make up about one-fifth of the world's population.

To reflect this geographical distribution and the cultural, social and religious diversity of the peoples of the Muslim world, *The New Cambridge History of Islam* is divided into six volumes. Four cover historical developments, and two are devoted to themes that cut across geographical and chronological divisions – themes ranging from social, political and economic relations to the arts, literature and learning. Each volume begins with a panoramic introduction setting the scene for the ensuing chapters and examining relationships with adjacent civilisations. Two of the volumes – one historical, the other thematic – are dedicated to the developments of the last two centuries, and show how Muslims, united for so many years in their allegiance to an overarching and distinct tradition, have sought to come to terms with the emergence of Western hegemony and the transition to modernity.

The time is right for this new synthesis reflecting developments in scholarship over the past generation. *The New Cambridge History of Islam* is an ambitious enterprise directed and written by a team combining established authorities and innovative younger scholars. It will be the standard reference for students, scholars and all those with enquiring minds for years to come.

General editor

MICHAEL COOK, CLASS OF 1943 UNIVERSITY PROFESSOR OF NEAR EASTERN STUDIES, PRINCETON UNIVERSITY

VOLUME 1
The Formation of the Islamic World
Sixth to Eleventh Centuries
EDITED BY CHASE F. ROBINSON

VOLUME 2
The Western Islamic World
Eleventh to Eighteenth Centuries
EDITED BY MARIBEL FIERRO

VOLUME 3
The Eastern Islamic World
Eleventh to Eighteenth Centuries
EDITED BY DAVID O. MORGAN AND ANTHONY REID

VOLUME 4
Islamic Cultures and Societies to the End of the Eighteenth Century
EDITED BY ROBERT IRWIN

VOLUME 5
The Islamic World in the Age of Western Dominance
EDITED BY FRANCIS ROBINSON

VOLUME 6
Muslims and Modernity
Culture and Society since 1800
EDITED BY ROBERT W. HEFNER

Grants made from an award to the General Editor by the Andrew W. Mellon Foundation, and from the National Endowment for the Humanities RZ-50616-06, contributed to the development of *The New Cambridge History of Islam*. In particular the grants funded the salary of William M. Blair who served as Editorial Assistant from 2004 to 2008.

THE NEW CAMBRIDGE HISTORY OF ISLAM

*

VOLUME 3

The Eastern Islamic World Eleventh to Eighteenth Centuries

*

Edited by

DAVID O. MORGAN

and

ANTHONY REID

CAMBRIDGE
UNIVERSITY PRESS

CAMBRIDGE
UNIVERSITY PRESS

Shaftesbury Road, Cambridge CB2 8EA, United Kingdom

One Liberty Plaza, 20th Floor, New York, NY 10006, USA

477 Williamstown Road, Port Melbourne, VIC 3207, Australia

314–321, 3rd Floor, Plot 3, Splendor Forum, Jasola District Centre, New Delhi – 110025, India

103 Penang Road, #05–06/07, Visioncrest Commercial, Singapore 238467

Cambridge University Press is part of Cambridge University Press & Assessment, a department of the University of Cambridge.

We share the University's mission to contribute to society through the pursuit of education, learning and research at the highest international levels of excellence.

www.cambridge.org
Information on this title: www.cambridge.org/9781107456976

First published 2010
4th printing 2015
First paperback edition 2023

A catalogue record for this publication is available from the British Library

ISBN 978-0-521-85031-5 Volume 3 Hardback
ISBN 978-0-521-51536-8 Set of 6 Hardback Volumes
ISBN 978-1-107-45697-6 Paperback

Contents

List of illustrations *page x*
List of maps *xi*
List of contributors *xii*
Note on transliteration *xv*
Chronology *xvi*
List of abbreviations *xxi*
Maps *xxii*

Introduction: Islam in a plural Asia *1*
DAVID O. MORGAN AND ANTHONY REID

PART I
THE IMPACT OF THE STEPPE PEOPLES

1 · The steppe peoples in the Islamic world *21*
EDMUND BOSWORTH

2 · The early expansion of Islam in India *78*
ANDRÉ WINK

3 · Muslim India: the Delhi sultanate *100*
PETER JACKSON

4 · The rule of the infidels: the Mongols and the Islamic world *128*
BEATRICE FORBES MANZ

5 · Tamerlane and his descendants: from paladins to patrons *169*
MARIA E. SUBTELNY

PART II
THE GUNPOWDER EMPIRES

6 · Iran under Safavid rule *203*
SHOLEH A. QUINN

7 · Islamic culture and the Chinggisid restoration: Central Asia in the sixteenth and seventeenth centuries *239*
R. D. McCHESNEY

8 · India under Mughal rule *266*
STEPHEN DALE

PART III
THE MARITIME OECUMENE

9 · Islamic trade, shipping, port-states and merchant communities in the Indian Ocean, seventh to sixteenth centuries *317*
MICHAEL PEARSON

10 · Early Muslim expansion in South-East Asia, eighth to fifteenth centuries *366*
GEOFF WADE

11 · Follow the white camel: Islam in China to 1800 *409*
ZVI BEN-DOR BENITE

12 · Islam in South-East Asia and the Indian Ocean littoral, 1500–1800: expansion, polarisation, synthesis *427*
ANTHONY REID

13 · South-East Asian localisations of Islam and participation within a global *umma*, *c.* 1500–1800 *470*
R. MICHAEL FEENER

14 · Transition: the end of the old order – Iran in the eighteenth century *504*
G. R. GARTHWAITE

PART IV
THEMES

15 · Conversion to Islam *529*
RICHARD W. BULLIET

16 · Armies and their economic basis in Iran and the surrounding lands, *c.* 1000–1500 *539*
REUVEN AMITAI

17 · Commercial structures *561*
SCOTT C. LEVI

18 · Transmitters of authority and ideas across cultural boundaries, eleventh to eighteenth centuries *582*
MUHAMMAD QASIM ZAMAN

Glossary *611*
Bibliography *620*
Index *681*

Illustrations

1 Mould for jewellery, bearing inscription 'Al-mulk li-llāhi / al-wahid / al-qahhar' *page* 371
2 A *tasbih* recovered from a mid-fourth/tenth-century shipwreck in the Java Sea 372
3 Mainstream South-East Asian mosque type before the twentieth century, exemplified in the multi-tiered roof of the seventeenth-century Indrapuri mosque in Aceh 442
4 The entrance to the tomb of Sunan Bonang, outside Tuban 451
5 Evidence of Shāfiʿī penalties for theft being applied in Aceh, as sketched by Thomas Bowrey in the 1660s 461
6 The artificial mountain (*Gunongan*) of Aceh 491

Maps

1	Western Asia in the Saljuq period	*page* xxii
2	The Mongol empire	xxiv
3	The empire of Tamerlane	xxvi
4	India and the Delhi sultanate	xxviii
5	Iran under the Safavids	xxix
6	Mughal India	xxx
7	The Indian Ocean as Islamic oecumene	xxxi
8	South-East Asia and southern China	xxxii
9	South-East Asia in the fifteenth to eighteenth centuries	xxxiii
10	Java in the fifteenth to seventeenth centuries	xxxiv

Contributors

REUVEN AMITAI is Eliyahu Elath Professor of Muslim History at the Hebrew University of Jerusalem. Among his works are *Mongols and Mamluks: The Mamluk–Ilkhanid War 1260–1281* (Cambridge, 1995) and *The Mongols in the Islamic lands: Studies in the history of the Ilkhanate* (2007).

ZVI BEN-DOR BENITE specialises in Chinese Islam and teaches in the Department of Middle Eastern and Islamic Studies and the Department of History at New York University. He is the author of *The Dao of Muhammad: A cultural history of Muslims in late imperial China* (2005) and *The ten lost tribes: A world history* (2009). He is currently working on a book entitled *Crescent China: Islam and the nation after empire.*

C. EDMUND BOSWORTH is Emeritus Professor of Arabic Studies at Manchester University and a Fellow of the British Academy. He was the British Editor of the second edition of *The encyclopaedia of Islam* (1960–2005), and is the author of several books on Arabic literature and on Islamic history and culture.

RICHARD W. BULLIET is Professor of Middle Eastern History at Columbia University in New York City. He is the author of *The patricians of Nishapur* (1972), *The camel and the wheel* (1975), *Conversion to Islam in the medieval period* (1979), *Islam: The view from the edge* (1994), *The case for Islamo-Christian civilization* (2004), *Hunters, herders, and hamburgers* (2005) and *Cotton, climate, and camels in early Islamic Iran* (2009).

STEPHEN DALE is Professor of South Asian and Islamic History at Ohio State University, specialising in the eastern Islamic world: South Asia, Afghanistan, Iran and Central Asia. His publications include *Islamic society on the South Asian frontier: The Mappilas of Malabar, 1498–1922* (1980), *Indian merchants and Eurasian trade, 1600–1750* (Cambridge, 1994), *The garden of the eight paradises: Babur and the culture of empire in Central Asia, Afghanistan and India, 1483–1530* (2004) and *The Muslim empires: Ottoman, Safavid, Mughal, 1300–1923* (Cambridge, 2010).

R. MICHAEL FEENER is Associate Professor in the Department of History and the Asia Research Institute, at the National University of Singapore. His books include *Muslim legal thought in modern Indonesia* (Cambridge, 2007); and as co-editor, *Islamic law in contemporary*

Indonesia: Ideas and institutions (2007), with Mark Cammack, and *Islamic connections: Muslim societies of South and South-East Asia* (2009) with Terenjit Sevea.

G. R. Garthwaite is the Jane and Raphael Bernstein Professor of Asian Studies and Professor of History at Dartmouth College. He is the author of *Khans and shahs: A documentary analysis of the Bakhtiyari in Iran* (Cambridge, 1983) and *The Persians* (2005).

Peter Jackson is Professor of Medieval History at Keele University. His previous publications include *The Cambridge history of Iran*, vol. VI: *The Timurid and Safavid periods* (as editor, 1986), *The mission of Friar William of Rubruck: His journey to the court of the Great Khan Möngke, 1253–1255* (trans. and ed., with D. O. Morgan, Hakluyt Society, 2nd series, 173: 1990), *The Delhi Sultanate: A political and military history* (Cambridge, 1999), *The Mongols and the West, 1221–1410* (2005), *The Seventh Crusade, 1244–1254: Sources and documents* (trans. and ed., 2007).

Scott C. Levi is Associate Professor of History at Ohio State University. He is the author of *The Indian diaspora in Central Asia and its trade, 1550–1900* (2002) and the editor of *India and Central Asia: Commerce and culture, 1500–1800* (2007).

R. D. McChesney is Emeritus Professor of Middle Eastern and Islamic Studies and History at New York University. He is the author of *Waqf in Central Asia* (1991), *Central Asia: Foundations of change* (1996) and *Kabul under siege* (1999) as well as numerous articles on the social history of the greater Persianate world in the sixteenth to nineteenth centuries.

Beatrice Forbes Manz is Professor of History at Tufts University and the author of two books: *The rise and rule of Tamerlane* (Cambridge, 1989) and *Power, politics and religion in Timurid Iran* (Cambridge, 2007) and one edited collection, *Central Asia in historical perspective* (1994).

David O. Morgan has been Professor of History and Religious Studies at the University of Wisconsin-Madison since 1999. Previously he taught the history of the Middle East and Central Asia at the School of Oriental and African Studies, University of London. He is the author of *The Mongols* (2nd edition, 2007) and *Medieval Persia 1040–1797* (1988), and is General Editor of Cambridge Studies in Islamic Civilization.

Michael Pearson is Emeritus Professor of History at the University of New South Wales, Sydney, Australia and Adjunct Professor of Humanities at the University of Technology, Sydney. Among his recent publications are *Port cities and intruders: The Swahili coast, India, and Portugal in the early modern era* (1998 and paperback edn 2003), (ed.) *Spices in the Indian Ocean world* (1996), *The Indian Ocean* (2003 and paperback edn 2007), *The world of the Indian Ocean, 1500–1800: Studies in economic, social and cultural history* (2005).

Sholeh A. Quinn is Associate Professor in the School of Social Sciences, Humanities and Arts at the University of California, Merced. She is the author of *Historical writing during the reign of Shah ʿAbbas* (2000) and co-editor of *History and historiography of post-Mongol Central Asia and the Middle East: Studies in honor of John E. Woods* (2006).

ANTHONY REID is a Southeast Asian Historian, currently Emeritus Professor and Visiting Fellow at the Research School of Pacific & Asian Studies at the Australian National University, where he was also employed 1970–99. In between he was founding Director (2002–7) of the Asia Research Institute of the National University of Singapore, and Professor of History and founding Director of the Center for SE Asian Studies at UCLA (1999–2002). He is a Corresponding Fellow of the British Academy and the Royal Historical Society. His more recent books include *Southeast Asia in the age of commerce*, 1450–1680 (2 vols., 1988–93), *Charting the shape of early modern Southeast Asia* (1999), *An Indonesian frontier: Acehnese and other histories of Sumatra* (2004), *Imperial alchemy: Nationalism and political identity in Southeast Asia* (Cambridge, 2009) and (as editor or co-editor) *Verandah of violence: The historical background of the Aceh problem* (2006), *Viet Nam: Borderless histories* (2006), *Islamic legitimacy in a plural Asia* (2007), *Chinese diaspora in the Pacific* (2008) and *Negotiating asymmetry: China's place in Asia* (2009).

MARIA E. SUBTELNY (Ph.D., Harvard University, 1979) is Professor of Persian and Islamic Studies in the Department of Near and Middle Eastern Civilizations at the University of Toronto. Her related publications include *Timurids in transition: Turko-Persian politics and acculturation in medieval Iran* (2007) and *Le monde est un jardin: Aspects de l'histoire culturelle de l'Iran médiéval* (2002).

GEOFF WADE is a Senior Research Fellow at the Institute of Southeast Asian Studies, Singapore. He researches diverse aspects of pre-modern and early modern intra-Asian interactions and comparative historiography. Key works include a database of Ming imperial references to South-East Asia (www.epress.nus.edu.sg/msl/) and the six-volume collection *China and Southeast Asia* (2008).

ANDRÉ WINK is Professor of History at the University of Wisconsin-Madison. He is the author of *Al-Hind: The making of the Indo-Islamic world*, 5 vols. (1990, 1997, 2004 and forthcoming) and *Akbar* (2008).

MUHAMMAD QASIM ZAMAN is Niehaus Professor of Near Eastern Studies and Religion at Princeton University. He is the author of *Religion and politics under the early ʿAbbāsids* (1997), *The ulama in contemporary Islam: Custodians of change* (2002) and *Ashraf ʿAli Thanawi: Islam in modern South Asia* (2008).

Note on transliteration

The transliteration of Arabic and Persian words is based on the conventions used by *The Encyclopaedia of Islam*, second edition, with the following modifications. For the Arabic letter *jīm*, *j* is used (not *d̲j*). For the Arabic letter *qāf*, *q* is used (not *ḳ*). Digraphs such as *th, dh, kh* and *sh* are not underlined.

Words and terms in other languages are transliterated by chapter contributors according to systems which are standard for those languages.

Place names that are Arabic in origin have diacritical points, except in some well-known instances (e.g. Baghdad, not Baghdād), or where there are standard Anglicised versions (e.g. Cairo).

Chronology

334/945	Būyids occupy Baghdad
376/986	Cham Muslims flee Vietnamese pressure to Hainan, south China
388/998	Maḥmūd of Ghazna takes power there
400/1010	Ashab mosque founded in Quanzhou, south-east China
411/1020	Death of Firdawsī, author of the *Shāh-nāma*
415/1024	Hindu Cōla attacks disrupt Muslim maritime network in southern Asia
421/1031	Accession of Masʿūd of Ghazna
431/1040	Ghaznavids defeated by Saljuqs at Dandānqān
447/1055	Saljuqs under Ṭoghrıl Beg occupy Baghdad: fall of Būyids
455/1063	Death of Ṭoghrıl Beg; accession of Alp Arslan
459/1067	Foundation of the Niẓāmiyya madrasa in Baghdad
463/1071	Saljuqs defeat Byzantines at Manzikert
464/1072	Death of Alp Arslan; accession of Malik Shāh
475/1082	Earliest-dated Muslim gravestone in Indonesia, in Leran, east Java
483/1090	Nizārī Ismāʿīlīs under Ḥasan-i Sabbāḥ take Alamūt
485/1092	Death of Malik Shāh and his Persian vizier Niẓām al-Mulk
505/1111	Death of al-Ghazālī
536/1141	Saljuq sultan Sanjar defeated on the Qaṭwān steppe by the Qara Khitay
552/1157	Death of Sanjar: effective end of Great Saljuq sultanate
602/1206	*Quriltai* in Mongolia acclaims Chinggis Khan. Foundation of the Delhi sultanate by Quṭb al-Dīn Aybak
604/1208	ʿAlāʾ al-Dīn Muḥammad Khwārazm Shāh takes Transoxania from Qara Khitay
616/1219	Mongols under Chinggis Khan invade the Khwārazm Shāh's empire

617/1220	Balkh and Nīshāpūr fall to the Mongols
618/1221	Death of ʿAlāʾ al-Dīn Khwārazm Shāh
624/1227	Death of Chinggis Khan
654/1256	Hülegü, first Mongol Ilkhan, takes Alamūt
656/1258	Hülegü takes Baghdad and executes the last ʿAbbāsid caliph
658/1260	Ilkhanid Mongols defeated at ʿAyn Jālūt by Mamlūks
662/1264	Qubilai becomes Great Khan of the Mongol empire after a four-year civil war
663/1265	Death of Hülegü
672/1273	Death of Jalāl al-Dīn Rūmī, Sufi master and poet
672f./1274	Muslim Pu Shougeng becomes maritime trade supervisor in Quanzhou
673/1274	Death of Naṣīr al-Dīn Ṭūsī
693/1294	Wijaya establishes Majapahit kingdom in Java, following Mongol invasion
694/1295	Accession of Ghazan Khan, first of the line of Muslim Ilkhans
695/1296	Accession of ʿAlāʾ al-Dīn Khaljī, sultan of Delhi
696/1297	Death of Sultan Malik al-Ṣāliḥ of Pasai (north Sumatra), earliest authenticated Muslim ruler in South-East Asia
703/1304	Death of Ghazan; accession of Öljeitü
718/1318	Rashīd al-Dīn, Ilkhanid minister and historian, executed
724/1324	Accession of Muḥammad Tughluq, sultan of Delhi
731/1331	Ibn Baṭṭūṭa describes flourishing Muslim port-states of Kilwa and Mogadishu, in East Africa
734/1334	Death of Shaykh Ṣafī al-Dīn Ardabīlī, founder of the Safavid order
736/1335	Death of Abū Saʿīd, last Ilkhan of the line of Hülegü. Birth of Tamerlane
738/1338	Independence of Muslim Bengal
744/1343	Ibn Baṭṭūṭa visits flourishing sultanates of Maldives and Pasai, respectively Mālikī and Shāfiʿī.
751/1350	Accession of Hayam Wuruk brings Majapahit to peak; conquest of Muslim Pasai
758/1357	Muslim 'Iṣfahān' rebellion in Quanzhou region; Muslim traders flee violence by sea to South-East Asia
769/1368	Chinese Ming dynasty replaces Mongol Yuan dynasty in China
791/1389	Death of Muḥammad Bahāʾ al-Dīn Naqshbandī, after whom the Naqshbandī Sufi order was named

801/1398	Tamerlane sacks Delhi
804/1402	Tamerlane defeats Ottomans at Ankara
805/1403	Independence of Muslim Gujarat
807/1405	Death of Tamerlane
807/1405	Voyages into Indian Ocean by China's Muslim admiral Zheng He begin, extending until 838/1435 and following Muslim trade routes to Hormuz and Aden
850/1447	Death of Shāh Rukh, Tamerlane's son and ultimate successor
871/1466	Accession of Uzun Ḥasan Aq Qoyunlu
872/1467	Uzun Ḥasan defeats Jahānshāh Qara Qoyunlu
873/1469	Accession of Sulṭān-Ḥusayn Bayqara, last Timurid ruler in Herat
876/1471	Vietnamese capture of Cham capital Vijaya creates Muslim diaspora
878/1473	Uzun Ḥasan defeated by Ottomans at Tirjan
882/1477	Death of Sultan Mansur, Melaka's strongest ruler
885/1480	Dated inscription in mosque of Calicut (Kerala, India)
903/1498	Vasco da Gama reaches Calicut (Kerala); Portuguese–Muslim trade competition in Indian Ocean
907/1501	Shāh Ismāʿīl, first shah of the Safavid dynasty, takes Tabrīz
910/1504	Bābur occupies Kabul
913/1507	Uzbeks occupy Herat after death of Sulṭān-Ḥusayn Bayqarā in previous year
916/1510	Shāh Ismāʿīl defeats the Uzbeks at Marv: Muḥammad Shibani Khan killed
917/1511	Albuquerque conquers Melaka; Malay capital moves to Johor
920/1514	Ottomans defeat Shāh Ismāʿīl at Chāldirān
921/1515	Portuguese capture Hormuz
930/1524	Death of Shāh Ismāʿīl: succeeded by Ṭahmāsp I
932/1526	Bābur defeats Ibrāhīm Lodī at Pānīpat, occupies Delhi, founds Mughal empire
933/1527	End of Majapahit kingdom; Muslims dominate Java
936/1530	Death of Sultan Ali Mughayat, unifier of Aceh (Sumatra)
937/1530	Death of Bābur; succeeded by Humāyūn
945/1538	Ottoman naval expedition into Indian Ocean against Portuguese
963/1556	Death of Humāyūn; succeeded by Akbar
972/1565	Alliance of four sultanates destroys Hindu Vijayanagara, south India

975/1567	Aceh–Ottoman alliance against Portuguese
978/1570	Portuguese murder of Sultan Hairun ensures rise of Muslim expansionist Sultan Baabullah in Ternate (east Indonesia)
984/1576	Death of Ṭahmāsp
987/1579	Muslim Banten crushes Hindu Pajajaran in west Java
996/1588	Accession of Shāh ʿAbbās I
1007/1598	Safavid capital transferred from Qazvīn to Iṣfahān
1014/1605	Conversion of Makassar (Sulawesi) to Islam
1014/1605	Death of Akbar; succeeded by Jahāngīr
1028/1619	Dutch East India Company (VOC) establishes Asian headquarters in Batavia (Jakarta)
1034/1625	Sultan Agung of Mataram conquers Surabaya, unifies Javanese on syncretic Muslim programme
1037/1628	Death of Jahāngīr; succeeded by Shāh Jahān
1038/1629	Death of Shāh ʿAbbās I
1038/1629	Military setbacks of Aceh against Portuguese Melaka, and Mataram against Batavia
1046/1636	Death of Sultan Iskandar Muda of Aceh; succeeded by son-in-law Iskandar Thani, patron of Nūr al-Dīn al-Rānīrī
1049/1639	Definitive peace between Safavids and Ottomans
1051/1641	Death of Sultan Iskandar Thani; accession of his widow Safiyyat al-Din as first of four Aceh queens
1056/1646	Death of Sultan Agung of Mataram; succession of Amangkurat I
1067/1658	Shāh Jahān imprisoned by his son Aurungzeb
1080/1669	VOC with Bugis allies conquers Makassar
1082/1671	Khoja Afaq spreads Naqshbandī Sufi order in north-west China
1090/1679	VOC crushes Islamic Trunajaya rebellion in Java, in alliance with weakened Mataram
1093/1682	VOC conquers Banten, and thereafter controls sultanate indirectly
1105/1693	Death of ʿAbd al-Raʾūf al-Singkili, scholar-saint of Aceh
1105/1694	Accession of Sulṭān Ḥusayn, last Safavid shah
1111/1699	Female rule ended in Aceh with help of *fatwā* from Mecca; Arab dynasty
1118/1707	Death of Aurungzeb
1134/1722	Afghans occupy Iṣfahān: effective end of Safavid rule

1148/1736	Nādir Khan declares himself Shāh of Iran
1152/1739	Nādir Shāh takes Delhi
1160/1747	Assassination of Nādir Shāh; foundation of kingdom of Afghanistan by Aḥmad Shāh Durrānī
1164/1751	Karīm Khan Zand becomes ruler in Shīrāz
1209/1795	Āghā Muḥammad Khan, founder of the Qājār dynasty, establishes the capital of Iran at Tehran

Abbreviations

EI^{2}	*The encyclopaedia of Islam*, 2nd edn (Leiden, 1960–2003)
EI^{3}	*The encyclopaedia of Islam*, 3rd edn (Leiden, 2007–)
EIr	*Encyclopaedia Iranica*
VOC	Verenigde Geoctroyeerde Oost-Indische Compagnie – (Dutch) United Chartered East India Company

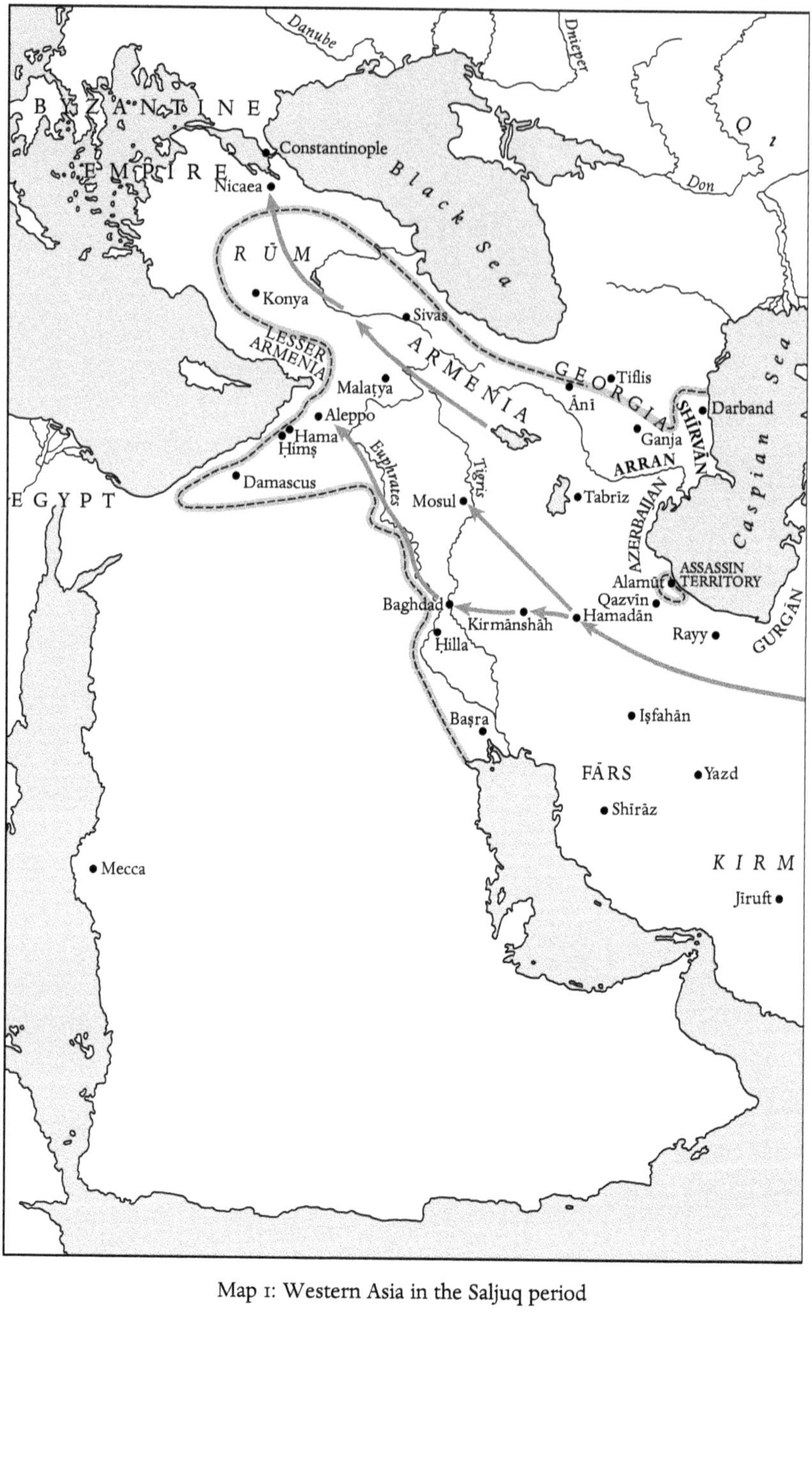

Map 1: Western Asia in the Saljuq period

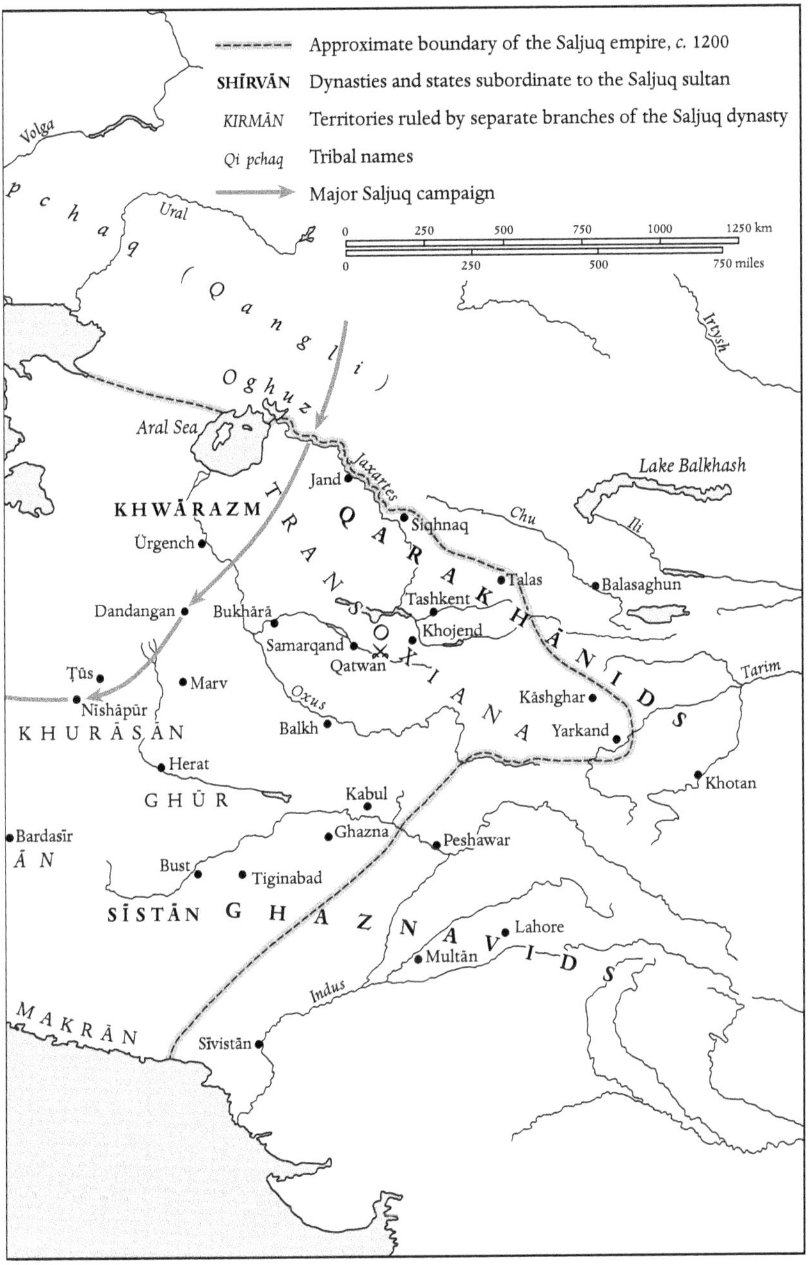
Approximate boundary of the Saljuq empire, c. 1200
SHĪRVĀN Dynasties and states subordinate to the Saljuq sultan
KIRMĀN Territories ruled by separate branches of the Saljuq dynasty
Qi pchaq Tribal names
Major Saljuq campaign
0 250 500 750 1000 1250 km
0 250 500 750 miles
Volga
Ural
pchaq (Qangli)
Oghuz
Irtysh
Aral Sea
Jaxartes
Jand
Lake Balkhash
KHWĀRAZM
TRANSOXIANA
QARAKHĀNIDS
Siqhnaq
Chu
Ili
Ürgench
Talas
Balasaghun
Tashkent
Dandangan
Bukhārā
Khojend
Samarqand
Qatwan
Ṭūs
Marv
Tarim
Kāshghar
Nīshāpūr
Oxus
KHURĀSĀN
Balkh
Yarkand
Herat
Khotan
GHŪR
Kabul
Bardasīr
Ghazna
Peshawar
ĀN
Bust
Tiginabad
SĪSTĀN
GHAZNAVIDS
Lahore
Multān
Indus
MAKRĀN
Sīvistān

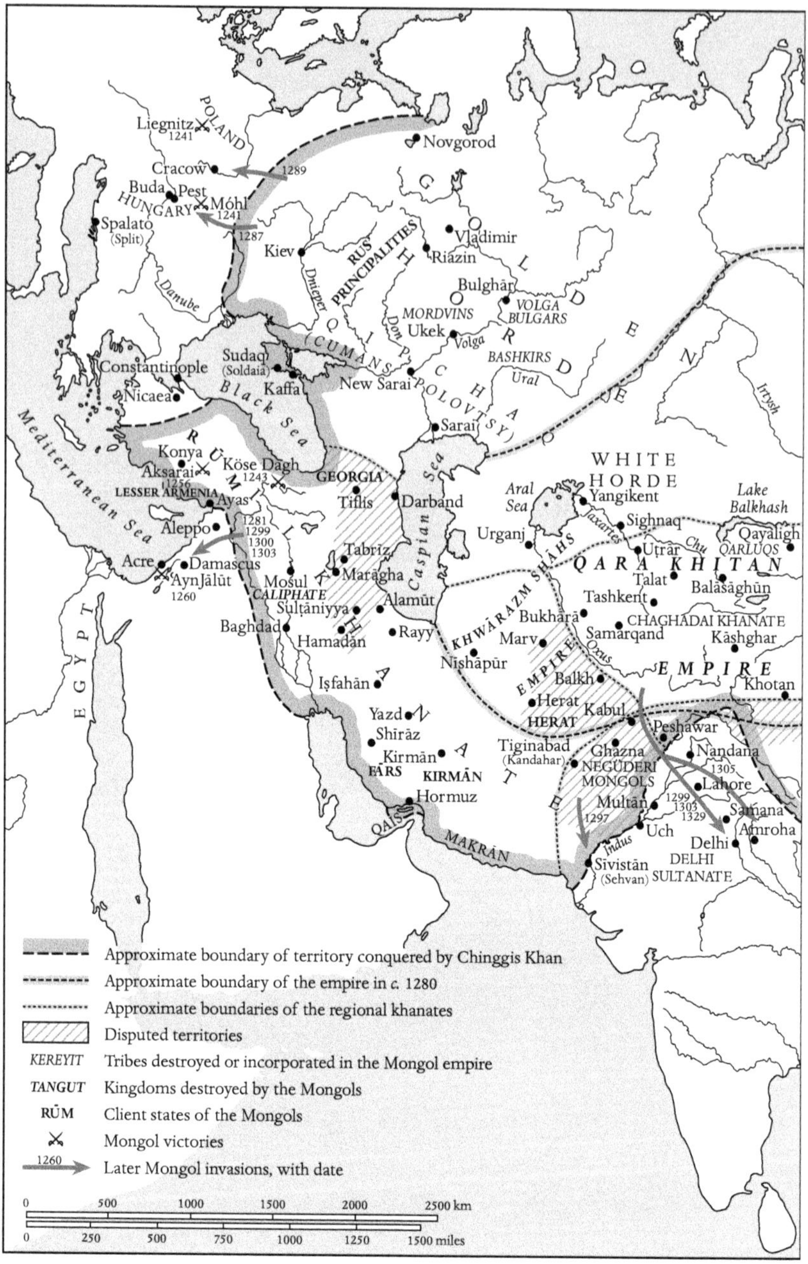

Map 2: The Mongol empire

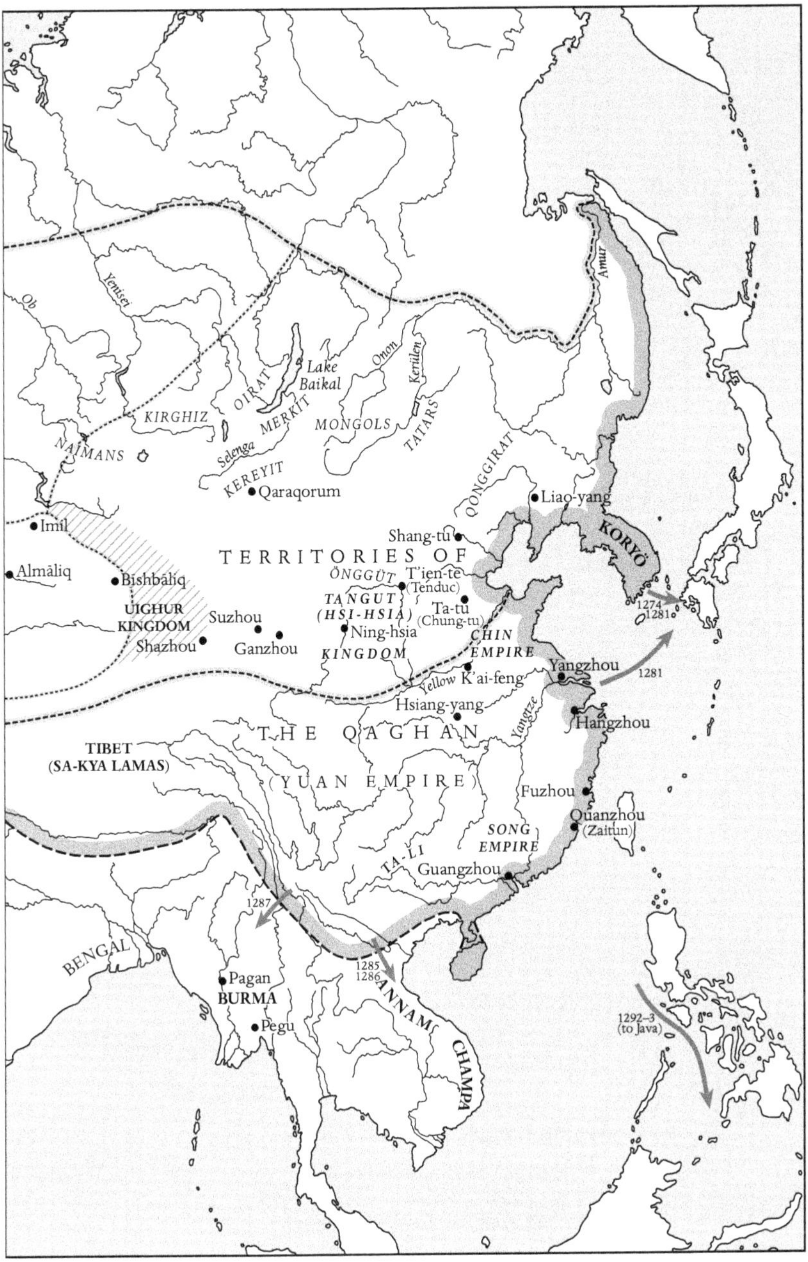

Amur
Ob
Yenisei
Lake Baikal
Onon
Kerülen
KIRGHIZ
OIRAT
MERKIT
Selenga
MONGOLS
TATARS
NAIMANS
KEREYIT
Qaraqorum
QONGGIRAT
Liao-yang
Imil
Shang-tu
KORYŎ
TERRITORIES OF
Almāliq
Bishbālïq
ÖNGGÜT
T'ien-te (Tenduc)
TANGUT (HSI-HSIA) KINGDOM
Ta-tu (Chung-tu)
1274
1281
UIGHUR KINGDOM
Suzhou
Shazhou
Ganzhou
Ning-hsia
CHIN EMPIRE
Yangzhou
1281
Yellow
K'ai-feng
Hsiang-yang
Hangzhou
THE QAGHAN
Yangtze
TIBET (SA-KYA LAMAS)
(YUAN EMPIRE)
Fuzhou
Quanzhou (Zaitun)
SONG EMPIRE
TA-LI
Guangzhou
1287
BENGAL
1285
1286
Pagan
BURMA
ANNAM
Pegu
CHAMPA
1292–3 (to Java)

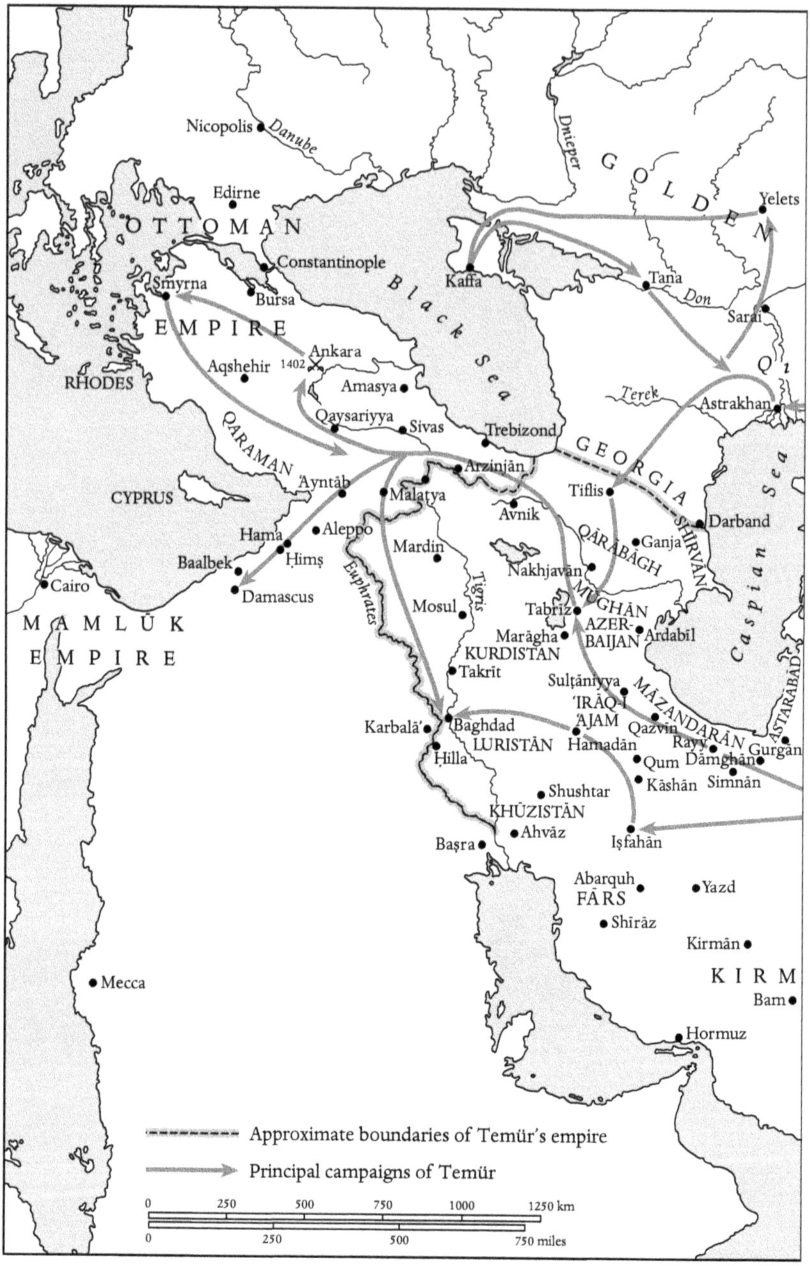

Map 3: The empire of Tamerlane

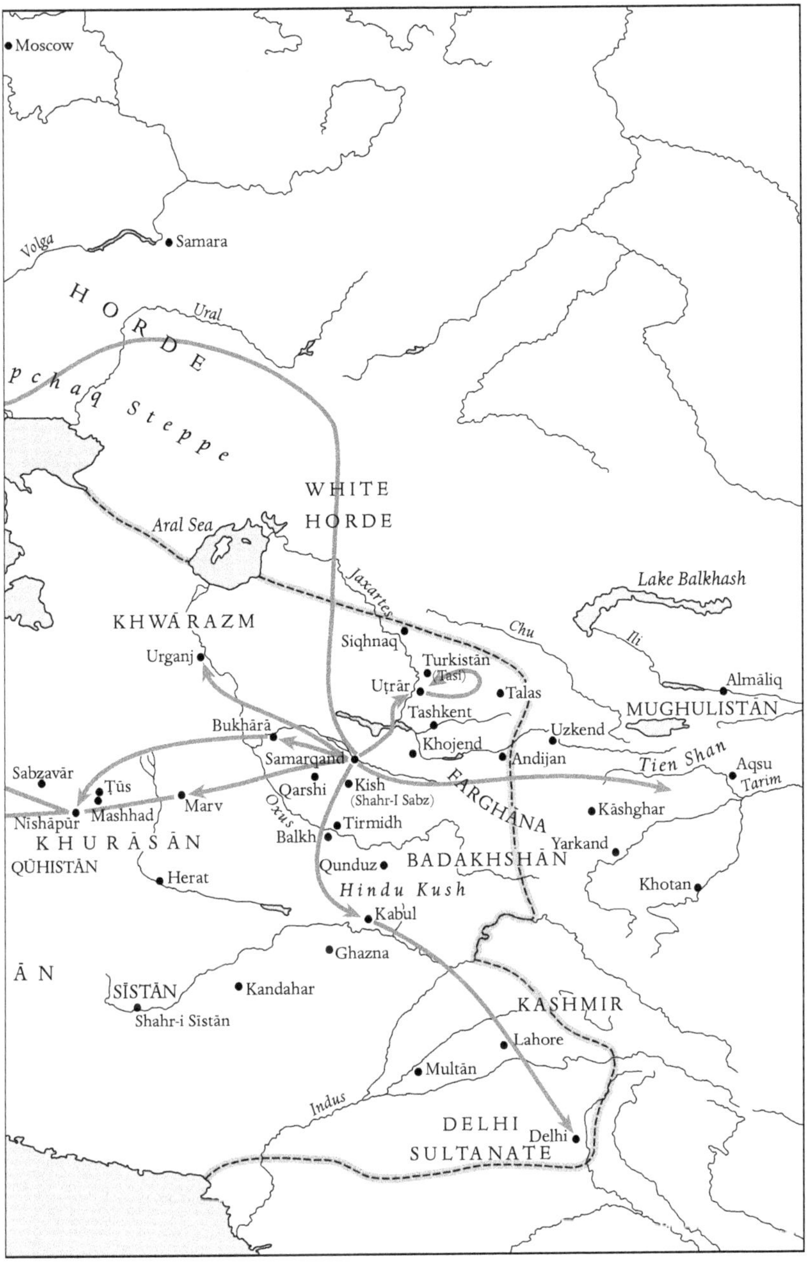
Moscow
Samara
Volga
HORDE
Ural
pchaq Steppe
WHITE
HORDE
Aral Sea
Jaxartes
Lake Balkhash
KHWĀRAZM
Chu
Ili
Siqhnaq
Urganj
Turkistān
(Tasi)
Uṭrār
Talas
Almāliq
Tashkent
MUGHULISTĀN
Bukhārā
Uzkend
Khojend
Samarqand
Andijan
Tien Shan
Sabzavār
Aqsu
Tarim
Ṭūs
Qarshi
Kish
(Shahr-I Sabz)
FARGHĀNA
Marv
Oxus
Kāshghar
Nīshāpūr
Mashhad
Tirmidh
KHURĀSĀN
Balkh
Yarkand
QŪHISTĀN
Qunduz
BADAKHSHĀN
Herat
Khotan
Hindu Kush
Kabul
Ghazna
ĀN
SĪSTĀN
Kandahar
KASHMIR
Shahr-i Sīstān
Lahore
Multān
Indus
DELHI
SULTANATE
Delhi

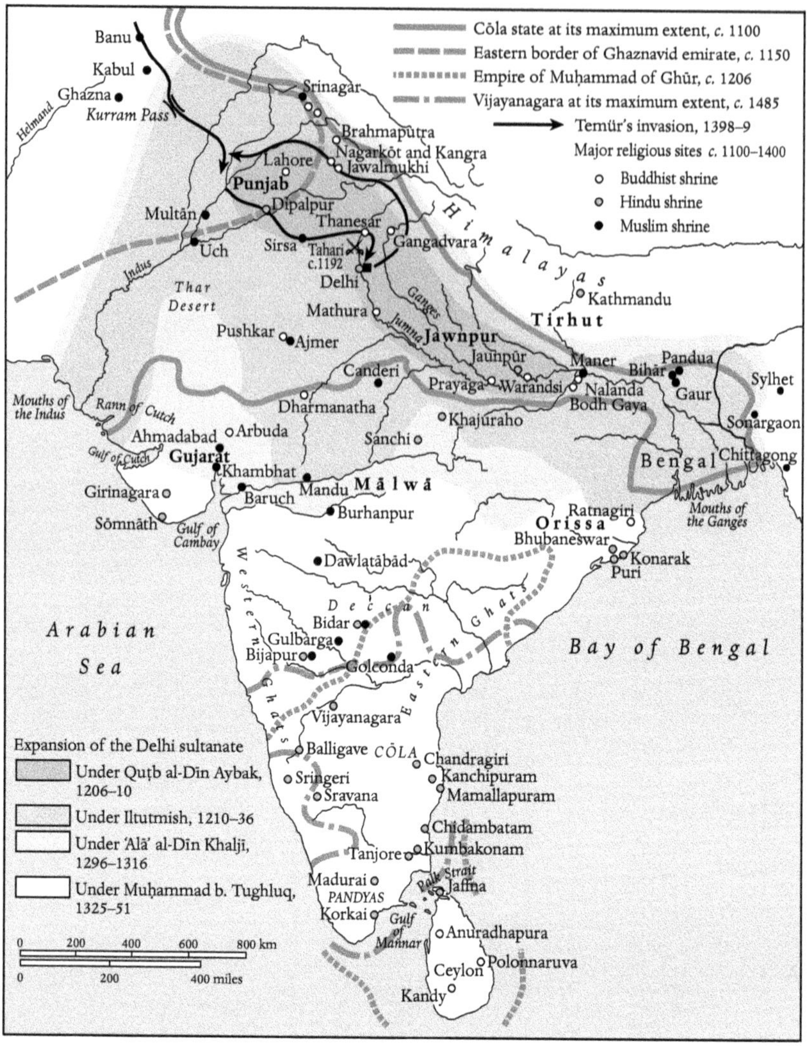

Map 4: India and the Delhi sultanate

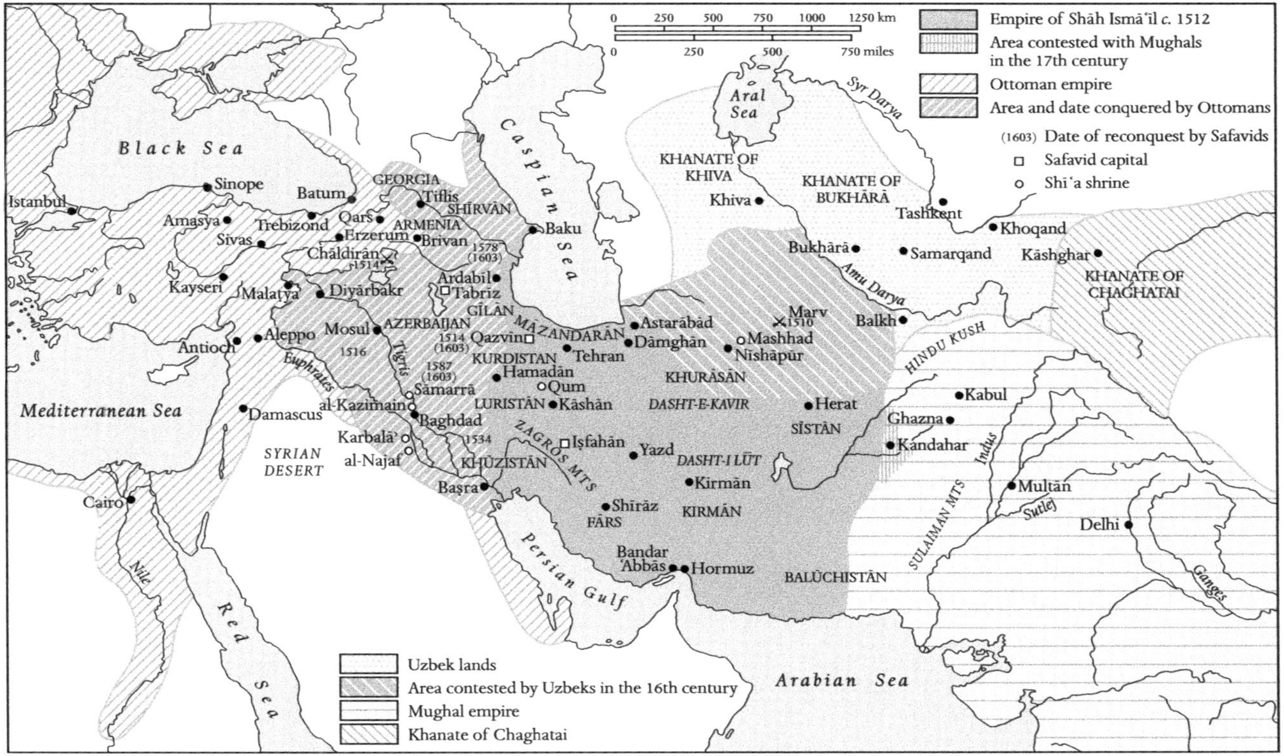

Map 5: Iran under the Safavids

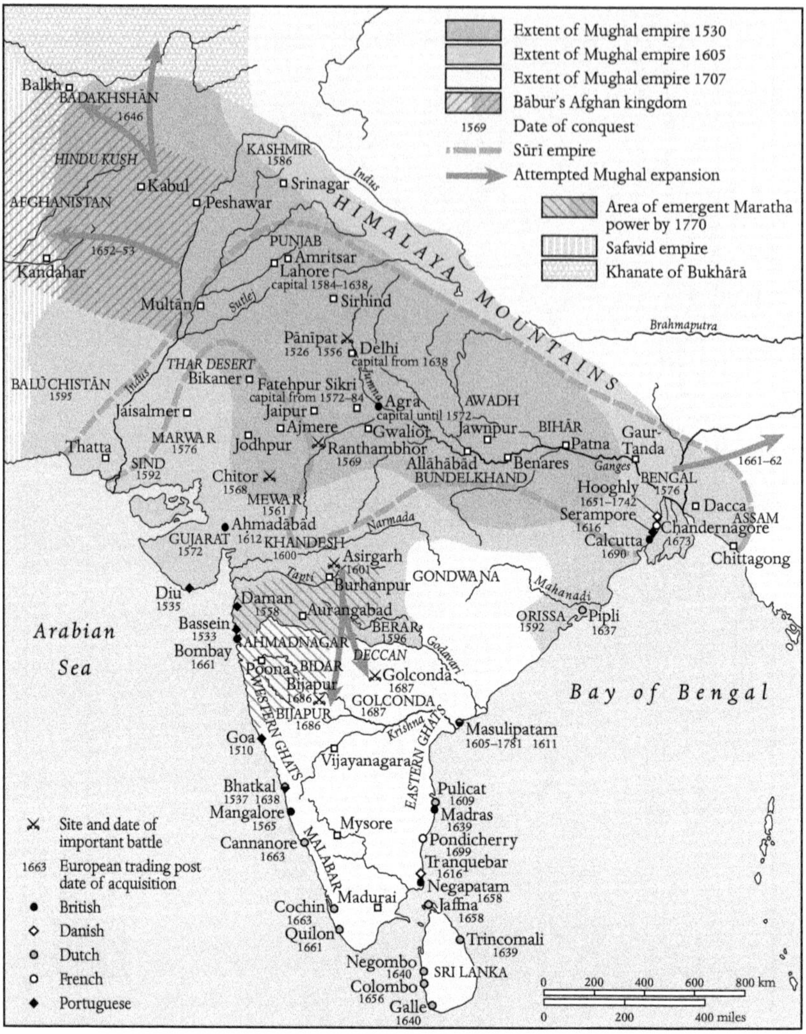

Map 6: Mughal India

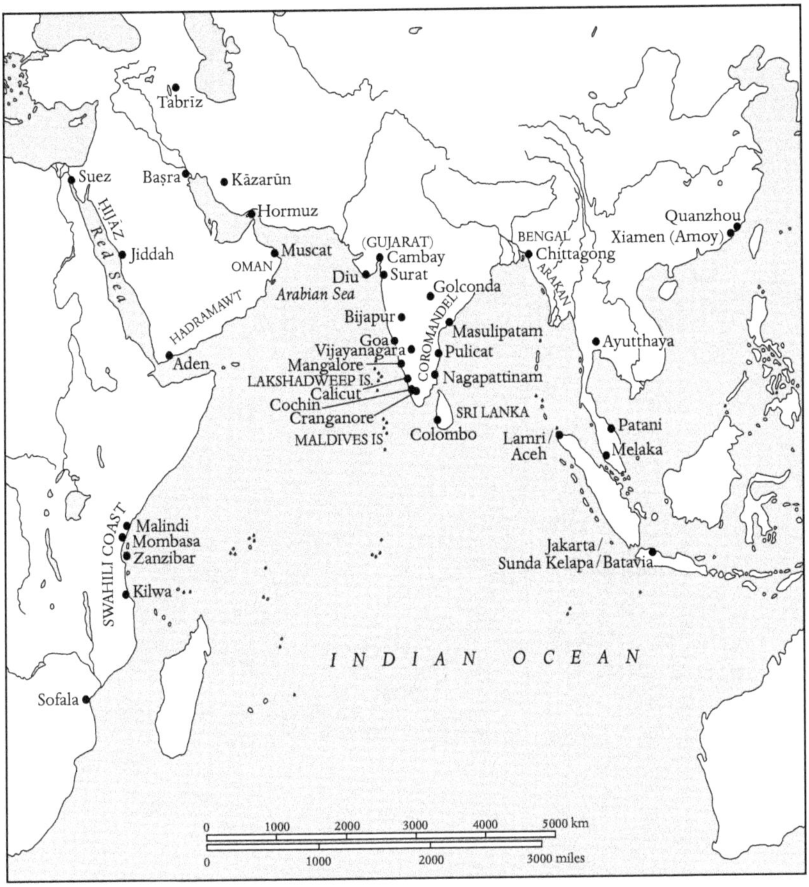

Map 7: The Indian Ocean as Islamic oecumene

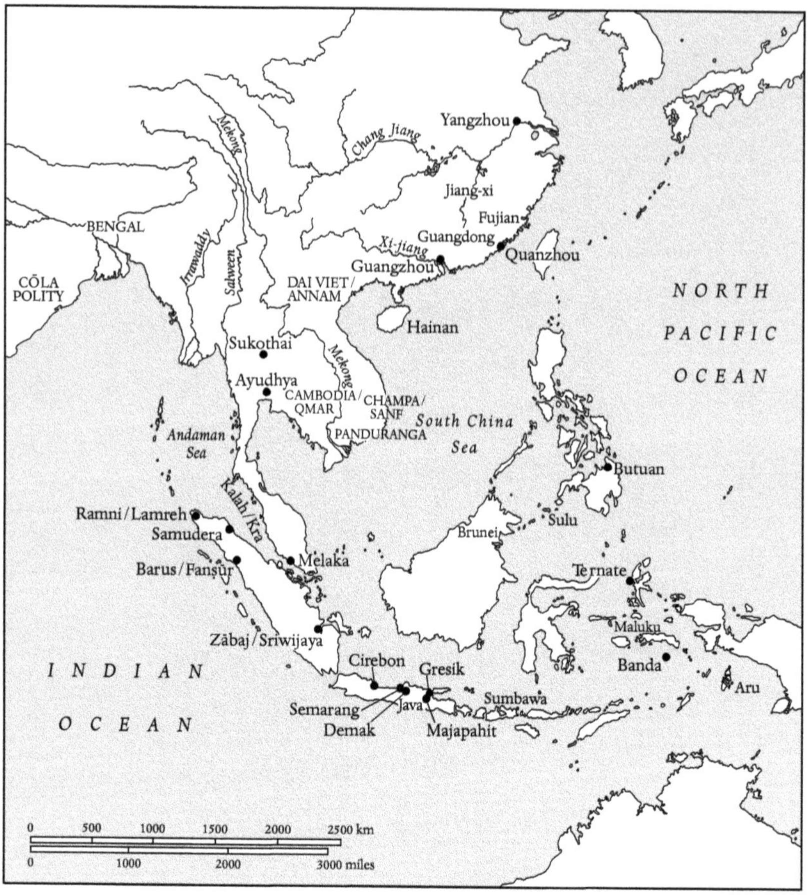

Map 8: South-East Asia and southern China

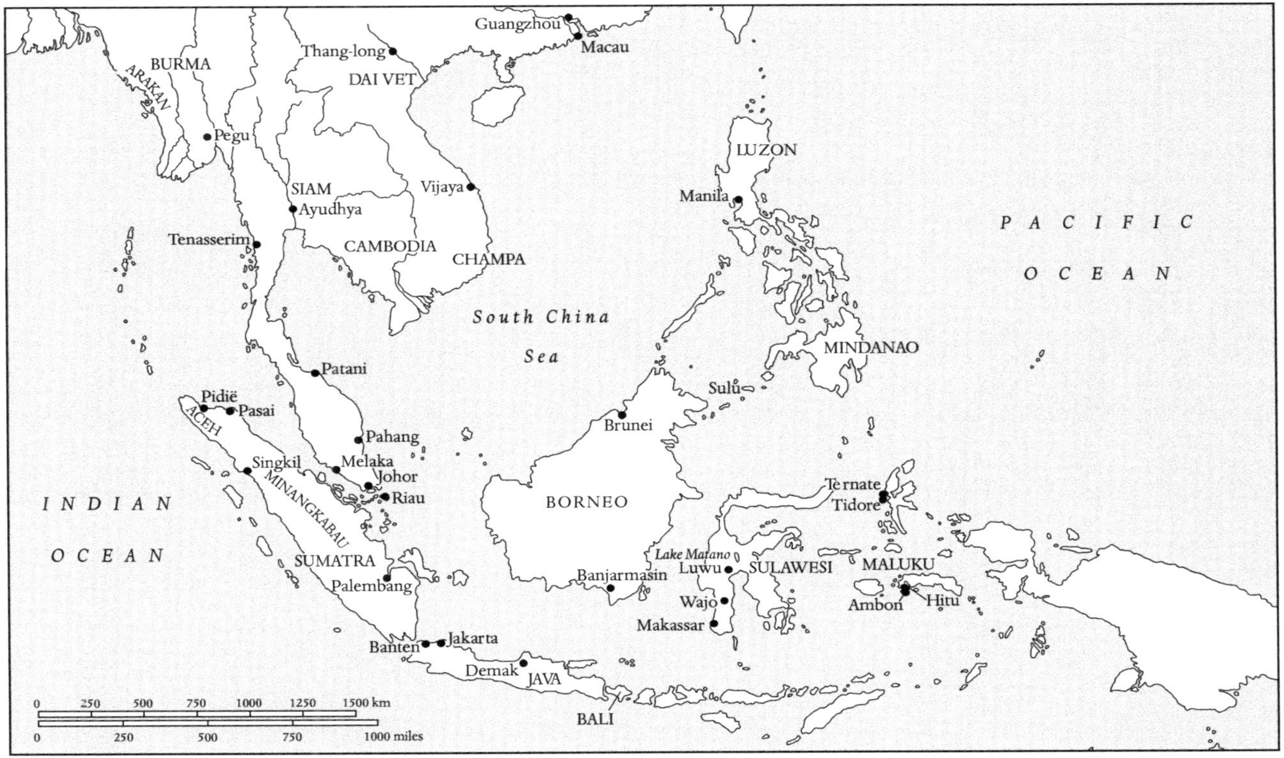

Map 9: South-East Asia in the fifteenth to eighteenth centuries

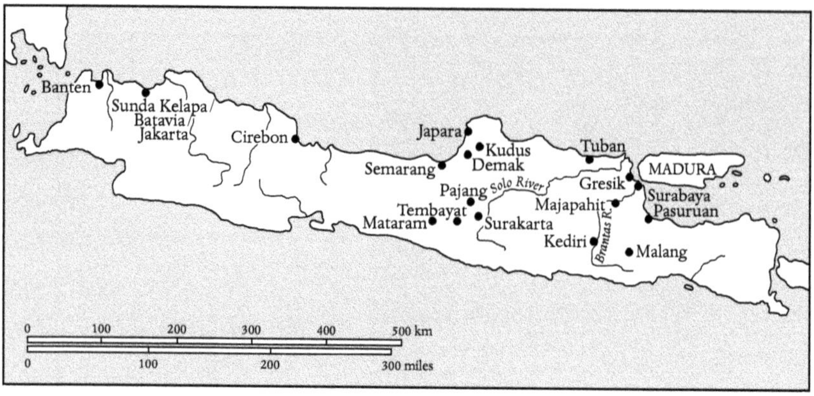

Map 10: Java in the fifteenth to seventeenth centuries

Introduction: Islam in a plural Asia

DAVID O. MORGAN AND ANTHONY REID

In writing the history of the Islamic world, there are two expedients which, sooner or later, become impossible to avoid: periodisation and geographical subdivision. These are bound to be, to a greater or lesser extent, arbitrary, but that does not imply that they are necessarily meaningless. It is possible to tell the story of early Islam, the mission of the Prophet Muḥammad, the first Arab Muslim expansion and the Umayyad and ʿAbbāsid caliphates as a single, integrated narrative. There is an essential unity to the historical evolution of the Muslim community, in its first four centuries, which lends itself to such an integrated treatment. From the eleventh century, and increasingly thereafter, this is no longer the case. The political unity represented by the early caliphates is no more. Though caliphs remained important for a time as local rulers, whether in Baghdad, Cairo or al-Andalus, and even more as instruments of legitimisation for Islamic regimes far and wide, real power passed to a multiplicity of sultans, *amīrs*, maliks and so on. There is nothing very surprising about this. At the point at which this volume commences, the Islamic world stretched uninterruptedly from Spain to Central Asia and northern India. Over the next few centuries it was to spread much further, deeper into India and to western China, and by oceanic routes to East Africa, coastal South Asia, South-East Asia and southern China. Not only does such an expanse defy central rule or co-ordination of any kind, the spread of Islam across such cultural and political diversity would also have been impossible if the Islamic lands had remained politically unified. The trader and the mystical order (*ṭarīqa*) became as important as the soldier and administrator in the further spread of Islam. As the faith crossed numerous cultural boundaries, distinctive Islamic idioms emerged in other great linguistic traditions beyond the Arabic – including Turkish, Persian, Swahili, Malay and Chinese.

That is some justification for commencing a volume of this history in the eleventh century, and for dividing the Islamic world into a western and an eastern half. It is convenient, and it is necessary. And as we shall see, the historical experience of the eastern Islamic world, from the time of the Saljuq incursions, is in many ways different from that of the western half. But there is a price to be paid, in that crudely severing the lands of Islam into two can easily generate the impression of much greater divergence than was in reality the case. We might mention just two examples. The Saljuqs, who ushered in the new era which, it will be argued, began in the mid-eleventh century, incontestably belong on the eastern side of the divide. Yet they ruled for a time in Syria, and for centuries in Anatolia, both of which fall on the western side of our divide, and therefore cannot be dealt with in this volume. Similarly, the ʿAbbāsid caliphs lived in Baghdad, within our geographical area. But whatever the limitations of their 'secular' power in this period, they were still acknowledged as the titular heads of the Muslim community, until the destruction of the caliphate by the Mongols in 1258, throughout much of the western Islamic world.

A terminal date at the end of the eighteenth century finds its justification in the relationship between Islam and modernity, as understood in both European and Islamic terms. The conventional periodisation of European history makes a crucial break, the division between 'medieval' and 'modern', somewhere around 1450–1500: the time of the Renaissance and the Reformation. There were changes in the Islamic world, too, around 1500: some of these will be discussed later. But they hardly match in their radical significance the changes that overcame Western Europe. By contrast 1800, or the century of which it marks the centre, sees the beginnings of the impact on the world's Muslims of the full weight of modernity in the guise of Western economic and military success in the nineteenth and twentieth centuries. Islamic modernism, though in most respects a quite different phenomenon from its European counterpart, had its origins in the same watershed, and can be considered a development (however internally varied) of the nineteenth and twentieth centuries.

There remains an argument for suggesting that for the older-established eastern lands of Islam, the period between the eleventh and eighteenth centuries – the period treated in this volume – has sufficient unity of character to be justly termed a 'middle' age. What sets it apart from the earlier and later periods, however, cannot be equated with what characterised the European Middle Ages. And in any case, for most of the Asian peoples who form the majority of contemporary Muslims, our period is not a 'middle' at all, but rather the foundational period of their Islam. This volume will therefore emphasise three major features which distinguish the time and place from both the earlier experience of Islam, and the universal modernity of the nineteenth and twentieth centuries. One with far-reaching consequences – still not wholly exhausted – was the impact on the Islamic lands of the steppe tribal peoples of Central Asia, especially though not exclusively the Turks. A second was the maritime expansion of Islam along the trade routes of the Indian Ocean and the South China Sea, which had a quite different character from the conquests of the heroic age. Related to both phenomena was a third, broader one. Until the eleventh century, Islam had expanded and developed in interaction primarily with Christianity and its Greco-Roman heritage, and with Judaism and Zoroastrianism. In the eastern lands thereafter, interactions became extensive with Asian spirituality, including what we today label Hinduism, Jainism, Sikhism, Buddhism, Taoism and Shamanism, as well as with Asian political and cultural forms.

Central Asia and the Turks

The Islamic lands had had relations, friendly and otherwise, with Turks beyond the borders for much of the period covered by volume 1 of this history. The at least partly Judaised Khazar empire had for long been an effective barrier to the spread both of Islam as a religion and of Muslim political rule north of the Caucasus. As the Central Asian frontiers of the *dār al-islām* were pushed forward into and beyond Transoxania, individual Turks were captured in battle or purchased as slaves. The ʿAbbāsid caliphs – most famously al-Muʿtaṣim, though the process was under way before his reign – came to value such slaves particularly for their martial qualities: a trained military force of Turks, newly converted to Islam and loyal to their caliphal master, looked an attractive, efficient and trustworthy alternative to reliance on the fractious Khurāsānī armies which had first brought the ʿAbbāsid dynasty to power. It is true that that loyalty did not last very long: not many years were to elapse before political power in Baghdad became a prize to be fought for between the Turkish generals, with the caliph becoming little more than a conveniently tame, if necessarily legitimising, figurehead. But Turkish slave soldiers (*mamlūks* or *ghulāms*) had come to stay. Even the Būyids, Persians from the Caspian provinces who ruled in western Iran and in Baghdad itself for a century from 945, had a substantial Turkish element in their army. The notable dynasty to the east which was for a time the Būyids' contemporary, the Persian Sāmānids of Bukhārā, were famed for their efforts not only in encouraging the spreading of the faith of Islam further into Turk-dominated Central Asia but also in trading extensively in Turkish slaves at the frontier markets. And it was one of their own dissident Turkish generals who set up the Ghaznavid empire in what is now Afghanistan and northern India.

But all of these developments, important though they certainly were, were changes internal to the *dār al-islām*. Whatever the power ultimately wielded by Turkish military slaves, they had all been brought into Islam, in both its religious and its secular aspects, as individuals. That, indeed, had been part of their appeal to their early masters: they had no local or family loyalties – such ties had been left behind in their Central Asian homeland – and thus it was supposed, initially with some justification, that their allegiance would be exclusively to their new Muslim owners. In the eleventh century, as this volume commences, all this was to change. *Mamlūk* soldiers were to remain crucially important in many Muslim states right to the end of our period. But many of the Turks who entered the *dār al-islām* from now on were not to be warriors acquired as individuals, but tribal hordes coming in *en masse*, their tribal organisation, social structure and nomadic way of life still intact, and their tribal leaders still very much in charge. It has sometimes been suggested, with a degree of exaggeration, that for much of the Middle East the period from the eleventh to the nineteenth centuries was one in which military, and hence political, power throughout most of the region was held either by Turks or by the descendants of Turks. Even at the beginning of the twentieth century, the two major independent Muslim powers in the Middle East were still ruled by Turkish dynasties: the Ottomans, of course, but the Qājārs of Iran were also, in origin, of Turkish descent. Indeed, it may be said that apart from the Zand interlude of the eighteenth century in part of the country, Iran as a whole had no ethnically Persian rulers from the arrival of the Saljuqs until the accession of Reza Shāh in 1925 – very nearly 900 years. In northern India, the first Muslim rulers (discounting the early Arab incursions into Sind), the Ghaznavids, had been of Turkish stock. The sultanate of Delhi, under whose rule the first real advances of Islam as a religion in India were made, was established by Turkish generals of the Ghūrids in what is now Afghanistan. The last and greatest Muslim dynasty, that of the Mughals, which ultimately if briefly reigned over almost the whole of the subcontinent and which did not finally disappear until the mid-nineteenth century, was of Turko-Mongol stock, the founder, Bābur, rejoicing in his descent from both Tamerlane (Temür) and Chinggis Khan.

What impact these incursions had has been much debated. From a strictly religious point of view, things could have been worse in that most of the nomads from the east were already converts to Islam by the time they entered the *dār al-islām*. This was true of the first such incursion, that of the

Qarakhānids, though in any case their arrival was of comparatively limited effect, in that they progressed no further westwards than Transoxania. Much more important, the Saljuqs had become Muslims before they crossed the frontier: though precisely what kind of Muslims is not as obvious as is sometimes assumed. What is usually said about the conversion to Islam of the tribal peoples of Central Asia is that it was the work of wandering Sufi missionaries – wild, wonder-working figures who were so similar to the shamans of traditional tribal society that the Turks and others were hardly able to tell the difference. There is sometimes, but not always, evidence that something of the sort occurred, but as a general explanation this should be viewed with a degree of scepticism. The Saljuqs are a classic example. If they had in fact been converted to a syncretic, Shamanism-like form of Sufi Islam, it is not immediately obvious why they should have become, once in power in Iran and Iraq, fervent champions of hardline Sunnī orthodoxy. The possibility remains that lurking in the pre-Islamic background may be the influence not so much of Shamanism as of either Nestorian Christianity, which was long to remain influential and widespread on the steppes, or, more probably, the Judaism of the Khazars.[1] That Judaism, it is thought, was probably rabbinic, and the step from rabbinic Judaism to Sunnī orthodoxy is perhaps smaller than one from wonder-working Sufism would have been. Evidence is lacking, but the names allegedly given to the four sons of the Muslim convert Saljuq, though respectably Islamic, have without exception a suggestively Old Testament look to them.

Still, there was no doubting the Saljuqs' Muslim credentials, by whatever route they may have arrived at them. The bigger problem was the Mongols, who ruled large parts of the Islamic world for many decades while still infidels. Chinggis Khan arrived in 1219, and it was not until 1295 that the Mongol rulers of Iran definitively went over to Islam. It was a basic presumption of Islamic political thought that the *dār al-islām* should expand, inexorably, at the expense of the *dār al-ḥarb*, until the whole world was under Muslim rule (though not necessarily entirely converted to Islam). There was no provision for the process to go into reverse, for Muslim lands to come under the rule of non-Muslims. There had already been some losses, notably in al-Andalus and in the Mediterranean. But the loss to the infidel of Iran and Iraq was a far more serious blow. The Mongols were unique in this respect until, in the modern period, large parts of the Islamic world came under the political domination of

1 Peter B. Golden, *An introduction to the history of the Turkic peoples* (Wiesbaden, 1992), p. 218.

European powers and Manchu China; but at least the Mongols, unlike those later powers, did come ultimately to acknowledge the truth of Islam.

The effect of the Turkish incursions on the fortunes of Islam as a religion was not, then, in any way catastrophic, except perhaps from the point of view of the Shīʿī communities. What was significant was the boost the Saljuqs gave to the Sunnī form of Islam. Prior to their arrival, much of the Middle East had been under Shīʿite rule, most notably but not only the Fāṭimids in Egypt and the Būyids in Iran and Iraq. Of the major Muslim powers of the region around 1000, only the Ghaznavids were Sunnī. It was the Saljuqs who restored Sunnī supremacy in the areas they came to rule; and the ultimate abolition of the Fāṭimid caliphate in Egypt by Saladin may be regarded as another long-term effect, since, as Claude Cahen once observed, Nūr al-Dīn and Saladin are not explicable without reference to the achievement of Ṭoghrıl Beg, the first Saljuq sultan, and Niẓām al-Mulk, the Saljuqs' great Persian administrator.

In other ways, too, the advent of the Saljuqs was epoch-making. They may not precisely have caused, but they certainly initiated, a marked change in the ethnic make-up of the region. Put simply, from the eleventh century onwards, there were a great many more Turks. This is, of course, most conspicuously the case in Turkey, a country the Saljuqs invented, albeit inadvertently. The collapse of the Byzantine eastern frontier after the emperor Romanus IV Diogenes's defeat at the hands of Sultan Alp Arslan, at Manzikert in 1071, allowed Turks to flood into Anatolia. Although some of the territories then lost were later recovered – for a time – by the Byzantines, the battle of Manzikert created the potential for Turkey, a potential which ultimately produced what has been called the last and greatest of the Muslim empires, that of the Ottomans. That, however, is not the concern of this volume. But the influx of Turks did not affect only Anatolia. It had permanent consequences for the ethnic population balance of much of the eastern Islamic world, especially Iran. To this day, a large proportion of the Iranian population is Turkish speaking, and much of that, presumably, is of Turkish ethnic origin. Whether or not that means that their ancestors entered Iran in the wake of the Saljuq invasion or during the Saljuq period is, however, another question: one about which there has been a good deal of discussion. The likelihood is that while the process of Turkish immigration did indeed begin, to a very significant degree, under the Saljuqs, the bulk of the Turks arrived later, particularly during the Mongol period and even after. The numbers quoted by historians of the Saljuq period for the sizes of tribal hordes are not enormous, unlike those routinely ascribed to the Mongol armies by those historians' later successors (which may perhaps suggest caution about assuming that medieval chroniclers invariably tend to exaggerate).

In terms, too, of the way of life of the peoples of the eastern Islamic world, the arrival of the Saljuqs and other Turks from Central Asia caused a major shift: in the balance of the population between sedentary and nomad. This was of permanent significance: the nomadic element in the population remained, from then on, of much greater importance, culturally and politically, than was the case in much of the rest of the *dār al-islām*. It was only in the twentieth century that a more or less successful attempt was made to curb the power and comparative independence of the nomadic tribes of Iran – and even then, the last major tribal revolt occurred as recently as 1963. The Saljuqs' followers in their migration across the Oxus were tribally organised nomads, and their military force, therefore, was essentially a classic tribal horde of cavalry archers, not dissimilar in most major respects from the better-known Mongols of the thirteenth century, though certainly not so disciplined and regulated as the armies of Chinggis Khan were to be. Indeed, the tribal Turkish hordes soon came to be something of an embarrassment to the newly respectable Saljuq sultans. Traditionally, a tribal khan was very far from possessing despotic powers in time of peace, though he was expected to command, and to command effectively, in warfare. Not all of the Turks who followed Ṭoghrıl Beg and Chaghrı Beg into Iran and Iraq took kindly to their transformation into, potentially, the subjects of much more powerful Muslim sovereigns. Hence many of them, seen increasingly as disorderly and disruptive by their leaders, voted with their feet. The Turkomans whose incursions into Byzantine eastern Anatolia precipitated the crisis that led to the battle of Manzikert in 1071 are one example. Similarly, the lifelong preoccupation of the last Saljuq sultan of the east, Sanjar (d. 1157), was the containment of the Ghuzz Turkish hordes who were endangering the stability of Khurāsān. It was not long before the Saljuqs found it necessary to provide themselves with a permanent, if fairly small, standing army to reduce reliance on the tribal contingents that had first brought them to power. Their great Persian vizier, Niẓām al-Mulk, in his handbook of government, the *Siyāsat-nāma*, recommended the recruitment of *mamlūks* as a reliable buttress for the state: he was clearly worried about the ungovernability of the Turkish tribes.

In military terms, the advent of the Turks marked the supremacy, for centuries to come, of the steppe cavalry archer. The Mongols are the most conspicuous example of this, but in principle the same factors, to a greater or lesser extent, worked to the advantage of other conquerors from Central Asia. In the field, in pre-modern times, an army composed of such warriors could expect to have a decisive advantage over the armies of the sedentary states they faced, richer and more populous though those states generally may have been (though when it came to siege warfare it was a different story, and nomadic invaders frequently had to avail themselves of the expertise of engineers from the sedentary world). Because of the close approximation between ordinary nomadic life, with its herding and hunting, and warfare, the tribesmen were in effect a permanently available mounted force, trained constantly in appropriate techniques since childhood. What is more, they were all available: no sedentary state could possibly mobilise so large a proportion of its manpower. And in the composite bow of the steppes, the nomads had a battlefield weapon which in terms of accuracy, rate of fire, range and power of penetration had no equal until long after the first appearance of firearms: it was centuries before a handgun existed which could hope to match the composite bow in effectiveness. We should not assume that with the invention of gunpowder, the traditional style of steppe warfare and its composite bow were immediately rendered obsolete.

Maritime expansion and cultural diversity

The second major theme of this volume will be the maritime expansion of Islam, accompanying the vessels that criss-crossed the Indian Ocean and travelled as far as the south-eastern coast of China. This pattern had very little in common with the advancing military and administrative frontiers of the heartlands of Islam and the steppes of Eurasia.

The forested tropical regions around the Indian Ocean were not favourable to the empires of marching armies or cavalry charges. Communication was much easier by water than by land. But the oceans of Asia also offered few examples of military expansion by sea until the advent of European naval power in 1498. Those few examples – the Tamil Cholas in the eleventh century, the Javanese of Majapahit in the fourteenth or the huge Chinese fleets of the early fifteenth – were not Islamic, except in so far as individual Muslims took leadership roles, as the Yunnan eunuch and admiral Zheng He (Cheng Ho) did in commanding the Chinese expeditions. The only explicit uses of central Islamic power in the Indian Ocean – that of the Ottomans in response to Portuguese naval attacks in the 1530s and again in the 1560s – were failures, even if significant ones.

Nevertheless, Muslims held certain advantages in navigation and maritime trade which gave them commercial dominance in the Indian Ocean from roughly the twelfth century to the sixteenth. Arabs, commanding the favoured Red Sea and Persian Gulf routes between the Mediterranean and Indian Oceans, had been sailing their dhows to India and beyond since pre-Islamic times. The egalitarian, commercial and legal ethos of Islam appeared well suited to the establishment of Islamic commercial communities in all the ports of that immensely diverse littoral. By the eighth century the Arab and Persian Muslim traders residing in Canton were rich and numerous enough to stage a revolt (758) which briefly took control of the city. By the end of the Tang dynasty in 907 Sinicised Muslims, the Hui, had become a permanent part of several coastal Chinese cities. From the ninth century we have the accounts of Arab geographers, describing the trading routes and ports between the Red Sea and China.

The major ports along this route were in south India and Sri Lanka, northern Sumatra, the isthmian ports of the Malayan peninsula, the north coast of Java and the Cham ports of what is now the central Vietnamese coast. In all these places, as in the Chinese ports themselves, a few Islamic tombstones bear witness to the beginnings of Islamic communities in the eleventh to fourteenth centuries. All began as enclaves and minorities, Islamic quarters in larger trading cities. Islamic law and the Arabic language made it easier for traders to move from one of the quarters to another, creating a kind of Muslim commercial oecumene even before the rise of Islamic political power.

The first Islamic states in South-East Asia which can be clearly documented from tombstones and travel accounts occurred on the northern coast of Sumatra in the 1290s. The most prominent of these was Samudera, later called Pasai, where Ibn Baṭṭūṭa in 1345 found a flourishing Sunnī polity following the Shāfiʿī school of law, as virtually all of South-East Asia does today. As Muslim merchants became more and more important a factor in the prosperity of the host of small river-ports in the archipelago, many of their rulers became Muslim in the following century, through conviction, force, marriage or a judicious choice of alliances.

An intriguing, still unresolved, issue is the extent of northern influences from China and Champa in this phase of Islamisation. The Mongol conquest of China in the late thirteenth century had brought a variety of Central Asian Muslims into the official and military service of China. They were particularly strong in Yunnan, which the Mongols added to the Chinese empire and placed under a Muslim governor. When the Mongols in turn were overthrown by the Ming dynasty in 1368, those Muslims who remained were Sinicised in language and much of their culture, but many remained in privileged positions. The great expeditions sent to South-East Asia and the Indian Ocean under the emperor Yongle were commanded by the Yunnan Muslim Zheng He, and many of his soldiers were also Muslim. Some traditions of Java attribute to these fleets an injection of Chinese Muslims into the affairs of the Java Sea, and the rise of Muslim port-states such as Gresik, Tuban, Japara, Demak and Cirebon, along the north coast of Java. Melaka on the peninsula, which replaced Pasai as the most important Malay Muslim trading state in the late fourteenth century, also got its start by cultivating these imperial Chinese fleets.

Once Javanese port-states had become predominantly Muslim, their superior arms, wealth and motivation came into play in the conquest of the Hindu–Buddhist kingdoms of the interior. The fall of Majapahit to Muslim arms is conventionally dated 1478, but was in any case complete by about 1527. But the hegemony of the Islamic coast was brief. Around 1600 a new Javanese kingdom arose at Mataram, centred near modern Yogyakarta. The great king of Mataram, usually known as Sultan Agung (1613–46), though he carried many titles both Hindu and Muslim, achieved what Akbar attempted in India, a synthesis of old and new religions. From his reign stems the idea that Java is a special case within Islam, a stable amalgam of Hindu–Buddhist mystical ideas, animist popular practices and Islamic externals. The controversy this idea has engendered will engage particular attention below.

As Islam became established so far from its roots, translations became necessary into a variety of languages. In the sixteenth century this process began with Malay and Javanese, and the fullest flower of Islamic literature in Malay occurred in the seventeenth century. Most of the most influential writers and teachers known to us in these traditions were Sufis, and many had studied in Mecca or Medina and become members of the Khaḍiriyya or Shaṭṭāriyya *ṭarīqa*. As they were throughout the Muslim world in this period, these Sufis were followed in life and revered in death, often more than they were read. They gave substance and life to the traditions of life and law the traders had brought.

The century from about 1540 to 1640 is a particularly interesting one in maritime Asia, because the reaction against Portuguese attacks on Islam produced a high point of rallying around the banner of political Islam. The Portuguese directed their attacks particularly against the Arab, Gujarati, south Indian and Malay traders who had dominated the pepper and spice trade from South-East Asia to the Red Sea. After severe initial disruption and the loss of many ports, a Muslim trading network was re-established in mid-century, linking Aceh in Sumatra to the Red Sea by way of the Maldives. In the 1560s Aceh envoys were taking their pepper to the Ottoman court and pleading for military assistance against the Portuguese. Military help was sent, but it was especially the idea of a unified counter-crusade in the name of Islam that was influential.

In Sumatra, the Peninsula, Maluku (the Spice Islands of eastern Indonesia), Sulawesi and even Siam and Cambodia, the sharp opposition between Muslim and Christian was at its peak in the following sixty years. We also see attempts at the literal application of *sharīʿa* law, including the amputation of hands and feet for theft, in several centres of South-East Asia in this period.

The direct Muslim trade link to the Arab ports of the Red Sea was cut in the first decades of the seventeenth century by more efficient Dutch and English shipping around the Cape of Good Hope. Pilgrimage to, and study in, the holy places became much more difficult. The antagonism between Muslim and Christian was also complicated by the ferocious competition between Dutch and Portuguese, Protestant and Catholic. The great Islamic trading states such as Aceh, Banten and Makassar were either conquered by the Dutch Company in the seventeenth century or lost their most profitable trade to it. One might see the period that followed in the late seventeenth and eighteenth centuries as one of localisation and the deepening of roots, with much less evidence of literalist applications of scriptural norms. The interplay between local and exotic models, syncretism and literalism, compromise and reform, will be the stuff of the chapters that follow.

Islam and Asian religions

The fact that Islamic dispersion in maritime Asia was often the work of traders and Sufi scholars rather than armies and administrators was not the only respect in which this Asian 'middle' period differed from its Middle Eastern analogue. In that Middle Eastern and Mediterranean world Islam had largely taken shape in interaction with Christianity and Judaism, sharing the scriptural emphasis and doctrinal exclusiveness of the Abrahamic faiths. But from the eleventh century its Asian expansion was largely in interaction with Asian spirituality, including the widespread acceptance of the idea that the ultimate inner reality could have many outer forms. Here the preoccupation of the Abrahamic monotheisms with guarding and enforcing orthodoxy was a very minor strain. The first great Islamic scholar to comment on the Indic world, Abū Rayhān al-Bīrūnī (973–1048), noted how radically it differed from Islamic (or Christian) civilisations: 'On the whole there is very little disputing about theological topics among themselves: at the utmost, they fight with words, but they will never stake their soul or body or their property on religious controversy.'[2] The inherent pluralism of Indic religious experience derived from this root, and made it seem

2 *Alberuni's India*, trans. E. Sachau; abridged edn, ed. A. T. Embree (New York, 1971), p. 19.

natural that different peoples would have different cults. A Thai king who presided over a particularly cosmopolitan seventeenth-century space expressed his surprise that King Louis XIV of France, in requesting him to become a Catholic Christian (following hard upon a Persian embassy urging him to become a Shīʿī Muslim), appeared to believe that his God required all his creatures to approach him in the same way. Since the Creator had made his creatures so very different, should we not rather assume, he asked, that He takes pleasure in being honoured by different rituals?

Religious architecture was one tangible area in which the influence of Asian ideas of the sacred was influential throughout our period. Much of the Indic tradition valued religious buildings as sacred sites rather than as places of assembly for the faithful. Many of the earliest places of Muslim devotion in Asia were also at holy tombs, or places of meditation and study, which had older roots of sacredness, gradually Islamised by the practice of Sufi masters. We naturally find the earliest Muslim buildings in China and in Java looking very much like pre-Islamic sacred sites, with pagoda-like minarets and cool courtyards, much as church architecture had influenced Islamic building in the Mediterranean area. The very prominent role throughout Asia of saints, *walīs* and shaykhs, renowned for their meditation and consequent miraculous powers, predated the formal organisation of Sufi *ṭarīqas* in most areas. Their tombs became centres of pilgrimage and meditation. As Muslim political empires weakened in the late seventeenth and eighteenth centuries, however, the Sufi orders became an important alternative model of social organisation, extending their reach throughout India, China and South-East Asia, and frequently operating in areas ruled by Hindus, Buddhists, Confucians or Christians.

There is plenty of evidence of Muslim communities drawing sharp boundaries to protect themselves from the dangers they saw in the other religious communities with which they coexisted in Asia. As subsequent generations of scholars combined an Islamic with an indigenous high civilisation, however, there were also remarkable works of synthesis, showing the truths of Islam to be compatible with Confucian morality, on the one hand, or Indian and Javanese ideas of non-duality, on the other.

In much of Asia this middle period is marked by great internal diversity, since non-Muslim rulers – whether Thai Buddhist, Malabari Hindu, Chinese Confucian or European port-rulers – had neither the legitimacy to impose uniformity on their Muslim subjects, nor any interest in doing so. Sunnī and Shīʿa and various schools of law coexisted and contended over much of the continent. In Malay-speaking South-East Asia, on the other hand, a remarkable uniformity of Sunnī Islam and Shāfiʿī law prevailed by the end of our period. One explanation of this may have to do with the prominence of these features in the Hadramawt and the Ḥijāz, the two major sources of learning and legitimacy for South-East Asia since the eighteenth century. Another may be the prominence of rulers 'below the winds' in setting the pattern for Islamic observance.

The Persian moment

Niẓām al-Mulk (d. 1092), chief minister for several decades to the early Saljuq sultans Alp Arslan and Malik Shāh, has already been referred to. He is an appropriate symbol for the beginnings of another critical development of the period covered in this volume: Persianisation, in both administration and culture. The Saljuqs were canny enough to realise that although they might have become the rulers of a substantial part of the central Islamic lands, and while they might well possess awesome military superiority over any likely rivals, they would not be well advised to try to run their empire as if it was merely an extension of their steppe tribal dominion. They had lived for some time on the borders of the *dār al-islām* before entering it – the time during which they had themselves become Muslims. They knew something about Islamic civilisation, agriculture and the life of cities. They knew enough, at any rate, to appreciate that they needed expert help in running their new empire. That help was available in the shape of the old Persian bureaucracy (of which Niẓām al-Mulk was a representative if exceptional member), which consciously drew on the administrative traditions of pre-Islamic Iran, the ʿAbbāsid caliphate, the Sāmānids and the Ghaznavids. There were, then, strong Islamic elements in the tradition, but it was in essence a Persian tradition of government. It has been argued for Iran at least, and not without justification, that the governmental pattern established by the Saljuqs, or by the Saljuqs' Persian servants, was the pattern that prevailed there, with changes in detail and terminology, till the nineteenth century. Such traditions were transplanted into India, and there, too, Persian became the language of government – so ineradicably that even in the nineteenth century it was still thought necessary to teach Persian to young British recruits to the service of the East India Company.

Culturally, Persian influence was even more pronounced. In a celebrated exchange of letters at the beginning of the sixteenth century, Shāh Ismāʿīl I, founder of Iran's great Safavid dynasty, wrote to the Ottoman sultan Selīm I in Turkish, but received the sultan's reply in Persian: even in Ottoman Istanbul, the language of a cultured and educated gentleman was Persian, not Turkish – let alone Arabic. This is not to say that Arabic lost its prestige: as the language of the Qurʾān, of law and of theology, its position was unassailable. But for literature, for poetry, for history, for civilised discourse generally, Persian became the language of choice over a vast geographical range, enormously larger than anything that might be considered to be Iran in a political or ethnic sense. This was, perhaps, only beginning during the Saljuq period. The historian of that epoch will still find that more of the sources are written in Arabic than in Persian. The decisive shift, it would seem, occurred under the Mongols. Not a people who were strikingly literate in any language, for them there was certainly no reason to have any truck with Arabic, since for the first seventy years or so of their rule in the *dār al-islām* they were not themselves Muslims. Arabic had no special status, whereas Persian was the language of the people they, like the Saljuqs, employed to help them run their empire. They were not as quick as the Saljuqs had been to appreciate the character and virtues of civilised life away from the steppes. They had arrived in vastly greater numbers, with no educational preparatory period on the borders. This may be part of the explanation for the ferocity of the first Mongol invasions: they had not yet understood that allowing agriculture and cities to continue in existence could be to their advantage as the new owners. But they soon caught on, took large numbers of experienced Persian bureaucrats into their service, and facilitated the further spread of Persian, which became something of a lingua franca throughout their empire – even in China.

This shift in a Persian direction throughout so great a proportion of the Islamic world has profound implications for how we see its overall history. It is not so long since it was still thought self-evident to depict Islamic history as a pattern of rise (early Islam and the first expansion; the Umayyad and early ʿAbbāsid caliphates), decline (the later ʿAbbāsids, the coming of the Turks, the final blow to civilisation inflicted by the perfidious Mongols) and revival (the beneficial effects of the impact of the West, from the beginning of the nineteenth century). Any such pattern, which seems to underlie even the first edition of this *History*, was definitively blown out of the water by Marshall Hodgson in his (regrettably posthumous) three-volume survey *The Venture of Islam*, published in 1974, a deservedly influential book which might have had even greater repercussions had its author commanded an accessible English style.

What Hodgson showed, among much else, was that the old rise-and-decline story only made sense if the historian's gaze was firmly fixed on a kind of Baghdad–Damascus–Cairo triangle. That there was a decline after the early Islamic centuries, in some sense, was undeniable, but it was an Arab and an

Arabic, not a general Islamic, decline. The young Albert Hourani asked Philip Hitti why his celebrated *History of the Arabs* of 1937 contained so little on the period between the Ottoman conquest and the nineteenth century. 'There was no Arab history then,' was the reply.[3] The centre of the Islamic world had shifted out of the old Arab heartlands, and so likewise should the attention of the historian. The centre shifted, in fact, to the Persian world. Hence the sixteenth and seventeenth centuries may not have been periods of triumph in terms of Arab culture and politics; but in the wider Islamic world, these two centuries could easily be seen as the apogee, in which the *dār al-islām* was dominated by three great and powerful empires, the Ottoman, the Safavid and the Mughal – all of them very much part of the Persian cultural area. This did not imply peace and unity: far from it. The Ottomans were bastions of Sunnī Islam, at constant loggerheads with the Safavids (though not solely for religious reasons), until some way into the seventeenth century. In Iran, Shāh Ismāʿīl and his successors had set up Twelver Shīʿism as the approved – indeed, compulsory – form of Islam, in contradistinction and opposition to their Sunnī neighbours, Ottomans to the west and Uzbeks to the east. The religious situation in Mughal India was more complex, but there too the approved variety of Islam was Sunnism; and there were other causes of Mughal–Safavid friction, notably the line of demarcation between the two empires in what is now Afghanistan.

By now, it would seem, most Muslims, not just lawyers and theologians, could tell the difference between Sunnī and Shīʿī Islam at a glance. This had not always necessarily been the case. Many Sunnīs in the fifteenth century had been sufficiently fervent in their devotion to ʿAlī and the Shīʿite imams to cause modern historians considerable confusion. It was not helpful, for example, that the Qara Qoyunlu sultan Jahānshāh should have minted coins which were Sunnī on one side and no less clearly Shīʿī on the other. The disappearance of the caliphate after the Mongols killed the last ʿAbbāsid of Baghdad in 1258 may have added to the prevailing religious turmoil. The tame ʿAbbāsid caliphate maintained by the Mamlūk regime in Cairo received little acknowledgement outside its own domains: most Sunnī Muslims found that they had to do without whatever stability and authority the caliphate, however politically weak it may have become, had still provided. Whether for this or for other reasons, the allegiance of enormous numbers of Muslims came in this period to reside not with the official machinery of the faith but in the increasingly organised and regularised Sufi brotherhoods: and there it has remained to this day. Sufism was,

3 A. Hourani, 'How should we write the history of the Middle East?', *International Journal of Middle East Studies*, 23 (1991), p. 129.

and is, much more a Sunnī than a Shīʿī phenomenon, which may be connected with the fact that the Twelver Shīʿism of Iran does have a kind of hierarchy, and it is a hierarchy which, as much in the twenty-first century as in the eighteenth, is by no means favourably disposed towards Sufism.

What was different after 1500?

As we have seen, the dominant powers in the Muslim world after 1500 were the Ottoman, Safavid and Mughal empires. These states were distinguished not only by their size, but also by their longevity. Since the decline in the central authority of the ʿAbbāsid caliphate, ruling dynasties, even formidable ones like the Saljuqs, the Mongols and the Timurids, rarely lasted for much more than a century, and often less. By 1500, the Ottoman dynasty, however, was already two centuries old (though hardly a major power for some time after its still mysterious appearance around 1300); and it was to last for a further 400 years. The other two great empires did not enjoy comparable longevity. Both were founded in the early sixteenth century, and they may be said to have survived as holders of effective power for a little over two centuries. This did not remotely approach the Ottoman record, but it was still twice what had been the norm before 1500.

What is the explanation for this? The most obvious point is that they were 'gunpowder empires'. The argument is that, with the increasing sophistication and expense of gunpowder weaponry, only large states could afford to keep up to date, which endowed such states with a decisive political and military advantage. By contrast, in the era of the dominance of the composite bow, which every nomad cavalryman possessed, any ambitious chieftain could attempt to put together a force which, when it reached a sufficient size, could hope to be the equal of any other. Hence in part, perhaps, the comparatively ephemeral nature of many pre-1500 states.

Whether or not a 'modern' army had such an inherent advantage depended to some extent on the type of warfare being waged. At Chāldirān in 1514, the Ottoman victory over the Safavids seems to a large extent to have been due to firearms; but what really counted was that the Ottoman Janissary musketeers were sheltered behind a wagon laager, and the cannons were chained together. This all provided an effective obstacle to the Safavid cavalry charge. But the Safavids learned their lesson. While they did use firearms to a degree, they kept clear of wagon laagers and relied on speed and manoeuvrability, which the Ottomans had inevitably sacrificed in their increasing reliance on gunpowder technology. Safavid Iran, it has been argued, 'succeeded in remaining independent because it did not allow itself to get drawn into the kind of war that only the Ottomans could win. Its reliance on cavalry instead of firearms was the secret to its survival.'[4]

Still, there can be little doubt that the efficient use of gunpowder technology did, ultimately, change things decisively. There were to be no more steppe empires after Tamerlane's, and the vast area that had produced the Turks and the Mongols was eventually divided between the sedentary empires of Russia and China. The most spectacularly successful post-Tamerlane conqueror in the region was Nādir Shāh (d. 1747): but his ephemeral conquests were the achievement of a thoroughly modern and up-to-date army, not a force made up of steppe cavalry archers.

Many other factors – religious, political, administrative, economic, cultural – distinguished the three great empires from their predecessors.[5] For example, Bernard Lewis argued that the introduction into the Muslim world by the Turks and Mongols of the steppe notion of family sovereignty and 'a workable principle of dynastic succession' made long-term political stability much easier to achieve.[6] Certainly much had changed, and in 1500 Muslim imperial 'decline' was a very distant prospect.

The period covered in this volume is one of great creativity and vitality in the Islamic world. It also had its share of disaster and suffering: whatever may be said about the positive impact of Mongol rule, for example – and there is now a great deal that can and should be said, not least with respect to the unprecedented opportunities for advancement with which Mongol rule across Asia provided Muslims – there is very little that can be done to rehabilitate the human rights records of Chinggis Khan or Tamerlane. Yet even so, it is a mistake to portray the centuries from the eleventh to the eighteenth as centuries of steady and unremitting decline, as has too often been the tendency of historians. Rather, we should see the period as one in which Islam became truly a world religion, dressed in the civilisational colours of Uzbeks, Uighurs, Bengalis, Gujaratis, Tamils, Malays, Javanese and Chinese. In its breadth and depth in the eighteenth century it bore little resemblance to the Arabic and Greek world of the eleventh. In looking to the classic or formative age of the Islamic experience of the Asians who dominate contemporary Islam, we must look to this fascinating era of plurality and expansion.

4 Kenneth Chase, *Firearms: A global history to 1700* (Cambridge, 2003), p. 127.
5 These elements are illuminatingly discussed in John Darwin, *After Tamerlane: The global history of empire since 1405* (New York, 2008), pp. 73–87.
6 'The Mongols, the Turks and the Muslim polity', in B. Lewis, *Islam in history: Ideas, people and events in the Middle East* (Chicago and La Salle, 1993), p. 205.

PART I

*

THE IMPACT OF THE STEPPE PEOPLES

I

The steppe peoples in the Islamic world

EDMUND BOSWORTH

I

Until the opening of the eleventh century CE, the eastern frontiers of the Islamic world had been fairly stable. The frontier region between what is now eastern Afghanistan and north-western India, essentially the Indus Valley, still remained fluid, and was now to form the springboard for Muslim expansion further into India under the Ghaznavids and Ghūrids. To the north-east, the ancient Iranian kingdom of Khwārazm on the lower Oxus and, above all, the equally Iranian Sāmānid emirate in Khurāsān and Transoxania, which flourished for almost two centuries, constituted bastions of Islamic faith and society against the peoples of the Eurasian steppes. See Map 1 for this chapter.

However, the years after *c.* 1000 CE witnessed for this region an irruption of peoples from the steppe and forest lands beyond these Islamic outposts of Khwārazm and Transoxania, first of Turks and then, in the second half of the twelfth century, of Mongols and Turco-Mongols in the shape of the Qara Khitay and then, after 1217, of Chinggis Khan's hordes. New ethnic elements were thus injected into the eastern Islamic world, hitherto dominated ethnically mainly by Iranians, and politically and culturally by a symbiosis of the Persian and Arabic literary and governmental traditions. These incursions from Inner Asia had effects on the older Islamic lands – in the case of the Mongol invasions, cataclysmic ones – but in the longer term, the perdurable, absorptive powers of Islamic religion and culture exercised their effects on the incomers.

Many of the Turks were recent converts to Islam when they arrived on the north-eastern margins of the Islamic world, and the pagan elements among them gradually followed suit. The Mongol Western Liao or Khitan, who arrived in Transoxania and eastern Turkistān in the middle decades of the twelfth century and became known to the Muslims as the Qara Khitay, retained their own animist and Buddhist beliefs but were content to leave their Muslim vassal rulers and subjects with the free and unimpeded exercise of their own cult (see below, p. 70). The Mongols of Chinggis and his family were initially hostile, at times strongly so, towards their Muslim subjects, but by *c.* 1300 the Mongol Ilkhanids of Persia had become Muslim and the process was repeated, rather more slowly, among the Chaghadayids of western and eastern Turkistān and the Golden Horde of the western Inner Asian steppes in the course of the fourteenth century.

In the religio-cultural sphere, Islamic society probably absorbed without difficulty a certain amount of extraneous influences; and certain syncretistic, even heterodox, elements have been discerned in the activities of certain Sufi orders in Transoxania and the adjacent steppelands, and in those of the dervish orders which came to flourish in the lands of the Rūm Saljuqs and those of the tribal chiefs, the *beyliks*, in Anatolia (see below, pp. 54–5). The Perso-Islamic governmental tradition, in which older Iranian ideas of kingship had been grafted on to Islamic concepts of authority, elevated the sovereign to a high position above his subjects, with his power buttressed by the support of a professional army, often a standing one and multiethnic in composition. This became speedily attractive to the Turkish and Mongol princes who installed themselves south of the Oxus river, if not to their tribal followers. Over the course of time, such rulers, above all the Turkish ones, began to assume a role of near-universal providers of military leaders and princes for virtually all the central and eastern Islamic lands, so that Turks could eventually be found ruling from Algiers through Syria and Yemen to Bengal: a phenomenon which waned only in the twentieth century with the bloodless disappearance of the Qājārs in Persia in 1925 and the line of Muḥammad ʿAlī in Egypt in 1953.

Turkish rulers thus fitted neatly into existing political and administrative structures, skilfully moulded by the Arab and Persian bureaucrats who had been responsible for the day-to-day running of the lands to which these Turks had recently fallen heir and whose services the Turks now eagerly sought. Only in parts of Central Asia and eastern Turkistān did the older tribal ways of life and tradition persist, explicable by the fact that the Turkish Qarakhānids and the Qara Khitay, who largely dominated these regions in the eleventh and twelfth centuries, remained resistant to the more authoritarian and hierarchical trends that came to dominate the lands south of the Oxus. The domination after *c.* 1040 of the Saljuq Turks, the line of Great Saljuqs in Persia and Iraq (with minor branches in regions like Anatolia, Syria and Kirmān), of their epigoni the atabegs, and then, after the Mongol interlude, of the various Turkmen lines controlling lands stretching from Anatolia to Afghanistan, had lasting effects, over the centuries, in the domains of demography, language and land utilisation, though these were not immediately felt (see below).

Within the lands which came to be dominated by the Saljuqs (i.e. the northern tier running from western Afghanistan through Khurāsān and north-western Persia to al-Jazīra, Syria, Armenia and Anatolia), the incoming Turkmens, above all composed of the various tribes of the Oghuz/Ghuzz, found that upland regions like northern Khurāsān, Azerbaijan, Arrān and the regions of the Zagros chain extending through Fārs towards the Persian Gulf shores, furnished especially attractive pasture lands for their herds of sheep and goats. These movements, and the resultant patterns of territorial occupation, set in train changes in land utilisation, demography and linguistic usage which were eventually wide-ranging. Lambton has noted that the initial effects of the influx of nomads were probably not extensive during the early Saljuq period, since their numbers were limited and their effects on the economy of Khurāsān, for instance, no worse than those of the Ghaznavid armies which had been trampling across it, to the distress of the local population. Given that the pastoralists now injected into the economies and industries of the towns dairy products, and wool and hides, their effects may even have been beneficial.[1] Bregel has attempted to estimate, from the sparse figures given in the sources, the numbers of Turkmens entering the Persian lands under the Saljuqs, and has agreed that these were comparatively modest.[2] It was most likely in post-Saljuq times, those of the Mongols and of the Timurids and the Turkmen dynasties which succeeded them, that the momentum of immigration into the Persian lands increased, with fresh waves of Turks involving continuing bands of Oghuz but also other tribal groups like the Qıpchaqs. The whole process had in fact already been set in train, for western Persia in particular, during the preceding Būyid times, by the system of *iqṭā*ʿs, grants of land by rulers for the support of their troops and civilian officials, which were theoretically revocable by the monarch. At first, these grants were made by the central administration from a position of strength, a means of reducing administrative expenses; but in practice, they could often not be reclaimed from over-mighty *iqṭā*ʿ holders, the *muqṭa*ʿs, and thus became

1 *EI*² 'Īlāt' (A. K. S. Lambton), vol. III, pp. 1098–9, and her chapter 'The *iqṭā*ʿ system and the Seljūqs', in A. K. S. Lambton, *Landlord and peasant in Persia: A study of land tenure and land revenue administration* (London, 1953), pp. 53–76; and Lambton, 'Aspects of Saljūq-Ghuzz settlements in Persia', in D. S. Richards (ed.), *Islamic civilisation 950–1150* (Oxford, 1973), pp. 105–25.

2 Yuri Bregel, 'Turko-Mongol influences in Central Asia', in Robert L. Canfield (ed.), *Turko-Persia in historical perspective* (Cambridge, 1991), p. 58.

virtually hereditary.[3] All these trends probably amounted to a long-term process of pastoralisation, although it is not clear whether existing agricultural lands, especially those in areas where dry farming was possible, were transformed into grassland or whether the nomads took over for their flocks lands which were marginal or until then underused, in which case the nomads were actually contributing to the economic development of these regions.

Whatever may have been the case here, in such areas as Arrān in eastern Transcaucasia; Azerbaijan; parts of Jibāl or north-western Persia such as the region of Khalajistān south-west of Tehran and west of Sāva; and the southern Zagros mountain region, later occupied by Turkmen tribes like the Qashqāʾī and the three Turkish tribes within the ethnically mixed Khamsa confederation, the concentration of Turkish elements, not least including the ruling elite there, was such that forms of the Turkish language took over in these areas and have largely prevailed there until the present day. In south-western Persia, a limited form of the nomadic way of life, or at least transhumance, persisted for the Qashqāʾī and other Turkish groups well into the twentieth century.

II

There had never been a completely hard-and-fast boundary between the Turkish peoples of Inner Asia on the one hand, and the lands of ancient Iranian civilisation such as Khwārazm, Sogdia and Farghāna on the other. The local princes of Sogdia had in the early second/eighth century allied with Turkish elements under their chiefs, the *yabghus* (*jabbūyas* of the Arabic sources), in the upper Oxus lands in order to oppose the advancing Arabs.[4] A century later, the ruler of the eastern provinces of the ʿAbbāsid caliphate, al-Maʾmūn, faced with a coming struggle for power with his brother, the caliph al-Amīn (r. 193–8/809–13), had to conciliate various potentates on the far eastern fringes of his governorate, described as the Yabghu, the Khaqan, the ruler of Tibet and the king of Kabul, some of whom at least must have been

3 Among a large literature on the *iqṭāʿ* at this time, see Cl. Cahen, 'L'évolution de l'iqtaʿ du IXe au XIIIe siècle', *Annales: Économies, Sociétés, Civilisations*, 8 (1953), pp. 25–52; A. K. S. Lambton, 'Reflections on the *iqṭāʿ*', in G. Makdisi (ed.), *Arabic and Islamic studies in honor of Hamilton A. R. Gibb* (Leiden, 1965), pp. 358–76; *EI*[2] 'Iḳṭāʿ' (Cahen); and a useful summary in D. O. Morgan, *Medieval Persia 1040–1797* (London, 1988), pp. 37–40.

4 H. A. R. Gibb, *The Arab conquests in Central Asia* (London, 1923), pp. 8–9; R. Grousset, *The empire of the steppes: A history of Central Asia* (New Brunswick, NJ, 1970), pp. 116–20; *EIr* 'Jabbuya. ii. In Islamic sources' (C. E. Bosworth).

themselves Turks or rulers over Turkish peoples.[5] From the caliphate of al-Ma'mūn (r. 198–218 / 813–33) and that of his brother and successor al-Muʿtaṣim (r. 218–27 / 833–42), Turks from the steppes formed an increasing element of slave soldiers (*ghilmān, mamālīk*) at the side of the remnants of the old Arab free *muqātila* and the Khurāsānian guards of the first ʿAbbāsids.[6] The Sāmānid emirate grew rich on the slave trade from the steppes, with markets at places like Isfījāb, Nakhshab and Bukhārā, and the *amīrs* exacted transit dues at the Oxus crossings for slaves forwarded to the caliphal heartland for military or domestic purposes.[7] The Arab geographers and compilers of 'road books' from the later third / ninth century onwards now began to differentiate between various tribes of the Turks; Ibn Khurradādhbih (wrote in the later third / ninth century) mentions Kimek, Türgesh, Qarluq, Toghuz-Oghuz, Kirghiz, Qıpchaq and Khazars. By *c.* 1050, the detailed account of Turkish peoples given by the Ghaznavid author Gardīzī in his history shows that Muslim knowledge of these peoples of the deep steppes, and even of Finno-Ugrian and Mongol peoples of the forest zone to their north, was quite extensive.[8]

Hence the coming of the Qarakhānids into the settled lands of Sāmānid Transoxania at the end of the tenth century CE may not have appeared to local Muslims of say Samarqand or Bukhārā as a cataclysmic event, an irruption of savage barbarians from beyond the imagined Inner Asian defensive wall against the Qur'ānic Gog and Magog. The precise ethnic origins of the Qarakhānids (a name coined, together with that of 'Ilek / Ilig Khans', by Western scholars in the nineteenth century; the contemporary Islamic sources simply call them 'the Khans', *al-Khāqāniyya, Khāniyān* or the *Āl-i Afrāsiyāb*, with a reference to the ruler of Tūrān, the foe of the Iranians, in Firdawsī's

5 al-Ṭabarī, *Ta'rīkh al-Rusul wa 'l-mulūk*, ed. M. J. de Goeje *et al.*, 15 vols. (Leiden, 1879–1901), vol. III, pp. 815–16, Eng. trans. M. Fishbein, *The History of al-Ṭabarī*, vol. XXXI: *The war between brothers* (Albany, 1992), pp. 71–2. The question whether there was any substantial infiltration of Turks into the borderlands of what became the Sāmānid emirate during the first three or four centuries of Islam has been much discussed but without any conclusive results; cf. Bregel, 'Turko-Mongol influences', pp. 54–8.

6 Among an extensive literature on this very important trend of medieval Islamic military history, see the works of David Ayalon, Patricia Crone, Daniel Pipes, etc., surveyed in Matthew S. Gordon, *The breaking of a thousand swords: A history of the Turkish military of Samarra (AH 200–275 / 815–889 CE)* (Albany, 2001), pp. 6–8 and passim; also EI^2. 'Ghulām. i. The caliphate. ii. Persia' (D. Sourdel and C. E. Bosworth).

7 See the geographers Ibn Ḥawqal and al-Maqdisī, cited in C. E. Bosworth, *The Ghaznavids: Their empire in Afghanistan and eastern Iran, 994–1040* (Edinburgh, 1963), pp. 208–9.

8 See the information on specific tribes in Peter B. Golden, *An introduction to the history of the Turkic peoples* (Wiesbaden, 1992), pp. 189ff.

Shāh-nāma) and their early history are shrouded in mystery, and various suggestions have been put forward. We can put aside the old view, recently revived by certain modern Chinese historians, that they stemmed from the Uighurs, who were originally located in what is now Mongolia and after 840 in eastern Turkistān. Much more feasible is the hypothesis of Omeljan Pritsak, that the Qarakhānid ruling house came from the tribal group of the Qarluq, which included associated tribes like the Chigil, Yaghma, Arghu and Tukhsı; it seems likely that, in the later eighth century, the Qarluq, under their chief who had the title of Yabghu, were forced westwards by the Uighurs into the Semirechye or Yeti Su, 'the land of the seven rivers' in the Chu and Ili river valleys–Issik Kol lake region (what is now the northern part of the Kirghiz Republic and the south-easternmost part of the Kazakh Republic). They thus acquired neighbours on their west in the shape of another great tribal group which was to have a great future in the eastern and central lands of Islam, the Oghuz (in Arabic sources, Ghuzz). By the mid-ninth century the Qarluq lands stretched from the territory of the Oghuz in the west to the confines of Tibet in the east, and from the lands of the Kimek on the Irtysh river in the north to the northern frontiers of the Sāmānid emirate.[9]

It is the transition from this Qarluq grouping to that of the Qarakhānids of the later tenth century that is obscure. But on the evidence of Islamic sources, it does seem that the Qarluq chiefs had assumed the exalted title of qaghan/khan and by *c.* 950 had become Muslim, an event crystallised in what is perhaps a semi-legendary tale of the conversion of a Qarluq chief who later became supreme qaghan/khan of his people, Satuq Bughrā Khan, who assumed on his conversion the Muslim name of ʿAbd al-Karīm.[10] The Islamisation of the western part at least of the Qarluq seems to have followed, although this was probably a slow and piecemeal process, one probably reflected in the story given in the sources (but with what must have been gross exaggeration) that in

9 Omeljan Pritsak, 'Von den Karluk zu den Karachaniden', *Zeitschrift der Deutschen Morgenländischen Gesellschaft*, 101 (1951), pp. 270–87; Pritsak, 'Die Karachaniden', *Der Islam*, 31 (1953), pp. 21–2; Peter B. Golden, 'The Karakhanids and early Islam', in Denis Sinor (ed.), *The Cambridge history of early Inner Asia* (Cambridge, 1990), pp. 354–7; Golden, *An introduction*, pp. 196, 214–15.

10 A prime source here is the Mongol-period writer on the *ʿulamāʾ* and scholars of Central Asia, Jamāl Qarshī (*fl.* later seventh/thirteenth century), used by F. Grenard, 'La légende de Satok Boghra Khan et l'histoire', *Journal Asiatique*, ser. 9, 14 (1900), pp. 5–79; W. Barthold, *Zwölf Vorlesungen über die Geschichte der Türken Mittelasiens* (Berlin, 1935), pp. 73–8; Pritsak, 'Von den Karluk zu den Karachaniden', pp. 291–3; Jürgen Paul, 'Nouvelles pistes pour les études karakhanides', in Vincent Fourniau (ed.), *Études karakhanides*, Cahiers d'Asie centrale 9 (Tashkent and Aix-en-Provence, 2001), pp. 19–22.

349/960, about 200,000 tents of Turkish tribesmen became Muslim.[11] Over the ensuing decades, the Qarluq, despite their status as new Muslims, made depredations into the northern borders of the Sāmānid emirate, now increasingly enfeebled by dynastic quarrels, financial crises and the indiscipline and rebelliousness of the army commanders.

In 382/992 Bughrā Khan Hārūn or Ḥasan, the grandson of Satuq Bughrā Khan, temporarily occupied the Sāmānid capital of Bukhārā, without the sources mentioning any serious show of resistance by the populace, no doubt by now war-weary and willing to give a trial to anyone who promised a degree of peace and order.[12] The definitive takeover of Bukhārā came a few years later, in 389/999, when another member of the Qarakhānid family, the Ilig (Tkish. *éllig*/*élig* 'holder of a territory', i.e. one subordinate to the supreme Khan) Naṣr b. ʿAlī of Özkend in the Farghāna valley marched into it unopposed. A last member of the Sāmānid family was to fight on bravely for a few more years, but the political map of the north-eastern Iranian lands was now changed decisively. Naṣr divided up the Sāmānid dominions with one of the dynasty's former Turkish commanders, Maḥmūd, whose father Sebüktegin had established himself some twenty years previously at Ghazna in what is now eastern Afghanistan, laying the foundation of what was to become under Maḥmūd (r. 388–421/998–1030) the mighty Ghaznavid empire.[13] The Oxus became in effect the boundary between the two new powers, although at the outset the Qarakhānids coveted the rich province of Khurāsān, while Maḥmūd was later, in 408/1017, to add the ancient kingdom of Khwārazm on the lower Oxus to his extensive dominions.[14] Both these empires, directed by Turks, were to persist, with varying fortunes, for some two centuries, but evolved into very different types of state. The Ghaznavid sultans developed to a high degree the Perso-Islamic ideal of a despotic monarch elevated far above his subjects, with a sharp division in society of the ruler and his supporting military and bureaucratic apparatus over against a docile, tax-paying

11 Miskawayh, *Tajārib al-umam*, ed. and trans. H. F. Amedroz and D. S. Margoliouth, *The eclipse of the ʿAbbasid caliphate*, 7 vols. (Oxford, 1920–1), vol. II, p. 181, trans. vol. V, p. 196; Ibn al-Athīr, *al-Kāmil fi 'l-taʾrīkh*, 13 vols. (Beirut, 1385–7/1965–7), vol. VIII, p. 532.

12 For the attitude of the Bukhārān people and the religious leaders at this time, see Hilāl al-Ṣābiʾ, cited in W. Barthold, *Turkestan down to the Mongol invasion* (London, 1928), pp. 258–9, 267; Richard N. Frye, *Bukhara, the medieval achievement*, 2nd edn. (Costa Mesa, CA, 1997), pp. 147–8.

13 Barthold, *Turkestan*, pp. 257–67; Muḥammad Nāẓim, *The life and times of Sulṭan Maḥmūd of Ghazna* (Cambridge, 1931), pp. 30–2, 42–8; Frye, ch. 'The Sāmānids', in R. N. Frye (ed.), *The Cambridge history of Iran*, vol. IV: *The period from the Arab invasion to the Saljuqs* (Cambridge, 1975), pp. 157–60; Frye, *Bukhara*, pp. 142–9.

14 Barthold, *Turkestan*, pp. 275–9; Nāẓim, *Sulṭān Maḥmūd*, pp. 56–60.

populace.[15] Such a trend towards autocracy was to become the norm in much of the Persian and Indo-Muslim lands south of the Oxus over the next centuries, a process from which the Saljuq tribal leaders were not, as we shall see below, to be immune.

For the Qarakhānid khans in Transoxania, the Semirechye and the western part of eastern Turkistān as far as the Tarim basin, development was to be otherwise. The khans never attempted to build up the lands they controlled into a unitary state of any kind, far less into a hierarchical state directed by a Turkish military elite, as did their Ghaznavid rivals. Rather, the Qarakhānids remained a tribal confederation, with various members of the family, often at odds with each other, possessing winter seats in established urban centres like Balāsāghūn, Özkend, Bukhārā and Kāshghar. The assemblage of lands that they came to control was regarded by the Qarakhānids as a family possession, rather than that of a single, individual ruler. There was a complex network of subordinate princes and chiefs under the great khan or khans, for after *c.* 1040 the united khanate split into a western one, controlling Sogdia with its cities of Bukhārā and Samarqand, and an eastern one, controlling the Semirechye and Eastern Turkistān with two capitals, Balāsāghūn (until the entry of the Qara Khitay into Sogdia in 536/1141) and Kāshghar, with Kāshghar latterly the sole capital. For a few decades, which cannot be closely delimited but which extended up to *c.* 609/1212f. and the expansionism of the Khwārazm Shāhs, there was a further line of khans in the Farghāna valley. Throughout Qarakhānid history, family members often held appanages, some quite limited in extent. Turkish names (many of animals or birds, perhaps reflecting an original totemistic significance of these) and titles (held side by side with Islamic ones) usually changed as people moved up the hierarchy of ruling power, creating great problems for anyone trying to construct a genealogical stemma of the dynasty or lists of individual rulers and their regnal dates. Given the very limited range of Islamic historical and literary sources, the legends on the numerous coin emissions of the Qarakhānids are of prime importance, and recent advances in our knowledge here have mainly stemmed from this type of evidence, adduced mainly by such Russian scholars as E. A. Davidovich, B. D. Kochnev and M. Fedorov, utilising coin hoards that have come on the market since the break-up of the Soviet Union in 1991.[16]

15 Barthold, *Turkestan*, pp. 291–2; Bosworth, *The Ghaznavids*, pp. 48–97; Frye, *Bukhara*, pp. 156–7.

16 On the territorial extent of the Qarakhānid lands, see B. D. Kochnev, 'Les frontières du royaume des Karakhanides', in Fourniau (ed.), *Études karakhanides*, pp. 41–8. On the

Within the towns and cities controlled by the Qarakhānids, we know of a certain amount of court life and of the existence of cultural circles, out of which arose significant monuments of early Turkish Islamic literature. The didactic poem, the *Qutadgu bilig*, 'Knowledge that brings happiness', was written by Yūsuf Khāṣṣ Ḥājib, an author who stemmed from Balāsāghūn but who in 462/1069f. completed his work at Kāshghar for the khan of the eastern branch there; and although Maḥmūd Kāshgharī compiled his great dictionary of the Turkish language at Baghdad (begun in 464/1072), he came from the Semirechye and had connections with the Qarakhānid ruling house.[17] The khans were clearly not gross barbarians. One of the rulers of the western branch, Shams al-Mulk Naṣr b. Ibrāhīm (d. 472/1080), built extensively at his capital Bukhārā, reconstructing the great mosque there after it had been burnt down and building a palace for his line outside the citadel of Bukhārā which he called Shamsābād and which had gardens and an enclosed parkland (*quruq*) for game and wild beasts. His brother Khiḍr Khan (r. 472–?479/1080–?1086) added to the complex of Shamsābād; the latter's son Aḥmad (r. ?479–88/?1086–95) built a new palace (*sarāy*) at Jūybār with elaborate gardens and a water supply for them, which a continuator of Narshakhī's local history of Bukhārā says was the centre of government at Bukhārā for thirty years; and Arslan Khan Muḥammad b. Sulaymān (r. 495–524/1102–30) had new palaces and baths constructed and built a new great mosque.[18]

Nevertheless, it seems that the Qarakhānids spent much of their time outside these urban centres, remaining in close touch with their tribal followers and aiming to stay attuned to their needs and aspirations, hence nomadising with them during the spring and summer months. Such contact was a necessity for them, since they apparently chose not to employ a professional army built up round a military slave nucleus but to utilise their fellow tribesmen when military necessity arose. A corollary of not having an

complexity of Qarakhānid onomastics and titulature, see Pritsak, 'Die Karachaniden', pp. 23–4. The present rapid evolution of our knowledge of their titulature and genealogy means that the section on the dynasty in C. E. Bosworth, *The New Islamic dynasties: A chronological and genealogical manual* (Edinburgh, 1996), pp. 181–4 no. 90, already needs correcting and updating; see Kochnev, 'La chronologie et la généalogie des Karakhanides du point de vue de la numismatique', in Fourniau (ed.), *Études karakhanides*, pp. 49–75.

17 See *EI*². 'Al-Kāshgharī, Maḥmūd b. al-Ḥusayn b. Muḥammad' (G. Hazai), 'Ḳutadghu bilig' (A. J. E. Bodroligeti) and 'Yūsuf Khāṣṣ Ḥādjib' (R. Dankoff).

18 Narshakhī, *Tārīkh-i Bukhārā*, ed. Mudarris Riḍawī (Tehran, n.d. [1939]), pp. 35–6, 60–1, Eng. trans. R. N. Frye, *The history of Bukhara* (Cambridge, MA., 1954), pp. 29–30, 50–2; cf. Barthold, *Turkestan*, pp. 100, 103, 319–20.

expensive standing army was that the expenses of running the state were low. Life in the urban centres went on little changed from Sāmānid times, with the religious classes retaining their power, so that influential hereditary lines like the *ṣadrs* or supreme Ḥanafī religious leaders in Bukhārā of the Āl-i Burhān could flourish under Qarakhānid and then Qara Khitay overall political control during the sixth/twelfth and early seventh/thirteenth centuries.[19] The local Iranian landed classses, the *dihqāns*, probably enjoyed a resurgence of power in Transoxania under the light yoke of the Qarakhānids. Narshakhī's continuator says that taxes were everywhere lightened when the Turks supplanted the Sāmānids; the fragmented authority that the Qarakhānids were content to exercise now reversed the trends under the Samanids towards state centralisation.[20]

When they first came into the Islamic lands, the number of Qarluq and other tribesmen in the Qarakhānids' following was probably not large, but elements, such as the Qıpchaq and Qanghlı, who had moved into the western Inner Asian steppes when first the Qarluq and then the Saljuqs had moved southwards into the Islamic lands, were gradually attracted into the Qarakhānid lands. The influx of Qıpchaq certainly accelerated under the Anūshteginid Khwārazm Shāhs (see below, p. 59), who recruited them extensively for their armies. In the absence of specific information, we can only assume that many of these newcomers to the major sedentary regions of Central Asia, that is, Khwārazm, Transoxania and Farghāna, remained nomadic in lifestyle, but some process of sedentarisation must gradually have taken place, contributing to an ethnic and linguistic turcisisation process in what had been originally the outer Iranian lands, *l'Iran extérieur* (the process in eastern Turkistān must have begun much earlier, in the period of Uighur domination there).[21] Persian was to retain its prestige as the media for cultural, intellectual and religious life, as it has done in the Central Asian cities almost till the present day, but the general population became more and more ethnically mixed, a trend accelerated by the great Turco-Mongol population movements of the thirteenth century onwards. Turkish ethnicity and language thus became preponderant; the indigenous Middle Iranian language of Khwārazm died out completely by the end of the fourteenth century, and Sogdian and other Iranian tongues of the eastern

19 See on these *ṣudūr*, Pritsak, 'Āl-i Burhān,' *Der Islam*, 30 (1952), pp. 81–96; *EIr* 'Āl-e Borhān' (C. E. Bosworth).
20 *Tārīkh-i Bukhārā*, p. 39 (with the text here corrected by Frye), trans. Frye, p. 33 and n.
21 Bregel, 'Turko-Mongol influences', pp. 56, 59–60.

Transoxanian fringes and Pamirs region survive today only as small, vestigial remnants.[22]

The history of the Qarakhānids' two centuries of existence is bound up, in the eyes of the Muslim historians, with their relations to neighbouring powers, and, especially, with those two that controlled the adjacent province of Khurāsān, the Ghaznavids and then the Saljuqs, and, in the sixth/eleventh century, especially with the Anūshteginid Khwārazm Shāhs and the Qara Khitay, until their demise on the eve of the Mongol invasions. Accordingly, the history of the western branch of the Qarakhānids is better known than that of the eastern one.[23] The sources have little to say on the internal political and social history of the khanates beyond adverting to internal dynastic disputes and tensions between the khans and the religious classes. In the course of these dissensions, an exemplar of Muslim rulers, Tamghach Khan Ibrāhīm (on whom see below, p. 32), executed an imam, Abu'l-Qāsim Samarqandī; and as result of family disputes and intrigues of the *'ulamā'* against him, Shams al-Mulk Naṣr's nephew Aḥmad b. Khiḍr, was eventually judicially murdered at Samarqand in 488/1095.[24] The sources also record various military forays of the khans northwards into the steppes, as far as the Manghıshlaq peninsula to the east of the Caspian Sea, in order to subdue recalcitrant tribesmen. Thus Arslan Khan Muḥammad b. Sulaymān led regular campaigns into the steppes, presumably against pagan Qıpchaqs, and brought back numerous slave captives, gaining the title of *Ghāzī*.[25]

The Ghaznavids' relations with the western Qarakhānids were not in general harmonious. Despite the formal division of the Sāmānid territories in 389/999, the khans coveted the rich province of Khurāsān, and in 396/1006 the Ilig Naṣr's forces invaded and occupied Nīshāpūr before retreating on

22 See *EIr* 'Chorasmia. iii. The Chorasmian language' (D. N. MacKenzie); *EI*² Suppl. 'Īrān. iii. Languages (d) Kh^{w}ārazmian, (e) Sogdian and Bactrian in the early Islamic period' (MacKenzie and N. Sims-Williams); J. R. Payne, 'Pamir languages', in R. Schmitt, *Compendium linguarum iranicarum* (Wiesbaden, 1989), pp. 417–44.

23 There is as yet no detailed monograph on the Qarakhānids, and the materials for this hardly exist. Hence one must have recourse to the relevant sections in Barthold, *Turkestan*, pp. 268ff., 305–22, 353–5, 364–6; Pritsak, 'Die Karachaniden' (political and dynastic framework only); Reşat Genç, *Karahanlı devlet teşkilâtı (XI. yüzyıl) (Türk hâkimiyet anlayışı ve Karahanlılar* (Istanbul, 1981) (internal structure and administration of the khanates); *EI*² 'Ilek-Khāns or Ḳarakhānids' (C. E. Bosworth); Golden, 'The Karakhanids and early Islam', pp. 343–70; E. A. Davidovich, 'The Karakhanids', in M. S. Asimov and C. E. Bosworth (eds.), *History of civilizations of Central Asia*, vol. IV: *The age of achievement: AD 750 to the end of the fifteenth century*, part 1: *The historical, social and economic setting* (Paris, 1998), pp. 119–43.

24 Muʿīn al-Fuqarā' Aḥmad b. Muḥammad, *Kitāb-i Mullāzāda*, cited in Barthold, *Turkestan*, p. 313, and Ibn al-Athīr, vol. X, pp. 243–4, cited in *Turkistān*, pp. 316–18.

25 Bundārī, *Zubdat al-nuṣra*, ed. M. T. Houtsma, in *Recueil de textes relatifs à l'histoire des Seljoucides*, vol. II (Leiden, 1889), p. 264.

Sultan Maḥmūd's return from India in 398/1008.[26] It became Maḥmūd's policy to encourage internal rivalries and dissidence within the Qarakhānid house. His acquisition of Khwārazm in 407/1017, bringing to an end the line of Ma'mūnid shahs there, enabled him to turn the flank of the khans. A particular thorn in the sultan's flesh was the ruler in Bukhārā and Samarqand, ʿAlī b. Bughrā Khan Hārūn or Ḥasan called ʿAlītegin (d. 425/1034), hence Maḥmūd allied with his more distant brother and rival, Qadır Khan Yūsuf of Kāshghar and Khotan, whom he met personally near Samarqand in 416/1025. The sultan sent a punitive expedition into Transoxania which drove out ʿAlītegin to the outer steppelands, and he negotiated marriage alliances between his children and those of Qadır Khan Yūsuf. Maḥmūd did not, however, envisage overthrowing ʿAlītegin in order to replace him by Qadır Khan Yūsuf as ruler of a much stronger, unified Qarakhānid kingdom. ʿAlītegin returned, and it was left to Maḥmūd's son and successor Masʿūd (r. 421–32/1030–41) to send an army into Sogdia in 423/1032 against ʿAlītegin and his Turkmen auxiliaries led by members of the Saljuq family. The fighting was indecisive, and the Ghaznavid army had to extricate itself with some difficulty. After ʿAlītegin's death, his sons carried on the struggle against Masʿūd, allying with the sultan's rebellious governor in Khwārazm Hārūn b. Altuntash.[27]

Masʿūd managed to secure control, exercised through rulers who were his vassals, of the principalities north of the upper Oxus of Chaghāniyān, Wakhsh and Khuttal. However, the Ghaznavid position here came under pressure in the late 420s/1030s from a new Qarakhānid foe, whom the Ghaznavid historians Gardīzī and Bayhaqī know by his totemistic name of Böritegin 'wolf-prince', but who was to have a more glorious future as Tamghach Khan Ibrāhīm, son of the Ilig Naṣr. Ibrāhīm crushed the sons of ʿAlītegin and secured the western khanate for himself, ruling in Transoxania for nearly thirty years till 460/1068 or shortly afterwards as a ruler distinguished, as several anecdotes in the collection of the later literary anthologist ʿAwfī relate, for his great piety and justice and for his solicitude regarding the welfare of his subjects (see further, below, pp. 47–8).[28]

26 ʿUtbī, *al-Kitāb al-Yamīnī*, Gardīzī, *Kitāb Zayn al-akhbār*, Bayhaqī, *Tārīkh-i Masʿūdī* and Ibn al-Athīr, cited in Barthold, *Turkestan*, pp. 272–3, and Nāẓim, *Sulṭān Maḥmūd*, pp. 48–52.
27 Gardīzī, Bayhaqī and Ibn al-Athīr, cited in Barthold, *Turkestan*, pp. 275–85, 294–8, and Nāẓim, *Sulṭān Maḥmūd*, pp. 52–60; Golden, 'The Karakhanids', pp. 362–5.
28 Barthold, *Turkestan*, pp. 311–13, citing Ibn al-Athīr and ʿAwfī's collection of anecdotes, the *Jawāmiʿ al-ḥikāyāt*.

After the victory of the Saljuqs over the Ghaznavid army at Dandānqān in 431/1040 (see below, p. 37), the external history of the western branch of the Qarakhānids becomes to a considerable degree intertwined with that of the Saljuqs, this linkage of fortunes including various marriage links between the two great powers, and it is to this last dynasty that we must now turn.

III

The Saljuq family sprang from the Oghuz tribal group of the Turks.[29] This was an anciently attested people of Inner Asia, mentioned by the Byzantine historians as the *Ouzoi*; in the Orkhon inscriptions as a component of the tribes making up the Eastern Turk empire, the *Oghuz*; and in Khazarian Hebrew as the *Turk* and in Rus' sources like the *Nestor Chronicle* as *Torki*. The actual name derives from a Turkish root *ōgh/uq* denoting a kinship group. They seem to have been a loose assemblage of related clans rather than a unified grouping, with constituents identified by numerals, such as the *Üch Oghuz* 'Three Tribal Groupings', *Toquz Oghuz* 'Nine Groupings', etc. After the disintegration of the Eastern Turk empire in 744, the Oghuz moved south-westwards from Mongolia, so that by the tenth century they were the western neighbours of the Qarluq group in the Eurasian steppelands.[30]

A prime source on their status and nature in the early tenth century, just before they began to be affected by Islam, is the caliphal envoy Aḥmad b. Faḍlān's account of his journey to the court of the recently Islamised king of Bulghār on the middle Volga in 309–10/921–2. He travelled through the lands of the Oghuz on his journey from Khwārazm, passing to the north of the Caspian Sea and crossing rivers like the Emba and the Ural. The Oghuz whom he met were at a low cultural level, animistic shamanists, living wretchedly and wandering 'like straying wild asses'. He met certain of their leaders, whose titles recur later in the Islamic history of the Saljuqs. Their chief was the Yabghu, bearer of the Orkhon Turkish title which had passed to the Oghuz when the chiefs of the Qarluq assumed the grander title of qaghan/khan (a title which the Oghuz and then the Saljuqs were never to arrogate to

29 The spelling Saljuq represents what is, linguistically, a hybrid convention. Islamic tradition (and Syriac authors borrowing from it) writes *s.l.jūq*, with back vowels; Kāshgharī's orthography in the *Dīwān lughāt al-turk* shows, however, that he read it with front vowels, i.e. Seljük. See Barthold, *Zwölf Vorlesungen*, p. 101; Golden, *An introduction*, p. 217.

30 See Golden, *An introduction*, pp. 205ff.

themselves), and his deputy the Külerkin or Kūdherkīn; the army leader, the *ṣāḥib al-jaysh*, held the title of Sü-bashı or Sü-begi; there was a subordinate commander called the Lesser Yınal; and there was another commander, the Ṭarkhan.[31] It is soon after this time that we first encounter the term *Türkmen* to denote the south-western Turks, whereas the Turks of the more easterly Qarluq group were simply called Turks. In *c.* 370/980 the geographer al-Maqdisī speaks of 'two frontier posts against the *Turkmāniyyūn*' in the region of Isfījāb on the middle Syr Darya; these had become converts to Islam 'out of fear' but had clearly not given up their old predatory habits.[32] In the next century, *Türkmen* comes to be used exclusively for the Oghuz followers of the Saljuqs, as by the Ghaznavid historians Gardīzī and Bayhaqī in their accounts of the overrunning of Khurāsān and then by the Saljuq vizier Niẓām al-Mulk in his 'mirror for princes', the *Siyāsat-nāma* (see on this, below, pp. 50–1) for the tribal followers of the Great Saljuq sultans who had remained nomads in Persia and the lands further west.

On the evidence of the Muslim historians and geographers, the Oghuz were already in contact with the borders of the Islamic lands in Khwārazm and Transoxania, often as raiders but also as traders and, increasingly, as auxiliary troops in the service of various of the Muslim powers there. They were clearly a loose, disorganised grouping, with the component clans pursuing their own interests, as indeed they continued to do when involved in the politics and warfare of Muslim Transoxania in the first decades of the fifth/eleventh century and as individual members of the Saljuq family did when they overran Ghaznavid Khurāsān. The Yabghu had no supreme authority over all the Oghuz, and the Yabghu of the the first years of the fifth/eleventh century, whose winter capital was at Jand on the lower Syr Darya, became completely sidelined by the vigorous and pushing Saljuqs (see below).

It is towards the middle of the tenth century that we learn something about the origins of the Saljuq family, who belonged to the Qınıq clan or sub-group (among some twenty-two to twenty-five of these named by Kāshgharī and other sources), and together with the Qayı and Bayandur apparently one of the leading clans of the group.[33] A prime source for Saljuq beginnings is an

31 *Riḥla*, ed. and Ger. trans. A. Z. V. Togan, *Ibn Faḍlāns Reisebericht* (Leipzig, 1939), text pp. 15–17, trans. pp. 28–31, cf. Excursus 33–6; Fr. trans. Marius Canard, 'La relation du voyage d'Ibn Fadlân chez les Bulgares de la Volga', *Annales de l'Institut d'Études Orientales de la Faculté des Lettres d'Alger*, 14 (1956), pp. 76–9.

32 *Aḥsan al-taqāsīm*, ed. M. J. de Goeje (Leiden, 1906), p. 274; cf. Bosworth, *The Ghaznavids*, p. 214.

33 Cl. Cahen, 'Les tribus turques d'Asie occidentale pendant la période seljukide', *Wiener Zeitschrift für die Kunde des Morgenlandes*, 51 (1948–52), pp. 179–80; Golden, *An introduction*, pp. 207–9.

anonymous *Malik-nāma* (so-called in imitation of the *Shāh-nāma*?), probably written for the prince Alp Arslan b. Chaghrı Beg just after 451/1059, now lost but known from extracts in later historians such as Ṣadr al-Dīn al-Ḥusaynī, Ibn al-Athīr, Barhebraeus and Mīrkhwānd. The ancestor of the family, Duqaq, known as Temür Yalıgh 'Iron bow' (bows and arrows being symbols of power among the Oghuz) from his courage and strength, and his son Saljuq were both in the service of the Oghuz Yabghu, with the latter holding the office of Sü-bashı, but relations became strained, with the ambitious Saljuq and his family challenging the Yabghu's authority.[34]

According to al-Ḥusaynī, Duqaq had opposed the Yabghu's plans to raid the Islamic lands, but this is clearly an attempt to push back in time the family's adoption of Islam and show them as motivated by the true light of faith.[35] It was more likely towards 382/992 that the family became Muslim, having moved from the inner steppes to Jand, whither they had expelled the Yabghu's representative. Saljuq's sons are found with Old Testament names like Mīkā'īl, Isrā'īl, Mūsā, etc., possibly the results of earlier contacts back in the steppes with Khazar Judaism or with Nestorian or Melkite Christianity. The hostility between the two branches of the Oghuz was to last into the 1040s when the brothers Ṭoghrıl Beg Muḥammad and Chaghrı Beg Dāwūd b. Mīkā'īl b. Saljuq finally got the upper hand over the Yabghu Shāh Malik (see below, p. 39). From *c.* 375/985 Oghuz bands served as auxiliaries of the Sāmānids along the northern frontiers of the emirate, and in 382/992 Arslan Isrā'īl b. Saljuq was aiding the *amīrs* against Bughrā Khan Hārūn or Ḥasan when he temporarily occupied Bukhārā; it seems that this Saljuq leader had at some point arrogated to himself the ancient title of Yabghu in defiance of the original holder of the title.[36]

Over the next thirty years, the Saljuqs and their followers were found as condottieri in the service of the Qarakhānids and Ghaznavids, allying with whoever could promise plunder and pasture for their herds; they became particularly close to 'Alītegin, ruler in Transoxania (see above, p. 32). Towards the end of the second decade of the eleventh century a long-distance raid of Turkmens under Chaghrı Beg as far as Azerbaijan and the frontiers of Rūm

34 Cl. Cahen, 'Le Malik-Nameh et les origines seljukides', *Oriens*, 2 (1949), pp. 41–3; Bosworth, *The Ghaznavids*, pp. 219–20.

35 *Akhbār al-dawla al-saljūqiyya*, ed. Muḥammad Iqbāl (Lahore, 1933), pp. 1–2.

36 Cahen, 'Le Malik-Nameh', pp. 42–6; Bosworth, *The Ghaznavids*, pp. 220–3; C.E. Bosworth, 'The political and dynastic history of the Iranian world (AD 1000–1217)', in *The Cambridge history of Iran, Vol. V: The Saljuq and Mongol periods*, ed. J. A. Boyle (Cambridge, 1968), pp. 17–18.

or Anatolia is reported in some sources, but this date seems rather early and the story more probably refers to raids of some ten or more years later.[37]

The Ghaznavid conquest of Khwārazm in 408/1017 brought Sultan Maḥmūd into immediate proximity of the Oghuz of the surrounding steppes, at a time when movements in the eastern part of Inner Asia, on the borders of the Khitan state in Mongolia, had initiated a series of tribal migrations which ultimately put pressure on the Oghuz to move southwards to the fringes of Khurāsān. There now begin complaints from the people of the towns on the northern rim of Khurāsān, such as Nasā, Abīvard and Farāva, concerning Oghuz depredations. Hence in 418/1027 Maḥmūd despatched against them a powerful army which hurled the Turkmens back into the steppes to Dihistān and Balkhān Kūh, and westwards into Persia, where they were enrolled as auxiliaries by the Ghaznavid governor of Rayy and Jibāl and by the Kākūyid ruler of Iṣfahān, ʿAlāʾ al-Dawla Muḥammad, but proved a continual source of violence and instability there (it was these Turkmens whom the Ghaznavid historians call the "ʿIrāqī' ones, from their penetration of northern Persia, ʿIrāq-i ʿAjam or Persian Iraq). After ʿAlītegin's death in 425/1034, the Saljuqs, now headed by Ṭoghrıl Beg, entered the service of the Khwārazm Shāh Hārūn b. Altuntash until Sultan Masʿūd procured the latter's death, after which Masʿūd's new ally, Shāh Malik of Jand, defeated and scattered the Oghuz, driving them into Khurāsān but thereby making the security system there worse.

The sultan launched punitive expeditions against these Turkmens, but a surprise defeat of his army on the road to Nasā in 426/1035 compelled him to make formal grants of the northern Khurāsānian towns to Ṭoghrıl, Chaghrı and Mūsā Yabghu. Inevitably, these concessions only emboldened the Saljuq leaders to demand more. They complained in 428/1036 that the pastures allotted to them were inadequate, and sought a grant of Marv, Sarakhs and Abīvard, strategic and commercial centres that the sultan could not possibly surrender. The Turkmens, disorganised though they were, gradually wore down the professional armies of the Ghaznavids, ill-equipped for the highly mobile type of warfare required along the steppe

37 Cahen, 'Le Malik-Nameh', pp. 50–1 (denying the historicity of an expedition at this early date); İbrahim Kafesoğlu, 'Doğu Anadoluya Selçuklu akını (1015–21) ve tarihî ehemmiyeti', in *Fuad Köprülü armağanı* (Istanbul, 1953), pp. 259–74, Eng. trans. Gary Leiser, in *Mésogeios/Méditerranée* (Paris), 25–6 (2005), pp. 27–47.

fringes; even if defeated in a pitched battle, the Turkmens could melt into the desert and re-form.[38]

The oasis towns of Khurāsān were suffering badly from Turkmen herds trampling their crops and from disruption of the caravan trade, were frustrated at the sultan's inability to protect them and were resentful of the heavy taxation he was requiring in order to keep his armies continuously in the field. They began to make the best of a bad job and to conclude local agreements with the Turkmens. Thus towards the end of 428/1037 the leading *ʿulamāʾ* and notables of Marv surrendered the city to Ṭoghrıl and Chaghrı on condition that the populace was not harmed. In 429/1038 the Saljuq leader Ibrāhīm Inal and then Ṭoghrıl entered Nīshāpūr and made an agreement with leading clerics and secular leaders; Ṭoghrıl sat down formally upon Masʿūd's throne (the sultan subsequently had this profaned object broken up) and seems to have been able to restrain the mass of Turkmens from plundering. Such occupations were only temporary, and the arrival of Ghaznavid troops caused the Turkmens to withdraw. But time was running out for Masʿūd. His army, heavily encumbered with war matériel, including elephants, but with totally inadequate supplies of food, fodder and water, set out from Sarakhs for Marv in spring 431/1040. At Dandānqān it was totally defeated, in one of the decisive battles of eastern Islamic history, by some 16,000 Turkmens. Ṭoghrıl was proclaimed *amīr* of Khurāsān on the battlefield and renewed his contacts with the caliph in Baghdad, sending an envoy to secure formal confirmation of his territorial acquisitions, since the whole of Khurāsān speedily passed under Saljuq control. The dispirited Masʿūd fled to Ghazna, and fearing (unnecessarily, as it proved) that his capital would fall to the Saljuqs, withdrew in the next year to India, where his troops, now devoid of confidence in him, mutinied and deposed him, soon after which he was killed. The Ghaznavid empire was to survive for over another century, but in a truncated form and now essentially oriented towards India.[39]

IV

The Saljuqs had for long had a great fear of Sultan Masʿūd and the Ghaznavid war machine, but this ended with the Dandānqān victory, which not only gave

38 Cahen, 'Le Malik-Nameh', pp. 55–60; Bosworth, *The Ghaznavids*, pp. 241–3; Bosworth, 'The political and dynastic history', pp. 18–20.

39 Cahen, 'Le Malik-Nameh', pp. 61–4; Bosworth, *The Ghaznavids*, pp. 243–68 (with a translation of the detailed passage in Bayhaqī on the first Saljuq occupation of Nīshāpūr); Bosworth, 'The political and dynastic history', pp. 20–3.

them control of Khurāsān but also laid open to them the lands further west. Northern and western Persia were at this time in the last phase of what V. Minorsky called 'the Daylamī interlude' of medieval Persian history.[40] Among the powers involved here, the Ziyārids were ruling in the lowland Caspian provinces of Gurgān and Ṭabaristān. *The amīrs* had latterly been vassals of the Ghaznavids, but after 433/1041f. the Saljuq became their overlords; in the middle decades of this century, the Ziyārid ruler ʿUnṣur al-Maʿālī Kay Kāwūs was the author of a celebrated 'mirror for princes', the *Qābūs-nāma*, named after his illustrious forebear Qābūs b. Vushmgīr. Other princes of the central Elburz region, such as the Iranian Bāvandid Ispahbadhs and the Daylamī Musāfirids of the region of Daylam itself, at the south-western corner of the Caspian Sea, were too inaccessible in their mountain fastnesses to be dislodged by the Saljuqs, and in general remained as tribute-paying vassals of the Great Saljuqs while these last continued dominant in western Persia.[41] There were various lines of Kurdish chiefs in Azerbaijan and the Zagros regions of Kurdistan and Luristān, but the main powers that the Saljuqs were to come up against were those of the Daylamī Būyids and Kākūyids. The heyday of the Būyid confederacy had been in the later fourth/tenth century under such forceful rulers as Fakhr al-Dawla of Rayy and ʿAḍud al-Dawla of Fārs and Iraq, but when the Saljuqs appeared in western Persia, the dynasty was in a state of some confusion and decay. The northern emirate, based on Rayy, had already been annexed by Maḥmūd of Ghazna in 420/1029, but now passed almost immediately under Saljuq control. However, the Būyids still had extensive lands in western and southern Persia, that is, Jibāl, Fārs, Kirmān and Iraq; the last of these, Jalāl al-Dawla (r. 416–35/1025–44), had styled himself *Amīr al-Umarāʾ* 'Supreme Commander' and in 429/1037f. assumed the ancient Sasanid title (regarded by strict Muslims as blasphemous) of *Shāhanshāh* 'King of Kings'[42]. Although

40 See his *La domination des Daïlamites*, Publications de la Société des Études iraniennes (Paris, 1932), repr. in *Iranica, twenty articles/Bīst maqāla-yi Minorsky* (Tehran, 1964), pp. 12–30.

41 For these petty dynasties, see Bosworth, 'The political and dynastic history', pp. 24–32, and for their chronology, Bosworth, *The New Islamic dynasties*, pp. 148–9, 164–7 nos. 71, 80–1.

42 For the Būyids of Persia, see EI^2 'Buwayhids' (Cl. Cahen); and Bosworth, 'The political and dynastic history', pp. 36–7; for those of Iraq, H. Busse, *Chalif und Grosskönig. Die Buyiden im Iraq (945–1055)* (Beirut and Wiesbaden, 1969) and J. J. Donohue, *The Buwayhid dynasty in Iraq 334H/945 to 403H/1012: Shaping institutions for the future* (Leiden and Boston, 2003); and for the chronology of the various branches of the dynasty, see Bosworth, *The New Islamic dynasties*, pp. 154–7 no. 75. For a special study of Jalāl al-Dawla's act of *lèse-majesté* towards the caliph, see H. F. Amedroz, 'The assumption of the title Shâhanshâh by Buwaihid rulers', *The Numismatic Chronicle*, ser. 4, 5 (1905), pp. 393–9.

theoretically a vassal of the Būyids, the able Daylamī ruler in Iṣfahān and Ḥamadān, ʿAlāʾ al-Dawla Muḥammad, called in the sources Ibn Kākūya (d. 433/1041), was able to pursue a skilful policy of self-interest, making peace with Ṭoghrıl when Saljuq pressure became overwhelming, which enabled his descendants to survive modestly within the Great Saljuq empire till well into the sixth/twelfth century.[43]

The two outstanding members of the Saljuq family, Ṭoghrıl Beg and Chaghrı Beg, seem to have made an informal division of power regarding the lands which were falling into their hands. Khwārazm was taken over when Ṭoghrıl led a campaign into it in 433/1041f. or shortly thereafter. The old enemy of the Saljuqs, and ally of Sultan Masʿūd of Ghazna, the original Yabghu Shāh Malik of Jand, did not long enjoy his dominion over Khwārazm. He was now defeated and driven out of the capital Gurgānj. It seems that he was unable to return to his old centre of Jand (presumably because it was now in alien hands, those of the Oghuz or Qıpchaq) and had to flee southwards through Khurāsān and eventually to Makrān, where he met his death.[44] Henceforth Chaghrı was in overall charge of the eastern lands, whose core was Khurāsān and its dependencies, while other members of the Saljuq family, Ertash and Mūsā Yabghu or Bıghu, campaigned in adjacent parts of Afghanistan, including Sīstān, which now, under its local princes, the so-called Maliks of Nīmrūz, became a Saljuq vassal state.[45]

Ṭoghrıl assumed responsibility for Saljuq expansion into the western lands, a task which he now set about putting into practice. After Maḥmūd of Ghazna's seizure of the Saljuq Arslan Isrāʾīl in 418/1027 (see above, p. 36), his Turkmen followers, the 'ʿIrāqī' ones, had scattered westwards and had become a turbulent element in the politics and society of western Persia. In the 1030s, the Būyids, Kākūyids, Ghaznavids and various local Kurdish princes all endeavoured to employ Turkmen bands against their opponents and rivals. As a result, the whole region became chronically insecure. The rich cities of western Persia were obvious targets for the Turkmen marauders, and it is around this time that town walls were built or rebuilt as a protective measure, for example at Iṣfahān

43 See Bosworth, 'Daylamīs in central Iran: The Kākūyids of Jibāl and Yazd', *Iran, Journal of the British Institute of Persian Studies*, 8 (1970), pp. 73–95, and for their chronology, Bosworth, *The New Islamic dynasties*, pp. 160–1 no. 78.

44 Ibn al-Athīr, vol. X, p. 506, under year 434; Ibn Funduq, *Tārīkh-i Bayhaq*, ed. Aḥmad Bahmanyār (Tehran, 1317/1938), p. 51, with the year 433 for Shāh Malik's flight; Omeljan Pritsak, 'Die Untergang des Reiches des Oğuzischen Yabğu', in *Fuad Köprülü armağanı*, p. 408.

45 C. E. Bosworth, *The history of the Saffarids of Sīstān and the Maliks of Nimruz (247/861 to 949/1542–3)* (Costa Mesa and New York, 1994), pp. 376–86.

by Ibn Kākūya and at Shīrāz by the Būyid *amīr* of Fārs, Khūzistān and Kirmān 'Imād al-Dīn Abū Kālījār.[46] The lands beyond were also affected, especially after the Saljuq leaders had imposed their control on the cities of Persia, as did Ibrāhīm Inal at Rayy and then Hamadān in 1033–4 and 1041–3, driving many of the "Irāqī' Turkmens into northern Iraq and al-Jazīra and even as far as Armenia and Diyārbakr in south-eastern Anatolia. It seems that Ṭoghrıl and the other leaders were already trying to exercise some control over their more anarchic followers, and that these last were resisting this. Later, it would become something like official policy of the Great Saljuq sultans to deflect uncontrollable elements to the farther western fringes, such as northern Syria, Armenia and Anatolia. In particular, Azerbaijan, an area particularly fragmented, politically, ethnically and confessionally, now became a concentration point for Turkmens attracted inceasingly from Inner Asia once the Ghaznavid and Būyid defences in northern Persia had crumbled. As noted above, Azerbaijan had upland pasture grounds suitable for the nomads' herds, and there were old-established traditions of *ghāzī* warfare there, aimed at such Christian powers as Armenia and Georgia, which the Turkmens, once they became Muslims of sorts, could adopt. It is these factors which came together and set in train the process whereby Azerbaijan became what it is today, ethnically and linguistically, Turkish (see above, p. 24). From the second half of the fifth/eleventh century onwards, Turkmens also infiltrated into Anatolia and founded there in the course of the following century *ghāzī* states like those of the Shāh-i Armanids, Dānishmendids, Mengüjekids and Saltuqids; but before these came into being, a member of the Saljuq family, Sulaymān b. Qutlumush or Qutalmısh, had already laid the foundations for the most important and longest-lasting of all of them, the Saljuq sultanate of Rūm (see below, p. 45).

Ṭoghrıl's immediate need, however, was gradually to establish Saljuq authority over northern and western Persia. This was facilitated by Ibn Kākūya's death. Under Saljuq suzerainty, his two sons Farāmurz and Garshāsp succeeded him in Iṣfahān and Hamadān respectively,[47] while Ṭoghrıl made Rayy his own base, until in 442/1050f. the Saljuq leader took over Iṣfahān from Farāmurz (who had tried to keep on good terms with both the Saljuqs and the Būyids of Fārs and Khūzistān), and moved his capital

46 For Shīrāz, see Ibn al-Balkhī, *Fārs-nāma*, ed. G. Le Strange and R. A. Nicholson (London, 1921), p. 133; and for Iṣfahān, Mufaḍḍal b. Sa'd Māfarrukhī, *Kitāb Maḥāsin Iṣfahān*, ed. Jalāl al-Dīn Ṭihrānī (Tehran, 1312/1933), pp. 81, 100–1, and Nāṣir-i Khusraw, *Safar-nāma*, ed. Muḥammad Dabīr-Siyāqī (Tehran, 1335/1956), pp. 122–3, Eng. trans. W. M. Thackston Jr (New York, 1986), p. 98.

47 Bosworth, 'Daylamīs in central Iran', pp. 81–2.

thither from Rayy.[48] The Būyids themselves were still powerful enough for Ṭoghrıl to treat diplomatically with ʿImād al-Dīn Abū Kālījār in 439/1047f. Ṭoghrıl promised to restrain Ibrāhīm Inal and the "ʿIrāqī' Turkmens from raiding Būyid territory, and a marriage alliance was arranged between a young Būyid prince and one of Chaghrı Beg's daughters.[49] This did not, however, prevent Chaghrı's son Qavurd raiding through Khurāsān into the Būyid province of Kirmān and taking it over, the beginning of a petty Saljuq principality which was to last for over a century (see below); this was in 440/1048, the point at which Abū Kālījār died before he could take steps to recover his lost province. Fārs now fell into the hands of the Shabānkāraʾī Kurdish chief Faḍlūya, who in 454/1062 killed the Būyid *amīr* there and ended the dynasty's line there, only in turn to bring down on himself Saljuq intervention and annexation of the province.[50]

The other surviving Būyid emirate, that in Iraq, was centred on Baghdad, a city now wracked with the violence of Turkish soldiery and of rival Sunnī and Shīʿite factions. As early as 426/1035 the Saljuq chiefs crossing the Oxus into Khurāsān (see above, p. 36) had styled themselves *Mawālī Amīr al-Muʾminīn* 'Clients of the Commander of the Faithful', conscious of the symbolic value of such claimed ties, and Ṭoghrıl had opened up diplomatic relations with the ʿAbbāsid caliphs when first he occupied Nīshāpūr. Although the Turkmens who later overran Anatolia were to contain within their ranks many heterodox religious elements, including messianic Shīʿite ones, it clearly suited Ṭoghrıl now to pose as protector of the caliph and defender of Sunnī orthodoxy as against a Būyid Shīʿite *Amīr al-Umarāʾ* there and Turkish commanders who were in touch with the Ismāʿīlī Fāṭimids, deadly enemies of the ʿAbbāsids, at the other side of the Syrian desert. In later times, pro-Saljuq historians would attempt an ideological justification for the coming of the Turks and their rule over so much of the Islamic world by adducing Ṭoghrıl's deliverance of the caliph from the Būyids and the Saljuqs' subsequent leadership in the *jihād* or holy war against the Byzantines in Anatolia.[51]

Ṭoghrıl marched into Baghdad in 447/1055, deposed the last Būyid *amīr* there, al-Malik al-Raḥīm Khusraw Fīrūz, restored order in the city and had the

48 Bundārī, p 9; Ibn al-Athīr, vol. IX, pp. 507–8.
49 Ibn al-Athīr, vol. IX, p. 536.
50 H. Bowen, 'The last Buwayhids', *Journal of the Royal Asiatic Society* (1929), pp. 233–43; Bosworth, 'The political and dynastic history', pp. 44–7, 49.
51 Cf. the words of Rāwandī (who dedicated his history to one of the Rūm Saljuq sultans), *Rāḥat al-ṣudūr*, ed. Muḥammad Iqbál (1921), pp. 17–18, cited in Bosworth, 'The political and dynastic history', p. 15.

khuṭba, with the caliph al-Qā'im's permission, made for himself.[52] Whether Ṭoghrıl's removal of the Būyids was regarded by him as a crusade to release the caliphs from Shīʿite tutelage is unclear; in the ensuing decades, the ʿAbbāsids were to find that the weight of Saljuq authority was at times as heavy as that of the Būyids had been. It is undoubtedly true that Ṭoghrıl's close advisers when he appeared in Iraq were all strong Sunnīs, such as the ʿAmīd al-Mulk Abū Naṣr Kundurī, and convinced Ḥanafīs in legal rite; when Ṭoghrıl gave Kundurī permission to curse the Shīʿa in the *khuṭba* of Khurāsān, the latter also added cursing of the Ashʿarīs, who were in general Shāfiʿīs in legal rite. Ṭoghrıl was not actually received by al-Qā'im until 449/1058, when he was awarded grandiloquent titles, including that of *Malik al-Mashriq wa 'l-Maghrib* 'King of East and West,' robes of honour in ʿAbbāsid black, and two crowns signifying rule over the Arabs and the ʿAjam. He seems to have glorified in his role as deliverer of the caliph, allegedly enthroning himself wiith great pomp and majesty.[53] However, it took much browbeating on Ṭoghrıl's part, including threats of cutting off finance, before the caliph would agree to an ʿAbbāsid princess, one of his own daughters, marrying a barbarian Turk, a situation which was soon resolved anyway since Ṭoghrıl died in 445/1063 before the marriage could be consummated.[54]

The appearance of Ṭoghrıl in Iraq with a powerful war machine which was clearly now going to be the dominating force in the caliphal heartlands, posed problems for the theologians and jurists of the time. These scholars had been able to ignore on religious grounds the realities of other leading powers of the age: for them, the Būyids had been military commanders only, and Shīʿites to boot (probably Zaydīs); the Fāṭimids styled themselves caliphs (and were in reality far more glorious rulers than the feeble ʿAbbāsids) but as Ismāʿīlī Shīʿites were beyond the religious pale. Now, as mentioned above, Ṭoghrıl vaunted his Sunnī credentials, so that the theorists had somehow to accommodate the sultan, as holder of secular power, alongside the caliph, theoretically the wielder of all power under God but, in practice at this time, the holder of a largely moral and religious influence only. The jurists of the later fifth/eleventh and sixth/twelfth centuries had reluctantly to wrestle with this

52 Busse, *Chalif und Grosskönig*, pp. 119–21.

53 Bundārī, pp. 13–14; Ḥusaynī, pp. 17–18; Pseudo-Ẓahīr al-Dīn Nīshāpūrī, *Saljūq-nāma*, Eng. trans. K. A. Luther (Richmond, 2001), pp. 41, 43; Ibn al-Athīr, vol. IX, pp. 633–4; Barhebraeus, *Chronography*, vol. I, Eng. trans. E. A. Wallis Budge (Oxford, 1932), pp. 201–2, 211–12.

54 Bosworth, 'Political and dynastic history', pp. 45–6, 47–9; Busse, *Chalif und Grosskönig*, pp. 121–7.

problem of reconciling these two elements within the secular Islamic world, seen for example in the works of Abū Ḥāmid al-Ghazālī (d. 505/1111) on this question, in particular his 'mirror for princes', the *Naṣīḥat al-mulūk*, written in Persian towards the end of his life.[55]

Whilst Ṭoghrıl was engaged in the west, Chaghrı Beg, from his capital at Marv, was consolidating Saljuq rule in the east. There were for a while fears of a Ghaznavid revanche to recover Khurāsān, under the vigorous Sultan Mawdūd b. Mas'ūd (r. 432–?440/1041–?1048), in alliance with the Qarakhānid ruler of Transoxania, Tamghach Khan Ibrāhīm (see above, p. 32). But Mawdūd's anti-Saljuq coalition fell apart on his death, and on his accession in 451/1059, the new Ghaznavid sultan Ibrāhīm b. Mas'ūd negotiated a peace settlement with Chaghrı which recognised the status quo in the east, with the upper Oxus principalities under Saljuq control but eastern Afghanistan, beyond Tirmidh and Balkh, left to the Ghaznavids.[56]

Thus at the deaths of Chaghrı in 452/1060 and of Ṭoghrıl three years later, there stood a vast Saljuq empire comprising Persia, Khwārazm and much of Iraq, and this had been accomplished without undue violence and disturbance, at least by the standards of the age, to the economies of those lands. The two brothers had worked in harmony, but the maintenance of the empire now demanded strong, unified rule, especially as there were strong centrifugal forces at work in the state. There had already been sporadic revolts by members of the Saljuq family who cherished an older Turkish, patrimonial view of the assemblage of the lands as the shared heritage of senior family members, that is, a 'collective sovereignty' rather than the view that supreme direction of the state was the personal property of a single, forceful individual. It was usually the eldest and most militarily prestigious member of the family who succeeded in enforcing his claim to the throne. However, this never precluded other ambitious family members from putting forward their claims, and there were always plenty of Turkmen malcontents on whom they could rely in a bid for power; these Turkmens were in any case unenamoured of the prospect of a strong centralised government which would entail encroachments on their personal freedom and, above all, result in the imposition of taxation.[57] Such challenges to

55 See G. Makdisi, 'Les rapports entre Calife et Sultân à l'époque saljûqide', *International Journal of Middle East Studies*, 6 (1075), pp. 228–36; A. K. S. Lambton, *State and government in medieval Islam: An introduction to the study of Islamic political theory: The jurists* (Oxford, 1981), pp. 103–29.

56 C. E. Bosworth, *The later Ghaznavids: Splendour and decay: The dynasty in Afghanistan and northern India, 1040–1186* (Edinburgh, 1977), pp. 25–30, 51–5; Bosworth, 'The political and dynastic history', pp. 49–53.

57 See Golden, *An introduction*, pp. 220–1.

the sultans' authority were to continue all through the life of the Great Saljuq sultanate, culminating in the role of the Oghuz nomads of northern Afghanistan and the upper Oxus region in procuring the downfall of Sanjar b. Malik Shāh in 548/1153 (see below).

A succession crisis ensued at the childless Ṭoghrıl's death, but the most able of Chaghrı's sons, Alp Arslan, was raised to the throne by a combination of several of the slave commanders of the Saljuq army, whose interests lay in the building up of a powerful, paid, professional army, and a statesman of genius, Alp Arslan's personal vizier, Abū ʿAlī al-Ḥasan Niẓām al-Mulk, forestalling an attempt by Ṭoghrıl's vizier Kundurī to install a palpably less suitable candidate.[58] The Khurāsānian official Niẓām al-Mulk, an archetypal representative of the Perso-Islamic administration but also a convinced proponent of orthodox Sunnī faith, was to guide the destinies of the Great Saljuq empire for the two reigns which were to form its apogee, those of Alp Arslan (r. 455–65/1063–73) and his son Malik Shāh (r. 465–85/1073–92), and it was not for nothing that Ibn al-Athīr styled these thirty years *al-dawla al-niẓāmiyya* (see further on Niẓām al-Mulk, below, pp. 49–51).

V

Alp Arslan's decade of rule, buttressed by Niẓām al-Mulk's guiding hands, saw expansion into new areas of the west, with unruly Turkmens directed into Armenia, Transcaucasia and Anatolia, and the consolidation of the sultanate in its heartlands of Persia and Iraq. In 456/1064 the sultan, accompanied by his son Malik Shāh and the vizier Niẓām al-Mulk, led an expedition into Arrān and Transcaucasia. He captured the old Armenian capital of Ānī and also Kars, and in a second campaign of 460/1068 ravaged Georgia and occupied Tiflis, although the capable king of Georgia, Bagrat IV (r. 1027–72), managed to retrieve the situation and retain control of his realm.[59]

For some time, Turkmen raiders had been operating within Byzantine Anatolia, although without any concerted plan or unified direction; at times they were even used by the Greek emperors as auxiliary troops (*foederati*) against other Turkmen bands. In the years 459–60/1067–8 Caesarea/Kayseri, Amorium and Iconium/Konya were sacked by the Turkmens, attacks which

58 Bundārī, pp. 26, 28; Ibn al-Athīr, vol. X, p. 29.

59 Ḥusaynī, pp. 34–8, 43–6; V. Minorsky, *Studies in Caucasian history* (London, 1953), pp. 64–7.

menaced Byzantine lines of communication and supply through the Taurus mountains and Cilicia to their possessions and their armies operating in northern Syria from such centres as Malaṭya, Antioch and Edessa. Hence in 462/1070, despite a probable truce that he had made with Alp Arslan, the emperor Romanus Diogenes (r. 1068–71) sent an army into Anatolia and northern Syria which menaced the Muslim emirate of Aleppo. In the spring of the next year, Romanus assembled a vast army at Erzerum and marched into Armenia, but was confronted by Alp Arslan's forces, decisively defeated by them at Manzikert/Malāzgird on a tributary of the upper Euphrates, and himself captured. The sultan was preoccupied with operations in Syria aimed at the Fāṭimids, and was content to release Romanus on payment of a ransom and some slight adjustments of territory. Alp Arslan's victory made him a Muslim hero, but one can infer from his release of the emperor that the sultan was not consciously leading a crusade and had no definite plan to overthrow Byzantine authority in Anatolia.[60]

Nevertheless, Alp Arslan's success here meant that most of Armenia now passed definitively into Muslim hands, with the Georgians remaining the only significant Christian power in the region. The perceived weakness of Byzantine defences in eastern Anatolia opened the floodgates for further Turkmen raids there. It is soon after the date of the Manzikert battle that we hear of the activities of the four sons of Qutlumush/Qutalmısh b. Arslan Isrāʾīl, the sultan's cousin, one of whom, Sulaymān, was to found the Saljuq sultanate of Rūm in central and western Anatolia.[61] These Turkmen raids were essentially acts of private enterprise rather than Saljuq state-directed ones. Both Alp Arslan and Malik Shāh were hostile towards the family of Qutlumush, since the ambitious Qutlumush had fruitlessly rebelled against Alp Arslan immediately after the latter's accession in 456/1064, dying then in mysterious circumstances.[62]

Events within the heartlands of the sultanate continued to concern Alp Arslan. Qutlumush's bid for power had been quashed, but it soon became clear that the sultan's own elder brother, Qara Arslan Qavurd, was dissatisfied with his circumscribed dominion over the province of Kirmān in south-eastern

60 Bundārī, pp. 38–44; Ḥusaynī, pp. 46–53; Pseudo-Ẓahīr al-Dīn Nīshāpūrī, trans. Luther, pp. 48–53; Ibn al-Athīr, vol. X, pp. 65–7; Cl. Cahen, 'La campagne de Mantzikert d'après les sources musulmanes', *Byzantion*, 9 (1934), pp. 621–5; Cahen, *Pre-Ottoman Turkey* (London, 1968), pp. 66–72; C. Hillenbrand, *Turkish myth and Muslim symbol: The battle of Manzikert* (Edinburgh, 2007), pp. 3–25.

61 Cahen, *Pre-Ottoman Turkey*, pp. 73–4.

62 Bundārī, pp. 28–9; Ḥusaynī, pp. 30–2; Ibn al-Athīr, vol. X, pp. 36–7; Barhebraeus, pp. 226–7.

Persia. The origins of Saljuq rule there are rather obscure, and the opening pages of the otherwise valuable local historian Muḥammad b. Ibrāhīm's history of the Kirmān Saljuqs are unfortunately missing. The Būyids had recovered Kirmān from a short-lived Ghaznavid occupation in the early 1030s, but the Ghaznavid debacle at Dandānqān allowed Oghuz raiders to move southwards through Khurāsān and harry the towns of Kirmān, the capital Bardasīr being attacked in 434/1042f. Kirmān remained in Būyid hands for a few more years, but just before the death in 440/1048f. of the *amīr* of Fārs, Khūzistān and Kirmān, Abū Kālījār, Bardasīr passed into Qavurd's hands.[63] There thus began some 140 years of Saljuq rule there under a line of Qavurd's descendants until this was extinguished by the irruption into Kirmān of unruly bands of Oghuz tribesmen in the later sixth/twelfth century. Under Saljuq rule, Kirmān was to enjoy a period of considerable prosperity. Qavurd, who reigned for thirty-four years, is said to have built caravanserais and cisterns along the trade routes, to have protected the people of the agricultural oases by directing his tribal followers to pasture their herds out on the steppes and granting them specific *iqṭā*ʿs, and to have led a punitive expedition against the predatory Kūfichī and Balūch mountaineers of south-eastern Kirmān and adjacent Balūchistān.[64] The province seems to have benefited by trade from India and beyond which had entered such Persian Gulf ports as Tīz, Sīrāf and Hormuz and now passed through Kirmān to Khurāsān and Central Asia. Chaudhuri has remarked that the prosperity at this time of cities like Kirmān (as Bardasīr now becomes styled) and Yazd is only explicable by income derived from artisanal activity and from services supplied to caravans of merchants passing through the region; the local historian mentions communities of foreign merchants, including Rūmīs and Indians, in a trading colony near the town of Jīruft, in the mid-sixth/twelfth century.[65]

Qavurd had accepted Alp Arslan's succession in 455/1063, but three years later rebelled against him. This required the sultan to lead an army into Kirmān against him (459/1067) which subsequently penetrated into Fārs, and, in a further campaign of 461/1069, the Shabānkāra'ī chief Faḍlūya, who

63 Afḍal al-Dīn Kirmānī, *ʿIqd al-ʿulā li 'l-mawqif al-aʿlā*, ed. ʿAlī Amīrī Nā'inī (Tehran, 1311/1932), pp. 68–9; Muḥammad b. Ibrāhīm, *Tārīkh-i Saljūqiyān-i Kirmān*, ed. M. T. Houtsma, in Recueil de textes relatifs à l'histoire des Seljoucides, vol. I (Leiden, 1886), pp. 2–3; Ibn al-Athīr, vol. IX, pp. 510–11, 547; Erdoğan Merçil, *Kirman Selçukları* (Istanbul, 1980), pp. 11–26.

64 Muḥammad b. Ibrāhīm, pp. 4–5, 6–8, 11–12; Merçil, *Kirman Selçukları*, pp. 27–68.

65 K. N. Chaudhuri, *Trade and civilisation in the Indian Ocean: An economic history from the rise of Islam to 1750* (Cambridge, 1985), p. 56; Muḥammad b. Ibrāhīm, p. 49.

had seized control of Fārs after the demise of the Būyids, was defeated and subsequently killed in 464/1071f.[66]

Alp Arslan never visited Baghdad in person but was careful, through Niẓām al-Mulk's diplomatic contacts with the ʿAbbāsid caliph al-Qāʾim's own viziers, Ibn al-Muslima and then Fakhr al-Dawla Ibn Jahīr, to maintain his influence in the caliphal capital at a time when the ʿAbbāsids were beginning tentatively to assert their political power in Iraq after the long years of subordination to the Būyid *amīrs*, a development which was gradually to accelerate and to form the background for Saljuq-ʿAbbāsid relations over the next century or so. For the moment, thanks to the skill of Niẓām al-Mulk (whose daughter married Ibn Jahīr's son ʿAmīd al-Dawla), relations were generally cordial. In 458/1066 the sultan secured caliphal approval for his designation of his son Malik Shāh as *walī al-ʿahd* or covenanted heir, a step which placed Alp Arslan's vision of rulership firmly within the Perso-Islamic succession procedure of primogeniture (or, at least, choice of the ruler's most capable son) and outside the old Turkish one of succession by seniorate within the whole ruling family; and the seal was set on these good relations when in 464/1071f. Alp Arslan's daughter was married to al-Qāʾim's son and heir, the later caliph al-Muqtadī.[67]

On the eastern fringes of the Saljuq empire were two still formidable powers, the Qarakhānids and the Ghaznavids. The Ghaznavid sultan Ibrāhīm was in general content to maintain the *modus vivendi* arrived at in 451/1059 by himself and Chaghrı Beg (see above, p. 43); specific information is totally lacking here, but it is probable that Ibrāhīm concerned himself mainly with India during these years.[68]

The Ghaznavid realm was distant, and the Saljuq sultanate had obviously reached a logical and sensible frontier, running as it did southwards through the mountain regions of what is now Afghanistan; an army advancing beyond it would have faced serious strategic and logistical problems. Relations with the Qarakhānids, neighbours of the Saljuqs just across the Oxus, were more immediate and therefore more delicate. The Qarakhānid Tamghach Khan Ibrāhīm had built up a powerful and flourishing kingdom in Transoxania and Farghāna, achieving a reputation during his reign as an exemplary just ruler, careful of the interests of his subjects. He had a special care for the economic and financial stability of his kingdom. Among other currency reforms, he introduced a *muʾayyadī dirham* of a guaranteed standard against gold, thus

66 Bundārī, pp. 30–1; Ibn al-Athīr, vol. X, pp. 71–2.
67 Bundārī, pp. 36, 45, 46–7; Ibn al-Athīr, vol. X, pp. 50, 70–1.
68 Bosworth, *The later Ghaznavids*, pp. 51–2, 61–2.

facilitating internal trade, and when he conquered Farghāna, which had previously been part of the eastern Qarakhānid khanate, he incorporated this into the currency area of the western khanate.[69] Ibrāhīm had certainly shown himself a skilful and tenacious field commander in his struggles with rival members of the Qarakhānid family in Transoxania and against Masʿūd of Ghazna in the upper Oxus region (see above, p. 32). Alp Arslan, still at this time his father Chaghrı Beg's deputy, was the aggressor here in 453/1061, sending an expedition across the Oxus, and causing Ibrāhīm to send a delegation to the ʿAbbāsid caliph with protests about this unprovoked attack. A further aspect of Alp Arslan's concern for the lands beyond the Oxus and Syr Darya, the sources of irruptions into the empire by indisciplined Turkmens, was a campaign in 457/1065, soon after he had become sultan, from Khwārazm into the lower Syr Darya steppes, bringing into subjection the ruler (a Qıpchaq tribal chief?) of Jand and Sawrān and visiting at Jand the tomb of his ancestor Saljuq b. Duqaq; and a punitive expedition against the Qıpchaq that took him as far as the Manghıshlaq peninsula is also mentioned.[70]

But after these shows of force, Alp Arslan adopted a more pacific attitude towards the Qarakhānids, and a series of marriage alliances was negotiated. The sultan himself married the widowed daughter of Maḥmūd of Ghazna's old ally, Qadır Khan Yūsuf; one of his own daughters married Tamghach Khan Ibrāhīm's son and successor Shams al-Mulk Naṣr; and his son Malik Shāh, the future sultan, married another Qarakhānid princess, who eventually, as the formidable Terken Khātūn, gave birth to the short-reigned Saljuq sultan of 485–7/1092–4, Maḥmūd (I). Tensions nevertheless arose between Alp Arslan and Shams al-Mulk Naṣr in 465/1072 towards the end of the sultan's reign. He crossed the Oxus on a bridge of boats with an army alleged to number 200,000, but the campaign was cut short when he was assassinated by a castellan whom he had condemned to death, and Shams al-Mulk Naṣr was therefore able to take the offensive by seizing Tirmidh and temporarily occupying Balkh.[71]

Although he had not added any significantly increased amount of territory to the Saljuq empire, Alp Arslan left it in a stable condition, certainly the strongest power in the central and eastern Islamic lands. When he had made Malik Shāh his heir in 458/1066, he had distributed to various members of the Saljuq family governorships on the eastern fringes of the empire, in

69 Davidovich, 'The Karakhanids', pp. 128–9.
70 Ḥusaynī, pp. 40–1; Ibn al-Athīr, vol. X, p. 49; Barthold, *Turkestan*, pp. 311–14.
71 Ḥusaynī, pp. 53–4; Ibn al-Athīr, vol. X, pp. 73–4; Barthold, *Turkestan*, p. 314; Bosworth, 'The political and dynastic history', pp. 64–5.

Khwārazm, Ṭabaristān and eastern Khurāsān, as appanages. It would appear from this that he was still mindful of traditional obligations to his kinsmen but also that he viewed the central and western parts of his empire, which he kept firmly within his own hands, as the centre of gravity in the state, hence the most deserving of his personal control.

Malik Shāh's twenty years' reign is often regarded as the zenith of the Great Saljuq empire before a 'time of troubles' ensued under his fractious and squabbling sons, one which was in turn followed by a *de facto* division of the sultanate into a western part, comprising essentially Iraq and western Persia, and an eastern part embracing Khurāsān and its dependencies. Malik Shāh consolidated and in many ways surpassed the achievements of his father, and under him, the directly administered Saljuq empire stretched from al-Jazīra and northern Syria to Khwārazm and the Oxus, with protectorates of varying degrees of effectiveness over the Turkmen bands in Anatolia and the Qarakhānid lands in the extreme east; while in the south, the Fāṭimids were cleared out of southern Syria and most of Palestine and successful expeditions were undertaken within the Arabian peninsula as far as Yemen and al-Aḥsāʾ.

This was a truly impressive achievement for a monarch who died at the comparatively early age of thirty-seven, but it could not have been secured without guidance from the wise and experienced Persian vizier, Niẓām al-Mulk, whom Malik Shāh inherited from his father, whose service to the two Saljuq rulers amounted to some thirty years.[72] Words are attributed to him, uttered just before his assassination in 485/1092, in which he boasted, with truth, that the security and florescence of the realm was due as much to himself as to his master,[73] and in effect he acted as an atabeg (Tkish. 'father-commander') or tutor to Malik Shāh, although this title and the institution only came into general use in the following century, when various young Saljuq princes were provided with *ghulām* or slave commanders as guardians and tutors.[74]

Niẓām al-Mulk directed state policy mainly through the Great *Dīwān*, the *Dīwān-i Wazīr*, which might accompany the sultan's *dargāh* or court on his progresses and campaignings (and Niẓām al-Mulk not infrequently led military campaigns himself) but often remained in the capital Iṣfahān.

72 Pending the appearance of a biography of this outstanding figure from Professor Carole Hillenbrand, see A. K. S. Lambton, 'The internal structure of the Saljuq empire', in *The Cambridge history of Iran*, vol. V: *The Saljuq and Mongol periods*, pp. 264ff.; *EI*² 'Niẓām al-Mulk' (H. Bowen and C. E. Bosworth).

73 Words given in their fullest form in Ibn al-Athīr, vol. X, pp. 205–6, trans. in Bosworth, 'The political and dynastic history', p. 68.

74 See *EI*² 'Atabak' (Cl. Cahen).

Niẓām al-Mulk filled other government departments with his partisans and protégés. For him, as with Admiral 'Jackie' Fisher in Britain over eight centuries later, favouritism was the secret of efficiency. During his own lifetime, his numerous sons filled many strategic posts; he even attempted (in this instance, unsuccessfully) to impose his son, Muʾayyid al-Mulk ʿUbaydallāh, as the ʿAbbāsid caliph al-Muqtadī's vizier. After his death, the influence of his sons and of the *Niẓāmiyya*, the body of his supporters and partisans, remained significant almost till the end of the Great Saljuq sultanate, especially as it was widely believed that skills, such as administrative ones, descended hereditarily (in regard to Niẓām al-Mulk's sons, this belief was only partly justified).[75]

Niẓām al-Mulk aimed at providing the formal administrative infrastructure of a typical Perso-Islamic state, with an array of specialised *dīwāns*, for what was still basically a Turkish dynasty only two or three generations away from their steppe origins and retaining many of the customs and attitudes of Oghuz tribal society.[76] He also aimed at training up a corps of scholars and officials inculcated with an orthodox Sunnī Muslim education who would enable the Saljuq state to equal the intellectual attractiveness and the material splendours of the heretical Ismāʿīlī Shīʿite state of the Fāṭimids in Cairo. The famed madrasas or colleges that he founded in the cities of al-Jazīra, Iraq and Persia, the *niẓāmiyyas*, were not the first of their kind, nor was he the sole founder of such institutions in his own time, but he took especial care to recruit for them leading intellectuals of the age, such as the jurist Abū Isḥāq al-Shīrāzī (d. 476/1083), chosen for the Baghdad *niẓāmiyya* which opened in 459/1067, and he later brought the celebrated theologian and mystic al-Ghazālī to lecture there.

However, Niẓām al-Mulk was more than just a motivator and encourager of others. His own treatise on statecraft, the *Siyāsat-nāma*, completed in 484/1091 just before his death, really delineates an administrative and military ideal that he had failed to achieve during his own lifetime and of whose necessity he had not succeeded in convincing his Turkish masters. The nub of the problem was, how could the newer Perso-Islamic ideal of autocratic government, with its administrative apparatus designed to overawe subjects

75 For this last body, see EI^2 'Niẓāmiyya' (C. E. Bosworth).

76 For the Saljuq administrative structures, see Bosworth, 'The political and dynastic history', pp. 68ff., and Lambton, 'The internal structure of the Saljuq empire', pp. 203–82; Morgan, *Medieval Persia 1040–1797*, pp. 34–40; and for the vizierate specifically, Carla L. Klausner, *The Seljuk vezirate: A study of civil administration 1055–1194* (Cambridge, MA, 1973).

and keep them from rebelling, be grafted on to the ways of a line of Turkish chiefs sprung from the steppes and with attitudes still going back to nomadic life (from which Malik Shāh was only two generations away), in which the chief had to cherish and respect the interests of his fellow tribesmen, his only support?[77] Hence although Niẓām al-Mulk chides his Saljuq masters for not keeping up the apparatus of repression and intelligence-gathering practised by former rulers like the Būyids and Ghaznavids, he recognises that the sultans still needed to conciliate their still non-sedentarised Turkmen kinsmen and supporters and to satisfy their needs. For one direction in which the Saljuqs had gone along the road of earlier rulers within the governmental mainstream of the Islamic heartlands, was to recognise the need for a professional, paid body of troops at the side of their tribal followers. The norm was for such an army to be built round a nucleus of Turkish *ghulām* troops, but there were also contingents in the Saljuq armies of free troops recruited from various groups to be found within the empire and on its fringes and regarded as warlike, such as Arabs, Armenians and Greeks. Niẓām al-Mulk specially commends the use of Daylamīs, Khurāsānians, Georgians and Shabānkāra'ī Kurds.[78] It seems to have been Ṭoghrıl who first tried to throw off exclusive dependence on his Turkmen followers, and Alp Arslan certainly had several highly competent slave commanders, like the eunuch Savtegin (d. 478/1085). This *ghulām* campaigned in Arrān in 460/1068 and again in 468/1075, securing that region for the sultan and extinguishing the main line of the local dynasty, probably Kurdish in ethnic origin, of the Shaddādids of Dvin and Ganja, and then went on to serve Malik Shāh, being temporarily appointed governor of Kirmān after the suppression of Qavurd's revolt in 465/1073 (see below, p. 52). In the sixth/twelfth century, as the personal power of the Saljuq sultans became enfeebled, it was members of this corps of *ghulāms* who assumed power in various parts of the realm, such as the founders of the Aḥmadīlī and Eldigüzid lines of atabegs in Azerbaijan and that of the Salghurids in Fārs (see below, p. 73). Professional armies were, of course, expensive, and the Saljuq ones had to be maintained partly by land grants, *iqṭā*'s, but also by taxation. The sultans welcomed the access of personal power that such armies brought, but were conscious of the need not to antagonise their subjects, and especially the Turkmens (totally unused to paying taxes at all), by undue financial burdens; hence Malik Shāh's

77 See for evidence of Malik Shāh's concern for his Turkish tribal retainers (including, e.g., the giving of periodic feasts for them), Bosworth, 'The political and dynastic history', p. 79.
78 *Siyāsat-nāma*, ed. Harold Darke (Tehran, 1340/1961), p. 128, Eng. trans. Darke, *The book of government or rules for kings* (London, 1960), pp. 100–1.

periodic fits of economy, strongly opposed by Niẓām al-Mulk, when soldiers were discharged from the army during periods of peace.[79]

The events of Malik Shāh's reign show him as an energetic warrior whose sphere of operations ranged from the Mediterranean shores of Syria to eastern Turkistān.[80] He had first of all to crush opposition to his accession to his father's throne from members of his own family, for whom the concept of hereditary succession, which seemed now to be fixed in the descent of Chaghrı Beg, was by no means obvious or desirable. When Alp Arslan was killed on the banks of the distant Oxus, his brother Qavurd – who had proved his military and administrative skills by governing Kirmān for around a quarter of a century and who had behaved there like an independent sovereign, with such regal attributes as a ceremonial parasol (*chatr*), the use of the traditional *tamgha* or emblem of the Saljuqs and exalted honorific titles – considered that he, as the senior capable member of the family, had the superior right. The two claimants met outside Hamadān in 465/1073. Malik Shāh emerged the victor in a closely fought battle in which the support for Malik Shāh of his *ghulām* commanders and Arab and Kurdish, that is, non-Turkish, auxiliary troops was decisive. The defeated Qavurd was strangled with a bowstring, presumably to prevent the shedding of royal blood. Kirmān was given to Savtegin to govern, but eventually restored to Qavurd's sons. It seems that one of them, ʿImād al-Dawla Tūrān Shāh (r. 477–90/1085–97), extended his power over the neighbouring province of Fārs, for, subsequently, Malik Shāh's son Berk-yaruq sent a military expedition to recover it for direct Great Saljuq rule.[81]

Another potential challenger to the succession, Malik Shāh's brother Ayaz, conveniently died at this point, so the sultan was able to grant out appanages in eastern Khurāsān, including Herat, Balkh and Walwālīj, to various other Saljuq family members. One of these, a further brother of the ruler, Shihāb al-Dīn Tekish, was later, in 477/1084f., tempted to rebel in Khurāsān while Malik Shāh was campaigning at the other end of the empire in al-Jazīra; the sultan hastened across Persia and quelled the outbreak, blinding and imprisoning

79 Bosworth, 'The political and dynastic history', pp. 80–1.

80 An anecdote much quoted in the sources to show the geographical extent of Malik Shāh's power (see, e.g., Pseudo-Ẓahīr al-Dīn Nīshāpūrī, trans. Luther, p. 59) has Niẓām al-Mulk writing out a financial draft for the boatmen at the Oxus crossing which will be honoured from the finances of Antioch.

81 Muḥammad b. Ibrāhīm, pp. 12–13, 21–5; Bundārī, pp. 48–9; Ḥusaynī, pp. 56–8; Rāwandī, pp. 126–8; Ibn al-Athīr, vol. X, pp. 78–9, 239; İbrahim Kafesoğlu, *Sultan Melikşah devrinde Büyük Selçuklu imparatorluğu* (Istanbul, 1953), pp. 23–6; Bosworth, 'The political and dynastic history,' pp. 87–90.

Tekish.[82] The firmness of the sultan and Niẓām al-Mulk in dealing with internal opposition contrasts with the more lenient policy of Alp Arslan towards malcontents like these, but the displays of force had their required effect, and Malik Shāh faced no more challenges from within the Saljuq family for the rest of his reign.

Malik Shāh was now free to deal with the rival power of the Qarakhānids across the Oxus. As noted above (p. 48), at the time of his assassination Alp Arslan had been engaged in hostilities with the khan of Transoxania, Shams al-Mulk Naṣr. The temporary vacuum of power had allowed the khan to cross the Oxus and invade Tukhāristān. Once he was firmly on his throne, Malik Shāh came eastwards in 466/1073f., drove the Qarakhānids out of Balkh, captured Tirmidh and pushed on to the khan's capital at Samarqand. The latter was forced to sue for peace, especially as he seems to have been involved, around this time, with the rival, eastern branch of the Qarakhānids, the descendants of Qadır Khan Yūsuf of Kāshghar and Khotan.[83] This success enabled Malik Shāh to exert considerable influence within the western Qarakhānid lands, and a further opportunity for intervention presented itself in 482/1089. The then ruler in Samarqand, Aḥmad b. Khiḍr Khan, nephew of both Shams al-Mulk Naṣr and Malik Shāh's Qarakhānid wife Terken Khātūn, was at odds with the orthodox religious institution in his capital. The latter appealed to Malik Shāh, who invaded Transoxania again, captured Bukhārā and Samarqand, deposed Aḥmad Khan and deported him to the Saljuq capital Iṣfahān. He then marched onwards to the Semirechye, where at Özkend he received the homage of the Eastern Qarakhānid ruler Hārūn b. Sulaymān, who now agreed to place Malik Shāh's name in the *khuṭba* of his lands. Internecine disputes within the Qarakhānid confederation nevertheless continued. Malik Shāh had to intervene again and play an intercessory role, and at some unknown date he returned Aḥmad Khan to Samarqand (where he was later, in 488/1095, to be deposed and executed by the influential body of orthodox *ʿulamāʾ* there on the grounds that the khan was showing Ismāʿīlī sympathies). In this way, the eastern khanate for a short period, and the western khanate for well over half a century, became subject to the Saljuqs, with strong rulers like Malik Shāh and Sanjar often intervening to place their own candidates on the throne in Samarqand; some

82 Ḥusaynī, pp. 58, 61, 63–4; Ibn al-Athīr, vol. X, pp. 76, 92–3, 118–19, 137–8; Kafesoğlu, *Sultan Melikşah*, pp. 57–9; Bosworth, 'The political and dynastic history', pp. 90–1.
83 Ibn al-Athīr, vol. X, p. 92; Barthold, *Turkestan*, pp. 314–15; Pritsak, 'Die Karachaniden', p. 46; Bosworth, 'The political and dynastic history', p. 91.

Qarakhānid coins of this period acknowledge the Saljuq sultans, but whether this vassal status ever involved the payment of tribute is not known.[84]

Further south, but still on the eastern fringes of the empire, in Sīstān the Maliks of Nīmrūz also remained Saljuq vassals; joint operations of the Maliks and Saljuq commanders against the Ismāʿīlīs of Quhistān are mentioned towards the end of Malik Shāh's reign.[85] The Ghaznavid sultan Ibrāhīm b. Masʿūd tried unsucessfully to take advantage of the troubled events around Malik Shāh's succession and to recover his lost territories in Badakhshān and Tukhāristān, but Malik Shāh had to treat on equal terms with him. There were marriage links between the two great Turkish houses; Ibrāhīm's son, the future sultan Masʿūd III (r. 492–508 / 1099–1115), married successively daughters of Alp Arslan and Malik Shāh, the latter being Gawhar Khātūn, famed in Ghaznavid history as the *mahd-i ʿirāq* 'bride from western Persia'. Saljuq cultural influence seems to have been strong around this time; at some point the sultans formally adopted the Saljuq title of *al-Sulṭān al-Muʿaẓẓam* 'Highly Exalted, Supreme Sultan'.[86]

At the other end of the Saljuq empire, Azerbaijan and Arrān retained their importance as concentration points for Turkmen bands operating in the Caucasus region and in Anatolia. The line of Shaddādid *amīrs* of Ganja and Ānī was already in vassalage to the Saljuqs, but soon after Malik Shāh's accession his armies extinguished this branch of the family (see above, p. 51). The sultan campaigned personally in Georgia in 471 / 1078f. Kars was recaptured from the Georgians and Turkmen commanders penetrated to the Black Sea coast in Lazistan and threatened the Byzantine city of Trebizond (according to one report, temporarily capturing it). The whole of the Araxes-Kur basin of Arrān seems now to have been parcelled out as *iqṭāʿ*s for the Turkmens and their commanders.[87]

The sons of Qutlumush had arrived in Anatolia at the opening of Malik Shāh's reign. Turkmen bands operating under their general leadership were now overrunning much of Byzantine Anatolia; they were able to take advantage of succession disputes within the imperial family at Constantinople which

84 Narshakhī, p. 34, trans. Frye, p. 29; Rāwandī, pp. 128–30; Ibn al-Athīr, vol. X, pp. 171–5, 243–4; Barthold, *Turkestan*, pp. 316–18; Pritsak, 'Die Karachaniden', pp. 47–8; Kafesoğlu, *Sultan Melikşah*, pp. 119–23; Davidovich, 'The Karakhanids', pp. 130–1.

85 C. E. Bosworth, 'The Ismaʿilis of Qūhistān and the Maliks of Nīmrūz', in Farhad Daftary (ed.), *Medieval Ismaʿili history and thought* (Cambridge, 1996), p. 224.

86 Bosworth, *The later Ghaznavids*, pp. 52–6.

87 Cl. Cahen, 'La première pénétration turque en Asie-Mineure,' *Byzantion*, 18 (1948), p. 49; Minorsky, *Studies in Caucasian history*, pp. 67–8; *EI*[2] 'Shaddādids' (C. E. Bosworth).

continued there until Alexius Comnenus (r. 1081–1118) emerged victorious. During these internecine struggles of the Greeks, Turkmens were recruited as auxiliaries by the various contenders, with the result that Sulaymān b. Qutlumush's raiders reached the Sea of Marmara shores by 474/1081 and captured Nicaea/Iznik.[88] The beginnings of the future Saljuq sultanate of Rūm may be placed here, based on Konya which the sultan Masʿūd b. Qılıch Arslan (r. 510–52/1116–56) adopted as his capital. It seems unlikely, as future Rūm Saljuq historiography of the seventh/thirteenth century was to assert, that Malik Shāh formally invested Qutlumush's sons (whom he regarded with suspicion and even hostility) with Anatolia as an appanage. Their assumption during his reign of the title of *sulṭān* seems to have been a unilateral act and was probably regarded by the Supreme Sultan Malik Shāh as derogatory to his own position.

Within the central lands of the Great Saljuq sultanate, Malik Shāh's concern was to secure the provinces of al-Jazīra and Syria as buffers against Fāṭimid intervention there (although Fāṭimid power in these regions was waning by this time) and to bring under control local Arab and Kurdish principalities, some of which were Shīʿite in sympathy. Roving Turkmen bands were already operating there, laying the groundwork for what was to be a permanent Turkmen ethnic element in northern Syria and Iraq. At the opening of his reign, Malik Shāh sent his brother Tutush to hold Syria as an appanage. Tutush and the commander Artuq b. Ekseb of the Döger clan of the Oghuz (whose progeny, the Artuqids, were to found a long-enduring Turkmen emirate in Diyārbakr) secured southern Syria and northern Palestine, and Artuq campaigned in eastern Arabia as far as al-Aḥsāʾ, attacking Carmathian sectaries there (469/1076f.).[89] The Kurdish Marwānids in Diyārbakr were extinguished by a joint campaign of the caliphal vizier Fakhr al-Dawla Ibn Jahīr and Saljuq commanders (477–8/1084), and the Arab ʿUqaylids of northern Syria and al-Jazīra were humbled, with the sultan campaigning there personally in 478–9/1085–6. The great cities of the region – Mosul, Aleppo, Antioch and Damascus – all thus came under Saljuq control.[90] Tutush's personal ambition was to end in his death in 488/1095 when he challenged the succession of his nephew Berk-yaruq (see below), but his sons Duqaq and Riḍwān managed, in the troubled decades after Malik Shāh's death, to establish a short-lived Saljuq sultanate of Syria, with themselves and their

88 Cahen, 'La première pénétration turque', pp. 35–6; Cahen, *Pre-Ottoman Turkey*, pp. 73–8.
89 Ibn al-Athīr, vol. X, pp. 111, 183–4; Kafesoğlu, *Sultan Melikşah*, pp. 31–9.
90 Kafesoğlu, *Sultan Melikşah*, pp. 40–59; Bosworth, 'The political and dynastic history', pp. 97–9.

sons in Damascus and Aleppo repectively, as theoretical vassals of the Great Saljuq sultans further east.[91]

Malik Shāh's relations with the ʿAbbāsids were at best correct and often hostile. Since Alp Arslan's time there had been in Baghdad a Saljuq *ghulām* governor, Gawhar-āyīn, as *shiḥna* or military commander for the maintenance of the sultan's authority and interests in the capital and in the wider region of Iraq.[92] Baghdad was at this time a maelstrom of hostile factions – Sunnī Ḥanbalīs, Shīʿites in their respective quarters of the city and *ʿayyārs*, bands of urban desperadoes, everywhere. The sultan tended to leave relations with the caliphs to Niẓām al-Mulk, and only came first to Baghdad after his Syrian campaign, that is, in the mid-1080s. Niẓām al-Mulk's contacts with the caliphate were, of course, conducted with the caliph's own viziers, which substantially meant with the Banū Jahīr.[93] Relations oscillated between frostiness and cordiality, the latter when Niẓām al-Mulk established a friendly relationship with ʿAmīd al-Dawla Ibn Jahīr, sealed by marriage alliances between the two families, and leading up to the events of 480/1087, when the caliph al-Muqtadī married one of Malik Shāh's daughters.[94] A son was speedily born, the short-lived Abū'l-Faḍl Jaʿfar, who became the sultan's favourite. But thereafter, relations rapidly deteriorated, and just before his death the sultan was planning to make Baghdad instead of Iṣfahān his winter capital, and extensive building operations were undertaken during the winter of 484–5/1091–2. When Niẓām al-Mulk was in 485/1092 murdered, ostensibly by Ismāʿīlī assassins, the sultan threw off all restraint and resolved to expel the caliph from his ancestral capital. It seems that he had the idea of setting up his infant grandson, Jaʿfar, as caliph, but any such plans were aborted by Malik Shāh's own sudden illness and death only fifty-three days after that of his minister.[95]

The death of Niẓām al-Mulk at the hands of Ismāʿīlī *fidāʾīs* or devotees (if this was not in fact procured, as rumour had it, by the sultan himself, an act which would have been paralleled by that three centuries before when Hārūn al-Rashīd rid himself of the Barmakids) highlights what was being felt at this

91 For the Saljuqs of Syria, see ʿAli Sevim, *Suriye ve filistin Selçukları tarihi* (Ankara, 1983); *EI*[2] 'Saldjūḳids. III. 4. The Saldjūḳs of Syria (471–511/1078–1117' (C. E. Bosworth).

92 Ibn al-Athīr, vol. X, pp. 70, 112.

93 See *EI*[2] 'Djahīr, Banū' (Cl. Cahen).

94 Bundārī, pp. 72–3; Ibn al-Athīr, vol. X, pp. 110, 120.

95 Bundārī, p. 70; Rāwandī, p. 140; Ibn al-Athīr, vol. X, pp. 199–200, 204–6; Barhebraeus, Eng. trans. Budge, p. 231; Kafesoğlu, *Sultan Melikşah*, pp. 203–13. For studies of the somewhat mysterious death of Niẓām al-Mulk, see M. T. Houtsma, 'The death of the Niẓām al-Mulk and its consequences', *Journal of Indian History*, 3 (1924), pp. 147–60; K. Rippe, 'Über den Sturz Nizām-ul-Mulks', *Fuad Köprülü armağanı*, pp. 423–35.

time as a threat to the fabric of Sunnī orthodox society by the Nizārī Ismāʿīlīs and the descendants of the earlier Carmathians. Several centres of Nizārī activity emerged around this time across the Saljuq empire, including northern Syria, the Elburz mountains region, Quhistān in Khurāsān, and the region around Iṣfahān in Fārs, brought into being by *dāʿīs* or propagandists connected with the Nizārī group in Fāṭimid Egypt. Ḥasan-i Ṣabbāḥ's seizure in 483/1090 of the fortress of Alamūt in north-western Persia, the region of Daylam, where there were long-established currents of Shiʿism and heterodoxy, gave the movement a base where a line of chiefs, the Grand Masters, who regarded themselves as the true heirs of Nizār and the rightful Ismāʿīlī Imams, were to endure till the appearance in Persia of the Mongol conqueror Hülegü in 654/1256. These Ismāʿīlīs were dedicated enthusiasts, even fanatics, but cannot have been all that numerous. Their chosen weapon was not so much action by large bodies of troops (although on several occasions in the sixth/twelfth century they fielded contingents in northern Persia) as selective political assassination which, in an age when so much depended on personal leadership and example, could have serious effects on the fortunes of states. It certainly engendered in the minds of orthodox Muslims something approaching a psychosis, the fear that orthodox Islam was in danger of subversion from within. The Ismāʿīlīs were never a major threat to the fabric of the Saljuq empire, although in the course of the sixth/twelfth century various military expeditions were to be sent against their mountain strongholds.[96]

VI

The Great Saljuq sultanate now entered upon a 'time of troubles'. Three generations of leaders, culminating in Malik Shāh, had provided inspired leadership and military success. They had been aided by dashing Turkish slave commanders and efficient Persian administrators, but the unity that they had achieved, dependent as it was on personal élan plus an ability to keep the nomadic elements either under control or with their energies directed to external expansion, was precarious. The greatest of all the Persian statesmen who served them, Niẓām al-Mulk, had had a view of an ideal Islamic state and society which he had urged his often reluctant masters to keep before their eyes and which had made the sultanate something more than a mere

96 M. G. S. Hodgson, *The order of Assassins: The struggle of the early Nizârî Ismâʿîlîs against the Islamic world* (The Hague, 1955), pp. 41–61; Morgan, *Medieval Persia*, pp. 43–6; Farhad Daftary, *The Ismāʿīlīs: Their history and doctrines* (Cambridge, 1990), pp. 324–42.

exploitative, robber state. The centrifugal tendencies inherent in a Turkish tribal society, with its notions of collective leadership where seniority in kinship, as well as experience in leading warfare, counted, had been kept in check by the first sultans, at times not without difficulty, and these notions continued in the consciousness of Saljuq family members, surfacing in times of uncertainty and crisis. It might have been expected that, on an Ibn Khaldunian analysis, three generations of expansion were now due to be followed by a period of decline and collapse, and this was to some extent true for the western lands of the sultanate, although the period of decline there was protracted and the sultanate was an inordinately long time dying (the last Great Saljuq, Ṭoghrıl (III) b. Arslan Shāh, was not killed until almost the end of the sixth/twelfth century).

Malik Shāh's sons Berk-yaruq and, especially, Muḥammad managed with difficulty to establish some degree of central control, but after 511/1118 their successors in western Persia and Iraq were embroiled in family dissensions and rivalries. This provided an opportunity, in regions like Azerbaijan and Arrān, al-Jazīra and Fārs, for the ambitions of Turkish slave commanders, the atabegs, who often arrogated to themselves the powers of the young Saljuq princes they were supposed to be nurturing and tutoring. Also, the ʿAbbāsid caliphate, after its years in the doldrums under the Būyids, enjoyed a revival of power and influence in the course of the sixth/twelfth century, so that the caliphs from al-Mustarshid (r. 512–29/1118–35) up to al-Nāṣir (r. 575–622/1180–1225) became major players in the military campaignings and power politics of Iraq and western Persia. Iraq was in effect lost to the Great Saljuqs by the early 1150s, but the last two generations of sultans in the west managed in very difficult circumstances to keep the sultanate alive for over three more decades. It was the misfortune of Arslan Shāh (r. 556–71/1161–76) and his son Ṭoghrıl (III) (r. 571–90/ 1176–94) to be squeezed between the ʿAbbāsids in the west and a new line of vigorous, expanding Khwārazm Shāhs of Anūshtegin's line who established a great empire in Transoxania and eastern Persia only to be overwhelmed in the end by the Mongols of Chinggis Khan.

However, while the descendants of Muḥammad b. Malik Shāh were squabbling in the western part of the sultanate, the eastern part enjoyed a remarkable period of some sixty years' comparative stability and governmental continuity under Malik Shāh's son Aḥmad Sanjar, who became governor of Khurāsān in 490/1097 and remained there until he died in 552/1157, being recognised after Muḥammad's death in 511/1118 as supreme head of the Saljuq ruling family. What put an end to Sanjar's power in the east was a combination of external pressures, from new political entities beyond the Oxus like the

Khwārazm Shāhs and Qara Khitay, and internal ones from discontented Oghuz tribesmen within Khurāsān, who were never reconciled to central control from Sanjar's capital at Marv and whose ranks were continually being replenished by fresh influxes of nomads from Inner Asia. As well as causing Sanjar's sultanate to end unhappily, these Oghuz were also responsible for the demise of the Saljuq line in Kirmān in *c.* 584/1188. Only in Anatolia did the name endure in the shape of the Rūm Saljuqs, who enjoyed a glorious existence in the sixth/twelfth century but after 641/1243 fell back into the status of vassals of the Mongols for the last sixty years or so of their existence.

With the support of the Niẓāmiyya, the youth Abū'l-Muẓaffar Berk-yaruq (Tkish. 'firm, strong brightness') was raised to the throne at Rayy on his father's death against a rival party in Iṣfahān of the Chief Secretary Tāj al-Mulk Abū'l-Ghanāʾim and Malik Shāh's Qarakhānid queen and widow Terken Khātūn, who favoured the latter's infant son Maḥmūd. Maḥmūd in fact conveniently died soon afterwards, and Berk-yaruq secured the sultanate for himself, being recognised in 487/1094 by the caliph al-Mustaẓhir, but was beset by a host of rival Saljuq claimants to the throne: Ismāʿīl b. Yāqūtī in Azerbaijan and, more seriously, two of his uncles, Arslan Arghun in Khurāsān (whose power there only ended with his death at the hands of his own *ghulāms* in 490/1097) and Tutush in Syria. Tutush (Tkish. 'he who grasps [power]') had a strong army at his disposal, and was soon in control of Baghdad, but Berk-yaruq met him in battle near Rayy and defeated him in 488/1095, and Tutush was slain. The seat of Berk-yaruq's power was essentially Iraq and western Persia, that is, Fārs and Jibāl, and in 490/1197 he appointed his half-brother Aḥmad Sanjar (Tkish. 'he who pierces, thrusts') as governor of Khurāsān, providing him with an atabeg and a vizier.[97] Berk-yaruq campaigned in Khurāsān against Arslan Arghun, and it was at this time that he had to send to Khwārazm his commander, the Amīr-i Dād ('chief justiciar') Ḥabashī, and who now appointed as governor there, with the title of Khwārazm Shāh, Quṭb al-Dīn Muḥammad, the son of Malik Shāh's governor there Anūshtegin Gharchaʾī. This was the origin of the last and most brilliant line of Khwārazm Shāhs, who were to become in the course of the sixth/twelfth century a major power in Turkistān and Khurāsān. After this time, distractions in the west compelled Berk-yaruq to leave Sanjar at Balkh substantially to govern the east on his own with the title of malik.[98]

97 Bundārī, pp. 82–6; Ḥusaynī, pp. 74–6; Rāwandī, pp. 140–3; Ibn al-Athīr, vol. X, pp. 229, 244–5, 262–5; Bosworth, 'The political and dynastic history', pp. 102–6.

98 Ibn al-Athīr, vol. X, pp. 265–8; Juwaynī, *Tārīkh-i Jahān-gushā*, Eng. trans. J. A. Boyle (Manchester, 1958), vol. I, pp. 277–8; Barthold, *Turkestan*, pp. 318–19.

Back in the west, Berk-yaruq's power remained uncertain, and outlying parts were never under his control. His half-brother Muḥammad Tapar (Tkish. 'he who obtains, finds') was in Arrān, but soon threw off the control of his atabeg and used north-western Persia as his base for a bid for the caliphate. Hence all the years left to Berk-yaruq, that is, 490–8/1097–1105, were taken up with a struggle against his rival Muḥammad, who by now had the support of most of the Niẓāmiyya and of his full brother Sanjar, who provided him with troops. In desperation, Berk-yaruq seems at times to have had to call on contingents of Ismāʿīlī troops from northern Persia for help. In 495/1102 he was compelled to cede to Muḥammad the title of malik and the provinces of Azerbaijan and Arrān, al-Jazīra, Syria and Diyārbakr, but Muḥammad soon repudiated this arrangement. Berk-yaruq besieged Muḥammad in Iṣfahān and defeated his army in Azerbaijan, but worn out by illness and continual campaigning, decided to make peace, with the provisions that each of the two half-brothers should have the title of sultan in his own right, Muḥammad to keep the provinces he had been allotted and Berk-yaruq to retain the heartlands of the empire, Iraq, Jibāl, Fārs and Khūzistān. In the next years, however, Berk-yaruq died at the age of only twenty-five, and Muḥammad succeeded by default to the whole of the lands west of Khurāsān and the title of Supreme Sultan.[99]

During the years of internecine warfare, the lands fought over were ravaged and plundered by each side; regular taxation could not be collected, and irregular, forced levies had to be made in order to pay armies. The Turkish *ghulām* commanders and tribal chiefs would, for their part, sell their services to either side, but had a vested interest in seeing that no strong, central power emerged from the struggle. Hence it is at this time that, out of the various appanages nominally held by Saljuq princes after Malik Shāh's death but in practice often ruled by their Turkish atabegs, various lines of the latter begin to emerge: the sons of Bursuq in Khūzistān, the Shāh-i Armanids at Khilāt in eastern Anatolia, the Artuqids in Diyārbakr and, slightly later, the Zangids at Mosul.

Muḥammad reigned for thirteen years as undisputed sultan (498–511/1105–18), while Sanjar remained as viceroy of the east, with his court and administration now established at Marv and with the title of malik. The sources praise Muḥammad as a just and pious ruler, although he does not seem to have been

99 Bundārī, pp. 87–9, 261; Ḥusaynī, pp. 76–8; Rāwandī, pp. 145–9; Ibn al-Athīr, vol. X, pp. 287–8, 329–31, 333–5, 369–72, 380; Bosworth, 'The political and dynastic history', pp. 108–11; and for a further connected account of Berk-yaruq's reign, M. F. Sanaullah, *The decline of the Saljūqid empire* (Calcutta, 1938), pp. 91–113.

a more capable military commander than Berk-yaruq was. He did, however, have the advantage of a period of peace. Hence he was able to give a small amount of help to the *amīrs* of Syria, such as the dispossessed prince of Tripoli, Ibn ʿAmmār, now challenged by the Frankish Crusaders, and he campaigned in Daylam and in the Iṣfahān region against the Ismāʿīlīs, who had been able, in the disturbed conditions of the time, to increase their power in those regions and in Quhistān; both lines of policy were calculated to give the sultan kudos in the eyes of the religious classes. Within central Iraq, Muḥammad strengthened his position by humbling the Shīʿite Arab Mazyadids of Ḥilla, and his good relations with the ʿAbbāsids were sealed by the marriage in 502/1108f. of Muḥammad's sister to the caliph al-Mustaẓhir. In western Persia, his governor in Fārs, Chavlı Saqāʾō, brought prosperity to his province by curbing the predatory Shabānkāraʾī Kurds.[100]

Muḥammad died in 511/1118, the last Great Saljuq to exercise substantial control over the western provinces of the sultanate. As his successor, he appointed his son Maḥmūd, who was to reign for fourteen years (511–25/1118–31), but there were four other sons of Muḥammad, sc. Masʿūd, Ṭoghrıl, Sulaymān Shāh and Saljuq Shāh, who at various times exercised power in different areas, all but the last actually gaining the title and authority of sultan. Muḥammad had held in check the tendencies to division and disunity, but these now had full play; the succession was permanently disputed, with up to three or four claimants at any one time. These royal aspirants to power could only gain support from the Turkish *amīrs* by alienating to them more and more land as *iqṭāʿ*s, thus reducing their own fiscal resources, and these commanders were now able to intervene even in the sultan's own administration. Thus Anūshirwān b. Khālid (whose Persian chronicle of his times, now lost, forms, via an Arabic version by ʿImād al-Dīn al-Iṣfahānī, the ultimate basis of Bundārī's Arabic epitome, the *Zubdat al-nuṣra*) served as vizier to the Saljuqs Maḥmūd and Masʿūd and to the ʿAbbāsid caliph al-Mustarshid, and accordingly had first-hand experience of affairs.[101] He lamented the parlous state of the realm: 'In Muḥammad's reign the kingdom was united and secure from all envious attacks; but when it passed to his son Maḥmūd, they split up that unity and destroyed its cohesion. They claimed a share with him in the power and left him only a bare subsistence.'[102]

100 Ibn al-Balkhī, *Fārs-nāma*, pp 165, 167; Bundārī, pp. 117–18; Ḥusaynī, pp. 81–2; Ibn al-Athīr, vol. X, pp. 244, 452–3, 471, 527–8; Sanaullah, *The decline of the Saljūqid empire*, pp. 114–32; Bosworth, 'The political and dynastic history', pp. 113–19.
101 See *EIr* 'Anūšervān Kāšānī' (C. E. Bosworth).
102 Bundārī, p. 134; Ibn al-Athīr, vol. X, pp. 525–7.

At the outset, Maḥmūd faced an invasion from his uncle Sanjar, who among other things alleged that Maḥmūd was encouraging the Qarakhānids to attack him in his rear. Sanjar's powerful army was said to have included four vassal kings with their troop contingents, and he had with him war elephants. Not surprisingly, Maḥmūd was defeated near Sāwa in Jibāl and Sanjar advanced as far as Baghdad; in the ensuing peace settlement, Maḥmūd had to cede to Sanjar territories south of the Caspian including the strategically highly important city of Rayy. Maḥmūd's brother Ṭoghrıl held lands in northern Jibāl, from where he rebelled against Maḥmūd's authority; while Masʿūd, in Mosul, al-Jazīra and Diyārbakr, and with support from local Turkmen bands and Kurdish chiefs, likewise refused allegiance. Maḥmūd was, however, able to maintain the Saljuq position, in part because of the ʿAbbāsids' fear of their powerful and hostile neighbour, the Mazyadid *amīr* Dubays b. Ṣadaqa. These troubles allowed Maḥmūd to give only intermittent attention to the external frontiers of the realm. In the north, the Georgians were resurgent under their forceful king David the Restorer (r. 1089–1125), who recaptured Tiflis and Ānī from the Muslims, threatened the lands of the Shīrvān Shāhs in eastern Transcaucasia and withheld tribute from the Saljuqs. Maḥmūd could do little against these actions, despite a personal appearance in the region, and later in his reign the Georgians were able temporarily to capture Ganja.[103]

Maḥmūd's death in 525/1131 brought further internal crises, with his young son Dāwūd proclaimed sultan in Hamadān but with parallel claims from Masʿūd in Iraq and Saljuq Shāh in Fārs and Khūzistān. As senior member of the dynasty, the mediation of Sanjar was sought, but he only now pushed the claims of his own protégé Ṭoghrıl. The threat of a Qarakhānid revolt in Transoxania prevented him from giving much aid to Ṭoghrıl, and when the latter died in 529/1134 after reigning in Azerbaijan alone as the sultan Ṭoghrıl (II), Masʿūd managed to secure the throne in Hamadān in the face of opposition from Dāwūd, now in Azerbaijan, and began a reign of almost twenty years (529–47/1134–52), the longest of any sultan in the west since Malik Shāh. His authority was nevertheless largely confined to Jibāl and central Iraq. Azerbaijan was the centre of Dāwūd's limited authority, but the province fell under the control of Turkish commanders, with Shams al-Dīn Eldigüz as atabeg for the young Arslan b. Ṭoghrıl (II) in Tabrīz and Aq Sonqur b. Aḥmadīlī in Marāgha; Fārs was dominated by Masʿūd's enemy, the *amīr*

103 Sources for the period and connected narrative are given in M. A. Köymen, *Büyük Selçuklu imparatorluğu tarihi, vol. II: İkinci imparatorluk devri* (Ankara, 1954), pp. 5–148, 164–73, and Bosworth, 'The political and dynastic history', pp. 119–24; see also W. E. D. Allen, *A history of the Georgian people* (London, 1932), pp. 96–100.

Boz-aba; and Zangī b. Aq Sonqur, son of a *ghulām* commander of Malik Shāh, from a base at Mosul built up a powerful principality in al-Jazīra, Diyārbakr and northern Syria.[104]

During his early years, Masʿūd had been able to curb the growing power of the ʿAbbāsids, capturing al-Mustarshid in a battle near Hamadān, shortly after which the caliph was murdered by Ismāʿīlī assassins.[105] The new caliph al-Rāshid was soon embroiled with the sultan over non-payment of tribute due to the Saljuqs, and Masʿūd's authority reached its peak when in 530/1136 he deposed al-Rāshid after the caliph had reigned only two years (529–30/1135–6).[106] But thereafter, the capable and energetic new caliph al-Muqtafī (r. 530–55/1136–60) built up his army with Armenian and Rūmī *ghulāms* instead of unreliable Turkish ones, strengthened the defences of Baghdad and was able on several occasions to defy the Saljuqs.[107]

In the middle and later parts of his reign, Masʿūd fell more and more under the influence of the Turkish *amīrs*. He was beset by over-mighty and ambitious commanders. Two of these, ʿAbbās of Rayy and Boz-aba of Fārs, who had in their care two young sons of the former sultan Maḥmūd, in 540/1145f. raised up a rebellion, which Masʿūd managed to quell, but he was not free of the threat from Boz-aba till the latter was killed during a further outbreak a year later. On his western flank, Masʿūd's authority had been eclipsed by the spectacular successes of Zangī, a Muslim hero after his capture of Edessa from the Crusaders in 539/1144; the threat from Zangī was only relieved by Zangī's death in 541/1146. The sultan was thus able at last to break out of the encircling grip of the Turkish atabegs and *amīrs*. He now relied much on his favourite, the *amīr* Khāṣṣ Beg Arslan b. Palang-eri, but this excessive dependence on Khāṣṣ Beg raised up in 543/1148 a coalition of excluded and discontented *amīrs*, who espoused as a candidate for the sultanate one of Maḥmūd's sons, Malik Shāh. Masʿūd was besieged in Takrīt, but the coalition then dispersed, and Masʿūd's temporary ally the caliph al-Muqtafī (both the sultan and the caliph feared Mazyadid dominance in central Iraq) had successfully defended Baghdad.[108]

Masʿūd died in 547/1152 without a direct heir. Ibn al-Athīr lamented that 'With him the fortunes of the Saljuq family died; after him, there was no banner

104 Bundārī, pp. 156–75, 184, 219–20; Ibn al-Athīr, vol. X, pp. 669–70, 674–8, 686–7. For connected narratives of the reigns of Ṭoghrıl and Masʿūd, see Köymen, *İkinci imparatorluk devri*, pp. 203–300, and Bosworth, 'The political and dynastic history', pp. 124–33.
105 Bundārī, pp. 176–8; Ḥusaynī, p. 107; Ibn al-Athīr, vol. XI, pp. 24–8.
106 Ibn al-Athīr, vol. XI, pp. 35, 42–3.
107 Bundārī, p. 235.
108 Bosworth, 'The political and dynastic history', pp. 130–4.

for them to rely upon or turn to – "Qays's death was not the death of a single man, but rather the collapse of a whole tribe's foundations.'"[109] There were several Saljuq princes, including a brother of Mas'ūd and various nephews, with claims to the succession. Muḥammad (II) b. Maḥmūd (r. 548–54/1153–9) is praised by 'Imād al-Dīn as 'the most majestic, the most learned and the most just of the Saljuqs', but two other ephemeral rulers were of mediocre capability. In 551–2/1157 Muḥammad had advanced on Baghdad, but after a prolonged siege of the city, had to withdraw on receiving news of a threat to his position in Jibāl from his brother Malik Shāh and Eldigüz.[110] Thus, after Mas'ūd's death, there was no longer a *shiḥna* of the sultan in Baghdad; al-Muqtafī appropriated all buildings and properties of the Saljuqs in the city, so that all Saljuq influence ended there.

VII

In contrast to the vicissitudes and difficulties of the Great Saljuqs in Iraq and western Persia, the eastern part of the empire, governed by Sanjar b. Malik Shāh since Berk-yaruq's time, enjoyed a continuity of administration for more than half a century, while the Saljuq *amīrs* in Kirmān, substantially untroubled in their comparative geographical isolation, were to survive almost till the end of the sixth/twelfth century (see below, p. 73). Constitutionally, Sanjar at first styled himself on his coins merely as *Malik* or *Malik al-Mashriq*, 'King of the East', and recognised his brothers Berk-yaruq and Muḥammad as Supreme Sultan, *al-Sulṭān al-Mu'aẓẓam*. But when Muḥammad died in 511/1118, Sanjar regarded himself, in accordance with the old Turkish principle of the seniorate, as the senior figure in the dynasty and immediately placed on his coins the title of Supreme Sultan, regarding his nephew Maḥmūd b. Muḥammad and his successors as subordinate to him.[111] His court at Marv paralleled those of his kinsmen in western Persia and Iraq at Iṣfahān and Hamadān, and he had a fully developed administration in Marv directed from a *dīwān-i a'lā* and presided over by a vizier (the names of several of these are known) and with a

109 Ibn al-Athīr, vol. XI, pp. 160–1.

110 Bundārī, p. 288; Ḥusaynī, pp. 134–9; Rāwandī, pp. 266–9; Pseudo-Ẓahīr al-Dīn Nīshāpūrī, trans. Luther, pp. 130–2; Ibn al-Athīr, vol. XI, pp. 312–55.

111 Bosworth, 'The political and dynastic history', pp. 135–6; C.E. Bosworth, 'The Saljuqs and the Khwārazm Shāhs. Part 3. The eastern Seljuq sultanate (1118–57) and the rise and florescence of the Khwārazm Shāhs of Anūshtegin's line up to the appearance of the Mongols (1097–1219)', in UNESCO, *History of the civilizations of Central Asia*, vol. IV: *The age of achievement: AD 750 to the end of the fifteenth century. Part 1, The historical, social and economic setting* (Paris, 1998), pp. 161ff. *EI*[2] 'Sandjar b. Malik Shāh' (C. E. Bosworth).

busy chancery under the Chief Secretary. We know quite a lot about the central and provincial administration exercised from Marv through the survival of copies of documents issued by this chancery, several of which concern the appointment of provincial governors. Thus an investiture document for Sanjar's nephew Masʿūd b. Muḥammad as governor of Gurgān stresses the importance of this region, at the south-eastern corner of the Caspian Sea, as a *thaghr* or frontier defence region against the infidel Turks of Dihistān and Manghıshlaq. He is enjoined to facilitate safe travel through his lands, to listen to complaints of oppression, to collect taxation only at the official rate laid down (i.e. he is not empowered to alter the official tax rates), to pay out the official salaries of his subordinates, and to consult with the leading men and the masses of people alike. It was recognised that the Turkmens were a special case and that they were a chronically unruly element. Thus other documents concern the appointment of a *shiḥna*, that is, in this context the official charged with administering tribesmen in a tribal area, in this instance, the Turkmens of Gurgān, and with keeping order among them.[112]

Sanjar's role in the events of Maḥmūd's reign and his support for Ṭoghrıl (II) b. Muḥammad in Azerbaijan have been mentioned above (p. 62), but after his intervention in western Persia of 526/1132 against Masʿūd b. Maḥmūd it was happenings in Khurāsān, Transoxania and Khwārazm which came virtually to monopolise his attention in the seat of his power, Marv.

The considerable Saljuq cultural influence within the later Ghaznavid sultanate has been noted. When the Ghaznavid sultan Masʿūd (III) b. Ibrāhīm died in 508/1115, a succession dispute between his two sons, Bahrām Shāh and Malik Arslan or Arslan Shāh, ensued, carried on at both the diplomatic and military levels. The former appealed to Sanjar for help. The Saljuq sultan led a powerful army to Ghazna, defeated Malik Arslan and placed Bahrām Shāh on the throne as his vassal. Apart from an episode in 529–30/1135–6 when Bahrām Shāh stopped paying tribute to Marv, bringing down on himself a second Saljuq attack on Ghazna which temporarily expelled him to his north-west Indian possessions, most of his four decades of rule was as Sanjar's liege, a dependence seen in the legends on Bahrām Shāh's coins minted at Ghazna.[113]

112 A. K. S. Lambton, 'The administration of Sanjar's empire as illustrated in the *ʿAtabat al-kataba*', *Bulletin of the School of Oriental and African Studies*, 20 (1957), pp. 376–8, 380–2 (the author of this collection of *inshāʾ*, official documents, was the head of Sanjar's chancery at Marv); Heribert Horst, *Die Staatsverwaltung der Grosselǧūqen und Ḫōrazmšāhs* (Wiesbaden, 1964), pp. 43–60.

113 Ibn al-Athīr, vol. X, pp. 504–8; Jūzjānī, *Ṭabaqāt-i nāṣirī*, ed. ʿAbd al-Ḥayy Ḥabībī (Kabul, 1342–3/1963–4), vol. I, pp. 241–2, Eng. trans. H. G. Raverty (London, 1881–99), vol. I, p. 107; Bosworth, *The later Ghaznavids*, pp. 89–98, 99–101.

Ghazna was on the remote periphery of Sanjar's dominions. Much more immediately acute for him were relations with the Qarakhānids of Transoxania and with Khwārazm. At the beginning of his governorship, Sanjar had to repel an attack by a Qarakhānid originally from the eastern branch of the family and a great-grandson of Qadır Khan Yūsuf, Jibrāʾīl b. ʿUmar (495/1102), whose troops captured Tirmidh and penetrated into Khurāsān.[114] Sanjar now took steps to place on the throne in Samarqand a more compliant vassal, a great-grandson of Tamghach Khan Ibrāhīm b. Naṣr, Arslan Khan Muḥammad b. Sulaymān, who was to enjoy a rule there of some thirty years (495–524/1102–30). He was further attached to the Saljuq cause by a marriage alliance with one of Sanjar's daughters, receiving military aid from the Supreme Sultan against a challenger to his succession. He regularly led slave raids into the steppes against pagan Qıpchaqs, earning the title of *Ghāzī*, and became known as one of the greatest builders of his dynasty, restoring the walls and citadel of Bukhārā, laying out palaces and an *ʿīdgāh* or open area for the celebration of the Muslim festivals, and erecting a splendid congregational mosque. Only at the very end of his reign, when Arslan Khan was a sick man and when the religious institution, which had a long history of antagonism towards the khans, caused discord in the state, did Sanjar again appear at Samarqand, plundering part of the city and deposing Arslan Khan (524/1130). Sanjar now placed various short-lived rulers on the throne, his choice finally in 526/1132 lighting on his own nephew (through his earlier marriage to a Qarakhānid princess) Maḥmūd, third son of Arslan Khan.[115]

Maḥmūd proved a faithful ally of the Saljuqs, and his fortunes were to be closely intertwined with those of the dynasty in Khurāsān. When Maḥmūd became at odds with unruly Qarluq tribesmen in his military following, he appealed to Sanjar for help, whereupon the Qarluq in turn called upon the new power which had just appeared in Turkistān, that of the Qara Khitay (see on them, below). It was this episode that provoked the Qara Khitay invasions of Transoxania and Khwārazm and led to Sanjar's crushing defeat of 536/1141 at the Qaṭwān steppe in Ushrūsana to the east of Samarqand, dealing a severe blow to the sultan's prestige in the east. Maḥmūd fled with Sanjar to Khurāsān and remained there, while in Transoxania the Qara Khitay set up one of his brothers, Tamghach Bughrā Khan Ibrāhīm (r. 536–51/1141–56), who likewise

114 Barthold, *Turkestan*, pp. 318–19; Pritsak, 'Die Karachaniden', p. 49.

115 Ibn al-Athir, vol. X, p. 350; Barthold, *Turkestan*, pp. 319–22; Pritsak, 'Die Karachaniden', pp. 50–2; Davidovich, 'The Karakhanids', p. 131.

later fell out with his Qarluq troops and was in the end defeated by them in battle and killed.[116]

Maḥmūd later fell heir to Sanjar's position in Khurāsān. One of Sanjar's perennial problems was controlling the pastoralist nomads who had become an increasingly significant element in the countryside of Khurāsān, with their numbers frequently replenished by fresh arrivals of Oghuz, apparently forced out of the Inner Asian steppes by pressure from the Qarluq; their increased numbers probably meant increased pressures on the sedentary population of Khurāsān and encroachments by the nomads upon the settled agricultural lands. Sanjar's frequent military campaignings placed a heavy financial burden on his subjects, and his tax-collectors had to resort to increasingly harsh measures. Eventually, in 548/1153, a group of Oghuz who nomadised on both sides of the upper Oxus, in Khuttal and in Tukhāristān, rebelled against these exactions. They had been accustomed to handing over an annual tribute of 24,000 sheep for the sultan's kitchens, but this had become exacted with increased brutality. Sanjar refused all compromise and led an expedition against these Oghuz, but was defeated and captured by them, after which the Oghuz swept through Khurāsān and sacked cities like Nīshāpūr, taking an especial vengeance on the sultan's officials and on members of the religious instition, whom they regarded as closely linked with the established order. Although the polite fiction was maintained that Sanjar was the guest of the Oghuz, he was in fact closely guarded (according to Juwaynī, they paraded him around on a throne during the day, but locked him up in a cage at night[117]), and only managed to escape three years later. His prestige was totally shattered; the leaderless army of Khurāsān had become accustomed to choosing its own *amīrs* as leaders, and, very soon after his liberation, Sanjar died (552/1157). While Sanjar had been in captivity, the Qarakhānid Maḥmūd Khan was recognised by the Saljuq army in Khurāsān as legitimate malik of Khurāsān. He had moved his own residence to Nīshāpūr and had left his son Muḥammad as regent in Transoxania; and after Sanjar's death and the extinguishing of Saljuq rule in the east, he continued to rule from Khurāsān till his own death in 557/1162.[118]

116 Ibn al-Athīr, vol. XI, p. 202; Barthold, *Turkestan*, p. 333; Pritsak, 'Die Karachaniden', p. 53; Davidovich, 'The Karakhanids', p. 132.

117 Juwaynī, trans. Boyle, vol. I, p. 285.

118 Bundārī, pp. 277–81; Rāwandī, pp. 172–4; Pseudo-Ẓahīr al-Dīn Nīshāpūrī, trans. Luther, pp. 88–95; Ibn al-Athīr, vol. XI, pp. 81–6, 183; Juwaynī, trans. Boyle, vol. I, pp. 285–6, 289; Barthold, *Turkestan*, pp. 326, 329–31; M. A. Köymen, 'Büyük Selçuklar imparatorluğunda Oğuz isyanı', *Ankara Üniversitesi Dil ve Tarih-Coğrafya Fakültesi Dergisi*, 5 (1947), pp. 159–73, Ger. trans. at pp. 175–86; Pritsak, 'Die Karachaniden', pp. 52–4.

The beginnings of the Khwārazm Shāhs of the line of Anūshtegin during the reigns of Malik Shāh and Berk-yaruq go back to the appointment of Quṭb al-Dīn Muḥammad as Shāh, as mentioned above (p. 59). Now, for the first and last time in its history, Khwārazm was to become under his descendants the centre of a military empire embracing large stretches of Central Asia and much of Persia. The basis for this success was not only the ambitions and the military skills of the Shāhs, which could come into play when the earlier great powers that had dominated the region, the Qarakhānids and the Saljuqs, were at best in a static if not declining state, but the fact that Khwārazm was an agriculturally rich region. It had a highly sophisticated system of canals and irrigation channels, and towns which flourished on trade between the Islamic lands and the Eurasian steppes, the Khwārazmians themselves always having been great travellers, attested by traces of their presence in the toponymy of south Russia and even Hungary.[119] Thus with a strong financial base, the shahs had the sinews of war at their disposal. It was to be their bad luck in the early seventh/thirteenth century to come up against a foe whose ruthlessness and violence were on a scale hardly known previously in the Islamic lands, the Mongols of Chinggis Khan.[120]

Quṭb al-Dīn Muḥammad (governor 490–521/1097–1127), as a Saljuq appointee, remained Sanjar's faithful vassal, with frequent attendance at his court in Marv and provision of troops for the Saljuq armies on various occasions. It is unclear why the sultans departed from the principle which, certainly in their heyday, they tried to follow elsewhere in the empire of avoiding the creation of hereditary lines of provincial governors. Sanjar was a far stronger monarch than his kinsmen further west, who had not the prestige or military strength to curb the formation of hereditary lines of local governors and atabegs. It may be that Khwārazm was adjudged a special case; it was almost an island of flourishing agriculture and civilised Islamic life jutting out into the steppes, a good number of whose tribal inhabitants were still pagan. On this analysis, it was sensible of Sanjar to send there commanders of proven ability who knew the local conditions and who could cope with the nomadic pressures that surrounded much of Khwārazm, even if this meant allowing a hereditary line to develop there, with all the attendant temptations to rebellion and independence.

119 A. Z. V. Togan, *The Khorezmians and their civilisation*, Preface to his facsimile edn. of Zamakhsharī's *Muqaddimāt al-adab* (Istanbul, 1951), pp. 20ff.

120 For histories of the shahs, see İbrahim Kafesoğlu, *Harezmşahlar devleti tarihi (485–617/1092–1229)* (Ankara, 1956); Z. M. Bunyatov, *Gosudstarstvo Khorezmshakhov Anushteginidov* (Moscow, 1986).

The next Shāh, ʿAlāʾ al-Dīn Atsız (governor 521–51 / 1127–56), was the real founder of his family's fortunes. Though nominally subject to Sanjar almost to the end and initially respectful, sending troops for Sanjar's campaigns, he pursued a calculated policy of securing as much autonomy as possible for Khwārazm, with independence as an ultimate goal. He secured his northern borders by extending control over the Oghuz and others of Manghıshlaq to the east of the Caspian and over the Qıpchaqs beyond the Aral Sea, recruiting many of them into his army, irrespective of whether they were Muslim or pagan. He intervened militarily, when occasion arose, in the affairs of his Qarakhānid neighbours, at a later date dealt cautiously with the Qara Khitay who came to control Transoxania (see below) and took advantage of Sanjar's difficulties with the Oghuz tribesmen in Khurāsān.

Atsız had unsuccessfully rebelled against Sanjar in 533 / 1138, but this flooding of the lower Oxus valley failed to Sanjar's advance; he defeated the Shāh and temporarily installed a Saljuq nominee in Gurgānj. But a further expedition of 538 / 1143f., provoked by Atsız's raids into Khurāsān as far as Bayhāq and Nīshāpūr, could not establish a permanent Saljuq presence in Khwārazm; the Shāh seems to have had solid support from his Khwārazmian subjects. Sanjar's defeat at the Qaṭwān steppe emboldened Atsız further to pursue his own ends, although during Sanjar's captivity at the hands of the Oghuz he showed remarkable restraint; and when Sanjar managed to escape after three years, his negotiations with the Qarakhānid ruler in Khurāsān, Maḥmūd Khan, for joint intervention against the Oghuz, were put on hold. Thus Atsız was still nominally a vassal of Sanjar when he died only a few months before the sultan himself.

The Qara Khitay have been mentioned, and this people of Far Eastern origin now played a part in the history of Islamic Transoxania, without their ever becoming Muslims. The Qara Khitay stemmed from the Khitan Liao, probably Mongolian in ethnos, who had been regarded by the Chinese Song emperors as a legitimate Chinese dynasty living north of the Great Wall. In the early twelfth century, under pressure from another people of the Siberian fringes, the Tungusic Jürchen of Manchuria, a part of the Liao migrated across the Altai and Tien Shan mountains into the Semirechye, founding there an empire based on an *ordo* or tented encampment near the Muslim town of Balāsāghūn. They then extended into eastern Turkistān, northwards into the upper Yenesei valley and westwards into Transoxania. The Qara Khitay were thus ostensibly one more wave of Inner Asian peoples into the settled Islamic lands, but with a difference from, for example, the Qarluq and Oghuz, who had taken over Turkistān and founded the Qarakhānid and Saljuq political groupings, or from the Mongols who succeeded them, with their policies of massacre and terror against all who opposed them. The Qara Khitay leader, the Tianyou, 'One protected by Heaven' in the Chinese context, or the Gürkhan, a new title meaning 'Universal Khan' in the Islamic one, was content to leave in place existing rulers, in practice the various branches of the Qarakhānids and the Khwārazm Shāhs, with free exercise of their own Islamic religion provided they handed over regular tribute to the Gürkhan. It seems that the Qara Khitay felt no attraction towards the Islamic religion because they lived outside the towns which were centres of Muslim life and because they regarded the Chinese-Liao position, which attached them to the Chinese religious and cultural world, as superior.[121]

Hence the appearance of the Qara Khitay in the Islamic lands did not make a great difference to life there. Their requirements of the local people were essentially fiscal; at least at the outset, their yoke was light, and Muslim sources regard them, for infidels, comparatively favourably.[122] They possessed, however, a powerful military machine, as they showed when in 536/1141 they humbled Sanjar (who seems deliberately to have provoked them). From the time of Il Arslan (r. 551–67/1156–72), the Khwārazm Shāhs at times chafed under Qara Khitay financial control, but the withholding of tribute usually provoked punitive expeditions into Khwārazm. The next Shāh, Tekish (r. 567–96/1172–1200), owed his succession to the throne to intervention by the Gürkhan's son-in-law Fuma (Chin. *fu-ma* 'son-in-law of the emperor'), but sought an early opportunity to throw off their control. The Islamic sources state that the Qara Khitay tax-collectors, who had originally behaved in an impartial and equitable manner, had become increasingly arrogant and oppressive. The looseness of power relationships within the ruling family of the Qara Khitay, and lax control over subordinates, may have contributed to this; but it may be that, latterly, the shahs raised the banner of *jihād* against the Qara Khitay on any pretext that came to hand in an attempt to pacify the orthodox religious classes aroused by the shahs' anti-ʿAbbāsid policies.

121 See histories of the dynasty in W. Barthold, *History of the Semirechyé*, in *Four studies on the history of Central Asia*, trans. V. and T. Minorsky (Leiden, 1962), vol. I, pp. 100–7; Barthold, *Zwölf Vorlesungen*, pp. 120–6; Denis Sinor, 'The Khitan and the Kara Khitay', in UNESCO, *History of civilizations of Central Asia*, vol. IV, part 1, pp. 227–42; Michal Biran, *The empire of the Qara Khitai in Eurasian history: Between China and the Islamic world* (Cambridge, 2005); *EI*² 'Ḳarā Khiṭay' (C. E. Bosworth).

122 A contemporary, Niẓāmī ʿArūḍī Samarqandī, speaks of the 'boundless justice' of the Gūrkhan in his *Chahār maqāla*, ed. Muḥammad Qazwīnī and Muḥammad Muʿīn (Tehran, 1333/1954), p. 38.

After Sanjar's capture by the Oghuz, Khurāsān entered into an administrative limbo. The Oghuz were too disorganised and unsophisticated to form an organised state there, and, after the sultan's death, power became divided out among the former Saljuq *amīrs* under the general overlordship of the Qarakhanid Maḥmūd Khan (see above, pp. 66–7). The most powerful of these was Sanjar's *ghulām* Mu'ayyid al-Dīn Ay Aba (d. 569/1174), who established himself at Nīshāpūr, eventually as a vassal of Maḥmūd Khan, and earned a reputation for his wise and just rule.

VIII

The Great Saljuqs of the west had almost forty years of continued life after Sanjar's death, but their power became more and more circumscribed. One significant factor here was the growing political and military power of the ʿAbbāsid caliphs, increasingly inclined now to assert their secular rights. Al-Muqtafī, as well as recruiting troops, excluded the Saljuq *shiḥnas* from Baghdad after the death of Sultan Masʿūd b. Muḥammad (see above, p. 64), and he was aided by a formidably energetic vizier, ʿAwn al-Dīn Yaḥyā Ibn Hubayra (d. 560/1165), accorded by his master the title of 'Sultan of Iraq' after the ejection of the *shiḥna* from the capital.[123] A wide-ranging ʿAbbāsid diplomatic policy was adopted; links were made, for example with the Sunnī hero of Syria, Nūr al-Dīn b. Zangī; and the caliphs themselves now took the field at the head of their armies. There was a strongly Ḥanbalī ethos at the heart of the caliphate in Baghdad, against the Shīʿite influence centred on the great Shīʿite shrine cities of central Iraq.

The peak of caliphal influence in Iraq and western Persia came under al-Nāṣir (r. 575–622/1180–1225).[124] Al-Nāṣir had a vision of a rejuvenated Islamic world and hoped to establish the caliphate once more as the spiritual and secular focus for the aspirations of all Muslims, whatever their sectarian loyalties, and certainly including the Sunnīs and moderate Shiʿites. An aspect of his ethical and moral policy here was his encouragement of a system of political alliances backed by membership of the

123 See on him Herbert Mason, *Two statesmen of medieval Islam: Vizir Ibn Hubayra (499-560AH/1105-1165AD) and Caliph an-Nâṣir li Dîn Allâh (553–622AH/1158–1225AD)* (The Hague and Paris, 1972), pp. 13–66; Angelika Hartmann, 'Ibn Hubaira und an-Nāṣir li-Dīn Allāh', *Der Islam*, 57 (1976), pp. 87–99.

124 See the magistral study of Angelika Hartmann, *An-Nāṣir li-Dīn Allāh (1180–1225). Politik, Religion, Kultur in der späten ʿAbbāsidenzeit* (Berlin and New York, 1975); EI^2 'al-Nāṣir li-Dīn Allāh' (Hartmann).

chivalric orders of the *futuwwa*.[125] He himself joined the Raḥḥāṣiyya order at Baghdad in 578/1182f. and personally introduced into it other potentates, including members of the Ayyūbid family, the Rūm Saljuqs and, at the other end of the Islamic world, the Ghūrid sultans. Although his efforts here in the central and eastern lands of Islam did not survive the Mongol cataclysm, the ideals and practices of *futuwwa* did have a a clear influence in the Anatolia of the later Saljuqs and the succeeding *beyliks*, in the shape of the *akhī* groups in the towns there.[126] The caliph undoubtedly scored a great success in orthodox Sunnī eyes by bringing back into the fold of orthodoxy the new Grand Master of the Ismāʿīlīs of Alamūt, Jalāl al-Dīn Ḥasan (III) b. Muḥammad (acceded to power in 607/1210), who publicly proclaimed his abandonment of the doctrine of *qiyāma*, the return of the Expected Imam just before Resurrection Day, and declared his adhesion to Sunnī Islam. On the Talisman Gate at Baghdad, which al-Nāṣir now erected (no longer extant), the great Swiss epigraphist Max Van Berchem interpreted the decoration showing a human figure with his hands on the heads of two dragons as representing the caliph's triumph over his two great enemies, the Ismāʿīlī Grand Master and the Khwārazm Shāh ʿAlāʾ al-Dīn Muḥammad.[127]

Al-Nāṣir's main enemy in western Persia was the remaining Great Saljuq, Ṭoghrıl (III), against whom he concentrated his efforts. In 583/1187 he ordered the old Saljuq palace in Baghdad, the symbol of tutelage by an outside regime, to be torn down.[128] The sources are not wholly explicit, although one at least, Ibn al-Athīr, does state that al-Nāṣir egged on the Khwārazm Shāh Tekish in order to dispose of Ṭoghrıl,[129] even though the Khwārazm Shāhs, with their long-term ambitions of conquering western Persia and pushing into Iraq, were known to be dangerous enemies of the caliphate (see below). It was more obviously in the natural interests of the caliphate that al-Nāṣir should incite against the Shāhs their opponents on the eastern fringes of Khurāsān, the Ghūrids. This line of chiefs from Ghūr, in the mountainous interior of what is now Afghanistan, had in the mid-sixth/twelfth century dealt a near-death blow to the surviving Ghaznavids, and under their forceful sultan Ghiyāth

125 See *EI*² 'Futuwwa' (Cl. Cahen).
126 See Cahen, *Pre-Ottoman Turkey*, pp. 195–200, 335–41; *EI*² 'Akhī' (Fr. Taeschner).
127 Hodgson, *The order of Assassins*, pp. 217–25; Daftary, *The Ismāʿīlīs: Their history and doctrines*, pp. 405–7. However, Hodgson (p. 223 n. 31) suggested that the figures depicted are simply astrological symbols.
128 Ibn al-Athīr, vol. XI, p. 560.
129 Ibn al-Athīr, vol. XII, p. 107.

al-Dīn Muḥammad (r. 558–99/1163–1202f.) were now vigorously expanding westwards into Khurāsān, inevitably coming up against the Khwārazm Shāhs.[130]

Another factor contributing to the demise of the Great Saljuqs was the shrinkage of their territories, hence financial resources, and their sphere of action through the growth of powerful atabeg and other Turkish commanders. In Azerbaijan, the Eldigüzids of Tabrīz and the Aḥmadīlīs of Marāgha were all-powerful, and through Shams al-Dīn Eldigüz's marriage to the widow of the ephemeral sultan Ṭoghrıl (II) b. Muḥammad, and other marriages linking his line with the Saljuq family, this atabeg was able to set up Ṭoghrıl's son Arslan as sultan and, inevitably, protégé of the Eldigüzids in Hamadān in 556/1161. Eldigüz's sons and successors maintained a close tutelage over the last two Saljuqs, and Ṭoghrıil (III) b. Arslan was only able to break out of this during the last years of his life. Fārs was under the Turkmen Salghurids, from the Oghuz tribe of the Salghur/Salur, while Khūzistān was controlled by another Turkmen, Shumla, from the Oghuz tribe of the Avshār, and his progeny. In Khurāsān, the Oghuz tribesmen remained a significant if disorganised force. They had brought about the eventual downfall of Sanjar, and in 582/1186 the Oghuz leader Malik Dīnār put an end to the Saljuq line in Kirmān. Malik Dīnār tried to legitimise his rule by marrying a Saljuq princess, and is actually praised in the sources for his just ten years' rule and his care for the prosperity of Kirmān and its subjects, an attitude uncharacteristic of Turkmens of his background; but after his death, his incompetent son and successor was unable to hold the Oghuz horde together, and when he in turn died the Oghuz had to submit to the Khwārazm Shāh Tekish and were incorporated into his army.[131]

Thus the last two sultans, Arslan and Ṭoghrıl (III), held no more than Jibāl, with their centres of power at Hamadān and Iṣfahān and occasionally at Rayy. Arslan ruled only nominally under the control of Eldigüz, who adopted the title of *Atabak al-Aʿẓam* 'Supreme atabeg,' and it was his son Nuṣrat al-Dīn Jahān-Pahlawān Muḥammad who in 571/1176 set up Ṭoghrıl as sultan when Arslan died. The sources commend this last of the Saljuqs for his intellectual as well as his martial qualities, but the odds were heavily stacked against him. Ṭoghrıl soon became restive under Jahān-Pahlawān's successor as atabeg, Qızıl Arslan, who treated him harshly, and he gathered together troops, assumed the initiative and defeated the forces of the caliph (now Qızıl

130 Bosworth, 'The political and dynastic history', pp. 163–5.

131 Bosworth, 'The political and dynastic history', pp. 169–75; Merçil, *Kirman Selçukları*, pp. 210–28.

Arslan's ally) at Dāy-marg near Hamadān in 584/1188. He nevertheless had to surrender to Qızıl Arslan in 586/1190, who imprisoned him and now proclaimed himself sultan, but he was mysteriously murdered so that Ṭoghrıl could obtain his freedom. He soon secured Jibāl for himself, but at this point came up against the Khwārazm Shāh Tekish. Although Ṭoghrıl captured Rayy from its unpopular Khwārazmian garrison, he was overwhelmed by the Khwārazmians' superior numbers in a battle with Tekish outside Rayy. He was killed at the age of only twenty-five, the last Saljuq to rule (590/1194), and his head sent by the Shāh to Baghdad. Western Persia was now divided up between a commander of the Eldigüzids and the caliph.[132]

The latter, however, now faced a much more redoubtable and powerful foe than the last Saljuq, especially since after 589/1193 Tekish was free of his brother and rival for power in Khurāsān, the deceased Sulṭān Shāh. Tekish considered himself as heir to the Saljuq empire, which involved control of western Persia, and, after his death, increased pressure was exerted on al-Nāṣir by Tekish's son and successor, the last Shāh to reign in Khwārazm, ʿAlāʾ al-Dīn Muḥammad (r. 596–617/1200–20). ʿAlāʾ al-Dīn demanded recognition of his claim to a vast empire which now stretched from Turkistān to the Indian Ocean shores, the justification for his assumed title of 'the Second Alexander', and required al-Nāṣir to place his name in the Baghdad *khuṭba*.

Al-Nāṣir could only seek to neutralise the Shāhs by giving moral support to the Ghūrids in their struggle with the Shāhs for possession of Khurāsān. ʿAlāʾ al-Dīn Muḥammad knew from documents captured at Ghazna that the caliph had earlier incited the Ghūrids against him and was now using Ismāʿīlī *fidāʾ*īs to remove his opponents. Questioning the whole legitimacy of the ʿAbbāsids as excluders of the ʿAlids from their rights, he secured a *fatwā* from compliant *ʿulamāʾ* declaring al-Nāṣir deposed, and nominated in his place a Ḥusaynid ʿAlid as anti-caliph, whose name he now placed in the *khuṭba* of the Khwārazmian lands and on his coins. He began to march on Baghdad in the winter of 614/1217f. but was halted in the mountains of Kurdistan by unusually heavy snowfalls; and hearing of the Mongols' appearance on the borders of Transoxania, he turned back to Khurāsān.[133]

132 Bundārī, pp. 301–3; Ḥusaynī, pp. 176–93; Rāwandī, pp. 339–74; Pseudo-Ẓahīr al-Dīn Nīshāpūrī, trans. Luther, pp. 151–3; Ibn al-Athīr, vol. X, pp. 24–5, 75–6; Juwaynī, trans. Boyle, vol. I, pp. 299–303; Barthold, *Turkestan*, pp. 366–7; Kafesoğlu, *Harezmşahlar devleti tarihi*, 116–19, pp. 123–6.

133 Ibn al-Athīr, vol. XII, pp. 106–8; Juwaynī, trans. Boyle, vol. II, pp. 364–7, 390–2; Barthold, *Turkestan*, pp. 373–5; Kafesoğlu, *Harezmşahlar devleti tarihi*, pp. 202–5, 214–20.

It is at this point that a totally new phase of Islamic history begins, with the appearance of the Mongols. Ruling houses familiar in the history of Transoxania had already disappeared. The last ruler of the western branch of the Qarakhānids, ʿUthmān b. Ibrāhīm (r. 600–9 / 1204–12), had borne grandiose titles like *Sulṭān al-Salāṭīn* 'Supreme Sultan' but was ill-equipped to withstand the Khwārazmian onslaught. He had rebelled in Samarqand against ʿAlāʾ al-Dīn Muḥammad, upon which the Khwārazm Shāh had come to ʿUthmān's capital, sacked it and executed him.[134] The Naiman Mongol leader Küchlüg had in autumn 1211 captured the Qara Khitay Gürkhan Chih-lu-ku / Zhilugu near Kāshghar and in effect taken over the Qara Khitay titulature and state apparatus for himself.[135] Such radical changes in the governmental pattern of eastern and western Turkistān facilitated the expansion to the west shortly afterwards of Chinggis Khan's hordes. According to a Western source, al-Nāṣir had been negotiating with the Mongols in order to delay the advance of the Khwārazmians, an allegation that Angelika Hartmann thought might well contain some truth.[136] At all events, the policies of provocation pursued by ʿAlāʾ al-Dīn Muḥammad brought down on his head the Mongols in 1217, with fateful consequences not merely for his own dynasty but for the Islamic lands in Asia as a whole.

IX

As has been seen (above, p. 21), the two centuries or so that we have covered brought new ethnic groupings and demographic trends into the eastern Islamic lands, with consequences in the linguistic field and in that of land tenure and utilisation. The question remains, were there significant reactions in the fields of culture and of literary and artistic expression, within the milieux of the Qarakhānids, the Saljuqs and Khwārazm Shāhs, as well as political, economic and demographic ones? It was noted (above, p. 29) that the earliest monuments of Turkish Islamic literature emanate from the Qarakhanid milieux of western and, especially, eastern Turkistān, either composed at the courts of the khans, as with the *Qutadghu bilig* and the moral and didactic treatise, the *ʿAtabat al-ḥaqāʾiq*, of Aḥmad Yüknekī, or written by an expatriate like Kāshgharī. Poetry, both of a folk nature and of a higher, court level,

134 Juwaynī, trans. Boyle, vol. II, pp. 392–5; Barthold, *Turkestan*, pp. 365–6; Pritsak, 'Die Karachaniden', pp. 56–7.
135 Ibn al-Athīr, vol. XII, pp. 269–71; Biran, *The empire of the Qara Khitai*, pp. 79–80.
136 *EI*² 'al-Nāṣir li-Dīn Allāh', at vol. VII, pp. 997–8.

continued to be composed, according to Kāshgharī.[137] There may also have been at this time the beginnings of a Sufi mystical literature in Turkistān, but the topic is shrouded in mystery. The shaykh Aḥmad Yasawī (i.e. from Yasi in the middle Syr Darya valley, the modern town of Turkistān in the southernmost part of the Republic of Kazakhstan; it is there that the shaykh's mausoleum, later known as 'the Kaʿba of Turkistān' and a great goal of Central Asian pilgrims, is situated) is often adduced as a significant figure here, but the death date given for him of 562/1167 is probably too early and the collection of Turkish mystical poetry attributed to him, the *Dīwān-i ḥikmet*, was almost certainly put together by other hands after his death.[138] Whether the Qarakhānid rulers ever became literate in the prestige Islamic languages of Persian and Arabic, let alone in Turkish itself, is unknown. Their close identification with their Turkish military backing, their loose system of governance hence lack of need for a complex bureaucracy of traditional Islamic type, and their lifestyle that was at least semi-nomadic, would seem to make this problematical; Turkish must have been the language which continued to loom largest in their mode of life and for their military and administrative needs. Yet perhaps this is too facile a judgement; the career at the Bukhārā court of a poet like Amʿaq (d. *c.* 543/1148f.) shows that a poet in Persian could secure honour and doubtless financial reward from the Qarakhānids.[139]

We have more information about the situation in the Persian lands. Here the ethnically Turkish Saljuq sultans and their provincial governors and atabegs became highly dependent on the bureaucracies that they inherited from their predecessors for running the complex administrative and fiscal structures which had evolved over the centuries. The personnel involved were almost wholly Persian, imbued with Arabo-Persian procedures and traditions of statecraft; they possessed the whole gamut of the Islamic sciences and, especially, polite learning, *adab*, and all these they placed at the disposal of their Turkish masters. Although we know that the Saljuqs' predecessors in Khurāsān, the Ghaznavids, became highly literate within one or two

137 Barthold, *Zwölf Vorlesungen*, p. 117.

138 See *EI*^{2}. 'Yasawiyya' (Th. Zarcone). Accepted ideas about the Yasawiyya are due for a radical reappraisal in the light of recently discovered texts on religious life in Islamic Central Asia which may bring the order's origins into the seventh/thirteenth century rather than in the previous one. See the Foreword by Devin DeWeese to Gary Leiser and Robert Dankoff (trans. and eds.), *Early mystics in Turkish literature: Mehmed Fuad Köprülü* (London and New York, 2006), pp. viii–xxvii.

139 See Alessio Bombaci, *Storia della letterature turca dall'antico impero di Mongolia all'odierna Turchia* (Milan, 1956), part III, ch. VII 'L'età qarakhanide (XI–XII sec.)', pp. 81–106.

generations from their Central Asian *ghulām* origins,[140] we have little firm information about the cultural and linguistic attainments of the Saljuq sultans themselves. Barthold's categorical assertion that the sultans 'were strangers to all culture' and that Sanjar was certainly illiterate requires more substantial proof than he adduced.[141] It does not seem likely that the contemporary ʿImād al-Dīn al-Iṣfahānī would praise the dead Muḥammad (II) b. Maḥmūd as 'the most learned of his house' (*awfarahum ʿilm*[an]) (see above, p. 64) if the sultan had been illiterate. Unlike the case with the Qarakhānids, no substantial body of Turkish lore and literature emanated from the Saljuq courts, so far as we know. The literature of their courts which *is* known to us is wholly in Persian and Arabic, with Persian poets of high calibre, such as Muʿizzī, the eulogist of Malik Shāh and Sanjar (d. between 519 and 521 / 1125 and 1127), and, a generation or so later, such poets at Sanjar's court as Adīb Ṣābir (d. between 538 and 542 / 1143 and 1148) and Anwarī (585 / 1189 or 587 / 1191). Of provincial courts, we find Khāqānī (d. 595 / 1199) at that of the Shīrvān Shāhs in Transcaucasia, while the Khwārazm Shāhs Atsız and Il Arslan had the services of an outstanding poet and epistolary stylist in Rashīd al-Dīn Waṭwāṭ (d. 578 / 1182f. or somewhat earlier).[142] It seems improbable that there was not some degree of Persianisation among the Turks at the court circles here, to which there had been some degree of predisposition, on the evidence of Maḥmūd Kāshgharī; he states that 'when the Oghuz mixed with the Persians they forgot many Turkic words and used Persian instead'.'[143] Although the course of Islamic history shows that rulers of Turkish origin clung much longer to their native tongue than is often (mainly from lack of explicit information) thought,[144] and Turkish must have remained a valuable tool for diplomacy and communication with Turkish tribesmen and chiefs remaining within the steppes, the attraction of Persian ways and customs at rulers' courts and the use of Persian governmental lore and practice in their administrations inevitably led to the formation of a composite culture combining Turkish vitality with Persian sophistication.

140 Bosworth, *The Ghaznavids*, pp. 129–30.
141 Barthold, *Turkestan*, p. 308.
142 See J. Rypka *et al.*, *History of Iranian literature* (Dordrecht, 1968), pp. 194–5, 197–9, 200, 202–8.
143 *Dīwān lughāt al-turk*, trans. R. Dankoff and J. Kelly, *Compendium of the Turkic dialects* (Cambridge, MA, 1982–5), vol. I, p. 115.
144 See *EI*² Suppl. 'Turks. III. Literature. 6 (a) Turkish literature in Muslim India' (B. Péri) on the use of Turkish in Mughal India up to the nineteenth century.

2

The early expansion of Islam in India

ANDRÉ WINK

In the wake of the Islamic conquests, trading activity between the Middle East and India appears to have expanded dramatically. Between the Hellenistic period and the first/seventh century, the Arabs had lost their predominance in this trade to the Ethiopians – Byzantium's trading partners in the Indian Ocean – and, to an even greater degree, to the latter's political and commercial rivals, the Sasanid Persians. The early Islamic conquests brought Byzantine/Sasanid rivalry to an abrupt end while bringing the Middle East into a single monetary exchange system and linking the Mediterranean to the Indian Ocean under the aegis of a single imperial polity. Gravitating towards Mesopotamia and the Persian Gulf, the trade with India became the major external source of wealth for Islam, at the same time that the overland route to China acquired much greater significance with the accession of the Tang dynasty in 618 CE. The Islamic trade with India was a trade in pepper (the 'black gold of India') and spices in the broadest sense, but included an almost infinite array of other items, from jewels to metallurgical products and ivory, to teakwood and textiles, which were exchanged against precious metals, horses and many manufactured products such as paper, glass and the like.

The India trade

There is significant evidence to show that the conquests in Makrān and Sind were, at least partly, motivated by the ambition to safeguard the India trade against the (semi-)nomadic tribes of these regions, such as the Jats and Mīds, whose predatory activities affected much of the western Indian Ocean, from the mouth of the Tigris up to the coasts of Sri Lanka. The early conquests in the eastern direction enhanced the power of the Azd ʿUmān at the expense of the tribes of the Sindian wastes. These Azdī of Oman were a thoroughly Persianised population of Arab seafaring merchants (Zoroastrians before the rise of Islam) which had been settled on the coasts of

Fārs and Kirmān–Makrān, and as far as Sind from the days of the first Sasanid emperor Ardashir (r. 226–41 CE) onwards.[1] The Azdī rise to power on the easternmost frontiers of the caliphate did not go unopposed (the notorious governor al-Ḥajjāj turned against them in the late first/seventh century) but demonstrates a strong link between the expansion of Islamic commercial interests and the conquests on the Indian frontier. This link persisted until about 447/1055, when the Saljuq Turks occupied Baghdad, the India trade was rerouted to the Red Sea and the Balūchī overran Makrān. Until that time, in Oman the ports of Ṣuḥār, Julfar, Daba and Masqaṭ rose to eminence under the Azdī trading network. Many other Persian Gulf cities became important after the conquest of Sind and the subsequent foundation of Baghdad, including Baṣra (newly founded by the Arabs), Kūfa, Wāsiṭ and al-Ubulla – the latter city attracting such a large part of the India trade that it came to be regarded as 'part of al-Hind'. The efflorescence of these cities is another strong indication of the importance, from ʿAbbāsid times onwards, of the Persian Gulf connection with India, and beyond, with Malaya and China, as well as with Africa. The Būyid dynasty (320–454/932–1062) boosted this trade still further, along the entire littoral, by effectively keeping the Balūchī tribes of Kirmān at bay.

Throughout the early centuries, the Ḥijāz and the Red Sea ports were completely eclipsed. Jiddah and Aden were not restored until the rise of the Fāṭimids (359–567/969–1171) and the Ayyūbids (567–650/1171–1250) in Egypt. By then the intercontinental trade route through Syria and Asia Minor, via Baghdad, to the Persian Gulf was subverted by the arrival of the Saljuq Turks, the subsequent devastation of Fārs by the Shabānkāra and other unhinged tribes elsewhere in the Gulf region (including the islands), the concomitant decline of the ʿAbbāsids and by the beginning of the Crusades in 485/1096. To some degree the decline of Baghdad, Shīrāz and of Baṣra and other cities in the Persian Gulf, was offset by the Saljuqs' policy of rerouting the India trade from Makrān to Hormuz and northwards to Jīruft and Bardasīr, in Kirmān, and as far as Yazd and the caravan route to Azerbaijan and Anatolia.[2] But the decline of the Persian Gulf and the rise to pre-eminence of the Red Sea and Egypt in the India trade were sealed by the fall of Constantinople in 600/1204, during

1 A. Wink, *Al-Hind: The making of the Indo-Islamic world*, vol. I: *Early medieval India and the expansion of Islam, 7th–11th centuries* (Leiden, 1990), pp. 45–53; G. F. Hourani, *Arab seafaring in the Indian Ocean in ancient and early medieval times* (Princeton, 1951), pp. 45–6; D. Hawley, *Oman* (London, 1977), pp. 17, 19.

2 J. Aubin, 'La ruine de Sīrāf et les routes du Golfe Persique aux XIe et XIIe siècles', *Cahiers de Civilisation Médiévale, X–XII* (1959), pp. 295–301; A. Wink, *Al-Hind: The making of the Indo-Islamic world, vol. II: The slave kings and the Islamic conquest of India, 11th–13th centuries* (Leiden, 1997), pp. 17–23.

the Fourth Crusade, and the destruction of the caliphate by the Mongols in 656/1258. From the Red Sea and Egypt, links with Malabar, especially with Calicut, and with the Coromandel were increasingly given emphasis over those with Gujarat and western India, although the latter areas were soon to regain an important role in trade, above all that in textiles.

Outside the conquered territories of Makrān and Sind, Zābul and Kabul, and parts of the Punjab, up to the eleventh century no permanent Muslim communities appear to have been founded in India beyond the coastal towns.[3] On the coasts, however, Muslim communities took root in innumerable locations, from Gujarat and the Konkan to Malabar, the Coromandel, Sri Lanka, Bengal and beyond, to the Malay–Indonesian archipelago and China; and everywhere their raison d'être was trade. Sustaining the emerging networks of Indian Ocean trade, we also find significant numbers of Hindus and Jains migrating to the Persian Gulf, Oman, Socotra, to the Red Sea and its islands, as well as to Indonesia, but in all likelihood these did not found permanent communities. If we can go by the later medieval and early modern evidence, Hindus and Jains, beyond India, remained sojourners.[4] It was the Muslim diasporas in the Indian Ocean that became numerically the most important and by the thirteenth century overshadowed all others, including the Jews and Parsis, not least because they routinely gave rise to mestizo communities, originally often through *muṭʿa* or 'temporary marriage' with women of low fishing and mariner castes, while living under Hindu domination. Up to about the tenth century the largest settlements of Muslim trading groups of this kind, mainly originating from the Persian Gulf region and Oman and to a lesser extent from the Hadramawt, were to be found on the coasts of Gujarat and the Konkan, in the domain of the Rashtrakuta or Ballaharā kings. Here the Arab element gradually submerged under the Turkish conquests from as early as the eleventh century but mostly from the late thirteenth century or, in the Konkan, under the expanding Bahmani dominion from the fourteenth century onwards. According to al-Masʿūdī, the largest settlement was that of about 10,000 Muslims in Saymur (south of present-day Mumbai).[5] In the tenth century, many of these were *bayāsira*

3 M. J. De Goeje (ed.), *Al-aʿlāq al-nafīsa of Ibn Rusta* (Leiden, 1892), p. 135.

4 Cf. C. D. Ley (ed.), *Portuguese voyages, 1498–1663* (London, 1947), p. 22; S. C. Levi, *The Indian diaspora in Central Asia and its trade, 1550–1900* (Leiden, 2002), pp. 261–2; A. Wink, *Al-Hind: The making of the Indo-Islamic world*, vol. III: *Indo-Islamic society, 14th–15th centuries* (Leiden, 2004), p. 200.

5 al-Masʿūdī, *Murūj al-dhahab*, 2 vols. (Cairo, 1948), vol. I, p. 170.

(sing. *baysarī*), that is 'Muslims born in al-Hind of Muslim parents'.[6] Particularly the Caulukya king Siddharaja (1094–1143) fostered the growth of coastal Muslim communities in Gujarat – which came to include more and more local converts and ran the gamut from wealthy traders and shipping magnates to sailors, oilmen and other manual labourers.[7] In the popular imagination, Siddharaja later became the founder of all important Muslim communities in Gujarat and he was reported to have been converted to their sects by the Bohras and the Khojas – Ismāʿīlī communities which became larger in Gujarat than anywhere else in India – and even by the Sunnīs who entered Gujarat from the Turkish-dominated areas of the north.

The Arab-Muslim trading communities of south India – the Nāvayat of the Canara coast, the Mappilas of Malabar and the Lappai or 'Labbai' (a corruption of *ʿArabī*) of the Coromandel – retained the Shāfiʿī legal orientation and assiduously fostered the Arab identity that they had brought with them from Baghdad and the Persian Gulf, as well as from Arabia, Yemen and Hadramawt, even though these same communities adopted important elements (such as the matriarchal customs of Malabar) from their Hindu host environment. They remained closely connected, through trade and continued migration, with the Muslims of the Middle East, and developed more important ties (also through intermarriage) with other Shāfiʿī-Muslim societies which sprang up in the tropical ecosystems of south India, Sri Lanka and the Indian Ocean island archipelagoes than with the 'Tartars' of continental India, whom they affected to regard as late converts and who were Ḥanafī.[8] With origins going back as far as the eighth century in some places, and some Mappilas in effect claiming to be refugees from the reign of terror of al-Ḥajjāj in Iraq at the end of the seventh century, the coastal Muslims of south India were clearly dominant in maritime commerce (especially long-distance) by the thirteenth century and had grown numerous in many ports. But the position of these south Indian Muslims among the politically empowered Hindu majority in south India always remained extremely ambivalent, especially in caste-conscious Malabar. Here, the Mappila and even the 'Pardeshi', or foreign Muslim element, while enjoying a privileged position among the Hindu military upper castes of Nāyars and Nambūtiri Brahmans, nonetheless

6 On this term, see J. C. Wilkinson, 'Bayāsirah and Bayādīr', *Arabian Studies*, 1 (1974), pp. 75–85.
7 S. C. Misra, *Muslim communities in Gujarat* (Baroda, 1964), pp. 7–13.
8 Cf. S. Bayly, 'Islam in southern India: "Purist" or "syncretic"?', in C. A. Bayly and D. H. A. Kolff (eds.), *Two colonial empires: Comparative essays on the history of India and Indonesia in the nineteenth century* (Leiden, 1986); Wink, *Al-Hind*, I, pp. 69–86.

remained separated from these by a ritual barrier of pollution.[9] Other groups of Muslims – of unknown provenance – found employment as mercenaries in the indigenous armies of south India, serving the kings of Malabar and Sri Lanka alike.[10]

The conquest of Zamīndāwar, Zābulistān and Kabul

By contrast, the sweeping victories in the north of the Indian subcontinent, in the frontier regions of Zamīndāwar, Zābulistān or Zābul, and Kabul (all of which are now in southern and eastern Afghanistan), as well as in Makrān, Balūchistān and Sind, allowed the Muslims to assume political power over a Hindu–Buddhist population which vastly outnumbered them but could, as revenue and tribute-paying subjects, be fitted into the easternmost administrative divisions of the caliphate. Zamīndāwar was the lowland region around Kandahar ('where people do not eat cows') and here the Zunbīl kings and their kinsmen the Kābulshāhs – who were probably descendants of a southern branch of the Chionite Hephthalites or 'White Huns' – had their winter residence, in the religious centre of their realm where the cult of the Shaivite god Zūn was performed on a hilltop. Zābul was the mountainous zone of the upper Helmand and Kandahar rivers where the Zunbīls had their summer residence. Partly due to the inaccessibility of their realm, the resistance of the Zunbīls was much more effective than that of other Indian kings who took up arms against the invading Muslims. In effect, the Zunbīls and the related Kābulshāhs were able to slow down the final conquest until as late as 256/870 – holding out for more than a century and a half after the remnants of Chionite-Hephthalite power were erased in the upper Amū Daryā valley, in Herat and the surrounding region of Bādhghīs, as well as in the region of what is now northern Afghanistan, and for as long after the Brahman kings of Sind had been overthrown at their first encounter with the Muslim armies.

The Zunbīls' tenacious resistance thwarted an attempted Muslim advance through Zābul and Kabul to the Indus Valley as early as 22/643.[11] Arab forces advanced to the shrine of Zūn in 32/652f., mutilating the icon (the shrine itself survived until as late as the third/ninth century), and after that date mounted frequent plunder and slave expeditions as far as Ghazna, Kabul and Bāmiyān, first from a base in Zarang, in Sīstān, and subsequently from Bust, a town to

9 Wink, *Al-Hind*, II, pp. 275–80.
10 *Ibid.*, pp. 268–9.
11 Wink, *Al-Hind*, I, pp. 119–28.

the east of Zarang which drew great numbers of volunteer *ghāzīs* but never became more than a turbulent frontier outpost.[12] The Zunbīl more than once struck back at the Arab positions in Sīstān – up to the end of the eighth century this remained the 'ill-omened frontier' of consolidated conquests. According to al-Mas'ūdī, 'the Zunbīl was that king of al-Hind who marched to Sīstān with the design to invade the kingdom of the Syrians'.[13] An army sent under al-Ḥajjāj, in 77/697f., to Zamīndāwar and almost as far as Kabul, was virtually destroyed. Arab infighting in Sīstān, exacerbated by Zunbīl interventions, brought the Islamic conquest to a halt, and for about one-and-a-half centuries no lasting military gains were made in the difficult terrain of the Zunbīl's dominions, although the latter, lying athwart the vital caravan route from Hind to Khurāsān, were frequented by Muslim merchants, as well as by renegades, especially Khārijites persecuted by al-Ḥajjāj, and although some Afghans living in the area were possibly converted at this early stage. In the first half of the eighth century, the Zunbīl instead chose to pay homage to the Tang emperor of China.

The military breakthrough in Zābul and Kabul (although not yet in mountainous Ghūr) occurred in the late ninth century CE, under the Ṣaffārids, a dynasty of local Sagzī provenance which had an intimate knowledge of the geographical and climatological conditions of these regions. By then the Buddhist 'Turk Shāhī' dynasty of Kabul had made room for a 'Hindū Shāhī' dynasty, founded by a Brahman vizier of the old dynasty in a new capital at Wayhind.[14] Under the Sāmānids, a Turkish slave general by the name of Alptigin set up his headquarters at Ghazna in 322/933, and then founded the dynasty of the Ghaznavids, which drove the Hindū Shāhī rulers further into the Punjab, and ultimately, in the early fifth/eleventh century, into Kashmir, thereby giving a new impetus to Islamic expansion in Hind.

The conquest of Makrān

From a military point of view, the first report received by the caliph 'Uthmān relating to the Indian borderlands of Makrān revealed conditions which were hardly more encouraging than those of the Zunbīl's dominions to the north: 'the water is scanty, the dates are bad and the robbers are bold; a small army

12 C. E. Bosworth, *Sīstān under the Arabs: From the Islamic conquest to the rise of the Ṣaffārids (20–250/651–864)* (Rome, 1968).
13 al-Mas'ūdī, *Murūj al-Dhahab*, I, p. 211.
14 Y. Mishra, *The Hindu Sahis of Afghanistan and the Punjab, AD 865–1026* (Patna, 1972).

would be lost there, and a large army would starve'.[15] This report essentially refers to the ancient *Gedrosia*, the barren territory where Alexander nearly lost his army in 325 BCE, on his march back from the Indus to Susa. Here the Greeks had been startled, after having become acquainted with the far more civilised barbarian kingdoms of the north-west frontier, by the primitive life of the *Ichthyophagoi*, or what the Persians called the *Māki-khorān* – the 'fish-eaters' of which the name Makrān is said to be a corruption.

It was an ancient convention to regard the satrapy of the *Gedrosi* (Makrān), with those of the *Arachotae* (Kandahar), *Arii* (Herat) and *Parapanisidae* (Kabul), as part of India. Al-Bīrūnī, in the fifth/eleventh century, similarly maintained that 'the coast of al-Hind begins with Tiz, the capital of Makrān, and from there extends in a south-eastern direction towards the region of Debal'.[16] From a physiographic point of view, Makrān is an extension of the Great Desert or Dasht-i Lūt of Persia, and the part that was Indianised and ruled by Indian kings lay to the east of a wholly arid tract, extending up to Tiz (the chief commercial centre of Makrān, on the Persian Gulf), and was called *Kīj-Makrān*, now constituting the south-western division of the province of Kalat, Balūchistān, with a coastline of 320 kilometres. *Kīj-Makrān* consisted largely of mountain ranges with cultivable tracts with towns and villages running from east to west, with Kīj being the largest inland town, on the great highway connecting India with Persia which in the early centuries of Islam was even more vital to the economic life of the caliphate than the route running through the Kabul river valley.

The Arabs first invaded Makrān, routing a large assembly of Indian troops and elephants, in 23/644, towards the end of the caliphate of 'Umar, almost three-quarters of a century before Muḥammad al-Qāsim conquered Sind and established the first Muslim settlement on the Indus.[17] Parties of horsemen began exploring the Makrān coastal regions during the caliphate of 'Uthmān (r. 23–35/644–56). Soon after, under 'Alī (r. 35–40/656–61) and Mu'āwiya (r. 41–60/661–80), military raids into the Makrān were resumed which took the Arabs as far inland as Qiqanan, and even beyond, as far as al-Ahwar (Lahore), but these resulted mostly in defeat. Later in the caliphate of Mu'āwiya, Makrān was 'conquered by force', and permanent garrisons were established which subdued the country as far as Qandabil, obtaining more regular flows of tribute and slaves, although not without reversals. Some of the main towns of Makrān had

15 al-Balādhurī, *Futūḥ al-buldān* (Cairo, 1932), pp. 420–1.
16 Pliny, *Natural history*, II (London, 1947), Book VI, XX.53–XXI.56, XXIII.78–9; al-Bīrūnī, *Kitāb fī Taḥqīqī mā li-l-Hind* (Hyderabad, India, 1958), p. 167.
17 Wink, *Al-Hind*, I, pp. 129–44.

to be subdued again by Muḥammad al-Qāsim when the latter launched the 'holy war against Sind and Hind' which was authorised by the caliph Walīd and which led to the conquest of Sind by Arab forces around 96/712.[18]

In Makrān, in the succeeding centuries, an unknown number of Arab Muslims, living in urban enclaves, appear to have asserted authority against largely unconverted and 'depraved' native tribes – Jat dromedary-men, an emerging population of Balūchīs, pastoral and seafaring Mīds preying on coastal traffic from Sind, and numerous other mobile groups which the Arabs had to contend with, often in violent encounters. Like Zābul, Makrān became a place of refuge for Khārijites and other extremists, following in the wake of Persian Mazdeans fleeing from Kirmān. But there was also the increasing number of Azdī Arabs, originating from Oman, which established an important mercantile presence in Makrān that lasted until the Balūchīs, under pressure from the Saljuqs, overran the province in about 447/1055 from the west. An important conduit of long-distance commerce, Makrān remained more or less under the effective control of the caliphate between 96/712 and 256/870. The authority of the Ṭāhirid, Ṣaffārid and Sāmānid dynasties of eastern Persia did not extend as far as Makrān, and we find that, by 256/870, Makrān was effectively controlled by a number of *mutaghalliba* chiefs who had 'usurped' power without being appointed by Baghdad but who still used the caliph's name in the Friday prayers in Kīj, and in a place called Mashki, on the Kirmān border, as well as elsewhere, without paying tribute. Even then however the commercial traffic through Makrān and along its coasts appears to have continued undiminished.

The conquest of Sind

Sind, the alluvial plain on both sides of the middle and lower course of the river Indus or 'Mihran', extending from Attock and the Salt Range to the coast, and with varying portions of the dry and hilly uplands, such as Qiqanan, adjoining Balūchistān, and of the Thar desert included, was conquered under al-Ḥajjāj, 'governor of 'Irāq and Hind and Sind' from 74/694 to 95/714. This occurred at a time of great expansionist ambition, amounting to an all-out reorientation of the caliphate in the eastern direction, towards Iraq and the Persian Gulf, towards Mā Wara' al-Nahr, and, above all, towards Hind.[19] Like

18 U. M. Daudpota (ed.), *Chachnāma* (Hyderabad, Deccan, 1939), p. 91; al-Balādhurī, *Futūḥ al-buldān*, p. 424.
19 Wink, *Al-Hind*, I, pp. 144–218.

Makrān, Sind had a mixed Hindu–Buddhist population, with some Zoroastrian elements. Most of Sind also had a pastoral-nomadic economy, and much of it was still wilderness, a land of deserts, marshes and reeds. It probably held no more than several hundred thousand people along the lower Indus, next to perhaps 50,000 in Balūchistān. In some places, especially in the areas around al-Manṣūra and Multān, it was considerably more densely settled by agriculturists, and it was generally more urbanised than Makrān, commensurate with its greater commercial importance. For the Arabs, Sind was overwhelmingly important as a thoroughfare of the India trade, both overland and maritime.

The first Arab naval expedition to Sind was undertaken in ʿUmar's reign, either in 15/636 or 23/644, but was unauthorised by the caliph, who was hesitant about naval expeditions at that time.[20] The Arab naval force came via Baḥrayn and Oman to Debal and then crossed the sea to Tanah, a port on the west coast of India, near present-day Mumbai.[21] The same caliph, having received reports that Sind was inaccessible, 'even worse' than Makrān, also prohibited an overland expedition from Makrān to Sind. ʿUthmān, too, prohibited his troops from invading Sind. Not until Makrān was occupied and the Mīds of the coast of Sind were brought to heel under Muʿāwiya was such hesitation set aside. The expeditionary force which was then, in 94/710, sent from Shīrāz in southern Persia under al-Ḥajjāj's nephew and son-in-law, the seventeen-year-old Muḥammad al-Qāsim, consisted of 6,000 Syrian cavalry and detachments from Iraq with the *mawālī*. These were military men who would not return to their places of origin but would settle down, with native women, in colonies which were known as *junūd* and *amṣār*, usually in or around the main towns of Sind. The conquest army that invaded Sind in 95/711 was not followed by a mass migration of Arab tribes, nomads or otherwise, as had been the case in Iraq between 17/638 and 25/656. Reinforcements, however, of camel riders were made along the way, and more troops were transferred by sea, while numberless volunteers soon began to arrive from Syria, and local forces of Jats and Mīds were swept up in the conquest army as well.

The port city of Debal was taken first, with great slaughter, and here the first mosque of the subcontinent was built. Other cities to the north of Debal capitulated to the conquest army, which then crossed the Indus for the

20 H. M. Ishaq, 'A peep into the first Arab expeditions to India under the companions of the Prophet', *Islamic Culture*, 19 (1945), pp. 109–14; B. M. B. K. As-Sindi, 'The probable date of the first Arab expeditions to India', *Islamic Culture*, 20 (1946), pp. 250–66.

21 al-Balādhurī, *Futūḥ al-buldān*, p. 420; Daudpota, *Chachnāma*, p. 73.

decisive engagement with Dahir, the Brahman king of Sind, who was killed in battle, his head, with those of 'the chiefs of Sind' and a fifth of the booty and slaves, sent to al-Ḥajjāj. The governor rightly surmised that this victory practically put all of Sind in his hands and, on the occasion, delivered a sermon in the great mosque of Kūfa congratulating his people on 'the conquest of Hind and the acquisition of immense wealth'.[22] The capital cities of Brahmānābād, Alor and Multān, with all fortresses in between, were now taken in quick succession, with, according to the sources, casualties on the Muslim side remaining low, while the enslavement of great numbers of women and children accompanied the killing of the 'fighting men' of Sind. Few chose to convert. But more mosques were built, and Friday prayers were held and coins were issued in the name of the caliph. The victorious Muḥammad al-Qāsim was executed in 96/715 as part of a purge undertaken against the relatives and protégés of al-Ḥajjāj, upon the latter's death, after having attempted to thwart the succession of the new caliph Sulaymān.

Subsequent Umayyad governors made repeated attempts to convert Dahir's son Hullishāh and other surviving members of the Sindian ruling elite, but with little lasting result. Apostasy and rebellion went hand in hand. The Arabs remained at war in Sind, even while conducting immensely lucrative raids, both by land and by sea, as far as Cutch, Gujarat and Rajasthan. Such raids, too, went not without reverses. An inscription in Sanskrit of the Gurjara-Pratihara king Bhoja I commemorates how Nagabhata, the founder of the dynasty, defeated a powerful 'Mleccha king' who had invaded his dominion.[23] In the last decades of the Umayyad caliphate, in fact, the position of the Arabs not only appears to have deteriorated in many parts of Sind, but they withdrew altogether from regions to the east and south.

This was also the time, however, when the two major stronghold towns were built of al-Maḥfūẓa and al-Manṣūra, on opposite sides of a now unknown lake 'which borders on al-Hind', and here the Arabs could secure their position.[24] Al-Manṣūra, which appears to have been built adjacent to 'old Brahmānābad', the former capital of the Brahman rajas, became the seat of the later governors. There are now three main masses of ruins in this area, approximately 75 kilometres to the north-east of modern Hyderabad. To none of these the name of al-Manṣūra is attached, the city having been destroyed, like its predecessor Brahmānābad and so many other cities of Sind and Hind, by an

22 Wink, *Al-Hind*, I, p. 205.
23 *Indian Antiquary* (Bombay, 1872–1923), 60 (1911), p. 240.
24 al-Balādhurī, *Futūḥ al-buldān*, pp. 430–1.

earthquake and shifts in the course of the river occurring at some time after the fifth/eleventh century. But it was from the secure bases of these twin cities that the early ʿAbbāsid governors, displaying varying degrees of loyalty to the caliphate, engaged in a new round of conquest activities, again both by sea and by land, and extending Arab control beyond previous limits, even, fleetingly, to the coasts of Gujarat and Kathiawar. They also regained control of Multān and the upper Punjab, subduing the Jats and Mīds in a range of localities, while at the same time building mosques of increasing size and number.

Sind, with Makrān, went its own way, under hereditary governing dynasties, by about the same time that the Ṭūlūnids in Egypt and the Ṣaffārids in Sīstān gained practical autonomy, and the Zanj revolt occurred in Iraq. *De facto* renunciation of caliphal control over Sind occurred in 256/870. By this time Sind, like Makrān, was parcelled out among a number of *mutaghalliba* chieftains who were under the authority of hereditary governors but sent them no revenue or tribute. Among the hereditary Arab governors of Sind the two most important ones in the fourth/tenth century were those of Multān and al-Manṣūra, both still mentioning the ʿAbbāsid caliph in their Friday prayers, although, as the century wore on, Multān appears to have paid allegiance to the Shāhī rulers rather than Baghdad. Multān became an Ismāʿīlī principality when it openly proclaimed the sovereignty of the fourth ruler of the Fāṭimid dynasty of Egypt, al-Muʿizz (r. 341–65/953–76), the anticaliph who was also known as 'the western one'. Al-Muqaddasī, visiting Sind in 375/985, observed: 'In Multān the khuṭba is read in the name of the Fāṭimid (caliph) and all decisions are taken according to his commands. Envoys and presents go regularly from Multān to Egypt. Its ruler is powerful and just.'[25] In Sind generally, the Fāṭimid *daʿwa* of missionary Ismāʿīlism – an organised Shīʿite Muslim sect with roots in western India and Sind going back to the ninth century but not officially embraced by any ruling dynasty until the Fāṭimids of Cairo espoused it – was extraordinarily successful and appears to have been related to the developments in trade.[26] When the Fāṭimids extended their control down the Arabian and African shores, the Red Sea route gained greatly in importance, eclipsing the Persian Gulf in the trade with India. By the mid-fifth/eleventh century, even Baghdad was temporarily held in the Fāṭimids' name. In Sind, Makrān and Balūchistān, Ismāʿīlī propaganda and Fāṭimid trade (which was supported by military

25 M. J. De Goeje (ed.), *Al-Muqaddasī, Descriptio imperii moslemici* (Leiden, 1906), p. 485.

26 B. Lewis, 'The Fatimids and the route to India', *Revue de la Faculté des Sciences Économiques de l'Université d'Istanbul* (Oct. 1949–July 1950), nos. 1–4, pp. 50–4; M. J. De Goeje, *Mémoire sur les Carmathes du Bahrain et les Fatimides* (Leiden, 1886).

intervention, as well as by the introduction of a Fāṭimid coinage) developed side by side, indicating that Sind remained the vital commercial hinge that it had become in the second/eighth century. When Maḥmūd of Ghazna conquered Multān in 400/1010, the Ismāʿīlī communities suffered a severe setback. They later revived significantly, only to be suppressed once more in 570/1175 by Muḥammad Ghūrī, but never entirely.

Throughout the three centuries of Arab-Muslim rule in Sind, it appears, urbanism increased. The pastoral and only lightly Indianised Jats and similar tribes which the Arabs encountered in the waste and swamp lands throughout lower and central Sind and which they generally described as 'highway robbers', 'thieves' and 'pirates',[27] were brought under the political authority of the Muslim state. They were either demilitarised and domesticated, or enlisted in protection rackets as caravaneers, dromedary-men, watchmen and the like, or directly enlisted in the armies. Significant groups of Jats were also deported as slaves to Iraq, or settled in the swamps of the Shatt al-ʿArab (a policy inherited from the Sasanids). Throughout these centuries, there also appears to have been a substantial, although by no means complete, shift away from the pastoral nomadism of lower Sind to a more settled, agricultural existence in the Multān area and the Punjab, particularly among the Jats. Even the notorious Mīds, who were especially numerous in south-eastern coastal Sind, do not seem to have engaged in large-scale piracy at sea between 221/836, when Arab attacks on them intensified, and the early fifth/eleventh century, although they held on to a pastoral existence. There is no evidence that conversion to Islam had proceeded very far by the fifth/eleventh and sixth/twelfth centuries anywhere in Sind, nor that the Buddhists converted.[28] In the early Islamic world, Arab Sind was, above all, important as a conduit of the India trade. The conquest, the quickened pace of commerce, and the increase of traffic between India and the heartlands of the Umayyad and ʿAbbāsid caliphates, as well as western Asia, Africa and Europe, also led to a noteworthy dissemination of numerous Indian crops – hard wheat, rice, sugarcane, new varieties of sorghum, banana, sour orange, lemon, lime, mango, as well as spinach, artichoke and eggplant/aubergine among them – and new agricultural techniques to parts of the

27 Daudpota, *Chachnāma*, pp. 61, 215; al-Balādhurī, *Futūḥ al-buldān*, p. 424.

28 As is maintained by D. N. Maclean, *Religion and society in Arab Sind* (Leiden, 1989). Maclean, like others before him, argues that Buddhists collaborated with the Arabs at an early stage and converted to Islam, lured by the prospect of being incorporated in a 'pan-Islamic international trade network'. Not only is there no evidence for this theory, but Buddhism and Hinduism occurred in blurred forms in Sind.

world far beyond India.[29] This process was relatively slow and less easily visible, but its results revolutionised agriculture and may well have been the most significant legacy of early Muslim rule in Sind over the long term.

The emergence of post-nomadic empires

The next, and most important, chapter in the history of the early expansion of Islam in India begins with the Turks, a people of Central Asian origin but no longer nomadic by the time of their arrival in the subcontinent in the late fourth / tenth and fifth / eleventh centuries. Due to the conquests of the Turks, by the seventh / thirteenth century more people would be living under Islamic imperial rule in India than anywhere else, even though it would be a long time before these numbers would be reflected in the numbers of converts. Meanwhile, the old Islamic heartlands, with only Egypt excepted, between the fifth / eleventh and seventh / thirteenth centuries, suffered nomad invasions on an increasingly large and devastating scale – first the Saljuqs, then the Mongols (with, in Iraq, Bedouin making destructive inroads into the breaches left open by the Mongols) – followed by extensive nomadisation and a concomitant long-term decline of the urban and economic infrastructure. India did not suffer from nomad devastation and already had a population at this time of around 100 million people, which was, moreover, continually increasing. With the majority of these living in the fertile northern plains – at the time one of the richest agricultural regions – which were now coming under Islamic rule, and with the Islamic heartlands in disarray but maritime trade with Egypt expanding, the Indian subcontinent moved to a central position within the Islamic world at large.

Nomads have never been able to establish empires in the monsoon climate of India.[30] The Turks who established their Islamic empire beyond Sind in the fifth / eleventh century, like their pre-Islamic predecessors (the Shakas, Kushanas and Hephthalites), are better designated as post-nomadic people, with origins in the steppes but no longer active practitioners of pastoral nomadism. The successive post-nomadic empires which they established were a quite specific adaptation to the ecological conditions of India. The Indian subcontinent, from a physiographic point of view, was a zone of transition between the nomadic world of the deserts and steppes which stretched from North Africa to Central

29 A. Watson, *Agricultural innovation in the early Islamic world: The diffusion of crops and farming techniques, 700–1100* (Cambridge, 1983).

30 Wink, *Al-Hind*, II, pp. 52–76 and *passim*; *Al-Hind*, III, pp. 118–69; J. J. L. Gommans, 'The silent frontier of South Asia, *c.* AD 1000–1800', *Journal of World History*, 9, 1 (1998), pp. 1–23.

and Inner Asia and the humid, equatorial parts of Asia where intensive rice agriculture was practised in alluvial river plains enclosed by rainforests. Because the arid zone of deserts and steppes had important extensions into India, the subcontinent was always closely linked to the nomadic world of the arid zone and it shared some of its features. Historically, it meant, above all, that the Indian subcontinent was conquered repeatedly by people of nomadic background and then colonised to varying degrees, but that it was never subjected to extensive nomadisation. Another branch of the Turks, the still nomadic Saljuqs, in the fifth/eleventh century, sponsored a significant pastoral immigration into Iran and Anatolia, but failed to do so in India. There are remains of Saljuq mausoleums and minarets in Afghanistan, but not beyond. On the Indian frontier, the incidental settlements of Saljuqs that may have occurred remained isolated, like in Baltistān (on the bank of the Indus, between Gilgit and Ladakh), where the rajas and viziers claim descent from Saljuq Turks who arrived here just before their fellow tribesmen pushed into Iran and Anatolia.[31] And there are some Saljuq families in the Juggaur district of Awadh who claim to be descendants of the brother of Nūr al-Dīn Muḥammad, the Artuqid ruler of Diyārbakr, and to have arrived there from Anatolia as part of the Ghūrid armies in 580/1184. But none of these were nomads. Later, in the seventh/thirteenth century, the Mongol nomadic hordes in their turn failed to establish themselves in India on a permanent basis. Only in areas like Binbān and the Kūh-i Jūd, on the north-west frontier of the subcontinent, did Mongol occupation lead to the devastation of agricultural land and large tracts of agricultural land being turned into pasture to sustain the Mongol cavalry. This did not happen in the plains. India was, for climatological and ecological reasons, unsuitable for Mongol-style nomadism. India's patchy pastoral economy of sheep, goats and cattle always stood in a competitive relationship with sedentary agriculture, and it could not accommodate large hordes of Turkish and Mongol nomads on account of its lack of good pasture-lands and appropriate fodder grasses, particularly for horses. The humid climate of most of the subcontinent was detrimental to the health of horses and did not provide good breeding conditions, outside a few areas that were an extension of the arid zone, as in the north-west, or in some parts of the Deccan. Generally, Turko-Mongol writing is pervaded by fear of India's hot and humid climate and concomitant unhealthy conditions for horses as well as men.

The Turkish conquest of India, then, did not significantly modify the equilibrium between nomadic and sedentary people. The Turks who

31 D. Murphy, *Where the Indus is young: A winter in Baltistan* (London, 1977), p. 185.

migrated to India from the steppe, like those who were in the vanguard of the military conquest, always left their nomadism behind. But, even though their numbers were dwarfed by the size of the domestic population of the subcontinent, the impact of the Turks was immensely important. For one thing, the Turks extended the rule of Islam across the Indian plains. For another, the Turks, straddling the arid north-west frontier from Afghanistan to the mouth of the Indus as well as the steppe lands, acquired a virtual monopoly of the regular supply of good warhorses that the subcontinent could not provide for itself. Most importantly, the Turkish conquest armies, consisting of regular and irregular recruits from the nomadic steppes and built around a core of *mamlūks* but never accompanied by sprawling nomadic hordes with their flocks and herds of sheep, with women and children in tow, brought about a revolution in warfare and military technique that would change the patterns of political and resource mobilisation of the subcontinent forever.

The inhabitants of the steppes, living in conditions which were optimal for horse breeding, in medieval times distinguished themselves by the practice of mounted archery, and this allowed the Turks to prevail militarily over their sedentary neighbours, in India as much as in Byzantium, Iran or China. For this reason the Turks could bring about a horse-warrior revolution in India even though they could not bring about a pastoral-nomadic one. The military differential between the Turks and the Indians, both social and technical in origin, was an essential factor in the early centuries of incessant conquest activity, especially because the Turks were relatively few in numbers and prone to be decimated by disease. While the co-ordinated deployment of mounted archers was essential for Turkish military victory, it appears beyond doubt that in India itself archery was left to infantry and a relatively small number of elephant-riders. Although horses and horsemanship had a long history here, India failed to develop mounted archery, and it was this failure which was exposed by the Turks coming from Central Asia.

The heavy (although never exclusive) reliance on horses and mounted archery by the post-nomadic Turkish empires is what set them apart not only from the Indians but also from the Muslim Arabs who preceded them in the conquest of the north-western frontier areas of the subcontinent. The battles of the Arabs in the first centuries of Islam were mostly fought by infantry, supported by archers. However, these infantry armies of the Arabs were not recruited from among the nomads but mostly from among the sedentary population of the towns and oases. The relatively minor nomadic element in the Arab armies was largely put to tactical use as light cavalry, especially in raiding excursions. What was essential in the Arab armies was superior mobility in the campaigns in the desert and the ability to concentrate forces over great distances by making use of the dromedary. The role of the dromedary was decisive in the early Arab conquests and explains, at least partly, why these conquests did not go much beyond Sind and the arid regions of the Thar desert. But in spite of the prominent role they gave to the dromedary, the Arab conquerors were clearly not nomads, nor did they introduce mounted archery to India, nor did they bring large numbers of nomadic pastoralists along at a later stage for relocation in Sind.

Post-nomadic expansion of the kind that the Turks undertook in India could normally only be consolidated in the interstices of the sedentary world, along India's inner frontier of arid and semi-arid habitats. Hence the Islamic globalisation of the economy, concomitant with the great increase of the offensive capabilities of mobile warfare in these centuries, followed the vagaries of the arid zone. As a result, in this period of post-nomadic empire formation, the role of horses, dromedaries and oxen increased considerably, enlarging India's capacity for warfare, transportation and cultivation simultaneously.

The importance of the domesticated elephant was, however, from now on gradually reduced in the new warhorse military economy. In India, elephants were kept in forested reservations outside the cultivated realm where they needed a transhumance circuit which included both elevated and lowland, even swamp-like, terrain. Such elephant forests, like grazing pastures for horses, stood in a competitive relationship with sedentary agriculture. Over time, with the agricultural realm expanding, the ecological situation of elephants in many parts of the subcontinent had come to resemble more and more that of horses. Horse-grazing, on the other hand, had the advantage that it could be done in non-contiguous areas, which were, moreover, not necessarily excluded from any other use, as elephant forests mostly were. The mobility of elephants was limited, while they had to be kept in a half-tamed or wild state in forest reservations, and was further impeded by the fodder problem. Horses were more mobile, being always tame, and could more easily be controlled, relocated, concentrated and deployed over long distances. Beginning with the post-nomadic empires of the Turks in the late fourth/tenth and fifth/eleventh centuries, the disadvantages of the keeping and use of horses relative to elephants were gradually reduced to the point that elephants were bound to become ever more obsolete in warfare. Horses proved to be tactically much more useful in mobile warfare, while elephants could only be deployed statically, in set battles.

In general, the evidence shows that the post-nomadic empires of medieval India were in an almost permanent state of military mobilisation, and that they relied specifically on mounted archers, much like nomadic empires. They were almost equally fluid and indeterminate in their institutional infrastructure (lacking, notably, a clear law of succession). The major difference was that they did not rely on pastoral nomadism but on agriculture as their means of subsistence. Post-nomadic armies were thus trimmed of their livestock, and unlike the nomadic armies mobilised by the Saljuqs and Mongols, did not move in conjunction with women, children and other non-combatants, while they were always broken up in smaller contingents and never moved *en masse*.

From Ghazna to Lahore

Al-Bīrūnī, in his *Kitāb al-Hind*, dates the beginning of 'the days of the Turks' from 'the time when they seized power in Ghazna under the Sāmānī dynasty, and sovereignty fell to Nāṣir al-Dawla Sabuktigīn'.[32] The dynasty of the Ghaznavids, which was then founded, was from the beginning preoccupied with the invasion of the major river plains, first of the Indus, then the 'five-river' land of the Punjab, and finally the 'two-river' land of the Ganges–Yamuna Dūāb. It would pursue these goals until 582/1186, when the dynasty was overthrown by the Ghūrids and their Turkish slave generals who, in their turn, would push the conquests as far as the eastern Ganges delta. Thus, for almost two centuries, the Turkish rulers of Ghazna played an important role in the expansion of Islam.[33] They were quick to proclaim themselves the caliphal defenders of Sunnī orthodoxy against the Shīʿite Būyids and the Ismāʿīlī principalities of Sind. Most importantly, they took it as their historic mission to conquer 'the infidels of al-Hind'.

Acutely conscious of their post-nomadic status, the Ghaznavids and their Turkish slaves recast themselves as a Perso-Islamic ruling elite with such zeal (adopting even non-Turkish names) that it is almost impossible to find significant reminders in the Persian historical record of their Turkishness, or of their former paganism, let alone their former nomadism. The fact remains that Turks from the steppes were the most important ethnic component of the Ghaznavid armies from beginning till end, especially of the *mamlūk* leadership and elite troops, even though these armies were at all times rather heterogeneous, including recruits from among the semi-nomadic Arab population of

32 al-Bīrūnī, *Kitāb al-Hind*, p. 16.

33 C. E. Bosworth, *The Ghaznavids: Their empire in Afghanistan and eastern Iran, 994–1040* (Edinburgh, 1963); Bosworth, *The later Ghaznavids: Splendour and decay: The dynasty in Afghanistan and northern India, 1040–1186* (Edinburgh, 1977); Wink, *Al-Hind*, II, pp. 112–35.

Khurāsān (which had become 'a second Arabia'), and now also from among the Afghans (still absent in the Arab armies), Daylamī infantry and cavalry (originally from the Caspian Sea area), Tājīks or 'Persians' from Khurāsān and various groups of Indians – soon enough Indian Muslims as well. According to contemporary sources (which arc almost certainly highly exaggerating), under Sultan Maḥmūd of Ghazna (r. 388–421/998–1030), these regular troops could number over 50,000, excluding provincial garrisons. Volunteer *ghāzīs*, who went unregistered and without salaries, living off plunder, are said to have joined in the *jihād* in even greater numbers.

Up to the end of Maḥmūd's reign, such Ghaznavid armies remained extremely mobile, undertaking raids into Hind, after the monsoon rains had subsided, on an almost annual basis, and then withdrawing to Ghazna with booty and slaves. From about 404/1013f., garrisons were beginning to be left behind and forts were conquered on a more permanent basis, while more and more petty Hindu rajas were beginning to be co-opted in the conquest state. Lahore gradually emerged as a second Ghaznavid capital in the Punjab but did not replace Ghazna until 555/1160, when the latter city was taken over by the Ghūrids. There were practically no permanent additions to the Ghaznavid conquests beyond Sind and the Punjab at any time, so that beyond these areas the pattern remained one of lightning raids into 'infidel' territory. Some of the major sacred sites of the Hindus, such as Kanauj, Mathura, Thaneshwar and Sōmnāth, were plundered, their icons destroyed or removed, while enormous amounts of treasure which had been accumulated over centuries (the figures given by many texts are astronomical) were transferred to the Ghaznavid capital and brought back into monetary circulation or, in their turn, carried off by the Saljuq armies when they temporarily seized Ghazna in 511/1118. Scores of mosques were erected with the rubble of smashed temples, with carefully selected fragments being remitted to Ghazna to be trampled by the faithful.

Demographic losses resulting from the destruction and killing concomitant with warfare, as well as from the large-scale deportation of war captives and slaves, were probably severely aggravated by the outbreak of a famine, followed by epidemic disease, in 423/1033, in the wake of several decades of prolonged campaigning, which seemed to indicate that the great age of Ghaznavid expansion was drawing to a close. According to a later historian, Firishta: 'This year of 423/1033 was remarkable for a great famine (*qaḥt*) in many parts of the world. The famine was followed by a pestilence which swept away many thousands from the face of the earth. In less than one month 40,000 people died in Iṣfahān alone. Nor did it rage with less violence in

Hindustān, where whole countries were entirely depopulated.'[34] In the Punjab, when the Hindu Shāhī ruler Anandapala was forced out (causing the Ismā'īlī *amīr* of Multān to flee as well), a great exodus of Brahmans appears to have occurred from the increasingly Muslim-dominated province towards the mountain valley of Kashmir, as well as to Varanasi and other areas still beyond the reach of the 'country-conquering Turushkas'. Among the invading Turks, the most substantial losses of manpower were probably caused by exposure to the almost entirely new disease pool – comprising malaria, smallpox, cholera, bubonic plague and a host of others – of the hot and humid climate of the densely settled plains of India rather than by warfare as such.

An investiture patent was sent from the caliphal office in Baghdad in 421/1030, officially recognising not only the Punjab as a Muslim domain under the Ghaznavids but also all the areas which they had conquered to the west, as far as Qasdar, Sibi or Walishtān, Qiqanan and Makrān. The dynasty held on to its possessions in northern and eastern Afghanistan, as well as its Indian conquests, for over a century more. Contemporary authors attached great significance to the establishment of Saljuq suzerainty over Ghazna in 511/1118, consequent upon the death of Mas'ūd. By that time, however, the real threat to the Ghaznavids' survival came not from the Saljuqs but from the Shansabānīs of Ghūr.

Mountains of Fīrūzkūh, plains of Hind

The Shansabānī dynasty superseded the Ghaznavids in the second half of the twelfth century. This dynasty was not of Turkish, nor even Afghan, but of eastern Persian or Tājīk origin, speaking a distinct Persian dialect of its own, like the rest of the inhabitants of the remote and isolated mountain region of Ghūr and its capital of Fīrūzkūh (in what is now central Afghanistan). Here it presided over a mainly agricultural rather than a nomadic population – a source of slaves for the Arabs – whose external commercial connections were alleged to have been in the hands of Jews since the time of Hārūn al-Rashīd.[35] As long as he remained a *Mālik al-Jibāl* or 'King of the Mountains', the Ghūrid ruler did not have a cavalry at his disposal but merely an army of footsoldiers

34 *Ta'rīkh-i-Firishta* (Lucknow, 1864), p. 41.

35 N. Lees (ed.), *Ṭabaqāt-i-Nāṣirī of Abū 'Umar al-Jūzjānī* (Calcutta, 1894), pp. 36–7; Wink, *Al-Hind*, II, pp. 135–49; C. E. Bosworth, 'The early Islamic history of Ghūr', *Central Asiatic Journal*, 6 (1961), pp. 116, 118; for a modern account, in Dutch, of Fīrūzkūh, see G. Mandersloot, *Firozkohi: Een Afghaans Reisjournaal* (Rotterdam, 1971).

equipped with long shields made of bullock-hide and cotton cloth. When Turkish and Mongol pastoral nomads did penetrate into Fīrūzkūh in the early seventh/thirteenth century they, eventually, under Ögedei, utterly destroyed it, bringing the Jewish presence to an end as well.

Islam had come to Ghūr, or at least to its capital, long before the Ghaznavids began to meddle with the Shansabānīs' dynastic disputes and, in the period leading up to the mid-sixth/twelfth century, began to prop up the dynasty against rival mountain chieftains. Gathering strength, the Shansabānī ruler acquired the title of sultan in return for tributary status. Soon after the mid-sixth/twelfth century, however, the Ghūrid sultan 'Alā' al-Dīn Jahānsūz (the 'world-burner') undertook to use his increased strength for the destruction of the city of Ghazna itself, as well as of the palaces at Bust which had been built by Maḥmūd. Now, under an agreement with the Saljuq sultan Sanjar, effective Ghūrid dominion was extended over neighbouring regions like Tukhāristān, Bāmiyān, Zamīndāwar, Bust and parts of Khurāsān, or as Jūzjānī, the chief chronicler of the Shansabānī dynasty, wrote, with some exaggeration, 'from Hindustān and the frontier of Chin and Mahachin to Iraq and from the Jihun river in Khurāsān to Hormuz'.[36] In the process, the composition and character of the Ghūrid armies changed entirely.

Not only did the geographic recruitment area of the Ghūrid army broaden in the second half of the sixth/twelfth century, but cavalry became all-important. In the Ghūrid cavalries that invaded India we find Afghans, Damghānīs from Qūmis in northern Iran, Tājīks from Khurāsān, Khalaj from Garmsīr and Zamīndāwar, Saljuq *amīrs* from Rūm, and innumerable 'Ghuzz Turks' who had arrived in Khutlan and Chaghaniyan around 511/1118 and in Tukhāristān, Ghazna, Kabul and Zābul after the mid-sixth/twelfth century. Moreover, when in 556/1161 Sayf al-Dīn Muḥammad succeeded to the throne of Fīrūzkūh, the Ghūrid state evolved from a local clan-based polity into an empire led by a Turkish *mamlūk* elite which was largely purchased in the steppes of Central Asia, thus coming very close to the post-nomadic model of the Ghaznavids who preceded them in the conquest of Hind. Having subdued the Ghuzz Turks at Ghazna, the Ghūrid Mu'izz al-Dīn (better known as 'Muḥammad Ghūrī') in 569/1173 'ascended the throne of Ghazna like Maḥmūd'. The Ghūrid conquest of Hind then became the work of Sultan Mu'izz al-Dīn, the ruler of the appanage of Ghazna from 569/1173 to 599/1203 and of Fīrūzkūh between 599/1203 and 602/1206, and three of his Turkish slaves, Quṭb al-Dīn Aybak, Nāṣir al-Dīn Qabācha and Tāj al-Dīn Yildiz, and

36 Lees (ed.), *Ṭabaqāt-i-Nāṣirī*, p. 76.

one non-slave, Ikhtiyār al-Dīn Muḥammad bin Bakhtiyār Khalajī. Without sons of his own, Muʿizz al-Dīn arranged for his Turkish slaves to become the heirs to his dominion after his death. Meanwhile he effectively used his prerogative to keep his own Shansabānī kinsmen out of his appanage of Ghazna, and by extension out of Hind, and could monopolise its by now diminished but still considerable wealth for himself.[37] In this way, Turkish predominance in the expanding empire was sealed.

The essential difference between the Ghūrids and their Ghaznavid predecessors did not lie in different military strategies or tactics – both relied heavily on mounted archery – but probably in the logistics of supplies. By the late sixth/twelfth century we first hear of the activities in north-western India of regular supply corps or commissariats, the roving bands of grain dealers with bullock trains which in later times were called *Banjāras*. These appear to have made their appearance with the Ghūrid armies at this time, some of them already converting to Islam, according to later tradition, under Muḥammad Ghūri.[38] The first nomadic Muslim caravaneers (*kārwānīyān*) supplying the Ghūrid armies in the field apparently came from the Multān area athwart the route of the earliest Ghūrid campaigns in India. Aiming to bypass the Ghaznavid dominion in the Punjab, Muʿizz al-Dīn in 570/1175 had taken the southern route through the Gomal Pass, and Multān was the first city he captured, followed by Uch, in upper Sind, leaving both in the hands of a governor. He returned in 573/1178 via the same route, proceeding through the desert towards Nahrwāla in Gujarat, still in an attempt to outflank the Ghaznavids. The defeat of his exhausted army by the Caulukya king Mularaja II induced him finally to give up the southern route. But the nomadic caravaneers of Multān, if later tradition can be relied on, accompanied the Ghūrids in many, perhaps all, subsequent campaigns.

These subsequent campaigns during the next five years resulted in the subjugation of Sind, as far as Debal and Makrān. Peshawar, Sialkot and, through strategem, Lahore were secured by 582/1186, bringing to an end Ghaznavid rule in the Punjab. Coming into a strategic position to advance into the plains of northern India, the Ghūrids then began to engage Pṛthivīrāja, the Cāhamāna 'King of the Earth'. Pṛthivīrāja, heading a powerful alliance of

37 S. Kumar, 'The emergence of the Delhi sultanate, 588–685/1192–1286', Ph.D. thesis, Duke University (1992), pp. 9–29.

38 M. A. Sherring, *Hindu tribes and castes*, vol. III (New Delhi, 1974; first published 1881), p. 80; H. M. Elliot, *Memoirs on the history, folk-lore, and distribution of the races of the north western provinces of India*, vol. I (London, 1869), p. 52; P. Carnegy, *Notes on the races, tribes and castes, inhabiting the province of Awadh* (Lucknow, 1868), p. 137.

Indian kings, initially prevailed in the so-called First Battle of Tara'in of 587/1191, forcing the 'army of Islam' back to Lahore. In the following year, however, Pṛthivīrāja's army was scattered and defeated in the Second Battle of Tara'in, in which the Ghūrid elite guard of 10,000 mounted archers appears to have played a decisive role.

In the events which then unfolded, Quṭb al-Dīn Aybak began his meteoric rise. The forts of Sarsatī, Hānsī, Sāmāna and Kahram, then Ajmer, Mīrath, Baran, Delhi and Kol, were all in his hands prior to 589/1193. Officially, it was still Muʿizz al-Dīn who received caliphal authorisation for these conquests and who built the first triumphal arches and Jāmiʿ Masjid in the emerging new Indo-Muslim capital of Delhi. But Aybak, the former slave, was about to ascend the throne of an independent sultanate of Delhi which was largely his creation – a watershed event that happened in 602/1206.

In the intervening years, the conquests were extended from Delhi: to Rajasthan, Varanasi and Bayana; to Gwalior, 'the pearl of the necklace of the forts of Hind'; up to Badā'ūn and Katahr, in the northern Dūāb, and as far as the frontier of the country of Ujjayn. The Candella forts of Kalanjar, Mahoba and Khajuraho were taken by Aybak in 598–9/1202–3. Badā'ūn became the starting point for the conquests of Awadh, Bihār and Bengal, by Muḥammad bin Bakhtiyār Khalajī, in Aybak's service. Bihār was extensively raided by his forces. Buddhist monks took flight, or were massacred, their monasteries turned into horse stables. Muḥammad bin Bakhtiyār took possession of the capital of Nadiya in 600/1204, bringing Sena rule to an end, leaving the city in desolation, and prompting an exodus of Brahmans to the remotest corners of Bengal, then transferring the seat of Muslim government to Lakhnawti, a former northern Sena capital on the Ganges, near Gaur. Here another provincial administration was set up, the *khuṭba* was read and coins were issued, still in Muʿizz al-Dīn's name, while mosques, madrasas and *khānaqā*s were founded all over the area. In real terms the conquest was now completed. Well over half a millennium after the beginning of the first campaigns, Muslim arms prevailed from the Indus to the mouths of the Ganges and Brahmaputra. The plains of Hind were no longer 'in darkness'.[39]

39 See C. Defrémery and B. R. Sanguinetti (eds. and trans.), *Voyages d'Ibn Batoutah*, 4 vols. (Paris, 1853–8), II, pp. 89–90.

3

Muslim India: the Delhi sultanate

PETER JACKSON

The emergence of an independent Muslim state in India

Following Muʿizz al-Dīn Muḥammad's assassination in 602/1206 the Muslim conquests in the Indo-Gangetic plain went their own way. While the Ghūrid heartlands, Ghūr and Fīrūzkūh, were contested among the various princes of his dynasty, further east the beneficiaries were the Turkish slave (*ghulām*; *banda*) commanders to whom the sultan had largely delegated authority.[1] Two of them – Tāj al-Dīn Yildiz in Ghazna and Quṭb al-Dīn Aybak in Lahore – were quick to establish their *de facto* autonomy. Aybak was acknowledged by the Khalaj rulers who succeeded Muḥammad b. Bakhtiyār at Lakhnawti in Bengal, and thus became the paramount ruler in Muslim India. But Aybak, who contested Ghazna with Yildiz, in turn recognised the overlordship of Muʿizz al-Dīn's nephew and successor, Ghiyāth al-Dīn Maḥmūd; numismatic evidence suggests that he bore no higher title than malik. After Aybak's death in 607/1210f., his heir Ārām Shāh was soon defeated and killed by Aybak's slave and governor in Budaon, Iltutmish, who had been set up at Delhi. Aybak's territories were now disputed among Iltutmish, Yildiz and another former Ghūrid slave lieutenant, Nāṣir al-Dīn Qubacha, who held Multān and Uchch in Sind.

If Aybak was the effective founder of an independent Muslim power in India, Shams al-Dīn Iltutmish (607–33/1210–36),[2] was the real architect of the Delhi sultanate. Although he was initially obliged to acknowledge Yildiz's sovereignty and to content himself with the title of malik, his fortunes

1 Irfan Habib, 'Formation of the sultanate ruling class of the thirteenth century', in Irfan Habib (ed.), *Medieval India 1: Researches in the history of India 1200–1750* (Oxford and Delhi, 1992), pp. 5–7.

2 The correct form of the name was established by Simon Digby, 'Iletmish or Iltutmish? A reconsideration of the name of the Dehli sultan', *Iran*, 8 (1970), pp. 57–64.

improved as a consequence of events beyond the Indus. In 612/1215f., the Khwārazm Shāh Muḥammad b. Tekish overwhelmed the last Ghūrid princes and seized Ghazna from Yildiz. Fleeing into the Punjab, Yildiz was defeated by Iltutmish on the historic battlefield of Tarā'in, captured and later put to death at Budaon. Then, in 617–21/1220–4, the Khwārazmian empire in turn was destroyed by the pagan Mongols under Chinggis Khan. Muḥammad's son Jalāl al-Dīn, defeated by the Mongols on the Indus (618/1221), spent three years in exile in the Punjab, where he carved out for himself a short-lived principality before returning to Persia. The Mongol forces sent in pursuit were unable to apprehend him and ravaged parts of Sind, besieging Multān for several weeks (621/1224); they did not touch the territory of Delhi. Iltutmish had at first made peace with Jalāl al-Dīn, though he seems subsequently to have assisted Qubacha against him.[3]

Qubacha's territories had therefore borne the brunt of the Khwārazmian and Mongol attacks; and this may have weakened him in the face of Iltutmish's assault in 625/1228, when Uchch and Multān fell and Qubacha drowned himself in the Indus to avoid capture. Within the next few years, Iltutmish expelled one of Jalāl al-Dīn's lieutenants from Kurramān and secured the submission of another, Ḥasan Qarluq, who ruled in Binbān. In 628/1230f. his son Nāṣir al-Dīn Maḥmūd overthrew the Khalaj ruler of Lakhnawti, who had assumed the title of sultan, and when a rebellion broke out on the prince's death soon afterwards Iltutmish crushed it in person and brought the Muslim-held regions of Bengal under his control (630/1232f.). Even prior to this, in 626/1229, he had received a patent from the ʿAbbāsid caliph al-Mustanṣir, investing him with the government of the whole of Muslim India. When he died (633/1236), his dominions extended from the river Jhelum almost to the Ganges delta.

Sultans and nobility, *c.* 1220–1295

The elite of the early Delhi sultanate comprised overwhelmingly first-generation immigrants from Persia and Central Asia: Persians ('Tājīks'), Turks, Ghūrīs and also Khalaj from the hot regions (*garmsīr*) of modern Afghanistan. Even if Fakhr-i Mudabbir, writing in 602/1206, exaggerates the improvement in their fortunes that immigrants could expect,[4] it is clear that

3 See Peter Jackson, 'Jalāl al-Dīn, the Mongols and the Khwarazmian conquest of the Panjāb and Sind', *Iran*, 28 (1990), pp. 45–54.

4 Fakhr-i Mudabbir, *Shajarat* [or *Baḥr*] *al-ansāb*, partial edn by Sir E. Denison Ross as *Taʿrīkh* [sic]-*i Fakhr al-Dín MubárakSháh* (London, 1927), p. 20.

from the time of the Ghūrid campaigns northern India exerted a strong attraction upon them. Such immigration grew in the wake of the Mongol campaigns of devastation, and Iltutmish is said to have encouraged it.[5] The majority of the newcomers, perhaps, would have been military men, but a later writer mentions also *sayyids* and *ʿulamāʾ*.[6] Among the latter class was the historian Jūzjānī, a refugee from Ghūr, who first entered Qubacha's service but deserted to Iltutmish on his invasion of Sind in 625/1228, and later rose to be three times grand *qāḍī* of the Delhi empire.

Like the Ghūrids, however, Iltutmish built up a corps of Turkish slave troops, known from the sultan's own *laqab* as the Shamsīs. The later historian Ḍiyā-yi Baranī (*fl.* 758/1357) refers to them by the term *chihilgānīs*: its significance is unclear, though the distributive form may well indicate that each commanded a group of forty *ghulāms*.[7] Baranī characterises Iltutmish's mostly short-lived successors as mere ciphers who watched helplessly while his Turkish *ghulāms* wrested power from the free nobles who had entered Muslim India during his reign.[8]

In some measure, this picture can be substantiated from the *Ṭabaqāt-i Nāṣirī* which Jūzjānī completed in 658/1260. Under Iltutmish's son Rukn al-Dīn Fīrūz Shāh (r. 633–4/1236) the Turkish household slaves massacred a great many Tājīk bureaucrats;[9] shortly afterwards they overthrew and murdered Fīrūz Shāh in a rising on behalf of his half-sister Raḍiyya (r. 634–7/1236–40). She in turn was deposed when she demonstrated signs of independence and showed excessive favour to her African (*Ḥabashī*) master of the horse; the Turks enthroned another son of Iltutmish, Muʿizz al-Dīn Bahrām Shāh (r. 637–9/1240–2). A number of Turkish *amīrs* who attempted to reinstate her as sultan were defeated, and Raḍiyya was killed by Hindus while in flight near Kaithal (637/1240). Following her deposition, considerable power was vested in a military officer who bore the style of *nāʾib* ('viceroy'); Bahrām Shāh's own enthronement was contingent on his acceptance of the Turkish *ghulām* Ikhtiyār al-Dīn Aybak in this position.[10]

5 Jājarmī, preface to his translation of al-Ghazālī's *Iḥyāʾ ʿulūm al-dīn*, British Library ms. Or. 8194, fo. 3v; Nazir Ahmad, 'Bérúní's Kitāb-aṣ-Ṣaydana and its Persian translation', *Indo-Iranica*, 14, part 3 (1961), p. 17; Jūzjānī, *Ṭabaqāt-i Nāṣirī*, ed. ʿAbd al-Ḥaiy Ḥabībī, 2nd edn, 2 vols. (Kabul, AH solar 1342–3), vol. I, pp. 440–1.

6 ʿIṣāmī (*c.* 1350), *Futūḥ al-salāṭīn*, ed. A. S. Usha (Madras, 1948), pp. 114–15.

7 Peter Jackson, *The Delhi sultanate: A political and military history* (Cambridge, 1999), p. 66; Gavin R. G. Hambly, 'Who were the Chihilgānī, the forty slaves of Sultan Shams al-Dīn Iltutmish of Delhi?', *Iran*, 10 (1972), pp. 57–62.

8 Baranī, *Tārīkh-i Fīrūzshāhī*, ed. Saiyid Ahmad Khán (Calcutta, 1861–2), pp. 27–8, 550.

9 Jūzjānī, vol. I, p. 456; cf. also vol. II, p. 36.

10 Jūzjānī, vol. I, p. 463.

Aybak's murder at the sultan's instigation prompted fears that he planned the wholesale annihilation of the Turkish slave commanders, and an army sent to defend the frontier following the Mongol sack of Lahore turned back and besieged Delhi. Bahrām Shāh was put to death and replaced by Fīrūz Shāh's son, 'Alā' al-Dīn Mas'ūd Shāh (r. 639–44/1242–6). We know relatively little of internal politics during Mas'ūd Shāh's reign, but a later writer ascribes his downfall to resentment at his reliance upon African (*Ḥabashī*) slave elements.[11] He was displaced in favour of Iltutmish's youngest son, Nāṣir al-Dīn Maḥmūd Shāh (r. 644–64/1246–66), a shadowy figure in our sources, who passed much of his relatively long reign under the tutelage of his viceroy (*nā'ib*), Iltutmish's former slave, Bahā' al-Dīn Balaban. On Maḥmūd Shāh's death, Balaban succeeded him as Sultan Ghiyāth al-Dīn Balaban (r. 664–85/1266–87).

Baranī clearly exaggerates the incapacity of Iltutmish's progeny. Raḍiyya and Bahrām Shāh both displayed signs of energy, and all four monarchs of Iltutmish's line appear to have tried to build up power bases of their own. The implication, moreover, that the Turkish slaves constituted a discrete or monolithic group is simplistic. No faction comprised exclusively Turkish slave officers. They are found collaborating with *amīrs* of Ghūrī and Tājīk origin as well as free Turkish nobles;[12] while the opposition to Balaban, which included prominent Turkish *ghulām* commanders, was fronted by an Indian slave *amīr*, 'Imād al-Dīn Rayhān.[13] It is possible, of course, that our perspective is distorted not only by Baranī but also by Jūzjānī, who was writing for Balaban, himself a Turkish *ghulām*. Turkish slave officers may only seem to dominate the political landscape because they are the principal focus of the penultimate section (*ṭabaqa*) of his work.

Moreover, far from eliminating immigrant notables the Turkish *ghulām* element ultimately lost out to them. Fugitives from the territories conquered by the Mongols continued to enter Muslim India during Balaban's reign, among them the Khalaj *amīr* and future sultan, Jalāl al-Dīn. From 659/1261, when the Mongol empire dissolved in civil war, even Mongol notables sought asylum in Delhi, where they became known as 'neo-Muslims' (*naw-musulmānān*), and a whole quarter of the old city was assigned to them.[14] Balaban has been accused

11 Yaḥyā' ibn Aḥmad Sirhindī, *Tārīkh-i Mubārakshāhī*, ed. S. M. Hidayat Hosain (Calcutta, 1931), p. 34.

12 Peter Jackson, 'The *Mamlūk* institution in early Muslim India', *Journal of the Royal Asiatic Society* (1990), pp. 347–9, and Jackson, *Delhi sultanate*, pp. 68–9.

13 Jackson, *Delhi sultanate*, pp. 71–3.

14 Firishta, *Gulshan-i Ibrāhīmī*, lithograph edn, 2 vols. (Bombay, AH 1247), vol. I, p. 131, citing the late eighth/fourteenth-century writer 'Ayn al-Mulk Bījāpūrī; Baranī, *Tārīkh-i Fīrūzshāhī*, p. 133.

of sapping the strength of the Turkish nobility by destroying many of his erstwhile Shamsī colleagues; but like his old master Iltutmish he clearly sought to promote his own Turkish *ghulāms* (known as 'Ghiyāthīs'), several of whom received high military command and lucrative assignments (*iqṭā*ʿs).

Balaban's elder son Muḥammad perished in battle with the Mongols (683/1284); and when the old sultan died, a party among the nobility ignored the claims of both Muḥammad's son Kaykhusraw and Balaban's younger son, Bughra Khān, and installed the latter's young and pliable son, Muʿizz al-Dīn Kayqubād (r. 685–9/1287–90). Kaykhusraw, who made an unsuccessful bid for Mongol support, was murdered. Bughrā Khan, who governed Lakhnawti, advanced west in a bid for the throne, but was reconciled with his son and contented himself with autonomy in Bengal. Kayqubād fell increasingly under the control of the powerful justiciar (*dādbek*), Niẓām al-Dīn, who destroyed many of Balaban's Turkish slave officers, and of the immigrant 'neo-Muslim' Mongol *amīrs*. After Niẓām al-Dīn's own murder, a faction deposed the ailing Kayqubād in favour of his infant son, Shams al-Dīn Kayūmarth (r. 689/1290), but lacked the strength to resist the Khalaj commander Jalāl al-Dīn, the governor of Sāmāna, who eliminated both Kayqubād and the child ruler and himself assumed the title of sultan as Jalāl al-Dīn Fīrūz Shāh (r. 689–95/1290–6).

During the seventh/thirteenth century the Muslim-held territories in western Bengal and Bihār were often in rebellion under ambitious governors; from Kayqubād's accession (685/1287) they formed an independent sultanate until their reconquest in 724/1324. The Delhi sultan's authority often barely extended beyond the lower and middle Indus Valley, the eastern Punjab, the towns of the Dūāb and parts of Awadh. Only a relatively small area, comprising Delhi and its environs (*ḥawālī*) and perhaps one or two other strongpoints such as Gwalior, was retained as *khāliṣa*, the 'reserved' territory, exploited directly by the sultan's own revenue officials. The monarch could do no more than grant out other territories to his officers as *iqṭā*ʿ: that is, the grantee (*muqṭa*ʿ) was responsible for extracting tribute from the local chiefs (*rānagān, muqaddamān*) and headmen (*khūṭān*), maintaining himself and a body of troops from the proceeds and, by the turn of the century, forwarding the surplus (*fawāḍil*) to Delhi. In Balaban's reign the appointment of an accountant (*khwāja*) to each *iqṭā*ʿ indicates the government's concern both to maximise its revenues and to rein in the ambitions of its leading *amīrs*.[15]

15 Baranī, *Tārīkh-i Fīrūzshāhī*, pp. 36–7; Irfan Habib, 'Agrarian economy', in Tapan Raychaudhuri and Irfan Habib (eds.), *The Cambridge economic history of India*, vol. I: *c.1200–c.1750* (Cambridge, 1982), pp. 69–70.

Warfare with the Hindu states

The struggles for power at the centre during the seventh/thirteenth century inevitably had an impact on the expansion of the sultanate. In stark contrast with the era of his lieutenancy on Muʿizz al-Dīn's behalf, Aybak's reign witnessed no recorded campaigns against independent Hindu kingdoms, and Iltutmish, during the first fifteen years of his reign, is known only to have headed one such expedition, against the Chauhan (Chāhamāna) kingdom of Jālōr. It is clear, moreover, that some of Aybak's conquests were lost after his death and had to be retaken by Iltutmish, only to pass out of Muslim hands again. Two examples will suffice. The great fortress of Ranthanbōr, seat of the senior line of the Chauhan dynasty, had been reduced to tributary status in 587/1191, but must have defied Iltutmish, who took it in 623/1226. Further east, Gwalior had yielded to Aybak in 597/1200f., but was subsequently lost, since Iltutmish recaptured it in 630/1233. Yet both towns were abandoned under Raḍiyya in 635/1237f. Ranthanbōr was repeatedly attacked (in 646/1248, 657/1259 and 691/1292) before its final reduction by ʿAlāʾ al-Dīn Khaljī. Gwalior's recovery at some point before 657/1259 was short-lived, and thereafter we cannot be sure that it was ever in Muslim hands prior to the eighth/fourteenth century. Even in the 1340s the Moroccan visitor Ibn Baṭṭūṭa describes this important strongpoint as 'an isolated and inaccessible castle in the midst of the infidel Hindus' and sets its garrison at 600 horsemen, who were constantly engaged in *jihād*.[16]

The north-western districts of the Punjab, as we shall see, lay within the penumbra of Mongol sovereignty; even much of the eastern Punjab was home to imperfectly subdued tribes like the Khokhars, the Bhattīs, the Jats and the Mandāhars of Kaithal. There were numerous *mawāsāt* (sing. *mawās*, 'refuge'), where the sultan's writ barely ran and could be enforced only by painstakingly hacking down the jungle.[17] During his reign, as in his final years as viceroy, Balaban's principal concerns appear to have been the reduction of the hilly tracts (*kūhpāya*) west of the capital, the erection of forts in the Dūāb

16 Ibn Baṭṭūṭa, *Tuḥfat al-nuẓẓār*, ed. Ch. Defrémery and B. R. Sanguinetti, 4 vols. (Paris, 1853–8), vol. III, pp. 188, 195, and trans. H. A. R. Gibb and C. F. Beckingham, *The travels of Ibn Baṭṭūṭa AD 1325–1354*, Hakluyt Society, 5 vols. (Cambridge and London, 1958–2000), vol. III, pp. 642, 645.

17 Ibn Baṭṭūṭa, vol. III, p. 389 (trans. Gibb and Beckingham, vol. III, pp. 741–2). For an example (Katehr), see Simon Digby, 'Before Timur came: Provincialization of the Delhi sultanate through the fourteenth century', *Journal of the Economic and Social History of the Orient*, 47 (2004), p. 302 and n. 5.

and punitive campaigns against the notoriously refractory Hindus of Katehr (now Rohilkhand).

Much of the campaigning by the seventh/thirteenth-century monarchs or their representatives, in fact, might seem to have had no purpose – and certainly no effect – beyond the temporary humiliation of Hindu potentates and the guarantee of annual tribute or the acquisition of large quantities of precious metals and impressive numbers of slaves, horses and elephants. Jūzjānī, it is important to note, suggests that the main purpose of warfare against Hindu kingdoms was to amass the resources which would enable the sultans to raise larger armies to resist the Mongols.[18] Whatever the case, in the wake of such swashbuckling and often risky campaigns, the spread of Muslim settlement, the construction of mosques and the regular extraction of land revenue (*kharāj*) from local Hindu chiefs were a less spectacular – and doubtless rather intermittent – process.

The Mongol threat in the thirteenth century

The reigns of Iltutmish's first successors witnessed a steady build-up of Mongol pressure beyond the Indus. Generals acting on behalf of the qaghan Ögedei (r. 1229–41) destroyed the residue of the Khwārazmian principality, driving Ḥasan Qarluq from Binbān into Sind, and reduced to obedience the other local rulers in present-day Afghanistan; they thereby secured the territories that had acted as the springboard for Ghūrid invasions of India half a century previously. Kashmir was invaded and reduced to tributary status in *c.* 632/1235. The first Mongol attack on the Delhi sultanate came in 639/1241, when they sacked Lahore. In 643/1245 they invested Uchch, necessitating a relief expedition under Sultan Masʿūd Shāh. From this point onwards Mongol raids upon the westernmost provinces became an annual occurrence. Nor were they an altogether unwelcome element in the politics of the sultanate. Sultan Maḥmūd Shāh's brother Jalāl al-Dīn took refuge with them in *c.* 1250, and on the orders of the qaghan Möngke (r. 1251–9) an army under Sali Noyan installed him as ruler of a territory that embraced Lahore, Nandana, Kūjāh (now Gujrat) and Sōdra.[19] We do not know what became of the prince,

18 Jūzjānī, vol. II, p. 57.

19 Karl Jahn, 'Zum Problem der mongolischen Eroberungen in Indien (13.–14. Jahrhundert)', in *Akten des XXIV. internationalen Orientalisten-Kongresses München … 1957* (Wiesbaden, 1959), pp. 617–19. I. H. Siddiqui, 'Politics and conditions in the territories under the occupation of Central Asian rulers in north-western India – 13th and 14th centuries', *Central Asiatic Journal*, 27 (1983), pp. 288–306.

though Küshlü Khan, the sultan's governor of Sind, likewise accepted client status in 653/1255; and by the time Jūzjānī wrote in 658/1260 there are signs of apprehension that the Delhi sultanate would fall under Mongol overlordship. In that very year Balaban, as Maḥmūd Shāh's viceroy, was in diplomatic contact with the qaghan's brother Hülegü, who was in overall command of Mongol forces in Persia. The object and outcome of these negotiations are alike unclear, and it is just at this juncture, regrettably, that Jūzjānī's narrative comes to a halt.

The sultanate undoubtedly owed the reprieve it now obtained not so much to diplomacy as to the disintegration of the Mongol empire. Following Möngke's death in 1259, civil war broke out in the Mongolian homeland. Other members of the dynasty took sides in this struggle, and a secondary conflict erupted between Hülegü, in Persia, and his cousin Berke, who commanded the Mongols of the Golden Horde in the Pontic and Caspian steppes. By the time that Qubilai emerged as undisputed qaghan in the Far East (1264), the empire had splintered into a number of rival khanates: the Ilkhanate, under Hülegü and his descendants in Persia; the khanate of the Golden Horde; the Chaghadayid khanate in Central Asia; and the dominions of Qubilai and his successors in Mongolia and China. The situation was further complicated, first, by the flight of Berke's troops from Persia into Afghanistan (*c.* 660/1262) under a commander called Negüder, who gave his name to a new, independent Mongol grouping; and second, by the emergence in Central Asia in 669/1271 of Ögedei's grandson Qaidu, who headed a confederacy of Mongol princes in opposition to the qaghan until his death in 1303. The empire did not again acknowledge a single head until Qaidu's son Chapar submitted to the qaghan Temür in 1304.

These upheavals enabled Balaban, early in his reign, to reassert the sultan's authority in Sind and to restore the fortifications of Lahore. Mongol pressure on the Punjab was naturally at its greatest when mounted by a major Mongol power drawing on the resources of the whole empire or at least of Central Asia. The Negüderi Mongols (or Qara'unas, as they were also known) did not fall within this category. Although they continued to raid the sultanate annually, they appear to have penetrated no further than Rupar, on the upper Sutlej,[20] or the Multān region, where they did, however, succeed in defeating and killing Sultan Balaban's son Muḥammad in 683/1285.

20 Baranī, *Tārīkh-i Fīrūzshāhī*, p. 82: for the corruption in the text here, see S. H. Hodivala, *Studies in Indo-Muslim history*, 2 vols. (Bombay, 1939–57), vol. II, pp. 85–6.

From the Khaljīs to the Tughluqids

The ethnic origins of the Khalaj are obscure; although early Arab geographers class them among the Turkish tribes, by the seventh/thirteenth century they were regarded as a separate people, distinct from the Turks.[21] Yet the significance of the so-called 'Khaljī revolution' does not lie so much in the transfer of power from a Turkish ruling elite to a non-Turkish one. It is true that Jalāl al-Dīn promoted to high office several of his numerous kinsfolk and other fellow Khalaj tribesmen, and that in 690/1291 he had to crush a rebellion by Balaban's nephew and supporters of the old dynasty. But Ghiyāthī *amīrs* were by no means excluded from the state apparatus. It was only after the sultan's assassination by his nephew 'Alā' al-Dīn (695/1296), the *muqṭa*' of Kara, that a marked change occurred in the composition of the ruling class.

Jalāl al-Dīn's youngest son, Rukn al-Dīn, was proclaimed sultan in Delhi, but fled to Multān, where he held out with his brothers until the city fell to his cousin's forces (696/1296). 'Alā' al-Dīn Muḥammad Shāh (r. 695–715/1296–1316) is said to have brought down the great majority of his uncle's *amīrs* and those who survived from the era of Balaban and Kayqubād. His most trusted servitors were close kinsmen and officers who had formed his entourage at Kara. But the example set by the new sultan was infectious, and during the early years of his reign he was confronted with a number of bids by relatives to murder him and seize the throne; even his brother, Ulugh Khan, was allegedly planning an unauthorised expedition to Tilang at the time of his sudden death.

Under 'Alā' al-Dīn Indian slave *amīrs* first appear to have held high military rank, and during the final stage of the reign one of these, the eunuch Kāfūr, attained a position of dominance, persuading the sultan to imprison his son Khiḍr Khan in Gwalior and to nominate as his successor one of his younger sons by the daughter of the Yadava king of Deogir. When 'Alā' al-Dīn died, this child was duly enthroned as Shihāb al-Dīn 'Umar (r. 715–16/1316) under Kāfūr's tutelage. 'Alā' al-Dīn's sons were blinded, with the exception of Quṭb al-Dīn, who engineered Kāfūr's murder and himself ascended the throne as Quṭb al-Dīn Mubārak Shāh (r. 716–20/1316–20). Quṭb al-Dīn was in turn murdered by his Indian favourite Ḥasan, on whom he had conferred the title Khusraw Khan and who now seized the throne. During his brief reign (720/1320), Nāṣir al-Dīn Khusraw Shāh – the only Indian convert, in fact, ever to become Sultan of

21 Baranī, *Tārīkh-i Fīrūzshāhī*, pp. 150, 171–2; C. E. Bosworth and Sir Gerard Clauson, 'Al-Xwārazmī on the peoples of Central Asia', *Journal of the Royal Asiatic Society* (1965), pp. 6, 8; repr. in Bosworth, *The medieval history of Iran, Afghanistan and Central Asia* (London, 1977); Aziz Ahmad, 'The early Turkish nucleus in India', *Turcica*, 9 (1977), pp. 99–109.

Delhi – had all ʿAlāʾ al-Dīn's sons killed. When one of ʿAlāʾ al-Dīn's officers, Tughluq, the *muqṭaʿ* of Dēōlpālpūr, overthrew the usurper with the ostensible aim of avenging his old master's dynasty, he himself was proclaimed sultan as Ghiyāth al-Dīn Tughluq Shāh (r. 720–4/1320–4).[22]

Tughluq, who was in all probability an immigrant of Turco-Mongol origin from the Qara'una (Negüderi) territories in Afghanistan,[23] came to power with the aid of officers who had served under him on the north-western frontier; and men from these regions would play a prominent role in the early years of Tughluqid rule. In 724/1324 the sultan personally intervened in a succession dispute in Muslim Bengal, where Balaban's line had died out earlier in the century,[24] and occupied Sunargaon, installing his own client at Lakhnawti. He died while he was on his way back to Delhi from this campaign later in the year, when a palace that had been erected for his reception at Afghānpūr by his son and heir Ulugh Khan collapsed on him. Ulugh Khan, who now succeeded as Sultan Muḥammad b. Tughluq (r. 724–52/1324–51), is nevertheless exonerated of the charge of parricide by the majority of contemporary sources and of modern historians.

The great Mongol invasions

ʿAlāʾ al-Dīn's reign witnessed a sharp escalation in Mongol attacks. From the 1280s the Negüderi territories had been under pressure from the Chaghadayid Mongols of Transoxiana and Turkistān. By *c.* 1295 the Chaghadayid khan Du'a, who was allied with Qaidu, had established his son Qutlugh Qocha as ruler of a large principality south of the Amu-darya (Oxus). Qutlugh Qocha and Qaidu's commanders were responsible for a series of major assaults, which penetrated more deeply into northern India than previous attacks. The most formidable occurred during ʿAlāʾ al-Dīn's absence from Delhi on campaigns against independent Hindu powers. In *c.* 699/1299f. Qutlugh Qocha in person headed a campaign which almost reached Delhi, although he was wounded and died during the retreat;[25] while in 703/1303 his general Taraghai was able to subject the capital to an investment lasting several weeks.

22 For the probable date of Tughluq's death, usually placed in 725/1325, see Jackson, *Delhi sultanate*, pp. 330–1.

23 R. C. Jauhri, 'Ghiyāthu'd-Dīn Tughluq – his original name and descent', in Horst Krüger (ed.), *Kunwar Mohammad Ashraf: An Indian scholar and revolutionary 1905–1962* (Berlin, 1966), pp. 62–6.

24 Abdul Majed Khan, 'The historicity of Ibn Batuta re Shamsuddin Firuz Shah, the so-called Balbani king of Bengal', *Indian Historical Quarterly*, 18 (1942), pp. 65–70.

25 See Jackson, *Delhi sultanate*, p. 222.

After this, the outbreak of civil war in Central Asia between Du'a and Chapar seriously impaired the Mongols' ability to mount major strikes against India for some time. ʿAlāʾ al-Dīn's *amīrs*, notably Tughluq at Dēōpālpūr, were able not only to defeat invading Mongol forces, who may in some cases have been fugitives, but even to take the offensive and launch campaigns beyond the Indus.[26] Ibn Baṭṭūṭa saw an inscription at Multān in which Tughluq laid claim to twenty-nine victories over the Mongols.[27]

Muḥammad b. Tughluq began his reign with an expedition to Peshawar, which lay on the very border of the Mongol dominions, and may thereby have provoked a large-scale invasion by the Chaghadayid khan, Du'a's son Tarmashirin, who threatened Delhi and advanced as far as Mīrat (Meerut) before withdrawing beyond the Indus. At one time the historicity of this attack was denied, on the grounds that the standard recension of Baranī's *Tārīkh* makes no reference to it; but it is in fact mentioned not only by another contemporary, ʿIṣāmī, but also in an earlier recension of Baranī's work and by an author writing in the Mamlūk empire, who dates it at the beginning of 730 / winter of 1329f.[28] Tarmashirin's attack was to be the last major assault on the sultanate prior to Temür's invasion.

The aims behind the Mongol invasions of India are difficult to assess. Elsewhere in Mongol-held territories the traditional aim of world conquest had not been jettisoned, but it is conceivable that in India the hot season acted as a significant deterrent to permanent occupation. For this reason the Mongols had abandoned the siege of Multān in 621 / 1224,[29] and those whom Jalāl al-Dīn Khaljī installed in the vicinity of Delhi in 691 / 1292 did not remain long because the climate was uncongenial to them.[30] On the other hand, such considerations do not seem to have prevented Mongol notables and their families from settling in India at other times, as during the reigns of Balaban and Kayqubād. The invading Mongol armies in 691 / 1292 and in *c.* 1306 were

26 According to a document found in Amīr Khusraw, *Rasāʾil al-iʿjāz*, lithograph edn, 5 vols. in 2 (Lucknow, 1876), vol. IV, pp. 144–56. See Jackson, *Delhi sultanate*, pp. 229–30.

27 Ibn Baṭṭūṭa, vol. III, p. 202 (trans. Gibb and Beckingham, vol. III, p. 649).

28 Shams al-Dīn Muḥammad al-Jazarī (d. 739 / 1338), *Ḥawādith al-zamān*, ed. ʿAbd al-Salām Tadmurī, 3 vols. (Beirut, AH 1419), vol. III, p. 377; Peter Jackson, 'The Mongols and the Delhi sultanate in the reign of Muḥammad Tughluq (1325–1351)', *Central Asiatic Journal*, 19 (1975), pp. 118–26, and Jackson, *Delhi sultanate*, p. 232.

29 ʿAlāʾ al-Dīn Aṭā Malik Juwaynī, *Tārīkh-i Jahān-gushā*, ed. Mīrzā Muḥammad Qazwīnī, 3 vols., Gibb Memorial Series, vol. XVI (Leiden and London, 1912–37), vol. I, p. 112, and trans. J. A. Boyle, *The history of the world-conqueror*, 2 vols. (Manchester, 1958, repr. in 1 vol., 1997), vol. I, p. 142.

30 Baranī, *Tārīkh-i Fīrūzshāhī*, p. 219.

certainly accompanied by women and children;[31] and during Muḥammad b. Tughluq's reign Mongol commanders, with their wives and offspring, would winter in the Punjab every year in anticipation of the sultan's largesse.[32] Qutlugh Qocha and Taraghai, at least, were probably intent on the plunder afforded by a wealthy city like Delhi. But other campaigns may have represented simply seasonal migrations in search of winter grazing-grounds.

The conquest of India

A change of tempo is also visible during ʿAlāʾ al-Dīn Khaljī's reign in the context of relations with independent Hindu kingdoms. As *muqṭaʿ* of Kara under Jalāl al-Dīn, he had led an audacious raid into the distant Yadava kingdom in the Deccan, sacking its capital, Devagiri (Deogir). Following his accession he launched an expedition against Gujarat (698f./1299f.), which sacked Sōmnāth, Anhilvāra (Patan) and Kanbhāya (Cambay); though the Chaulukyas were not finally overthrown until *c.* 710/1310 and even thereafter Muslim rule was confined to the eastern parts of their kingdom. ʿAlāʾ al-Dīn then embarked upon the reduction of Rajasthan and the far south. While the sultan himself captured Ranthanbōr (700/1301) and Chitōr (703/1303), his generals took Sevana and Jālōr (708/1307f.) and overthrew the Paramāra kingdom of Mālwā (705/1305). As a consequence, an inscription of 1309f. in the vicinity of Chandērī could describe the 'Mlecchas' as having overrun the earth in ʿAlāʾ al-Dīn's time and strongholds such as Dhār, Mandū, Chandērī and Ērach could be granted out as *iqṭāʿ*s.[33]

The sultan's Indian slave lieutenant, Malik Kāfūr, was especially prominent in campaigns further to the south. His first expedition reduced the Yadava king Rāmadēva to client status (706/1307). Rāmadēva was brought to Delhi and treated with honour by ʿAlāʾ al-Dīn, who then sent him back to the Deccan as his subordinate. The value of this relationship was demonstrated in the considerable assistance that Rāmadēva furnished for Kāfūr's subsequent campaigns; his successor, however, would repudiate Delhi's overlordship, necessitating a fresh campaign by Kāfūr against the Deccan (*c.* 714/1314f.).[34] In further expeditions Kāfūr exacted tribute from the Kakatiya kingdom of Tilang (709/1309f.) and the Hoysala kingdom of Dvārasamudra (710/1310f.). An assault on the

31 *Ibid.*, pp. 219, 321–2.
32 *Ibid.*, p. 499.
33 Michael D. Willis (ed.), *Inscriptions of Gopakṣetra: Materials for the history of central India* (London, 1996), p. 22; Baranī, *Tārīkh-i Fīrūzshāhī*, p. 323.
34 Kishori Saran Lal, *A history of the Khaljis AD 1290–1320*, 3rd edn (Delhi, 1980), pp. 255–7.

Pāndya kingdom of Maʿbar (710/1311) secured plunder, though not submission. In the north, meanwhile, by stages that are largely concealed from us, the subjugation of regions like Bundelkhand and Awadh was accelerated.

Expansion into peninsular India continued under ʿAlāʾ al-Dīn's successors. Quṭb al-Dīn headed a successful expedition against the rebellious Deccan (717/1317), and his favourite Khusraw Khān conducted a wide-ranging campaign against Maʿbar; though the reduction of much of the country seems to have been left until the reign of Ghiyāth al-Dīn Tughluq (*c.* 1323) or perhaps that of Muḥammad b. Tughluq (*c.* 1327).[35] It was Muḥammad who, as Ulugh Khān's and his father's heir apparent, had defeated the recalcitrant Kakatiya monarch, Rudradēva II, and asserted direct rule over Tilang (*c.* 721/1321f.). While in pursuit of the rebel Bahāʾ al-Dīn Garshāsp in 727/1327, Muḥammad's generals overthrew the kingdom of Kampila and annexed it to the sultanate.

The spectacular expansion of ʿAlāʾ al-Dīn's reign rested upon the successful imposition of a system of direct taxation within northern India (see below). But more general circumstances underlying Muslim military superiority need to be taken into consideration. One must have been the sultans' access to a larger supply of good warhorses – via the overland route from Central Asia and from the Golden Horde territories in the steppes north of the Black Sea and the Caspian – than was available to their Hindu opponents in peninsular India, who were dependent on the seaborne trade in horses from Fārs and the Arabian peninsula. The Delhi sultans' cavalry often outnumbered that of their antagonists, and the readiness of Hindu princes to pay high prices for good-quality warhorses was notorious.[36]

The sultans' armies may also have enjoyed an advantage in siege technology. It is widely accepted that the late seventh/thirteenth century witnessed the introduction into the subcontinent of the counterweight trebuchet (*maghribī*) from Muslim regions to the west. This represented a major advance on the older type of catapult (*manjanīq*; *ʿarrāda*), since it was capable of throwing a projectile at least four times as heavy over a distance at least twice as great.[37] The role played by gunpowder is less clear. The Mongols had

35 N. Venkataramanyya, *The early Muslim expansion in south India* (Madras, 1942), pp. 70, 122–5.

36 Simon Digby, *War-horse and elephant in the Dehli sultanate: A study of military supplies* (Oxford and Delhi, 1971), pp. 29–32; Ranabir Chakravarti, 'Horse trade and piracy at Tana (Thana, Maharashtra, India): Gleanings from Marco Polo', *Journal of the Economic and Social History of the Orient*, 34 (1991), pp. 159–82; André Wink, *Al-Hind: The making of the Indo-Islamic world*, vol. II: *The slave kings and the Islamic conquest of India, 11th–13th centuries* (Leiden, 1997), pp. 83–7.

37 Jos Gommans, 'Warhorse and gunpowder in India *c.*1000–1850', in Jeremy Black (ed.), *War in the early modern world* (London, 1999), pp. 112–13.

been acquainted with gunpowder since their campaigns of the 1230s in China and had apparently been using it in Persia in the 1250s; and from the very limited evidence found in contemporary Indo-Muslim sources a case has been made for the introduction of gunpowder-based devices into northern India before 1300, perhaps through the agency of Mongol renegades.[38]

Administrative developments under ʿAlāʾ al-Dīn and his successors

Both the successful resistance to major Mongol attacks during ʿAlāʾ al-Dīn's era and the pronounced territorial expansion over which he presided were made possible by administrative measures which, in the first place, greatly extended the area under the sultan's direct control and subjected it to a uniform system of land-tax. Unlike the *kharāj* previously levied, which was simply tribute by another name, that imposed by ʿAlāʾ al-Dīn was a percentage of the value of the crop or, in some regions, of the crop itself, required on the basis of measurement and at the time of the harvest (*bar sar-i kisht*). The rate was 50 per cent, the maximum permitted by the Ḥanafī school which was dominant in the sultanate. Baranī, who is our principal source for these measures, presents them at one point as an expedient designed to bring low the rural Hindu chiefs, an aim with which he himself was stridently in sympathy.[39] But he also makes it clear that the impulse behind them was militaristic[40] – to enable the sultan to raise considerably larger armies, in order, presumably, both to repel the Mongols (see below) and to conquer the Hindu kingdoms of central and southern India. It is a measure of the government's enhanced effectiveness that the land-tax proper could be levied in both newly conquered Jhāyin (near Ranthanbōr) and in Kābar (in the hitherto turbulent territory of Katehr).

The second arm of ʿAlāʾ al-Dīn's policy was the enforcement of low prices and wages in Delhi and its environs and possibly in some other regions also. Doubt has been expressed regarding the reliability of the data supplied by Baranī, who is our principal source for these measures; but Irfan Habib has

38 Iqtidar Alam Khan, 'The role of the Mongols in the introduction of gunpowder and firearms in South Asia', in Brenda J. Buchanan (ed.), *Gunpowder: The history of an international technology* (Bath, 1996), pp. 33–44; Khan, 'The coming of gunpowder to the Islamic world and north India: Spotlight on the role of the Mongols', *Journal of Asian History*, 30 (1996), pp. 27–45; Khan, *Gunpowder and firearms: Warfare in medieval India* (Oxford and Delhi, 2004), pp. 17–40 *passim*.

39 Baranī, *Tārīkh-i Fīrūzshāhī*, pp. 287–8.

40 *Ibid.*, pp. 304, 323–4.

shown both that they were intimately linked with the taxation policy and that Baranī's material is corroborated by other authors.[41] The chief priority was that prices for grain and other foodstuffs should be kept at a level which would enable the sultan to pay his troops at a fixed and relatively modest rate.

We are told that ʿAlāʾ al-Dīn's price-control measures did not survive him.[42] But the growth of centralised control at the expense of the sultan's representatives in the provinces undoubtedly continued after his death. Although under Ghiyāth al-Dīn Tughluq the *muqṭaʿ* still had access to that portion of the *iqṭāʿ* revenue which was earmarked for the stipends of his troops, a further erosion of the *muqṭaʿ*'s rights occurred during the reign of his son and successor. We know from an external observer that there was now a direct link between the revenue department and the ordinary trooper, that is, that the allocation to the *muqṭaʿ* of the funds to pay his troops, and hence his capacity to bind them to his own interests, had ceased.[43] Ibn Baṭṭūṭa reveals that within the province of Amroha, for instance, there was now ensconced, alongside the military commander, a financial officer (*wālī al-kharāj*) answerable directly to the sultan.[44] It has been plausibly suggested that this encroachment may have fostered the discontent among the military class that characterised the latter years of Muḥammad's reign.[45]

The reigns of Muḥammad b. Tughluq and Fīrūz Shāh

At the accession of Muḥammad b. Tughluq (r. 724–52/1324–51), the Delhi sultanate embraced a larger area than at any time previously. The sultan's reputation as a formidable holy warrior and victor over the Mongols reached Persia and Mamlūk Egypt,[46] and according to Ibn Baṭṭūṭa, who visited India during Muḥammad's reign, even the rulers of the Maldives feared him.[47] He seems to

41 See Irfan Habib, 'The price regulations of ʿAlāʾuddīn Khaljī – a defence of Ẓiāʾ Baranī', *Indian Economic and Social History Review*, 21 (1984), pp. 393–414.

42 Baranī, *Tārīkh-i Fīrūzshāhī*, pp. 383–6.

43 Ibn Faḍl-allāh al-ʿUmarī (d. 749/1348), *Masālik al-abṣār fī mamālik al-amṣār*, partial edn by Otto Spies, *Ibn Faḍlallāh al-ʿOmarī's Bericht über Indien* (Leipzig, 1943), Arabic text p. 13 (German trans. pp. 37–8), and trans. I. H. Siddiqi and Q. M. Ahmad, *A fourteenth-century Arab account of India under Sultan Muḥammad bin Tughlaq* (Aligarh, 1975), pp. 37–8.

44 Ibn Baṭṭūṭa, vol. III, pp. 436, 439 (trans. Gibb and Beckingham, vol. III, pp. 762, 763).

45 Habib, 'Agrarian economy', pp. 72–3.

46 Shabānkāraʾī, *Majmaʿ al-ansāb*, ed. Mīr Hāshim Muḥaddith (Tehran, AH 1363 solar), pp. 87–8, 287; Ibn Faḍl-allāh al-ʿUmarī ed. Spies, p. 29 (German trans., p. 55); trans. Siddiqi and Ahmad, p. 54; partial edn by Klaus Lech, *Das mongolische Weltreich*, Asiatische Forschungen, 22 (Wiesbaden, 1968), Arabic text p. 40 (German trans., p. 118).

47 Ibn Baṭṭūṭa, vol. IV, p. 158 (trans. Gibb and Beckingham, vol. IV, p. 843).

have been a man of boundless ambition. Baranī, who for seventeen years was a member of his entourage, asserts that the sultan would not tolerate a single island or closet remaining outside his authority.[48] The same author pays tribute to the efficiency of the revenue department, during Muḥammad's early years, in levying the *kharāj* from an unprecedented number of far-flung provinces.[49]

The successive crises which afflicted the sultanate under Muḥammad were accordingly all the more perplexing. Here we should bear in mind two circumstances. In the first place, the recent imposition of direct rule over so much of the south entailed both the forfeiture of plunder and new fiscal commitments in terms of maintaining garrisons and a civil administration in formerly enemy territory. And second, in the 1330s the Ilkhanate and the Chaghadayid khanate in Central Asia entered upon a period of upheaval, while the Egyptian Mamlūk sultanate underwent a series of monetary crises. We cannot dismiss the possibility, therefore, that in Muḥammad's time the sultanate and its neighbours and major trading-partners were engulfed in a common economic turbulence.

Baranī, however, blames the upheavals on the sultan's own policies: the establishment of Dawlatābād (Deogir), in the Deccan, as the second capital; the so-called 'Khurāsān project'; a sharp increase in the government's revenue demand from the Dūāb cultivators; and the introduction of a 'token' currency.[50] It will be argued here that these various measures were closely linked and that they were by no means as chimerical as Baranī claimed.

Baranī provides inconsistent definitions of the region of 'Khurāsān', which Muḥammad planned to invade, and has thereby misled modern historians. It is clear that the expedition was directed against the old enemy, the Mongol Chaghadayid khanate in Transoxiana and present-day Afghanistan; indeed, at one point Baranī specifies that Mā Warā' al-Nahr (Transoxiana) was the target. A large force – set at 475,000 in an earlier recension of Baranī's work and at 370,000 in the standard text – was mustered specifically for the purpose, but had to be disbanded owing to a lack of money to pay the troops in the second year. In an attempt to keep the troops in training and doubtless also for the sake of plunder, a part of this army was despatched into an unspecified region of the sub-Himalaya (termed Qarāchīl in our sources), but with disastrous consequences.

From this point onward, the sultan and the Chaghadayid rulers seem to have been on amicable terms. Muḥammad is said to have corresponded with

48 Baranī, *Tārīkh-i Fīrūzshāhī*, p. 458.
49 *Ibid.*, pp. 468–9.
50 *Ibid.*, p. 471.

Tarmashirin, whose offspring took refuge with him after their father's overthrow and death in 735/1334f., and subsequently played host to a fresh wave of Mongol notables and their followers during the upheavals that convulsed the Chaghadayid polity. He jettisoned military confrontation with the Mongols in favour of using the vast patronage at his disposal to win over individuals and groups.[51] By his last years, he was on friendly terms with the *amīr* Qazaghan, the effective ruler of the western Chaghadayid khanate in Transoxiana, who was of Qara'una origin (as Muḥammad's own dynasty may have been): Qazaghan would furnish him with a body of Mongol auxiliaries for his final campaign in Sind in *c.* 751/1350.

Closely connected with the Khurāsān expedition was the establishment of a second capital at Dawlatābād; and one author hints that they coincided.[52] The broader impulse behind the choice of Deogir seems to have been twofold: to implant Islam more securely in the newly conquered Deccan province and to create a more suitably situated administrative centre for the greatly extended sultanate. But the nature and timing of the project, which was launched in 727/1326f., have been obscured. The aim was not to abandon Delhi completely. It was the principal residents only of the old city of Delhi (the *Qil'a-yi Rāī Pithūrā*, i.e. the city of Prthviraja, captured by Aybak in 589/1193) and their households who were moved south. The newer 'cities' in the Delhi complex, like Sīrī, Hazār Sutūn and Tughluqābād, were not affected; at this very time Muḥammad was engaged in ambitious construction projects in the region, including a new fortress, 'Ādilābād, near Tughluqābād, and a wall that linked the old city of Delhi with Sīrī to enclose an area henceforward known as Jahānpanāh.[53] And Baranī's statement that the *amīrs* and maliks and their troops were with the sultan in Delhi while their families were in Dawlatābād shows that Muḥammad was turning the old city into a vast military encampment.[54]

The increase in taxation in the Dūāb was also intimately linked with the needs of the enormous 'Khurāsān' force. Baranī, again, has helped to confuse the question by using the phrase *yakī ba-dah wa-yakī ba-bīst* ('tenfold and

51 *Ibid.*, first recension, Bodleian ms. Elliot 353, fo. 199b; Jackson, *Delhi sultanate*, pp. 233–5.

52 Mīr-i Khwurd, *Siyar al-awliyā'*, lithograph edn (Delhi, AH 1302), p. 271.

53 H. Waddington, ''Ādilābād: A part of the "fourth" Delhi', *Ancient India*, 1 (1946), pp. 60–76; A. Welch and H. Crane, 'The Tughluqs: Master builders of the Delhi sultanate', *Muqarnas*, 1 (1983), pp. 128–9.

54 Baranī, *Tārīkh-i Fīrūzshāhī*, p. 479; Peter Jackson, 'Delhi: The problem of a vast military encampment', in R. E. Frykenberg (ed.), *Delhi through the ages: Essays in urban history, culture and society* (Oxford and Delhi, 1986), pp. 24–6, and Jackson, *Delhi sultanate*, pp. 258–60.

twenty-fold') for the rise. Any enhancement in the revenue demand, following so swiftly on Tarmashirin's devastation of the province, would have caused unrest. But if we piece together the scraps of information in our sources, it seems that the *kharāj* was now demanded partly in cash, that the basis of assessment was a standard (and not the actual) yield, that the value of the crop was calculated according to decreed (and not current) prices and that a number of other taxes were simultaneously imposed on them.[55] The cultivators were being required to pay, as well as provision, the unprecedentedly large army that Muḥammad had amassed. That the remuneration of the troops placed a strain on the sultan's finances is also clear from other evidence: the abandonment of ʿAlāʾ al-Dīn's system, with a partial reversion to the assignment of *iqṭā*ʿs to pay the troops;[56] and the issue of a low-denomination currency from 730/1329f. onwards. This latter measure, like the reduction of the silver content of the *tanga* since 727/1326f., was designed to remedy an acute shortage of silver in the Delhi sultanate.[57]

The reign appears to be dominated by revolts. The two earliest (727–8/1326f.) – those of Küshlü Khān, governor of Sind, and Bahāʾ al-Dīn Garshāsp, governor of Sāgar in the Deccan – were the work of men closely associated with Tughluq's seizure of power in 720/1320, and were seemingly sparked off by the Dawlatābād project. Küshlü Khan was allegedly stung into rebellion by the arrogance of an officer sent to oversee the transfer of his family to the south, and Garshāsp may have been concerned about the establishment of a new bastion of central power so close to his own territory. Both were crushed, as was an insurrection by Ghiyāth al-Dīn Bahādur Būra, a scion of the former ruling dynasty in Bengal, in 730/1329f.

The revolt of the Dūāb cultivators, which lasted from 732/1331f. to 734/1333f. and necessitated campaigns by Muḥammad in person to suppress it, served to ignite a series of further risings throughout the sultanate as Muslim *amīr*s and Hindu chiefs alike sought to profit from the sultan's embarrassments, and thus led to the permanent loss of a number of distant territories. In the far south, Maʿbar seceded (734/1334) under an officer who assumed the title of Sultan Jalāl al-Dīn Aḥsan Shāh. In 735/1334f. Muḥammad led an army south to recover the province, but was obliged to retreat by the outbreak of an epidemic which severely reduced the number of troops under his command. This crisis

55 Baranī, *Tārīkh-i Fīrūzshāhī*, pp. 473, 479; also first recension, Bodleian ms. Elliot 353, fo. 192b; Sirhindī, pp. 101–2; Jackson, *Delhi sultanate*, pp. 262–3.
56 Baranī, *Tārīkh-i Fīrūzshāhī*, pp. 476–7.
57 Simon Digby, 'The currency system', in Raychaudhuri and Habib (eds.), *Cambridge economic history of India*, vol. I, pp. 97–8.

sparked off further revolts. Two Hindu chiefs formerly in the sultan's service established the new state of Vijayanagara with its nucleus in Kampila, and another Hindu warlord seized power in Tilang (*c.* 736/1335f.). In the same year, a rebel named Fakhr al-Dīn ('Fakhrā') seized control in Bengal following the assassination of Muḥammad's governor. When fresh troops failed to arrive from Delhi, a loyal officer named ʿAlī Mubārak himself assumed the title of sultan at Lakhnawti in opposition to Fakhrā. From *c.* 743/1342f. both men were confronted by a third claimant, Shams al-Dīn Ilyās Shāh, who would emerge victorious by the early 1350s.[58]

The secession of these provinces prompted Muḥammad to make greater demands on the territories he still controlled, and this in turn provoked further risings by Muslim officers, probably *c.* 740/1339f. Niẓām Māʾin and Nuṣrat Khān, who had farmed the revenues at Kara and at Bidar respectively, both rebelled when they were unable to amass the enormous sums which they had contracted to raise. ʿAyn al-Mulk Ibn Māhrū, the governor of Awadh, rebelled under the false impression that Muḥammad planned his recall and execution. There is also evidence that resentment against the sultan's pagan Hindu servitors underlay some insurrections, such as that in Sīvistān (Sehvan) in *c.* 742/1341f., when a Hindu officer whom Ibn Baṭṭūṭa calls Ratan was killed, and that of ʿAlī Shāh Kar ('the Deaf') in Bidar slightly later, when the chief victim was a Hindu tax-farmer named Bhiran.[59] These revolts were all suppressed.

The sultan, whose relations with many representatives of the religious class, especially the Chishtiyya, were strained, seems to have tried to win their support by securing confirmation of his title from the puppet ʿAbbāsid caliph maintained by the Mamlūk sultans at Cairo. He was the first Delhi ruler to win caliphal recognition, in all likelihood, since Raḍiyya and certainly since the sack of Baghdad in 656/1258; the arrival of an official envoy with a diploma in 745/1344f. was attended by considerable ceremony. At this point Muḥammad still retained the allegiance of the great majority of the military class, but in 745/1344f. new revenue-raising arrangements for the Deccan and for Gujarat met with determined opposition from the *amīrān-i ṣada* ('*amīrs* of a hundred') in the two provinces. Muḥammad defeated the Gujarat rebels and then moved to Dawlatābād, where he was again victorious. But on his

58 A. H. Dani, 'Shamsuddīn Ilyās Shāh, Shāh-i Bangālah', in H. R. Gupta *et al.* (eds), *Essays presented to Sir Jadunath Sarkar*, 2 vols. (Hoshiarpur, 1958), vol. II, p. 55.

59 K. A. Nizami, 'Sultan Muḥammad bin Tughluq (1324–51)', in M. Habib and K. A. Nizami, *A comprehensive history of India*, vol. V: *The Delhi sultanat AD 1206–1526* (New Delhi, 1970), p. 565.

withdrawal to deal with a fresh rising in Gujarat by his Turkish *ghulām*, Taghai, insurrection flared up in the Deccan once more, and in Rabīʿ II 748/August 1347 the province seceded under Ḥasan Gangū, the founder of the Bahmani dynasty (748–933/1347–1527). The sultan died on the banks of the Indus on 21 Muḥarram 752/20 March 1351 after spending his last three years in Gujarat and Sind in a vain attempt to eliminate Taghai, who was not killed until a few weeks later.[60] The sultanate now wielded no authority south of the Narbada river.

Muḥammad's cousin Fīrūz Shāh (r. 752–90/1351–88), who was proclaimed sultan by the army commanders in Sind, had first to deal with a mutiny by Mongol detachments which had formed part of the late ruler's army. Then he advanced slowly on Delhi, where a faction centred on the vizier, Khwāja Jahān, had enthroned an alleged infant son of Muḥammad. The opposition melted away, and although Khwāja Jahān submitted he was shortly put to death at the instigation of the *amīrs*. A later conspiracy to replace Fīrūz Shāh with Muḥammad's sister's son came to nothing. The legitimacy of the regime was boosted by the arrival of successive embassies from the ʿAbbāsid caliph at Cairo from 754/1353 onwards, bringing diplomas that recognised Fīrūz Shāh as the only Muslim ruler in the subcontinent and indeed over a still wider area that included Sarandib (Sri Lanka), the Maldives, Java and Sumatra.

In military terms, Fīrūz Shāh's reign was undistinguished. The sultan declined an invitation from elements in Maʿbar to intervene there, and the shortlived sultanate of Maʿbar would be snuffed out by Vijāyanagara in 779/1377f. Fīrūz Shāh also abandoned a projected expedition against the Bahmani regime at Dawlatābād. Two attacks on Bengal, the first against Ilyās Shāh (754/1353) and the second against his son Sikandar Shāh (760/1359), achieved little more than the acquisition of elephants and other items of tribute; Bengal would remain independent until the tenth/sixteenth century. Of the two expeditions which the sultan headed into Sind in the late 1360s with the purpose of avenging Muḥammad's humiliation, the first failed and the second was hardly more effective. His most successful campaign, against the fortress of Nagarkōt (*c.* 766/1365), resulted in the submission of its raja; the region would serve as a base for his son Muḥammad in the civil wars that followed the old sultan's death.

In order to prevent a repetition of the unrest that had plagued his cousin's reign, the new sultan made concessions to the *amīrs*, the military class and even the cultivators. *Iqṭāʿ*s, including the smallest assignments made to

60 *Sīrat-i Fīrūzshāhī*, School of Oriental and African Studies ms. 283116, pp. 19, 27–8.

individual troopers, and administrative posts were made hereditary. In *c.* 759/1358 the revenue demand for the whole empire was fixed at 67,500,000 *tangas* for the duration of the reign. Fīrūz Shāh, a man of undoubted if conventional piety, also made efforts to retain the support of the religious class, abolishing the uncanonical taxes imposed by Muḥammad and setting aside a total of 3,600,000 *tangas* for *ʿulamāʾ*, shaykhs and other holy men. In strictly political terms, these measures appear to have paid off. We know of only one revolt during the reign, that of Shams al-Dīn Dāmghānī in Gujarat (782/1380f.), which was put down by the local *amīrān-i ṣada*. It is clear, nevertheless, that such tranquillity was achieved at a price. The policy of hereditary *iqṭāʿ*s risked the creation of autonomous principalities in an era of lesser security; and at the fiscal level, the government failed to benefit from a general increase in agricultural production, to which, incidentally, Fīrūz Shāh's own measures to extend cultivation had contributed. The military consequences of this decline in the government's resources, accentuated by a decade of internecine strife, would become evident when Temür attacked Delhi in 801/1398.

Hindu–Muslim relations within the Delhi sultanate

The era of the Delhi sultanate witnessed the first implantation of Islam within a vast region lying east and south-east of the Indus Valley. The sultans' attitudes towards 'Hinduism', their treatment of their non-Muslim subjects, and the way in which those subjects viewed Islam and Muslim rulers, are accordingly matters of some moment; but discussion of these issues has been bedevilled by preconceptions born of modern communalism. Admittedly, literary sources such as the voluminous works of Amīr Khusraw Dihlawī (d. 726/1325) furnish numerous examples of opprobrious comment about 'Saturnian' or 'crow-faced' Hindus.[61] Yet it is clear that beneath such polemic lay a substratum of everyday intercourse between Hindus and Muslims. Muḥammad b. Tughluq, who gained a reputation for fraternising with Hindus,[62] was possibly only the most eminent Muslim figure to take part in Hindu festivities. And against epigraphical evidence that denounces the barbarian (*mleccha*) Muslim invaders and celebrates their defeat at the hands of Hindu kings must be set those Sanskrit inscriptions which, like the Palam Baoli inscription of 1276, simply locate the Muslim

61 Annemarie Schimmel, 'Turk and Hindu: A poetical image and its application to historical fact', in Speros J. Vryonis, Jr (ed.), *Islam and cultural change in the Middle Ages* (Wiesbaden, 1975), pp. 107–26.
62 ʿIṣāmī, *Futūḥ al-salāṭīn*, p. 515.

sultans within a sequence of ruling dynasties and utilise the symbolism and motifs of an earlier era to depict their rule.[63] Even in the far south, where the sultans' faith was rejected along with their sovereignty, the culture and titulature of the court of Vijayanagara retained the imprint of several years' subjection to the Delhi sultanate.[64]

The complexity of the relations between the sultans and their Hindu subjects can be illustrated with reference to two questions: the fate of Hindu religious establishments and the imposition of the *jizya* (the Islamic poll-tax). Muslim conquerors and rulers have often been charged with the wholesale desecration or destruction of Hindu temples, and hence with fanatical hostility towards Hinduism. Admittedly, whatever doubts attach to the claims of the early seventh/thirteenth-century author Ḥasan-i Niẓāmī that Aybak uprooted 'idolatry' and destroyed idol-temples in a number of centres (including a thousand in Varanasi), architectural remains endorse his statement that the materials from demolished temples were incorporated in newly constructed mosques, as for instance in the Quṭb Minār at Delhi and the Arhai Din ke Jhompra mosque at Ajmer.[65] But recent research suggests that such actions sprang less from Muslim iconoclasm than from an awareness of Indian political tradition. That is to say, Muslim rulers were actuated by precisely the same considerations as were the plundering attacks by Hindu kings on temples in the territories of their Hindu rivals – namely, further to undermine the legitimacy of the defeated sovereign by severing the intimate link between his authority and the religious complex over which he presided.[66] Moreover, the situation in the immediate wake of the Muslim conquest and the impact of Muslim rule, once established, might well differ sharply. In much the same way as Hindu kings had patronised Muslim mosques within their dominions,

63 Brajadulal Chattopadhyaya, *Representing the Other? Sanskrit sources and the Muslims (eighth to fourteenth century)* (New Delhi, 1998), pp. 48–54. But cf. Peter Hardy, 'The authority of mediaeval Muslim kings in South Asia', in Marc Gaborieau (ed.), *Islam et société en Asie du Sud*, Collection Puruṣārthe, 9 (Paris, 1986), p. 39.

64 Philip B. Wagoner, '"Sultan among Hindu kings": Dress, titles, the Islamicization of Hindu culture at Vijayanagara', *Journal of Asian Studies*, 55 (1996), pp. 851–80; also Wagoner, 'Harihara, Bukka, and the sultan: The Delhi sultanate in the political imagination of Vijayanagara', in David Gilmartin and Bruce B. Lawrence (eds.), *Beyond Turk and Hindu: Rethinking religious identities in Islamicate South Asia* (Gainesville, FL, 2000), pp. 300–26.

65 Ḥasan-i Niẓāmī, *Tāj al-ma'āthir*, India Office ms. 15 (Ethé, *Catalogue*, no. 10), fos. 53a, 74b, 134b, 185a; Robert Hillenbrand, 'Political symbolism in early Indo-Islamic mosque architecture: The case of Ajmīr', *Iran*, 26 (1988), pp. 105–17.

66 Richard M. Eaton, 'Temple desecration and Indo-Muslim states', *Journal of Islamic Studies*, 11 (2000), pp. 293–302; repr. in Gilmartin and Lawrence (eds.), *Beyond Turk and Hindu*, pp. 254–60.

and continued to do so even when under attack from Delhi, the sultans and their officers can also be found extending their protection, and donating funds, to Hindu (or Jain) religious establishments.[67] Of the numerous documents conferring land and tax exemptions on Brahmans, Jains, jogis and Parsis, issued by the Mughal emperors or by the rulers of the successor-states to the Delhi sultanate, some clearly represent the renewal or extension of grants made in the sultanate period.[68]

The Muslim legal texts which enjoyed authority throughout the wider Islamic world make no mention of Hindus among the *dhimmīs* ('protected peoples'), those non-Muslims who were liable to pay the *jizya* (a graduated poll-tax); although an obscure reference in the Qur'ān to a people called the 'Sabians' had enabled the early Arab conquerors to admit Zoroastrians to *dhimmī* status. By the eighth/fourteenth century a good many Indo-Muslim authors and one legal text composed within the sultanate, the *Fatāwā-yi Fīrūzshāhī*, were prepared to refer to the sultan's Hindu subjects as *dhimmīs*. Kūfī's *Chach-nāma* (*c.* 613/1216f.), which purports to be a Persian translation of an earlier (lost) work in Arabic, speaks of the levying of the *jizya* on the conquered population of Sind at the time of the Muslim conquest in the early second/eighth century. This is quite anachronistic, and it has been suggested that this kind of statement was used to justify what had become standard practice in Sind by the time the *Chach-nāma* was written.[69] References to seventh/thirteenth-century conditions in India seem to show the term *jizya* (sometimes *kharāj wa-jizya*) being used of the tribute rendered by Hindu potentates. The occasional allusion by Baranī raises the slight possibility that the poll-tax was levied on the Hindu populace within Muslim-held towns in northern India.[70] But the earliest incontrovertible evidence for the imposition of the *jizya* as a discriminatory tax on individual non-Muslims dates from the reign of the Tughluqid Fīrūz Shāh; though it is difficult, even so, to see how the measure could have been enforced outside the principal urban centres.

67 Carl W. Ernst, *Eternal garden: Mysticism, history and politics at a South Asian Sufi center* (Albany, NY, 1992), pp. 32–3, 48–50; Eaton, 'Temple desecration', pp. 302–3 (and in Gilmartin and Lawrence, p. 261).

68 B. N. Goswamy and J. S. Grewal (eds.), *The Mughals and the Jogis of Jakhbar* (Simla, 1967), pp. 20–1. For the Lodī period, see also Iqtidar Husain Siddiqi, 'Wajh-i Ma'ash grants under the Afghan kings (1451–1555)', *Medieval India: A miscellany*, 2 (1972), pp. 36–7.

69 Peter Hardy, 'Is the *Chach-nama* intelligible to the historian as political theory?', in Hamida Khuhro (ed.), *Sind through the centuries* (Oxford and Karachi, 1981), pp. 116–17.

70 Baranī, *Tārīkh-i Fīrūzshāhī*, p. 217; Baranī, *Fatāwā-yi Jahāndārī*, ed. Afsar Saleem Khan (Lahore, 1972), p. 167.

The civil wars and Temür's invasion

During his last years Fīrūz Shāh had associated with him first his youngest son Muḥammad Shāh and then Tughluq Shāh, the son of his grandson Fatḥ Khan who, after enjoying quasi-sovereign status in the empire in the 1350s and early 1360s, had died in 778/1376.[71] Tughluq Shāh II (r. 790–1/1388–9), who duly succeeded his great-grandfather, was able to hold off Muḥammad, but was himself murdered by a cousin, Abū Bakr Shāh (r. 791–2/1389–90). There now ensued a duel for the throne between Muḥammad, who commanded the support of the majority of the provincial governors, and Abū Bakr, who was based in Fīrūz Shāh's new residence of Firūzābād and backed by the old sultan's numerous slaves. It was only when a significant number of these slave officers, for unknown reasons, transferred their allegiance to Muḥammad that Abū Bakr was expelled from the Delhi complex, enabling his rival to enter the capital and to order the execution of all the Fīrūzshāhī slaves in the opposition party. Abū Bakr was subsequently captured (793/1390f.) and died in captivity in Meerut.

Muḥammad's triumph was a hollow one. He was able to replace the rebellious governor of Gujarat (793/1391), but otherwise his brief reign was spent endeavouring to enforce obedience on Hindu princes rather closer to the capital, notably the *muqaddams* of Gwalior and Etāwa, and Bahādur Nāhir, the chief of the Meos (Mīwāt) immediately south-west of Delhi, who had been a steady adherent of Tughluq Shāh and Abū Bakr Shāh. Muḥammad was preparing a campaign to suppress Shaykhā, the Khokhar chief, who had rebelled and occupied Lahore, when he died in 796/1394; his son and successor, Humāyūn Shāh, followed him to the grave a month later. Another son of Muḥammad, the ten-year-old Maḥmūd Shāh (r. 796–815/1394–1412), was thereupon proclaimed sultan.

The new reign began auspiciously, when Sārang Khān, the newly appointed governor of Dēōlpālpūr, dislodged Shaykhā from Lahore, while the vizier Khwāja Jahān Sarwar was given the title of *malik al-sharq* and entrusted with the government of an enormous tract extending from the Dūāb to Bihār, with its centre at Jawnpur. But antipathy between the principal *amīrs* at court, Muqarrab Khān, the sultan's deputy, and Saʿādat Khān, the *bārbek* (military chamberlain) and a former slave of Muḥammad Shāh, and the

71 For coins in Fatḥ Khān's name, see H. Nelson Wright, *The coinage and metrology of the Sulṭāns of Dehlī* (Delhi, 1936; repr. New Delhi, 1974), pp. 186–8; and for the precise genealogy of these princes, Jackson, *Delhi sultanate*, p. 332.

intrigues of Mallū Khān, Sārang Khān's brother, paralysed the regime. Sa'ādat Khan was ousted and retaliated by proclaiming as sultan at Firūzābād Nuṣrat Shāh, a brother of Tughluq Shāh II (797 / 1394f.). Sa'ādat Khan shortly fled from Firūzābād to Delhi, where Muqarrab Khan put him to death; but the opposition centred on the person of Nuṣrat Shāh continued. The forces of the two sultans – Nuṣrat Shāh commanding the allegiance of the districts between the Dūāb, Sambhal, Pānīpat and Rohtak, while Maḥmūd Shāh was acknowledged in Delhi and Sīrī – fought numerous engagements but were unable to dislodge each other from their respective power bases. This was the situation when the Central Asian conqueror Temür 'the Lame' (*Timür-i lang*, 'Tamerlane') invaded northern India.

The turbulence that afflicted the Chaghadayid khanate from Tarmashirin's reign onwards had lasted for over a quarter of a century, and had led to its division into a western khanate, centred on Transoxiana, and an eastern, embracing the more nomadic lands and known as Mughulistān. Although the Punjab and Sind suffered minor forays early in the reign of Fīrūz Shāh, these are likely to have been the work of small groups of fugitives dislodged from Transoxiana in the struggles that followed Qazaghan's death in 759 / 1358 and preceded the rise of Temür in the late 1360s. Once he had become from 771 / 1369f. *de facto* master of the western khanate, which he ruled through a puppet khan of Ögedei's line, Temür embarked on a career of conquest that pitted him against the khans of the Golden Horde, the various local princes who had taken over the lands of the Ilkhanate in Persia, and the Delhi sultanate, so frequently invaded by Chaghadayid armies in the past.

One source alleges that Temür and Fīrūz Shāh had corresponded, and that Muḥammad Shāh, during his struggle with Abū Bakr Shāh in 792 / 1390, had set out for Samarqand to seek Temür's assistance when he was summoned to Delhi to take the throne.[72] Temür himself claimed that as a good Muslim he was impelled by the duty to punish the rulers of Delhi for having allowed such latitude to their pagan Hindu subjects; though as it transpired the victims of his Indian campaign would be overwhelmingly Muslims. In any case, Temür needed no pretext for attacking India. His military operations were ostensibly designed to recreate the world empire of Chinggis Khan, who had entered India briefly in *c*. 1223.

Temür's advance forces, commanded by his grandson Pīr Muḥammad, who governed Kabul, took Multān in 800 / 1397. Temür himself moved

72 Muḥammad Bihāmadkhānī, *Tārīkh-i Muḥammadī*, British Library ms. Or. 137, fos. 422b–423a, 442b; trans. M. Zaki (Aligarh, 1972), pp. 32, 59–60.

through Multān and the Punjab by way of the Ghaggar river, to do battle with Sultan Maḥmūd Shāh and Mallū Khan in the plain outside Delhi on 7 Rabīʿ II 801/16 December 1398. Despite a spirited resistance, the Delhi army was routed; Mallū and the sultan fled, and the Chaghadayid forces plundered the city for several days. The rival sultan, Nuṣrat Shāh, abandoned Fīrūzābād for the Dūāb, where the conqueror soon followed him. After storming Meerut, however, Temür began a gradual withdrawal westwards across the Indus. His triumph can be attributed to the fact that he had welded the Chaghadayid nomads into a formidable military machine and drew, in addition, on contingents supplied by client rulers beyond the Chaghadayid boundaries. Nevertheless, the weakness of the opposition must also be taken into account. Against the invaders Mallū and the sultan had been able to muster only 10,000 horse, 20,000 foot and 120 elephants,[73] a pitiful force compared with those available to ʿAlāʾ al-Dīn Khaljī, to Muḥammad b. Tughluq or even to Fīrūz Shāh.

The truncated sultanate

While Mallū re-established himself in Sīrī, where he was rejoined after a time by Maḥmūd Shāh, and brought back under control the Dūāb and the environs (*ḥawālī*) of the capital, what remained of the Delhi sultanate underwent an irrevocable fragmentation. Autonomous states emerged under Khiḍr Khan in Multān, Ẓafar Khan Wajīh al-Mulk in Gujarat, ʿAmīd Shāh (Dilāwar Khan) in Mālwā, Shams Khan Awhadī in Bhayāna, Khwāja Jahān Sarwar in Jawnpur and Maḥmūd Khan b. Fīrūz Khan in Kalpī. It should be noticed that all these rulers except the last had been nominees and supporters of Muḥammad Shāh (r. 792–6/1390–4); and even Maḥmūd Khan of Kalpī, whose father had been vizier to Tughluq Shāh II, had submitted to Muḥammad after Abū Bakr's downfall and received an increase in his territory. All, again with one exception, were slow to declare their independence of Delhi and appear to have done so only after Temür's attack. The exception was Khiḍr Khan, who, expelled from Multān by Sārang Khan, had thrown in his lot with Temür and had been reinstated in the city as his lieutenant. It was Khiḍr Khan who defeated and killed Mallū Khan in 808/1405f. Maḥmūd Shāh maintained a shadowy authority

73 Ghiyāth al-Dīn ʿAlī Yazdī, *Rūz-nāma-yi ghazawāt-i Hindūstān*, trans. A. A. Semenov, *Dnevnik pokhoda Timura v Indiiu* (Moscow, 1958), p. 115; Niẓām-i Shāmī, *Ẓafar-nāma*, ed. Felix Tauer, *Histoire des conquêtes de Tamerlan*, 2 vols., Monografie Archivu Orientálního, 5 (Prague, 1937–56), vol. I, p. 189.

in Delhi until his death in 815/1412; then, following the brief reign of the *amīr* Dawlat Khān, Khiḍr Khan occupied the capital (817/1414).

Under Khiḍr Khān's dynasty – known, in view of their alleged descent from the Prophet Muḥammad, as the Sayyids (817–55/1414–51) – the sultanate had shrunk to being just one of a number of competing principalities in the north. Khiḍr Khan (r. 817–24/1414–21) at no point assumed the title of sultan, but contented himself with the style of *rāyat-i aʿlā* ('exalted standard'). He, his son Mubārak Shāh (r. 824–37/1421–34) and the latter's nephew Muḥammad Shāh (r. 837–49/ 1434–45) acknowledged the sovereignty of Temür's son, Shāh Rukh (d. 850/1447), who ruled in Herat, though this did not afford them security against further attacks by that monarch's kinsmen and lieutenants in Kabul.[74] The Sayyid rulers' own military energies were absorbed in attempts to extract the land revenue from the Meos, the Dūāb, Katehr, Etawa and Gwalior and by the need to defend their territories against threats from the sultanates of Mālwā, Gujarat and, especially, Jawnpur. In the west, Multān, Khiḍr Khān's old base, seceded under the dynasty of a local shaykh (847/1443). In the east, Jawnpur denied the sultanate access both to important sources of elephants and to some of the most fertile of its former territories. A historian writing in the Mughal era immortalised a contemporary ditty that saluted the last Sayyid, ʿAlāʾ al-Dīn ʿĀlam Shāh (*shāh-i ʿālam*, 'world-king'), as ruler only from Delhi as far as Pālam.[75]

Afghan immigrants, who had first attained prominence among the *amīrs* during the Khaljī era, formed a high proportion of the nobility and the military officers under the Sayyids, and in 855/1451 one of their chiefs, Bahlūl Lodī, displaced the feeble ʿĀlam Shāh and ascended the throne. Under the Lodī dynasty (855–932/1451–1526) the sultanate enjoyed something of a renaissance. Bahlūl (r. 855–94/1451–89) conquered the sultanate of Jawnpur (884/1479). His son and successor, Sikandar (r. 894–923/1489–1517), reduced Bihār and Nagaur, terminated Awhadī rule in Bhayāna (898/1492f.) and recovered territory both from the Hindu ruler of Gwalior and from the Muslim sultan of Mālwa. It is a measure of his preoccupation with his southern frontiers that in 911/1505 he transferred his capital from Delhi to Agra.

Afghan immigration continued apace under the Lodīs, and although Bahlūl had been content to be simply *primus inter pares*, his successors were concerned to impose their will upon the Afghan chiefs. Sikandar achieved this by

74 Ḥāfiẓ-i Abrū, *Zubdat al-tawārīkh*, ed. Sayyid Kamāl Ḥāj Sayyid Jawādī, 2 vols. (Tehran, AH solar 1372), vol. II, pp. 408–9, 641–2, 680–1, 755, 798–9.
75 Aḥmad Yādgār, *Tārīkh-i Shāhī*, ed. M. Hidayat Hosain (Calcutta, 1939), p. 5.

diplomatic means, but the more high-handed tactics of his son Ibrāhīm (r. 923–32/1517–26) provoked sharp opposition. One Afghan *amīr* rebelled in Bihār, while another, Dawlat Khan Lodī, governor of the Punjab, made overtures to Bābur, a descendant of Temür who since 910/1504 had ruled in Kabul and who had already invaded the Punjab three times. Bābur took Lahore (930/1524), and two years later advanced on Delhi. On 8 Rajab 932/20 April 1526, despite the numerical superiority of the Delhi forces and thanks in some measure to Bābur's artillery, Ibrāhīm was defeated and killed at Pānīpat and Bābur supplanted the Lodīs.

The victory at Pānīpat marked the establishment of the Mughal empire. Although many historians now regard the expulsion of Bābur's son Humāyūn by Shīr Shāh, and the brief reassertion of Afghan rule in Delhi under the Sūr dynasty (947–62/1540–55), as introducing a restoration also of the Delhi sultanate, this episode is best reserved for a later chapter.

In its early stages, the Delhi sultanate survived upon raids against independent Hindu kingdoms, which yielded plunder and tribute and enabled it to withstand pressure from the Mongols in the north-west. From the time of ʿAlāʾ al-Dīn Khaljī, a successful attempt was made to field more formidable armies by maximising the appropriation of the agrarian surplus. At the same time, however, the balance of military priorities changed, and the sultans followed a policy of imposing direct control over Hindu states in Rajasthan and the south. This shift brought in its wake administrative and economic problems, with the result that the sultanate forfeited first its more distant territories in Bengal and the south and then those closer to Delhi. Temür's attack effectively delivered the *coup de grâce*; but the Delhi polity still survived for more than a century as one of a number of rival states in northern India.

4

The rule of the infidels: the Mongols and the Islamic world

BEATRICE FORBES MANZ

The formation of the Mongol empire

The Mongol period was a watershed for the Islamic world, as it was for most of Eurasia. The ferocity of the conquest and the confusion of early rule exacerbated an agricultural decline already deepened by decades of internal warfare. For artisans and merchants, however, the period brought significant new opportunities. As foreign nomads, the Mongols were not a novelty, and eastern regions had already experienced the rule of the non-Muslim Qara Khitay. However, the Mongols replaced the familiar caliphate with a new imperial ideal and administrative methods conceived and tested in Mongolia and China. While the Chinggisid rulers were quick to adopt the bureaucratic practices of conquered territories, they did so within a framework conceived at the beginning of Chinggis Khan's rule; thus steppe traditions lay at the base of Mongol administration.

The political and economic connections of the Mongolian plateau reached from northern China to western Turkistān (see Map 2). Its southern sections were closely involved with China and the Silk Road and sometimes in contact with powers to the west. In the northern forest region many tribes lived from hunting and fishing or reindeer herding, while in the steppe pastoral-nomadism prevailed. There were also agricultural settlements. Two related languages, Turkic and Mongolian, predominated, sometimes spoken within one confederation. The most powerful populations were the pastoral nomads, and it is probably not by chance that the Mongols set their myth of origin in the time and place of their transition to pastoralism.[1] Their main animals were those that predominate among the nomads of Iran and Afghanistan – sheep, goats, horses, cattle and camels. The most important political unit was the

1 Thomas T. Allsen, 'Spiritual geography and political legitimacy in the eastern steppe', in Henri J. M. Claessen and Jarich G. Oosten (eds.), *Ideology and the formation of early states* (Leiden, 1996), p. 118.

tribe, usually based on a combination of real and fictive kinship. Tribes grew or shrank according to economic and military conditions; they could break up into small units but could also develop into confederations or states. The region had been the centre of several steppe empires, most notably the Turkic (Tü-chüeh) empire which dominated the eastern steppes from 552 to 745 CE. The Turkic state developed an imperial ideology, a written language and a set of administrative institutions which survived long beyond its rule.

When leaders of the Mongolian plateau lost their positions, as the more ambitious often did, they took refuge within neighbouring tribes and states. In the twelfth century northern China was ruled by the Jurchen Chin dynasty (1115–1234), which was closely involved in the politics of the Mongolian plateau. In the Ordos and the Gansu corridor the Tangut or Hsi-Hsia state (982–1227) ruled over a multiethnic population. From the northern Tarim river basin to the northern Tien Shan the major power was the Uighur kingdom which had preserved the traditions of the Turkic empire in a partly sedentary state. In about 1130, the Uighurs became vassals of a new power, the Qara Khitay state founded by the Khitan Liao dynasty, whose realm extended from the western Tarim river basin to Transoxiana, where its rulers competed with the Khwārazm Shāhs.

The strongest steppe powers were the Naiman in the Altai and the Kerait in the upper Orkhon. Although probably largely Mongolian in language, both were of Turkic origin and remained attached to Turkic political traditions. The Naiman had adopted the Uighur script for their chancellery and financial administration. Most of the ruling lineage was Buddhist, and Nestorian Christianity had also gained a following. The Kerait rulers were Nestorian Christians and had developed a central court with elements of state organisation. Their ruling lineage had the advantage of controlling the Orkhon river valley, the sacred centre of earlier steppe empires. In the eastern region tribes were less organised. Among them were the Mongols, part of a loose coalition centred in the region of the Onon and Kerulen rivers. Further east were the Tatars; both tribes had lineages which claimed the title khan, but they were often controlled by several competing leaders.[2]

Temüjin – the man who became Chinggis Khan – was born into the Kiyan-Borjigin section of the Mongol tribe, probably about 1167. In 1147 the Tatars

2 Paul Ratchnevsky, *Genghis Khan, his life and legacy*, trans. and ed. Thomas N. Haining (Oxford, 1992), pp. 1–8; Isenbike Togan, *Flexibility and limitation in steppe formations: The Kerait khanate and Chinggis Khan* (Leiden, 1998), pp. 75–7, 117–18; Thomas T. Allsen, 'The rise of the Mongolian empire and Mongolian rule in north China', in Herbert Franke and Denis Twitchett (eds.), *Cambridge history of China*, vol. VI (Cambridge, 1994), pp. 323–6, 331–2; Allsen, 'Spiritual geography', pp. 124–6; Rashīd al-Dīn Hamadānī, *Jāmiʿ al-tawārīkh*, ed. A. A. Ali-zade (Moscow, 1968–80), vol. I, pp. 249–51, 289.

had defeated the Mongols, and in Temüjin's youth his tribe was in disarray. Temüjin's father Yesügei was killed by Tatars when Temüjin was eight or nine years old and newly betrothed to his chief wife, Börte. The histories recount Temüjin's youth as a tale of hardship: a widow with her children abandoned by the tribe. This led the young man to a classic steppe solution, gathering a band of personal followers from outside his own tribe. In the early 1180s he collected his bride, Börte, and attached himself to the leader of the Keraits, To'oril – best known by his Chinese title Ong Khan – who had been an ally of Temüjin's father and apparently enjoyed authority over part of the Mongol tribe. As a leader attempting to centralise and enlarge his confederation, Ong Khan offered Temüchin an excellent opportunity for advancement.[3] By the mid- to late 1180s, Temüjin had become well known, and he was chosen as the head of the Borjigin. He rewarded his personal followers with offices, creating patriarchal positions – cook, falconer, equerry – which also involved wider duties. Temüjin's rapid advancement and Ong Khan's assertion of power aroused resentment, and soon both men disappeared from sight for almost ten years. During this time Ong Khan was with the Qara Khitay to the west, and Temüjin may have been in China.[4]

In 1195–6 Ong Khan regained his throne with Temüjin's help and for the next several years the two men collaborated to defeat their rivals, using an unusual level of violence against their enemies. The *Secret History of the Mongols*, written for the Chinggisid dynasty, claims that in 1203 Ong Khan pushed out his own son, making Temüjin his adopted son and heir apparent. However, within a short time Temüjin was at war with Ong Khan, who was killed by the Naiman while fleeing after a defeat. Instead of massacring the Kerait, as he did other defeated tribes, Temüjin appropriated their prestige and presented his victory as a legitimate succession to the rule of the Kerait confederation. For a while he recognised Ong Khan's brother as co-ruler and formed marriage alliances with him; he took one daughter himself and chose another, Sorqaqtani Beki, for his youngest son Tolui. His new administration incorporated the Turkic institutions of the Kerait and Naiman. He reorganised his army on the decimal system and created a central regiment, the *keshig*, recruited from his personal followers. In a campaign lasting from May 1204 into 1205 he broke the power of the Naiman and Merkid and became master of the Mongolian plateau.[5]

3 Togan, *Flexibility*, pp. 68–76.
4 Ratchnevsky, *Genghis*, pp. 45–9; Allsen, 'Rise', p. 337.
5 Ratchnevsky, *Genghis*, pp. 52–88; Allsen, 'Rise', pp. 338–42.

In 1206 Temüjin convoked a *quriltai* – a gathering of tribal leaders – at the source of the Onon river. His followers raised his white standard bearing nine horse or yak tails, combining the colour and number associated with good fortune. The Turkic concept of God-given fortune attached to the ruler became a central part of Mongol imperial ideology. Temüjin now received the title Chinggis Khan. The term has been translated as 'Oceanic', but Igor de Rachewiltz recently argued for the meaning 'fierce, hard, or tough'[6] The new khan had a scribe from the Naiman adapt the Uighur alphabet for Mongolian and teach it to his sons. The *keshig* grew to 10,000 men; its members served as chamberlains, supervisors of households and herds, and major military commanders. Another office was that of chief judge (*yeke jarghuchi*), with two tasks: to oversee the apportionment of subject peoples and to preserve Chinggis Khan's legislative pronouncements, known as *jasagh*s.

Chinggis Khan seems to have adopted the centralising policy of Ong Khan, who had asserted the power of the dynasty over tribal leaders.[7] Most tribes were divided among contingents commanded by personal followers.[8] Another tactic that Chinggis shared with Ong Khan was the increase in violence, particularly the massacre of defeated tribesmen, and the selective use of extreme violence remained part of his strategy throughout his career. Chinggis now moved rapidly towards expansion. In 1209 he conquered the Tangut and from 1211 to 1215 mounted campaigns against north China and Manchuria. By 1216, the Mongols had taken the Chin capital.

Western conquests

Islamic Central Asia had long been connected to the eastern steppe. The Khwārazmian cities traded with China and Mongolia, and Temüjin had several Muslim merchants among his early followers. Soon after his enthronement he encouraged his eldest son Jochi to campaign on the northern and western frontiers. In 1207–8 two commanders, Jebe and Sübetei, pursued fugitives west and they apparently clashed with the Khwārazm Shāh Sultan Muḥammad (r. 596–617/1200–20f.) in Semirechye in 1209–10.[9] Circumstances

6 Igor de Rachewiltz, 'The title Cinggis Qan/Qa'an re-examined', in W. Heissig and Klaus Sagaster (eds.), *Gedanke und Wirkung: Festschrift zum 90. Geburtstag von Nikolaus Poppe*, Asiatische Forschungen, 108 (Wiesbaden, 1989), pp. 281–8.

7 Togan, *Flexibility*, pp. 86, 90–1, 102–3.

8 Allsen, 'Rise', pp. 346–7.

9 Paul D. Buell, 'Early Mongol expansion in western Siberia and Turkistan (1207–1219): A reconstruction', *Central Asiatic Journal*, 36, 1–2 (1992), pp. 4–16.

favoured the Mongol advance: the Qara Khitay had recently increased their exactions on subject people, and had alienated several vassals. The Uighur ruler sent gifts to Chinggis Khan in 1209, then arrived in person in 1211 and was rewarded with high status. The Qarluq chiefs of the Ili valley likewise submitted voluntarily.[10] Meanwhile the rulers of Samarqand and Bukhārā reacted to Qara Khitay pressure by inviting in the Khwārazm Shāh.

In 1208, after Chinggis Khan defeated the Naiman, their prince Güchülüg took refuge at the Qara Khitay court, where he rose quickly and then allied with Sultan Muḥammad to seize power over the kingdom in 1211. Soon, however, he was attempting to expand into the regions of Kāshghar and Kulja and threatening the Khwārazm Shāh. The Khwārazmians and Mongols now shared a common enemy and Sultan Muḥammad sent an embassy and trading caravan to Chinggis Khan. However, the Mongols' western advance soon strained relations. In 1216 Chinggis Khan sent his senior commander Jebe against Güchülüg, and by the end of 1218 the Qara Khitay realm was under Mongol control. In the meantime Jochi moved west to put down an uprising of the Siberian tribes. The Khwārazm Shāh now faced the Mongols directly. A Mongol embassy arrived in Transoxiana proposing trade relations, to which Sultan Muḥammad assented, but when the caravan reached Uṭrār the city governor executed its merchants and seized their goods, probably with Sultan Muḥammad's encouragement. When Chinggis Khan sent an envoy to protest, the Khwārazm Shāh had him killed. This incident provided justification for western conquest. Chinggis Khan left a force in northern China and enlarged the western army with foot soldiers and cavalry from the Uighurs, Qarluq and the ruler of Almāliq. In the summer of 1219 the army gathered on the Irtysh river. Sultan Muḥammad held a large realm, but he faced serious internal political problems.[11] He therefore retreated along with his major commanders and left the defence of Transoxania, Khwārazm and Khurāsān to its cities and their garrison troops.[12]

Even if the Khwārazm Shāh had stood firm, it is not clear how he could have organised a successful defence. As usual, Chinggis Khan divided his forces so that Transoxiana suffered attack simultaneously by four separate armies. One contingent was sent under Jochi to take Sighnaq, Ūzkand and Jand.[13] A small

10 Thomas Allsen, 'The Yuan dynasty and the Uighurs of Turfan in the thirteenth century', in Morris Rossabi (ed.), *China among equals* (Berkeley, 1983), pp. 246–7.

11 W. Barthold, *Turkestan down to the Mongol invasion* (London, 1968), pp. 374–80, 393–9.

12 'Alā' al-Dīn 'Atā-Malik Juwaynī, *The history of the world conqueror*, trans. John A. Boyle, 2 vols. (Manchester, 1958), pp. 373–8.

13 Barthold, *Turkestan*, p. 415; Buell, 'Early Mongol expansion', p. 27.

army went against Banākath and Khujand, while Chinggis Khan's second and third sons, Chaghadai and Ögedei, conquered Uṭrār, then joined the main army with a levy of men from the city. Chinggis and his youngest son Tolui headed against Bukhārā, where they arrived in February 1220. After three days of fighting most of the garrison fled. The next day the population opened the city gates but since resistance continued in the citadel the Mongols attacked it for twelve days, during which much of the city was destroyed by fire. Once the garrison was conquered, the Mongols massacred the surviving soldiers, destroyed the city walls and took a levy of men. They then marched against Samarqand, where the civilian section of the city surrendered after four days.

The methodology of Mongol campaigns is well known. When cities submitted they were subjected to a tax and assigned a Mongol official. In most recorded cases, the garrison troops resisted, often backed up by the population for one or two days. The population was then taken out of the town, which the army looted. The walls were destroyed, the garrison massacred, and the Mongols conscripted military levies and craftsmen before allowing people to return to the city. Craftsmen were immediately put to use, either in the army or as skilled labour in Mongol workshops.[14] Not all of these actions were new – the massacre of soldiers after battle, permitted looting and the destruction of fortifications were all familiar. It was in the systematic organisation of conquered populations that the Mongols stood out, and in the ferocity with which they punished recalcitrant cities. In such cases the population was divided up among the soldiers to be killed, with the exception of women and children to be enslaved, young men for levies, craftsmen and the religious classes, who were spared. The historians report figures for the dead that far exceed the actual city populations and illustrate the horrid fascination of Mongol actions.

After taking Samarqand Chinggis Khan again divided his army, sending a contingent against Khujand and Farghāna and one to Wakhsh and Ṭalaqān. Jebe, Sübetei and Chinggis Khan's son-in-law Taghachar pursued the Khwārazm Shāh who abandoned Nīshāpūr in spring 617/1220. Jebe and Sübetei headed west as Sultan Muḥammad fled to an island in the Caspian, where he died in the winter of 617/1220f. The troops chasing the sultan were reportedly ordered not to attack cities. There was nonetheless considerable destruction, but it appears that the contingent overlooked minor acts of

14 Thomas T. Allsen, *Commodity and exchange in the Mongol empire: A cultural history of Islamic textiles* (Cambridge, 1997), pp. 31–6.

aggression in the interest of efficient pursuit.[15] Taghachar remained in Khurāsān and was killed putting down an uprising in Nīshāpūr.

Considering the consequences of resistance, it is remarkable how many cities opposed the Mongols. Rebellions are often attributed to the lower classes, but in many cities members of the elite were also involved, and there was often internal disagreement.[16] It is probable that the extraordinary level of destruction in Khwārazm and Khurāsān was due to the resistance of their cities, based partly on factionalism and partly on a miscalculation of Mongol strength. In both provinces early Mongol armies were sometimes small enough for local forces to defeat. The fact that Chinggis Khan could send out small contingents in different directions is a testament to the exceptional loyalty of the Mongol army; the defeat of one army did not threaten Chinggis Khan's control over his followers. This sort of discipline was a phenomenon unknown in the recent experience of Iranian cities. The Mongols moreover enlarged their army through local alliances and levies – some levies rebelled, but others fought efficiently and participated enthusiastically in punitive massacres.[17]

In 1220 Chinggis Khan remained north of the Oxus while Jebe and Sübetei wintered in western Iran, and in their absence the people of Khurāsān and Khwārazm lost some of their fear of the invaders. Khwārazmian *amīrs* retook Yangikent from Jochi's governor, and Sultan Muḥammad's sons Jalāl al-Dīn Mangubirni and Uzlaq-shāh returned to Khwārazm. The most active centre of unrest was Marv, whose leaders disagreed over Mongol rule. The anti-Mongol party attacked Sarakhs for accepting a Mongol governor, then, joined by some Turkmens and other remnants of the Khwārazm Shāh's army, they defeated a small Mongol contingent. In triumph, they paraded their prisoners through the town.[18] At the end of winter 1221, Chinggis Khan attacked Balkh and at about the same time Jebe and Sübetei defeated the Georgians in Transcaucasia, while Jochi, Chaghadai and Ögedei besieged Urganj. Tolui was assigned the pacification of Khurāsān. His first major goal was Marv, where he arrived in Muḥarram 618/February 1221. He brought a Mongol contingent significantly enlarged by levies from Khurāsānian cities, including

15 Barthold, *Turkestan*, pp. 421–7; Juwaynī, *History*, pp. 143–7, 383–6.
16 Jürgen Paul, 'L'invasion mongole comme révélateur de la société iranienne', in D. Aigle (ed.), *L'Iran face à la domination mongole*, Bibliotèque Iranienne 45, (Tehran, 1997), pp. 46–9; I. P. Petrushevskiĭ, 'Pokhod mongol'skikh voĭsk v Sredniuiu Aziiu v 1219–1224 gg. i ego posledstviia', in S. L. Tikhvinskiĭ, (ed.), *Tataro-Mongoly v Azii i Evrope* (Moscow, 1970), p. 114.
17 Juwaynī, *History*, pp. 162, 168, 178.
18 *ibid.*, pp. 150–9.

Sarakhs, and he took Marv in eight days. He then attacked Nīshāpūr, which suffered a massacre in revenge for the death of his brother-in-law Taghachar.

The new offensive did not extinguish opposition. The Khwārazm Shāh's son Jalāl al-Dīn Mangubirni, who had regrouped near Ghazna, succeeded in defeating a small Mongol force. Chinggis sent an army under his chief judge, Shigi Qutuqu, but once again Jalāl al-Dīn was victorious, and his success ignited a number of insurrections in Khurāsān. Together with Chaghadai, Ögedei and Tolui, Chinggis defeated Jalāl al-Dīn after a fierce battle near the Indus in autumn 618/1221. According to Persian histories, Jalāl al-Dīn fought bravely and then plunged into the river, watched by the admiring Mongols; this event became a favourite subject for Persian miniatures. Jalāl al-Dīn spent the next three years south of the Indus and some leaders in Khurāsān continued to trust in his future. Several months after Tolui took Herat in the spring of 618/1221 local people rebelled and killed the city's Mongol official. Chinggis sent out his commander Eljigidei, who took Herat after a siege of six months and ordered a general massacre. Marv and Sarakhs also rose against the Mongols, and the movement spread to other cities, notably Nisā. The Mongols probably did not restore control until late summer 619/1222.[19] At the end of 1222 Chinggis Khan moved to Transoxania and in early 1223 the main army departed for the east.

The successors of Chinggis Khan

Chinggis Khan died in August 1227, leaving an empire in the process of formation. He had made several grants of land and troops to relatives during his life – perhaps designed to placate people unhappy with the growth of central power – but it is not clear what provisions he had made for the future of his empire.[20] The sources which describe his division of territory, troops and responsibility were all written considerably later and show signs of distortion.[21] As things turned out, Chinggis Khan's sons Jochi, Chaghadai, Ögedei and Tolui, borne by his principal wife Börte, became the progenitors of the four recognised branches of the dynasty. The larger part of the empire

19 *ibid.*, pp. 164–8; Barthold, *Turkestan*, p. 448.

20 *Men-da Beĭ-lu ('Polnoe opisanie Mongolo-Tatar')*, ed. and trans. N. Ts. Munkuev (Moscow, 1975), pp. 55–9; Peter Jackson, 'From *ulus* to khanate: The making of the Mongol states *c.* 1220–*c.* 1290', in Reuven Amitai-Preiss and David O. Morgan (eds.), *The Mongol empire and its legacy* (Leiden, 1999), pp. 15–20.

21 Peter Jackson, 'The dissolution of the Mongol empire', *Central Asiatic Journal*, 22 (1978), pp. 188–91; Dorothea Krawulsky, *Mongolen und Ilkhâne – Ideologie und Geschichte: 5 Studien* (Beirut, 1989), pp. 65–85.

and its army fell to their descendants and although borders were frequently disputed, the central territories are clearly described. They are designated by the term *ulus*, signifying both land and its population. The north-west, including the Russian steppes, was the *ulus* of Jochi; since he died before his father, this region went to his sons. The Altai was Ögedei's *ulus*, the Semirechye and Turkistān went to Chaghadai, while as the youngest Tolui kept the heartland of Mongolia and became regent on his father's death. Chinggis's third son, Ögedei, was enthroned as supreme khan – *qaghan* – by the Mongol princes at a *quriltai* near the Kerulen river in autumn 1229.

Expansion was one of Ögedei's first concerns and an important tool in asserting power. In 1230 he sent a commander to retake Khurāsān and western Iran; this campaign will be described later. He sent an army to the Russian steppes, an expedition which reached into Hungary and was ended by his death in 1241. These lands became part of Jochi's *ulus*. In the east Ögedei mounted campaigns against Korea and northern China, where the Mongols overthrew the Chin dynasty in 1234. The Mongols were well aware of the importance of their settled territories. Chinggis Khan had appointed governors known as *darughas* in many cities and had created administrations in northern China and Transoxiana. Ögedei transformed these into jointly owned branch secretariats under civilian governors, a system later extended into Iran. Turkistān was put under the Khwārazmian Maḥmūd Yalavach and northern China under the Khitan Yeh-lü Ch'u-ts'ai.

Centralisation was a priority for the new qaghan, but, like his father, he had to placate his relatives. The qaghan's officials in the branch secretariats were accompanied by representatives of the Jochid, Chaghadayid and Toluid houses. In this way the qaghan maintained his claim on the settled territories while acknowledging the interests of family members. In the armies sent on major campaigns, the lines of the four brothers were likewise represented. These troops were known as *tamma*, and since some remained as garrison troops, each area of the empire had armies representing the four dynastic branches. Mongol princes and princesses furthermore had holdings outside their own *ulus*. Many held appanages – lands whose income was to go to an individual – and retained rights to income from cities and artisans granted during conquest, usually managed by their own agents.

Ögedei attempted to increase government revenues without further damaging the population, who were suffering from dues levied by innumerable people connected to the government or to the Mongol elite. In China Yeh-lü Ch'u Ts'ai abolished most irregular dues and from 1230 to 1235 introduced a tax on adults and on households. Additional income came from government monopolies on salt, liquor, vinegar and yeast. There was a tax on trade, the *tamgha*, while Mongols and other nomads were taxed at a rate of one animal per hundred.[22] In 1234–6, the Mongols carried out a census in north China and began the military recruitment of Chinese. There were censuses in Māzandarān, Khurāsān and Sīstān in 1239–42.[23] The qaghan reorganised the official post – a system of stopping places and horses for official business throughout the empire – and in 1235 began the construction of the capital city Qaraqorum in Mongolia.[24]

Towards the end of his life, Ögedei was incapacitated by alcoholism, and power went to his wife, Töregene Khatun, who became regent on his death in December 1241. During her long regency princes and *amīrs* expanded their power in the settled regions at the expense of the government and the population. By this time rifts had opened within the dynasty and indeed it is possible that Tolui's death in 1232 was at Ögedei's command.[25] Relations between the Ögedeyid and Jochid houses were particularly strained, since Güyüg – the son of Ögedei and Töregene – had quarrelled bitterly with Jochi's son and successor Batu on the western campaign. In 1246 Töregene nonetheless managed to arrange Güyüg's enthronement as qaghan. Like his father, Güyüg began his reign with measures to increase central control, sending armies against China, the Tangut regions and the Middle East. He cancelled all orders and grants given since his father's death and ordered new censuses in China and the Middle Eastern territories.[26] Güyüg however died in the summer of 1248, possibly on his way to confront Batu. Once more the empire was ruled by a regent, Güyüg's widow Oghul Qaimish. In the twenty-four years between Chinggis Khan's death and Möngke Khan's enthronement in 1251, the Mongol empire was without a ruler for ten years, enough to undo much of the systematisation achieved by the qaghans.

22 Thomas Allsen, *Mongol imperialism: The policies of the Grand Qan Möngke in China, Russia and the Islamic lands, 1251–1259* (Berkeley, 1987), pp. 159–62, 169; Igor de Rachewiltz, 'Yeh-lü Ch'u Ts'ai (1189–1243); Yeh-lü Chu (1221–1285)', in Igor de Rachewiltz, Hok-lam Chan, Hsiao Ch'i-ch'ing and Peter W. Geier, (eds.), *In the service of the khan: Eminent personalities of the early Mongol-Yuan period* (Wiesbaden, 1993), pp. 150–1.

23 Ann K. S. Lambton, *Continuity and change in medieval Persia: Aspects of administrative, economic and social history, 11th–14th century*, Columbia Lectures on Iranian Studies, 2 (Albany, NY, 1988), p. 201.

24 David O. Morgan, 'Reflections on Mongol communications in the Ilkhanate', in Carole Hillenbrand (ed.), *Studies in honour of Clifford Edmund Bosworth*, vol. II: *The Sultan's turret: Studies in Persian and Turkish culture* (Leiden, 2000), pp. 376–9.

25 Joseph Fletcher, 'The Mongols: Ecological and social perspectives', *Harvard Journal of Asiatic Studies*, 46 (1986), p. 36.

26 Ho-dong Kim, 'A reappraisal of Güyüg Khan', in Reuven Amitai and Michal Biran (eds.), *Mongols, Turks, and others: Eurasian nomads and the sedentary world* (Leiden, 2005), pp. 327–9; Allsen, 'Rise', p. 387.

The Islamic lands in the early Mongol empire

Until 1259, the Mongol territories of the Middle East were part of an empire ruled from Mongolia. At this period, Transoxania was the only province directly under Mongol control and it fared better than other Islamic lands. In the region of Samarqand and Bukhārā, Chinggis Khan appointed the Khitan Yeh-lü A-hai, referred to in Persian sources by his title, T'ai-shih, as *darugha*. Yeh-lü began reconstruction, importing Chinese, Khitan and Tangut agriculturalists to offset depopulation; the Chinese Taoist Ch'ang-ch'un, who visited Samarqand in 1221, stated that its population had been reduced to one-fourth. On Yeh-lü A-hai's death, *c.* 1223, his position went to his son, Yeh-lü Mien-ssu-ko, who held it until about 1239.[27] Transoxania was joined with the other regions of the Silk Road and in 1229 Ögedei appointed Maḥmūd Yalavach to be in charge of the regional administration. Maḥmūd repaired irrigation systems and implemented a tax reform, probably the model for that of Yeh-lü Ch'u-ts'ai in China, with a poll-tax on adult males called *qubchur* and a land-tax called *qalan*. Other taxes were abolished, at least in theory. Maḥmūd had to contend with attempts by Chaghadai, whose territory adjoined Transoxania, to assert authority. In 636/1238f., the rebellion of Maḥmūd Tārābī in Bukhārā brought a punitive assault, but Maḥmūd was able to prevent a massacre by an appeal to Ögedei. Perhaps to placate Chaghadai, Ögedei moved Maḥmūd to China and replaced him by his son Mas'ūd, with no change in policy. Contemporary observers and numismatic evidence suggest that by 1260 Central Asia had nearly regained its earlier prosperity.[28]

The situation was very different in Iran, where Chinggis Khan made no attempt to install systematic administration.[29] Some eastern cities had Mongol officials but most simply remained under earlier rulers: the atabegs of Fārs in southern Iran, the Khwārazm Shāh's son Ghiyāth al-Dīn in Rayy, and in Azerbaijan, the Saljuqid atabegs. Kirmān was seized in 619/1221f. by Baraq Ḥājib, a former servitor of the Khwārazm Shāhs, who gave allegiance to the Mongols and founded the Qutluq-Khanid dynasty. Most rulers offered submission to the qaghan and many travelled to the central court. Describing

27 Paul D. Buell, 'Sino-Khitan administration in Mongol Bukhara', *Journal of Asian History*, 13, 2 (1979), pp. 122–5, 134–41; and Buell, 'Yeh-lü A-hai (*ca.* 1151–*ca.* 1223); Yeh-lü T'u-hua (d. 1231)', in de Rachewiltz *et al.* (eds.), *In the service*, pp. 118–19.

28 Buell, 'Administration', pp. 139–47; Thomas Allsen, 'Maḥmūd Yalavac (?–1254); Mas'ūd Beg (?–1289); 'Alī Beg (?–1280); Buir (*fl.* 1206–1260)', in de Rachewiltz *et al.* (eds.), *In the service*, pp. 122–7.

29 Paul D. Buell, 'Tribe, "*Qan*" and "*ulus*" in early Mongol China: Some prolegomena to Yuan history', Ph.D. thesis, University of Washington (1977), p. 154.

Güyüg's enthronement in 1247, Juwaynī mentions rulers or their relatives from Anatolia, Georgia, Mosul and Aleppo, along with envoys from Fārs, Kirmān, the caliph in Baghdad and the Ismāʿīlīs of Alamūt.[30] The exception was the Khwārazm Shāh's son Jalāl al-Dīn. After Chinggis Khan's departure he left India, defeated his brother Ghiyāth al-Dīn in central Iran and set out against the caliph and the atabeg of Azerbaijan. He took Tabrīz in 622/1225 and then attacked the Georgians and campaigned towards Kirmān. The pillage he allowed his army soon turned rulers and populations against him, and he headed east to fight the Mongol forces of Khurāsān.

In the summer of 627/1230 Ögedei sent an army under the commander Chormaghun to assert Mongol control over Iran. Jalāl al-Dīn retreated and was subsequently killed by Kurds in Shawwāl 628/August 1231. Chormaghun's army subdued most of northern and central Iran including the Mūghān plain, from this time on the Mongols' regular winter pasture. The Georgians and the Armenians became faithful allies. When Chormaghun became incapacitated, his second-in-command, Baiju, took over and extended Mongol power into northern Syria and Anatolia. On 6 Muḥarram 641/26 June 1243, Baiju defeated the armies of the Saljuqid sultan of Rūm, Kaykhusraw II (r. 1237–46), at the battle of Köse Dagh. Kaykhusraw retained the throne as a vassal but many of the important posts in Anatolia went to Mongol *amīrs*.

The allocation of command within Iran is not entirely clear. Although Chormaghun was given overall authority, he was active primarily in the west and appointed Chin-Temür, governor of Khwārazm for Jochi's son Batu, over Khurāsān and Māzandarān, along with representatives from the qaghan and the other Chinggisid houses. Chin-Temür's authority probably covered only north-western Khurāsān, since Ögedei sent a separate army to the southern region stretching from Bādhghīs to the Indian borderlands.[31] Mongol officials soon began to fight among themselves and to ally with competing Iranian rulers. There was no one cause for Mongol rivalries; the presence of agents from all four *ulus*es contributed, but regional and personal tensions were also important. Chin-Temür came into conflict with Dayir, a commander of the southern army stationed in Bādhghīs. Ögedei had ordered Dayir to pacify Nīshāpūr, and Dayir used the directive to claim control of Khurāsān with Chormaghun's backing. Chin-Temür countered by sending two regional rulers (*maliks*) to Ögedei's court, thus winning both imperial

30 Juwaynī, *History*, p. 250.
31 *Ibid.*, p. 487; Juwaynī, *Tārīkh-i jahān-gushā*, ed. Mīrzā Muḥammad Qazwīnī, Gibb Memorial Series XVI (Leiden, 1912–37), vol. II, p. 223; Jean Aubin, 'L'éthnogénèse des Qaraunas', *Turcica*, 1 (1969), p. 70.

favour and local allies. His protégés received patents for their regions and Ögedei confirmed Chin-Temür as governor of Khurāsān, independent of Chormaghun. The vizier Bahā' al-Dīn Juwaynī, father of the historian 'Aṭā Malik, joined Chin-Temür as *ṣāḥib dīwān*. Dayir however remained strong in the south along with another *amīr*, Qara Noyan, in alliance with Rukn al-Dīn Marghanī who held the fortress of Khaysār in Ghūristan.[32] On Chin-Temür's death in 633/1235f., Ögedei appointed Batu's agent Nosal as governor but Chin-Temür's ambitious chamberlain, Körgüz, gained actual power and succeeded Nosal on his death in 1239f. A rival party developed around the candidacy of Chin-Temür's son Edigü Temür. This split combined with tensions among the *maliks* of Khurāsān and Māzandarān and divided both Mongols and Persians into rival camps. Ögedei sent his official Arghun Aqa to investigate and summoned the combatants to Qaraqorum, where the Mongol commanders and officials – *noyans* – took different sides in the dispute. Körgüz maintained his position and was appointed to take over from Chormaghun in the west, but his authority was undermined by the influence of Arghun Aqa, allied with Edigü Temür's party.

Herat, which lay within the sphere of the southern commanders, was also affected by regional and dynastic rivalries. Ögedei entrusted its reconstruction to the former head of the city weavers, 'Izz al-Dīn, who arrived back in 635/1237f. He, and his son after him, worked in collaboration with a Mongol governor appointed by Qara Noyan of the southern army. However, their power was challenged by another Iranian, who appealed for help to Batu and Körgüz, both happy to use local rivalries to their own advantage. Batu's candidate took power and showed consistent favour to the agents of Batu and Körgüz, but after some years he was murdered – perhaps with the help of Arghun Aqa. In 643/1245f. the governorship of Herat went to the protégé of Dayir and Qara Noyan, the Ghūrid Malik Shams al-Dīn Kart, founder of the Kartid dynasty.[33]

32 Juwaynī, *History*, pp. 485–7; Sayf b. Muḥammad b. Ya'qūb al-Harawī Sayfī, *Tārīkh-nāma-i Harāt*, ed. Muḥammad Zubayr al-Ṣiddiqī (Calcutta, 1944), p. 151; Rashīd al-Dīn Hamadānī, trans. J. A. Boyle, *The successors of Genghis Khan* (New York, 1971), pp. 51–3; Jean Aubin, *Émirs mongols et vizirs persans dans les remous de l'acculturation*, Cahiers de Studia Iranica (Paris, 1995), p. 14.

33 Mu'īn al-Dīn Zamchī Isfizārī, *Rawḍāt al-jannāt fī awṣāf madīnat Harāt*, ed. Sayyid Muḥammad Kāẓim Imām (Tehran, AH solar 1338), vol. II, pp. 107–21; Sayfī, *Tārīkh-nāma*, pp. 117–40; Lawrence G. Potter, 'The Kart dynasty of Herat: Religion and politics in medieval Iran', Ph.D. thesis, Columbia University, 1992, p. 41; George Lane, *Early Mongol rule in thirteenth-century Iran* (London, 2003), pp. 154–8; Aḥmad b. Jalāl al-Dīn Faṣīḥ Khwāfī, *Mujmal-i faṣīḥī*, ed. Muḥammad Farrukh (Mashhad, solar 1339), vol. II, p. 314.

Shortly after Ögedei's death Körgüz was killed by the Chaghadayids, whom he had insulted, and Arghun Aqa took his place. Coming into office during the interregnum, Arghun faced major difficulties but through energy, competence and frequent visits to the central court he maintained this position.[34] After Ögedei's death Batu increased his influence, particularly over western Iran and Anatolia, and it was from his court that the official patent for Kaykhusraw arrived. During his brief reign in 1246–8, Güyüg attempted to assert authority, sending Arghun Aqa west to take over Georgia, but shortly after Möngke took power in 1251 Baiju regained command. Arghun Aqa retained overall authority but had difficulty asserting his power over Baiju in the west.[35]

The restoration of agriculture in Khurāsān began during Ögedei's reign. In 1239–40 Körgüz began to restore buildings and agriculture in the region of Ṭūs and Rādkān where he centred his administration. Arghun Aqa continued the development of Ṭūs and also restored Marv. However, the constant infighting hampered progress. The qaghan controlled conflicts by summoning those involved to the central court (*yarghu*). While officials and rulers were away, their rivals often gained ground, but if they returned with a decision in their favour, the situation was abruptly reversed. Confusion increased during the interregnums as the princes sent their agents to demand taxes without regard to legality. Under these conditions, orderly administration was impossible to maintain.

Möngke and the Toluid coup

The reign of Möngke marked at once the apogee and the end of unified Mongol rule. Möngke was a man of great intelligence and will who expanded the empire beyond earlier borders while mobilising its resources to an extent that was extraordinary for the medieval period. However, he did not ease tensions within the dynasty. Möngke came to the throne through a coup against the line of Ögedei. During Töregene's regency Batu had allied with Tolui's widow Sorqaqtani Beki, the niece of the Kerait Ong Khan, a powerful woman and a bitter enemy of Töregene. After Güyüg's death Sorqaqtani collaborated with Batu to arrange the election of her son Möngke at a *quriltai* west of Mongolia attended primarily by Jochid and Toluid princes. The choice was confirmed in

34 George Lane, 'Arghun Aqa: Mongol bureaucrat', *Iranian Studies*, 32, 4 (1999), pp. 459–82; *EIr* 'Arghun Aqa' (Peter Jackson).
35 Juwaynī, *History*, pp. 507–9.

another *quriltai* in summer 1251. Shortly after his accession Möngke discovered an assassination plot by Ögedeyid and Chaghadayid princes, and opened his reign with a series of trials of men and women who had opposed his election. Rulers from settled territories who had taken the wrong side suffered appropriately. The Ögedeyid and Chaghadayid lines both endured numerous executions and from this time on power lay with the Toluids and Jochids.

Möngke undertook a series of reforms to rationalise taxes and mobilise resources for the central government. In Iran the poll-tax became a progressive one, from 7 *dīnārs* for wealthy men to 1 *dīnār* for the poor; it was revised in 654–6 / 1256–8, when rates were reduced for the people of moderate means and increased for the rich. The tax continued to be resented, in part due to its similarity to the *jizya* tax for non-Muslims. We should remember also that it fell most heavily on the wealthy class, which included the historians on whom we rely.[36] In 1252 Möngke organised a new census, covering many areas not counted before. Registration began in China in 1252; the next year marked its beginning in Iran, and 1254 in the Caucasus. In the Golden Horde, where little had previously been done, the census lasted from 1254 to 1259. It seems likely that Möngke's reign also brought new taxes along with monopolies – a Chinese practice – in West Asia. The Armenian historian Kirakos mentions the *tamgha* tax on trade and taxes on fishermen, miners and craftsmen as a recent hardship; he also relates the seizure of the salt mines of Transcaucasia.[37] The population was further liable for corvée duties, onerous for Mongols and settled subjects alike. One purpose of the census was the mobilisation of troops. The population was divided into decimal units from 10 to 10,000, of which some served as soldiers and others provided for the army's needs. The system is best known in China, where auxiliary formations served also as territorial administrative units. In the Middle East, these armies were known as *cherig* and contained both cavalry and footmen, conscripted from all segments of the population.

In 1252 Möngke organised military expeditions under the leadership of his younger brothers, sending Qubilai against China and Hülegü to the Middle East. From this time Qubilai was based in north China, though the regional secretariat remained in existence under Maḥmūd Yalavach. It is clear that Möngke allowed Qubilai only limited independence, and there was frequent friction over his authority. In 1256 when Möngke attacked the Song dynasty of southern China, he led the campaign in person.

36 Allsen, *Mongol imperialism*, pp. 166–7.
37 *Ibid.*, pp. 116–43, 161–3.

Hülegü and the founding of the Ilkhanid dynasty

For Möngke the existing state of balanced conflict in Iran was no longer acceptable. Hülegü was ordered to subjugate three powers seen as troublesome: the tribes of Luristān, the Ismāʿīlīs in Qūhistān, the Caspian region and Syria, and the caliph. These powers had previously reached an accommodation with the Mongols but relations had since soured.[38] Advance forces prepared the route from western Mongolia to Azerbaijan and informed populations along the path of the supplies they must provide. The experienced commander Ked-Buqa served as advance guard.[39] He crossed the Oxus in 651/1253, and campaigned in Qūhistān, Rayy and the region of Alamūt before Hülegü arrived at Samarqand in 653/1255. By this time it was clear that the region was to become more fully integrated into the empire, and local rulers were ordered to provide supplies and to accompany the army. It is not surprising that some people who had previously shown obedience should balk at new conditions. Since the Ismāʿīlī grand master Rukn al-Dīn Khurshāh of the Maymūn-Diz fortress near Qazvīn was unwilling to meet Hülegü's terms, the army took the fortress on 29 Shawwāl 654/19 November 1256. They destroyed many other fortresses including the centre at Alamūt, from which astronomical instruments and part of the famous library were saved. The astronomer Naṣīr al-Dīn Ṭūsī, who had been in the service of the Ismāʿīlīs, joined Hülegü's camp.

For the assault on Baghdad Hülegü called in Mongol armies under Baiju and Jochid commanders. The caliph refused Mongol conditions, so the armies converged on the city along with local forces including Armenians, Georgians and the atabegs of Shīrāz and Mosul. The assault began on 22 Muḥarram 656/29 January, 1258 and the caliph surrendered on 4 Ṣafar/10 February. Although the inhabitants laid down their arms they were systematically slaughtered and the city was sacked for seven days; the scene echoed the massacres of the first Mongol conquest, apparently at Möngke's orders. On 14 Ṣafar/20 February the caliph was killed, probably by being rolled in a carpet and kicked, a sign of respect since it avoided the shedding of blood.

In the autumn of 656/1258 Hülegü invaded Syria, accompanied by the Saljuq sultans of Rūm, the ruler of Mosul, King Het'um of Armenia, and Het'um's son-in-law, Bohemond VI of Antioch. Ked-Buqa went ahead as

38 Juwaynī, *History*, pp. 250, 256; Timothy May, 'A Mongol–Ismâʿîlî alliance?: Thoughts on the Mongols and Assassins', *Journal of the Royal Asiatic Society*, ser. 3, 14, 3 (2004), pp. 231–9.

39 Juwaynī, *History*, pp. 608–10.

advance guard. The subjugation of Syria appeared to pose little challenge, since the Ayyūbid dynasty was in disarray and most of its princes had declared submission. In Egypt the Mamlūks had not yet consolidated power and were continually threatened by the remaining Ayyūbid rulers of Syria, most notably al-Nāṣir Yūsuf in Damascus. Aleppo capitulated after a week; the citadel surrendered about a month later, on 11 Rabīʿ I 658/25 February 1260, and the city was subjected to pillage and massacre. Hama, Homs and Damascus submitted without a struggle. By the beginning of summer the army had reached Gaza, where Hülegü learned of the struggle over succession to Möngke and turned back, leaving behind a small army under Ked-Buqa.[40]

For some time the campaign continued smoothly. However, the situation in Egypt had changed with the accession of the Mamlūk Quṭuz in late 657/1259. He came to power on an anti-Mongol platform and attracted a number of important *amīrs*, including the gifted Baybars. They gathered a force significantly larger than that of Ked-Buqa and when the armies joined battle at ʿAyn Jālūt on 3 September 1260, Ked-Buqa was killed and the Mongols fled.[41] Quṭuz proceeded north to restore local rule in Damascus and Aleppo. The battle at ʿAyn Jālūt was not the first defeat of Mongol forces, though it was an exceptionally severe one. What gave it lasting importance was lack of Mongol resolve. The Mongols undertook another campaign later that year but after a defeat near Homs in 658/1260 they evacuated much of Syria. Most importantly the Mamlūk victories provided instant prestige to their nascent state. In 660/1261 the new sultan Baybars welcomed a fugitive ʿAbbāsid, thus acquiring a shadow caliph, and from this time on the Mamlūks presented their rule as a bulwark of Islam against the infidels.

The founding of the Ilkhanate

Möngke's death on 12 August 1259 led to the establishment of independent Mongol states in Iran and China. During his reign the increase in revenue from agriculture and trade had changed the balance of power between the steppe and settled regions, making central power more difficult to maintain. The struggle that developed between his brothers Ariq Böke, based in Mongolia, and Qubilai in north China, offered Hülegü a valuable opportunity. Although Qubilai had himself enthroned as khan, Hülegü was the only important ruler

40 Reuven Amitai-Preiss, *Mongols and Mamluks: The Mamluk–Īlkhānid war, 1260–1281* (Cambridge, 1995), pp. 16–28; R. Stephen Humphreys, *From Saladin to the Mongols: The Ayyubids of Damascus, 1193–1260* (Albany, NY, 1977), pp. 330–63.

41 Amitai-Preiss, *Mongols*, pp. 39–45.

to recognise him. He was rewarded in 1262 when Qubilai's envoys invested him with the title *ilkhan* and official power over the Mongol Middle East. The Ilkhanate became a separate state, though not equal in prestige to the Golden Horde, Mongol China or the Chaghadayid khanate. Formal recognition by Qubilai and his successors remained a source of legitimation up to the fourteenth century and the two khanates maintained close relations.[42] There is continuing controversy over whether Hülegü's assumption of power accorded with Möngke's intentions, as the historians of Iran and China assert, or was a coup contravening the testament of Chinggis Khan, as the khans of the Golden Horde contended.[43] It is possible that the truth is in between, and that Hülegü was given a position of limited independence similar to that of Qubilai in China. During his campaign the joint regional secretariat continued under Arghun Aqa, but the foundation of an observatory at Marāgha suggests the intention to remain.[44]

Hostilities between Hülegü and the Jochids broke out in 1261–2 over control of north-western Iran, claimed by both khanates. Berke, who had succeeded Batu in the Golden Horde, began to advance through the Caucasus probably in 660/late 1261; in 661–2/1262, the Ilkhanids repulsed his army, though in attempting to chase Berke they were defeated.[45] Berke had converted to Islam and he now initiated an alliance with the Mamlūks. The Mongols had for some time been in contact with the pope and European rulers, and Hülegü sent a mission in 660/1262 to King Louis IX of France, proposing joint action against the Mamlūks.[46] These two opposing alliances lasted through much of the Ilkhanid period. Hülegü also had to cope with two attempts at independence. One was from the new Zangid atabeg in Mosul, who allied with the Mamlūks. Ilkhanid troops took the city in 660/1262 and put an end to the dynasty. In Fārs, the death of the atabeg Abū Bakr in 658/1260 brought a succession struggle and attacks on Mongol functionaries. Hülegü installed Abū Bakr's young granddaughter Abish and arranged for her marriage to his son Möngke-Temür.

42 Thomas T. Allsen, 'Changing forms of legitimation in Mongol Iran', in Gary Seaman and Daniel Marks (eds.), *Rulers from the steppe: State formation and the Eurasian periphery*, Ethnographic Monograph Series, 2 (Los Angeles, 1991), pp. 226–32; Allsen, 'Notes on Chinese titles in Mongol Iran', *Mongolian Studies*, 14 (1991), pp. 27–39.

43 Jackson, 'Dissolution', pp. 208–27; Aubin, *Émirs*, pp. 17–19; Allsen, *Mongol imperialism*, pp. 46–51.

44 Juwaynī, *History*, p. 519.

45 For variant analyses and chronology see J. A. Boyle, 'Dynastic and political history of the Īl-Khāns', in *Cambridge history of Iran*, vol. V (Cambridge, 1968), p. 353; Lane, *Early Mongol*, pp. 75–6; Jackson, 'Dissolution', pp. 233–4.

46 Jean Richard, 'D'Äljigidäi à Ġazan: La continuité d'une politique franque chez les Mongols d'Iran', in Aigle (ed.), *L'Iran*, pp. 62–3.

The early Ilkhanid dynasty

Hülegü died on 19 Rabīʿ II 663/8 February 1265. The realm he left his successors was potentially rich but appallingly difficult to rule. Several decades of conflict had left the region riddled with local rivalries. Many personnel from outside Chinggisid *uluses* remained in Iran, and members of the other Chinggisid branches still had possessions within Ilkhanid domains.[47] The early Mongol commanders – Körgüz, Chormaghun, Baiju and Arghun Aqa – left behind offspring with inherited land, alliances and expectations of continuing power. Mongol *noyans* were personally involved in administration alongside Persian bureaucrats who were their allies or clients.[48] The role of Mongol dynastic women added yet another complication. Royal women had their own entourage (*ordo*), including armed retainers, and they had independent sources of income in taxes, trade and workshops. In the early Ilkhanate, two of Hülegü's widows, Khutuy Khatun and Öljei Khatun, held very considerable political power.[49] Since so many of the elite had rights to local income, it was almost impossible for the central government to collect the money it needed. The inclusion of both women and *noyans* in state deliberations was formalised in the accession ceremonies for new rulers.[50] In addition many local rulers were closely involved in Mongol politics, and were familiar with Mongolian culture and language.[51] The most powerful were the Kartids in Herat (1245–1381), the Qutluq-Khanid dynasty of Kirmān (1222–1305/6) and the Salghurids of Fārs (1148–1280). The dynasties of Fārs and Kirmān both married princesses to the dynasty.[52]

Because so many different groups were politically active, conflicts within any one sphere pulled in people from other ones. Struggles within subordinate dynasties, within the *dīwān* and, most importantly, issues of succession produced factions which included local rulers, bureaucrats, *amirs* and members of the dynasty. The transfer of loyalty from one ruler to the next was complicated by the institution of the *keshig*, which survived in Iran and

47 Thomas T. Allsen, *Culture and conquest in Mongol Eurasia* (Cambridge, 2001), pp. 46–9.
48 David O. Morgan, 'Mongol or Persian: The government of Īlkhānid Iran', *Harvard Middle Eastern and Islamic Review*, 3, 2 (1996), pp. 62–76; Judith Pfeiffer, 'Conversion to Islam among the Ilkhans in Muslim narrative traditions: The case of Aḥmad Tegüder', Ph.D. dissertation, University of Chicago (2003), pp. 226–7.
49 Pfeiffer, 'Conversion', pp. 224–5.
50 Rashīd al-Dīn Hamadānī, *Jāmiʿ al-tawārīkh: Compendium of chronicles: A history of the Mongols*, trans. Wheeler Thackston, Sources of Oriental Languages and Literatures, Harvard University (Cambridge, MA, 1998–9), pp. 519, 548–9, 562–3, 580.
51 Aubin, *Émirs*, pp. 25–6.
52 Lane, *Early Mongol*, pp. 96–175.

combined a concept of service and loyalty to the individual ruler with the expectation of inheriting office.[53]

Hülegü was succeeded by his son Abaqa (r. 1265–82), apparently chosen without opposition. He was enthroned on 3 Ramaḍān 663/19 June 1265 and within a month had sent an army to counter an invasion from the Golden Horde. His troops were successful, in part probably due to the death of Berke Khan. At about this time the Mamlūks began a series of raids on Armenia, which lasted several years. In 665/1266 Abaqa opened relations with European kings to arrange joint campaigns against the Mamlūks, but the Ilkhans offered their Armenian allies essentially no protection, even allowing Antioch to be taken in 666/1268.[54] The major reason for Mongol inaction in the west was the Chaghadayid threat in the east. Baraq Khan (r. 1266–71) claimed that the region from Bādhghīs to Ghazna belonged to the Chaghadayids. He pillaged from Badakhshān to Nīshāpūr and ordered the ruler of Herat, Malik Shams al-Dīn Kart, to put the resources of the city at his disposal. Malik Shams al-Dīn took refuge in the fortress of Khaysār while Abaqa led his army east and achieved a decisive victory over Baraq's forces near Herat in 668/1270.[55] The eastern Ilkhanate nonetheless remained insecure in part because of the Qara'unas, a group originating from the Mongol *tamma* troops in the region from Bādhghīs to the borders of India. These troops had remained largely intact and constituted a significant force. One contingent had become the personal property (*injü*) of Hülegü and had moved west, but most remained in the eastern borderlands and gradually came under Chaghadayid control. The section previously attached to the Jochid prince Negüder, known as the Negüderī, were particularly active and constituted a constant danger to the southern regions of Iran.[56]

The greatest threat in the west came in 675/1277, when the Mamlūk sultan Baybars took over Kayseri, the capital of the Rūm sultanate, and began minting coins in his own name. Baybars had support from several local officials, including the powerful Parwāna Muʿīn al-Dīn Suleymān, who had risen to prominence through the favour of Baiju. Baybars retreated to Syria as Abaqa approached with his army. Abaqa viewed the battlefield where his forces had been defeated and punished those judged responsible; the Parwāna

53 Charles Melville, 'The *keshig* in Iran: The survival of the royal Mongol household', in Linda Komaroff (ed.), *Beyond the legacy of Genghis Khan* (Leiden, 2006), pp. 136–41, 145–50.

54 Amitai-Preiss, *Mongols*, pp. 94–138.

55 Michal Biran, 'The battle of Herat (1270): A case of inter-Mongol warfare', in Nicola Di Cosmo (ed.), *Warfare in Inner Asian history (500–1800)* (Leiden, 2002), p. 190.

56 Aubin, 'L'éthnogénèse', pp. 65–94.

he took back with him and executed.[57] In 680/1281 Abaqa sent an army into Syria which was defeated by the Mamlūks near Homs on 30 October; he planned to invade again, but died of delirium tremens on 20 Dhū' l-Ḥijja 680/1 April 1282. In general his reign, one of the longest in the Ilkhanate, was a time of peace and recovery.

Abaqa's brother and successor Tegüder Aḥmad reigned only two years before his defeat and execution. His experience provides an illustration of the problems facing Ilkhanid rulers attempting to keep the loyalty of members of the dynasty, *noyans*, bureaucrats and vassals. Before coming to the throne Tegüder had converted to Islam and taken the name Aḥmad, and some historians have attributed his fall to his promotion of Islam. There were however many other reasons for his failure. On Abaqa's death support of royal women, princes and *noyans* was fairly evenly divided between Aḥmad and Abaqa's son Arghun. Arghun ceded the election but asserted his rights to the inheritance of valuable property and troops as Abaqa's son. He collected half the taxes of Khurāsān and in addition laid claim to shares in the wealth of Shīrāz and Baghdad.[58] Aḥmad's prominent *dīwān* officials, the Juwaynī brothers Shams al-Dīn and ʿAtā Malik, were undermined by a rival, Majd al-Mulk of Yazd, attached to Arghun. Aḥmad ended fighting in the *dīwān* by executing Majd al-Mulk, but was less successful with the Mongol elite.[59] The Jalayir *noyan* Buqa, powerful under Abaqa, initially favoured Arghun, and Aḥmad was able to win his service only by giving him a level of power which alienated other *noyans*.[60] In Fārs, already disturbed by recent moves against corruption, local officials withheld taxes and played the *noyans* against each other.[61]

Two courses of action connected to Aḥmad's religion probably did contribute to his downfall. He chose as his closest advisers two Muslim shaykhs rather than the Mongol *noyans*, notably Soghunchaq and Shiktür, who held high positions and expected to wield primary influence. Furthermore, against the advice of his entourage, he attempted to improve relations with the Mamlūks and the Golden Horde.[62] Had the Mamlūks welcomed his overtures, the policy might have succeeded, but they met his advances coldly.

57 Amitai-Preiss, *Mongols*, pp. 157–77; Claude Cahen, *The formation of Turkey: The Seljukid Sultanate of Rūm: Eleventh to fourteenth century*, trans. P. M. Holt (Harlow, 2001), pp. 196–207.

58 Pfeiffer, 'Conversion', pp. 149–59, 204–10, 230.

59 Lane, *Early Mongol*, pp. 197–206; Pfeiffer, 'Conversion', pp. 216–18.

60 Pfeiffer, 'Conversion', pp. 153, 228–9; Rashīd al-Dīn, *Compendium*, pp. 40, 541, 548, 554.

61 Denise Aigle, *Le Fārs sous la domination mongole: Politique et fiscalité (XIIIe–XIVe s.)* (Paris, 2005), pp. 126–32; Lane, *Early Mongol*, pp. 141–4.

62 Pfeiffer, 'Conversion', pp. 182–4; Peter Jackson, *The Mongols and the West, 1221–1410* (Harlow, 2005), pp. 168–9.

As Aḥmad tried to assert power, increasing numbers of *noyans* and princes went over to Arghun, who wrote to Qubilai Khan to complain about Aḥmad's abandonment of the 'old ways'. What was meant by this phrase is not explained. When Aḥmad attacked Arghun his *amīrs*, under the leadership of Buqa, switched sides; he was defeated in battle near Qazvīn and executed on 25 Jumādā I 683/9 August 1284.

Arghun was enthroned on 27 Jumādā I/11 August; his accession spelled the end of the Juwaynī viziers as ʿAṭā Malik died of a stroke in 1283 and Shams al-Dīn was executed a few months into Arghun's reign. Buqa Jalayir, whose help had been decisive in Arghun's victory, became the chief administrator and sent to Qubilai Khan for official approval – this arrived in early 684/1285, and Arghun staged an official enthronement.[63] Arghun returned to the policy of alliance with Europe and enmity to the Mamlūks, but as usual no action resulted. The Mamlūk border remained relatively quiet and two invasions from the Golden Horde, in spring 1288 and 1290, were easily repelled. In Fārs Arghun ended the reign of the Salghurid princess Abish, associated with Aḥmad, and instituted more direct Mongol control.

Over the course of Arghun's reign the rivalries of Mongol *noyans* came to dominate political life. The first problem came from Buqa Jalayir and his brother Aruq, governor (*shaḥna*) of Baghdad. Their power aroused resentment among other senior *amīrs*. The vizier Ṣadr al-Dīn Zanjānī, employed by Amīr Taghachar who commanded the Ilkhanid Qara'unas troops, accused Buqa of withholding the revenue of Fārs, and there were similar accusations about Tabrīz and Baghdad. As Buqa lost power he formed a conspiracy to enthrone a different member of the dynasty; this failed, and he was executed in 687/1289. Arghun now chose as the head of his *dīwān* the Jewish physician Saʿd al-Dawla who had helped to investigate Buqa's brother Aruq. Over the next years Saʿd al-Dawla expanded his power and that of his family, thus becoming a target of animosity in his turn.

Buqa's execution led to an insurrection by Nawrūz, the son of the earlier governor, Arghun Aqa. Nawrūz had inherited great wealth in land and flocks centred in Rādkān and held the emirate of Khurāsān, thus sharing control of the region with Arghun's son Ghazan. Several princes were implicated in his plot and executed, and Nawrūz fled to the Chaghadayid regions, from which he invaded Khurāsān in 690/1291. As Arghun became seriously ill that year, a group of *noyans* including Taghachar conspired to eliminate their enemies,

63 Aubin, *Émirs*, pp. 37–8; Allsen, 'Changing forms', p. 229.

bringing about a series of executions of rival *noyans* and of Saʿd al-Dawla with his family. On 7 Rabīʿ I 690/10 March 1291, Arghun died.

The two major candidates for the throne were Arghun's brother Geikhatu and his cousin Baidu. Geikhatu was chosen and enthroned on 24 Rajab 690/23 July 1291. Among his major supporters was Amīr Choban, a great-nephew of the *noyan* Soghunchaq, who had died in 689 / 1290. Geikhatu was persuaded to forgive the *noyans* who had destroyed Saʿd al-Dawla; thus Taghachar remained active and his protégé Ṣadr al-Dīn Zanjānī became head of the fiscal administration. Geikhatu attempted a set of fiscal reforms modelled on those of Qubilai Khan, probably with the help of Bolad Ch'eng Hsiang, a Khitan administrator with a distinguished record of service in China, who had come to Iran with Qubilai's embassy in 684/1285.[64] The programme is remembered for the experiment with paper money, known by its Chinese name, *ch'ao*. Its introduction was carefully planned, proclaimed in Ramaḍān 693/August 1294, and implemented a month later, but the population refused to accept it. Commerce shut down and violence erupted on the streets, so the experiment was cancelled. Only a few months later Geikhatu's *amīrs* conspired to install Baidu, with Taghachar again among the leaders. Geikhatu was killed on 6 Jumādā I 694/24 March 1295 and Baidu was enthroned the next month but he ruled only until 23 Dhū 'l-Qaʿda/4 October when Ghazan had him put to death. These events had a devastating effect on the dynasty in Kirmān, which was divided into two factions, one allied by marriage with Geikhatu and the other with Baidu. In the course of their reigns the leaders of both factions took sides in central politics and were killed, bringing the province into disorder.

Ghazan and the later Ilkhanids

Ghazan Khan is remembered primarily for his conversion to Islam and the reforms he promulgated with the help of the famous vizier and polymath Rashīd al-Dīn Hamadānī. Ghazan's reign was long seen as the crucial moment for Mongol assimilation and adaptation to Islamic society. However, he did not abandon his Mongol heritage and recent scholarship has brought into question the extent of actual change he achieved.[65]

Ghazan had made peace with the rebellious Nawrūz in late 693/1294, and when some of Baidu's *amīrs* defected to Ghazan, the two men prepared to

64 Allsen, *Culture*, pp. 72–4.

65 For example, Reuven Amitai, 'Ghazan, Islam and Mongol tradition: A view from the Mamlūk sultanate', *Bulletin of the School of Oriental and African Studies*, 59, 1 (1996), pp. 1–10.

make a bid for power. Nawrūz, who was Muslim, suggested that Ghazan convert. Since many Mongols in the army were already Muslim, Ghazan would be attractive to them as well as to the subject population.[66] His conversion was an official one, and after Baiju's defeat, Nawrūz destroyed churches, synagogues and Buddhist monasteries in Tabrīz, but Ghazan put an end to the destruction when he returned to Tabrīz a few months after his enthronement on 23 Dhū 'l-Ḥijja 694/3 November 1295. Ghazan did not reverse foreign policy; he wrote inimical letters to the Mamlūks and friendly ones to the European powers. His title – *pādishāh-i Islām* – expressed independence within the Mongol tradition and claims to pre-eminence in the Islamic world. In accord with this, he worked to gain influence in the Holy Cities.[67] Ghazan however had little success against the Mamlūks. He undertook a series of expeditions to Syria from 1299 to 1303 but although his forces took Homs and Damascus temporarily, within a few months the Mamlūks had reoccupied Syria, and further campaigns in 700/1300 and 702/1303 were failures, though for a time in 700/1300 all Mamlūk forces were driven from Syria.

Ghazan's two predecessors had been unseated by the Mongol *noyans*, and he owed his throne to Nawrūz. It is not surprising therefore that his reign was marked by purges of powerful commanders. One victim was Taghachar, who had deserted Geikhatu for Baidu, and then Baidu for Ghazan.[68] Soon Nawrūz's power also became unacceptable, and he was executed in 696/1297. Bloodshed continued through Ghazan's reign and reached into the *dīwān*. In 1298 Ṣadr al-Dīn Zanjānī was executed, partly due to accusations by Rashīd al-Dīn, who took his place as *ṣāḥib dīwān* with Saʿd al-Dīn Sāwajī as partner.

Rashīd al-Dīn was born into a Jewish family of doctors in 647 or 648/1249–51 and probably began his career at court quite young. He was close to Ghazan and seems to have served him in a personal capacity as well as an administrative one. His enormous wealth appears to have come partly as reward for his scholarly works and his service as administrator (*mutawallī*) of Ghazan Khan's *waqf*.[69] In his history, the *Jāmiʿ al-tawārīkh*, Rashīd al-Dīn describes Ghazan Khan's reforms and gives the texts of many decrees. Land-taxes were to be collected regularly, according to fixed rates written on plaques attached

66 Charles Melville, 'Pādshāh-i Islām: The conversion of Sultan Maḥmūd Ghāzān Khān', *Pembroke Papers*, 1 (1990), pp. 159–77; Amitai, 'Ghazan', pp. 1–3.
67 Charles Melville, '"The year of the elephant": Mamluk–Mongol rivalry in the Hejaz in the reign of Abū Saʿīd (1317–1335)', *Studia Iranica*, 21, 2 (1992), pp. 198–9.
68 Rashīd al-Dīn, *Compendium*, pp. 586, 625–6, 632.
69 Birgitt Hoffmann, *Waqf im mongolischen Iran. Rašīduddīns Sorge um Nachruhm und Seelenheil*, Freiburger Islamstudien, 20 (Stuttgart, 2000), pp. 59–72.

to the walls of buildings. Numerous extraordinary taxes were repealed and neither envoys nor military were allowed to demand lodging at will. Other measures promoted the restoration of abandoned land and systematised currency, weights and measures. To support the army, grants of land were distributed to Mongol soldiers according to rank; these were to be farmed, probably by slaves or subjects, as was the case in China.[70] Rashīd al-Dīn claimed credit for the reforms in his history and in the correspondence attributed to him; however, the correspondence has been shown to be a later composition, and recent scholarship has questioned Rashīd al-Dīn's pre-eminence in the programme.[71] Like earlier reforms, Ghazan's measures show similarities to many of Qubilai Khan's programmes; one should note that Bolad Ch'eng Hsiang, who had served under Qubilai, was still at court.[72]

Ghazan Khan died on 5 Shawwāl 703/11 May 1304 and was succeeded by his brother Kharbanda, who took the name Öljeitü when he was enthroned on 15 Dhū 'l-Ḥijja/19 July with the traditional Mongol rites. He became disenchanted with Sunnism, supposedly after a particularly acrimonious debate between Ḥanafī and Shāfiʿī *ʿulamāʾ*, and he adopted ʿIthna ʿasharī (Twelver) Shīʿism in 1309–10, but made no effort to impose it. Öljeitü was in an unusually comfortable position, since Ghazan had executed the most powerful *amīrs* and had left no male offspring. Furthermore Öljeitü lived in a rare period of harmony among the Mongol states; he wrote optimistically to Philip the Fair of France in spring 1305 that the Mongol empire had been restored.

Öljeitü faced a number of challenges from the smaller powers within his realm and on its borders. Early in 706/1306 he sent an expedition against Herat whose ruler, Malik Fakhr al-Dīn Kart, had failed to congratulate him on his accession or send tribute, and was harbouring the Negüderī who habitually raided Kirmān and Fārs. When the Kartids murdered the Ilkhanid commander another army was sent out, which seized Herat. In 706/1307 Öljeitü undertook a major expedition against Gīlān which foundered with the defeat and death of his chief *amīr* Qutlugh Shāh; this initiated the rise of Amīr Choban, who

70 Shihāb al-Dīn Aḥmad al-ʿUmarī, *Das mongolische Weltreich. Al-ʿUmarīs Darstellung der mongolischen Reiche in seinem Werk Masālik al-abṣār fī mamālik al-amṣār*, ed. and trans. K. Lech (Wiesbaden, 1968), p. 155; Ch'i-ch'ing Hsiao, *The military establishment of the Yuan dynasty*, Harvard East Asian Monographs, 77 (Cambridge, MA, 1978), pp. 20–2, 46.

71 A. H. Morton, 'The letters of Rashīd al-Dīn: Ilkhanid fact or Timurid fiction?', in Amitai-Preiss and Morgan (eds.), *Mongol empire*, pp. 155–99; David O. Morgan, 'Rašīd al-Dīn and Ġazan Khan', in Aigle (ed.), *L'Iran*, pp. 185–7.

72 Thomas T. Allsen, 'Biography of a cultural broker, Bolad Ch'eng-Hsiang in China and Iran', in Julian Raby and Teresa Fitzherbert (eds.), *The court of the Il-khans 1290–1340* (Oxford, 1996), pp. 7–22.

dominated the later Ilkhanate.[73] In autumn and winter 707/1307f., Öljeitü attacked the Mamlūk fortress Rabāṭ al-Shām but withdrew on meeting resistance. In 713/1313f. the truce with the Chaghadayids broke down when the Ilkhan annexed Negüderī territories, and a Chaghadayid army chased Ilkhanid troops almost up to Herat. As Öljeitü set out against them they withdrew, but the Chaghadayid prince Yasa'ur defected and Öljeitü rewarded him with the rich region of Bādhghīs.

Öljeitü died 1 Shawwāl 716/17 December 1316 of a stomach problem probably related to drinking. His twelve-year-old son Abū Saʿīd succeeded him but actual power lay with Amīr Choban. There was bitter rivalry within the *dīwān* where Rashīd al-Dīn and his partner Tāj al-Dīn ʿAlī-Shāh had become so inimical that Öljeitü had divided the administration, with Rashīd al-Dīn in charge of central and southern Iran and ʿAlī-Shāh in charge of the north-west, including Mesopotamia and Asia Minor. ʿAlī-Shāh engineered Rashīd's execution with other family members on 17 Jumādā I 718/17 July 1318.

Early the next year Yasa'ur attacked Māzandarān while the Jochid Uzbek Khan (r. 1313–41) invaded through the Caucasus. The Ilkhanid forces pushed Yasa'ur to the south, where he was later killed by the Chaghadayid khan Kebeg. In the Caucasus, Abū Saʿīd headed against Uzbek Khan with insufficient forces and his advance guard was put to flight. A little later he reversed the situation, aided by Choban. Choban punished the *amīrs* who had failed to stand against Uzbek Khan; a few months later these *amīrs* waylaid him and he had to flee to the court for safety. The rebellious *amīrs* gained support from Abū Saʿīd's uncle Irenjin and marched on Tabrīz, but were defeated near Miyāna in 719/1319.

For some years Choban and ʿAlī-Shāh worked cooperatively and it was they who achieved peace with the Mamlūks in 1320–3. However, even though Choban was married to Abū Saʿīd's sister Sati Beg, from the mid-1320s he encountered increasing hostility, due in part to the behaviour of his son Dimashq Khwāja who served as his representative at court. When Choban failed to heed complaints, Abū Saʿīd encouraged members of the court to kill Dimashq Khwāja in 727/1327. Furthermore, Abū Saʿīd had fallen in love with Amīr Choban's daughter, married to another *amīr*, and Choban refused to arrange her divorce. Eventually Choban began an open revolt and fled to Herat, where the Kartids, reluctant to break with the Ilkhans, killed him.[74]

73 Charles Melville, 'The Īlkhān Öljeitü's conquest of Gīlān (1307): Rumour and reality', in Amitai-Preiss and Morgan (eds.), *Mongol empire*, pp. 73–125.

74 Charles Melville, *The fall of Amir Chupan and the decline of the Ilkhanate 1327–1337: A decade of discord in Iran* (Bloomington, IN, 1999), pp. 11–27.

There were further conspiracies in 1328 and 1329, leading to the execution of many of the *amīrs* involved in the fall of Dimashq Khwāja. The *dīwān* was entrusted to Rashīd al-Dīn's son Ghiyāth al-Dīn but many *noyans* disliked him and dissidents gathered around the deposed governor of Shīrāz, Maḥmūd-Shāh Injü, so that the governor whom Abū Saʿīd sent to Fārs in 735/1334f. was unable to take over for some time. The Golden Horde again advanced, and Abū Saʿīd headed against them but died on 13 Rabīʿ II 736/30 November 1335. Since he was childless and no other strong members of the dynasty survived, his death initiated a protracted struggle.

Mongol patronage

The Mongol period was one of high achievement in fields which interested the Mongol ruling class, whose familiarity with Chinese and Central Asian culture affected the production of the artists and scholars working for them. Outside influences initiated a period of extraordinary cultural efflorescence for Iran. The Mongols showed a predilection for practical scientific knowledge such as astronomy, medicine, agronomy and geography. When Chinggis Khan conquered the Middle East he brought along Chinese astronomers, one of whom was in charge of an observatory in Samarqand by 1222. The Khitan Yeh-lü Ch'u Ts'ai used Middle Eastern astronomical tables to revise Chinese calendars and produced a new calendar for the Mongol rulership.[75] Hülegü came to Iran with Chinese doctors and astronomers and employed Naṣīr al-Dīn Ṭūsī (1201–74), who became supervisor of *waqf* endowments, some of which he diverted to promote his own intellectual interests. Soon after taking Baghdad Hülegü founded an observatory in Marāgha, with Middle Eastern and Chinese astronomers. Here Ṭūsī composed an influential work on planetary astronomy and his team produced the *Zīj-i Īlkhānī* star tables used for centuries thereafter. The Mongols also brought Middle Eastern scholars to China. Qubilai Khan (1215–94) established several institutes for Middle Eastern sciences, including the Office of Western Medicine in 1263 and a Muslim astronomical observatory in 1271. In 1285 he commissioned a geographical compendium including information from Middle Eastern maps.[76]

Textile production was among the earliest concerns of Mongols, who set up workshops in Iran, Mongolia and China to produce luxury cloth combining Iranian and Chinese motifs. Ceramics and metalwork also flourished with a

75 Allsen, *Culture*, pp. 165–6.
76 *Ibid.*, pp. 108, 150, 166–7.

liberal admixture of Chinese decorative themes like the dragon, phoenix and peony, which remained part of Persian art thereafter. The Ilkhans founded their state just after the demise both of the caliphate and of a united Mongol empire, and in crafting their legitimation they turned to Iranian traditions. One illustration of the new ideology was Abaqa Khan's palace at Takht-i Sulaymān, situated on the site of a royal Sasanian city. Conspicuous among the decorative motifs were verses and illustrations of the Persian epic, the *Shāh-nāma*; like earlier nomad dynasties, the Ilkhans were identified with the Turanian king Afrāsiyāb. The palace also contained references to Chinese symbolism.[77] Production of luxury manuscripts became one of the marks of Ilkhanid patronage, with the creation of magnificent Qur'āns, and later illustrated histories and epics.[78]

Arghun Khan's major architectural undertaking was a suburb of Tabrīz called Arghuniyya, completed in 690/1291. Conversion to Islam brought increased patronage of religious architecture, while the interest of Ghazan and Rashīd al-Dīn in Mongolian and Chinese traditions introduced a period of intense cultural borrowing. Abandoning the custom of secret burial, Ghazan built his mausoleum in a *waqf* complex which constituted a whole suburb near Arghuniyya, and included a mosque, madrasas, a *khānaqā*, observatory, library, hospital, hospice for *sayyids* and a kitchen to feed the poor.[79] In 713/1313f. Öljeitü completed a mausoleum in the town of Sulṭāniyya which became the necropolis and second capital for the Ilkhanids. The mausoleum, still standing, is a masterpiece of Islamic architecture. Rashīd al-Dīn built a charitable foundation in Tabrīz similar to Ghazan's, known as the Rabʿ-i Rashīdī. In addition to religious buildings and a hospital, he endowed a scriptorium where his works would be regularly copied to ensure their diffusion.[80] In the later Ilkhanid period numerous people endowed mausoleum complexes on a smaller scale – referred to by scholars as 'little cities of God', which became a standard feature of the urban landscape. The rise of Sufi organisations continued

77 Tomoko Masuya, 'Ilkhanid courtly life', in Stefano Carboni and Linda Komaroff (eds.), *The legacy of Genghis Khan: Courtly art and culture in western Asia, 1256–1353*, (New York, 2002) pp. 84–5; A. S. Melikian-Chirvani, 'Conscience du passé et résistance culturelle dans l'Iran mongol', in Aigle (ed.), *L'Iran*, pp. 145–59.

78 Masuya, 'Ilkhanid courtly life', p. 79; Stefano Carboni, 'Synthesis: Continuity and innovation in Ilkhanid art', in Carboni and Kamaroff (eds.), *Legacy*, p. 203; Robert Hillenbrand, 'The arts of the book in Ilkhanid Iran', in Carboni and Komaroff (eds.), *Legacy*, pp. 135, 143.

79 Hoffmann, *Waqf*, p. 112.

80 Birgitt Hoffmann, 'The gates of piety and charity: Rašīd al-dīn Faḍl Allāh as founder of pious endowments', in Aigle (ed.), *L'Iran*, p. 196.

under the Mongols and their *khānaqās* became a locus for cultural activity, including the production of fine manuscripts.[81]

Rashīd al-Dīn was the author – at least the planner and editor – of several encyclopaedic works. His treatise on agronomy was novel in its practical bent and in the inclusion of numerous plants from outside, particularly from China. His greatest work was the monumental world history, the *Jāmiʿ al-tawārīkh*, begun for Ghazan Khan and completed about 710/1310f. He made use of information from Indian and Buddhist scholars, Ghazan's knowledge of Mongol lore, and Bolad Ch'eng Hsiang's expertise in Chinese and Mongolian history to put earlier histories of the Islamic world into a new frame encompassing the Mongols, Europeans, Chinese and others. The history was illustrated – a practice new with the Ilkhans – and the paintings show strong Chinese and Central Asian elements. Within a few years luxury copies of the *Shāh-nāma* were being illustrated, and by the 730s/1330s, the time of the 'Great Mongol' (Demotte) *Shāh-nāma*, a new Persian style of painting had begun. The new fashions set by the Ilkhans affected their vassals and neighbours. In the fourteenth century, Shīrāz became a centre for the production of illustrated manuscripts, including several *Shāh-nāmas*, and Armenian manuscripts of the period show Chinese motifs. Even the Mamlūks took inspiration from their Mongol enemies.

The economic impact of the Mongols

It is difficult to form an accurate picture of economic developments under the Mongols. The most detailed study on agriculture is the book of I. P. Petrushevskiĭ, who was constrained by Soviet policies which dictated a negative assessment of Mongol rule;[82] his conclusions can no longer be accepted without critical examination.[83] More recent scholars vary in their opinions, but some common revisions emerge. The decline in agriculture is no longer attributed only to the Mongols and greater importance is given to restoration before

81 Sheila S. Blair, 'Calligraphers, illuminators, and painters in the Ilkhanid scriptorium', in Komaroff (ed.), *Beyond the legacy*, pp. 170–1.

82 I. P. Petrusheveskiĭ, *Zemledelie i agrarnye otnosheniia v Irane XIII–XIV vekov* (Moscow and Leningrad, 1960). Parts are summarised in 'The socio-economic condition of Iran under the Īlkhāns', in *The Cambridge history of Iran*, vol. V, pp. 483–537.

83 Lambton, *Continuity*, p. 219; Jean Aubin, 'Réseau pastoral et réseau caravanier: Les grand'routes du Khurassan à l'époque mongole', *Le Monde Iranien et l'Islam*, 1 (1971), pp. 107–8; and Aubin, 'La propriété foncière en Azerbaydjan sous les Mongols', *Le Monde Iranien et l'Islam*, 4 (1976–7), p. 130.

Ghazan Khan.[84] The Mongols entered a region where agriculture was already in decline and their conquest precipitated a crisis. The seriousness of the situation did not escape notice; Chinggis Khan began restoring Transoxiana before his departure. Rebuilding continued under the Great Khans and the Ilkhanids, but recovery was hampered by the difficulty of asserting central control.

In addition to the *qubchur*, *qalan* and *tamgha*, the Mongols collected numerous taxes for the support of specific services. However, only a portion of what the population handed over reached the central government. Private income sources and the stipends of princes, princesses and *amīrs* were sometimes collected directly from the population. Furthermore, local governors and maliks often bribed Mongol collectors, thus enriching both groups at the expense of the population.[85] The situation may have been even worse in areas ruled through local powers, where the regional dynasty provided an additional level of consumption and corruption. Fārs provides an illustration of the difficulties facing the Ilkhanid tax administration. Under several different khans officials arrived with a reform agenda only to suffer attack and speedy demotion.[86] The oppression of the agricultural population was not due to preferential treatment of nomads. During the struggle preceding Ghazan's accession to the throne, when taxes were increased and demanded in advance, a levy of 20 per cent was raised from livestock, thus bringing the nomadic tribes into disorder, at least in Fārs.[87] In Rashīd al-Dīn's description of abuses preceding Ghazan's reign he describes the impoverishment of common soldiers in the Mongol army, a problem that also plagued the Yuan.[88]

Trade and production were of particular interest to the Mongols. The *tamgha* tax provided significant income, some perhaps going directly into the dynasty's private treasury.[89] The leadership also engaged directly in international commerce through partnerships known as *ortoq*, in which money was entrusted to merchants in return for a share of profits. There

84 Aubin, 'Propriété', pp. 79–81, 129–32; Lambton, *Continuity*, p. 144; Peter Christensen, *The decline of Iranshahr: Irrigation and environment in the history of the Middle East 500 BC to AD 1500* (Copenhagen, 1993), p. 12 and *passim*.

85 Thomas Allsen, 'Sharing out the empire: Apportioned lands under the Mongols', in A. Wink and A. Khazanov (eds.), *Nomads in the sedentary world* (Richmond, 2001), pp. 177–81; Aubin, 'Propriété', p. 94; Aigle, *Fārs*, pp. 152–3.

86 A. K. S. Lambton, 'Mongol fiscal administration in Persia', part II, *Studia Islamica*, 65 (1987), pp. 100–21; Lane, *Early Mongol*, pp. 133–41; Aigle, *Fārs*, pp. 92, 104, 120, 127.

87 Lambton, 'Fiscal administration', II, pp. 109–10.

88 Rashīd al-Dīn, *Compendium*, pp. 232, 739–40; Hsiao, *Military*, pp. 29–31.

89 Philip Remler, 'New light on economic history from Ilkhanid accounting manuals', *Studia Iranica*, 14, 2 (1985), pp. 170–3; Ḥamd Allāh Mustawfī Qazwīnī, *The geographical part of the Nuzhat al-qulūb*, ed. G. Le Strange, Gibb Memorial Series (London, 1915–18), text, pp. 50, 56, 59, 78, 116.

was thus a close relationship between the Mongol government and international merchants, who benefited from significant privileges. *Ortoqs* existed under the Ilkhans and provided additional income for the dynasty and elite.[90] A number of merchants served the administration, particularly as holders of tax farms. The most notable examples were the wealthy merchants of Qays in the Persian Gulf, who for some time managed the taxes of Fārs.[91]

Tabrīz and Sulṭāniyya were international trading centres where the land routes through Central Asia connected with those of the Golden Horde and the sea trade of the Persian Gulf. After about 1275 the Genoese dominated Black Sea commerce from Kaffa, the major port for the Golden Horde, and from about 1280 into the middle of the fourteenth century they maintained a colony in Tabrīz.[92] In the south two small mercantile powers, Qays, usually allied with Fārs, and Hormuz, closer to the Qutluq Khanids of Kirmān, competed in the rich trade with India and China. For the sea trade, horses and pearls appear to have been the major exports but for other regions textiles were more important, and it is notable that the production of silk and cotton is said to have increased.[93] The Ilkhans were active in protecting trade routes in both the Black Sea and the Gulf.[94] Mongol interest in trade promoted the growth of the middle classes. Skilled craftsmen seem to have risen in status, while practical and linguistic skills provided a path to advancement within government. The success of people from the lower classes is a frequent lament of Ilkhanid bureaucrat historians.[95]

The Mongol legacy in Iran

It is hard to define the end of the Mongol period in the Middle East. Despite strong separate identities, Mongols and Iranians intermarried and became closely connected both culturally and politically.[96] While Mongolian

90 Thomas Allsen, 'Mongolian princes and their merchant partners, 1200–1260', *Asia Major*, 3rd ser., 2 (1989), pp. 94–121.
91 Lambton, 'Fiscal administration', II, pp. 105–6, 114.
92 Jacques Paviot, 'Les marchands italiens dans l'Iran mongol', in Aigle (ed.), *L'Iran*, pp. 73, 78.
93 Lambton, *Continuity*, p. 181.
94 Paviot, 'Les marchands', p. 84; Jean Aubin, 'Les princes d'Ormuz du XIIIe au XVe siècle', *Journal Asiatique*, 241 (1953), pp. 85, 92–3.
95 Oliver Watson, 'Pottery under the Mongols', in Komaroff (ed.), *Beyond the legacy*, pp. 330–3; Bernard O'Kane, 'Persian poetry on Ilkhanid art and architecture', in Komaroff (ed.), *Beyond the legacy*, p. 353; Aubin, 'Propriété', p. 129.
96 al-ʿUmarī, *Mongolische Weltreich*, p. 159; Tatiana Zerjal, Yali Xue, *et al.*, 'The genetic legacy of the Mongols', *American Journal of Human Genetics*, 72 (2003), pp. 717–21.

remained the chancery language, by the fourteenth century the ruling class spoke Turkic, like earlier steppe dynasties. Many bureaucrats and local rulers were familiar with Mongolian culture and depended on Mongol legitimacy for their own prestige. Thus when Abū Saʿīd Khan died childless on 30 November 1335, the first reaction was to prop up Chinggisid rule. Ghiyāth al-Dīn b. Rashīd al-Dīn installed a new khan within hours of Abū Saʿīd's death, but was soon defeated. In the northern regions the competing powers were families of *noyans* who had married into the royal family over several generations. Ḥasan Beg Jalayir, a grandson of Öljeitu married to a Chinggisid woman, soon promoted his own candidate. In early 739/July–August 1338, the descendants of Choban made a bid for power, using Abū Saʿīd's sister Sati Beg – Choban's widow – as candidate. The Jalayirids (1336–1432) based themselves in Baghdad and the Chobanids (1336–56) in Tabrīz, with constantly shifting borders.

For several years vassal states in southern Iran continued to give nominal allegiance to the khans of the Jalayirids or Chobanids. The Injuid dynasty in Fārs soon lost out to Mubāriz al-Dīn Muẓaffar, who had begun his career under Abū Saʿīd and later allied with the Chobanids. The Muẓaffarid dynasty took over much of southern and central Iran, including Kirmān and Iṣfahān. The eastern centre of the Ilkhanate lay in Khurāsān. Here *noyans* gathered with Iranian rulers and religious figures in the summer of 737/1336 and elected as khan Taghay Temür, a descendant of Chinggis Khan's brother Jochi Qasar.[97] The most powerful *noyan* in Khurāsān was Arghunshāh, who was descended from Arghun Aqa and led the family's hereditary troops. His dynasty and that of Taghay Temür however soon lost territory to the Iranian Sarbadārid dynasty of Sabzawār (1337–86), while the Kartid dynasty of Herat became the pre-eminent power of the region. For some time after Abū Saʿīd's death rulers included the name of one or another Chinggisid khan on their coinage, then in the mid-740s/1340s a few began to issue coins anonymously. It was only in the 1350s that some rulers looked to new sources of legitimacy. In 755/1354 Mubāriz al-Dīn Muẓaffar requested a patent from the shadow caliph in Egypt, and in 759/1358, following the demise of the Chobanid dynasty, the Jalayirid sultan Uways claimed power in his own name.[98]

There is no sign of an exodus of Mongol population and we find Mongol tribes and populations active well into the fifteenth century. The Iranian armies (*cherig*) organised by the Mongols remained an important element of

97 Jean Aubin, 'Le quriltai de Sultân-Maydân (1336)', *Journal Asiatique*, 279 (1991), pp. 175–97.
98 Steven Album, 'Power and legitimacy: The coinage of Mubāriz al-Dīn Muḥammad ibn al-Muẓaffar at Yazd and Kirmān', *Le Monde Iranien et l'Islam*, 2 (1974), pp. 158–68.

military power for more than a century. Mongol influence continued in government structures as well. Turkic and Mongolian words entered into Persian vocabulary and several Mongol institutions, such as the military governor – *darugha* – and the imperial guard, the *keshig*, lasted through the Safavid dynasty.[99] A more contentious element of Mongol tradition was the *yasa* (Mongolian: *jasagh*), usually translated as 'law' or 'code'. Scholars disagree over whether or not the *yasa* was a specific set of laws existing as a written document. The precepts preserved deal primarily with military and administrative matters which were tried in the Mongol court, the *yarghu*. By the fourteenth century however the term *yasa* was a general one, encompassing both law and custom (*yosun*). There was considerable disagreement over how much the *yasa* and the *sharīʿa* conflicted. For rulers who adhered to both the Mongol and the Islamic order, like Ghazan Khan and later Tamerlane, there was apparently no contradiction, while scholars hostile to Mongol rule considered the two systems mutually exclusive. Whatever the reality of the *yasa*, as a marker of identity it remained central to Turco-Mongolian government.[100] For centuries the Mongol empire continued to set the standard of imperial power against which all dynasties had to measure themselves, and reference to Mongol ancestry was used in Islamic lands into the nineteenth century.

The Chaghadayid khanate

Transoxania and the Silk Road cities lay within the Chaghadayid khanate, about which we have distressingly little information since the area produced almost no indigenous historical writing. Most of the settled regions were included in the satellite administration created by Ögedei in 1229, which remained in existence for some time after Qubilai's accession.[101] The families of the early officials Maḥmūd Yalavach and Yeh-lü A-hai retained their positions for decades; that of Yalavach until after 1302.[102] Their long tenure suggests that the Chaghadayid administration did not suffer from the vicious bureaucratic infighting that plagued Iran. Political history presents a strong

99 Melville, '*Keshig*'.

100 For recent discussion see: Denise Aigle, 'Le grand *jasaq* de Gengis-Khan, l'empire, la culture mongole et la *sharīʿa*', *Journal of the Economic and Social History of the Orient*, 47, 1 (2004), pp. 31–79; David Morgan, 'The "Great *yasa* of Chinggis Khan" revisited', in Amitai and Biran (eds.), *Mongols, Turks and others*, pp. 291–308.

101 The census conducted in Bukhārā about 1265 was at his orders. (Michal Biran, *Qaidu and the rise of the independent Mongol state in Central Asia* (Richmond, 1997), p. 35.)

102 Biran, *Qaidu*, p. 98; Allsen, 'Maḥmūd Yalavac', pp. 122–36.

contrast. The khanate was constantly embroiled in wider politics and succession was often imposed from outside. When Güyüg came to the throne in 1246, he replaced Chaghadai's grandson Qara Hülegü b. Mö'etüken (r. 1242–6) with Chaghadai's son Yesü Möngke (r. 1246–51). Because the Chaghadayids opposed Möngke's accession, Yesü Möngke was executed along with other Chaghadayids. Qara Hülegü died before he could resume the throne, but until 1260 his widow Orghina Khatun served as regent for her young son Mubārakshāh. She held great prestige as a granddaughter of Chinggis Khan, a member of the Oirat tribe and a close relation of the wives of several Mongol khans.[103]

After Möngke's death the struggle between Ariq Böke and Qubilai offered a new chance for the Chaghadayids. Ariq Böke offered the throne to Alghu (r. 1260–6), and in 1261 sent him to gather supplies. Instead, Alghu enlarged the Chaghadayid territories and sent his own agents to Samarqand and Bukhārā, still under joint administration. His actions led to open warfare with Ariq Böke in 661 / 1262f.; Alghu prevailed and cemented his position by marrying Orghina Khatun.[104] In 664 / 1266, after Alghu's death, Orghina Khatun enthroned her Muslim son Mubārakshāh, who was soon deposed by his first cousin Baraq (r. 1266–71).

The Jochids were likewise interested in Chaghadayid politics. Berke Khan allied with Qaidu, a grandson of Ögedei working to restore Ögedeyid rule in Central Asia, and promised him the Chaghadayid throne. Qaidu's attempt to overthrow Alghu in about 663 / 1264f. failed, but, after Alghu's death, he managed for a while to take over the regions of Talas and Almāliq. Pushed west by Qubilai, he defeated Baraq Khan in 1268 near Khojand. Baraq retreated to Samarqand and Bukhārā and began plundering them. Qaidu proposed peace, and in 1269 organised a *quriltai* at which the rulers agreed that Transoxiana would be divided – two-thirds to Baraq and one-third to Qaidu – and both would remain outside the agricultural areas. Tiring of Baraq, Qaidu encouraged him to invade Khurāsān with a number of commanders who were secretly ordered to desert. On 1 Dhū 'l-Ḥijja 668 / 22 July 1270 Abaqa's army defeated Baraq outside Herat. About a year later Baraq died, and Qaidu became khan over a combined realm.

By this time the Chaghadayids were beginning to expand control towards Ghazna, where the Qara'unas increasingly came under their command. After

103 Rashīd al-Dīn, *Compendium*, pp. 55–6; Karin Quade-Reutter, '... *denn sie haben einen unvollkommenen Verstand'. Herrschaftliche Damen im Grossraum Iran in der Mongolen- und Timuridenzeit* (c. *1250–1507*) (Aachen, 2003), p. 316; Rashīd al-Dīn, *Successors*, pp. 109–10.

104 Rashīd al-Dīn, *Successors*, pp. 150–1; Biran, *Qaidu*, pp. 21–2.

the defeat of Baraq, the deposed khan Mubārakshāh b. Qara Hülegü joined the Ilkhans, and Abaqa appointed him to the command of the Negüderī, whose allegiance soon passed to the Chaghadayids. Another contingent of Qara'unas near Ghazna was commanded by the descendants of Chaghadai's son Baiju. This was an important post, allowing involvement in the politics of Khurāsān and Kirmān and profitable raids on the Delhi sultanate.[105]

On Baraq's death Qaidu enthroned Buqa Temür (r. 1272–82), from a different dynastic line. Over the next eleven years Transoxiana suffered uprisings and plunder by princes of the lines now excluded – the sons of Alghu and Baraq – and from 1277 to 1279 Qaidu was also at odds with Buqa. The situation improved in 1282 when Qaidu enthroned Du'a b. Baraq (r. 1282–1307). The two men spent several years fighting the Yuan, thus giving Transoxiana a welcome rest. With the rebellion of Amīr Nawrūz in 688/1289, Qaidu and Du'a turned west and from 1290 to 1295 they again threatened Khurāsān. After 1295 their attention turned east until Qaidu's death in 701/1301.[106]

Du'a Khan now emerged as the major power in the combined Ögedeyid and Chaghadayid realm, with Qaidu's son Chapar as the subordinate khan. Du'a made peace with the Yuan but he and Chapar were almost immediately at war.[107] Du'a prevailed, resulting in an exodus of Chapar's troops into the Ilkhanate in 1306.[108] Chapar submitted to the Yuan in 1310 and most Ögedeyid territories were divided between the Chaghadayids and the Yuan. Since many of the Chaghadayids' eastern migration routes now included Yuan territory, the border became a constant source of friction.[109] After Du'a's death in 706/1307 the throne rotated rapidly among his sons.[110] The next major power was Du'a's son Kebek, who enthroned his brother Esen Buqa (r. 1310–18), keeping for himself the administration of Farghāna and Transoxania, centred in Nakhshab. Kebek took the throne himself about 1318 and ruled until 727/1327. He is famous for his currency reform; the silver *dīnār* he minted took his name and remained the standard for currency in Transoxiana and eastern Iran for over a century.

105 Aubin, 'L'éthnogénèse', pp. 82–4; Kazuhide Katō, 'Kebek and Yasawr: The establishment of the Chaghatai-Khanate', *Memoirs of the Research Department of the Toyo Bunko*, 49 (1991), p. 104.
106 For the date: Biran, *Qaidu*, p. 69.
107 *Ibid.*, pp. 72–3.
108 Russell G. Kempiners, 'Vaṣṣāf's *Tajziyat al-amṣār wa tazjiyat al-a'ṣār* as a source for the history of the Chaghadayid khanate', *Journal of Asian History*, 22, 2 (1988), p. 177.
109 Biran, *Qaidu*, p. 77; Yingsheng Liu, 'War and peace between the Yuan dynasty and the Chaghadaid khanate (1312–1323)', in Amitai and Biran (eds.), *Mongols, Turks and others*, pp. 340–41.
110 Biran, *Qaidu*, p. 77; Michal Biran, 'The Chaghadaids and Islam: The conversion of Tarmashirin Khan (1331–34)', *Journal of the American Oriental Society*, 122, 4 (2002), p. 750.

Kebek was followed on the throne by three brothers, Eljigidei (r. 1327–30), Döre Temür (r. 1330–1) and finally Tarmashirin (r. 731–5 / 1331–4).[111] It is Tarmashirin who is credited with the Islamicisation of the western part of the Chaghadayid khanate. He converted to Islam probably shortly before he came to the throne, and as ruler he promoted conversion; according to Muslim sources, he abrogated the *yasa* in favour of the *sharīʿa*. This move is seen as a reason for his fall – he was blamed for giving up the annual convocation and for failing to visit his eastern territories. According to one source, he also attempted to push his Mongol followers into practising agriculture. Other problems probably contributed to his downfall, most notably the recent devastation of Transoxiana and increasing dynastic discord. In 735 / 1334 Tarmashirin was deposed by a coalition including several of his nephews, based apparently in the eastern regions.[112]

Two of Tarmashirin's nephews succeeded in turn to the throne after which the chronology of rule becomes confused. It seems likely that the realm had begun to divide into eastern and western sections, with separate khans claiming power in each.[113] While the khans immediately after Tarmashirin were probably not Muslim, it is clear that Islamicisation of the nomads in Transoxiana had begun before Tarmashirin, and his overthrow did not interrupt the process. In 747 / 1346f., Qazan Khan b. Yasa'ur was killed by the *amīr* of the Qara'unas troops, who took power in the name of a puppet khan and ruled over the western section of the khanate, which came to be known as the Ulus Chaghatay. The eastern section stayed under the rule of Chinggisid khans, and Islam was not established there until the conversion of Tughluq Temür Khan in 755 / 1354. The two sections remained largely separate though it appears that the situation was viewed as temporary up to the fifteenth century.[114]

The expansion of Islam

Anatolia

Although the Mongol conquest put many Muslims under the rule of infidels, Mongol rule eventually resulted in a massive expansion of the *dār al-islām*.

111 The dates of these reigns have been corrected by Biran, 'Chaghadaids', pp. 744–5.

112 *Ibid.*, pp. 749–50; Ibn Baṭṭūṭa, *The travels of Ibn Baṭṭūṭa, AD 1325–1354*, trans. H. A. R. Gibb, Hakluyt Society (Cambridge, 1971), vol. III, pp. 560–1.

113 Biran, 'Chaghadaids', p. 750; Peter Jackson, 'The Mongols and the Delhi Sultanate in the reign of Muḥammad Tughluq (1325–1351)', *Central Asiatic Journal*, 19, 1–2 (1975), p. 144 n. 129; Jean Aubin, 'Le khanat de Čaġatai et le Khorassan (1334–1380)', *Turcica*, 8, 2 (1976), pp. 22–4.

114 Ho-dong Kim, 'The early history of the Moghul nomads: The legacy of the Chaghatai khanate', in Amitai-Preiss and Morgan (eds.), *Mongol empire*, pp. 302–3.

Muslims became predominant in western Anatolia and much of the western Eurasian steppe, while large Muslim minorities formed in parts of China. In Anatolia, the Mongols accelerated a process already under way. Oghuz Turkic tribes had entered Asia Minor in the Saljuq period, and by the beginning of the thirteenth century the Saljuq sultanate of Rūm controlled most of central and eastern Anatolia, though for some time much of the population probably remained Christian. From 1230 on, Mongols moved into the pastures of Azerbaijan and crowded out nomad Turks, many of whom migrated into Anatolia. In 675/1277 the sultanate of Rūm was incorporated into the Ilkhanate, and as central rule weakened in the fourteenth century, Turkmen nomads sought opportunities on the western borders, thus expanding their territory at the expense of the remaining Christian kingdoms. By the end of the century the population of Anatolia was largely Turkic and Muslim.

The Golden Horde

It was under Mongol rule that Islam began to take hold among the Turks of the western steppes. Muslim merchants had long been active in the Volga region and Islam had become formally established there with the conversion of the Bulghār kingdom in the tenth century. When the Mongols set out to incorporate the Qıpchaq steppe, they began in 1231–2 with the Bulghār region – thus many of their first subjects were Muslim. The Golden Horde capital Sarai was built on the lower Volga, important for both pasture and trade. It is not surprising then that the second major khan of the Golden Horde, Berke (r. 1257–67), became Muslim, reportedly through the influence of the Bukhārān shaykh Sayf al-Dīn Bukhārī.[115] Berke did not impose Islam as a state religion, and since his religious orientation aided his alliance with the Mamlūks, the importance of Islam for him and his followers may be exaggerated in histories and correspondence.[116] However, the European friar William of Rubruck states that pork was not allowed within his court and it appears that many of his followers converted. The khans who followed Berke adhered to other religions, but the *amīr* Nogay, the greatest power in government from 1267 to his death in 1299, was Muslim.

115 István Vasáry, '"History and legend" in Berke Khan's conversion to Islam', in *Aspects of Altaic civilization III: Proceedings of the thirtieth meeting of the Permanent International Altaistic Conference, Indiana University, Bloomington, Indiana, June 19–25, 1987* (Bloomington, IN, 1990), pp. 235–6, 239–48.

116 Vasáry, 'History and legend', p. 250; Devin DeWeese, *Islamization and native religion in the Golden Horde: Baba Tükles and conversion to Islam in historical and epic tradition* (University Park, PA, 1994), pp. 83–5.

The official Islamicisation of the Golden Horde came with Uzbek Khan (r. 1313–41). Like many other khans who promoted Islam, Uzbek attempted to increase central power at the expense of Mongol *noyans*, and his early rule was marked by resistance and widespread purges.[117] During his reign the ruler of the eastern section of the Jochid realm, Irzan Khan (r. 720–45/1320f.–1344f.), also converted and built mosques, madrasas and *khānaqās* in the northern Jaxartes region. Islamicisation was a gradual process; Ibn Baṭṭūṭa noted in his travels that Christianity was still more popular than Islam among most Turkic tribes.[118] Legends quickly grew up around the conversion of the Jochid rulers and over time combined with native Turkic religion to form origin myths for new communities. Thus conversion became a self-perpetuating process. The succession states which emerged in the fifteenth and sixteenth centuries were ruled largely by Muslims, and many of their followers were likewise believers.

China

By the twelfth century China had a sizeable Muslim population concentrated in port and trading cities.[119] The first immigrants in the Mongol period came as captured artisans and military conscripts. Several workshops staffed by captives became colonies in Mongolia and China.[120] The use of foreign soldiers continued into the reign of Qubilai; thus Muslim troops were among the garrison armies which eventually became permanent settlements.[121] The Mongols brought in merchants from eastern Iran and Central Asia, many of whom entered into *ortoq* partnerships. To the disgust of elite bureaucrats, the khans recruited merchants to serve in administration, particularly in financial affairs. In 1239, when Ögedei faced a pressing need for income, the merchant ʿAbd al-Raḥmān proposed tax-farming and received the tax collection of north China. For some years the taxes of northern China were often farmed out to *ortoq* merchants. When peasants were unable to pay, the same men offered them credit at exorbitant rates. *Ortoq* merchants continued to exploit tax collection until the reign of Möngke, who abolished the worst abuses but

117 G. A. Fedorov-Davydov, *Obshchestvennyĭ stroĭ Zolotoĭ Ordy* (Moscow, 1973), p. 104.
118 Ibn Baṭṭūṭa, *Travels* (Cambridge, 1962), vol. II, p. 470; DeWeese, *Islamization*, p. 131.
119 Donald D. Leslie, *Islam in traditional China: A short history to 1800* (Belconnen, 1986), pp. 53–5.
120 Allsen, *Commodity*, pp. 30–45.
121 Thomas T. Allsen, 'Ever closer encounters: The appropriation of culture and the apportionment of peoples in the Mongol empire', *Journal of Early Modern History*, 1, 1 (1997), pp. 8–9; Michael Dillon, *China's Muslim Hui community: Migration, settlement and sects* (Richmond, 1999), pp. 21–3.

allowed merchants to continue their money-lending activities, and their practices contributed to the Chinese dislike of Muslims in the Mongol period.

From Möngke's reign onwards much of China was under the oversight of Qubilai. Like Möngke, he attempted to rein in the power of the *ortoq* merchants, but after a rebellion in 1261 which involved Chinese officials he turned to foreigners to staff his administration. Qubilai instituted a systematic classification of population according to ethnicity: Mongols had the highest status, western and Central Asians (*se-mu*) came second, then northern Chinese. In theory, the highest offices were reserved for the Mongols and *se-mu*, who also enjoyed tax privileges and the right to bear arms. We cannot tell what proportion of offices were held by Muslims, but it is clear that they remained active through the Yuan period, especially in the financial sphere. The highest financial position, control over the Central Secretariat of north China, went to the Muslim Aḥmad, who remained in office for over twenty years and succeeded in raising revenue at the cost of his own popularity. He was murdered in 1282 and is recorded in Chinese historiography as an evil minister. One should note however that his non-Muslim successors were equally unpopular.

Another Muslim official won the opposite reputation; this was Bukhārān Sayyid Ajall (d. 1279), whom Qubilai appointed governor of the border region Yunnan in 1274. While he is remembered for introducing Chinese culture into Yunnan, he also presided over an influx of Muslim people, who created a sophisticated irrigation system. He was succeeded in office by his son, who remained to 1291, and from this time on Yunnan contained a significant Muslim minority.[122] In 1279 Qubilai received help from the Muslims of the southern cities in conquering the Southern Song. The Muslim official Pu Shougeng, who had gone over from the Song into Qubilai's service, was appointed supervisor of maritime trade for Kwantung and Fukien.[123]

Despite the usefulness of Muslims, Qubilai was not immune to public feeling against them, particularly after 1278, when rebellions began along the north-western frontier. In 1280 he forbade circumcision and made the slaughter of animals according to *sharīʿa* rites a crime punishable by death. In 1287 however he was persuaded to rescind many restrictions on the grounds that they would discourage the western merchants needed for China's prosperity. Swings in policy continued after his death in 1294, and the enthronement of a

122 Paul D. Buell, 'Saiyid Ajall (1211–1279)', in de Rachewiltz *et al.* (eds.), *In the service*, pp. 474–9.

123 Morris Rossabi, 'The Muslims in the early Yuan dynasty', in John D. Langlois (ed.), *China under Mongol rule* (Princeton, 1981), pp. 270–5.

new emperor often meant a change in the position of Muslims. By 1368, when the Ming dynasty overthrew the Yuan, China had a sizeable Muslim population spread over several provinces. During the Ming the community continued to grow and at this time many intermarried with Chinese and began to adopt Chinese language and culture.[124] Only in the north-west did most Muslims retain a separate linguistic identity.

Conclusion

Within the Islamic regions the Mongols brought at once devastation and new initiatives. In their attempts to centralise administration, the khans faced determined resistance from the Mongol elite, particularly in fiscal affairs. The constant political contests after Chinggis Khan's death exacerbated similar tendencies in the Middle East. Since neither Islamic nor Mongolian tradition favoured primogeniture, there were frequent succession struggles, and the Mongol period was one of particularly intense factionalism. Not many men of power, whether bureaucrats or commanders, died of natural causes. The only way to achieve an orderly administration was to rule for a long time, and here Mongol rulers were handicapped by their excessive consumption of alcohol. Leadership required constant feasting, accompanied by the drinking of both fermented and distilled alcohol. The resulting alcoholism was a common cause of death, and both the Great Khans and the Ilkhans had unusually short reigns.

Mongol rule marks the end of what might be called the classical age of Arab-Muslim culture and Islamic societies emerged from it more diverse and more expansive. As Mongols centred themselves in the north, trade routes changed and new regions came to the fore. Mongol rule did not extend into Syria or Egypt, thus creating a separation between Iran and the Arab cultural region of the Mamlūk sultanate.[125] From this time on, the Middle East remained divided into three major cultural zones, one primarily Arab, one primarily Iranian and one primarily Turkish. Like the Saljuqids, the Mongols entered through eastern Iran and gave a central place in their administration to Persian bureaucrats; they also adopted elements of Iranian legitimation. The promotion of Persian traditions combined with cultural borrowing to create new Persian

124 Dillon, *China's Muslim*, pp. 27–9.
125 Bert Fragner, 'Ilkhanid rule and its contributions to Iranian political culture', in Komaroff (ed.), *Beyond the legacy*, pp. 68–80.

styles increasingly distinct from Arab culture. As the Islamic religion spread to new areas, it was often marked by Persian as well as Mongol influence.

By destroying the central caliphate, the Mongols inaugurated a new era in which it was possible to assert sovereign rule over one part of the Islamic world. This act made possible the great empires of the early modern period – the Ottomans, Safavids, Mughals and Uzbeks, each of which fostered a unique cultural complex, while sharing many elements of the mixed culture that developed under the Mongols.

5

Tamerlane and his descendants: from paladins to patrons

MARIA E. SUBTELNY

Introduction

The nearly simultaneous dissolution of the Mongol successor states of the Ilkhans in Iran, the Chaghadayids in Central Asia and the Golden Horde in the Qıpchaq, or Eurasian, steppe during the fourteenth century was paralleled in the far east by the unravelling of the Mongol Yuan dynasty in China, and in the far west by the eventual displacement of the Bahri Mamlūk state in Egypt by its Circassian counterpart. These political developments following the period of the great *pax mongolica*, which under the Chinggisid dispensation had brought together east and west, Turk and Iranian, Arab and Mongol in a vast international mercantile and cultural enterprise, resulted in the creation of what has traditionally been viewed as a political vacuum, particularly in the eastern Islamic world, and they mark the transition between the beginning and end of what Marshall Hodgson referred to as the Islamic Later Middle Period (1250–1500).[1] See Map 3 for this chapter.

With the death of the last Ilkhanid ruler, Abū Saʿīd, in 736/1335, greater Iran and Central Asia became the arena for competing political factions, some of which succeeded in establishing local control in the form of dynastic states. Originally a Mongol tribe in Ilkhanid service, the Jalayirids established themselves in north-western Iran and Iraq, eventually prevailing over their rivals, the Chopanids. The Muzaffarids, who were of Arab descent, carved out a political niche for themselves in southern and western Iran, in the process absorbing the short-lived dynasty of the Injuids, who ruled over Fārs. In western Khurāsān, the revolutionary Shīʿī state established by the Sarbadar rebel movement, which was centred on Sabzavār, managed to maintain itself for about fifty years despite a highly unstable and confused chronology. And in

1 Marshall G. S. Hodgson, *The venture of Islam: Conscience and history in a world civilization*, vol. II: *The expansion of Islam in the Middle Periods* (Chicago, 1974), pp. 371–3.

eastern Khurāsān, the Kart (or Kurt) kings ruled lavishly, albeit precariously, from what would later become the great Timurid capital of Herat (in present-day north-western Afghanistan). These independent and semi-independent polities were in constant flux, their political fortunes waxing and waning, and even when they encroached on the territories of their neighbours they often lacked sufficient power to sustain control over them. The prevailing climate was thus one of political instability and social ferment, which was aggravated by the general decline of the agrarian economy as a result of the Mongol invasions of the previous century.

The restoration of political order and the re-establishment of balance in the eastern Islamic world was the result of the ruthless empire-building strategies of the nomadic warlord Tamerlane (Turkic form, Temür; Persianized form, Tīmūr or Taymūr) during a thirty-five-year period lasting roughly from 1370 until his death in 807/1405. All of the aforementioned states would at some point towards the end of the fourteenth century be conquered or annexed by Temür in his drive to create a neo-Mongol empire in terms of both geographical extent and Chinggisid ideology. Like most so-called nomadic empires, Temür's fell apart almost immediately after his death, as he had made few provisions either for an orderly succession or for the establishment of a bureaucratic administration, having spent most of his life conducting military campaigns. Despite the initial political chaos, Temür's descendants, referred to collectively as the Timurids, managed to rule important fragments of the empire for an entire century and their concern for fiscal administration and agricultural development, sophisticated court culture and patronage of the arts and architecture assured them pride of place in the cultural history of the eastern Islamic world.

Temür: charismatic authority and Chinggisid tradition

Temür's authority was based on the Turko-Mongolian concept of leadership based on charisma, which according to the typology developed by Max Weber represents one of the forms of legitimate domination in history. Extremely adept at manipulating his own image, Temür adopted the title *ṣāḥib-qirān*, meaning one whose manifest destiny is governed by the auspicious conjunction of the planets Jupiter and Venus, and he linked himself genealogically not only to Chinggis Khan (d. 1227), the founder of the Mongol empire, but also to ʿAlī b. Abī Ṭālib (d. 661), the first Shīʿī imam and foremost member of the family of the Prophet Muḥammad.[2] A powerful psychological portrait of Temür was drawn by Ibn ʿArabshāh in his polemical Arabic history, *ʿAjāʾib al-maqdūr fī nawāʾib Taymūr*, completed in 839/1435.[3] In an effort to portray himself as the new avatar of the Chinggisid dispensation, Temür fostered an elaborate personal myth that had many similarities with the legends surrounding the youth and early career of Chinggis Khan. Timurid historians even assigned to him a birth date designed to coincide with the year of the death of the last Ilkhanid, Abū Saʿīd, thereby suggesting an unbroken continuum of Chinggisid rule in West Asia.[4] Temür's marriage to a Chinggisid princess (the daughter of Qazan Khan) gave him the right to use the title *kürgän*, or imperial son-in-law, which was also adopted by several of his descendants, and he attempted to revive the Chinggisid house through the elevation of puppet khans in the Ulus Chaghadai.[5]

Temür's claims to a Chinggisid connection have often been dismissed by scholars as pretensions inadequate to satisfy the requirement of Chinggisid descent that had become the main legitimating factor in Central Asian politics. Although he may not have been of direct Chinggisid descent, Temür was nevertheless the scion of a prominent Mongolian tribal family – the Barulas (Turkic form, Barlas) – that had been closely associated with the house of Chinggis Khan's second son, Chaghadai. As recent research has demonstrated, the Barlas had belonged to Chinggis Khan's *keshig*, or imperial guard corps, which was a central institution of imperial Mongol rule, and Temür's tribal ancestor Qarachar Noyon, who figures prominently in Timuro-Chinggisid genealogical history, had apparently been the head of the guard corps assigned to Chaghadai, whose appanage included the region of Transoxania.[6] In accordance with the model of the Mongol patrimonial household, whereby

2 Maria E. Subtelny, *Timurids in transition: Turko-Persian politics and acculturation in medieval Iran* (Leiden, 2007), pp. 11–13.

3 J. H. Sanders (trans.), *Tamerlane or Timur the Great Amir: From the Arabic life by Ahmed Ibn Arabshah* (London, 1936); and R. D. McChesney, 'A note on the life and works of Ibn ʿArabshāh', in Judith Pfeiffer and Sholeh A. Quinn (eds.), *History and historiography of post-Mongol Central Asia and the Middle East: Studies in honor of Professor John E. Woods* (Wiesbaden, 2006), pp. 205–49.

4 Abū Saʿīd died on 13 Rabīʿ II 736/30 November 1335, and the date of Temür's birth is sometimes given as 25 Shaʿbān 736/8 April 1336.

5 Jean Aubin, 'Le khanat de Čaġatai et le Khorassan (1334–1380)', *Turcica*, 8, 2 (1976), p. 54; Beatrice Forbes Manz, *The rise and rule of Tamerlane* (Cambridge, 1989), pp. 14–15; and John E. Woods, 'Timur's genealogy', in Michel M. Mazzaoui and Vera B. Moreen (eds.), *Intellectual studies on Islam: Essays written in honor of Martin B. Dickson* (Salt Lake City, 1990), pp. 108–9.

6 S. M. Grupper, 'A Barulas family narrative in the *Yuan Shih*: Some neglected prosopographical and institutional sources on Timurid origins', *Archivum Eurasiae Medii Aevi*, 8 (1992–4), pp. 21–38, 60–1 and 77–81; and Shiro Ando, *Timuridische Emire nach dem Muʿizz*

members of the imperial guard corps were appointed to the highest ranks of government administration, Qarachar Noyon became Chaghadai Khan's chief administrator as well as chief judge of the *yarghu*, or court of investigation, through which Mongol law was enforced.[7]

The Barlas tribe thus occupied an important position in Transoxiana, where it had held the hereditary command of the *tümen* of Kesh still from Qarachar Noyon's time.[8] This, incidentally, provides an explanation for Temür's customary title *amīr* ('commander') or *amīr-i buzurg* ('the great commander'), which may be interpreted as an abbreviation of *amīr-i tümen*, referring to his command of this former Mongol military-administrative district. As the descendant of the head of Chaghadai Khan's *keshig*, Temür would have remained loyal not only to the house of Chaghadai but also to the *yasa*, or Chinggisid customary law, of which Chaghadai had been designated official custodian by his father and of which Qarachar Noyon had been *yarghuchi*, or chief judge, in the Ulus Chaghadai.

Yasa vs *sharī'a*: Turko-Mongolian custom and Islamic law

Transoxania belonged to that part of the Ulus Chaghadai that had been Islamicised for some time, and Temür was himself a Muslim, if only nominally. Because he came to exercise control over a significant portion of the Islamic world, Temür's attitude towards Islam and *sharī'a* law became a question of considerable import and even urgency. Although he did not hesitate to invoke Islamic legality whenever it was to his advantage to do so, Temür generally favoured the *yasa* over the *sharī'a*, which prompted Islamic jurists at one point to declare him an infidel.[9]

Exactly what legal precepts constituted the *yasa* is still a matter of scholarly debate. In its Timurid elaboration, the *yasa* was usually referred to as the *törä* or 'the *törä* of the Lord of the auspicious conjunction' (*törä-i ṣāḥib-qirānī*), that is, Temür. In a nutshell, it represented Turko-Mongolian customary law as

al-ansāb. Untersuchung zur Stammesaristokratie Zentralasiens im 14. und 15. Jahrhundert (Berlin, 1992), pp. 68–9. For the term *keshig* or *keshik*, see Gerhard Doerfer, *Türkische und mongolische Elemente im Neupersischen*, 4 vols. (Wiesbaden, 1963–75), vol. I, pp. 467–9.

7 For this interpretation of Qarachar's role in the Ulus Chaghadai, see Subtelny, *Timurids in transition*, pp. 18–24.

8 Manz, *Rise and rule of Tamerlane*, p. 156; and Woods, 'Timur's genealogy', p. 96. For the term *tümen*, which denoted a military district capable of supplying a contingent of 10,000 men, see Doerfer, *Türkische und mongolische Elemente*, vol. II, pp. 632–42.

9 Aḥmad b. Muḥammad Ibn 'Arabshāh, *'Ajā'ib al-maqdūr fī nawā'ib Taymūr*, ed. Aḥmad Fā'iz al-Ḥimṣī (Beirut, 1407), p. 455.

practised by Temür and his Chaghadai followers. The Timurids cultivated the *törä* as a means of maintaining their nomadic military ethos and Chaghatay identity as distinct from the culture of the Muslim, largely Iranian (Tājīk), sedentary population over which they ruled.[10] Just as there appears to have been no written exposition of the precepts of the Chinggisid *yasa*, which can only be partially reconstructed from the sources, so too is the nature of the Timurid *törä* known only through random references in the contemporary Persian, Arabic and Turkish sources that identify specific customs and practices as belonging to it, often through negative comparison with Islamic prescriptions. Probably the single most important feature of the *törä* that conflicted with *sharī'a* law was the *yarghu*, or Turko-Mongolian court of investigation. Although it was supposedly abolished during the reign of Temür's son Shāh Rukh, the *yarghu* continued to exist, along with many other Turko-Mongolian practices, until the end of the dynasty's rule in Iran.

Temür's early career and conquests

Politically, the western Ulus Chaghadai where Temür began his political career represented a confederation of old Mongolian and Turko-Mongolian tribes (such as the Suldus, Barlas, Arlat, Jalayir, Yasa'uri and Apardi), local commanders with their own tribal armies (such as the Khuttalani *amīrs*), and métis Qara'unas tribes, all of whom vied with each other for power, under the nominal rule of Chinggisid khans of the line of Chaghadai. The political turmoil of the period lent itself to the emergence of a series of strong men, most of whom were tribal commanders of non-Chinggisid background. Temür emerged in the political arena around 761/1360 when he was appointed head of the Barlas tribe to replace Amīr Ḥājjī Beg, who had fled the Ulus at the time of the invasion of the eastern Chaghadayid (Mughul) khan Tughluq Temür. When Temür was granted control of the ancestral *tümen* of Kesh, he allied himself with the powerful Qara'unas leader Amīr Ḥusayn in his bid to become head of the western Ulus. But when Ḥājjī Beg Barlas returned from exile, and the troops of the Kesh *tümen* deserted Temür, he returned his allegiance to Ḥājjī Beg. Another invasion by the Mughuls in the following year, and the appointment of Ilyās Khwāja Khan as ruler of western Chaghadai, put an end to Ḥājjī Beg's political ambitions. Temür again allied himself with Amīr Ḥusayn and even helped him gain a military victory over the Mughuls, but the two soon found themselves in competition, and when Amīr

10 For the term *törä*, see Doerfer, *Türkische und mongolische Elemente*, vol. I, pp. 264–7.

Ḥusayn seized control of the Uluṣ in 767/1366 in the name of a Chinggisid puppet khan, Temür was forced to seek refuge in the region around Marv where he spent the next two years freebooting, as a political vagabond.

Temür has often been portrayed as a common brigand or horse thief before coming to power in the Ulus, but such a characterisation does not do justice to the importance in steppe politics of the period of *qazaqliq* (Persianized form, *qazāqī*), or political vagabondage, during which an aspiring tribal leader assembled a loyal following and forged political alliances that were often strengthened by marriage and commercial ties.[11] The socio-political institution of *qazaqliq* was informed by the patrimonial and highly personal nature of relations in the early Timurid state, and those who supported Temür during his period of political vagabondage were subsequently appointed to leading military-administrative positions.

By 771/1369 Temür had assembled a military force, which included the aristocracy of the Barlas tribe, and defeated Amīr Ḥusayn, who was later executed by Timurid *amīrs*. After being confirmed as leader of the Ulus at a *quriltai*, or tribal gathering, in the spring of 771/1370, Temür set himself up in the capital city of Samarqand, ruling through a Chinggisid puppet khan from the line of Ögedei. Temür's control over the tribes of the Ulus would remain precarious for over a decade, however, and the campaigns of conquest which he launched almost immediately were designed primarily to harness these tribal energies and channel them into his evolving political enterprise.

During the 1370s Temür asserted his authority over the eastern part of the Ulus Chaghadai in a series of short campaigns against Mughulistān, Khwārazm and the Qıpchaq steppe. By 777/1375 he annexed the Farghāna valley region and appointed his son ʿUmar Shaykh governor of Andijan. After installing a governor in Kāshghar in 779/1377f., he maintained his claim to the region by campaigning as far as the Irtysh and Yulduz rivers. Repeated campaigns were made against the Qungirat Sufi dynasty of Khwārazm in 773–4/1372–3. Temür's first expedition to the Qıpchaq steppe took place in 778–9/1376–7 on behalf of Toqtamish, a pretender to the leadership of the Blue Horde, whom Temür had set up in 777/1376 in the region of Uṭrār north of the Syr Darya river. Even after Temür Malik, the son and successor of the Jochid

11 See Annemarie von Gabain, 'Kasakentum, eine soziologisch-philologische Studie', *Acta Orientalia Academiae Scientiarum Hungaricae*, 11, 1–3 (1960), p. 162; Stephen F. Dale, *The garden of the eight paradises: Bābur and the culture of empire in Central Asia, Afghanistan and India (1483–1530)* (Leiden, 2004), pp. 98–100; and Subtelny, *Timurids in transition*, pp. 29–32. For Temür's marriage alliances during this period, see Manz, *Rise and rule of Tamerlane*, pp. 46 and 57.

khan Urus, defeated Toqtamish, the latter remained khan in Sighnaq in accordance with Temür's wishes. In 779/1377f., Toqtamish captured leadership of the Blue Horde from Temür Malik and by 784/1382 he extended his control over the Golden Horde after defeating its ruler, Mamay, in 782/1380 and raiding the Russian principalities as far as Moscow, which he sacked in 784/1382.

Temür's first campaigns against Iran began in 1380–1 with incursions into the agriculturally rich, eastern province of Khurāsān, and he appointed his son Mīrānshāh its governor in 782/1380. Although the Kart kings, who ruled from Herat, were initially allies, Temür occupied the city in 783/1381. Later, after a major rebellion in Herat in 785/1383, the Kartid ruler was removed and his territory annexed. Also in 783/1381 Temür took over the region of Kalāt and Ṭūs, which had been held by the Turko-Mongolian Ja'un-i Qurban tribe, who eventually surrendered to him, and he accepted the submission of the Sarbadar state of Sabzavār, whose chiefs rallied to his support. In 785/1383 he conquered Sīstān. He then turned to the western regions of Iran. In 786/1384 he took Astarābād in Māzandarān, which he entrusted to the Ilkhanid prince Luqmān b. Togha Temür, and he expelled the Jalayirid dynasty from Sulṭāniyya in Azerbaijan. The goal of this first phase of operations against Iran, which did not result in the establishment of firm administrative control over the conquered regions, appears to have been to extract ransom money and acquire booty for Temür's treasury and for rewarding his troops.

Toqtamish's attack on Tabrīz in 787/1385f. occasioned Temür's campaign against western Iran and the Caucasus and inaugurated a decade-long contest between the two nomadic warlords, which was reminiscent of the rivalry between the Golden Horde of the Qıpchaq steppe and the Ilkhanids of Iran. This three-year campaign, as it was dubbed by the Timurid historians, which began in 788/1386, was the first of Temür's major campaigns against Muslim West Asia. In 788/1386, he campaigned in Luristān, wrested Tabrīz from the Jalayirids and subjugated Georgia after taking Tiflis by storm. In 789/1387, he sent his son Mīrānshāh to Azerbaijan to counter Toqtamish, who was defeated. Temür then campaigned in the Lake Van region against the Qara Qoyunlu, as well as in Kurdistan. In the same year he secured the submission of Iṣfahān, which was under the rule of the Muzaffarids, but a revolt of the population occasioned a general massacre in which 70,000 were estimated to have been killed. News of the massacre facilitated the capture in the same year of Shīrāz, which was entrusted to a Muzaffarid vassal.

In response to the pillaging of Transoxania in 789/1387 by Toqtamish, who had gained the support of the Qungirat Sufi dynasty and the eastern

Chaghatayids, Temür launched a series of punitive campaigns against him and his allies during the years 789–98/1387–96. In 789/1387 he seized and sacked the city of Urganj in Khwārazm, which had been ruled by the Sufi dynasty, and deported its population. Two campaigns were waged against Khiḍr Khan, the ruler of Mughulistān. Temür then turned to the Qıpchaq steppe and in 793/1391 defeated Toqtamish north of the Samara river, installing a new khan in the Golden Horde. Toqtamish recovered control of the Golden Horde, however, and in the following year raided the region of Shīrwān in the Caucasus. Temür finally defeated Toqtamish in 797/1395 at the Terek river. After a looting spree along the Volga river, then down to the Crimea, then back up again along the Don, he ended up in the northern Caucasus, where he campaigned against the Circassians and Alans. In the winter of 798/1395, he sacked the Golden Horde capital of New Saray near the Volga, as well as Ḥājjī Tarkhan (Astrakhan). He left the Qıpchaq steppe in 798/1396 and, although he did not establish permanent control, the Golden Horde never fully recovered from his depredations.

At the same time, Temür inaugurated the so-called five-year campaign against Iran, which lasted 794–8/1392–6, with attacks against Māzandarān, while Luristān and Kurdistan were pacified by his sons. In 795/1393 he extinguished the Muzaffarid dynasty in southern Iran and appointed his son ʿUmar Shaykh governor of the region. He appointed his other son Mīrānshāh governor of western Iran (ʿIraq-i ʿAjam) and Iraq (ʿIraq-i ʿArab), and having secured the support of the Aq Qoyunlu, he proceeded to oust the Jalayirids and Qara Qoyunlu who still held sway here. In 795/1393 he captured Baghdad from the Jalayirids and appointed a Sarbadar chief as governor. (However, Sultan Aḥmad Jalayir recovered control of the city a year later.) In 796/1394, Diyārbakr and al-Jazīra were taken. In 798/1396, on his way back from his final expedition against Toqtamish, Temür campaigned in Georgia, Azerbaijan and Fārs.

Temür's next campaign was directed against northern India and in 800/1397 he sent his grandson Pīr-Muḥammad, who ruled in present-day Afghanistan, ahead to the Punjab. He set off himself in 800/1398 and in the winter of 801/1398 sacked Delhi, after which he campaigned along the Ganges.

After returning to Samarqand in the spring of 801/1399, Temür decided to swing back to the west again and in 802/1399 inaugurated the seven-year campaign, which would be his longest, lasting 802–7/1399–1404. It was occasioned by Mīrānshāh's apparent inability to deal with unrest in Azerbaijan and his growing independence in the region. Temür removed Mīrānshāh, whom he transferred to his own retinue, and restored order there himself. After wintering in Qarābāgh, he again campaigned against Georgia, storming Tiflis in 802/1400 and confirming the vassalship of the Georgian king.

On account of his involvement in Turkmen, Kurd and Arab tribal politics, Temür came into conflict with both the Ottomans and the Mamlūks. Relations with the Mamlūks were already strained. They had murdered Temür's ambassador to Cairo and given refuge to his Jalayirid and Qara Qoyunlu opponents; moreover, they had attempted to form an anti-Timurid alliance with the Golden Horde. In 803/1400, Temür attacked Aleppo, which surrendered, and later that same year (803/1401) he took Damascus, which was pillaged by his soldiers and its population massacred or deported. It was at his camp near the city that he was supposedly visited by the historian Ibn Khaldūn, who was acting as envoy from the Mamlūk sultan al-Malik al-Nāṣir Faraj.[12] Taken by storm in 803/1401 from Sultan Aḥmad Jalayir's commander, Baghdad was destroyed and its population massacred.[13] While it has been demonstrated that Temür's treatment of the towns he captured was generally motivated by a desire to extract booty or ransom money, there can be no doubt that his use of terror tactics, such as the wholesale slaughter of civilian populations and the erection of towers of decapitated human heads, was meant not only to deter popular resistance but also to enhance his image as a neo-Mongol conqueror.[14]

As for Temür's relations with the Ottomans, the extension of Ottoman control over the eastern Anatolian principalities, as well as Ottoman support of both Aḥmad Jalayir and Qara Yūsuf, provided Temür with enough reasons to conduct an expedition against Anatolia. In 802/1400 he took Sivas and in the summer of 804/1402, after wintering in Qarābāgh, he defeated the Ottoman sultan Bāyezīd I Yıldırım at Chubuq Ovası near Ankara, taking him prisoner. (Bāyezīd died in captivity at Aqshehir in 805/1403.) Temür's grandson Muḥammad-Sulṭān was entrusted with the capture of Bursa, which he burned to the ground in 805/1402. Campaigning deep into Ottoman territory, Temür reached as far as Izmir (Smyrna) on the Aegean coast. He obtained the submission of the Byzantine emperor at Constantinople, and later on that of Bāyezīd's son Süleymān. Temür's invasion disrupted Ottoman territorial expansion and consolidation, but because no permanent administrative structures had been put in place, the Ottomans soon resumed their empire-building

12 Walter J. Fischel, *Ibn Khaldūn and Tamerlane: Their historic meeting in Damascus, 1401 AD (803 AH): A study based on Arabic manuscripts of Ibn Khaldūn's 'Autobiography'* (Berkeley and Los Angeles, 1952).

13 Jean Aubin, 'Tamerlan à Baġdād', *Arabica*, 9 (1962), pp. 303–9.

14 Jean Aubin, 'Comment Tamerlan prenait les villes', *Studia Islamica*, 19 (1963), pp. 83–122.

strategies, eventually becoming the paramount power in the region. Turning east again, Temür passed through Qarābāgh (where he wintered in 806/1403f.), Georgia (which he again laid waste) and Māzandarān (where he put down a major rebellion), returning to Samarqand in 807/1404.

Temür's last and most ambitious campaign was launched against China right after the great *quriltai* held in Samarqand in 807/1404, which was attended by many foreign embassies, including a Spanish one headed by Ruy Gonzáles de Clavijo, who left a detailed account.[15] But the project was abandoned when Temür died upon reaching Uṭrār in 807/1405.

It appears that Temür was originally supposed to be buried at Kesh (Shahr-i sabz) in the *quruq*, or royal preserve, where his sons ʿUmar Shaykh and Jahāngīr had already been buried in the funerary structures connected to the Aq Saray complex. He was eventually buried in Samarqand, however, in what came to be known as the Gūr-i Amīr, which he had constructed in 807/1404, and which was transformed into a dynastic mausoleum thanks largely to the efforts of Shāh Rukh's son Ulugh Beg. Also buried there, besides Temür's sons Shāh Rukh and Mīrānshāh, his grandson Ulugh Beg, and his favourite nephew, Muḥammad-Sulṭān, was his spiritual adviser, Sayyid Baraka.[16]

The Timurid state and administration

The Timurid state (the term is applied loosely here) was predominantly military in character. It was based on a tribal military elite and supported by nomadic cavalry forces. The army was characterised by the use of Turko-Mongolian titles, the Chinggisid ranking of military offices, and adherence to Mongolian battle formations. Offices and titles such as *beg* and *noyon* ('commander'), *tovachi* ('troop inspector'), *yasaul* ('sergeant-at-arms'), *yurtchi* ('quartermaster') and *akhtachi* ('equerry') reflected long-standing Turko-Mongolian practice. Besides the paramount Barlas tribe with its various branches, the main tribes represented in the Timurid army and military administration were the Arlat, Jalayir, Arghun, Qungirat, Turkmen, Tarkhan, Uzbek, Ilchikday and Uighur, among others. Whereas some of

15 [Ruy González de] Clavijo, *Embassy to Tamerlane, 1403–1406*, trans. Guy Le Strange (London, 1928; repr. 2005).

16 V. V. Bartol'd, 'O pogrebenii Timura', in V. V. Bartol'd, *Sochineniia*, vol. II, part 2, ed. Iu. È. Bregel' (Moscow, 1964), pp. 423–54; and Robert D. McChesney, *Timur's tomb: Politics and commemoration*, Central Eurasian Studies Lectures, 3 (Bloomington, IN, 2003).

these enjoyed hereditary positions, others achieved dominance under particular rulers or became prominent only during the later Timurid period.[17]

Like all states based on Turko-Mongolian concepts of socio-political organisation, the Timurid polity was essentially patrimonial in nature, personal service to the ruler being one of its defining features. Many official titles, such as *qorchi* ('quiver-bearer'), *bökävül* ('taster'), *suchi* ('cup-bearer') and *qushchi* ('falconer'), denoted household positions. In point of fact these were important military-administrative positions that reflected an individual's trustworthiness and proximity to the ruler in the patrimonial household. There were also various categories of individuals who enjoyed special privileges and had direct access to the ruler, such as the *tarkhans*, who were exempt from taxation and judicial prosecution, and the *ichkis* ('insiders'), who were members of the household establishment with close personal ties to the ruler, often through the institution of foster-brotherhood (*kökältashī*).[18]

Since the Timurid empire was established in the sedentary oases of Central Asia and Iran, the organisation of military affairs was adapted to the existing Arabo-Persian administrative system of the *dīwān*, which was concerned with the organisation of financial and bureaucratic affairs. The resulting administrative structure was a dichotomous one that distinguished between the military and civilian spheres, thereby reflecting the cultural division between the Turkic and Tājīk (Iranian) segments of society, with the former responsible for the conduct of military affairs and the latter in charge of bureaucratic administration. The distinction between the military and bureaucratic branches became blurred, however, as Tājīk (Iranian) bureaucrats became increasingly powerful in the financial administration of the state and were even granted membership in the Timurid household establishment.[19]

The overarching administrative structure of the *dīwān* consisted of two branches, the *dīwān-i tovachi*, which dealt with military affairs, and the *dīwān-i a'lā* (also *dīwān-i buzurg* or *dīwān-i māl*), which dealt with administrative and financial matters as well as with non-Islamic judicial matters, such as the *yarghu* court. The highest-ranking personnel of both *dīwāns* held the title *amīr*, although the officers of the *dīwān-i tovachi* traditionally had precedence over those of the *dīwān-i a'lā*. An *amīr* could be appointed concurrently to both *dīwāns*. Collectively, the *amīrs* of both *dīwāns* were referred to as 'the great

17 Ando, *Timuridische Emire*, pp. 66ff.
18 *Ibid.*, pp. 245–52; and Subtelny, *Timurids in transition*, pp. 33–5.
19 H. R. Roemer, 'The successors of Tīmūr', in Peter Jackson and Laurence Lockhart (eds.), *The Cambridge history of Iran*, vol. VI: *The Timurid and Safavid periods* (Cambridge, 1986), pp. 131–2; and Subtelny, *Timurids in transition*, pp. 68–70.

commanders' (Persian, *umarā-yi buzurg*; Turkish, *ulugh begler*), and their respective heads held the title of chief *amīr* (*amīr al-umarā'*). Other *amīrs* were appointed as provincial governors (*ḥākim, wālī, darugha*).

The *dīwān-i a'lā* or *dīwān-i māl* was staffed by Iranian bureaucrats (often referred to as *dīwānīyān* or *aṣḥāb-i dīwān*), who exhibited a remarkable continuity of indigenous administrative traditions, as their positions were often hereditary. Because of the wide scope of its financial and administrative responsibilities, the *dīwān-i a'lā* appears to have been organised into several departments, including the *dīwān-i inshā'* (chancery), *dīwān-i amlāk-i khāṣṣa* (privy purse) and *dīwān-i ṣadārat* (or *dīwān-i awqāf*), which was presided over by the *ṣadr*, the supervisor of pious endowments and religious appointments. The head of the *dīwān-i a'lā* was the chief vizier, and the overseer of the viziers was called the *mushrif*. Although the main language of the Timurid chancery was Persian, the Tājīk scribes, or *nawīsandagān-i Tājīk*, had their Turkic counterparts in the *nawīsandagān-i Türk*, who belonged to the *dīwān-i tovachi*. Many of these Turkish scribes, who were proficient in the use of the Uighur script, had Uighur scribal (*bakhshi*) backgrounds. Other important bureaucratic positions were the *parwānachī*, who was responsible for issuing financial orders, and the *muhrdār*, or keeper of the seal, who had the right to authorise various types of orders by using a particular type of seal. As had always been the case in Persian chancery practice, the use of seals was widespread, the most important being the royal seal (*muhr-i buzurg, muhr-i kalān, muhr-i humāyūn*), the seal of the *parwānachī* (*muhr-i parwāna*) and the seal used for tax vouchers (*muhr-i barāt*).[20]

The struggle for succession and the emergence of Shāh Rukh

Although the goal of Temür's conquests appears to have been the restoration of the Mongol world empire, his far-flung realm fell apart soon after his death in 807/1405. Like Chinggis Khan, Temür had divided his empire into four parts, each governed by one of his sons or the son's descendants: the eldest, 'Umar Shaykh (d. 796/1394), and his sons held central and southern Iran;[21] Jahāngīr's (d. 777/1376) son Pīr-Muḥammad governed Kabul in the south-east; Mīrānshāh (d. 810/1408) held the western regions with his sons Khalīl-Sulṭān

20 See Ando, *Timuridische Emire*, pp. 223ff.
21 On the question of who was the eldest son of Temür, see John E. Woods, *The Timurid dynasty*, Papers on Central Asia, 14 (Bloomington, IN, 1990), p. 14 n. 34.

(d. 814/1411) in Armenia and Georgia (later in Rayy), ʿUmar (d. 809/1407) in Azerbaijan, and Abā Bakr (d. 811/1409) in ʿIraq-i ʿArab and Kurdistan; and the youngest, Shāh Rukh, and his sons held Khurāsān and the region of Transoxiana to the north and east. Temür did not designate any of his sons as his successor during his lifetime, but rather his grandson Muḥammad-Sulṭān b. Jahāngīr, who died in 805/1403, and then another grandson, Pīr-Muḥammad b. Jahāngīr. But even before the latter's murder in 809/1407, a succession struggle ensued that lasted fifteen years and involved not just immediate members of Temür's family and the Timurid *amīrs* but also the tribal society of the Ulus Chaghadai, as well as local dynasts and vassal rulers, some of whom took advantage of the opportunity to assert their independence. Internecine warfare among the Timurid princes, and encroachment by outside powers, including the Golden Horde, Jalayirids and Qara Qoyunlu, resulted in significant territorial losses in Khwārazm, ʿIraq-i ʿArab and Azerbaijan.

Shāh Rukh, who had been governor of Khurāsān since 799/1396f., was engaged from the time of Temür's death in putting down rebellions by Temür's former vassals and in countering the centrifugal tendencies of powerful Timurid *amīrs* who sought to reassert their authority at his expense. By 811/1409, however, he managed to extend his authority to Transoxania where he installed his son Ulugh Beg as governor in Samarqand. In 815/1413, his powerful *amīr* Shāh-Malik recovered Khwārazm from the Golden Horde. Campaigns against the sons of ʿUmar Shaykh in Fārs in 817–18/1414–15 resulted in the appointment of another son, Ibrāhīm, as governor in Shīrāz. But despite several successful campaigns against the Qara Qoyunlu in ʿIraq-i ʿAjam and Azerbaijan, these and other regions were eventually lost to the Timurid empire, which was essentially reduced to the two large regions of Khurāsān, with its capital Herat, and Transoxiana, with Temür's former capital Samarqand. Although Transoxania was the principal site of the succession struggles after Temür's death, with Shāh Rukh's emergence as the leading power in 811/1409 the focus of the Timurid realm shifted south to Khurāsān.

Shāh Rukh was faced with the task of transforming what remained of the Timurid nomadic empire, which had been fuelled by a 'booty economy', into an Islamic polity based on the regular taxation of revenues derived from agriculture and trade. This was dictated as much by fiscal necessity as it was by a desire to legitimate Timurid rule over a predominantly sedentary Muslim population that was becoming increasingly restive. In 813/1411 Shāh Rukh officially abrogated the *törä* and abolished the *yarghu* court of investigation in favour of a 'return' to *sharīʿa* law and Islamic practices, although the effectiveness of these measures remained limited. The Sunnī religious revival initiated by Shāh Rukh was supported by the Muslim religious intelligentsia, who portrayed him as the 'renewer of Islam'. Styling himself *pādishāh-i Islām*, he even had pretensions to be recognized as caliph of the entire Muslim world, a claim that was challenged by the Mamlūk sultan. Shāh Rukh's Islamicising policies included the prohibition of prostitution and the drinking of wine in the capital city of Herat, as well as the promotion of Islamic missionary activity in such regions as Qūhistān, a traditional Ismāʿīlī enclave. Notwithstanding these policies, Shāh Rukh's reign witnessed the growth of heterodox movements of socio-religious opposition, some of which espoused extremist and messianic views, often with a Shīʿī colouring, such as the cabalistic Ḥurūfiyya, whose adherents even made an unsuccessful attempt on his life in 830/1427.

The chief means by which Shāh Rukh sought to promote Islamic doctrinal orthodoxy were the madrasas he and his wife, Gawharshād (d. 861/1457), constructed in Herat in 813/1410f. and 820–7/1417–24. The mandate of these educational institutions, which were staffed by prominent Sunnī scholars and jurists, was to ensure the dominant position of the Ḥanafī and Shāfiʿī schools of legal interpretation. The curriculum of Islamic higher learning established at this time continued to be followed in madrasas in pre-Safavid Iran and in Uzbek Central Asia.[22] On the popular level, Shāh Rukh tapped into the widespread practice of the visitation of tombs of Muslim saints by reviving the burial place of the eleventh-century Ḥanbalī traditionist and patron saint of Herat, Khwāja ʿAbd Allāh Anṣārī (d. 481/1089), known as Pīr-i Harāt, which he developed architecturally into a large shrine complex that became a venue for ceremonial events of a political nature. The Anṣārī shrine and cult continued to be patronised by Shāh Rukh's successors, reaching a high point under the last Timurid ruler of Herat, Sulṭān-Ḥusayn, who even claimed descent from ʿAbd Allāh Anṣārī and used his shrine as a dynastic burial place.[23] The tombs of other famous Sufis and important Muslim religious figures were also accorded attention, chief among these being the shrine of ʿAlī b. Mūsā al-Riḍā, a descendant of ʿAlī b. Abī Ṭālib and the eighth Shīʿī imam, at Mashhad, which was developed and endowed principally by Gawharshād and her son Baysunghur.[24] Timurid patronage of the Mashhad shrine, which included the

22 Maria Eva Subtelny and Anas B. Khalidov, 'The curriculum of Islamic higher learning in Timurid Iran in the light of the Sunni revival under Shāh-Rukh', *Journal of the American Oriental Society*, 115, 2 (1995), pp. 211–36.

23 Maria Eva Subtelny, 'The cult of ʿAbdullāh Anṣārī under the Timurids', in Alma Giese and J. Christoph Bürgel (eds.), *Gott ist schön und Er liebt die Schönheit/God is beautiful and He loves beauty: Festschrift in honour of Annemarie Schimmel* (Bern, 1994), pp. 388–92.

24 Lisa Golombek and Donald Wilber, *The Timurid architecture of Iran and Turan*, 2 vols. (Princeton, 1988), vol. I, pp. 328ff.

construction of a spectacular congregational mosque, was not motivated simply by a desire to appease the Shīʿī population of the region, as has sometimes been argued; rather, it represented a reassertion of the long-standing Sunnī tradition of veneration of the *ahl al-bayt*, or family of the Prophet, in Iran and Central Asia, as well as an expression of the deep reverence Turko-Mongolian dynasts had for saints and holy men of all religious stripes.

An important legacy of Shāh Rukh's reign was the professionalisation of the financial administration. Under the chief vizier, Ghiyāth al-Dīn Pīr-Aḥmad Khwāfī, who headed the *dīwān* from 820/1417 until Shāh Rukh's death in 850/1447, standard bureaucratic procedures such as the use of accounting notation (*siyāqat*) and the keeping of ledger books (*daftar*) were introduced.[25] Ghiyāth al-Dīn Pīr-Aḥmad subsequently served in the administrations of several other Timurid princes (including ʿAbd al-Laṭīf, ʿAlāʾ al-Dawla, Sulṭān-Muḥammad and Abūl-Qāsim Babur) until his death in 857/1453. His son Majd al-Dīn Muḥammad Khwāfī followed in his footsteps, beginning his career in the chancery of Sulṭān-Abū Saʿīd and eventually becoming chief executive officer in the administration of Sulṭān-Ḥusayn Bayqara in 876/1472, until his dismissal in 895/1490. Thus, for roughly three-quarters of a century, two generations of the Khwāfī family exerted a profound influence on the financial administration of the Timurid state, which they attempted to centralise on the Perso-Islamic model.[26]

During Shāh Rukh's reign, regular diplomatic and trade relations were established between the Timurid state and the Ming dynasty. The items exchanged consisted largely of silk fabrics, paper money and porcelains provided by the Chinese in return for such commodities as jade and horses. Although Shāh Rukh expressed hope that the Ming emperor would convert to Islam, facilitating trade appears to have been the main concern on both sides.[27]

Ulugh Beg: scientific achievement

Shāh Rukh's death in 850/1447 precipitated another struggle for power among the Timurid princes, as most of his sons had predeceased him. His only remaining son, Ulugh Beg, born Muḥammad Taraghay, who had been

25 Ghiyāth al-Dīn b. Humām al-Dīn Khwāndamīr, *Dastūr al-wuzarāʾ*, ed. Saʿīd Nafīsī (Tehran, 1317; repr. 2535/1976), pp. 353–7; and Sayf al-Dīn Ḥājjī b. Niẓām ʿUqaylī, *Āthār al-wuzarāʾ*, ed. Mīr Jalāl al-Dīn Ḥusaynī Urmawī ʻMuḥaddithʼ (Tehran, 1337), pp. 342–3.

26 For Majd al-Dīn Muḥammad Khwāfī, see below.

27 Ralph Kauz, *Politik und Handel zwischen Ming und Timuriden. China, Iran und Zentralasien im Spätmittelalter* (Wiesbaden, 2005), pp. 93–143.

governor of Samarqand since 811/1409, eventually succeeded him after defeating his nephews Abā Bakr b. Muḥammad Jūkī (d. ?852/?1448) and ʿAlāʾ al-Dawla b. Baysunghur (d. 865/1460) in 852/1448 in Khurāsān. However, because he preferred to remain in the original Timurid seat of power in Transoxania, Ulugh Beg failed to consolidate his victory. When he was called to the defence of Samarqand, he left Herat in the hands of his son ʿAbd al-Laṭīf, who was unable to hold on to it for more than a few months. Ulugh Beg thus lost control of Khurāsān, which by that time had come to be regarded as key to Timurid hegemony.

Concentrating his political and cultural efforts on Transoxania, Ulugh Beg ruled Samarqand in a semi-independent manner until 853/1449. During the early part of his father's reign, he had helped reaffirm Timurid authority in such regions as Farghāna and Mughulistān. In 830/1427, however, he was defeated on the Syr Darya by the khan of the Blue Horde, and in 1435 the eastern Chaghadayids took back Kāshghar. A much more significant threat was posed by the nomadic Uzbek confederation that had been created in the Qıpchaq steppe under the leadership of the Jochid ruler Abūl-Khayr Khan, who during the 1440s established himself in the northern Syr Darya region and in 852/1448 launched a raid into Transoxania, looting and burning the region around Samarqand. Abūl-Khayr Khan took advantage of the struggles among the Timurid princes to intrude into Transoxanian politics. After two years of fighting following the death of Shāh Rukh, the already fractured Timurid empire was further divided into three principal parts: Transoxania under Ulugh Beg; ʿIraq-i ʿAjam and Fārs under Muḥammad b. Baysunghur; and Khurāsān under Abūl-Qāsim Babur. In 853/1449 Ulugh Beg's son ʿAbd al-Laṭīf, who was governor of Balkh and with whom he had strained relations, rebelled against him, and after a humiliating defeat Ulugh Beg was forced to submit. In an act that occasioned universal disapproval, ʿAbd al-Laṭīf had his father murdered. In 854/1450, after a brief rule in Samarqand, he was himself killed by Ulugh Beg's *amīrs*.

Ulugh Beg has come to be known primarily for his scientific interests and organisation of advanced scientific study at Samarqand. A competent astronomer himself, who had been tutored in his youth by the famous astronomer Qāḍīzāda Rūmī (d. *c.* 840/1436) of Bursa, Ulugh Beg assembled a large group of scientists, including the Persian mathematician Ghiyāth al-Dīn Jamshīd Kāshī (d. 832/1429) and the astronomer ʿAlāʾ al-Dīn ʿAlī Qushchi (d. 879/1474), at his court. In 823/1420 he oversaw the foundation of an astronomical observatory, probably modelled on the famous Ilkhanid observatory at Marāgha, the most conspicuous feature of which was its meridian transit instrument, which had a radius of approximately 40 metres. The most celebrated and lasting achievement of the Samarqand observatory was the completion (in 1437–48) of a new set of astronomical tables (*zīj*), which contributed greatly to knowledge in the field of theoretical astronomy. Impressive advances were also made in the field of computational mathematics, including the calculation of π and the application of the decimal place-value system to fractions, and in the trigonometric tables of Ulugh Beg's *zīj*, with their prodigiously accurate sine table.[28]

Ulugh Beg has sometimes been portrayed as ruling Transoxania more in the neo-Mongol style of his grandfather, Temür, than in accordance with the Islamicising policies of his father, Shāh Rukh. Although this is to some extent true, it rather reflects the often uneasy coexistence of Turko-Mongolian and Perso-Islamic customs that characterised the early Timurid period as a whole. Deeply concerned with Chinggisid genealogical history, Ulugh Beg was apparently responsible for the composition of a history of the Chinggisids, entitled *Tārīkh-i arba' ulūs*, which is an important source for the chronology of the later Chaghadayids. In what appears to have been an attempt to assert the primacy of Samarqand in Timurid dynastic culture, he transferred his father's body from Herat to the Gūr-i Amīr mausoleum in 852/1448. At the same time, he was also the founder of important madrasas in Samarqand and Bukhara. Despite his efforts, however, he was unable to gain the support of the religious establishment. His difficult relationship with his sons, military defeats, as well as the disintegrating state of Timurid politics, all contributed to his demise.[29]

Sulṭān-Abū Sa'īd: administrative continuity

The Timurids were never able to implement a policy of the rational transfer of power based on the principle of primogeniture because they adhered to the concept of corporate sovereignty, which held that every male member of the paramount clan was eligible to succeed the previous holder of power. With four competing Timurid lines and scores of uncles, cousins and grandsons, the Timurid polity was plunged with predictable regularity into internecine warfare. After the death of 'Abd al-Laṭīf in 854/1450, Sulṭān-Abū Sa'īd, a grandson of Mīrānshāh, emerged as the next leading candidate for the contested Timurid throne.[30]

28 E. S. Kennedy, 'The exact sciences in Timurid Iran', in *The Cambridge history of Iran*, vol. VI, pp. 568–80.

29 V. V. Bartol'd, 'Ulugbek i ego vremia', in Bartol'd, *Sochineniia*, vol. II, part 2, pp. 25–196.

30 'Sulṭān' is a component of this double name, not a political title. The Timurids often used the title *mīrzā*, an abbreviated form of *amīrzāda*, meaning 'descended from the *amīr*' (i.e. Temür).

Sulṭān-Abū Saʿīd, who had earlier been in the service of Ulugh Beg, succeeded in capturing Samarqand in 855/1451 with the aid of the Jochid Abu'l-Khayr Khan. Another Timurid contender, Abūl-Qāsim Babur, who was of the line of Shāh Rukh, challenged him by invading Transoxania in 858/1454 from his base in Khurāsān. Sulṭān-Abū Saʿīd took advantage of the anarchic situation following Abu'l-Qāsim Babur's death in 861/1457 to occupy Herat, at which time he had Shāh Rukh's widow, Gawharshād, executed for allegedly conspiring against him. After a brief Qara Qoyunlu interregnum in 862/1458, Sulṭān-Abū Saʿīd took Herat again and in 863/1458 formally occupied the throne for a second time. His defeat of a coalition of Timurid princes in 863/1459 resulted in the elimination of a significant number of rivals.[31]

Although he ruled over Khurāsān, Transoxania, Māzandarān and parts of Afghanistan, Sulṭān-Abū Saʿīd's hold on these territories was precarious, as he was pressured on the one hand by incursions on the part of the Uzbeks and the eastern Chaghadayids, and on the other by another rising Timurid contender, Sulṭān-Ḥusayn Bayqara, of the line of ʿUmar Shaykh, who in 865/1461 made an attempt to capture Herat. Because of the continual warfare, agricultural activity in Khurāsān had been interrupted, and a terrible famine ensued in Herat and its dependencies in the winter of 863/1458. As for areas to the west of Khurāsān, the Qara Qoyunlu leader Jahānshāh, who had been kept in check in Azerbaijan by Shāh Rukh, extended his power over central and western Iran, effectively putting an end to Timurid control over these regions. A modus vivendi was eventually established with the Timurids, but this came to an abrupt end in 872/1467, when Jahānshāh was killed and the Qara Qoyunlu confederation was destroyed by the Aq Qoyunlu under the leadership of Uzun Ḥasan. The need to stem the growing power of the Aq Qoyunlu resulted in an ill-fated campaign against Azerbaijan, in the course of which Sulṭān-Abū Saʿīd was captured and handed over to yet another Timurid pretender to the throne of Herat, Yādgār-Muḥammad, who put him to death in 873/1469 in order to avenge the murder of Shāh Rukh's widow, Gawharshād.[32] From now on, the ever-shrinking Timurid realm would be reduced to the two main provinces of Khurāsān and Transoxania.

Although it began badly, Sulṭān-Abū Saʿīd's eleven-year reign in Herat was by all accounts a beneficial one. Thanks largely to the efforts of competent administrators, in particular the vizier Quṭb al-Dīn Ṭā'us Simnānī, who

31 Ghiyāth al-Dīn b. Humām al-Dīn al-Ḥusaynī Khwāndamīr, *Ḥabīb al-siyar fī akhbār afrād-i bashar*, ed. Jalāl al-Dīn Humāʾī, 4 vols. (Tehran, 1333; 3rd repr. 1362), vol. IV, pp. 67–77.

32 Khwāndamīr, *Ḥabīb al-siyar*, vol. IV, pp. 87–93.

focused his energies on the agricultural development of Khurāsān and the construction of major irrigation works, Sulṭān-Abū Saʿīd laid the foundation for the agricultural prosperity that characterised the reign of his eventual successor, Sulṭān-Ḥusayn Bayqara.[33]

Sulṭān-Ḥusayn Bayqara: from political vagabond to princely patron

Sulṭān-Ḥusayn Bayqara, a great-grandson of ʿUmar Shaykh, started his career in the retinue of his cousin Abūl-Qāsim Babur in Herat. After the latter's death in 861/1457, he entered the service of his cousin Sanjar (d. 863/1459) in Marv. A falling out with Sanjar forced him into the first of several periods of political vagabondage (*qazaqliq*) in the region around Marv and in the deserts of Khwārazm. In 862/1458, he succeeded in taking Astarābād from the Qara Qoyunlu, but he soon clashed with Sulṭān-Abū Saʿīd, who retook it from him in 864/1460, forcing him to flee. Sulṭān-Ḥusayn now began another period of political vagabondage in Khwārazm, during which he tried to gain the support of Muṣṭafā Khan, the Uzbek ruler of the region. In 865/1461, he was able to recapture Astarābād again, after which he made an ambitious bid for Herat, to which he laid siege. But he was forced to retire to Astarābād and again fled to Khwārazm before Sulṭān-Abū Saʿīd's approaching army. In 866/1461, he made yet another unsuccessful attempt to conquer Khurāsān but was again forced into a long period of *qazaqliq*, which lasted seven and a half years. It was not until Sulṭān-Abū Saʿīd's death in 873/1469 that Sulṭān-Ḥusayn was finally able to capture Herat and proclaim himself ruler. In order to re-establish order as quickly as possible and gain the support of the religious intelligentsia, he proclaimed his intention to govern Timurid Khurāsān according to Islamic principles.[34]

Sulṭān-Ḥusayn's first period of rule in Herat, which lasted only about fifteen months, was challenged by Yādgār-Muḥammad, a great-grandson of Shāh Rukh, who had been supported first by Jahānshāh Qara Qoyunlu against Sulṭān-Abū Saʿīd and then, after Jahānshāh's death, by the Aq Qoyunlu *amīr* Uzun Ḥasan. Yādgār-Muḥammad managed to take the city for a short while in 875/1470 before being captured and executed by Sulṭān-Ḥusayn, who acceded to the throne of Herat for a second time.[35] Sulṭān-Ḥusayn thus ruled Herat for

33 M. E. Subtelny, 'A medieval Persian agricultural manual in context: The *Irshād al-zirāʿa* in late Timurid and early Safavid Khorasan', *Studia Iranica*, 22, 2 (1993), pp. 184–9.

34 Khwāndamīr, *Ḥabīb al-siyar*, vol. IV, pp. 115–35.

35 *Ibid.*, pp. 146–52; and Subtelny, *Timurids in transition*, pp. 43–67.

roughly thirty-seven years, from 873/1469 until his death in 911/1506.[36] A determined and gifted political leader, his long, uninterrupted rule in Herat represented a period of political and economic stability that was conducive to the creation of the so-called Timurid cultural renaissance.

At the beginning of his reign, Sulṭān-Ḥusayn was faced with the urgent task of restoring fiscal stability to a region whose main tax base had become eroded due to a decline in agricultural production. Further financial pressures were created by the cost of rewarding old retainers and recruiting new personnel to his fledgling state. At the time of his accession, Sulṭān-Ḥusayn made several key appointments of individuals who had earlier served in the administrations of Abūl-Qāsim Babur and Sulṭān-Abū Saʿīd. He was soon also joined by ʿAlīshīr (also known as Mīr ʿAlīshīr and ʿAlīshīr Nawāʾī), the scion of an Uighur family of *bakhshis*, or Turkic chancery scribes, who were connected to the Timurid house by ties of foster-brotherhood (*kökältashī*). Although he subsequently held several official appointments, such as *amīr* of the *dīwān-i aʿlā*, ʿAlīshīr was an *ichki*, or member of the Timurid household establishment, who until his death in 906/1501 served Sulṭān-Ḥusayn primarily as a trusted adviser.[37]

In 876/1472, Sulṭān-Ḥusayn appointed Majd al-Dīn Muḥammad Khwāfī, the son of Shāh Rukh's chief vizier, Ghiyāth al-Dīn Pīr-Aḥmad Khwāfī, as head of the financial administration, granting him unprecedented powers to implement fiscal and bureaucratic reforms. Majd al-Dīn's appointment turned out to be a controversial one, and he was removed from office in 883/1478, only to be reinstated again in 892/1487. During his second tenure in office, Majd al-Dīn attempted to centralise the Timurid fisc by purging the *dīwān* of corrupt officials and instituting a reform of the taxation system that included curtailing the system of land grants with tax immunity, called *soyurghal*, whose main beneficiaries were members of the Timurid military elite and household establishment.[38] Accustomed to a more decentralised form of government, the Turko-Mongolian *amīrs* were particularly opposed to Majd al-Dīn's centralising policies and they conspired to have him removed from office.[39] Leading the coalition against Majd al-Dīn were ʿAlīshīr and his brother

36 Muʿīn al-Dīn Muḥammad Zamchī Isfizārī, *Rawḍāt al-jannāt fī awṣāf madīnat Harāt*, ed. Sayyid Muḥammad Kāẓim Imām, 2 vols. (Tehran, 1338–9), vol. II, p. 368.

37 Maria Eva Subtelny, ''Alī Shīr Navāʾī: *Bakhshī* and *beg*', *Harvard Ukrainian Studies*, 3–4 (1979–80), part 2, pp. 799–802; and *EI*[3] ''Alī Shīr Navāʾī' (M. E. Subtelny).

38 For the system of landholding and taxation under the Timurids, see Bert Fragner, 'Social and internal economic affairs', in *The Cambridge history of Iran*, vol. VI, pp. 491–567.

39 Maria Eva Subtelny, 'Centralizing reform and its opponents in the late Timurid period', *Iranian Studies*, 21, 1–2 (1988), pp. 130–49.

Darwīsh-ʿAlī Kökältash. A wealthy landowner who enjoyed access to the Timurid *dīwān*, ʿAlīshīr would have been hit hard by Majd al-Dīn's reforms. V. V. Bartol'd speculated that ʿAlīshīr's extensive building activities may have contributed to the financial difficulties the Timurid treasury was experiencing. This appears to be borne out by the fact that ʿAlīshīr temporarily fell out of favour with the court and in 892/1487 was forced to leave Herat for a while to assume the governorship of Astarābād.[40] The coalition of *amīrs* finally prevailed, and Majd al-Dīn was dismissed in 895/1490. (He died in 899/1494, most likely having been murdered.)

Following Sulṭān-Ḥusayn's death in 911/1506, intractable fiscal problems and political uncertainty due to the uneasy co-regency of Sulṭān-Ḥusayn's sons Badīʿ al-Zamān Mīrzā and Muẓaffar-Ḥusayn Mīrzā prompted invasion by the Uzbeks, who under the leadership of Abūl-Khayr Khan's grandson Muḥammad Shibani captured Herat in 913/1507, thereby bringing Timurid rule in Khurāsān to an end.

The agrarian economy

During Sulṭān-Ḥusayn's reign, the agriculture of the core Timurid region of Khurāsān reached a high level of development. Thanks to the construction and reconstruction of major irrigation works and the restoration of agricultural production under Shāh Rukh and Sulṭān-Abū Saʿīd following the disruption caused by Temür's conquests, the area under cultivation in Khurāsān was expanded considerably during the second half of the fifteenth century. Agricultural production consisted mainly of fruits (including many varieties of grapes), garden vegetables, herbs and flowers (including roses for the production of rose water), and various types of cereal grains. A rich source of information about the intensive agriculture practised in the Herat region is the Timurid agricultural manual, *Irshād al-zirāʿa*, composed in 921/1515 by Qāsim b. Yūsuf Abū Naṣrī.[41]

The Timurids appreciated the economic value of agriculture, which represented the chief source of tax revenues in Khurāsān. Although trade and commerce were also important, long-distance trade along the so-called Silk Road declined with the increasing decentralisation of the Timurid empire, political pressure from the Turkmen dynasties in the west and the growing power of the Uzbeks to the north-east. During the fifteenth century, there was

40 V. V. Bartol'd, 'Mir Ali-Shir i politicheskaia zhizn'', in Bartol'd, *Sochineniia*, vol. II, part 2, pp. 238–9.

41 Subtelny, 'Medieval Persian agricultural manual', pp. 184–9.

an increase in lands belonging to Islamic pious endowments (*awqāf*), particularly those connected with the many shrine complexes that had been constructed and developed throughout Khurāsān by members of the Timurid elite. Besides the shrines of ʿAbd Allāh Anṣārī and ʿAlī Riḍā, which were developed under Shāh Rukh at Herat and Mashhad, respectively, the shrine complex based on the purported tomb of ʿAlī b. Abī Ṭālib, which was miraculously 'rediscovered' in 885/1480f. in a village (today Mazār-i Sharīf) located on the Hazhdah Nahr ('Eighteen canal') irrigation network in the Balkh region, was agriculturally and commercially developed by Sulṭān-Ḥusayn and members of the Timurid elite.[42] It appears that the Timurids systematically established and endowed such complexes and by staffing them with professional personnel made them into efficient vehicles for managing the intensive irrigated agriculture of Khurāsān.[43] The same management model was applied, albeit on a smaller scale, by members of prominent Sufi orders, such as the Naqshbandiyya, to their own agricultural enterprises.[44]

The Timurid renaissance

The upsurge in cultural activity in Iran and Central Asia under Timurid patronage coincided roughly with the Renaissance in Europe, and even though there was no historical connection between the two cultural phenomena and no shared philosophical basis, historians of Timurid art and culture dubbed it the 'Timurid renaissance', a designation that continues to be used even as some scholars have demonstrated its inappropriateness.[45] It cannot be denied, however, that there was something extraordinary about the way in which a large number of artistic and literary talents came together with wealthy patrons and elaborated a culture whose impact on the subsequent development of almost every field of artistic endeavour, in both the eastern and western Islamic world, was entirely out of proportion to the Timurid dynasty's relatively limited duration and geographical scope.

An insightful explanation for the increase in cultural patronage and the creativity it fostered is the notion of the 'military patronage state', put forward by Marshall Hodgson, who argued that while a state ruled by a privileged

42 R. D. McChesney, *Waqf in Central Asia: Four hundred years in the history of a Muslim shrine, 1480–1889* (Princeton, 1991), pp. 21–45.
43 Subtelny, *Timurids in transition*, pp. 198–219.
44 Jürgen Paul, *Die politische und soziale Bedeutung der Naqšbandiyya in Mittelasien im 15. Jahrhundert* (Berlin, 1991), pp. 89–112.
45 Jean Aubin, 'Le mécénat timouride à Chiraz', *Studia Islamica*, 8 (1957), p. 72.

military family did not necessarily increase the amount of patronage of high culture, it did provide a different framework for its distribution.[46] A closer examination of the socio-economic bases of the Timurid state would appear to support this hypothesis, as the fragmentation of political authority due to incessant dynastic and internecine struggles went hand in hand with the fiscal decentralisation that resulted from the granting of benefices and tax immunities to the many Timurid princes and military commanders whose growing power and independence only reinforced the prevailing centrifugal tendencies. Such a situation, often regarded by historians as signalling a period of decadence or decline, appears in fact to have stimulated the production of culture by creating multiple centres with competing courts and patrons.[47]

Literature

The literary output of the Timurid period was exceedingly rich and varied, with works composed in three languages – Persian, Arabic and Chaghatay Turkish. Persian, which was spoken by the vast majority of the indigenous Iranian population of Khurāsān and Transoxania, was the main literary language, used for historical writing, chancery correspondence, and poetry and prose. Although Arabic continued to be used for works on the religious and exact sciences, Persian increasingly exerted its dominance in these areas as well. Under Timurid patronage, Chaghatay, a Middle Turkic language, became a full-fledged literary language used in a growing corpus of poetic and prose works that often closely followed Persian models.

As was generally the case in classical Persian literature, poetry predominated over prose. Timurid biographical sources, such as ʿAlīshīr Nawāʾī's *Majālis al-nafāʾis* (completed 897/1491f.), devoted largely to contemporary poets writing in Persian and/or Turkish, and Dawlatshāh Samarqandī's *Tadhkirat al-shuʿarā* (completed *c.* 892/1487), provide an idea of the extent of poetical activity as well as information about contemporary literary tastes. A rare glimpse of the poetic activity of women is provided by Fakhrī Harawī's *Jawāhir al-ʿajāyib*.[48] The favoured poetical forms were the *ghazal*, or lyric poem in monorhyme, which was utilised for mystico-erotic themes, and the *mathnawī*, consisting of rhyming couplets, which was used for epic or

46 Hodgson, *Venture of Islam*, vol. II, pp. 404–10.

47 Maria Eva Subtelny, 'Socioeconomic bases of cultural patronage under the later Timurids', *International Journal of Middle East Studies*, 20, 4 (1988), pp. 479–505.

48 Maria Szuppe, 'The female intellectual milieu in Timurid and post-Timurid Herāt: Faxri Heravi's biography of poetesses, *Javāher al-ʿajāyeb*', *Oriente Moderno*, n.s. 15, 2 (1996), vol. I, pp. 119–37.

romantic tales, often having an ethical or mystical intent.[49] The poetry of the period was characterised by rhetorical embellishment and stylistic intricacy, with a penchant for the innovative imitation of earlier poetic models. Reflecting the literary tastes of the period, such verse forms as the palindrome, the chronogram and the enigma (*mu'ammā*) enjoyed great popularity.[50] Music was closely associated with poetry and the literary gathering (*majlis*), and in addition to the works of musical theorists and composers like 'Abd al-Qādir al-Marāghī (d. 1435), the descriptions of performances by singers and musicians in contemporary sources attest to the vitality of the Timurid musical tradition.[51]

The most important Persian poet of the period was 'Abd al-Raḥmān Jāmī (d. 898/1492), who is sometimes unjustifiably referred to as the last classical poet of Iran. A disciple of the Naqshbandī spiritual master Sa'd al-Dīn Kāshgharī and a close friend of 'Alīshīr Nawā'ī, Jāmī is best known for his *Haft awrang*, a compendium of seven *mathnawīs* composed largely in imitation of the *Khamsas* ('Quintet') of Niẓāmī and Amīr Khusraw, although with a mystico-ethical interpretation, and entitled *Silsilat al-dhahab, Salāmān wa-Absāl, Tuḥfat al-aḥrār, Subḥat al-abrār, Yūsuf wa-Zulaykhā, Laylī wa-Majnūn* and *Iskandar-nāma* (or *Khirad-nāma-i Iskandarī*). Jāmī was also the author of three *dīwāns* of poems. His interpretations were entirely in keeping with Islamic theosophical conceptions as these had been elaborated from the twelfth century, and his poetic works attest to a high level of spiritual sensibility and rhetorical sophistication. He was also the author of several prose works, mostly on mystical and related topics, including *Lawā'iḥ, Shawāhid al-nubuwwa, Bahāristān* and the popular Sufi hagiography *Nafaḥāt al-uns*.[52]

Jāmī's close friend and spiritual disciple 'Alīshīr Nawā'ī (d. 906/1501) is perhaps the most imposing cultural figure of the period, as he was not only an outstanding poet himself in both Turkish and Persian, but also the main patron and prime mover of literary and cultural activity at Sulṭān-Ḥusayn's court. Although he was not the 'founder' of the Chaghatay literary language, he was certainly its greatest representative. Despite the fact that New Persian (*Fārsī*) had been the literary language par excellence in Iran and Central Asia

49 For an overview, see Jan Rypka, *History of Iranian literature*, ed. Karl Jahn, trans. P. van Popta-Hope (Dordrecht, 1968), pp. 279–90; and Ehsan Yarshater, 'Persian poetry in the Timurid and Safavid periods', in *The Cambridge history of Iran*, vol. VI, pp. 965–85.

50 Maria Eva Subtelny, 'A taste for the intricate: The Persian poetry of the late Timurid period', *Zeitschrift der Deutschen Morgenländischen Gesellschaft*, 136, 1 (1986), pp. 56–79.

51 Owen Wright, 'On the concept of a "Timurid music"', *Oriente Moderno*, n.s. 15, 2 (1996), vol. II, pp. 665–81.

52 Evgenii Èduardovich Bertel's, *Navoi i Dzhami* (Moscow, 1965), pp. 209–78.

since the tenth century, 'Alīshīr championed the cause of Turkish (*Türkī*), which he argued could not only vie with Persian as a poetic language but in some respects was superior to it. Following the lead of earlier Timurid poets such as Luṭfī, Sakkākī and Gadā'ī, he shaped Chaghatay Turkish into a supple instrument of poetic expression, composing almost thirty works under the pen name Nawā'ī. He also wrote several works in Persian under the pen name Fānī. His chief works are the *Khamsa*, modelled on the works of Niẓāmī, Amīr Khusraw and Jāmī, which comprise *Ḥayrat al-abrār*, *Farhād wa-Shīrīn*, *Laylī wa-Majnūn*, *Sab'a-i sayyār* and *Sadd-i Iskandarī*. He also wrote *Lisān al-ṭayr* in imitation of 'Aṭṭār's mystical masterpiece, *Manṭiq al-ṭayr*. Of great originality and subtlety are his lyric poems, collected under the general title *Khazā'in al-ma'ānī*, which in fact comprises four *dīwāns*. His prose works include *Muḥākamat al-lughatayn*, *Maḥbūb al-qulūb*, *Nasā'im al-maḥabba*, *Mīzān al-awzān* and *Waqfiyya* (which in spite of its title is in fact his apologia).[53]

Another Chaghatay author who cannot escape mention is the Timurid prince Ẓahīr al-Dīn Muḥammad Babur (d. 937/1530), founder of the Timurid (Mughal) state in India. His prose memoirs, known as the *Babur-nāma*, are a masterpiece of concise and straightforward Chaghatay prose, revealing an endearingly complex personality who lived in difficult political times.[54]

But a figure who perhaps best captures the spirit of the late Timurid period is Kamāl al-Dīn Ḥusayn Wā'iẓ-i Kāshifī (d. 910/1504f.). A popular preacher by profession, Kāshifī reputedly wrote forty works of a compilative nature covering the entire spectrum of learning in medieval Iran at the turn of the sixteenth century. Written mainly in Persian, they encompassed the Islamic religious sciences, the exact sciences, literature and ethics, as well as various popular esoteric sciences. His best-known work is the 'Alid martyrology *Rawḍat al-shuhadā'*, which achieved near-canonical status under the Shī'ī Safavid dynasty. However, he was almost equally well known for *Anwār-i Suhaylī*, which was based on the *Kalīla wa-Dimna* animal fables; *Akhlāq-i Muḥsinī*, a treatise on ethics and statecraft; and *Mawāhib-i 'Aliyya*, a Qur'ān commentary popularly known as *Tafsīr-i Ḥusaynī*. Kāshifī's works on magic (*Asrār-i Qāsimī*), chancery correspondence (*Makhzan al-inshā'*), astrology (*Sab'a-i Kāshifiyya*) and rhetorics (*Badāyi' al-afkār fī ṣanāyi' al-ash'ār*) are only beginning to be subjected to scholarly analysis.[55]

53 *EI*³ art. ''Alī Shīr Navā'ī' (M. E. Subtelny); and Maria Eva Subtelny, 'The *Vaqfīya* of Mīr 'Alī Šīr Navā'ī as apologia', *Journal of Turkish Studies*, 15 (1991), vol. II, pp. 257–86.

54 Wheeler M. Thackston (trans. and ed.), *The Baburnama: Memoirs of Babur, prince and emperor* (New York, 1996); and Dale, *Garden of the eight paradises*, pp. 23–66.

55 Maria E. Subtelny, 'Husayn Va'iz-i Kashifi: Polymath, popularizer, and preserver', *Iranian Studies*, 36, 4 (2003), pp. 463–7.

Historical writing and chancery prose

The Timurids contributed to the further development of the eastern Iranian tradition of historical writing, which was heavily influenced by Persian literary conventions. Temür had an acute sense of his historical mission and engaged secretaries to document his utterances and conquests. The *Ẓafar-nāma* ('Book of conquests'), completed by Niẓām al-Dīn ʿAlī Shāmī in 806/1404, which chronicled Temür's early career and military conquests, formed the basis for later Timurid histories. Under Shāh Rukh, the court-sponsored historiography sought to portray Temür in a more positive, Islamic light and by the same token legitimate Shāh Rukh's claim to the Timurid heritage. Continuations of Shāmī's history included Tāj al-Salmānī's *Shams al-ḥusn*, which covered the period 807–11/1404–9, and Ḥāfiẓ-i Abrū's *Dhayl-i Ẓafar-nāma-i Shāmī*, composed in 814/1412. In order to situate the history of the Timurid dynasty within the larger Islamic framework, several universal histories were composed at this time, chief among them being Muʿīn al-Dīn Naṭanzī's *Muntakhab al-tawārīkh-i Muʿīnī*, completed 817/1414, and Ḥāfiẓ-i Abrū's *Majmaʿ-i tawārīkh*, which covered the period to 830/1427.[56] Sharaf al-Dīn ʿAlī Yazdī's *Ẓafar-nāma*, completed in 832/1424f., represented an expanded version of Shāmī's work, with which it shared the same title.[57] A number of important illustrated manuscripts of this work have survived from the Timurid period.[58]

The main source for the history of the period to 875/1470 is the *Maṭlaʿ-i saʿdayn wa-majmaʿ-i baḥrayn* by ʿAbd al-Razzāq Samarqandī, who drew on the work of Ḥāfiẓ-i Abrū. The most widely utilised work for the history of the Timurid dynasty as a whole, but particularly for the second half of the fifteenth century, is Khwāndamīr's *Ḥabīb al-siyar*, which represents a continuation of Mīrkhwānd's universal history, *Rawḍat al-ṣafā*, up to the year 930/1524.[59] Other sources containing valuable biographical information relating to the careers of Timurid administrators are Khwāndamīr's *Dastūr al-wuzarāʾ*, completed *c.* 915/1509f., and Sayf al-Dīn ʿUqaylī's *Āthār al-wuzarāʾ*, completed in 883/1478f.[60]

56 *EIr* art. 'Ḥāfeẓ-e Abru' (Maria Eva Subtelny and Charles Melville).

57 John E. Woods, 'The rise of Tīmūrid historiography', *Journal of Near Eastern Studies*, 46, 2 (1987), pp. 81–108; and Shiro Ando, 'Die timuridische Historiographie II. Šaraf al-dīn ʿAlī Yazdī', *Studia Iranica*, 24, 2 (1995), pp. 219–46.

58 See, for example, Thomas W. Lentz and Glenn D. Lowry, *Timur and the princely vision: Persian art and culture in the fifteenth century* (Los Angeles, 1989), pp. 100–5 and 264–7.

59 Khwandamir, *Habibu's-siyar: Tome three*, trans. W. M. Thackston, 2 parts (Cambridge, MA, 1994), part 2.

60 For an overview of historical sources for the Timurid period, see Ch. A. Stori [C. A. Storey], *Persidskaia literatura: Bio-bibliograficheskii obzor*, trans. and rev. Iu. È. Bregel', 3 vols. (Moscow, 1972), vol. I, pp. 339–93 and vol. II, pp. 787–843.

Other sources for Timurid history are the compilations of official documents and chancery correspondence, such as *Mansha' al-inshā'*, which contains documents composed by 'Abd al-Wāsi' Niẓāmī Bākharzī, and *Sharaf-nāma* by 'Abd Allāh Marwārīd, both of whom were connected with the court of Sulṭān-Ḥusayn.[61] *Makhzan al-inshā'*, a manual for chancery scribes, was composed in 907/1501f. by Ḥusayn Wā'iẓ-i Kāshifī.[62] Mention may also be made of the correspondence of Sufi shaykhs and spiritual leaders, such as Jāmī and 'Ubayd Allāh Aḥrār, which are a rich source of information about the social and economic history of the period.[63]

Painting, calligraphy and the arts of the book

The literary legacy of the Timurid period was inextricably linked with the production of book manuscripts, many of which were sumptuously illustrated and illuminated. It is no exaggeration to state that, judged by any standards, the arts of the book were raised under Timurid patronage to the highest levels of artistic accomplishment. In fact, the illustrated manuscripts produced during this period have in many respects come to represent 'Islamic' painting as a whole. It should be noted, however, that the painting of the Timurid period was based on a long-standing Iranian tradition of figural representation, which was heavily influenced by Chinese painting during the post-Mongol period. Among the main literary works illustrated were the Persian epic, *Shāh-nāma*, and the *Khamsas* of Niẓāmī and Amīr Khusraw, which included such favourites as the tales of *Laylī wa-Majnūn*, *Khusraw wa-Shīrīn* and the Alexander romance. A stunning example of what may be termed religious art is an illustrated Islamic ascension narrative (*mi'rāj-nāma*), which dates from the period of Shāh Rukh.[64]

Probably the most important contribution to the development of painting and the arts of the book under Timurid patronage was the institution of the *kitābkhāna*, which functioned as a library, scriptorium and artistic atelier, in which an impressive array of painters, gilders, calligraphers, bookbinders and other craftsmen worked under court sponsorship on the production of

61 For a partial translation of the latter, see Hans Robert Roemer (ed. and trans.), *Staatsschreiben der Timuridenzeit. Das Šaraf-nāmä des 'Abdallāh Marwārīd in kritischer Auswertung* (Wiesbaden, 1952).

62 Colin Paul Mitchell, 'To preserve and protect: Husayn Va'iz-i Kashifi and Perso-Islamic chancellery culture', *Iranian Studies*, 36, 4 (2003), pp. 485–507.

63 A. Urunbaev (ed. and trans.), *Pis'ma-avtografy Abdarrakhmana Dzhami iz 'Al'boma Navoi'* (Tashkent, 1982); and Jo-Ann Gross and Asom Urunbaev (eds. and trans.), *The letters of Khwāja 'Ubayd Allāh Aḥrār and his associates* (Leiden, 2002).

64 Marie-Rose Séguy (ed.), *The miraculous journey of Mahomet: 'Mirâj nâmeh', Bibliothèque Nationale, Paris (Manuscrit Supplément Turc 190)*, trans. Richard Pevear (New York, 1977).

illustrated manuscripts and other luxury items for use by the Timurid court elite. Although the *kitābkhāna* was not a Timurid invention, a number of princely and elite patrons, notably Shāh Rukh's son Baysunghur (d. 837/1434), made it the focal point of what has been referred to as 'the Timurid cultural complex'.[65] Baysunghur also appears to have initiated the development of the Persian album, in which calligraphic specimens, paintings and drawings were assembled together and used for presenting artistic collections and workshop designs.[66] Besides Herat, other important Timurid centres of cultural and scientific patronage in the first half of the fifteenth century were Shīrāz (especially under the princes Iskandar b. 'Umar-Shaykh and Ibrāhīm-Sulṭān b. Shāh Rukh), Iṣfahān, Yazd and Samarqand.[67]

The undisputed locus of cultural activity in the second half of the fifteenth century was the court of Sulṭān-Ḥusayn Bayqara in Herat. The manuscripts produced under his patronage and that of members of the Timurid elite are among the most outstanding specimens of the arts of the book in Islamic cultural history.[68] The painters of this period included Shāh-Muẓaffar, Mīrak Naqqāsh and the extraordinarily gifted Bihzād (d. 1535).[69] As for calligraphers, it would appear that the pinnacle of the calligraphic arts in the eastern Islamic world was attained by the likes of Sulṭān-'Alī Mashhadī and Mīr-'Alī al-Harawī, both of whom were attached to the Timurid scriptorium. Among the favoured manuscripts copied and illustrated during this period were the works of the poets 'Alīshīr Nawā'ī, Niẓāmī, Jāmī and Amīr Khusraw, Rūmī's *Mathnawī* and Ḥusayn Kāshifī's *Anwār-i Suhaylī*.[70]

Architecture

Temür appreciated the legitimating function of architecture, and his architectural legacy reflects a taste for monumentality that was part of an ideological

65 Lentz and Lowry, *Timur and the princely vision*, pp. 50 and 159ff.

66 David J. Roxburgh, *The Persian album, 1400–1600: From dispersal to collection* (New Haven, 2005), pp. 37ff.

67 Aubin, 'Le mécénat timouride', pp. 75–88; and Francis Richard, 'Un témoignage inexploité concernant le mécénat d'Eskandar Solṭān à Eṣfahān', *Oriente moderno*, n.s. 15, 2 (1996), vol. I, pp. 45–72.

68 Oleg Akimushkin *et al.*, *The arts of the book in Central Asia, 14th–16th centuries*, ed. Basil Gray (London, 1979), pp. 179–214.

69 Abolala Soudavar, *Art of the Persian courts: Selections from the Art and History Trust collection* (New York, 1992), pp. 95ff.; and Michael Barry, *Figurative art in medieval Islam and the riddle of Bihzâd of Herât (1465–1535)* (Paris, 2004), pp. 133ff.

70 Hamid Sulaimon and Fozila Sulaimonova, *Alisher Navoii asarlariga ishlangan rasmlar, XV–XIX asrlar / Miniatiury k proizvedeniiam Alishera Navoi XV–XIX vekov / Miniatures illustrations of Alisher Navoi's works of the XV–XIXth centuries* (Tashkent, 1982); and Soudavar, *Art of the Persian courts*, pp. 85–125.

programme of self-aggrandisement. Unfortunately, many buildings in this 'imperial Timurid style', such as the Bībī Khanum congregational mosque and the Aq Saray palace in Samarqand, were often erected hurriedly and either collapsed or soon fell into ruin. Others, like the shrine of Aḥmad Yasawī in Turkistān, loom large on the horizon or are enveloped in gloomy splendour, as in the case of the Gūr-i Amīr mausoleum in Samarqand. In the popular imagination, Temür's monuments were connected with the memory of his brutal conquests and the forcible transfer of architects, engineers and artisans to Samarqand. After Temür's death, the Iranian architect Qawām al-Dīn Shīrāzī (d. 842/1438) was instrumental in creating a distinctive style which architectural historians have labelled 'metropolitan Timurid'. Characterised by geometric complexity, it featured barrelled vaults (*aywān*), large dome chambers (*gunbad*) and rectangular halls with transverse tripartite vaults articulated with plaster stalactite compositions (*muqarnas*). Probably the most representative building constructed by Qawām al-Dīn Shīrāzī that is still standing is the congregational mosque of Gawharshād at the shrine of Imām Riḍā in Mashhad.[71]

An integral feature of Timurid architecture was its decoration, including polychrome surface revetments in mosaic faience, glazed or unglazed brick, cuerda seca and painted plaster, which utilised a wide array of geometric, ornamental and epigraphic designs of great intricacy and abstract beauty. The practical aspects of geometrical patterning, such as the interlocking star- and polygon patterns in two and three dimensions (called *girih*), have been preserved in architectural drawings and design scrolls dating from this period.[72]

Timurid architecture favoured complexes and ensembles, particularly the pairing of madrasa and *khānaqā*, and funerary monuments, especially in the form of the domed mausoleum, were constructed largely under the patronage of elite Timurid women.[73] Another characteristic aspect of Timurid architecture was its close connection with garden design. Temür constructed a large number of garden residences in Samarqand, with names like Bāgh-i dilgushā ('The heart-expanding garden') and Bāgh-i jahānnumā ('The world-revealing

71 For a comprehensive description of surviving Timurid architectural monuments, see Golombek and Wilber, *Timurid architecture*, vol. I, pp. 187–216 and 224–457.

72 Gülru Necipoğlu, *The Topkapı scroll – geometry and ornament in Islamic architecture* (Santa Monica, 1995), pp. 29–57 and 349–59.

73 Maria Eva Subtelny, 'A Timurid educational and charitable foundation: The Ikhlāṣiyya complex of 'Alī Shīr Navā'ī in 15th-century Herat and its endowment', *Journal of the American Oriental Society*, 111, 1 (1991), pp. 42–6; and Subtelny, *Timurids in transition*, pp. 151–2.

garden'). Shāh Rukh's royal garden residence in Herat was called Bāgh-i zāghān ('The ravens' garden'), and Sulṭān-Ḥusayn constructed the Bāgh-i jahānārā ('The world-adorning garden') to serve as his seat of government.[74] Sulṭān-Ḥusayn, who reputedly had a great interest in horticulture and arboriculture, had in his employ a master landscape architect named Mīrak-i Sayyid Ghiyāth (d. *c.* 1550), whose design of the quadripartite garden (*chahārbāgh*) had a profound influence on the architecture of Central Asia and Mughal India.[75]

The decorative and artisanal arts

As in the case of painting, the decorative and artisanal arts of the Timurid period were greatly influenced by Chinese aesthetics. This was probably most evident in ceramics, since large quantities of Ming porcelains had been brought to Central Asia and Iran during the many trade embassies exchanged between the Timurids and the Ming dynasty during the first half of the fifteenth century. A taste for the signature blue-and-white Ming porcelain vessels resulted in the production of 'chinoiserie ceramics' during the Timurid period. These were not mere imitations of Chinese models but imaginative reinterpretations of such traditional Chinese design motifs as the peony or chrysanthemum, the cloud-point, the dragon motif and the classic scroll patterns, which were adapted to the Timurid penchant for repetitive arabesque patterns known as *islīmī*.[76] The most important ceramic workshops operating during the Timurid period were in Nīshāpūr, Samarqand and Mashhad; Herat does not appear to have figured as a centre of ceramic production, although it was certainly a consumer of blue-and-white ceramic objects, as attested by the frequent illustrations of various kinds of porcelain vessels, such as bowls, plates and decanters, in manuscripts produced by the Timurid atelier. Great strides in the study of Timurid ceramics have been made in recent years thanks to the application of petrographic analysis techniques to the body fabric of ceramic wares, thereby permitting the

74 Lisa Golombek, 'The gardens of Timur: New perspectives', *Muqarnas*, 12 (1995), pp. 137–47; and Golombek and Wilber, *Timurid architecture*, vol. I, pp. 174–83.

75 Maria Eva Subtelny, 'Agriculture and the Timurid *chahārbāgh*: The evidence from a medieval Persian agricultural manual', in Attilio Petruccioli (ed.), *Gardens in the time of the great Muslim empires: Theory and design*, (Leiden, 1997), pp. 115–18; and Subtelny, *Le monde est un jardin: Aspects de l'histoire culturelle de l'Iran médiéval* (Paris, 2002), pp. 101–25.

76 Lisa Golombek, Robert B. Mason and Gauvin A. Bailey, *Tamerlane's tableware: A new approach to the chinoiserie ceramics of fifteenth- and sixteenth-century Iran* (Costa Mesa, 1996), pp. 58–9; and Bernard O'Kane, 'Poetry, goemetry and the arabesque: Notes on Timurid aesthetics', *Annales Islamologiques*, 26 (1992), pp. 76–8.

identification of centres of production.[77] Many specimens of Timurid chinoiserie ceramics were preserved in porcelain collections, particularly the collection formerly housed at the Safavid shrine in Ardabīl.[78]

The decorative arts of the Timurid period displayed great interdependence, and architectural decoration and the design motifs featured on chinoiserie ceramics were also found on textiles, carpets, bookbindings, wood carvings and metalwork of the period. The few surviving fabrics and textiles produced by Timurid workshops betray strong Chinese influence. The most desirable fabrics were silk and silk brocade, which were used for ceremonial robes, such as the exquisite cloud collar preserved in the Armoury Chamber of the Moscow Kremlin.[79] The elaborate tents, royal parasols and sumptuous canopies utilised by Temür and the Timurids in their outdoor audiences and entertainments are frequently depicted in paintings.[80] Only tiny fragments of carpets have survived, but again representations in Timurid paintings provide an idea of their intricate designs.[81] Among objects that have survived in greater quantities, mention may be made of those fashioned from jade, which was highly esteemed by the Timurids for its reputed talismanic properties. Many objects, such as candlesticks, basins and ewers were made from metals such as copper and brass, which were frequently inlaid with silver and gold. The most spectacular example of Timurid metalwork is the huge bronze cauldron commissioned by Temür for the shrine of Aḥmad Yasawī.[82] In general, Timurid aesthetics reflected a preoccupation with geometric symmetry, decorative intricacy and artistic refinement that found expression in all areas of cultural creativity.

Conclusion

It was thanks to the rich cultural legacy of the Timurids that this Turko-Mongolian dynasty, which became increasingly marginalised politically towards the end of the fifteenth century, achieved a renown in the Islamic

77 Robert B. Mason, 'The response I: Petrography and provenance of Timurid ceramics', in Golombek, Mason and Bailey, *Tamerlane's tableware*, pp. 16–56.
78 T. Misugi, *Chinese porcelain collections in the Near East: Topkapi and Ardebil*, 3 vols. (Hong Kong, 1981).
79 See Lentz and Lowry, *Timur and the princely vision*, p. 216.
80 Bernard O'Kane, 'From tents to pavilions: Royal mobility and Persian palace design', *Ars Orientalis*, 23 (1993), pp. 249–68.
81 Lentz and Lowry, *Timur and the princely vision*, pp. 220–1.
82 Linda Komaroff, *The golden disk of heaven: Metalwork of Timurid Iran* (Costa Mesa, 1992), pp. 17ff.

world that far exceeded its geopolitical significance. The Timurid court of Herat in particular served as a model for subsequent Islamic dynasties, including those of the Uzbeks, Safavids, Mughals and Ottomans, who aspired to the same level of sophistication in their own court culture and patronage of the arts.[83] In more recent times, the charismatic figure of Temür and the Timurid cultural legacy have become of great relevance to the construction of their national identity by the modern Uzbeks of the post-Soviet republican period.[84]

83 Stephen Frederic Dale, 'The legacy of the Timurids', *Journal of the Royal Asiatic Society*, 3rd ser., 8, 1 (1998), pp. 43–58; and Eleazar Birnbaum, 'The Ottomans and Chagatay literature: An early 16th century manuscript of Navāʾī's *Dīvān* in Ottoman orthography', *Central Asiatic Journal*, 20, 3 (1976), pp. 157–90.

84 Maria Eva Subtelny, 'The Timurid legacy: A reaffirmation and a reassessment', *Cahiers d'Asie Centrale*, 3–4 (1997), pp. 14–17.

PART II

*

THE GUNPOWDER EMPIRES

6

Iran under Safavid rule

SHOLEH A. QUINN

Safavid origins

The Safavid dynasty traces its origins to a fourteenth-century Sufi order established in the northern Iranian city of Ardabīl, located in the province of Azerbaijan (see Map 5). Iran at this time was witnessing one of its not so uncommon periods of political fragmentation and decentralisation, and control of Ardabīl was in the hands of either the post-Ilkhanid Mongol Jalayirids or Turcoman Aq Qoyunlus. As a result of the Mongols placing increasing importance on Tabrīz, and transferring the capital to Sulṭāniyya, both in northern Iran, Azerbaijan was increasingly becoming an important Islamic centre.[1] In Ardabīl, the eponymous founder of the Safaviyya *ṭarīqa*, Shaykh Ṣafī al-Dīn Iṣḥaq Ardabīlī (650–735 / 1252–1334) and his followers lived what approximated to a 'typical' Sufi existence. Even during his lifetime, Shaykh Ṣafī was highly respected and well known in Ardabīl. Adepts of the Safaviyya order, according to Ibn Bazzāz's massive hagiographical source, the *Ṣafvat al-ṣafā*, written during the lifetime of Shaykh Ṣafī's son and successor, Shaykh Ṣadr al-Dīn Mūsā, engaged in prayer, fasting, *dhikr* sessions and other activities. Ibn Bazzāz narrates the many miraculous events of Shaykh Ṣafī's life, all designed to portray him as a devout and pious Sufi. The Safaviyya was just one of many Sufi orders that flourished in post-Mongol Iran and Anatolia. During the time of Shaykh Ṣafī, the order was decidedly Sunnī – although like many contemporary orders it may have professed special love and devotion to the family of ʿAlī – as evidenced by an anecdote from the *Ṣafvat al-ṣafā*, where Ibn Bazzāz relates on the authority of Shaykh Ṣadr al-Dīn that one day, Shaykh Zāhid, who was Shaykh Ṣafī's *pīr* or *murshid*, was communicating with God. When his followers asked him where he had been, he said that his heart had travelled

1 Michel Mazzaoui, *The origins of the Safawids: Šīʿism, Ṣūfism, and the Gulāt* (Wiesbaden, 1972), p. 43.

the entire world in order to choose an appropriate spot for a centre for Shaykh Ṣafī. He decided upon Ardabīl, because the people were pure in their faith (*ṣafā-yi īmān*) and stated that 'in this place (i.e. in Ardabīl), except for the *sunna* and *jamāʿa*, there has not been and there is no dispute and diversity of opinion of the schools (*madhāhib*) such as the ʿAshariyya, Muʿtazila, Qādiriyya, Mushabbaha, Mujassama, Muʿaṭṭala and others'.[2]

The followers of the Safavids were known pejoratively by the Ottomans as Qizilbāsh, literally 'Red Heads', for the colour of their turbans. These were the Turcoman tribal groups, most of which originated in eastern Anatolia, supported the Safaviyya and became their religious followers. There were many different Qizilbāsh tribes; some, such as the Afshārs and the Qājārs, eventually seized power after Safavid rule came to an end. Other groups included the Rūmlūs, the Ustājlūs and the Dhū'l Qadrs. The Qizilbāsh adhered to the same sort of *ghulāt* Shīʿism as their shaykhs.

The next two leaders of the Safaviyya, Shaykh Ṣadr al-Dīn Mūsā (d. 794/1391f.) and Shaykh Khvāja ʿAlī (d. 832/1429), continued in Shaykh Ṣafī's footsteps while the prestige and influence of the order grew in significant ways. Under Shaykh Ṣadr al-Dīn Mūsā, Jalayirid officials acknowledged the influence of the Safaviyya, and even issued *firmāns* acknowledging the influence of the order.[3] Although during this time the order experienced some persecution and difficulties, it managed to survive these and emerge even more prosperous and influential under Shaykh Khvāja ʿAlī.[4] At the same time, Iran's political landscape was changing, and leaders of the Safaviyya not only married into ruling families but also had interactions with political powers in the region. It is interesting to note that later Safavid chroniclers highlighted and in some cases exaggerated or reinvented these relationships. For example, although not mentioned in any Timurid source, several Safavid chroniclers of the sixteenth and seventeenth centuries narrate an account of either Shaykh Ṣadr al-Dīn or Khvāja ʿAlī's meetings with Temür (r. 771–807/1370–1405).[5] For example, according to the well-known chronicler of Shāh ʿAbbās, Iskandar Beg Munshī, in the first two of three encounters, Shaykh Khvāja ʿAlī first met Temür when the famous conqueror crossed the Oxus on his way to Transoxiana. Apparently, in this meeting, a vision

2 Ibn Bazzāz Tavakkul ibn Ismāʿīl, *Ṣafvat al-ṣafā*, ed. Ghulām Riẓā Ṭabāṭabā'ī Majd (Ardabīl, [1373] 1994), p. 178. This passage (with slight modifications) is translated in Mazzaoui, *Origins of the Safawids*, p. 49.

3 Mazzaoui, *Origins of the Safawids*, p. 53.

4 *Ibid.*, p. 54.

5 Woods has listed, according to the early Timurid sources, the important religious individuals and shrines that Temür visited around this time. They number nearly thirty, and none of them are Safavid. Personal communication from John E. Woods.

of Shaykh Khvāja ʿAlī appeared to Temür, and presented him with his whip that had fallen into the water. Temür interpreted this as a good omen. The dervish told him, 'My home is Ardabīl, the place where I shall appear is Dezful, and the place where I shall be buried is Jerusalem.'[6] In the second meeting, Temür was on his way from Baghdad to Khūzistān when a dervish appeared wearing a black Sufi robe. He told Timür that he was the dervish who had given him the whip which had fallen into the Oxus, and stated that they would meet again in Ardabīl.[7] Iskandar Beg's account of the third meeting describes how Temür came to release Anatolian prisoners. He also adds a section on the discovery of a *waqf* (endowment) document, now considered a forgery, indicating that Temür endowed the revenues of a parcel of land for the benefit of the Safavid family.[8] While it is probable that such meetings never took place, they indicate something of the standing that the early Safavid shaykhs had for later dynastic writers.[9]

The activities of the Safaviyya during the leadership of Junayd (d. 893/1460) started to change when the order became involved in *ghāzī* warfare against Byzantine Trebizond and the Georgian Caucasus.[10] By this time, too, the order had taken on many of the beliefs associated with *ghuluww*ism, or exaggerated religious beliefs. The history of *ghuluww* expression in Islamicate history is complex. In previous centuries, *ghuluww* thinkers had become known for their ideas about the nature of the imam; this includes the idea that the imam was, if not divine, then at least of the rank of prophethood and with the authority that accompanied that status. They also expounded ideas that suggested the anthropomorphism of God, resurrection, reincarnation and the transmigration of souls. Influences from certain varieties of Zoroastrianism, Judaism and Christianity also informed the development of *ghuluww* notions.[11] By the Safavid period, such beliefs had already been absorbed into forms of Imamism, and many Sufi orders, though not necessarily Shīʿī, showed particular reverence for ʿAlī and displayed *ghuluww* tendencies. The religious, Sufi and associated esoteric factions that shared some common characteristics with the Safaviyya in the fifteenth century included the Ahl-i Ḥaqq, the Mushaʿshaʿ, the Ḥurūfiyya, the Bābāʾis and others. These groups all

6 Iskandar Beg Munshī, *Tārīkh-i ʿālam-ārā-yi ʿAbbāsī*, 2nd edn, 2 vols., ed. Īraj Afshār (Tehran, 1350 [1971]), vol. I, p. 15; trans. Roger Savory as *History of Shah ʿAbbas the great (Tarik-e ʿalamara-ye ʿAbbasi)*, 3 vols., Persian Heritage Series, 28 (Boulder, CO, 1978), vol. I, p. 27 (hereafter cited as 'trans.').

7 Iskandar Beg Munshī, *ʿĀlam-ārā-yi ʿAbbāsī*, p. 15, trans., p. 27.

8 See Heribert Horst, *Timur und Hôgä ʿAli. Ein beitrag zur geschichte der Safawiden* (Mainz, 1958).

9 See *ibid.*

10 See Mazzaoui, *Origins of the Safawids*, p. 74.

11 See *EI*[2] 'ghulāt' (Marshall Hodgson).

shared certain similar features, including the propagation of *ghuluww* beliefs through charismatic leaders, a number of whom made messianic claims or claims of divinity for themselves, and they enjoyed widespread popular appeal.[12] The Safavid Junayd appears to have presented himself as something of a divine incarnation. The hostile Aq Qoyunlu writer Faẓl Allāh b. Rūzbihān Khunjī, author of the *ʿĀlam-ārā-yi Amīnī*, states that 'they openly called Shaykh Junayd "God" and his son "Son of God"'.[13] At the same time that the Safaviyya was displaying *ghuluww* proclivities, Safavid leaders continued to forge marital alliances with the ruling families of the time. For example, Junayd married the Aq Qoyunlu ruler Uzun Ḥasan's sister, and Junayd's son Ḥaydar (d. 893/1488) married Uzun Ḥasan's daughter.

Shāh Ismāʿīl's rise to power and subsequent reign

The Safavid family continued to involve themselves in Aq Qoyunlu politics, including succession struggles, until Ismāʿīl (r. 907–30/1501–24) took the throne and crowned himself king. As Aq Qoyunlu power weakened, however, and in the political confusion that ensued during this time, Ismāʿīl and his brother Ibrāhīm were smuggled away to Gīlān, in the Caspian Sea region.[14] Ismāʿīl was tutored and protected by the Shīʿī Sufis of Lāhījān. Eventually, he marched out from Lāhījān with his followers, taking advantage of Aq Qoyunlu civil war and general weakness, and started moving into Arzinjān in Anatolia, and then on towards Ardabīl. He continued to gather supporters and after waging successful campaigns in Shīrvān and Bākū, he finally headed for Tabrīz.[15]

When he reached Tabrīz, Ismāʿīl crowned himself king, or Shāh, in 907/1501. At the same time, he declared Twelver Shiʿism the official state religion. The early Safavid chronicler Ghiyāth al-Dīn Khwāndamīr explains how 'a regal decree was issued that all preachers in the realm of Azerbaijan pronounce the *khuṭba* in the name of the Twelve Imams'. Furthermore, the muezzins were ordered to add the phrase 'And I profess that ʿAlī is the Friend of God' to the call to prayer.[16]

The whole issue of Shāh Ismāʿīl's religious policies has received a great deal of scholarly attention. Ismāʿīl's own religious persuasion before this time was

12 For more information on this process, see Kathryn Babayan, *Mystics, monarchs, and messiahs: Cultural landscapes of early modern Iran* (Cambridge, MA, 2002), pp. 245–81.

13 See Mazzaoui, *Origins of the Safawids*, p. 73.

14 *Ibid.*, p. 80.

15 *Ibid.*, pp. 81–2.

16 Ghiyāth al-Dīn ibn Humām al-Dīn Khvāndamīr, *Tārīkh-i ḥabīb al-siyar*, 4 vols., ed. Jalāl al-Dīn Humāʾī ([Tehran], 1333 [1954]), vol. I, p. 468; trans. Wheeler Thackston as *Habibu's-siyar*, 2 vols. (Cambridge, MA., 1994), vol. I, p. 576.

marked by significant *ghuluww* concepts, as his poetry attests. In his *dīwān*, where he refers to himself as 'Khaṭā'ī', Ismā'īl makes numerous high prophetological, imamological, messianic and related claims, where he suggests that he is the Mahdī, the return of Christ, and other religious and political figures of the past, as seen in the following poem:

> Shāh Ismā'īl is my name, I am the mystery of Truth / Of all of these Ghazis I am the commander
> Fāṭima is my mother, 'Alī is my father / Of the Twelve Imams I am the Pir
> Upon Yazīd I revenged my father's blood / Know well that I am of Ḥaydarian essence
> The living Khiḍr and Jesus son of Mary / The Alexander of the people of the age
> Behold Yazīd and the polytheists and the damned! / Quit am I of the Qibla of the hypocrites
> With me is Prophethood (*nubuvvat*) and the secret of successorship (*vilāyat*) / Successor am I to Muḥammad Muṣṭafā
> With my sword have I subdued the world / I am the Qanbar (menial slave) of 'Alī Murtaḍā
> Ṣafī is my grandfather, Ḥaydar is my father / Of the people of courage, truly I am Ja'far
> Ḥusaynid am I – my curse upon Yazīd! / Khaṭā'ī am I, a servant of the shāh[17]

The establishment of Shī'ism as the official state religion

Shāh Ismā'īl's early religiosity raises certain questions in light of the fact that the most significant policy change that he instituted once he crowned himself king was the proclamation of Shī'ī Islam as the official state religion. The chroniclers themselves are not particularly forthcoming about the matter; Iskandar Beg Munshī simply states the following: 'The practice of the Twelver rite of shi'ism was made public. The pulpits in the mosques resounded with sermons in which the exalted names of the Shī'ite Imams were commemorated. The dinars were stamped with the inscription, "There is no god but God; Mohammad is the Prophet of God, and 'Alī is the favorite friend of God", and with the name of that chosen One of his descendants (Esma'il himself).'[18] The reason behind this decision has been the subject of some debate and

17 Shāh Ismā'īl, *Il Canzoniere di Šāh Ismā'īl Ḫaṭā'ī*, ed. Tourkhan Gandjeï (Naples, 1959), no. 16, trans. Robert Dankoff in 'Readings in Islamic civilization: From the rise of Islam to the beginning of the 10th/16th century', Robert Dankoff, gen. ed., unpublished ms. Slightly modified.

18 Iskandar Beg Munshī, *'Ālam-ārā-yi 'Abbāsī*, pp. 27–8; trans., p. 44.

discussion. Some have suggested that Ismāʿīl wanted to distinguish his new state from Sunnī neighbours to the east and west, and therefore he chose to convert Iran to Shīʿism.[19] Another possible reason could be that while *ghuluww* Shīʿism was an acceptable form of religious expression for Ismāʿīl's Qizilbāsh supporters, he needed something that provided more formal organisation for ruling a state. Whatever his reasons, the changes he imposed on Iran were successful, for today the majority of Iran's population is Shīʿī, unlike the Sunnī majority in Iran at the time of Shāh Ismāʿīl.

The question of outside influences

Although Shāh Ismāʿīl used many Persians who had been administrators during previous dynasties to run the bureaucracy of the new empire, in order to promote Shīʿism, he invited scholars and experts from Qum, a traditional Shīʿī centre in Iran, and southern Lebanon, in particular the Jabal ʿĀmil region, which had been a centre of Shīʿism since the tenth century, to travel throughout Iran and promote Shīʿism.[20] He also appointed such individuals to be muezzins and prayer leaders in mosques. There has been considerable discussion surrounding the migration of Shīʿī clerics to Iran in the Safavid period. Debate has surrounded the question of which Shīʿī scholars from outside Iran, in particular Jabal ʿĀmil, came to Iran, and how many there were. The standard view was that the numbers were quite large, but it has been recently argued that individuals such as the famous ʿAlī ibn ʿAbd al-ʿAlī al-Karakī (d. 940/1534), the first Shīʿī from Jabal ʿĀmil who went to Iran, were more the exception than the rule.[21] At this point, it remains uncertain exactly how many scholars came to Iran, why they came, how long they stayed and what their activities were once they arrived.[22] What does seem to be the case is that although most of the Shīʿī scholars in Iran were not from Jabal ʿĀmil, many of the Shīʿī scholars in the Jabal ʿĀmil region did in fact leave for Safavid Iran, resulting in a 'brain drain' of sorts.[23]

19 See, for example, *EI*[2] 'Ismāʿīl I' (Roger Savory).

20 For details on Shāh Ismāʿīl's early administration, see Jean Aubin, 'Études Safavides I – Sah Isma'il et les notables de l'Iraq Persan', *Journal of Economic and Social History of the Orient*, 2 (1959), pp. 37–8. For the movement of scholars from Jabal 'Āmil to Iran, see Albert Hourani, 'From Jabal 'Āmil to Persia', *Bulletin of the School of Oriental and African Studies*, 49 (1986), pp. 133–40.

21 Andrew J. Newman, 'The myth of the clerical migration to Safawid Iran: Arab Shiite opposition to 'Ali al-Karaki and Safawid Shiism', *Die Welt des Islams*, 33 (1993), pp. 66–112.

22 Devin J. Stewart, 'Notes on the migration of 'Amili scholars to Safavid Iran', *Journal of Near Eastern Studies*, 55 (1996), p. 3.

23 *Ibid.*, p. 4.

In terms of the impact these Shīʿī experts had in Iran, it appears that they were in fact quite influential. For example, al-Karakī was the leading Shīʿī authority in Iran during his time, and, furthermore, the leading jurists during the first 120 years of the dynasty were from Jabal ʿĀmil.[24] Moreover, the influx was not immediate or early, as the bulk of the migrations took place after the reign of Shāh Ismāʿīl in the second half of the sixteenth and the seventeenth centuries.[25]

Once these individuals arrived in Iran, they received prestigious court positions. Al-Karakī and others were instrumental in converting Iran to Imāmī Shīʿism, as distinct from the earlier Safavid Qizilbāsh form of Shīʿism that was tinged with *ghulāt* beliefs. However, not all jurists who settled in Iran agreed with each other over religious matters; indeed, robust debates took place as early as the reign of Shāh Ṭahmāsp, when, for example, al-Karakī and his former student Amīr Niʿmat Allāh al-Hillī the *ṣadr* debated whether or not Friday prayers should take place in light of the absence of the twelfth imam.[26] Al-Karakī was powerful and influential enough to garner opposition from *ṣadr*s and other notables as he gained increasingly important positions from the king.[27] The king sided with al-Karakī, who ended up finding support from among the Qizilbāsh. The Qizilbāsh seemed to favour the king's policies of further establishing a Shīʿī orthodoxy in Iran.[28] Al-Karakī and his colleagues gradually helped to 'invent' a new Shīʿī identity for the Safavids that included practices that helped to differentiate the Shīʿī Safavids from their Ottoman enemies. Popular expressions of religiosity included the ritual cursing of the first three Sunnī caliphs, and others developed over time.

Ismāʿīl's initial conquests resulted in his taking over most of Iran, what had been former Aq Qoyunlu territory, part of Ottoman territory in eastern Anatolia, Baghdad and Khūzistān.[29] He later challenged the Uzbeks, killed Muḥammad Shaybānī (Shibani) Khan the Uzbek leader in 916/1510, and took over Herat the same year. Although this did not end the Uzbek threat and one of Ismāʿīl's generals was in fact defeated by the Uzbeks in 918/1512, essentially the Uzbeks were kept behind their border. Of all his enemies, it was the Ottomans who posed the greatest threat and danger to Safavid rule. The

24 *Ibid.*, p. 6.
25 *Ibid.*, p. 7.
26 Rula Jurdi Abisaab, *Converting Persia: Religion and power in the Safavid empire* (London, 2004), p. 17.
27 *Ibid.*, pp. 17–18.
28 *Ibid.*, p. 20.
29 This summary is based on the very useful overview of Ismāʿīl's conquests in Hans R. Roemer, 'The Safavid period', in Peter Jackson and Laurence Lockhart, (eds.), *The Cambridge history of Iran*, vol. VI: *The Timurid and Safavid periods* (Cambridge, 1986), pp. 189–350.

Ottomans were worried, of course, about the possibility of rebellion and defection on the part of eastern Anatolian Turcoman Qizilbāsh to the Safavid cause. This fear was well founded, for in 917/1511, a rebellion led by a Qizilbāsh named Shāh Qulī Khan took place in the province of Teke-Ili. His death in turn led to further rebellions within Ottoman territory, most notably in Rūm. When Sultan Selīm succeeded to the sultanate after the abdication of his father Bāyezīd in 918/1512, he persecuted Qizilbāsh in Anatolia and eventually led a campaign against Shāh Ismāʿīl in 920/1514. This was the famous battle of Chāldirān, greatly celebrated in Ottoman chronicles, where Ismāʿīl and his army suffered a decisive defeat.

The vicissitudes of Ṭahmāsp's reign and after

Although the Safavids experienced military defeat at Chāldirān, the political outcome of the battle was a stalemate between the Ottomans and Safavids, even though the Ottomans ultimately won some territory from the Safavids. The stalemate was largely due to the 'scorched-earth' strategy that the Safavids employed, making it impossible for the Ottomans to remain in the region.[30] Nevertheless, the defeat was a personal setback for Ismāʿīl, who appears to have spent the rest of his life thereafter involved only in the internal affairs of his state.

It was not until Ismāʿīl's son, Ṭahmāsp (r. 930–84/1524–76), took the throne that the policies his father established were fully enforced and started to become integrated into Iranian society. Ṭahmāsp was ten years old when he came to the throne on Monday, 19 Rajab 930/23 May 1524, and therefore could not immediately establish himself as king. A co-regency was established consisting of Dīv Sulṭān Rūmlū and Kapak Sulṭān Ustājlū.[31] The two factions represented by these individuals came into conflict that eventually led to outright civil war between the Rūmlūs and their supporters and the Ustājlūs and their backers. Although the civil war kept the various Qizilbāsh factions at bay, during the early years of Shāh Ṭahmāsp's reign, Qizilbāsh leaders still managed to become extremely powerful and for all practical purposes ruled the various provinces under their control independently. It took Shāh Ṭahmāsp some nine years to re-establish his authority.

30 See *EI*² 'Caldiran' (J. R. Walsh).

31 Martin B. Dickson, 'Sháh Tahmásb and the Úzbeks: The duel for Khurásán with 'Ubayd Khán (930–946/1524–1540)', Ph.D. dissertation., Princeton University (1958), p. 52.

Externally, Shāh Ṭahmāsp had to face the Uzbek challenge coming from the east and the Ottomans to the west. The Uzbeks were first to take advantage of Ṭahmāsp's initial weakness when he ascended the throne. The research of Martin Dickson has shown that there were actually two distinct Uzbek states bordering on Khurāsān that the Safavid monarch had to contend with: the Yādgārid Uzbeks of Khwārazm and the 'Abū'l Khayrid Uzbeks of Mā Warā' al-Nahr. It was the latter, led by 'Ubayd Khan, that posed the greatest threat to the Safavids.[32] Although Ṭahmāsp was successful in retaking Herat at one stage, the Uzbeks posed a fairly constant threat to the eastern borders of the Safavid state, invading Safavid territory a total of five times during Ṭahmāsp's reign.[33]

Ṭahmāsp also had to deal with external threats from the Ottomans, in particular when Sultan Süleyman 'kānūnī' (law-giver), or 'the Magnificent' as he is known in the West (r. 926–74/1520–66), came to power. Despite four campaigns against the Safavids, the Ottomans were never able to make significant inroads into Safavid territory, for several reasons. First of all, they were trying to expand their empire in a westward direction as well as towards the east, and so their resources were thinly stretched. Second, the route from Istanbul to Iran was long and difficult. It involved crossing mountain passes which became covered with snow and impossible to penetrate in the winter. Furthermore, the previously mentioned 'scorched-earth' strategy that the Safavids employed deprived the Ottomans of any resources that they might have acquired from the land on the passage to Iran. Hostilities against the Ottomans came to an end with the signing of the treaty of Amasya, which fixed the north-west border of the Safavid state and divided Georgia between the Safavids and the Ottomans.[34] Although the Safavids were successful in keeping back the Ottomans, in 962/1555 Shāh Ṭahmāsp nevertheless transferred the Safavid capital from Tabrīz to Qazvīn, which better protected the Safavid capital from any future Ottoman threats.

Of all Ṭahmāsp's neighbours during this period, the Mughals perhaps presented the least danger to the Safavid state. The Mughal emperor Humāyūn, facing problems both externally and internally, was forced to flee India and in 951/1544 sought refuge at Shāh Ṭahmāsp's court. In an act of great humiliation, he was forced to acknowledge his loyalty to Shīʿī Islam. After presenting Ṭahmāsp with handsome gifts, including a large diamond

32 *Ibid.*, p. 23.

33 These took place in 930/1524, 930–2/1524–6, 933–5/1526–8, 935–7/1529–31, 937–41/1531–4 and 941–4/1535–8. See *ibid.*, pp. 1–4.

34 *EI*[2] 'Ṭahmāsp', (Roger Savory).

that weighed, according to the Safavid sources, approximately three-quarters of a pound, Humāyūn was sent on his way back to India with support troops.[35]

Shāh Ṭahmāsp's religious policies

Ṭahmāsp was a very different character from his father. He did not want to be regarded as a semi-divine figure, and he took steps to crush any sort of religious expression that considered him a messianic figure thereby transfiguring notions of Safavid kingly legitimacy. This took some time to accomplish; the Italian traveller Michele Membré, who visited Ṭahmāsp's camp when it was near Marand, describes how Anatolian Turcomans came to join Ṭahmāsp: 'Thus, there were of those Turcomans, horsemen, with their arms and lances, to the number of 600, who were stationed over against the court of the said Sophy, at a distance, riding round and round; all together they kept crying "Allāh, Allāh"... until the Shah came forth from his apartments, at the entrance.'[36] Furthermore, although Shāh Ṭahmāsp may have suppressed groups who proclaimed him as the Mahdī, he continued to promote the notion that he had a special relationship with this figure.[37] Membré describes how Shāh Taḥmāsp would not allow one of his sisters to marry 'because, he says, he is keeping her to be the wife of the Mahdi. This Mahdi is a descendant of ʿAli and Muhammad, and he says he keeps her on the grounds that he is the court and the true place of Muhammad. Thus, too, he has a white horse, which he keeps for the said Mahdi ... no one rides this horse and they always put it in front of all his horses.'[38] In addition to downplaying the *ghuluww* tendencies exhibited during Ismāʿīl's reign and earlier, during Ṭahmāsp's reign, both *ghuluww* expressions of religiosity and Sunnism were persecuted, leading to many individuals leaving Iran for Mughal India. Ṭahmāsp further solidified Iran's new Shīʿī identity by formally including within his military corps groups of *tabarrāʾiyān*. These individuals were in charge of ensuring that the practice of ritual cursing of the first three Sunnī caliphs was carried out throughout Iran, and they also engaged in surveillance activities in an attempt to detect any Sunnī activity. They received the direct support of Ṭahmāsp himself.[39]

35 Iskandar Beg Munshī, *ʿĀlam-ārā-yi ʿAbbāsī*, p. 99; trans., p. 164.
36 Michele Membré, *Mission to the Lord Sophy of Persia (1539–1542)*, trans. A. H. Morton (London, 1993), p. 18.
37 Moojan Momen, *An introduction to Shiʿi Islam* (New Haven, 1985), pp. 109–10.
38 Membré, *Mission to the Lord Sophy*, pp. 25–6.
39 Rosemary Stanfield-Johnson, 'The Tabarra'iyan and the early Safavids', *Iranian Studies*, 37 (2004), pp. 48–9.

Despite this relative difference in Ismāʿīl and Ṭahmāsp's relationship with the Qizilbāsh with regards to their messianic position, Ṭahmāsp continued the practice of marrying into prominent Qizilbāsh families. Recent scholarship on the Safavid family has traced kinship ties with the Safavids and the Tekelu Qizilbāsh tribe, and shown that the Safavids pursued this policy in order to broaden their base of support and enjoy continued Qizilbāsh loyalty.[40] Although this policy changed by the end of the sixteenth century, during the reigns of Shāh Ismāʿīl and Shāh Ṭahmāsp, it brought advantages to the Qizilbāsh in terms of wealth and prestige for the offspring of these alliances and Qizilbāsh loyalty and an ever-growing kinship network for the Safavid royal family.

Early Safavid political legitimacy, until the time of Shāh ʿAbbās, rested on three pillars: the king as the shadow of God on earth in line with pre-Islamic Persian notions of kingship; the king as the shaykh of the Safaviyya Sufi order; and the king as the representative of the seventh imam, Mūsā al-Kāẓim, from whom the Safavids claimed descent. This ideological platform is reflected in both Safavid historical writing and painting. During Shāh Ṭahmāsp's reign, chroniclers rewrote the Safavid past in order to show that the Safavid Sufi founders had always been practising Twelver Shīʿīs. For example, Amīr Maḥmūd, son of a well-known late Timurid/early Safavid chronicler Khwāndamīr, used his father's *Ḥabīb al-siyar* as a model which he rewrote in significant ways for his own history, known as the *Dhayl-i ḥabīb al-siyar*. For example, in his *Ṣafvat al-ṣafā*, Ibn Bazzāz describes in detail the illness, death and burial of Shaykh Zāhid, Shaykh Ṣafī's *pīr/murshid* (Sufi guide). Amīr Maḥmūd transformed the account of rituals performed before the burial, and the burial itself, into a specifically Twelver Shīʿī funeral. The following parallel passages illustrate the process of historical revision reflecting the religious transformation that Iran was undergoing during Shāh Ṭahmāsp's rule:

> *Ṣafvat al-ṣafā*
> Shaykh Ṣafī performed all of the religious, customary and ceremonial duties that were necessary and if the Shaykh forgot something because of fear, the spirit of Shaykh Zāhid taught him until he did it, and he assisted and helped him in all that he did and did not do until the necessary duties and customs were completely finished. Then he performed a formal burial in his luminous, fragrant sepulchre.[41]

40 See Maria Szuppe, 'Kinship ties between the Safavids and the Qizilbash amirs in late sixteenth-century Iran: A case study of the political career of members of the Sharaf al-Din Oghli Tekelu family', in Charles Melville (ed.), *Safavid Persia: The history and politics of an Islamic society* (London, 1996), pp. 79–104.

41 Ibn Bazzāz, *Ṣafvat al-ṣafā*, p. 248.

> *Ḥabīb al-siyar*
> Shaykh Ṣafī al-Dīn proceeded with the necessities of preparing and shrouding [the body], and performed the customs of mourning.[42]
> *Dhayl-i ḥabīb al-siyar*
> Shaykh Ṣafī al-Dīn commanded that his pure body be washed according to the custom of the Prophet and in conformity with Twelver practice, and shrouded him, and offered prayers at his blessed funeral; and they buried him in a suitable place in that region, and proceeded to build a tomb for that unique one of the age.[43]

As seen in these passages, the original episode in *Ṣafvat al-ṣafā* describes how after Shaykh Zāhid died they buried him, thus completing the requisite duties of a formal burial (*dafn-i sūrī*). In Amīr Maḥmūd's chronicle, Shaykh Ṣafī washed the body according to the customs of the Prophet (*sunnat-i rasūl*) and in conformity with Twelver practice.[44] Historians writing during Shāh ʿAbbās's reign reproduced this particular version of the narrative in their accounts, and in this way they continued to propagate the notion that the early Safavids were practising Twelver Shīʿīs.

In 940/1533, Shāh Ṭahmāsp himself commissioned a certain Abū al-Fatḥ al-Ḥusaynī to 'update' the *Ṣafvat al-ṣafā* in certain ways. Al-Ḥusaynī altered the preface which contained the genealogy, and the epilogue. This royal command to revise the *Ṣafvat al-ṣafā* reflects the Safavids' preoccupation with their earlier history and legitimising principles. However, even before al-Ḥusaynī made his revisions, changes had been made to the Safavid genealogy which extended Fīrūz Shāh's ancestry back to the seventh imam of the Imāmī Shīʿa, Mūsā al-Kāzim, and added the title 'sayyid' to the names of the shaykhs and their ancestors. Indeed, as Roger Savory has pointed out, reworkings of the Safavid genealogy included the addition of four unknown individuals simply named 'Muḥammad' to extend the genealogy back to Mūsā al-Kāzim.[45]

As the borders of the Safavid state expanded, and as Safavid historiography evolved to reflect changing notions of politics, kingship and religion, so too did Safavid artistic achievements. For example, Safavid miniature painting during this time found its greatest expression in the form of a *Shāh-nāma* completed during the reign of Shāh Ṭahmāsp. Shāh Ismāʿīl initially commissioned the work as a gift for his nine-year-old son, Prince Ṭahmāsp. The manuscript eventually

42 Khwāndamīr, *Ḥabīb al-siyar*, p. 417.
43 Amīr Maḥmūd ibn Khwāndamīr, *Īrān dar rūzgār-i Shāh Ismāʿīl va Shāh Ṭahmāsb Ṣafavī*, ed. Ghulām Riżā Ṭabāṭabāʾī (Tehran, 1370 [1991]), p. 42.
44 *Ibid.*
45 Roger Savory, *Iran under the Safavids* (Cambridge and New York, 1980), p. 3.

found its way to the Ottoman empire, where it may have been presented to the Ottoman sultan Murād III (r. 982–1003/1574–95) as a coronation gift from Shāh Ṭahmāsp in 984/1576.[46] Martin Dickson and Stuart Cary Welch, in their massive undertaking to study this important illuminated manuscript, were able to identify at least four senior painters and five younger artists who worked on the 'Houghton *Shāh-nāma*' as it is sometimes called, although only two of the paintings are actually signed.[47] In this great manuscript, often groups of artists worked on individual paintings, although some of the finest illustrations were executed by one artist.[48] It was probably the great artist Sulṭān Muḥammad who directed the project at first, assigning specific illustrations to particular artists, depending on their abilities.[49] He was then succeeded by Mīr Musawwir, who was replaced by Āqā Mīrak.[50] Some artists specialised in backgrounds, others in portraits, and still others in battle scenes or tragic events. Completed pages of illustrations were then passed on to specialists who gilded and framed the pages and added various ornaments to the pages.[51] This particular *Shāh-nāma* contains perhaps the greatest and certainly the most famous miniature painting in all of Persian art: Sulṭān Muḥammad's 'The Court of Gayūmars'. According to Welch and Dickson, the painting represents a combination of Tabrīz Turcoman and Timurid Herati artistic traditions. The painting shows the first king of Iran, Gayūmars, seated on a mountain top. On either side of him stand two lines of individuals dressed in leopard skins. The rocks and mountains in the background of the painting contain hidden pictures of people and monsters, perhaps 'earth spirits'.[52] It is no coincidence that the Safavid kings would choose to direct their royal patronage to a *Shāh-nāma*; ever since the Mongols invaded Iran, the production of illustrated *Shāh-nāmas* was an important way in which kings legitimised their rule. For the Mongols in particular, who were ruling as outsiders, producing a *Shāh-nāma* helped legitimise rule over their Iranian subjects. And the Safavids, who claimed in part to be ruling as the shadow of God on earth in line with pre-Islamic notions of kingship, were no exception.

Although some Safavid artists, namely painters, found patronage with the first two Safavid kings, others, whether out of religious conviction, or religious

46 Stuart Cary Welch, *A king's book of kings: The Shah-nameh of Shah Tahmasp* (New York, 1972), pp. 16–17. See also M. B. Dickson and S. C. Welch, *The Houghton Shahnameh* (Cambridge, MA, 1981).

47 *Ibid.*, p. 21.

48 *Ibid.*, p. 25.

49 *Ibid.*, p. 20.

50 *Ibid.*

51 *Ibid.*, p. 21.

52 *Ibid.*, pp. 88–91.

persecution, or the promise of higher salaries, left Iran for neighbouring Mughal India. For example, the late Timurid/early Safavid historian Khwāndamīr, who was a Zaydī Shīʿī, went to India in 935/1528 and met Bābur (r. 932–7/1526–30). Bābur, whom Khwāndamīr often accompanied on various campaigns, mentions Khwāndamīr's presence in his autobiographical memoirs, the *Bābur-nāma*.[53] Shortly after their meeting, Bābur died and was succeeded by his son Humāyūn, to whom Khwāndamīr dedicated his *Humāyūn-nāma*, also known as the *Qānūn-Humāyūnī* (940/1534).[54] Khwāndamīr enjoyed great prestige under Humāyūn, who eventually made him the *amīr-i muwārrikh*, or 'chief chronicler'.[55] As a result, Khwāndamīr bridged the historiographical traditions of the Safavids and the Mughals by writing for both dynasties.

During Akbar's reign (r. 963–1014/1556–1605), Mughal historians utilised, or at least were familiar with, Mīrkhwānd's *Rawżat al-ṣafā*, a late Timurid work, because a certain Mīr Ghiyāth al-Dīn ʿAlī 'Naqīb Khan' had apparently committed to memory the seven volumes of *Rawżat al-ṣafā*, thus reflecting the popularity that this work enjoyed in at least some Mughal circles.[56] Naqīb Khan came from a well-known family that had originally served the Safavids. His father was Mīr ʿAbd al-Laṭīf Qazvīnī, one of Akbar's tutors, and his uncle was Mīrzā ʿAlā al-Dawla 'Kāmī' Qazvīnī, author of the *Nafāʾiṣ al-maʾāthir*, a biographical dictionary of Persian poets.[57] Naqīb Khan's grandfather was Yaḥyā ibn ʿAbd al-Laṭīf Ḥusaynī Qazvīnī. The latter lived in Iran during the reign of Shāh Ṭahmāsp, and wrote the *Lubb al-tavārīkh*. Ḥusaynī Qazvīnī, a Sunnī, was eventually put in prison by Shāh Ṭahmāsp and died there two years later in 962/1555. Ten years later, his family left Iran for India (in 973/1565), at Humāyūn's invitation.[58]

Safavid society under Shāh Ismāʿīl and Shāh Ṭahmāsp

After Shāh Ismāʿīl established his rule over Iran, the Turkic Qizilbāsh tribes (*uymāq*) that supported him in his bid for power were granted significant posts

53 See Babur, *The Baburnama: Memoirs of Babur, prince and emperor*, trans. and ed. Wheeler M. Thackston (New York, 1996), pp. 403, 442.
54 Khvāndamīr, *Qānūn-i Humāyūnī*, ed. M. Hidayat Hosain (Calcutta, 1940).
55 *Ibid.*, p. xv.
56 Khaliq Ahmad Nizami, *On history and historians of medieval India* (New Delhi, 1982), p. 225.
57 See D. N. Marshall, *Mughals in India: A bibliographical survey of manuscripts* (London, 1967; repr. New York, 1985), p. 54.
58 C. A. Storey, *Persian literature: A bio-bibliographical survey*, 3 vols. (London, 1927), p. 111; rev. and trans. Yu E. Bregel as *Persidskaya literatura: Bio-bibliograficheskii obzo*, 3 vols. (Moscow, 1972), p. 399.

in the new government. In particular, they held the position of *amīr al-ʿumarā*ʾ, or 'chief Qizilbāsh leader', a term that was interchangeably used with *wakīl* (deputy). Prominent Qizilbāsh leaders furthermore received prestigious provincial governorships and the responsibilities of controlling that province and mobilising their troops at the request of the king.[59] All together, they formed what could be called a 'military/governing elite' in the new Safavid state. In addition to prominent Qizilbāsh, the other main element in Safavid society consisted of the Persian-speaking elite who formed the administrative classes under previous ruling dynasties. The most important positions within this social group were the vizier, or chief administrator, and the *ṣadr*, who was the chief religious figure.[60] Although the oft-repeated quote by Minorsky that these two groups, the so-called 'Turks and Tājīks', mixed 'like oil and water' and that their spheres of power were quite separate may have held true to some degree, there were certainly significant exceptions.[61] These included, for example, the famous court secretary and historiographer Iskandar Beg Munshī, who was a Turcoman. Ḥasan Beg Rūmlū, another important chronicler from the era of Shāh Ṭahmāsp, was also of Qizilbāsh background, as evidenced by his name 'Rūmlū'.

After Shāh Ṭahmāsp's reign of fifty-two years, the longest reign of any Safavid or indeed any Persian king of the Islamic period, he was succeeded by his son Ismāʿīl II (r. 984–5/1576–7), who is best known for having attempted to return Iran to Sunnī Islam. Safavid chroniclers do not have very many good things to say about Ismāʿīl II's religious policies. For example, Iskandar Beg certainly shows little admiration for this king in his chronicle. He accuses him of being 'guilty of a number of forbidden practices', such as 'associating with certain crazy fools among the qizilbāsh'.[62] In narrating the death of Ismāʿīl II, he states that 'since most people had suffered as a result of the evil actions of Shāh Ismāʿīl II, no one was particularly disturbed by his death, and the transfer of power was effected without any disturbances'.[63] Ismāʿīl II did not stay in power for very long – only one year, approximately, until a group of Qizilbāsh with the assistance of his sister, Parī Khan Khānum, poisoned him.[64] He was succeeded by his brother, the nearly blind Sulṭān Muḥammad Khudābanda. During this

59 See Dickson, 'Sháh Tahmásb and the Úzbeks', pp. 11–13.

60 *Ibid.*, p. 14.

61 *Tadhkirat al-mulūk*, trans. and ed. V. Minorsky (London, 1943), p. 188. See also Savory, *Iran under the Safavids*, pp. 31–2.

62 Iskandar Beg Munshī, *ʿĀlam-ārā-yi ʿAbbāsī*, p. 294; trans., p. 199.

63 *Ibid.*, p. 221; trans., p. 330.

64 See Savory, *Iran under the Safavids*, p. 68.

king's reign, real power lay in the hands of his wife, Mahd-i 'Ulyā', and his sister, Pari Khan Khānum. After Mahd-i 'Ulyā' orchestrated the murder of Parī Khan Khānum, she reigned supreme, much to the dismay of the Qizilbāsh. The fact that 'harem politics' and Qizilbāsh supremacy had become a major feature of Safavid politics at this time reflects the decentralised nature of the Safavid state in the aftermath of Shāh Ṭahmāsp's reign, and indeed, during the reigns of Ismāʿīl II and Sulṭān Muḥammad Khudābanda, Iran again lapsed into political fragmentation as individual Qizilbāsh leaders became increasingly powerful. They successfully conspired to murder Mahd-i 'Ulyā' and they chose the next king, ʿAbbās.[65] They also enjoyed governorships of important Iranian cities and provinces. At the same time, the neighbouring Uzbeks and Ottomans encroached upon Safavid territory, eager to take advantage of a weakened Safavid Iran. It was not until the reign of Shāh ʿAbbās (r. 996–1038/1588–1629) that centralised rule became re-established in Iran.

The reign of Shāh ʿAbbās: changes in the military and administrative structure of the state

Shāh ʿAbbās came to the throne in 996/1588 in a succession where a Qizilbāsh chief, Murshid Qulī Khan Ustājlū, played the most important role, for he was the one who chose the seventeen-year-old ʿAbbās to be king.[66] Shāh ʿAbbās goes down in history perhaps as Safavid Iran's most successful and famous monarch. However, at the beginning of his reign, he faced the challenge of 'reconquering' Iran before dealing with the ever-present external threats to the Safavid state. The chronicler Iskandar Beg Munshī characterises Shāh ʿAbbās's challenges in the following manner:

> He [Shāh ʿAbbās] was confronted by two powerful monarchs, the problem of Qizilbash disunity had not been solved, and he was faced by domestic revolts … and by rebellions on the part of the semi-independent rulers on the borders of the Safavid empire, who had taken advantage of fifteen years of weak Safavid rule since the death of Shāh Tahmasb to shake off Safavid suzerainty and assert their independence.[67]

65 See *Ibid.*, pp. 70–5.

66 *Ibid.*, p. 75.

67 Iskandar Beg Munshī, *ʿĀlam-ārā-yi ʿAbbāsī*, pp. 409–10; trans., p. 587. This is at the beginning of Iskandar Beg's section on the Year of the Ox, 998/1589–90, in reality 997 and the third regnal (*julūs*) year, according to McChesney's corrected dating system. See Robert D. McChesney, 'A note on Iskandar Beg's chronology', *Journal of Near Eastern Studies*, 39 (1980), p. 62.

Shāh ʿAbbās addressed these challenges by implementing a twofold strategy that consisted of destroying rebellious and disobedient Qizilbāsh leaders on the one hand and, on the other, raising a new army consisting of *ghulāms*, or slaves, who had been brought into Iran from the Caucasus, and transforming them into a new elite. In his attempt to suppress Qizilbāsh power, the monarch systematically removed those Qizilbāsh who were rebelling against his rule, and replaced them with *ghulām* leaders who would show allegiance to the monarch alone.

Perhaps the most dramatic example of ʿAbbās's contest against the Qizilbāsh can be seen in his dealings with Yaʿqūb Khan (d. 998/1590), the Dhū'l Qadr governor of Shīrāz. The chroniclers of Shāh ʿAbbās narrate this episode in great detail, giving it more attention than nearly any other episode in the early period of his reign. One historian, the chronicler Afūshta-yi Naṭanzī, even stated that this was the event that inspired him to write his history: 'When the news of this manifest victory spread far and wide throughout Iran, it became a source of astonishment to the masters of knowledge because the fortress of Istakhr, by virtue of its strength, had been a source of glory to the Eastern kings ... The strangeness of this wonderful incident and the good fortune of the ʿAlid king became the reason for the limping pen to hasten in writing this story.'[68] Yaʿqūb Khan was the governor of Fārs who was effectively ruling the region independently when Shāh ʿAbbās came to power. He also controlled Kirmān, Abarqūh and Yazd, and therefore posed a threat to the king.[69] Prior to his rebellion, Yaʿqūb Khan associated with members of the Niʿmatullāhī Sufi order, in particular Mīrmīrān Yazdī and his son Shāh Khalīl Allāh, who was allied with Yaʿqūb Khan for some time.[70] The khan surrounded himself with a number of Qizilbāsh rebels of various tribes, including Mukhtār Sulṭān of the Sharaf al-Dīn branch of the Tekelu Qizilbāsh.[71] In order to avoid what would have been certain execution, Yaʿqūb Khan sought refuge in the fortress of Iṣṭakhr in Shīrāz. Shāh ʿAbbās tried to use diplomacy both before and after Yaʿqūb Khan entered the fortress, and sought a meeting with the khan, but was unsuccessful in doing so. He was successful, however, in persuading him to leave the fortress. Yaʿqūb Khan eventually made his way to the king's court, where he was ultimately executed in 998/1590.

While the episode of Yaʿqūb Khan perhaps symbolically marked the victory of the king over the Qizilbāsh, at the same time, in order to bypass the

68 Maḥmūd ibn Hidāyat Allāh Afūshtah-yi Naṭanzī, *Naqāvat al-āthār fī dhikr al-akhyār*, ed. Iḥsān Ishrāqī (Tehran, 1350 [1971]), pp. 7–8.

69 See Szuppe, 'Kinship ties', p. 93.

70 See Said Amir Arjomand, *The shadow of God and the hidden imam: Religion, political order, and societal change in Shi'ite Iran from the beginning to 1890* (Chicago, 1984), pp. 116–17.

71 Szuppe, 'Kinship ties', pp. 92–3.

Qizilbāsh problem militarily, Shāh ʿAbbās developed a new 'pillar of legitimacy' whereby he called for the direct loyalty of the *ghulām* elite that formed his new army. By issuing the call for *shāhsevān*, or 'love for the king', ʿAbbās attempted to bypass the Qizilbāsh altogether. The fact that Shāh ʿAbbās needed to raise this new army at all reflects some of the political problems that he faced when he came to power. Most notably, Shāh ʿAbbās found it difficult to make legitimising claims on the basis of being the representative of the hidden imam, because the clerical classes had become increasingly powerful and were acknowledging the fact that genealogical descent from the imams was irrelevant in officially representing the hidden imam. Furthermore, as the Sufis had increasingly fallen out of favour, claims on the part of the king to be the head of the Safavid Sufi order also did not carry much weight. Thus, in addition to appealing to the notion of *shāhsevān*, Shāh ʿAbbās's chroniclers added another new theme to the legitimising platform: drawing connections between Shāh ʿAbbās and Temür. These shifts in political currents are reflected in chronicles such as Siyāqī Niẓām's *Futūḥāt-i humāyūn*, a history of Shāh ʿAbbās's campaign to Khurāsān (1007/1598). In this history, Siyāqī Niẓām goes to considerable lengths to connect Shāh ʿAbbās's name with Temür's. In his preface, Siyāqī Niẓām includes an interesting passage in which he links, by alphabetical and numerological (*abjad*) means, the Safavid and Temurid dynasties. Here, Siyāqī Niẓām states that, since Shāh ʿAbbās was a descendant of the Twelve Imams, there were twelve major events in his reign. He then compares this to Temür's reign, noting that even though Temür, the 'supreme lord of the fortunate conjunction (*ṣāḥibqirān-i aʿlā*)' did not pay attention to whether the time was auspicious or not, his undertakings nevertheless occurred at auspicious times.[72] Thus, Siyāqī Niẓām attempts to link the twelve great events in Shāh ʿAbbās's reign (he does not state what they were) – which numbered twelve because of his being a descendent of the Twelve Imams – with the auspiciousness of the events of Temür's reign.

Other evidence of this new Timurid emphasis as a legitimising factor exists in Iskandar Beg Munshī's chronicle, where he too refers to Shāh ʿAbbās as *ṣāḥibqirān* and explains why he does so:

> It will not have escaped the notice of perspicacious persons that the title of *saheb-qeran* (lord of the auspicious conjunction of planets) has, in the past, frequently been bestowed on princes by secretaries wishing to flatter their masters. In the case of Shāh ʿAbbas, however, it is verifiable by fact. From the time of his birth up to the present day, there has occurred the conjunction of

72 Siyāqī Niẓām, *Futūḥāt-i humāyūn*, ed., trans. and ann. Chahryar Adle as 'Fotuhat-e homayun: Les victoires augustes, 1007/1598', Ph.D. dissertation, University of Paris (1976), p. 334.

various celestial bodies, the prognostications of which corroborate events in the life of Shah ʿAbbas. According to the calculations of astrologers, each of these conjunctions foretells the appearance of a powerful and fortunate prince.[73]

Religion during the reign of Shāh ʿAbbās

Despite the new Timurid emphasis, Shāh ʿAbbās still presented himself as a devout Shīʿī. One of his chroniclers, Jalāl al-Dīn Munajjim Yazdī, referred to him as the *kalb-i āstān-i ʿAlī* ('the dog of ʿAlī's threshold'), to express the king's great humility before Shīʿī holy figures. Shāh ʿAbbās's displays of religiosity were public and designed to attract attention. Aside from erecting beautiful and expansive mosques in his new capital city of Iṣfahān, as will be discussed below, in 1010/1601 he undertook a pilgrimage on foot to Mashhad in order to visit the shrine of Imām Riẓā (d. 203/818).[74] It took him approximately two months to complete the trip. Although the reason that he gave for making the pilgrimage was to fulfil a vow, we do not know the specifics of this vow, and the actual rationales were complex and included diplomatic, political and religious motivations.[75] The political motive may have been to reassert the legitimacy of the Safavid monarchy after the instability that followed the death of Shāh Ṭahmāsp, and to claim Mashhad for the Safavids after conflicts with the Uzbeks over the city.[76] At the same time, by establishing Mashhad as a place for his Shīʿī subjects to visit, Shāh ʿAbbās may have been trying to redirect the pilgrimage to Mecca, which at this time, as a result of conflicts with the Ottomans, posed major challenges to those living in Iran.[77] It may also be that he was inspired by the neighbouring Mughal emperor Akbar, who also undertook pilgrimages on foot several times during his reign.[78]

Shīʿī religiosity was not just the domain of the king. During this time, Shīʿī scholars and clerics continued to expound the doctrines and beliefs of the state religion. Perhaps the most important religious figure during the reign of Shāh ʿAbbās was Shaykh Bahāʾ al-Dīn al-ʿAmilī, sometimes known as Shaykh Bahāʾī (d. 1031/1622). Iskandar Beg pays glowing tribute to him in his section on 'Sayyids, Shaykhs and Divines', and 'Notable Deaths', saying that he was 'profoundly learned in all branches of knowledge, particularly jurisprudence'.

73 Iskandar Beg Munshī, *ʿĀlam-ārā-yi ʿAbbāsī*, p. 1102; trans., p. 519.
74 Charles Melville, 'Shah ʿAbbas and the pilgrimage to Mashhad', in Charles Melville (ed.), *Safavid Persia: The history and politics of an Islamic society* (London, 1996), pp. 191–229.
75 *Ibid.*, p. 191.
76 *Ibid.*, pp. 197–8.
77 *Ibid.*, pp. 215–16.
78 *Ibid.*, p. 193.

He also refers to him as 'the foremost scholar of his age', noting that he enjoyed a great deal of royal favour: 'The shah kept him constantly at his side; both when he was in the capital and when he was making a journey somewhere, the shah would visit his dwelling to enjoy his company.'[79] Although Iskandar Beg does not say so, some considered him to be the *mujaddid*, or 'renewer' of the eleventh/seventeenth century.[80] Shaykh Bahā'ī was appointed to the post of Shaykh al-Islām of Iṣfahān, a position which he held for a short time.[81] He was extremely prolific and wrote on a diverse variety of topics, including scientific works such as treatises on mathematics, numerology and astrolabes; traditional Islamic sciences such as *tafsīr* and *ḥadīth*, and books of poetry, which reflect his Sufi tendencies. He was teacher to several famous scholars, including Mullā Muḥsin al-Fayż al-Kāshānī (d. 1091/1680) and Mullā Ṣadrā (d. 1050/1649), both of whom were significant Shīʿī writers and philosophers in their own right. Shāh ʿAbbās respected him greatly, and the shaykh accompanied the king on various diplomatic and political missions, or went on such trips on his own as the king's representative. For example, several chroniclers, including the court astrologer and historiographer Jalāl al-Dīn Munajjim Yazdī, Qāẓī Aḥmad Qummī and Naṭanzī all note several instances in which Shaykh Bahā'ī was sent on various missions on Shāh ʿAbbās's behalf. These include the shaykh's bringing the rebellious vizier Yulī Beg out of the fortress of Tabarak, and his trip to Gīlān and elsewhere for the purpose of arranging temporary marriages.[82] One chronicler, Mīrzā Qāsim Beg Junābādī, even stated that he was involved in retrieving Yaʿqūb Khan, the rebellious Dhū'l Qadr Qizilbāsh leader, from the fortress in Iṣṭakhr.[83]

Another important Shīʿī philosopher-theologian from this period was the famous philosopher Sayyid Muḥammad Bāqir Astarābādī, better known as Mīr Dāmād (d. 1040/1630f.), who is widely regarded as the founder of the so-called 'school of Iṣfahān'. Astarābādī received the title 'Dāmād' or 'son-in-law' as a result of his marriage to the daughter of the famous theologian Shaykh ʿAlī b. Ḥusayn Karakī. Although like Shaykh Bahā'ī, Mīr Dāmād wrote on a variety of topics, his main interest was in the field of philosophy, where he attempted to

79 Iskandar Beg Munshī, *ʿĀlam-ārā-yi ʿAbbāsī*, p. 157, trans., p. 249.
80 See *EIr* 'Bahā' al-Dīn ʿĀmelī (E. Kohlberg).
81 *Ibid.*
82 See Mullā Jalāl al-Dīn Munajjim Yazdī, *Tārīkh-i ʿAbbāsī yā rūznāma-yi Mullā Jalāl*, ed. Sayf Allāh Vaḥīd Niyā ([Tehran], 1366 [1987]), pp. 87, 109, 244–5, 268, 301 and 347; Qāẓī Aḥmad Munshī Qummī, *Khulāṣat al-tavārīkh*, ed. Iḥsān Ishrāqī (Tehran, 1363 [1984]), vol. II, p. 1086; Naṭanzī, *Naqāvat al-āthār*, pp. 334–5, 566.
83 Mīrzā Beg Junābādī, *Rawżat al-ṣafaviyya*, ed. Ghulām Riżā Ṭabāṭabā'ī-majd (Tehran, 1378 [1999]), p. 719.

bring together the philosophies of Avicenna (Ibn sīnā) (d. 428/1037) and Suhrawardī (d. 587/1191).[84] He also had an interest in the philosophies of time, and the terminology that earlier philosophers used to describe time-related phenomena. Mīr Dāmād was an important figure at the courts of Shāh ʿAbbās I and his successor Shāh Ṣafī I (r. 1038–52/1629–42), and at least one of his works, the Persian *al-Jadhawāt*, was written at the command of the former.

On a popular level, Shīʿī rituals and practices also evolved and developed considerably during the time of Shāh ʿAbbās. These practices were, like the king's own expressions of religiosity, quite public in nature and often promoted by the king himself. These included, for example, the development of the commemoration of Muḥarram into an elaborate public festival.[85] Such festivals included mourning processions, gatherings and pageants. These especially expanded after the capital was transferred to Iṣfahān. At the same time, the people of Iran, including the king, commemorated traditionally Persian festivals such as the feast of *Nawrūz* (new year), which under ʿAbbās was celebrated for several weeks. Aspects of this festival and other pre-Islamic Persian festivities had an influence on not only observations of Muḥarram, but also *ʿĀshūrāʾ*.[86]

Both internal and external sources also point to other expressions of popular culture, some of which are just now beginning to receive scholarly attention. Shāh ʿAbbās apparently was responsible for instituting festivals of 'lights' which involved firework displays and the burning of lights whenever he entered a particular city or on other occasions.[87] The king also encouraged neighbourhood factionalism between two different groups known as the Ḥaydarīs and the Niʿmatīs. The names come from earlier medieval Sufi shaykhs, and the practice of civic factional competition or strife also dates back to earlier centuries. According to one traveller's account, Shāh ʿAbbās promoted these conflicts in order to 'divide and rule' and to make sure that expressions of violence were safely contained within the context of these opposing groups fighting each other with sticks and stones.[88]

The era of Shāh ʿAbbās was therefore one in which notions of legitimacy had changed and evolved from the early Safavid period. ʿAbbās developed new ways to legitimise his rule and, in doing so, transformed the monarchy.

84 See *EIr* 'Dāmād, Mir-(e), Sayyed Moḥammed-Bāqer' (A. Newman).
85 Jean Calmard, 'Shiʿi rituals and power II: The consolidation of Safavid Shiʿism: Folklore and popular religion', in Melville (ed.), *Safavid Persia*, p. 143.
86 *Ibid.*, p. 150.
87 *Ibid.*, p. 148.
88 *Ibid.*, p. 145. See also Hossein Mirjafari, 'The Haydari–Niʿmati conflicts in Iran', trans. and adapt. J. R. Perry, *Iranian Studies*, 12 (1979), pp. 135–62.

These developments are reflected in Safavid art and culture, as can be generally seen in the area of architecture and specifically in the city of Iṣfahān.

Safavid art and culture: the city of Iṣfahān

The greatest expression of Safavid artistic achievement during the era of Shāh ʿAbbās was no doubt the city of Iṣfahān. ʿAbbās moved the capital city to Iṣfahān from Qazvīn in 1005/1596f. to make the capital safer from potential Ottoman attack. Iṣfahān was a planned city, designed to become the commercial and political centre of the Safavid state. The entire city was designed to reflect the power and legitimacy of the king. Symbolically, we may also view Iṣfahān as a reflection of Shāh ʿAbbās's successful efforts at transforming the Safavid state into one that reflected the international power of the dynasty, the increasing importance of the royal household and a new style of kingship that, in a very tangible way, reflected the Shāh's power.

Shāh ʿAbbās's Iṣfahān was built around a large square, known as the Maydān-i naqsh-i jahān. The square was constructed with shops on both sides of the two-storey perimeter walls. This construction was done in two phases. The initial phase and purpose of the square, undergone in 998–1003/1590–5, was for royal entertainment and sports. The second phase, begun in 1011–12/1602–4, expanded or transformed the square into a commercial centre.[89] Each side of the square had an important building. These included the ʿAlī Qāpū palace, a five-storey edifice with a large balcony from which the king watched polo tournaments and other events taking place in the square. On another side was the Masjid-i Shāh, the congregational mosque, which was covered with turquoise tiles. Work on this mosque started approximately seven years after the commercial renovation of the square.[90] There was definitely a commercial motivation even in the building of this mosque, because it was strategically situated at a site whereby visitors had to cross the market area twice in order to enter the mosque.[91] The Shaykh Luṭf Allāh mosque, or the Great Dome mosque, the last major undertaking on the royal square, was not completed until after the king's death. This mosque was intended for the monarch's own private worship. Like the Masjid-i Shāh, the Shaykh Luṭf Allāh mosque is decorated on the exterior with beautiful painted tiles. Finally, at the other end, opening on to the square, was the Qaysariyya bazaar, one of the earliest structures to be built

89 Robert D. McChesney, 'Four sources on Shah ʿAbbas's building of Isfahan', *Muqarnas*, 5 (1988), pp. 114–15.

90 *Ibid.*, p. 120.

91 *Ibid.*

on the maidan, which became the centre of Safavid trade and commerce. The Qaysariyya represents the king's attempt to modernise commerce in the city. This bazaar included separate sections for various types of goods such as carpets, silks and others. The Qaysariyya complex also included caravans, mosques and bathhouses, and the entire bazaar complex took up some 11 square miles. Other features of the capital city included the *chahār bāgh*, or four gardens complex. This suburban neighbourhood included a great garden, a boulevard, a bridge and a district known as the Tabrīzī district.[92]

Safavid poetry

Safavid poetry has historically received much less attention than what is considered 'classical' Persian poetry, and what attention it has received has been negative. This is largely due to the fact that it has been placed within the context of a later literary development known as the *bāz gasht-i ʿadabī* (return) movement, whereby both Iranian and Western scholars viewed the poetry from this period as qualitatively worse than classical poetry.[93] It has also been traditionally seen as the poetry of 'decline'. This idea is often still repeated today.[94] Because much of this poetry was written in India, scholars referred to Safavid poetry using the problematic phrase *sabk-i hindī*, or the 'Indian style', and pointed out its negatively unique features of 'metaphorical conceits, personification proverbs, poetic etiology, unusual imagery, colloquialisms, tangled syntax, ellipses and so forth'.[95] Such assessments of Safavid poetry have also extended into prose writing, in particular historiography.[96] Many reasons have been given for the migration of Iranian poets to Mughal India. Earlier assessments suggested that religious persecution and concern with developing a Shīʿī orthodoxy left Safavid kings, Shāh Ṭahmāsp in particular, uninterested in promoting poetry. More recently, however, such theories have been discarded in favour of economic explanations, which show that Safavid poets went to India due to financial

92 *Ibid.*, p. 124.
93 Paul E. Losensky, *Welcoming Fighānī: Imitation and poetic individuality in the Safavid-Mughal Ghazal* (Costa Mesa, 1998), p. 2.
94 For a new approach to understanding Safavid poetry, see Paul E. Losensky, '"The allusive field of drunkenness': Three Safavid-Moghul responses to a lyric by Baba Fighani', in Suzanne P. Stetkevych (ed.), *Reorientations/Arabic and Persian poetry* (Bloomington IN, 1994), pp. 227–62.
95 Losensky, *Welcoming Fighānī*, p. 3.
96 See Sholeh A. Quinn, *Historical writing during the reign of Shah ʿAbbas: Ideology, imitation and legitimacy in Safavid chronicles* (Salt Lake City, 2000).

incentive; India was wealthier and, furthermore, due to the fact that Mughal emperors were Persian speaking, they promoted Persian language and culture.[97] In addition to re-examining reasons for Persian poets moving to India, recent scholarship has also re-evaluated Safavid poetry and historiography, and this has led to new appraisals of its quality. In particular, Safavid poets took earlier models that they used as a basis for innovation. Thus, like its historiographical counterpart, Safavid poetical writing was imitative in nature, as poets took earlier metres, themes and other aspects of classical poems, reworking them in innovative ways.[98]

Some of the most important Safavid poets included Bābā Fighānī (d. 925/1519), 'Urfī Shīrāzī (d. 999/1590f.), Shānī Takallū (d. 1023/1614), Ḥakīm Shafā'ī of Iṣfahān (d. 1037/1627f.) and Ṣā'ib Tabrīzī (d. 1087/1676f.).[99] Rather than referring to themselves as proponents of the *sabk-i hindī*, these poets and others considered themselves to have developed a 'fresh style', or *tāza-gū'ī*, suggesting the innovative and new nature of this poetry. Among the features of this new style of poetry was the importance of the 'unexpected turn of thought' or 'startling connection between image and idea'.[100] Although currently there exists a lively debate regarding the value of such poets and their work, particularly in comparison with their classical predecessors, there is no doubt that during the Safavid period itself, promoters of the 'new style' were popular, enjoyed patronage of various Safavid rulers and were in many cases extremely prolific writers.[101]

Social and economic developments

Perhaps the most significant of all Shāh 'Abbās's economic policies and reforms was his establishment in 1028/1619 of a royal monopoly out of the silk industry. Like the construction of Iṣfahān, this policy was carried out in more than one phase. It started with his bringing the silk-producing regions of Gīlān and Māzandarān under his control early on during his reign. Then, in the 1590s, he transformed these provincial areas into crown lands. After the forced immigration of Armenian communities into New Julfa, he monopolised the silk industry.[102]

97 For an overview of these issues, see Stephen Frederic Dale, 'A Safavid poet in the heart of darkness', in Stephen Frederic Dale, *Safavid Iran and her neighbors* (Salt Lake City, 2003), pp. 64–8.
98 See Losensky, *Welcoming Fighānī*.
99 See *ibid.*, ch. 5.
100 See *EIr* 'Ṣāeb Tabrīzī' (Paul E. Losensky).
101 See *ibid.*
102 Rudolph P. Matthee, *The politics of trade in Safavid Iran: Silk for silver, 1600–1730* (New York, 1999), p. 84.

In order further to promote trade, in 1012/1604, Shāh ʿAbbās brought Armenians from Julfa, very much against their will, to live in Iṣfahān, where they settled in a neighbourhood called 'New Julfa'. This population transfer took place at a time when the Ottomans and Safavids were at war with one another. The Armenians were allowed to construct their own churches and worship as they pleased, and they became prosperous and powerful merchants in Iṣfahān, where they enjoyed special privileges from the state. In particular, they became very much involved in silk production and export, and, along with the *ghulāms*, they profited greatly from the silk trade.[103]

In addition to the Armenian merchants, the same *ghulāms* who served in Shāh ʿAbbās's new army also formed part of the new elite that developed in the wake of the Qizilbāsh decline. While the famous *ghulām* Allāh Verdī Khan was known and celebrated as a great general serving under the king, he also sponsored important building projects in the Shīrāz area, such as a bridge, a double dam, a fort, royal house and a madrasa.[104] Others of the new elite *ghulām* class also participated in such projects, thus indicating that this social group engaged in a range of activities beyond the military. These included Ganj ʿAlī Khan Zek, who built a maidan complex in Kirmān, as well as accompanying the king on military campaigns and serving as governor of Kirmān.[105] The most famous *ghulām* patron of the Shāh ʿAbbās period was Mīrzā Muḥammad 'Sārū' (blonde) Taqī, who sponsored the construction of entire towns and roads, and contributed to the upkeep of Shīʿī shrines.[106] Allāh Verdī Khan (d. 1022/1613) and his son Imām Qulī Khan (d. 1042/1633) were also involved in sponsoring other Safavid arts. The latter, in particular, patronised calligraphy, painting and poetry, as did Sārū Taqī and the Armenian *ghulām* Qaracahqay Khan, who supported the Safavid shrine in Ardabīl.[107]

The land reforms that the king instituted consisted primarily of transforming significant amounts of state land into crown land. This practice continued under ʿAbbās's successors. It was initiated in order to pay the new *ghulām* army. Qizilbāsh were traditionally paid through land grants known as *tiyūl*, which gave them considerable independence, but once Shāh ʿAbbās consolidated his own power, he decided to pay the *ghulāms* through his own crown lands.[108]

103 S. Babaie, K. Babayan, I. Baghdiantz-McCabe and M. Farhad, *Slaves of the Shah: New elites of Safavid Iran* (London, 2004), p. 52.
104 *Ibid.*, p. 93.
105 *Ibid.*, p. 94.
106 *Ibid.*, pp. 97–8.
107 *Ibid.*, pp. 120–6.
108 *Ibid.*, p. 9.

Travellers in the Safavid era

During the Safavid period, relations and interactions with Europe reached a new peak of activity. Many Europeans, with the encouragement of the Safavid kings, came to Iran in hopes of establishing trading houses, engaging in commerce, spreading Christianity, seeking alliances against the Ottomans and searching for adventure.[109] Numerous such individuals wrote extensively about their experiences in Iran and their travel narratives became well known and read in Europe. They provided pen portraits of the various Safavid kings and transmitted details about customs and practices not found in other sources. These merchants and missionaries include Jean Chardin, Tavernier and others.

Many Safavid kings engaged in diplomacy with European rulers, and European travellers helped facilitate the forging of such diplomatic contacts. These came in the form of correspondence, embassies and other types of interactions. The Portuguese sent embassies to Iran as early as 1523. Their main interest was protecting their naval base on the island of Hormuz, which they had occupied since 1515.[110] Shāh Ismāʿīl was also involved in efforts to forge alliances with European powers, in particular Emperor Charles V and Ludwig II of Hungary, against the Ottomans. Ismāʿīl's efforts to correspond with Charles V were inconclusive due to his death in 930/1524, but relations with European powers continued during Shāh Ṭahmāsp's reign. By this time, European powers had been successful against the Ottomans at sea, and the current pope, Pius V (d. 1572), contacted Shāh Ṭahmāsp, requesting that the Safavids attack the Ottomans. Ṭahmāsp, however, was not interested and did not respond positively to the pope's letter.[111] Another pope, Gregory XIII (d. 1585), also tried unsuccessfully to instigate interest in a Safavid–European alliance against the Ottomans and sent an ambassador to Iran. Again, the Safavid state was internally weakened by the time the ambassador returned to Europe in 1587 and did not come to Europe's assistance.

European relations with Iran reached their peak during the reign of Shāh ʿAbbās. The most famous travellers to Iran during this period were the Sherley brothers, Anthony and Robert. They travelled to Iran as part of yet another attempt to gain Iran's assistance against the Ottomans, this time sponsored by the British earl of Essex, who sent Anthony and his brother to

109 Laurence Lockhart, 'European contacts with Persia, 1350–1736', in Peter Jackson and Laurence Lockhart (eds.), *The Cambridge history of Iran*, vol. VI: *The Timurid and Safavid periods* (Cambridge, 1986), p. 374.

110 *Ibid.*, pp. 380–1.

111 *Ibid.*, p. 384.

Shāh 'Abbās. The Shāh sent Anthony back to Europe in order to gain further support against the Ottomans. This return embassy went to Prague, Rome and Valladolid, where they met the Emperor Rudolph (d. 1612), Pope Clement VIII (d. 1605) and Philip III (d. 1621), respectively.[112] Both the Emperor Rudolph and the pope sent return embassies to Persia, thereby increasing Europe's knowledge about Safavid Persia. And Shāh 'Abbās in turn sent envoys laden with gifts back to Europe.

Commerce was another strong motivation for European interactions with the Safavids. A trade route was established through Russia for merchants heading to Persia, and this led to numerous contacts and companies seeking to establish bases in Persia. One of the earliest parties to visit Iran consisted of the English merchants Anthony Jenkinson and Richard and Robert Johnson. Other merchants also passed through Iran, notably merchants from the Russia Company. When the Sherley brothers went to Iran, they too were interested in promoting trade. Eventually, both the East India Company and the Dutch Oost-Indische Compagnie vied against each other for favour from Persia. When the Safavids were at their peak of political power, kings concluded treaties with these companies in order to promote trade. These agreements, or 'capitulations', provided protection, tax breaks, living expenses and other incentives in order to encourage them to engage in trade in Persia. Although such agreements had disastrous effects in the later period, at the time they were concluded they worked to the Safavids' advantage.

Religious missionaries also went to Iran in hopes, sometimes, that the monarch would convert to Christianity. This was nothing new; missionaries entertaining similar hopes had visited the Mongols, but were never successful in their endeavours. Nevertheless, the number of religious figures making the trip to Iran was impressive. They included Carmelites, Portuguese Augustinians, Jesuits, Capuchins and many others. Shāh 'Abbās appears to have been particularly interested in these religious visitors and even allowed some, such as the Portuguese Augustinians, to build churches in Iṣfahān.[113] Some of these individuals have recorded their accounts of visiting Persia. The Carmelites, for instance, described their audiences with Shāh 'Abbās, recounting the religious discussions they had with him about the differences between Catholicism and Protestantism. Here, Shāh 'Abbās comes across as a king deeply interested in religious matters, discussing, according to Father Vincent's account of his meeting

112 *Ibid.*, p. 387.
113 *Ibid.*, p. 389.

with the king, four related topics, including Roman Catholicism and the role of the pope, fasting, the Cross and free will.[114] These missionaries also included other sorts of information in their accounts; Father Simon, for example, includes a valuable physical description of ʿAbbās and his court.[115]

Finally, some individuals went to Iran for personal reasons, such as to search for adventure or better health. The most notable of these included Pietro della Valle, who apparently travelled eastward to the court of Shāh ʿAbbās for a variety of reasons, including 'glory', adventure and possibly to get over a broken heart.[116] Pietro della Valle (d. 1652) wrote extensively of his travels. Others who sought adventure and delighted in travel included Jean-Baptiste Tavernier (d. 1689) and Jean de Thevenot (d. 1667).

Shāh ʿAbbās's conquests and campaigns

As for external relations, early on in his career, when he was still dealing with the Qizilbāsh threat, Shāh ʿAbbās lost a significant amount of territory, including Tabrīz, Azerbaijan, Qarābāgh, Baghdad and elsewhere to the Ottomans as a result of the 'Peace of Istanbul', which was concluded in 998/1590. For strategic reasons, Shāh ʿAbbās decided to turn towards the Uzbeks first, and in 1007/1598f. he embarked on a campaign for Khurāsān, accompanied by the famous *ghulām* general Allāh Verdī Khan. This campaign won back for the Safavids Herat, Mashhad, Balkh, Marv and Astarābād. The campaign was celebrated in a chronicle devoted entirely to this event: Siyāqī Niẓām's *Futūḥāt-i humāyūn*. Other chroniclers who wrote more general histories, after having to justify and explain years of defeat to the Ottomans, could now narrate a Safavid victory, and thus they seem to have taken special pleasure in describing the events of this particular year of Shāh ʿAbbās's reign, when Dīn Muḥammad Khan, the Uzbek ruler, died in the aftermath of the battle at Rabāt-i Pariyān, near Herat.[117]

After his victories against the Uzbeks, Shāh ʿAbbās then turned to the Ottomans, and by 1012/1603f., he was able to retake Azerbaijan, Nakhjavan and Erevan, and, approximately ten years later, conclude a new treaty with the

114 *The Islamic world*, ed. William H. McNeill and Marilyn Robinson Waldman (Chicago, 1973), p. 383.
115 *Ibid.*, pp. 377–8.
116 Lockhart, 'European contacts', p. 394; John Gurney, 'Pietro della Valle: The limits of perception', *Bulletin of the School of Oriental and African Studies*, 49 (1986), p. 103.
117 For more details on Uzbek–Safavid relations, see Robert. D. McChesney, 'The conquest of Herat 995–6/1587–8: Sources for the study of Ṣafavid/Qizilbāsh–Shībānid/Uzbak relations', in Jean Calmard (ed.), *Études Safavides* (Paris and Tehran, 1993), pp. 69–107.

Ottomans.[118] Late in his reign, in 1031/1622, ʿAbbās was able to bring Kandahar back into Safavid hands after having been part of the Mughal empire since Akbar the Mughal emperor captured it in 1003/1594f., and, the following year, he recovered Mesopotamian territories, including the city of Baghdad.

The late Safavid period

Shāh ʿAbbās died at his summer palace in Māzandarān in 1038/1629. The period after the death of Shāh ʿAbbās until the end of the dynasty has traditionally been seen as a period of 'decline', as in the case of traditional periodisations of Ottoman history. But as in the Ottoman case, use of this problematic term has rendered it difficult to understand the transformations that were taking place in Iran in the later Safavid period.

Of these changes, the most significant actually started at the time of Shāh ʿAbbās. This was the practice of confining the royal princes to the palace. Instead of succeeding to the throne with experience as governors of provinces or cities, these sheltered princes knew only the confines of the palace harem. This practice sometimes resulted in kings having difficulties distinguishing between important and trivial matters, and not being particularly effective. Judgement impairments were further exacerbated by increasing incidences of alcoholism. Courtiers were all too eager to indulge kings in drinking and other entertainment in order to gain further power and control for themselves. These changes certainly indicate a transformation of power to the palace. Harem politics became increasingly important as mothers of kings and their favourite wives also tried to gain power either by influencing the current king or by ensuring that their own sons came to power at the point of succession.

The approximate half-century following the death of Shāh ʿAbbās saw Iran ruled by his grandson, who took the name Shāh Ṣafī (r. 1038–52/1629–42), and his great-grandson, ʿAbbās II (r. 1052–77/1642–66). These two kings were different monarchs in many respects, but in other ways they both carried forward certain of ʿAbbās I's policies, in particular his practice of transferring provincial land into crown territories. Shāh Ṣafī has suffered from a negative reputation in Western assessments of his reign. He was the first king to have succeeded to the throne without any experience and having been confined to the harem. He ruthlessly eliminated any potential rivals both within his own family and without. He was incompetent enough to lose territory, though not a great deal of it, to rival Ottomans, Mughals,

118 Roemer, 'The Safavid period', pp. 266–8.

Uzbeks and Georgians. It must however be kept in mind that in many ways he was a product of the changes that were instituted by ʿAbbās I, most notably the practice of isolating the royal princes and by extension their families in the harem. Ṣafī I did not receive the valuable experience of having been ruler of an important province or city before he came to the throne. His reign marks the beginning of the transformation of the Safavid dynasty into one that was centred in the palace and power falling into the hands of the grand vizier and various other courtiers. Numerous individuals gained power and influence during Ṣafī I's reign; probably the most influential figure was his grand vizier, the above-mentioned Sārū Taqī.[119] It was Sārū Taqī who advised Ṣafī I to convert Fārs to crown land, because Qizilbāsh were no longer needed to ward off external enemies.[120] *Ghulāms* also continued to play an important role in the state; Imām Qulī Khan, son of Allāh Verdī Khan, was another important military figure. He was responsible for the governorship of Fārs and had a great deal of influence and control over southern Iran, but he and his family were subsequently executed by the king.[121] It has been suggested that part of the reason for Shāh Ṣafī's poor reputation was due to statements made by Fr Krusinski, who noted that his rule was 'cruel and bloody', and a reference to the episode of Imām Qulī Khan in Carmelite accounts.[122]

Shāh Ṣafī's coronation

An examination of Shāh Ṣafī's coronations indicates how Safavid religious policies and foci of power had evolved by this time. By the time Shāh Ṣafī (r. 1038–52/1629–42) succeeded to the throne, the religious classes were enjoying much greater power than at the time of Shāh Ismāʿīl I or II. In particular, the Safavid kings' claim to be ruling in the name of the hidden imam was seen by the clerics as illegitimate, and accounts of Shāh Ṣafī's coronation reflect this shift.[123] This shift can be seen in the main official who participated in the coronations: in the sixteenth century, after the reign of Shāh Ismāʿīl, the Mujtahid of the Age (*mujtahid-i zamān*), a descendant of the Shīʿī scholar al-Karakī, participated in the coronations of Ismāʿīl II and Muḥammad Khudābanda (r. 985–95/1578–87). But by the seventeenth century, the Shaykh al-Islām of Iṣfahān had this duty.[124]

119 *Ibid.*, pp. 282–3.
120 Savory, *Iran under the Safavids*, p. 228.
121 *Ibid.*, p. 229.
122 *Ibid.*
123 Momen, *An introduction to Shiʿi Islam*, p. 112.
124 Arjomand, *Shadow of God*, p. 177.

Although during his lifetime Shāh ʿAbbās had caused any potential rivals to the throne to be blinded, he had apparently made provisions for the succession, appointing his grandson Sām Mīrzā (later known as Shāh Ṣafī) as his heir. There was concern, of course, that the succession plan would be challenged, and so leading government officials tried to hold Sām Mīrzā's coronation ceremony as soon as possible. This was achieved in Iṣfahān with Sām Mīrzā taking the throne in 1038/1629 and changing his name to Shāh Ṣafī.[125] It was during Shāh Ṣafī's coronation that the prayer carpet (*sajjāda/qalīcha*) of the Safavid Sufi order, a central item used in Safavid coronations, was used for the last time; the fact that it was subsequently discontinued reflects the declining power of the Qizilbāsh.[126]

Shāh Ṣafī apparently had two coronation ceremonies; the second one took place in order to accommodate a very important individual who was unable to attend the first coronation. This was the philosopher and founder of the Ishraqi school of philosophy, or the 'school of Iṣfahān', Mīr Dāmād (*c.* 969–1040/1561f.–1630f.), mentioned earlier.[127] A later Safavid chronicler, Maʿsūm ibn Khwājagī Iṣfahānī, author of the *Khulāṣat al-siyar* (1052/1642), also notes that they used Shāh Ismāʿīl's belt and sword in the coronation ceremony. The practice of bestowing a sword upon a ruler goes back at least to the Saljuq period, when Ṭoghrıl Beg (d. 455/1063) was girded with a sword by the caliph.[128] In mentioning the sword and belt of Shāh Ismāʿīl, Iṣfahānī could be emphasising the early history of the Safavid dynasty without raising the religious and political implications of the Sufi/Qizilbāsh prayer carpet. At the same time, this Safavid practice could have been established in order to counter, or at least keep up with or compete with, Ottoman legitimising forces. Ottoman sultans took the throne by the 'girding of the sword' ceremony, a tradition which went back to the reign of Murād II (824–48; 850–5/1421–44; 1446–51).[129] As Ottoman coronation ceremonies became increasingly elaborate, so did those of the Safavids, who could claim that their king, too, was enthroned with a significant sword: that of their dynasty's founder. Iṣfahānī lists other coronation rituals as well, in particular the sounding of the drum and the flute. The beating of drums was an ancient Iranian practice

125 For more information on Shāh Ṣafī in general, see Roemer, 'The Safavid period', pp. 278–9.

126 Arjomand, *Shadow of God*, p. 180.

127 For more background on Mīr Dāmād, see S. H. Nasr, 'Spiritual movements, philosophy and theology in the Safavid period', in Peter Jackson and Laurence Lockhart (eds.), *The Cambridge history of Iran*, vol. VI: *The Timurid and Safavid periods* (Cambridge, 1986), pp. 669–75.

128 *EI*[2] 'Marāsim' (J. Burton-Page).

129 *Ibid.*

rooted in Mithraism, and it was performed on various occasions such as the king's birthday and other important religious holy days and commemorative events.[130]

After a reign of approximately thirteen years, Ṣafī I died at the age of thirty-two, in 1052/1642, probably from weakness due to opium and alcohol addiction. He was succeeded by his son, ʿAbbās II (r. 1052–77/1642–66). ʿAbbās II continued many of his father's policies, in particular the practice of bringing provinces that were traditionally governed by Qizilbāsh leaders under direct crown control. Specific provinces that came under crown control included the northern regions of Azerbaijan, Gīlān, Māzandarān and Qazvīn, the southern regions of Yazd and Kirmān, and the eastern region of Khurāsān.[131] ʿAbbās II has been compared to his great-grandfather ʿAbbās I and indeed may have modelled his reign on that of his illustrious ancestor. He continued to expand and embellish the city of Iṣfahān with new building projects such as the Āqā Nūr mosque and the madrasa of Mullā ʿAbd Allāh.[132] He also completed projects that ʿAbbās I had started, such as the Chihil Sutūn palace, or the palace of forty pillars, and repaired older buildings that needed renovation, such as the Masjid-i Shāh.[133] ʿAbbās II died in 1077/1666, and was succeeded by Shāh Ṣafī II (Sulaymān), whose rule lasted from 1077 (1078)–1105/1666 (1668)–1694.

The reign of Shāh Sulaymān

The economic situation of Shāh Sulaymān's reign can be financially characterised as broke. When Shāh Sulaymān came to the throne, the royal treasury was 'nearly empty' and, out of necessity, the court had to be extremely frugal in its spending practices.[134] The situation was so severe that the Shāh's grand vizier, Shaykh ʿAlī Khan, implemented a strict financial policy that resulted in cutting down court spending, and courtiers, include the *ghulāms*, had to rely on the king's personal financial generosity.[135] Shaykh ʿAlī Khan was a strict Muslim who disapproved of, or at least did not himself participate in, the popular

130 *Ibid.*
131 Savory, *Iran under the Safavids*, p. 228.
132 Robert Hillenbrand, 'Safavid architecture', in Peter Jackson and Laurence Lockhart (eds.), *The Cambridge history of Iran*, vol. VI: *The Timurid and Safavid periods* (Cambridge, 1986), p. 796.
133 Savory, *Iran under the Safavids*, p. 232.
134 Rudolph P. Matthee, 'Administrative stability and change in late-17th-century Iran: The case of Shaykh 'Ali Zanganah (1669–89)', *International Journal of Middle East Studies*, 26 (1994), pp. 82–3.
135 *Ibid.*, pp. 83, 88.

pastime of drinking parties at the palace, and was disliked at the palace for his fiscal measures.

Late Safavid historiography

It was during this late Safavid period that we see a new trend in historical writing in the form of popular histories emphasising the heroic aspects of the early Safavid kings, perhaps to forget about the troubled times in which they were living, or to provide their audiences with a strong contrast to the contemporary period. Nearly all of these texts are of unknown authorship, although recent scholarship has identified one author as Bījan, the 'reciter of the Safavid story' (*qiṣṣa-yi Ṣafavī-khwān*), or 'reciter of Safavid history' (*tārīkh-i Ṣafavī-khwān*), and also uncovered the title of Bījan's history as the *Jahān-gushā-yi khāqān-i ṣāḥib-qirān*. For many years this chronicle was thought to be dated to the period of Shāh Ismāʿīl himself, but now its composition can be placed to the period of Shāh Sulaymān. Although there are connections between these texts and earlier standard chronicles such as Ḥasan Beg Rūmlū's *Aḥsan al-tavārīkh*, these authors employ a style which is, overall, direct, unadorned and straightforward.[136] Furthermore, although early accounts representative of this tradition do not exist today, its origins might well go back at least to the time of Shāh Ṭahmāsp.[137] The fact that these histories emphasise the origins and rise of the Safavid dynasty supports the notion that at least some elements within late Safavid society were looking back, perhaps with a certain amount of nostalgia, to the past. More evidence supporting this theory can be seen in the example of Shaykh Ḥusayn ibn Shaykh Abdāl's *Silsilat al-nasab-i Ṣafaviyya*, a hagiography drawing heavily on the *Ṣafvat al-ṣafā* (composed 759/1358, updated 940/1533), dedicated to Shāh Sulaymān.[138] Although this work does not form the same tradition as the anonymous popular histories, its emphasis on Safavid origins and its late composition date support the notion of a revival of early Safavid history during this time.

Certain aspects of Shāh Sulaymān's rule could also provide an explanation for the general characteristics of the late Safavid popular chronicles. The first

136 See A. H. Morton, 'The date and attribution of the *Ross Anonymous*: Notes on a Persian history of Shah Isma'il I', in Charles Melville (ed.), *Pembroke papers I* (Cambridge, 1990), pp. 185 and 188, for instance, for a discussion of the connections between Bījan's history and Ḥasan Beg Rūmlū's *Aḥsan al-tavārīkh*.

137 See A. H. Morton, 'The early years of Shah Isma'il in the *Afzal al-tavarikh* and elsewhere', in Charles Melville (ed.), *Safavid Persia: The history and politics of an Islamic society* (London, 1996), pp. 44–5.

138 Shaykh Ḥusayn Pīrzāda Zāhidī, *Silsilat al-nasab-i Ṣafaviyya* (Berlin, 1924), p. 9.

has to do with the changing nature of kingship in the late Safavid period. As princes were increasingly confined to the harem, the inner palace became a centre of focus and power.[139] Rudi Matthee has outlined the basic features of this harem system, in which Shāh Sulaymān relied heavily on a 'secret council of eunuchs' for advice.[140] It is therefore not surprising that Morton concluded that Bījan's history may have been commissioned by Āqā Muḥammad Riḍā Beg, most likely a court eunuch who ordered Bījan to insert portions of a text similar to the *ʿĀlam-ārā-yi Ṣafavi*, a history of the genre under discussion here, into his history. If this is the case, we might conclude that the audience for this particular strand of historical writing was in the palace, and quite possibly the inner palace, and consisted chiefly of eunuchs and *ghulāms*.[141] Indeed, it is possible that in the late seventeenth century, this 'altered and distorted' tradition of historical writing was even the dominant one, as testified by the fact that we have many surviving copies of these anonymous histories. Furthermore, the fact that many of them were illustrated, some by famous artists of the time, suggests that these texts enjoyed a certain level of popularity and prominence.[142]

Ultimately, Shāh Sulaymān enjoyed a peaceful reign. His administration was marked by an expansion of the tendencies that had displayed themselves during the reigns of previous post-ʿAbbās I kings. In particular, the strengthening position of the vizier, as exemplified in the career of Sārū Taqī, continued and reached its pinnacle in the career of Shaykh ʿAlī Khan, who enjoyed tremendous power and prestige for some thirty years (1669–89) before his dramatic fall from power.[143] He put great effort into attempting to address the financial difficulties that the state was facing, and became known as an official who would not resort to bribery.[144]

Shāh Sulaymān did not officially nominate a successor and so the succession was determined apparently by his aunt, Princess Maryam Begum, who was a partisan of Sulaymān's son, Sulṭān Ḥusayn, who was crowned king in 1105/1694.[145] Sulṭān Ḥusayn ruled for twenty years, during which time the Safavid state witnessed the consolidation of power on the part of the religious

139 See Matthee, 'Administrative stability and change', pp. 77–98.
140 *Ibid.*, p. 89.
141 *Ibid.*; Morton, 'Date and attribution', p. 185.
142 See Eleanor Sims, 'A dispersed late-Safavid copy of the *Tarikh-i Jahangusha-yi Khaqan Sahibqiran*', in Sheila R. Canby (ed.), *Safavid art and architecture* (London, 2002), pp. 54–7.
143 Matthee, 'Administrative stability and change', pp. 78–9.
144 *Ibid.*, p. 83.
145 Roemer, 'The Safavid period', p. 311.

clerics. This trend is epitomised by the life and career of the famous jurist Muḥammad Bāqir Majlisī (1037–1110/1627–98). Majlisī, the son of the renowned Shīʿī *ʿālim* Ḥājjī Muḥammad Taqī Majlisī, was one of the most eminent and powerful clerics of the later Safavid period, and received the highest support from both Shāh Sulaymān, who conferred upon him the position of Shaykh al-Islām, and Shāh Sulṭān Ḥusayn, who made him Mullā Bāshī. These two positions were among the highest religious positions in the state, and Majlisī repaid both kings for the honour by dedicating books to them and praising them to the highest degree.[146] Majlisī is widely regarded as an outstanding *ḥadīth* scholar and Shīʿī polymath of the seventeenth century. He wrote numerous books in both Arabic and Persian. His monumental *Biḥār al-anwār* consists of no less than 110 printed volumes. This work is basically a Shīʿī encyclopaedic compilation of Imāmī Shīʿī traditions and all aspects of doctrine and history from cosmology and the lives of the imams to visitation accounts and essays on messianism and eschatology. It also includes information on medicine that indicates Majlisī was influenced and positively disposed to aspects of Galenic medicine.[147] His other works include the Persian *Ḥayāt al-qulūb*, which gives biographies of the lives of the prophets, the story of Muḥammad and the lives of the imams, as a sort of Shīʿī 'salvation history'. He also wrote shorter pieces against Sufism, treatises on various aspects of Shīʿī legalism, legalistic compilations and much more.

The end of the Safavid dynasty

The Safavid dynasty came to a final end as Safavid rule became increasingly weak and power became increasingly decentralised. Shāh Sulṭān Ḥusayn was an ineffectual ruler who grew up in the harem. He was devoutly religious, receiving the nickname of 'Mullā Ḥusayn'. The Safavid state at this time was facing threats from all of its non-Shīʿī border areas. One of these, Kandahar, was taken over by Ghilzais, who opposed and rebelled against Safavid-sponsored Georgian oppression. Eventually, a Ghilzai Afghan by the name of Maḥmūd was able to take over Kirmān while the Safavid army was occupied in dealing with takeovers of Safavid territories in the Persian Gulf. Although the king eventually turned to the east and Kandahar, there was so much opposition to such a campaign that they were unable to meet Maḥmūd

146 See *EI*² 'Madjlisī, Mullā Muḥammad Bākir' (Abdul-Hadi Hairi).
147 See Andrew Newman, 'Bāqir al-Majlisī and Islamicate medicine', in Andrew J. Newman (ed.), *Society and culture in the early modern Middle East: Studies on Iran in the Safavid period* (Leiden, 2003), p. 381.

there. Instead, Maḥmūd and his army started marching towards Iṣfahān. The Safavid troops first met Maḥmūd and the Afghans outside the village of Gulnabad. Although Maḥmūd's forces were outnumbered, they defeated the Safavids and continued their advance on Iṣfahān, attacking New Julfa. The king remained in Iṣfahān, rejected the opportunity for negotiation and did not allow people to leave the city. This resulted in a devastating famine. The king finally gave in and abdicated to Maḥmūd, who entered the city in 1722. Maḥmūd and his family did not remain in power for long, as eventually Russian and Turkish designs on Safavid territory carved deeper into the Safavid state. Although Maḥmūd's invasion of Iṣfahān marks the end of central Safavid rule, Safavid pretenders continued to exercise power in various ways in a politically fragmented Iran until 1087/1773. Against the backdrop of Afghan, Afshārid, Zand and Qājār rule, such individuals served as symbolic 'rallying-points' of opposition to the Afghans and those who later ruled Iran, such as Nādir Shāh.[148]

Conclusion

Although notions that the Safavid state was an early example of a 'nation state' in the Middle East, or even a 'proto-nation state' have long been dispelled, the Safavids made a long-lasting impact on Iran's political, religious and cultural landscape. As mentioned above, the fact that most of Iran's population subscribes to the Twelver or Imāmī form of Shīʿism is a direct outcome of Shāh Ismāʿīl's 1501 religious policy. Many of the clerics who now hold extremely powerful positions in Iran, and who helped bring about the overthrow of the Pahlavi dynasty, are the spiritual and physical descendants of those clerics who rose to power in the Safavid era.[149] In terms of historical geography, although the borders of Iran today are smaller than those of the Safavid empire, nevertheless, the general outline of the nation today reflects Safavid borders. Finally, although contact between the Western world and Iran is taken for granted now, it was during the Safavid period that Iran became involved with Western Europe on a large scale, and vice versa.

148 J. R. Perry, 'The last Safavids, 1722–73', *Iran*, 9 (1971), pp. 59–69.
149 See Momen, *An introduction to Shiʿi Islam*, pp. 132–4.

7

Islamic culture and the Chinggisid restoration: Central Asia in the sixteenth and seventeenth centuries

R. D. McCHESNEY

At the beginning of the sixteenth century, the Timurids were ousted from Central Asia and a new era of Chinggisid politics began. Although the Timurids had nominally recognised the sovereign rights of descendants of Chinggis Khan, that recognition had waned as the fifteenth century progressed. Chinggisid rule was restored in Transoxania and Cisoxania (Mawarannahr and Balkh) by a direct descendant of Jochi the eldest son of Chinggis Khan, Muḥammad Shibaq (var. Shāhī Beg, Shāh Bakht, Shaybak), but better known by his *nom de plume* of 'Shībānī'. His line went back to Jochi through the latter's third son, Shībān, hence the dynastic name Shibanid. Muḥammad Shibani's clan took its name, Abu'l-Khayrid, from his grandfather. A collateral (and rival) line of Shībānids, the 'Arabshāhid, established itself in Khwārazm at about the same time. The Shībānids of Māwarānnahr and Balkh ruled until 1599 at which point another Jochid line, claiming descent from the thirteenth son of Jochi, Tuqāy Temür, took power and remained sovereign there until the mid-eighteenth century. The 'Arabshāhids remained sovereign in Khwārazm until the early eighteenth century.[1]

During these two and a half centuries, the Chinggisids operated within an appanage system of government in which every male member of the ruling clan was entitled to a share in the territory held by the clan. Presiding over the entire polity was a khan, chosen on the basis of seniority and with little real

1 For details of the political history of the sixteenth and seventeenth centuries see R. D. McChesney, 'Central Asia vi. In the 10th–12th/16th–18th centuries', *EIr*, vol. V, pp. 176–93; Audrey Burton, *The Bukharans: A dynastic, diplomatic and commercial history, 1550–1702* (Richmond, 1997); Yuri Bregel, *An historical atlas of Central Asia* (Leiden, 2002), pp. 48–60; and Bregel, ''Arabshāhī', *EIr*, vol. II, pp. 243–5. For the Khwārazm Chinggisids during the first half of the sixteenth century see Martin B. Dickson, 'Sháh Tahmásb and the úzbeks: The duel for Khurásán with 'Ubayd Khán (930–946/1524–1540)', Ph.D. dissertation, Princeton University (1958), Appendix 1 'The Khwārazmian Uzbeks (930–946)', pp. I–XLIV.

authority outside his own appanage. The appanages, initially all held by Abu'l-Khayrid Shibanids, centred on the cities of the region – Tashkent, Samarqand, Bukhara and Balkh. For the first half of the sixteenth century, Bukhārā was held by the Shāh Budāqid sub-clan, Samarqand by the Kūchkunjids, Balkh and Karmina by the Jani-Begids, and Tashkent by the Suyunjuqids. In the second half of the century, the Jani-Begid sub-clan emerged pre-eminent. In Khwārazm two great appanages slowly emerged, the so-called 'riverside', following the lower reaches of the Oxus river (Amū Daryā) and the 'mountainside', along the northern flanks of the Kopet Dagh.

The appanage system worked best when new territory was being incorporated. When campaigns to expand the territory ceased being productive and march areas between the Chinggisid territories and those of their Iranian and Indian competitors became static, the dynamics of the appanage system led to internal struggles and the re-formation of appanages. In the latter half of the sixteenth century, success in such warfare brought the Jānī-Begid sub-clan of the Abu'l-Khayrid Shībānids to a predominant position which lasted about two decades. When its last and greatest khan, 'Abd Allāh (r. 1583–98) died, the resulting struggle among surviving Jānī-Begids brought about the rise of the Tuqāy-(Toghay) Timurids.

The end of the appanage system came about over the course of the seventeenth century as territorial expansion at the expense of the comparatively powerful states of Safavid Iran and Timurid (Mughal) India proved impossible. Unable to expand, both the Chinggisids and their Uzbek *amīrs* invested their political capital in holding on to what they had and wherever possible taking the territory of their appanage neighbours. The seventeenth century is marked by the formation of two great appanages, that of Bukhārā and Balkh, ruled successively by pairs of Tuqāy-Timurid brothers (Imām Qulī and Nadhr Muḥammad from 1611 to 1641 and Nadhr Muhāmmad's sons, 'Abd al-'Azīz and Subḥān Qulī from 1651 to 1681). Within these great appanages subinfeudations were created for their amirid supporters and these grants gradually became seen as belonging to the tribes of those *amīrs*. Thus by the middle of the eighteenth century one finds Badakhshān considered the patrimony of the Qataghan *amīrs*, Maymana that of the Mīng, Bukhārā belonging to the Mangghit, Khoqand to the Yūz, and the Kulāb region to the Keneges (Kanīkas), a situation that persisted well into the nineteenth century.

In Khwārazm, the 'Arabshāhid clan of the Shībānids had a much longer tenure but with different consequences for the cultural history of the region.[2]

2 The main sources on the politics of the 'Arabshāhid Shībānids are: Abu'l-Ghāzī Bahādur Khān, *Shajara-i Turk*, ed. and trans. Petr I. Desmaisons as *Histoire des Mongols et des Tatares par*

The Abu'l-Khayrid Shībānids and the Tuqāy-Timurids were thoroughly urbanised, living in garden-estates and palaces in the towns of Mawarannahr and Balkh and forging close ties with the elites of their appanages, whereas in Khwārazm, the members of the royal clan and their supporters maintained a nomadic lifestyle, lived in tents and used the towns primarily as fortresses when threatened by outsiders.[3] They felt little need to cultivate townsmen, to forge alliances with intellectuals, merchants and other city leaders and so, in marked contrast to their contemporaries in Māwarānnahr and Balkh, have left little in the way of an urban legacy of cultural patronage.

Society in the Chinggisid era

The reinstitution of Chinggisid political control in Central Asia had little impact on society as a whole, simply substituting one Turko-Mongol ruling organisation for another. The newcomers in the sixteenth century did introduce one new feature – probably more important to the political elite than to the ordinary subject – and that was the marked distinction between the khanly family and its military supporters, the 'Uzbek' *amīrs*. The title of khan (*khāqān*) was reserved for the senior member of the Chinggisid family. The male members of the royal clan suffixed the title *sulṭān* to their names. The leaders of the various tribal groups, subsumed under the generic term 'Uzbek' used the title *amīr*. That distinction between khans and *amīrs*, between those who could rightfully claim supreme authority and those who could not, no matter how individually powerful, remained central to political philosophy and practice through the entire period. In Central Asian sources of the period, the *amīrs* are usually identified by a tribal name (e.g. Dūrman, Naiman, Jalāyir, Arlāt, Kanīkas, Mīng, Manghghit, Yūz, Qaṭaghan, Qunghrāt, Barlās, Bahrīn, Qushjī, etc.) never as 'Uzbek', a generally derogatory or condescending term applied to an unlettered person, a bumpkin or rustic. It was outsiders who used the term 'Uzbek', and often in a pejorative sense, to refer to the entire state, its rulers and their military supporters.

The Chinggisid revival notwithstanding, there was much societal continuity from the Timurid to the Shībānid and Tuqāy-Timurid eras. This was especially true in the case of cultural issues, but even in the political sphere, where the Shibanid regime had displaced and assumed the prerogatives of its

Aboul-Ghâzi Béhâdour Khân (St Leonards and Amsterdam 1970 repr. of St Petersburg 1871–4 edn); and Mu'nis, Shīr Muḥammad Mīrāb and Muḥammad Rizā Mīrāb Agāhī, *Firdaws al-iqbāl: History of Khorezm*, ed. and trans. Yuri Bregel (Leiden, 1999).

3 Yuri Bregel, ''Arabshāhī', *EIr*, vol. II, p. 244.

Timurid predecessors. Many Timurid supporters, as long as they had committed no unforgivable offences against the incoming power, were accommodated in the new order. For the rest of the population, social hierarchies and cultural norms remained more or less as they had evolved during previous centuries. To the extent that we can speak of classes or distinct social groups, Central Asian society comprised first of all the general populace of farmers, sharecroppers, herders, shopkeepers, artisans, slaves and labourers – men, women and children – those whose names occasionally appear in written records and then often in conjunction with the doings of the more wealthy and powerful. But property ownership was something of a leveller and ownership of real estate was common to all social groups, with the possible exception of slaves. Supported by the general population was a group privileged by birth, education or position, and this group may broadly be divided between a shaykhly and learned caste, a military-civil officialdom comprised mainly of Uzbek *amīrs*, and the relatively small group of royals, the Chinggisids.

Except for membership in the Chinggisid clan, the boundaries between any of the other groups are blurred and permeable. Learned *amīrs* were common as were non-Uzbeks who had made careers in the military. The fact that there were no restrictions on the ownership of real estate, including agricultural land, opened a path to building wealth and thereby improving one's social status. Property ownership was certainly widespread. Sources from the sixteenth and seventeenth centuries such as the documents of the Jūybārī family (family biographies, deeds of sale and *waqf-nāmas*), along with the thousands of *waqf* deeds in the Uzbek and Tājik archives, reveal the names of a multitude of small landowners. The access to property made the accumulation of capital possible and so far as one can tell the *sharīʿa* laws on property were applied without distinction as to class, ethnic affiliation or gender. In the case of women, some 30 per cent of the more than 3,000 owners of property in and around Bukhārā mentioned in the property deeds of the Jūybārī family alone[4] were women, either as parties to the transactions with the Jūybārīs, or as owners of adjacent properties.

Occasionally one finds recorded instances of utterly unpredictable and rare strokes of fortune which suddenly enriched a person and elevated them to local prominence. Such an instance is the probably apocryphal case of the founder of one of Bukhārā's most famous teaching institutions, the Muḥammad Sharīf

4 E. Bertel's (ed.), *Iz arkhiva Dzhuibari* (Leningrad, 1938). On the actual editor and translator of this work, Fedor Borisovich Rostopchin, see R. D. McChesney, 'Some observations on "garden" and its meanings in the property transactions of the Jūybārī family in Bukhara, 1544–77', in Attilio Petruccioli (ed.), *Gardens in the time of the great Muslim empires* (Leiden, 1997), pp. 105 n. 11 and 107 n. 29.

madrasa. An early twentieth-century Bukhārān source reports that Mullā Muḥammad Sharīf was born poor and became a disciple of a certain Mawlānā Imlā'. During the Iranian siege of Bukhārā in 1740, the Chinggisid ruler, Abu'l-Fayz Khan, and his *amīrs* decided they should seek terms from the Iranians and chose Mawlānā Imlā' to negotiate on their behalf. He took his disciple with him to meet Nādir Shāh, the leader of the Iranian force, and, was received with great honour. Nādir Shāh gave Mawlānā Imlā' a priceless jewel and he in turn passed it to Muḥammad Sharīf. With the jewel, Muḥammad Sharīf 'banished the word "ascetic" from his vocabulary' and became a great merchant. After the death of his mentor, he built a number of buildings including a madrasa and mosque near the Ghāziyān reservoir in honour of his master, all from the proceeds of the sale of the jewel.[5] This madrasa, alternately known as the Ghāziyān madrasa, became one of the chief teaching centres of Bukhārā and had a renowned library.[6]

But such incidents were of course extremely rare and for a person not born to wealth, into the royal clan or into one of the amirid organisations, prestige and status came through personal effort: as a soldier, farmer, merchant or, as above, through connection to a prominent teacher or shaykh.

Patronage patterns

The Abu'l-Khayrid Shībānids, the Tuqāy-Timurids, and the military and intellectual supporters of both Chinggisid lines (but not the ʿArabshāhids of Khwārazm) are noteworthy for their continuation of the Timurid model of artistic and scholarly patronage. Indeed, much of the material and intellectual legacy of the Timurid period – from architecture to Arabic grammar – was maintained, preserved and encouraged by the wealthy of the appanage regimes of the sixteenth and seventeenth centuries.

The Chinggisid rulers and their leading *amīrs* were well-educated men and, in the fashion of the time, prided themselves on their skills in poetry. Many of them were well known, and in a few cases even well regarded, for their poetry as well as for their support of poets and other producers of literature. In addition, they devoted substantial resources to promoting scholarship

5 Tamkin, *Maṭāliʿ al-fākhira wa maṭālib al-ṭāhira*, Tashkent IVAN ms. 8245, fos. 410b–411b. The late seventeenth-century *Muzakkir al-aṣḥāb* however places Muḥammad Sharīf and his madrasa, also known as the Ghāziyān madrasa, in the late seventeenth century, fo. 119a. Tamkin may have been relying more on oral tradition. The story could well be apocryphal but is nonetheless illustrative of what people thought possible.

6 Edward A. Allworth (ed.), *The personal history of a Bukharan intellectual: The diary of Muḥammad Sharīf-i Ṣadr-i Ẓiyā* (Leiden, 2004), *passim*.

through direct stipends to scholars, in the form of judgeships and other judicial positions and indirectly through endowments paying salaries for professorships. Those with the means also lavished their wealth on great public works projects to support education, the cult, commerce and the hydraulic needs of an agrarian society.

In their literary endeavours, most Chinggisids were able to compose in both Persian and Turki and some, like Shībānī Khan and the late sixteenth-century ʿAbd Allāh Khan, could write in at least passable Arabic as well. These men of power were also very often conversant in the Qurʾānic disciplines. To further the Islamic sciences, they invested much of their surplus wealth in building madrasas, the typical venue for encouraging intellectual life. In addition, they presided over literary assemblies (*majālis, maḥāfil, mushāʿarāt*) and encouraged creativity by awarding monetary prizes as well as salaried positions.

The support of intellectual and artistic activity was influenced, of course, by both economic and political conditions. The turbulent first half of the sixteenth century was marked by the struggles between the Shībānid, Safavid and Indian Timurid (Mughal) polities until a balance of power was reached which left the Hindu Kush as the frontier between the Shībānids and the Indian Timurids, and the Harī Rūd and Murghāb basins as the relatively stable marches between the Shībānids and the Safavids. During this transitional period, existing patronage ties were broken and many artists, architects, literary figures, scholars and entertainers migrated (or were forcibly moved) and found new patrons.

The artistic and intellectual community that had formed at Herat with the financial support of men like Mīr ʿAlī Shīr Nawāʾī, Sulṭān-Ḥusayn Mīrzā Bāyqarā and Amīr Shaykh Aḥmad al-Suhaylī dispersed to Ottoman territory, Māwarānnahr and India as a consequence not only of the warfare between the last of the Timurids, the Safavids and the new Chinggisids but also because of the new and divisive ideological element introduced by the Shīʿite Qizilbāsh supporters of the Safavid family and the Ḥanafī Sunnī reaction it produced. Over time, the flow of patronage-seekers became increasingly channelled towards India as the Mughal regime there extended its hold over the country and increased its resources. By the end of the sixteenth century, 25–30 per cent of the biography-worthy officials of the Mughal state were first-generation immigrants from Iran alone[7] and we can assume that another substantial

7 Masashi Haneda, 'Emigration of Iranian elites to India during the 16th–18th centuries', *Cahiers d'Asie Centrale*, 3–4 (1997), p. 131.

percentage, perhaps not quite of this magnitude, was represented by first-generation job-seekers from Central Asia.

The attraction of India as a destination for patronage-seekers took some time to develop and did not much affect those caught up in the Shībānid–Safavid–Timurid struggles in the first half of the century. A good example of a highly skilled artisan affected by the problems of that period is the landscape architect Mīrak-i Ghiyāṡī, who worked for Sulṭān-Ḥusayn Bāyqarā until the latter's death in 1506, at which time he was about thirty years old. He then worked under the Shibanids when they captured the city in 1507. When the Safavids retook it in 1510, he was imprisoned and was finally forcibly removed to Bukhārā when the Shibanids once again captured Herat in 1513. He eventually peregrinated between Samarqand, Herat, Agra and Bukhara, spreading Timurid garden-design ideas and leaving known examples of his work in Herat, Agra and Bukhārā before disappearing from the scene in the late 1550s.[8]

Other examples of the effect of international politics on scholars are found in the contrasting cases of Faẓl Allāh b. Rūzbihān Khunjī Iṣfahānī (d. *c.* 937/1530) and Amīr Ṣadr al-Dīn Sulṭān Ibrāhīm 'Amīnī' (d. 941/1535). The former, born in Shīrāz into an upper-class family with a long Shāfiʿite Sunnī heritage, was a well-travelled young man before offering a book and his services to the Aq Qoyunlu sultan Yaʿqūb, the son of Uzun Ḥasan (d. 1490). After the latter's death Khunjī Iṣfahānī briefly served some of the last Timurids in Iran. As the Safavid Shīʿite movement grew, he wrote *Ibṭāl nahj al-bāṭil*, a polemical anti-Shīʿī work, which reportedly made it impossible for him to live in the Safavid domains. He chose the court of Shibani Khan and after the latter's death in 1510 lived at Samarqand, eventually being invited to join the court of ʿUbayd Allāh in Bukhārā (r. 1512–40) for whom he wrote a treatise on government, *Sulūk al-mulūk*.

Sulṭān Ibrāhīm 'Amīnī', on the other hand, typifies intellectuals moving in the opposite direction. Like Iṣfahānī, he was born into privilege, became a noted scholar and was attached to the court of a son of Sulṭān-Ḥusayn Bāyqarā, Muẓaffar Ḥusayn, who briefly governed Herat after his father's death in 1506. When Shibani Khan took Herat in 1507, Amīnī was persecuted and his properties confiscated but these were restored when Shāh Ismāʿīl occupied the city in 1510. Ten years later Amīnī joined Ismāʿīl's court in Tabrīz where he began work on a verse history of the shāh, *Futuḥāt-i shāhī*.[9]

8 Maria E. Subtelny, 'Mīrak-i Sayyid Ghiyās and the Tımurid tradition of landscape architecture', *Studia Iranica*, 24 (1995), pp. 19–60.

9 C. A. Storey, *Persidskaya literatura: Bio-bibliograficheskii obzor*, rev., trans., and updated Yuri E. Bregel, 3 vols. (Moscow, 1972), vol. II, p.850.

Probably more often it was economic, rather than political or ideological, circumstances which fuelled the migration of intellectuals and artists. Whatever the reason, these migrations produced a new flowering of cultural activity in Central Asia, India and Iran. The memoirist-anthologist Zayn al-Dīn Wāṣifī paints a vivid picture of the intellectual life at the Bukhārān court of ʿUbayd Allāh Khan. Many of the literary figures he describes were refugees from Timurid Herat and Safavid Iran.

In art as well as literature, changing economic and ideological circumstances led to the flowering of new centres. Shaykhzāde, a pupil of the great Bihzād, left Iran sometime after 1532. This probably was connected to Shāh Ṭahmāsp's public 'repentance' and his highly publicised effort to 'promote virtue and prohibit vice', which was followed by a puritanical clampdown on cultural activity. In Bukhārā, ʿAbd al-ʿAzīz, the son of ʿUbayd Allāh Khan, welcomed Shaykhzāde and for two decades or so the artist and his pupils produced manuscripts in ʿAbd al-ʿAzīz Khan's scriptorium (*kitābkhāna*) and created what is known as the 'Bukhara school' of miniature painting.[10]

Through the sixteenth and seventeenth centuries the ruling circles' support of scholarship, art and religious life is well recorded not just in the chronicles they commissioned to memorialise themselves but in the biographical anthologies (*tazkiras*) written by those who usually depended on their patronage. Through the whole period there is a nearly unbroken chain of anthological writing, one author building on the work of a predecessor. For the sixteenth century, these writers include Wāṣifī (writing between 1517 and 1532), Fakhrī Harawī (writing in the years 1551–5), Ḥasan-i Nithārī Bukhārī (writing between 1566 and 1572) and Muṭrībī Samarqandī (chronicling the literary scene down to 1605). The seventeenth-century anthologists are less well known because they remain unpublished. But these include Muḥammad Samī ʿSamarqandī, whose work covered the period from 1583 (the accession of ʿAbd Allāh Khan) to 1644 (the abdication of Nadhr Muḥammad Khan), and Muḥammad Badīʿ Samarqandī, author of *Mudhakkir-i aṣḥāb*, which he tells us he first conceived in 1669 and which covers the period up to 1693.

10 See the following works by Yves Porter, 'Remarques sur la peinture à Boukhara au XVIe siècle', *Boukhara La Noble; Cahiers d'Asie Centrale*, 5–6 (1998), pp. 147–67; Porter, 'Farhad le peintre: À propos des ateliers de peinture de Boukhara à l'époque de ʿAbd al-ʿAziz Khan (1645–1680)', *L'héritage Timouride: Iran–Asie centrale–Inde XVe–XVIIIe siècles; Cahiers d'Asie Centrale*, 3–4 (1997), pp. 267–78; Porter, 'Le *kitâb-khâna* de ʿAbd al-ʿAzîz Khân (1645–1680) et le mécénat de la peinture à Boukhara', *Patrimoine manuscrit et vie intellectuelle de l'Asie centrale islamique; Cahiers d'Asie Centrale*, 7 (1999), pp. 117–36. Also see Barbara Schmitz, "Bukhara VI. The Bukharan school of miniature painting', *EIr*, vol. IV, pp. 527b–530a.

While these anthologies show us that composing poetry was a universal phenomenon and did not seem to require any particular preparation, attaining recognition as a scholar (*'ālim*), on the other hand, required formal training. The credentials of individual scholars were recorded in *ijāzas* (licences to teach certain books), *istījāzas* (requests for *ijāzas*) and *mashyakhahs* (lists of authorities[11]). Other indications of scholarly accomplishment are also to be found in book-endowment lists and in the biographical notices of scholars found in a wide variety of sources.

What is remarkable about sixteenth- and seventeenth-century scholarship is its debt to the work of Timurid-era scholars, although pre-Timurid scholarship was central to the curriculum as well. In this latter category, most prominent are Bahā' al-Dīn al-Marghinānī (d. 1197) and the extensive tradition of legal commentary and glossing to which his great work of jurisprudence, *al-Hidāya*, gave rise; Ibn Ḥājib (d. 1249) and his treatise on Arabic syntax, *al-Kāfiya*; Bayżāwī's (d. 1286) commentary on the Qur'ān, *Anwār al-tanzīl*; the *Mishkāt al-maṣābīḥ* in the recension of Kātib Tabrīzī (*fl.* 1340), a favoured work on *ḥadīth*; and al-Nasafī's (d. 1142) statement of belief, *al-'Aqā'id*. These works all figure prominently in the lists of book collections that survive from the sixteenth and seventeenth centuries.

Yet it is Timurid-era works that predominate in these catalogues and book lists. The body of scholarship left by such Timurid-sponsored intellectuals as Sa'd al-Dīn Mas'ūd b. 'Umar al-Taftāzānī (d. 1390), the 'Sayyid al-Sharīf' 'Alī b. Muḥammad al-Jurjānī (d. 1413), Shams al-Dīn Muḥammad al-Jazarī (d.1429) (all three of whom were at Temür's court), Nūr al-Dīn 'Abd al-Raḥmān Jāmī (d. 1492) and Kamāl al-Dīn Ḥusayn b. 'Alī 'al-Wā'iẓ' al-Kāshifī (d. 1504) (at the late fifteenth-century court of Sulṭān-Ḥusayn Mīrzā) was canonised in the madrasa curricula of the Shībānids and Tuqāy-Timurids. Being versed in the works of the Timurid period as well as in the Marghīnānī tradition of legal scholarship qualified an individual for posts in judicial administration (as *qāḍī*, *muftī* and *ra'īs*) as well as for the madrasa professorships (*tadrīs*) that often seemed to go along with judicial appointments. An example of the kind of education a middle-level judicial appointee would typically have is that of Muḥammad Badi' of Samarqand, known to us today as the compiler of an anthology of poets. Born in 1050 or 1053/1640 or 1643, he followed in his father's footsteps to become a *muftī* in Samarqand. He says that he spent the

11 On these credentials see Maria E. Subtelny and Anas B. Khalidov, 'The curriculum of Islamic higher learning in Timurid Iran in the light of the Sunni revival under Shāh-Rukh', *Journal of the American Oriental Society*, 115 (1995), pp. 210–36.

first thirty years of his life under his father's tutelage studying logic, theology, astronomy and *ḥikmat* (which at this point probably meant Galenic medicine). When his father died *c.* 1670, the Tuqāy-Timurid khan, ʿAbd al-ʿAzīz (r. 1651–81), gave him his father's salary and office. After a three-year trip to Iṣfahān, he spent seven years in Bukhara and Samarqand acquiring competence in Arabic, jurisprudence (*fiqh*), Qurʾānic commentary (*tafsīr*) and the discipline of *ḥadīth* criticism. He was never recognised as an *ʿālim* but his education was considered advanced enough that in 1100/1690 (at the age of fifty) he was offered the post of *qāḍī* of Samarqand and given a professorship at the Shībānī Khan madrasa as a stipend.[12]

The politicians who made the appointments learned of credentials like these through word of mouth, and sometimes through public contest, at assemblies where a person of power would pose a legal or theological problem and often reward the person who provided the best answer with money or a position. (Khunjī Iṣfahānī's *Mihmān-nāma-i Bukhārā* (The Bukharan Guestbook) contains many accounts of just such assemblies under Shībānī Khan, and, a century later, Maḥmūd b. Amīr Walī describes numerous such gatherings in the *Baḥr al-Asrār*.)

Shībānid khanly patrons and their works

The founder of the Māwarānnahr lineage of the Abu'l-Khayrid Shibanids, Muḥammad Shibani Khan, is portrayed by his contemporaries as a man of some learning and more importantly as a friend and patron of scholars and an active supporter of intellectual life. According to those who knew him best, Shībānī had formal instruction himself in at least one Islamic discipline, the science of *qirāʾa*, the variant readings of the Qurʾān.

The above-mentioned Iranian refugee, Khunjī Iṣfahānī, was commissioned by Shībānī Khan to memorialise him and devotes much of his work, *Mihmān-nāma-i Bukhārā*, to the scholarly debates over which Shībānī Khan presided and which he apparently used to resolve some of the legal problems raised by the ouster of the Timurids. These included the issue of ownership of abandoned property and questions relating to inheritance.[13] His interest in the law also led to the khan's sponsoring the compilation of a collection of *fatwās* named in his honour.[14] He is

12 Muḥammad Badiʿ, *Muzakkir al-aṣḥāb*, ms. 610, fos. 256–9; ms. 4270, fos. 221a–225a.
13 Ken'ichi Isogai, 'Yasa and Shariah in early 16th century Central Asia', *L'héritage Timouride: Iran–Asie centrale–Inde XVe–XVIIIe siècles; Cahiers d'Asie Centrale*, 3–4 (1997), pp. 91–103.
14 ʿAli b. Muḥammad ʿAli al-Khwārazmi, *Fatāwā al-Shībāni*, Uzbek IVAN ms. 11282.

remembered as well for a love of calligraphy, having pride in his own hand and for promoting the Turki (or Chaghatay) literary revival usually associated with the name of Mīr ʿAlī Shīr Nawāʾi. He himself wrote a poetry collection (*dīwān*) in Chaghatay or Turki, a mixture of political and devotional verses, riddles (*muʿammās*) and *ghazals*.[15]

Bahāʾ al-Dīn Ḥāsan Nithārī Bukhārī, writing about a generation after Shībānī Khan's death, portrays him as a devotee of the Naqshbandī Sufi way, composing devotional poetry in Persian in honour of Bahāʾ al-Dīn Naqshband.[16] But the fact that he is credited with also composing a chronogram in Persian commemorating the death of Najm al-Dīn Kubrā suggests an affiliation or at least sympathy with the Kubrāwiyya as well; and 125 years later, Maḥmūd b. Amīr Walī, in a section of his work devoted to naming the great shaykhs who were the principal spiritual advisers of the Chinggisid khans, identifies Kamāl al-Dīn Ḥusayn Khwārazmī, the early sixteenth-century reviver of Kubrāwiyya fortunes, as the most significant spiritual influence on Shībānī Khan.[17] The two might have met when Shībānī conquered Khwārazm in 1505 but Ḥusayn Khwārazmī did not come to Samarqand until five years after Shībānī's death and none of the Bukhārān-centred sources mention the connection. Nonetheless that such a tradition survived for more than a century suggests there was something to it. It should also be noted that Shībānī Khan's *dīwān* contained eulogies of the Yasavī Sufi tradition as well. In any event these accounts are an indication of a well-known phenomenon, the competition among the Sufi *ṭarīqas* for the patronage of the ruling circles. And Shībānī Khan's religious sentiments were not exclusively focused on Sufis. Fakhrī Haravī, also writing in the 1550s, notes that the campaign which brought Shībānī Khan to Mashhad prompted him to compose a *qaṣīda* in honour of the Eighth Imam, symptomatic of the universal reverence for the family of the Prophet and for Ḥusayn's line in particular.

Shībānī Khan's interest in promoting Islamic culture was given more monumental form in the Madrasa-i ʿĀliyya-i Khāniya which was under construction when he was killed in 1510. The madrasa was completed by Muḥammad Temür Sulṭān, the eldest of his three sons, and the latter's wife,

15 See H. Hofman, *Turkish literature: A bio-bibliographical survey*, Section III: Part 1 (Authors) (6 vols. in 2) (Utrecht, 1969), Part 1, vol. V, pp. 222–33.

16 Khwāja Bahāʾ al-Dīn Ḥasan Nithārī Bukhārī, *Mudhakkir-i aḥbāb*, ed. Syed Muḥammad Fazlullah (New Delhi, 1969), pp. 15–22; also editor's introduction, pp. 14–15

17 Maḥmūd b. Amīr Walī, *Baḥr al-asrār fī manāqib al-akhyār*, vol. VI, part (*rukn*) 4, India Office Library ms. 575, fo. 141a.

Mihr Sulṭān Khānum, left a large endowment for it. The madrasa continued to operate until the late nineteenth century.[18]

The pattern of Shībānī Khan's support for the cultural life of Central Asia was continued by his successors. The next reigning khan, his uncle Kūchkunjī (or Kūchūm Khan, r. 1512–30), whose appanage centre was Samarqand, has left few literary traces, but a contemporary, Wāṣifī, who completed his work in 1538–9, relates that he 'honoured and exalted scholars and intellectuals' and that he renovated and reconstructed 'madrasas, *khānaqās*, hermitages (*ṣawāmiʿ*), mosques and shrines which had fallen into ruin'.[19] Wāṣifī also notes that he endowed ten professorships for the Ulugh Beg madrasa-*khānaqā*, as it was known at the time, as well as four more for Shībānī Khan's madrasa, the subjects to be taught by these professors being (Arabic) grammar, medicine and law.[20] In addition, Kūchkunjī commissioned work on a congregational mosque built by the Timurid *amīr* Alīkah Kūkaltāsh, adding a stone minbar to replace a wooden one destroyed by fire and making other alterations.[21]

Shībānī Khan's nephew, ʿUbayd Allāh b. Maḥmūd Sulṭān (r. 1533–40), won wide acclaim, even from his enemies, for his literary abilities and his generous patronage. When not engaged in one of his numerous campaigns against Herat and Khurāsān, he composed well-regarded poetry in Arabic, Persian and Turkī under the pen name ʿUbaydī and supported an extensive company of scholars, artists and architects. His own artistic and scholarly accomplishments were summed up by Mīrzā Ḥaydar Dughlāt, writing about ten years after ʿUbayd Allāh's death and certainly no friend of the Abu'l-Khayrid Shībānids. In lauding ʿUbayd Allāh Khan's personal qualities, Ḥaydar Dughlāt wrote,

> It is my claim that during this period of a hundred years in all the realms of the world where there have been padishahs, of those who have been heard of and seen, there has been none like him. First of all he was a Muslim padishah, religious, pious, and abstinent. In all matters of religion and the nation, in state, military, and civilian affairs, he made his decisions in accordance with the religious law and he never tolerated even an iota of transgression. In the

18 On the madrasa and its endowment see R. G. Mukminova, *K istorii agrarnykh otnoshenii v Uzbekistane XVI v.: Vakf-name* (Tashkent, 1966), pp. 9–13.

19 Zayn al-Dīn Wāsifī, *Badāʾiʿ al-waqāʾiʿ*, ed. Aleksandr Boldyrev, 2 vols. (Moscow, 1961), vol. I, p. 11a.

20 *Ibid.*

21 Sharaf al-Dīn b. Nūr al-Dīn Andījānī, *Tārīkh-i Mīr Sayyid Sharīf Rāqim*, Royal Asiatic Society ms. 163, fos. 116a–b.

forest of courage, he was a lion-hunting tiger; in the sea of generosity his hand rained pearls.[22]

Ḥaydar Dughlāt, as well as others, states that ʿUbayd Allāh excelled in writing the *naskh* script and copied a number of Qurʾāns which he sent as gifts to Mecca and Medina. Besides poetry, ʿUbayd Allāh composed music and some of his songs were still being sung in Dughlāt's time. Nithārī Bukhārī adds that the khan was a student of *ḥadīth* and *fiqh*, that he translated from Persian into Turkī and wrote a work on *qirāʾa*, coincidentally the same Qurʾānic science that Shībānī Khan studied. Nithārī lists twenty-one famous scholars, religious figures and artists who enjoyed ʿUbayd Allāh Khan's patronage. Among them was the calligrapher Mīr ʿAlī Harawī, the great master of the *nastaʿlīq* script, whose career began in the Timurid secretariat (*dār al-inshāʾ*) in Herat in the 1490s. In Bukhārā, Mīr ʿAlī spent sixteen years under the patronage of first ʿUbayd Allāh and then his son, ʿAbd al-ʿAzīz, and trained a generation of master calligraphers as director (*malik al-kuttāb*) of the royal scriptorium (*kitābkhāna*).[23] ʿUbayd Allāh Khan was also patron of the landscape architect Mīrak-i Ghiyāsī, who designed a public garden for him in Bukhārā and then went on to greater fame and fortune in India.

The 1530s and 1540s saw the major Abu'l-Khayrid cities of Bukhārā, Samarqand and Balkh thrive as centres of cultural activity, distinguished by much new architecture. Nithārī calls Samarqand a 'science centre' (*dar al-ʿilm*) under Kūchkunjī Khan's son and successor as khan, ʿAbd al-Laṭīf (r. 1540–52).[24] The latter was particularly noted for his support of astronomy. He refurbished Ulugh Beg's observatory and sponsored research there.[25] At the same time in Bukhārā, ʿUbayd Allāh Khan's son, ʿAbd al-ʿAzīz (d. 1550), maintained his father's cultural legacy as appanage ruler of Bukhārā, although he never became supreme khan himself. He composed poetry under the pen name ʿAzīzī in both Persian and Turkī and sponsored much new monumental architecture, including a mosque inside the 'old walls' (*ḥiṣār-i qadīm*) of Bukhārā and a madrasa situated in the south-west quadrant of Bukhārā, a madrasa known today as 'The Khan's Mother's Madrasa'.[26] He also built the great *khānaqā* which still stands at the tomb of Bahāʾ al-Dīn Naqshband just to

22 Mirza Muḥammad Haidar Dughlat, *Tārikh-i Rashidi: A history of the khans of Moghulistan*, Eng. trans. and ann. W. M. Thackston (Cambridge, MA, 1996), p. 182a.
23 P. P. Soucek, 'ʿAlī Heravī, also known as Mir ʿAli Kāteb Hosaynī', *EIr* vol. I, pp. 864–5.
24 Nithārī, *Mudhakkir-i aḥbāb*, p. 45.
25 *Ibid.*, pp. 44–5.
26 Bakhtiyar Babajanov, 'Datation de la mosquée Vâlida-ye ʿAbd al-ʿAzîz Xân à Boukhara', *Studia Iranica*, 28 (1999), pp. 227–34.

the east of the city.[27] Another project of his was the expansion of the city walls which were referred to in later documents as the 'new walls' (*ḥiṣār-i jadīd*).

Balkh was first taken by Shībānī Khan after a siege in late 1506, then retaken by the Timurids in 1516 and finally regained once and for all by the Shibanids in 1526. The Jānī-Begid Shībānid, Kīstan Qarā Sulṭān, ruled Balkh from then until his death in 1547 or 1548 and during his rule the city underwent major renovation and development. This was contemporary with 'Ubayd Allāh Khan's work in Bukhārā and that of the Kūchkunjids in Samarqand. He rebuilt walls, erected a palace (*'imārat*) in the citadel (*arg*), restored the congregational mosque built by the Timurid Sulṭān-Ḥusayn Bāyqarā, and added a public bath to its endowment.[28] None of this survives today, at least above ground.

Another architectural complex of the same period, the shrine and madrasa of the Parsā'ī family, suffered a kinder fate, surviving to the present time though in drastically truncated and altered form. In the first half of the sixteenth century, a new madrasa was built at that site and at the very end of the century the complex underwent extensive renovation.[29]

The deaths of 'Abd al-'Azīz at Bukhārā in 1550 and 'Abd al-Laṭīf at Samarqand in 1552 opened an era of inter-appanage warfare that lasted for the next three decades and ended with the Jānī-Begid clan as the paramount Abu'l-Khayrid Shībānid clan in Transoxania and Balkh. The cousin-clans – the Kūchkunjids, Suyūnjukids and Shāh Budāqids – were all eliminated in this period. Cultural investments came increasingly to be concentrated in the Jānī-Begid centre, Bukhārā, although some work was still done in Samarqand and Balkh. Royally sponsored work for the most part is associated with the name of 'Abd Allāh b. Iskandar, the paramount figure of the Jānī-Begids. Although he only became khan in 1583 he was the unquestioned leader and policy-maker of the clan from the mid-1550s onwards, and probably disposed of most of the family's surplus wealth as well. Besides the khan, the great patrons of the time were 'Abd Allāh's right-hand *amīr*, Qul Bābā Kukaltash, and the shaykhly family of the Jūybārīs who had assisted him and his father to power in Bukhārā.

27 Nithārī, *Mudhakkir-i aḥbāb*, pp. 78–9; Sharaf al-Dīn, *Tārīkh-i Mīr Sayyid Sharīf Rāqim*, fos. 131b, 132a, 138a.

28 Sulṭān Muḥammad b. Darwīsh Muḥammad, *Majma' al-gharā'ib fi bayān al-'ajā'ib*, IVAN, Uzbekistan, ms. 1494, fos. 16a–16b; Sharaf al-Dīn, *Tārīkh-i Mīr Sayyid Sharīf Rāqim*, fos. 116b, 127a; Anon., *Tazkirah-i tawārīkh*, IVAN, Uzbekistan, ms. 361/VI, fo. 128a.

29 R. D. McChesney, 'Architecture and narrative: The Khwaja Abu Nasr Parsa shrine', (Part One) *Muqarnas*, 18 (2001), p. 105.

The records of ʿAbd Allāh Khan's public works are extensive and probably explain his later legendary status as a builder – comparable in the region to Chinggis Khan's mythic reputation as a destroyer. The Abu'l-Khayrid Jānī-Begid khan built at least four madrasas, two in Bukhārā and one each in Balkh and Nasaf (Qarshī). He is also credited with a congregational mosque in Bukhārā and several parish mosques in various towns of the region. A great deal of commercial infrastructure was also erected under his auspices – bridges, large cisterns (*sar ḥawż*), caravanserais, warehouses (*tīms* and *ribāṭs*) and retail markets (*chārsūs*) such as the three still-surviving *ṭāqs* in Bukhārā.[30] He was a great patron of architecture on behalf of shrine centres, the Jūybārī shrine at Chār Bakr outside Bukhārā being the most notable beneficiary of his support.[31] His principal chronicler, Ḥāfiẓ-i Tanīsh, attributes to him a *chahār bāgh*, a *khānaqā*, a mosque and a madrasa at the site[32] but it is clear that the Jūybārī shaykhly family was also involved in and responsible for at least the mosque. In any event the khan and the head of the family, Khwāja Saʿd Jūybārī, were such intimates that sponsorship of the Chār Bakr buildings was in all likelihood a joint endeavour.

Amirid patronage in the sixteenth century

Like their Chinggisid overlords, the Uzbek *amīrs* played a major role in furthering Muslim culture. The *amīrs* were not an undifferentiated mass and their prominence as patrons depended on their personal ties to the Chinggisid ruling clan. Hierarchies of *amīrs* are found in Bannā'ī's *Shībānī-nāma* for the early part of the sixteenth century and in Maḥmūd b. Amīr Walī's *Baḥr al-asrār* for the early seventeenth century. Bannā'ī begins his biography of Shibani Khan, the reviver of Chinggisid fortunes in Mawarannahr and Balkh, with a chapter on those '*amīrs* and heroes (*bahādurān*)' who aided Muḥammad Shibani in empire-building, primacy of place being given to those who banded with him during his *qāzāqī*, his period of freebootery, when he had no territory of his own and his sword was for hire.[33] From a different age and reflecting a

30 G. A. Pugachenkova and E. V. Rtveladze, 'Bukhara V. Archeology and monuments', *EIr*, vol. IV, pp. 526b–527b and R. D. McChesney, 'Economic and social aspects of the public architecture of Bukhara in the 1560s and 1570s', *Islamic Art*, 2 (1987), pp. 224–30.

31 Bakhtyar Babajanov and Maria Szuppe, *Les inscriptions persanes de Chār Bakr, necropole familiale des* khwāja *Jūybārī près de Boukhara, corpus inscriptionum iranicarum*, Part IV: *Persian inscriptions down to the early Safavid period*, vol. XXXI: *Uzbekistan* (London, 2002).

32 Ḥāfiẓ-i Tanīsh, *Sharaf-nāma-i Shāhī*, ed. and trans. M. A. Salakhetdinova (vols. 1 and 2 only of four projected) (Moscow, 1983–9), fos. 103b–104b, pp. 225–7 (Russian trans.).

33 Kamāl al-Dīn Bannā'ī (Binā'ī), *Shaybānī-nāma*, ed. Kazuyuki Kubo (Kyoto, 1997), pp. 5–7.

different political reality, the *Baḥr al-asrār* divides its discussion of the *amīrs* between those who were affiliated with the khan in Bukhārā and those affiliated with the author's patron in Balkh. Further differentiations are made based on office held, with the 'father-surrogate' or 'tutor' (*atālīq, atāka*) and the 'milk brother' (*kūkaltāsh*) representing the pinnacle of amirid proximity to the Chinggisid clan. The leading *amīrs* at least had resources at their disposal comparable to those available to the Chinggisid ruling clan. One of Kīstan Qarā Sulṭān's *amīrs*, Kamāl al-Dīn Qunāq (*fl.* 1540), for example, built and endowed an extensive congregational mosque and madrasa complex in Balkh just outside the inner city walls.[34] Nithārī tells of his own study of astronomy at Kamāl al-Dīn Qunāq's madrasa.[35] Yet today, except for the tombs of Kistan Qara and a woman, possibly his daughter, Sharīfa Sulṭān Khānum, no trace of either his or Kamāl al-Dīn Qunaq's extensive architectural legacy has survived.[36]

Another great amirid patron of literature and architecture was Qul Bābā Kūkaltāsh (d. 1598), ʿAbd Allāh b. Iskandar's chief *amīr* and leading administrator of his regime. Besides leading the army on numerous campaigns, he oversaw the work of ʿAbd Allāh's chancellery as *mushrif-i dīwānī*. He also had charge of the judicial administration (*ṣadārat-i khānī*) and in this capacity apparently was assigned to probate ʿAbd Allāh Khan's father's estate.[37] Qul Bābā was also a great patron of architecture, some of which survives. He is best known today for his great Bukhārān madrasa of 160 cells (*ḥujras*) which stands on the north side of the Lab-i Hawz (see below). According to its endowment deed, it was built in 976/1568. and probably housed more than 300 students in its heyday. He is also said to have built madrasas in Samarqand, Tashkent, Herat and Taluqan. And while he was governor of Samarqand (after the ouster of the last Kūchkunjid there in the spring of 1578) he devoted many of his resources to restoring and refurbishing Timurid buildings in the city. According to Ḥāfiẓ-i Tanīsh this was done at the instructions of ʿAbd Allāh Sulṭān after his visit in January 1580.[38] Like his khan, Qul Bābā is also

34 For a description and the endowment of this complex see R. D. McChesney, 'Reconstructing Balkh: The *Vaqfiya* of 947/1540', in Devin DeWeese (ed.), *Studies on Central Asian history in honor of Yuri Bregel* (Bloomington, IN, 2001), pp. 187–243.

35 Nithārī, *Mudhakkir-i aḥbāb* (New Delhi, 1969), pp. 373–4.

36 For a photograph of Kīstan Qarā's tomb see Bernard O'Kane, 'The Uzbek architecture of Afghanistan', *La mémoire et ses supports en Asie central; Cahiers d'Asie Centrale*, 8 (2000), pp. 122, 128.

37 Ḥāfiẓ-i Tanīsh, *Sharaf-nāma-i Shāhī*, India Office Library ms. 575, fo. 311a.

38 *Ibid.*, India Office Library ms. 574, fos. 234b, 276b.

credited with the building of commercial structures, including a serai in Bukhārā and a *ribāṭ* near Balkh.[39]

Qul Bābā was a man who loved literature and compiled a large library which he donated to his madrasa in Bukhārā. He hosted literary assemblies and took the pen name 'Muḥibbī'. Muṭribī Samarqandī, who knew him personally, relates an occasion on which Qul Bābā offered him 1,000 *tangas* if he could compose five lines of poetry that would appropriately complete an opening line (*maṭla*ʿ) which he gave him. But Mutrībī felt the number of possible rhyming syllables was limited and, 'the horse of his mind having come up lame in running back and forth searching for those words', he had to excuse himself.[40]

Shībānid-era shaykhly patronage

Under Abu'l-Khayrid auspices, the descendants of Khwāja 'Ubayd Allāh Aḥrār, Khwāja Aḥmad Kāsānī and Khwāja Muḥammad Pārsā, all Naqshbandīs, flourished in their respective centres (the Aḥrārīs in Tashkent and Samarqand, the Kāsānīs or Dahbīdīs in Dahbīd outside Samarqand and the Pārsā'īs in Bukhārā and Balkh). One shaykhly family in particular, the Jūybārīs, stands out for its political influence and its wealth. Its transformation from a modest family of shrine caretakers (responsible for the Chār Bakr shrine west of Bukhārā City) to an extraordinarily wealthy dynasty of kingmakers was completed in the second half of the sixteenth century. Along with this transformation came the acquisition of enormous wealth. An outsider, Anthony Jenkinson, was mightily impressed by the founder of the family's fortune, Khwāja Muḥammad Islām, when he reached Bukhārā in December of 1558:

> There is a Metropolitane in this Boghar who causeth this lawe (Sharīʿa) to be straightly kept, and he is more obeyed than the King and will depose the king, and place another at his will and pleasure as he did by this king that reigned at our being there.[41]

The basis of the Jūybārī family's landed wealth is richly documented but where the capital originated remains something of a mystery. Land and other real estate in and around Bukhārā were purchased in astonishing amounts

39 *Ibid.*, fos. 311b, 456b; Muḥammad Badīʿ Samarqandī, *Muẕakkir al-aṣḥāb*, IVAN, Uzbekistan, ms. 4270, fo. 44b.
40 Muṭribī Samarqandī, *Tazkirat al-shuʿarā* (Tehran, 1377/1998), pp. 460–1.
41 E. Delmar Morgan and C. H. Coote (eds.), *Early voyages and travels to Russia and Persia by Anthony Jenkinson and other Englishmen*, (New York repr. of London 1886 edn), vol. I, pp. 83–84.

over a thirty-year period between 1544 and 1577.[42] The Jūybārīs (Muḥammad Islām 'Khwāja Jūybārī', his son Khwāja Sa'd 'Khwāja Kalān Khwāja' and subsequent generations) used this wealth to make themselves major patrons of architecture, scholarship and art from the second half of the sixteenth century down to the early nineteenth,[43] building madrasas and mosques, patronising painters and calligraphers, and commissioning biographies of the family. This tradition was carried on by their descendants through subsequent centuries. Their best-known surviving monuments are the Gāwkushān Madrasa and Friday Mosque complex straddling the main canal (the Rūd-i Shahr) that bisects Bukhārā, the Kalabad madrasa in the eastern part of the city and the Chār Bakr complex. The greatest builder in the family was the Khwāja Sa'd al-Dīn (aka Khwāja Kalān Khwāja, d. 1589) son of the founder of the family's wealth. He has been credited with at least seventy-five major public works including parish and congregational mosques, madrasas, *khānaqās*, *chahār bāghs*, public baths, caravanserais, canals and underground cisterns (*sardāba*). No other figure in either the sixteenth or seventeenth century approached this level of public building.

The Tuqāy-Timurid era: 1599–1747

In 1598–9, the Shībānid Chinggisids in Māwarānnahr and Balkh succumbed to internecine struggles and external pressures. A new Jochid-Chinggisid family, the Tuqāy-Timurid, found the needed amirid support to oust the last of the Jānī-Begid Shībānids from Bukhārā and take power.

As their resources permitted, the Tuqay-Timurids followed the established pattern of their Shībānid predecessors in sponsoring public works projects. No building activity or other cultural patronage is yet associated with the name of the first Tuqāy-Timurid khan, Jānī Muḥammad (r. 1599–1606), but his sons, Bāqī Muḥammad and Walī Muḥammad, on the other hand are both well memorialised as builders. The former sponsored the construction of a Friday mosque and a madrasa in Bukhārā, both of which survived into the nineteenth

42 *Iz arkhiva Dzhuibari*, ed. [F. B. Rostopchin] and E. E. Bertel's (Leningrad, 1938) contains some 400 deeds of sale for properties throughout Central Asia but mostly concentrated in Bukhara City and the Bukharan oasis. In addition, collections of individual sale deeds as well as deeds of gift to the Jūybārīs and endowments they created are found in the archives of Uzbekistan and Tajikistan.

43 James B. Fraser, *Narrative of a journey into Khorasan in the years 1821 and 1823* (1984 repr. of London 1825 edn), Appendix B, 83 calls the Jūybārīs of his day 'the greatest of these holy personages (i.e. the ulema)' who could be considered 'independent of the king' due to their immense wealth.

century, along with a *chahār bāgh*, the location of which is no longer known. In Samarqand, which he briefly held in 1598–9, he is remembered for an assembly hall (*kūrnīsh-khāna*) and a holiday prayer ground (*ʿīd-gāh*).

Walī Muḥammad, who held Balkh before he became khan, is remembered for his patronage of the shrine ʿAlī b. Abī Ṭālib to the east of the city. He had an avenue (*khiyābān* – usually implying landscaping with trees and gardens as well as a road) laid out between Balkh and the village (now the city of Mazār-i Sharīf) where the shrine was situated. At the shrine itself, he renovated and expanded part of the shrine building. He also had a 50-acre *chahār bāgh* of eighteen parterres (*chaman*) constructed.[44]

Imām Qulī Khan, who ruled Bukhārā from 1611 to 1641, has left virtually no record of patronage. A single madrasa in Bukhārā and a large canal at Tāshqurghān are the only projects attributed to him in the textual record. His brother, Nadhr Muḥammad, on the other hand, who ruled independently south of the Oxus river during the same period, was a very active builder. In the detailed history of his reign at Balkh, the *Baḥr al-aṣrār fi manāqib al-akhyār* (which he commissioned), Nadhr Muḥammad is depicted as a major patron of architecture. In the outer city, he built a large madrasa of fired brick (begun in 1021/1612) with four lecture halls and many dormitory rooms and a library of 2,000 volumes. He also built a palace district (*dawlat-khāna*) in several (the cosmological number 'twelve' is given) sections (*darband*) in a garden-estate that had once belonged to a Jani-Begid-era *amīr*, Mīr Jān Kildi Bi. Although no trace of it remains today, all evidence indicates the complex was brought to completion. The Mughal historian ʿInāyat Khan, author of the *Shāh Jahān-nāma*, mentions its existence in 1056/1646 when a Mughal army occupied the city.[45] The Tuqāy-Timurid ruler of Balkh also constructed a congregational mosque in Qunduz. In addition, seven hunting lodges or palaces are also attributed to him and these may well have been inspired by descriptions he heard of the hunting palaces constructed by Shāh Jahān in India.

His sons and subsequent successors to the khanate, ʿAbd al-ʿAzīz and Subḥān Qulī, both left major madrasas with rich endowments as monuments to their reigns. The ʿAbd al-ʿAzīz Khan madrasa today stands opposite the madrasa of Ulugh Beg in the Goldsmith's Quarter of Bukhārā but only a

44 R. D. McChesney, *Waqf in Central Asia: Four hundred years in the history of a Muslim shrine 1480–1889*, (Princeton, 1991), pp. 88–90.

45 Ināyat Khan, *The Shāh Jahan Nama*, trans. A. R. Fuller, ed. and completed W. E. Begley and Z. A. Desai (Delhi and New York, 1990), p. 350.

remnant, the entryway, remains of the Subḥān Qulī Khan madrasa in Balkh, which was built opposite the Abū Naṣr Pārsā shrine.

Uzbek amirid patronage under the Tuqay-Timurids

The leading *amīrs* of the seventeenth century, men like Nadr Bī Dīwānbegī Arlāt and Yalangtūsh Bī Alchīn, have left a substantially richer record of patronage than their Tuqay-Timurid masters. Like their sixteenth-century predecessors, they cultivated shaykhly and scholarly figures by building and endowing madrasas and *khānaqās*. Today much of the architectural legacy of Nadr Bī Arlāt and Yalangtūsh Bī Alchīn survives in Samarqand and Bukhārā.

Nadr Bī Arlāt had the nickname 'Taghāy', a kinship name referring to the fact that his aunt was Imām Qulī Khan's mother.[46] He was Imām Qulī's most trusted *amīr* and held the position of *dīwānbegī*, chief financial officer. He took a special interest in the Aḥrārī legacy in Samarqand, erecting a madrasa (recently renovated) at the tomb of Khwāja Aḥrār as well as a tomb enclosure (*ḥaẓīra*), presumably around the platform (*ṣuffa*) on which Aḥrār's tombstone now stands. Work on the madrasa began in 1630 and was completed in 1635–6. South of the city he built a hostel (*khānaqāh*) at the shrine called ''Abdī Bīrūn'. The building that survives there today does not, however, seem to be the hostel. In Bukhārā, Nadr Bī sponsored the building of what has become the centre of the old city, the Lab-i Ḥawż (Cistern's Edge). His constructions there included a madrasa and *khānaqāh* facing each other across a huge stone reservoir (*ḥawż*). All three works are intact and have been recently refurbished. The north side of this complex is flanked by the Qul Bābā Kūkaltāsh madrasa. Both the Nadr Bī and Qul Bābā Kūkaltāsh madrasas were important educational centres from the time of their construction well into the Soviet period.

Nadr Bī was the leading *amīr* under Imām Qulī Khan and was called the 'guiding vizier and the righteous *amīr*' by Maḥmūd b. Amīr Walī. Besides his marital connection to the khan, he had also married one of his daughters to a Jūybārī scion and another to Khusraw, the second son of Imām Qulī's brother, Nadhr Muḥammad. Intermarriage between khanly, shaykhly and amirid families was common throughout the two centuries discussed here and served to meld the interests and the constituencies of the three elite groups.

46 Maḥmūd b. Amīr Walī, *Baḥr al-asrār*, vol. VI, part 4, fos. 124a–b. Also see L. Z. Budagov, *Sravnitel'nyi slovar' turetsko-tatarskikh narechii* (St Petersburg, 1869), *ṭāgha, taghāy, ṭaghāy* 'uncle on the mother's side (elder or younger brother of the mother)'.

Yalangtūsh Bī Alchīn was very much a self-made man. His given name was Jatāy Bahādur and he left Shighnaq in the Qıpchaq steppe at the age of twelve to link his fortunes to the Tuqāy-Timurids. He may have come south with his father, Bāy Khwāja Bī, but we know nothing of the latter. Yalangtūsh offered his services to Dīn Muḥammad apparently during the Shībānid/Uzbek occupation of Herat and the Tuqay-Timurid campaigns in Quhistān, that is in the early to mid-1590s, and was given the title 'Yalangtūsh' ('bare-chested'[47]) by Dīn Muḥammad for heroic action. He was known by this name from then on. Once the Tuqāy-Timurids came to power in Transoxania, he was assigned first to one of the collateral branches of the family and spent a few years fighting the Qazāq threat in the east. He then was with Imām Qulī in Samarqand during Walī Muḥammad's reign (1606–11). It was in those years that he not only acquired extensive properties in the Samarqand region but also forged close ties to the Dahbīdī Naqshbandī shaykhs. By the early 1620s he was with Nadhr Muḥammad in Balkh and had been assigned control of the marches to the south. He built two very large madrasas in Samarqand on the Rigistan; these madrasas were popularly known as the Shīrdār/Shayrdār ('lion-possessing', for the depictions of lions on the spandrels) and the Ṭillā Kār ('gilded', for the decoration). They flank the east and north sides of the Rigistan square respectively. The Shīrdār, on which work proceeded from 1619 to 1636 under the supervision of the architect Mullā ʿAbd al-Jabbār, faces the Ulugh Beg madrasa across the square. The Ṭillā Kār madrasa, constructed a decade after the Shīrdār, at some point came to serve as the main congregational mosque, probably due to the dilapidation of the great Friday mosque of Temür, known today as the Bībī Khānum mosque.

Outside Samarqand at Dahbīd, the shrine centre of the 'Makhdūm-i Aʿzam' Khwājagī Aḥmad-i Kāsānī (d. 1549) and the centre of the missionary organisation that was carrying Naqshbandī Sufism eastward into China, Yalangtūsh Bī constructed a *khānaqā*, no longer extant. He also planted an avenue of plane trees (*chinār*) so that the members of the order could travel to Samarqand in shade. According to Maḥmūd b. Amīr Walī, the endowment for the two madrasas in Samarqand was a 'gift' for the Dahbīdī shaykhs.

Yalangtūsh Bi's wealth in land was considerable. The Uzbek State Archives contain at least eight documents relating to his properties, including two endowment deeds. A land survey undertaken by the tsarist government in

47 I am grateful to Florian Schwarz for this information. Maḥmūd b. Amīr Walī may have been referring to a fight in which the warrior went into battle without armour.

the 1870s revealed that the endowment lands for his madrasas exceeded 5,300 *ṭanābs* or about 2,700 acres.[48]

These few examples typify the building activity of the elites of Mawarannahr and Balkh and serve to represent the hundreds of other public building projects – *chahār bāghs*, parish mosques, canals, bridges, prayer grounds (*ʿīdgāhs*), assembly halls (*kürnush-khānas*), cisterns (*sar ḥawż* and *sardāba*) and commercial structures (*tīms*, serais, *ribāṭs*, caravanserais), etc. for which records exist. Building construction as we know it from texts seems to have peaked in the last half of the sixteenth century and this would accord with what is known about the trajectory of the region's economy, fuelled perhaps by New World silver until the early seventeenth century and then subsiding, in part because of the decline of the precious metal exports from South and Central America that eventually found their way to Central Asia via the Philippines and India, and in part perhaps because of the unusual climatic conditions of the seventeenth century (the so-called 'cold century'). Whatever the causes, after 1650 at the latest, major construction projects are no longer recorded at the rate sketched above.

Islamic scholarship

Although monographic studies of the intellectual history of sixteenth- and seventeenth-century Central Asia have yet to be written, certain trends and patterns may be discerned in the literature of the time. For one thing, scholars showed a degree of regional loyalty, not surprising considering that Central Asia was the nursery of Ḥanafī legal studies, and Ḥanafī Islam was the nearly universal legal tradition followed by Central Asian scholars of the period. Works by authors of Central Asian origin or by authors who had spent a considerable part of their lives working in the madrasas, law courts and political courts of the region but who had immigrated (sometimes involuntarily) from elsewhere dominate the book lists of this era, whether these lists are found in book endowments, in the curricula vitae of scholars or in licences to teach (*ijāzāt*). In addition to the geographical focus, a Timurid-era provenance of a majority of the books found in the book lists of the seventeenth century is evidence of the creation and canonisation of a madrasa curriculum

48 Gosarkhiv Uzbekistana, *Kollektsiia vakufnykh dokumentov*, Tashkent, 1983, nos. 1180/9, 1197/1–6, 1203/9. See also O. D. Chekhovich, *Dokumenty k istorii agrarnykh otnoshenii v Bukharskom khanstve XVI–XIX vv.*, Tashkent, 1954, documents 1, 2, 6, 9 and 13.

under Timurid auspices. As noted above, the five most important scholars of the Timurid period in terms of producing the texts underlying the madrasa curriculum of later centuries were al-Taftāzānī, al-Jurjānī (al-Sayyid al-Sharīf), al-Jazarī, Jāmī and Kāshifī. The first three were either invited or transported to Temür's court in Samarqand while the last two were part of the Herat court scene under Sulṭān-Ḥusayn Mīrzā and the 'Maecenas of the age', Mīr ʿAlī Shīr Nawāʾī. Their original works as well as their commentaries, glosses and superglosses make up a substantial part of the lists of books donated to madrasas or cited as the books a well-educated person should know. For example, in one endowment of books to the Ulugh Beg madrasa in Bukhārā eight of the seventy books in the list were titles by al-Taftāzānī alone.[49]

The lives of many scholars bridged the unsettling transition from Timurid to Shibanid rule, as already noted. As an example of the importance attributed to that period for contemporary scholarship, Maḥmūd b. Amīr Walī devotes several pages to the great scholars who migrated to Transoxania in the early sixteenth century from Timurid lands and left a legacy of works which students in his own day, a century later, were still studying. One such example is the philologist ʿIṣām al-Dīn Ibrāhīm b. Muḥammad al-Isfarāʾīnī (d. 1537). Al-Isfarāʾīnī taught in Herat at the Shāh Rukh Mīrzā madrasa during the reign of Sulṭān-Ḥusayn Bayqara but left in 1520 for Bukhārā where he enjoyed the patronage of ʿUbayd Allāh Khan until his death.[50] One of the books Maḥmūd mentions that students of his time were reading was Isfarāʾīnī's gloss (*ḥāshiya*) on ʿAbd al-Raḥmān Jāmī's *al-Fawāʾid al-Ziyāʾıyah*, in turn a commentary (*sharḥ*) on Ibn Ḥājib's work on Arabic syntax, *al-Kāfiya*.[51] Other standard works by al-Isfarāʾīnī on the madrasa curriculum were a commentary on Nasafī's famous creed, a supergloss (*ḥāshiya ʿalā ḥāshiya*) on Jūrjānī's gloss on Taftazānī's commentary on Khatīb al-Dimashqī's abridgement of al-Sakkākī's work on rhetoric, *Miftāh al-ʿulūm* and a gloss on Kāshifī's commentary on the Qurʾān.

Support for scholars and scholarship

Thanks to the observant eye and detailed records kept by Maḥmūd b. Amīr Walī and later historians of the seventeenth century, the outlines of academic (as distinct from mystical) scholarship as well as scholarly life are fairly distinct.

49 Uzbek State Archives fond I-323, document no. 114/2.
50 Khwāndamīr, *Ḥabīb al-siyar*, 3/3: 358.
51 Maḥmūd b. Amīr Walī, *Baḥr al-asrār*, vol. VI, part 4, fos. 149aff.

Besides endowed professorships at madrasas, scholars seeking a stipend to support their work had a number of government offices to aspire to. Those to which people of learning were appointed and which were not reserved for certain families included: *ṣadr, qāḍī, qāḍī-ʿaskar, muftī, muftī-ʿaskar, raʾīs* and *raʾīs-iʿaskar*. The exact functions of all these offices must be inferred from the context in which they appear. What seems clear is that the titles suffixed with '-*ʿaskar*' were connected to the court of the appanage khan while every town with a *sharīʿa* court would have had a *qāḍī, muftī* and *raʾīs*. In addition, by the beginning of the seventeenth century one finds the honorary title of *aʿlam al-ʿulamāʾ* ('most learned of the learned'). By all accounts conferral of these offices and titles was based on merit, although being the son of such an office-holder was a definite advantage if one aspired to the same career.

The offices of *shaykh al-islām* and *naqīb*, on the other hand, were reserved for individuals from specific families and were not strictly speaking associated with scholarship. In this period, every major city had a *shaykh al-islām* while the office of *naqīb* seems to have been restricted to the khanly court. Efforts have been made to determine the role of the *shaykh al-islām* in Timurid times[52] but the term occurs there in different contexts and all one can say for certain is that it was considered the most prestigious title for those connected with Sufi traditions. During the sixteenth and seventeenth centuries, the title was reserved for specific shaykhly families. In Jānī-Begid Bukhārā (i.e. after 1556) the office of *shaykh al-islām* belonged by right to the Jūybārī family. In Samarqand it was granted to the Aḥrārīs, in Balkh it had been given to the Parsāʾīs in Shāh Rukh's time (r. 1409–47), according to Maḥmūd b. Amīr Walī, and was still held by them in the mid-seventeenth century. Throughout Transoxania and Cisoxania, the office of *naqīb*[53] was held by either members of the Sayyid Atāʾī family itself or members of the Sayyid Atāʾī order, an offshoot of the Yasawiyyah.[54] When the Tuqāy-Timurids came to power (1599 in Transoxania and 1601 in Balkh) those privileges were all reviewed. In Samarqand by the end of the seventeenth century, the office of *naqīb* (*niqābat*) was in the hands of the Dahbīdīs where it seems to have remained, and in Balkh, a Sayyid Atāʾī was dismissed from the post in 1634 and replaced by a Naqshbandī, a shaykhly line connected with the shrine centre at Bukhārā.

52 Shiro Ando, 'The *shaykh al-islam* as a Timurid office: A preliminary study', *Islamic Studies*, 33 (1994), pp. 253–80.

53 Devin DeWeese, 'The descendants of Sayyid Ata and the rank of *naqīb* in Central Asia', *Journal of the American Oriental Society*, 115 (1994); pp. 612–34.

54 Devin DeWeese, 'Atāʾīya order', *EIr*, vol. II, pp. 904–5.

All offices were subject to the approval of the appanage khan, whose right of appointment and dismissal was absolute. Qualifications were made known to him by the recommendations of others or by a kind of competitive interview process over which the khan presided and at which supplicants were asked to discuss and debate a particular question. Sometimes the credentials became known to the khan at his more informal assemblies where extemporaneous skills were challenged: to produce or answer a riddle, for example, or to compose a verse after being given the *maṭlaʿ* (the two opening hemistichs of a poem). Notable scholars themselves held assemblies at which budding talent emerged. One of the *qāḍīs* of Balkh, a man known as Khwāja Mullā-yi Qāḍī, is a case in point. His father left Khurāsān for Māwarānnahr probably following one of ʿUbayd Allāh's forays there. He entered the service of Iskandar Khan the Jānī-Begid and then worked for ʿAbd Allāh, Iskandar's son and successor as khan. We are told he frequented the salons of individual scholars and it was through this avenue that he came to the attention of ʿAbd al-Muʾmin, ʿAbd Allāh's son, who took him to Balkh and appointed him *qāḍī* and professor at the ʿAbd Allāh Khan madrasa. (The frequency of joint appointments of *qāḍīs* to professorships suggests the endowed professorship may have been the source of the salary.)

The *ʿulamāʾ* proper, that is those who might have sought credentials for, and eventually aspired to, the formal position of *aʿlam al-ʿulamāʾ* (or *aʿlamī* for short), by and large tended not to be from shaykhly backgrounds. But not unlike the shaykhly families, the pre-eminent scholars of the time tended to have a regional importance only and did not generally move from city to city. In Bukhārā the pre-eminent *ʿulamāʾ* of the seventeenth century were, first, Mawlānā Yūsuf Qarābāghī (dates of his death vary from 1624 to 1645) and after him Mullā Muḥammad Sharīf al-Bukhārī (d. after 1699). Qarabāghī's and Bukhārī's work followed the same disciplines – glosses on Qurʾānic commentaries (Bayżawī especially), on works of Ḥanafī jurisprudence and on works of logic (particularly those of Taftāzānī and Jalāl al-Dīn Dawānī). The library of the Biruni Institute of Oriental Studies in Tashkent, Uzbekistan contains two separate glosses on Bayżawī's commentary on the *Sūrat al-fatḥ* and a gloss on Dawānī's (d. 1502) commentary on al-Ījī's (d. 1335) *al-Mawāqif fī ʿilm al-kalām*, an extraordinarily popular handbook on theology, all by Qarābāghī.

The scholarly career of al-Bukhārī is somewhat more accessible than Qarabāghī's and as his work follows the same path – he in fact wrote a gloss on *al-Mawāqif* avowedly to bring to completion the Dawānī-Qarābāghī commentary – it is not unreasonable to think that Bukhārī was Qarābāghī's student and that therefore we can infer something about Qarābāghī's career from Bukhārī's. Both were connected to the politicians of their time: Qarābāghī reportedly supported Imām Qulī Khan (r. 1611–41 at Bukhārā) in his successful bid to take the khanate from Walī Muḥammad Khan (r. 1606–11) and although al-Bukhārī's direct involvement in politics is unknown, he did dedicate his commentary on *al-Mawāqif* to the Tuqāy-Timurid khan at Bukhārā, ʿAbd al-ʿAzīz (r. 1645–81). When the latter's brother assumed the khanate at Bukhārā in 1681, al-Bukhārī resigned his position as *aʿlam al-ʿulamāʾ* and his professorships (perhaps in anticipation of losing these to scholars favoured by the incoming khan) and retired to his *khānaqā*.

Mullā Muḥammad Sharīf al-Bukhārī's list of known works again reflects the very powerful influence of Timurid scholarship on later writing and is most notable for its similarity to the work of al-Isfarāʾīnī a century and a half earlier. He wrote a gloss on Jāmī's commentary *al-Fawā'id al-żiyā'īya* on Ibn Ḥājib's popular Arabic grammar *al-Kāfiyah fi'l-naḥw*; the above-mentioned gloss on Dawānī's and Qarābāghī's glosses on *al-Mawāqif* and also a supergloss on his own gloss on those works, and finally a gloss on Taftāzānī's widely used textbook on logic, *Tahdhīb al-manṭiq*.

At Balkh, the *aʿlam al-ʿulamāʾ* of the first half of the seventeenth century was Mawlānā Ḥasan Qubādyānī, a very influential teacher whose students went on to fill the offices of *qāḍī*, *muftī* and *ra'īs* throughout the region. At the end of the sixteenth century he was studying in Bukhārā, and early in the seventeenth came to Balkh at the request of the appanage khan there, Nadhr Muḥammad. By virtue of his brilliant performances at the assemblies for scholars presided over by the khan he won a professorship at the ʿAbd Allāh Khan madrasa. When Nadhr Muḥammad's own madrasa was completed (sometime after 1612) a professorship there was also given to him. Later Qubādyānī set out on the *ḥajj* pilgrimage via India and was received by Shāh Jahān but died soon after at Agra without reaching the Holy Cities. His son was one of his students and was appointed professor at the ʿAbd Allāh Khan madrasa in Balkh.

For scholars and shaykhly figures alike, styles of living should not be confused with their particular career paths. Individuals could be, and were, *ʿulamāʾ* in the traditional 'transmitted' disciplines of jurisprudence, Qurʾānic commentary and *ḥadīth* and yet follow a life of asceticism more commonly associated with mystics or Sufis. For example, a certain Mawlānā ʿAlī Beg was described as learned in *fiqh*, *tafsīr* and *ḥadīth*, wore the clothing 'of the people of poverty and annihilation' (*faqr wa-fanā*), and avoided contact with 'worldly people' (*abnā al-zamān*). Another man described as 'an extreme mystic who became a *malāmatī*, a term indicating behaviour or professed belief outside the norm, held a professorship at the Qul Bābā Kūkaltāsh madrasa and was at one point named to the post of *qāḍi-ʿaskar*. On the other hand many of those primarily known for their prominence in the Naqshbandī Sufi sub-orders were renowned and indeed celebrated for their affluence and luxurious lifestyles. Typical is an Aḥrārī from Samarqand, Khwāja Abu'l-Qāsim, who 'paraded in the garments of a possessor of great wealth as a means of concealing the face of the *mysterium*'. The narratives indicate that society could separate a person's learning and what that qualified them for from their personal religious beliefs and practices.

To sum up, scholarship in the sixteenth and seventeenth centuries followed and built on the scholarship of the Timurid era. Intellectuals were dependent on the government for positions in judicial administration and teaching for the living that would provide them the means to carry on their work. Politicians in turn looked to the output of the great madrasas of Bukhara, Samarqand and Balkh to staff not only their *sharīʿa* courts but to confirm their own roles as defenders of Islam and as continuators of the great scholarly traditions of Central Asia.

The Chinggisid restoration petered out in Khwārazm, Māwarānnahr and Balkh by the middle of the eighteenth century, although vestiges of Chinggisid norms and practices survived, and in Bukhārā and Balkh as nominal khans were kept in public view for a time. Eventually however, the *amīrs* used their power as the military support for Chinggisid claims to dispense entirely with the Chinggisid lines. But, during the restoration, due in no small part to the economic resources available during that period, the Chinggisids, both Shībānids and Tuqāy-Timurids, oversaw the continuation and expansion of Timurid Islamic culture.

8

India under Mughal rule

STEPHEN DALE

Introduction

In 1526 Ẓahīr al-Dīn Muḥammad Bābur (888–937/1483–1530) successfully invaded north India and founded the Mughal empire (932–*c.* 1152/1526–*c.* 1739) (see Map 6). Bābur, as he is generally known from his personal name – meaning leopard or tiger – was a Turco-Mongol, Ḥanafī Sunnī Muslim native of western Central Asia. He was descended from two Central Asian conquerors. These were the Barlas Turk Temür (736–807/1336–1405), known in Persian as Tīmūr-i leng, 'Tīmūr the lame', or in European parlance Tamerlane, and Chinggis Qan (*c.* 563–625/*c.* 1167–1227), or in Persian spelling Chingiz Khan. As a patrilineal descendant of Temür he thought of himself in ethnic, social and dynastic terms as a Turk and a Timurid, but he also revered his matrilineal Mongol connections traced through Chinggis Khan's second son Chaghadai. Raised as an observant Sunnī Muslim in the lush Farghāna valley east-south-east of Tashkent, Bābur was also born into the Naqshbandī Sufi order, a doctrinally conservative but politically active devotional order long connected with Temür's descendants. Bābur both wrote and spoke Turkī, the language common to most contemporary Turks and Mongols, but like many other well-educated men of the region he also knew Persian, the lingua franca and dominant literary language of the Iranian plateau and the cities of Central Asia and north India in the early modern era.

Bābur invaded India for two interrelated reasons. First, he was an ambitious warrior aristocrat of impeccable lineage, and second, he lacked a decent kingdom after the Uzbeks expelled him from Central Asia in 909/1504. Thus as a descendant of Temür and Chinggis Khan, he possessed, what he ingenuously describes in his autobiographical memoir, the *Vaqāʾiʿ*, as 'kingdom-seizing' ambitions. His descendants were similarly motivated, although they rarely expressed themselves so baldly. Then as he looked around from his impoverished base in Kabul, where he took refuge and ruled from 909/1504 to

932/1525, Bābur saw in north India a politically vulnerable and wealthy agrarian heartland that offered the economic basis for a respectable empire. He could also claim to be a legitimate ruler of the territory he identifies as Hindustān, a legacy of Temür's invasion of India and sack of Delhi in 800/1398. It is quite likely that Temür's example, commemorated by paintings and buildings in Samarqand, might have prompted Bābur to see India as a potential target for his ambition even before 925/1519, by which time he had decided on an invasion. By defeating the army of his fellow Muslims, the Afghan Lodīs, at the Pānīpat battlefield north of Delhi in 932/1526, Bābur initiated the Timurid renaissance, a dynasty whose eclectic culture was formed from the mutual influence of Bābur's Central Asian heritage and the indigenous traditions of his Indian empire.

In addition to its Central Asian and South Asian strains, the Mughal empire, or as it is variously known, the Indo-Timurid or Timurid-Mughul empire, should also be understood within the context of the other three contemporary early modern Islamic powers: the Ottoman and Safavid empires and the Uzbek confederation. These states were linked with and influenced Bābur and his descendants in a variety of ways. All three states were connected to Mughal India by well-established trading patterns and the circulation of literary, religious and scientific elites. However, apart from those common ties, the Ottomans, who shared the Mughal's Ḥanafī Sunnī orthodoxy, were particularly influential in Mughal India as experts in military tactics and fire-arms technology. The Safavids, a militantly Shīʿī dynasty, exported human capital to India in the form of Persian-speaking artists, bureaucrats and literati, even when the Safavid shahs were fighting Mughal armies for control of the wealthy and strategic city of Kandahar in south-central Afghanistan. The Uzbeks, a Ḥanafī Sunnī tribal confederation, were both the revanchist focus of Mughal imperial nostalgia and the homeland of the Mughal's Naqshbandī Sufi order. In addition Uzbek lands functioned as a source of military immi-grants and a reservoir of cavalry horses for the Mughal army. Thus Mughal India continued to function throughout its history as an interconnected regional variant of a broader Central Asian and Middle Eastern Islamic world. However, compared to the Ottomans, Safavids and Uzbeks, the Mughal empire's ultimate legacy was muted. Unlike those states, which ultimately gave way to ethnically recognisable successors with predominantly Muslim populations, the Mughals left behind a Muslim minority within an overwhelmingly non-Muslim environment ruled by a European trading com-pany. In that respect it is perhaps appropriate that the Tāj Mahal, Mughal India's most exquisite architectural artefact, is a tomb, although it is also particularly ironic that the Tāj Mahal has come to symbolise India for outsiders in modern times.

The Central Asian background

The Mughal empire's Central Asian heritage is a habitually neglected aspect of its history. It is common to begin accounts of the empire with the reign of Akbar (r. 963–1014/1556–1605), largely ignoring both Bābur and his son, Humāyūn (r. 937–47, 962–3/1530–40,1555–6). Yet the Mughal empire was in its origin a late-Timurid, Central Asian state and aspects of this heritage are visible throughout the dynasty's Indian history. That heritage involved, first of all, a dynastic culture characterised by a supremely confident sense of legitimacy and a perennially unstable succession tradition. The Mughals' confidence in their family's prestige is exhibited prominently in Bābur's memoirs, where he exhibits a casual arrogance and assumption of sovereignty – over any territory he fancied – born of his impeccable Turco-Mongol lineage. Contemporaries and such rulers as the Safavids generally accepted Babur's political conceit and that of his son Humāyūn. This recognition sustained both men during their tumultuous careers that were replete with near-death political experiences. Throughout the later history of the Mughal dynasty its rulers constantly reminded themselves and their courtiers of their genealogy in histories, paintings, inscriptions and royal titles, and, in truth, no earlier or contemporary Muslim rulers in India possessed imperial traditions of comparable grandeur.

If the Mughals' impeccable lineage distinguished them in India, that was partly because few other Timurids or Chinggisids of note survived the debacle of the Uzbek conquest to challenge their rule in Hindustān. During his Central Asian years, 888–909/1483–1504, Bābur had been just one among many Timurids and Chinggisids who struggled for power in what was an atomised, fragmented political 'system'. However, it was not just the multitude of legitimate claimants that fuelled the internecine wars of the late Timurid era. These conflicts were also the product of traditional Turco-Mongol inheritance and succession customs that were also noted features of Mughal dynastic history.

In Turco-Mongol states any son could legitimately compete for power, a principle institutionalised in the appanage system, in which Timurids and Chinggisids parcelled out territories among their sons, each one of whom could and usually did compete for their father's patrimony – during his lifetime and thereafter. Sons were sent to their appanages with military guardians when they were young boys, where each of them developed mini-courts and a sense of their own independence. The competition among them intensified when, as was common, they were sons of different mothers. As these boys usually matured apart from their brothers and half-brothers they also lost a sense of family identity or, in Ibn Khaldūn's terms, social solidarity, which understandably atrophied over the time and distance they spent apart from their natal household. Unlike the Ottomans and Safavids, Mughal rulers retained these traditions throughout the history of the dynasty, with the result that sons habitually rebelled against their fathers, whose deaths often triggered bloody civil wars among their male descendants.

The Mughals' history of internecine dynastic warfare implicitly raises one other facet of the dynasty's Central Asian heritage, their military tactics. Knowledge of these tactics is especially important for understanding Bābur's pivotal victories in north India in 932–3/1526–7. Bābur fought his battles utilising highly structured traditional Central Asian battle formations and tactics. While cavalry raids were a perennial feature of Turco-Mongol military encounters, major confrontations did not usually feature free-flowing cavalry encounters over miles of open steppe, but set-piece battles on prepared fields. Bābur himself describes how he and his men dug ditches in a meadow outside Samarqand before confronting Shibani Khan Uzbek in 906/1501, when he suffered the catastrophic defeat that led to his eventual flight from Central Asia in 909/1504. In the late fifteenth century such battles were often decided by disciplined, highly mobile cavalry, as Bābur himself acknowledges was the case in the Uzbek victory. Swift flanking cavalry manoeuvres were the signature Turco-Mongol military tactic, which Mongol detachments used to secure Bābur's Indian victories first at Pānīpat and then in the following year at Kanwā against the Hindu Rajputs. Later, sieges became common in an Indian countryside dotted with formidable fortresses, but Mughal heavy cavalry always remained the principal striking force of the regime's formidable armies.

Despite their Turco-Mongol political and military traits, as late Timurids the Mughal emperors espoused the values of the eastern Islamic world, that is, the norms of Perso-Islamic culture. They saw themselves as sedentary Muslim 'just sultans', men who encouraged agrarian development, valued urban life and protected lucrative, taxable commerce. All identified Islam with urban life – and vice versa. The late Timurids' cultural vision of themselves is most obvious in their Sunnī Muslim orthodoxy and reverence for the Naqshbandī and Chishtī Sufi orders and respect for Persian literary culture. Bābur's own religious tutor, Khwāja Maulānā Qāḍī, was a descendant of the important

ʿālim Burhān al-Dīn ʿAlī Qilich al-Marghīnānī, who, like Bābur, was a Farghāna valley native. This man was the author of the *Hidāya*, a book that became a standard reference of orthodox Ḥanafī practice widely known throughout the Sunnī Muslim world, including the fourteenth-century Delhi sultanate. Al-Marghīnānī personified the dominance of Ḥanafī Sunni orthodoxy that was characteristic of theologians in Bukhārā and Herat in both the pre-Mongol and Timurid eras. Khwāja Maulānā Qāḍī was also a Naqshbandī Sufi, and this was virtually a dynastic Timurid devotional order, although Temür's descendants were also respectful of the Chishtīyya, itself, in origin, a Central Asian order. Indeed, one of the first shrines Bābur visited when he arrived victorious in Delhi in 1526 was a tomb of a Chishtī *pīr* or shaykh who was a native of Bābur's homeland, the Farghāna valley.

As was typical of other Timurids of this era, Bābur also brought with him to India a profound respect for and extensive knowledge of Persian poetry and historical prose. Two centuries earlier many Delhi sultanate rulers and officials had participated in the Persianate culture that enjoyed such high prestige in Central Asia and India. Ibn Baṭṭūṭa testifies to the welcome that Iranians received when they arrived in sultanate territories in the early fourteenth century. Yet the late fifteenth century witnessed an especially important florescence of Persian culture in Timurid Central Asia and Khurāsān. Temür's descendants generally and Sulṭān-Ḥusayn Bayqara of Herat (r. 873–911/1469–1506) in particular, patronised Persianate culture to the degree that Samarqand and Herat became the most important centres of Persian artistic and literary activity in the eastern Islamic world. While Bābur wrote both prose and poetry in Turkī, the language known in nineteenth-century Europe as Chaghatay Turkish, it was Persian rather than still undeveloped Turkī that he revered as the canonical literary tradition. In his memoirs he always cites Persian-language poets when he wishes to use aphorisms to legitimise observations or actions not specifically connected with the Islamic morality or piety. That is, while Islam was for him and most of his followers the categorical religious authority, classical Persian poets such as Saʿdī (610–90/1213–91), Rūmī (604–72/1207–73), Amīr Khusrau Dihlavī (651–726/1253–1325) and Ḥāfiẓ (720–92/1320–89) provided cultural sanctions of nearly equal weight.

The conquest of Hindustān

Bābur marched out of Kabul in 932/December 1525 intent on conquering Hindustān. At the time he had already seized Lahore and its wealthy hinterland, using some of its funds to secure the loyalty of his allies in northern Afghanistan as he marched into India's heartland. Bābur's victory over the Afghan Lodīs in April represented a Timurid dynastic conquest that was undertaken solely to provide an imperial base for his family and their Chaghatay Mongol kin. Islamic ideology played no discernible part in Bābur's initial campaign, and even later when he had to confront formidable Hindu, Rajput armies he invoked religion only as a tactical device to bolster morale. Even while Aurungzeb, the last great Mughal emperor (r. 1069–1118/1658–1707), consciously, sincerely and publicly ruled as a conservative Sunnī monarch, the Mughals and their servants generally adopted a pragmatic, *laissez-faire* attitude towards religious observance similar in some respects to policies adopted by the British East India Company during the initial period of its rule. As for Bābur's army, it consisted of a melange of Turco-Mongol, Badakhshāni and Afghan troops whose total number of actual combatants probably did not exceed 8,000 men. Many of the estimated 12,000 men who accompanied him – and whom he had counted when they crossed the Indus – were camp followers: merchants, *ʿulamāʾ* and others. Bābur's victory over the Lodīs at Pānīpat did not represent the triumph of a gunpowder empire, although he employed at least two types of firearms in the battle. Based upon his own detailed account, which is also the sole description of the battle, his success represented the triumph of an experienced and perhaps charismatic Turco-Mongol dynast, a man who fought a traditional cavalry battle using Mongol flanking detachments on a field where his foot soldiers were arrayed defensively behind carts according to Ottoman military practice.

Following his victory at Pānīpat, Bābur occupied the Lodī capital at Agra and began to consolidate his conquests. His military and political strategy is evident from his memoirs, but little is known of his administrative policies. In military terms Bābur set about subduing major fortresses in the Agra region, believing, as he convincingly observes in the *Vaqāʾiʿ*, that defeating his most imposing enemies would trigger a cascade of submissions by lesser figures. However, even as he began to successfully implement this policy against surviving Afghan commandants in 933–4/1526–7, he was suddenly confronted by a far more formidable coalition of Hindu Rajputs, who controlled a broad swathe of territory stretching in an arc from the south of Agra north-west into the Rajasthan desert. As Rajput forces approached Agra in February 933/1527, Bābur's tenuous sovereignty unravelled almost overnight as recently cowed Afghans quickly repudiated their submission.

Bābur confronted the Rajputs near Sikri, later the site of his grandson Akbar's great sandstone capital, Fatehpur Sikri. In a tumultuous, epic battle in which his Mongol flanking cavalry again seems to have played the same key role it did at Pānīpat, he was victorious. In the few remaining years of his life, Bābur was never again seriously threatened with defeat, although he constantly campaigned against both Rajput and Afghan forces in order to consolidate his fragile hegemony in Hindustān. That hegemony consisted of the imposition of rule of a Turco-Mongol military class over a disparate collection of Muslim and Hindu rulers, most of whom accepted Timurid legitimacy only to the degree that superior military force dictated. Bābur's descendants rarely tried to eradicate these indigenous ruling lineages, but only coerced their submission to a regime that needed to extract land revenue to support the Timurid-Mughal ruling elite and their military, religious and cultural camp followers.

Bābur saw himself as a Central Asian founder of an Indo-Afghan state, which he far preferred to rule from Kabul rather than Agra. He and many of his men were appalled by the environment and society of India. In fact, many of his *begs* or commanders fled back to the temperate climate of Kabul immediately after their Rajput victory. Bābur himself did not have that luxury, and in his memoirs he recorded his acerbic evaluation of his conquests. Noting, first of all, that the trans-Indus region known as Hindustān was a 'strange-kingdom ... a different world' where even the rocks were unique, he went on to indicate that the only thing he liked about Hindustān was its wealth and its seemingly limitless human and material resources. He particularly hated north India's flat, featureless landscape, with its lack of geometrically precise gardens bisected by waterways, and despised much of what he knew of Hindu society. Many of his most provocative critiques are contained in one brief passage, in which he writes that:

> The people of Hindustān have no beauty; they have no convivial society, no social intercourse, no character or genius, no urbanity, no nobility or chivalry. In the skilled arts and crafts there is no regularity, proportionality, straightness or rectangularity.[1]

Apart from a certain racial prejudice and homesickness for life in Kabul or Central Asia, two elements in this passage are profoundly meaningful as markers along the social boundaries between Muslim and Hindu societies or at least Bābur's perception of the fundamental differences between his preferred Turco-Mongol, Perso-Islamic society of Central Asia and the society

1 Stephen F. Dale, *The garden of the eight paradises: Bābur and the culture of empire in Central Asia, Afghanistan and India (1483–1530)* (Leiden and Boston, 2004), p. 369.

and culture of north India. First of all, by criticising the lack of 'convivial society' and 'social intercourse' Bābur remarked on the distinction between his own society, where social equals regularly gathered together to eat, drink and recite poetry or to govern, from Hindu caste society, where religious pollution rules prevented the kind of interaction that was common in most Mediterranean and Middle Eastern communities. Second, in criticising the lack of 'regularity, proportionality, straightness or rectangularity' in Indian arts and crafts, Bābur signalled his own membership in a Greco-Islamic culture that valued geometrical symmetry and, in the case of such Greco-Islamic philosophers as al-Bīrūnī (363–*c*. 442/973–1050), regarded Aristotle's logic, whose reasoning was exemplified by geometrical axioms and theorems, as the foundation of a truly scientific civilisation.

Despite Bābur's distaste for the culture of his newly conquered territories, he remained in India until his death in 937/December 1530. While almost nothing is known of his administration, it is clear from his memoirs that he governed Hindustān through a fairly standard type of early modern Islamic military feudalism. He retained some territories in India as *khalīsa*, demesne or crown land that supplied income directly to the regime in Agra. Other territories were parcelled out to his *begs* or *amīrs* as military fiefs to support themselves and the troops under their command. These fiefs seem to have been similar to those he knew as *tiyūl* in Afghanistan and Central Asia, that is, temporary and revocable grants similar to the *iqṭā*'s common to pre-Mughal India, Iran and other regions of the Middle East. Such assignments were the precursors of the elaborate system which his grandson, Akbar, established in the late sixteenth century to support the military class. The major difference between the two systems was that in his grandson's era assignments were usually based on geometric surveys and knowledge of local soil conditions. The quality of Lodī revenue records is not known, but it is important to understand that Bābur himself was familiar with complex commercial and agrarian revenue systems from reading the *Hidāya* text of al-Marghīnānī.

The apparent reason why so little is known about the details of Bābur's administration in India is that the first period of Mughal rule lasted only until 1540, when resurgent Afghan forces drove his son and heir, Humāyūn, from India. Led by Shīr Shāh Sūrī, Afghans reasserted control over north India, establishing a sophisticated revenue system and road network that were probably a continuation of Bābur's and Humāyūn's policies. Humāyūn's difficulties were partly due to the the Turco-Mongol appanage system, in which his brothers competed for regional power or outright sovereignty in the

Indian heartland. What can never be known is the degree to which his own military skills were responsible for his loss to Afghan forces, some of whom he had defeated earlier in his reign. Between 947/1540 and 962/1555 Humāyūn was first a wandering refugee in the Indian–Afghan borderlands and then a guest of the Safavid Shāh Ṭahmāsp. He apparently purchased Ṭahmāsp's cooperation with lavish presents of jewels that may have included the famous *kuh-i nūr* diamond, and a possible promise of conversion to Shīʿī Islam. In this he may have reprised an alliance that Bābur had concluded with Ṭahmāsp's father, the Safavid founder, Shāh Ismāʿīl, when in 917/1511 Bābur needed Safavid military aid to retake Samarqand for the third and last time from his Uzbek enemies. Using Safavid troops Humāyūn appeared outside Kandahar in 952/1545 to begin the decade-long process of reclaiming his patrimony, first from his recalcitrant brothers in Afghanistan and then from the Sūrīs themselves. However, Humāyūn survived only a year in India before accidentally dying in an accident, tripping on the steep stone steps of his library and possibly fracturing his skull as he hurried to evening prayers.

Akbar and the formation of empire

Humāyūn's young son Akbar succeeded to the Mughal throne in 963/1556 in his twelfth year. Initially it was his guardian or tutor, the Qara Qoyunlu Turk Bayram Khan, who directed the affairs of the resuscitated Mughal state during the first four years of Akbar's rule. Only in 1560 did Akbar, then no longer a child but an assertive adolescent, dismiss Bayram Khan, presaging his emergence as the effective ruler of the state a year later. During the period of Bayram Khan's *de facto* regency and the early years of Akbar's direct rule up to 975/1567, Mughal armies were preoccupied with recapturing the central core of territory held by Bābur at the time of his death in 937/1530. This comprised Lahore and much of the Punjab, the Delhi–Agra axis and Gwalior to the south, the western and central Gangetic valley and eastern Rajasthan. Just as Bābur had first fought the Lodīs, his descendant began by attacking the formidable remnants of the Afghan Sūrī coalition that had retreated down the Ganges valley following Humāyūn's victory. Akbar defeated the last major Sūrī leader near Jawnpur in 968/1561, although Afghan resistance continued in eastern India for many years. Afterwards, Akbar, like Bābur before him, secured his eastern flank with campaigns in 974/1567 and 976/1569 against Chitōr and Ranthambor, the two most formidable Rajput fortresses. These latter campaigns illustrate that by the mid-sixteenth century the Mughal dynasty had indeed become a gunpowder empire to the extent that Akbar defeated his

Rajput opponents by besieging their stone fortresses with cannons and sapping the walls with mines.[2]

In between these Afghan and Rajput campaigns Akbar was preoccupied with dissent and sometimes open rebellion within his own nobility and by competition from his two most legitimate and therefore formidable rivals. It was especially Uzbek members of his military coalition who revolted in the mid-1560s, but whatever the motivations of specific individuals, this kind of activity was a common feature of Timurid and early Mughal history. However, unless they were actual descendants of the Chinggisid founder of Uzbek power, Shibani Khan, Uzbek nobles were less of a threat to Akbar's long-term prospects than were the challenges posed by Timurids, who possessed legitimacy as valid as Akbar's own. These were his half-brother Mīrzā Ḥakīm, long the governor of Kabul, and the Timurid Muḥammad Sulṭān Mīrzā, a grand-nephew of Sulṭān-Ḥusayn Bayqarā (d. 911/1506), the last Timurid ruler of Herat. The assumption of shared inheritance and the Turco-Mongol appanage system lay behind these men's activities, depicted in Mughal sources as rebellions. Muḥammad Sulṭān Mīrzā had fought alongside Bābur, but he often challenged Humāyūn's sovereign claims. Along with Humāyūn's brothers and another Timurid, Muḥammad Zamān Mīrzā, he had contributed to Humāyūn's defeats and expulsion from India. In 974/1566, however, Akbar defeated Muḥammad Sulṭān Mīrzā after a campaign in which he drove the Mīrzā Ḥakīm back to Kabul, following the latter's invasion of the Punjab.

Akbar enjoys an almost unreservedly positive image in the historiography of India, whether or not written by Muslims, Hindus or Westerners. This is due to a number of factors, but most of all to his military success, political skills, administrative acumen, spiritual experiments and liberal religious policies. He is, first of all, acknowledged to have been an exceptionally effective military leader, one who rarely suffered a serious defeat as he went about re-establishing and then enlarging the Mughal empire. During his long reign he never ceased campaigning, as he steadily expanded the circumference of Mughal power outward from its Delhi–Agra node in all directions until his small north Indian state became the Mughal empire of legend. Second, in political and administrative terms Akbar was, first of all, an effective monarch because he ruled himself, and not through viziers or other intermediaries as became the enervating practice in the Ottoman and Safavid empires. Personal

2 For an introduction to Mughal administrative and political history from Akbar's reign to the collapse of the empire see John F. Richards, *The Mughal empire* (Cambridge, 1993).

rule was the custom of Akbar's successors as well. He also effectively integrated non-Muslim groups into the elite ranks of the empire and either created or at least formalised the basic administrative structures of the regime that endured in one form or another until its collapse in the eighteenth century. Third, Akbar's inquisitive mind, eclectic religious interests and patronage of both Islamic and non-Muslim Indian culture have not only appealed to scholars who write India's history, but also seem to have engaged the sympathy of contemporary Hindus as well.

Akbar personally commanded the Mughal armies throughout most of his reign; he was still on campaign in 1011/1602, when his son Salīm, the future Jahāngīr, rebelled against his father's authority in the traditional Turco-Mongol manner. After his early campaigns against Sūrī forces in the eastern Ganges region and successful assaults on the two major Rajput fortresses, Akbar conquered the wealthy province of Gujarat with its pivotal seaport of Surat in 980/1572. Subsequently he and then later his generals, including his Hindu finance minister, Todar Mal, commanded a series of difficult campaigns against Afghan forces in Bihār and Bengal in the 1570s and 1580s. In one of these campaigns in 987/1579 Akbar fought against a particularly dangerous coalition of Afghans, who had allied themselves with Mughal rebels. The coalition challenged Akbar's legitimacy, and orthodox *ʿulamāʾ*, who objected to Akbar's religious experiments, sanctified these men's actions. The Mughal nobles involved also arranged to have Mīrzā Ḥakīm (d. 993/1585) proclaimed emperor, whom Akbar now finally deposed as ruler of Kabul after a rapid march to the Afghan capital. The eastern provinces were then gradually pacified in a series of hard-fought battles by the late 1580s, when Akbar sent one of his premier Rajput allies, Man Singh, to administer them. Finally, in the 1590s Akbar turned his attention to the Muslim sultanates of the Deccan. He first demanded their submission in 999/1591, and then attacked the Ahmednagar sultanate in 1003/1595. After a successful siege in 1599, he integrated Ahmednagar into the empire. No less than Bābur, Akbar and his successors possessed inbred, that is Timurid and Chinggisid, 'kingdom-seizing ambitions'.

As the evidence of some of his early campaigns demonstrate, Akbar co-opted important Hindu lineages into his regime early in his reign. Todar Mal, for example, his famous finance minister who also commanded Mughal armies in the east, was a Punjabi Khatri. The Khatris were and are one of the most important north Indian commercial castes, whose members were concentrated in the Punjab and settled as a mercantile diaspora in Afghanistan, Iran, Central Asia and, by the mid-seventeenth century, even in Moscow.

Todar Mal provided the regime with financial expertise, just as many Mughal nobles relied on Hindu advisers to manage their private investments. Man Singh, the other highly visible Hindu general in Akbar's campaigns, was a Rajput, and his role reflected the critical military service that these formidable Hindu chiefs provided to the empire. Rulers of earlier north Indian Muslim states had previously employed Hindus. Indeed, the fourteenth-century historian Ziā' al-Dīn Baranī complained bitterly in his work *Fatāwā-yi Jahāndārī*, that the Delhi sultanate could hardly be considered a Muslim state at all, for Hindus were so prominent and the sultans acted more like pre-Islamic Iranian emperors than committed Muslims. Akbar liberalised and systematised the use of Rajput lineages, appointing defeated or intimidated rajas to high ranks in the Mughal nobility, while also allowing them to retain their historic estates.

The degree to which Akbar co-opted Rajput lineages and his appreciation of their military importance is reflected in the enumeration of Rajput clans that Abū'l Faḍl 'Allāmī, his amanuensis and companion, provided in the *Ā'īn-i Akbarī*, his gazetteer of the Mughal empire that he finished in the late sixteenth century:

> I record the names of a few of the most renowned [Rajputs] that are now in His Majesty's service. 1. The Rāthor; there are several tribes of this clan in service. They number sixty thousand cavalry and two hundred thousand infantry. 2. The Chauhān are divided into several branches, viz., Sungira, Khichi, Deora, Hādā, and Narbān. The troops of the clan number fifty thousand cavalry and two hundred thousand infantry. 3. The Panwār. In ancient times, of this tribe was the royal dynasty in Hindustān, and it numbered many clansmen. At the present time their force consists of twelve thousand cavalry and sixty thousand foot.[3]

While these troop figures are probably, like so many such estimates, exaggerated, the passage simultaneously conveys Mughal respect for these ancient Hindu lineages and publicises the power of Akbar's empire. It also illustrates how vitally important these Rajput lineages were for the Mughal state.

Akbar's intimate involvement with the Rajputs had begun when he returned from a pilgrimage to the Chishtī Sufi shaykh at Sikri, west of Agra, in 969/1561. He accepted the offer of marriage to a Rajput princess, whose father wanted imperial assistance against a local Mughal governor. He married the girl in Agra. Not only was she allowed to retain her own religion, but

3 Abū'l Faḍl 'Allāmī, *Ā'īn-i Akbarī*, trans. Colonel H. S. Jarrett, ed. Sir Jadunath Sarkar (New Delhi, repr. 1988), vol. III, p. 131.

also other Rajput princesses who were later brought into the harem were allowed to erect temple structures for their own devotions. Simultaneously with this first marriage Akbar enrolled the Rajput father, his son and grandson in Mughal service, presaging the future recruitment of the princely heads of important Rajput lineages. The influence of Akbar's new Hindu wife and in-laws may have led him two years later to abolish the pilgrimage tax levied on Hindus and subsequently to issue other regulations that allowed Hindus to repair their temples and forbade the forced conversion of non-Muslim captives.

Later Akbar enlisted the princely heads of major Rajput lineages named above in the imperial service, where they were not only given ranks equal to Muslim officers, but, in fact, were accorded special status. That is, unlike most imperial officers whose assignments to military fiefs were changed periodically, Rajput officers were allowed to retain their historic family territories as their permanent fiefs. This policy essentially recognised the entrenched power of these Rajput lineages and their military value to the Mughal empire. It would have been prohibitively expensive to eradicate these families and hundreds of other well-entrenched Hindu rajas. The survival and indeed the prosperity of the Rajput kingdoms is only the most prominent example of a phenomenon that explains why, when Mughal centralised power decayed in the early eighteenth century, its authority and presence could evaporate overnight in many areas, often leaving behind as the imperial tide receded only the architectural remnants of a great empire.

By 987/1580 Akbar had appointed nearly forty Rajputs to commands within the imperial forces, whose economic basis of agrarian fiefs was fundamental to the success of the empire. The basic organisation was a decimal one that reflected the Mughals Turco-Mongol heritage. Chinggis Khan, his descendants, Temür and the Timurids, including Bābur, divided up their predominantly cavalry forces into commands of 10, 100, 1,000 10,000, etc. Bābur and Humāyūn, and initially Akbar also, commanded semi-autonomous *begs* or *amīrs*, to whom they assigned large parcels of villages and agricultural land to support both their families and the troops under their command. In this early Mughal period such commanders constituted more of a military coalition than a centrally controlled army. However, as Akbar gradually extended his control over the Indian heartland he developed a sophisticated military-feudal structure known as the *mansabdārī-jāgīrdārī* system that was formally instituted in 982/1574f. In essence each commander – of 100, 500, 1,000, 5,000, etc. was assigned a *mansab*, a rank, which he *dār*, held. At the same time nearly every commander was paid, not in cash, but through an assignment of agricultural land known as a *jāgīr*, which he also held from the emperor. Most Muslim officers of varying ethnic identities were treated as imperial servants who were not allowed to own land, but only to hold *jāgīrs* temporarily, before being moved at intervals to other assignments, as a way of preventing them from becoming an entrenched class of regional feudatories. Rajput officers were also both *mansabdārs* and *jāgīrdārs*, but as a sign of their special military status they held their own small kingdoms as *watan* or homeland *jāgīrs*. Some were also granted temporary but lucrative assignments outside their historic territories, thus helping to ensure their loyalty and prevent inter-Rajput warfare.

While the *mansabdārī-jāgīrdārī* system served the empire well enough for more than a century to provide the heavy cavalry core of the imperial armies, it did not automatically function as the Mughal equivalent of a deist clock, sprung perfectly operating from the mind of Akbar and remaining functionally unchanged thereafter. Like any complex administrative system it was subject to the influence of personal ambition, family ties, political faction and local interests. In fact almost immediately after he formally initiated the system Akbar had to adjust it to conform to the realities of the *mansabdārs*' ambitions and acquisitive instincts. Among other problems, *mansabdārs* only rarely kept up their specified troop levels, a fact that Abū'l Faḍl acknowledged when he noted that 'The monthly grants made to the Mansabdārs vary according to the condition of their contingents.'[4] Abū'l Faḍl's orthodox critic and jealous competitor, ʿAbd al-Qādir b. Mulūk Shāh, known as al-Badāunī, went further and wrote scathingly of the *mansabdārs* that:

> As they were wicked and rebellious, and spent large sums on their stores and workshops, and amassed wealth, they had no leisure to look after their troops or to take an interest in the people. In cases of emergency, they came themselves with some of their slaves and Moghul attendants to the scene of war; but of really useful soldiers there were none.[5]

A system of branding, troop musters and formal military reviews was devised to ensure minimum compliance with the system. Akbar's son and successor, Jahāngīr, describes one such review, which took place on 4 April 1618, albeit in this case for his father-in-law, who was also one of his most important ministers:

4 *Ibid.*, p. 248.
5 al-Badāunī, *Muntakhabu-'t-Tawārīkh by ʿAbdu-l-Qādir Ibn-i-Mulūk Shāh known as Al-Badāonī*, ed. and trans. W. H. Lowe, rev. B. P. Ambashthya (Patna, repr. 1973), vol. II, p. 193.

> On the twenty-fifth [4 April], I'timad ud-dawla's troop passed for review in the field beneath the jharoka [audience window]. There were two thousand fine horsemen, mostly Moghuls [Mongols], five hundred foot soldiers armed with bows and guns, and fourteen elephants. The bakhshis [military accountants] counted them and reported that the troop was fully equipped and appeared to be formed according to regulation.[6]

According to al-Badāunī, however, if anything the abuses during Akbar's reign grew steadily worse, observing: 'But notwithstanding this new regulation ... the Amirs did as they pleased.'[7] Al-Badāunī undoubtedly identified real problems, but he was so angry and biased his description cannot be assumed to be based on a comprehensive knowledge of all *mansabdārs* and, indeed, may refer to a specific campaign. If the entire system was as corrupt as he suggests, Akbar could have scarcely remained in power, much less conquered a great empire. In fact, many of these officers and their descendants, including Rajputs, are known to have loyally served the Timurid house with distinction and sometimes even sacrificial devotion.[8] However flawed in practice, the system could still produce tens of thousands of troops for campaigns in the early eighteenth century. It is reasonable to suppose but impossible to prove that the abuses Badāunī describes varied directly with the *mansabdārs*' geographic distance from Agra, where contingents of the great nobles of the courts could be evaluated with relative ease.

The *mansabdārī-jāgīrdārī* system generated, by necessity, a large bureaucracy to survey and register lands that became part of the pool for assignments. These officials represented only one dimension of a complex administrative system that also included a bifurcated provincial administration of governorships and financial officials established after 979/1572. Thus at the level of the individual province two different officials, both appointed by the emperor, were responsible for political and military control and financial administration. Governors controlled administrative and military affairs while provincial *dīwāns* or revenue officers drew revenues directly from *khalīsa* or crown lands for the central administration. The relations among *mansabdār-jāgīrdārs*, the *subahdārs* or governors and *dīwāns* varied with each individual instance. Despite the theoretical rotation of *jāgīrdārs* around the empire and the division of political and financial powers, sometimes *mansabdārs* might be repeatedly appointed to the same province, or relatives or clients of powerful individuals

6 Jahāngīr, *The Jahangirnama: Memoirs of Jahangir, emperor of India*, ed. and trans. Wheeler M. Thackston (Washington, DC, 1999), p. 219.
7 al-Badāunī, *Muntakhabu-'t-Tawārīkh*, vol. II, p. 193.
8 Richards, *The Mughal empire*, pp. 107–9.

might be appointed to the same province and on occasions one man might simultaneously hold both political and financial posts. An additional complicating factor was the presence of varying numbers of entrenched, semi-independent lineages or autonomous rajas designated by the Mughals as *zamīndārs*, that is, holders of *zamīn* or land. A map of the administrative and political situation in any particular Mughal province might reveal a patchwork of crown, *jāgīr* and *zamīndār* territory, sometimes with *zamīndārs* located within a *mansabdār's jāgīr*. The interconnected political and financial authority of its governors, financial administrators and *mansabdār-jāgīrdārs* constantly shifted according to the personalities of individual officials, the dynamism of the imperial government and the ambitions of *zamīndārs*.

Akbar: religion and culture

If Akbar's success as a ruler can be attributed to his military leadership, recruitment of local elites and the possession of a systemising intelligence that led him to construct an effective administration, his later reputation among the Indian public and both Indian and foreign intellectuals stems in large measure from his intellectual curiosity and religious experiments. Like his father and grandfather before him, Akbar exhibited a strong attachment to Sufi devotionalism. He showed a particular preference for the Chishtī order. Even though like the Naqshbandī it originated in Central Asia, the Chishtīyya was a well-established order in Hindustān before Bābur's invasion, with major shrines in Delhi, Ajmir and Sikri, near Agra, and in the Ganges valley. From the 1570s on Akbar seems to have been increasingly absorbed in pantheistic Sufi doctrines that evolved into a profound belief in the essential oneness of all religions. Nonetheless, an attachment to Sufism hardly seems a sufficient explanation for the evolution of Akbar's religious interests and state policies from an unremarkable Islamic piety in the early years of his reign to increasingly latitudinarian beliefs and, in the opinion of some Muslims, heretical religious experiments. The possible factors that may have contributed to this change include his own, well-documented intellectual curiosity, a seemingly restless intelligence reminiscent of his grandfather, the influence of his Rajput marriages and incorporation of Rajput princes into the regime, his exposure to Christian ideas following his conquest of Gujarat and contact with the Portuguese on the Indian Ocean coast, the very likely influence of Buddhist or Jain ideas of non-violence prevalent in the same region, his knowledge of Zoroastrian doctrine and, finally, a possible desire to define his sovereignty in Iranian imperial rather than just Timurid and Islamic terms. The most intractable problem in this regard is the difficulty, the impossibility really, of accurately determining how Akbar's personal religiosity influenced state policy and vice versa.

Lacking a religious autobiography of the order of Gandhi's work *The Story of My Experiments with Truth*, it is only possible to point to several events or periods that date and document Akbar's religious policies or interests. First is his initial Rajput marriage, followed so shortly by the abolition of the Hindu pilgrimage tax and other measures that seem to reflect a growing sensitivity to his Rajput allies. These include the well-known elimination of the *jizya*, the so-called poll-tax on non-Muslims that Akbar's historian, Abū'l Faḍl, claims was done in 1564, but may not have been formally implemented until fifteen years later. Second, Akbar attributed the birth of his first son Salīm, later the emperor Jahāngīr, in 1569 to the prayers of Shaykh Salīm Chishtī at Sikri in Rajasthan. This intensified Akbar's devotion to an order and a shrine in nearby Ajmir that he visited for five consecutive years between 971/1564 and 977/1569. Third, the presence of the Chishtī shrine and the residence of Salīm Chishtī at Sikri was probably one reason why Akbar constructed a new capital at Sikri in 978/1571, halfway between Ajmir and Agra. However, it is also worth recalling that Bābur won his great battle against the Rajputs nearby in 933/1527, where he also later built a Garden of Victory to commemorate the epic battle. Akbar may have taken the name for his new city, Fatehpur, the 'city of victory', from this event. Fourth, this new capital of Fatehpur Sikri became, in 1575, the site of the famous religious debates that Akbar sponsored, initially between Muslims and later involving Jains, Zoroastrians and, finally, in 1580, some Christians. Fifth, it was also during this period that Akbar had an epiphany that seems like a distant but indistinct echo of the conversion to Buddhism of the great Mauryan emperor, Ashoka (273–232 BCE), one perhaps influenced by Akbar's contact with Jains in the Sikri religious debates. In Ashoka's case the slaughter of thousands of enemies in Orissa prompted him to embrace non-violence and the ethical code of Gautama Siddhartha's Indian disciples. Akbar reacted to the slaughter of thousands of animals during a typical Central Asian-style royal hunt in 1578 by prohibiting the killing of animals on certain days and by adopting a modified form of vegetarianism.

Finally, during the same period Akbar instituted measures that first of all, in 987/1579, proclaimed his authority to be the final arbiter in Islamic religious matters. He apparently asserted this right of *ijtihād* or interpretation of Muslim law after becoming disenchanted with the sterile, intolerant religious debates among Muslim clerics at Fatehpur Sikri. In the decree announcing this decision, Akbar was described as the *imām-i ʿadl* or the just *imām*, a Shīʿī title but perhaps also an echo of the concept of *insān-i kāmil*, the perfectly enlightened Sufi. At the same time his principal religious ideologue at court, Shaykh Mubarak, the author of this document, suggested that Akbar embodied the *farr*, the divine light of kingship known from pre-Islamic Iran. Then two years after making these religious claims that shocked and alienated some members of the *ʿulamāʾ* and helped to legitimise the combined Afghan–Mughal rebellion in 1579, Akbar initiated a royal cult known as the *dīn-i ilāhī* or *tauhīd-i ilāhī*, literally 'the faith of God', or 'the divine unity', in which he enrolled a small number of disciples who pledged to him an absolute devotion reminiscent also of Sufi disciples' unconditional commitment to their spiritual masters.

It was especially Akbar's implied claims to spiritual authority that convinced al-Badāunī, the disaffected courtier and religious critic of Akbar's reign, to consider Akbar an apostate. Even some Rajputs, it might be noted, thought that Akbar's innovations were quite odd and refused to participate. Reacting to the controversy over Akbar's religious inclinations and court cult, Abūʾl Faḍl repeatedly defended his master's practices, remarking in one passage that also revealed how infrequently Akbar visited major Friday mosques, such as the one he had built at Fatehpur Sikri:

> Ardently feeling after God, and searching for truth, His Majesty exercises upon himself both inward and outward austerities, though he occasionally joins public worship, in order to hush the slandering tongues of bigots of the age. But the great object of his life is the acquisition of that sound morality, the sublime loftiness of which captivates the hearts of thinking sages, and silences the taunts of zealots and sectarians.[9]

Continuing on to discuss Akbar's known reverence for the sun, which might have been connected with his regard for Zoroastrian ideas and Hindu fire sacrifices, Abūʾl Faḍl first convincingly remarks that Akbar 'passed every moment of his life in self-examination or in adoration of God'. He continues, saying that the emperor 'especially does so at the time, when morning spreads her azure silk, and scatters abroad her young golden beams, and at noon when the light of the world-illuminating sun embraces'. And why not, Abūʾl Faḍl continues. After all:

> It is incumbent upon us, though our strength may fail, to show gratitude for the blessings we receive from the sun, the light of all lights ... This is

9 Abūʾl Faḍl ʿAllāmī, *Āʾīn-i Akbarī*, vol. I, p. 163.

> essentially the duty of kings, upon whom ... the sovereign of heaven sheds an immediate light. And this is the very motive, which actuates his Majesty to venerate fire and reverence lamps.[10]

Akbar's personal religious experiments and imperial cult had no perceptible legacy in the Mughal court of his descendants. In retrospect they seem to be quixotic manifestations of his restless intellect and heartfelt spiritual quests. When it came to Mughal court culture, however, Akbar's policies were as formative and substantial as his administrative innovations. It was Akbar, first, who formally instituted Persian as the official language of the court, thereby turning away from Bābur's Chaghatay Turkic heritage and embracing Persian as the high court and literary culture of Mughal India. He also actively recruited Persian-speaking literati, thus encouraging Iranians increasingly to leave the relatively impoverished Safavid state to enjoy the patronage of the stunningly wealthy Mughal empire. After Bayram Khan wrote his *dīwān*, or collected verse, in Turkī, almost no texts were composed in that language in Mughal India. Akbar's son Jahāngīr claimed to know Turkī, but his claim, even if true, has the air of an exceptional, self-conscious achievement. Indeed, in the seventeenth century scholars had to compile Persian–Turkī glossaries to explain the now obscure Central Asian vocabulary. Persian was the language of all the great histories written during Akbar's reign, the Persian verse of Sa'dī and Ḥāfiẓ continued to be valued as *the* classical literary canon, as indeed it had been by Bābur, and both Iranian émigrés and Indians composed Persian verse in the late Timurid style known as *sabk-i hindī*. Iranian influence was also noticeable in other spheres at this time. Akbar adopted the Iranian or Zoroastrian solar calendar for administrative reasons, and Iranian ideas of kingship, widely known for centuries if not millennia among Persian-speaking literati and military throughout Central Asia and India, were absorbed by the Mughal dynasty.

Apart from Persian, the focus of Akbar's patronage is both suggestive of his self-image and intellectually engaging as a complex fusion of Perso-Islamic, Indian and European elements. Akbar was as influential in patronising architecture, literature, music and painting as he was in shaping the Mughal administrative and military systems. He was a great systemiser in every respect, echoing in highly practical ways the systemising intelligence that Bābur displays in his memoirs. The nature and scope of his patronage offer compelling implicit evidence that he saw himself as the architect of a great

10 *Ibid.*

empire. Akbar visibly manifested Mughal grandeur, or, more accurately, his own grandiose ambitions, for the first time in 968/1562 when he ordered the construction of a monumental tomb for Humāyūn. Completed eight years later in 1570 and combining both Timurid and Hindu design elements, it dwarfed Temür's tomb in Samarqand. A year later he began construction of the massive new city Fatehpur Sikri, whose red sandstone buildings echoed the design of Muslim wooden buildings in Gujarat. Fatehpur Sikri remained his capital until he moved to Lahore in 993/1585.

In the last two decades of the sixteenth century Akbar systematically set about creating a historical memory of the now imposing Timurid renaissance that Bābur had consciously recorded in the 1520s. He explicitly linked himself to his Timurid past in several ways. Not only did he commission several illustrated manuscript versions of Bābur's *Vaqāʾiʿ* and a history of Temür himself, the *Temür-nāma*, but he decreed that anyone who had personal knowledge of Bābur and Humāyūn should record their recollections, and from his order came the second major autobiographical work of the dynasty. This was the Persian-language memoir of Bābur's daughter Gulbadan Begim, a detailed and often touching evocation of a Timurid woman's world and of the author's humanity. Just as Bābur's autobiography is a unique work by a founder of an Islamic empire – of any period – so his daughter's memoir is equally remarkable for offering an aristocratic woman's account of her life. No comparable text exists for any princess or concubine of the Ottoman or Safavid regimes at any period in their history. Akbar himself seems to have been at best only semi-literate, some think dyslexic, and so he did not write an autobiographical account of his long reign. Therefore he enlisted his companion and courtier, Abūʾl Faḍl ʿAllāmī to commemorate his achievement in two great historical and statistical works. These were the narrative history of his reign, the *Akbar-nāma* and the massive gazetteer of the empire, the *Āʿīn-i Akbarī*.

If Akbar had been merely preoccupied with his legitimacy and imperial grandeur he would be a far less interesting man, but he had a passionate interest in music and painting in addition to his lifelong spiritual search. In 969/1562, the same year that he began Humāyūn's tomb, he forced the most renowned singer-musician of his day, Miyān Tansen, to leave the court of his Rajput patron and join Akbar where he remained until his death in 994/1586. Tansen was a Hindu and his music was based in the raga tradition of classical Indian music. He was especially known for his mastery of the *Drupad* form of singing, a classical court genre rendered in local languages and/or Sanskrit and associated especially with the Rajput court of Gwalior, located south of Agra.

Nonetheless like the great Persian-language poet and musician of the thirteenth and early fourteenth centuries, Amīr Khusrau Dihlavī, he was one who evidently moved in a world of both Hindu and Muslim devotionalism, that is *bhaktī* and Sufism, and he may have been a disciple of the renowned sixteenth-century Sufi, Muḥammad Ghaus Gwaliorī. Yet Tansen was only the most prominent of the musicians who performed at Akbar's court, many of whom were Muslims from Iran and Central Asia.

The eclectic musical atmosphere at the court was visibly echoed in the massive output of Persian-style miniature paintings, most of them done to illustrate literary or historical texts. This art form was based initially on the expertise of two Persian artists, Mīr Sayyid ʿAlī and ʿAbd al-Samad, men whom Humāyūn had brought to India in 962/1555 after his enforced exile. They initially supervised the production of such works as the eclectic *Tūtī-nāma* (the *Tales of the Parrot*) and the fourteen-volume *Hamza-nāma*, completed between 969/1562 and 985/1577 with 100 illustrations per volume, an undertaking so enormous that no other illustrated texts are known to have been produced in these years. Even these early works illustrate how quickly Mughal miniature painting departed from the restrictive, stylised confines of Iranian aesthetics, and integrated Hindu techniques into this all-important court art form. Later, Mughal artists – and architects – experimented with European stylistic influences, derived from their examinations of paintings first introduced by Jesuits from Goa.[11] Not only did biblical scenes now occasionally emerge from the Mughal atelier, but miniature paintings sometimes also exhibited Renaissance perspective and the shading technique known as chiaroscuro.

Most of the well-known later productions of Akbar's well-organised studio were done after he moved to Lahore in 1585. These included Bābur's memoirs, the *Tārīkh-i alfī*, the history of Islam's first millennium, the *Akbar-nāma* itself, a Hindu text, the *Harivamsa* and a number of illustrated manuscripts of classical Persian verse, a reminder of Mughal India's dominant Persian literary culture. Single artists usually did these later works, in which the verse was rendered in beautifully rendered *nastaʿliq* calligraphy, itself a major art form at the Mughal court throughout its history. The most elegant of these texts were the illustrated editions of the works of renowned Persian-language poets such as the *Khamsa* of Nizāmī and the *Khamsa* of Amīr Khusrau Dihlavī. One of the

11 Ebba Koch, 'The baluster column: A European motif in Mughal architecture and its meaning', in Monica Juneja (ed.), *Architecture in medieval India: Forms, contexts, histories* (Delhi, 2001), pp. 328–51.

most engaging features of the mature style of Akbarī paintings is the prevalence of a naturalism in portraying both animals and birds as well as people, a characteristic that contrasted strongly with the stereotypical art that predominated in both traditional Hindu painting and also Persian miniature art of Safavid Iran. Even when they rendered busy court scenes, Mughal artists painted recognisable individuals in distinct costumes.

Economy and trade in 1009/1600

Akbar's construction of Humāyūn's tomb and Fatehpur Sikri and his lavish patronage of artists and musicians hint at the acquisition of wealth that by the late sixteenth century distinguished the Mughal empire from its Ottoman and Safavid contemporaries. By the end of his life Akbar had subdued a territory that may have included more than 100 million people, nearly comparable to the population of Ming China, the only contemporary state that rivalled Mughal India in territory, population and wealth. At about the same time the populations of the Ottoman and Safavid states comprised an estimated 22 and 10 million people respectively, while Uzbek territories probably held no more than 5 million. The lavish wealth that many European observers remarked on when they visited the Mughal court was derived from two principal sources, the agricultural tax and a foreign trade surplus. Mughal India, like most pre-industrial states, was in socio-economic terms an overwhelmingly agrarian society. It depended for the bulk of its income on the effective extraction of wealth from the countryside. The social structure of Mughal-controlled rural society varied tremendously from region to region. In some cases the land was controlled and farmed by landholding peasant castes such as the Jats, whose extensive corporate lineages were especially numerous, cohesive and even militarily formidable in the Delhi–Agra region and in the Punjab. In other cases ruling clans or extended family lineages that the Mughals uniformly classed as *zamīndārs* controlled whole districts' worth of villages.

Yet whether Mughal officials collected agricultural taxes directly from cultivators or from *zamīndārs*, they may have taken as much as one-third to two-fifths of the produce, an amount consistent, so far as it is possible to estimate, with pre-Mughal revenue demands. The precise percentage of Mughal land-revenue collections is, however, not documented and remains a source of dispute. However, what distinguished Mughal agrarian policy was the regime's thorough study of agrarian conditions, including crop yields, price data and land-measurement surveys. Abū'l Faḍl gives the state's idealised view of the agrarian taxation system, a balance of imperial and agrarian interests, in the *Āʿīn-i Akbarī*, where he describes the duties of the revenue collector as one who:

> Should be a friend of the agriculturalist ... He should consider himself the representative of the lord paramount ... He should assist the needy husbandman with advances of money and recover them gradually ... He should ascertain the extent of the soil in cultivation and weigh each several portion in the scales of personal observation and be acquainted with its quality. The agricultural value of the land varies in different districts and certain soils are adapted to certain crops. He should deal differently with each agriculturalist and take his case into consideration.[12]

Part of this official's duties was to see that the cultivator brought wasteland under cultivation, thereby increasing the revenue of the empire.

Precise land measurement was hardly a novelty in the history of Muslim agrarian policy; careful geometric land surveys, for example, were practised during the period of the ʿAbbāsid caliphate (132–656/750–1258). Bābur himself was familiar with agrarian revenue based upon field surveys. However, the Mughal system was distinguished by its officers' detailed local knowledge of agrarian conditions in the wealthy north Indian heartland and beginning around 988/1580 Akbar's Khatri revenue minister and sometime general, Todar Mal, resumed all the *mansabdārs' jāgīr* holdings and, based upon these data, gradually reassigned them five years later. By this time the Mughal treasury demanded its collections in cash, which was paid in either copper or silver coinage. The increasingly monetised Mughal economy saw enormous funds flow into the Mughal treasury from demesne or *khalīsa* lands and stable income fund the *jāgīrdārs*' troop contingents. From the 1580s to the end of Aurungzeb's reign in 1118/1707 the amount of land surveyed rose by nearly 50 per cent, even though Kabul, Sind, Bengal and Orissa were never included in this system. Apart from the Punjab, the Ganges–Yamuna Dūāb and the central Gangetic valley, where treasury officials steadily increased the amount of land surveyed, most of the new territories included were in the northern Deccan, although this did not begin to occur until a half-century after Akbar's death.

The breadth and thoroughness of the Mughal revenue settlement in Hindustān had a number of unquantifiable implications for the nature of the Mughal state. These include the enormous drain of wealth from the

12 Abū'l Faḍl ʿAllāmī, *Āʿīn-i Akbarī*, vol. II, p. 46.

peasantry, the enrichment of the Tīmīrids and the Mughal service class, the increased demand for luxury and craft products to serve these officers' acquisitive instincts, and the increased size and prosperity of towns and cities such as Agra, whose population may have reached three-quarters of a million people in the mid-seventeenth century, at least when the court was in residence. Not the least of these questions for its historical significance is the relatively high degree of centralised control that Mughal emperors exercised in the north Indian heartland.

Apart from their ability to extract revenue by fiat from the Indian peasantry in these regions, the Mughals' level of control is partly also indicated by the standardisation, purity and stable value of coinage throughout the empire. Just as Akbar regularised so many other aspects of Mughal administration so he standardised coinage. From the late 1570s on, coins of equal value and identical design were issued from mints from Gujarat to Lahore, from Bengal to Fatehpur Sikri, and the Mughals enforced an order that all precious metals entering their territories be recast at mints into Mughal coins. Both Akbar and his son, Jahāngīr, also personally saw to their coins' aesthetic appeal. Akbar, who appointed as mint master 'Abd al-Samad, the Iranian calligrapher and painter who oversaw the royal atelier, and Jahāngīr, whose artistic interests often seem to have taken precedence over governance, each supervised the production of coins. In purity, aesthetic standards and precision of design Akbar and Jahāngīr's issues were superior to any other Muslim coins in the early modern era – or Muslim coinage of any pre-modern era. Coinage as an art form reached its zenith in Jahāngīr's zodiac coins and imperial portrait medals that he presented to loyal courtiers.

By the later years of Akbar's reign issues of square silver rupees had become the standard circulating coin within Mughal territories, a fact that by itself testifies to the regime's second major source of wealth, the flow of foreign specie into its territories. This in turn was due to India's perennial trade surplus with lands throughout the Indian Ocean and, after 1498, with Western Europe. No significant silver deposits were located within Mughal territories. Silver for Mughal coins entered India primarily through north-western and western Indian mint towns and reflected the degree to which India remained, as it had been since Roman times, a metallurgical 'black hole' for precious metals exported from the West. Much of the silver for Mughal coinage came, in fact, from South American silver mines, and after entering the European economy substantial sums of silver coins flowed eastward and either reached India directly in European ships or arrived in Mughal territories after circulating in the Ottoman empire or in Safavid Iran. Those two latter empires, like Mediterranean and Western European countries, ran a perennial trade deficit with India. And only after the industrial revolution did Europe finally gain the financial upper hand with India – and China. Apart from the indirect benefit to the dynasty of a wealthy commercial class and a thoroughly monetised economy, the Mughal treasury directly profited from mint fees on the massive but unquantifiable volume of imported specie.

Europeans may have come to India initially for 'Christians and spices,' as one of Vasco da Gama's officers is said to have remarked to a North African Muslim upon coming ashore near Calicut in 903/1498. They found both commodities in abundance in Calicut and in other port towns along India's south-west coast. This region, known as the Malabar coast and now incorporated within Kerala state, was, however, one of the few areas of the subcontinent that Mughal armies never reached. Mughal India's favourable trade balance was primarily based upon the production of cotton cloth, which had been sold throughout the Indian Ocean and in the Mediterranean region since Roman times. Medieval hoards of this cloth have been found in Egypt. Indeed, when Indian Muslims went on *ḥajj*, they often financed their journeys with sales of Indian textiles. North Indian merchants also sold Indian silk, slaves, sugar and medicinal herbs in Afghanistan, Central Asia and Iran, but cloth continued to be the most valuable export commodity until the industrial revolution. Indeed, the cost of Indian cotton cloth in a self-consciously mercantilist era was one of the economic stimuli for English cotton manufacturing in the eighteenth century.

One sign of India's regional economic dominance in the Mughal era was the presence of an Indian mercantile diaspora whose representatives were prominent in Iran and Central Asia, and who, after the mid-sixteenth century, even reached Moscow. This diaspora reflected both the strength of India's export economy and the financial sophistication – or ruthlessness, depending on one's point of view – of India's mercantile/financial castes. It was also facilitated by the solicitous concern shown to merchants by early modern Islamic states: all three empires protected trade routes, knowing they would derive substantial economic benefits thereby. During the last years of Akbar's reign the Indian mercantile diaspora in Iran alone may have numbered as many as 10,000 individuals. Most of these men were Punjabi Khatris; that is, they were from the same large caste group as Akbar's finance minister, Todar Mal. They evidently controlled India's foreign trade with Iran as well as functioning as bankers or moneylenders in the Iranian economy. In the late sixteenth and seventeenth centuries some of these Khatri merchants migrated from north-western Iran to newly conquered Russian territory in the former

Astrakhan khanate along the lower Volga, eventually making their way to Moscow. A few Khatris eventually sought permission to trade as far west as Poland. Members of the same caste group resided in such Central Asian cities as Samarqand. In Central Asia some Khatris transformed themselves from exporters to producers by establishing a local putting-out system to produce cloth utilising local cotton. There and in Iran they operated through what were family firms of the type known in Italian Renaissance city states. Their presence in Iran, Russia and Central Asia at a time when European seaborne trade with India was steadily growing helps to balance the Eurocentric historiography of the Mughal era by reminding everyone concerned of the financial strength and mercantile sophistication of just one portion of the Indian merchant class. Other such castes, such as the Chettis from India's south-east or Coromandel coast, carried on extensive trade with South-East Asia in the early modern era, just as centuries and even millennia earlier their predecessors had spread widely throughout this region.

It is important to appreciate the economic vibrancy of the Indian economy as a whole and that of Mughal territories in particular. Not only were Indian merchants expanding their trade and financial activities overland, just as the Europeans were arriving by sea in greater numbers, but many of these mercantile caste groups increased their wealth and influence within Mughal India as the Mughals extended their authority and sophisticated extraction techniques to larger areas of agrarian production. Such well-known mercantile caste groups as the Oswals, natives of the region of Rajasthan known as Marwar, were especially effective in exploiting the new opportunities offered by the monetised agrarian economy and the relative security provided by Mughal power. The Oswals and other commercial castes became bankers for the empire. Indeed, when the Europeans arrived in India they discovered a sophisticated banking system that allowed merchants or government officials to transmit funds from Bengal to Delhi or further to Afghanistan, Iran, Central Asia, Iran and Russia via *hundis* or bills of exchange. The presence of financially astute, well-capitalised Indian mercantile castes and the existence of their elaborate trade and financial networks facilitated European commerce in South Asia and the contiguous regions.

By the time Akbar died in 1605 the three major European seaborne powers had arrived in India: the Portuguese in 1498, the Dutch and British as united commercial companies in 1600 and 1602. Initially, as has been noted, the Portuguese as well as their northern European competitors were preoccupied with the spice trade, and therefore focused their attention on the Malabar coast, well away from Mughal territories. However, even before Dutch and

English merchants arrived in India in any numbers, the Portuguese had begun to reduce the amount of pepper shipped to Europe in favour of indigo and textiles. In the 1580s this shift was fairly modest, but in the early seventeenth century as Dutch and British ships began carrying spices to Europe, the price of pepper and other spices fell precipitously, and the Dutch and the British, who had quickly usurped the primacy of Indian Ocean commerce from the Portuguese, increasingly purchased Indian textiles, not only cotton but also silk from Bengal.[13]

By the 1680s textiles, both cotton and raw silk, which were produced in north as well as south India, became the most important Indian exports to Europe, with most spices arriving from Dutch bases in Indonesia and the Moluccas. Indian textiles also had become critical for Dutch trading in South-East Asia and Japan. The British and Dutch had established commercial posts in Gujarat at Surat in 1022/1613 and 1038/1628 respectively, and by the 1630s they had both opened 'factories', that is warehouses, in Bengal. Both Gujarat and Bengal were by then Mughal territories, and the Mughal economy thus directly and indirectly profited from this ever-increasing volume of commerce with Europe that the British, Dutch and others largely paid for with specie. The state directly profited from mint charges and tolls, and Mughal officials, *mansabdār-jāgīrdārs*, peasants and craftsmen benefited from increased demand for local agricultural and manufactured goods. Whether this huge influx of specie produced significant price inflation in Mughal territories is difficult to determine, any more than it can be done for the Malabar coast after Vasco da Gama's arrival there in 903/1498. Nonetheless, there seems to have been only modest price inflation in Mughal territories during the seventeenth century.

Throughout the seventeenth century Europeans acted as traders and, politically, petitioners with Mughal officials. Not until the Mughal empire had ceased to exist and become a mere city-state in Delhi in the 1740s did the English become a military and territorial power within Mughal dominions. In consequence, the history of the Mughal empire from the time of Akbar's death until the death of the last great Mughal emperor, Aurungzeb, in 1707, is primarily an Indian rather than a European matter. There are two major aspects to this narrative: the Mughal emperors and their policies, and indigenous developments that were sometimes outside or beyond their control. First of all, the personalities and policies of individual emperors have to be

13 For an introduction to European seaborne commerce see especially Om Prakash, *European commercial enterprise in pre-colonial India*, The new Cambridge history of India (Cambridge, 1998).

studied seriously, for nothing is more obvious from Bābur's autobiography and Akbar's exceptionally well-documented reign than the fact that the emperors determined how the state functioned. In such an imperial system the emperor was the linchpin, the capstone, the *deus ex machina*. A study of both Bābur's and Akbar's reigns demonstrates a pattern of unremitting activity, campaigning during the dry season and personally overseeing every possible administrative, political and cultural detail. Second, in studying the history of the Mughal empire it is always important to remember that indigenous religious and social movements that threatened the empire often developed independently or at the very least were only indirectly caused by a particular ruler's actions. One of the most obvious cases in point was the evolution of the Sikhs from a syncretic religious movement to a social and political power led by Khatris and staffed by Jats that threatened Mughal control over the wealthy and strategically crucial Punjab province.

Jahāngīr: the aesthete as emperor

The reign of Akbar's successor Salīm or Jahāngīr, the 'World-seizer' (r. 1014–37/1605–27), vividly illustrates the importance of idiosyncratic personality while it also witnessed the beginnings of Sikhism as a social and political force. Jahāngīr, like Bābur, wrote an autobiography, and while it seems to reveal a shallower individual than his great-grandfather the work is nonetheless still a rich, complex text that combines an explicit proclamation of imperial values as well as implicitly offering an intriguing psychological self-portrait. Jahāngīr intended it to be a kind of 'mirror for princes' work in which he presents himself as the cultured 'just sultan' who ruled over a fabulously wealthy kingdom that, as he is careful to note, far exceeded the wealth of his neighbours. By neighbours he seems to have had especially in mind the Safavids of Iran, with whom he shared a language and culture. It is especially in Jahāngīr's *Twelve Decrees*, proclaimed, evidently, in 1016/1607, and which he included in his memoirs, that he revealed much about both his principles of government and his self-indulgent personality.

The first four of these decrees dealt with economic measures designed to protect merchants and increase trade. These included encouraging *jāgīrdārs* to build caravanserais and emphasising the sanctity of private property, whether belonging to Muslims or 'infidels'. In a related edict Jahāngīr also forbade the quartering of troops in private houses. Several other measures concerned social policy. These included the prohibition of mutilation as a punishment, the construction of hospitals in large cities, the requirement that the 'deserving poor' should be brought before him daily, by implication, for alms, an order against the slaughter of animals on certain days – a continuation of Akbar's custom – and the prohibition against *jāgīrdārs* and provincial revenue officials seizing peasant lands and cultivating the land themselves. This last measure may have been designed to guard against *jāgīrdārs* becoming entrenched landlords or local chiefs as much as it was intended to protect cultivators. This is certainly true of the next edict, which forbade *jāgīrdārs* from intermarrying with the local population without royal permission. Then, in a series of edicts designed to secure his political position, Jahāngīr confirmed the appointment of his father's *jāgīrdārs* – later substantially raising their *mansab* ranks – and confirmed also the grants to those who 'formed the army of prayer'. He also substantially increased the stipend of women in the harem. Finally, in the one edict, number five, that does not fall under any of these categories, Jahāngīr outlawed the manufacture of wine, spirits or intoxicants of any kind.[14]

This latter stipulation, which on the evidence of its opening sentence might be seen merely as a further means to impress the 'army of prayer' with his piety, seems from the remainder of the very long passage more immediately the consequence of his own well-known and here, openly exhibited, alcoholism. This was not unusual for members of either the Mughal or the Safavid ruling class, many of whom were alcoholics and, like Jahāngīr, opium addicts. Bābur himself drank profusely for about a fifteen-year period before he quit in 1527. It is only one of many personal revelations that Jahāngīr provides in his memoirs. He writes about this prohibition:

> This despite the fact that I myself commit the sin of drinking and have constantly persisted in doing so from the age of eighteen until my present age of thirty-eight ... sometimes I began to drink three or four hours before the end of the day. Sometimes I drank at night, and occasionally I drank during the day. Until the age of thirty this is how it was. After that I decided that I would only drink at night. These days I drink solely to promote digestion.[15]

Jahāngīr later reports that he had begun drinking during a hunting trip along the Indus and 'liked the feeling he got'. Later, however, wine didn't affect him enough so he began drinking hard liquor. 'Things got so bad', he writes, 'that in my hangovers my hands shook and trembled so badly I couldn't drink myself but had to have others help me.'[16] While reducing his

14 Jahāngīr, *The Jahangirnama*, pp. 26–7.
15 *Ibid.*, p. 26.
16 *Ibid.*, p. 185.

wine consumption he gradually substituted opium, which, he says, at age forty-six, he took both day and night.

It is tempting to see Jahāngīr's debilitating addictions as symptoms of a weak, dependent personality, if drinking had not been such a common vice among rulers and military aristocrats in India, Iran and Central Asia at this period. And yet while Jahāngīr constantly invokes his father's policies and achievements, he rested on Akbar's laurels rather than trying to win his own. While he possessed the dynastic arrogance and cultural sensibilities of his forebears, by the evidence of his own writing he had little taste for actual combat. He relied instead on the imposing imperial foundation that his father had erected and on Akbar's experienced commanders for the continuous military activity seen by them as a prerequisite for long-term political survival. Jahāngīr awarded promotions, received embassies, hunted and drank, visited Muslim and Hindu ascetics, admired and patronised miniature painting, saw to the design of new coinage and recorded memories of his own emotional sensitivity and personal attachments that humanise him. Having just reported, for example, the death of his mother-in-law, he describes how his minister and father-in-law, Iʿtimād ud-dawla, never recovered from the grief he felt over his wife's death:

> No husband has ever had the affection and attachment for his spouse that Iʿtimād ud-dawla had for her. One can imagine what befell the poor, grief-stricken old man ... Although Iʿtimād ud-dawla kept himself externally under control and exhibited forbearance in order to please me, given the attachment he had for her, forbearance could not replace her as a companion ... From the day his spouse passed away he no longer took care of himself and wasted away day by day ... He suffered inwardly from loneliness until he died three months and twenty days later.[17]

Iʿtimād ud-dawla left behind at least forty-one children, whom Jahāngīr consoled, as he notes, with robes of honour.

Mughal women

Jahāngīr's ability to convey the pathos of human emotion is unmatched in the literature of early modern Muslim rulers, including that of his great-grandfather, Bābur. However, his feeling for his in-laws was genuine and unusually strong, springing probably in the first instance from his passionate

17 *Ibid.*, p. 369.

attachment to his favourite wife, Nūr Jahān, whom he had married as a young widow of a Mughal officer in 1019/1611. By every sign Jahāngīr was deeply in love with and probably emotionally dependent on this beautiful Iranian woman, a guess about marital relations that cannot be hazarded about most other Muslim rulers in pre-colonial times. Nūr Jahān seems to have been his almost constant companion, including accompanying him on many hunting expeditions, as in the spring of 1026/1617:

> On the seventeenth [16 April] after the elapse of two watches and three gharis, the scouts had cornered four lions. I set out with the ladies of the harem to hunt them. When the lions came into view, Nurjahan Begam said, 'If so commanded, I will shoot the lions.' I said, 'Let it be so,' She hit two of them with one shot each and the other two with two shots.[18]

Nūr Jahān even had coins and imperial decrees issued in her name and until the death of her father she acted as part of a triumvirate with her father and brother, Asaf Khan. Together the three effectively ran the empire for long periods, especially during the prolonged periods when Jahāngīr was incapacitated with alcohol and opium. However, the family's supremacy did not presage an Ottoman-style administration where the emperor retired from active administration and ceded power to a series of viziers. When Jahāngīr's son, Shāh Jahān, came to the throne the new emperor again took direct control of Mughal affairs.

Nūr Jahān's highly visible role and the importance of her entire family serve as reminders of two important aspects of Mughal court culture: the active role of women and the increasing numbers of Iranians in India. Nūr Jahān was one of the most visible and powerful individual women among the Mughal nobility – visible at least to historians – but she was far from the only influential and identifiable woman at court. The time is long since past when it was possible to think of the Mughal harem – or the woman's quarters of any early modern Islamic state – as an undifferentiated society of passive pleasure objects.[19] First of all it is important to note two things about the identity and status of royal women: many were themselves Timurids or Chinggisids, that is, sisters, daughters or nieces of the emperors, and many of the emperors' numerous wives were members of Muslim or Hindu aristocratic or ruling families. Therefore, unlike the Ottoman harem, with its legions of concubines or slaves, who were often, no doubt, exceptionally

18 *Ibid.*, p. 219.
19 See for example Ruby Lal, *Domesticity and power in the early Mughal world* (Cambridge, 2005).

powerful individuals, a large if indeterminate number of Mughal women were of high status and highly educated. Timurid and Chinggisid women and favourite wives like Nūr Jahān had their own households and often their own houses as well.

Women in Turco-Mongol tribal and nomadic societies, while certainly subordinate individuals to a dominant male ethos, nonetheless were both far more physically visible and also politically influential than wives, sisters and daughters in great urban empires. Temür's wives were present at his receptions and drank and got drunk with men present, even with the Spanish ambassador Clavijo in 808/1405. Whether shared intoxication translated into political influence is not known, as Temür left no verifiable memoir, but five generations into the evolution of Timurid society with Bābur, women were known, by Bābur's own testimony, to act as his advisers. When describing events in his Farghānah homeland in 899/1494, shortly after inheriting his father's appanage, he remarks that his grandmother, Isen Devlat Begim, 'was an exceptional advisor and counsellor. She was extremely intelligent and prudent. Most affairs were settled with her advice.'[20] It is especially noticeable that in his *Vaqā'i'* Bābur carefully publicises his respect for three groups of individuals: Turco-Mongol aristocrats, that is, Timurids and Chinggisids; descendants of Khwāja Ahrār, his Naqshbandī 'patron saint' who died in 895/1490; and Timurid and Chinggisid women. According to his own testimony Bābur almost ostentatiously showed such women his regard by visiting them – as he did male Timurids and Chinggisids and Ahrārī Naqshbandīs – rather than calling them into his presence.

Bābur's daughter, Gulbadan Begim (*c.* 929–1012/1523–1603), herself personified the high status and influence of Timurid women – influence in the Mughal house and with posterity. She composed at Akbar's request her own remarkable memoir that not only has a powerful emotional content, but also rescues many other Timurid and Chinggisid women from anonymity. Speaking for example of her reaction at age ten to the death of her foster mother in 1533, Gulbadan writes that 'I felt lonely and helpless ... and night and day would weep, grieve and mourn.'[21] Then a few pages later Gulbadan writes that after the period of mourning Humāyūn celebrated two splendid feasts, the so-called 'Mystic' or talismanic feast celebrating Humāyūn's accession and a marriage feast for Humāyūn's brother, Mīrzā Hind-al. She

20 Dale, *The garden of the eight paradises*, p. 63.
21 Gul-Badan Begam, *The history of Humāyūn (Humāyūn-nāma)*, trans. and ed. Annette S. Beveridge (Delhi, repr. 1972), fo. 23b.

names more than eighty women who attended, some of whom were simply nurses, but most were important Timurids and Chinggisids, and she manages to bring the court alive by conveying the excitement of the lavish celebratory occasion. Writing of the events within the 'Mystic House' on the bank of the Ganges, Gulbadan recalls that:

> First there was a large octagonal room with an octagonal tank. In the centre, and again, in the middle of the reservoir an octagonal platform on which were spread Persian carpets. Young men and pretty girls and elegant women and musicians and sweet-voiced reciters were ordered to sit in the tank ... [Later after gifts were distributed] His majesty [Humāyūn] was pleased to say [to Khanzadah Begim [his grand-aunt], 'Dearest Lady, if you approve, they might let water into the tank.' She replied: 'Very good,' and went herself and sat at the top of the steps. People were taking no notice, when all at once [?] the tap was turned and water came. The young people got very much excited. His Majesty said 'There is no harm; each of you will eat a pellet of anise and a bit of comfit [*maʿjūn*, an intoxicant or confection – or both] and come out of there.'[22]

Women's agency, at least within the imperial family, is evident from events in 946/1539. When Humāyūn was fleeing before the Sūrī Afghan Shīr Khan, he asked Gulbadan, then perhaps seventeen, to ride to nearby Alwar to make peace with Humāyūn's brother Mīrzā Hind-al. Citing Gulbadan's youth, her mother went instead. Then in 983/1575 Gulbadan, at the time a mature woman in her early fifties, led the pilgrimage to Mecca, accompanied by a number of her female relatives and wives and relatives of other important Mughal women. They returned to Fatehpur Sikri only in 990/1582.

It is evident from Gulbadan's memoirs and Nūr Jahān's activities that Mughal women were literate, assertive individuals. In fact, daughters of the Mughal house after the time of Gulbadan Begim were literate in Persian and often competent in Arabic, with a sophisticated knowledge of both Persian verse and Sufi religious literature. Zīb al-Nisā, one of Aurungzeb's daughters, is a prime example, and probably as influential in her way as Nūr Jahān. One of at least three Mughal princesses who wrote a *dīwān*, or collection of poetry, Zīb al-Nisā was tutored by Ashraf Māzandarānī, a highly educated and socially prominent member of the religious literati class in the Safavid capital, Iṣfahān. In fact, Māzandarānī, who reached Agra in 1658/9, was related by marriage to the famous Majlisī family of theologians in Iṣfahān. He was also acquainted with the eminent poet Sā'ib and the calligrapher Daylāmī, both of whom had

22 *Ibid.*, fos. 24a, 28a.

served the Mughal court before returning to Iṣfahān. Daylāmī, in fact, had been tutor to Dārā Shikuh, Shāh Jahān's eldest son and designated heir. Zīb al-Nisā became one of the principal religious and literary patrons during Aurungzeb's early reign. Her activity was all the more important because Aurungzeb's own ascetic habits led him to turn his back on the lavish artistic and architectural patronage of his predecessors in favour of piety and conquests. Indeed, it was at Zīb al-Nisā's initiative that the famous compilation of Islamic legal decisions, the *Fatāwa-yi ʿAlamgīrī*, was translated from Arabic to Persian, although she herself had also studied Arabic grammar. Zīb al-Nisā's literary and religious interests offer just a fleeting insight into the sophisticated cultural world of Mughal women who, even if they lived relatively confined lives, could, if they were so inclined, cultivate vibrant intellectual interests.

Indo-Persian literature

The fact that Zīb al-Nisā studied with an Iranian who was as well connected as Ashraf Māzandarānī is a reminder of the degree to which Mughal India had become an integral part of the Persianate cultural sphere. Akbar's recruitment of Iranians, the disparity between the wealth of Mughal India and the relative poverty of Safavid Iran and Safavid persecution of Sufis stimulated a migration of historic proportions from Iran to India. Nūr Jahān and her family were part of this movement of Iranians to India, which continued largely unabated until the Safavid regime collapsed in 1134/1722 and the Mughal empire gradually atrophied during the same period. Many of the Iranians who settled in India wrote poetry and were part of what the modern Iranian scholar, Gulchīn-i Maʿānī, has termed the 'Caravan of Hind'.[23] Maʿānī has identified more than 700 such individuals who immigrated to Mughal territories or the Deccan states during the Mughal era. Most of these men were not court poets, but administrators, warriors, teachers or *ʿulamāʾ* who wrote poetry in their leisure time, as was so common among educated Iranians.

Māzandarānī was not the most influential émigré poet to write Persian verse in India, but he is memorable for the 'exile' verse he wrote in which he expressed his conflicted feelings about the subcontinent. 'Among destitute Iranians', he observed, 'there is nothing but desire for India.' The contrast between the wealth of the two kingdoms was so great that:

23 Gulchīn-i Maʿānī, *Karvān-i Hind*, 2 vols. (Tehran, 1369/1970).

> Whoever comes from Iran to India imagines,
> That in India gold is scattered like stars in the evening sky.[24]

Yet despite Mughal India's attraction for impoverished Iranians, Māzandarānī, at least, was not entirely happy there. First of all he was simply homesick:

> I do not know why there is naught in me but grief,
> Since the means of happiness have fallen to me in India.[25]

Not only did he dislike the climate, but like many Iranians he also regarded Indo-Persian culture as a pale imitation of the Iranian original. Playing on the common Iranian and Central Asian image of India and Indians as black or dark, he wrote:

> How can you compare the soil of Hind with the land of Iran?
> Do not equate black soil with a rose garden …
> How can you compare the Indian kingdom to Iran?
> As the copy can never be equal to the original.[26]

Most twentieth-century Iranian and Western literary scholars also felt that the quality of Indo-Persian verse was a poor, debased imitation of the original, that is, of the poetry of Saʿdī and Ḥāfiẓ, the two great 'classical' Persian poets. Generally known as *sabk-i hindī*, the Indian style has been widely considered to be a unique hothouse variant of Persian verse, characterised by extraordinary or bizarre imagery and highly intellectualised and obscure conceits. By the late twentieth century, however, scholars had actually begun to devote serious attention to Indo-Persian verse rather than just repeating stereotypes, and a consensus has now emerged that the 'Indian style' was in fact a product of literary developments in greater Khurāsān, Central Asia and India. It is seen as peculiarly 'Indian' in modern Iran because Iranians had then turned their backs on the innovative literary developments of the Safavid–Mughal period in a *bāzgasht* or 'return' to classical traditions. Nonetheless, some of the poets associated with the Indian style were born in India and did produce verse that was, in certain respects, distinctly more Indian than the poems written by expatriate Iranians.

The first poet who is usually seen as a practitioner of what he and others saw as a 'new' style that went beyond the verse of Jāmī of Herat was Bābā Fighānī of Shīrāz (d. 925/1519).[27] In fact, Fighānī and other poets now associated with the Indian style worked with a thorough knowledge of verse of the

24 Stephen Frederic Dale, 'A Safavid poet in the heart of darkness: The Indian poems of Ashraf Mazandarani', *Iranian Studies*, 36, 2 (2003), p. 197.

25 *Ibid.*, p. 206.

26 *Ibid.*, p. 207.

27 See Paul Losensky, *Welcoming Fighānī: Imitation and poetic individuality in the Safavid-Mughal ghazal* (Costa Mesa, 1998).

Timurid period. Fighānī himself, interestingly enough, might be also considered to be 'Indian', although he lived and died in Iran, because he wrote a number of 'imitations', that is, innovative variations, on the verse of the first great Indo-Persian poet, Amīr Khusrau. Two important Mughal practitioners of Fighānī's new style were 'Abū'l Faiz Faizī (954–1004/1547–95), who was Abū'l Faḍl's older brother and one of a few Indian-born poets associated with this style, and Jamāl al-Dīn Muḥammad 'Urfī (957–99/1550–91), a native of Shīrāz. Faizī, as he is known by his pen name, was, apart from stylistic matters, an 'Indian' poet in the sense that he sometimes used Hindu sources – the *Mahabharata* and *Bhagavad Gita* – for his verse. However, the most famous of the *sabk-i hindī* writers were Sā'ib (1010–89/1601–78), an Iṣfahān native, and Bedīl (1054–1133/1644–1721), who was born in India at Patna.

A native speaker of Bengali, Bedīl is the pre-eminent example of a poet whose *sabk-i hindī* verse was not just part of Persian literary evolution, but was identifiably Indian in certain ways. Bedīl, who like so many other Persian-language poets was spiritually attracted to Sufism, is known for his elaborate conceits and ambiguity and for employing colloquialisms and using Indian vocabulary not found in the verse of other Persian-language poets of the era. The difficulty of his verse is probably more immediately due to his Sufi piety and his sense of the inexpressible quality of his relationship with God. He, more than any other than Indo-Persian writer in Mughal India, became famous beyond Hindustān, particularly in Central Asia and Afghanistan, and remains extremely popular in Afghanistan and Tājīkistan to this day.

While Persian remained the dominant court and literary language at the Mughal court it is also important to recall that much of what is now considered classical Hindi or Hinduwī verse was written during the Mughal era and that many Mughal emperors and princes both during and after Akbar's reign patronised Hindi verse as well as Indian music. This fact also serves as a reminder not only that the bulk of Mughal India's population always remained Hindu, or at least non-Muslim, but also that fundamentally important cultural and socio-economic changes were occurring in the mid-seventeenth century among the majority population that altered the social and political topography of the Mughal empire. One such fundamental change was the rise of the Sikh movement.

Internal unrest: Sikhs and Naqshbandīs

Sikhism grew out of a syncretistic movement that borrowed both from Sufism and *bhaktī* or Hindu devotionalism. Sikhism was monotheistic, protestant both in its scathing criticism of Brahman priests and Muslim '*ulamā*', and in its egalitarian ideology at the petty bourgeoisie and peasant level. It was founded by a Punjabi Khatri, a member, that is, of the same large caste group as Todar Mal, Akbar's revenue minister. This man, Guru Nanak (b. 1469), strongly criticised the Lodī predecessors of the Mughals as unjust rulers who discriminated against non-Muslims, but he also railed against Hindu caste and social distinctions. Guru Nanak preached that God could only be understood by absorbing the teaching of the divine teachers or *gurus*, thus initiating a line of sacred disciples, who became the leaders of the community.[28]

Many of the early Sikhs were, like Guru Nanak, Khatris of modest wealth and status, small merchants and shopkeepers, but cultivators were also prominent among his followers, and many of these agriculturalists were Jats. Part of Sikh ideology was a proud proclamation of their members' middling social status. By the time Guru Nanak died in 1539 members of the sect had begun to coalesce into a new social group, publicly proclaimed by their disciples' commensality. When Jahāngīr came to the throne the Sikhs had evolved into a self-consciously separate and increasingly well-organised community, distinct from Muslims and Hindus, concentrated in the Punjab, especially in and around Lahore. However, when the fourth Guru Arjan blessed Jahāngīr's rebel son Khusrau in 1605, Jahāngīr responded quickly to the growing Sikh movement and had Guru Arjan arrested and executed. This prompted the Guru's son to begin transforming the order into an armed sect that by the 1670s was successful in converting large numbers of Jats and also some Muslims to the new faith and society. When Aurungzeb executed the Sikh Guru Tegh Bahadur in 1086/1675 on grounds of blasphemy, the Mughals earned the undying hatred of a community that had long since become a state within a state in the Punjab. This was the wealthy and militarily strategic province that Shāh Jahān's historian, ʿInāyat Khan, described as the 'choicest portion of the imperial dominions'.[29] A new conflict erupted following Aurungzeb's death, and while Mughal armies were able to defeat poorly armed Sikh forces in 1127/1715, leading to hundreds of additional executions, the Sikhs quickly extended their influence in the Punjab as Mughal power atrophied in the 1730s and 1740s.

Jahāngīr, whose execution of the fourth Guru initially provoked the alienation of Sikh followers from the Mughal regime, was a man who was suspicious of all popular religious movements that seemed to threaten public order

28 J. S. Grewal, *The Sikhs of the Punjab*, vol. II, part 3 of *The new Cambridge history of India* (Cambridge, 1990), 'Introduction' and ch. 2 'Foundation of the Sikh Panth'.

29 W. E. Begley and Z. A. Desai (eds.), *The Shah Jahan Nama of ʿInayat Khan* (Delhi and New York, 1990), p. 121.

or Mughal supremacy. He publicly revered Hindu and Muslim ascetics, but was hostile to charismatic or activist figures of any religious stripe. In 1028/1619 he arrested Shaykh Aḥmad Sirhindī, an Indian-born member of the Naqshbandī Sufi order that Bābur had brought with him from Central Asia. Sirhindī was a student of a Naqshbandī from Kabul, Baqī Billah Birang, who was probably an Ahrārī Naqshbandī on his mother's side. Baqī Billah had arrived in Delhi in 1602 after visits to the Naqshbandī homeland in the Samarqand region. Little is known about his teachings in India, but Sirhindī claimed for himself a semi-divine status as an incarnation of the Companions of the Prophet Muḥammad and the 'Renewer of the Second Millennium of Islam', which had begun in 1000/1591. Like many other conservative Muslims Sirhindī had been offended by Akbar's religious policies and encouragement of Hindu participation in the Mughal state, and his affiliation with the conservative and largely orthodox Naqshbandīs probably reflected his orthodox views. However, not only was Jahāngīr publicly proud of his father's latitudinarian policies but also he was suspicious of Sirhindī's claims and the enthusiasm he generated among the populace. As he wrote:

> Also during these days it was reported that a charlatan in Sirhind named Shaykh Aḥmad had spread a net of deceit and deception in which he had trapped many unspiritual worshippers of externality. He had also sent into every city and region those of his devotees whom he called khalifas, who were best versed in setting up shops in which mysticism could be peddled and people hoodwinked ... I saw that the only thing to do with him was to let him spend a few days in prison.[30]

Later he released Sirhindī, who, while apologising for his extreme religious claims, went on to establish the Naqshbandīs as a vital, if conservative, Sufi order in India. From there as the *Mujaddidī*, or 'Renewal', form of the Naqshbandī order it expanded outward – back to Afghanistan and also to the Ottoman empire, where it survived to become influential among upper-class Turks in the twentieth and twenty-first centuries.

In certain ways Jahāngīr personified the goal of Bābur's original conquest. As his memoirs attest, he enjoyed being emperor of a wealthy kingdom where he could indulge his sophisticated artistic interests. And here was Hindustān, a wealthy refuge for urbanised, culturally sophisticated Timurids and Chaghatay Chinggisids who were formally observant Sunnī Muslims with a strong attachment to Sufi spiritualism. In retrospect Jahāngīr's reign seems a

30 Jahāngīr, *The Jahangirnama*, p. 304.

kind of aesthetic interregnum, a pause in the history of a regime that evolved to become more formally imperial and openly orthodox under the rule of the last two emperors, Shāh Jahān and Aurungzeb. Yet Jahāngīr ruled in a political system where he faced the same difficulties that he had earlier, as a prince, visited upon Akbar. In 1622 one of his sons, Prince Khurram, the future Shāh Jahān, revolted, fearing that one of his brothers had gained ascendancy in the early manoeuvring to succeed Jahāngīr. His revolt precipitated a series of hard-fought campaigns as imperial forces chased Prince Khurram from the Deccan to Bengal to the middle Ganges region. Khurram apparently intended to depose his father, had he been victorious, but ultimately he failed and accepted a brokered peace, according to which he remained as governor of the Deccan. Khurram's rebellion highlights the persistent tensions of the Turco-Mongol inheritance and appanage system that first the Ottomans and then the Safavids had solved by incarcerating potential heirs to the throne in the harem. The question remains: why did the Mughals never follow their lead?

Shāh Jahān: the Second Temür

Jahāngīr – or Nūr Jahān and her brother, Asaf Khan – ruled for another five years before the emperor died near Lahore in 1037/October 1627. After Asaf Khan came out openly in support of Prince Khurram and defeated one of his brothers, Khurram was proclaimed emperor and, before reaching Agra, ordered the execution of his brother and four surviving Timurids who could possibly claim the throne. In a way his victory justified chaotic Mughal inheritance practices, even if it doesn't answer the question posed above. That is, Khurram, now enthroned as Shāh Jahān, was an experienced military leader and practised diplomat in the dangerous world of imperial court politics. He was quite likely the most qualified man to rule. In personality, a complete contrast to his father, Jahāngīr, he was an able, conscientious, aggressive individual who took and retained direct control of the state. He was also an openly conservative Sunnī Muslim in the mould of al-Badāunī and Shaykh Aḥmad Sirhindī. A European observer said, indeed, that in religious matters, Shāh Jahān 'was everything unlike his father'.[31] Shāh Jahān turned his back on Akbar's and Jahāngīr's sympathetic attitude towards non-Muslims, and he also exhibited little of the relentless intellectual curiosity of Akbar or the deeply emotional artistic sensitivity of Jahāngīr. Yet the nature of his

31 Quoted in Milo Beach and Ebba Koch, *The King of the World: The Padshahnama*, trans. Wheeler Thackston (London, 1997), p. 59.

intellect, emotions and religious convictions can only be inferred from his public actions. Neither did Shāh Jahān write or dictate a memoir like Bābur and Jahāngīr, nor are there the kind of eyewitness reports for his reign that make Akbar seem so human and such a humane individual. Apart from his actions, inscriptions and monuments, Shāh Jahān has to be viewed through the panegyric rhetoric of court historians, whose prose obscures individuality in favour of formal presentation of an imperial and imperious figure.

When viewed against the military activities of Shāh Jahān's reign, al-Badāunī's scathing indictment of *mansabdārs* seems even more the bilious critique of a disaffected courtier and orthodox Sunni Muslim. Whatever the day-to day problems with the *mansabdārī-jāgīrdārī* system it survived Jahāngīr's intoxicated inertia to be revivified by another strong emperor. Shāh Jahān continuously used troops that the system supplied and throughout his reign exerted military pressure both within the boundaries of the empire and on its frontiers. Internally, Mughal troops were dispatched to annex kingdoms and pressure others, particularly in Rajasthan. Externally, Shāh Jahān sent troops on the missions into: the Deccan in the 1630s, the upper Brahmaputra valley in 1045/1636 and Baltistān or 'Little Tibet' in 1046/1637; against Balkh in the 1640s and Kandahar in 1059/1649. He was successful in the Deccan, Bengal and Baltistān but failed completely after long sieges and arduous campaigns to capture and secure Balkh and Kandahar, both cities whose climates and locations made campaigns difficult for Mughal armies. Despite the expenses of his campaigns he was able to replenish the treasury that the self-indulgent Jahāngīr had nearly exhausted by substantially increasing the revenue demand, adding new territory and by systematic efforts to expand cultivation. He also increased the amount of *khalīsa* or state revenue that flowed directly into the treasury to equal one-seventh of the total collections.

Shāh Jahān's brief occupation of Balkh in the 1640s is but one indication of his heightened sense of his exalted lineage, for this campaign was driven by the revanchist nostalgia that he shared with his predecessors. According to the historian 'Abd al-Ḥamīd Lahorī, Shāh Jahān had his ancestors' exploits read aloud to him when he retired for the evening:

> So that His Majesty may fall into a sweet sleep, the eloquent members of the assembly read behind the veil works on biography and history, containing accounts of prophets and saints as well as events of the reigns of former kings and emperors – which are memoirs of vigilance for the blessed who take warning, and reminiscences of pardon for the enlightened who are fortunate. Especial favourites are the *Tuzuk* ('Memoirs') of the Emperor Babur and the *Zafar Nama* – which contains annals and conquests of the reign of His

> Majesty's illustrious ancestor the emperor Timur, the Lord of the Auspicious Planetary Conjunction (*Sahib-i-Qiran*).[32]

Shāh Jahān, who consistently called himself by the Timurid title that Jahāngīr occasionally used, the second *Sāhib-i Qirān*, showed that he took his heritage seriously when he dispatched his sons to occupy Balkh in northern Afghanistan in the 1640s. The conquest of Balkh was meant to provide the staging ground for the restoration of Timurid banners in Samarqand, Temür's capital. Jahāngīr, when describing his visit to Bābur's tomb in Kabul, had himself declared his intention to reconquer the Timurid homelands, but being Jahāngīr, never mounted such an arduous campaign. That Shāh Jahān made the attempt even when it was known that it would cost more to conquer these regions from the Uzbeks than the Mughals could recoup in revenue for many years, is but one of many testaments to his self-image. However, his sense of grandeur is more easily seen in the architectural monuments of his reign. Grandeur is actually an inadequate term to characterise Shāh Jahān's personal involvement in architectural projects calculated publicly to dramatise the stature of the imperial Mughal state.

Architecture and empire

One of the earliest signs of Shāh Jahān's lofty ambition was the construction of the Peacock Throne, a gem-encrusted monument that was commissioned in 1037/1628 and completed seven years later. The throne came to symbolise the Mughal empire, and when the Iranian usurper Nādir Shāh Afshar invaded India and plundered the throne in 1739, it signalled the empire's denouement – the actual end came only with a prolonged whimper more than a century later in 1859. In the 1630s and 1640s, however, that pathetic conclusion was unimaginable as Shāh Jahān constructed two other spectacular monuments testifying to the success of the Timurid Renaissance, the Tāj Mahal and a new capital in Delhi, Shāhjahānābād.

Following the death of his favourite wife, Mumtāz Mahal, in 1040/June 1631 while he was campaigning in the Deccan, Shāh Jahān ordered a memorial tomb constructed in Agra on the banks of the Yamuna river. Laid out within a classic Timurid *chahār bāgh* or four-part garden, the Tāj is part of an elaborate complex that also includes two smaller, relatively unobtrusive structures, a mosque and caravanserai. In architectural terms the Tāj is most immediately a

32 Quoted in Begley and Desai (eds.), *The Shah Jahan Nama of 'Inayat Khan*, p. 573.

Timurid building, an exquisite reformulation of the ideas that shaped Humāyūn's tomb in Delhi, whose garden setting manifested the *hasht bihisht* or 'eight paradise' model developed in Timurid Iran.[33] The eschatology of this concept was appropriate for a garden setting that in pre-Islamic Iran was already identified with paradise, the word itself being the Persian term for an enclosed garden. Then to reinforce these associations the calligraphic inscriptions on the Tāj suggest that the tomb represents an architectural metaphor for the resurrection. It is described by 'Ināyat Khan, who also informs his readers that the entire complex, a city in itself, as he points out, was sustained by an elaborate *waqf* or endowment of some thirty villages in the environs of Agra as well as by rent and sales from its bazaars:

> On the 17th Zi'l Qa'da this year 1052 [21 January 1643], the twelfth anniversary (*'urs*) of Her Late Majesty the Queen's death was celebrated in the customary manner. His majesty repaired in person to the sacred enclave congregated in the gardens around her radiant tomb, and distributed both that night and on the morrow, vast sums of money in charity among the deserving of both sexes ...
>
> Let it not be concealed that the recently completed mausoleum had been erected in the course of twelve years, at a cost of 50 lakhs of rupees [5 million rupees]; that its gardens were surrounded by squares, serais and bazaars; and that a great number of substantial workshops were established behind the serais ... To maintain the mausoleum and its garden, His Majesty established an endowment consisting of the annual revenues of 30 hamlets ... and an identical amount is also realized from the annual rent and proceeds of the bazaars and serais.[34]

Even as the Tāj Mahal was being built Shāh Jahān began the construction of a new fortress city in Delhi, Shāhjahānābād, a complex comprising ceremonial buildings, harem apartments, bazaars and gardens that cost a further 6 million rupees. Women, most noticeably Shāh Jahān's sister, the influential Jahān-ārā Begim, constructed some of the buildings within the fortress; she was responsible for a large serai and *hammām* or bath. Opposite this great city Shāh Jahān constructed the monumental Jāmi' Masjid, the largest mosque in India, an open-air building similar to the one Akbar constructed at Fatehpur Sikri. The foundations for the new city were laid on 29 April 1639, a date chosen by astrologers, and the emperor ceremonially entered the newly constructed city on 18 April 1648. In summarising the history of the Shāhjahānābād – 'whose

33 Lisa Golombek, 'From Tamerlane to the Taj Mahal', in Monica Juneja (ed.), *Architecture in medieval India* (Delhi, 2001), pp. 21–5.
34 Begley and Desai (eds.), *The Shah Jahan Nama of 'Inayat Khan*, pp. 299–300.

Paradise-resembling edifices have been constructed along the banks of the river Yumuna' – 'Ināyat Khan wrote that:

> Several years before, the thought came to His Majesty's omniscient mind that he should select some pleasant site on the banks of the aforesaid river, distinguished by its genial climate, where he might find a splendid fort and delightful edifices. In accordance with the promptings of his noble nature, he envisioned that streams of water should be made to flow through the proposed fort ... [and the newly constructed canal] was designated as the Nahr-i Bihisht ('Stream of Paradise').[35]

Given the geographic, economic and political distance that Mughal rulers had come since Bābur's day, they might be excused for their profligate expenditure of cosmological metaphors, including one of Shāh Jahān's inscriptions on his new fortress, a literal echo of Amīr Khusrau's panegyric verse:

> Agar firdaws bar rū-yi zamīn ast
> Hamīn ast, hamīn ast, hamīn ast.
>
> If there is paradise on earth,
> It is this, it is this, it is this.

It is nowhere noted whether or not Shāh Jahān had a fine sense of irony to match his sophisticated architectural sensibilities. If so he might have used it to compose verse contrasting these paradises with his imprisonment in Agra fort from 1658 until his death eight years later. In essence Shāh Jahān became the victim of the Mughal appanage system previously exemplified by his own succession. Thus, when in September of 1657 he fell seriously ill and designated his eldest son, Dārā Shikuh, as heir apparent, his other three sons began in traditional fashion to seek the throne for themselves. The fact that Shāh Jahān improved dramatically by the time he reached Agra in October, where he had gone in hope that the change of scene would improve his health, did nothing to halt the military preparations of the three sons who were provincial governors and experienced commanders, each with loyal households and reliable troops. These three initially became temporary and uneasy allies against Shāh Jahān and Dārā Shikuh in Agra. Eventually, however, the war of succession devolved into a contest between Dārā Shikuh and Aurungzeb, who in 1657 commanded the imperial armies in their assault on Bījāpūr, a continuation of the perennial Mughal campaigns to conquer the Deccan.

35 *Ibid.*, pp. 406–7.

In Indian historiography the warfare among these four Mughal princes is often portrayed as a Manichean conflict, pitting the culturally sensitive and religious eclectic Dārā Shikuh against the personally austere, religiously orthodox Aurungzeb. Sometimes by implication, at other times more explicitly, historians argue that a victory for Dārā Shikuh, an intellectually inquisitive, Akbar-like figure, would have solidified the Mughal empire as a multicultural edifice, whose legacy would have been Muslim–Hindu amity and therefore, in 1947, a peaceful, united transition from British rule to an undivided, communally peaceful, independent Indian state. In this view Aurungzeb's military triumph, capture and execution of Dārā Shikuh set India on a path to the tragedy of partition.

The appanage system, however, rewarded cunning intelligence, ruthless determination and superior military skills. Contemporary as well as modern intellectuals might have preferred a cultured, religiously syncretistic aesthete. Both may also have been, like Ashraf Māzandarānī, shocked by Aurungzeb's usurpation of Shāh Jahān's throne. Māzandarānī, for example, ostensibly addressing Iranians planning to follow him to India, wrote:

> O you who have come from our country to India;
> In your region have you not heard the news of India? …
> The Indian-born intent on killing his father;
> Have you not heard this story on the Indian journey?[36]

However, Aurungzeb, like his father, whose orthodox religious outlook he shared, was, if nothing else, an intelligent, indefatigable man and an experienced military leader dedicated to the efficient administration and continuous expansion of the Mughal state.

Aurungzeb and the Marathas

Aurungzeb ruled longer than any of his predecessors, dying at ninety years of age in 1118/1707. Even more than his father he persisted in his effort to expand Mughal control over the border regions of the empire, in his case to Bengal, Afghanistan and, eventually in the area he knew best, the Deccan. In the 1660s and 1670s he dispatched his generals to wage war in east Bengal and habitually unstable Afghanistan. He was modestly successful in both areas, which were economically valuable for the empire: Bengal for its productive agriculture and Afghanistan as a commercial crossroads and trading entrepôt.

36 Dale, 'A Safavid poet in the heart of darkness', pp. 208–9.

Simultaneously Aurungzeb engaged in what appears to have been a conscious policy to reduce Rajput influence in the Mughal state and exert greater control over the Rajput principalities west of Agra. The Mughal emperor never repudiated the well-established Mughal policy of utilising Rajput military prowess, but he reduced the number of Rajputs in the imperial service and interfered much more aggressively in Rajput succession disputes. At the same time Aurungzeb alienated some Rajput nobles with his increasingly intrusive Muslim orthodoxy, reimposing the *jizya* tax on non-Muslims, destroying Hindu temples during campaigns and preventing temple construction at other times. In the late 1670s and 1680s Rajput discontent led some chiefs to persuade Aurungzeb's son, Akbar, to ally with them, rebel against his father and seize the throne. With the support of his cultured sister, Zīb al-Nisā, Akbar proclaimed himself emperor in 1091/January 1681, but he was outmanoeuvred by his father in a confrontation near Ajmir, the old Mughal pilgrimage site. Akbar then fled south to the Deccan, where he joined forces with the confederation that had by then become the greatest threat to Mughal authority, the Marathas of the western Deccan.

The rise of the Hindu Maratha kingdom was, like the growth of the Sikh community in the Punjab, the appearance of a threat to Mughal dominance and presumptions of sovereignty over the subcontinent that had not existed at the time of Bābur's initial conquest. As was true of their relations with the Sikhs, Mughal policies partly catalysed the growth of Maratha power and its increasingly anti-Mughal and even anti-Muslim tone. However, the Marathas had become a formidable regional power in their home territories, the rugged mountainous regions north and south of Bombay known as the Western Ghats, well before Aurungzeb laid siege to Bijapur as his father's deputy in 1656. Led by the ruthless and charismatic Shivaji, a man of low ritual status in the Hindu caste hierarchy, the Marathas first served with and then confronted the increasingly enfeebled Bijapur sultanate that was, by 1656, on the verge of being conquered by the Mughals. Shivaji first came into direct conflict with Mughal power in 1663 when he defeated a Mughal general who had earlier occupied the important Maratha town of Puna. Then in the following year the Maratha chief plundered the vitally important port of Surat, the single most important Mughal link with trade in the Arabian Sea and with Europe. While Mughal forces succeeded in defeating Shivaji and forcing him into Mughal vassalage in 1076/1665, by 1081/1670 he broke with his nominal overlords and resumed raids into imperial territories, once again that same year, successfully occupying and plundering Surat. Four years later Shivaji had himself declared a *kshatriya*, in fact a Rajput, using compliant Brahmans to ritually eradicate his low-caste status, and in a spectacular, expensive ceremony he was crowned as a Chatrapati, a traditional Hindu ruler, implicitly claiming universal dominion.

Shivaji was an audacious, skilled military leader, an intelligent, efficient administrator and a clever ideologue, who, in his coronation, defined himself as a Hindu alternative to the Mughal emperors. While his newly created state fragmented soon after his death in 1091/1680, both he and his successors posed a formidable, unrelenting threat to the Mughal state. By institutionalising raids into Mughal territories as state policy, Shivaji financed the expanding Maratha enterprise in the Deccan and south India and drained resources from Mughal territories. The fact that Aurungzeb's rebellious son, Akbar, had taken refuge with the Marathas in 1681 lent greater urgency to the Maratha crisis. Therefore, following a peace with the Rajputs of Mewar, Aurungzeb marched into the Deccan in 1092/1681 with his main field army and a host of officials, government clerks and camp followers. He remained there for most of the rest of his reign. Initially his campaigns were directed against the Marathas, but the difficulty of ever finally destroying them in the difficult hill country of the Western Ghats led Aurungzeb to turn his attention back to a long-time personal and dynastic goal, the conquest of the two surviving Deccan sultanates, Bijapur and Golconda. In campaigns partly financed by the surplus revenues of Bengal, both of these kingdoms fell to Mughal armies between 1096/1685 and 1099/1688, with most of their Muslim nobles then integrated into the Mughal *mansabdārī-jāgīrdārī* system. Aurungzeb then climaxed these triumphs with the capture and execution of Shivaji's son and successor, Shambhaji.

Aurungzeb's dramatic successes in 1688 did not, however, have the intended effect of eliminating Maratha resistance. Instead, the executed Maratha ruler's brother, Rajaram, fled to the formidable fortress of Ginji on India's south-east coast, which the Mughals failed to seize until ten years later. In the meantime Marathas in their homelands in the Western Ghats opposite Bombay led multiple plundering campaigns against Mughal territories. Even though Aurungzeb remained in the Deccan throughout these years until his death, directing imperial forces, and despite the many successes he and his commanders enjoyed in seizing Maratha forts, they were never able to suppress what had become a hydra-headed monster. As Aurungzeb's reign drew to a close Maratha forces slowly but inexorably extended their raids further north and by 1111/1700 were regularly raiding Gujarat and Mālwa, across the Narmada river, the traditional boundary between north India and the Deccan. As the Mughal empire atrophied during the first half of the eighteenth century, Marathas founded a series of independent kingdoms, most notably at Gwalior, the strategic fortress south of Agra, and raided east as far as the British commercial settlement of Calcutta. By mid-century they had penetrated deep into the Punjab with full-scale armies. But for the intrusion of the Afghans and the British the Marathas might have occupied the wealthy and strategic heartlands of the Mughal empire. However, Afghans shattered a confederated Maratha army at Bābur's famous Pānīpat battlefield in 1174/1761, and in the late eighteenth and early nineteenth century British military power prevented further Maratha expansion.

The seemingly endless campaigns in the difficult conditions of the Deccan placed an enormous strain on the heart of the Mughal imperial system, the *mansabdārī-jāgīrdārī* institution. Old trusted nobles were frustrated and exhausted, and resentful at the influx of new Muslim nobility from Bijapur and Golconda, who were given extraordinarily high ranks and preferable *jāgīrs*. Many *mansabdārs* simply refused to fight or made private arrangements with Maratha raiders. Nor was Aurungzeb able to co-opt Marathas as Akbar had done with the Rajputs, even though nearly 100 were appointed to the imperial service at this period, another source of resentment for older Mughal *amīrs*. His failure to assimilate Maratha chiefs, despite conscious efforts to do so, may have been due to many factors, two of which seem particularly important. First, unlike the desiccated terrain of Rajasthan, where rajas or lesser lineage chiefs ruled from isolated and ultimately vulnerable fortresses – much like Central Asian terrain where the seizure of a city often meant the conquest of a province – Marathas lived scattered through the isolated, forested regions of western India, where the narrow valleys and rugged mountains of the Western Ghats gave them shelter. Second, unlike Rajput clans, with their relatively cohesive hierarchies, Maratha society was far more decentralised or fragmented. Aurungzeb's armies defeated Marathas on many occasions, but were unable to halt Maratha raids, which became an institutionalised feature of Maratha culture and at times, as in the late 1750s, evolved into organised campaigns of conquest.

The imperial denouement

Aurungzeb's death in 1118/1707 is justifiably seen in hindsight as the beginning of the end of the Mughal empire. However, despite its manifold problems the empire and its institutions were still intact in that year, drawing substantial revenues from its core Punjabi and Gangetic provinces that, despite the extraordinary drain of the Deccan wars, provided a hoard in the central Agra treasury of more than 240 million rupees. Despite these reserves the empire slowly disintegrated between 1118 and 1152/1707 and 1739, when the invasion of the Iranian usurper, Nādir Shāh Afshar, acted as the *coup de grâce*, and left the empire as a tattered remnant, no longer an empire, but a weak north Indian state. There were several underlying, interrelated causes for the prolonged imperial death rattle. These were dynastic crises, the consequent disintegration of the imperial system and the seemingly intractable political and military challenges to Mughal authority throughout the empire.

The dynastic crises were most immediately the result of Aurungzeb's own longevity and the Mughal appanage system. Thus Bahādur Shāh, the victor in the inevitable succession struggle that erupted at Aurungzeb's death, was sixty-five years old when he came to the throne. It is impossible to gauge how much his age affected his ability to govern, and he was an active commander throughout his brief reign. However, his death in 1123/1712 disrupted the empire once again with a prolonged and inevitably expensive war of succession that essentially lasted from January 1712 until January 1713. In the first phase Bahādur Shāh's most powerful noble, Zulfiqar Khan, enthroned a new Timurid ruler, Jahāndār Shāh. This was followed by a bloody and distinctly un-Mughal purge of *amīrs* who had supported the losing princes. Jahāndār Shāh's brief, drunken and self-indulgent year-long reign ended when Farruksiyar, the son of one of Jahāndār Shāh's defeated younger brothers, was enthroned with the support of two powerful brothers from the important Sayyid lineage of Barha, a well-entrenched Muslim family long settled north of Delhi. His victory was also marked by the execution of nobles and Timurid princes, including his own young brother.

Farruksiyar's brief reign of six years was marked by further dramatic erosion of imperial authority as the emperor's conflicts with his erstwhile supporters, the Sayyid brothers, dominated imperial affairs until the brothers succeeded in seizing, blinding and eventually strangling the emperor in 1719. This act, an unimaginable event in the days of Shāh Jahān and Aurungzeb, accelerated the downward spiral of the dynasty. The lingering prestige of the Timurid house dissipated even further in the following year, during which the Sayyid brothers ruled through two Mughal puppets, both of whom died of tuberculosis. Finally, a third Timurid prince, a grandson of Bahādur Shāh, crowned as Muḥammad Shāh, was able to break free of the Sayyid brothers' control with the help of a group of Mughal loyalists, who evidently saw their own fate tied to the integrity of the Timurid house. However, by this time the empire was coming apart and, as events were to prove, Muḥammad Shāh was not capable of restoring even a fragment of its power and grandeur.

The memoirs of Bābur and the histories of Akbar's reign illustrate how personal qualities – intelligence, dynamism, relentless military campaigns and direct administration – created and sustained the early Mughal empire. Early modern empires depended, in the first instance, on the quality of the monarch, and especially after 1123/1712, no member of the Timurid house exhibited the qualities of their great predecessors: Bābur, Akbar, Shāh Jahān and Aurungzeb. As the character of the emperors deteriorated and the court and central administration were damaged with purges and vicious partisan conflicts the entire imperial system fragmented. Fragile ties of loyalty that bound Muslim and Rajput officers to the Timurid house frayed, imperial orders were ignored – or not given – and local officials had to fend for themselves or took the opportunity of the chaotic state of imperial affairs to seize regional power. This process by which emperors gradually lost control over their empire was also partly the consequence of indigenous groups asserting their own independence. Bahādur Shāh faced Rajput, Sikh and Maratha challenges as soon as he was crowned, and while he enjoyed some success in Rajasthan and the Punjab, the Marathas moved inexorably north. Jat lineages in the Agra region that had rebelled in Aurungzeb's day also asserted their independence. As affairs deteriorated during Farruksiyar's disastrous reign, Rajputs and many *zamīndārs* seized *de facto* control of territories previously under Mughal suzerainty. Some Rajput chiefs now re-emerged as independent magnates. *Watan jāgīrs* became kingdoms once more. Muslim governors turned inward, away from Agra and the atrophied empire, and became provincial rulers – the Nawābs of Bengal or the Niẓāms of Hyderabad.

Loss of Mughal control meant loss of revenue. Loss of revenue meant the reduction in military strength. The reduction in military strength meant the inability to reassert control over revenue resources. The pathetic state of the Mughal system was marked, finally, by the successful invasion of the ruthless Iranian tribal leader Nādir Shāh in 1152/1739. His invasion and rout of a dispirited, factionalised Mughal army and subsequent seizure of the Mughal treasury and the Peacock Throne, made it impossible for the Mughals to recover. In 1179/1764 the British East India Company itself defeated a fragment of the old Mughal army and, in consequence, became the *dīwān* of Bengal. The Company then used its power without responsibility to plunder the wealthiest province of the empire, impoverish the population and precipitate a famine that may have killed 10 per cent of the population. Never did Temür's legacy seem more irrelevant as the Mughals' kingdom-seizing ambitions atrophied to be replaced in the minds of Indian Muslims by an impotent nostalgia.

PART III

★

THE MARITIME OECUMENE

9

Islamic trade, shipping, port-states and merchant communities in the Indian Ocean, seventh to sixteenth centuries

MICHAEL PEARSON

Introduction

This chapter consists of surveys of the following regions: the Swahili coast, the Maldive islands, Malabar, Coromandel and Sri Lanka (see Map 7). The period to be covered is from the seventh to the sixteenth centuries. The concern will be to describe the arrival of Islam in these areas, the process of conversion and the state of Islam towards the end of this period. First, however, it is necessary to provide an overall sketch of trade, shipping and seafaring in the Indian Ocean, in the period from before Islam to the end of the sixteenth century, and then, before getting to specific areas, to consider some area-wide themes.

Pre-Islamic Indian Ocean trade

The sea, more precisely the Arabian Sea, plays a large role in the story.[1] Travel by sea, facilitated or sometimes circumscribed by the monsoon wind pattern, has a very long history in this area. The earliest boats were canoes made of reeds, still to be seen today in the marsh areas of the Tigris–Euphrates delta. Wooden boats, which gain their buoyancy from enclosed air, mark a major technological step forward. They go back at least some 5,000 years, to the time of the Indus Valley Civilisation.

The rise of early civilisations in the Tigris–Euphrates area and in north-west India, that is those of Mesopotamia and the Indus Valley, had profound effects for trade by sea. For the first time there were relatively routine maritime connections established, and indeed these extended to the third great early

1 See Michael Pearson, *The Indian Ocean* (London, 2003), pp. 46–61 for this and subsequent paragraphs.

civilisation, in Egypt. Most of this trade was carried on by small craft hugging the coastline, and carrying not only 'luxury' products like beads, gold, silver, pearls and ivory, but a vast quantity of humble goods: timber, foodstuffs, cloths.

In the first millennium BCE, after the decline of these two early civilisations, Arabian Sea trade became focused on India, which is to be seen as the fulcrum of Indian Ocean trade from very early on. By this time participants included very diverse people: those described as Greek or Roman, people from the Arabian peninsula, as well as from India. By this time there were connections far down the Swahili coast, and across all of the Indian Ocean to the Malay world. Longer connections were facilitated by sailors slowly learning how to use the monsoon wind system to their advantage. This had begun by at least 1000 BCE. From around 400 BCE there is evidence of Indian and Arab sailors going direct from the mouth of the Red Sea to India.

Unlike seas with constant trade winds, the way in which the monsoons reverse during the year made return voyages in the Indian Ocean relatively routine. Put most simply, in the Arabian Sea monsoon area, north of about 10°S, winds from the south-west prevail from June to October, and from the north-east from November to March. As a result, a passage from say Mombasa to India would take place during the south-west monsoon, and the return trip while the north-east wind prevailed.

In the third to the fifth centuries CE trade in the Indian Ocean was affected positively by the rise of the Sasanian empire in Persia. Traders from Persia dominated trade in the Gulf and even the western Indian Ocean. Some may even have reached South-East Asia and China.[2] More usually western Indian Ocean ships used Sri Lanka as a transhipment place. Persians, and Axumites from the Axum port of Adulis on the south-west coast of the Red Sea, met traders from East Asia there. Similarly linking the eastern and western oceans was the south-east coastal area of Coromandel: for example, there is evidence of Tamil products on the Red Sea coast of Egypt, and an inscription in Thailand from the early part of the Common Era.[3]

2 Valeria Fiorani Piacentini, 'International Indian Ocean routes and Gwadar Kuh-Batil settlement in Makran', *Nuova Rivista Storica* (May–Aug. 1988), p. 308 and *passim*, pp. 307–44; R. A. Donkin, *Beyond price: Pearls and pearl fishing, origins to the age of discovery* (Philadelphia, 1998), p. 95.

3 George F. Hourani, rev. and expanded by John Carswell, *Arab seafaring in the Indian Ocean in ancient and medieval times* (Princeton, 1951, 1995), pp. 40–9; Philip Snow, *The star raft: China's encounter with Africa* (Ithaca, 1989), p. 3; K. Rajan, 'Early maritime activities of the Tamils', in Himanshu Prabha Ray and Jean-Francois Salles (eds.), *Tradition and archeology: Early maritime contacts in the Indian Ocean* (New Delhi, 1996), pp. 97–108.

Navigation in this period, before the arrival of Islam, could be described as wayfinding. It was a craft, something passed on from generation to generation. Sailors learnt to 'read' the stars, sun, winds, ocean swells, the colour of the sea and the flight of birds. The magnetic compass came late to the Indian Ocean as compared with Chinese practice, but the astrolabe was used in the Indian Ocean from quite early times. By observing stars, this made finding a ship's position much more precise.[4]

Islam and trade in the western Indian Ocean: ships and navigation

Arabs played a role in Indian Ocean trade, alongside many others. From the seventh century these Arabs were converts to the new faith. In religious terms this of course marks a fundamental break, but trade, navigation and seafaring in general were little affected. Arabs, now become Muslims, kept on doing what they had been doing for some centuries, and kept on sailing to the same places: the Swahili coast, the Gulf, the Arabian Sea islands, especially the Maldives, above all India, and then sometimes further east.

By this time there is better information about the ships which sailed in the Indian Ocean. Generically these are called, at least by westerners, dhows.[5] While there were and are very substantial variations within this overall nomenclature, for simplicity's sake it seems best to write merely of dhows *tout court*. The hull was made of teak from Malabar in south-west India, producing a hull using the carvel method, held together by coir-fibre stitching. There were no keels. They had sternpost rudders, and usually only one mast and a sail made of matting from coconut. These were the famous triangular lateen sails. The hulls were double ended rather than having square, transom, sterns. On the largest dhows there may have been a raised poop deck, with cabins underneath, but most often the holds were open and there was no deck. Remarkably heavy cargo, camels, horses, even elephants, could be carried.

The navigator of the dhow in this period, such as at the time of the famous ninth/fifteenth-century sailor Ibn Mādjid, was the *muʿallim*, who sailed the

4 R. A. L. H. Gunawardana, 'Changing patterns of navigation in the Indian Ocean and their impact on pre-colonial Sri Lanka', in Satish Chandra (ed.), *The Indian Ocean: Explorations in history, commerce and politics* (New Delhi, 1987), pp. 61, 77 and *passim* for a very useful overview. B. Arunachalam has published extensively on traditional Indian navigation. See for example 'Traditional sea and sky wisdom of Indian seamen and their practical application', in Ray and Salles (eds.), *Tradition and archeology*, pp. 261–81.

5 Pearson, *Indian Ocean*, pp. 63–71.

ship and was responsible for what happened on board. He checked the fitting out, the stores, gear and loading. He was in charge of the crew and passengers, looked after their safety and health, and solved their quarrels. All this was laid down in the contract drawn up before the ship left. It was required to take a set number of passengers, and a set quantity of their effects. There were also bills of lading governing the cargo. His duty of care ended when he got the ship back to its home port.[6]

How did captains find their way over the ocean? There is a contrast here between blue-water sailing and finding one's way in more restricted waterways. To a considerable extent oceanic navigation was still wayfaring. Ibn Mādjid for example provides detail on land sightings for guidance into a port. He also relied on sightings of the sun and the stars. His work is an example of the pilot guides and navigational literature which were commonplace in the ocean from both the Chinese and the Arab side. It may be that practical navigational charts were not known before the Europeans, but there certainly were maps. It seems that Arab empirical methods were more than adequate to determine latitude quite accurately. Yet there is no doubt that Chinese navigational expertise, at its height from about 1000 to 1400 CE, was more advanced, including especially the use of the marine compass.

Chinese ships were also very different from the dhows. Once around Cape Comorin there were huge ships, which will be described in another chapter, in the Bay of Bengal. However, this was a rather temporary presence. They came south to the Malay world only from the twelfth century, and may have been displaced for a time in the mid-fourteenth century when the powerful Javanese state of Majapahit was at its height. Under the Ming, from 769/1368 onwards, Chinese ships re-entered South-East Asian waters, reaching a massive peak with the Zheng He expeditions of the early ninth/fifteenth century. Soon after this, long-distance Chinese voyaging in these monsters ended.[7] Thus for a time Chinese ships had competed with Muslim-owned shipping in the eastern Indian Ocean. Once the Chinese withdrew, Muslims dominated here, as they had done all the time in the western ocean. This dominance was next challenged when the Portuguese arrived at the early tenth/late fifteenth century.

6 G. R. Tibbetts, *Arab navigation in the Indian Ocean before the coming of the Portuguese* (London, 1971), pp. 59, 192–5.

7 Anthony Reid, 'The rise and fall of Sino-Javanese shipping', in V. J. H. Houben, H. M. J. Maier and W. van der Molen (eds.), *Looking in odd mirrors: The Java Sea* (Leiden, 1992), pp. 177–211.

Trading networks and products

By at least the end of the first millennium CE there were sophisticated and complex trading relations all around the Indian Ocean, and indeed far afield to China and the Mediterranean, and even Russia and Scandinavia. The most famous trade product was spices – that is, pepper, a bulk commodity, and the rarer and more expensive fine spices: mace, nutmeg, cloves and cinnamon. The last named came only from Sri Lanka, the other three fine spices from the distant Maluku islands. Pepper was found in parts of the Malay world, but most came from India's west coast, from Malabar. A typical passage for a spice from the Malukus involved a relay trade. If the destination was the Mediterranean, then the spice would go via an entrepôt in the Malay world – from the ninth/fifteenth century this was Melaka – then on to the west coast of India, then across the Arabian Sea to the Red Sea, and so to Alexandria and waiting Venetian merchants. Remembering however that three-quarters of spices were consumed within Asia, this journey is much longer than a more typical one, which for example would involve merely taking pepper or ginger up to China. The great Islamic ʿAbbāsid empire centred on Baghdad consumed vast quantities of spices from the second/eighth century onwards, as also later did the Islamic states in northern India.[8]

Spices are the best example of a trade in luxuries. Similar was the trade in coined precious metals, which was revolutionised from the middle of the eleventh/sixteenth century by the arrival of floods of gold and then silver from the Americas. The slave trade, especially from East Africa to the ʿAbbāsid empire, similarly was a luxury trade, as was that in ivory from the same region. Other trades were in humble essentials, such as cloths and food. One example here was another form of currency, more widespread than gold or silver. This was the cowry shells from the Maldives, used all around the ocean and even further afield, for example to Yunnan or West Africa, as basic currency.

The structure of long-distance trade changed fundamentally during the period under discussion. Around 290/900 there were direct passages from the Gulf to China in one ship, though other trade was done in several ships. By the end of the eleventh century direct trade in one ship had ended. The trade became segmented, with one merchant and ship doing the Arabian Sea part to south India, where the goods were exchanged, and then taken on by other

8 Detail on the spice trade in M. N. Pearson (ed.), *Spices in the Indian Ocean world* (Aldershot, 1996), pp. xvi–xxxiv.

ships and merchants to South-East Asia, where there was another exchange, and so to China. South India and Sri Lanka were always places where there was a halt, and exchange, but the difference is that in the earlier time sometimes the same merchant and ship kept going beyond there, while later none did this.

In the earlier period, from say the second/eighth century, the very long-distance trade from the Gulf to China was handled by Muslim merchants from Persia. It was based on the wealth and stability of the ʿAbbāsid empire from 132/750, and of Tang China (618–907 CE). Both had a large demand for foreign luxuries. In the Gulf, Sīrāf, on the east bank, was the main centre, where were to be found goods from all over the Indian Ocean, including East Africa. Later Julfar, on the west coast, was important, and later still Hormuz. Another old centre was Daybul, in present-day Pakistan. Arabs also took part in this trade, and soon became more important than the Persians. Later some Chinese ships also, from the sixth/twelfth century and particularly in the eighth/fourteenth, traded into the Arabian Sea. However, from the end of the seventh/thirteenth century the direct passage from Baghdad to Canton declined, and instead emporia rose. Shorter routes connected the major port cities of Baghdad, Hormuz, Cambay, Calicut, Melaka and Canton, with many minor routes from for example the Bay of Bengal feeding into this network.

From the sixth/twelfth century or a bit later, then, there were three segments: the Arabian Sea, the Bay of Bengal and the South China Sea. Chinese and Indians went to Melaka, Persians and Arabs only to India. This important move towards segmentation was partly a result of unsettled conditions at both ends of the route as powerful empires declined, and partly because traders realised that the direct passage in the same ship was inefficient, given that they had to wait for monsoons at several places. South India seems to act as a fulcrum in this very long-distance connection. Later in this period other Indians joined in, this time Muslims based in the many emporia on the west coast, and in the major Islamic state of Gujarat from the thirteenth century. Increasingly the trade east from India was controlled by Indian Muslims, while Arabs, and a few Persians, were restricted to the Arabian Sea. For many centuries Gujarati merchants, both Muslim and Hindu, were especially prominent. Hindus from Gujarat tended to settle in port cities on the Indian Ocean littoral, while Muslims had a flourishing trade north and west to the Gulf and Red Sea, and east and south to Malabar and South-East Asia. These merchants were based in the port cities in the Gulf of Cambay, of which Cambay itself was the most important.

Port cities in the Indian Ocean

There are several ways to categorise ports around the Indian Ocean at this time. Some owed much to geography, either because they were located on choke points, or because they had productive hinterlands. Some were pure exchange centres, others had some industry of their own. Some were subordinate to a larger inland state, while others were port city states, or perhaps, to borrow the South-East Asian term, port-polities. All of them were by definition cosmopolitan, much more so than the inland.

Where were the major port cities in the Indian Ocean area at this time?[9] Starting in East Africa, in the far south, Sofala provided gold and ivory from the interior. The gold was mined or washed in the inland Mutapa state in present-day Zimbabwe and brought to the coast at Sofala to be taken on to Kilwa and exchanged for cloth and other manufactures from India and the Middle East. Kilwa was the great emporium on the coast between roughly 648/1250 and 730/1330, from which time a great mosque and palace date, the latter being the largest roofed stone building south of the Sahara until modern times. By 957/1500 the greatest port city was Mombasa, an important centre of exchange for ivory and gold from the south with manufactures from the east and north. Malindi was a smaller centre at this time, but Mogadishu benefited from its proximity to the Red Sea and the Hadramawt to be another important port.

Moving along the coast, Aden was usually a great port city because of its location at the entrance to the Red Sea. There were several ports within the Red Sea, but the greatest certainly was Jiddah. It was the central mart in the Red Sea, with goods coming down from Cairo, and up from the whole Indian Ocean. It also had an important religious function as the maritime gateway to the Holy Cities.

The situation in the Gulf varied from time to time. At the beginning of this period, around 184/800 when the ʿAbbāsid empire was flourishing, Sohar was an important port, with contacts up the Gulf and across to Africa. After it was sacked by the Buyids from Oman it was replaced by Sīrāf, on the east coast of the Gulf south of Shīrāz, where large boats were unloaded and their goods taken in smaller ships to the great cities further north. Going south, ships went from Siraj to Muscat and Sohar, then either to Daybul or ports in Malabar, then around Sri Lanka to Melaka, then up to Canton or Quanzhou. Typically, this trade at first was handled in its entirety by Muslim traders, some Persians

9 Pearson, *Indian Ocean*, pp. 92–4.

but increasingly Arabs, and from about 390/1000 became more segmented, with Chinese coming some of the way, and Muslim Indians also involved as goods were transhipped and sold on at one or other of these entrepôts.[10] The other great port in the Gulf in late ʿAbbāsid times, in the fifth/eleventh and sixth/twelfth centuries, was Qeys, Qais or Kish, on a small island down the Gulf from Sīrāf. Here Indians brought in spices, and people from Yemen, Iraq and Fārs provided silks and cloths, wheat, barley and millet. There also was a large slave trade, and ivory, gold, wood, skins and ambergris from East Africa. Horses were sent out to the Deccan. Pearls were another export from this major port, while there have been many finds of Chinese ceramics.

Hormuz, located on the choke point at the entrance to the Gulf, was always an important exchange centre, but rose to greater prominence in the ninth/fifteenth century. Most of the great marts described so far were independent of any exterior political authority at this time, and most had no major productive role, nor extensive hinterland. Rather they were hinges linking areas to the north with those to the south and east.

Moving south-east from the Gulf there are variations on this pattern. Ports in the area around the Indus delta drew on a large and quite productive hinterland. Daybul, or Bambhore, at the mouth of the Indus, was a very old emporium, which declined from the fifth/eleventh century as a result of silting. It was replaced by Lahori Bandar.

The great ports of Gujarat were certainly major centres of exchange, but they were located on the maritime fringe of important production centres for such products as indigo, saltpetre and especially a vast variety of cotton cloths. The greatest was Cambay. From the seventh/thirteenth century Cambay, and many other ports within and around the gulf, were not independent city states: rather they were part of the important Muslim sultanate of Gujarat. Here were huge volumes of trade, skilful merchants and a very well articulated network of production and exchange and credit.

The ports further down India's west coast were less important, in part because the interior was less productive. The next major group of port cities were in Malabar, now the Indian state of Kerala. The dominant port here from the late fifth/eleventh century was Calicut, ruled by a powerful and independent ruler, the *Samudri raja* or Zamorin. It was an exchange centre for a host of 'foreign' goods. Equally important, it was a great collection and

10 Moira Tampoe, *Maritime trade between China and the West: An archaeological study of the ceramics from Siraf (Persian Gulf), 8th to 15th centuries AD* (Oxford, 1989), p. 124; Hourani, *Arab seafaring*, p. 69.

distribution centre for the pepper which was harvested in abundance in the interior. Several other port polities were important at different times in this region. One of them was Cranganore, some 25 kilometres inland from the seashore and located on several rivers. There was a vast array of merchants there dealing in spices.[11] None of these Malabar ports were centres for manufacturing, yet neither were they merely exchange centres. In these cases, location – that is, that they made obvious stopping places for trade from west to east and back again – joined with an interior where much pepper was found to ensure that for many centuries there would be major ports in this region. The main traders in Malabar were Muslims from the Gulf, and later from the Red Sea. Traders from other areas of India were also present, such as those from Coromandel and Sri Lanka, who had ethnic and religious ties with the Malabar locals. However, the most important Indian visitors to Malabar were those from Gujarat, both Hindu and Muslim. The rulers were Hindu, but they encouraged trade, whether by Muslims or anyone else, because trade brought them customs revenues.

This also applies quite exactly to Sri Lanka, and its major port of Colombo, for its location paralleled that of the Malabar ports, while the island was the only place where true, fine cinnamon was produced. Moving around to the Bay of Bengal, towards the end of the period on the Coromandel coast the major port was Pulicat, which drew on production, especially textiles, from the great Hindu kingdom of Vijayanagara, but was little affected politically by it. There were, however, a host of others; Kayal, for example, was an important centre for pearl fishing. In Bengal the most important port was Chittagong, which similarly was little controlled from the political centre of Gaur. The last major port relevant to the discussion was Melaka, which rose to prominence in the ninth / fifteenth century both as a great trade centre, maybe the greatest of all in the second half of this century, and as a dissemination centre for Islam.

Politics in the port cities

The rulers of the port cities in Malabar, Coromandel and Sri Lanka were not Muslim; in the other areas they were, that is on the Swahili coast and in the Maldives. Nevertheless, in all of them merchants, mostly Muslim but some others also, enjoyed a very large degree of autonomy. Muslims from specific

11 A. Vallavanthara, *India in 1500 AD: The narrative of Joseph the Indian* (Kottayam, 1984), pp. 152–5.

areas lived together, and had their own heads. These heads usually settled any points of contention within the group on their own, or perhaps after taking advice from some sort of council of more senior members of the community. Disputes between members of two groups were settled by negotiation between the respective heads. It was very rare indeed for the political authority, the sultan of Melaka or the *Samudri raja* of Calicut, to be involved even in criminal cases, and almost never in commercial disputes.

Many historians used to claim that the trade of the Indian Ocean in this period was increasingly handled by Muslims: the ocean was a 'Muslim lake'. There is certainly much truth in this, even if Hindus, Armenians and Jews also participated. Nor is this a matter for wonder, for Islam had spread from the heartland of the Red Sea all around the Indian Ocean over water. One could predict then that coastal people were most likely to be converted first, and indeed this was the case. However, there was an important change during the period, for while earlier it was Muslims from the Gulf, and then Muslim Arabs from the Red Sea and Egypt who dominated Indian Ocean trade and its markets, later it was local converts from such coastal areas as Gujarat and Bengal, and Middle Eastern Muslims who often had migrated to the Indian Ocean area, who had the cream of the trade, especially that going past India to the Bay of Bengal and beyond. Many of these Muslim traders were part of far-flung networks, these being based often not only on trade but also on adherence to a particular religious leader or sect. Merchants and religious specialists worked hand in hand, indeed could be the same person, in that a trader could well adhere to a particular Sufi order, and a religious specialist would trade on his own behalf. One example is traders based in the Iranian town of Kāzarūn, whose community solidarity was based on locality as well as common religious practice. This particular network had people in Cambay, Calicut, Quilon, and Canton in China. We will say more about this particular Sufi order presently.[12]

Islam and trade

The focus now moves to a description of these scattered Muslims in the areas under discussion, stressing their religious activities. Before attempting an area-by-area survey, certain general themes can be sketched. Relatively easy and even routine maritime links made possible the creation of an Islamic littoral

12 Ibn Baṭṭūṭa, *The travels of Ibn Battuta*, trans. H. A. R. Gibb, 4 vols. (London, 1958–94), p. 320. (The volumes are paginated consecutively.)

community all around the shores of the Arabian Sea, and indeed further east also. Travel by religious specialists was something new in this area. Previous travellers had been exclusively traders, apart from an occasional and very unusual military expedition. Now some travellers were primarily concerned to inculcate or rectify Islam, though, as is well known, many also traded on the side. To allocate priority to one or the other motive is hazardous and of dubious validity anyway. The connection is important, for Muslim traders necessarily travelled in order to trade, and so could influence widely scattered areas around the ocean rim. Risso notes that 'Islam is often described as especially well suited to merchants who needed to conduct complex transactions, and to travel. Islam not only sustained minority Muslim merchant communities in non-Muslim regions, but also attracted many merchant converts.' She then sounds a warning that 'Islam cannot be reduced to commerce, and commerce in the Indian Ocean region cannot be reduced to Muslims.'[13] Certainly the religion as such had a positive attitude to trade and making profits, deriving no doubt from the Prophet's own early history as a trader.

The oceanic context is important, for arguably it dictated a particular sort of Islam. Ross Dunn has put the contrast between coastal Islam and that of the heartland very well:

> In the Middle East an individual's sense of being part of an international social order varied considerably with his education and position in life. But in the Indian Ocean lands where Islam was a minority faith, all Muslims shared acutely this feeling of participation. Simply to be a Muslim in East Africa, southern India, or Malaysia in the fourteenth century was to have a cosmopolitan frame of mind.

This was reinforced by the coastal location and the fact that most of them were traders, and so had to be aware of distant markets and people and places.[14]

The spread of Islam

In most of these littoral areas Islam was at first represented by visiting Arab traders. It is possible to sketch a continuum, to the extent the data allow. First was the arrival of Arab Muslim traders to the various coastal areas, these to be seen as merely continuing an existing and long-established Arab trade from long before Islam in most areas. The first mosques were built to service them.

13 Patricia Risso, *Merchants and faith: Muslim commerce and culture in the Indian Ocean* (Boulder, CO, 1995), pp. 6, 7.
14 Ross Dunn, *The adventures of Ibn Battuta* (Berkeley, 1986), p. 116.

It was in the sixth/twelfth century that there was a wave of conversions, as seen by the larger mosques, though why this occurred in so many places at roughly the same time remains something of a mystery. Several of the areas covered in this chapter have firmly held origin narratives to do with the conversion of a local ruler thanks to some miracle, or the arrival of a particularly persuasive Arab exemplar. The ruler converted and then others followed him.

Parkin has suggested that it is more accurate to write of the

> 'acceptance' of Islam, which is likely to take longer and to be reciprocally inscribed in pre-existing custom and cosmology. The term conversion presupposes a shift from one to another unambiguously defined religion. Acceptance is less visibly dramatic and does not mean abandonment of a pre-existing cosmology. Yet it may well typify much Islamisation in the region in allowing for Islamic and non-Islamic traits to inter-mingle steadily.[15]

This means that there was additive change much of the time, as opposed to substitutive change. The former implies that an existing body of belief is added to, while the latter means existing notions are cast aside and replaced. Conversion then was a process rather than an event, and might extend over several generations.

Muslim travellers to areas already nominally Muslim often found what they considered to be deviations and lax practice in some of the areas they visited. Either by example, or more proactively by exhortation, they worked to improve the quality of Islam around the shores of the ocean. Ibn Baṭṭūṭa, whose travel account will be copiously used in this chapter, was one such. (While the reliability of his account of South-East Asia has been questioned, his observations on the coasts of the Arabian Sea are usually confirmed by other sources, and can be considered to be authentic.)The work of exemplars like him again points to conversion being a process rather than an event. Normative Islamic observance may have taken some generations to be fully implemented; indeed this process continues today. This is not, however, to decry the continuance of local practices, some of which may not have been completely in accord with the *sharīʿa*. It is not a matter of erecting some monolithic and unchangeable model of 'pure' Islam against which local practice can be evaluated, or even condemned. Susan Bayly correctly asked, 'what do we actually mean by the terms "purist" and "syncretic" and are these

15 David Parkin and Stephen C. Headley (eds.), *Islamic prayer across the Indian Ocean: Inside and outside the mosque* (London, 2000), p. 3.

really useful categories to apply to the historical study of Asian Muslim communities?'[16]

Travelling religious authorities

Most of the normative travellers came from the area conventionally perceived to be the Muslim heartland, often from southern Arabia, and especially the Hadramawt region. Many men left this impoverished and infertile homeland to settle abroad, carrying with them notions about true Islamic observance. Martin in fact finds discrete waves from this area: to India after 596/1200, to East Africa after 648/1250 and fifty years later to South-East Asia.[17] This emigration continues today. This is not, however, to say that they were the only traders and proselytisers: in a major port city like Calicut Muslims hailing from Morocco to Sumatra were present. There was a constant flow of people around the Arabian Sea coasts. Some of this was local, men for example going from one southern Indian coast to another, or down to Sri Lanka. Other intra-oceanic circulation consisted of men travelling on circuits all around the shores. Some routes were more directed, especially back and forth to southern Arabia, and further north to the Holy Cities, and to Cairo and Baghdad. Religious exemplars came out from the perceived heartland, some 'locals' visited there for instruction and to undertake the *ḥajj*. This religious circulation often mirrored the major trading patterns in the Indian Ocean which have already been sketched.

The continuing prestige of Arabs, however defined, is well shown in the way many local converts insisted on an Arab ancestry somewhere in the past. Objectively such claims are problematic, to say the least, for it seems that almost no free married Arab women moved to these areas. Thus even when people claimed an Arab background, their progeny over several generations became less and less Arab. So much more for local converts, who in South Asia and Sri Lanka at least came from lower areas of society; even so they often claimed Arab descent. It is notable that the many origin narratives in the area link the origins of Islam to the Prophet or his family, or more vaguely to Arabia, and not to inland powers like the Mughals or Turks.

16 Susan Bayly, 'Islam in southern India: "Purist" or "syncretic"?', in C. A. Bayly and D. H. A. Kolff (eds.), *Two colonial empires: Comparative essays on the history of India and Indonesia in the nineteenth century* (Leiden, 1986), p. 36.

17 B. G. Martin, 'Arab migration to East Africa in medieval times', *International Journal of African Historical Studies*, 7 (1975), p. 370.

We have described the trade and economic role of the great port cities strung around the Indian Ocean littoral, and the way shifts in long-distance trade routes influenced importantly their rise and fall. They were where the Islamic elite lived, and where impressive *jāmiʿ masjids* were located. They were distinctive from the interiors economically, and in terms of being much more cosmopolitan. This distinctiveness also applies to religion. First, the port cities were largely Muslim, or had important Muslim groups within their populations. This did not apply to the interiors of any of the areas to be discussed in this chapter. Second, a vital connecting link which set off the coast from the interior was the dominance of the Shāfiʿī *madhhab* on the coast, as opposed (in India) to the Ḥanafī interior. It may be that the Shāfiʿī school fitted better doctrinally with the needs of travellers and traders, and men living in areas not part of *dār al-islām*. This school, named after Muḥammad ibn Idris al-Shāfiʿī (d. 204/820), was very influential in the Islamic heartland in the centuries preceding the emergence of the Ottoman empire, and indeed up to the sixteenth century. Today it is the dominant school in East Africa, the Comoro and Maldive islands, the west coast of India, Indonesia, and also in part of Egypt and in its original home, the port towns of southern Arabia and the Gulf. While it is important not to overemphasise differences between the four orthodox Sunnī *madhhabs*, the Shāfiʿī school was much more relaxed about Muslims living in areas ruled by non-Muslims, while in theory at least Mālikī Muslims should avoid this completely. Yet Ibn Baṭṭūṭa, a Mālikī, wrote positively about the favourable treatment that the Hindu rulers of Malabar gave to their Muslim residents and visitors.

It was during this period, from around the fifth/eleventh century, that followers of the mystical Sufi path gradually became integrated into normative, book-based, Islam. From this time various Sufi orders were present and influential. The Qādiriyya order was prominent around the shores of the ocean, and seems to have had a close relationship with the Shāfiʿī *madhhab*. Ibn Baṭṭūṭa also found much evidence of an influential, though now extinct, Sufi order based on the Persian town of Kāzarūn.

This chapter will by and large be concerned with slow-moving change, a gradual accretion of numbers of Muslims and changes in their practice. However, there seem to be two more dramatic gaps. The change in long-distance trading patterns which was mentioned above marks one important caesura in the period. In particular, the end of the direct route between Baghdad and Canton led to the rise of several port cities, especially Calicut, where goods were exchanged. This in turn led to Muslim settlement in, as opposed to visits to, these port cities; the consequences for the spread of Islam are obvious. The other is the arrival of the Portuguese at the end of the ninth/fifteenth century, which is covered in detail in Chapter 12. For economic and religious reasons their hostility was focused precisely on Muslims. Nevertheless, they had very limited success in their attempts to take over existing Muslim-dominated trade routes, or in blocking access to the Holy Cities. Preaching, conversions and solidification of the faith kept going under their noses. They fulminated against the way people they called 'cacizes' travelled around the ocean with impunity, spreading Islam as they went and indeed having much more success than did Portuguese missionaries. Some of them even took passage on Portuguese ships.[18]

The arrival of Islam on the Swahili coast

Arab traders from Yemen and further along the southern Arabian coast had been visiting the Swahili coast since about the beginning of the Common Era.[19] When they converted they continued to trade, and from the second/eighth century in the northern port city of Shanga and other places there is evidence of rudimentary mosques, made of timber and mud, which serviced these visitors. No doubt there was interaction, and intermarriage, with the local Bantu population, but the earliest Muslim accounts of East Africa reflect very clearly that the locals had not converted. The fourth/tenth-century 'Wonders of India', a collection of Arab stories, describes 'Zanj' as a strange, uncouth place, with sorcerers, cannibals, strange birds and fishes.[20] Al-Bīrūnī in the early fifth/eleventh century still found East Africa to be a wild and largely un-Islamic place.[21]

Beginning in the sixth/twelfth century, or a few decades before, large-scale conversions took place among the indigenes. In material terms this can be seen in the way the mosque at Kilwa, the most important port city from about 648/1250 to 730/1330, was enlarged and now constructed in stone. By around 700/1300 it measured some 12 metres by 30 metres, implying a very large

18 A *caciz* is a Muslim religious specialist. For details see M. N. Pearson, *Pious passengers: The hajj in earlier times* (Delhi and London, 1994), pp. 71–2.

19 For an earlier discussion of Islam on the Swahili coast see my 'Gateways to Africa: The Indian Ocean and the Red Sea', in Nehemia Levtzion and Randall Pouwels (eds.), *The History of Islam in Africa* (Athens, OH, 2000), pp. 37–59. By far the best modern survey is Mark Horton and John Middleton, *The Swahili: The social landscape of a mercantile society* (Oxford, 2000).

20 Buzurg ibn Shahriyar, *The book of the wonders of India* [*Kitab al Ajaid al Hind*], trans. and ed. G. S. P. Freeman-Grenville (London, 1981), pp. 10, 31–6, 38, 102, 105.

21 al-Biruni, *Alberuni's India*, trans. and ed. Edward Sachau, 2 vols. (Delhi, 1964), vol. I, p. 270.

Muslim resident population.[22] By this time there were more than thirty communities on the coast which had one mosque, and many had several.[23]

These mosques were located in the port cities strung down the East African coast, over a length of some 3,000 kilometres from north to south. Some of them, especially in the south, drew in goods from the interior: gold, ivory and slaves were the main products. These were exchanged for imported goods, for there was little manufacturing on the coast. Cotton cloths from India were overwhelmingly important as imports, though obviously they have left few traces as compared with considerable finds of pottery, and even porcelain from far distant China. The Swahili in the port cities seem to have played a comparatively passive role. There is no evidence of their sailing far, except up the coast to southern Arabia and the Red Sea. Nor did they travel inland to collect goods for export: rather, particular tribes, none of them Muslim, brought goods to the coast. Certainly they were mediatory not only in economic terms but in other ways also: between Asia and Africa, between Islam and non-Islam. The Swahili were essentially Bantu, and a trickle of visitors and settlers from Arabia did not change this. Yet they were set apart from their fellow Africans by their exposure to a wider Indian Ocean world. Their port cities were much more cosmopolitan than the interior, as indeed were other port cities located on coasts with much more advanced civilisations close inland, such as those in India. Conversion led to them becoming more isolated from their Bantu kin. Before the coming of Islam they were quite small settlements, with little trade. Over the centuries covered in this chapter they became much bigger, richer and more cosmopolitan. Most important, their inhabitants were now followers of a great tradition religion, and so were set off from the interior Bantu.

The conversion of these port-city dwellers was a slow process, really an accretion of Islamic practice, something which applies in all the areas under discussion. Nurse and Spear provide a succinct account of Swahili motivations:

> Many townspeople … operated in a wider world than the microcosm of the village, living in towns with other peoples, sailing from town to town along the coast, and trading with people from across the Indian Ocean. These people lived in a macrocosmic world inhabited by peoples speaking different languages, having different ancestors, and working in different occupations.

22 John Sutton, *A thousand years of East Africa* (Nairobi, 1990), pp. 67–8.

23 Randall Pouwels, 'The East African coast, *c.* 780 to 1900 CE', in Levtzion and Pouwels (eds.), *Islam in Africa*, p. 252.

In this world the beliefs of the microcosm were too parochial; what was needed were beliefs that were universal. And so townspeople began to adopt Islam, and in so doing they adopted a set of beliefs and a framework for action that were held in common by others in the town, by people in other towns, and by people from the whole Indian Ocean world.[24]

This was very much a reciprocal process, not a matter of an imposition of a new faith from outside. Horton some time ago produced a strong statement which reflects well the current scholarly consensus:

The East African coast was always inhabited by African communities, who in time gradually absorbed the culture and teachings of Islam as they were drawn into contact through commercial dealings and missionary activities. The archaeological evidence shows how first material culture, then architecture, and finally religion itself was grafted from the Islamic world onto the East African coast. There was no interest in either conquest or settlement but rather in the establishment of reliable local trading partners.[25]

The Swahili coast and a wider world

Muslims from the heartland, from Yemen, Hadramawt and Oman, moved south to East Africa for various reasons. Often they were traders, for the strong nexus between trade and the spread of Islam has been much noted all over the Indian Ocean world. Some moved as a result of push factors, in other words they exchanged a life of poverty in the inhospitable regions of southern Arabia for the more benign region of East Africa. But what may be the very first Muslims to move to the far south seem to have been people escaping religious persecution. These were the followers of Ibāḍī Islam, part of the heterodox Khārijī group, originating from Oman and further into the Gulf. This group moved further and further south, and by the eighth/fourteenth century the coast was thoroughly Shāfiʿī Muslim. The decline (until the early thirteenth/late eighteenth century) of Omani influence may have been a result of changes in Indian Ocean trading patterns. When Baghdad was at its height, from about 132/750 to 442/1050, trade with East Africa linked in to the great Baghdad–Canton route. As this declined East African trade became oriented to southern Arabia, especially the Red Sea and Hadramawt area. Nevertheless, several of the ruling dynasties of the coastal port cities proudly

24 D. Nurse and T. T. Spear, *The Swahili: Reconstructing the history and language of an African society, AD 500–1500* (Philadelphia, 1984), pp. 94–5.

25 M. C. Horton, 'Asiatic colonisation of the East African coastline: The Manda evidence', *Journal of the Royal Asiatic Society*, 2 (1986), p. 211.

claimed to come from Shīrāz: Kilwa from the fourth/tenth century, and also Mombasa, Malindi and Zanzibar.[26] These rulers shared a common narrative of origin, and had lineage ties with each other. The claim of a direct link with Shīrāz, or the Gulf in general, can be discounted. It is revealing of the change from Omani influence to that from further west along the southern Arabian coast that from late in the seventh/thirteenth century the rulers of Kilwa, the dominant port city at the time, were a family, the Mahdali, of *sharīfs* from Yemen. One of them did the *ḥajj* in 813–14/1410–11, and then spent time at home in Yemen before returning to Kilwa. The ruler of Mozambique was a *sharīf* who claimed kinship with the ruling families of the Somali coast and Kilwa. Also in the seventh/thirteenth century the Nabhani rulers of Pate arrived from Oman, and continued in power into the thirteenth/nineteenth century. Over time these ruling families indigenised, giving something to the people they ruled and getting much from these same subjects. They rapidly became merged into the Swahili world. In other words, through acculturation and intermarriage they became another element, albeit a politically important one, in the Swahili world.

These rulers, and the many other anonymous sojourners or settlers from Arabia, especially Yemen, brought with them very considerable prestige. They of course brought the Shāfiʿī *madhhab*. They also brought with them, if they were *sharīfs* or *sayyids*, very considerable *baraka*, or prestige, based on their claim to be direct descendants of the Prophet. As an twelfth/eighteenth-century Hadramī *sharīf* wrote rather self-servingly,

> They are the guarantee of the earth from fear
> Guides of the People along Right Paths
> Take refuge with them from catastrophe
> Ask God's help through them.[27]

Such men were very influential by the middle of the seventh/thirteenth century at least, though this was never a matter of large-scale migration. Some were reformers who tried to end non-Islamic practices in coastal religion, while others merely integrated into local coastal society. This learned elite retained important ties back to their homeland and its famous Islamic centres.

It was also from the seventh/thirteenth century that contact with, and migration from, the Hadramawt flourished, over time perhaps becoming more important than that from Yemen further west. Coastal towns in the

26 On the Shirazi matter the best modern summing up is Horton and Middleton, *Swahili*, pp. 52–61.
27 Martin, 'Arab migration', p. 390.

Hadramawt such as al-Shiḥr and al-Mukallạ, and also inland towns, connected to the Swahili coast. As Martin noted, 'Sometimes the appearance of a sharif triggered a religious revival or led to acceleration of the process of ongoing islamization.' A prestigious migrant might marry the daughter of a local sultan, and over generations the Arab 'blood' was diluted and the lineages' *baraka* diminished. Then another migrant might come in from Yemen or Hadramawt with fresh new *baraka* and he would take over. An example of an influential lineage is that of Abu Bakr bin Salim, whose tomb is at Inat, near Tarīm in Hadramawt. This famous saint died in 992/1584. His sons moved to East Africa during his lifetime, to Pate. Later members of the dynasty spread as far as the Comoro islands, Lamu, Mombasa and Zanzibar.[28] Indeed, it may have been a member of this lineage that a Portuguese observer noted in Pate about 978/1570. He wrote that Pate 'has considerable trade with Mecca [sc. the Red Sea] and other parts. The town is very large and has many buildings. It was here that a Moorish *caciz*, the greatest in the entire coast, resided.'[29]

There is almost no contemporary information on any Sufi presence in East Africa during this period. However, all over the world of Islam most of the great scholars and *ʿulamāʾ* were also members of Sufi orders. This being the case, it would be extraordinary indeed if the scholars on the Swahili coast were not also Sufis. There is a much clearer picture of the situation during the colonial period, and it may not be completely invalid to 'read back' from here to this period. In the colonial period the most influential brotherhood was the austere ʿAlawiyya one, whose main shrine was at Inat. There is some detail on this and other brotherhoods only from the thirteenth/nineteenth century, though there is no doubt that the ʿAlawis had been tied in with the various *sharīf* lineages for centuries before this. The same is probably true for the Qādiriyya order, followers of ʿAbd al-Qādir, whose adherents in the colonial period were scattered from West Africa to Indonesia. As we noted earlier, there is a strong link between jurists of the Shāfiʿī school and Sufis who follow the Qādiriyya order.

The Portuguese, who were firmly opposed to these Muslims, even so provide important information which particularly reinforces the link between trade and religion. In 903/1498 the first Portuguese fleet, under Vasco da Gama, in Mozambique found a Muslim who came from near Mecca, and was a pilot on one of the ships. Later in his voyage he received an ambassador from the sultan of Malindi, who he noted was a white Moor, as compared with a local convert, and also a *sharīf*, that is, according to the Portuguese, a priest.

28 *Ibid.*, pp. 378–82.
29 Quoted in Pearson, 'Gateways to Africa', p. 49.

A letter to the Portuguese king from Mozambique in 914/1508 claimed that 'these others who do the damage are merchants and foreigners, one from Ormuz, another from Aden, others from other parts and they are men of knowledge who have traded all their lives and these are the ones who should be expelled'.[30]

The much-quoted travel account of Ibn Baṭṭūṭa can give us something of the flavour of this very cosmopolitan interchange in the mid-fourteenth century, when this prestigious and experienced Muslim scholar was on the coast. In 731/1331 he arrived at Mogadishu. He was immediately singled out as a person of importance, perhaps even one with *baraka*. 'When the young men came on board the vessel in which I was, one of them came up to me. My companions said to him "This man is not a merchant, but a doctor of the law," whereupon he called out to his friends and said to them "This is the guest of the *qāḍī*."' He went ashore and was told, 'It is the custom that whenever there comes a jurist or a *sharif* or a man of religion he must first see the sultan before taking a lodging.' Arriving at the sultan's residence, 'one of the serving boys came out and saluted the *qāḍī*, who said to him "Take word to the intendant's office and inform the Shaikh [sc. sultan] that this man has come from the land of al-Hijaz."' He was given robes, including a tunic of Egyptian linen, a furred mantle of Jerusalem stuff and an Egyptian turban. He leaves a picture of a very Islamic town, where the sultan, who spoke Arabic although his first language was Maqdishi, used a type of ceremonial parasol which was introduced by the Fāṭimids in Egypt and which spread all over the Muslim world. There were many jurists, *sharīfs* and people who had done a *ḥajj*, and shaykhs. Ibn Baṭṭūṭa said little about Mombasa, but in Kilwa, then at its height of power and riches, he found the sultan to be very generous. He often raided in the black interior, and set aside one-fifth of the booty for the purposes set out in the Qur'ān: 'whenever he was visited by *sharīfs* he would pay it [this fifth] out to them, and the *sharīfs* used to come to visit him from al-Iraq and al-Hijaz and other countries'.[31]

The nature of Islam on the coast

The description earlier of how becoming Muslim is a process rather than an event, a matter of adding on Islamic ideas to existing beliefs, raises the

30 Quoted in Michael Pearson, *Port cities and intruders: The Swahili coast, India, and Portugal in the early modern era* (Baltimore, 1998), p. 61.

31 Ibn Baṭṭūṭa, *Travels*, pp. 374–81.

controversial matter of the 'purity' of Islam at this time. Ibn Baṭṭūṭa, who was critical enough in other places he visited, cast no aspersions on Swahili Islam. Horton and Middleton claim there is little evidence of syncretism; for example, the importance of spirits in coastal Islam is a later development, beginning from the end of slavery. However, they also note that there are really two religious trends: *dīn*, religion, and *mila*, custom. While not completely separate, the former includes the Qur'ān, the *ḥadīth* and learned writings, all of this in Arabic, while the latter predates Islam, and is often communicated orally in the local language.[32]

Testimony from the early Portuguese must be used with caution, given their anti-Muslim attitudes. They took malicious delight in finding fault. Yet it is perhaps revealing that they noted many examples of what they claimed to be lax Islam on the coast in the sixteenth century. In 903/1498 the ambassador of the ruler of Malindi was 'a white Moor and sharif, that is priest, and at the same time a great drunkard'. One Jesuit debated with a senior Islamic scholar, who believed that Muḥammad was the first man created by God. In 949/1542 in Malindi the Jesuit missionary Francis Xavier was told by an Islamic notable that the locals were quite unobservant. Once there had been sixteen mosques, but now only three, and these little frequented and badly served.[33]

What influence did the Portuguese political presence on the coast have on Islam? While they had friendly relations with the ruler of Malindi, their main effort in the sixteenth century was further south, below Cape Delgado. There is no doubt that in this area Muslim trade was disrupted to an extent, and no doubt contact with Islamic areas further north was hindered, if not broken. It may even be that this contributed not only to a diminution of contacts, but flowing on from this that the 'quality' of Islam was changed, or in other words Islam in the south was more indigenised precisely because contact with the normative centre was blocked. The malicious comments from Portuguese on the quality of Islam which were quoted above may bear this out. There is another example of what may well be the effects of Portuguese hostility on the quality of Islam in the south. An account of Sofala, in the far south, from 996/1588 noted that:

> The Mahometans that at this present doe inhabite those Countries, are not naturally borne there, but before the Portugals came into those quarters, they Trafficked thither in small Barkes, from the Coast of Arabia Felix. And when the Portugals had conquered that Realme, the Mahometans stayed there still,

32 Horton and Middleton, *Swahili*, pp. 180–1.
33 Pearson, *Port cities and intruders*, p. 61 and sources there cited.

> and now they are become neither utter Pagans, nor holding the Sect of Mahomet.[34]

Late in the tenth/sixteenth century, in response to the threat of Ottoman attacks, the Portuguese established a strong base further north in Mombasa, where Fort Jesus was built. The result seems to be that contact with the perceived heartland was reinforced further north again, in the Lamu and Pate area, partly as this area was closest to the centre anyway, and partly as Portuguese power was seldom evident this far north. The broad pattern in this early modern period seems to be of Pate and Lamu maintaining close contacts, and, once the power of the Portuguese had waned late in the eleventh/seventeenth century, spreading their ideas further south to areas which had been to an extent cut off from the heartland. Yet although the Portuguese, for both religious and economic reasons, opposed the Muslims, it is important not to exaggerate their success. Horton and Middleton point out that there were many mosques, tombs and houses built in the tenth/sixteenth century.[35]

Islam reaches the Maldive islands

The Maldives consist of about 1,200 islands, though fewer than 200 of them are permanently inhabited. Lying as they do astride the major route from the Red Sea and southern Arabia to India and Sri Lanka, they have long served as places to trade, or merely to take on food and water. The only products of any note are the many uses of the coconut palm (coir thread from the Maldives was considered to be especially strong), and cowry shells, which served as humble currency for many centuries all around the shores of the Indian Ocean, and indeed as far as West Africa. This connection with the trade of the Indian Ocean is typical of all the coastal regions covered in this chapter. There is also evidence of continuing ties with the heartland of Islam. Another theme is the importance of a conversion narrative, that is, that Islam was brought to the islands by a particular historic person at a particular time. Finally, Ibn Baṭṭūṭa, the main authority, went to some lengths to praise the quality of Islam while he was resident, though he and others also mention some practices which may not be completely 'orthodox', in Swahili terms *mila* perhaps as compared with *dīni*.

34 Quoted in Pearson, *Indian Ocean*, p. 176.
35 Horton and Middleton, *Swahili*, p. 84.

The first authenticated settlers in the Maldives were Sinhalese, who arrived from around 500 BCE. Archaeological remains show that from around 300 CE Theravada Buddhism was supreme, as shown in numerous monasteries and stupas. A reminder of this Sinhala Buddhist past is seen in the language of the Maldivians, which is Divehi, an Indo-European language closely related to Sinhalese, and which used to be written in a script like early Sinhalese scripts.[36]

The Maldives lie on the direct route between India and southern Arabia, so one can assume that they were visited by Arabs and others long before Islam, indeed probably once the monsoon wind system had been worked out.[37] It is likely that the first Muslims arrived very soon after the life of the Prophet, if not during his lifetime. Certainly the charts in Tibbetts's work on Arab navigation show the Maldives were well known and visited.[38] Some Muslims settled and intermarried. However, it was only in the twelfth century that the local population was converted to Islam.

The Maldivian origin narrative

The traditional version of how Islam arrived is best told by Ibn Baṭṭūṭa, who spent eighteen months in 744–5/1343–4 in the islands. His account constitutes an excellent example of an origin narrative, one which is widely and officially accepted in the islands today.[39] There are however several variant versions of the narrative, and these will be noted below as examples of how Muslim communities can modify and change historical events according to present circumstances.

Trustworthy people told Ibn Baṭṭūṭa that the islanders used to be infidels. Each month a jinn would come from the sea. The islanders would take a virgin girl to the idol (Buddhist) temple on the seashore, and when they came back in the morning they would find that she had been violated and killed by the jinn. Each month they drew lots to see whose daughter was next to undertake this melancholy task. Then in 548/1153 a man from the Maghrib came among

36 Clarence Maloney, *People of the Maldive islands* (Bombay, 1980), p. 104; *EI*[2] 'Maldives' (Andrew Forbes). The fundamental study of Maldivian Islam for this period is Andrew D. W. Forbes, 'Southern Arabia and the Islamicisation of the central Indian Ocean archipelagos', *Archipel*, 21 (1981), pp. 55–92.

37 Albert Gray's long appendix 'Early notices of the Maldives' in François Pyrard, *The voyage of Francois Pyrard of Laval to the East Indies, the Maldives, the Moluccas and Brazil*, trans. and ed. Albert Gray, Hakluyt Society, nos. 76, 77, 80, 2 vols. (London, 1887–9), vol. II, part 2, pp. 423–508 shows copious Muslim knowledge of, and visits to, the Maldives before their conversion to Islam.

38 Tibbetts, *Arab navigation*, *passim*.

39 Ibn Baṭṭūṭa, *Travels*, pp. 829–30.

them, called Abū'l-Barakāt al-Barbarī, who could recite by heart the holy Qur'ān. He lodged in the house of an old woman. One day she was very upset, because her only daughter had been chosen. Having made his ablutions, Abu'l-Barakāt, being beardless, went in her place, and spent the night reciting the Qur'ān. When the *jinn* came he heard the recital and plunged into the sea. The old woman and her relatives came in the morning, expecting to have to collect a body and burn it. Instead they found Abū'l-Barakāt alive and well, still reciting the Qur'ān. He was taken before the king, and expounded Islam to him to explain the miracle. Impressed, the king promised to convert if Abū'l-Barakāt could repeat his performance next month. He did so, and the king, his family and courtiers all converted, as did the rest of the islanders soon after. By the seventh/thirteenth century Buddhism had been totally replaced by Islam, of the Mālikī *madhhab*, which was what Abū'l-Barakāt, and also Ibn Baṭṭūṭa, followed.

There are some minor variations and additions to Ibn Baṭṭūṭa's account, which do not however alter the basic story in any important respect. Different names, and places of origin, are given to the sage. Rizwan Aḥmad quotes the version from the *Ta'rīkh*, the Maldivian state chronicle. The agent was Maulana Shaykh Yusuf Shams-ud-din of Tabrīz. He arrived in the Maldives but failed to convert the locals, who wanted him to perform a miracle to demonstrate his credentials. The sage obliged by showing a great man whose head nearly touched the sky. The terrified king and local inhabitants converted at once, and the king also forcibly or otherwise got the population of all the islands to convert. He was given the title of Sultan Muḥammad. This occurred in 548/1153, when he had reigned thirteen years, and he reigned another thirteen years as a very pious and observant Muslim, after which, in 561/1166, he set off on *ḥajj*. Shaykh Yusuf died and was buried in Malé and his tomb is greatly venerated.[40] Some versions name the king who converted as Kalaminja when he was a Buddhist, and subsequently Sultan Muḥammad al-ʿĀdil. He had reigned for twelve years as a Buddhist, but the times were bad. After the conversion, peace and happiness prevailed. In 561/1166 he set off on a *ḥajj*, and never returned; this is a common part of most such origin narratives, where the original convert leaves for the holy places after some time. Another variant has the sage accompanying the virgin to the Buddhist temple and protecting her by chanting the Qur'ān.[41] A very confused popular

40 Quoted in Rizwan A. Ahmad, 'The state and national foundation in the Maldives', *Cultural Dynamics*, 13 (2001), pp. 295–6, and *passim* for various versions.

41 V. Vitharana, *Sri Lankan–Maldivian cultural affinities* (Polgasovita, 1997), pp. 5–12, 192.

version on one website says that it was Ibn Baṭṭūṭa who confronted the *jinn*, and as a result was made *qāḍī*, and married the sultan's sister![42] Yet another version, widely believed today, has it that it was the king who raped and killed the young girls. The story of an arrival from the sea was a subterfuge. It has even been claimed that a saint called Shaykh Barkhandle, who spread Islam in the interior of the Horn of Africa between 700 and 900 years ago, and whose religious name was Shaykh Yusuf al Kawneyn, is the same saint whom the people in the Maldives call Saint Abū'l-Barakāt al-Barbarī.[43] However, the tomb of this Somali saint is in Somalia, while the tomb of Abū'l-Barakāt is in the grounds of the Hukuru mosque in the capital of Malé. Built in 1066/1656, this is the oldest mosque in the Maldives. The tomb is an object of great veneration and pilgrimage.

Sultan Muḥammad al-ʿĀdil succeeded in initiating a series of six dynasties consisting of eighty-four sultans and sultanas that lasted until 1351/1932. There followed a puppet sultan controlled by the British, then a revolution and then a new sultan who was deposed in 1388/1968. In our period the only caesura occurred between 965/1558 and 981/1573, when the Portuguese occupied Malé. Their vigorous anti-Muslim activities had an important consequence for the islands. Many of the Mālikī *ʿulamāʾ* were killed by them. After they were driven out a famous shaykh from Hadramawt, Shaykh Muḥammad Jamal-ud-din, arrived. He was received by the sultan with great honours. He had spent fifteen years in Arabia studying at Shāfiʿī centres, and he introduced the Shāfiʿī *madhhab* to the islands. Then he retired to become a recluse.[44] A century later his work was carried on by another Hadramī, Sayyid Muḥammad Shams al-Dīn, who acted just like Ibn Baṭṭūṭa earlier as a classic rectifier and also as an example of a peripatetic Muslim authority. He had studied in Cairo and Mecca, and then went to Malabar and made many converts. After a visit to Aceh, he was on his way home when he stopped off at Malé in 1097/1686. For a time he was treated with great honour, and instituted reforms. Every man was to grow a beard, and every woman must be veiled. He ended up in Hugli after being expelled from the Maldives, but returned when a new sultan took power. Indeed, the *sayyid* himself became sultan for one year, in 1103/1692.[45] Thus the Maldivians joined the rest of the population of the Indian Ocean littoral as followers of the Shāfiʿī school.

42 www.soc.soton.ac.uk/OTHERS/CSMS/OCHAL/ibn.htm.

43 Musa H. I. Galaal, 'Historical relations between the Horn of Africa and the Persian Gulf and the Indian Ocean islands through Islam', in UNESCO, *Historical relations across the Indian Ocean* (Paris, 1980), p. 24.

44 *EI*² 'Maldives' (Forbes).

45 Forbes, 'Southern Arabia and the Islamicisation', pp. 89–90.

Islam in the Maldives

Knowledge of Islamic practice in the Maldives is based on the accounts of the Muslim visitor Ibn Baṭṭūṭa, who was a *qāḍī* in the Maldives, in the capital Malé, for eighteen months in 744–5/1343–4, and the Frenchman Pyrard de Laval, who was there for five years from 1011/1602 to 1016/1607. In the former time the dominant *madhhab* was, as noted, Mālikī, and in the latter Shāfiʿī, but it is unlikely that this change affected the lives of most of the islanders, apart from the *ʿulamāʾ* who administered the *sharīʿa*.

Ibn Baṭṭūṭa had good things to say about Islam in the Maldives. He wrote that 'The people of these islands are upright and pious, sound in belief, and sincere in purpose; they keep to lawful foods, and their prayers are answered.' There were beautiful mosques on all the islands, mostly made of wood. Islamic authorities were greatly venerated. Not that they were perfect. He was scandalised that the women went around naked from the waist up, and refused to eat with their husbands.[46]

He had good cause to comment on the islanders' respect for authority, for he became the *qāḍī* in Malé. This is a very common occurrence, that is, of an authority from the heartland receiving respect, and important positions, simply because they can present themselves as cynosures of Islam. Indeed, as noted, this happened to Ibn Baṭṭūṭa on the Swahili coast, and he also was much patronised when he was in Delhi, where Muḥammad b. Tughluq made him an ambassador. He not only commanded respect, he also acted as a classic rectifier, trying to bring the islanders closer to what he considered to be normative Islam, that is, in Swahili terms to have less *mila* and more *dīni*. 'I strove my utmost to establish the prescriptions of the Sacred Law. Lawsuits there are not like those in our land.' He stopped divorced women from staying on in the house of their previous husband, made sure prayers were observed and 'I compelled the salaried prayer-leaders and muezzins to be assiduous in their duties and sent letters to all the islands to the same effect. I tried also to determine how women dressed, but I could not manage this.'[47]

Pyrard left an extremely detailed account which, although by an outsider, nevertheless confirms many of Ibn Baṭṭūṭa's claims.[48] He describes the teaching of Arabic, though the home language was Divehi. Overall he confirms that this was a deeply rooted faith in an observant community. He comments on prayers, circumcision, the observance of Ramaḍān, Friday prayers, strictly observed

46 Ibn Baṭṭūṭa, *Travels*, pp. 822–4.
47 *Ibid.*, pp. 840–1.
48 Pyrard, *Voyage*, vol. I, pp. 123–207.

social divisions, legal matters and the administration of justice, the seclusion of women, *ḥalāl* slaughtering of animals, and respect for the learned and for dignitaries in general. Those who had done the *ḥajj* were especially esteemed; they were allowed to wear their beards in a particular way:

> Those who have been to Arabia, and have visited the sepulchre of Mahomet at Mecca [*sic*, but a very common European error at this time], are held in high respect by all the world, whatever be their rank, and whether they be poor or rich; and, indeed, a great number of the poor have been there. These have peculiar privileges: they are called Agy; and in order to be recognised and remarked among the others, they all wear very white cotton frocks, and on their heads little round bonnets, also white, and carry beads in their hands without crosses; and when they have not the means to maintain themselves in this attire, the king or the nobles supply them, and fail not to do so.[49]

Both observers also noted some practices which seem to lie a little outside the bounds of normative Islam. On one occasion Ibn Baṭṭūṭa gave a banquet, which the sultan attended:

> The food was served, and when the guests had eaten the *Qur'an* readers chanted in beautiful voices. The poor brethren [Muslims from Malabar whom Ibn Baṭṭūṭa had looked after] then began their ritual chants and dances. I had made ready a fire and they went into it, treading it with their feet, and some of them ate it as one eats sweetmeats, until it was extinguished.[50]

Pyrard has a quite lengthy discussion of the widespread use of charms by the islanders. They were kept in boxes and carried under people's clothes. Most of them were multipurpose, for example offensive and defensive, making well and making sick and so on.[51]

They also commented on sexual matters. Ibn Baṭṭūṭa prudishly tried to get the local women to cover up, yet he also complacently wrote about how the products of the local coconut palm and fish

> have an amazing and unparalleled effect in sexual intercourse, and the people of these islands perform wonders in this respect. I had there myself four wives and concubines as well, and I used to visit all of them every day and pass the night with the wife whose turn it was, and this I continued to do the whole year and a half I was there.[52]

49 *Ibid.*, pp. 110, 165.
50 Ibn Baṭṭūṭa, *Travels*, p. 836.
51 Pyrard, *Voyage*, vol. I, pp. 178–80.
52 Ibn Baṭṭūṭa, *Travels*, pp. 822–3.

Pyrard was much less relaxed about this. He wrote a long account of their 'lasciviousness': 'Adultery, incest, and sodomy are common, notwithstanding the severity of the law and penalties.'[53]

The Maldives were emphatically part of a wider Muslim world. Ibn Baṭṭūṭa's account is full of notices of contact with far places: Quilon, Macassar, Coromandel, Mogadishu and the Islamic heartland. The respect paid to those who had done the *ḥajj*, who had undertaken this long, dangerous and expensive voyage, shows another distant connection. Abū'l-Barakāt may have been a Maghribi, but soon after his time Hadramī influence became most important.[54] No doubt this was reinforced once the Shāfiʿī *madhhab* became dominant. Just as in East Africa, many of these migrants or visitors were shaykhs or sayyids, learned men with much *baraka*. Ibn Baṭṭūṭa was one such, and Pyrard noticed another example, a 'Cherife of Arabia, that is, one of a family the most respected and noble among these people as being of the race of Mahomet. He was a very good man, and was greatly beloved of the king.'[55] This person had come from Aceh, and was on his way back to Arabia; like Ibn Baṭṭūṭa he fulfilled some judicial functions while he was in the islands. Some of the visitors may have had Sufi connections also. Forbes says that while there is no firm evidence of Sufi influences in the Maldives, many of the learned visitors were probably members of the Qādiriyya Sufi order. Ibn Baṭṭūṭa once stayed in a hospice built by the pious Shaykh Najīb, but there is no indication of which order he belonged to.[56] The most intimate connections may have been with the Malabar coast, from where came the fire walkers that Ibn Baṭṭūṭa described. Most immigrants, and visitors, were males who formed local alliances, just like Ibn Baṭṭūṭa, but the Mappilas, who will be described in detail soon, came in families, as Pyrard noted: 'Malabars [sc. Mappilas] come there frequently with their wives, children and servants. These are permitted to traffic everywhere, like the folk of the country, and are subject to the same police and regulations.'[57]

The Lakshadweep islands

The Lakshadweep islands, formerly the Laccadives, have a rather different, and much more obscure, history. They consist of twenty-seven islands, of which ten are inhabited. Like the Maldives, they lie on the direct trade route

53 Pyrard, *Voyage*, vol. I, pp. 195–7, and more on this topic pp. 304–7.
54 See especially Forbes, 'Southern Arabia and the Islamicisation', *passim*.
55 Pyrard, *Voyage*, vol. I, p. 304.
56 Ibn Baṭṭūṭa, *Travels*, p. 835.
57 Pyrard, *Voyage*, vol. I, p. 300.

from Arabia to India. The original settlers were Hindus from the north Malabar coast, who arrived perhaps as early as the second century CE. They were conquered by the expansionist Cōla south Indian state in the fourth/tenth century, though there is no evidence of close control. It seems that the islands were converted to Islam in the sixth/twelfth or seventh/thirteenth century. However, according to the island origin narrative the founder was ʿUbaid Allāh. He was a grandson of Abū Bakr, a companion of the Prophet and his immediate successor as head of the Muslim community. It is claimed that ʿUbaid Allāh was shipwrecked on the islands in 43/663. Initially he was met with hostility, but after he performed a series of miracles all the islanders converted. His tomb in Androth is venerated up to today. In the mid-tenth/sixteenth century the islands were conquered by a Mappila ruling family from Cannanor. Concentrated western Indian influence is reflected in the language of the islands, which is Malayalam, but with some Arabic words and written in the Arabic script, and in the importance of 'caste' divisions, which are almost identical with the Hindu practice from which they are derived. Like the Maldives, they are Sunnī Muslims and follow the Shāfiʿī *madhhab*. Two Sufi orders are especially important, the Qādiriyya and the Rifaʿiyya. Both were introduced to the islands in the sixth/twelfth century by a visiting Sufi *sayyid*, who married a descendant of ʿUbaid Allāh. However, while in the Maldives succession is orthodox, that is patrilineal, the Lakshadweep islands are matrilineal, with descent traced through the mother. This seems to be another example of influence from the Malabar region, where, as we will see, matrilineal succession is not uncommon among both Muslim and Hindu communities.[58]

Malabar

The Malabar coast stretches some 400 kilometres from Cannanor to Quilon, and is more or less coterminous with the coast of the modern Indian state of Kerala. According to Ibn Baṭṭūṭa it was two months' journey from Sandabur to Quilon.[59] This region shares many characteristics with the other areas described in this chapter. Dale notes that its geography is more like the

58 This account relies on *EI*² 'Laccadives,' (Andrew Forbes); Forbes, 'Sources towards a history of the Laccadive Islands,' *South Asia*, 2 (1979), pp. 130–50; Geneviève Bouchon, *'Regent of the sea': Cannanore's response to Portuguese expansion, 1507–1528* (Delhi, 1988), pp. 39–50; and especially Theodore Gabriel, 'Islamic mystics of the Lakshadweep islands, India', in Theodore P. Gabriel and C. H. Partridge (eds.), *Mysticisms east and west* (Carlisle, 2003), pp. 44–53.

59 Ibn Baṭṭūṭa, *Travels*, pp. 805–7.

South-East Asian Malay world than the rest of India, and this notion could easily be extended to the Swahili coast, to the Maldives, and to the coasts of Sri Lanka and Coromandel. All are more outward looking, international, cosmopolitan, than are the interiors. Malabar however is different in two respects. Unlike all the other littorals, its near interior boasted copious supplies of a very important early modern trade product, that is, pepper. To Arabs the region was known as *Bilad al-fulful*, the land of pepper. Pepper was by far the main spice traded in this period, being the only one which was consumed *en masse*, unlike the 'fine spices' of mace, nutmeg, cloves and cinnamon. Malabar thus was a focus for international trade. Indeed, its major port cities, of which Calicut was the most important from the sixth/twelfth century, not only funnelled pepper from the interior towards distant markets, but also was a major transhipment port, where goods from further east, west and north, as far as China and Europe, were landed, broken up and sold, and sent on to their markets. As an example, those fine spices from the Malukus (mace, nutmeg and cloves) which were bound for the Middle East or the Mediterranean and so Europe, proceeded from Melaka to Calicut and so on across the Arabian Sea.

The second way in which Malabar is different to the other coasts for Muslims is that while Muslims dominated much of the trade of the coast, inland they encountered a very sophisticated different great tradition religion, Hinduism. To an extent Sri Lankan Muslims were in a similar situation *vis-à-vis* the Buddhist interior, but this does not apply to the Maldives or to the Swahili coast. There was a major difference between interior and coastal Muslims. North India was ruled by Muslim dynasties which were Ḥanafī and Persianised, but coastal Muslims were Arabicised and Shāfiʿī.[60] However, the majority of the population of Malabar remained Hindu, while only two of the many port cities, Cannanor and Honavar, both rather minor ports in this period, were ruled by Muslims. All the other rulers were Hindu.

The Malabari origin narrative and the arrival of Islam

The local Muslim community in Malabar, the Mappila Muslims, have their own origin narrative to explain the arrival of Islam in their area. Like similar ones elsewhere, there is considerable variation in the details and it is very

60 Stephen F. Dale, *Islamic society on the South Asian frontier: The Mappilas of Malabar, 1498–1922* (Oxford, 1980), pp. 5–11.

difficult for the modern historian to separate 'fact' from 'fiction'. In any case, the real point is that this narrative is accepted by the community then and now. There are two main versions, though both involve a ruler of the Hindu Cera dynasty called Cheraman Perumal. In one version this ruler dreamed that the moon had split. Soon after a group of Muslims arrived at Cranganore, on their way to visit Adam's Peak in Sri Lanka,

> and intelligence of their arrival having reached the King, sending for them into his presence, he manifested towards them much kindness, conversing with them without reserve: and enquiring of them their circumstances and condition, the Shaykh, encouraged by the King's condescension, related to him the history of our prophet Mahomed (upon whom may the divine favour and blessing ever rest!), explaining also to the monarch the tenets of Islamism; whilst, for a confirmation of their truth, he narrated to him the miracle of the division of the moon [which purportedly the Prophet had done]. Now, conviction of the Prophet's divine mission, under the blessing of Almighty God, having followed this relation, the heart of the King became warmed with a holy affection towards Mahomet (on whom be peace!)

and he and later many others converted to Islam.[61] A variant is that after Perumal decided to convert to Islam he divided up his kingdom. When the pilgrims came back from Sri Lanka he accompanied them back to Arabia in 210/825. He died there, but he charged his companions to return to Malabar, where they gained many conversions and built nine mosques. Another version relates how the Cera ruler had a dream about the splitting of the moon at the same time as the Prophet actually did this. He went off to Arabia and met the Prophet himself, dying in 2/624. It is notable that the tenth/sixteenth-century local historian Shaykh Aḥmad Zayn al-Dīn rejects this version, even though it is widely believed by local Muslims. He says the visit to Arabia occurred some two centuries after the death of the Prophet.[62] Yet another variant is recounted by a scribe who accompanied a Persian traveller/ambassador, who was on the coast in the 1090s/1680s. He was told by the locals that a ruler in Malabar saw with his own eyes the division of the moon by the Prophet. He and his family then set out for the Ḥijāz. However, the ship encountered a storm and was in danger of sinking. In a dream the raja was

61 Zayn al-Dīn, *Tohfut-ul-Mujahideen*, trans. M. J. Rowlandson (London, 1833), pp. 48–50.

62 R. E. Miller, *Mappila Muslims of Kerala* (Madras, 1976), pp. 46–51; Dale, *Islamic society*, p. 12; Zayn al-Dīn, *Tohfut*, pp. 48–56. For a long analysis see Geneviève Bouchon, 'Les Musulmans du Kerala à l'époque de la découverte portugaise', *Mare Luso-Indicum*, 2 (1973), pp. 21–4. See also A. P. Ibrahim Kunju, 'Origin and spread of Islam in Kerala', in Asghar Ali Engineer (ed.), *Kerala Muslims: A historical perspective* (Delhi, 1995), pp. 17–23 for a good discussion based on Hindu, Muslim and Portuguese sources.

told that blood must be shed if the boat was to survive. None in his entourage volunteered to be sacrificed. However, one of his sisters pointed out that a small cut on her son's leg would produce enough blood to satisfy the requirement. Sure enough, a little blood was shed, the storm abated, and the raja went on to meet the Prophet. His sister's sagacity made the raja decree that accession to the throne should go to the son of the sister of the ruling raja. The scribe then notes that the rulers of Cochin soon lapsed; matrilineal succession however continued.[63]

Ibn Baṭṭūṭa relates another story of miraculous conversions. In Dharmapatam, where there was a large *ba'in* (tank) and a congregational mosque, the head of the Muslims was called Kuwail. His ancestor had been converted thanks to a miracle. Beside the mosque was a tree, and in the autumn of each year a single leaf fell from the tree, and written on this leaf was the *shahāda*. Ibn Baṭṭūṭa said that the jurist Husain and other trustworthy people had seen this happen, and read the words. At the time that it fell various trustworthy people both Muslim and infidel sat under the tree, and when the leaf fell the Muslims took half, and the other half was placed in the treasury of the infidel ruler, and they used it for healing of the sick. This tree was the cause of the conversion of the ancestor of Kuwail, the one who constructed the tank and mosque. He was able to read Arabic, and when he read the *shahāda* he embraced Islam. 'His story has been handed down amongst them by many witnesses.'[64]

A more sober, though less interesting, version of the conversion of many coastal people to Islam, thus creating the Mappila community, would note that Arabs, along with others, had been visiting this area long before Islam. According to the first-century CE *Periplus*, Cranganore was the main international port at the time, much frequented by ships from Arabia, which often then went on to Sri Lanka and China.[65] Just as elsewhere, these Arab traders continued to visit when they became Muslims, so that the first Muslims in Malabar must date from the time of the Prophet, or very soon afterwards. Barbosa early in the tenth/sixteenth century claimed that Muslims arrived in the area 610 years ago, that is, early in the fourth/tenth century,[66] but this

63 Ibn Muḥammad Ibrāhīm, *The ship of Sulaimān*, trans. John O'Kane, Persian Heritage Series, 11 (London, 1972), pp. 219–23.

64 Ibn Baṭṭūṭa, *Travels*, pp. 810–11. The text is rather confused; this seems to be the right account.

65 André Wink, *Al-Hind: The making of the Indo-Islamic world*, 3 vols. (Leiden, 1990–2004), vol. I, p. 67, vol. II, p. 276.

66 Duarte Barbosa, *A description of the coasts of East Africa and Malabar in the beginning of the 16th century*, trans. Henry E. J. Stanley, Hakluyt Society, 35 (London, 1866), p. 102, and generally pp. 101–60.

seems to be far too late an estimate. Rather, this was the earliest Muslim community, however small, in South Asia, predating by a good margin the arrival of Muslim armies in Sind in 92/711. The earliest extant Muslim remains which can be dated include a tomb from the 170s/780s near Calicut. Shokoohy's excellent study of mosques in Malabar notes that many of the early ones were destroyed by the Portuguese in the tenth/sixteenth century. The Jāmiʿ Masjid in Calicut has an inscription from 885/1480f. in very elegant *naskh* script, and this mosque must have been maybe a century old already. Others in Calicut and Cochin date from the tenth/sixteenth century, while an early Shīʿa mosque in Quilon is probably a century or so earlier than this. Tradition claims that there was one in Cranganore which was founded in 8/630. The locals accept this tradition as authentic. Interestingly, it is associated with the legend of the conversion of Raja Cheraman Perumal by an Arab saint.[67]

Again in familiar fashion, some of these Arabs settled and intermarried. Certainly by the third/ninth century there were many Muslim settlements on the coast. The result of this interbreeding, along with many conversions of local Hindus, produced the local Mappila community, which is to be distinguished from the *Pardesi*, 'foreign', Muslim group. A detailed Portuguese account from the early tenth/sixteenth century explains why so many local Hindus converted. The central claim, one familiar to anthropologists though not always now accepted by them, is that oppressed low-caste people are likely to convert to a religion perceived to be more egalitarian. Correia's account describes both the mix of trade and religion which proved so successful, and the way the Islamic stress on the equality of all believers fostered conversions, producing the indigenous Muslim Mappila community. He described the dominance of the Nayyars in this area, and the degraded position of the lower castes. Muslims, presumably from the Red Sea area given that this was the major trading area for Malabar, pointed out to the (Hindu) rulers that the low-caste porters were unable to move about freely in the area, because if they ran into Nayyars they would be killed. But if these low-caste Malabaris converted to Islam 'they would be able to go freely where they wished, because once they became Muslims they were immediately outside of the law of the Malabaris, and their customs, and they would be able to travel on the roads and mingle with all sorts of people'. This argument,

67 Mehrdad Shokoohy, *Muslim architecture of south India: The sultanate of Ma'bar and the traditions of the maritime settlers on the Malabar and Coromandel coasts (Tamil Nadu, Kerala and Goa)* (London, 2003), pp. 137–44.

plus a few bribes, convinced the rulers, who gave their consent. The actual conversion of these much oppressed people was easy, for they then could live where they pleased and eat what they wanted. They also received clothing from the Muslims. The result was a great success for this Muslim-conversion drive, which in turn spilt over into trading success, especially in the spice trade to the Red Sea.[68] It is to be noted that this account by an outsider shows clearly that most local converts came from lower levels of Hindu society in Malabar. Shaykh Aḥmad Zayn al-Dīn confirms this.

Pardesi Muslims

The *Pardesi* Muslims resident in or visiting Malabar were a very diverse group, who however could claim more or less 'pure' Arab ancestry. Their primary differentiator from the locals was that they were essentially sojourners, or at least that they looked back to their place of origin as their real home, regardless of how long they had been in Malabar or how well they had done there. Barbosa, who generally is well informed, wrote that there were many foreign Muslims in Calicut, 'These are Arabs, Persians, Guzarates, Khurasanys, and Decanys: they are great merchants, and possess in this place wives and children, and ships for sailing to all parts with all kinds of goods.'[69] There is a textual matter to note here. The more recent edition of Barbosa reads, 'they gathered here in great numbers with their wives and sons'.[70] The difference is of some importance, for if they indeed brought their families with them this implies that they were settled, and also this would reduce the possibility of having local wives and children. Contrariwise, if they came as single men they would be much more likely to interbreed, thus increasing the number of local Muslims. The general history of Muslim diasporas around the Indian Ocean littoral usually stresses that only men moved, and even they would retain ties to their homeland and try to return there for domestic matters from time to time. Thus on this occasion it seems prudent to favour the earlier translation of Barbosa, which implies that the wives and children were locals.

The Mappilas claimed Arab ancestry, too, but with much less credibility, for even if there was an Arab somewhere in their background this ethnicity had

68 Gaspar Correia, *Lendas de India*, 4 vols. (Coímbra, 1921–31, Lisbon, 1969), vol. I, pp. 75–6.
69 Barbosa, *A description*, p. 147.
70 Duarte Barbosa, *The book of Duarte Barbosa: An account of the countries bordering on the Indian Ocean and their inhabitants*, trans. and ed. Mansel Longworth Dames, Hakluyt Society, ser. 2, nos. 44, 49, 2 vols. (London, 1918–21), vol. II, p. 76.

been radically diluted by intermarriage with local Hindu women. In any case many of them were converted Hindus *tout court*. This said, there is really a continuum of 'arabness' rather than a bipolar situation; nevertheless, for heuristic reasons the Mappila/*Pardesi* division will be followed here.

There are available copious descriptions of the *Pardesi* Muslims. They came primarily for trade, to participate in and even dominate the lucrative spice trade to the Red Sea. Some Mappilas were also able to enter this trade, but not nearly to the extent of the foreigners. The internal economy was controlled by other people: some local Christians played a role in the collection and transportation of pepper, but the two main groups were Gujarati *Vanias* and Coromandel Chettyars, both of these of course being Hindu and not native to Malabar. All of these 'foreign' groups lived in the Hindu-ruled port cities under conditions of considerable autonomy. One account of the *Pardesi* noted that 'They have among them a Moorish governor who rules over and chastises them, without the king meddling with them.'[71] Most legal matters, especially commercial ones, were settled within the group, or by negotiation between the heads of several groups: for example, a debt owed by a Cairo merchant to a Gujarati would be arbitrated between the heads of the two groups. The Hindu rulers were appreciative of the customs revenues these wealthy traders brought in, and by and large left them alone, or even actively encouraged them to call. Another account, which mirrors what Ibn Baṭṭūṭa found in Mogadishu and other places, describes how 'The king gave to each one a nair to guard and serve him, a Chety scribe for his accounts, and to take care of his property, and a broker for his trade. To these three persons such a merchant would pay something for their maintenance' and they also received a commission from those who sold goods to the *Pardesi* merchant.[72]

The rulers had to treat visiting merchants well, for the *Pardesi* did have choices. There were a host of competing port cities up and down the coast. Curiously, almost none of these ports had adequate harbours. Except for Cochin, they all were open, and often dangerous, roadsteads where cargo had to be perilously transhipped to lighters which took the goods to the shore. Yet despite having no harbour, Calicut had been dominant from soon after its founding in the late fifth/eleventh century. As noted, this rise seems to have been a result of a fundamental shift in trading patterns, consequent on the decline of the direct trade between Baghdad and Canton. The result was the rise of entrepôts such as Calicut and later Melaka.

71 Barbosa, *A description*, p. 147.
72 *Ibid.*, p. 148.

A contemporary Portuguese account gives some detail on the *Pardesi* trade of Calicut in the early tenth/sixteenth century, before the Portuguese had affected it. After a description of their ships, it goes on to say:

> And in this manner ten or twelve ships laden with these goods sailed every year in the month of February, and made their voyage to the Red Sea, and some of them were for the city of Aden, and some for Jiddah the port of Mekkah, where they sold their merchandise to others, who transported them thence in other smaller vessels to Turkey and to Suez, and thence by land to Cairo, and from Cairo to Alexandria.[73]

The *Pardesi* came from very diverse places. There were Persians, Turks, Arabs from Egypt, Arabia, Syria and Tunis, an important 'nation' from the Maghrib, and also some refugees from Granada. After the collapse of Baghdad, Egyptian merchants from Cairo, the Karimi merchants, were especially important. From early in the seventh/thirteenth century Hadramīs flowed in. Other *Pardesi* came from Ethiopia, Sumatra and Pegu.[74]

These wealthy traders lived in some style. ʿAbd al-Razzāq was in Calicut in 846/1442f. and said it was a prosperous trading town, with two mosques to service the resident Muslim community. There was a *qāḍī*, and a 'priest', and most of them were followers of the Shāfiʿī *madhhab*. 'As to the Mussulmauns, they dress themselves in magnificent apparel after the manner of the Arabs, and manifest luxury in every particular.' Another account says: 'These are white men and very gentlemanlike and of good appearance, they go well dressed, and adorned with silk stuffs, scarlet, cloth, camlets and cottons; their head-dress wrapped round their heads. They have large houses and many servants: they are very luxurious in eating, drinking, and sleeping.'[75] They were joined by fellow Muslims, especially from Gujarat, and also by Jews and Hindu merchants, *Banias*.

Muslim exemplars and Sufism

We have so far presented these *Pardesi* as successful merchants. However, there were among them other foreign Muslims, many of whom seem to be

73 *Ibid.*, p. 147.

74 Wink, *Al-Hind*, vol. II, pp. 276–80; Geneviève Bouchon, 'Quelques aspects de l'islamisation des régions maritimes de l'Inde à l'époque médiévale (XIIe–XVIe s.)', *Purusartha*, 9 (1986), p. 32; Bouchon, 'Les Musulmans du Kerala', p. 50.

75 ʿAbd al-Razzāq's account in R. H. Major (ed.), *India in the fifteenth century: Being a collection of narratives of voyages to India in the century preceding the Portuguese discovery of the Cape of Good Hope; from Latin, Persian, Russian, and Italian sources, now first translated into English*, Hakluyt Society, 22 (London, 1857), pp. 13–17; Barbosa, *A description*, p. 148.

more settled, whose primary interest was not trade but religion, remembering however again that 'piety and pelf' (property) could easily coexist. From around 600/1204 many of the religious authorities in Malabar were Hadramī. It will be remembered that there seem to be a series of outflows from this inhospitable area. Thus was created a network of Shāfiʿī scholars not only from the Hadramawt but also from Yemen, Oman, Baḥrayn and Baghdad who had connections with, and travelled between, all the Muslim communities around the shores of the Indian Ocean. Many of these men were *sayyids* and *sharīfs*, and were learned in Shāfiʿī jurisprudence. There were close ties to the Hadramawt and, just as on the East African coast, people went back there to study.[76]

Ibn Baṭṭūṭa's account from the 740s/1340s reveals prosperous, substantial and pious Muslim communities up and down the coast, many of them like him of foreign origin. Like Shaykh Aḥmad Zayn al-Dīn two centuries later, he stressed mostly friendly ties with the local Hindus, including the rulers, except that Muslims and Hindus did not eat together, or go into each other's houses. It is worth noting that Ibn Baṭṭūṭa, being from Morocco, was Mālikī, and so in theory should have been opposed to Muslims living under non-Muslim rule; yet this seems in no way to colour his observations of Malabar, which are mostly very positive.

A brief summary of his travels down the coast in the early 740s/1340s will give a picture of the *Pardesi* community at this time: he says little about Mappilas.[77] In Panderani, near Calicut, the *qāḍī* and preacher was from Oman, and the *amīr* of the merchants in Calicut was from Baḥrayn. This man was also the *shāhbandar*, the main port official, and all the merchants used to gather and eat at his table. The factor on one of the ships was from Syria. In Quilon the chief Muslim merchant was from Iraq and was a Shīʿa. The *qāḍī* originated in Qazvīn. There was a great Jāmʿi Masjid there, constructed by a merchant. 'Muslims are honoured and respected there.'

The ruler in Honavar was a Muslim. The people were Shāfiʿī. He met various shaykhs and jurists and the *qāḍī*. The women were modest and beautiful. They all knew the Qurʾān by heart. There were thirteen schools for girls and twenty-three for boys, 'a thing which I have never seen elsewhere'. The ruler was very pious. He would come to the mosque before daybreak and read the Qurʾān until dawn, when he would do his first prayers of the day. He fasted when the moon was full, and wore silks and fine linen.

76 Wink, *Al-Hind*, vol. II, pp. 276–80.
77 Ibn Baṭṭūṭa, *Travels*, pp. 803–19.

In Mangalore, north of Malabar proper, Ibn Baṭṭūṭa found 4,000 Muslims serviced by a very distinguished *qāḍī*. Then he went on to Hili, where there was a large mosque of great blessedness. It had a rich treasury under the control of the preacher Husain and the chief of the Muslims, Hasan al-Wazzan. Also in the mosque were several students of religious science who got stipends from its revenue, and a kitchen where all travellers and poor Muslims could get food. He also found in Hili a pious jurist from Mogadishu called Sa'id, 'of fine figure and character. He used to fast continually, and I was told that he had studied at Mecca for fourteen years and for the same length of time at al-Madina, had met Abu Numayy the Amir of Mecca and Mansur b. Jammaz, the Amir of al-Madina, and had travelled in India and China.' Another example of widespread connections came from Cannanore, where he met a jurist from Baghdad, who had charge of his deceased brother's children, and was going to take them to Baghdad. Finally, in Panderani there were three Muslim quarters or localities, and each had a mosque, one of them very fine. The *qāḍī* and preacher was from Oman.

Ibn Baṭṭūṭa's *baraka* is shown many times all around the shores of the Arabian Sea. We saw how he was looked after in Mogadishu and the Maldives. Similarly on the Malabar coast. During his travels his ship was attacked by pirates:

> They took everything I had preserved for emergencies; they took the pearls and rubies that the king of Ceylon had given me, they took my clothes and the supplies given me by pious people and saints. They left me no covering except my trousers. They took everything everybody had and set us down on the shore. I returned to Qaliqut [Calicut] and went into one of the mosques. One of the jurists sent me a robe, the qadi a turban and one of the merchants another robe.[78]

Ibn Baṭṭūṭa also gives us some information on Sufism on the coast. When he was in southern Iran, at Kāzarūn, he stayed in the hospice of the Shaykh Abū Isḥāq. He was highly venerated by the people of India and China. When travellers in the sea of China got a bad wind or feared pirates they would make a vow to him and write down how much their obligation was. When they reached land people from the hospice would come on board and collect the vows. 'There is not a ship that comes from China or from India but has thousands of dinars in it vowed to the saint, and the agents on behalf of the intendant of the hospice come to take delivery of that sum.' Poor believers could come to the head of the hospice and get a written order for a certain

78 *Ibid.*, p. 865.

amount. The mendicant then found someone who owed a vow and collected the money from him, and gave him a receipt. Once a king of India vowed ten thousand *dīnārs* to the shaykh, and when one of the poor brethren at the hospice in Kāzarūn heard of this he went off to India and collected that money.[79]

This hospice in Kāzarūn was the original home of the early Sufi order called Kāzarūniyya, founded in southern Iran by the eminent Shaykh Abū Isḥāq Ibrāhīm b. Shāhriyār of Kāzarūn (d. 426/1033). It spread widely, and was very influential in the eighth/fourteenth and ninth/fifteenth centuries. The home *khānaqā* was suppressed early in the tenth/sixteenth century by the Safavids, and the order seems to have died out.[80] In Ibn Baṭṭūṭa's time it was quite widespread. It had a hospice in Calicut, whose superior was Shaykh Shihab al-Dīn of Kazarun, 'to whom are the offerings made in vows by the people of India and China to the Sheikh Abu Ishaq, God profit us by him'. Then in Quilon, Ibn Baṭṭūṭa stayed at another hospice of this order, run by Shaykh Fakhr al-Dīn, the son of Shihād al-Dīn. There was yet another hospice of the same fraternity in Quanzhou (Polo's Zaitun).[81] However, it seems that the dominant Sufi order in Malabar was again the Qādiriyyas, who established numerous hospices and were influential in the region.[82]

Overall the picture is of a dynamic and pious *Pardesi* Muslim community on the coast, one with widespread ties all around the shores of the ocean. It is appropriate to close this account with a nice little vignette, which is Ibn Baṭṭūṭa's own account of what he did while he was delayed in Honavar:

> I spent most of my time in his [the sultan's] mosque and used to read the *Qur'an* through every day, and later twice a day, beginning the first recital after the dawn prayer and ending it in the early afternoon, then after making fresh ablutions I would begin the second recital and end it about sunset. I continued to do this for the space of three months, during which I went into retreat for forty days.[83]

The Mappila Muslims

Ibn Baṭṭūṭa says little about indigenous Muslims, the Mappilas, and none of it is very positive. His praise is reserved for those who like himself were Arabs from the heartland, and indeed he always commented on their presence, while

79 *Ibid.*, p. 320.
80 EI^2 'Kāzarūnī'. (H. Algar).
81 Ibn Baṭṭūṭa, *Travels*, pp. 812–13, 895.
82 Kunju, 'Origin and spread', pp. 23–8
83 Ibn Baṭṭūṭa, *Travels*, p. 819.

either ignoring or belittling the locals. Typical was his experience in the backwaters when he was travelling from Calicut to Quilon. The trip took ten days, and they anchored at night and stayed in villages. It was not a pleasant trip. 'There was no Muslim on board the boat except the man I had hired, and he used to drink wine with the infidels when we went ashore and annoy me with his brawling.'[84] Much of what is known about the Mappila community in this period comes from Portuguese sources, which have their own biases and prejudices. Bouchon's detailed and elaborately referenced survey covers well their economic and political roles, but says little about their religion. Miller's survey is a rather unscholarly account of their history which stresses that before the Portuguese this was an irenical age, which the Portuguese destroyed.[85] It certainly was, by say 905/1500, a substantial community, perhaps 10 per cent of Malabar's total. In modern times they make up some 20 per cent of the total population of Kerala. Ludovico di Varthema claimed there were 15,000 or more in Calicut, and indeed it seems that the bulk of the Muslim population lived in the north of the region, in areas controlled by the Zamorin. Barbosa left an invaluable account of them:

> In all this said country of Malabar there are a great quantity of Moors, who are of the same language and colour as the gentiles of the country. They go bare like the nairs, only they wear, to distinguish themselves from the gentiles, small round caps on their heads and their beards fully grown. So that it appears to me that these people are a fifth part of all the inhabitants that there are in this country. They call these Moors Mapulers, they carry on nearly all the trade of the seaports: and in the interior of the country they are very well provided with estates and farms.[86]

The tenth/sixteenth-century Muslim authority Shaykh Aḥmad Zayn al-Dīn noted how even though they studied and were apparently pious, their succession customs, just as in the Laccadive islands, were matrilineal. He noted matrilineal succession among Nayyars, and this 'has been adopted by the greater part of the Mahomedans of Cannanore, and those who are dependent on them ... although there are not wanting among them, who read the Koran, treasure up its maxims, and study it with apparent zeal, being seemingly desirous to improve themselves by science, and who are regular in the performance of religious worship'. Thus even apparently orthodox Mappila still practised distinctly unorthodox matrilineal succession.[87] This

84 *Ibid.*, p. 816.
85 Bouchon, 'Les Musulmans du Kerala'; Miller, *Mappila Muslims*.
86 Barbosa, *A description*, p. 146.
87 Zayn al-Dīn, *Tohfut*, p. 63.

matrilinearity seems to apply mostly to Mappila groups in the north, where at least some of them were converted Nayyars. In the south many of the converts came from other castes, and did not follow matrilineal custom.

The quotation from Barbosa stresses their continuing much Hindu Malabari practice, and this is shown in other ways also. Their language was Malayalam, with some Arabic additions. The mosques in Malabar, though always remembering that many of the oldest ones which Ibn Baṭṭūṭa described were destroyed by the Portuguese, were quite different from those in the rest of the subcontinent. Curiously Ibn Baṭṭūṭa, who spent so much time in them, says nothing about this, but merely notes that some were very grand and blessed. In Malabar they used timber in the upper storeys, which often had elaborate wood carving. The roofs were tiered or peaked, as are many secular buildings in the region.[88]

In economic terms the Mappilas were a subaltern group, who engaged in local trade up and down the west coast of India and to the interior, or served in local navies. Some apparently reached higher levels, taking part, along with the *Pardesi*, in oceanic trade. Their maritime role may have been advantaged by changes in Hinduism at this time. In south India the third/ninth-century Hindu reformer Sankara was influential. His stress on orthodoxy, or what he considered to be orthodox, meant that Hindus became much less likely to travel by sea, over the Black Water, considering this to be ritually polluting. Marco Polo in the seventh/thirteenth century wrote that Hindus in Coromandel did not drink wine, 'so shameful would it be thought that his evidence would not be accepted in court. A similar prejudice exists against persons sailing the sea, who, they observe, must be desperate, and whose testimony in court ought not to be admitted.'[89] Thus the field was left open for Muslims. It is notable that while Hindus from Gujarat sometimes did travel by sea, and even settle overseas, it seems that Malabar Hindus did not.[90]

Portuguese in Malabar

The arrival of the Portuguese in 903/1498 led to profound changes in Malabari Islam. Yet how to interpret this is a bit of a minefield. Shaykh Aḥmad Zayn al-Dīn stressed tolerance and good relations between Hindus and Muslims, as also does the modern author Miller with his description of relations as being irenical. Can it be said that with the Portuguese, religious intolerance entered

88 See K. J. John, 'The Muslim-Arabs and mosque architecture in Malabar', in Engineer (ed.), *Kerala Muslims*, pp. 47–55.
89 Marco Polo, *The travels of Marco Polo* (New York, 1961), p. 251.
90 Bouchon, 'Les Musulmans du Kerala', pp. 9–14.

Malabar *de novo*? This matter will be covered in detail elsewhere in this volume, but certainly their virulent anti-Muslim actions, resulting from both economic and religious competition, caused the *Pardesi* to move off to safer places even as early as 921/1515. Easy enough for them to do this, given the widespread connections we have noted so often. The Mappilas of course, being local people, did not have this option. Some accommodated to the Portuguese, others resisted, especially by continuing the coastal trade in pepper which they had been doing for so long. The main naval opponents of the Portuguese, the famous Kunj ʿAlī Marakkars, or Kunhali Marakkars, a dynasty of guerrilla naval commanders, came from a family of legists in Cochin who, when this became a Portuguese vassal port, moved on to Calicut, where throughout the tenth/sixteenth century they opposed the Portuguese, sometimes in alliance with the Zamorins, sometimes not. The tenth/sixteenth-century Muslim writer Shaykh Aḥmad Zayn al-Dīn called on the Mappilas to undertake a *jihād* against the Portuguese; implicitly he saw Malabar as *dār al-islam*, and being attacked by the Portuguese from *dār al-ḥarb*. When Aceh was attacked by the Portuguese in the sixteenth century they were helped by Muslims from various areas, including southern Arabia, but also by Mappilas from Malabar. Later, when they opposed the pretensions of the Dutch and English, a Hadramī chronicle praised the Mappilas for their courage: they are 'people of great courage and zeal for Islam', even though 'they have few scholars among them, and [know] no more of Islam than the merest name of it'.[91]

This denigration of their religious purity points to another consequence of Portuguese hostility. They tried, with some success, to control trade and navigation in the Arabian Sea. One of the effects of this was that the sort of dense circulation of religious authorities which have been described in such detail was now hindered. Mappila access to the heartland, to the *ḥajj* and to authorities from there, was reduced, and there seems little doubt that, as the Hadramī chronicle noted, the quality of Islam suffered. It is an open question whether this should be seen as a negative, a falling away from normative practice, or rather a healthy process of indigenisation, or Indianisation. Perhaps in its isolation Mappila Islam stressed *mila* more than *dīni*, though if this be so, it is also worth remembering that even before the Portuguese, local Islam in Malabar was distinctive, as noted, in terms of succession matters, mosque architecture and the continuing influence of some pre-Islamic practices.

91 Dale, *Islamic society*, pp. 51, 53.

Sri Lankan Muslims

Sri Lanka's Muslim population makes up less than 10 per cent of the island's total today. They are conventionally divided into two groups, the so-called Moors and the Malays.[92] The latter, despite some claims for an ancient past, in fact arrived only under Dutch rule, primarily in the late eleventh/seventeenth and twelfth/eighteenth centuries. They make up about one-fifth of the total Muslim population, and speak a language which includes some Malay elements mixed in with local Sinhalese dialects.

The term 'Moor' is a derogatory one, being used by the Portuguese to describe all their Muslim adversaries. However, in Sri Lanka it appears to be sanctioned by custom, and will be used here. Their history has, as one would expect, many similarities with that of the other coastal Muslim communities already discussed. They claim descent from Arab traders who arrived very early in the Muslim period, and some claim that in terms of ethnicity they are more Arab than Sinhalese. Certainly Sri Lanka was known to Arab and other traders long before Islam, being a source of precious stones, pearls from the Gulf of Mannar (or Fishery coast), between south-east India and Sri Lanka, and cinnamon, and serving as a convenient way station for east–west and vice versa trade. These Arab traders knew the island as Serendip, an indication then of its appeal to them, for this is the root of the English word 'serendipity'. One can then assume that when Arabs converted they continued to call at Sri Lanka, and that there they intermarried with local women, both Sinhalese and Tamil, thus forming a *mestizo* Muslim population, though one which over time became less and less 'Arab' in terms of ethnicity. These descendants of foreign merchants merged into the majority of the Muslim population, who were Sinhalese by ethnicity, and usually from lower levels in the society. Their main settlements were on the north-east, north and west coasts, such as Jaffna, Colombo and Galle.

Apart from trade, the main attraction of the island for Muslims was the presence in the interior of Adam's Peak, where it was believed an indentation in the rock was the footprint of Adam himself. (Buddhists believe it is that of Gautama the Buddha.) It will be remembered that the legendary facilitators of the conversion of Malabar were a party of Arab pilgrims bound for Adam's Peak. A later pilgrim was Ibn Baṭṭūṭa, in 745/1344, who left an impression of a quite flourishing Muslim community. As he ascended he noticed several

92 Generally see Wink, *Al-Hind*, vol. I, pp. 80–1; EI^2 'Ceylon' (A. M. A. Azeez). and the rather unsatisfactory Vasundhara Mohan, *Muslims in Sri Lanka* (Jaipur, 1985).

Muslim-associated places, and especially a mosque of a shaykh from Shīrāz, whose tomb was nearby and was venerated by all. However, his account gives none of the useful detail which he provides for other places already commented on.[93]

It appears that relations with the majority Buddhist rulers in Sri Lanka were cordial, as also with the Hindu rulers in the north. The Muslims with their international trading connections brought in much needed customs revenues, and goods from far away. Thus they were patronised and encouraged. A good deal of interaction between the three religions is to be expected, and among other things is shown by the home language of the Moors, which is overwhelmingly Tamil though with the addition of a large number of Arabic words. In this period there was some writing in Arabic script but it seems that Tamil was more common, and this points to close ties with Tamil-speaking Muslims in Coromandel, especially focused on the pearl fisheries, along with their location in Sri Lanka, which was often in Tamil-speaking areas.

Sri Lankan Muslims operated in two zones, one local, one very extensive. They had closest ties with their fellow Shāfiʿī Muslims in Malabar and Coromandel. This area made up a distinctive commercial region, where the main trade products were pepper from Malabar, cinnamon from Sri Lanka and pearls from the Gulf of Mannar. Indeed the way in which the pearl fisheries lay between Sri Lanka and Coromandel, and were shared by the two areas, plus the fact that Mappilas tried to stop the Portuguese from interfering in them, typifies the interconnectedness of these three areas. There was considerable interchange of people and products in what was a defined trading arena. To separate out Muslims from any one of these regions as distinctive would be to ignore the dense interaction, intermingling and intermarriage which in fact occurred. Local Muslims from the three areas collected the products, and fed them into the wider Indian Ocean circuit, indeed into a worldwide circuit, for these three products had universal appeal.

Some authors see the period up to 905/1500 as a golden age for Sri Lanka's Moors, when they prospered and had good relations with local rulers. This changed dramatically with the arrival of the Portuguese, who extended their anti-Muslim activities to Sri Lanka as well as India. In the sixteenth century they attacked Muslim traders on sight, and later occupied much of the Sri Lankan coast. When the Dutch took the island in the middle of the eleventh/seventeenth century they instituted a monopoly policy over cinnamon, thus again detrimentally affecting the Moors.

93 Ibn Baṭṭūṭa, *Travels*, pp. 847–56.

Coromandel

We have much less data on the Muslim presence in Coromandel and the Tamil interior. It is impossible to describe them in the comparative depth which was available for other littoral areas, and what we do know is bedevilled by considerable terminological confusion in the existing literature. For our purposes the area under discussion is essentially the same as the coastal area of the present Indian state of Tamil Nadu. Arab writers knew this region as Maʿbar, though confusingly sometimes this term refers to part of the Malabar coast.

The first evidence of Muslims on the Coromandel coast comes from an inscription of 261/875. The area was known to Arab geographers from very early.[94] Muslims became a more substantial presence only from the fifth/eleventh century, and conversions on the coast reached any great numbers only from the seventh/thirteenth.[95] Alone of the areas under discussion in this chapter, the Coromandel region was conquered early in the eighth/fourteenth century by Muslim armies from the north, that is, those of the Delhi sultanate. It seems that these northerners were unimpressed by the quality of Islam that they found in Coromandel.[96] Their incursion was soon ended, though it did result in a short-lived Muslim sultanate in Madurai (733–80/1333–78), which was taken over by the Hindu kingdom of Vijayanagara. From the last decades of the tenth/sixteenth century, after the defeat of Vijayanagara by Muslim armies, Coromandel was again subject to Muslim rule. However, here and elsewhere we must avoid any communal tinge in our discussion; thus Muslims happily served in the armies of Hindu rulers such as the Pandyas.

Any discussion of the Muslim communities of the Coromandel coast and Tamil interior must first try to make sense of a very complex matter of terminologies. There are both collective and specific terms in use, but some of these have changed over time, as have the fortunes of the various groups. Since the British began to categorise people in the late nineteenth century four distinct groups within the Tamil Muslim community have been recognised. However, this does not necessarily apply to the early modern period. Some authorities refer to Labbai as a generic term which encompasses all four.

94 S. Muḥammad Husayn Nainar, *Arab geographers' knowledge of southern India* (Madras, 1942).

95 Wink, *Al-Hind*, vol. I, pp. 78–80, vol. II, p. 280. See also Shokoohy, *Muslim architecture of south India*, pp. 275–90.

96 J. B. P. More, *Muslim identity, print culture and the Dravidian factor in Tamil Nadu* (New Delhi, 2004), pp. 10–11.

It may be that this is a modern usage. Alternatively, according to Arasaratnam the term Chulia was a collective one which included all four groups. Chulia is not an indigenous word, and may be a corruption by Europeans of the local name for the area: Cholamandalam. However, Ibn Baṭṭūṭa in Quilon found very wealthy merchants whom he called Suli, that is Chulia. For the early Europeans the Hindu traders of the Coromandel coast were Klings, later often called Chetties, more correctly Chettyars, who were Hindu, while the Muslims were Chulias.[97]

The four divisions for the community, used once censuses began to make inchoate divisions firmer, are Maraikkayar, Kayalar, Rawther and Labbai. The Maraikkayar and Kayalar groups are Sunnī, and follow the Shāfiʿī *madhhab*. They were and are merchants who lived on the southern part of the Tamil Nadu coast and traded extensively in South East Asia. The Rawther and Labbai groups are also Sunnī, but Ḥanafī. They live inland in the northern areas, and are much poorer than their coastal co-religionists. The division between inland Ḥanafī and coastal Shāfiʿī is one found generally in South Asia at this time.

The coastal Maraikkayar today claim that they are descended from Arab traders, and are more Arab than Tamil. According to them the interior two groups are mere converts, and not very observant Muslims at all. Susan Bayly makes clear that this exclusiveness and intolerance is a nineteenth-century development. In previous times, including the period under discussion, there was less differentiation, and all Coromandel Muslims were syncretic. In terms of literature, 980/1572f. is the year in which the earliest extant complete Islamic poem in the Tamil language, the *Āyiramacalā*, was composed. From that point onward, we have texts written by Tamil Muslims in both Tamil and Arabic on Islamic topics, using both the Tamil and Arabic scripts for the Tamil language.[98] However, while some recent writers stress interaction between Hindus and Muslims, such as common worship at Muslim *dargāhs* (shrines), and grants to them from local Hindu rulers, we have very little contemporary evidence of this. Bayly discusses the shrine of a Qādiriyya Sufi master in Nagore. He established a *khānaqā* in 950/1543. His *dargāh* was a focus of worship for both Hindus and Muslims, with a lot of practices taken from Hindu worship.[99]

97 Sinnappah Arasaratnam, *Merchants, companies and commerce on the Coromandel coast, 1650–1740* (Delhi, 1986), p. 219; Ibn Baṭṭūṭa, *Travels*, p. 816.

98 This section owes almost everything to Torsten Tschacher, then of the South Asian Studies Program at the National University of Singapore. He provided help with bibliography, and extensive comments on my first draft. Space limitations dictated that I could not use much of what he provided, but I am grateful even so.

99 See Bayly, 'Islam in southern India', pp. 35–73 for an account which perhaps relies too much on nineteenth- and twentieth-century sources to tell the story of earlier periods.

This saint used a common religious vocabulary, derived from Hindu, Muslim and Christian ideas. His shrine received donations from the Hindu elite and even from Europeans, as well as Muslims. In the early twelfth/eighteenth century the famous Labbai poet Umaru Pulavar wrote a 5,000-stanza epic called *Sirapuranam* on the life of the Prophet based on the Tamil version of the *Ramayana*. Subrahmanyam emphasises the lack of religious particularism at this time, and earlier. None of these men saw themselves as being forced to choose between an Arab-Islamic culture and a Tamil one.[100]

The Maraikkayar in the early modern period had important trading connections in their immediate area, that is, to Sri Lanka, to the pearl fisheries in the Gulf of Mannar and around the corner to Malabar, where there were close connections with the Mappilas. In the 930s and 940s/1520s and 1530s Mappila fleets led by the Kunjali Marakkars of Malabar operated in southern Coromandel, too, to support the Tamil Maraikkayars and to oppose (ultimately unsuccessfully) the Portuguese attempt to take over the pearl fisheries in the Gulf of Mannar. In these lucrative diving areas the Maraikkayar worked as divers and also as entrepreneurs.[101] Their most important centres at this time, in the early sixteenth century, were Kayalpatnam and Kilakkarai. They married into families with similar Shāfiʿī allegiance from Malabar and Sri Lanka rather than with the Ḥanafī of the interior, despite having a common language of Tamil with the latter.

These ties with contiguous areas seem to have existed from early on in the history of the Coromandel Muslim merchant presence. However, it may be that their more extensive trading role began around the middle of the ninth/fifteenth century with the rise of the Melaka sultanate. They became an important element in the very diverse mercantile world of this port city, and played a major role in the Malay world in general both in trade and in the process of the conversion of the Malays to Islam. In the eleventh/seventeenth century Tamil commercial groups were important traders in Johor, Banten and Perak. Chulia traders moved in to Aceh once the Gujaratis left this port to concentrate on the trade to the Red Sea. In the

100 See Sanjay Subrahmanyam, 'Diversity in South Asian Islam', *Akhbar*, 5 (2002); David Shulman and Sanjay Subrahmanyam, 'Prince of poets and ports: Citakkati, the Maraikkayars and Ramnad, ca 1690–1710', in Anna Libera Dallapiccola and Stephanie Zingel-Avé Lallaemant (eds.), *Islam and the Indian regions*, vol. I (Stuttgart, 1993), pp. 497–535.

101 Barbosa, *The book of Duarte Barbosa*, vol. II, pp. 116–25; Sanjay Subrahmanyam, 'Noble harvest from the sea: Managing the pearl fishery of Mannar, 1500–1925', in Burton Stein and Sanjay Subrahmanyam (eds.), *Institutions and economic change in South Asia* (Delhi, 1996), pp. 134–72.

second half of the eleventh / seventeenth century they had a massive trade in Aceh. Everywhere they functioned as key middle merchants and brokers. One family called Lebbe, who were Chulia Muslims, were prominent commercial advisers to the sultan of Johor towards the end of the seventeenth century.[102]

Knowledge of religious practice, perhaps visits from heartland shaykhs, or religious connections with the wider Shāfiʿī world, is very slight. However, the Coromandel coast was an important source of textiles, and we have just noted extensive trade by Muslims from this coast with Sri Lanka, Malabar and especially the Malay world. It would then be extraordinary if there did not exist the sort of mingling of commerce and religion which we have found in other areas. The dominant Sufi order was the Qādiriyya. The usually informative Ibn Baṭṭūṭa tells us little, except to point to a group of *faqīrs* in an obscure town: this points to an active Muslim community. He was with a ruler called Ghiyāth al-Dīn, who was part of a short-lived Muslim dynasty in Madurai. In Fattan, an unidentified port near Madurai, he noticed a fine stone-built mosque, and met there the pious Shaykh Muḥammad of Naisabur, one of the distraught *faqīrs* who let their hair grow down to their shoulders. He had about thirty *faqīrs* with him.[103]

Conclusion

It would be tempting to see the Muslim communities strung around the shores of the Arabian Sea, and further to Coromandel, as existing in a golden age of peace and prosperity which was rudely ended by the arrival of fanatical Portuguese. Another chapter in this volume considers the role of the first Europeans to operate extensively in our area; generally the literature today tends to belittle the impact of the Portuguese in the region. What is more important is to stress several themes which have been prominent in this chapter. In most of these areas conversion narratives have been important. These attribute the conversion of local people resulting from the *baraka* of a visitor from the Arab world. This points to wide connections back and forth between the heartland of Islam and its outposts in the Arabian Sea littoral. This interplay continued, and continues today. Scholars and saints travelled widely, resulting first in conversions and then attempts to inculcate a more

102 Sinnappah Arasaratnam, 'The Chulia Muslim merchants in Southeast Asia, 1650–1800', in Sanjay Subrahmanyam (ed.), *Merchant networks in the early modern world* (Aldershot, 1996), pp. 159–77.

103 Ibn Baṭṭūṭa, *Travels*, p. 862.

'orthodox' version of the religion. The cosmopolitan nature of these coastal Muslims must be emphasised in terms of both their trading activities and their religious ties to Arabia. They were thus very largely set off from their inland neighbours. Yet some at least of their religious practice continued to draw on themes and motifs which lay deep in the coastal soil, and which long predated Islam. In none of this are Arabian Sea Muslims unusual within the wider world of Islam; all of these themes are to be found in most other areas which today are Muslim.

10

Early Muslim expansion in South-East Asia, eighth to fifteenth centuries

GEOFF WADE

Introduction

Islam was to come to the polities and societies of South-East Asia by sea, along the girdle of trade which extended from the Middle East through the ports of southern Asia, to South-East Asia and onwards to the southern extensions of the Chinese world in the East China Sea.[1] Islamic influences extended into South-East Asia from both ends of this trade route in different periods. In examining historical processes, periodisation is often a helpful tool, and it is thus proposed that we examine the extension of Islam to South-East Asia up until the ninth/fifteenth century in three major stages: (1) The period from the emergence of Islam until the Cōla invasions of South-East Asia in the fifth/eleventh century; (2) The end of the fifth/eleventh century until the seventh/thirteenth century; (3) The eighth/fourteenth and ninth/fifteenth centuries, following the establishment of the first Islamic South-East Asian polities in the seventh/thirteenth century. The reconstruction of the earlier periods is of course restricted by the dearth of sources, but newly available materials from Chinese texts and the archaeological record help to extend the existing histories of the religion in the South-East Asian region. The intimate interactions between this region and the ports of southern China demand that the latter also be considered in any study of the emergence of Islam in the area we today term South-East Asia.

From the emergence of Islam until the Cōla attacks on South-East Asia in the fifth/eleventh century

There is little doubt that the earliest introduction of Islam to South-East Asia was by Muslim merchants who travelled along the maritime routes which, for

1 The author wishes to thank Azyumardi Azra, James Chin, Edmund Edwards-McKinnon, Michael Feener, Michael Laffan, Elizabeth Lambourn, Li Tana, Pierre-Yves Manguin, John Miksic, Michael Pearson, Anthony Reid, Merle Ricklefs, Claudine Salmon and Torsten Tschacher for comments and suggestions.

at least a millennium earlier, connected the two ends of the Eurasian continent. The foundation of the urban centre of Baghdad in 145/762 –with Baṣra as its outlet to the Arabian Sea – was a major impetus in the transformation of trade and the development of commerce between the Persian Gulf and East Asia.[2] The early importance of the maritime vector is still evident today, as it is in maritime rather than mainland South-East Asia that the major Muslim communities reside. The specific activities of the early Persian and Arab traders[3] in South-East Asia are poorly documented, but at least one Chinese source notes contact between a South-East Asian polity and Arab people during the first/seventh century. The *New History of the Tang* notes in its account of He-ling, likely located in Java:

> During the *shang-yuan* reign (54–5/674–5) the people of the country promoted a woman as their ruler, and she was entitled *Xi-mo*. Her stern majesty ensured that society was strictly ordered so that not even things lost on the road were picked up by others. A prince of the Arab lands[4] heard of this and placed a bag full of gold in her suburbs. There it remained for three years without pedestrians touching it. Once the crown prince kicked it while passing and *Xi-mo* was greatly angered and was going to behead him, but the assembled ministers strongly urged her against that action. *Xi-mo* then said 'The fault lies with your feet. They need to be cut off.' Again the ministers urged her not to pursue this action, so in the end she just cut off his toes as a warning. Those of the Arab lands heard of this, and in fear, dared not attack them.[5]

It may well have been that the 'prince of the Arab lands' described resided in Sumatra, as Sumatran ports were long known as transit points on the maritime routes described above, as well as entrepôts for trading the products from the hinterland of that island. From Arab texts we glean further knowledge of the extent of these trade routes, extending to destination ports in southern China. In the third/ninth century, for example, Ibn Khordadbeh recorded the trade ports at the furthest extension from the Arab world as *Lūqīn* (likely Loukin, situated in what is today Vietnam), *Khānfū* (Guangzhou/Canton),

2 Pierre-Yves Manguin, 'The introduction of Islām into Champa', in Alijah Gordon (ed.), *The propagation of Islām in the Indonesian–Malay archipelago* (Kuala Lumpur, 2001), pp. 287–328. See p. 311 n. 12.

3 The 'Persian and Arab traders' referred to here is a generic reference to peoples from the Middle East trading on ships crewed by people of a likely diverse range of ethnicities and religions.

4 The term translated here as Arab lands is Da-shi (大食), a term deriving from the Persian name *Tazi*, referring to a people in Persia. It was later used by the Persians to refer to the Arab lands. The Chinese used the term from the Tang dynasty until the sixth/twelfth century to refer to the Arabs.

5 Ouyang Xiu *et al.*, *Xin Tang Shu* [*New history of the Tang dynasty*], (Beijing, 1975), *juan* 222.

Khānjū (Quanzhou), with *Qānṣū* (Yangzhou) marking the end of the maritime route (see Map 8). In the middle of the same century (141/758), following the An Lu-shan rebellion in China, the major Chinese port of Guangzhou was sacked by 'Arab' people.[6] By a century later, there was evidence in the same city of a quite large Islamic community. Sulaymān, who visited Guangzhou in 236/851, noted that the city had a Muslim community governing itself according to the *sharīʿa* under a *qāḍī*, whose appointment had to be confirmed by the Chinese authorities. It is likely that this was the port from which the Arab/Indian ship wrecked off Belitung island in about 210/826 and carrying southern Chinese cargo seemingly bound for western Asia had sailed.[7] The foreign community in Guangzhou was quite large in the ninth century, as Abū Zayd reports that some 120,000 Muslims, Jews, Christians and Parsis were killed when the city was taken in 264/878 by Huang Chao, a rebel against the ruling Tang dynasty.[8] The reasons behind the massacre are not clear, and it is not recorded whether similar depredations were inflicted on Islamic communities in the ports further north. Given that Guangzhou's early Muslim and other foreign communities would have arrived by sea, they would probably have been connected with similar communities in South-East Asia at this time. Flight from the massacre would thus have undoubtedly been towards South-East Asia. The successive Arab geographers wrote of many places in South-East Asia between the second/eighth and third/ninth centuries, many experienced at first hand by their informers, suggesting that Islamic traders were regularly passing through and perhaps sojourning in the port-polities of South-East Asia.[9]

The fourth/tenth century saw the development of further linkages between the Middle East and South-East Asia through the ports of the Indian subcontinent,[10] and at the same time there is much evidence of Islamic connections between China and South-East Asia. During this early

6 Again 'Da-shi'. See Liu Xu *et al.*, *Jiu Tang shu* [*Old history of the Tang dynasty*], (Beijing, 1975), *juan* 10.

7 Michael Flecker, 'A ninth-century AD Arab or Indian shipwreck in Indonesia: First evidence for direct trade with China', *World Archaeology*, 32, 3 (Feb. 2001), pp. 335–54.

8 Note, by comparison, the 10,000 Muslim population of Chaul (=Saymur), the main port for the Konkan coast as given by al-Maʿsūdī. Wink suggests that the exodus of Arabs from China at this time was responsible for the rise of the major ports in the Thai isthmian region, particularly Kalāh. See André Wink, *Al-Hind: The making of the Indo-Islamic world*, (Leiden, 1990), vol. I, p. 84.

9 See G. R. Tibbetts, *A study of the Arabic texts containing material on South-East Asia* (Leiden, 1979).

10 As detailed in André Wink's contribution above, Chapter 2, and his *Al-Hind*, vol. I, pp. 67–83.

period, Chinese texts record the arrival at the Northern Song court (at Kaifeng) of envoys from Da-shi (the Arab lands), the Cōla empire, Zābaj/ Zābag[11] (likely Sriwijaya) and Champa, all bearing names which can be reconstructed as being Muslim. These arrivals reflect the great maritime trade route which connected the Arab lands with China, passing through southern India, Zābaj/Sriwijaya in Sumatra and Champa in what is today central Vietnam. It thus appears that during this century, the more prominent Muslim communities in South-East Asia likely resided in or traded out of the capital of Zābaj (either Palembang or Jambi) and the capital of Champa.

The listing of the names of the envoys who arrived in China in the fourth/ tenth and fifth/eleventh centuries (see Appendix 1, at the end of this chapter) suggests a number of salient points. That the envoys to China from the polities of Zābaj and Champa during this period were Muslim is undoubted, and verified by their names. The 'tribute' missions to China were often the only way to obtain trade concessions in China, and it is thus obvious why merchants desired to be recognised as representatives of South-East Asian polities in coming to the Song court.[12] Whether these merchants were trading on their own account, acting as agents for local rulers or some combination of the two remains unknown, but we can say with some certainty that Muslim merchants were well ensconced in South-East Asia by the fourth/tenth century. The names borne by these people, or at least the Chinese equivalents which the texts ascribed to them, are interesting in themselves, and the repetition of the same names often associated with different states suggests that these merchants were acting as 'envoys' for a range of polities. Some also appear to have become part of the ruling structure. The viceroy of Champa in 357/968 was named in Chinese sources as Li Nou, which might be tentatively reconstructed as ʿAli Nūr. It is also apparent, again from Chinese texts, that Muslim traders were operating into China through Brunei in Borneo and Butuan in the modern Philippines by the early fifth/eleventh century.[13] Further, in one of the few references to Muslims in the Cambodian court, in

11 For details of which see Michael Laffan, *Finding Java: Muslim nomenclature of insular Southeast Asia from Śrîvijaya to Snouk Hurgronje*, Asia Research Institute Working Paper Series, 52, Singapore (Nov. 2005).

12 Elizabeth Lambourn's research (e.g. 'Tombstones, texts and typologies – seeing Sources for the early history of Islam in Southeast Asia', *Journal of the Economic and Social History of the Orient*, 51, 2 (2008), pp. 252–86) suggests that, at least in the subcontinent, some Muslim merchants were formally integrated into the administrative structures of coastal polities and thus did operate as formal envoys of those polities.

13 Friedrich Hirth and W. W. Rockhill, *Chau Ju-Kua* (St Petersburg, 1911; repr. Taipei, 1970), p. 157.

about 290/903, Ibn Rusta wrote that an Arab merchant, Abū ʿAbd Allāh Muḥammad bin Isḥāq, had spent two years at the court of the Khmer ruler, presumably at Angkor.[14] And in a recently excavated shipwreck found in the ocean 100 kilometres north of Java and dated to approximately 349/960, there was discovered a stone mould for casting dual medallions, both bearing an Islamic inscription which has been tentatively identified as reading in three lines ʿAl-mulk li-llāhi / al-wahid / al-qahhar' (Fig. 1).[15] The function of such medallions remains unknown, but the ship's cargo suggests a regional trading vessel touching at a range of South-East Asian ports.[16] Arab texts also provide us with details of the South-East Asian ports visited by Middle Eastern traders during this period.[17]

What are particularly notable about the envoys from South-East Asian ports to China during the fourth/tenth and fifth/eleventh centuries are their names. The vast majority of them, according to the Chinese sources, bore a 'surname' – either Li (李) or Pu (蒲), followed by phonetic representations of names which are obviously Islamic. The likelihood of all these people being of the same two families is almost negligible. These merchants, some of whom were apparently Sino-Arab, had thus either adopted a surname to accord with

14 P.-Y. Manguin, 'The introduction of Islam into Champa', in Alijah Gordon (ed.), *The propagation of Islam in the Indonesian–Malay archipelago* (Kuala Lumpur, 2001), p. 293, after Gabriel Ferrand, *Relations de voyages et textes géographiques, arabes, persans et turks relatifs à l'Extrême-Orient du VIII au XVIII siècles* (Paris, 1912).

15 'Allah, the Possessor of all Sovereignty, the One and Only, the Dominator'. The transcription follows a reading by Elizabeth Lambourn.

16 This tenth-century wreck, assigned the name *Five Dynasties Wreck*, was excavated in 2005. Much Middle Eastern glass as well as a huge range of Chinese ceramics and South-East Asian commodities were found on the wreck. Another tenth-century wreck discovered in the Java Sea, and known as the *Intan*, has also been excavated and analysed. For details, see Michael Flecker, 'The archaeological excavation of the 10th century Intan wreck', Ph.D. thesis, National University of Singapore (2001). Published in the BAR International Series 1047 (Oxford, 2002). For details of the cargoes of these wrecks, see http://maritime-explorations.com.

17 Including the work of Abū Zayd (303/916) which mentions Zābaj and Qmār; the *Murūj al-dhahab* of Maʿsūdī (fourth/tenth century) which mentions Zābaj, China, India, Kalāh, Sirandīb, Sribuza and the sea of Ṣanf; the work of Abū Dulaf (*c.* 330/940) which recorded Sandābil, China, Kalāh and Qamrūn; the work of Ibn Serapion (*c.* 340/950) which mentions Kalāh, Zābaj, Harang and Fanṣūr; the work of Ibn al-Nadīm (378/988) which notes Qmār, Ṣanf and Lūqīn; the *ʿAjā'ib al-Hind* (*c.* 390/1000) which mentions Malāyu, China, Ṣanf, Mā'it, Sribuza, Zābaj, Lāmurī, Fanṣūr, Kalāh and Qāqulla; the *Mukhtasar al-ʿajā'ib* (*c.* 390/1000) which records Ṣanf, Kalāh, Jāba, Salāhit and Zābaj; Bīrūnī's *India* (early fifth/eleventh century) which records Zābaj and Qmār; the work of Marwazī (*c.* 515/1120) which records Zābaj and Lankabālūs; and the text of Idrīsī (of the mid-sixth/twelfth century) which lists Zābaj, Karimata, Rāmnī, China, Qmur, Niyān, Bālūs, Kalāh, Harang, Jāba, Salāhit, Mā'it, Tiyūma, Ṣanf, Qmār, Lūqīn and China. See Tibbetts, *A study of the Arabic texts* and Gabriel Ferrand, *Relations de voyages et texts rélatifs à l'Extrême Orient*, 2 vols. (Paris, 1913–14). See also, for some new interpretations, Laffan, *Finding Java*.

1 Mould for jewellery, bearing inscription 'Al-mulk li-llāhi / al-wahid / al-qahhar'. This was recovered from a mid-fourth/tenth-century shipwreck in the Java Sea and is one of the earliest known physical vestiges of Islam in South-East Asia.

Chinese expectations, or provided an 'origin' or 'genealogy' name which was then used as a surname either by themselves or by the Chinese chroniclers or both. It is now accepted that 'Li' derived from "Ali' and 'Pu' represents Abū.

As can be seen from the listing in Appendix 1, envoys to China from maritime polities and bearing the 'surname' Li are recorded regularly in Chinese texts beginning in the 350s/960s. This is not to say that such people had not been travelling to Chinese ports and polities prior to that. It is just that these are the earliest of such detailed sources available to us. During the fourth/tenth century, the majority of these Li-'surnamed' envoys came from San-fo-qi/Zābaj and Champa, with some from the Arab lands and one from Butuan in the southern Philippines.

2 A *tasbih* recovered from a mid-fourth/tenth-century shipwreck in the Java Sea and one of the earliest known physical vestiges of Islam in South-East Asia.

Zhao Ru-gua's (趙汝适) *Zhu-fan-zhi* (諸蕃志) ('Account of the various *fan*') of 622/1225 also includes references to envoys 'surnamed' Li during the fourth/tenth century. He notes, for example,

> In the fourth year of the *shun-hua* period [383/993], they [the country of Da-shi] sent tribute through the Assistant Envoy Li-a-wu (李亞勿) ['Ali Aḥmad], who stated, at an audience granted him in the Ch'ung-Chong Hall [of the palace], that his country bordered on Ta-ts'in, and that it produced ivory and rhinoceros horns. The Emperor T'ai-tsung asked him how rhinoceros and elephants were captured. He replied, 'To capture elephants, we use decoy elephants to get so near them that we can catch them with a big lasso. To catch a rhinoceros, a man with a bow and arrow climbs a big tree, where he watches for the animal until he can shoot and kill it. The young rhinoceros are not shot as they can be caught.'[18]

A reference to this mission is also included in *juan* 490 of the *Song Shi*, where it is recorded that the head of the mission was Pu Xi-mi (Abū Ḥāmid?), the master of an Arab vessel. It noted that, as Pu Xi-mi was old and sick, he sent his assistant Li Ya-wu with his credentials to the court on his behalf. The mention of methods for capturing rhinoceros and elephants suggests that at least the 'Da-shi' deputy envoy – 'Ali Aḥmad – was domiciled in Sumatra or Champa.

While not all of the names of these Li-'surnamed' envoys can be reconstructed, and some of those from Champa may actually be Chinese or Viet in

18 Hirth and Rockhill, *Chau Ju-kua*, pp. 117–18.

origin, there are sufficient names which can be firmly reconstructed to conclude that the people who bore them were Muslims. That this name represented ''Ali' is widely acknowledged. The question then arises as to why so many of these Islamic envoys should have borne the name ''Ali' or have had it assigned to them by the Chinese chroniclers.

One possibility is that the people who adopted or were assigned the 'Li' surname were those who traced their religious origins to ʿAli ibn Abī Ṭālib, the son-in-law of the Prophet, and who thus were ʿAlids/Shīʿa.[19] Did they perhaps move into South-East Asia as a result of persecutions in the Arab lands? An eighth/fourteenth-century Arab source suggests that was indeed the case. The description of Ṣanf (Champa) from Mehren's edition of Dimashqī (pp. 168–9) has been translated from the Arabic by Mike Laffan, and notes:[20]

> the city of Ṣanf is on the coast and its people are Muslims, Christians and idolaters. The Islamic call (*daʿwa*) reached them in the time of Uthman (may God be pleased with him).

An interpolation from a variant edition continues:

> The ʿAliyyūn fleeing from the Bani Ummaya and al-Ḥajjāj[21] settled there and entered the Sea of Ziftī[22] and settled on [p. 169] the island for which they are known to this day.[23]

Even though this is from an eighth/fourteenth-century text, it suggests a tradition that ʿAlids had been in the South-East Asian region from the time of the third caliph ʿUthmān, who died in 35/656.[24] It also provides powerful

19 On the emergence and evolution of the Shīʿites (more formally *shīʿat ʿAlī*, 'the party of ʿAlī'), see Chase F. Robinson's 'The rise of Islam, 600–705' (*The new Cambridge history of Islam*, vol. I, ch. 5).

20 Personal correspondence, June 2005. Mehren, August Ferdinand, *Manuel de la cosmographic du moyenâge traduit de l'arabe 'Nokhbet ed-dahr fi 'Adjaib-il-birr wal-bahr' de Shems ed-Din Abou-ʿAbdallah* Chapter 2 *Moh'ammed de Damas, et accompagné d'éclaiteissements* (Copenhagen, 1874).

21 For al-Ḥajjāj, see www.princeton.edu/~batke/itl/denise/hajjaj.htm. In his chapter above, André Wink notes that some of the Mappilas of the Malabar coast also traced their origins to those who fled from al-Ḥajjāj.

22 Laffan assumes that Ziftī (زفتي) should be read as Zanqī or Zanqay (زنقي) and that the following insular reference is to Hainan.

23 Pierre-Yves Manguin provides another translation of this from Ferrand's French version: 'the country of Champa, with its principal town of the same name ... is peopled by Muslims, Christians and idolators. The Muslim religion went there in the time of Othman ... and the Alids, expelled by the Omeyyads and by Hajjaj, took refuge there.', Manguin, 'The introduction of Islam into Champa', pp. 290–1.

24 Similar claims were made by Marvazī (sixth/twelfth century) and ʿAufī (seventh/thirteenth century). See D. D. Leslie, *Islam in traditional China* (Canberra, 1986), p. 39 and S. Q. Fatimi, *Islām comes to Malaysia* (Singapore, 1963), pp. 53–6.

support for the thesis that the people surnamed 'Li' in the Chinese texts were descendants of refugee ʿAlids,[25] who adopted that 'surname' through their religious affiliation with ʿAli ibn Abī Ṭālib. We can also draw comparisons with the names of the Muslim rulers of Kilwa on the East African coast, albeit of a slightly later date.[26]

What is also worth noting is that we observe no more confirmed Islamic envoys to China bearing the Li 'surname' after the first two decades of the fifth/eleventh century, suggesting that perhaps the Cōla attacks on maritime South-East Asia in 415/1024,[27] which were obviously quite traumatic for the region, affected the traders who bore this 'surname'.[28] This further suggests that these traders/envoys had been based at the port/s of Sriwijaya.

A selection of envoy names which included the Pu 'surname', extracted from Chinese texts relating to the tenth–twelfth centuries, is provided in Appendix 2. Again, given the reconstructions, there can be little doubt that the majority of the envoys bearing these names were Muslims. The list of polities represented overlaps a great deal with those from which the 'Li' envoys came – San-fo-qi/Zābaj, Champa and the Arab lands – but with occasional envoys noted from Bo-ni/Brunei, Java and Zhu-nian/the Cōla empire. In one case, comprising two references, we can identify the envoy from 'the Arab lands' as having had (or having been assigned) a name which can be reconstructed as Abū Maḥmūd Tabrīzī – suggesting that he was either from or was associated with the city of Tabrīz.

Some other interesting elements are notable. One envoy, Pu Ma-wu (蒲麻勿) – whose name can be reconstructed, with Hokkien or Cantonese pronunciation, as Abū Maḥmūd – is recorded as being an envoy of the Arab lands in 466/1073 and as a representative of Champa in 479/1086. Does this suggest a wide-ranging trader who represented a variety of people or polities in the tribute-trade with Song China?

25 For whom, see *EI*[2] 'Alids' (Bernard Lewis).

26 The period from the fourth/tenth century to the fifth/eleventh century was a key period in the introduction of Islam to the East African coast. The founder of Kilwa was known as ʿAli ibn al-Hussain ibn ʿAli, while the frequency of the name ʿAli among subsequent rulers suggests that the name had a special significance for some Islamic communites in this period. Joäo de Barros, *Da Asia*, four *Decadas* in 9 vols. (Lisbon, 1777), I: Livro VIII: Cap. VI notes, from the chronicle existing at that time, rulers of Kilwa with the names Alé Bumale, Alé Bufoloquete, Alé Bonebaquer, Alé Ben Daúte and Alé Boni.

27 For which see G. Coedès, *The Indianized states of Southeast Asia* (Honolulu, 1968), pp. 141–4, and Hermann Kulke, K. Kesavapany and Vijay Sakhuja (eds.), *Nagapattinam to Suvarnadwipa: Reflections on the Chola naval expeditions to Southeast Asia* (Singapore, 2009).

28 The last Muslim envoy from San-fo-qi to China in the first half of the fifth/eleventh century was Abū Abd Allāh in 419/1028. The next envoy was Di-hua-jia-luo (Dewakara) in 468/1077. This fifty-year hiatus seems to suggest that the Cōla attacks on the Sriwijayan realm had quite serious repercussions.

As noted above, the frequency of the appearance of Li-'surname' trader-envoys in Chinese texts declined after the first few decades of the fifth / eleventh century, but those bearing the Pu 'surname' seem to have continued their links with the Chinese court, almost as many arriving in China during the fifth / eleventh century as in the fourth / tenth. It was also people bearing the Pu 'surname' who were to later settle in China and become important in the maritime trade relations of the Southern Song, of which more below.

From whence came the Pu 'surname'? In their translation and study of the account of San-fo-qi[29] in Zhao Rugua's *Zhu-fan-zhi*, Hirth and Rockhill record that 'a large proportion of the people of the country are surnamed "P'u" (蒲)'. A similar claim was made for Hainan at about the same time. These translators also drew attention to the likely equivalence between 'Pu' and the Arabic *kunya* element Abū.[30] Today it is widely accepted that the Chinese Pu, as used as a 'surname' for maritime traders, indeed derives from the Arabic 'Abū'. But, while the 'surname' Pu was apparently derived from the Arabic *kunya* element Abū, it was used in a very different way within the Chinese texts in assigning names to these Muslim traders.

That the activities of those Muslim maritime traders who were 'surnamed' Pu in the Chinese records were not greatly affected by the Cōla attacks of the early fifth / eleventh century suggests that a large number were based in the ports of Champa rather than Sriwijaya. But their links with China were to grow ever closer over the ensuing centuries. In 292/904, the head of the foreigners in Guangzhou / Canton was recorded as Pu Ho-li (Abū 'Ali).[31]

In 376/986, a member of the Pu clan – Pu Luo-e (Abū Nūr?) – led members of his community from Champa to Hainan to escape what is described in the *Song Hui-yao* as pressure from Jiaozhou (the early Viet polity).[32] Two years later, another Muslim from Champa, Hu-xuan (Ḥusayn), reportedly led 300 members of his clan to Guangzhou.[33] This suggests, first, that these Muslim

29 The Chinese transcription of the name Zābaj / Zābag, for which see Laffan, *Finding Java*.

30 Hirth and Rockhill, *Chau Ju-kua*, p. 60. Their note to this part of the text (p. 64 n. 3) suggests: '*P'u* stands for *Bū*, an abbreviation of *Abū* "father", which precedes so many Arabic names. The phrase 多姓蒲 "many are surnamed P'u", occurring here and there in Chinese ethnographical literature may safely be taken to indicate Arab settlements. Hirth, *Die Insel Hainan* 487, note.'

31 Wang Bu *et al.*, *Tang Hui-yao* [*Collected statutes of the Tang*] (Beijing, 1957), *juan* 100, p. 1799. See Leslie, *Islam in traditional China*, p. 38.

32 See Geoff Wade, *Champa in the Song Hui-yao*, Asia Research Institute Working Paper Series, 53 (Singapore, Nov. 2005).

33 See Appendix 3 below. See also Manguin, 'The introduction of Islam into Champa', p. 292.

groups in Champa were quite large and, second, that in the late fourth/tenth century, they had began to establish Islamic communities in the ports of Hainan and Guangzhou.

The Champa Muslims who settled in Hainan appear to have been key links between Islamic communities in Champa and those in China. An eleventh/seventeenth-century Chinese encyclopaedia, *Gujin tushu jicheng*, which brings together much earlier material, informs us of the following about Aizhou, which was located on the southern coast of Hainan:

> The foreigners [here] were originally from Champa. During the Song and Yuan dynasties [tenth–thirteenth centuries], because of great disorder, they brought their families in ships and came to this place. They settled along the coast and these places are now called 'foreigners' villages' or 'foreigners' coast'. The people now registered in Sanya village are all of this tribe. Many of them are surnamed 'Pu' and they do not eat pork. Within the home, they do not worship their ancestors, but they have a deity hall, where they chant scriptures and worship their deity. Their language is similar to that of the Hui-hui[34]... They do not marry the natives and the latter do not marry them.

Here, then, we have strong evidence of a Muslim community, including many members of the Pu clan, tied to both Champa and China and situated on the maritime route linking the two.[35] Little is heard of these communities during the fifth/eleventh century, but we do have an account from *Dongnan jiwen* (東南記聞), a Yuan work which refers to Song dynasty events. It notes of the period: 'Many Sea Lao (海獠) lived scattered about in Canton. The most prominent among them was a man surnamed Pu (蒲) who was by birth a noble of Chan-ch'öng [Champa]. Later on, he took up his permanent residence in China, to attend to his import and export trade. He lived inside the city where his home was furnished in the most luxurious fashion, for in wealth he was the first of the time.'[36] This was the beginning of the Pu clan in China – a major element in the story of Islam in the maritime realm which connected South-East Asia and South China, and of which more below.

34 Referring mainly to Islamic peoples of Central Asia.

35 Hirth also cites from the *Tushu jicheng* (*juan* 1380) a fourteenth-century reference to a temple at the port of Liantang on Hainan, where the deity was known as *Bo-zhu* (舶主), or Master of the Ship, where pork was forbidden and where everyone referred to the temple as the *fan-shen-miao* (番神廟), or 'temple of the foreign deity'. See Kuwabara Jitsuzō, 'On P'u Shou-kêng', *Memoirs of the Research Department of the Toyō Bunko*, 2 (1928), p. 21.

36 Hirth and Rockhill, *Chau Ju-kua*, p. 16 n. 2. See also Kuwabara, 'On P'u Shou-kêng', 1, p. 44 for full text.

Another mystery of this period relates to the polity of Kalāh/Killah/Kra, which was, according to the Arab geographers, an entrepôt, a place marking the border of India, 'the general rendezvous of the ships of Sīrāf and Oman, where they meet the ships of China', a producer of tin, and a place frequented by Indians. The conditions described are all met by a polity centred on the portages linking the western coastal region of what is today the southern Thai peninsula, and its eastern seaboard, with tin being found throughout the Phuket and Kedah areas, and trans-peninsular portage available between 'the ships of Sīrāf and Oman' and the ships of China. In the Chinese texts, the polity was named Gu-luo[37] and in these texts it is noted that Gu-luo controlled twenty-four subordinate polities and had a sizeable army. In the story of Islam in South-East Asia, this must have been one of the main ports frequented by ships from the Arab and Persian worlds from the second/eighth to fourth/tenth centuries, and in fact it was the South-East Asian polity most frequently mentioned in the Arab texts. Its precise identification, location and extent remain to be ascertained, but its centre likely lay near Takuapa on the peninsula. The excavation in Sungei Bujang, Kedah, of two silver coins issued by the ʿAbbāsid caliph Al-Mutawakkil (r. 232–47/847–61) suggests that Kedah was not outside this trade zone in the third/ninth century.[38]

We also need to examine the Sumatran port-polity of Barus for what it tells us of Islamic traders in the fourth/tenth and fifth/eleventh centuries. References to Barus/Fanṣūr, famed as a port for camphor exports, date back to the second/eighth century.[39] Barus was also already well known to the Arab geographers in the fourth/tenth century as a source of excellent camphor, the Fanṣūrī camphor.[40] We can certainly thus assume that Islamic merchants traded through this port during its heyday in the third/ninth to fifth/eleventh centuries in their quest for camphor and other Sumatran

37 Likely 'Kra'.

38 For further details, see Tibbetts, *A study of the Arabic texts*, pp. 118–28. The Middle Eastern ceramics found in the area are described in Bennet Bronson, 'Chinese and Middle Eastern trade in southern Thailand during the 9th century AD', in Amara Srisuchat (ed.), *Ancient trades and cultural contacts in Southeast Asia* (Bangkok, 1996), pp. 181–200. For the two silver coins see H. G. Quaritch-Wales, 'Archaeological researches on ancient Indian colonization in Malaya', *JMBRAS*, 18, 1 (1940), pp. 32–3.

39 Under the early name Po-lu-shi and Po-luo-suo (sometimes obviously confused in Chinese texts with Bo-si or Persia) and later under the names Bin-su, Bian-shu and Bin-cuo for Pansur/Pancur. See Roderich Ptak, 'Possible Chinese references to the Barus area (Tang to Ming)', in Claude Guillot (ed.), *Histoire de Barus, Sumatra: Le site de Lobu Tua, I – Études et documents*, Cahier d'Archipel 30 (Paris, 1998), pp. 119–38.

40 See Tibbetts, *A study of the Arabic texts*, pp. 92–3, 95–6, 114–15, 140–3. Jane Drakard has also studied these sources in her 'An Indian Ocean port: Sources for the earlier history of Barus', *Archipel*, 37 (1989), pp. 53–82.

products.[41] The third/ninth- to fifth/eleventh-century Islamic glass and ceramics excavated at the site also suggest linkages with the Middle East[42] and these correlate with the Chinese ceramics of the same period discovered there.[43] An important piece excavated in Barus is a glass seal of the fourth/tenth to fifth/eleventh centuries, likely deriving originally from Iran, and bearing a Kufic-style inscription 'Allāh.Muḥammad'.[44] This and the other Middle Eastern trade products certainly suggest an Islamic presence in west Sumatra during these centuries. Separately, it appears that Islamic influence continued in Champa. Zhao Rugua noted that in 377/987 the Cham polity of Panḍuranga brought tribute to the Chinese court, in the company of those of Da-shi (Arabs).[45]

Two political events affecting Muslims in South-East Asia stand out from the available records of the fourth/tenth and fifth/eleventh centuries. As noted above, some hundreds of Muslims removed in the 370s/980s to Hainan and Guangzhou to escape political turmoil in Champa. It is likely that it was these people who formed the nucleus of the Muslim community at Sanya on the southern coast of Hainan, which has continued into the present day.[46] The other event, reflected in the listings of Muslim envoys to the Song court, was the Cōla attacks on South-East Asia. The reasons for these attacks are not clear, but the possibility that the Cōla ruler Rājēndra I wished to take control of the trade passing through the Straits of Malacca should not be excluded. Raids are suggested for 408/1017 and 416/1025. While missions to China from Da-shi (the 'Arab lands') saw a hiatus from 410/1019 until the 440s/1050s, Champa missions to China led by Muslims continued during this period. It thus appears that Islamic trading links with the Straits were affected by the attacks on, and probable capture of, the major ports in the region by Cōla forces. These military activities likely permanently changed the patterns of Middle Eastern

41 The links between Barus and the various ports of the Middle East are discussed in Claude Guillot (ed.), *Histoire de Barus, Sumatra: Le Site de Lobu Tua, II – Étude archéologique et Documents*, Cahier d'Archipel 30, (Paris, 2003), 'Ch. II – 'Conclusions historiques', pp. 45–6 and 60–2.

42 Claude Guillot and Sonny Ch. Wibisono, 'Le verre à Lobu Tua: Étude préliminaire', in Guillot (ed.), *Histoire de Barus I*, pp. 189–206; and Guillot (ed.), *Histoire de Barus II*, ch. V – 'Céramique du Proche-Orient', pp. 171–96.

43 Marie-France Dupoizat, ch. IV – 'Céramique chinoise', in Guillot (ed.), *Histoire de Barus II*, pp. 103–69.

44 Guillot (ed.), *Histoire de Barus II*. See 'ch. VII – Verre', p. 268, plate 58. See also Ludvik Kalus, 'Le plus ancienne inscription islamique du monde malais?', *Archipel*, 59 (2000), pp. 23–4.

45 Hirth and Rockhill, *Chau Ju-kua*, p. 51.

46 For one of the few historical reports on this community, see Chen Da-sheng and Claudine Salmon, 'Rapport preliminaire sur la découverte de tombes musulmanes dans l'Ile de Hainan', *Archipel*, 38 (1989), pp. 75–106.

trade to the archipelago. We certainly have evidence of the likely related rise of the Tamil guilds in Barus during that century.[47] Muslims resident in Champa, however, continued to operate their tribute-trade missions to China.

Islam in South-East Asia from the eleventh to the thirteenth centuries

By the second half of the fifth/eleventh century, envoy-merchants from the Middle East were again arriving in China by sea, through South-East Asia. This period also saw a major shift in the region's maritime trade, with the Fujian port of Quanzhou eclipsing the former trade centre of Guangzhou. Quanzhou quickly became the site of mosques[48] and Tamil temples, as the maritime merchants from lands extending all the way to West Asia brought trade products to China and took Chinese products on their return journeys. On this voyage, it is clear that Champa was a major staging post. As noted above, Muslim traders were leading Champa missions into China throughout the fourth/tenth and fifth/eleventh centuries. A Chinese official text – the *Song Hui-yao* – records the following of Champa in the fifth/eleventh or sixth/twelfth century: 'There are also mountain cattle, but they cannot be used for ploughing. They are only killed in sacrifice to the spirits. When they are about to be slaughtered, a medium is instructed to offer prayers, which sound thus: "Allāhu Akhbar". In translation, this means: "May he be early reborn."' Here then we have a Chinese account which, although somewhat erroneous in interpretation, clearly records that an important element of animal slaughter in at least part of Champa society was the affirmation of the supreme greatness of Allāh. The same work notes: 'Their customs and clothing are similar to those of the country of Da-shi [the Arab world].' In that the Chinese chronicler considers these to have been aspects of Champa society, there must have been a considerable Islamic community residing in at least the major trade port of that polity during this period. The provenance of two Kufic inscriptions earlier ascribed to Champa has been shown to be very suspect,[49] but are now not needed for us to demonstrate an Islamic community in Champa at this time. That the Islamic communities of China and South-East Asia were intimately

47 See, for example, Y. Subbarayalu, 'The Tamil merchant-guild inscription at Barus: A rediscovery', in Guillot (ed.), *Histoire de Barus I*, pp. 25–33. The inscription is dated to the equivalent of 1088 CE.

48 The oldest mosque in Quanzhou – the Qingjing mosque – reputedly dates from the eleventh century when the port began to rise in importance.

49 Ludvik Kalus, 'Réinterprétation des plus anciennes stèles funéraires islamiques nousantariennes: I. Les deux inscriptions du "Champa"', *Archipel*, 66 (2003).

tied during the sixth/twelfth century is apparent from a comment by al-Idrīsī (493–560/1100–65), who stated that when China was convulsed by troubles, the (Muslim) merchants would descend to the harbours of a place they called Zābaj.[50] This was a reference to the ports of Sumatra and surrounding areas.

Halfway around the globe, in and near the Red Sea, the sixth/twelfth and seventh/thirteenth centuries saw Yemeni ports developing their links with regions to the east under the aegis of the Ayyūbids (566–648/1171–1250) in Egypt and subsequently the local Rasulid dynasty (625–858/1228–1454). This revitalised the luxury and spice trades with India and ports further east, providing further avenues for Muslims to travel to and interact with people from the South-East Asian realm, as well as further reasons for South-East Asians and Chinese to travel to the major Islamic centres in the Middle East.

Quanzhou thus became the end port for the long journey from the Arab and Persian lands, as well as a key port for those Muslims trading from South-East Asia. From the sources we have available, more than half of the foreign trade into Quanzhou appears to have been controlled by Muslims in this period. By the seventh/thirteenth century, when the Mongols ruled over China, it appears that Quanzhou was being administered as a Muslim polity, funded through its trade with South-East Asia and beyond. The boom in maritime trade during the sixth/twelfth and seventh/thirteenth centuries underwrote Islamic power in Quanzhou, and in this, Pu Shougeng and his family were major players.

Islamic links between Quanzhou and Brunei during this period are evidenced by material remains. A grave of a Song-dynasty official surnamed Pu and likely from Quanzhou has been found in Brunei. Dated to the equivalent of 662/1264, it is the earliest Chinese-script gravestone in South-East Asia as well as one of the earliest Muslim gravestones.[51] The Pu clan was a major element in the story of Islam in the maritime realm which connected South-East Asia and south China. One account suggests that an unnamed Pu

50 al-Idrīsī, *Opus geographicum*, ed. E. Cerulli *et al.*, 2 vols. (Rome, 1970), vol. I, p. 62. Cited in Laffan, *Finding Java*, p. 22 n. 65.

51 The assumption is that this official surnamed Pu was, like other members of the Pu clan, a Muslim. There exists in Leran, east Java an Islamic gravestone dated 475/1082 of a woman, the daughter of Maimun. However, there is no firm evidence that the gravestone originated in Java, and it has been suggested that it was possibly brought there as ballast. See Ludvik Kalus and Claude Guillot, 'Réinterprétation des plus anciennes stèles funéraires islamiques nousantariennes: II. La stèle de Leran (Java) datée de 475/1082 et les stèles associées', *Archipel*, 67 (2004), pp. 17–36.

ancestor had originally come to Guangzhou from somewhere in the Arab world and was appointed as the headman of the foreign quarter in that city, eventually becoming the richest man in the entire region. Another version suggests that this person was a noble from Champa which, as noted above, does not preclude him from having been an Arab. Could he have been a descendant of the Pu Luo-e who led his family members to Hainan from Champa in 376/986 following political disturbance in that place? The fact remains that during the sixth/twelfth century a person 'surnamed' Pu, a Muslim, was one of the richest men in the city of Guangzhou, and behind whose residence was a giant 'stupa' that was unlike Buddhist ones. This was likely the minaret of the Huai-sheng-si, the famous mosque of Guangzhou. The wealth of the family, however, declined, and the son of the Guangzhou foreign headman, named Pu Kaizong (蒲開宗), removed the family to Quanzhou,[52] as that port rose to dominate the trade with South-East Asia and beyond. It was his son, Pu Shougeng (蒲壽庚), who was to become famed in the histories of Quanzhou, Chinese Islam and maritime trade with South-East Asia.[53] Reputedly for his assistance in suppressing pirates in the region of Quanzhou, Pu Shougeng was rewarded by the Song court in 672/1274 with the position of maritime trade supervisor in the port. All maritime trade through Quanzhou was subject to his control, and as this was the major port of the entire polity, the opportunities for gain would have been enormous. He and his brother also operated many ships. Pu Shougeng was subsequently appointed to even higher office with a provincial post, only a few years before the Yuan armies crushed the Southern Song capital at Hangzhou and the Song dynasty came to an end.

Even before they took Hangzhou, the Yuan generals had recognised the power of Pu Shougeng and his brother in south-eastern China and had sent envoys to invite them to side with the Yuan. The Pu brothers knew where their future lay, and they gave their allegiance to the incoming Mongols, probably by 674/1276. The importance of this to the Yuan was enormous, as it provided them with a local regime possessing access to the sea, something which the Mongols had never commanded. Their new ally subsequently massacred the Song imperial clansmen who resided in Quanzhou, showing his allegiance to the Mongols. The Yuan rulers richly rewarded those who had assisted them and Pu Shougeng was appointed as the Grand Commander of

52 This is noted in He Qiaoyuan, *Min Shu* (閩書) [*An account of Fujian*] (Fuzhou, 1994), *juan* 152.

53 For the most detailed account of Pu Shougeng, see Kuwabara, 'On P'u Shou-kêng', 2, pp. 1–79, and 7 (1935), pp. 1–104.

Fujian and Guangdong, and subsequently as a vice minister of the Fujian administration. Pu was tasked with assisting the Mongols in both promoting maritime trade and providing ships and personnel for some of the Mongol invasions of overseas polities. It is not surprising that the first countries to respond to Pu Shougeng's invitation to resume trade were Champa in South-East Asia and Ma'abar on the subcontinent – both major trading polities with large Muslim populations. One of the latest reports we have of Pu Shougeng, dating from 680/1281, notes that he had been ordered by the Yuan emperor to build 200 ocean-going ships, of which 50 had been finished.

The arrival of the Yuan forces in southern China in the 670s/1270s and the violence which accompanied that arrival had apparently spurred some Muslims to leave Chinese ports and, as in the past, flee south. Li Tana has examined the Vietnamese annals on this point and found reference to Muslim refugees from China arriving in the Vietnamese polity in 672/1274.[54] This date fits well with the last-ditch Song defence of Yangzhou during the Yuan attack on that city in 673/1275. Yangzhou was a very cosmopolitan city and it would not have been surprising if some of the Muslims resident there would have opted for safer climes to the south prior to the attack.[55]

At approximately the same time, on the other side of the archipelago, we begin to see evidence of the emergence of Muslim rulers in South-East Asia. An Islamic gravestone is reported for a Sultan Sulaymān bin ʿAbd Allāh bin al-Baṣīr of Lamreh dated 608/1211.[56] The dating of the gravestone remains controversial, but if confirmed this will be the first evidence of a Muslim ruler in the Nusantaran world. Separately, in the account of his return journey by sea from China, Marco Polo reported in the 690s/1290s that the Sumatran city of Pĕrlak/Ferlec was Muslim,[57] but neighbouring urban centres named Basman and Samara were not. The latter polity was more than likely Samudera, where a gravestone of the reputed first Islamic ruler of that

54 Personal communication from Li Tana. For original text, see Chen Ching-ho, 陳荊和(編校)校合本 '大越史記全書' (3 本), (*Đại Việt sử ký toàn thư*) (Tokyo, 1985–6), pp. 348–9.

55 One apparent victim of the battles at this time was Pu Ha-ting, a *sayyid* of the sixteenth generation and builder of the Xianhe mosque in Yangzhou, who died in 673/1275. See Leslie, *Islam in traditional China*, p. 48.

56 Suwedi Montana, 'Nouvelles données sur les royaumes de Lamuri et Barat', *Archipel*, 53 (1997), pp. 85–96. See p. 92. There remains much dispute over the dating and other aspects of this gravestone.

57 'This kingdom, you must know, is so frequented by the Saracen merchants that they have converted the natives to the Law of Mahommet – I mean the townspeople only, for the hill people live for all the world like beasts.' Henry Yule (trans. and ed.), *The book of Ser Marco Polo*, 2 vols., 3rd edn (London, 1929), vol. II, p. 284.

polity – Sultan Malik al-Ṣāliḥ – dated 696 / 1297 has been found.[58] In the 680s / 1280s, two envoys came to the Yuan court from Samudera (Su-mu-da), and they bore patently Islamic names – Ḥasan and Sulaymān. These phenomena suggest a new age in the relationship between Islam and South-East Asia, with rulers of polities adopting the new religion. That the rise of these Islamic polities was linked with the rise and expansion of the Mamlūks (648–923 / 1250–1517) in Egypt is suggested by the adoption by Samuderan sultans of the title *al-Malik al-Ẓaḥir*, an apparent commemoration of the Mamlūk sultan al-Malik al-Ẓaḥir Rukn al-Dīn Baybars al-Bunduqdārī (r. 658–76 / 1260–77) of Egypt and Syria, who had defeated the Seventh Crusade sent by Louis IX, as well as the Mongol forces at ʿAyn Jālūt in Palestine in 658 / 1260. The indigenous tradition relating to these earliest Islamic polities in Sumatra was later recorded, somewhat anachronistically, in *Hikayat Raja-raja Pasai*.[59]

More direct links between Samudera and the ports of western India are evidenced by the material remains of the age. The cemeteries of Samudera have a range of gravestones, some with *bismillāhs* in Kufic script, and these have been shown to be linked with the gravestones of Cambay in Gujarat. These stones were seemingly imported from Cambay, but were carved locally with local artistic elements.[60] Muslim traders from the Arab world had long traded through Cambay, and Elizabeth Lambourn provides a revealing study detailing the pre-conquest regional networks of Islamic judges and clerics connecting Rasulid Yemen with the ports along the western coast of India.[61] It was only in the early eighth / fourteenth century however that Gujarat was taken by the Khaljīs and Islamic rule was instituted in the region. The links between Gujarat and the archipelago strengthened through the eighth / fourteenth and ninth / fifteenth centuries, with 1,000 Gujarati merchants residing in Melaka in the early

58 For further details of the gravestones, see Elizabeth Lambourn, 'The formation of the *batu Aceh* tradition in fifteenth-century Samudera-Pasai', *Indonesia and the Malay World*, 32 (2004), pp. 211–48.

59 See A. H. Hill, 'Hikayat Raja-raja Pasai', *Journal of the Malaysian Branch of the Royal Asiatic Society*, 33, 2 (June 1960).

60 More details can be found in Lambourn, 'The formation of the *batu Aceh* tradition'. See also Lambourn, 'From Cambay to Pasai and Gresik – the export of Gujarati grave memorials to Sumatra and Java in the 15th century AD', *Indonesia and the Malay World*, 31, 90 (2003), pp. 221–89; and Lambourn, 'La production de marbre sculpté à Cambaye au Gujarat et son exportation dans l'Océan Indien (XIIIe–XVe siècles Ap. J. C.)', in J. M. dos Santos Alves, C. Guillot and R. Ptak (eds.), *Mirabilia Asiatica: Produtos raros no comércio marítimo. Produits rares dans le commerce maritime. Seltene Waren im Seehandel* (Wiesbaden and Lisbon, 2003), pp. 209–52.

61 Elizabeth Lambourn, 'India from Aden: *Khuṭba* and Muslim urban networks in late thirteenth-century India', in Kenneth R. Hall (ed.), *Secondary cities and urban networking in the Indian Ocean realm c. 1400–1800*, (Lanham, MD, 2008), pp. 55–98.

tenth/sixteenth century when the Portuguese arrived there. Such connections drew Kern to note: 'The gravestones erected on Malik al-Ṣāliḥ's grave were brought in ready-made from Cambay.[62] This is then where we must look for the source of the spiritual and material links which joined Samudera to the world of Islām.'[63] This opinion is disputed by other scholars. Marrison, for example, proposes that south India was a far more obvious source, given the long-term existence of Islamic communities there, the local title Perumal used in both southern India and Pasai, along with the dominance of the Shāfiʿī school, something which was not the case in Gujarat.[64] Marrison was, in some ways, repeating the arguments put earlier by Snouk Hurgronje.[65] The arguments hinge on the emergence of Islam in Kerala, but the chronology of this remains a disputed issue. While there are Islamic gravestones there dated as early as the second/eighth century, the tradition of local adherents appears to date only from the early sixth/twelfth century.[66]

The new appearance of the name 'Java' in Arab sailing itineraries (with the concurrent decline of the earlier generic term Zābaj) in the early part of the seventh/thirteenth century, and the description of Jāwa as 'one of the lands of China', suggests new trade routes at this time, resultant from changes both in China, where maritime trade was being encouraged by the Southern Song dynasty, and in South-East Asia and India. These changes were also reflected in the patterns of the spread of Islam.

Islam in South-East Asia in the fourteenth and fifteenth centuries

Why Islamic polities should have emerged in northern Sumatra in the seventh/thirteenth century remains an enigma. It is obvious that Muslim traders had been passing and stopping at these port-polities for centuries before this. It is likely that the rise of Islamic states in Sumatra was linked with the decline of the Cōla dynasty in southern India, the collapse of that country into war and the end

62 Lambourn dismisses this and notes that these gravestones were in fact ninth/fifteenth- or tenth/sixteenth-century local remakes of earlier stones, perhaps commissioned by the Acehnese after their conquest of Samudera-Pasai in 1524.

63 R. A. Kern, *De Islam in Indonesië* (The Hague, 1947), p. 9.

64 G. E. Marrison, 'The coming of Islam to the East Indies', *Journal of the Malaysian Branch of the Royal Asiatic Society*, 24, 1 (Feb. 1951), pp. 28–37.

65 G. W. J. Drewes, 'New light on the coming of Islam to Indonesia?', *Bijdragen tot de Taal-, Land- en Volkenkunde*, 124 (1968), p. 441.

66 A. P. Ibrahim Kunju, 'Origin and spread of Islam in Kerala', in Ashgar Ali Engineer (ed.), *Kerala Muslims: A historical perspective* (New Delhi, 1995). See pp. 18–21. See also Chapter 9 in the present volume by Michael Pearson.

of the integrated regional economy which incorporated the northern Sumatran polities. With the rise of the more domestically oriented Vijayanagara in southern India, the linkages of the Hindu–Buddhist polities of Sumatra with the subcontinent would have declined, as would have the Tamil guilds, likely providing new avenues for religious conversion. However, the ports of the Malabar coast and Sumatra continued to be meeting places and commercial marts for traders from Yemen, South-East Asia and China. The expansion of Islamic trading networks, and some have suggested Sufi guilds, along these maritime trade routes appears to have thus burgeoned.

From the eighth/fourteenth century we see growing evidence of the expansion of Islam in South-East Asia. In Sumatra (or al-Jāwa as he referred to it), Ibn Baṭṭūṭa recorded what he, or his informants, observed when passing through the port-polity of Samudera in 746/1345 and 747/1346. He noted that the ruler – one Sultan al-Malik al-Ẓāhir – was 'a Shāfiʿī in *madhhab* and a lover of jurists' who 'often fights against and raids the infidels'. It was further noted that 'the people of his country are Shāfiʿī who are eager to fight infidels and readily go on campaign with him. They dominate the neighbouring infidels who pay *jizya* to have peace.'[67] Through the account provided, we see a polity whose ruler was engaged in frequent *jihād*, who sent missions to Delhi and to Zaitun/Quanzhou, and who, at home, was surrounded by viziers, secretaries, *sharīfs*, jurists, poets and army commanders, and who obviously had close links with Islamic societies to the west, and direct sea links with Quilon. The Shāfiʿī school which the sultan followed has remained important throughout Indonesia and in the coastal areas of India. We should not, however, consider this to have been simply a Middle Eastern society or ruling structure transplanted to South-East Asia. It has been remarked that Ibn Baṭṭūṭa likely concentrated excessively on the cosmopolitan Arab/Iranian aspects of the court, and ignored the Indic and local elements unfamiliar to him. Certainly, the *batu Aceh* of the period reflect a strong indigenous element to the polity.[68]

Ibn Baṭṭūṭa then visited Mul Jāwa, the 'country of the infidels', which is accepted to mean that Islam had not gained any real foothold in the island of Java by the mid-eighth/fourteenth century. The only other major stop on the voyage to China was Ṭawālisī, which has never been definitively identified. The long-standing importance of Champa as a stop on the Islamic trade route to China, however, makes it the leading candidate. This supposition is

67 H. A. R. Gibb, *The travels of Ibn Battuta AD 1325–1354*, trans. with revisions and notes from the Arabic text, ed. C. Defrémery and B. R. Sanguinetti, completed with annotations by C. F. Beckingham, Hakluyt Society (London, 1994), vol. IV, pp. 876–7.

68 Lambourn, 'The formation of the *batu Aceh* tradition'.

supported by Yamamoto Tatsuro's equation of Kailūkarī, the name of the largest city in Ṭawālisī according to Ibn Baṭṭūṭa, with the Cham name Klaung Garai.[69]

The earlier West Asian links of Champa are manifested in the princess whom Ibn Baṭṭūṭa met in this polity, who spoke to him in Turkish, who was literate in Arabic and who wrote out the *bismillāh* in the presence of the visitor. The polity itself, however, he considered to be outside of Islam. He then travelled on to China, where Ibn Baṭṭūṭa noted the option of staying with Muslim merchants resident there, and that in Zaitun/Quanzhou, the 'Muslims live in a separate city'. There he met Muslims from Iṣfahān and Tabrīz. It thus appears that, for Ibn Baṭṭūṭa in the mid-eighth/fourteenth century, all the areas between the Islamic polity at Samudera and China remained outside Islam.

Events which occurred in southern China not long after the visit by Ibn Baṭṭūṭa, however, were to have major effects on Islam in South-East Asia. The port of Quanzhou was controlled by Muslims during this period, the Mongol Yuan rulers including them within the *semu*[70] group of Central Asian and Middle Eastern officials who exercised Yuan power over the Chinese inhabitants. The two major groups competing for power over the city and its foreign trade were the locally born Islamic families, including that of Pu Shougeng, and the newly arrived Iṣfahān group of Persians, both merchants and troops, who had come to the area with the Yuan armies. In the 750s/1350s, a descendant of Pu Shougeng, named Na-wu-na, controlled the local maritime trade supervisorate for the Yuan court, while the Persians were represented by two people – Sai-fu-ding and A-mi-li-ding – both holding military positions as brigade commanders. At a time when the Yuan was in steep decline, and when rebellions against the Yuan administration were occurring widely throughout China, it is not surprising that the tensions in Quanzhou also spilled over. The *Yuan History* tells us: 'In the spring of the seventeenth year of the Zhi-zheng reign [758/1357], the local brigade commanders Sai-fu-ding and A-mi-li-ding rebelled and took control of Quanzhou.' This so-called Iṣfahān[71] rebellion was to last for ten years. It is possible that the prominent merchant

69 The name of a Cham temple complex (Po Klaung Garai) located at Phanrang in what is today Ninh Thuan province. It comprises three towers dating back to about 700/1300, built during the reign of Cham king Jaya Siṃhavarman II. See Tatsuro Yamamoto, 'On Tawalisi as described by Ibn Battuta', *Memoirs of the Research Department of the Toyo Bunko*, 8, 1936, p. 117.

70 A reference to people from Central Asia and West Asia.

71 Chen and Kalus, following Maejima Shinji, suggest an alternative – that the Chinese term 'yi-xi-ba-xi' should be reconstructed as *ispāh* and that it derives from the Persian

Sharaf al-Dīn of Tabrīz, whom Ibn Baṭṭūṭa met in Quanzhou and from whom he noted that he had borrowed money in India, was the same 'Sai-fu-ding' who is mentioned in the Yuan text.[72]

By 763/1362, the forces of Sai-fu-ding controlled much of the area around the provincial capital Fuzhou, but were then defeated by Yuan forces and fled back to Quanzhou, where it is reported that A-mi-li-ding was killed by the maritime trade supervisor Na-wu-na, who seized control of the Iṣfahān forces. He was in turn killed and his forces destroyed in 767/1366. It has been suggested that the members of the Pu Shougeng clan and others from earlier Arab and Cham inflows into Quanzhou were Sunnī, while the Iṣfahān forces were Shīʿite. This possibly intra-Islamic struggle in Quanzhou also quickly involved Mongol forces of the Yuan and then the Chinese themselves who felt that they had been maltreated under Yuan rule. The breakdown of dynastic order gave an opportunity to a more powerful contender for regional power – Chen Youding, a former Yuan general, who was appointed governor of Fujian province. With the assistance of Jin Ji, a general of Persian origin, he began methodically murdering Sunnī followers, as well as destroying Sunnī graves, mosques and residences. It appears that initially the purge was directed at Sunnī followers, but that it was later expanded by some of the forces into a broader anti-Islamic campaign, with the depredations lasting for almost a decade after Chen Youding captured Quanzhou. Those who escaped the purge either fled into the mountains or set sail. This flight of Muslims by sea from Quanzhou and elsewhere in Fujian into South-East Asia in the 760s/1360s greatly stimulated the development of Islam in the latter region. Those who remained in Quanzhou, including the prominent Guo clan, appear to have been descendants of the Persian Shīʿites.

Not much more than a decade after the first massacres in Fujian, Muslim tombs began to appear in Java. Most of these were devoted to elite figures apparently intimately involved with the administration of the Majapahit state. These gravestones (*maesan*) began appearing at Trowulan and Trayala near ancient Majapahit in the 770s/1370s and their dates extend well into the second half of the ninth/fifteenth century.[73] They were inscribed with the *Saka* year in ancient Javanese script on one side of the stone, and with pious

term *sepāh*, meaning 'great army'. See Chen Da-sheng and Ludvik Kalus, *Corpus d'inscriptions arabes et persanes en Chine, 1. Province de Fujian (Quanzhou, Fuzhou, Xiamen)* (Paris, 1991). See p. 45 n. 151.

72 It is also likely not coincident that another senior person whom Ibn Baṭṭūṭa met in Quanzhou was Shaykh al-Islām Kamāl al-Dīn, 'a pious man' who indeed came from Iṣfahān. Was he the other leader of the rebellion, 'A-mi-li-ding' (= Kamāl al-Dīn)?

73 See Louis-Charles Damais, 'Études javanaises: Les tombes musulmans datées de Tralaya', *Bulletin de l'École Française d'Extrême Orient*, 48 (1956), pp. 353–415. See listing and dates of the graves on p. 411.

Islamic inscriptions in Arabic on the other. Given what we know of the situation in Quanzhou in the 760s/1360s and the links already established between Champa and Quanzhou in this period, the existence of the tomb of *Puteri Cĕmpa* (the Champa princess) in Trowulan,[74] dated to 852/1448, underlines the likelihood that these graves belong to Muslims who fled the conflagrations in southern China in the 760s/1360s, and were then engaged in various capacities by the Majapahit court, maintaining links with both Champa and the southern Chinese ports. The sudden appearance of a group of Muslims, possibly Sunnī, intimately tied to the Javanese administration is otherwise difficult to explain. It is possible that this *Puteri Cĕmpa* was Haji Ma Hong Fu's wife, whom Parlindungan's 'Annals of Semarang and Cirebon' tell us, 'had passed away and was buried in Majapahit according to Islamic rites' in or just before 853/1449.[75] Earlier references in these annals tell us that Haji Ma Hong Fu, who had his origins in Yunnan, had been married to the daughter of Haji Bong Tak Keng, who had been appointed by the Chinese in Champa.[76] At Surabaya, the *pĕcat tanda*, that is, the 'head of the market', at Terung was also a Chinese person employed as an official by the Majapahit court, and it was he who protected a young Muslim who had come from Champa and who would later become Raden Rahmat.[77] While Damais and others believe that the people interred in the Trowalan and Trayala graves were Javanese, the possibility should thus also be considered that these were people from abroad who had given their allegiance to the Majapahit polity. New polities on Java also suggest new arrivals at this time. Demak on the northern Javanese coast first appeared in the historical record in 779/1377, and is recorded as having sent 'tribute' to the Ming court in 796/1394. The possible founding of this *pesisir* (coast) polity by refugees in the 760s/1360s or 770s/1370s conforms to all that we know of it. Javanese texts also record Muslim leaders coming to Java from Champa, and settling in the three most important early centres of Islamic propaganda – Surabaya

74 The grave remains today an Islamic pilgrimage site.

75 H. J. de Graaf and G. Th. Pigeaud, *Chinese Muslims in Java in the 15th and 16th centuries: The Malay Annals of Sĕmarang and Cĕrbon*, ed. M. C. Ricklefs, Monash Papers on Southeast Asia, 12 (Melbourne, 1984), p. 20. I am assigning this text more veracity than hitherto accorded to it for reasons detailed below. For Parlindungan see pp. 396–7.

76 *Ibid.*, p. 14. This fits precisely with the date of the Trowulan tomb, but those who are suspicious of the Parlindungan source might point to the fact that Damais's article on the tombs was published in 1956, while Parlindungan's work *Tuanku Rao* within which the 'Annals' are contained, was only published in 1964, allowing for the information on the tombs to be incorporated in the latter work.

77 Denys Lombard and Claudine Salmon, 'Islam and Chineseness', in Gordon, *The Propagation of Islām*, p. 184. See also the correlation in Javanese texts between Champa and the spread of Islam as detailed by Manguin in 'The introduction of Islām into Champa', pp. 294–5.

(Ngampel), Gresik (Giri) and Cirebon (Gunung Jati). By the early ninth/fifteenth century, Gresik had over 1,000 'Chinese' families, likely including the Muslim people of diverse ethnic origins who had fled from Fujian.

Evidence from Sumatra also supports the argument for a flight of hybrid Persian–Arab–Cham–Chinese Muslims out of southern China into maritime South-East Asia during the 760s/1360s. Recent archaeological surveys and excavations in Barus reveal that the earliest Islamic tombstone found there dates from 772/1370,[78] which fits excellently with the chronology proposed above. The name of the woman buried beneath the tombstone – Suy – may be Chinese, while the inscription itself contains Persian grammar and Arabic terms. Thus, the 760s/1360s likely saw the return of an Islamic community to Barus following the driving out of the earlier community in the fifth/eleventh century by the Cōlas. By the beginning of the tenth/sixteenth century, Tomé Pires spoke of Barus as being a wealthy port and well known to the Gujaratis, Persians, Arabs, Tamils and Bengalis.

Brunei's adoption of Islam in this period is reflected in the gravestone of a eighth/fourteenth-century sultan, named 'Mahārājā Brunī', found in the Residency cemetery in Bandar Seri Begawan. Links between that community and China are indicated by the fact that the gravestone was certainly manufactured in Quanzhou and transported to Brunei, as it is almost identical to those carved in China and, like them, is also made of diabase and inscribed completely in Arabic. In Terengganu, a stone inscribed in Malay written in Arabic script and dating from the eighth/fourteenth century suggests that Islamic law was being promoted in at least this estuary of the Malay peninsula. In both these places, there is evidence that Islam had been a recent arrival, and the process of adjustment was still taking place. The Brunei ruler, for example, was still being entitled maharaja[79] while the Terengganu inscription referred to the Almighty by the Sanskritic name 'Dewata Mulia Raya' alongside the name Allāh. In addition, the Terengganu law code provided for differentiated fines depending on social rank, a practice unknown to more orthodox Islam. Kern suggested that 'we have here a stone inscription from a convert, undoubtedly assisted by someone learned in the law, among a population yet to be converted'.[80] The same phenomenon is manifested in two late

78 Ludvik Kalus, ch. XIV 'Les sources épigraphiques musulmanes de Barus', in Guillot (ed.), *Histoire de Barus II*, pp. 303–38. For the tombstone cited, see pp. 305–6. John Miksic drew my attention to this artefact.

79 The title maharaja was still in use for the ruler of Brunei in the early fifteenth century.

80 R. A. Kern, 'The propagation of Islām in the Indonesian–Malay archipelago', in Gordon (ed.), *The propagation of Islām*, p. 36.

eighth/fourteenth-century gravestones at Minye Tujuh in north Sumatra for the daughter of Sultan al-Malik al-Ẓāhir,[81] which have inscriptions in both Arabic and in Old Malay written in an Indic-inspired Sumatran script. That sometimes political power in the Islamic polities of South-East Asia reverted to persons who were not Muslims is suggested by the fact that in the early tenth/sixteenth century, the governor of Melaka wrote to the king of Portugal noting that 'the king of Brunei is a pagan, the traders are Moors'.[82]

Thus, the eighth/fourteenth century can certainly be seen as a period of wider extension of Islam within South-East Asia. Apart from those manifestations noted above, Chinese texts note the existence of other Islamic rulers including Sultan 'Melayu Da-xi', ruler of Samudera in 785/1383, and Sultan Zayn al-ʿĀbidīn, who had assumed the rulership of that polity by 822/1419, Sultan Ḥusayn, the ruler of Aru in 814/1411, and Muḥammad Shāh, the ruler of Lambri in 815/1412. Thus, by the beginning of the ninth/fifteenth century, the northern and eastern coasts of Sumatra were the location of at least three Muslim polities. Was the extension of the presence of Islam the result of the raids by Sultan al-Malik al-Ẓāhir and his successors, as suggested by Ibn Baṭṭūṭa? If so, can we assume that these polities also followed the Shāfiʿī school?

Samudera remained a cosmopolitan centre of Islam in the early ninth/fifteenth century. The grave of Naina Ḥusām al-Dīn, son of Naina Amīn, dated Shawwāl 823/Oct 1420, is headed by a gravestone which bears verses in Persian, apparently from *Tayyibat*. These Sumatran polities were the intellectual and cultural centres of Islam in ninth/fifteenth-century South-East Asia, thanks to their location, linking through maritime routes with the subcontinent and the Middle East. Links with Gujarat appear to have been close and regular, with cemeteries at Samudera having some representations of gravestones from Cambay.[83]

From the meagre evidence available, it also appears that Sufi influences came to South East Asia through Sumatra. A predecessor of the famous ninth–tenth/fifteenth–sixteenth-century Sumatran mystic Ḥamzah Fanṣūrī – bearing the *nisba* 'al-Jāwī', which suggests a South-East Asian and likely Sumatran origin – appears in a ninth/fifteenth-century collection of Sufi biographies.[84]

81 Either the same sultan whom Ibn Baṭṭūṭa had met in the 1340s, or his son.

82 Kern, 'The propagation of Islām', p. 66.

83 Lambourn also describes booming local tombstone production during this period. See Lambourn, 'The formation of the *batu Aceh* tradition'.

84 See R. Michael Feener and Michael F. Laffan, 'Sufi scents across the Indian Ocean: Yemeni hagiography as a source for the earliest history of Southeast Asian Islam', *Archipel*, 70 (2005), pp. 185–208.

Abū ʿAbd Allāh Masʿūd b. Muḥammad al-Jāwī is recorded as having been involved with major mystics and jurists in Aden and elsewhere in the Yemen during the seventh/thirteenth century, at a time when links with South-East Asia were growing. The great shaykhs of Yemen, and their spiritual guide – the famous Ḥanbalī mystic ʿAbd al-Qādir al-Jīlānī (469–561/1077–1166) – subsequently featured in the spiritual genealogy of many South-East Asian Muslims, in Sumatra and beyond. The name of al-Jīlānī was, for example, later evoked in edicts issued by the Acehnese sultans.

By the end of the eighth/fourteenth century, it appears that the influx of Muslims from southern China and the links with the Indian subcontinent had already begun to change the religious nature of Nusantara. It was at this juncture, following the coming to power in China of the usurping Ming emperor Yongle, that another southward push from China was to occur. The voyages of the eunuch Muslim admiral Zheng He, which extended over the period 807/1405 to 838/1435, have attracted a wide range of explanations as to their impetus and functions. The most appealing is that the usurping emperor Yongle needed to boost his legitimacy by extending Ming power over as great an area as possible.[85] The sending of these vast armadas under the command of Zheng He and other eunuch officials was intended to bring the known maritime world to submission. Thereby, a *pax Ming* could be established, trade nodes and routes to the West could be controlled, and both political and economic power would reside in the hands of the Ming emperor. It was thus that these missions proceeded along the trade routes which the Arabs and Persians had been using for centuries, all the way to the east coast of Africa.

The prominence of Muslim traders and Muslim polities along the existing trade routes may have influenced the decision to have Muslims lead these massive missions, each of which comprised up to hundreds of ships and up to 30,000 troops. Like Zheng He, some of the other senior commanders were Muslims, as were some of the soldiers and seamen who accompanied the missions. It was thus at this time, in an effort to soothe the remaining Muslims of Fujian, to aid the conscription of interpreters and pilots for the eunuch-led armadas and to facilitate links with those who had fled southwards, that the Yongle emperor issued a proclamation in 810/1407 ordering that no more violence was to be perpetrated against Muslims. 'No official, military or

85 The claim that Yongle and other Ming emperors were secret Muslims is unsubstantiated by any accepted source.

civilian personnel shall despise, insult or bully [Muslims] and whoever disobeys this order by doing so shall bear the consequences.'[86]

The Zheng He-led navies established bases in the Straits of Malacca – at Melaka itself and at Samudera – in order to be able to control trade through that narrow waterway. The newly emergent polity of Melaka provided the Ming forces with a useful base, while the Ming forces provided Parameswara, the first ruler of Melaka, with the protection necessary to prosper without concern about the continuing threats from the Siamese and the Javanese. The Ming missions were certainly not intended by the Ming court to have a religious proselytising function, but given the religious affiliations of many of the senior members of the missions, it would not have been surprising if there had been efforts to encourage the adoption of a new religion among some of the political leaders met on the voyages. These missions had the added unintentional effect of linking together the major Muslim communities in southern China, and those throughout South-East Asia and India, with the societies of the great Islamic centres of West Asia. Many of the rulers, or at least senior envoys, from places visited in South-East Asia and beyond were carried in the Ming ships to the Chinese capital together with envoys from Islamic polities further west – Cochin, Hormuz, Aden, Dhofar and even Mecca. Awareness of the extent and influence of Islam in these areas may have contributed to the ongoing Islamisation in South-East Asia.

Two urban areas – Melaka and the northern coastal cities of Java – provide helpful data about the adoption of Islam among South-East Asians during the first half of the ninth / fifteenth century. Ma Huan, a Muslim who accompanied Zheng He on some voyages, recorded much about the ports and peoples visited during these voyages at the beginning of the ninth / fifteenth century. He is known to have accompanied the voyages of 816–18 / 1413–15, 824–5 / 1421–2 and 834–6 / 1431–3. These descriptions he collected into a volume entitled *Ying-yai sheng-lan* (or 'Supreme Survey of the Ocean Shores'). Of Java, which he visited on the 816–18 / 1413–15 mission, he noted:

> The country contains three classes of persons. One class consists of the Muslim[87] people; they are all people from every foreign kingdom in the west who have flowed to this place as merchants; and in all matters of dressing and eating, they are all very clean. One class consists of T'ang

86 Chen Da-sheng (chief ed.), (*Quanzhou Yisilan jiao shike* (Islamic stone inscriptions from Quanzhou) (Quanzhou, 1984). See pp. 11–13.

87 The term used was 'Hui-hui', likely derived from Hui-gu, the term by which the Chinese knew the Uighurs.

> people,[88] and they are all people from Guangdong and from Zhangzhou and Quanzhou and such places, who fled away and now live in this country; the food of these people, too, is choice and clean; and many of them follow the Muslim religion, observing the precepts and fasting. One class consists of the local people; they have very ugly and strange appearance, tousled hair and go in bare feet. They are devoted to devil worship, this country being among the 'devil countries' spoken of in Buddhist books. The food which these people eat is very dirty and bad.

Of the new polity of Melaka, Ma Huan specifically states that: 'The king of the country and the people of the country all follow the Muslim religion, fasting, doing penance and chanting liturgies.'

Further to the north, of Aru near Deli in Sumatra, Ma's text notes: 'The king of the country and the people of the country are all Muslim,' while of Lambri on the northern coast of Sumatra, he recorded: 'This country lies beside the sea and the population comprises only something over a thousand families. All are Muslims and they are very honest and genuine ... The king is also a Muslim.' Even further north, in reference to the Bengal kingdom, the account reads:

> As to the dress worn by the king of the country and the chiefs, they all observe the ordinances of the Muslim religion, and their headwear and clothes are very neat and elegant ... there are also some people who speak the Fārsi language ... The customs of the people, and the rites relating to coming of age, funerals, sacrifices and marriages all conform with the regulations of the Muslim religion.

A number of points emerge from Ma Huan's account. The first is that by the early part of the ninth/fifteenth century, there were already quite a large number of Muslims, both Chinese and those from further west, resident in Tuban, Gresik, Surabaya and Majapahit on the northern coast of Java, but the 'local people' had not adopted the religion. The second, is that many of the Chinese Muslims in Java had 'fled' from China, endorsing the thesis that they had fled the repercussions of the 'Iṣfahān rebellion' in Quanzhou.

The process of the introduction of Islam to Melaka is worthy of a little further attention.[89] Who was this king whom Ma Huan wrote of as being a Muslim? Ma Huan visited Melaka several times from 816/1413 to 836/1433, and

88 An endonym for Chinese people.

89 Christopher Wake has made a detailed study of the complexities of this process in his 'Melaka in the fifteenth century', in Kernial Singh Sandhu and Paul Wheatley (eds.), *Melaka: The transformation of a Malay capital c. 1400–1980*, (Kuala Lumpur, 1983), vol. I, pp. 128–61.

over these twenty years there had been a number of rulers. The first ruler, Parameswara, who had come to Melaka from Sumatra, appears to have retained this Indic title until his death, which occurred sometime about 816/1413. While he was probably not Muslim, he certainly employed Muslims in his relations with the Ming. The envoy he sent to China in 811/1408, for example, was named ʿAbd Allāh Ḥasan. Parameswara was succeeded by his son Megat Iskandar Shāh in about 817/1414, who, like his father, also travelled to the Ming court with the Zheng He missions.[90] His successor, known by the title Sri Mahārājā, likewise travelled to the Ming court, with Ma Huan in 836/1433. By 849/1445, the Melakan ruler being recorded in Chinese texts was Sri Parameswara Dewa Shāh, also a distinctly Indic title. Rivalry between Islamic and non-Islamic contenders for the throne thus seems possible.[91] It might be posited that Islamic rule in Melaka, perhaps up to the 830s/1430s, was underwritten by the power of the Ming forces who maintained a base in the city, and that when the Ming withdrew from South-East Asia from the late 830s/1430s, the power of those who had been supported by the Ming declined. This was certainly the case with the Ming-installed Chinese rulers of Palembang over the same period. However, the re-emergence of an Indic-titled ruler in Melaka appears to have been a brief interregnum, as by the 850s/1450s we read of a new ruler bearing a distinctly Islamic name – Sultan Muẓaffar Shāh. His is the first reign we can firmly associate with any coinage, with the coins he minted bearing the legend: 'Muẓaffar Shāh al-Sultān / Nāṣir al-dunyā wa'l-Dīn'.

The expansion of Islam within the peninsula is likely to have been stimulated by the existence of the sultanate at Melaka, and the spread of Malay people throughout this region. The monuments at Pĕngkalen Kĕmpas not far

90 *Ibid.*, p. 143. Tomé Pires's account of the history of Melaka, which he collected during the early sixteenth century, specifically states that Iskandar Shāh, whom he noted as Parameswara's son, was initially not a Muslim. The account relates that only at the age of seventy-two did he agree to marriage with some of the daughters of the ruler of Pasai and at the same time to accept the Islamic faith. See Armando Cortesão, *The Suma oriental of Tomé Pires*, Hakluyt Society (London, 1944), vol. II, pp. 241–2.

91 The questions of conversion and naming are hugely complex, and when one examines the situations in these polities, we observe much hybridity in the situations of early Islam in South and South-East Asia. The question of how the Muslim trade communities related to their host polities is an integral element of this. The term 'sultan' was Sanskritised and adopted by Hindu rulers, Muslim governors administered for Hindu kings, Hindus adopted Islamic garb and so forth. The complexities of the gradual process of Islamisation thus require much more detailed and specific studies than is allowed by this general overview. The various works of Wink, Eaton, Lambourn and Feener are useful for elucidating the issues of Islamic hybridity in South Asia, the Indian Ocean and South-East Asia.

from the sultanate's core suggest that this region was in transition to Islam in the 860s/1460s,[92] while the first sultan of Pahang, who died in 880/1475, was a son of the sultan of Melaka,[93] suggesting a spread of the religion to the east of the peninsula. The role of South-East Asians in this continuing spread of the religion in the region should not be ignored.

How important then were the Zheng He voyages in stimulating conversion or otherwise promoting the spread of Islam in South-East Asia? As noted, the purges in Fujian in the 760s/1360s had created an earlier influx of Muslims and therefore potential agents of Islamic conversion into South-East Asia. It appears that the Ming voyages in the early ninth/fifteenth century made use of these people and their connections with Fujian, with South-East Asia and with areas to the west. Anti-Islamic violence had continued in Quanzhou and elsewhere in Fujian until the beginning of the ninth/fifteenth century, as evidenced by the 810/1407 edict by the Yongle emperor forbidding any harassment of Muslims.[94] The emperor also needed the Quanzhou Islamic connections with South-East Asia to assist with these voyages. Navigators, translators and specialists in the Islamic societies of the Indian Ocean could be found in Quanzhou, which thus became an important port of call for the Chinese voyages to the Western Ocean.

The Ming naval forces definitely became engaged in the politics of Java in the early part of the ninth/fifteenth century. Chinese texts inform us that two competing rulers of Java – a Western king and an Eastern king – were both in contact with the Ming state in the early years of the century. The Ming naval forces were apparently in close contact with the Eastern ruler before he was killed by the Western ruler in 809/1406. A further 170 Ming troops involved with the Eastern kingdom were also killed, and as compensation for these people, the Ming court demanded 60,000 ounces of gold. As the Western king was the ruler of Majapahit, we may well surmise that the Eastern king ruled a newly emergent coastal polity, probably in Semarang-Demak,[95] where a new

92 See *Journal of the Federated Malay States Museums*, 9, 3 (1921), which contains Ivor H. N. Evans, 'A grave and megaliths in Negri Sembilan with an account of some excavations'; W. A. Wallace, 'Plans of the Negri Sembilan grave and megaliths with notes'; and C. Boden Kloss, 'Notes on the Pengkalan Kempas tombstone'. See also R. J. Wilkinson, 'The Pengkalan Kĕmpas "saint"', *Journal of the Malayan Branch Royal Asiatic Society*, 9, 1 (1931), pp. 134–5.

93 The gravestone, which is extant, is an example of the *batu Aceh* tradition.

94 See Chen, *Quanzhou Yisilan jiao shike*.

95 Demak first appeared in Ming texts (under the name *Dan-ba*) in 779/1377, which gels well with the thesis that it emerged as a base for the Muslim refugees who had fled from southern China in the 760s/1360s. See Geoff Wade (trans.), *Southeast Asia in the Ming Shi-lu: An open access resource*, http://epress.nus.edu.sg/msl/entry/1883.

power base had arisen around the Muslim refugees who had fled from Fujian to South-East Asia in the 760s / 1360s and subsequently. This group would have had connections with the forces commanded by Zheng He, and been able to draw them into support for the new *pesisir* polity, resulting in the friction with the Western king – the ruler of Majapahit.[96]

This scenario lends credence to the otherwise quite contentious Malay-language *Peranakan* chronicles of Semarang and Cirebon 'discovered' and published by Mangaradja Parlindungan in the 1960s. Parlindungan's account, supposedly derived from the Chinese community archives in these cities, depicts a wide-ranging early ninth / fifteenth-century network of Chinese Ḥanafī Muslims, spread throughout South-East Asia, and tightly connected to Ming agents such as Zheng He. These Chinese Ḥanafī communities were supposedly established in Palembang, Sambas, Melaka and Luzon, as well as all along the north coast of Java – at Ancol, Cirebon, Lasem, Tuban, Semarang, Gresik and Joratan. The account further assigns Chinese origins to some of the Islamic saints of Java, including Sunan Ngampel and Sunan Giri, as well as to Njai Gede Pinatih, the Great Lady of Gresik.[97]

It must be affirmed that much of the Parlindungan account is in accord with the evolution of the Chinese Muslim communities overseas as reflected in the foregoing history. People did flee from Quanzhou to various ports in South-East Asia in the late eighth / fourteenth-century, and the links which Parlindungan suggests are congruent with other sources he was unlikely to have known. The ninth / fifteenth-century *Xi-yang fan-guo-zhi* actually stated that all of the Chinese in Java were Muslims,[98] and within Java there are traditions of Chinese involvement in the Islamisation of Java.[99] The Sino-Javanese envoy Ma Yong-long (Ma Yong-liang) is well attested in other sources, but, most interestingly, another of the leaders of the Javanese Ḥanafī community as reported in Parlindungan's work – Gan Eng Cu – is found to have a correlate only in the Ming veritable records (*Ming shi-lu*) which would not have been available to Parlindungan. Of Gan Eng Cu, the Parlindungan account reads:

96 Relevant materials can be gleaned from the *Ming Shi-lu*, *Ming-shi* and *Shu-yu-zhou-zi-lu*. The last of these works notes that the Chinese who sojourned in Java were generally Muslims.

97 See de Graaf and Pigeaud, *Chinese Muslims in Java*; D.A. Rinkes, *Nine saints of Java* (Kuala Lumpur, 1996); and Tan Yeok Seong, 'Chinese element in the Islamisation of Southeast Asia', *Journal of the South Seas Society*, 30, 1 and 2 (1975).

98 Lombard and Salmon, 'Islam and Chineseness', p. 183.

99 Slamet Muljana, *Runtuhnja keradjaan Hindu-Djawa dan timbulnja negara-negara Islam di Nusantara* (Jakarta, 1968), as quoted in Lombard and Salmon, 'Islam and Chineseness', p. 184.

> 1423: Haji Bong Tak Keng transferred Haji Gan Eng Cu from Manila/Philippines to Tuban/Java to control the flourishing Ḥanafīte Muslim communities in Java, Kukang and Sambas. At that time, Tuban was Java's main port, with the kingdom of Majapahit as hinterland. Haji Gan Eng Cu became a kind of consul-general of the Chinese government, the Ming Emperor, having control of all Muslim Chinese communities in the southern Nan Yang countries including Java, Kukang and Sambas.[100]

In the Ming veritable records, we read of Gong Yong-cai (龔用才 – in Hokkien 'Giong Eng-cai'), a Chinese person acting as an envoy from Java, travelling to the Ming court in 832/1429, and receiving robes from the Chinese emperor, exactly as was recorded of Gan Eng Cu in Parlindungan's work.[101] This reference opens up the possibility that these annals do provide us with new factual material on Sino-Javanese Islamic networks of the ninth/fifteenth century.

Regardless of the veracity of this account, we do observe in this period the beginning of a new age of Islamisation along the Javanese northern coast.[102] We have evidence of Islam in Gresik by 822/1419,[103] and further indications of the religion's gradual growth along this coast. These *pesisir* communities were to become some of the most powerful agents of Islamic expansion in South-East Asia both during the ninth/fifteenth century and beyond. Demak is depicted in some accounts as having waged *jihād* against other *pesisir* polities through the ninth/fifteenth century.[104]

Further north, we also observe changes in the religious topography of the western littoral of the South-East Asian mainland during the early ninth/fifteenth century, which were also to affect maritime South-East Asia. Bengal had become part of the Delhi sultanate following its capture by Turkish forces under Muḥammad Bakhtiyār in the early seventh/thirteenth century, after which the *khuṭba*, diverse elements of Islamic administration and mosques were introduced to that place. Repeated attempts to throw off the controls of Delhi saw successive military expeditions against the region by Delhi, bringing ever more Muslim forces into the Bengali cultural region. In the middle of the eighth/fourteenth

100 De Graaf and Pigeaud, *Chinese Muslims in Java*, p. 15.

101 *Ibid.*, pp. 15–16.

102 For further details of which, see Lombard and Salmon, 'Islam and Chineseness', pp. 115–17.

103 J. P. Moquette, 'De datum op den grafsteen van Malik Ibrahim te Grisse', *Tijdschrift voor Indische Taal-, Land- en Volkenkunde*, 54 (1912), pp. 208–14. Again the gravestone derived from Cambay.

104 De Graaf and Pigeaud, however, write of a tradition which holds that the first Muslim ruler of Demak (who was of Chinese origin) did not emerge until the last quarter of the ninth/fifteenth century. See H. J. de Graaf and Th. Pigeaud, *Islamic states in Java, 1500–1700* (The Hague, 1976), pp. 6–8.

century, Shams al-Dīn Ilyās Shāh (r. 743–58/1342–57) established his own Bengal sultanate free of Delhi. The mid-eighth/fourteenth-century historian Shams-i Ṣirāj ʿAfif referred to him as the 'sultan of the Bengalis' and the 'king of Bengal', while his coins called him: 'The just sultan, Shams al-dunȳa wa al-dīn, Abū'l Muẓaffar Ilyās Shāh, the sultan: The second Alexander, the right hand of the caliphate, the defender of the Commander of the Faithful'.[105]

This rising polity promoted Islam as a state-sponsored religion in a pan-Islamic spirit. Later rulers also drew on imperial Persian symbols of authority, and tried to attract great poets from Shīrāz to grace their courts. It was towards the end of the eighth/fourteenth century that a new force appeared in Bengal politics – Sufis of the Chishtī and Firdausi orders. Championing a reformed and purified Islam, they insisted that the state's foreign and Islamic identity not be diluted by admitting Bengalis into the ruling class.[106] Similar influences were felt to the south, in the coastal polities of Sumatra and beyond.

The history of early Bengali Islam aids an understanding not only of that South-East Asian borderland itself, but also of the Islamic links and influences exerted on its many trading and political partners to the south-east. Arakan, for example, was certainly influenced by the Bengal polity, politically and otherwise, during the ninth/fifteenth century, even if Bengal's support for the Arakanese king Naramithla in his battles with Ava remains unproven. Arakanese expansion was always northwards towards the ports of Bengal and it is likely through such temporary control over ports where Islam would have been most influential that the religion would come to have increasing influence within Arakan society.[107]

In addition, early tenth/sixteenth-century accounts show Bengali merchants spread widely across the ports of the archipelago. In the peninsula and Sumatra, while tenth/sixteenth-century rulers were already called sultan, as in Bengal, further east the title raja or patih was used. Tomé Pires noted in addition that 'the people of Pase are for the most part Bengalees and the natives descend from this stock'.[108] He expanded: 'Pase used to have heathen kings, and it must be a hundred and sixty years now since the said kings were worn out by the cunning of the merchant Moors there were in the kingdom of

105 Richard M. Eaton, *The rise of Islam and the Bengal frontier, 1204–1760* (Berkeley and Los Angeles, 1993), p. 41.
106 *Ibid.*, p. 50.
107 For further details, see the various contributions to Jos Gommans and Jacques Leider (eds.), *The maritime frontier of Burma: Exploring political, cultural and commercial interaction in the Indian Ocean world, 1200–1800* (Leiden, 2002).
108 Cortesão, *The Suma oriental of Tomé Pires*, p. 142.

Pase, and the said Moors held the sea coast and they made a Moorish king of the Bengali caste, and from that time until now the kings of Pase have always been Moors.'[109] If we are to assign credence to Pires's dates, we can say that his account supports the supposition which is suggested by other evidence, that Pasai was actually originally a separate polity from Samudera, and that, on the latter's demise, Pasai incorporated Samudera's history into its own *hikayat*.[110] The Samudera–Bengal connection in the middle of the ninth/fifteenth century is also evidenced by Chinese texts which record that Ai-yan, the nephew of Song Yun, who had travelled to the Ming court in the 840s/1440s as an emissary of Bengal, was at the time based in Samudera.[111] S. Q. Fatimi based his argument that Islam came to the Straits of Malacca from Bengal mainly on the claims of Pires.[112] Hooker has suggested that this is unlikely, given that the Ḥanafī school was predominant in Bengal, whereas throughout the archipelago it is the Shāfiʿī school which dominates.[113] However, the envoy Song Yun mentioned above was likely at least partly Chinese and it may be significant that both the Bengali and early South-East Asian Chinese versions of Islam were Ḥanafī, which were later overwhelmed or surpassed by that of the Shāfiʿī school.

When Tomé Pires wrote his unparalleled account of South-East Asia in the early tenth/sixteenth century, he reported a situation where Islam had become a very integral part of the region.[114] The ruler of Bengal was recorded as 'a faithful Mohammedan'. Of Siam, Pires noted that while it did not have many 'Moors', there were Arabs, Persians, Bengalis and Klings found in the trade ports. Champa was said to have no Muslims, while Cochin China was reportedly unfriendly to Muslims. Of Sumatra, he noted: 'The land of Palembang used to have heathen kings of its own and it was subject to the *cafre* king of Java, and after the Moorish *pates* of Java had made themselves masters of the sea coasts, they made war on Palembang for a long time and took the land, and it had no more kings, only *pates*.' This suggests an extension to Sumatra of the *jihād* which had been waged along the northern coast of Java during the early ninth/fifteenth century. The rulers of Aru, Arcat, Siak, Kampar and Jambi, all on the island of Sumatra, are also noted as being

109 *Ibid.*, p. 143.
110 For which see Hill, 'Hikayat Raja-raja Pasai'.
111 *Ming Ying-zong shi-lu*, *juan* 54.7b of 843/1439 and *juan* 141.1a of 850/1446. Song Yun was later killed in China by one of the Javanese envoys, but whether there was any political intent in the killing remains unknown.
112 Fatimi, *Islām comes to Malaysia*, pp. 12–29.
113 M. B. Hooker, 'Introduction: The translation of Islam into South-East Asia', in M. B. Hooker (ed.), *Islam in South-East Asia* (Leiden, 1983), pp. 1–22. See p. 6.
114 Cortesão, *The Suma oriental of Tomé Pires*, *passim*.

Muslims, while Palembang itself was controlled by *Pate Rodim*, 'lord of Demak', and Bangka and associated islands were under the control of *Pate Unus*, 'a Javanese Moor'. Muslims were, however, reportedly forbidden by local lords from travelling to the gold mines of Minangkabau. Aceh had already begun its rise and its ruler was noted by Pires as being 'a Moor'.

On the island of Java itself, 'the kingdom of Sunda does not allow Moors in it, except for a few, because it is feared that with their cunning they may do there what has been done in Java, because the Moors are cunning and they make themselves masters of countries by cunning, because apparently they have no power'. Muslim populations are recorded for the north-coast port-polities of Chi Manuk (Chemano), but *Guste Pate*, the viceroy and chief captain of the king of Java, is said to have been 'always at war with the Moors on the seacoast, especially with the lord of Demak'. The port of Tuban was controlled by Daria Timã de Raja, 'a Moor who is the vassal of the said king'.

In describing the 'Mohammedan *pates* who are on the seacoast' of Java, Pires claimed that: 'These lord *pates* are not Javanese of long-standing in the country, but they are descended from Chinese, from Parsees and Kling', a suggestion well in accord with the sources cited above. The succession of Muslim ports along the northern Javanese coast are then enumerated – Chiremon, controlled by Lebe Uça, vassal of *Pate Rodim*, lord of Demak; Japura, the *pate* of which was a cousin of *Pate Rodim*; Tegal, controlled by an uncle of *Pate Unus*; Samarang, controlled by *Pate Mamet*, uncle of *Pate Rodim*; Demak itself, controlled by *Pate Rodim*, chief *pate* of Java; Tidunan, under the charge of *Pate Orob*, uncle of *Pate Unus*; Japara, controlled by *Pate Unus*; Rembang under *Pate Morob*, also an uncle of *Pate Unus*; Tuban, the nearest port to the inland capital of Daha / Daya, which was under *Pate Vira*, who was subject to the anti-Islamic *Guste Pate*. Next along the coast was another Islamic port-polity, Sidayu, with a lord named *Pate Amiza*, cousin of *Pate Unus*, but the population of which was mainly heathen. To its east lay Grisee / Grisik, 'the best trading port in Java', divided between two rival Muslim lords, one intimately linked with Melaka, and trading into the Moluccas and Banda, and the other closely tied to the Javanese aristocracy. Thence one arrived at Surabaya, controlled by *Pate Bubat*, a vassal of *Guste Pate*, but 'closely related to the Moorish *pates*'. The next port-polity was Gamda, under the control of *Pate Sepetat*, a heathen, son of *Guste Pate*, and son-in-law of the ruler of Madura. Pires noted that *Pate Sepetat* had, with the help of his father-in-law, 'prevented the Moors from passing beyond Surabaya for a long time'; then followed the smaller polities of Cantjam, Panarukan and Pajarakan, and finally Blambangan, whose lord was known as *Pate Pimtor*, and was a nephew and ally of *Guste Pate*. A phenomenon recorded in Java by Pires was that of 'tapas', which he says means 'observants', apparently some kind of religious ascetics, numbering, according to the Portuguese scribe, 50,000 in the island. These people, he claimed, were 'also worshipped by the Moors'. This suggests another element of the syncretism which has long marked Javanese Islam – the *agama Jawa* described by Brakel.[115]

On the islands further east, Pires also noted the dispersed presence of Muslims. Of Banda, he recorded, 'Those along the seacoast are Moorish merchants.' That they were fairly recent arrivals was apparent: 'It is thirty years since there began to be Moors in the Banda islands.' In respect of the Moluccas, Pires declared: 'According to what they say, Mohammedanism in the Molucca islands began fifty years ago. The kings of the islands are Mohammedans, but not very deeply involved in the sect. Many are Mohammedans without being circumcised and there are not many Mohammedans. The heathens are three parts and more out of four.' The king of Ternate was known as sultan, while other local rulers were termed simply raja. The island of Gillolo (Jeilolo) was also noted as having a 'Mohammedan ruler'.

Regarding Melaka, the *Suma oriental* provides a great amount of information. Pires recounts, obviously on the basis of local accounts, how Xaquem Darxa (Iskandar Shāh), the son of Paramjçura (Parameswara), the founder of Melaka, provided great hospitality to Islamic merchants as he endeavoured to build his polity, and eventually also converted to Islam upon marriage to the daughter of the sultan of Pasai. This account needs to be read in conjunction with the analysis of Islam in Melaka provided above. The later sultan Manṣūr Shāh is lauded as a great ruler and as the builder of a 'beautiful mosque which used to be where now is the famous fortress of Melaka, and which was the finest known in these parts'. Manṣūr Shāh is also noted as having employed non-Muslim officials, reminding one of the Bengali sultans who were very cosmopolitan in their outlook and actions. The recorded links between Melaka and the diverse polities up and down the Straits of Malacca in *Suma oriental* suggest that Melaka was indeed the major centre of commerce and likely intellectual and religious intercourse in the region during the latter part of the ninth/fifteenth century.

Tomé Pires's overview of the archipelago at the beginning of the tenth/sixteenth century is a fitting way by which to conclude this chapter. We observe, at this time, Islamic polities already established up and down both sides of the Straits of Malacca and all along the northern coast of Java – the latter albeit engaged in rivalry with non-Muslim polities, both coastal and

115 L. F. Brakel, 'Islam and local traditions: Syncretic ideas and practices', *Indonesia and the Malay World*, 32, 92 (2004), p. 12.

inland. There were also the beginnings of Islamic states in the eastern islands of the archipelago. Thus was the stage set for a renewed expansion of Islam in tenth/sixteenth-century South-East Asia, a period which was also to see the arrival of a new religious competitor – the Christianity of the Portuguese and the Spanish.

The history of Islam in South-East Asia obviously cannot be understood without examining the component phenomena on a global scale. When we look back at the three periods discussed above, we see in the period up until the fifth/eleventh century the emergence of Islamic trading communities along the southern coast of China, in Champa, undoubtedly in Sumatra and possibly in Brunei or what is today the southern Philippines. These were tied to the Indian subcontinent and thence on to the Middle East. It is quite possible that Shīʿa influence was quite strong during this period. With the breaking of the trade routes through the Cōla attacks in the early fifth/eleventh century, a certain independence and innovation occurred within the Muslim communities in South-East Asia. At that time, the Muslim community in Champa was obviously large enough for the Chinese envoy to see it as being representative of Champa *per se*. Muslim communities appeared in Hainan and Brunei, and the first Islamic polities began to be observed in seventh/thirteenth-century northern Sumatra. It must be affirmed that the eighth/fourteenth and ninth/fifteenth centuries constituted an important period in the spread of Islam through South-East Asia, particularly in the Islamisation of *pesisir* Java. While the Sumatran states were developing their links with polities and rulers in the Middle East and the subcontinent, Muslim refugees from disturbances in Quanzhou and other major Islamic centres of southern China began to flow into South-East Asia in the 760s/1360s and 770s/1370s, becoming key catalysts in the emergence and growth of coastal Javanese Islamic polities.

During these periods, Muslim traders appear to have been the most usual carriers of Islam. With the importance of the Sufis in the development of Islam in Bengal, and the existence of al-Jawi (probably Sumatran) Sufis from possibly the seventh/thirteenth and definitely the eighth/fourteenth century, we can affirm that during the eighth/fourteenth and ninth/fifteenth centuries, Sufis[116] were an important channel for transmission of the faith in South-East Asia, a phenomenon discussed by both Johns[117] and Fatimi.[118]

116 Here Sufi is not intended as an absolute category. A Sufi could have been a soldier, an administrator, a cleric or a trader.

117 A. H. Johns, 'Sufism as a category in Indonesian literature and history', *Journal of South-east Asian History*, 2, 2 (July 1961), pp. 10–23.

118 Fatimi, *Islām comes to Malaysia*, pp. 23–4, *passim*.

Throughout these processes of Islamic expansion a multitude of changes took place in the physical as well as mental topographies of the region. New ideas of law and jurisprudence emerged, along with new moralities. New forms of dress, new types of tombs and new forms of architecture also appeared. The Malay languages of the archipelago began to absorb the terminology of Islamic theology and law, as well as the new Arabic-based script, together with the many new external links this world religion provided them with. Iconography diminished greatly in the archipelago, and the Hindu–Buddhist style of architecture went into decline. The processes by which these aspects were continued or arrested will be discussed in the succeeding chapters.

Appendix 1 *Envoys and others with Li 'surname' from maritime polities to China tenth to early twelfth centuries*

Date (CE)	Name	Proposed reconstruction	Polity affiliation	Source and remarks
960	Li Shu-ti (李 庶帝)	'Alī Shadi	San-fo-qi	*Song Shi juan* 489
962	Li Li-lin (李 麗林)	'Alī Leyli	San-fo-qi	*Song Shi juan* 489
	Li Ya-mo (李 鵶末)	'Alī Aḥmad		
963	Li Ban (李 半) (alt. Lie Mie 李 咩)		Champa	*SHY FY* 4: Champa
968/9	Li Ban (李 半)		Champa	*SHY FY* 4: Champa
	Li Bei-qiang (李 被瑲)			*Song Shi* gives second name as Li Bei-cuo (李 被磋)
971	Li He-mo (李 何末)	'Alī Ḥāmid	San-fo-qi or the Arab lands	*SHY FY* 7 *Yu Hai juan* 154
971/2	Li Nou (李 ?)	'Alī Nūr	Champa	*SHY FY* 4: Champa Deputy king of Champa

Appendix 1 (*cont.*)

Date (CE)	Name	Proposed reconstruction	Polity affiliation	Source and remarks
977	Envoy Li Pai (李 牌); deputy envoy Li Ma-na (李 麻 那), and administrator Li Tu (李 屠)	ʿAlī Bahij (?)	Champa	*SHY FY* 4: Champa
979/80	Li Mu-zha-duo (李 木吒哆)	ʿAlī Muẓaffar	Champa	*SHY FY* 4: Champa
980	Li Fu-hui (李 甫誨)		San-fo-qi (A merchant)	*Song Shi juan* 489
986	Li Chao-xian (李 朝 仙)		Champa	*SHY FY* 4: Champa Possibly a Viet or Chinese name
990	Li Zhen (李 臻)	ʿAlī Zayn (?)	Champa	*SHY FY* 4: Champa
993	Li-a-wu (李 亞勿)	ʿAlī Aḥmad	The Arab lands	*SHY FY* 7
995	Li Bo-zhu (李 波珠)	ʿAlī Bashīr (?)	Champa	*SHY FY* 4: Champa
	Li He-san (李 訶散)	ʿAlī Ḥasan		
	Li Mo-wu (李 磨勿)	ʿAlī Maḥmūd		
997	Li Bu-liang (李 補良)	ʿAlī ...	Champa	*SHY FY* 4: Champa
999	Li Gu-lun (李 姑倫)	ʿAlī ...	Champa	*SHY FY* 4: Champa
1003	Li Jia-pai (李 加排)	ʿAlī ...	San-fo-qi	*SHY FY* 4: San-fo-qi
	Li Nan-bei (李 南悲)	ʿAlī ...		
1003	Li Yi-han (李 ? 罕)	ʿAlī ...	Butuan	*SHY FY* 4: Butuan
1008	Li Mei-di (李 眉地)	ʿAli Badī	San-fo-qi	*SHY FY* 7: Possibly same person as the Ya-li Bai-di mentioned

Appendix 1 (*cont.*)

Date (CE)	Name	Proposed reconstruction	Polity affiliation	Source and remarks
				under date 1011 in Appendix 3
1011	Li Yu-xie (李于燮)	'Alī Yūsuf	Butuan	*SHY FY* 4: Butuan
1029	Li Pu-sa (李菩薩)	'Alī …	Champa	*SHY FY* 4: Champa
1030	Li Pu-sa (李菩薩)	'Alī …	Champa	*SHY FY* 4: Champa
1071	Li Pu-sa (李蒲薩)	'Alī …	Champa	*SHY FY* 4: Champa
1105	Li-zhan-pa (力占琶)	'Alī Champa (?)	Champa	*SHY FY* 4: Champa

FY = *Fan-yi* (a section of *SHY*)
SHY = Xu Song, *Song Hui-yao* (Shanghai, 1995)
Yu Hai= Wang Yinglin, *Yu Hai* [*Sea of jade*] (thirteenth century), (Shanshai, 1987)

Appendix 2 *Envoys and others with Pu 'surname' from maritime polities to China tenth to twelfth centuries*

Date (CE)	Name	Proposed reconstruction	Polity affiliation	Source and remarks
960/1	Pu He-san (菩訶散)	Abū Ḥasan	Champa	*SHY FY* 4: Champa
961	Pu Mie (蒲蔑)	Abū Mat	San-fo-qi	*Song Shi juan* 489
972	Pu He-san (菩訶散)	Abū Ḥasan	Champa	*SHY FY* 4: Champa
975	Bu Luo-hai (不囉海)	Abū …	The Arab lands	*SHY FY* 7
976	Pu Xi-mi (蒲希密)	Abū Ḥāmid	The Arab lands	*SHY FY* 7
976	Pu Tuo-han (蒲陁漢)	Abū …	San-fo-qi	*Song Shi juan* 489

Appendix 2 (*cont.*)

Date (CE)	Name	Proposed reconstruction	Polity affiliation	Source and remarks
977	Pu Ya-li (蒲亞里)	Abū ʿAlī	Bo-ni (Brunei)	*SHY FY* 7
977	Pu Lu-xie (蒲盧歇)	Abū Yūsuf (?)	China/ Bo-ni	*Song Shi juan* 4
977	Pu Si-na (蒲思那)	Abū Cina	The Arab lands	*SHY FY* 7
	Pu Luo (蒲羅)	Abū Nūr		
983	Pu Ya-tuo-luo (蒲押陁羅)	Abū ʿAbd Allāh	San-fo-qi	*SHY FY* 7
986	Pu Luo-e (蒲羅遏)	Abū Nūr (?)	Champa	*SHY FY* 4: Champa (Led 100 members of clan to Hainan)
988	Pu Ya-tuo-li (蒲押陀黎)	Abū ʿAbd Allāh	San-fo-qi	*SHY FY* 7
990	Pu He-san (蒲訶散)	Abū Ḥasan	Champa	*SHY FY* 4: Champa
992	Pu Ya-li (蒲亞里)	Abū ʿAlī	Java	*SHY FY* 4: She-po
993	Pu Xi-mi (蒲希密)	Abū Ḥāmid	The Arab lands	*Song Shi*: Da-shi (Master of ship) 舶主
995	Pu Ya-tuo-li (蒲押陁黎)	Abū ʿAbd Allāh	The Arab lands	*SHY FY* 7: (Master of ship) 舶主 See Kuwabara I p. 78
998	Pu Ya-ti-li (蒲押提黎)	Abū ʿAbd Allāh	The Arab lands	*SHY FY* 4
1004	Pu Jia-xin (蒲加心)	Abū Qāsim	The Arab lands	*SHY FY* 7
1008	Pu Ma-wu Tuo-po-li (蒲麻勿陁婆離)	Abū Maḥmūd Tabrīz	The Arab lands	*Xu Zi-zhi-tong-jian chang-bian*, *juan* 69.9a (Master of ship) 舶主
1008	Pu Po-lan (蒲婆藍)	Abū Burhān	San-fo-qi	*SHY FY* 7 San-fo-qi
1011	Pu Ma-wu Tuo-po-li (蒲麻勿陁婆離)	Abū Maḥmūd Tabrīz	The Arab lands	*SHY FY* 7

Appendix 2 (*cont.*)

Date (CE)	Name	Proposed reconstruction	Polity affiliation	Source and remarks
1015	Pu Jia-xin (蒲加心)	Abū Qāsim or Abū Ḥasan	Zhu-lian (Chola)	*SHY FY* 7
1017	Pu Mou-xi (蒲謀西)	Abū Mūsī	San-fo-qi	*SHY FY* 7
1019	Pu Ma-wu	Abū Maḥmūd	The Arab lands	*SHY FY* 4
	Tuo-po-li (蒲麻勿陁婆離)	Abū Tabrīz		And *FY* 7
	Pu Jia-xin (蒲霞辛)	Abū Ḥasan		
1028	Pu Ya-tuo-luo-xie (蒲押陀羅歇)	Abū ʿAbd Allāh	San-fo-qi	*SHY FY* 7
1033	Pu Ya-tuo-li (蒲押陁離)	Abū ʿAbd Allāh	Zhu-lian (Chola)	*SHY FY* 7
1053	Pu Si-ma-ying (蒲思馬應)	Abū Ismāʿīl (?)	Champa	*SHY FY* 4: Champa
1055	Pu Sha-yi (蒲沙乙)	Abū Sayyid	The Arab lands	*SHY FY* 7
1060	Pu Sha-yi (蒲沙乙)	Abū Sayyid	The Arab lands	*SHY FY* 7
1068	Pu Ma-wu (蒲麻勿)	Abū Maḥmūd	Champa	*SHY FY* 4: Champa
1073	Pu Ma-wu (蒲麻勿)	Abū Maḥmūd	The Arab lands	*SHY FY* 7
1086	Pu Ma-wu (蒲麻勿)	Abū Maḥmūd	Champa	*SHY FY* 4: Champa
1087	Pu Xia-xin (蒲霞辛)	Abū Ḥusayn	Champa	*Luan-cheng-ji* (欒城集) 28.6a
1137	Pu Ya-li (蒲亞里)	Abū ʿAlī	Unknown	*SHY* See Kuwabara I p. 56

FY = *Fan-yi* (a section of *SHY*)
Kuwabara I = see n. 53
Luan-cheng-ji = Su Shi, *Luan Cheng ji* (Shanghai, 1987)
SHY = *Song Hui-yao*
Xu Zi-zhi-tong-jian chang-bian = Bi Yuan, *Xu zizhi tongjian changbian* (Beijing, 1957)

Appendix 3 *Other envoys with Islamic names from maritime polities to China, tenth to eleventh centuries*

Date (CE)	Name	Proposed reconstruction	Affiliation or sent by	Source and remarks
977	Ge-xin (哥心)	Qāsim	Bo-ni (Brunei)	*SHY FY* 7
977	Mo-he-mo (摩訶末)	Muḥammad	The Arab lands	*SHY FY* 7
988/9	Hu-xuan (忽宣)	Ḥusayn	Champa	*SHY FY* 4: Champa Led 300 members of clan to Guangzhou
997	Ya-tuo-luo-pan-si (押陀羅潘思)	ʻAbd Allāh Pansur	Champa	*SHY FY* 4: Champa
1008	Ma-he-wu (麻訶勿)	Muḥammad	San-fo-qi	*SHY FY* 7
1011	Ya-li Bai-di (亞里白地)	ʻAli Badī	San-ma-lan-guo (possibly Zamboanga)	*SHY FY* 4 Possibly same person as the Li Mei-di mentioned in Appendix 1 under date 1008
1017	Ma-si-li (麻思利)	Masrī	Arab merchant	*SHY* *Shi-bo-si* section
1088	Hu-xian	Ḥusayn	San-fo-qi	*Wen-xian tong-kao juan* 332

FY = *Fan-yi* (a section of the *SHI*)
SHY = *Song Hui-yao*

11

Follow the white camel: Islam in China to 1800

ZVI BEN-DOR BENITE

Introduction

The inhabitants of Jiezi, a Muslim village of the Salar ethnic group in Qinghai, China, tell an interesting story about the circumstances of their migration from Central Asia many centuries ago. As the story goes, they had left Samarqand centuries earlier, fleeing injustice and tyranny. They had moved generally eastward – to 'China, the Land of Peace and Harmony' – but arrived in the specific location of Jiezi 'following the lead of a white camel with a Qur'ān strapped to its head for guidance'.[1] The white camel in this story is noteworthy. Recall that the caliph 'Umar entered Jerusalem on a white camel, thereby sending a message of peace and harmony; more importantly, the Prophet Muḥammad determined the spot of his mosque in Medina by letting his white camel loose and following it until it stopped to rest. The implications of the story are quite clear: the journey of Muslims from Samarqand to China – outside the 'House of Islam' – was justified and even divinely approved. It was to be seen as akin to other significant events in Islamic history: the making of Jerusalem part of the Islamic world, and the very creation of the first Islamic polity. One could take it even a step further: the journey to Jiezi was nothing less than a re-enactment of the *hijra*. Just as Muḥammad had fled tyranny and injustice, so too the Muslims from Samarqand. Just as he used a white camel to transform Yathrib into Medina, so too the Muslims of Jiezi. This story is but one piece of a broader Chinese Muslim strategy of making China home to Muslims and transforming it

1 Mi Yizhi, *Sala zu shi* (Chengdu, 2004), pp. 6–8; Ma Jianzhong, 'Stone camels and clear springs: The Salar's Samarkand origins', *Asian Folklore Studies*, 55 (1996), pp. 287–98. For issues of space I refer the reader to an excellent bibliography on Islam in China: Donald Daniel Leslie, Yang Daye and Aḥmad Youssef, *Islam in traditional China: A bibliographical guide* (Nettetal, 2006).

into an 'Islamic space' in spite of the fact that it actually lies outside the *dār al-islām*.[2]

Grasping this duality – between China being 'distant' and China being an Islamic home – is crucial to the understanding of the history of Islam and Muslims in China. It reflects the sense of 'diasporic homeland'[3] that resulted from an acute sense of distance from the Islamic world among Chinese Muslims and the need for conscious negotiation of the place of Islam and Muslims within Chinese society and culture. This process of negotiation eventually gave rise to an Islam that is uniquely Chinese in its self-perception, and to a Muslim community that, while emphasising the 'foreign' origins of its religious tradition, considers itself specifically Chinese.

The historical, as opposed to mythical, circumstances of the Muslims' migration to and arrival in China contribute significantly to their subsequent history. Furthermore, the distance and the sporadic and disorganised nature of Muslim migration to China created different, and sometimes separate, Muslim communities within Chinese territory. Until, perhaps, the twentieth century and the creation of the Republic and the People's Republic, there is no truly unified history of 'Islam in China' to speak of.[4] Only the modern Chinese state was able to classify the Muslims of China as members of several distinct collectivities known to be Muslim. Even though Chinese Muslims within China's old territories ('China Proper') tend to believe and understand their history to be one unified historical trajectory of a 'Muslim nationality', this was certainly not the case. However, the main Muslim community in China was already engaged during the seventeenth and eighteenth centuries in creating what would later become a more unified, transregional Chinese Muslim identity. In many respects, though, it is more accurate to speak of histories of Islam and of Muslims in China, rather than of a singular historical trajectory, 'Islam in China'.

Another important point to bear in mind is the fact that the term 'China' was itself profoundly transformed several times over the course of the period discussed in this essay. Politically speaking, 'China' moved from a huge

2 Zvi Ben-Dor Benite, '"Even unto China": Displacement and Chinese Muslim myths of origin', *Bulletin of the Royal Institute for Inter-Faith Studies*, Winter, (2003), pp. 93–114.

3 This term is my own. Other scholars in the field might have slightly different ways to describe this condition. Jonathan Lipman implies another meaning when he speaks of 'Familiar Strangers'. Jonathan Lipman, *Familiar strangers: A history of Muslims in north-west China* (Seattle, 1997). Also see Zvi Ben-Dor Benite, *The Dao of Muḥammad: A cultural history of Muslims in late imperial China* (Cambridge, 2005), pp. 12–20.

4 Dru C. Gladney, *Muslim Chinese: Ethnic nationalism in the People's Republic* (Cambridge, MA, 1991), pp. 36–60.

empire during Tang times (618–907); to a small and embattled empire during Song times (960–1279); to be part of a huge Mongol khanate known as the Yuan (1279–1368); to a rather strong empire (though much smaller than the khanate) during Ming times (1368–1644); to a huge empire twice the size of its predecessor during Qing times (1644–1911). Geographically speaking, these transformations meant that at certain times different Muslims were or were not under Chinese rule. For instance, Central Asian Muslim communities that were under the yoke of the khan in Khanbaliq (Beijing) during Yuan times were not subjects of China during the Ming. Similarly, the Qing conquests in Central Asia during the eighteenth century brought many more communities that were Muslim into the fold.[5] From a cultural point of view, China itself was also transformed by these shifts. In Tang times, it tended to be quite open about its affinities with Central Asia. During Song times, it was 'Chinese', but during Yuan times, it became a multilayered society with Mongols at the top. During Ming times it was a Chinese polity striving for a greater degree of homogenisation and seeking to revive an imagined pure 'Han' Chinese past. Finally, during Qing times, China became part of a consciously multiethnic empire again ruled by a non-Chinese people.

As we shall see, these transformations had a tremendous impact on the history of Islam in China. These transformations are also important because they allow us to understand the various possible periodisations of its history. Given the multiple trajectories of Chinese Islamic history over the years, it is impossible to offer a simple unified periodisation. Joseph Fletcher offered an approach that divided Chinese Islamic history into 'tides', each connected to the 'influence and impact of individuals who entered China during critical periods of exchange with the outside world'.[6] However, the dramatic changes and wealth of research in the field since Fletcher's untimely death mandate that internal developments and transformations within Chinese Islamic society, as well as the 'general' trajectory of Chinese history, be taken into account as well. This essay therefore offers an 'unfastened' periodisation, divided into 'phases' (rather than strict stages) that highlight the main features of each period in the history of Chinese Islam. The phases are organised in a loose chronological order, and for simplicity's sake each carries the name of

5 For a bibliographical manual of Chinese history see Endymion Wilkinson, *Chinese history: A manual* (Cambridge, 2000).

6 Gladney, *Muslim Chinese*, 36; Joseph Fletcher, *Les 'voies' (turuq) soufies en Chine* (Paris, 1986). See Gladney's elaboration on each tide in Gladney, *Muslim Chinese*, pp. 6–59; Joseph Fletcher, *Studies on Chinese and Islamic Inner Asia*, ed. Beatrice Forbes Manz (London, 1995).

significant locations that mark turning points in Chinese Islamic history. I should caution readers that the division into phases does not mean that all Muslims in China had similar historical experiences at the same time. Such a condition does not exist in China even today, when there is an unprecedented degree of homogeneity in Chinese Islam. In fact, during the pre-modern era in many areas of China one phase continued well after another phase had already started elsewhere. Therefore, the locales I choose as titles for each phase are best seen as marking the highlight of a specific era.

Phase one: Chang'an and Quanzhou

The first significant marker of Muslim presence in China is the Great mosque in Xian (then Chang'an). The original structure was built on what was apparently a Buddhist site, according to tradition in 742 CE (but certainly at least somewhat later).[7] This period precedes the designated scope of this chapter, but a brief summary is crucial for the understanding of subsequent periods. The location of the first mosque in Xian should not be surprising at all. Chang'an was then the capital of the Tang dynasty (618–907), and a major world and Asian commercial centre. The Tang empire at that time stretched its long 'arm' to Central Asia reaching as far west as the north-eastern provinces of today's Iran. The Tang emperors, themselves related to the Turkic tribes which they often fought, maintained complex military and commercial relationships with various Central Asian nomadic groups as well as with Sasanid Iran. The Tang also had similar diplomatic ties with the Islamic empire that replaced the Persians.[8] The Muslim presence in the region was felt in China in different ways during the early eighth century. Already, during the 710s, the Arab general Qutayba arrived at the Tang borders with his armies. The event was recorded in both Arab and Chinese histories of the time, but no major military clash took place.[9] In 751, a large Muslim force clashed with and defeated a much smaller Tang garrison at the battle of Talas, thereby triggering the long retreat of the Tang from Central Asia.[10]

7 Wu Jianwei (ed.), *Zhongguo Qingzhensi Zonglan* (Yinchuan, 1995), pp. 304–5.
8 Denis C. Twitchett (ed.), *The Cambridge history of China*, vol. III: *Sui and T'ang China, 589–906* (Cambridge, 1979), pp. 279–81. See also Tazaka Kōdō, *Chūgoku ni okeru Kaikyō no denrai to sono kōtsū* (Tokyo, 1964), pp. 261–90.
9 Donald Leslie, *The integration of religious minorities in China: The case of Chinese Muslims* (Canberra, 1998), p. 5.
10 Twitchett (ed.), *The Cambridge history of China*, pp. 34–8.

Muslim armies did not arrive in China following the battle, but Muslim merchants did, as part of the increasing presence of Muslims in various locations along the 'Silk Road'. Soon after, Arab merchants arrived in the Central Asian trade posts on the Silk Road. Some of them came to the Tang capital of Chang'an, where they joined countless other people of many ethnicities, religions and locations from the old world. Chang'an, the capital of the entire East Asian region, with over a million people, was the easternmost and most significant location on the Silk Road. The establishment of the mosque in the city suggests the creation of a more stable community.[11] At about the same time, or shortly thereafter, Muslim merchants, mainly from the Gulf, began arriving in China via Indian Ocean trade routes. These early connections with the Islamic world gave rise to several significant Muslim communities in China: the aforementioned Chang'an in the north-west, and the port cities of Canton (Guangzhou) in the south, and Quanzhou on the south-eastern coast of China. New communities subsequently emerged in other central cities along major communication lines. Hangzhou and Kaifeng, major commercial hubs on the Chinese Grand Canal, and later Song capitals; and Yangzhou on the northern banks of the Yangzi river, are good examples. All of these housed large sojourner populations of merchants, soldiers and mercenaries, refugees and adventurers of all sorts. The rapid rise of these Islamic communities, it is very important to note, was also a quintessential sign of the high degree of cosmopolitanism and openness that characterised particularly the early Tang empire.[12] These features allowed Muslim communities to prosper. A rather rare case is cited of one Li Yansheng, identified in Tang sources as 'an Arab' (*Dashiguo ren*), who passed the civil service exams in 847, and was recommended to a post at the palace. The incident sparked a debate among Chinese scholars about the meaning of 'being Chinese' in the wake of this appointment. Li's achievement in passing the exams and gaining the court attention shows the degree of integration into Chinese society and culture that could be attained by individual Muslims if so desired. Chinese Islamic memory many centuries later would 'translate' this cosmopolitanism of the Tang into a perception of friendship and hospitality between the Tang and Islamic empires.

11 Lipman, *Familiar strangers*, pp. 24–31. For a more detailed summary based on Chinese sources see Li Xinghua, Huibin Qin, Jinyuan Feng and Qiuzhen Sha, *Zhongguo Yisilan jiao shi* (Beijing, 1998), pp. 3–57; Qiu Shusen, *Zhongguo huizu shi* (Yinchuan, 1996), pp. 2–30.

12 Charles Holcombe, 'Immigrants and strangers: From cosmopolitanism to Confucian universalism in Tang China', *T'ang Studies*, 20–1 (June 2002), pp. 71–112; see also Marc Abramson's careful assessment of that question: Marc Samuel Abramson, *Ethnic identity in Tang China* (Philadelphia, 2008).

The Muslims in China maintained contacts with the wider Islamic world. In this key regard, Muslims were different from the other sojourning populations. Nestorian Christians, for instance, had arrived in Chang'an as part of a general migration eastward following persecution in the Middle East. The Muslims, in contrast, had an increasingly strong and dominant Islamic world 'behind them', as external referent. This meant that so long as trade routes with China were dominated by Muslims, more and more Muslims came to dwell in the country. It also meant that, as the Islamisation of Central Asian peoples prevailed, more and more Muslims arrived in China. Thus, while the original community of Indian Buddhists that had resided in Quanzhou since well before the Muslims became greatly diminished, Muslims dominated this centuries-old city, and even gave it an Arab name, Zaitun.[13] Similarly, the Jewish community of Kaifeng always remained small, whereas the Muslim community in the city kept increasing, and thus in the seventeenth century was to become a major centre of Islamic learning.[14] The increasing size of China's Islamic communities also meant that Muslim wealth could sustain communal life and its institutions. This phase saw the construction of several important mosques in various communities. China's 'Four Ancient Mosques' – the Huaisheng mosque in Canton, the Qingjing mosque in Quanzhou (Masjid al-Ashab), the Xianhe mosque in Yangzhou and the Fenghuang mosque in Hangzhou – were all constructed or purchased during the period of the Tang and Song dynasties. The Quanzhou Muslims (who had been particularly dominant) left an impressive cemetery with beautiful inscriptions in Arabic on tombstones and on mosque tablets. Smaller monuments and tombs of this kind can be found elsewhere in China.[15]

Quanzhou/Zaitun was certainly the most significant community, and was so for centuries. It bore the key hallmarks of Islamic presence in China between the eighth and thirteenth centuries: a maritime community of merchants, with close and frequent commercial ties to the Islamic world to ensure a steady migration of Muslims. An examination of the aforementioned inscriptions shows that most of the Muslims in the city came from the Persian Gulf, or from locations with access to the Indian Ocean, such as Yemen.

13 Tansen Sen, *Buddhism, diplomacy, and trade: The realignment of Sino-Indian relations, 600–1400* (Honolulu, 2003).

14 Donald Leslie, *The survival of the Chinese Jews: The Jewish community of Kaifeng* (Leiden, 1972).

15 Fujian sheng Quanzhou haiwai jiatongshi bowuguan, *Quanzhou Yisilan jiao yan jiu lun wen xuan* (Fuzhou, 1983); Chen Dasheng and Ludvik Kalus, *Corpus d'inscriptions arabes et persanes en Chine, vol. I: Province de Fu-Jian (Quanzhou, Fu-zhou, Xia-men)* (Paris, 1991).

However, a few also came from Central Asian locations, suggesting that the city also attracted Muslims who were part of a different trade system. By the end of the Song period, during the thirteenth century, Muslim dominance in the city was such that Muslims were appointed by the state as officials in the Trade and Customs office. Most well known is the case of Pu Shougeng, whose family moved to the city from Canton, and who served as superintendent (*tiju*) of the office from 1250 to 1280.[16] Evidently, this appointment signified not only the importance of the Muslims in the city, but also their crucial role in China's dealings with other regions of the southern and western oceans.The Song dynasty was less cosmopolitan and confident than its Tang predecessor, but by its time Muslim communities were so significant that they were at the very least tolerated and accepted.

The Islamic communities in China attracted attention in the Islamic world, mainly because of the supposed 'enchantedness' of China and its distance from the core Islamic regions. The famous *Akhbār al-Ṣin wa-l-Hind* (published *c.* 915) tells of large Arab communities in southern China; even though the numbers are undoubtedly exaggerated, they clearly reflect sizeable communities.[17] The distance of China had always to be accounted for in tales of adventures of the Arabs going there. For instance, al-Sīrāfī's account tells of one Ibn Wahb al-Quraishi who was originally from Baṣra but left this city for Sīrāf after it was sacked by rebels (probably in 898 by Qarāmiṭa), and 'found himself on a boat going to *al-Ṣin*'. The description of the journey to China reflects the reality: a constant movement back and forth to China from various ports in the Islamic world, taking along merchants and merchandise and the occasional adventurer like Ibn Wahb.

Even though Arab accounts such as those of al-Sīrāfi or the later Ibn Baṭṭūṭa, who toured China in the fourteenth century (whose depictions of Muslim life focus mostly on merchants in the port cities), describe a degree of communication and interaction with the local Chinese population, it is quite clear that most Muslims lived in secluded neighbourhoods in the large cities where they could maintain a more '*ḥalāl*' culture – free from idols and pork, but quite autonomous in every other regard, as well.[18] Ibn Baṭṭūṭa, serious cleric that he

16 Jitsuzō Kuwabara, 'On P'u Shou-keng', *Memoirs of the Research Department of the Toyō Bunko*, 2 (1928), pp. 1–79, and 7 (1935), pp. 1–104. For this appointment in the context of China's maritime history see Gang Deng, *Maritime sector, institutions, and sea power of premodern China* (Westport, CT, 1999), pp. 120–2.

17 Sulaymān al-Tājir and Abū Zayd Ḥasan ibn Yazīd Sīrāfī, *Akhbār al-Ṣīn wa-l-Hind* (Cairo, 2000), pp. 54–61. See more on this in Ben-Dor Benite, 'Even unto China', pp. 99–101.

18 Lipman, *Familiar strangers*, pp. 28–33.

was, reflects this sequestration nicely: 'China, for all its magnificence, did not please me. I was deeply depressed by the prevalence of infidelity and, when I left my lodging, I saw many offensive things that distressed me so much that I stayed at home and went out only when necessary.'[19] Far away from home, the Muslims Ibn Baṭṭūṭa encountered were very hospitable: 'they are delighted when a Muslim arrives among them and they say, "He has come from the land of Islam" and give then *zakat* ... so that he becomes as rich as one of them.'[20] In 'Khansa' (Hangzhou), Ibn Baṭṭūṭa stayed with "Uthman ibn 'Affān the Egyptian, ... one of the important merchants who became fond of this city and settled [here]'. In Zaitun, he stayed with a 'a merchant from Iṣfahān'. In Guangzhou (Sin-kalan), he lodged with 'Awhad al-Din from Sinjar, a distinguished, important and very wealthy man'. These wealthy merchants could easily support the religious life of their communities and hire teachers, *imāms* and clerics for their mosques and madrasas, so that Ibn Baṭṭūṭa kept meeting people like 'a *qāḍī* from Ardabīl', or 'a shaykh from Kazarun'. His claim that 'in every one of their [the Muslims'] quarters there is a Shaykh al-Islām' is probably an exaggeration, but certainly it reflects an image of rich and self-sustaining religious life.[21] The wealth of Islamic literature – religious books of all sorts and Qurʾāns – from that period that was preserved in China suggests that the Muslim communities of the time were major consumers and importers of Islamic education and educators.[22]

Despite the comfort and wealth, it is clear that Muslim life in China was perceived more as a matter of sojourn and tenancy rather than permanent habitation. The terminology used by the Song state to define Muslims certainly reflects this in calling their neighbourhood 'foreigners' quarters' (*fanfang*) and insisting on using the term 'guests' (*ke*) in reference to them. Thus, for instance, we can find designations such as 'native-born foreign sojourners' (*tusheng fanke*) or 'fifth-generation foreign sojourners' (*wushi fanke*).[23] Even after more than a hundred years in China, one was still not 'Chinese'. This was the quintessential 'merchant diaspora', and the numerous references in Ibn

19 Abū 'Abd Allāh ibn *Baṭṭūṭa, Rihlat Ibn Baṭṭūṭa* (Beirut, 1997), p. 639. Translations are from Ibn Baṭṭūṭa, The *travels of Ibn Baṭṭūṭa,* trans. and ed. H. A. R. Gibb, Hakluyt Society (London, 1994), p. 900, with my minor amendments.

20 Ibn Baṭṭūṭa, *Rihla*, p. 633. In Gibb, *Travels*, pp. 894–5.

21 Ibn Baṭṭūṭa, *Rihla*, pp. 633–5. In Gibb, *Travels*, pp. 894–7.

22 M. J. Shari'at, 'The library of the Tung-his [*sic*; i.e. Tongsi] mosque at Peking', *Asian Affairs*, 11, 1 (1980), pp. 68–70; Donald D. Leslie and Mohamed Wassel, 'Arabic and Persian sources used by Liu Chih', *Central Asiatic Journal*, 26, 1–2 (1982), pp. 78–104.

23 Yang Huaizhong, 'Tangdai de fanke'; 'Songdai de fanke', in Yang Huaizhong, *Huizushi lungao* (Yinchuan, 1991), pp. 50–128.

Baṭṭūṭa to merchants, on the one hand, and to the acute sense of distance from the Islamic world, on the other, account for both parts of this term.[24]

Phase two: Khanbaliq and Yunnan

The Mongol conquest of China, completed in the second half of the thirteenth century, dramatically transformed Muslim presence and Islamic life in China. In many regards, the 'Quanzhou phase' was not disrupted and was even further intensified in the wake of the Mongol unification of Asia and the effects of the 'Pax Mongolica'. More merchants than ever before came to China – many of them from the Islamic world.[25] They also became stronger politically. The aforementioned Pu Shougeng, the Song-appointed official in Quanzhou, surrendered the city to the Mongol armies in 1276, and offered them naval forces. He remained in office until 1280, and the grateful khan, Qubilai, made him responsible for all trade in southern China, including Canton. He passed away peacefully in 1296.[26] During the Yuan period, a third of the superintendents of trade ships in Fujian were Muslims, located in several ports.

The bigger change, however, came with the different type of Muslims and Muslim settlements introduced to China during the Mongol period. The Mongols created in China a 'professional diaspora', in which Muslims were the largest element, by bringing in technocrats, scientists, administrators, soldiers, musicians and artisans of all sorts, to settle and help govern and administer China.[27] (It is important to note, however, that Muslims had served in various Mongol courts from early on, even before the conquest of China.)[28] This professional diaspora did not replace the merchant diaspora but added an important layer to it. The massive influx of Muslims during the period also created rural Muslim communities particularly, but not only, in north-western and south-western China. Migrants and discharged Muslim soldiers were encouraged to settle and farm areas that were depopulated after the wars, so as to revive the economy and enhance the control over the local population. This policy helped create a large rural Muslim population.[29] Finally, just

24 Ben-Dor Benite, 'Even unto China'.

25 See Yang Zhijiu, *Yuan dai Hui zu shi gao* (Tianjin, 2003), pp. 77–125; also see Jerry Bentley, *Old world encounters: Cross-cultural contacts and exchanges in pre-modern Times* (New York, 1993).

26 Kuwabara, 'On P'u Shou-keng'.

27 Yang, *Yuan dai Hui zu shi gao*.

28 Morris Rossabi, 'The Muslims in the early Yuan dynasty', in J. Langlois (ed.), *China under Mongol rule* (Princeton, 1981), pp. 257–94. See also Yu Zhengui, *Zhongguo li dai zheng quan yu Yisilan jiao* (Yinchuan, 1996), pp. 76–114.

29 Yang, *Yuan dai Hui zu shi gao*, pp. 149–89, 237–62; and Lipman, *Familiar strangers*, pp. 34–5.

as Muslims had been introduced to China, the Mongols introduced China to the world. 'China' was now part of the 'Yuan khanate' and was incorporated with other territories, among them Central Asia, Mongolia, Tibet, northern Vietnam, and the kingdom of Dali in the south-west. This meant that more Muslims, particularly in the Islamised and Islamising Central Asian territories, were now sharing the same rulers with the Chinese and coming into closer contact with China.

Thus, in addition to the 'Quanzhou' Muslim merchant, semi-secluded in the Muslim quarter in port cities, we now encounter figures like ʿAbd al-Raḥmān, Fāṭima, or Aḥmad, the all-powerful minister at the Mongol court in Khanbaliq (future Beijing) who appears in Marco Polo's travelogue. Marco Polo's account of this man is quite hostile. Its mention of Aḥmad's sexual voraciousness suggests that Polo was influenced by European images of the Prophet Muḥammad when he was writing. But, the basic description of the 'saracen named Ahmac' (A-ha-ma in the Chinese sources), 'a crafty and bold man, whose influence with the Grand Khan surpassed that of all others', reflects the power that certain Muslims had at the court. This Aḥmad was a finance and treasury man, like numerous other, less important, Muslims at all levels of the Yuan treasury and tax administration.[30] Other wings of the Yuan government such as medicine and engineering housed large numbers of Muslims as well. The official records of the Yuan dynasty tell us of two – Aḥmad and Ismāʿīl – who came from Mosul to China at the invitation of Qubilai to make cannons. It was also at this time that Ibn Sīnā's studies in pharmacology arrived in China.

But perhaps more interesting than the political figures at the court were the Muslim scientists and other learned men. Perhaps more than the previous rulers of China, the Mongols considered astronomy and calendar-making to be important tools of power. They populated their newly built observatory in Khanbaliq with astronomers brought in from the Islamic world, where astronomy and mathematics were the most advanced in the world. The records of the period mention men like Jamāl al-Dīn, a Persian astronomer in charge of the most significant calendar reform in China in centuries. Soon after the establishment of the Yuan dynasty, Jamāl presented the court with his 'Thousand Year Calendar'. Islamic astronomy was so important in the court that the Mongols created a 'Bureau of Muslim Astronomy' (*Huihui si tian jian*) alongside the regular office of astronomy. An independent office was certainly necessary since the Muslim astronomers introduced new tools and new

30 Marco Polo, *Travels* (London, 1929), pp. 275–8; Lipman, *Familiar strangers*, pp. 31–2.

methods to Chinese astronomy.[31] Jamāl al-Dīn also introduced new methods of geography and mapmaking and was very instrumental in producing the first 'all national record' (*da yi tongzhi*), encompassing all of China's geography.[32] As we shall see, one of the most important projects during the Ming would be the translation of this knowledge into Chinese. In any event, from the early Yuan period on, until the arrival of Jesuit astronomers in the seventeenth century, Islamic astronomy would play an important role in the history of Chinese science.

Alongside the Khanbaliq scientists and administrators came massive numbers of Muslims in the military system who settled elsewhere in China. As is well known, the Mongol armies that conquered and governed China included many non-Mongols and Muslims. After the conquest, the Mongols used these soldiers in garrisons all over China and encouraged them to settle in different regions – in eastern, as well as north-western China. The rather high numbers of Muslims in Chinese military organisations later on is partially connected to this policy. The most significant activity, however, was in what was to become the south-western Chinese province of Yunnan. This large region, originally not part of China, was incorporated with the khanate, and its inhabitants 'civilised' for the Mongols, by Shams al-Dīn 'Umar (1211–79). 'Umar, a nobleman and a *sayyid* from Bukhārā, had a long career in the Mongol military after the surrender of Bukhārā to the Mongols during the wars of Central Asia. In China, he held a number of high military appointments in the Mongol government before taking over as governor of the newly conquered Yunnan in 1274. 'Umar was responsible not only for the successful 'stabilisation' of Yunnan, which meant by and large bringing Chinese administration, agriculture and farming as well as culture to the province, but also for its (perhaps unintended) Islamisation. There is some controversy among Western scholars concerning the depth of Shams al-Dīn's faith in Islam. But there should be little doubt that this Bukhārān prince is at least partially responsible for the influx of Muslims into the province during this period, an immigration that created a vibrant Muslim community in Yunnan.[33] Two of 'Umar's sons succeeded him as governor and this family of Muslims dominated the province well into the Ming period, when the government forced

31 Benno van Dalen, 'Islamic astronomy in China during the Yuan and Ming dynasties', *Historia Scientiarium*, 7 (1997), pp. 11–43. Also, Tazaka Kōdō, 'An aspect of Islam [*sic*] culture introduced into China', *Memoirs of the Research Department of the Toyō Bunko*, 16 (1957), pp. 75–160.

32 Yang, *Yuan dai Hui zu shi gao*, pp. 303–14.

33 *Ibid.*, pp. 347–55.

Han settlers to move to the province. During the nineteenth century, Yunnan was an important centre of Islamic activity – political, cultural and military.

The Yunnan–Khanbaliq phase was crucial as a transition away from the Tang–Song relative isolation of 'non-Chinese' Muslims living in China. In addition to the merchants, we now had also Muslims who were soldiers, farmers, artisans, administrators and scientists – all professions that require greater and more intensive contacts with the population at all levels. During the Tang and the Song periods, cases of Muslims who adopted Chinese names and/or were intimately familiar with Chinese culture, such as the 'Arab mandarin' Li Yansheng, or the Pus of Quanzhou, were quite rare. During the Yuan period, this began to change. Mongol policies had generally tended to keep the different populations under their control separate, and Ibn Baṭṭūṭa's description of the Muslim communities reflects a picture of Muslims living in distinct quarters within large cities. Now, the presence of Muslims in the government and the administration meant, in the long run, that more and more Muslims became increasingly familiar with Chinese culture, styles and norms. This was probably true towards the end of the Yuan dynasty, when its Mongol rulers themselves became acculturated to Chinese culture to a considerable degree.

One can understand this process on different levels – administrative, economic and cultural. First, the various designators with the *ke* (guest) character to them that prevailed during the previous periods disappeared. Instead, the state used a new administrative term for identifying its foreigners (and therefore Muslims): *semu* (lit. 'coloured eyes'), which meant 'people of various categories'.[34] Furthermore, the term 'huihui' became exclusively associated with Muslims.[35] *Huihui* has its origins in the Tang period, and to this day it is not quite clear why it became associated with Islam and Muslims. Nevertheless, it became the most common designator for Muslims during the Yuan period, as the aforementioned title of the Islamic bureau of astronomy and the numerous figures identified in the official records as 'huihui' testify. *Huihui* also developed several variations – *huimin* (hui people), *huizei* (Muslim bandits), *huijiao* (hui teaching; that is, Islam) and *huizu* (Muslim national), to name a few, and became the first word used for Islam in Japanese as well (*kaikai*, and *kaikyō*). Finally, in terms of culture, the Yuan period saw the first instance of Muslim literary activity in Chinese – most notably Chinese poetry. Traditionally less socially and culturally rigid a field than classical learning,

34 Lipman, *Familiar strangers*, pp. 32–5.
35 Zhang Yingsheng. *Yuan dai Hui zu wen xue jia* (Beijing, 2004), pp. 1–29.

Chinese poetry already had one great hero of non-Chinese descent, the Sogdian Li Bai (701–62). During the Yuan his successors were the Muslims Gao Kegong (1248–1310), Saadulla (1272–1355), Ma Zuchang (1279–1338), Ma Jiugao (1268–1350), Nai Jian (1309–68), Qin Buhua (1304–52) and many others. It should be noted that with the exception of the first poet, all the others were born in China after the founding of the Yuan.[36]

Phase three: Nanjing

The Nanjing phase, which corresponds quite closely to the rise of the Ming dynasty in the fourteenth century, is the most dramatic turning point in the Chinese Muslim history sketched here. Just as the transformation of the state and the empire during the Song–Yuan transition had a tremendous impact on China's Muslims, the transition from the Yuan, a huge multiethnic empire headed by Mongols, to the smaller and Chinese Ming had its impact. Simply put, it marks the ideational transformation of 'Muslims in China' into 'Chinese Muslims', as the Muslims living in China adopted Chinese culture. The other side of this process was the disappearance of Arab and Persian culture and language, leaving 'Islam' as the most significant element in the 'Islamic' side of the new emerging Chinese-Islamic identity. For instance, Arab and Persian language and names disappeared, giving way to Chinese names or Chinese variations on Arab names – Maḥmūd and Muḥammad turned into 'Ma'. Similarly, Middle Eastern and Central Asian styles of clothing and architecture also gave way to Chinese styles. Other Islamic practices were modified. Finally, towards the end of the Nanjing phase we see the rise of a specific form of Islam that was particularly Chinese. And next to the term *Huihui*, we now see the rise of two more terms designating Islam and Muslims: 'Qing Zhen' (lit. Pure and True, which should be read as 'authentic *ḥalāl*'), and 'Tian Fang' (lit. 'Heavenly Square', referring to the Kaʿba). The term *semu* disappeared with the Yuan state that created it. The Nanjing phase also marks the decisive end of the Quanzhou phase. Of course, Muslim merchants did not disappear. But the Arabic- or Persian-speaking merchant who had traded quite freely with the Islamic world was now gone. This development also had to do with changes in trade in the Indian Ocean. But within China, Nanjing – the first capital of the Ming dynasty – played the key role in such processes.

Muslims were greatly affected by the rebellions that eventually drove the Mongols out in the mid-fourteenth century and created the Ming dynasty. The

36 *Ibid.*, pp. 51–297.

strong Muslim military presence and their basic alliance with the Mongol state were both key in this transition. On the one hand, a Yuan garrison of Muslim soldiers near Quanzhou fought against the Ming armies when they arrived in the region after having defeated the Mongols elsewhere. This episode resulted in harsh Ming policies against the Muslims of Quanzhou after the 'rebellion' was crushed, and many families left the city and migrated elsewhere.[37] On the other hand, however, some prominent members of the Ming founder's original warband were Muslim. These men, like the Ming founder Zhu Yuanzhang (1328–98) himself, all hailed from a region in Anhui province where the Mongols had previously settled many Muslim soldiers.[38]

This duality affected Ming policies towards the Muslims. On the one hand they were suspect, on the other they were recognised as a social force to reckon with. Thus, for instance, when all 'foreign' religions were banned after the rise of the Ming, Islam was not. But the regime, striving for greater homogeneity along (imagined) 'authentic Chinese' cultural norms, dictated a much less conspicuous Islamic presence in the public sphere. As a result, minarets disappeared from Chinese mosques, and the call for prayer was abolished. Zhu Yuanzhang's son, Zhu Di (r. 1402–24), permitted and even sponsored the renovation of several mosques all over China. Similarly, at first, Zhu Yuanzhang sought to isolate the Muslims by banning intermarriage and the adoption of Chinese names. Soon thereafter, however, both were encouraged by the regime. At the court itself, the Muslim presence continued as, famously, the Ming rulers sponsored the translation of Islamic scientific knowledge into Chinese, a project that produced some of the most important Chinese works in astronomy and medicine.[39] Later on, such policies would give rise to the image of the Ming dynasty as a 'patron of Islam' and to the persistent claim that Zhu Yuanzhang himself was a 'secret Muslim'.[40] Soon enough, sizeable and highly acculturated Muslim communities emerged in Nanjing itself and elsewhere in eastern China. Many members of these communities began to compete for official positions through participation in the Chinese civil service examination system.[41]

37 Shinji Maejima, 'The Muslims in Ch'uan-chou at the end of the Yuan dynasty', *Memoirs of the Research Department of the Toyō Bunko*, 31–2 (1973–4).

38 Zvi Ben-Dor Benite, 'The Marrano emperor: The mysterious bond between Zhu Yuanzhang and the Chinese Muslims', in Sarah Schneewind (ed.), *Long live the emperor!: Uses of the Ming founder across six centuries of East Asian history*, Ming Studies Research Series, 4, Minneapolis, 2008, pp. 292–3.

39 *Ibid.*, pp. 281–4.

40 Ben-Dor Benite, 'The Marrano emperor'.

41 Ben-Dor Benite, *Dao of Muḥammad*.

Another important aspect of Ming policy that greatly affected Muslims was its attitude of 'conciliate and control' *vis-à-vis* Central Asia and its Muslims. The collapse of the Yuan khanate effectively created a border between the Muslim communities of Central Asia and the Muslims of China, particularly those of the north-west, which the Ming rulers tried hard to keep sealed. Nevertheless, Muslims kept migrating from Central Asia to China. Two centuries after the founding of the Ming, the Jesuit Matteo Ricci (1552–1610) gives us an invaluable testimony that reflects this situation and the results of the Ming transformation. Accounting for a wide range of forms of Muslim life in China and reflecting the condition of 'co-habitation' between Chinese law and Islamic ritual, Ricci writes:

> since in the far western regions China borders on Persia, at various times many followers of Mohammedan faith entered this country, and their children and descendants multiplied so much that they have spread over all China with thousands of families. They are residing in nearly all provinces, where they have sumptuous mosques, recite their prayers, are circumcised, conduct their ceremonies ... and live subject to Chinese laws ... For these reasons, they are treated as native Chinese, and not being suspected of plotting rebellion, they are allowed to study and enter the ranks of [the] bureaucracy. Many of them, having received official rank, abandon their old beliefs, retaining only their prohibitions against eating pork, to which they have never become accustomed.[42]

The most important outcome of the Nanjing phase was produced by a group of people located socially somewhere between the highly acculturated bureaucratic elite and the mosque-goers. The *Han Kitab*, a hybrid of Chinese and Arabic words that means 'The Chinese Book', is a huge collection of books and treatises on Islam, in classical Chinese, by scholars educated both in the Confucian classics and in Islamic textual tradition. Few Han Kitab scholars had passed through the official Chinese examination system. Most came from a unique education system, one that combined classical Chinese studies with Islam, which began emerging in the late 1500s. The system originated in the Muslim communities of north-western China, but it really gained ground and prospered after its second generation of teachers moved eastward, and settled within the highly acculturated urban communities of the Yangzi delta – Nanjing in particular. Even scholars from as far away as Yunnan, such as Ma Zhu (d. *c.* 1680), a descendant of the aforementioned Shams al-Dīn, spent time in the city teaching.[43]

42 Cited in Jonathan Spence, *The memory palace of Matteo Ricci* (New York, 1984), p. 118. Translation is Spence's with some of my own edits and amendments.
43 Ben-Dor Benite, *Dao of Muḥammad*, pp. 26–71, 115–62.

Drawing heavily on Chinese norms of scholarship and transmission of knowledge, the Han Kitab scholars understood themselves as a 'school of scholarship' within the wider community of Chinese scholars, a school whose traditional teaching was Islam. Accordingly, the study of Islam was defined as the study of the 'Dao of Muḥammad', that is, the 'Way' that originates in Muḥammad's teachings. As an originator of knowledge, the prophet was compared to great Chinese sages of antiquity so as to legitimate the study of his teachings by his followers in China.[44] The Han Kitab books consisted at first mostly of translations of Islamic (Persian Sufi) texts. From the mid-seventeenth century, shortly after the rise of the Manchu-Qing dynasty in 1644, scholars also began producing original works – mostly highly sophisticated combinations of Sufi and classical Chinese thought. The purpose of learning (*xue*) was *renzhu* ('Knowledge of the Lord'), an adaptation of the Sufi *maʿrifa*/*ʿirfān*. In this way, not Islam *per se*, but the *study of Islam* was rendered compatible with the Neo-Confucian definition of the purpose of learning, which tended to assign it mystical dimensions.[45] It is important to note that the Manchu-Qing dynasty's 'multiethnic' imperial policies had a direct impact on the identitarian tone that Han Kitab books began taking on from the later seventeenth century. As opposed to the 'China-centred', homogenising policies of the Ming, the Manchus, 'foreigners' themselves, redefined the empire as a multiethnic and diverse entity over which they presided. Their policies did not specifically single out Chinese Muslims, but they certainly enabled Han Kitab scholars to articulate a specific Chinese-Islamic identity in their writing, and to offer a unifying narrative for the history of Islam in China and its relationship with the wider Islamic world. These efforts were crucial during the emergence of the new 'national' Chinese-Muslim identity in the twentieth century.[46]

Phase four: Lanzhou and Xinjiang

Whereas the Nanjing phase of Chinese Islamic history was mostly cultural in nature, the final phase discussed in this essay is marked by a mixture of cultural shifts, military activity and violence. The heading, the place name

44 *Ibid.*, pp. 163–213.

45 Sachiko Murata, *Chinese gleams of Sufi light* (Albany, NY, 2000); Murata, William C. Chittick and Weiming Tu, *The sage learning of Liu Zhi: Islamic thought in Confucian terms* (Cambridge, MA, 2009).

46 Ben-Dor Benite, *Dao of Muḥammad*, pp. 1–20, 214–38; Ben-Dor Benite, 'From "Literati" to "ʿulama"': The origins of Chinese Muslim nationalist historiography', *Nationalism and Ethnic Politics*, 9, 4 (Winter, 2003/4), pp. 83–109.

'Lanzhou', the provincial capital of Gansu, or 'China's Mecca', derives from the fact that beginning in the mid-eighteenth century it emerged as a major regional centre for the numerous Muslims living in China's north-west. The transformations of Muslim life in the region are closely connected to the Qing expansion to the almost entirely Muslim region of eastern Turkistān, which came to be known after its conquest by the term Xinjiang, or 'new dominion'. More specifically, Xinjiang refers to the several oasis towns along the old Silk Road – such as Urumqi, Kāshghar, Turpan and Hami – all populated mostly with Muslims of various Turkic ethnicities, most notably people who are known today as 'Uighurs', a name taken from an ethnicity that has lived in this region since antiquity. Whereas the Ming severed the strong ties that north-western Muslims had with the inhabitants of Xinjiang's oases, the Qing's expansion to the region greatly affected their lives. The conquest and creation of the province of Xinjiang brought into the empire a whole new group of Muslims that was culturally different from the Muslims of 'China proper'. In this regard, a whole new chapter of the history of Islam in China began in the 1760s (and has not yet ended).[47] More specifically, the conquest of Xinjiang gave rise to a distinction between the Chinese Muslims across the border with Xinjiang, who came to be known as 'inner-land' Muslims (*neidi hui*), and the Turkic-speaking Muslims of Xinjiang.[48] More importantly, Uighur resistance to the Qing conquest became a source of constant friction and tension between Muslims and the government and often affected the relationship between Muslims and an increasingly hostile and suspicious government. Up until the 1780s, relations between the state and the Muslims in the north-west were relatively peaceful. But the tension and the violence between Muslims and the state in Xinjiang triggered a bloody history of tension that swept up Muslims from both sides of the provincial border. It largely ended only with the rise of the Communist state in 1949; in the case of Xinjiang the tensions are very much ongoing.

The second significant result of renewed connections with Central Asia was the introduction of Naqshbandī Sufi *ṭarīqas* to north-western Chinese Muslim communities. Initial Sufi paths to China had been forged already at the end of the seventeenth century, when Central Asian Sufi leaders came to the Muslim north-west seeking new followers. But the phenomenon really gained

47 Peter C. Perdue, *China marches west: The Qing conquest of central Eurasia* (Cambridge, MA, 2005).

48 James A. Millward, *Beyond the pass: Economy, ethnicity, and empire in Qing Central Asia, 1759–1864* (Stanford, 1998); Millward, *Eurasian crossroads: A history of Xinjiang* (New York, 2007).

momentum when local charismatic individuals imported the new practices to the region. Two stand out in this history: Ma Laichi (1681–1766), a disciple of a disciple of the Kāshghari master Afāq Khōja (d. *c.* 1694), who founded the Khaffiya order and had sojourned in China himself; and Ma Mingxin (1719–81), founder of the Jahriyya order. As opposed to the doctrinal Sufism that helped create a school of scholarship in eastern China, the much more rural northwest engaged in practical Sufism. The coming of Sufi orders to the region greatly transformed Muslim life, both socially and religiously. The form of Islam practised in the area before the coming of Sufism, adhered to now by only a small part of the population, came to be known as *gedimu* (from *qadīm*, that is, 'old', or 'original'). More importantly, the orders reorganised the Muslim society in the region, forming groups of adherents around certain figures who were treated as saints. The saints and the lineages they started became major loci of power that often competed with each other, and, crucially, with the suspicious state. Quarrels between followers of these orders led to the brutal execution of Ma Mingxin by the government of Lanzhou in 1781, triggering repeated major waves of violence between Muslims and the state that lasted for over a century and devastated the Muslim population of the region.[49]

The subsequent two Islamic centuries in China were quite different phases in terms of intensity, magnitude, nature of events and transformations, and in terms of the scope and nature of Chinese Muslim relationships with the state and with the Islamic world. Yet the phases discussed in this essay still resonate and their traces can be seen in the intensely diverse forms of Muslim life in China today.

49 Lipman, *Familiar strangers*, pp. 59–71.

12

Islam in South-East Asia and the Indian Ocean littoral, 1500–1800: expansion, polarisation, synthesis

ANTHONY REID

Over the past half-century historians have endeavoured to moderate the exaggerated importance long attached to 1498 and the arrival in the Indian Ocean of a small band of Portuguese. The Portuguese introduced consistent reportage in a language still relatively accessible, and in this sense 1498 may stand as a turning point in the literature. Asia was henceforth linked to Europe directly, and the exchange of ideas and technologies was possible without Arab or Central Asian mediation. Apart from an aggressive naval strategy and more effective technologies of navigation, time-keeping and warfare, however, the Portuguese had little more to offer by way of modernisation of commerce, science and technology. They made the great effort to join the maritime trade of the Indian Ocean precisely because it was already highly developed, delivering spices to Europe through Alexandria and Venice, and using some sophisticated financial techniques unknown to the Portuguese.

To this Muslim-dominated trade the Iberians initially brought only plunder and disruption, and were naturally seen as a scourge. In the longer term the establishment of a direct maritime route of trade around the Cape of Good Hope was profoundly important in depriving the Islamic commercial networks of their monopoly of east–west trade and intellectual mediation. It also introduced to the world of the Indian Ocean a sharp polarisation between Islam and its rivals from which the maritime world had previously been spared.

The 'Muslim lake' of the late fifteenth century

The carriage of goods between the various key centres of production in maritime Asia – coastal China, the islands of South-East Asia, India and the Middle East – grew in sophistication as southern Chinese, Javanese, Tamils and Arabs became more active in it. The movement of population southward in

China, together with the great prosperity of the Song dynasty there (960–1279), helped China replace India as the largest single market for South-East Asian tropical produce. But the prosperity of the countries at the opposite end of Eurasia, in Europe, following their recovery from the fourteenth-century Black Death, made this the other great magnet of long-distance trade in the fifteenth century.

Exotic items of food, aromatics and medicine, along with the universally prized gold, silver and jewels, were still the most important items of the long-distance trade in the fifteenth century. Within the Indian Ocean world more bulky items – cloth, rice, ceramics, cowry shells – already dominated in volume if not in value. If Muslim traders had been crucial all along the trading route to China since the eighth century CE, it was only the fifteenth-century European infatuation with eastern spices that took them to the extremity of the commercial Eurasian world, the Maluku archipelago of eastern Indonesia. Cloves were then harvested for export only in the tiny rival volcanic islands of Ternate and Tidore (north Maluku) and nutmeg in the cluster of five volcanic islands of Banda (south-east Maluku). (See Map 8.)

The key feature of these commercial carriers of Islamic beliefs and customs was that they were trading communities, not representatives of states. They were often effective warriors, with some of the same superiorities of weapons and motivation as the Europeans who followed them. But unlike either the expanding khanates of central Asia or the Portuguese, Dutch and English, they did not fight in the name of a distant state or receive reinforcements over the long term from a power centre. Only in the sixteenth century did states become the major factor in Islamic expansion also in maritime Asia.

Communities of traders of diverse ethnolinguistic background had earlier found in Islam a powerful rallying point as small minorities in the vast countries they linked through trade. Like Hindu, Jewish and Nestorian merchants, they received from Indian, South-East Asian and Chinese rulers the rights to build their place of worship and to apply their own rules in matters of marriage, inheritance and business contracts. Traders could not operate alone and could not expect the local state to intervene on their behalf to recover debts and so forth. In this world the commercial communities which flourished were those which had an internal mechanism for enforcing contracts, somewhat like the medieval *natio* of Europe or the millet of Turkey.[1] For Arabs, Persians, south Indian Muslims and 'Malays' of various

1 R.J. Barendse, *The Arabian seas: The Indian Ocean world of the seventeenth century* (New York, 2002), pp. 88–93.

origins, the Muslim identity was more useful in this regard than their ethno-linguistic one. Where the Muslims were small minorities, even Sunnī–Shīʿa distinctions were generally subordinated to the advantages of solidarity with those who shared an Islamic sense of propriety and acceptable food. Ibn Baṭṭūṭa, for example, made no mention of Sunnī or Shīʿa, Malay or Persian, in a lengthy description of Quanzhou and other maritime Chinese cities, where 'there is a quarter for Muslims, in which they live by themselves, and in which they have mosques both for the Friday services and for other religious purposes. The Muslims are honoured and respected.'[2]

Of course ports governed by Muslims offered more attractive opportunities, and there are numerous examples of the Muslim commercial minority playing a major role in putting a Muslim ruler on the throne. By around 1500, the major Indian Ocean ports for the long-distance trade were Muslim-ruled (see Map 7) – Jiddah, Aden, Baṣra and Muscat in the Arab world, Cambay in Gujarat, Melaka on the peninsula and Pasai, Pidië (Pedir) and Aceh competing in northern Sumatra (see Map 9). Even in Hindu-ruled Java the Muslim ports of the north coast – Gresik and Japara (see Map 10) – had asserted their independence of Hindu Majapahit. But the Muslim commercial minority was almost as much at home in ports such as Calicut in Malabar (Kerala), where Muslim writers like Ibn Baṭṭūṭa in the fourteenth century and Abdul Razzaq in the fifteenth appreciated the strict justice and security offered by its Hindu rulers – 'Security and justice are so firmly established in this city' – that every vessel was treated with the same strict honesty no matter what the religion or provenance of its owner.[3] In the Cham ports of what is today the Vietnamese coast, in Siam, Pegu (Burma), Cambodia and Brunei, as in China, the Muslim traders were rich and powerful enough in their respective quarters to be treated with respect and care.

The Muslim spice trade was particularly flourishing around 1500, when over 100 tons of Malukan spices (cloves, nutmeg, mace) were arriving each year on the docks of Venice. Though small items of trade in comparison with pepper, sandalwood and cinnamon, these were valuable and well documented, and travelled the whole route from easternmost Asia to the Mediterranean. The system worked in sectors, hinged around the great entrepôts just mentioned where the items would be sold and redistributed to onward markets. Javanese and Bandanese Muslims would carry the spices from Maluku to Java, particularly its Muslim ports; Javanese and Malays

2 *Ibn Baṭṭūṭa: Travels in Asia and Africa, 1325–1354*, ed. H. A. R. Gibb, Hakluyt Society (London, 1929, repr. New Delhi, 2001), p. 283.

3 'Journey of Abd-er-Razzak', in *India in the fifteenth century, being a collection of narratives of voyages to India*, ed. R. H. Major, Hakluyt Society (London, 1857), p. 14.

would carry them onward to Melaka, whence a variety of Chinese, Ryukyuan, 'Luzon' (hybrid Muslim Filipinos) and Malays would take them to north-east Asia, while Gujaratis, predominantly Muslim south Indians (known locally as Klings), Malays and assorted others would take them to Calicut and Cambay. Gujaratis, Persians and Arabs (notably the Karimi merchant guild from Hadramawt) dominated the onward trade to the Red Sea and Persian Gulf, while Venetian galleys plied the last stage of this maritime route, from Alexandria and Beirut to the chief European market for eastern spices in Venice. Virtually the whole route from Maluku to the Mediterranean was in Muslim hands. Each stage of the route was travelled when the annually alternating monsoon winds were in the correct direction, so that the entrepôts that formed the hinges of the system saw huge crowds of traders from diverse communities mingling for a period of months as they awaited the monsoon change.

The key to these ports was cosmopolitanism. Their lifeblood was in welcoming different kinds of merchants, each group playing its necessary role in the trade. Even though Muslim shipping was dominant, every port needed also its Hindu financial castes, the south Indian Chettyars and Gujarati Sarrafs, to provide finance and letters of credit on other ports. With them came the Hindu temples essential to their operations. In South-East Asia all welcomed the Chinese merchants with their religious traditions. Of Melaka at this time it was said that eighty-four languages could be heard in its streets. Frequently voyages were equipped using crews who were Muslim and Buddhist, and finance capital that might be Hindu or Jewish. The Arab pilot Shihāb al-Dīn Aḥmad ibn Mājid complained of Melaka at its Muslim height that 'The infidel marries Muslim women while the Muslim takes pagans to wife. You do not know whether they are Muslim or not … They drink wine in the markets and do not treat divorce as a religious act.'[4]

Portuguese disruption, Muslim regrouping and the rise of Aceh

The Portuguese brought to the Indian Ocean a different kind of naval warfare, motivated by ethnic and religious solidarities of a new kind. A tight fit between national self-interest and religious zeal had propelled the Portuguese southward in a long series of battles with Islam, first to complete the reconquest of Portugal

4 *Hawiyat al-Ikhtisar fi Ilm al-Bihār* (1462), trans. G. R. Tibbetts in *A study of the Arabic texts containing material on South-East Asia* (Leiden, 1979), p. 206.

itself, and then to carry the fight to the coast of Africa. Once into the Indian Ocean in 1498 their objective was to locate the sources of pepper and spices and seize control of them from the Muslim traders by whatever means it took. It was less a missionary imperative than a crusading one, which justified plunder in terms of a military-political struggle with Islam.

The first two Portuguese fleets, of Vasco da Gama (1498–9) and Cabral (1500–1), seized or sank enough Muslim shipping to make their intentions plain. The Muslim traders of Calicut and Gujarat appealed through their partners in Cairo to the Mamlūk rulers of Egypt to send a military force to combat this new threat. A forty-galley Mamlūk fleet reached Calicut in time to do battle against the third Portuguese expedition, in 1502, but was defeated by da Gama's cannons. A second Mamlūk fleet sent out in 1504 to stiffen Muslim resistance in Gujarat and the south was more successful in a battle off Sri Lanka, but was eventually routed off Diu by Almeida in 1509. They could not prevent the Portuguese entrenching themselves in fortified strategic points, initially at Calicut (where the Muslim population became their bitter enemies, making nearby Cochin a more satisfactory base), then at Goa (1510), Melaka (1511) and Hormuz (1515). In the first fifteen years of the new century the flow of Indian Ocean spices along the Muslim route to the Mediterranean faltered and almost died.

This onslaught forced the trade of the Indian Ocean to adjust in a variety of ways. Hindu and Buddhist actors quickly worked out modes of operating with the Portuguese. But the dominant Muslim trade was obliged to arm itself more effectively, and to regroup around stronger rulers able and willing to confront the Portuguese threat. The Portuguese capture of Melaka, at that time the largest entrepôt of South-East Asia, was particularly disruptive. Although the Javanese tried for a time to continue their strong relation with the city, the other major sectors of the Islamic trade had to attach themselves to different entrepôts. The long-term beneficiary was Aceh, but many also shifted their operations to Johor, Patani or Palembang. In Kerala the Mappilas eventually made Calicut impossible as a Portuguese base, but from nearby Cochin the Portuguese remained able to form local alliances and to take a share of the pepper crop.

The key political institution of Indian Ocean trade in the fifteenth century had been the city state, a cosmopolitan autonomous polity dedicated to trade and dependent on it. Polities such as Calicut, Pulicat (Coromandel coast), Melaka, Pasai, Japara and Gresik tried to stay aloof from the warfare of continental powers, buying their autonomy when necessary by sending tribute to those in a position to threaten. Dependent for even their rice staple on imports by sea, they were potentially vulnerable to the kind of naval attack launched by the Portuguese.

It was precisely such port-states that the Portuguese sought to overpower, and in the first years of the century they achieved amazing success in doing so. Virtually all of the port-states on which the Muslim trade depended in southern India and the archipelago were threatened. It was as Muslims that the traders had been attacked, and it needed to be as Muslims that they responded. Their complex links with Hindu rulers or financiers were called into question by the Portuguese challenge, and they transferred their support to rulers strong enough to defend them against Portuguese attack. As Barros acknowledged in mid-century in regard to Sumatra, since the Portuguese arrival many of the numerous port-states 'have been absorbed into the territory of their most powerful neighbours'.[5]

The origins of the Aceh sultanate at the mouth of the Aceh river in north-western Sumatra appear no older than the late fifteenth century, although Muslims were well placed since the thirteenth century in the older port of Lamri, 50 kilometres further east. The advent of a group of prominent merchants and aristocrats from the Champa capital, after that city fell to the Vietnamese in 1471, appears to have been the stimulus for a new Islamic dynasty to form in Aceh and incorporate Lamri. Nevertheless it was not sufficiently established as a port-state to attract the initial attention of the Portuguese, who from 1509 sought a foothold in the two older and larger ports of northern Sumatra – Pidië (modern Sigli) and Pasai, which since its conversion around 1292 had been the beacon of South-East Asian Islam. The Portuguese establishment of fortified strongholds in both ports and interference in their succession disputes increased the instability to which they were already prey, and particularly alienated the Indian and Arab merchants. Only in 1518 did a Portuguese fleet rashly attempt a raid on Aceh, lured by stories of a 'heathen temple' (possibly Chettyar) stocked with gold there. Aceh's defeat of this raiding party and seizure of many of its weapons set it on the road to driving the Portuguese from Pidië and Pasai in the early 1520s, no doubt with the support of Muslim merchants. By 1530 Aceh had unified the whole north Sumatran coast under a militantly anti-Portuguese dynasty. From that point Aceh provided a secure base for Muslim traders, who gradually developed new routes avoiding the centres of Portuguese power. Throughout the remainder of the century, it was the most consistent and militant enemy of

5 João de Barros (1563), *Decadas da Asia* (Lisbon, 1777, repr. 1973), Dec. 3, Livro V, 1.

the Portuguese, laying siege to the fortress of Melaka itself on multiple occasions.

The rise of Banten, eventually the strongest maritime sultanate in Java, has a similar origin. West Java was still Hindu at the Portuguese arrival, including its main port of Sunda Kelapa, modern Jakarta. The Portuguese saw it as a promising source of pepper and slaves and made an alliance with it in 1522. A backlash occurred against them at about the same time as Aceh conquered the Portuguese strongholds in northern Sumatra. The founder of Islamic power on the west Java coast, through the two west Java sultanates of Cirebon and Banten, is known in Javanese tradition as Sunan Gunung Jati. While it is possible that the military conquest of Banten and Sunda Kelapa was the work of his son-in-law Fatahillah (for whom there is a Cirebon grave dated 1570, quite distinct from that of Gunung Jati dated 1568), most sources attribute everything to Sunan Gunung Jati himself.

This *wali* or apostle (from Ar. *walī*, saint) was by origin a Sumatran from Pasai. Angered by the intrusion of the Portuguese in Pasai, he travelled to Jiddah and Mecca with the spice ships around 1515, and spent about three years as a religious student there. When he returned the Portuguese were still entrenched, and he moved on to the principal Muslim stronghold in Java, the port-state of Demak. There he reputedly married the sister of the ruler, Sultan Trenggana, and encouraged him to use his power to expand Islam on the island. Presumably learning of the Portuguese beachhead in the west, Gunung Jati obtained Demak assistance to go there and establish Muslim control at Banten, west of Jakarta. From there he conquered the main Sundanese (west Java) port of Sunda Kelapa in 1527, and renamed it Jakarta. His descendants became the sultans of Banten, developing in the coastal strip of west Java a substantial port and polity, distinct by its Javanese language and its literal Islam from the Sundanese of the interior, but also a formidable rival of the Javanese state centred eventually in Mataram. Once again, Portuguese intervention had provoked a strong Islamic riposte.

In southern India it was the Mappilas who emerged as the implacable Muslim opponents of the Portuguese, even though they had initially been more localised trade rivals of the Arabs and Gujaratis. The Mappilas were indigenous or hybridised Malayalam-speaking Muslims, who dominated the regional trade around the coasts of southern India and Sri Lanka. Virtually throughout the 1520s and 1530s they were at war with the Portuguese, fighting particularly over the pearl-fisheries and the trade in pepper and cinnamon. Like the Acehnese they adopted the language of *jihād*, laying siege to Portuguese forts in Calicut (where they forced its abandonment), Kollam and Colombo. Of major ports they were strongest in Calicut, and enabled its rulers to hold off the Portuguese, who made their major Kerala base for the pepper trade in Cochin further south. But they never controlled a state, and had a difficult relationship even with their prime protector, Hindu-ruled Calicut.

The rise of a few powerful 'gunpowder empires' in the sixteenth century at the expense of less defensible commercial ports was a wider phenomenon than the Indian Ocean world, and Christian–Muslim rivalry was by no means the only factor at work. The military revolution making more effective use of cannon and other technologies spread unevenly, and assisted some military innovators in becoming unprecedentedly strong. Portugal's invasion of the Indian Ocean coincided with the rise of two mighty Turkish empires. The Ottomans expanded towards the Indian Ocean by annexing Egypt in 1517, and extended their rule to the Ḥijāz and Hadramawt in the subsequent years. In India the victory of Babur's armies at Pānīpat inaugurated Mughal rule, which quickly came to dominate all of northern India.

The Ottoman Turks were far the more important of the two as a maritime factor. Their claims on the caliphate, their control of the land passages of the old Islamic spice route and their wars with the European powers made them the only conceivable leaders of any concerted Islamic response to the Portuguese threat. The first Asian maritime state to contact them and support their claim to the caliphate was the Bahmani sultanate of the Deccan, then master of the west coast around Goa. Its sultans exchanged letters with the Ottomans as early as the 1480s, despite the obstruction of the Mamlūks in Egypt. After the fall of the Bahmanis in 1527, these contacts appear to have been revived by Bijapur, the Muslim successor state in that section of the coast.

Gujarat, independent at the time under Muẓaffar Shāh II (r. 1511–26), had much more intimate commercial relations with the Red Sea and Persian Gulf ports as they fell under Ottoman control. In 1518 Muẓaffar Shāh congratulated the Ottoman sultan Selīm I (r. 1512–20) on his victories and sought his assistance against the accursed Portuguese. Turks were prominent in Gujarat's armed forces, and Gujarat became the first strategic partner of the Ottomans in their attempts to become an Indian Ocean power.[6]

6 Naimur Rahman Farooqi, 'Mughal–Ottoman relations: A study of political and diplomatic relations between Mughal India and the Ottoman empire, 1556–1748', Ph.D. dissertation, University of Wisconsin, (1986), pp. 20–3. This was subsequently published with the same title in Delhi in 1989.

By 1537, when the strongest of Ottoman rulers, Süleyman 'the Magnificent' (r. 1520–66), was ready to initiate a new phase of concerted anti-Portuguese action, Aceh was established as another enthusiastic strategic partner. Aceh's pepper, still grown chiefly in the formerly independent Pasai and Pidië regions, had mostly been destined to China during the fifteenth century. But Portuguese disruption of Muslim export from the south-west coast of India led Gujarati and Arab shippers to seek new supplies from Aceh, now firmly anti-Portuguese. By the mid-1530s, a new Islamic route was well established, probably shipping pepper directly from Aceh-ruled Pasai via the Islamic Maldives to the Red Sea. This quickly came to rival the Portuguese route in the volume of pepper shipped to Europe. It also established direct relations between Aceh and the Ottoman-ruled ports of Jiddah, Aden and Suez, and gave Aceh its claim to be 'the verandah of Mecca' (*serambi Mekkah*), the place of departure for South-East Asian pilgrims making the *ḥajj*.

Sultan Süleyman received petitions from Indian Ocean littoral states pleading for protection of shipping, and appealing to the Ottoman role as 'servitor of the Holy Cities' (*Khādim al-Ḥaramayn*). In 1537 he sent envoys to Gujarat and other Indian Ocean ports to gain their support for the attack on the Portuguese.[7] We do not know if these envoys also went as far as Aceh, but it seems likely that the first Acehnese attack on Portuguese Melaka, in 1537, was partly motivated by the Ottoman initiative. From this point onward, Portuguese sources are full of references to Turkish soldiers and weapons playing a key role in Aceh's campaigns, against both the neighbouring Hindu/animist Bataks and the Portuguese in Melaka. Mendes Pinto, more valuable for his evocative detail than for his accuracy with numbers, portrayed 300 Turkish troops, together with others from Gujarat and Malabar (Kerala), turning the tide in Aceh's contest with the Batak king, who was for his part bolstered by presumably non-Muslim auxiliaries from other parts of Sumatra and Borneo, and from Portuguese Melaka.[8]

However, the naval expedition under the Ottoman governor of Egypt, 20,000 men strong, proved a dismal failure. Its attempt to besiege the Portuguese fortress in Diu in September 1538 was defeated, and the Ottoman–Gujarat alliance broke up. Since many of this large army reportedly 'dispersed because the people of India had induced them away',[9] they must

7 R. B. Serjeant, *The Portuguese off the South Arabian coast, Hadhrami chronicles* (Oxford, 1963), pp. 76–7, 79–80.

8 *The travels of Mendes Pinto*, ed. Rebecca Catz (Chicago and London, 1989), pp. 21, 26.

9 Hadramī chronicle *al-Sana al-Bahir*, quoted in Serjeant, *The Portuguese*, p. 97.

have played a role nevertheless in subsequent attacks on Portuguese around the littoral.

The anti-Portuguese activities of Aceh in the period 1537–9 were probably the work of the warlike local ruler of Pasai, Ala-ud-din Ri'ayat Shah al-Kahar, brother and successor of the Aceh sultan. His control of the then major pepper port probably made him also the recipient of the additional Turkish military assistance which came with these ships. This may have enabled him both to lead the first expedition against Melaka, and to topple his brother and seize the throne sometime in the period between 1537 and 1539. Al-Kahar then ruled until 1571, and became the major scourge of the Portuguese in the Malacca Straits. Alliances between the Portuguese and Aceh's rivals in northern Sumatra, syncretically Muslim Aru and a non-Muslim Batak federation, increased the militant quality of al-Kahar's rhetoric. Acehnese remembered him as the one who established the Turkish alliance and first employed the *ghāzī* ideal of 'fighting all the unbelievers',[10] while Portuguese sources portrayed him as a bloodthirsty exponent of pure *jihād*. Pinto included the interesting detail that al-Kahar took special pride in a title of holy warrior against the infidels, bestowed by the *sharīf* of Mecca in acknowledgement of the annual gifts of two golden lamps that he sent to the Holy City.[11]

Süleyman the Magnificent must have been discouraged by the defeat in 1538, and subsequently directed his attention to Europe and the Mediterranean. Aceh also encountered some local setbacks in the 1540s. The only substantial Turkish fleet sent into the Indian Ocean in the remainder of Süleyman's reign was that of Piri Bey in 1551, destroyed by the Portuguese in the Persian Gulf. Even that ineffective thrust may have stimulated another anti-Portuguese coalition in the Islamic Far East. The Portuguese reported that Johor, one of Aceh's usual rivals, tried to rally Japara, the leading Java port and Portugal's main rival in the Maluku spice trade, into a holy war against Portuguese Melaka in 1550–1.[12] More fundamentally, the important Muslim states all along the Indian Ocean trading route, including the Mughals, Bijapur and Golconda in India, the Mappilas in Kerala and the port-states of South-East Asia, became committed in this period to orthodox Sunnī Islam, with implicit or overt acceptance that the *umma* ought to be a political community united behind a caliph in Turkey.

10 '*ghāzī dengan segala kafir*'; Nuru'd-din ar-Raniri, *Bustanu's-Salatan Bab II, Fasal 13*, ed. T. Iskandar (Kuala Lumpur, 1966), p. 32.

11 *The travels of Mendes Pinto*, p. 30.

12 H. J. de Graaf, 'De regering van Panembahan Senapati Ingalaga', *Verhandelingen van het Koninklijk Instituut*, 13 (1954), pp. 33–4.

The peak of this great power rivalry in the Indian Ocean came in the 1560s, probably also the peak for the Islamic trading route from Aceh to Jiddah. By this time Aceh's pepper production had greatly expanded on the west coast of Sumatra, while the Muslim share of the spices of Maluku was also expanding through commercial strongholds in Japara and Banda. In this period Venetian, Portuguese, Turkish and Acehnese sources all make note of the diplomatic and military ties expanding along the trade route between the Ottoman realm and Muslim South-East Asia.

The chief initiatives this time came from Aceh. There were Venetian and Portuguese reports as early as 1561–2 about well-endowed Aceh embassies to the Turkish capital. Sultan Süleyman sent out eight Turkish gunners in response to this early request. A later and better-documented embassy of the Acehnese envoy Husain, however, carried a still-extant letter from al-Kahar, appealing for the sultan's help as caliph to protect Muslim pilgrims and merchants on the way to the holy places. This arrived only after Süleyman had died in 1566. The new Ottoman sultan, Selīm II, began with enthusiasm to aid these distant tributaries. In decrees of September 1567 he commanded an expedition of seventeen vessels equipped with guns and gunsmiths to proceed to assist Aceh to crush the Portuguese and take Melaka. An ambassador was despatched to Aceh to carry the royal response. Three centuries before its time, Selīm commanded the investigation of a route for a canal to link the Mediterranean and the Red Sea, to make it easier for Turkish naval power to be projected into the Indian Ocean.[13]

The fleet never reached Aceh; it was diverted to suppress a rebellion in Yemen. Selīm II, like his predecessor, soon lost interest in Oceanic enterprises. But both Portuguese chroniclers and Acehnese memory insist that some Turkish help arrived in Sumatra. In the period leading up to a major Aceh attack on Melaka in January 1568 the Portuguese were convinced not only that 500 Turks arrived to strengthen Aceh, but that the Sumatran sultanate galvanised further support for a concerted *jihād* against the Portuguese by the rulers of Calicut, Masulipatam (Coromandel or Tamil coast), the local Gujarati ruler at Broach, and Demak in Java.[14] While most of this was rhetoric, there was an undoubted peak of militancy at this period. In 1565 Bijapur, Golconda and other Muslim states of the Deccan combined to destroy the Hindu empire of Vijayanagara. In 1570 there was another Acehnese siege of

13 Anthony Reid, *An Indonesian frontier: Acehnese and other histories of Sumatra* (Singapore, 2004), pp. 78–86; Farooqi, 'Mughal–Ottoman relations', pp. 267–9.

14 Diogo do Couto, *Da Asia* (Lisbon, 1778–88, repr. 1973–4), Decada 8, cap. 21, pp. 130–2.

Melaka and attacks at the same time by Calicut, Bijapur and Gujarat against Portuguese possessions in India. This was one of the most difficult moments for the Portuguese in Asia. Even as far east as Ternate in Maluku, the Portuguese were ejected from their fort when a militant Muslim for the first time assumed the Ternate throne.

It is rightly said that Islam came to these maritime realms by sea and by trade, interacting with and adapting to local beliefs as it made converts among the local commercial population. In this early stage force was seldom of much utility, and the community was essentially a commercial one living as an enclave minority in a very plural world. The sixteenth century, however, brought a quite different quality to political Islam. In a number of areas holy war was embraced as the appropriate response to the Portuguese onslaught, and then extended to local non-Muslims. New gunpowder empires arose on the back of trade wealth and firearms, and adopted a militant vision of Islam as the rationale for their expansion. In such areas the line between Muslim and unbeliever became explicitly political.

Crossing the line had clear political as well as behavioural consequences. Some groups who felt themselves the victims of this militant period, including al-Kahar's Batak rivals, the Hindu Balinese and some Torajans of Sulawesi, developed their sense of modern identity in consequence as specifically non-Muslim. Other communities, like the pearl-fishers of southernmost India or one of the two traditional moieties of Ambon, consolidated their identity by allying with the Portuguese as Christians against this political Islam of mid-century.

Sixteenth-century consolidation of Muslim institutions

Much energy has been expended pushing back the first indications of Islamic presence in one place or another, usually in the form of a tombstone or a name in the Chinese record. Too little has been given to the crucial process by which Islam extended its reach from harbour communities to major states, essentially in the sixteenth and early seventeenth centuries. At the beginning of this 'age of commerce' in the fifteenth century Pasai was probably the only state which espoused and institutionalised Islam as a central part of state identity. By its end in the mid-seventeenth century Islam had occupied most of its modern extent in South-East Asia, mosques and religious schools were built at substantial settlements, most Muslim rulers had ensured that pork was not eaten and that funerals and key public ceremonies were Islamised, while a few had imposed what they believed to be Islamic law in their capitals.

Writing around 1515, Tomé Pires pointed out that although the king of the Minangkabau (Sumatra's most numerous people) had accepted Islam when he married the Melaka sultan's sister, many said he was not truly Muslim. 'The truth is that he is a Moor [Muslim], with about a hundred of his men; all the other people are heathens'. 'In Borneo there were Muslims only at the Brunei capital, where the king had recently converted; in northern Maluku, the bastion of Islam in eastern Indonesia, the kings of Ternate and Tidore were Muslims 'but not deeply involved', while 'three parts and more out of four' were still heathen.[15]

The chronicle of Patani, in the Thai–Malay borderlands on the east coast of the peninsula, tells the story of that kingdom's Islamisation in two stages. Sometime in the early 1500s the king promised to become a Muslim if miraculously cured of an illness by a visiting shaykh from Pasai. After twice reneging on his promise, he finally submitted to the shaykh's requirements. He recited the *shahāda*, accepted an Islamic name and instructed all his court likewise to become Muslim. In his lifetime, 'all the people within the town adopted Islam, but of the people outside the town area not one accepted Islam. And although the raja accepted Islam, the only habits he abandoned were worshipping idols and eating pork. Apart from that he changed not one of his heathen habits.' It was only considerably later in the reign of his son Mudhaffar (d. 1564) that another shaykh from Pasai visited and complained that 'if there is no mosque [in a country] there is no sign of the Islamic religion'. So a mosque was built, and only then the country people too became Muslim and permanently accepted the laws of the Prophet. Although they in turn abandoned pork and the worship of idols (*berhala*), perhaps as a Hindu cult, they continued to worship stones, trees and spirits.[16]

In Pasai there were certainly mosques at the time of Ibn Baṭṭūṭa's visit in 1345, and in Melaka 'the beautiful mosque ... the finest known in these parts' was built by Sultan Mansur Shah (r. 1459–77).[17] In his time there was also a *qāḍī* of Melaka, as there had been earlier in Pasai. But outside the quarters of the traders from 'above the winds' (Persia, Arabia and India), there was little

15 *The Suma oriental of Tomé Pires*, trans. Armando Cortesão, Hakluyt Society (London, 1944), pp. 132, 213, 248.

16 *Hikayat Patani: The story of Patani*, ed. A. Teeuw and D. K. Wyatt (The Hague, 1970), vol. I, pp. 75, 78–9. An English translation, somewhat different from mine, is given in vol. II, pp. 151–2, 154–5.

17 *Suma oriental of Tomé Pires*, p. 249.

evidence of Islamic scholarship in South-East Asia before the sixteenth century. Only then do we begin to read of *ʿulamāʾ* spreading out from strongholds such as Pasai to teach in other ports. The political polarisation referred to above encouraged rulers who aligned with the Islamic side of the contest to seek out religious teachers and embrace their new ways of thinking as a bulwark against the Portuguese, and at the same time a justification for expanding their realms.

Muslims and Christians developed their institutional arrangements for proselytising South-East Asia in tandem with each other, and often provoking each other into further efforts. The initial crusading impetus of the Portuguese had left little room for preaching or proselytising. Only in mid-century with the Jesuit mission of Francis Xavier were there serious efforts at conversion for its own sake, rather than as a sign of political loyalty. Xavier went first (1542) to the impoverished Paravas of the pearl-fisheries opposite Sri Lanka, who had sided with the Portuguese in the bitter Christian–Muslim fighting over the pearl trade in the 1530s. He laid the basis for a permanent Tamil-speaking Christian community there, and a Malay-speaking one in eastern Indonesia, notably Ambon. The Spanish, colonising the Philippines after the full effect of the Catholic Counter Reformation, put a higher priority than the Portuguese on sending missionaries to convert the islanders.

From mid-century, then, the competition between Muslim and Christian also took on a proselytising quality. Centres such as Aceh, Demak, Gresik, Brunei and Ternate sent learned *ʿulamāʾ* on the trading ships to frontier areas, to set up schools and communities. In the first stage up to the fifteenth century the lingua franca of Islamic commercial communities around the Indian Ocean had been Arabic, but Malay now became established as the language of South-East Asian Islam. The Melaka chronicle noted that the people of fourteenth-century Pasai all spoke Arabic, whereas in fifteenth-century Melaka the chief lingua franca was Malay, with Arabic script. The Melaka chronicle, in its story of the Portuguese conquest of 1511, mentions the *Hikayat Muḥammad Hanafiah* and the *Hikayat Amir Hamza*, versions of two famous Arab stories of warrior heroes of the Prophet's time rendered into Malay verse. On the eve of battle the young Melaka nobles asked the sultan to have the first of these read to stir their courage, while he initially offered instead the latter.[18]

18 'Sejarah Melayu or "Malay Annals"', trans. C. C. Brown, *Journal of the Malaysian Branch of the Royal Asiatic Society*, 25, parts 2 and 3 (1952), p. 168.

Evidence for the development of a corpus of theological and mystical writing in Malay comes later. The earliest of the great Malay writers known by name, Hamzah Fansuri, was thought to have flourished around 1600 until a copy recently came to light of a gravestone in Mecca of one Ḥamza ibn Abdullah al-Fanṣūrī, dated 1527.[19] He felt the need to say that he was writing his mystical text in Malay so that the Muslims who did not know Arabic or Persian could understand it. If such writing was then still relatively rare, it reached its flowering within a century. Many of the key writers of the seventeenth century read and quoted Hamzah, and like him taught and wrote in Aceh, the principal domesticator of Arabic and Persian ideas into the Malay world.

The most prolific of these Malay writers, the Gujarati-born Nūr al-Dīn al-Rānīrī, recorded some of the history of this process. Some noted scholars arrived in Aceh from the Arab world on the pepper-ships, and began to teach in this new frontier. The Egyptian Muḥammad ʾAzhari Shaykh Nūr al-Dīn came from Mecca in the 1570s and taught inferential theology (*māqulat*). In the 1580s two more well-known *ʿulamāʾ* came from Mecca to teach *fikh* and *uṣūl* respectively. A little later al-Rānīrī's uncle, Shaykh Muḥammad Jailani, arrived from Gujarat to teach *fikh*, *uṣūl* and *taṣawwuf*.[20] While these learned men presumably taught and wrote in Arabic, their students and successors, including al-Rānīrī himself, were masters of Malay. One of the most prolific was the Pasai-born Shams al-Dīn al-Sumaṭrānī al-Pasāʾī, who composed many texts in Malay and Arabic advocating a mystical monism influenced by the Naqshbandī Sufi order. His chief tool for proselytisation was a Malay catechism of 1601, in the form of 211 questions and answers, the *Mīrat al-Mūmin*. He is also widely thought to have been the *qāḍī* or Shaykh al-Islām ('bishop') of Aceh who was able to use his Arabic to discuss matters with James Lancaster's first English fleet in 1602.

The direct political and economic connection between Aceh and the Ottoman-ruled Arabian peninsula, in other words, laid the basis for Aceh's emergence as the intellectual centre of Islamic South-East Asia (Fig. 3). We shall return below to the main preoccupations and debates of the schools of Islamic writing that developed there.

19 Claude Guillot and Ludvik Kalus, 'La stèle funéraire de Hamzah Fansuri', *Archipel*, 60 (2000), pp. 3–24.
20 Nuru'd-din ar-Raniri, *Bustanu's-Salatin*, pp. 32–3.

3 Mainstream South-East Asian mosque type before the twentieth century, exemplified in the multi-tiered roof of the seventeenth-century Indrapuri mosque in Aceh, on a base which may well have supported an earlier Buddhist shrine (photo: Anthony Reid)

The conversion of Java

As home of the only substantial Indianised kingdoms in South-East Asia that subsequently became Muslim, Java is especially interesting. Almost the whole of Javanese-speaking (central and east) Java became nominally Muslim in the long sixteenth century, with some of the Hindu elite taking refuge in Bali. This contrasts not only with Bali and the eventually Buddhist states of mainland South-East Asia, but with India itself, where major Hindu communities continued in those parts of India which were conquered by Muslims. Even in other parts of South-East Asia where Islam made an early and deep impression, there remained large interior communities that resisted Islam, as with the Batak case mentioned above. The key to Java's distinctiveness appears paradoxically to lie in the very strength of the older Hindu–Buddhist tradition exemplified by Majapahit, on to which Islam was successfully grafted. Warfare played a major part in the Muslim conquest, but a creative process of selecting and filtering the new religious and cultural elements was equally important. Akbar's synthetic project in Mughal India of developing a religious system which could carry all his subjects with him was a failure, but the analogous project in Java may be said to have prevailed under the Mataram kings.

The political conquest

The long sixteenth century was critical for this process in Java, even more decisively than elsewhere in the archipelago. Around 1500, according to Portuguese reports, Islam was still limited to the coastal trading cities of what had been the Majapahit kingdom – that is Javanese-speaking central and east Java. As the previous chapter has made clear, these were cosmopolitan trading centres, which owed their Islam partly to the (partly Ḥanafī) trade and tribute connection with Champa, Canton and Quanzhou, and partly to the (principally Shāfiʿī) Islamic spice trading route to the west, through first Pasai and Palembang, but after about 1460 primarily Melaka, to the Indian Ocean world beyond.

Demak was by 1500 the strongest of these Muslim port-states, while its erstwhile patron, Hindu Majapahit, was in disarray. Dynastic upheavals after 1486 led to the move of its capital further inland, to Kediri, where it lost influence over all the coastal ports except Tuban. The wealth of Demak had been built in the last quarter of the fifteenth century by a very successful Sino-Malay trader from Palembang, in some chronicles called Ko Po. He built a fleet of ships trading around the Java Sea, dominating the spice trade from Maluku and the supply of Java rice to Melaka. He had reputedly spent time in Gresik, an older Islamic centre and port for Majapahit, but as Majapahit crumbled he moved his base of operations to Demak, and central Java became the centre of Javanese rice exports. He was not himself a ruler as much as a politically astute merchant, who married his daughters to several of the key coastal kings. His descendants became rulers of Demak, and made it the clear leader of the Islamic alliance and the major power of the Java Sea. He or his son must have been one of the historical identities whose memory went into the construction of the legendary Javanese hero Raden Patah ('the conqueror'). In the eighteenth-century Mataram historical epic, *Babad Tanah Jawi*, this figure was used to legitimate the non-Javanese or mestizo Muslim coastal rulers as appropriate heirs of Majapahit. He was made the son of the last Majapahit Hindu ruler by a Chinese princess, banished to Palembang as a child and brought up by a client ruler there. His conquest of Majapahit, in the also legendary year 1478 (the Javanese year 1400, thought appropriate for a change of dynasty), could therefore be seen as a restoration of the Majapahit lineage.

The first firmly historical ruler of Demak was known posthumously as Sultan Trenggana. Son or grandson of the Sino-Malay shipping magnate, he may have come to the throne around 1505. He patronised the building or rebuilding of the great mosque of Demak, in 1507, and presumably the casting of the great cannon Ki Jimat, dated to 1527/8 and bearing the inscription 'the supreme result is the triumph of the faith'.[21] He may have patronised some of the semi-legendary holy men (*wali*) of Java, such as Sunan Kalijaga, whom popular tradition credits with the conversion of much of interior central Java. This king appears to have ruled until his death on the battlefield in 1546, though eclipsed during part of his youth by his forceful brother-in-law Patih Yunus of Japara, another successful shipowner who took over some of Demak's maritime networks and confronted the Portuguese in the second decade of the century.

Trenggana's long reign coincided with the transition of Javanese Islam from a cosmopolitan commercial enclave situation to an aggressive competitor for power in Java. The challenge of the Portuguese, vividly experienced by refugees from Melaka and Pasai, must have been connected with this transition, as we saw above in the expansion westward to Cirebon and Banten in the 1520s. Already a few years after the fall of Melaka to the Portuguese, the ruler of Tuban, Majapahit's only remaining coastal dependency, told Tomé Pires that Majapahit was 'always at war with the Moors on the sea-coast, especially with the lord of Demak'.[22] Muslims who had experienced the Indian Ocean contest with the Portuguese identified Trenggana as the likeliest leader of the political expansion of the *dār al-islām* in Java. Sunan Gunung Jati, notably, is remembered as having bestowed on him the title sultan after his return from Mecca, perhaps seeing it as a legitimation for military expansion. Demak finally succeeded in taking the Hindu capital at Kediri around 1527, in a campaign portrayed in Javanese sources as a holy war supported by several Muslim port-states and such spiritual leaders as the master of the sacred place Kudus (al-Quds), a little to the east of Demak.

The defeat of Majapahit did not lead directly to a Muslim kingdom taking its place. In the power vacuum at the centre of Java Demak was now well placed, but it remained a coastal metropolis long separated from the politics of the

21 Denys Lombard, *Le carrefour javanais: Essai d'histoire globale* (Paris, 1990), pp. 179–81, 378 n. 945.
22 *Suma oriental of Tomé Pires*, p. 176.

interior, and still interested above all in its trade. The following decades saw Sultan Trenggana sending the vital military and spiritual aid to one faction of a succession dispute in Banjarmasin, in return for conversion. According to the Banjarmasin chronicle, this intervention secured the Islamisation of Banjarmasin and enabled it to become the principal Muslim state of southern Borneo, initially under Demak patronage. In the 1540s Trenggana led a military campaign eastwards, against the Hindu kingdom of Pasuruan. Mendes Pinto claims to have followed the campaign in 1546, and refers to Turkish and Aceh assistance with artillery, and detachments of soldiers from Banten, and from the 'Luzons' (Muslim Filipinos) exiled from the Manila area. Pinto's account of this contest is free of the holy war rhetoric he used for Aceh's campaigns, however. Even though one side is Muslim, these contestants were both part of the same Javanese moral universe.

Sultan Trenggana was killed during this war against Pasuruan, and so it was presumably his successor who in 1548 alarmed a visiting Jesuit with his aggressive plans to spread Islam around the neighbouring peoples, and 'become another Sultan of Turkey'.[23] On the contrary, however, Java after Trenggana's death became again a patchwork of local chiefdoms. The commercial centrality his grandfather had built up had long passed to other centres with better ports. References in the most reliable Javanese chronicle to *wong mati Selam* (people who die for Islam, or martyrs), fighting furiously on the winning side in battles for interior centres in the 1570s,[24] suggests that the multiethnic Muslim shock troops who had fought for Islam under Demak's banner continued to be decisive in the following decades. But all sources agree that whatever unity there was on the Muslim side during Demak's heyday was lost to a variety of newly Muslim contenders by the 1460s. Pajang, near contemporary Surakarta, claimed authority over much of central Java including Demak itself in the third quarter of the century, and hence a primacy over the lords of Java.

According to the Javanese chronicles, it was a military commander of Pajang's forces who was given the fertile Mataram area around modern Yogyakarta as a fief. His son, Panembahan Senopati Ingalaga, emerges more fully into history as a conquering king of Mataram from about 1584. As portrayed by an acute Dutch visitor in the following century, he was remembered as having used Islam to make a clean break with the old Hindu dynasty,

23 Mendes Pinto from Melaka, 7 December 1553, in Joseph Wicki (ed.), *Documenta Indica* II (Rome, 1950), p. 423.

24 Babad ing Sangkala, 1738, in M. C. Ricklefs, *Modern Javanese historical tradition: A study of an original Kartasura chronicle and related materials* (London, 1978), p. 24.

kill all potential rivals from that quarter and stake his claim to a new kind of legitimacy based on upholding the new religion. After establishing an independent base in Mataram he 'made war until the end of his life', which came in 1601.[25] By then he had subdued the older centres of Pajang and Demak, and taken possession of items of regalia held to confer legitimacy since the time of Majapahit. He had also extended his power to Kediri and Madiun.

Senopati was remembered as the founder of the last strong Javanese state; a great conqueror who returned power to the interior by mastering the new type of warfare introduced by Muslims, Portuguese and Chinese on the coast. The Mataram he effectively founded laid claim to legitimacy in Islamic as well as Javanese terms. Senopati sought to compensate for his lowly origins by marrying various royal ladies, while subsequent historians saw him as successor to Majapahit through Demak and Pajang. We know almost nothing about the nature of his Islamic commitment, or the extent to which Islam was practised. Javanese legend has one of the coast-based *wali*, Sunan Kalijaga from the Demak holy place of Ngadilanggu, as his adviser, but no mosque is attributed to him. Senopati's Mataram appears in fact to have been a pioneering military camp in a fertile but underpopulated area, with most of its early population forced to shift there as soldiers or captives from other areas.

Unlike its Muslim predecessors Mataram was not dependent on the Muslim commercial communities of the Javanese *pesisir* (coast), though it needed their support if it was to grow and flourish. The centres of the old Majapahit culture were far away in east Java, and its leaders killed or fled to the remotest east at Balambangan. The models both for Islamic learning and for the partially Islamised Javanese court culture were now in the *pesisir*. With the decline of the central Java ports, the centre for both moved to Surabaya, including its nearby port area of Gresik in which sat the Islamic 'holy hill' of Giri. If Mataram applied just as much Islam as its ruler saw fit, Surabaya inherited from Demak the leading role of seeking to build a new civilisation which could reconcile the needs of international Muslims of the port communities with those of Javanese aristocratic tradition.

Senopati failed in his attempts to incorporate the Surabaya area. This task fell to his grandson, Sultan Agung (r. 1613–46), who defeated Surabaya in a series of campaigns in 1620–5. It was the reign of this Javanese sun-king that created the synthesis between the old Java of Majapahit and the new Java of the Muslim coastal cities. The eclipse of the Muslim coastal cities, under the

25 Rijklof van Goens, 1656, cited in Anthony Reid, *Southeast Asia in the age of commerce 1450–1680*, vol. II: *Expansion and crisis* (New Haven, 1993), p. 177.

military pressure of Mataram and the commercial inroads of the Dutch and English into the formerly lucrative spice trade of the *pesisir*, brought an end to a remarkable chapter in Javanese history. During the long sixteenth century Java had been as exposed to the cosmopolitan and commercial influences of the Muslim oecumene as had other parts of the Indian Ocean littoral. By the end of Agung's reign those influences were limited and controlled, and a Javanese synthesis was in place that could bring even the most Hinduised elements of Javanese society along with it.

The spiritual synthesis

The story just told is one of kings and battles, and the way in which the old order of Majapahit, centred 60 kilometres up the Brantas valley in east Java, was supplanted first by an avowedly commercial and cosmopolitan Islamic order, and then in turn by an interior kingdom in south-central Java. Another story must be told, closer to that of the Javanese traditions, about a spiritual transformation attributed to a number of miracle-working holy men, mystic saints as well as warriors.

The older religious order had comprised both a Hindu ritual in the courts, intended to safeguard the supernatural legitimacy of kings, and a popular spirituality of holy men and holy places – ascetics and hermits in their *dharma* or *pertapaan* (hermitages). The former was seemingly destroyed in the battles of the long sixteenth century, so that no Brahmans survived to minister to the needs of the court as they did in Buddhist Siam and Cambodia. The latter was much more resilient. Tomé Pires described how vigorously the older pattern of ascetics (*tapa*) survived the first stage of Islamisation even in the *pesisir* of Java:

> There are about fifty thousand of these in Java. There are three or four orders of them. Some of them do not eat rice nor drink wine: they are all virgins, they do not know women. They wear a certain headdress which is full a yard long ... And these men are also worshipped by the Moors, and they believe in them greatly; they also give them alms; they rejoice when such men come to their houses.[26]

The popular success of the new doctrine in Java lay in its ability to penetrate this ascetic world and gradually give it a more Islamic flavour, rather than seeking to condemn and confront it directly. The *wali* beloved of Javanese Islamic tradition are depicted as men who through meditation and self-denial

26 *Suma oriental of Tomé Pires*, p. 177.

had penetrated to the inner unities of being, and could thereby demonstrate superior spiritual powers. There are stories of their visiting the ancient mountain hermitages such as Mantingan near Demak, or Pulasari near Banten, and being accepted by the adepts (*santri*) there. The earliest Javanese guide to Islamic behaviour, from the *pesisir* of the sixteenth century, itself adopted the same term *tapa* for its model Muslim. But 'the stronghold of the *tapa* is to stay in the mosque, to perform the five daily prayers and to recite the Quran'. The line was drawn against the *tapa* of the unbelievers and their yogic practices.[27]

This document certainly comes down to us from a Javanese urban milieu where Islam was still contested, even if supported by the local ruler. Muslims had to be warned against honouring idols, praising the more generous behaviour of non-Muslims and answering questions about religious identity by denying one's Islam or suggesting it made no difference. Suggestive of the upper hand of Muslims in the city, however, was the warning against killing a non-believer in order to take possession of his property, rather than for religious motives.[28] The earliest Dutch expedition to Java, from 1597, also received the impression that it was still only the coast that was predominantly Muslim.

Legends about the spreading of the faith among the people of central Java are associated with one of the best-loved *wali*, Sunan Kalijaga, and his disciple, Ki Pandan Arang. The latter was supposed to have come from the former rulers of Java, and in one version was in reality the last king of Majapahit. Kalijaga converted him to the ascetic life through various miracles, however, after which Ki Pandan Arang travelled about central Java performing his own miracles and converting notable people as well as ruffians to the true faith. He ended his life by teaching and meditating at the small hill of Tembayat, in the Mataram area just south of modern Klaten. This appears to have been a pre-Muslim sacred place, judging from its architecture and inscriptions on the site. In Muslim times however its sacredness was attributed to the tomb of Ki Pandan Arang there, known after his death as Sunan Tembayat. Islamic prayers and interpretations provided an added source of sacred power for one of the holy places of the Mataram area. The former *tapa* became known as *santri*, and their *dharma* as *pesantren*, autonomous centres of study, meditation and often martial arts, both geographically and politically remote from the

27 G. W. J. Drewes (ed.), *An early Javanese code of Muslim ethics* (The Hague, 1978), pp. 15, 35.
28 *Ibid.*, pp. 36–9.

centres of royal power, and guaranteed immunity from taxes and levies like their Hindu–Buddhist predecessors.[29]

Sunan Kalijaga is also attributed with the creation of the Javanese shadow puppets (*wayang kulit*), despite the Hindu subject matter of their stories from the *Mahabharata* and the *Ramayana*. Modern students of this most central and semi-sacred of Javanese arts tend to agree that it attained its modern form in the Islamised *pesisir* around the sixteenth century, and was not part of the older repertoire of theatrical forms. It may indeed have seemed a cultural compromise, depicting not human forms, exactly, but shadows. A Javanese legend has Sunan Kalijaga telling the king of Demak that 'the *wayang* is indeed a reflected image of the One, so to speak, the image of the Law. The *wayang* represents all humanity, the *dalang* [puppeteer] corresponds to Allah, creator of the universe.'[30] Some monist texts saw the *dalang* as absolute being, the puppets as relative being and the screen as the outer world of essences where formal religion had its place. The screen on which the shadows played thereby represented the hiddenness of the ultimate reality of unity.[31] Yet the shadow puppets were never used for the cycle of stories (*menak*) inspired by the Islamic tradition, which were played on wooden puppets also perhaps developed in the coastal cities of the sixteenth century.

The aspect of the Islamic spiritual tradition which most appealed in Java, as to a lesser extent throughout maritime Asia, was the monism of authors such as al-Hallāj and especially the Andalusian Sufi Ibn al-ʿArabī (1165–1240). The strain of Sufism that stressed a progression through seven layers of meaning, towards the ultimate hidden one-ness, appealed to the ascetic and meditative strand of Hindu–Buddhist Java. Many from the Javanese *tapa* tradition believed they saw in the Sufi ideas filtering to them through an Indian lens another avenue of approaching this ultimate one-ness. Of course more orthodox versions of mysticism propounded by the greatest of Arab theologians, al-Ghazālī (1059–1111), also reached South-East Asia and gradually established the boundaries of orthodoxy there as elsewhere. The violent confrontation between the two strands was well documented in Aceh (see below), but in Java it is only through the *wali* legends that we know how a similar battle may have been played out.

Many of these legends concern Siti Jenar, whose life and death suggest some influence from the Arabic stories about al-Hallāj. At a famous meeting of

29 This argument is made most persuasively by Lombard, *Carrefour javanais*, II, pp. 114–20.
30 D. A. Rinkes, *Nine saints of Java*, trans. H. M. Froger (Kuala Lumpur, 1996), p. 130.
31 P. J. Zoetmulder, *Pantheism and monism in Javanese Suluk literature: Islamic and Indian mysticism in an Indonesian setting*, trans. M. C. Ricklefs (Leiden, 1995), pp. 163–5.

the *wali* in the mosque of Demak all gave their views about the true nature of unity. They were concerned that Siti Jenar was growing very popular by teaching the secret knowledge which should not be publicly revealed, and that in consequence his followers neglected the Friday prayer as unimportant. When they summoned Siti Jenar to join them he insisted that Siti Jenar did not exist, only God existed. When they criticised his followers for not attending Friday prayer he replied that 'there is no Friday, and there is no mosque'. Sunan Kalijaga, the warrior *wali*, then beheaded him with his sword, giving rise to various miraculous stories about his disappearance.[32]

We cannot know whether Siti Jenar had an existence in history as well as in the abundant stories about his life and death. But the fact that these stories end with his death, as do similar stories about four other popular radical monists, two more placed in the sixteenth century, one in Agung's reign and one in the eighteenth century, makes it very likely that the orthodox of the coastal cities did seek to condemn to death those they identified as pantheist heretics. The fact that they were all portrayed in the stories as miracle-workers who had attained ultimate knowledge, and erred if at all only in revealing it, shows the popularity of this manner of thinking in Java's transition to Islam.

It appears that the battle over spiritual legitimacy in this critical period was especially fought over sacred sites, and the charismatic spiritual eminences associated with them. Each of the nine *wali* is associated with a sacred place where they were thought to have taught, and where their tomb (if, unlike Siti Jenar, they have one) is located (Fig. 4). The leader of the *wali* in some versions was Sunan Giri, and the port-complex of Gresik-Surabaya over which Giri presided was sufficiently wealthy and well connected to ensure that Giri remained throughout the sixteenth and most of the seventeenth centuries the most prestigious Muslim site in Java. It became even more the spiritual opposite pole to Mataram during the long resistance of the Surabaya complex of cities to Sultan Agung's campaigns in the 1620s. Surabaya was eventually starved into submission in 1625, and the cultivated heir to its throne, Pangeran Pekik, was forced to become an ascetic at Surabaya's oldest mosque of Ampel. But Giri continued to represent the greater centrality of Islamic norms and leadership in the *pesisir* than in Mataram, and was therefore seen as an alternative and challenge by the king.

Sultan Agung's most explicit steps towards synthesis were coterminous with his campaign to incorporate Giri and co-opt its legitimacy in the 1630s. Reliance on military resources alone was not convincing after his armies had

32 Rinkes, *Nine saints*, pp. 15–48; Zoetmulder, *Pantheism and monism*, pp. 296–308.

4 The entrance to the tomb of Sunan Bonang, one of the nine semi-legendary apostles (*wali*) of Java, located just outside Tuban. It is in the style of the elevated entrances (*gapura*) to sacred places in Hindu Java and Bali, representing a syncretic phase in Muslim architecture (photo: Michael Feener)

met a spectacular defeat in attempting to expel the Dutch from Batavia in 1629. Soon after this disaster the nearby sacred hill of Tembayat appeared to pose a threat to the king, and he sent an army to conquer it. Whatever transpired with the *santri* there persuaded him to make amends in the form of a personal pilgrimage to the site in 1633, and the reconstruction of its massive gateway in old-Javanese style. At the same time he brought Pangeran Pekik to court from his internal exile in Ampel, and co-opted his charisma by royal marriages – Pekik married Agung's sister while Pekik's daughter married the heir to the Mataram throne. Pangeran Pekik was renowned not only for his heritage from Surabaya and Ampel, but for his literary skills in incorporating the new Muslim knowledge into acceptable Javanese poetry. He is often credited with the 'civilising' of Mataram by bringing to it the best of court culture from the old Majapahit as filtered through the new *pesisir* centres. Perhaps under his influence Sultan Agung established a uniquely complex Javanese calendar, which incorporated the Islamic calendar with its weekly cycle and lunar basis for establishing festivals, into the older Indian-derived *Saka* calendar.[33]

In 1635 Pangeran Pekik was placed in charge of the reconquest of Giri, which had presumably continued to see itself as an autonomous sacred place as well as a haven for internationally connected *ʿulamāʾ*. The expedition was successful and the Sunan Giri was brought to Mataram to make his obeisance to the king, even if the wanderings of *santri* refugees from Giri became the stuff of later legends. In the remainder of his reign Agung seemed determined to ensure that he was the sole source of spiritual as well as political power. He sent an embassy to Mecca that brought him back the title of sultan in 1641, a step his rival in Banten had taken earlier. He began building his mausoleum at Imogiri that explicitly evoked the kind of hybrid Javano-Islamic shrine architecture hitherto devoted to the tombs of the *wali*. Later Javanese chronicles gave him the title of king-priest (*prabu pandita*) also bestowed on some of the *walis*, and claimed that he had such spiritual power that 'each Friday the king went to Mecca to pray'.[34] Dutch envoys are witness to his success in domesticating Islam effectively into a royal cult in which they 'consider their king so proudly that they respect him as a god' even while insisting that they were good Muslims 'and curse all others'.[35] Challenges from the more literal Islamic world would return from time to time, most effectively in the twentieth century, but Sultan Agung had established a synthesis that allowed almost all Javanese to become Muslims without sacrificing their rich heritage.

The boundaries of Islam in the eastern archipelagos

Prior to the sixteenth century Muslim influences had travelled to those trade centres of the eastern islands best connected with trade routes to southern China on the one hand and to the clove-producing centres of northern Maluku on the other. The undated genealogies of Sulu have been interpreted to mean that a Muslim trader and adventurer from Sumatra began an Islamic lineage there around 1400. Brunei, Sulu and Manila were the three easternmost tributaries of Ming China in the early 1400s, perhaps because Muslim traders

33 See further in following chapter.

34 Babad Tanah Djawi, *Javaanse Rijkskroniek*, ed. W. L. Olthof (Dordrecht, 1987), p. 122.

35 H.J. de Graaf (ed.), *De Vijf Gezantschapsreizen van Rijklof van Goens naar het hof van Mataram, 1648–1654* (The Hague, 1956), p. 263.

from Quanzhou had settled in each of them. In Maluku it appears that Javanese buyers of the precious clove crops of Ternate and Tidore, and the nutmeg of Banda, began to establish stable Muslim communities there in the late fifteenth century.

When the Portuguese reached Maluku in 1512, and the Spanish of Magellan reached Cebu and Brunei in 1522, Islam had already begun to make converts among those who dealt with the trade. Tomé Pires explained that the great majority even of key centres like Ternate were still animist, and the king of Ternate seemed willing to switch from Muslim to Christian 'if it seemed good to him'.[36] The five small islands of the Banda group were a kind of merchant oligarchy where the Javanese and Malay Muslim merchants were held in great respect. In Brunei Pigafetta described a flourishing sultanate seeking to dominate trade along the whole route from Manila to Melaka. In Cebu (central Philippines) a Muslim trader was on hand to warn the local raja against the aggressive 'Franks'.

In none of these sites, however, did Islam present an obstacle to the favourable reception of the Europeans. They were at first welcomed everywhere as alternative buyers of the local spices, driving up the price and increasing the flow of Indian cloth into the region in exchange. Only as the Europeans sought local domination or monopoly, or like Magellan tried to impose Christianity at the first encounter, did the lines gradually become established between those who supported the Europeans and those who supported Islam.

As indicated above, the lines became more firmly drawn in mid-century throughout the Indian Ocean region, and the numerous local conflicts in Maluku were rapidly drawn into this Christian–Muslim dichotomy. The most useful chronicle of the events from the Muslim side, the *Hikayat Tanah Hitu*, portrayed the second half of the sixteenth century as one of continual holy war against the Portuguese, with those falling on the Muslim side described as martyrs (*shahīd*). The tenuous Portuguese alliance with the nominally Muslim kings of Ternate, leaders of one side of age-old rivalries throughout Maluku, finally broke down completely in 1570. The Portuguese murdered their supposed ally Sultan Hairun, and his son Baabullah led an effective Muslim alliance to throw the Portuguese out of Ternate and to impose Islam as the principal symbol of loyalty to Ternate rather than the Portuguese. He reigned until 1583, and the Europeans credited him with patronising numerous Arab and Persian preachers (*muballigh*), and with

36 *Suma oriental of Tomé Pires*, pp. 213–15.

spreading the faith as far as Buton, Selayar (both in southern Sulawesi) and southern Mindanao.

The permanent Spanish presence in the Philippines, beginning with Legazpi's expedition of 1565, ultimately established the northern boundary of Muslim expansion. Legazpi's seizure of Manila (1571) from the hands of an incipient Muslim port-state made of the city the opposite pole to Baabullah's Ternate. Alarmed at the sending of Islamic teachers to Mindanao by Ternate and the older Islamic trade centre of Brunei, Spanish Manila sent expeditions to Mindanao and Sulu, and in 1578 succeeded in sacking Brunei and curbing that city's role as a hub of trade and Islamisation for the Philippines. Henceforth the sultanates based in the island of Sulu and the Pulangi river basin of Magindanao would be the primary political upholders of Islam and of resistance to the Spanish in the Philippines. For both states the greatest strength was an intense pluralism, which made it impossible for the Spanish to turn their military superiority and periodic victories into permanent influence. Only the long reign of Sultan Qudrat in Magindanao (*c.* 1619–71) produced a strong political centre for Islam in this period, partly thanks to Dutch commercial support.

In this eastern frontier of Muslim/Christian competition, the Muslim side was far more successful in enrolling the support of local rulers. The port-kings who emerged as competition grew for spices and other products readily allied with the Muslim traders, patronised them and gave them daughters in marriage, while drawing on the charisma of a new faith as a justification for expanding their territories. Unlike the situation in Java, Bali, Siam or Cambodia, kingship had not in these regions embraced a specifically Hindu pattern of legitimation. Yet power remained profoundly spiritual, and no king could be strong who did not command supernatural support for his rule. Islam is rightly seen as having brought individualist ('bourgeois') and rational elements into the world of Indic and animist religion. But it could not have succeeded if it had directly subverted, as Iberian Catholicism did, the rulers' need to be the pre-eminent mediators with the supernatural. In Counter Reformation Catholicism the celibate clergy had a monopoly of sacramental power, and hence there could be no successful Christian kings. Many rulers in Sulawesi and Maluku were attracted to Christianity and Iberian assistance, but misunderstandings put an end to every Christian kingdom after a few years.

By contrast, even the most orthodox of South-East Asian sultans, Iskandar Thani of Aceh (r. 1636–41, see below), claimed in his diplomatic letters to be a supernaturally powerful world ruler endowed with magical regalia. The Malay-language culture of kingship found an Islamic vocabulary to express this royal transcendence. Arabic *dawla* (dynasty or state) became the term for the profoundly mystical essence of Malay sovereignty, expressed in the self-abasing acknowledgement of royal charisma, *'daulat Tuanku!'* Persian *nau-bat* (nine drums) became not only the orchestra restricted to royal use, but the term (*nobat*) for enthronement itself, by virtue of the sacred powers of the music. Arabic *waḥy* to express the divine inspiration of the Prophet, became the magical power unique to kings (especially in Java).

The Islamisation of south Sulawesi, the populous, rice-growing south-western arm of the island, is a particularly interesting case. Although situated in the east, beyond any substantial Brahmanic influences, the Bugis and Makassar peoples before their Islamisation in the early seventeenth century had developed great reverence for their heaven-descended royal lineages, a written culture in an Indic script closest to those of Sumatra and the Philippines, and a priesthood of transsexual *bissu* as special mediators between the kings and the upperworld of the gods, whose prehistory was elaborately described in the La Galigo epic. Although not an essential part of the spice-trading route, south Sulawesi's ports could deliver a rice surplus helpful for traders travelling to rice-deficient Maluku, while the iron of the Lake Matano area appears to have been important for both Java and Maluku. The abundant Chinese, Vietnamese and Thai ceramics buried in grave sites of the fifteenth and sixteenth centuries indicate that it was already integrated into a trading world. At least by the 1540s, both Muslim and Portuguese traders began calling in these ports, and encouraging converts. A few of the scores of local rulers experimented with Christianity, while the Malay traders of the Makassar area were permitted to build a mosque around 1580. But the major kings resisted conversion to either faith if it would diminish their supernatural status, not to mention interfering with their pattern of religious feasting with pork and palm-wine.

In the short period 1603–11, on the other hand, all the Makassar and Bugis kings accepted Islam. Local Muslim traditions associate these conversions with three Minangkabau missionaries, seemingly linked with the rulers of Aceh and Johor. The consummate politician of Makassar, Karaeng Matoaya, later told the Portuguese that he had adopted Islam out of largely political motives, and after failing to get any response from Melaka to his request for priests to be sent. The royal chronicles, however, suggest a pattern of consultation among the rulers with the greatest reputation for wisdom and high birth. The most ancient lineage of Luwu was the first to accept Islam formally, and Karaeng Matoaya led Makassar into the new faith very quickly thereafter (probably September 1605) to ensure that he would not be outflanked. After carefully securing the support of the Makassar nobles for the new religion, Matoaya proceeded to attack those Bugis states that resisted his request to follow him into Islam. The chronicles suggest that it was a mixture of this forceful pressure and the generous terms on which the autonomy of each state was guaranteed under Makassar's leadership that won them all over within a few years. Although Makassar, like Aceh, Banten, Demak and Banjarmasin, profited from the expansion of trade and the new firearms to rise to unprecedented prominence, it differed sharply from them in respecting most traditional autonomies, and almost all of the older aristocratic culture.

Bissu remained to celebrate the enthronements, weddings and funerals of courts of the Bugis and Makassar kings. Their lineages continued to be regarded as descended from the upperworld and surrounded with supernatural mystique. While the elaborate death rituals still to be seen among the upland Toraja of south Sulawesi were wholly Islamised, and pork abolished, other rituals of the life cycle, kingship and agriculture survived with an Islamic addition. In each state a *qāḍī* and an *imām* for the state mosque were appointed, though usually from among the aristocracy who could be relied upon not to overturn the *adat* (custom). Some old palm-leaf texts even developed a syncretic origin myth, in which the gods of the La Galigo cycle were descended from Adam and Eve, and the hero of that cycle, Sawerigading, became a prophet foretelling the Qur'ān. The story is probably apocryphal, but is nevertheless suggestive, that Shaykh Yūsuf (see below) returned to Makassar in the 1660s, and appealed in vain to the rulers to impose Islamic principles, but they 'were unwilling or unable to prohibit gambling, cock-fighting, arrack drinking, opium smoking and the like. They in fact promoted superstitious practices such as giving offerings to the spirit of ancestors in the hope that the latter would bring them prosperity.'[37]

The cosmopolitan port and capital of Makassar was, until it fell to the Dutch in 1669, a remarkable beacon of tolerance of all faiths, presenting itself in that period as the free antithesis of the monopolistic Dutch. While Catholic worship was forbidden in the Dutch settlements, there were three Catholic churches in mid-century Makassar, and a well-regarded Portuguese trading community of several thousand.

South Sulawesi's most learned and revered *'ālim*, Muḥammad Yūsuf al-Maqassārī (known today as Shaykh Yūsuf, *c.* 1627–99), left his homeland

37 Azyumardi Azra, *The origins of Islamic reformism in Southeast Asia: Networks of Malay-Indonesian and Middle Eastern 'ulama' in the seventeenth and eighteenth centuries* (Sydney, 2004), p. 94.

for further studies in his late teens, and probably never returned. His life and writings are more fully dealt with in the following chapter. He represents, however, two points that should be noted here. First, he is the best-documented South-East Asian example of the political Sufi who returned from his studies in Arabia to become not only the charismatic populariser of various *ṭarīqas*, but also the chief *qāḍī* upholding the *sharīʿa* and the soul of armed resistance after the Dutch conquered Banten's capital in 1682, leading a guerrilla force of perhaps 4,000 men. Second, he offers a refreshing corrective to the presumption that Islamic knowledge and authority always flowed eastward, with the role of South-East Asians only to adopt and adapt. His travels, sometimes involuntary, circled the Indian Ocean, and he left disciples in Sri Lanka, Arabia and South Africa as well as Indonesia.[38]

Further frontiers: Siam and Cambodia

The Asian maritime frontier of Islam expanded markedly in the sixteenth century, and in some sense reached its peak in the seventeenth before the boundaries consolidated. The Muslim commercial oecumene in the time of Ibn Baṭṭūṭa had stretched as far as China, but had little purchase on the littoral beyond the enclave ports. In the sixteenth-century contest with the Portuguese, important states became the champions of the Muslim side, but the Chinese arm of the original oecumene withered. Non-Muslim Chinese were definitively in charge of their own commerce in the South China Sea from at least 1567. By the mid-seventeenth century Muslims had lost most of the high points of maritime commerce, and even pilgrims from South-East Asia to Mecca travelled most of the way in European ships. Yet as an alternative to the aggressive Europeans, Islam still had gains to make on distant frontiers.

One of these was the Theravada Buddhist world of mainland South-East Asia. In this world the Cham ports along the major routes to China provided the earliest converts to Islam, particularly in the Phan-rang area left to the Chams after their 1471 defeat. There was a Muslim commercial minority here since the eleventh century, but they made rapid converts from the late sixteenth century until by 1670 the king and most of the coastal population were declared to be Muslim. This community established commercial and religious links with the Malay states of the peninsula, and a new frontier for Muslim commerce in Cambodia.

38 See the following chapter for a fuller account of Shaykh Yūsuf.

Cambodia in the half-century after 1594 was a battleground of foreign communities. Expanding Viet and Thai polities constantly threatened from east and west respectively, while well-armed Cham, Malay, Iberian, Chinese and Japanese minorities sought to protect their commerce by holding the king hostage in their mutual conflicts. By killing a group of Spanish and Portuguese adventurers in 1598 and opposing the subsequent Siamese intervention, the Malay and Cham commercial group positioned itself as one of the options for greater Cambodian independence. In 1642 they supported a coup against an unusually ruthless king, and the following year led a massacre of forty men of the Dutch mission which had been asking for monopoly trading rights. The new king, Cau Bana Chand, increasingly dependent on the Muslims to protect him against Dutch and other retaliation, embraced Islam, imposed it on his court, married a Malay woman and used the title Sultan Ibrahim when dealing with foreigners. Although Cambodian memory has marginalised this figure, his reign (1642–59) was one of the most stable of this turbulent century, and was only ended by a ruinous Vietnamese invasion that imposed a half-Viet king.

Islamic influence in Siam also peaked in the mid-seventeenth century, both in Sunnī and Shīʿa forms. The Sunnī were more numerous, at least in the southernmost Malay dependencies and among the Malay, Makassar and Cham refugees who appreciated Siam's tolerance. But it was Shīʿa Muslims from Persia and India who were far more influential at the capital. Their annual Ḥasan-Ḥusayn procession was one of the highlights of the Siamese calendar in the 1670s, with 2,000 Shīʿites reportedly participating. This festival had provided cover for the Persian-assisted coup that brought King Narai to power in 1657, and in gratitude the king had paid for the annual festival thereafter. A cultivated Persian merchant, Āqā Muḥammat Astarābādī, became Narai's chief adviser in commercial and foreign affairs, engineering a Siamese embassy to Persia in 1668, and placing (mainly Shīʿa) Muslims in control of all the key ports – Tenasserim, Mergui, Phuket and Bangkok. Narai was an intellectually curious renaissance man, intrigued by Persian civilisation as he later was by that of the Europeans, but was never likely to adopt either of the foreign faiths that were urged upon him.

Muslim political influence declined with the death of Astarābādi in 1679, and the prominence of Constance Phaulcon at court in the 1680s. It ended when a coup attempt by Makassar and Cham Muslim refugees was suppressed with French help in 1686. The example of these Theravada Buddhist countries reveals, however, both the strength of Islam in the maritime world at this time, and the factors ranged against its further expansion. The former included an association with commerce, military prowess and a kind of cosmopolitan modernity at a time when local certainties were under threat; the latter included even better-armed antagonists from Europe and north-east Asia, an ever-present anti-foreign sentiment and the capacity of the Buddhist monkhood (*sangha*) to create strong popular loyalties beyond anything known to the Hindu-influenced animist worlds of the islands.

Sharīʿa and Sufi in the seventeenth century

In South-East Asia, as in India, the carriers of the Islamic literary and philosophical tradition were primarily Sufi masters, who accepted to some degree a lineage of esoteric and literary learning to their particular teacher and beyond that to a chain of other masters of the tradition. Azyumardi Azra has at last provided the first comprehensive survey of these Sufi networks linking Indonesia to the broader Indian Ocean world, making use of their own habit of establishing the legitimacy of their writings by describing the chain of teachers before them.

In India these Sufi masters often showed an interest in the yogic mystical techniques long practised in the subcontinent, as in Java they could recognise the strengths of the older ascetic tradition. As we have seen in the Java case, the Sufi recognition of different stages of consciousness was in turn attractive to ascetics accustomed to self-denial and meditation to attain the inner essence of knowledge beyond the surface of law and requirements. Some of the earlier Sufis may indeed have seemed relatively indifferent to the legalistic tendency of *sharīʿa*. In the eyes of their later seventeenth-century critics, the great Malay poet Hamzah Fansuri (Ḥamza al-Fanṣūrī) and the possibly mythical Javanese Siti Jenar crossed the line into heretical pantheism. Yet even Hamzah Fansuri warned the faithful, in one of his favourite maritime metaphors, 'Uphold the *sharīʿa* … If the rope of your anchor is attached to something other than the *sharīʿa*, it will be difficult to reach the harbour of gnosis.'[39]

Azyumardi has pointed out that in the seventeenth century, the leading Sufi masters 'ardently believed that only by way of total commitment to the *sharīʿa* could the extravagant features of earlier Sufism be controlled.'[40] He stresses the harmony between the two trends, while earlier writers have perhaps excessively focused on the conflicts. The persecutions of al-Rānīrī were indeed

39 *The poems of Hamzah Fansuri*, ed. G. W. J. Drewes and Lode Brakel (Dordrecht, 1986), p. 92.
40 Azyumardi, *The origins of Islamic reformism*, p. 3.

of critical importance, but they are the only well-documented case of using the Islamic *murtad* (apostasy) laws to execute Sufis judged to have strayed too far from *sharīʿa*. These occurred in the reign of South-East Asia's greatest patron of the *sharīʿa*, Sultan Iskandar Thani of Aceh (r. 1637–41). He excluded Chinese traders from Aceh because of their pork-eating habits, executed scores of Portuguese who refused to accept Islam (including their French priest, Pierre Berthelot, subsequently beatified as a martyr by the Catholic Church) and entrusted religious authority to the stern and prolific upholder of the centrality of *sharīʿa*, Nūr al-Dīn al-Rānīrī. Having failed to convince the previous ruler, Iskandar Muda, to support his views, al-Rānīrī now prevailed, and had the books of Hamzah Fansuri and Shams al-Dīn al-Sumaṭrānī (d. 1630) burned in front of the great mosque. Their disciples who refused to renounce the proscribed views were executed for apostasy, including the popular Shaykh Jamāl al-Dīn.

A consensus may be said to have developed in Aceh and elsewhere that, although al-Rānīrī's numerous writings were extremely valuable in clarifying for the Malay reading world the dangers of the *wujūddiyya* mysticism, and the nature of *sharīʿa* and *fiqh*, his extremism was as unacceptable as the excesses he condemned. After al-Rānīrī's royal protector died in 1641, Sayf al-Rijal, a Minangkabau disciple of the executed shaykh, returned to Aceh from his studies in Arabia, and bitterly attacked al-Rānīrī's views and actions. As al-Rānīrī himself put it,

> Sayf al-Rijal ... held debates with us over the matters which had been discussed before. We ask: 'How could you approve of the people who assert that "man is Allāh and Allāh is man"?' He answers: 'This is my belief and that of the people of Mecca and Medina.' Then his words prevail, and many people return to the wrong belief'.[41]

In effect the crowd decided in favour of Sayf al-Rijal, the Aceh establishment accepted the popular view and in 1643 the learned Gujarati fled back to his birthplace in Gujarat.

The Aceh elite had earlier spurned his advice by putting a woman on the throne, and were so pleased with the results that they enthroned three subsequent women, covering in all the period 1641–99. In this they emulated the strategy of two other contemporary commercially inclined sultanates, Patani (from 1564) and the Maldives, who also showed a repeated preference for female rule not previously known in the region. This raises the question

41 al-Raniri, *Fath al-Mubin*, as translated in *ibid.*, pp. 60–1.

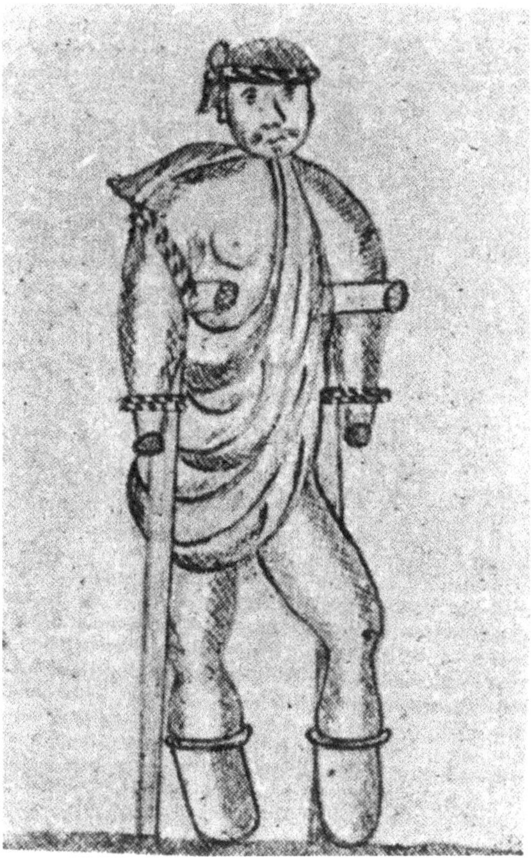

5 Evidence of Shāfiʿī penalties for theft being applied in Aceh, as sketched by Thomas Bowrey in the 1660s

whether the conventional disbarring of women from exercising religious authority was seen as an advantage for the queens by contrast with the pressures of office al-Rānīrī had been able to impose on Iskandar Thani. It may have been seen as a means to avoid pushing disagreements to the ultimate limit, and effectively legitimating, by default of a sole religious authority, the pluralism that was essential to stable commerce. Azyumardi points out that the queen, Safiyyat al-Din, 'wisely refused' to resolve the debate on the grounds that she had no authority on religious matters.[42]

42 *Ibid.*, p. 61.

Under the queens the Chinese returned, a Franciscan mission served the small Christian community, commerce prospered and Aceh's most beloved Sufi master, Shaykh ʿAbd al-Raʾūf al-Singkili, established a new and healing consensus.

ʿAbd al-Raʾūf was probably born about 1617 in Singkil, a west-coast dependency of Aceh, and departed for study in Arabia in 1642, just after the Rānīrī purges. As set out in the following chapter, he was inducted into the Shaṭṭāriyya and Qādiriyya orders by Aḥmad al-Qushāshī and studied philosophy, *fiqh* and *sharīʿa* with Ibrāhīm al-Kūrānī, the two great masters of his day. He returned to Aceh in 1660 as the best-connected and most authoritative of any Indonesian *ʿulama*ʾ, and was quickly appointed chief religious authority as *Kadi Malikul Adil* by the queen. In his own copious writings in Arabic and Malay he never condemned either Hamzah Fansuri or al-Rānīrī, but clearly sought a synthesis which would reconcile a commitment to *sharīʿa* with the appreciation of the inner knowledge of Sufi masters. It seems clear that it was he who appealed to the prominent Meccan shaykh Ibrāhīm al-Kūrānī for a ruling whether it was legitimate for a sultan to have executed a *wujūddiya* ṣūfī, accused of heresy by another *ʿulamā*ʾ, when the ṣūfī in question responded that he could not repent as his argument had not been understood. He received the answer he no doubt anticipated, that such executions were very grave errors, and that a statement which could be interpreted in multiple ways could not be held as evidence of heresy.

The conflict of the 1630s and 1640s was the most spectacular indication of a peaking in the trend to a rigid scriptural interpretation of *sharīʿa*, after which a more inclusive and indigenous synthesis was established. Regularly constituted *sharīʿa* courts were set up at least in Aceh in the first half of the seventeenth century. In the 1630s there were two such courts functioning, one to enforce the observance of fasting, prayer and religious orthodoxy, and the other for issues of debt, marriage, divorce and inheritance. Although Iskandar Muda (r. 1607–36) frequently interfered arbitrarily in the working of these courts, his successor Iskandar Thani supported the system devoutly, and even decreed that the ancient South-East Asian method of trial by ordeal be replaced by Islamic requirements for witnesses. Under the early period of female rule, at least, these courts continued to function. Foreign observers were quick to notice also that the Shāfiʿī penalties for theft were applied in seventeenth-century Aceh as rigorously as anywhere in the world, with numerous people being seen on the streets with their hands or feet amputated (Fig. 5). To a lesser extent, the same phenomenon was noted in Brunei in the 1580s, and Banten in the 1660s.

South-East Asian localisations

One may take the year 1629 as a striking military turning-point, after which the further expansion of Muslim political power was qualified by the ominous factor of superior European power at least by sea. In that year, coincidentally, massive attempts were made by the strongest South-East Asian Muslim powers to finally eject the Portuguese from their stronghold of Melaka, and the Dutch from theirs in Batavia (Jakarta). Iskandar Muda of Aceh sent 236 ships and 20,000 men against Melaka, 'the finest fleet that had ever been seen in Asia',[43] and the last Acehnese *tour de force*. It was largely destroyed by superior Portuguese naval tactics and timely assistance from Aceh's Malay rivals. The same year marked the last attempt by Java's most powerful ruler, Sultan Agung, to take Batavia in a siege by a vast army poorly equipped with modern siege techniques. After it too was destroyed, largely by hunger and disease, Javanese rulers found ways to legitimise the Dutch as part of Javanese history, working with them more often than against. Although it was much too early to speak of European military superiority on land, from this point Europeans held a naval advantage which was accepted as a fact of South-East Asian life.

The direct link between the archipelago and the Islamic heartland was also broken, as the greater capacity of the English and Dutch companies to ship spices and pepper around the Cape of Good Hope rendered the Muslim network uneconomic. By the 1620s the ships were no longer travelling directly between Aceh and the Red Sea. Gujarati shippers, with their own relatively direct links to the Holy Land, sailed to the archipelago in decreasing numbers, securing the route to Mecca and Medina via Gujarat taken by Shaykh Yūsuf in 1644. About eight Gujarati ships reached Aceh every year at the beginning of the century, three in the 1630s, one or two after 1660 and none at all after 1690.[44] Thereafter it was Dutch and English ships that provided the most comfortable passage to Mecca and Madina even by way of the main Gujarati port of Surat. Muslim traffic remained dense across the Bay of Bengal, but the chief Muslim connections outside South-East Asia came again to be with south India, and especially the Tamil coast, a world of similar localisations to those in South-East Asia.

43 Roque Carreiro 1630, trans. C. R. Boxer, 'The Achinese attack on Melaka in 1629, as described in contemporary Portuguese sources', in *Malayan and Indonesian studies: Essays presented to Sir Richard Winstedt on his 85th birthday*, ed. John Bastin and R. Roolving (Oxford, 1964), p. 113.

44 Reid, *Age of commerce* II, p. 28.

The result was a greater reliance on local resources and ideas, and a consensus that retreated from both extremes of the earlier debate.

Diffusions of Muslim power

The major centres of Islamic learning, translation and propagation in seventeenth-century South-East Asia – Aceh, Banten, Makassar, Ternate – were also newly strong 'gunpowder empires' and centres of the spice trade. The Dutch Company (VOC) at first allied with them in its attack on the Portuguese, but soon sought to dominate or defeat them in its quest for a monopoly of the supply of spices. The Muslim centres in Maluku (the Moluccas) were the first to fall under Dutch control. The sultan of Ternate was effectively a Dutch client from the 1620s, and the Muslim hold-out of Hitu in Ambon was defeated in the 1640s. Makassar then became a goad to the Dutch as the remaining free port of the eastern archipelago where the spices which eluded Dutch controls were sold to English, Portuguese and Muslim buyers. It was too strong for the Dutch alone, but they engineered an alliance with a Bugis coalition led by Arung Palakka, resentful of the unprecedented autocracy introduced by Makassar's Sultan Hasanuddin. Makassar fell in 1669. Power in south Sulawesi was again dispersed under multiple small states, as in the pre-Islamic sixteenth century, but with the difference of a strong Dutch naval presence in the fort of Makassar, able often to act as referee between them.

Aceh under its queens was alone able to retain its complete independence. The Dutch succeeded only in removing its productive pepper-producing areas on the west coast of Sumatra, and limiting its naval reach in the Straits of Malacca. Internally the sultans were never again as powerful as those of the early seventeenth century had been. The military leaders rewarded with fiefdoms by Iskandar Muda became hereditary chiefs, small rajas, and united with the capital only under religious exhortation or the threat from outside. The substantial party opposing the queens, who lost the contest in the succession dispute of 1688, won the day in 1699 with the aid of a *fatwā* from Mecca condemning female rule. But the new Arab dynasty was even less successful than the queens had been in imposing its will on the country.

In the pepper sultanates of south Sumatra, the Dutch established a monopoly in Palembang after sacking the city in 1659, though they continued to have problems in neighbouring Jambi. Banten remained a strong competitor of Dutch Batavia until the 1680s, with English, French and Danish companies, and a major Chinese presence, all using it as a base to take a share of the pepper from the VOC. As explained in the following chapter, Islamic literalism peaked in Banten under Sultan Abdulfatah Ageng (r. 1651–82), who patronised Shaykh Yūsuf al-Maqassārī and sent the heir to the throne on a pilgrimage to Mecca. Batavia's opportunity to crush this rival came in 1680, when the more pro-Dutch son, known as Sultan Haji, sought to take power from the old sultan. The VOC intervened in the civil war in 1682, and the old king capitulated a year later. The Banten sultanate became a kind of puppet thereafter, though often disturbed by bitter individual attacks on Dutchmen.

The conflict between Islamic-oriented port and agricultural hinterland, which played its part in these defeats for international Islam, had already been decided by Sultan Agung's Java in the 1620s in favour of a self-sufficient policy founded on rice-growing. But the battle was rejoined under Agung's less capable successors. The arbitrary cruelties of Amangkurat I (r. 1646–77) managed to unite all his enemies under an Islamic banner. He had massacred 2,000 prominent *'ulamā'* soon after his accession, and killed the king of Madura after bringing him to court.

A son of this royal victim, Prince Trunajaya, obtained the blessing of Java's major Muslim holy places, Tembayat and Giri, for his rebellion in the 1670s against Amangkurat. It was joined by a formidable group of Makassar refugees from the loss of their capital, for whom Amangkurat appeared another compromiser with the hated Dutch. By February 1677 Amangkurat I had so few supporters left that he signed a humiliating treaty with the VOC which legitimated their seizure of Surabaya.

When the king died soon after, his son saw no better option than to become a client of the Dutch, as Amangkurat II (r. 1677–1703). The better-organised Dutch forces managed to eliminate his chief rivals by 1680 – not only Trunajaya himself but the Islamic leadership of both Giri and Tembayat. The VOC could in this way keep the king on his throne but not enforce his will. The Javanese heartland knew little peace in the century between the death of Sultan Agung and the Dutch-sponsored Giyanti Treaty of 1755 which finally divided it into two kingdoms. The religious synthesis established under Sultan Agung nevertheless withstood various challenges and largely defined the way Javanese would face the new waves of Islamic reform with which they had to deal in the nineteenth and especially twentieth centuries.

The specifically Malay type of polity, the Malay-speaking *kerajaan*, had not experienced the 'gunpowder empire' phase of power concentration in the sixteenth and seventeenth centuries. Arguably its genius was necessarily based on a diffusion of power, with each raja occupying the lower reaches of a particular river, and mediating trade up the river to largely non-Islamic food producers and foragers whose forest products they exported. Relations between the different river systems were always unstable, with the primacy of any one port, such as Sriwijaya, Melaka or Riau, always dependent on attracting a diversity of traders. The shifting capitals of Riau-Johor in the Singapore area, and Patani in the Thai–Malay borderland, were the most substantial Malay centres in the seventeenth century, and Riau continued in the eighteenth.

Malay-language Islamic scholarship was sustained in the sixteenth and seventeenth centuries primarily in strong port-polities in which Malay was not the vernacular – Aceh, Banten and Makassar. The defeats suffered by these states in the latter part of the seventeenth century opened the door to a different type of millenarian Islamic resistance, especially with the approach of a new *hijra* century (AH 1100 began in 1688 CE). In this climate, states could be imagined rather than defended. One self-styled Sultan Ahmad Shah bin Iskandar, a miracle-working Minangkabau based on the island of Belitung, claimed in 1685 that he was the rightful king of Minangkabau and descendant of Alexander, commissioned by God to expel the Dutch from Muslim lands. He gained the support of thousands of dispossessed warriors – Makassarese, Bantenese, Malays and Minangkabaus – to threaten Dutch interests in south Sumatra and the Malacca Straits. The kings of Jambi and Palembang appeared to support him, and even Dutch ally Amangkurat II invited him to Java for the holy war. The Dutch sent numerous expeditions against him which regained control of the major commercial centres by 1690, though they never found him in the Sumatran interior. The most frightening moment for the Dutch came in August 1689, when they discovered evidence that the Muslim Ambonese Captain Jonker, their most trusted Indonesian lieutenant in numerous past military campaigns, had joined the cult and made preparations to massacre the Europeans of Batavia. The Dutch were merciless in pursuing him and his men to Kartasura, where Amangkurat II at first gave them refuge, and made Jonker's gruesome death an example to other potential rebels.

New networks of the eighteenth century

If the gunpowder empires had been the main proponents of Islam in the period 1550–1650, the eighteenth century was a time when Muslim devotional and scholarly life depended more on networks. The Dutch had demonstrated that they were the single strong power remaining in the archipelago, though not in a position to rule directly as the Spanish did in their comparatively underpopulated islands. Military technologies also shifted, with the key weapons no longer the royal cannons that had terrified the elephants and pikemen of an older generation of opponents. Muskets and soon the flintlock rifle became generalised everywhere in the islands (the Malay term for rifle, *senapang*, being derived from Dutch for flintlock), not only widely sold by English and Portuguese but also manufactured at centres in Sumatra, Borneo and Bali. With this the military balance shifted to smaller networks of armed individuals, who could evade the pressures the Dutch could mobilise against maritime states.

While the multiethnic followers of Trunajaya and Ahmad Shah had demonstrated these new possibilities, it was the Bugis who proved most adept in the long term at utilising the new conditions. In particularly the commercially minded Bugis of Wajo, having seen their senior partner and trade centre Makassar humbled by a Dutch–Bugis alliance, and the subsequent Bugis world dominated by neighbouring rival Bone, perceived little virtue in strong states. They developed an individualistic ethos approaching a doctrine of personal freedom (to travel, to gather, to speak, to own property) in their homeland, yet cooperated effectively outside their borders to establish new port-states. They particularly sought commercial bases in the sparsely populated but strategic Peninsula, settling in the Selangor area in the late seventeenth century.

Johor-Riau entered a period of crisis when the last scion of the old Melaka royal line was murdered in 1699. Both Minangkabau and Bugis adventurers moved in to support conflicting sides, but by 1721 the Bugis were clearly on top. They installed one of the Malay contenders as senior ruler (Yangdipertuan Besar), but one of their own, Daeng Marewa, became the first 'junior king' (Yangdipertuan Muda) and effective ruler of the most successful polity of the Straits area. Its headquarters were now on the island of Bintan, just south of Singapore, conveniently situated to become a hub for Chinese, Malay and Bugis trade. The most formidable of the Bugis junior kings, Raja Haji, took the fight to the Dutch in 1783–4 in a spirit of Islamic revival sparked by another imminent *hijra* century (AH 1200 began in 1785 CE). He laid siege to Dutch Melaka before being killed by a strong fleet sent out for the purpose from Holland. Riau thereafter was better known as a centre of Malay scholarship than as a serious challenger to Dutch power.

Among the other networks which became effective in the eighteenth century were those originating in China and India. Following the massacre of Chinese in Batavia in 1740, and the exclusion of further Chinese migration to Manila soon thereafter, Chinese trade showed more inclination to support smaller ports not controlled by Europeans. Among the Muslim ports which benefited from this shift were Riau itself, Trengganu on the east coast of the peninsula, Brunei (before its own attacks on the Chinese) and especially Sulu. Sulu, situated on an island chain at the margins of Spanish, Dutch, British and Chinese spheres of influence, became the archetype of the anti-state or pirate lair. The Spanish occasionally punished the Sulu capital, but its sultan was but one of the chiefs in a very plural polity, never susceptible to indirect rule. Sulu was able to become in the period 1760–1820 not only the gathering-place for sea produce for the Chinese market, but the largest slave market in South-East Asia, financing slave raids by its Illanun allies throughout the central Philippines and as far as Sumatra to the west. In this period the 'Moro scourge' became embedded in the Filipino psyche, with the heritage of Spanish plays about the *reconquista* of the peninsula being transplanted and indigenised into the Philippine locale.

Indian traders from Gujarat, the Tamil area and Bengal had all been bringing their cotton cloth to supply the South-East Asian markets since at least the fifteenth century. In the seventeenth century the English, Dutch and Danish companies realised they too could only do well in the South-East Asian spice trade if they brought Indian cloth for sale. Hence they established their collecting centres in each of the three areas and gradually came to dominate the supply. Gujarati and Bengali ships had virtually ceased to come to South-East Asia by 1700, as we noted above, though individual cloth traders and financiers from these communities were still active. It was the Tamil Muslims, known locally as Chulias, who became the chief Indian Muslim presence in South-East Asia in the eighteenth century, sailing out of Sao Tome, Porto Novo and Cuddalore. Many became influential advisers and ministers for the rulers of Aceh and the Peninsula.

The following chapter explains the new prominence of Hadramī networks in the eighteenth century, and their links with a number of states outside Java. The Hadramīs came in European or Indian ships, not their own, but made their way as financiers, investors, small traders and religious teachers. The *sayyids* among them were especially honoured as descendants of the Prophet. Many were able to intermarry with the ruling families of Sumatra, Borneo and the Peninsula, and their descendants even to become rulers in Aceh (from 1799) and Siak in Sumatra, Pontianak and Mempawa in west Borneo. Although the earliest census of them was only in 1859, this suggested that the biggest concentrations of Arabs were in Aceh and Palembang (1,764 in 1859),

Pontianak (800 in 1859), Banjarmasin and the colonial centres of Batavia and later Singapore.[45]

Though less direct and state-centred than the contacts of the sixteenth and seventeenth centuries, these Arab networks played their part in re-establishing dialogue between South-East Asia and the Arab world. The Palembang authors discussed in the next chapter, such as ʿAbd al-Ṣamad al-Palimbānī, began a new phase of reformist thinking that would influence the following centuries.

45 L. W. C. van den Berg, *Le Hadhramaut et les colonies Arabes dans l'Archipel Indien* (Batavia, 1886), pp. 108–9.

13

South-East Asian localisations of Islam and participation within a global *umma*, c. 1500–1800

R. MICHAEL FEENER

Situated as it is in geographic distance from the so-called 'central lands' of Islamicate civilisation in the Middle East, South-East Asia has often been regarded by modern scholarship as an 'exceptional' case, with discussions tending to focus on issues such as 'syncretism'.[1] While some of the forms that Islamic thought and practice take in various parts of the region may be distinctive, however, it would be mistaken to assume from this that somehow the religious texts and traditions of the region are necessarily 'less Islamic' than those of Muslim societies in the Middle East, or that Islam was merely a 'thin, flaking veneer' upon more solid foundations of Indic and local cultures. Often implicit in such views are ahistorical and essentialised understandings of 'Islam' conceptualised in relation to a rather limited range of modern reformist conceptions that persist across various academic fields, as well as in popular perceptions.

There are rich traditions of Islamic religious thought and practice throughout South-East Asia, comprising a diverse array of local expressions. Mainland Muslim communities, including Cham, Malay and other ethnic minority populations in what are today the nation states of Vietnam, Cambodia, Thailand and the Philippines have complex histories in which the mutual interaction of Islamicate, Indic and indigenous cultural forms have been dynamically negotiated. However, due to constraints of space, this chapter will focus on developments in the Indonesian archipelago. This choice of focus has been determined by the fact that the islands and adjacent Malay peninsula have historically been home to the vast majority of Muslims in South-East Asia, and because the bulk of the textual documentation for the history of Islam during the period originates from, or relates to, this area.

1 I would like to thank Nico Kaptein, Henk Maier, Tony Reid, Azyumardi Azra, Geoffrey Wade, Michael Pearson, Jon Miksic and Barbara Andaya for their helpful comments on an earlier draft of this chapter.

This chapter provides an overview of Islam in the Indonesian archipelago during the early modern period that presents a balance to prevalent understandings of the extent of localisation involved in the centuries-long processes of 'Islamisation' in the region by also highlighting the ways in which local Muslim populations came to actively participate in developments within the wider world of Islam. As a complement to the material presented by Anthony Reid in the preceding chapter on political and economic aspects of these social transformations, these pages will focus on the ways in which developments in local intellectual and cultural histories between 1500 and 1800 reflect localisations of Islam in the region as well as the engaged involvement of South-East Asian Muslims within a global, cosmopolitan community of Islamic religious scholarship.

Early developments of Islamic religious thought and culture in South-East Asia

Scattered references in Chinese court chronicles and epigraphic evidence from the region hint at the presence of Muslims in the ports of the Indonesian archipelago from the first centuries of Islamic history. However, it is not until the end of the thirteenth century that we have reports of quantitatively significant local conversions to Islam, and then apparently only among the political and mercantile elites of select maritime entrepôts. During this same period, we also have the earliest surviving evidence for the involvement of a Sufi shaykh associated with South-East Asia in the cosmopolitan scholarly circles active in the Middle East. This comes in an Arabic-language work of Sufi historiography containing notices of one Abū ʿAbd Allāh Masʿūd b. ʿAbd Allāh al-Jāwī. Al-Jāwī was a teacher in the Yemeni port of Aden who was highly regarded by his famous Arabian pupil ʿAbd Allāh b. Asʿad al-Yāfiʿī (d. 1367), the author of the work in which historical data on al-Jāwī first appears, and a pivotal figure in the early development of the Qādiriyya Sufi order.[2]

The Qādiriyya tradition came to have a lasting impact on the development of South-East Asian Islam, and is clearly reflected in one of the oldest surviving works of a Muslim author from this region, Ḥamza Fanṣūrī. Ḥamza hailed from the west Sumatran port of Barus, and a recent epigraphic discovery

2 For a discussion of the relevance of this source for understanding medieval Sufi connections between the Arabian peninsula and the Indonesian archipelago, see R. Michael Feener and Michael F. Laffan, 'Sufi scents across the Indian Ocean: Yemeni hagiography and the earliest history of Southeast Asian Islam', *Archipel*, 70 (2005), pp. 185–208.

suggests that he died at Mecca in 1527.[3] His surviving poetry demonstrates remarkable accomplishment in translating aspects of Sufi thought that were first developed in the Middle East into an evocative symbolic vocabulary forged in an Islamicised idiom of Malay and composed in a new genre that came to be known as *syair*:

> Listen, young reciter of the Qur'ān,
> Do not look too far afield
> Passing by the water unwittingly …
>
> The whale is casting about
> In the ocean in search of water.
> Yet the sea is clearly manifest
> To the pious and the profligate.[4]

Like al-Jāwī's student al-Yāfiʿī before him, Ḥamza combined affiliations with the way of ʿAbd al-Qādir Jīlanī with an affinity for the cosmological conceptions of the thirteenth-century Andalusian mystic Ibn al-ʿArabī.[5] Energetic debates over the interpretation of the latter's writings were to comprise a significant part of the broader developments in Islamic learning and literature in South-East Asia over the centuries that followed.

Following the Mongol conquest of Baghdad and the formal end of the ʿAbbāsid caliphate in the thirteenth century, Muslim trading networks across the Indian Ocean linking the Middle East with South-East Asia expanded dramatically. By the fifteenth century, a number of the heretofore small and often temporary populations of Muslim migrants from South Asia and the Middle East settled in various South-East Asian ports were evolving into significant local Muslim communities. The processes through which such changes came about were complex and involved specific local considerations on the part of both indigenous populations and immigrant Muslims, including shared economic interests, the building of political alliances and patterns of intermarriage. These developments led to the establishment of regional centres in which a range of local Muslim cultures emerged and from which elements of their respective 'styles' of Islam spread to other areas of the archipelago. Some of the ways in which the acceptance of Islam was

3 Claude Guillot and Ludvik Kalus, 'La stèle funéraire de Hamzah Fansuri', *Archipel*, 60 (2000), pp. 3–24.

4 G. W. J. Drewes and L. F. Brakel (eds.), *The poems of Hamzah Fansuri* (Dordrecht, 1986), Malay text, p. 140. Unless otherwise credited all translations in this chapter are my own.

5 Alexander Knysh, *Ibn ʿArabi in the later Islamic tradition: The making of a polemical image in medieval Islam* (Albany, 1999), pp. 118–19.

conceptualised in such contexts can be traced through the development of local traditions of Islamic learning during the sixteenth and seventeenth centuries.[6]

For example, one text from the period of transition to Islam on Java demonstrates an extensive engagement with broader Islamic conversations about the definition of confessional and communal boundaries:

> It is unbelief when people involved in a lawsuit and invited to settle the dispute according to the law of Islam, refuse to do so and insist on taking it to an infidel judge. Likewise it is unbelief to dress like an infidel and to speak highly of these clothes ... It is unbelief to say, 'Which is the better religion, Islam or the religion of the Javanese?' It is a pious act to give definite precepts with regard to eating and drinking. It is unbelief to praise a particular idol, maintaining that it is powerful; all this provided one was warned against it.[7]

The dynamics of working out such redefinitions of religion and society has been described by Marshall Hodgson as the 'naturalization of Islam' in South-East Asia.[8] Such a vision of the complex, and by no means teleological, negotiations between broad ranges of imported religious ideas and practices as well as myriad local traditions provides a useful heuristic for appreciating the ways in which the Indonesian archipelago came to be one of the most populous and dynamic lands of Islam over the past six centuries.

One important factor in this was the role played by an evolving canon of Arabic texts that both linked local scholars to discussions current in the broader Muslim world and provided the basis for emerging bodies of vernacular Islamic scholarship. By at least the sixteenth century, Islamic religious texts in Arabic were being translated and adapted into South-East Asian languages, early examples of which in Malay appear to date from the late sixteenth century in the form of vernacular adaptations of the creed of al-Nasafī (d. 1142), and the 'Mantle' poem (*Burda*) in praise of the Prophet by al-Buṣīrī (d. 1296). The oldest surviving examples of analogous developments in Javanese date from a few decades earlier in the sixteenth century and draw considerably upon the works of al-Ghazālī (d. 1111). The sharp critiques of

6 For richly illustrated introductions to local Islamicate manuscript traditions in the Arabic, Malay, Javanese, Acehnese, Sundanese, Sasak, Bugis and Makassarese languages, see Ann Kumar and John H. McGlynn (eds.), *Illuminations: The writing traditions of Indonesia* (Jakarta, 1996).

7 G. W. J. Drewes (ed. and trans.), *An early Javanese code of Muslim ethics* (The Hague, 1978), p. 37.

8 Marshall G. S. Hodgson, *The venture of Islam: Conscience and history in a world civilization* (Chicago, 1974), vol. II, p. 548.

established local practices elaborated in such texts point to the fact that during this period Islam was by no means the dominant paradigm in all sectors of society. At the same time, however, these works and other surviving examples from early stages in the development of Islamic learning in the archipelago all draw on the same scholarly and Sufi authorities recognised by Muslims all across the Middle East, Africa and Asia during this period. This aspect of such works attests to the extent to which a literate Muslim elite in South-East Asia had become participants in a broader Islamicate oecumene during that period.

The primary texts referenced in these far-flung scholarly circles were in Arabic, the language of the Qurʾan and the pre-eminent medium of established religious learning in medieval Islam. However, participation in such discourses did not necessarily involve 'Arabisation' in the sense of non-Arab writers necessarily having to abandon vernacular languages and literary traditions upon their conversion to Islam. In fact, beginning with the Persian renaissance of the tenth century, the spread of Islam beyond the Arabian peninsula stimulated the reinvigoration of and new formulations of a number of languages from vastly different linguistic families. By the early modern period, for example, there is evidence of remarkable developments in Islamicate forms of languages ranging from Bantu-derived Swahili to Indo-European Urdu, Dravidian Tamil, Altaic Turkic and a number of Austronesian languages in the Indonesian archipelago. Such transformations of these diverse traditions often involved both the incorporation of a considerable body of Arabic vocabulary, and the adaptation of some modified form of the Arabic script.

Tracking such developments in South-East Asia from the sixteenth through the eighteenth centuries opens up vistas on to a vivid mosaic of vernacular styles of Muslim cultural expression, including those articulated in languages including Malay, Javanese, Bugis and Makassarese. The pages that follow will introduce aspects of these diverse forms of Muslim culture in discussions focused upon developments in different geographic areas, as well as in relation to broader regional patterns associated with the diffusion of Malay Muslim culture and Arabic textual traditions across the archipelago. In reading through them it should be kept in mind that these various 'styles' of Islamic expression were by no means self-contained systems and in fact interacted with each other in dynamic ways over extended periods of time. Over the course of the seventeenth century, for example, a number of Javanese Islamic texts were adapted from Malay models, and a renowned Makassarese Sufi shaykh established himself as a prominent figure at the court of the sultanate of Banten. The rubrics employed in the following sections are thus intended only as one means of attempting to conceptualise the array of modalities through which Islam took root in the region.[9]

Pesisir and palace developments of Javanese-Islamicate culture

Over the fifteenth and sixteenth centuries, a distinct style of regional Islamicate culture developed on the north Java coast (*pesisir*) in which elements from the traditions of Muslim South Asia and the Middle East, as well as from China and diverse areas of the Indonesian archipelago combined with local traditions to form new, cosmopolitan cultural patterns among the merchant elite of what was at that time a dynamic maritime borderland of Muslim expansion. The early history of translating – in the most literal sense – Islamic teachings into a Javanese cultural milieu can be seen in surviving manuscripts that contain religious texts in Arabic, accompanied by interlinear glosses in Javanese.[10] It is texts of this type that provide some of our best evidence for the early stages of the 'Islamisation' of Java, and the 'localisation of Islam' there.

In popular understandings, the early Islamisation of Java is often attributed to the work of nine saints, known in Javanese as the *wali sanga*. Reliable historical documentation of their lives and work remains elusive. Nevertheless, local traditions circulating since at least the nineteenth century are rich with narratives describing the ways in which the *wali sanga* were believed to have won local populations over to Islam through their skilful manipulation of Javanese cultural forms. This appears all the more remarkable given that in popular imaginings of the *wali sanga* only one of them – Sunan Kalijaga – is regarded as being 'Javanese', the other eight being ascribed 'foreign' origins spanning the Muslim world from North Africa and Iran to Champa and China.

The Dutch scholar of Javanese literature Th. Pigeaud once suggested that the Islamicising agendas of the *wali sanga* 'loosened an ancient bond of sacral secrecy and secularized several elements of pre-Islamic religious ritual. In consequence some ancient religious texts may have developed into

9 The importance of examining 'modalities' of Islamisation in South-East Asia was first highlighted by A. H. Johns in 'Islam in Southeast Asia: Reflections and new directions', *Indonesia*, 19 (1975), p. 34.

10 See T. E. Behrend, 'Textual gateways: The Javanese manuscript tradition', in Kumar and McGlynn (eds.), *Illuminations*, p. 165.

semi-profane or popular literature.'[11] That is, he argues that as established religious traditions gave way to Islam, the boundaries of esoteric exclusivism constructed around cultural forms that may have once been the sacred preserve of a royal or religious elite crumbled. This in turn could make mass, rather than restricted, participation in or emulation of those forms of aesthetic expression possible.

Popular histories of various Javanese cultural art forms would appear to corroborate such an impression, with legendary narratives telling, for example, of the carving of a set of wooden masks for the *wayang topeng* dance dramas by Sunan Kalijaga (one of the *wali sanga*),[12] and attributing stylistic shifts in the appearance of *wayang kulit* shadow puppets to the work of another of the *walis*, Sunan Giri.[13] Later Javanese literary works such as the early nineteenth-century *Serat Centhini*[14] emphasise the harmony of Islam with local cultural expression through images such as the 'marriage' of the traditional *gamelan* percussion orchestra with Islamic religious knowledge (*ngelmu*): 'the sound of the *dhikr* prayer is analogous with the clanging of *gamelan* instruments'.[15] Elsewhere, the physical arrangement of a shadow puppet (*wayang*) performance is used as an analogy to describe a form of Sufi cosmology:

> Kidang Wiracapa spoke slowly, 'Younger brother Kulawirya, regarding perfection of insight, the deeper meaning of the *wayang*, the inner reality: the perfect person makes this into a symbol, an indication of God. He gives *dalang* [puppeteer] and *wayang* their true place [meaning] as depictions of the various ways in which God acts. He makes this comparison: "the screen is the visible world. The *wayang* puppets which are set up to either side of the screen are

11 Th. Pigeaud, *Literature of Java* (The Hague, 1967), vol. I, p. 93.

12 Soedarsono, *Wayang wong: The state ritual dance drama in the court of Yogyakarta* (Yogyakarta, 1990), p. 13.

13 James R. Brandon (ed.), *On thrones of gold: Three Javanese shadow plays* (Honolulu, 1993), p. 6.

14 This encyclopaedic work is thought to have originated from east Javanese *pesisir* tradition and consists of a series of religious instructions alternating with elaborate accounts of the amorous adventures of wandering Muslim students descended from one of the *wali sanga*. The current recension of the text dates from the early nineteenth century, but appears to be based on an older, now lost, *suluk*. Pigeaud, *Literature of Java*, vol. I, p. 229. For a condensed presentation of this work's contents in both Romanised Javanese and a modern Indonesian translation, see Sumahatmaka, *Ringkasan Centini – Suluk Tambanglaras* (Jakarta, 1981). A very helpful Dutch summary of the work is also available: Th. Pigeaud, 'De *Serat Tjabolang* en de *Serat Tjenṭini*: Inhoudsopgaven', *Verhandelingen van het Bataviaasch Genootschap*, 72, 2 (1933). Some of its Islamic religious content is discussed in Soebardi, 'Santri religious elements as reflected in the book of Tjentini', *Bijdragen tot de Taal-, Land- en Volkenkunde*, 127 (1971), pp. 331–49.

15 Trans. in Sumarsam, *Gamelan: Cultural interaction and musical development in central Java* (Chicago, 1995), p. 24.

the categories of God's creatures. The banana trunk (into which the puppets are stuck) is the earth. The *bléncong* [oil lamp] is the lamp of life.'"[16]

However, nearly all such texts are of comparatively recent provenance, and tell us more about evolving local understandings of the role of Islam in Javanese society during the early modern period than they do of earlier historical developments.

Another popular genre of Muslim literature and performance in the archipelago can be traced to significantly earlier: the *Menak* epic of narratives concerning the Prophet's kinsman Amīr Ḥamza, and its related story cycles. Its Javanese forms appear to combine characters and events apparently known through Malay texts with established local literary forms such as that of Pañji tales.[17] Developing first on the north coast of Java in the sixteenth century, the *Menak* later became known in Sundanese areas of west Java, where *Menak* stories were performed with three-dimensional rod puppets (*wayang golek*) in a form of theatre whose invention has been popularly ascribed to another one of the *wali sanga*, Sunan Kudus. As Javanese forms of Islam spread east to the island of Lombok, analogous developments also took place there, with *Menak* stories coming to serve as the foundation for the traditional repertoire of the local form of shadow puppet theatre (*wayang Sasak*).

Other heroes from Islamic sacred history were also incorporated into Javanese literature in the seventeenth and eighteenth centuries. For example, adaptations of Malay narratives – themselves based on elements of the extensive Arabic and Persian literatures of 'stories of the prophets' (*qiṣāṣ al-anbiyā*) – became popular in Javanese works referred to as *Serat Anbiya* and *Tapel Adam*.[18] However, perhaps the most elaborate treatment in Javanese of any Islamic prophet other than Muḥammad can be found in textual traditions associated with Yūsuf (Joseph). Throughout the seventeenth, eighteenth and early nineteenth centuries the courts of several Javanese sultans commissioned versions of the *Serat Yusup*, which was believed to be a work of particular supernatural potency.[19] These Javanese verse narratives of

16 P. J. Zoetmulder, *Pantheism and monism in Javanese suluk literature: Islamic and Indian mysticism in an Indonesian setting*, ed. and trans. M. C. Ricklefs (Leiden, 1995), p. 245.

17 Pigeaud, *Literature of Java*, vol. I, p. 213. For a short introduction to the Pañji tale genre, see S. O. Robson, *Waṇbaṇ Wideya: A Javanese Pañji romance* (The Hague, 1971), pp. 11–15.

18 Pigeaud, *Literature of Java*, vol. I, pp. 130–1.

19 M. C. Ricklefs has called attention to the importance of these royal copies of *Serat Yusup* and two other Javanese Islamic texts (the *Carita Sultan Iskandar* and the *Kitab Usulbiyah*) for the perceived religious and political authority of Javanese rulers since the reign of Sultan Agung. M. C. Ricklefs, *Mystic synthesis in Java: A history of Islamization from the fourteenth to the early nineteenth centuries* (Norwalk, CT, 2005), *passim*.

Joseph's near seduction and eventual vindication became incorporated into elaborate contexts of ritual recitation in Java and Madura, some of which have continued to be practised through the end of the twentieth century.

Alongside such literary narratives, however, Javanese textual production continued to adapt treatises in the technical Islamic religious sciences from Arabic during this period. One of the most influential such adaptations in the seventeenth century was based upon the work of the contemporary South Asian Sufi Muḥammad b. Faḍl Allāh al-Burhānpūrī (d. 1620) entitled, *al-Tuḥfa al-mursala ilā rūḥ al-nabī*. This Arabic text was composed in Gujarat in 1590, and soon thereafter began to make its impact in the Indonesian archipelago through a Javanese verse rendering,[20] as well as through the media of Malay and Arabic-language works produced by the Acehnese Sufi Shams al-Dīn Pasāʾī.[21] Muslims across South-East Asia were attracted to al-Burhānpūrī's 'seven grade' model of Sufi cosmology in the seventeenth century, and on the island of Buton Sultan Dayanu Iḥsān a'Dīn (r. 1598–1631) even used elements of its symbolism to elaborate the ranking of official offices in the state structure of his realm.

Aside from systematic treatises, Javanese literary expressions of Sufism were also expressed in poetry, particularly in a verse genre known as *suluk* composed in metres facilitating performative recitation. *Suluk* appear as an increasingly popular literary form from the seventeenth century when these mystical poems were apparently sung, sometimes perhaps even to the accompaniment of music and dance.[22] Some *suluk* deal specifically with the *wali sanga* and their teachings, or with other prominent Javanese mystical figures, including controversial mystical teachers such as Seh Siti Jenar and Sunan Panggung, who were executed by decree of religious councils in order to prevent (apparently unsuccessfully) the dissemination of their potentially disruptive doctrines.[23] Alongside such distinctively Javanese tropes, however, other *suluk* texts reveal a deep involvement with systematic Arabic grammar and its technical terminology.[24] *Suluk* were composed and performed in court circles of some Javanese sultanates including Cirebon (west Java) in the eighteenth century, and became popular in the interior as well as on the

20 A. H. Johns, *The gift addressed to the spirit of the Prophet* (Canberra, 1964).

21 Published editions of some of these texts, along with critical apparatus and some partial Dutch translations, can be found in C. A. O. van Nieuwenhuijze, *Samsu'l-Dīn van Pasai: Bijdrage tot de Kennis der Sumatraansche Mystiek* (Leiden, 1945), pp. 245–406.

22 Pigeaud, *Literature of Java*, vol. I, p. 85.

23 G. W. J. Drewes, 'Het Document uit den Brandstapel', *Djåwå*, 2 (1927), pp. 97–109.

24 G. W. J. Drewes, 'Javanese poems dealing with or attributed to the saint of Bonaṇ', *Bijdragen tot de Taal-, Land- en Volkenkunde*, 124 (1968), pp. 209–40.

coast (*pesisir*). The move inland reflected a significant shift in Javanese Muslim history following the decline of the coastal empire of Demak and the rise of the Javanese agrarian Muslim kingdom of Mataram in the latter half of the sixteenth century.

The construction of a Javanese Muslim identity for Mataram was most energetically developed during the reign of Agung (r. 1613–46). This archetypical ruler of Muslim Java is most often referred to as Sultan Agung, the title received in 1641 in response to a request that he had sent with a delegation to Mecca. The taking of this Arabic title, however, is only one aspect of the ways in which Agung pursued his agenda of Islamising Java (and Javanising Islam). In 1633 he inaugurated the hybrid *Saka* calendrical system that continued the established Indic Javanese practice of counting its 'year one' from 78 CE; however, from the year of Sultan Agung's decree forward each subsequent year was reckoned according to the strictly lunar months of the Islamic *hijrī* calendar.[25] Another example of the ways in which Sultan Agung worked to both Islamicise local traditions and to Javanise Islam can be seen in his mystical 'marriage' to Ratu Kidul, the 'Goddess of the Southern Ocean' from indigenous Javanese tradition. As M. C. Ricklefs has recently argued, through his deft manipulation of multiple symbolic idioms, Agung managed to cast a lasting image of himself as simultaneously, 'the lover of the distinctly non-Islamic Javanese deity Ratu Kidul, as a monarch with supernatural powers, and as a pious Muslim'.[26]

Complex adjustments of universal Islamic religious ideas and traditional Javanese cultural institutions have been characteristic of Muslim history in the region ever since. However, when trying to understand such long-term processes of Islamisation it must be kept in the mind that the model is not one of teleological progression towards some 'essential' perfection of Islam imagined in terms of present dominant conceptions of orthodoxy. Rather, historical developments actually reveal more of a pattern of flux, as has been evocatively demonstrated by Ricklefs in his history of Javanese Islam during the reign of Pakubuwana II (1726–49).[27]

In this way distinctly 'Javanese' expressions of Islam developed in dynamic interaction with surrounding Muslim cultures. At different periods between the sixteenth and eighteenth centuries, different forms of Javanese Muslim

25 H. J. de Graaf and Theodore G. Th. Pigeaud, *Islamic states in Java, 1500–1700* (The Hague, 1976), pp. 9–23, 45.
26 Ricklefs, *Mystic synthesis in Java*, p. 35.
27 M. C. Ricklefs, *Seen and unseen worlds in Java: History, literature, and Islam in the court of Pakubuwana II, 1726–1749* (Honolulu, 1998).

tradition had variously influenced, and been influenced by, the development of other regional Islamicate cultures in surrounding areas, including the sultanate of Banten, the Muslim communities of Lombok and especially the archipelagic networks of Malay Muslim culture. Even in such distant eastern reaches of the archipelago as Maluku (the Moluccas), elements of Javanese Muslim culture interacted with models of Malay practice, Middle Eastern influences and indigenous traditions in the formation of new local styles of Islam at the courts of the sultanates of Ternate and Tidore.[28]

South Sulawesi styles of Islam

One of the other major modes of Islamicate cultural patterning that came to be influential in the eastern half of the archipelago was that which was first developed in Makassar, located on the south-western tip of Sulawesi. There the ruler of Gowa formally converted to Islam in the early seventeenth century, and soon thereafter launched a series of campaigns of military conquest and religious conversion towards the surrounding Bugis states – long the most prominent local ethnic rivals of the Makassarese on the island.[29] In less than two decades, Makassar established itself as a powerful Muslim sultanate in south Sulawesi and thence continued its campaigns of expansion to other islands, most notably to Sumbawa.[30] The style of Islam that emerged there in the sultanate of Bima over the centuries following these conquests reflects Makassarese as well as Malay and Javanese models in matters ranging from court regalia and literary traditions to the design of Muslim burial markers.[31]

Local historiographic traditions credit three Malay Muslim preachers from west Sumatra with the conversion of Gowa's king, but in south Sulawesi, as elsewhere across the Muslim world, Islam came to take on its own distinctive

28 Leonard Y. Andaya, *The world of Maluku: Eastern Indonesia in the early modern period* (Honolulu, 1993).

29 J. Noorduyn, 'De Islamisering van Makassar', *Bijdragen tot de Taal-, Land- en Volkenkunde*, 112, 3 (1956), pp. 247–66.

30 J. Noorduyn, 'Makassar and the Islamization of Bima', *Bijdragen tot de Taal- Land- en Volkenkunde*, 142, 2–3 (1987), pp. 312–42.

31 Many other factors and cultural influences have been present in this eastern Indonesian state since the seventeenth century, including Chinese and European. For a concise overview of the cosmopolitan character of Bima, see Henri Chambert-Loir, 'État, cité, commerce: Le cas de Bima', *Archipel*, 37 (1989), pp. 83–105. Confluences of models from Makassarese and Malay literary traditions can be found in one of Bima's distinctive Malay-language literary productions of the seventeenth and eighteenth centuries, known as *Kitāb Bo'*.

local forms. As local populations came to identify as Muslims, teachings based upon the Qur'an and the *sunna*, as well as the works of Muslim scholars and Sufis, were transmitted in verse forms that were adapted from poetic genres with traditions of public performance well established before the Islamisation of the Makassarese and Bugis cultural areas. Examples of this can be found in works such as the Bugis poem *Surek Pangngajakna Nabita Muhammad nennia Abdul Ibadi*, which opens:

> This is advice for the wise man of learning,
> Expert in the science of *fiqh* and
> Master of the mystics.
> A man of exemplary behaviour,
> A man of pure heart,
> Who implements the Shari'a and
> Undertakes the discipline of the Sufi way.[32]

This text was originally recorded in what is commonly referred to as the *lontarak* script, because it was used on palm-leaves (*lontarak*). Before the coming of Islam to this part of the archipelago, the two major languages of south Sulawesi – Makassarese and Bugis – had well-developed literary traditions, including texts in a number of genres written in local forms of a syllabic script.[33] In the seventeenth and eighteenth centuries, this literature came to be supplemented with works in the Islamic religious sciences including Qur'ānic translation and exegesis written in this script. However as with Javanese and other South-East Asian languages of this period, Islamic religious works and other texts in the Makassarese and Bugis languages also came to be recorded using a modified form of the Arabic script. In addition to this we find a rather unusual development in south Sulawesi of an alternative 'cipher script', based upon the forms of Arabic numerals, that was used to record some extant texts of Bugis poetry.[34]

Among Muslim scholarly circles in south Sulawesi, a more straightforward adaptation of the Arabic script was more commonly used for certain kinds of Bugis and Makassarese texts in the seventeenth century. William Cummings has made a valuable contribution to our understandings of the symbolic, ritual

32 Abdul Kadir Mulya (ed. and trans.), *Surek Pangngajakna Nabita Muhammad SAW nennia Abdul Ibadi* (Jakarta, 1991), p. 1. This edition includes a translation of the Bugis poem into Indonesian.
33 Samples can be seen in B. F. Matthes (ed.), *Makassaarsche Chrestomathie* (Amsterdam, 1883).
34 B. F. Matthes, *Eenige Proeven van Boegineesche en Makassaarsche Poëzie* (The Hague, 1883), p. 20.

and institutional significances of the outward forms of Arabic-script texts in the history of Makassarese Islam.[35] Aside from these important aspects relating to their 'outsides' as artefacts, the actual contents of some such writings were also significant in local understandings and implementations of Islamic religious teachings in south Sulawesi.

This is evidenced, for example, during the reign of Sultan La Maddaremmeng in the Bugis state of Bone (r. 1631–44), who enacted a sweeping new legal order appealing to the *sharīʿa* in prohibiting pre-Islamic religious practices, attempting to abolish the traditional 'third gender' *bissu* priesthood and emancipating slaves.[36] Alongside these *sharīʿa*-oriented reforms, Sufi texts and practices also underwent a period of extensive development in south Sulawesi during the seventeenth century. Around 1620, an Arab *sayyid* named Jalāl al-Dīn al-ʿAydīd settled in the Makassarese town of Cikoang to begin teaching, alongside *fiqh*, a way of Sufism that became known locally as the *ṭarīqa baḥr al-nūr*.[37] Al-ʿAydid's most famous student at Cikoang was an associate of the royal house of Gowa who came to be known as Shaykh Yūsuf 'Taj al-Khalwatī' al-Maqassārī (d. 1699).

After completing his introductory studies in south Sulawesi, Yūsuf pursued more advanced studies of Islam in Banten, west Java (discussed below) and thence on to major centres of learning in Yemen, the Ḥijāz and Syria. Much of al-Maqassārī's studies were concentrated in Sufism as he was initiated into the Qādiriyya, Naqshbandiyya and Shaṭṭāriyya *ṭarīqas*. In Damascus he was elevated to become a master of the Khalwatiyya Sufi order.[38] After two decades of study in the Middle East, al-Maqassārī returned to the Indonesian archipelago in 1664, settling not in his native south Sulawesi, but rather in Banten, where he was attracted by the patronage of Sultan Ageng Tirtayasa. There he composed the Sufi manual *Zubdat al-asrār fī taḥqīq baʿḍ mashārib al-akhyār* and other works in Arabic.[39] However, his mode of Sufism was not that which is often imagined as typical of pre-modern South-East Asian Islam – no spiritualist syncretism facilitating concessions to indigenous or

35 William Cummings, 'Scripting Islamization: Arabic texts in early modern Makassar', *Ethnohistory*, 48, 4 (2001), pp. 559–86.

36 Christian Pelras, 'Religion, tradition, and the dynamics of Islamization in south Sulawesi', *Archipel*, 30 (1985), p. 124.

37 G. Harmonic, 'Le fête de grand Maulid à Cikoang: Traces d'influence Shīʿite en Pays Makassar', *Papers from the III European Colloquium on Malay and Indonesian Studies* (Naples, 1988), pp. 95–107.

38 al-Maqassārī, *Safīnat al-najā* in Tudjimah (ed.), *Syekh Yusuf Makassar: Riwayat dan Ajarannya* (Jakarta, 1997), pp. 194–204.

39 Nabilah Lubis, *Syekh Yusuf Al-Taj Al-Makassari Menyingkap Intisari Segala Rahasia* (Bandung, 1996), Arabic text pp. 72–126.

Hindu–Buddhist religious practices. As expressed in a letter attributed to al-Maqassārī addressed to the sultan ʿAbd al-Ḥāmīd Karaeng Karangreng of Makassar, 'Our way is the *ṭarīqa* of those Sufis who hold fast to the Qurʾān and *sunna*. Whoever does not adhere strictly to the Qurʾān and *sunna* have strayed from the true and praiseworthy path.'[40]

During the years al-Maqassārī spent in Banten, the Dutch East India Company (VOC) was growing increasingly wary of the potential for charismatic teachers returning from the Middle East to disrupt Dutch designs for control of the archipelago. In 1664 the VOC refused to allow the landing of three returning Bugis 'Hajjis' and transported them to exile at the Cape of Good Hope, arguing that they would become a disruptive influence among the Muslims of the East Indies.[41] Eventually al-Maqassārī found himself in conflict with the Dutch in Banten when he rallied to the support of Sultan Ageng Tirtayasa against the encroachments of the Dutch East India Company in 1682. After leading a local resistance movement for nearly two years, al-Maqassārī was captured by the Dutch, and exiled to the VOC outpost in Sri Lanka. Al-Maqassārī continued to compose Arabic works on Sufism there, 'in that place famous by the name of Sarandib, a foreign land and place of exile for insurgents'.[42]

From his Sri Lankan exile al-Maqassārī also used his pen to continue advocating resistance against the Dutch via correspondence with the Muslim communities of the archipelago at a time when opposition to European incursion into the region was increasingly expressed in an Islamic idiom. In 1685, the Minangkabau leader Aḥmad Shāh Ibn Iskandar was engaging his co-religionists from other regions of Sumatra, the Malay peninsula and even Makassar to join in his crusade against the 'un-believing' Europeans.[43] Such developments drove the Dutch to an increasingly active surveillance of communications between local Muslim communities,[44] and in

40 Tudjimah (ed.), *Syekh Yusuf*, p. 189. This Arabic document is preserved in an eighteenth-century manuscript compilation from Makassar; however, the precise dating of this particular letter is problematic as it both purports to have been written in Banten, and mentions Sri Lanka and one of the Sufi texts that al-Maqassārī is reported to have written there (*Safīnat al-najā*).

41 J. Vredenbregt, 'The Hadjdj: Some of its features and functions in Indonesia', *Bijdragen tot de Taal-, Land- en Volkenkunde*, 118 (1962), p. 96.

42 *al-Minḥat al-Saylāniyya fī'l-minḥat al-raḥmāniyya*, in Tudjimah (ed.), *Syekh Yusuf*, p. 205.

43 J. Kathirithamby-Wells, 'Ahmad Shah Ibn Iskandar and the late 17th century "holy war" in Indonesia', *Journal of the Malay Branch of the Royal Asiatic Society*, 43, 1 (1970), pp. 54–5.

44 On the contemporary Dutch reactions to similar 'subversive messages' circulating among Muslim courts in west Sumatra, see Jane Drakard, *A kingdom of words: Language and power in Sumatra* (Selangor, 1999), pp. 182–92.

1693 some of al-Maqassārī's missives were intercepted by the VOC. In an attempt to remove him from the lines of communication maintained by Muslim scholars and pilgrims between Arabia and the Indonesian archipelago, al-Maqassārī was re-exiled to the Cape of Good Hope where he remained until his death in 1699, becoming a founding figure of the Muslim community in South Africa.[45]

Banten: Islamic scholarship and state institutions

The career of Shaykh Yūsuf al-Maqassārī provides a dramatic view of the interactions between various parts of the Indonesian archipelago and the wider Muslim world. References to teachers and places deployed throughout his Arabic writings detail his links with prominent scholars all across the Muslim world, as well as with emerging regional centres of Muslim culture in South-East Asia such as the west Javanese sultanate of Banten. That area had previously been under the control of the Hindu state of Pajajaran until its major port, Sunda Kelapa, was captured by Sunan Gunung Jati, who established his son Ḥasan al-Dīn as sultan in 1527. Over the sixteenth century this western end of the Javanese coast was increasingly integrated into the rapidly developing maritime Muslim culture of the region, emerging as an important centre for trade, politics and religion.

The lucrative pepper trade passing through this port on the Sunda Straits provided revenues to support the patronage of Islamic learning and culture. Ḥasan al-Dīn laid out a new capital along Javanese lines, transforming a holy site previously venerated by Hindus into a destination of Muslim pilgrimage and the seat of his throne. He also used his resources to attract foreign Muslim scholars to his realm, increasing its prestige and strengthening connections between this South-East Asian state and Muslim centres in the Middle East.

In 1630, Banten sent an embassy to Mecca that carried copies of controversial Sufi texts written in Malay along with a request to the *sharīf* that he send a Meccan scholar to Banten in order to provide guidance on Islamic learning there.[46] Over the decades that followed, Banten experimented with a range of

45 He has remained an important figure in the historical memory of Muslims on both ends of the Indian Ocean littoral. For an overview of his importance in modern Indonesia, see R. Michael Feener, 'Shaykh Yusuf and the appreciation of Muslim 'saints' in modern Indonesia', *Journal for Islamic Studies*, 18 (1999), pp. 112–31.

46 *Sejarah Banten*, Canto 37. Cited in Drewes and Brakel (eds.), *Poems of Hamzah Fansuri*, p. 11.

ideas and institutions as it sought to define itself in relation to a broader Muslim *umma*. Sultan Ageng Tirtayasa (r. 1651–82), friend and patron of al-Maqassārī, encouraged the establishment of such formal indicators of Islamic identity as the prohibition of opium and the adoption of what were considered to be 'Arab' forms of dress. State sponsorship of Islam in the Banten sultanate included the founding of the mosque school at Kasunyatan as well as the establishment of the office of *Pakih Najmuddin* which served as both the chief *qāḍī* and a major political adviser to the sultan.[47] Such developments in Banten can be seen as reflecting broader trends throughout the archipelago during this period in which several local rulers made it a point of policy to cast local rule in the idiom of the *sharīʿa*.

Malay Muslim religious and literary cultures

The origins of a Malay 'style' of Islam stretch back to the late thirteenth century when the ruler of the north Sumatran port of Samudera-Pasai converted to Islam. In the centuries that followed its influence spread to other centres in the region and it continued to serve, symbolically at least, as a point of authoritative reference for later Malay Muslim communities.[48] This was particularly the case for the 'Malay' port of Melaka whose rulers first accepted Islam during the fifteenth century. This cosmopolitan port city located at a key point on the straits between Sumatra and the Malay peninsula became a thriving hub of commerce, in which Muslims from all around the Indian Ocean rim and beyond came together with non-Muslims from all across Asia and Africa in exchanges of ideas and social practices, as well as commercial goods. Among the polyglot merchant population of the port in the early sixteenth century, the Portuguese Tomé Pires listed:

> Moors from Cairo, Mecca, Aden, Abyssinians, men of Kilwa, Malinidi, Ormuz, Parsees, *Rūmes*, Turks, Turkomans, Christian Armenians, Gujeratees ... Merchants from Orissa, Ceylon, Bengal, Arakan, Pegu, Siamese, men of Kedah, Malays, men of Pahang, Patani, Cambodia, Champa, Cochin China, Chinese ... Moluccas, Banda, Bima, Timor, Madura, Java, Sunda, Palembang, Jambi ... Pase, Pedir, [and the] Maldives.[49]

47 Martin van Bruinessen, '*Shariʿa* court, *tarekat* and *pesantren*: Religious institutions in the Banten sultanate', *Archipel*, 50 (1995), pp. 165–200.
48 R. Roolvink, 'The Answer of Pasai', *Journal of the Malay Branch of the Royal Asiatic Society*, 38, 2 (1965), pp. 129–39.
49 Armando Cortesão (trans.), *The Suma oriental of Tomé Pires* (London, 1944), p. 268.

A number of the male Muslim merchants in Melaka apparently married local women in port, and the children of such unions were often polyglot pioneers of Islamic expansion into other ports across the region. Elements from all these various streams of Islamicate civilisation came together with others from China and diverse local traditions of the archipelago in contributing to the development of a new Malay Muslim culture.

This included not only the formation of a language of communication, study and trade, but also of evolving Malay Muslim styles of dress, diet, court ceremonial, literary tastes and conceptions of gender roles in society.[50] The new Malay Muslim cultural forms developed at Melaka spread throughout large areas of South-East Asia, and in the process the Malay language came to serve as a medium of Muslim learning to a number of nascent Muslim communities across the region. In fact, many of the other Islamicate literary traditions of the archipelago, ranging from Javanese to Makassarese, as well as the Cham Muslim texts produced on the mainland, developed rich traditions of adapting religious and literary works from Malay into local languages and genres.

The Malay Muslim religious and cultural superstratum tied such geographically distant and ethnically distinct areas as northern Sumatra, Patani (now southern Thailand), coastal Kalimantan (Borneo), Java and the 'Spice Islands' of Maluku into a cosmopolitan network of trade, travel and religious scholarship. The spread and diffusion of Melaka's Malay Islamicate culture even accelerated after the Portuguese conquest of that important trading port in 1511, which scattered elements of its Muslim community throughout the region. Over the century that followed their ways of speaking, patterns of social behaviour, styles of dress and eating habits, court ceremonial and religious practices – the building blocks of a Malay Islamicate culture – were further dispersed to coastal centres around the archipelago, several of which evolved into regional sultanates over the course of the seventeenth and eighteenth centuries.

Koster has characterised the common identity of 'Malayness' expressed in these settings as predicated upon a constellation of shared political concepts, customs and rituals, and the religion of Islam as well as a common language and textual tradition that linked under a cultural rubric the disparate petty

50 For more on the last of these cultural transformations, see Barbara Waston Andaya, 'Delineating female space: Seclusion and the state in pre-modern island Southeast Asia', in Barbara Waston Andaya, *Other pasts: Women, gender and history in early modern Southeast Asia* (Honolulu, 2000), pp. 231–53.

sultanates of the region.[51] Malay Muslim courts produced a wide range of texts in forms of Malay that were loaded with Arabic and Persian vocabulary and written almost exclusively in a modified form of the Arabic script (*Jāwī*). These included literary chronicles such as the *Sejarah Melayu* and the *Hikayat Raja Pasai*, as well as narratives involving important Islamic religious figures in the Malay *hikayat* genre.[52] Prose texts of this latter type offer vivid, embellished accounts of the lives of Sufi saints like Ibrāhīm b. Adham, and episodes from Muḥammad's life, ranging from the cutting of his hair to the delivery of his last words from his deathbed. Some of the earliest of surviving Malay *hikayat* appear to have been adaptations from Persian originals, such as the *Hikayat Muḥammad Ḥanafiyya* and the *Hikayat Amīr Ḥamza*.[53]

Other Malay texts concerned with Islamic religious themes were composed not in prose *hikayat*, but rather in the verse genre known as *syair*. These range from poetic romances such as the *Syair Bidasari* to non-narrative religious texts such as the *Syair Baḥr al-Nisāʾ* produced by an anonymous poet at the court of Aceh in the late sixteenth or early seventeenth century. *Syair* and *hikayat*, however, comprise only a part of the textual history of Malay Islamicate literature. Among the other productive genres from the fifteenth through nineteenth centuries was that of the Malay legal digests known as *undang-undang*. These are digests of customary law that can include articles in which rulings are stated in relation to both established local practice and more globalising *sharīʿa* norms. For example, the *Undang-undang Melaka* contains the following ruling on a rather particular type of killing:

> [If an adulterous woman's illicit lover] runs into someone's compound and is pursued by the cuckold, who then becomes involved in a fight with the owner of the compound ... and the pursuer is killed, the latter simply dies and there shall be no legal penalty. This is the custom (*ʿada*) of the country, however according to the law of God (*ḥukum Allāh*), he who kills shall also be killed. This follows the directives of the Qurʾan and is in accordance with enjoining the right and forbidding the wrong (*al-amr biʾl-maʿrūf waʾl-nahy ʿan al-munkar*).[54]

51 G. L. Koster, *Roaming through seductive gardens: Readings in Malay narrative* (Leiden, 1997), p. 15.

52 For an overview of these Malay narratives, see Teuku Iskandar, *Kesusasteraan Klasik Melayu Sepanjang Abad* (Jakarta, 1996), pp. 116–21.

53 See L. F. Brakel, *The Hikayat Muḥammad Ḥanafiah* (The Hague, 1975), and Ph. S. van Ronkel, *De Roman van Amir Hamzah* (Leiden, 1895).

54 Liaw Yock Fang (ed.), *Undang-undang Melaka/The laws of Melaka* (The Hague, 1976), Malay text p. 70.

Alongside the *undang-undang* texts, however, there were other Malay writings on law that would be more recognisable to students of Islamic jurisprudence elsewhere in the Muslim world.

One of the major characteristics of South-East Asian history during the sixteenth and seventeenth centuries was the region's rapidly accelerating involvement with expanding networks of global commerce. Anthony Reid has called attention to the relationship between this increased economic interaction and the development of increasingly self-conscious assertions of Islamic identity in the politics of South-East Asian societies.[55] In his groundbreaking survey of Muslim scholarly networks connecting South-East Asia to the Arabian peninsula, Azyumardi Azra has also characterised the period as one of lively development involving new participants and new agendas among Muslims from the Indonesian archipelago.[56]

Over the course of the seventeenth century an increasing number of Muslim states across the archipelago were integrating emerging understandings of Islam into their most basic institutions, including the political, legal and educational systems of a number of regional sultanates. This was manifest, for example, in the staging of elaborate state rituals to mark Muslim religious observances and in the interpretation of Sufi cosmological theories in ways that developed local models of political power and cultural capital. The same period also saw an Islamicising transformation in the legal systems of a number of South-East Asian sultanates. Examples of this have been pointed to even in areas such as the island of Muna in south-east Sulawesi, where Raja Sangia Latugho is reported to have 'implemented Islamic law' from 1671 to 1715.[57] However, the interpretation of just what this may have meant in such a context still requires further research.

Local interpretations and implementations of 'Islamic law' differed from place to place in the Indonesian archipelago (as across the Muslim world as a whole). However, despite considerable diversity of formal doctrines and structures, it is clear that during the seventeenth century a number of regional polities established localised traditions of law and jurisprudence that were

55 Anthony Reid, 'Islam and the state in seventeenth-century Southeast Asia', in Taufik Abdullah (ed.), *Proceedings of the international seminar on Islamic civilization in the Malay world* (Istanbul, 1997), pp. 67–84.

56 Azyumardi Azra, *The origins of Islamic reformism in Southeast Asia: Networks of Malay-Indonesian and Middle Eastern 'ulamā' in the seventeenth and eighteenth centuries* (Crows Nest, NSW, 2004).

57 *Laporan Hasil Penelitian Tentang Masuknya Islam di Sulawesi Tenggara*, Departemen Agama: Badan Penelitian dan Perkembangan Agama, Balai Penelitian Lektur Kegamaan. Ujung Pandang, 1986/7, p. 59.

self-assertively 'Muslim'. The very appeal to such external symbols of legal order comprises a significant marker of the ongoing processes of the Islamisation of social institutions in the region.

Islamic scholarship in the sultanate of Aceh

During the first half of the seventeenth century, and especially under the royal patronage of Sultan Iskandar Muda (r. 1607–36), Aceh became the leading regional centre of Islamic learning. Iskandar Muda launched campaigns for the Islamisation of the neighbouring Gayo and Minangkabau regions of Sumatra, and staged elaborate observances of Friday prayers and other Islamic religious observances. He also appears to have adopted various symbols and institutions from the contemporary Mughal and Ottoman empires to bolster his authority as a ruler of Muslims, including official state seals and insignia[58] and even an institution reminiscent in some ways of the office of the Sehülislam.[59] Iskandar Muda and his successors devoted considerable patronage to Islamic learning and literature as well, as attested to by both European visitors' accounts of Aceh and the legacy of influential Muslim texts from the seventeenth-century produced there that have survived to this day.

The earliest surviving evidence for a tradition of Acehnese literature written in a modified Arabic script comes from the late seventeenth century; however, most written texts in that language were produced in the eighteenth and nineteenth centuries. Rather than Acehnese, the predominant language of both the royal court and Islamic religious scholarship in the sultanate of Aceh in the seventeenth and eighteenth centuries was Malay. In fact, the power and prestige of the Acehnese court in the seventeenth century enabled it not only to take up the mantle of Muslim Malay culture rooted in the earlier tradition of Melaka, but also to significantly transform it. The extent to which this was the case has been demonstrated by Leonard Andaya in arguing that, 'Aceh came to offer new standards of Malayness based on Islamic models in literature and in court administration and behaviour.'[60]

Nevertheless the Malay Muslim character of the sultanate of Aceh was, like that of all other Islamicate cultures of the medieval and early modern period,

58 James Siegel, *Shadow and sound: The historical thought of a Sumatran people* (Chicago, 1979), pp. 24–5.

59 Takeshi Ito, 'The world of the Adat Aceh: A historical study of the sultanate of Aceh', (Ph.D. thesis, Australian National University (1984), pp. 259–62.

60 Leonard Y. Andaya, 'Aceh's contribution to standards of Malayness', *Archipel*, 61 (2001), p. 45.

complex in its relationship to pre-Islamic traditions. Thus the records of the period reveal that a number of ideas and institutions rooted in the earlier history of the region were transmitted and transformed within the sultanate's Islamicised idioms of symbolic power and social order. Perhaps the most striking example of this is a structure located in the inner precincts of the sultan's palace known as the *Gunongan* (Fig. 6). This was an artificial mountain located in the royal gardens, whose descriptions suggest that it resembled replicas of Mt Meru known from other South-East Asian courts, both Muslim and non-Muslim. The name of the garden in which this powerful Hindu–Buddhist image was situated was *Taman Ghayra*, through which flowed a river known as the *Dār al-ʿishq*, on the banks of which was a mosque called *ʿIshq Mushāhada*.[61] The Arabic terminology employed here is thick with Sufi valences, and points to the important role of *taṣawwuf* in expressions of the religious and political culture of the sultanate.

One of the most influential figures active in both the religious and political spheres of life in Aceh during the reign of Sultan Iskandar Muda was the Sufi shaykh Shams al-Dīn b. ʿAbd Allāh al-Sumaṭrānī al-Pasāʾī (d. 1630), whose presence is recorded in the works of European visitors to the court of Aceh, and who has left behind a considerable corpus of writings in both Malay and Arabic, some of which also contains quotations in Persian. In his work entitled *Nūr al-Daqāʾiq*, which is transmitted in both Arabic and Malay recensions, Shams al-Dīn presents one of the earliest Malay expositions of the 'seven grade' emanationist cosmology developed by al-Burhānpūrī. However, court tastes changed and eventually Shams al-Dīn's models of Islamic mysticism lost favour in the face of virulent critiques of the Sufi doctrine of the 'unity of Being' (*waḥdat al-wujūd*) by a newcomer to the Acehnese court, Nūr al-Dīn al-Rānīrī.

Al-Rānīrī was a Gujarati Muslim of south Arabian descent who was born into a family with far-flung connections in the commercial and cultural networks across the Indian Ocean littoral. His uncle had spent extended periods of time in Aceh where he taught the Islamic religious sciences in the late sixteenth century.[62] Al-Rānīrī himself benefited from a rich Islamic education under the direction of a number of highly mobile, ethnically hybrid teachers from various countries along the Indian Ocean littoral.[63] In his own writings,

61 Robert Wessing, 'The *Gunongan* in Banda Aceh, Indonesia: Agni's fire in Allah's paradise', *Archipel*, 35 (1988), pp. 157–94.
62 Azra, *Origins of Islamic reformism*, pp. 54–5.
63 Tudjimah (ed.), *Asrār al-Insān fī Maʿrifat al-Rūḥ wa'l-Raḥmān* (Jakarta, 1961), p. 2; S. N. al-Attas, *Raniri and the Wujudiyyah of 17th century Aceh* (Singapore, 1966), pp. 13–14.

6 The artificial mountain (*Gunongan*) of Aceh, built as a centrepiece of a Sufi-inspired royal garden (photo: Michael Feener)

al-Rānīrī brought a good deal of these cosmopolitan traditions of Muslim scholarship into his Malay compositions. His dexterity in adapting techniques and materials from global traditions of Arabic-language scholarship comes across clearly in the construction of his arguments in such works as the intra-Sufi polemics *Ḥujjat al-ṣiddīq li dafʿ al-zindīq* and the *Tibyān fī maʿrifat al-adyān*.

After he had established himself at the Acehnese court in 1637, al-Rānīrī initiated a radical campaign of religious reform that sought to discredit the mystical cosmologies popularised in the region by Ḥamza Fanṣūrī and more recently Shams al-Dīn to replace them with what he considered to be more 'orthodox' doctrine. Al-Rānīrī's ambitious programme of reform was carried out through the creation of a remarkable corpus of works written in Malay that strove to redefine Aceh's Malay Muslim tradition in the fields of jurisprudence, mysticism, theology, literature and history. His Malay works became the standard references for many South-East Asian Muslim students over the following centuries and were studied well beyond Aceh in places including the Malay peninsula and Kalimantan (Borneo), with translations and adaptations made into Bugis and other regional vernaculars.

Of all his writings in these various fields, however, it has been al-Rānīrī's work of *fiqh* that has proved of greatest longevity. The contents of this book, entitled *Ṣirāt al-Mustaqīm*, present striking images of the extent to which emerging traditions of Islamic religious scholarship in Malay during the seventeenth century had become engaged with contemporary conceptualisations of a global Sunnī normativity. For instead of raising specific issues immediately relevant to the lives of South-East Asian Muslims of that period, this monumental Malay-language work on *fiqh* includes rulings on such things as the eating of camel (*ḥalāl*) and giraffe (*ḥarām*).[64] That is, what is characteristic about a popular Malay teaching text such as this is not its exotic, local vision of a distinctly South-East Asian Islam, but rather its overwhelming uniformity with analogous *fiqh* manuals produced around the world in Arabic during its day. Parallel developments can be found in seventeenth-century Malay works of other fields of Islamic religious scholarship as well, including Qur'ānic exegesis.

The most significant Malay work of this type was produced by a scholar active at the court of Aceh following al-Rānīrī's abrupt fall from favour in 1643.[65] ʿAbd al-Ra'ūf al-Singkeli's (d. 1693) *Tarjumān al-mustafīd* was the most extensive and popular text of Malay-language *tafsīr* extant for almost 300 years and went through several print editions in the late nineteenth and early twentieth centuries. Through a painstaking study of this work Peter Riddell has demonstrated the overwhelming extent to which the *Tarjumān al-mustafīd* is based upon the *Tafsīr jalalayn*, which was composed by two Egyptian scholars in the sixteenth century, and ever since has served as a standard introductory text to the field.

The scholarly career of the author of the *Tarjumān al-mustafīd*, ʿAbd al-Ra'ūf al-Singkeli, provides an illuminating contrast to that of his predecessor at the court of Aceh, al-Rānīrī, in several respects. Most significantly, perhaps is the

64 Nūr al-Dīn Muḥammad Jīlānī b. ʿAlī b. Ḥasanjī b. Muḥammad b. Ḥumayd al-Rānīrī, *Ṣirāt al-Mustaqīm fī fiqh madhhab al-Shāfiʿī* (Cairo, 1937), p. 336.

65 Takeshi Ito, 'Why did Nuruddin ar-Raniri leave Aceh in 1054 AH?', *Bijdragen tot de Taal-, Land- en Volkenkunde*, 134, 4 (1978), pp. 489–91.

fact that ʿAbd al-Raʾūf was a locally born scholar who had returned to Aceh after decades of study and scholarship in Duḥā, the Yemen and the Ḥijāz. Seen alongside the career paths of al-Rānīrī others like him who came from South Asia and the Middle East to teach Islam in the Indonesian archipelago, the professional trajectories of ʿAbd al-Raʾūf and his contemporary colleague Yūsuf al-Maqassārī demonstrate that the movement of Muslim scholars and their works between Arabia and South-East Asia was by no means unidirectional.

A considerable amount of information about ʿAbd al-Raʾūf's period of study in the Middle East (1641–61) can be gleaned from an autobiographical codicil appended to his Sufi treatise entitled *ʿUmdat al-Muḥtājīn*. That section of the text documents his position within the Muslim scholarly circles of his day through detailed listings of the teachers that he studied with, especially those affiliated with the Qādiriyya and Shaṭṭāriyya Sufi orders.[66] Of all of these teachers, the most directly influential were the highly distinguished and influential shaykhs Aḥmad al-Qushāshī (d. 1661) and Ibrāhīm al-Kūrānī (d. 1690).[67] Among South-East Asian Muslims this pair of Ḥijāz-based Naqshbandī Sufi shaykhs became more popularly known as teachers of the Shaṭṭāriyya order, and their particular appeal for students from the Indonesian archipelago seems to have been in part due to their combination of affinities for the teaching of Ibn ʿArabī and the defence of the practice of vocalised *dhikr* (*jahr*) according to the Shāfiʿī school of jurisprudence.[68]

Educated in these prestigious Sufi circles of the Ḥijāz, ʿAbd al-Raʾūf appears to have considered Sufism to be a special preserve of a scholarly and spiritual elite, rather than a phenomenon of popular syncretism. As he maintained in his Malay treatise entitled *Daqāʾiq al-Ḥurūf*, 'those who do not understand the technical language [of the Sufis] ... should leave discussions of such to them [the Sufis]'.[69] Thus delimiting the sphere for such discussions, ʿAbd al-Raʾūf was able to make more refined arguments and subtle distinctions in elaborating his position on the controversial subject of *waḥdat al-wujūd*, quoting appreciatively from Ibn ʿArabī but maintaining a careful ontological distinction between God (*al-Ḥaqq*) and everything else in creation.

66 Peter Riddell, *Transferring a tradition: ʿAbd Al-Raʾuf Al-Singkili's rendering into Malay of the Jalalayn commentary* (Berkeley, 1990), pp. 223–38.

67 For more on his connection to Kūrānī, see A. H. Johns, 'Friends in grace: Ibrahim al-Kurani and ʿAbd al-Rauf al-Singkeli', in S. Udin (ed.), *Spectrum: Essays presented to Sutan Takdir Alisjahbana on his seventieth birthday* (Jakarta, 1978), pp. 469–85.

68 Dina Le Gall, *A culture of Sufism: Naqshbandīs in the Ottoman world, 1450–1700* (Albany, 2005), pp. 101–2.

69 A. H. Johns (ed.), '*Daḳāʾiḳ al-Ḥurūf* by ʿAbd al-Raʾūf of Singkel', *Journal of the Royal Asiatic Society* (1953), Malay text p. 59.

In addition to his works on Sufism and Qur'ānic exegesis, ʿAbd al-Ra'ūf composed books in a number of other fields, including *ḥadīth* studies and jurisprudence. Much of this work was produced under the patronage of the Acehnese court after his return from two decades of study in the Middle East. Notable among these compositions is the *Mir'āt al-ṭullāb fī tashīl maʿrifat al-aḥkām al-Sharʿiyya lil-mālik al-wahhāb*, in which he advanced a *sharīʿa*-based argument for the legitimacy of a female to serve as the head of a Muslim state (*khalīfa*).[70] For ʿAbd al-Ra'ūf, this was not an abstracted, hypothetical ruling, but rather a concrete reference to the situation in Aceh during his day, as the sultanate was ruled by a succession of four *sulṭānas* between 1641 and 1699.

Beyond his written work, ʿAbd al-Ra'ūf's lasting influence on the further development of Islamic thought in South-East Asia has been exercised by the legacy of his Sufi teachings passed down through his disciples hailing from various parts of the archipelago. Some of the most important among them were Shaykh Burhān al-Dīn (d. 1692) of Ulakan in west Sumatra, Tok Pulau Manis of Trengannu on the Malay peninsula (d. *c.* 1736), ʿAbd al-Muhyī of Banten in west Java and Baba Da'ūd b. Ismāʿīl al-Rūmī – who is believed to have been a descendant of Ottoman gunsmiths who had come to Sumatra to aid the Acehnese in their struggles with the Portuguese in the sixteenth century. Over the century that followed, the significance of such intersections of trans-regional Sufi lineages and opposition to European advances in the Indonesian archipelago were to become more pronounced.

New networks and European encroachment in the eighteenth century

In the early decades of the eighteenth century, attempts by the Dutch East India Company (VOC) to strengthen its control over commerce and political affairs in the Indonesian archipelago were challenged by various forms of local resistance, a number of which were pursued or perceived as being advanced in the name of Islam. In reaction to such challenges to their authority, real and imagined, the Dutch took steps to disrupt the development of opposition movements, particularly those which they feared from native Muslim leaders. In 1716 the VOC issued a prohibition on the use of Company ships to transport Muslim pilgrims from the archipelago on their return voyages from Mecca.[71]

70 Amirul Hadi, *Islam and state in Sumatra: A study of seventeenth-century Aceh* (Leiden, 2004), p. 60.
71 Vredenbregt, 'The Hadjdj', p. 96.

Later in the same decade, the Dutch began to sense other religiously inspired threats that originated not in Arabia, but in Java itself in the form of documents circulating under the title of 'Predictions of Jayabaya'.[72] These predictions of the overthrow of tyranny and the ascension to power of a messianic figure (*mahdī*) or a 'just king' (*ratu adil*) were seen by some among both the colonisers and the colonised as supporting various millenarian movements in the eighteenth century.

In 1721 these spectral menaces took on a new face for the Dutch population of Batavia with the uncovering of an 'Islamic plot' allegedly engineered by a baptised German-Siamese Eurasian by the name of Pieter Erberveld. He was arrested that December on charges of distributing Islamic religious amulets containing Arabic-script formulae (*jimat*) and plotting to put an end to VOC control by slaughtering the Christian population of Batavia. Soon thereafter he, along with a number of his associates, was executed and his head was displayed on a pike. A gruesome monument to his fate with inscriptions in Dutch and Javanese was set up as a constant reminder of the price to be paid for threatening the colonial order.

Aside from polyglot, highly mobile and eclectic individuals like Erberveld, there were during the eighteenth century increasing numbers of people in motion across the archipelago who could at various times identify themselves as members of different ethnic groups. Engseng Ho has described this period as one of expanding and interconnected diasporas impacting upon the histories of a number of port-polities in the archipelago. The two most influential Muslim diasporas in the region during the eighteenth century were those of the Bugis and Arabs from the Hadramawt in southern Arabia. While the Bugis integrated themselves into the highest levels of Malay courts around the Straits, the Hadramīs had an even wider range of influence. A Hadramī dynasty known as the Jamal al-Layl established itself at Aceh at the expense of the last sultana of Aceh in 1699, and in the decades that followed, other Hadramī creole migrants established themselves at Siak, Mempawa, Matan, Kubu and Pontianak.[73]

In many of these places, the ascendancy of 'Hadramī Arabs' within local religious and political elites contributed to the further incorporation of Islamic

72 H. J. de Graaf, 'South East Asian Islam to the eighteenth century', in P. M. Holt, Ann K. S. Lambton and Bernard Lewis, *The Cambridge history of Islam* (Cambridge, 1970), vol. II, p. 152.

73 Engseng Ho, 'Before parochialization: Diasporic Arabs cast in creole waters', in Huub de Jonge and Nico Kaptein (eds.), *Transcending borders: Arabs, politics, trade, and Islam in Southeast Asia* (Leiden, 2002), pp. 11–36.

elements in the symbols of political power in South-East Asian states. In certain ways these developments mark the acceleration and proliferation of processes that had been at work in the region for some time. As a result of such collaborations, cosmopolitan creole Arab Muslim immigrants came to assume primary leadership roles in numerous communities stretching across the archipelago.

Such patterns of close association between Arab immigrants and local elites were reproduced with variations across the region in the eighteenth century. For example, in 1711 two Arab *sayyids* arrived in Buton and were given permission by the sultan to establish two religious schools, one in the neighbourhood of the royal palace and one near the grand mosque at Bau-Bau.[74] In 1737, a Javanese royal embassy to Batavia returned to the court of Pakubuwana II, bringing with them an Arab shaykh named Sayyid Alwi. This new arrival at the central Javanese capital quickly rose to prominence, being granted one of the sultan's concubines for a wife and charge over religious affairs for the realm.

Islam in eighteenth-century Java

Pakubuwana II's reign (1726–49) was marked by a series of dramatic transformations in the religious and cultural character of Java. His elderly grandmother, Ratu Pakubuwana, had in the early years of his reign attempted to strengthen the sultanate through the cultivation of Islam, particularly by means of sponsoring the production of Islamic religious and literary works in Javanese. These texts included narratives of Alexander the Great (*Carita Sultan Iskandar*) and the prophet Yūsuf (*Carita Nabi Yusuf*), as well as the *Kitab Usulbiyah*, which details a mythic encounter between Jesus and Muḥammad. During the early years of his reign, Pakubuwana II appears to have embraced trends towards the further Islamisation of Javanese court life, and attempted to construct an image of himself as a crusading warrior of Islam against the 'Christian' Company of the Netherlands East Indies. However, after a dramatic reversal of military fortune in the joint Chinese–Javanese campaign against the VOC, he abruptly dropped such pretence and sought reconciliation with the Dutch. This decision was accompanied by radical reorientation of the *kraton* elite towards Javanist modes of asceticism and court aesthetics, and away from explicitly Islamic identifications.[75]

74 La Ode Zaenu, *Buton dalam Sejarah Kebudayaan* (Surabaya, 1985), p. 89.
75 Ricklefs, *Seen and unseen worlds in Java*.

The complex negotiations of defining Islam in relation to Javanese culture during this period are reflected in the literary as well as in the historical record. For example, another episode in which issues of establishing particular, court-approved conceptualisations of Islam in Java is purportedly described in the well-known work of Javanese Sufi literature *Serat Cabolek*. This later text vividly narrates the story of an unruly mystic who was reportedly brought before an assembly of Muslim scholars in eighteenth-century Java for divulging esoteric doctrines to the uninitiated. While initially boasting of his 'superior' knowledge of the faith gained under the tutelage of Yemeni teachers, Haji Amad Mutamakin is eventually humbled by the way in which one of the scholars sitting in judgment over him is able to interpret the 'proper' Islamic mystical meanings contained within Old Javanese 'Hindu' texts such as the *Bhima Suci*.[76]

With more precise dating and historiographic reliability for the latter half of the eighteenth century, we are fortunate enough to also be able to view some other aspects of the continuing dynamics defining Islam in relation to the culture of the Javanese court through writings in an altogether different genre than *suluk* and formal religious treatises. This is due to the survival of a manuscript written by a woman employed as a member of the sultan's elite female guard (*prajurit estri*) that includes descriptions of a number of religious rituals as they were observed at the court of Mangkunegara I from 1781 to 1791. For example, we get a sense of the concrete ways in which Javanese aesthetic and performance traditions were integrated into celebrations of the Muslim feast day commemorating Abraham's near sacrifice of his son (Jv. *Garebeg Besar* / Ar. ʿĪd al-āḍḥā):

> In the evening and through the night before Friday
> A vigil was kept by the army of the senior Pangeran Dipati who circled the courtyard.
> They placed bets on their skills at archery, while the *kaum* [pious Muslim] soldiers said their *dikir* in unison.
> There was singing, and playing a *gamelan*
> Of gongs and drums, and there was a meal at midnight.
> Some performed a [dance performed by ornately costumed archers known as] *tayungan*.
> In the morning they went to the prayer once again.[77]

76 S. Soebardi, *The book of Cabolek: A critical edition with introduction, translation and notes* (The Hague, 1978).

77 Ann Kumar, 'Javanese court society and politics in the late eighteenth century: The record of a lady soldier, part 1 – The religious, social, and economic life of the court', *Indonesia*, 29 (1980), p. 14.

More formal works of Javanese Muslim literature were produced at about the same time by the celebrated court poet of Solo, Raden Ngabehi Yasadipura I (d. 1803). Among his major works are modern Javanese verse renderings of *Menak* stories, a guide for rulers entitled *Taj al-Salāṭīn* and a collection of narratives of the lives of the prophets from Adam to Muḥammad. In his masterful survey of the history of Islam in early modern Java, M. C. Ricklefs has demonstrated that by the time of Yasadipura I's death in the early nineteenth century, a dominant mode of religious and cultural identity had formed in Java out of a long-developing 'mystic synthesis' incorporating elements of indigenous, Indic and Islamic traditions.[78] Yasadipura I's work, and that of the court poets Yasadipura II and Ronggowarsito who followed him, helped to create sophisticated works of local Muslim literature that reflected and further influenced the changing religious culture of the courts of Java's sultans. These latter works, however, are characteristic of a different era of the history of Islam in Java, one beyond the scope of this essay.

Malay Muslim scholarship in the eighteenth century

Outside Java, developments of religious and cultural dynamics in the region were also vibrant in other parts of the archipelago during this period. For example, in the mid-eighteenth century, a considerable number of Arab migrants came to be integrated into the political and cultural elite of the south Sumatran sultanate of Palembang, contributing to significant developments in the history of Islam there.[79] Manuscript holdings preserve the work of a number of local scholars active in Palembang at that time, including Shihāb al-Dīn b. ʿAbd Allāh Muḥammad and his younger contemporary Kemas Fakhr al-Dīn (d. 1763). Shihāb al-Dīn's work is preserved in three surviving texts presenting simplified outlines of a Sufi theology that eschews what he sees as the excesses of the 'seven grade' system of speculative emanationist cosmology that had been so popular in the archipelago since the early seventeenth century. Kemas Fakhr al-Dīn devoted a considerable amount of his scholarly output to Malay translations of Arabic works, ranging from an expanded treatment of Raslān al-Dimashqī's (d. 1146) classic statement of 'sober Sufism' *Riṣala fī'l-tawhīd*, to selections from the Arabic historiographical tradition dealing with the early Muslim conquest of Syria

78 Ricklefs, *Mystic synthesis in Java*, pp. 221–34.
79 Barbara Andaya, *To live as brothers: Southeast Sumatra in the seventeenth and eighteenth centuries* (Honolulu, 1993), pp. 220–1.

(ps.-Wāqidī's *Mukhtaṣar Futūḥ al-Shām*). The rendering of such texts into Malay testifies to the increasing involvement of the South-East Asian Muslim scholars in the world of Arabophone learning spanning the Indian Ocean during that period.

Within these contexts, the ongoing and deepening Islamisation of the archipelago underwent some remarkable developments during the eighteenth century. In many ways these were related to broader trends making themselves felt across the Muslim world as a whole. For at this time a new surge in internally oriented Islamic reform movements was sweeping across Africa and Asia. Perhaps the one with the most name-recognition today is that of ʿAbd al-Wahhāb which succeeded in becoming the 'official' form of Islam in Saudi Arabia. However, Wahhābism is only one manifestation, and a somewhat atypical one at that, of broader trends in Islamic religious reform in the eighteenth century. Many of the reform movements from this period combined a renewed emphasis on the study of *ḥadīth* with a re-evaluation of Sufi tradition within various newly established or reformulated Sufi orders, such as the Naqshbandiyya and the Shaṭṭāriyya.

In the mid-eighteenth century the Banten scholar ʿAbd Allāh b. ʿAbd al-Qahhār studied the Shaṭṭāriyya and Naqshbandiyya Sufi orders in Mecca, and returned carrying with him a manuscript of one of ʿAbd al-Raʾūf Singkeli's works. Later in the eighteenth century other *ṭarīqas* began attracting adherents in west Java, particularly the Rifaʿiyya and Sammāniyya orders.[80] Well beyond the localities of the archipelago, however, South-East Asian Sufis were deeply involved with contemporary currents of Sufi reform, as can be seen from the example of Shaykh Aḥmad Khatīb Sambās in the nineteenth century. Although born in Kalimantan, he spent most of his life at Mecca, where he played a formative role in the systematisation of a new Sufi order combining elements from the Qādiriyya and Naqshbandī traditions.

Before these developments, however, the most influential South-East Asian Sufi and Muslim scholar active in Arabia during the eighteenth century was ʿAbd al-Ṣamad al-Palimbānī (al-Jāwī). Like a Fakhr al-Dīn Kemas and Shihāb al-Dīn, ʿAbd al-Ṣamad hailed from Palembang. However, after coming to the Middle East to pursue his religious education, he never returned to South-East Asia, and died of old age in Ṭāʾif after a lifetime of study, teaching and writing in Yemen and the Ḥijāz. His writings were carried back to South-East Asia by his students where they had a tremendous impact on the evolving Islamic

80 van Bruinessen, 'Banten sultanate', pp.182–5.

intellectual history of the region. ʿAbd al-Ṣamad is known to be the author of a number of works in both Malay and Arabic on a broad range of topics.

ʿAbd al-Ṣamad wrote one of the earliest Malay works on the subject of *perang sabil* ('war in the way [of God]') against increasing European encroachment in the archipelago. This work draws on classical *fiqh* discussions of *jihād* and came to be used as a source for the subsequent development of local literatures on the subject in poetry and prose genres of Malay and Acehnese. Similar sentiments are reflected in letters ʿAbd al-Ṣamad sent from Arabia to Javanese leaders that were intercepted by the Dutch in 1772[81] – reminiscent of episodes from the career of Yūsuf al-Maqassārī a century earlier.

Today ʿAbd al-Ṣamad is best known for his Malay adaptations of al-Ghazālī's works, entitled *Hidāyat al-Sālikīn* and *Sayr al-Sālikīn*. His role as a teacher of Ghazālī's *ʾIḥyāʾ ʿulūm al-dīn* was valued not only by readers of Malay works, but also by Arab scholars, including such luminaries as ʿAbd al-Raḥmān b. Sulaymān al-ʾAhdal (d. 1835), who studied under ʿAbd al-Ṣamad in the Yemeni town of Zabīd. Al-ʾAhdal later wrote a biographical (*ṭabaqāt*) entry on ʿAbd al-Ṣamad that provides a striking depiction of a South-East Asian Muslim in the role of teacher to a prominent *sayyid* scholar in the Arabian peninsula:

> When our scholar arrived at Zabīd, he continued to increase his exhortations towards the study of Ghazālī's *ʾIḥyāʾ*, and I read under him, thanks be to God, the first quarter of every chapter. I asked him for an *ijāza* [document of certification] in this book to relate that which is good in it and to benefit from its knowledge. He wrote for me in his own noble hand a very long *ijāza*, it being his way that if a student came to him asking detailed questions and he saw something good in the student, he would lengthen his praise of the student in the *ijāza*. He would also explain to the student about law and literature to increase his adherence to it, and the student would see clearly that which was presented to him. The shaykh continued to explain for me the literature of legal decisions and the requirements of a *muftī*: it is not enough only to inquire [into the facts of a certain case] but if he has knowledge of the situation he must call attention to it in the writing of his decision.[82]

These lines provide not only a sense of the respect that ʿAbd al-Ṣamad commanded from his Yemeni Arab colleagues, but also of the way in which Sufism and the study of Islamic law were integrally related at the time.

81 G. Drewes, 'Further data concerning ʿAbd al-Samad al-Palimbani', *Bijdragen tot de Taal-, Land- en Volkenkunde*, 132, 2–3 (1976), pp. 267–92.
82 ʿAbd al-Raḥmān b. Sulaymān al-ʾAhdal, *al-Nafas al-yamānī* (Ṣanʿāʾ, 1979), pp. 139–40.

At Zabīd, ʿAbd al-Ṣamad was fully integrated into the heart of a network of Arabophone Muslim scholars that extended across the entire range of the Indian Ocean littoral and beyond, from West Africa to China. It is important to note, however, that he was far from being the only South-East Asian scholar in Arabia during the eighteenth century. Others notably included ʿAbd Allāh al-Raḥmān al-Batāwī al-Maṣrī, ʿAbd al-Wahhāb al-Bugisī and Muḥammad Arshad b. ʿAbd Allāh al-Banjārī.[83] Upon returning to his native Kalimantan in 1773, Arshad al-Banjārī (d. 1812) served the sultan of Banjar as an authoritative interpreter of what was considered legitimate Islamic teaching in the realm.[84] It was in this position that he composed his most celebrated work, the *Sabīl al-Muhtadīn*, which was commissioned in 1779 as a request to produce a Malay text of Shāfiʿī *fiqh* in a style of language more accessible than al-Rānīrī's *Ṣirāt al-Mustaqīm*. The close association of these two Malay *fiqh* works has persisted to this day, with currently available editions of the *Sabīl al-Muhtadīn* having al-Rānīrī's text printed in its margins.

Another scholar of Banjar contemporary with Muḥammad Arshad was Shaykh Muḥammad Nafīs b. Idrīs b. Husayn al-Banjārī, whose *al-Durr al-Nafīs* was completed in 1785. This work of Sufi thought draws on a wide range of authorities and entertains speculative cosmological musings on the pre-existent essence of Muḥammad while also acknowledging the importance of pursuing the Sufi path within the parameters established by the *sharīʿa*. Texts like these written in Arabic-script Malay comprise the Malay *kitāb* tradition – often referred to in modern Malay and Indonesian as *kitab jawi* or *kitab kuning*. These texts, and the institutional settings of the schools in which they were taught (*pesantren*), played a central role in the continuing development of Islamic thought and Muslim culture in South-East Asia throughout the nineteenth and twentieth centuries.[85]

One of the most prolific early masters of the Malay *kitāb* tradition who was also to enjoy some of the most widespread and long-lasting popularity in *pesantren* circles was Dāwūd b. ʿAbd Allāh al-Faṭānī.[86] He was a prolific author

83 Azra, *Origins of Islamic reformism*, pp. 118–19.

84 Azyumardi Azra, 'Opposition to Sufism in the East Indies in the seventeenth and eighteenth centuries', in Frederick de Jong and Bernd Radtke (eds.), *Islamic mysticism contested: Thirteen centuries of controversies and polemics* (Leiden, 1999), p. 685.

85 For an overview of these later developments, see: Martin van Bruinessen, 'Pesantren and kitab kuning: Continuity and change in a tradition of religious learning', in W. Marschall (ed.), *Texts from the islands: Oral and written traditions of Indonesia and the Malay world* (Berne, 1994), pp. 121–46.

86 For more on this author and his place in the ongoing tradition of *kitāb* scholarship in Patani, see Virginia Matheson and M. B. Hooker, 'Jawi literature in Patani: The maintenance of an Islamic tradition', *Journal of the Malay Branch of the Royal Asiatic Society*, 61, 1 (1988), pp. 1–86.

of Malay *kitāb* who hailed from the region that is today southern Thailand, and after a period of study in Aceh spent much of the rest of his long life in Arabia, where he apparently died sometime in the 1840s.[87] He was a younger colleague of ʿAbd al-Ṣamad and his cohort in Arabia, and from across the Indian Ocean he made remarkable contributions to Malay traditions of Islamic scholarship, through his popular and oft-printed works in the fields of *fiqh*, *taṣawwuf* and *kalām*, and other works such as his treatise on Muḥammad's 'night journey' (*mʿirāj*) and ascension (*ʾisrāʾ*).

Recognising the remarkable degree to which religious developments in South-East Asia were integrated into broader dynamics of intellectual and cultural change in the Middle East and other Muslim societies can help us to avoid the misperceptions that often accompany an overemphasising of the 'unique' nature of South-East Asian Islam. The Indonesian archipelago is home to a number of distinctive forms and expressions of Islamicate civilisation. However, the processes of 'naturalising' Islam in this region have not been in any sense categorically different from those at work in the history of other Muslim societies as they developed elsewhere, including in various cultural subregions of the Arab Middle East. For over the past fourteen centuries, Muslims all across the world have engaged in complex cultural negotiations in their striving to root the eternal message of the Qurʾān within the historical contingencies of their own day and age, and this has always involved the selective adaptation of traditional ideas and institutions to evolving interpretations of Islamic religious and legal ideals. In his recent survey of Muslim societies in African history, David Robinson has spoken of the complex and ongoing processes of Islamisation on that continent as 'making the faith universal and local at the same time'.[88] A similar perspective on the development of Islam in South-East Asia can help us to recognise the fact that its complex history involves the study of Arabic grammar as well as *gamelan*, and *waqf* as well as *wayang*.

Over the course of the nineteenth century the situation in South-East Asia and other lands of Islam became even more complex with the development of new dynamics of reform within Muslim communities, as well as the increasingly intense intrusions of modern European colonialism into various parts of Africa and Asia. By the 1820s, for example – while Dāwūd al-Faṭānī was composing his Malay works of traditionalist scholarship at Mecca – the Indonesian archipelago was experiencing considerable upheavals in the form

87 Azra, *Origins of Islamic reformism*, pp. 114, 122–6.
88 David Robinson. *Muslim societies in African history* (Cambridge, 2004), p. 201.

of militant movements of resistance to European control expressed in the idiom of Islam. Foremost among them were the so-called 'Diponegara war' in central Java and the rise of the *Padri* movement in west Sumatra. These very different campaigns can yet be seen as extensions of both the dynamics of internal Islamic reformism and the advancement of Dutch economic and military dominance characteristic of the eighteenth century in South-East Asian Muslim history. By the middle of the nineteenth century, however, changes were getting under way that were to dramatically transform Muslim cultures across the archipelago and around the world.[89]

89 I discuss major aspects of these transformations in *The new Cambridge history of Islam*, vol. VI, Chapter 2.

14

Transition: the end of the old order – Iran in the eighteenth century

G. R. GARTHWAITE

The nineteenth century in European history is often characterised as the 'long' century, which probably holds true for Iran, too, with the reign of the Qājārs from the late eighteenth century until 1925. Can the eighteenth century be seen as the 'short' century in Iran's history? Very short, indeed, if the period begins in 1722 with the Safavid collapse[1] and ends with Āghā Muḥammad Khan Qājār's consolidation of power a half-century later. Iran's eighteenth century is easily characterised by its dynastic fragmentation, when no fewer than five dynasties ruled Iran in that period: the Safavids, Afghans, Afshārs, Zands and Qājārs. There are the larger historical questions, too: on what basis does one era end and another begin? The Safavid era comes to its end in the eighteenth century and the Qājār period begins, but what about that arbitrarily designated period in between?

While there were dynastic changes, there was continuity in the eighteenth century in terms of political culture. Short-lived dynasties did result in weakened government institutions and in weakened, competing centres of power, which in turn directly affected Iran's territorial integrity and debilitated Iran in face of both internal and external threats. Internally and parallel with the decline of central government was not just its inability to maintain order, but its administrative ineffectiveness and a corresponding strengthening of tribal power[2] that further limited power at the centre.

Perhaps, the most significant change occurred in the increasing authority of the religious institution, the *ʿulamā*', a process begun late in the Safavid period and that would be more fully realised in the Qājār period, including not only new clerical roles but new identities for Iranian themselves as they responded to the challenges of the nineteenth century. Consequently, the eighteenth

1 Andrew J. Newman, *Safavid Iran: Rebirth of a Persian empire* (London, 2006).
2 A. K. S. Lambton, 'The tribal resurgence and the decline of the bureaucracy in the eighteenth century', in Thomas Naff and Roger Owen (eds.), *Studies in eighteenth century Islamic history*, (Carbondale, IL, 1977), p. 108.

century[3] marks more than a conventional time period indicated merely by the use of that date as a marker and more than simply a transition from the Safavids and to the Qājārs, although the changes that occurred were incremental rather than sudden.

After Shāh Sulṭān Ḥusayn's reign (1694–1722) came to an end – he was the last of the Safavids to rule – two Safavid puppets in particular continued the dynastic name, Ṭahmāsp II (r. 1722–32) and ʿAbbās III (r. 1732–49). Moreover, there were some eight additional Safavid pretenders in the eighteenth century that suggest the importance of Safavid descent as a legitimating principle; consequently, dynastic descent did give that century a certain unity.[4] Moreover, at the end of the century, Āghā Muḥammad Khan Qājār (whether his reign starts in 1779 or later) and Fatḥ ʿAlī Shāh Qājār (r. 1797–1834) can be characterised as Safavid successors, despite the fact that the Qājārs claimed no direct Safavid descent.

What is striking about the eighteenth century is not so much discontinuity in dynasties and government despite the principle of Safavid descent, but continuity in Iran's political culture,[5] a political culture that long predated the eighteenth century and provided for the essential transition in Iranian history not only into the nineteenth century, but into the twentieth century, as well, to the reign of Riżā Shāh Pahlavi (r. 1926–41). Iran and Central Asia's political culture of the eighteenth century, and long before it, had been characterised by weak centres of government and autonomy accorded to whole regions and, particularly, to tribal groups. In addition, dynastic power had always been established from a tribal base until the Pahlavis. While the Safavids initially emerged as leaders of a Sufi order, they utilised various Turkic tribes to achieve dynastic power and, initially, to maintain it.

An essential basis in Iran's political culture was geography and area, regardless of territorial borders, and geography was the critical determinant to its economy that combined agriculture, pastoral nomadism and trade. While the vast majority of the population resided in the countryside and produced crops and animals for their own consumption, small agricultural surpluses, other commodities and some handicraft production allowed for exchanges on a regional and international basis. Regional cities played key roles here, and these urban centres were centres of government, culture and learning. Increased trade with Europe, along with diplomatic contact, had

3 P. Avery, G. R. G. Hambly and C. Melville (eds.), *The Cambridge history of Iran*, vol. VII: *From Nadir Shah to the Islamic Republic* (Cambridge, 1991).
4 John Perry, 'The last Safavids, 1722–1773', *Iran*, 9 (1971), pp. 59–69.
5 Gene R. Garthwaite, *The Persians* (Oxford, 2005), pp. 9–11.

emerged in the Safavid period as an increasingly important factor and continued to grow in the eighteenth century. Notables were to be found in cities – including high-ranking government officials, large landowners, religious leaders and merchants – and from among the various tribal federations. That administration was traditionally embedded in bureaucratic families, and these families provided for continuity despite eighteenth-century decentralisation. While taxes were imposed from the centre, given fragmentation of government, provincial capitals did not remit them: that in turn exacerbated decentralising forces. A new elite, foreigners, began to play political, diplomatic and economic roles, especially at the end of the eighteenth century and increasingly in the nineteenth century.

Rulership[6] was a critical component of Iran's political culture, and an important factor in continuity. The shah stood at the apex of Iran's traditional political culture to rule on behalf of God, with the appropriate self-affirming titles. His role was to uphold and defend the community of believers and to establish and maintain justice and order. While in practice his authority and power were unchecked, his arbitrariness was checked by the ruler's reach, which was directed largely at notables and limited by Iran's expanse and autonomy of its regions and groups. At the same time that arbitrariness affected all Iranians. Moreover, the eighteenth century was beset with political fragmentation and fluidity that further limited the ruler's effectiveness and that was compromised by rival claimants, typically from the same family, for the throne.

Religion was an additional factor in continuity in political culture and rulership. Shīʿism as the state faith, and along with the development of the Shīʿī *ʿulamāʾ*, continued in the eighteenth century despite a possible mid-century attempt at change. Given fragmentation of power and government discontinuity, the *ʿulamāʾ* constituted one institution that not only provided continuity but gradually asserted its role over and against royal authority, a process begun in the late Safavid period, which constituted a change that resonated, and increased, through the nineteenth century – down to the present.

There is a continuity, too, in terms of other key factors for change that so profoundly affected the nineteenth and the twentieth centuries, changes that also began in the Safavid era and continued through the eighteenth century, only to be compounded in the Qājār period. Those factors would include European political, economic and cultural impacts and corresponding

6 *Ibid.*, pp. 11–21.

consequences and Iranian responses. Issues of the nature of government, national sovereignty, identity and economy become increasingly intertwined and evident. While rulership, political culture and the European impact can be separated out, in their historical contexts they were intertwined, and out of necessity the political context will be emphasised here.

Perhaps because of the eighteenth century's dynastic discontinuity and because this century has been viewed as one of transition, the period has failed to attract recent attention and scholarship let alone the recent intense interest in the Safavid era or that of the Qājārs.[7] Even important eighteenth-century rulers such as Nādir Shāh[8] or Karīm Khan Zand[9] have received little attention in the past quarter-century, with a very few exceptions. History in any of its categories – social, cultural, economic or political – has been all but neglected for the eighteenth century, this thin filling of that short century sandwiched between the Safavids and the Qājārs.

Eighteenth-century political history is commonly divided by dynasties and approximately by quarters: Safavids, 1501–1722, along with the subsequent, seven-year Afghan interlude; the Afshārs, 1736–48, and to 1795 in Khurāsān; the Zands, 1750–81, or, in various regions, 1794; and the Qājārs, 1779–1926. Notions of the Safavid ideal continued throughout the century, and, significantly, both the Afshārs and the Qājārs had played important roles from the beginning, and throughout the Safavid era, and both conceived of their dynasties as Safavid successors. Moreover, both the Afshārs and Qājārs eclipsed other important Central Asian confederations, notably the Uzbeks, who now fade from Iranian history. Capitals shifted with each dynasty from Iṣfahān, to Mashhad, to Shīrāz and finally to Tehran (see Map 5), where the centre of political power has continued to the present day.

The last Safavid rulers, Shāh Sulṭān Ḥusayn and especially the puppet Shāh Ṭahmāsp II (r. 1722–32), fall short in comparison with Shāh ʿAbbās (r. 1588–1629) who stood at the apogee of Safavid rule. Sulṭān Ḥusayn succeeded his father, who was known initially as Shāh Ṣafī II and then recrowned as Sulaymān (r. 1666–94). Already Sulaymān had sought *ʿulamāʾ* favour as a means of shoring up his authority, which also further strengthened *ʿulamāʾ*

7 For notable examples of recent scholarship on the Qājārs see *The new Cambridge history of Islam*, vol. V.

8 Lawrence Lockhart, *Nadir Shah: A critical study* (London, 1938), has long stood as the standard biography and is now replaced by Ernest Tucker, *Nadir Shah's quest for legitimacy in post-Safavid Iran* (Gainesville, FL, 2006) and Michael Axworthy, *The sword of Persia: Nader Shah from tribal warrior to conquering despot* (London, 2006).

9 John Perry's *Karim Khan Zand: A history of Iran, 1747–1779* (Chicago, 1979) remains the standard for the Zand period.

authority and power, particularly those *ʿulamāʾ* who were opposed to the Sufi and philosophically inclined *ʿulamāʾ*, the other leading school in the late Safavid period. While there was something akin to an official Shīʿism – especially under the domination of Mullā Muḥammad Bāqir Majlisī, appointed Shaykh al-Islām of Iṣfahān in 1686 – Safavid shahs played a balancing act between the competing schools. These ongoing religious disputes continued throughout the eighteenth century and would subsequently shape the *ʿulamāʾ*'s relationship with all subsequent governments.

Shāh Sulṭān Ḥusayn faced serious challenges to his sovereignty in the last years of his reign with revolts in the Caucasus, Kurdistan, Khūzistān, the Persian Gulf, Kandahar and Khurāsān. In addition, the Ottomans, and increasingly the Russians, posed an ongoing threat. There was also a potential coup from within the Safavid family, not to mention disloyal factions among military and administrative leaders, particularly in Herat and Kandahar. Consequently, in 1722, Maḥmūd, a Ghilzai Afghan from Kandahar, formed a confederation that defeated Safavid forces and then laid siege to Iṣfahān at great human and economic cost to its population. During the seven months before Iṣfahān capitulated, its population suffered great losses due to disease and starvation.

Even though Ṭahmāsp Mīrzā, the designated successor, escaped from the capital to Qazvīn to declare himself Shāh Ṭahmāsp II, Sulṭān Ḥusayn abdicated and named Maḥmūd Ghilzai as shah. The fall of the Safavids to the Afghans was as much a surprise to the Afghans as to the Safavids. The Afghans' initial, if limited, success was due to their political and tactical leadership. Safavid ineptitude, on the other hand, was the very absence of political and military leadership despite dynastic legitimacy. Other critical factors in the Safavid collapse were the decimation of Iṣfahān's population, the Safavids' critical centre, and the political fragmentation and autonomy of Safavid provinces. In similar circumstances earlier in Safavid history there had been dynastic recovery, but such a recovery was not to be repeated at the end of the first quarter of the eighteenth century. Even though the Safavid dynastic principle still held, it would be usurped by successive tribal leaders only to prove continuity in Iran and Central Asia's political culture.

The Afghans were to rule Iran, and then but a portion of it, for only seven years, and represented a transitional interlude from the Safavids to the Afshārs, the second of the four eighteenth-century dynasties. All of the subsequent rulers of eighteenth-century Iran failed to solve the challenges of contested power and legitimacy, which was exacerbated by weak support beyond the ruler's own provinces and by Ottoman and Russian power and expansionism. Maḥmūd had attempted to assert Afghan control over central Iran but when Qazvin successfully revolted, Maḥmūd feared that the Iṣfahānis too would rebel, and he ordered the execution of key administrative and military leaders, and Safavid princes. After three short years, Maḥmūd himself was overthrown in 1725 and killed by a kinsman, Ashraf Ghilzai.

Meanwhile, Ṭahmāsp II had vainly sought a Safavid restoration with Ottoman support, yet a joint Ottoman–Russian alliance for the division of north-western Iran was averted only by Peter the Great's death in 1725. The Ottomans, on the other hand, promised to restore Sulṭān Ḥusayn to the throne, but he too was murdered by Ashraf. Ṭahmāsp II rallied his forces when he won the support of two important tribal confederation leaders, first from Fatḥ 'Alī Khan Qājār and then more critically from Nādir Qulī Khan Afshār, and was able to inflict successive losses on Ashraf, who in 1729 attempted to return to Kandahar, only to be assassinated by a member of his own family. Descent in the Safavid family – and the family itself fought each other for control over that legacy – was still a prerequisite to rule Iran in the first half of the eighteenth century. Nādir Qulī Khan Afshār then entered Iṣfahān to enthrone Ṭahmāsp II in the Safavid capital. Only ten months later, however, Nādir replaced Ṭahmāsp with his infant son, 'Abbās, as 'Abbās III, and in 1736 Nādir freed himself from even a boy-puppet to proclaim himself shah. Nādir Shāh's reign (1736–47), and that of the other Afshārs, can be characterised as Safavid successors even though they, too, ruled over only a portion of Safavid Iran, and from Khurāsān rather than Iṣfahān.

Purportedly, Mīrzā 'Abd al-Ḥusayn, the *mullābāshī*, was executed by the soon to be crowned Nādir, when he uttered: 'Everybody is in favour of the Safavid dynasty.'[10] Nādir Qulī's own base was centred on his role as an Afshār tribal leader in northern Khurāsān and on the initial idea as upholder of Safavid legitimacy. Often styled as the last of the great Central Asian conquerors, like his predecessors he commanded others through demonstrated military and political leadership skills to build a confederation and to achieve and then maintain power. Nādir mastered his opponents through tactical and strategic alliances, including marriage. Like earlier leaders, he too seemed to sweep across vast distances at great speed with mounted tribesmen to defeat his opponents and to plunder their wealth. What legitimacy he possessed was based initially in the province of Khurāsān, fractious as a consequence of Safavid instability, and the promise of booty and the restoration of Central Asian trade. He represented himself under the mantle not only of Safavid

10 Roger Savory, *Iran under the Safavids* (Cambridge, 1980), p. 253.

legitimacy but of the earlier Timurids. And he sought late in his reign to accommodate Shīʿism to Sunnism, possibly to broaden, or strengthen, his legitimacy, or as a means possibly to stifle any Shīʿī radicalism or of a Safavid revival, or to advance his own imperial ambitions.

Nādir Qulī, while still nominally under the suzerainty of Ṭahmāsp II, was entitled Ṭahmāsp Qulī (servant/slave of Ṭahmāsp). Ṭahmāsp II then assigned him the key governorships of Khurāsān, Māzandarān, Kirmān and Sīstān on the strategically important northern and eastern frontiers. Nādir's power increased, and he even minted coins in his own name, which undercut Ṭahmāsp II's legitimacy as ruler. Nevertheless, Nādir continued to serve Ṭahmāsp with both military and diplomatic victories. The Ottomans were forced from western Iran and Azerbaijan in 1730, and two years later Nādir's army reached Baghdad, despite continuing Iranian anarchy and opposition. After their Baghdad defeat, the Ottomans agreed to the boundary terms of the earlier 1639 Treaty of Ẕuhāb. Subsequently, Nādir forced the Russians to withdraw from parts of northern Iran. With such military success – and it was in 1732 that Nādir had deposed Ṭahmāsp II for his infant son, ʿAbbās III – he assembled tribal leaders, notables and *ʿulamāʾ* who proclaimed him shah in 1736 at a great assembly, *quriltai*, on the Mughān plain. This *quriltai*, that hearkens back to Mongol practice, legitimised Nādir's rule and family that lacked actual Safavid descent.

From 1737 to 1740, Nādir Shāh gained his fame as an Asian conqueror. He first campaigned to take Kandahar and then continued on deep into India with its fabled wealth and infamously plundered Delhi in 1738, but seemingly without the intent of adding it to his realm. In 1740, however, he extended Iran's boundary to the Amū Daryā, which represented an extension of Khurāsān. Importantly, after this defeat of the Uzbeks, they begin to disappear from Iran's history, although not from Central Asia's. Iṣfahān, with its Safavid past, was further marginalised when Nādir chose Mashhad, Khurāsān's major city and the location of the shrine of the imam Riżā, the Ithnā ʿAsharī's eighth imam, as his capital. In Safavid and time-honoured practice, Nādir relocated tribal populations such as the Kurds and Bakhtiyārī in Khurāsān and in the other eastern provinces. For the last time, Iran's centre of power was shifted east towards Central Asia, and as a consequence a significant Sunnī population was incorporated into what until then had been a largely Shīʿī state. Moreover, Nādir had potential rivals killed, including three Safavid pretenders, and in 1741 had his own heir, Riżā Qulī, blinded.

While Nādir's military exploits and his political skill in forming an effective military force and in rallying his great *quriltai* are undoubted, yet his motives and purpose continue to elude us. Even less explicable is the purpose behind his religious proposals to bring Shīʿism more in accord with Sunnism. Nādir called for acceptance of Shīʿism as a fifth Sunnī school of law, to be called the Jaʿfarī school, after the sixth imam, Jaʿfar al-Ṣādiq. In addition, the Shīʿa would abandon their practice of cursing the first three caliphs who had preceded ʿAlī, who, from the Shīʿī perspective, was the rightful first caliph, or successor to the Prophet Muḥammad following his death. Did Nādir's proposed change represent some accommodation to the Sunnīs newly added to the empire that now extended into Central Asia? Or accommodation to the Sunnī Ottomans? Or the contrary, to appeal to the religiously mixed population of eastern Anatolia? Or did this attempted change represent an expression of Nādir's own broader religious views? Possibly, Nādir was attempting to strengthen his own legitimacy, or to reassert government control over the *ʿulamāʾ*.

Iran and Central Asia had a long, ancient tradition of universal, or simultaneous, rulership[11] – regardless of religious tradition, and Islamicised after the Islamic conquests and conversions there – as the basis for rulership; it was a rulership in which the sovereign represented himself as the equipoise between the cosmos and his realm. In this case, too, there were practical implications: in representing himself as that universal ruler, Nādir provided a new basis by appealing to Sunnīs – and as that universal ruler he was not only challenging the Ottoman sultan in particular, but also the Mughals of India – or in abandoning that position, he could appeal to the Shīʿa. In drawing back from his proposed changes, he was recreating new constituencies, the *ʿulamāʾ* and Iranians in general; Nādir Shāh may have sought to placate the elites who were becoming alienated as a consequence of his increasingly arbitrary and oppressive rule.

Elite alienation had appeared as early as 1741, when Nādir's son, Riżā Qulī, was implicated in an attempt to assassinate his father; as a result, he was blinded. Indeed, in 1747 Nādir's paranoia was borne out when he was assassinated by Afshār and Qājār leaders. Nādir was immediately succeeded by two nephews, and then his grandson, Shāh Rukh, who was able to maintain Afshār rule, but only over Khurāsān, from 1748 to 1796.

Nādir's legacy, if in the short term, consisted in reunifying Safavid Iran and providing some continuity in its institutions, and in successfully defending Iran from the Ottomans and the Russians. While he commanded

11 Garthwaite, *The Persians*, pp. 11–21; Pamela Kyle Crossley, 'The rulerships of China', *American Historical Review*, 97 (Dec. 1992), pp. 1468–83. In addition see Crossley, *A translucent mirror* (Berkeley, 1999), pp. 9–29.

Iran's political culture from his own tribal base, he was also its victim with the continuing challenges to his legitimacy, disloyalty of those whom he had appointed to high positions, and widespread fragmentation and instability. He maintained his power through his military and political skills, ruthlessness and promise of booty from his many campaigns. His purpose, aside from maintaining his own power, continues to be unresolved, and if it was to be the world conqueror, he lacked the means and resources to achieve, let alone maintain, it. Here the collapse of the Safavids, critically its economy, contributed to Nādir's problems, but these were exacerbated by his own maladministration. And even the central institution of rulership within his family would be short-lived. Nādir's contemporaries may have feared his ruthlessness, but had expectations that with it he could establish stability. His personality and even some of his idiosyncratic ideas and policies, including his notions regarding Shīʿism, were critical in shaping assessment of his rule. Emphasis on his failures and continuing instability in Iran, however, would be recorded by those who valued order and continuity.

Nādir's immediate successors were two nephews, ʿAlī Qulī Khan, who reigned as ʿAdil Shāh (r. 1747) and then Ibrāhīm (r. 1748). ʿAlī Qulī, following Nādir's death, raced to Mashhad and eliminated all possible Afshār claimants, save for Shāh Rukh, whose mother had descended from within the Safavid family. In addition to problems in Kurdistan and Ḥasan Khan Qājār's rivalry, ʿAdil Shāh had to face an internecine challenge from his brother Ibrāhīm, who had support from dissident Afshārs. And when Ibrāhīm declared himself shah, he was bested by Shāh Rukh, who possessed greater legitimacy and power from his base in Khurāsān, and his supporters there included Ḥasan Khan Qājār. Both ʿAdil Shāh and Ibrāhīm were executed in Mashhad in 1750. Shāh Rukh himself was deposed, blinded and then restored to a truncated kingdom as a consequence of Aḥmad Shāh Durrānī's need to protect his newly established Afghanistan – formed immediately after Nādir's death from his eastern holdings – from any potential changes that might emanate from central Iran.

Power and the capital of a continuingly fragmented Iran shifted from Khurāsān back to the centre of the Iranian plateau under the leadership of yet two other tribal leaders, Karīm Khan Zand and ʿAlī Mardan Khan Bakhtiyārī. When this brief diarchy ended, another dynasty, the third in the eighteenth century – the Zand – would emerge. While both Zands and Bakhtiyārī shared the Turkic tribal title of khan, their respective tribal confederations were Iranian, unlike the Turkic Afshārs and Qājārs. The Zand originated from Luristān in the west-central Zagros, and the Bakhtiyārī lived further to the south-west, in the central Zagros mountains and Khūzistān.

Notably, too, the pattern of Iran's political culture continued and the great tribal confederations – notably, of course, the Qājārs, but also the Bakhtiyārī, Qashqāʾī and Shāhsavan[12] – played roles that presaged their growing importance in the nineteenth century. Some 3,000 Bakhtiyārī families had been resettled in Khurāsān by Nādir Shāh for having threatened his rule – other Bakhtiyārī had participated in his Delhi campaign – and after his death 2,000 of these families are recorded as having returned to the Bakhtiyārī. In the anarchy following Nādir's assassination, ʿAlī Mardan Khan initially supported ʿAdil Shāh, but then gave his support to Ibrāhīm. Finally, along with Karīm Khan Zand, and in the face of Bakhtiyārī factionalism, ʿAlī Mardan Khan and Karīm Khan established joint suzerainty over central and western Iran in the name of Ismāʿīl III, yet another Safavid puppet.

The continuing importance of Safavid legitimacy for ʿAlī Mardan Khan was demonstrated in coins that were struck with *'bandah-ye Ismāʿīl'* ('slave / servant of Ismāʿīl') and in his use of the title, *Vakīl-i Ismāʿīl* ('regent of Ismāʿīl') that had been used earlier by Nadīr Qulī before he had became shah. The diarchy ended in 1754 after only some four years when Karīm Khan killed ʿAlī Mardan Khan, and defeated other former tribal commanders of Nādir's army, including Muḥammad Ḥasan Khan Qājār and Azād Khan, a Ghilzai but whose power was now located in Azerbaijan. Then in 1759, Karīm deposed Ismāʿīl III, but did not assume the title of shah; instead he first assumed ʿAlī Mardan's title *Vakīl-i dawlat* ('regent / deputy of government'). Karīm Khan moved his capital to Shīrāz where in 1765 he took the unusual title of *Vakīl-i raʿāyā* ('regent / deputy of the people').[13] After this, Karīm Khan is customarily known as Vakīl, which suggests a kind of populism; moreover, Karīm Khan in so doing inverted the notion of universal rulership of Nādir Shāh, the Safavids, and earlier Iranian and Central Asian rulers in which the shah as the equipoise between the cosmos, or God, and their realm allowed for absolutism. Karīm's rule, too, until his death in 1779 was more akin to earlier Islamic notions of the just ruler than the monarchical and arbitrary universal ruler. His period of rule was characterised by a kind of modesty that was reflected in the buildings he had constructed in Shīrāz and, importantly, he patronised Shīʿism there, although by now the *ʿulamāʾ* were increasingly independent of the ruler.

12 Lois Beck, *The Qashqa'i of Iran* (New Haven, 1986); G. R. Garthwaite, *Khans and shahs: A documentary analysis of the Bakhtiyari in Iran* (Cambridge, 1983); and Richard Tapper, *Frontier nomads of Iran: A political and social history of the shahsevan* (Cambridge, 1997).

13 Perry, *Karim Khan Zand*, pp. 215–17. See also Lambton, 'Tribal resurgence', pp. 116–20.

Once Karīm Khan had eliminated his rivals, atypically for an eighteenth-century ruler he only once attacked the Ottomans and maintained a defensive military posture rather than an offensive one. And in that one instance – against Baṣra – the Vakīl may have sought to develop trade in the Persian Gulf and to assure Bushire, with its close proximity to Shīrāz, as its dominant port.

Following Karīm Khan's death, the Zands competed among themselves for succession. His immediate successor was Ṣādiq (r. 1779–81), the Vakīl's youngest brother; Ṣādiq was succeeded by his grandson, Luṭf ʿAlī (r. 1789–94), the most competent of the Zand successors. In turn, Luṭf ʿAlī was killed by Muḥammad Khan Qājār, and with his death not only was the short-lived Zand dynasty brought to its end, but with it the last link to Safavid Iran under the guise of puppet shahs.

Until the advent of the Zands, the Qājārs had been eclipsed by the Afshārs, but they still counted as a significant tribal power – and not only in Gurgān and Māzandarān. And the shifting alliances and power among rival mid-century tribal groups – including Afshārs, competing Qājār federations of the Develū and Qūyūnlū (Āghā Muḥammad's tribe), Zand, Bakhtiyārī and the Afghan Ghilzai and Durrānī – while often confusing, exemplify the nature of Iran's political culture, especially in the absence of a strong centre. During the short reign of Ṭahmāsp II, Fatḥ ʿAlī Khan Qājār rivalled Nadīr Khan Afshār and had been given the title of *Vakīl-i dawlat*, the same title assumed next by Nādir and then by ʿAlī Mardan Khan. Fatḥ ʿAlī Khan Qājār was murdered in 1726, and his Qājār branch continued support for the Safavid pretender and for Nādir. Qājār power shifted from the Qūyūnlū to the Develū's Muḥammad Ḥusayn Khan, who was challenged for dominance over the whole of the Qājār confederation even before Nādir Shāh's assassination, by Fatḥ ʿAlī's son Muḥammad Ḥasan Khan Qūyūnlū.

Muḥammad Ḥasan also fought against Nādir as the proponent of yet another Safavid pretender, Sām Mīrzā, and, during the Afshār internecine struggle for the throne, against ʿAlī Qulī Khan (ʿAdil Shāh, Nādir's nephew). In this mid-century period, Muḥammad Ḥasan was the dominant power in central and northern Iran, and played a role there, too, as a Safavid successor, including political and cultural patronage. Meanwhile, Muḥammad Ḥasan had fathered (Āghā) Muḥammad in 1742, who was captured and castrated by ʿAdil Shāh in *c.* 1748, but then returned to his family, where he participated in his father's reconsolidation of Qājār power in the Caspian provinces during the early Zand period – and would later emulate his father's military and political leadership roles and consolidation of power in the north. In 1755, Muḥammad Ḥasan Khan not only defeated the Abdālī Afghans under Aḥmad Khan, subsequently Aḥmad Shāh Durrānī, but continued south to occupy Iṣfahān – where coins were even struck in his name – and went north again. During the next two years, Muḥammad Ḥasan re-established control of Iṣfahān and proceeded to Shīrāz to confront unsuccessfully Karīm Khan, and in the ensuing aftermath lost the loyalty of key tribal allies and was killed in 1759. Āghā Muḥammad was eventually seized and taken to Shīrāz along with his brother Ḥusayn Qulī Khan.

When Karīm Khan Zand died in 1779, Āghā Muḥammad escaped from Shīrāz to Māzandarān to begin the process of consolidation of Qājār power – hence the often cited date rather than his coronation date of 1796 for the beginning of his reign – from its northern base, which he accomplished by 1785, primarily against ʿAlī Murād Khan Zand, Karīm Khan's successor, and then against Jaʿfar Khan Zand.

Āghā Muḥammad's military and political achievement in re-establishing Safavid Iran in terms of institutions and approximate borders is overshadowed by his reputation for brutality and rapacity, but the shape of modern Iran owes much to him. He was born into a turbulent and fragmented Iran, learned military and political survival skills campaigning with his father, and had mastered tribal and regional politics. Ḥusayn Qulī's appointment as governor of Dāmghān by Karīm Khan, his captor and rival, and then Āghā Muḥammad's ability to escape Shīrāz were due to family alliances. Āghā Muḥammad established his always uneasy paramountcy within the Qūyūnlū and then over the Develū federation to consolidate the Qājār confederation. From his strengthened position within Māzandarān, he encountered and outwitted the Russians, who were intent on establishing a base at the south-eastern corner of the Caspian Sea, and established control of Gīlān.

While Āghā Muḥammad was preoccupied in Gīlān, an opposition emerged in Māzandarān, including a half-brother who had thrown his support to ʿAlī Murād Khan Zand, and Āghā Muḥammad's defeat of the Zands in Māzandarān in February 1785 opened west-central Iran to him. He pursued Jaʿfar Khan, who fled Iṣfahān, and after taking that city, Āghā Muḥammad turned north to seize Tehran, only to learn that Jaʿfar had reoccupied Iṣfahān. A Qājār alliance with the Valī of Ardalan succeeded in forcing the Zands back to Shīrāz, and this alliance would prove to be critical in maintaining Qājār control over north-western Iran, and during 1786–7 Zanjān and Gīlān would have to be rewon. Russia again was a destabilising factor here. Throughout the late 1780s tribal and regional leaders, often appointees, were able to assert their autonomy over against both Zands and the Qājārs, and Āghā

Muḥammad was unable to establish Qājār control over the south even when Ja'far was assassinated in January 1789, to be succeeded by Luṭf 'Alī Zand (r. 1789–94).

Both the Zands and the Qājārs, while competing with each other in the eighteenth century, also had to contend with challenges from within their respective families, which was especially acute for Āghā Muḥammad since he had no direct heir, although he had favoured his nephew Fatḥ 'Alī, even before Āghā Muḥammad's brother, Ḥusayn Qulī Khān, died in 1779. In 1790, he had ordered the execution of another brother, Ja'far Qulī Khān. Had he expected to accede to Qājār leadership, or did Āghā Muḥammad fear for an internecine battle that might result in the loss of Qājār hegemony? Āghā Muḥammad Shāh appointed Fatḥ 'Alī to important positions, and he co-opted tribal leaders and potential rivals to the succession by assigning them to a variety of governorships. Dynastic concern, issues of succession and legitimacy, and perhaps even piety were factors in Āghā Muḥammad's decision to make pilgrimage to the Safavid Ardabīl shrine and burial place.

Luṭf 'Alī took advantage of Āghā Muḥammad's absence in the north in 1790 and attacked Fatḥ 'Alī in an attempt to retake Iṣfahān, but Luṭf 'Alī lost Shīrāz in a coup to Ḥājjī Ibrāhīm, of Fārs, and faced insurrection in his own army. The coup instigators proffered support to Āghā Muḥammad, and Ḥājjī Ibrāhīm's willingness to hand over Shīrāz allowed Āghā Muḥammad finally to seize the Zand family, their property and Fārs itself. Luṭf 'Alī staged something of a comeback but in the end fled to Ṭabas. Āghā Muḥammad entered Shīrāz in July 1792. Ḥājjī Ibrāhīm was appointed *beglerbegī* (governor) of Fārs, hostages were taken – including members of Ḥājjī Ibrāhīm's family – and Karīm Khan Zand's body was disinterred and taken to Tehran. Given the impregnable walls of Shīrāz's Arg (fortress) and the many Qājār attempts to breach them, Āghā Muḥammad had the outer ones destroyed along with the Arg itself. Luṭf 'Alī, from a base first in Tabas and then Kirmān – where he had coins struck as *pādishāh* – managed to elude Āghā Muḥammad for over two years. He was finally captured and tortured, and died in Tehran; the Zand threat to Qājār sovereignty was essentially ended. At the end of 1794/early 1795, Āghā Muḥammad designated Fatḥ 'Alī *beglerbegī* of Fārs and Kirmān, for he had helped establish Qājār authority there. Ḥajjī Ibrāhīm was made vizier and entitled *I'timād al-Dawla*.

The borders of Safavid Iran, save for the Caucasus, were basically re-established at this point in time, and with that precedent in mind Āghā Muḥammad set out in 1795 with a large army of some 60,000 to take the region north of the Aras river, Qārābāgh, Ganja, Shīrwān and Georgia. Georgia was not only a former Safavid dependency, but as Christian its reconquest allowed for *jihād* and religious legitimacy in addition to the national one – reportedly, the *Shāh-nāma* was recited at the siege of Tiflis.

The Caucasus, however, was a changing world and increasingly affected by an expansionist Russia. Iran and the Qājārs would be irrevocably challenged by this powerful neighbour to the north. The Qājārs had fruitlessly sought support from Georgia and Russia in the stand-off against the Zands. Georgia, which had become a protectorate of Russia in 1783, could only be apprehensive with Āghā Muḥammad's military success and consolidation of Qājār power, particularly after his 1791 subjection of Azerbaijan. In 1795, Russia did not send support to Tiflis and dismissed the Qājār threat. Āghā Muḥammad advanced towards Georgia and reminded its ruler of Safavid precedent for Georgia's dependency status. After suffering serious damage, the besieged Tiflis fell to Āghā Muḥammad's forces in September. The city was sacked and its inhabitants were massacred, and some 15,000 Georgians were sent back to Iran as slaves. After several days, Āghā Muḥammad returned south to the Mughān plain for the winter and then to Tehran. In the spring of 1796 – the other commonly accepted date for the beginning of his reign – he accepted the crown pressed upon him by notables.

From Ḥasan-i Fasā'ī's contemporary account, Āghā Muḥammad clearly possessed a historical consciousness and a sense of destiny. His court reminded him, in proposing his coronation, of his determination and success in ridding Iran of all enemies and rebels save for Khurāsān. He responded: 'If, according to your desire, I put the crown on my head, this will cause you, in the beginning, toil and hardship, as I take no pleasure in bearing the title of king as long as I am not one of the greatest kings of Persia. This petition will not be granted but by toil and fatigue.'[14] The Kīyānī crown was placed on his head, the great diamond-studded armbands clasped to his arms and pearl necklaces were draped around his neck. These jewels had been part of Nādir Shāh's booty and treasury, but even more important in the legitimating coronation the Safavid sword 'with the blessing of the shrine of Shāh Ṣafī at Ardabīl' was girt around his waist. Similarly, the next day he wore the sword once again at a banquet and as he distributed alms.

Āghā Muḥammad pressed on to take Khurāsān, whose titular and long-term ruler was Shāh Rukh, Nādir's grandson. Power in this strategic province was held by a variety of autonomous and rival tribal leaders and magnates,

14 Hasan-i Fasa'i, *History of Persia under Qājār rule* (*Fārsnāma-ye Naseri*), trans. Heribert Busse (New York, 1972), p. 68.

almost all of whom submitted, and Khurāsān fell to the Qājārs with almost no bloodshed in May 1796. When the army reached Mashhad, Shāh Rukh and the leading *mujtahid* came to the Qājār camp to acknowledge Āghā Muḥammad's suzerainty, and he himself entered this city of the shrine of the Imām Riżā as a humble pilgrim on foot following the precedent of Shāh ʿAbbās I:

> with pious intention and in pure faith, he dismounted, and walking a distance on foot entered the city ... displaying signs of weakness, poverty, humility, and submissiveness, and shedding tears, he walked to the shrine and kissed the blessed soil. For a space of twenty-three days he was engaged on this sanctified soil in serving God, acting obediently, and offering prayers. During the time of his pilgrimage he served like a servant of the blessed shrine of the venerable Emam.[15]

As he had done in Shīrāz with Karīm Khan Zand's bones, Āghā Muḥammad had Nādir Shāh's bones disinterred to be reburied in Tehran. Shāh Rukh died as he was being escorted from Mashhad to Māzandarān. Consequently, the primacy of the Qājār dynasty over the Afshārs and the Zands was finally realised.

With Khurāsān now under Qājār control, the borders of Safavid Iran were re-established save for Herat, disregarding the short period that Baghdad had been part of their realm. While in Mashhad, Āghā Muḥammad may have considered regaining Herat or even going further into Central Asia. Changes in Russia and the Caucasus, however, intervened once again. Catherine the Great died in November 1796, and her son and successor, Paul I, ended her expansionist policy and withdrew Russian forces sent there at her behest. Āghā Muḥammad, nonetheless, turned to the Caucasus determined to lead his troops into it, if, for nothing else, as a show of force to forestall its governors from closer Russian ties. Shūsha capitulated to him and he entered the city; while there, Āghā Muḥammad was assassinated on 16 June 1797 by two servants, whose execution had been postponed, and by a third.

Succession in the eighteenth century was always problematic, but especially so with assassination and without a designated successor, even though Āghā Muḥammad had favoured Fatḥ ʿAlī. With the announcement of Āghā Muḥammad Khan Shāh's death, family claimants and others along with their supporters raced to Tehran to secure the capital, but its governor closed it off to await Fatḥ ʿAlī from Shīrāz. By the time of his arrival, he had won over most rivals, but had his uncle ʿAlī Qulī blinded, and then at Qazvin defeated Ṣādiq

15 *Ibid.*, pp. 69–70.

Khan Shaqāqī, who was pardoned in return for the royal regalia that he had acquired. Āghā Muḥammad's body was disinterred at Shūsha, taken first to Tehran and then to Najaf for final burial at the shrine of ʿAlī, the first imam.

Āghā Muḥammad's contribution should not be underestimated nor should it be overshadowed by his brutality; the portrait of his beardless and wizened face has become emblematic of that cruelty. That he emerged triumphant from internecine rivalry and from all of his family's enemies, especially the Afshārs and the Zands, including his own traumatic treatment by them, represents no small achievement. First and foremost, his triumph was based on his ability to manoeuvre among and manipulate tribal and regional politics to lead in the process of confederation building. Second, he possessed comparable military skills and successfully dominated most of Iran. Out of necessity and the nature of eighteenth-century Iranian political culture, Āghā Muḥammad was on a permanent military footing. Even after his coronation and the institutionalisation of his rulership, Āghā Muḥammad's personal political and military qualities commanded awe, if not fear, rather than authority derived from legitimacy. Aside from mounted Qājār tribesmen personally loyal to him, and the Turkic tribes of Azerbaijan,[16] the key military units were made up of cavalry from Gurgān and infantry from Māzandarān, regions that supported Āghā Muḥammad throughout his life. Typically, too, these two provinces provided their forces in lieu of taxes. His personal leadership style as well as his confidence in the loyalty of his troops are evident in the report that he slept among his troops at critical points.

At the height of his power in the Georgian campaigns, it is asserted that he could muster some 50,000 regular troops, largely cavalry. His army also included a small number of cannons and light artillery. These numbers could be augmented by irregular levies and requisition of tribal levies, but only when Āghā Muḥammad was successful. His military forces were most effective in what we know as guerrilla tactics: he avoided confronting directly troops of greater number, or better equipped, than his own. Above all his forces relied on mobility and speed and lived off the land. He exploited intertribal and regional rivalries in pursuit of particular military goals across northern and western Iran, just as he did not hesitate to compromise or even to entrust a specific responsibility to leaders whom he knew could not be trusted in the long run. Diplomatic skill and political and military judgement can be seen in forming tribal and marriage alliances, and in retaining hostages and removing whole peoples to new areas for strategic objectives. Āghā

16 Lambton, 'Tribal resurgence', p. 111.

Muḥammad's tactics reflected his careful and pragmatic assessment of the capability of both his own forces and his enemies. His overall military strategy, if he had one, was to maintain and expand his own power, and in Iran's political culture that was a zero-sum game. After the defeat of the Zands, Āghā Muḥammad's goal was the re-establishment of Safavid Iran.

Safavid Iran was re-established in terms of borders and rulership. The monarchy was once again instituted, but in the Qājār line. The Qājārs lacked spiritual descent from either Sufi leaders or the imams, but Āghā Muḥammad was raised in a *sayyid* family and was outwardly pious and observant. His legitimacy as an Islamic ruler was further strengthened by titles and symbols – his name was linked with the imams on his coins. As an Islamic ruler – and in the Safavid tradition – he patronised the *ʿulamāʾ*, constructed mosques, patronised the arts and restored the shrine of the Imām Riżā in Mashhad, where he demonstrated his piety after he secured its submission to him. That his body was reinterred at Najaf suggests, too, his successors', and possibly even his own, concern for traditional religious legitimacy. Furthermore, he led his troops in *jihād*. And his national credentials were reinforced not just by the recreation of borders but also by utilisation of the *Shāh-nāma* to rally his troops – again, on the Safavid basis. Tehran replaced Iṣfahān – and then Shīrāz – as the realm's capital. Āghā Muḥammad initially relied on a most rudimentary bureaucracy of two officials whose primary responsibilities were two: to collect revenues and to dispense them for military maintenance. In the end, he re-established a bureaucracy utilising Zand officials, in particular, and maintained the loyalty of such notables as Ḥājjī Ibrāhīm Khan, *Iʿtimād al-Dawla*, who functioned as prime minister. Administration across Iran followed Safavid practice, including regional and administrative divisions, each with its historic autonomy. After the turbulence and misrule of the eighteenth century, responsible, if at times ruthless, government was re-established, which contributed to Qājār legitimacy. Modern Iran is as much a Qājār construction as a Safavid one.

Āghā Muḥammad, of course, had no male issue. Even before the death of his only full brother, Ḥusayn Qulī Khan, Āghā Muḥammad seems to have preferred his first son, Fatḥ ʿAlī, over him. Equally important and indicative of Āghā Muḥammad's dynastic concern and for an unchallenged succession, he secured Fatḥ ʿAlī's marriage to a woman from the Develū clan, rivals of his own Qūyūnlū one, in 1781. Similarly, in the next generation, another Develū bride was arranged for ʿAbbās Mīrzā. No sooner crowned, however, in March 1797, Fatḥ ʿAlī Shāh (r. 1797–1834) was forced to deal with a challenge from his own brother, Ḥusayn Qulī Khan, *beglerbegī* of Fārs, as well as another from the troublesome Ṣādiq Khan and from Kurdish leaders.

While Fatḥ ʿAlī maintained his hold on the throne from family claimants, his greatest challenge would be from Europe and then from his own subjects, who would challenge his legitimacy as a consequence of lost territory and diminished sovereignty. The changed relationship with Europe was marked not only by an asymmetry in military and economic power but by the Qājār's seeming inability to recognise this imbalance. Iran's strategic location – and its decentralisation – meant that British, French and Russian governments could compete among themselves there at relatively low cost in terms of winning imperial gains in the Middle East and India.

The impact of Europeans on Iran's economy had begun to be felt in the Safavid era, but the force of Europe's military and political power and rivalries, combined with European economic interests, took on ever-greater importance at the beginning of the nineteenth century. Despite eventual Russian and then British support for succession within the Qājār ruling family, the Qājārs would be forced to relinquish claims over the Caucasus and eastern Khurāsān to suit Russian and British imperial aims. Moreover, Qājār impotence and misrule coupled with territorial losses resulted in the emergence of a kind of cultural nationalism linked with Shīʿī Islam that included a significant role for religious leadership that had begun early in Fatḥ ʿAlī Shāh's reign and would express itself throughout the nineteenth century.

The asymmetry in power and inability to recognise it and the reliance on irregular troops and tribal levies resulted not just in permanent territorial losses but a crushing indemnity as a consequence of an ill-conceived attempt to recover them that Iran's economy could hardly afford. One significant and long-standing consequence of the indemnity and territorial losses was the emergence of anti-foreign populism that was *ʿulamāʾ* led and motivated by the long-standing tradition of *jihād*, or *ghazā*, in the Caucasus. Territorial losses, the capitulations and increased European interference in Iranian domestic affairs reinforced through direct experience the symbolic aspects of *jihād* and added the new psychological ones of national and religious humiliation – and a role for the *ʿulamā*ʾ in rallying opposition to Iran's losses.

The roots for *ʿulamāʾ* political activism go back to the Safavid era,[17] and was represented in their challenge to the shah, to Iran's historic tradition of rulership, in which the ruler was God's representative and responsible for maintaining and protecting right religion – Shīʿī Islam, in the case of the Safavids and subsequent rulers. The challenge operated both theoretically and

17 Andrew Newman, 'Toward a reconsideration of the Isfahan school of philosophy: Shaykh Baha'i and the role of the Safawid ulama', *Studia Islamica*, 15, 2 (1986), pp. 165–99.

theologically as well as in actuality in reaction to government failure and politics, or the loss of legitimacy to rule. The eighteenth century, once again, provided for its transition.

The anarchy and fragmentation of late eighteenth-century Iran recalls the late fifteenth century, but Iran's reunification would then be brought about by the Qājārs, which would be the last dynasty in Iran's history to be formed from a tribal base. While the Qājārs were one of the Qizilbāsh tribal confederations that early supported the Safavids, the Qājārs, unlike the Safavids, had neither claim to religious authority nor to Safavid descent. Descent within the Qājār confederation and their political and military success were initially critical in establishing their dominance, but to rule the larger Iranian polity, the Qājārs had to legitimise themselves as Islamic rulers in the eyes of their subjects, particularly the Shīʿī *ʿulamāʾ*. And it was the *ʿulamāʾ* that had undergone a transformation in the Safavid period. Essentially, competing schools of Shīʿī thought had resulted in the domination of the Uṣūlī, or Mujtahidī, school that would increase its authority in the nineteenth century within the *ʿulamāʾ* and with increasing tension with the monarch.

The issue of religious versus royal authority would result in a weakening of the shah's legitimacy in both the eighteenth and the nineteenth centuries. In the eighteenth century, however, royal authority was further weakened by fragmentation and competition for power and authority, and incompetent government. In the nineteenth century, these factors would be compounded in the face of European domination, and the emergence of new ideas and identities.

Eighteenth-century fragmentation mirrored the sixteenth, but without the centralisation of government and institutionalisation of Shīʿī *ʿulamāʾ* authority that followed in the seventeenth century. Shīʿism, too, with its hierarchical nature and organisation allows for competing leadership. In addition, that leadership was further divided by legal, theological and philosophical differences over the nature of *ʿulamāʾ* authority; such differences were accentuated by Sufism and popular religion.

From the beginning of the sixteenth century, high-ranking Shīʿī *ʿulamāʾ* enjoyed a mutually privileged position with the Safavids that reinforced their legitimacy. Government appointments were important forms of state patronage, a role not neglected by eighteenth-century rulers, especially so since they individually lacked the legitimacy of the Safavids. In the Safavid period, the very basis of their rulership would even be questioned by some *ʿulamāʾ*: that the shah embodied both political and religious authority. Initially, too, in the Safavid period, the shah was seen in popular religion as representing the infallible imam. Some rulers linked their dynastic descent with descent from the imams and with notions of just rule. *ʿUlamāʾ*, too, took issue with popular Islamic expressions. Safavid shahs periodically stepped back from aggravating the *ʿulamāʾ*, who played important stabilising roles, especially in urban society.

While ideas on authority were contested, the most significant theological-legal dispute centred on sources and their interpretation between two emerging schools of thought: the Akhbārīs and the Uṣūlīs / Mujtahidīs. Central were the interpretation of two principles of jurisprudence (*fiqh*): *taqlīd* and *ijtihād*; the former articulated the authority of those most learned in jurisprudence, and the latter required the exercise of rational judgement, or disciplined reasoning, again of those most learned in jurisprudence.[18] Both principles recognised the authority vested ultimately in those in the hierarchy who exercised *ijtihād*, hence holders of the rank of *mujtahid*, or the most learned of jurists.

The Akhbārīs rejected the use of both principles and based their interpretations and rulings only on the traditions – *akhbār* or *ḥadīth* – transmitted by the imams, and the Uṣūlīs – *uṣūl*, roots / principles (of jurisprudence) – allowed for reinterpretation of the traditions by *mujtahids*. Furthermore, the Akhbārīs argued that *ijtihād* was restricted to the imams. The Uṣūlīs emerged as dominant in late Safavid history, and as an elite within the *ʿulamāʾ* to reflect a hierarchical view of authority and of society. And the Uṣūlīs are the ones to challenge the shahs' authority, although like the Akhbārīs they historically acquiesced to the reality of the shah's *de facto* power. Uṣūlī domination was assured late in the Safavid period, although the role of the great *mujtahid* Muḥammad Bāqir Majlisī (d. 1700) in this process has been challenged by recent scholarship.[19] Majlisī's writings and power within the establishment allowed for a frontal attack on the Akhbārīs, philosophers, Sufis and popular Islam in general.

A third *ʿulamāʾ* group emerged in the Safavid period as well, and these were philosophers – notably Mīr Dāmād (d. 1631) and Mullā Ṣadrā (d. 1640) – whose mystical and philosophical bases could put them at odds with the Uṣūlīs in particular. Like the Akhbārīs, the philosopher-mystics were politically

18 Andrew Newman, 'The nature of the Akhbari / Usuli dispute in late-Safawid Iran. Part One: 'Abdallah al-Sahahiji's "Munyat al-Mumirisin",' *Bulletin of the School of Oriental and African Studies*, 55, 1 (1992), pp. 22–51; Newman, 'The nature of … Part Two: The conflict reassessed', *Bulletin of the School of Oriental and African Studies*, 55, 2 (1992), pp. 250–61.

19 Juan Cole, 'Ideology, ethics and philosophical discourse in eighteenth century Iran', *Iranian Studies*, 22, 1 (1989), pp. 7–34; Cole, 'The world as text: Cosmologies of Shaykh Aḥmad al-Ahsa'i', *Studia Islamica*, 80 (1994), pp. 1–23.

quiescent, but were also given high religious offices. A philosopher-mystical school in the mid-eighteenth to early nineteenth century emerged as the result of the teachings of Shaykh Aḥmad Aḥsāʾī (1753–1826),[20] who left Baḥrayn to study in Najaf and Karbalāʾ and then travelled widely in Iran where he enjoyed acclaim, including royal and notable patronage. His followers became known as the Shaykhīs, and during his lifetime he claimed direct communication with the imams through his mystical practice; after his death, his followers became increasingly radical in their dissent and activism.

A case for political activism, however, was advocated as early as the reign of Shāh Ṭahmāsp (1524–76), by the important *mujtahid* Shaykh ʿAlī b. Ḥusayn b. ʿAbd al-ʿAlī al-Karakī (d. 1534), who was even given the authority to make key clerical appointments.[21] This idea seems to have been expressed when Ismāʿīl II addressed the *mujtahid* at his coronation in 1576: 'This kingship (*ṣaltanat*) in truth belongs to the *imām*, the *ṣāḥib al-zamān* [Lord of the Age] … and you are the *nāʾib* [deputy] appointed in his place … to put into operation the decrees of Islām and the *sharīʿa*. You spread the carpet for me and seat me on the throne … so that I may sit on the throne of government and rule by your decision and will.'[22] And the *mujtahid* was quoted as muttering that he was no one's servant; if so, this underscores the tension between competing authorities. This tension was expressed by Sir John Chardin late in the seventeenth century: 'The highest throne of the universe is only fit for a *mouchtehed* [*mujtahid*], someone who possesses more holiness and knowledge than common people. Since the *mouchtehed* is holy, and consequently a peaceable person, a king is needed who can wield the sword to exercise justice, but he can only be his [the *mujtahid*'s] minister and must be dependent on him.'[23]

Moreover, the emergence of increased ʿ*ulamāʾ* authority also meant greater political, economic and social power for them within Iran and without. For example, after the loss to the Ottomans of the shrine cities (ʿ*Atabat*) of Iraq, notably Najaf and Karbalāʾ, they became vital centres of Shīʿī learning and authority independent of Iranian governments. In addition, the collection of

20 Cole, 'The world as text.'

21 Andrew Newman, 'The myth of the clerical migration to Safawid Iran: Arab Shiʾite opposition to ʿAli al-Karakī and Safawid Shiʾism', *Die Welt des Islams*, 33 (1993), pp. 66–112; Said Amir Arjomand, 'Two decrees of Shah Tahmasp concerning statecraft and authority of Shaykh ʿAli al-Karaki', in Said Amir Arjomand (ed.), *Authority and political culture in Shiʾism* (Albany, 1988), pp. 250–62.

22 Ann K. S. Lambton, *State and government in medieval Islam: An introduction to the study of Islamic political theory: The jurists* (Oxford, 1981), p. 277.

23 Cited in Heinz Halm, *Shiʾism* (Edinburgh, 1991), p. 95.

khums (one-fifth) by the *ʿulamāʾ* helped to make them economically independent of government as well.

As the Safavid state withered in the eighteenth century, the one institution that carried Iran into the nineteenth century was the *ʿulamāʾ*, who had become centralised and increasingly independent of government – both in theory and out of necessity – under the *mujtahids*. *ʿUlamāʾ* continuity over that period was typified by the lifespan of the great *mujtahid* Āghā Muḥammad Bāqir Wahid Bihbahanī (*c.* 1705–91), who was responsible for the ultimate Uṣūlī victory over the Akhbārīs in the *ʿAtabāt*. The Akhbārīs virtually disappeared; however, something of an amalgam of Akhbārī thought with Safavid mystical philosophy would emerge in the early nineteenth century with the Shaykhīs. Despite the *ʿulamāʾ*'s disapproval of Sufism and popular religion, most Iranians found comfort in their many forms.[24] While the martyrdoms of the early imams had long been commemorated, dramatic expression of them, *taʿziya*,[25] emerged in this period of transition from the Safavids to the Qājārs. The use of the various Safavid pretenders throughout most of the eighteenth century also represented the popular appeal of descent and of rulership legitimised by both religion and tradition. In this instance, too, Karīm Khan Zand's appropriation of the title, *Vakīl-i raʿāyā*, 'representative of the people', possibly relates to the government's inherent responsibility to its populace. At the beginning of the nineteenth century, populism would express itself in religious terms, but at the end of the century nationalism would indicate a new direction for Iranian identities. In the end, continuity and transition in the eighteenth century were to be found in the land of Iran and its peoples and political culture. In the nineteenth, Iran's political culture would undergo continuing change, but the most profound change would come in the twentieth century with the emergence of the first non-tribally based dynasty, the Pahlavis, who would ultimately be confronted by revolution and by radical religious thought, whose origin goes back to the late seventeenth and eighteenth centuries.

24 Juan Cole, 'Shi'i clerics in Iraq and Iran, 1722–1780: The Akhbari-Usuli conflict reconsidered', *Iranian Studies*, 18, 1 (Winter 1985), pp. 3–34.

25 Peter J. Chelkowski (ed.), *Taz'iyeh, ritual and drama in Iran* (New York, 1979).

PART IV

*

THEMES

15

Conversion to Islam

RICHARD W. BULLIET

Introduction

Though it is self-evident that over the centuries many millions of people have changed their religious identity from non-Muslim to Muslim, a majority of them since the turn of the twelfth/sixth century in lands east of Iran, scholars understand the word 'conversion' in a variety of ways and use differing approaches in their studies of these changes. One person considers conversion to involve a deeply felt personal change in religious belief; another simply counts the growth over time in the number of people who consider themselves, or are considered by others, to be Muslims and infers that conversion has taken place. One person collects stories or legends about conversion experiences; another analyses social and economic circumstances to explain the growth of the Muslim community. The method chosen sets limits on the conclusions that can be reached. Just as stories about individuals cannot be relied on to explain mass phenomena, economic data and quantitative modelling say nothing about spiritual experience.

Complicating the matter still further, studies of conversion often take it for granted that converts to Islam move from one known entity to another, while in fact both Islam and the religions from which new converts come change over time and in response to their relative position in society. A person who is among the first in a community to convert to Islam is in a very different position from the person who is the last in the community to change religions, and almost certainly acts from a different motivation. Furthermore, Islam itself, even with an unchanging scripture and a fairly constant theology, appears different when it has newly arrived in a locality from the way it appears when it has been a common social identity for several centuries. In the first instance, for example, it may be the religion of a conquering elite or of a wandering holy man, whereas in the second it is considered part of tradition.[1]

1 Richard W. Bulliet, 'Process and status in conversion and continuity', in Michael Gervers and Ramzi Jibran Bikhazi (eds.), *Conversion and continuity: Indigenous Christian communities in Islamic lands, eighth to eighteenth centuries* (Toronto, 1990), pp. 1–12.

Finally, studies of conversion often assume that the religious identities of individuals and groups are clear-cut and that change from one identity to another is as unambiguous as turning an electric switch on or off. Yet there is ample evidence that some people waver between religions, adopting one identity in one situation or at one moment in time and another when the situation changes. And it is similarly apparent that there are halfway houses between religions in which beliefs from more than one tradition mix together.

In addition to all of these complications, the study of conversion to Islam is burdened by tales and assumptions that have little basis in fact. Fortunately, the 'conversion by the sword' stereotype has largely died away. But the notion that new converts are normally zealots, like the contradictory notion that new converts are insincere and not really Muslim, is still encountered.

Given these problems, no general history of the whens, hows and whys of conversion is possible. In the place of such a history, an assessment of current analytical approaches and of the types of conclusions that can be reached through different methods – quantitative, economic, literary and institutional – must suffice.

Quantitative analysis

Despite modern censuses, no one knows today how many Muslims there are in the world, much less the demographic breakdown between Sunnīs and Shīʿites. How much more difficult it is for historians of earlier periods to find reliable census data. Thus quantitative approaches usually depend on analytical modelling rather than counting heads. Some models derive from patterns of growth that have been observed in modern studies of innovation diffusion.[2] S-shaped curves portray conversion as beginning slowly and then accelerating into a bandwagon surge of conversion in the middle portion of the curve only to taper off as the number of people left to convert diminishes. The logic behind this model assumes that each individual makes a decision to change religion based on access to convincing information or persuasion by an influential personal contact. Early growth proceeds slowly because, in the absence of broad literacy and mass media, word of mouth is the primary source of information, and persuasion and informants are few. Language barriers slow diffusion yet further, a factor that accentuates the role of non-Muslim women, whether wives or concubines, who have children with

2 Richard W. Bulliet, *Conversion to Islam in the medieval period* (Cambridge, 1975) pioneered this approach.

Muslim men. The bilingual offspring of such unions are considered Muslim in Islamic law and are often better equipped than their fathers to explain the faith to potential converts.

Historians who take this innovation diffusion model as a hypothesis rely on data that can be interpreted as fitting the slow early phase, the bandwagon middle phase or the tapering-off phase of the curve.[3] But data are seldom abundant or systematic enough over a long period of time to demonstrate the validity of the model directly. Moreover, the model's assumptions that people decide individually on conversion, as opposed to changing religious identity as part of a community, and that conversion normally takes place in the definitive and unambiguous fashion of an off–on switch, may not be valid for many societies.

Another kind of diffusion model visualises conversion radiating outward from nodes of initial Muslim presence, such as royal courts, military camps, urban centres or Sufi shrines.[4] The assumption behind this model is that people who live close to such nodes feel pressure to convert, see opportunities in conversion or gain access to information about the new faith sooner than people who live in more remote locales. The growth of the convert community can thus be modelled as a series of chronologically sequenced concentric circles emanating from each node until the circles from different nodes eventually overlap. Unfortunately, few bodies of data contain the chronological and geographical specificity needed to demonstrate the validity of this model. Moreover, the model cannot easily accommodate collective change of religious identity by an entire community. Thus it is generally more useful for orienting the historian of conversion than for guiding empirical research.

Economic analysis

Traditional approaches to the economic dimension of conversion involved either the idea that economic opportunities available to new converts induce them to abandon their original faith, or that the head tax (*jizya*) collectible by Muslim governments from 'people of the book' – primarily Jews and Christians, but sometimes including Zoroastrians, Hindus or others – prompted conversion as a form of tax avoidance. Biographical accounts of government officials or military officers whose careers necessitated conversion to

3 See, for example, Anton Minkov, *Conversion to Islam in the Balkans: Kisve bahası petitions and Ottoman social life, 1670–1730* (Leiden, 2004).

4 Richard W. Bulliet, 'Conversion-based patronage and onomastic evidence in early Islam', in M. Bernards and J. Nawas, *Patronate and patronage in early and classical Islam* (Leiden, 2005), pp. 246–62.

Islam substantiate the first of these scenarios in particular cases, but it is difficult to prove a general link between conversion and economic opportunity. As for the second scenario, concrete evidence is generally lacking, and there is no way of determining why some people remain steadfast in their ancestral religion while others in the same community are willing to renounce it for economic gain. A third scenario, in which the Muslim government, or local Muslim communities, offers financial rewards for conversion, does appear in the historical record;[5] but it seems to be uncommon.

A more sophisticated economic approach that has a strong foundation in quantifiable data involves the growth of the Muslim community in east Bengal.[6] Richard M. Eaton has demonstrated a link between religious conversion and the spread of rice farming in that area. *Zamīndārs*, Mughal government officials entitled to collect the revenues from specific tracts of land, engaged local religious figures to assemble workers, establish a village, clear the land of jungle and plant rice. A few of these entrepreneurs were Hindus, but most were Muslims, and they used religion to advance their activities. The locally available labourers typically worshipped gods and goddesses from their tribal traditions. Eaton found that the inhabitants of the new rice villages adopted the religion of the entrepreneur, even though their understanding of that religion included many features of their previous cults, such as viewing Muḥammad as an incarnation of Vishnu. In this way, east Bengal became home to one of the largest populations of Muslims in India, but the content of the Islam practised there was initially quite eclectic.

It is unlikely that east Bengal was the only place where agricultural development, or some economic activity associated with Muslims, correlated directly with conversion to Islam; but examples of such developments cannot be expected to apply beyond specific subregions.

Literary analysis

The Islamisation of the Turkic societies of Central Asia has long been a historical conundrum. However, a detailed folkloristic analysis by Devin DeWeese has reframed the question in a stimulating new way.[7] In 712/1313 Uzbek Khan became the ruler of the Golden Horde, a Mongol state

5 See for example the Ottoman practice of giving a sum of money (*kisve baha*) to new converts in Minkov, *Conversion*.

6 Richard M. Eaton, *The rise of Islam and the Bengal frontier, 1204–1760* (Berkeley, 1996).

7 Devin DeWeese, *Islamization and native religion in the Golden Horde: Baba Tükles and conversion to Islam in historical and epic tradition* (University Park, PA, 1994).

established in southern Russia by a grandson of Chinggis Khan. Tribal traditions among Central Asian peoples who trace their descent from the Golden Horde agree that Islamisation became common during Uzbek's reign, even though the fourth Golden Horde ruler, Berke, had personally converted half a century earlier. Early literary sources attribute Uzbek's conversion to a Sufi named Sayyid Ata, just as they say that Berke converted at the hands of a Sufi named Sayf al-Dīn Bākharzī. Nothing substantial is known of either of these individuals, but their legends support the idea that Sufis were important agents of conversion in the Turkic world. At the time these events took place, Sufi brotherhoods had not yet formed, so these holy men, whose presence in Mongol camps is attested to by European Christian travel accounts, were presumably acting individually.

DeWeese's work concentrates not on these early tales, but on a more detailed legend of a person named Baba Tükles that gradually gained enough popularity to become the dominant conversion story by the tenth/sixteenth century. In that story, four Muslims who had been inspired by God to convert Uzbek arrived at his coronation and disrupted the traditional rituals. Uzbek's shamans and diviners urged him to kill the Muslim intruders, but he proposed a test instead. Two ovens would be stoked. A Muslim would enter one, and one of the diviners the other. Baba Tükles volunteered for the test on the Muslim side while the diviners simply tossed in one of their fellows, who was promptly incinerated. Baba Tükles put on his chain armour and entered the oven reciting his Sufi chant (*dhikr*). Then, according to the tenth/sixteenth-century text:

> When it was presumed that the sheep's flesh [suspended over the oven] was fully cooked, they opened the mouth of the oven; and Baba, wiping the sweat from his blessed face, came out of the oven, saying 'Why did you hurry? If you had held off for a time, my business [of reciting the *dhikr*] would have been finished.' They saw that the armor was blowing red hot, but by the power of God most high not a hair of the Baba's body was burned. When all the people, beginning with the Khan, saw this situation, they at once grasped hold of the hems of the *shaykhs'* [Muslim holy men's] garments and became Muslims; praise be to God for the religion of Islam![8]

DeWeese recognises that these (and other) conversion narratives preserved in literary sources have little value as historical fact, but he finds them valuable objects of study nonetheless:

> We are thus not so much concerned with the extent to which the narrative elements ... 'accurately' reflect historical events or practices ... Rather, we will

8 *Ibid.*, pp. 155–8.

> assume that the themes evoked in the narrative reflect religious counterpoints in the meeting of Islam and indigenous traditions, not 'as they were,' but *as they were imagined* among later generations. It is in light of this assumption that we may fully explore the religious meaning provided by the conversion narrative for Islamic, or Islamizing, communities in Inner Asia, without being inordinately troubled by the lack of *historical* evidence ... In the final analysis, even though we may find signs of the 'practical' encounter of Islam and indigenous traditions, our chief concern is with the narrative *response* to that encounter. We want to know how the communities most directly affected by the simultaneous confrontation and assimilation of the two traditions talked about the process and made sense out of it, ... this, after all, was a substantial, though too little appreciated aspect of the 'practical' encounter of Islamic and Inner Asian traditions, with quite real historical consequences.[9]

What this approach to conversion highlights is the importance of interaction, in areas of large-scale conversion, between Muslim and non-Muslim communities and traditions, and of the way that interaction became inscribed in literary texts, sometimes long after the events. For eastern regions that experienced such waves of conversion between the fifth/eleventh and twelfth/eighteenth centuries – Central and Inner Asia, China, India, peninsular and island South-East Asia and the Philippines – demographic and chronological questions, some of them long debated, pale beside the question of the way Islam accommodated local traditions, or vice versa. Thus this literary approach using manifestly legendary materials holds great promise for understanding the texture of conversion and community building.

Institutional analysis

Institutional analyses focus on networks of people who are believed to play a role in conversion. Travelling merchants, Sufis or scholars are the groups most commonly mentioned. With respect to the latter two, the character of the Islam communicated plays a role in many analyses. Inasmuch as the particular teachings or orientations of Sufi brotherhoods and scholarly networks are often known, looking at them as agents for changing religious belief sometimes involves the conversion of Muslims from one type of Islam to another, rather than non-Muslims to Islam. In the Muslim heartland of the Middle East and North Africa, this type of activity would be treated as part of the history of sectarian development. But in more eastern lands where questions have been

9 *Ibid.*, p. 162.

raised by both Muslims and non-Muslims about the genuineness of the Islam professed by new converts, the efforts of these networks to upgrade or purify Islam can be woven into the history of conversion.

South-East Asia serves as a microcosm for studying these approaches, though other regions offer parallel cases. Historians have speculated about the coming of Islam to Indonesia, where there is no history of conquest or of sharing a land border with a Muslim state. Scraps of information drawn from narrative sources, tombstones and rulers' names, and inferences from the dominant position of the Shāfiʿī law school, have been interpreted to pinpoint Gujarat in north-west India, Bengal in north-east India or southern Arabia as the original source of Islam in the archipelago. But these scanty data do not explain how and why Islam spread from a few coastal locales.

Since Muslim trade with South-East Asia, like trade with southern China, is attested from very early in Islamic history, some analysts surmise that travelling merchants spread Islam, persuading coastal rulers that their conversion to Islam would benefit their seaports and even intermarrying with the rulers' families. Unfortunately, for the period prior to the tenth/sixteenth century, too little is known about the organisation of trade to flesh out these surmises; and there is little concrete evidence that Muslim merchants took a particular interest in spreading the faith. The early Muslim merchants who took up residence in southern China, for example, seem not to have triggered a wave of conversion, though they were part of the same commercial networks that traded with Indonesia. In Central Asia, where merchants have also been suggested as agents for the spread of Islam, no one has produced concrete evidence that proselytising was an important or systematic activity.

The case for Sufi brotherhoods proselytising in Indonesia and elsewhere is much stronger because unlike merchants – except when the merchants themselves were also Sufis – the Sufis made religion their main calling and focused their efforts on building faith communities. However, fully developed Sufi brotherhoods did not appear in the Middle East until the seventh/thirteenth century, and there must certainly have been a time lag before Sufi networks reached lands as far away as Indonesia or China. Once they arrived, their activities can sometimes be traced. But whether the followings they attracted were new converts to Islam, or people who already considered themselves Muslim, is difficult to determine. In the Muslim heartland, after all, the great preponderance of those who were attracted to the Sufi way of life were already Muslims, and in both China and Indonesia fragmentary evidence shows that some sort of Muslim community was already present several centuries before the eighth/fourteenth century. In addition, Sufism cannot be considered a uniform phenomenon, for the brotherhoods differed substantially in their rituals, organisational complexity and interpretations of Islam.

In his overview of the history of Islam in China, Joseph Fletcher identified three tides, the first two of which are relevant here.[10] The first tide stretched from the first/seventh to the eighth/fourteenth century and consisted of small, independent communities clustered around a mosque. These communities descended from Muslim traders, military men and officials of various ethnicities, many of whom entered China during the Mongol Yuan dynasty in the seventh/thirteenth century. The degree to which conversion of the local population played a role in the establishment and survival of these communities is indeterminable.

Fletcher's second tide began with the activities of Sufi brotherhoods, probably in the eighth/fourteenth century, but did not make a major impact on Islam in China until the late eleventh/seventeenth century. Sources are available to study the spread of these Sufi networks from roots in the Middle East, but, as in Indonesia, it is hard to distinguish their proselytising activities from their reinvigoration of pre-existing Muslim communities. Thus while the general role of Sufis in spreading Islam is unquestioned, data for making direct connections with conversion are seldom readily available.

Turning to the role of scholarly networks, the work of Azyumardi Azra on the spread of reformist Islam to Indonesia stands out.[11] Samudera-Pasai, a kingdom in northern Sumatra, became a centre for Muslim learning in the late seventh/thirteenth century, some 200 years after the dates on the earliest Muslim tombstones found in the archipelago. Despite the efforts of pious monarchs, however, formal religious learning did not spread widely. Azra demonstrates that Indonesia did not become fully integrated into the world of Islamic scholarship until the eleventh/seventeenth century when pilgrims returning from several years of study in Mecca, often involving initiation into a Sufi order, set about teaching Islam in a more authoritative fashion. The sources he draws upon are voluminous, but it is not clear how the activities of this network should be interpreted from the standpoint of conversion. Just as

10 Joseph Fletcher, 'Les voies (*turuq*) soufites en Chines', in A. Popovic and G. Veinstein (eds.), *Ordres mystiques dans l'Islam: Cheminements et situation actuelle* (Paris, 1986). An excellent discussion of Fletcher's work is contained in Dru C. Gladney, *Muslim Chinese: Ethnic nationalism in the People's Republic* (Cambridge, MA, 1991), pp. 36–59.

11 Azyumardi Azra, *The origins of Islamic reformism in Southeast Asia: Networks of Malay-Indonesian and Middle Eastern 'ulama' in the seventeenth and eighteenth centuries* (Crows Nest, NSW, 2004).

DeWeese argues that an analysis of how a community remembers the conversion stories of bygone rulers can be used to diagnose the evolving relationship between Islam and non-Islam, as cultural traditions, if not demonstrably as faith communities, so Azra maintains that the propagation from Mecca of this more authoritative 'reformist' version of Islam relates significantly to how an earlier Islamic current that was more accommodating to local tradition evolved over time.

Conclusion

The original spread of Islam in the Middle East, North Africa and Andalusia took four to five centuries. Those who became Muslim in the first/seventh century clearly were joining a different religion from the one other converts joined three centuries later. However, because the elaboration of Sunnī and Shīʿite Islam, the Sunnī law schools and a variety of sects is normally treated as a separate historical subject, it is usually taken for granted that the simple fact of a change in religious identity is the central question in the history of conversion. By the sixth/twelfth century, when this first wave of conversion had plateaued in the heartland, most of the major institutional and intellectual developments within Islam had become manifest, though the elaboration of Sufi mystical experiences into full-blown brotherhoods was still on the horizon, as was the revival of neo-Platonist philosophy in Iranian Shīʿism. Thus the Islam that spread far to the east from the sixth/twelfth century onward was no longer a 'work in progress' as it had been several centuries earlier.

The sense that Islam was a known and fully developed entity during this later period has obscured the fact that the same sort of accommodation with local tradition that occurred when the legacy of Hellenistic culture entered and altered Islam during the early Islamic centuries was bound to be mirrored in the regions where Islam entered into its growth curve relatively late. The types of analysis summarised above tacitly recognise this. Even if the sources were available to determine the precise percentages of Muslims in the Central Asian, Chinese, Indian or south-eastern populations at any point in time, the characteristics of the faith professed by those Muslims would be seen to change over time, to such an extent that modern observers sometimes disparage segments of the earlier (and even the present) Muslim communities as merely 'nominal' adherents to Islam. (The term 'nominal' might well have been applied to segments of the Middle Eastern, North African and Andalusian Muslim communities in the ninth/fifteenth century.) One of the values of the approaches of Eaton, DeWeese, Fletcher and Azra is that conversion is seen not just as a demographic matter, but as an accommodation over time between Islam and the peoples it is drawing into its orbit. The process of accommodation, and the organisational forms by which accommodation comes about, represent the frontier of conversion studies in the lands of the east.

16

Armies and their economic basis in Iran and the surrounding lands, *c*. 1000–1500

REUVEN AMITAI

Who hath raised up one from the East,
At whose steps victory attendeth?
He giveth nations before him,
And maketh him rule over kings;
His sword maketh them as the dust,
His bow as the driven stubble. Isaiah, 41:2

One salient theme in the military, political and social history of the eastern Islamic world of the late Middle Ages and early modern period is the alteration and even tension between nomadic and standing armies. By the first mentioned, I am referring to armies that are based primarily on soldiers who normally live as pastoral nomads and can be called up to serve at need, as opposed to the latter, armies based in cities, composed of more-or-less professional soldiers. The former mainly receive their livelihood from their pastoral occupations while the latter draw either salaries or revenues derived directly from land allocations under their control. This chapter will revolve around this alternating military situation in various regimes and territories, looking also at the way armies were paid or otherwise supported.

Geographically, Iran – more-or-less defined as the country within the boundaries of the present Islamic Republic, but also including a wide swathe of northern modern Afghanistan and all of Turkmenistan – is at the heart of our discussion. At the same time, the effective influence (and thus the arena for the activities of the military) of these states based in Iran could extend much further to the east, north or west. Thus under the Saljuqs and Mongols we must include most of Anatolia, al-ʿIrāq, al-Jazīra (Upper Mesopotamia) and the southern Caucasus region as part of our canvas, and for the Timurids, we cannot forget their original stomping grounds, Transoxania. With the Safavids, however, we approach a territory enjoying something like the modern borders of Iran (see Map 5).

Even a casual student of Islamic history will note that the Turkish involvement with the region's history did not begin with the arrival of the Turcoman tribes under Saljuq leadership in the early eleventh century. Already from the first half of the ninth century the ʿAbbāsid caliphs had employed Turkish slave troops, known generally then as *ghilmān* (plural of *ghulām*, literally a 'youth'). Modern scholars are far from holding a consensus about the origins and early development of military slavery in the Islamic world, but there is no denying its importance in the military, political, social and economic life of the caliphate, and its contribution to the increasing crisis in these areas from the mid-ninth century onward. Military slaves, again mostly Central Asian Turks (also referred to as *mamālīk*, plural of *mamlūk*, an 'owned one'), also played an important role in the armies of the various successor 'states' to the united caliphate, from Egypt to the east. Without denying their significance and even prominence, however, *mamlūks* (to which we will henceforth conveniently, if at times anachronistically, refer to these slave troops) were never alone in any army, composed also of other professional soldiers, civilian militias and other volunteers, and nomadic auxiliaries. Yet, we can state that a clear trend can already be discerned in the ninth and tenth centuries which would come to fruition in the subsequent eras: the increasing status and then predominance of troops of Central Asian provenance be they nomads or professional soldiers, the latter mostly of slave origin or status.

The title of this chapter should be noted. There can be no discussion of the military without an examination of its financial basis: how were the officers and soldiers equipped and paid? At the same time, we should remember that probably the main recipient of the tax revenues of a pre-modern state (and not just in the Middle East) was the army. Often, as will be seen below, the officers themselves directly managed the collection of taxes from land and elsewhere, which went straight into their coffers for the upkeep of their households and units. The subjects of military history and tax policy (and by extension the system of land tenure) are therefore inextricably connected.

The Saljuqs

Under the aegis of the Saljuq family, relatively large numbers of Turkish tribal groups crossed the Syr Darya (Jaxartes) river from the Eurasian steppe region from the early eleventh century onward, then spreading into Iran and adjacent regions. These tribal groups, mostly of the Oghuz (Arabic: Ghuzz) tribe, converted to Islam at some point (probably on the whole before entering the Muslim world), maintained their tribal framework and pastoral nomadic lifestyle, and were known by the name of Turcoman (Arabic: *turkumān*; often rendered in the plural *tarākima*; cf. modern Turkish: *türkmen*).[1] Like Inner Asian invaders and raiders before and after them, the early successes of the Saljuq princes were based on the use of disciplined masses of mounted archers, the hallmark of Inner Asian warfare for probably two millennia before the advent of this dynasty.[2] Before proceeding to examining the early Saljuq army, it would be instructive to cite one Muslim author who commented on the military abilities, especially the archery, of the Turkish nomads (although from almost two centuries before the arrival of the Turcomans in the Islamic world). The Baghdadi belletrist al-Jāḥiẓ (d. 869) wrote in his essay on the 'Virtues of the Turks', where *inter alia*, the Turkish warrior is compared to the Arab Khārijite rebel:

> [The Turk] shoots [with his bow], while he lets his mount go at full gallop, riding backwards and forwards, right and left, going up and down. He lets off ten arrows, before the Khārijī can lift even one arrow [to his bow string]. The Turk rides his mount down off the hill or down into the valley better than the Khārijī can do on flat ground. The Turk has four eyes: two in the front and two in the back ... [The Turk] hits with his arrow when he faces backwards, as he does when he faces forward ... The Turk on a raid has with him everything that he will for himself, his armour, his beast and the apparatus of his beast. His endurance for riding and continuous travel, for night-long journeys and crossing the country are truly amazing ... And if – at the end of a Turk's life, one were to calculate his days, one would find that he sat on the back of his mount more than he had spent sitting on the earth.[3]

Of course, we should remember that this is from a polemical text, part of the discussion in mid-ninth-century Iraq about the role of the Turks, and there

1 For the etymology of this term, see B. Kellner-Heinkele, 'Türkmen', EI^2, vol. X, p. 682; P. B. Golden, *An introduction to the history of the Turkic peoples: Ethnogenesis and state-formation in medieval and early modern Eurasia and the Middle East* (Wiesbaden, 1992), pp. 212–13.

2 On the military abilities of the Turks, as well as the Eurasian Steppe nomads in general, see D. Sinor, 'The Inner Asian warriors', *Journal of the American Oriental Society*, 101 (1981), pp. 133–44; P. B. Golden, 'War and warfare in the pre-Čінggisid western steppes of Eurasia', in N. Di Cosmo (ed.), *Warfare in Inner Asian history (500–1800)* (Leiden, 2002), pp. 105–72, as well as the editor's comments in the 'Introduction', pp. 1–12.

3 Abū 'Uthmān b. Baḥr al-Jāḥiẓ, *Talāth rasā'il* (Leiden, 1903), pp. 28–9; cf. the translation in C. T. Harley Walker, 'Jahiz of Baṣra to al-Fath ibn Khaqan on the "Exploits of the Turks" and the army of the khalifate in general', *Journal of the Royal Asiatic Society* (1915), pp. 666–7. See the discussion in M. V. McDonald, 'Al-Ǧāḥiẓ and his analysis of the Turks', in U. Vermeulen and J. M. F. van Reeth (eds.), *Law, Christianity and modernism in Islamic society* (Leuven, 1998), pp. 27–38. The Khārijī refers to a member of the revolutionary sect in early Islam, mainly composed of Arab tribesmen, known collectively as Khawārij.

is no question of the pro-Turkish perspective of the author. But although there may have been questions about the contributions of the Turkish slave troops to the political instability of the capital (as well as resentment from other military elements at their power and prestige), there is no doubting their military abilities.[4]

Composed of such hardy mobile fighters possessing great 'firepower', the Saljuq armies were able to advance virtually unimpeded, from the Oxus river across Iran to Baghdad in 447/1055. We have few exact figures for the size of these mostly Turcoman armies, but they probably numbered not much more than 10,000 at a given time, since it is unlikely that significantly more than several tens of thousands of nomadic families actually immigrated into the Muslim world in the first half of the eleventh century. At Dandāqān in 431/1040, the Saljuq army under the princes Ṭoghrıl Beg and Chagrı Beg reportedly contained about 16,000 men, which was able to outmanoeuvre the larger and better equipped (but exhausted) Ghaznavid force that included over a hundred elephants. The Ghaznavid force was led into the dry plain north of Marv, where it met its demise, thus sealing the fate of the Ghaznavid state in Khurāsān.[5]

Virtually nothing is known of the organisation of the early Saljuq army, although it probably remained arranged according to earlier tribal organisation under traditional chiefs. The troops would have appeared to have maintained themselves by their own herds, supplemented by booty resulting from battle and raiding. There is no indication of any type of salary being paid to the common troops, but chiefs and senior officers surely were awarded presents of various types to tie them to the ruling house, and some of this wealth may have percolated down the ranks. There appears at first to have been little thought given to siege warfare. '[T]he fortifications and walls of the towns of Iran, like Ray and Isfahan did not have to be directly stormed by the Turkmen

4 For the positive characteristics of the Turks, as well as their perceived uncouthness and barbarity, see U. Haarmann, 'Ideology and history, identity and alterity: The Arab image of the Turk from the 'Abbasids to modern Egypt', *International Journal of Middle Eastern Studies*, 20 (1988), pp. 175–96; Golden, 'War and warfare in the pre-Čінggisid western steppes of Eurasia', pp. 123–8; Y. Frenkel, 'The Turks of the Eurasian Steppes in medieval Arabic writing', in R. Amitai and M. Biran (eds.), *Mongols, Turks and others: Eurasian nomads and the sedentary world* (Leiden, 2005), pp. 201–41. See also the discussion on the Mongols, below.

5 For this battle and its importance, see D. S. Richards, *The Annals of the Saljuq Turks: Selections from al-Kāmil fī'l-Ta'rīkh of 'Izz al-Dīn Ibn al-Athīr* (London, 2002), pp. 39–40; W. Barthold, *Turkestan down to the Mongol invasion*, 3rd edn (London, 1968), p. 303; C. E. Bosworth, 'The political and dynastic history of the Iranian world', in J. A. Boyle (ed.), *The Cambridge history of Iran*, vol. V (Cambridge, 1968), pp. 21–2.

when the tramplings of their horses and the nibblings of their flocks could devastate the towns' agricultural hinterlands and hamstring their commerce.'[6]

But what worked for the Saljuq rulers in their *Drang nach Westen* was to become increasingly inappropriate and unwieldy as they found themselves at the head of a large, mainly sedentary empire. The Turcoman tribesmen and chiefs had increasingly different interests from the sovereign (perhaps as early as 1040 known as *sulṭān*) and his inner circle. The tribesmen were interested in pastureland, raids and booty, and did not take kindly to the restrictions placed on these by the central government, now concerned about trade, revenues from agriculture, and general political and economic stability. The growing crisis can also be seen as a disagreement over the nature and extent of the ruler's authority. What had been acceptable in the steppe milieu and the period of conquest, where the ruler (*beg* or *khan*) was basically the leader of a war-party with limited authority over other affairs, was seen – to the chagrin of the nomads – as inappropriate for the situation in which the sultan and his entourage found themselves, where a more centralised regime and powerful ruler was called for. In order to head off tension and potential conflict, a *modus vivendi* was worked out to the benefit of both sides: the majority of Turcoman nomads moved to the area of Azerbaijan (comprising much of north-western Iran of today, the southern Caucasus and even some of eastern Turkey), where already some Turcoman had already taken up residence. There they found ample pastureland, a climate appropriate for their lifestyle, distance from the central authorities and ample opportunity to raid (against Georgians, Armenians and, most importantly, the Byzantines) in the name of Islam. The Saljuq authorities thus got their Turcomans out of their hair (but they were not too far if they were needed for a campaign), without having to resort to violence; they themselves, it should be remembered, were only a generation or two out of the steppe, and thus would have wanted to preserve a civil relationship with their nomadic 'cousins'.[7]

Of course, now that the Turcoman troops were somewhat far away, the Saljuqs needed a dependable force to preserve order from within, and wage warfare against enemies from without. Their solution was to resort to the now well-entrenched institution in the Muslim world, military slavery. Thus a large

6 C. E. Bosworth, 'Army, ii. Islamic, to the Mongol period', *EIr*, vol. II, p. 501.

7 This is a summary of the discussion in C. Cahen, *Pre-Ottoman Turkey*, trans. J. Jones-Williams (London, 1968), pp. 22–7. See also D. Morgan, *Medieval Persia, 1040–1797* (London, 1988), pp. 28–9.

formation of Turkish military slaves (usually still called *ghilmān*), was probably created already around the time of the taking of Baghdad. When exactly this force, which seemingly numbered between 10,000 and 15,000 troops, was established is uncertain; it would seem that the immediate precedent for this initiative was the Ghaznavid army, although as the Saljuqs moved west they would have encountered other Turkish slave units which should have strengthened their resolve to create and maintain such a force.[8] The role of Persian-speaking bureaucrats in conveying this long-established military tradition and assisting in its re-establishment under a Saljuq aegis should not be underestimated. Perhaps the greatest, and certainly the most famous, of these officials was Niẓām al-Mulk (d. 1092), the vizier of the sultans Alp Arslan and Malik Shāh, who left explicit instructions on the matter in his famous mirror for princes, *Siyāsat-nāma*: military slaves (*ghulāmān*, the Persian plural of *ghulām*) were to be taken from the Turcomans, and they 'should be enrolled and maintained in the same way as military slaves of the palace. When they are in continuous employment they will learn the use of arms and become trained in service. Then they will settle down with other people and with growing devotion serve as military slaves, and cease to feel that aversion [to settled life] with which they are naturally imbued.'[9] Of course, there is always the question when reading Niẓām al-Mulk's work whether he is being descriptive or merely prescriptive, reflecting his own views as a senior bureaucrat. But in this case, at least, his testimony is largely borne out by the historical record (see below). This author also states that the army should contain other ethnic elements (*az har jins*) besides Turks: Daylamīs, Khurāsānīs, Georgians and Shabānkāra'īs (from Fārs). This reflects the reality of a mixed army of cavalry (predominantly Turcomans and Turkish *ghilmān*) and infantry, primarily of Persian provenance. Kurdish and Arab tribesmen were also used as auxiliary forces; additional groups (Hindus, Rūmīs and others) were apparently found in smaller numbers.[10]

8 Cahen, *Pre-Ottoman Turkey*, pp. 22–7; Morgan, *Medieval Persia*, pp. 28–9; Bosworth, 'The Iranian world', pp. 80–1; A. K. S. Lambton, 'The internal structure of the Saljūq empire', in *Cambridge history of Iran*, vol. V, pp. 228–30 (with some details of weapons, logistics and tactics).

9 Niẓām al-Mulk (Abū 'Alī b. Ḥasan Ṭūsī), *Siyar al-mulūk* (=*Siyāsat-nāma*), ed. H. Darke (Tehran, 1962), p. 131; trans. taken, with some changes, from H. Darke, *The book of government or rules for kings*, 2nd edn (London, 1978), p. 102. Darke mistranslates the term *ghulām* as 'page', when it is clearly meant for military slave, i.e. *mamlūk*. Niẓām al-Mulk may well be mistaken when he states that the *ghulāms* were to be taken from among the Turcoman tribes, as opposed to Turkish tribes still out on the steppe. See the discussions in the studies cited in the previous note, as well as Barthold, *Turkestan*, p. 309.

10 Niẓām al-Mulk, p. 128 (=trans. pp. 103–4).

The important role of Turkish military slaves in the Saljuq army is seen in the following citation from the chronicle of Sibṭ ibn al-Jawzī (d. 654/1256), who describes the victory of Alp Arslan over the Byzantines at the battle of Manzikert/Malāzgird in 463/1071, as follows:

> Alp Arslan's army deserted him. Those who stayed were 4000 *ghulāms*. An army of 10,000 Kurds also joined him, but he relied, after his reliance on God, may He be exalted, on those 4,000 who stayed with him.[11]

The whole army was supervised, at least with regard to its income and equipment, by the *dīwān-i ʿarḍ* ('military inspection office', also called *dīwān-i jaysh*: 'army office'), headed by a bureaucrat, *ṣāḥib al-jaysh* or *ʿāriḍ*. It is clear that this civilian official could not hope to oversee effectively training or preparedness for war, even if theoretically he was in charge of organising training sessions. The 'commander-in-chief' was a Turkish officer known as chief *ḥājib* (chamberlain) or *ispāhsalār*. The extent of his responsibility and authority is unclear, since at least up to the time of Sultan Malik Shāh usually the ruler himself went out on major campaign at the head of his troops.[12]

One important area overseen by the Army Office, which in modern terms would be understood as 'the office for military payments and supplies', was the *iqṭāʿ* system used to pay much of the army, certainly the *ghulām* troops. This system had been adopted most probably from the Būyids, who had ruled previously in Iraq and western Iran, and had developed out of the attempts to find solutions to pay the army in the chaotic times – characterised by chronic financial crises – in Iraq in the late ninth and early tenth centuries. Here, at least, the Saljuqs did not look to the Ghaznavids as their institutional model.[13] The key concept behind this institution was that a senior commander would receive a large swathe of agricultural land over which he had the right to collect taxes, which he would use for the upkeep of himself, his household and his troops (the border between the last two not always clear). In theory, at least, the *muqṭaʿ* (a possessor of an *iqṭāʿ*) did not have any fundamental

11 Sibṭ ibn al-Jawzī, *Mir'āt al-zamān* (Ankara, 1968), p. 148, cited and trans. (upon which this is based) in D. Ayalon, 'The Mamlūks of the Seljuks: Islam's military might at the crossroads', *Journal of the Royal Asiatic Society*, 3rd ser., 6 (1996), p. 324. This article (pp. 305–33) contains other important information on the *mamlūks* of the Saljuqs, as well as a selection of citations regarding the appreciation in the Arabic sources of Turkish military qualities.

12 C. E. Bosworth, 'Recruitment, muster, review in medieval Islamic armies', in V. J. Parry and M. E. Yapp (eds.), *War, technology and society in the Middle East* (London, 1975), pp. 69, 75–7; Bosworth; 'Army', pp. 501–2; Lambton, 'Internal structure', p. 226.

13 See the comments by C. E. Bosworth, *The Ghaznavids: Their empire in Afghanistan and eastern Iran 994–1040*, 2nd edn (Beirut, 1973), pp. 66, 125.

administrative or governmental authority over this land, or the right to pass it on to his heirs. It was not private property (*milk*), but, essentially, the right to collect agricultural taxes (*kharāj*) at source. As such, it certainly cannot be confused with medieval European feudalism, and the use of the term 'fief' to translate *iqṭāʿ* should be eschewed. Where, as in earlier times, it had been hoped that from the income that the *muqṭaʿ* received he would pay the *ʿushr* ('tithe') to the state treasury (this type of *iqṭāʿ* being known as *iqṭāʿ tamlīk*, '*iqṭāʿ* of possession'), in reality, in most cases the officer in question just kept all of the revenues for his own uses. Eventually, this usage was recognised by the bureaucrats, and received the name *iqṭāʿ istighāl* ('*iqṭāʿ* of usufruct'). This latter form of the institution was that adopted in the Saljuq empire.[14] We also find another form of the *iqṭāʿ* institution, which became more pronounced with the weakening of the authority of the Saljuq state (starting at the end of the twelfth century, in the aftermath of the death of Niẓām al-Mulk and Malik Shāh). This was what has been referred to in modern scholarship as 'administrative' *iqṭāʿ*, whose holder received not only the right to collect taxes in a particular area but also governing powers as a representative of the central government. In times of weakening central authority, these governorships could even be transferred by inheritance. In one Saljuq successor state, the Zangid principality of Mosul and Aleppo, this right of inheritance was even institutionalised (although this was short-lived, and under their Ayyūbid successors there was a reversion to the non-hereditary *iqṭāʿ*).[15]

The Mongol invasions and the Ilkhanate

With the advent of the Mongol period in Iran, we again encounter an army of Inner Asian origin, with both similarities and differences between it and the original Turcoman army of the Saljuqs. The main similarity would have been the general character of the armies, based on masses of light horse archers. The

14 A. K. S. Lambton, 'Reflections on the *iqṭāʿ*', in G. Makdisi (ed.), *Arabic and Islamic studies in honor of Hamilton A. R. Gibb* (Leiden, 1965), pp. 358–76; Lambton, 'Eqṭāʿ', *EIr*, vol. VIII, pp. 520–3; see Lambton, 'Internal structure', p. 234, for other – albeit related – uses of the term *iqṭāʿ* under the Saljuqs; C. Cahen, 'L'évolution de l'iqṭāʿ du IXe au XIIIe siècle: Contribution à une histoire compare des sociétés médiévales', in C. Cahen, *Les peuples musulmans dans l'histoire médiévale* (Damascus, 1977), pp. 231–69 (originally published in *Annales: Économies, Sociétés, Civilisations*, 8 (1953), pp. 25–52); Cahen, 'Iḳṭāʿ', *EI*^{2}, vol. III, pp. 1088–91.

15 Lambton, 'Reflections', pp. 369–73; Cahen, 'L'évolution de l'iqṭāʿ', pp. 247, 256–9; R. Amitai, 'Turco-Mongolian nomads and the *iqṭāʿ* system in the Islamic Middle East', in A. N. Khazanov and A. Wink (ed.), *Nomads in the sedentary world* (Richmond, 2001), pp. 156, and notes 17–19.

differences were the size of the armies (the Saljuq army numbering perhaps several tens of thousands of horsemen, the Mongols probably more than a hundred thousand), the superior discipline of the Mongol troops and their obedience to the central authorities, and the greater destruction wrought by the Mongols in the conquered lands, certainly during the campaigns of conquest, and in specific areas in their aftermath. The Mongols introduced a larger scale of armies and fighting, and this in turn influenced at least some of their enemies, not the least the Mamlūks of Egypt and Syria, who were one of their main adversaries in the Middle East in the period after 1260.

Two main subjects will be investigated in this chapter: the Mongol army as first formed in the Inner Asian steppes,[16] and the Mongol army in the post-Hülegü period.[17] Brief comments will also be made regarding the size and nature of Hülegü's forces.

We can start by citing some passages from contemporary notices as to the nature of the Mongol forces while still primarily an army of the steppe, although after a generation or two as a unified, conquering empire. Thus writes John of Plano Carpini, the papal envoy to the court of the Great Khan Güyüg in 1246:

> It should be known that when the [Mongols] come in sight of the enemy they attack at once, each one shooting three or four arrows at their adversaries; if they see that they are not going to be able to defeat them, they retire, going back to their own line. They do this as a blind to make the enemy follow them as far as the places where they have prepared ambushes … When however they are going to join battle, they draw up all the battle lines just as they are to fight … Other columns of stronger men they dispatch far off to the right and the left so that they are not seen by the enemy and in this way they surround them and close in and so the fight begins from all sides … It should be known that if they can avoid it, the Tartars [=Mongols][18] do not like to fight hand to hand but they wound and kill men and horses with their arrow; they only

16 See these previous studies: H. D. Martin, *The rise of Chingis Khan and his conquest of north China* (repr. New York, 1971, of Baltimore, 1950), pp. 11–47; S. R. Turnbull, *The Mongols*, Men-at-Arms Series, 105 (London, 1980); R. W. Reid, 'Mongolian weaponry in *The secret history of the Mongols*', *Mongolian Studies*, 15 (1992), pp. 85–96; W. Świętosławski, *Arms and armour of the nomads of the great steppe in the times of the Mongol expansion* (Lodz, 1999), pp. 103–10.

17 This topic has been explored systematically in B. Spuler, *Die Mongolen in Iran: Politik, Verwaltung und Kultur der Ilchanzeit 1220–1350*, 4th edn (Leiden, 1985), pp. 30–48; D. O. Morgan, 'The Mongol armies in Persia', *Der Islam*, 56 (1979), pp. 81–96. Other relevant studies are mentioned below.

18 For the equivalence of the names Mongols and Tatars, in spite of the fact that the latter were originally a separate tribe, see the comments of J. A. Boyle, in *The history of the world-conqueror by ʿAlā-ad-Dīn ʿAṭā Malik Juvainī* (Manchester, 1958), vol. I, p. 20, n. 4.

come to close quarters when men and horses have been weakened by arrows.[19]

The mass nature of the Mongol army is noted by the Persian historian Juwaynī (d. 1283), who served the Mongols as governor of Baghdad. He writes: 'It is also a peasantry in the guise of an army, all of them, great and small, noble and base, in time of battle becoming swordsmen, archers and lancers and advancing in whatever manner the occasion requires.'[20] The discipline of the Mongol soldiers is also vaunted: 'On the day of review, also, they display their equipment, and if only a little be missing, those responsible are severely punished … Their obedience and submissiveness is such that if there be a commander of a hundred thousand between whom and the Khan there is a distance of sunrise and sunset, and if he but commit some fault, the Khan dispatches a single horseman to punish him after the manner prescribed: if his head has been demanded, he cuts it off, and if gold be required, he takes it from him.'[21]

The vast majority of the Mongol army at this stage was clearly composed of light cavalry, meaning horsemen who were lightly armoured (with armour mainly composed of cloth and leather, but sometimes with iron components, with partially metal helmets; some had iron armour), carrying bow and arrows and some basic weapons for hand-to-hand warfare,[22] and mounted on small, but sturdy steppe ponies.[23] The Mongol trooper would set off on campaign with a string of such ponies, apparently around five, in order to change mounts during both long-distance travel and battle (and perhaps provide meat also for himself and his fellow soldiers).[24] The tactic of choice was wave after wave of cavalrymen advancing while firing, and then wheeling around to permit the advance of another wave of similar troops.[25] This might

19 John of Plano Carpini [Giovanni di Pian di Carpine], 'History of the Mongols', in C. Dawson (ed.), *The mission to Asia* (London, 1980), pp. 36–7.
20 Juwaynī, trans. Boyle, vol. I, p. 30.
21 *Ibid.*, pp. 30–1. This information, derived from Juwaynī, is also found in the section on the Mongols by Ibn Faḍl Allāh al-ʿUmarī, *Das Mongolische Weltreich: Al-ʿUmarīs Darstellung der mongolischen Reiche in seinem Werk Masālik al-abṣār fī 'l-mamālik al-amṣār*, ed. and trans. K. Lech (Wiesbaden, 1968), pp. 10–11 (Arabic text), where there is more on the army's discipline. See also Carpini, 'History of the Mongols', ed. Dawson, p. 33.
22 See Carpini, 'History of the Mongols', ed. Dawson, pp. 33–5, for their armour (and that of their horses) and weapons.
23 For these horses, see J. M. Smith, Jr, 'ʿAyn Jālūt: Mamlūk success or Mongol failure', *Harvard Journal of Asiatic Studies*, 44 (1984), pp. 336–40.
24 Morgan, 'The Mongol armies in Persia', pp. 85–6.
25 Timothy May usefully compares this to the *caracole* ('charge and shoot') manoeuvre of sixteenth-century European pistol-wielding cavalry; see his 'The training of an Inner Asian nomad army in the pre-modern period', *Journal of Military History*, 70 (2006), pp. 627–8.

be accompanied by an attempt to encircle the enemy, facilitated by both the large numbers and the mobility of the Mongols.[26] The aim was to break the will and formation of the enemy by these repeated attacks, and only then to engage in hand-to-hand combat or to chase after them if they fled, in either case probably inflicting greater casualties than the previously mentioned barrages. Related to this technique was permitting encircled enemy troops to 'escape' their predicament and then pursuing them to kill and capture.[27] Another favourite tactic was the feigned retreat, during which the Mongol troops would turn around on their saddles, shooting behind them as they rode. Here the aim was to draw the enemy into an ambush, meanwhile exhausting their mounts and breaking up their formations.[28]There is nothing especially Mongol in these formations, but just a use of classic Inner Asian tactics, refined through practice,[29] efficient command and communications, discipline and large numbers. In fact, the size of the Mongol armies is noted by the sources,[30] and was certainly an important factor in their successes in the Middle East and elsewhere.[31] Certainly in the aftermath of the Mongol invasion of the region, armies tended to get larger, surely to meet the challenge of the Mongols. The Mamlūks of Egypt and Syria, in any event, had a significantly bigger army than their Ayyūbid predecessors.[32]

One adoption of a traditional Inner Asian military institution[33] was the decimal system of organisation, starting from units of 10, who were subsumed in companies of 100, which in turn were part of 'brigades' of 1,000 and these finally were part of divisions of 10,000, known as a *tümen* (in the singular).[34]

26 See the passage from John of Plano Carpini, cited above.

27 The Mongols used this tactic at the siege of Bukhārā in 1220; al-Nasawī, *Sīrat al-sulṭān jalāl al-dīn mankūbirtī* (Cairo, 1953), pp. 100–1; cf. Juwaynī, trans. Boyle, vol. I, p. 103. For this incident and additional similar ones, see May, 'Training', p. 620 and n. 5.

28 This was done at the battle of Köse Dagh in Anatolia against the Saljuqs; C. Cahen, 'Köse Dagh', *EI*², vol. V, p. 271.

29 Including the use of the massive, long-distant hunting circle (*nerge*); see Juwaynī, trans. Boyle, vol. I, pp. 27–9; May, 'Training', pp. 620–1; D. Morgan, *The Mongols*, 2nd edn (Oxford, 2007), pp. 74–5.

30 See, e.g. al-ʿUmarī, ed. Lech, p. 10.

31 See the comments in Smith, "Ayn Jālūt', p. 345; John M. Smith, Jr, 'Mongol manpower and Persian population', *Journal of the Economic and Social History of the Orient*, 18 (1975), pp. 271–99; also Morgan, 'The Mongol armies in Persia', pp. 82–8.

32 R. Amitai-Preiss, *Mongols and Mamluks: The Mamluk–Ilkhanid war, 1260–1281* (Cambridge, 1995), pp. 71–2.

33 See the comments in Smith, 'Mongol manpower', p. 298 n. 86; I. de Rachewiltz (trans. and ed.), *The secret history of the Mongols* (Leiden, 2004), vol. I, pp. 409–10, vol. II, pp. 689–90.

34 Carpini, 'History of the Mongols', ed. Dawson, pp. 32–3; Juwaynī, trans. Boyle, p. 30; al-ʿUmarī, ed. Lech, p. 11. See the discussion in Morgan, 'The Mongol armies in Persia', pp. 88–9.

Unlike earlier Inner Asian states, however, in the case of the Mongols this structure entailed the breaking up of many tribes, and men (and thus their families) were moved hither and fro. The idea behind this reorganisation was that the traditional system of loyalty and leadership was largely disrupted, permitting the erection of a framework guaranteeing more obedience to Chinggis Khan, his family and his officers.[35] Here and there, however, some tribes appear to have survived this exercise in social engineering, and continued to exist both in the period of the united empire and even during the rule of the successor states and beyond (the Oirats are the notable example, in both East and West Asia).[36] The decimal organisation of course greatly facilitated logistics, communications, and the strategic and tactical control of the troops. Whether the *tümens* actually were able to maintain their strength around 10,000 men over time remains an open question.[37] The attrition of a long-term campaign would certainly have taken its toll. Commanders of *tümens* were known, at least from the mid-thirteenth century, as *noyad* (plural of *noyan*),[38] a term which in an earlier period appears to have referred to chiefs, and later to princes.

An interesting and effective military institution of the Mongols, perhaps even their innovation, is the *tamma* system, which was used for both long-term occupation duty and long-distance campaigning. Basically, the idea was to create expeditionary forces composed of contingents from the armies of the different branches of the Chinggisid family. The concept behind this institution was twofold: first, to provide sufficient manpower for the military needs of the empire, and to spread this burden throughout the various princely appanages (*uluses*); and, second, to guarantee the unity of the imperial family by involving princes and forces from all branches in these campaigns (and, perhaps, these princes would function as would-be hostages to forestall disloyalty in the future).[39] The forces in the Middle East commanded by the

35 Morgan, *The Mongols*, pp. 79–80.

36 De Rachewiltz, *The secret history*, vol. I, pp. 164 (sec. 239), 519; vol. II, pp. 849, 852. For the later Oirats in the Ilkhanate, see D. Ayalon, 'The Wafidiyya in the Mamluk kingdom', *Islamic Culture* (1951), pp. 99–101.

37 Smith, ''Ayn Jālūt', p. 310, believes so, but cf. Hsiao Ch'i-ch'ing, *The military establishment of the Yuan dynasty* (Cambridge, MA, 1978), pp. 170–1, n. 27, as well as the remark by de Rachewiltz, in his commentary to *The secret history*, vol. I, p. 409.

38 This is the way that the term is defined by al-ʿUmarī, ed. Lech, p. 93; see the discussion in R. Amitai, 'An Arabic biographical notice of Kitbughā, the Mongol general defeated at ʿAyn Jālūt', *Jerusalem Studies in Arabic and Islam*, 33 (2007), p. 227 n. 35.

39 Morgan, *The Mongols*, pp. 82–3; P. D. Buell, 'Kalmyk Tanggaci people: Thoughts on the mechanics and impact of Mongol expansion', *Mongolian Studies*, 9 (1980), pp. 41–59; cf. D. Ostrowski, 'The *tamma* and the dual administrative structure of the Mongol empire', *Bulletin of the School of Oriental and African Studies*, 61 (1998), pp. 262–77.

Mongol viceroys Chormaghun (1229–42) and Baiju (1242–*c*. 1256) are referred to by the later pro-Mongol historian (and vizier) Rashīd al-Dīn (d. 1318) as *tamma* forces, both based in the environs of Azerbaijan.[40]

Essentially such an army, albeit a much larger one, was sent by the Great Khan Möngke with his brother Hülegü to the lands of Islam in the early 1250s. Juwaynī writes that he was sent with two out of every ten Mongol soldiers,[41] a statement which perhaps does not have to be taken literally but does clearly imply a very big army and also hints at its composition from different parts of the army. Rashīd al-Dīn gives us the name of certain princes from various *uluses*, perhaps most importantly that of the Jochids (the so-called Golden Horde).[42] The army, which was probably composed also of many Turkish nomads, may have included non-nomadic troops such as Alans from the northern Caucasus,[43] as well as 1,000 households of Chinese military technicians.[44] No less important, the officers and troops were accompanied by their families and herds.[45] Unlike Chinggis Khan's campaign of 1219 to Transoxania and north-east Iran, Hülegü's march entailed the migration of a significant section of the Mongols, as well as other steppe peoples.

Once Hülegü crossed the Syr Darya, and began campaigning in the Muslim world, first against the Nizārī Ismāʿīlīs (the so-called Assassins), then against

40 W. M. Thackston (trans. and ed.), *Rashiduddin Fazlullah's Jami'u't-tawarikh (Compendium of chronicles)* (Cambridge, MA, 1999), vol. II, p. 478. Rashīd al-Dīn does not mention here the command of Eljigidei (1248–51), who had replaced Baiju at the order of the Great Khan Güyüg (r. 1246–8) and continued into the following interregnum. With the arrival of Hülegü on the scene in the mid-1250s, Baiju and his troops vacated Azerbaijan and moved into Anatolia; P. Jackson, 'Bāyjū', *EIr*, vol. IX, p. 1.

41 Juwaynī, trans. Boyle, vol. II, p. 607; this information appears in Rashīd al-Dīn, trans. Thackston, p. 478. For a discussion of the size and composition of Hülegü's army, see T. T. Allsen, *Mongol imperialism: The policies of the Grand Qan Möngke in China, Russia, and the Islamic lands, 1251–1259* (Berkeley, 1987), pp. 203–7.

42 Juwanī, trans. Boyle, vol. II, p. 608; cf. Rashīd al-Dīn, trans. Thackston, pp. 487, 793; for the untimely end of these princes, see *ibid*., pp. 506, 511.

43 Allsen, *Mongol imperialism*, p. 208.

44 Juwaynī, trans. Boyle, vol. II, p. 608: '[Möngke] sent to Cathay [*khiṭāy*] to bring mangonel [*majanīq*] experts and naphta [*naft*=Greek fire] throwers.' A thousand of these households (*khāna*) of such specialists were dispatched. Cf. Rashīd al-Dīn, trans. Thackston, p. 478, who adds – probably gratuitously – 'crossbow men' to this list. See the discussion in T. T. Allsen, 'The circulation of military technology in the Mongolian empire', in Di Cosmo (ed.), *Warfare in Inner Asian history*, p. 278, for a discussion of this passage. The 'Cathay' referred to here must be northern China and not the Khitan people, its former rulers.

45 This statement has recently been called into question by J. M. Smith, Jr, 'Hülegü moves west: High living and heartbreak on the road to Baghdad', in L. Komaroff (ed.), *Beyond the legacy of Genghis Khan* (Leiden, 2006), pp. 111–34, who sees a much smaller Mongol army setting out with Hülegü, without herds and families, some of whom joined up with their menfolk at a later date.

the caliph in Baghdad as well as recalcitrant vassals and finally in Syria, his army was swelled by the addition of two important elements: first, the Mongol troops who had already been serving in the area, be it in north-eastern or north-western Iran; and, second, by a substantial number of auxiliaries from subservient rulers. These included Armenians, Georgians, Iranians (*tājīk* or *al-ʿajam*) and troops from al-Jazīra (northern Mesopotamia) and nearby Saljuq Rūm (Anatolia).[46] Those from al-Jazīra and Rūm, at least, appear to have been largely professional soldiers of Turkish origin, i.e. *mamlūks*, and thus cavalrymen. The Armenians and Georgians, who usually accompanied the Mongols in their campaigns into Syria, were probably a mixed force of cavalry and infantry.[47] If not professional soldiers, they were certainly highly trained militiamen. As for the 'Iranians', many of these were surely the professional soldiers of the local vassal rulers but they may have included militiamen of some type. Tājīk infantrymen were ordered to be used, at least during the reign of Ghazan (1295–1304), in guarding mountain passes and 'difficult places on the frontiers'.[48]

Some idea of the composition of the army is seen in two examples from the campaigns against the Mamlūks of Egypt and Syria, during the war which began with the Mongol defeat at ʿAyn Jālūt in 1260 and lasted for some sixty years.[49] In 1281, the Mamlūk sultan Qalawun received intelligence reports of an advancing Mongol army that numbered 80,000 soldiers and was composed of 50,000 Mongols (*al-mughul*), the remainder being Georgians, Saljuq Rūmi troops, Armenians, Franks and renegades (*al-murtadda*).[50] The Armenians, from Cilicia, and the Georgians were led by their kings. The 'renegades' may well be Muslim troops from al-Jazīra or elsewhere, even Iran (some

46 See the discussion in Allsen, *Mongol imperialism*, pp. 203–7.

47 For the role of the Armenian troops from Cilicia in Syria, sometimes even acting alone, as well as Georgians, see Amitai-Preiss, *Mongols and Mamluks*, pp. 26, 40, 54, 183, 189 (Saljuq and Iranian troops also mentioned in this campaign), pp. 195–6. On the army of Saljuq Rūm, see the comments in Cahen, *Pre-Ottoman Turkey*, pp. 230–4; for more on the Armenians, see Allsen, *Mongol imperialism*, pp. 205–6.

48 Rashīd al-Dīn, trans. Thackston, vol. II, p. 735; these troops were to be organised in units of 100 and 1,000, and were supposedly to be supported by *iqṭāʿ*s. For a discussion of local Iranian dynasties and their armies, see B. F. Manz, 'Military manpower in late Mongol and Timurid Iran', in M. Szuppe (ed.), *L'héritage timouride: Iran – Asie centrale – Inde XVe–XVIIIe siècles*, published as *Cahiers d'Asie Centrale*, 3–4 (1997), pp. 43–6. See also below.

49 See Amitai-Preiss, *Mongols and Mamlūks*, *passim*; Amitai-Preiss, 'ʿAyn Jālūt revisited', *Tārīḥ*, 2 (1992), pp. 119–50; R. Amitai, 'The resolution of the Mongol–Mamluk war', in R. Amitai and M. Biran (eds.), *Mongols, Turks and others* (Leiden, 2005), pp. 359–90.

50 Ibn al-Furāt, *Taʾrīkh*, vol. VII, ed. Q. Zurayk (Beirut, 1942), p. 215; Baybars al-Manṣūrī, *Zubdat al-fikra*, ed. D. S. Richards (Beirut, 1998), pp. 195–6. Rashīd al-Dīn, trans. Thackston, vol. II, p. 544, does not mention any of these non-Mongol forces, only the names of several Mongol officers, evidently *tümen* commanders.

sources mention soldiers from *al-ʿajam*), who would have been traitors in the Mamlūks' mind. The Franks are of unknown provenance, but could have been mercenaries, or troops from the castles of the military orders in north Syria and Cilicia. Unfortunately, there are no details of how these different contingents were used on the battlefield or subsequently behaved. The impression from the sources is that the actual fighting was mainly, if not exclusively, a cavalry affair.[51]

The second example is the battle of Wādī al-Khaznadār north of Homs in Syria, in December 1299, the one major field battle in which the Mongols were successful. We do not have here any information regarding non-Mongol (or rather, non-Mongol or Turkish) contingents. Only the names of Mongol commanders (certainly of *tümens*) are given by the contemporary Rashīd al-Dīn, who was present and provides a detailed order of battle.[52] In addition, another contemporary, Waṣṣāf, states that for this campaign, five out of every ten Mongols had been ordered out, and each of them was required to bring five mounts.[53] This is compelling testimony that the Mongols were still functioning as light cavalry, maintaining the fighting methods of their forefathers who had entered the Middle East two or three generations before.[54] Other information from this battle strengthens the view that there was a great deal of continuity in Mongol fighting methods. Originally, the Mongol troops in the centre had met the initial Mamlūk attack dismounted, apparently to improve the accuracy of their archery, but also perhaps to take cover behind their horses. Thereupon they remounted, and attacked the Mamlūks 'in the Turkish fashion' (*bar īshān turk tāz kardan*), which should probably be understood to mean the traditional steppe tactic of a unified cavalry assault, with the

51 For the battle, which ended in a Mongol defeat, see Amitai-Preiss, *Mongols and Mamluks*, pp. 187–201; cf. Smith, ''Ayn Jālūt', p. 329 n. 63; A. P. Martinez, 'Some notes on the Īl-Xānid army', *Archivum Eurasiae Medii Aeivi*, 6 (1986), pp. 159–65.

52 Rashīd al-Dīn, trans. Thackston, vol. II, pp. 645–6. This is, however, incomplete evidence. As we have just seen above, Rashīd al-Dīn provides no evidence on the various non-Mongol unit contingents that the Mamlūk sources mention for the battle of Homs in 1281.

53 Waṣṣāf, *Ta'rīkh* (Bombay, 1269/1852–3), p. 373.

54 The battle is discussed, as are the implications for the nature of the Mongol army in Iran, in R. Amitai, 'Whither the Ilkhanid army? Ghazan's first campaign into Syria (1299–1300)', in Di Cosmo (ed.), *Warfare in Inner Asian history*, pp. 220–64. A different view, holding that indeed the Mongols deliberately made a transition from 'light' to 'medium' cavalry in the first decades of their rule, is presented in Martinez, 'Some notes,' pp. 129–242, esp. p. 176. Morgan, 'The Mongol armies in Persia', pp. 90–6, also discusses the changing nature of the Mongol army *c.* 1300. Smith, ''Ayn Jālūt', tacitly assumes a continuity of the basic nature of the Mongol and then Ilkhanid army, its equipment and fighting methods.

troops letting off barrages of arrows.[55] Apparently at a later stage, when fresh Mongol troops approached, archery was effectively employed against the Mamlūk horses,[56] indicating the ongoing importance of this traditional nomadic weapon. We thus see that *c.* 1300, it appears on the whole that the Mongol armies in Iran and the surrounding countries were still based on the tactics derived from the preponderance of light cavalry.[57] While there is no explicit evidence that this is the case in the following decades, there is also no clear information that anything of substance had changed in the nature of the Mongol army. We can assume, therefore, that until the break-up of the Ilkhanate state in the 1330s, the mainstay of its army was the light cavalryman of Eurasian steppe provenance.

Originally, following the classical steppe pattern, the Mongol officers and troops in Iran did not receive salaries or other payments, except booty and occasional gifts. Perhaps even more surprisingly to those used to standing armies, the Mongol soldiers were expected to pay taxes; for the Mongol, military service was just another obligation towards the ruler. Juwaynī writes: 'It is an army after the fashion of a peasantry, being liable to all manner of contributions (*mu'an*), and rendering without complaint whatever is enjoined upon it, whether *qubchur*, occasional taxes (*'awāriḍāt*), the maintenance (*ikhrājāt*) of travellers or the upkeep of the post system (*yām*) with the provisions of mounts (*ulāgh*) and fodder (*'ulūfat*).'[58] I will just note here that *qubchur* refers to a yearly tax of a certain number of livestock that the Turco-Mongolian nomad *cum* soldier would pay to the authorities.[59]

Of course, the vast majority of the population was settled, and these continued to pay the land-tax (*kharāj*) as before. Apparently, at least as long as the khans had yet to convert to Islam, the *jizya* tax paid by *dhimmīs* was abolished.[60] In its place, however, was a bewildering array of taxes, duties and payments, often demanded on a capricious schedule, exacerbated by different

55 Rashīd al-Dīn, *Geschichte Ġāzān-Ḫān's aus dem Ta'rīḫ-i-Mubārak-i-Ġāzānī* ..., ed. K. Jahn (London, 1940), p. 128; cf. the translation by Thackston, vol. II, p. 646, where this phrase is not rendered.

56 Baybars al-Manṣūrī, *Zubda*, p. 331.

57 Certainly, this was what has been found for the Ilkhanid and Chaghadayid armies of a generation before. See M. Biran, 'The battle of Herat (1270): A case of inter-Mongol warfare', in Di Cosmo (ed.), *Warfare in Inner Asian history*, pp. 175–219, esp. pp. 205–12.

58 Juwaynī, trans. Boyle, vol. I, p. 30, with slight changes.

59 Morgan, *The Mongols*, p. 80; cf. Boyle, in his translation of Juwaynī, vol. I, p. 30 n. 12. Later on *qubchur* is used as a general term for tax or payment.

60 For the temporary reversal of this abolition during the short reign of Tegüder Aḥmad, see R. Amitai, 'The conversion of Tegüder Ilkhan to Islam', *Jerusalem Studies in Arabic and Islam*, 25 (2001), pp. 26–7.

authorities calling for various taxes. In general, it appears that the demands of the Mongol administration were quite onerous, and contributed in many places to a decline in the economy, agricultural and urban.[61]

For the Mongols, there is an often-cited piece of evidence that appears to show that radical changes were in the offing towards the end of the thirteenth century in the realm of payment and land tenure, indicative perhaps of the substantial transformation of Mongol society and with significant implications for the future. This is the passage found in the chapters devoted to the reforms enacted by his patron, the Ilkhan Ghazan – Rashīd al-Dīn writes:

> At this time [*c.* 1300], most of the soldiers had the desire for estates (*amlāk*) and [the practice of?] agriculture. Upon acquiring *iqṭāʿ* land (*milkī iqṭāʿī*), they will have reached their goal.[62]

Several scholars have accorded this passage much credence and seen it as unequivocal evidence for the sedentarisation process of the Mongols.[63] It is my opinion, however, that the evidence is problematic.[64] To start with, the edict regarding the *iqṭāʿ* was promulgated late in Ghazan's reign, leading one to wonder how much it was actually carried out by this khan and then by his successors. Second, the mention of actual *iqṭāʿāt* in the sources is few and far between, to put it mildly. Third, this institution, which is somewhat different from the *iqṭāʿ* of the Saljuqs (e.g. Ghazan's 'neo-*iqṭāʿ*' was to be allocated to common soldiers, not only officers, and could be passed on by inheritance), would not, even if implemented, have entailed the sedentarisation of the Mongols. Officers and soldiers could enjoy the fruits of agriculture without settling down and practising it. One of the most important pieces of evidence regarding land use by the Mongols and their continued practice of the pastoral

61 For Mongol taxation, see: A. K. S. Lambton, *Continuity and change in medieval Persia* (New York, 1988), pp. 199–220; I. P. Petrushevsky, 'The socio-economic condition of Iran under the Il-Khans', in *Cambridge history of Iran*, vol. V, pp. 529–37.

62 Rashīd al-Dīn, ed. Jahn, *Geschichte Gāzān–Hān's*, p. 302. The addition within the square brackets is from Morgan, 'The Mongol armies in Persia', p. 93. Cf. the translation in Thackston, vol. III, p. 731: 'since in this era most of the soldiers have a desire to own land and farm, when they get land in fief, they will have what they want'. For the text of Ghazan's *farmān* (royal order), see *ibid.*, pp. 731–5.

63 Morgan, 'The Mongol armies in Persia', pp. 91–6; but see Morgan, *The Mongols*, p. 148; A. M. Khazanov, *Nomads and the outside world*, 2nd edn (Madison, WI, 1994), pp. 251–5; J. Aubin, 'Le témoignage d'Ebn-e Bazzâz sur la turquisation de l'Azerbaydjan', in C. H. de Fouchécour and Ph. Gignoux (eds.), *Études Irano-Aryennes offertes à Gilbert Lazard* (Paris, 1989), pp. 5–17 (esp. pp. 8–9).

64 The following paragraph is a summary of the argument in Amitai, 'Turco-Mongolian nomads and the *iqṭāʿ* system', pp. 156–65.

nomadic lifestyle is provided by al-ʿUmarī, writing towards the middle of the fourteenth century:

> Every tribe has land to reside in and the descendants inherit it from the forefathers since Hülegü conquered the country. Their abodes (*manāziluhum*) are in it. They have in it crops for their substance, but they do not live by tilling and sowing.[65]

It appears, then, that there was nothing new in Mongol tribes having control over large swathes of agricultural land, from which they enjoyed at least some of its produce. This had thus nothing to do with a desire for agriculture, before, during or after Ghazan's time, and we should be wary of seeing a desire for sedentarisation in Rashīd al-Dīn's famous passage. The above parenthetical 'the desire for ... [practice of] agriculture' could probably be better replaced by 'the desire for ... [the fruits and revenues of] agriculture'. The corollary of this evidence is that if the Mongols remained nomads, there is little reason to assume that they changed their methods of warfare which were directly derived from their nomadic pastoral lifestyle. This conclusion fits the evidence presented above to this effect.

Three issues related to the Mongols remain to be briefly discussed. The first of these is the question of employment of gunpowder by the Mongols in the Middle East. While there is some evidence that the Mongols had brought some knowledge of gunpowder technology (probably as a means of causing a rapid combustion, not so much as a way to send a projectile)[66] with them into south-west Asia, it may be going too far to see this as an effective 'weapons-system' at this stage.[67] In fact, a careful analysis of a series of Mongol sieges against Mamlūk fortifications along the Euphrates and in Syria shows that there is absolutely no evidence of anything resembling gunpowder being used, and the major siege weapon of the Mongols was the *manjanīq*, literally mangonel, but surely in this context a trebuchet, both of the traction and counterweight variety.

A second matter relates to the logistic difficulties and limitations of the Ilkhanid army, a point independently raised and discussed by D. O. Morgan[68] and J. M. Smith, Jr,[69] in the framework of their analyses of the Mongol

65 al-ʿUmarī, ed. Lech, p. 95.
66 Allsen, 'The circulation of military technology', p. 281.
67 Cf. Iqtadar Alam Khan, 'The coming of gunpowder to the Islamic world and India: Spotlight on the role of the Mongols', *Journal of Asian History*, 30 (1996), pp. 27–45.
68 'The Mongols in Syria, 1260–1300', in P. W. Edbury (ed.), *Crusade and settlement* (Cardiff, 1985), pp. 229–35.
69 ''Ayn Jālūt', *passim*; John M. Smith, Jr, 'Nomads on ponies vs. slaves on horses', *Journal of the American Oriental Society*, 118 (1998), pp. 154–62.

invasions of Syria. The main thrust of their argument was that the Mongols were repeatedly stymied by the difficulties of feeding and watering their large number of horses whenever they entered Syria with a big army, particularly as they drew close to the summer, and thus had no choice but withdraw most of their forces after just a few months in the country. Related to this issue is Smith's suggestion that the Mongols were basically inferior soldiers (at least compared to their Mamlūk enemy), amateurs who made up for small horses, home-made weapons and haphazard training by mobility (facilitated by each trooper having several mounts), 'firepower' and numbers. Thus, if Syria put logistical limitations on the Mongols, they had no choice but to leave small armies (composed of inferior troops) there, after withdrawing their larger forces. The Mongols were thus doomed in their war with the Mamlūks over control of Syria. This is a compelling argument, but I feel that it is too deterministic and reductionist. Without going here into a detailed comparison of Mongols and Mamlūks, one should note that it is doubtful that with mediocre soldiers Chinggis Khan and his descendants would have conquered much of the known world. Second, logistical difficulties, while presenting real problems, were not necessarily insurmountable: the grasslands and fields of greater Syria were far from being exploited during any of the Mongol campaigns into Syria. Third, the Mongols kept coming back, so either they were unaware of these logistical difficulties, or they thought that they could be dealt with. Finally, the Mongols were not alone: the Mamlūks themselves had their own logistical problems, which could contribute – as in the battle of Wādī al-Khaznadār near Homs in 1299 – to a Mongol victory.[70]

Finally, it is worth noting that unlike the Saljuqs, and some other dynasties of Eurasian nomadic provenance (what some have called 'post-nomads'), the Ilkhans never adopted the institution of military slavery, that is, they had no regiments of *mamlūks* or anything that resembled them. Rather, they preferred to maintain large armies of mounted horse archers (supplemented by infantry and cavalry auxiliaries that included some *mamlūk* units of local rulers). This military tradition was to be basically continued by the Turcoman federations that rose in north-western Iran and the surrounding regions and also by Temür (Tamerlane) and his successors, to which we will now briefly turn.

70 See Amitai-Preiss, *Mongols and Mamluks*, pp. 214–29; R. Amitai, 'Some more thoughts on the logistics of the Mongol–Mamluk war (with special reference to the battle of Wādī al-Khaznadār)', in J. Pryor (ed.), *Logistics of war in the age of the Crusades* (Aldershot, 2006), pp. 25–42.

Armies in post-Mongol Iran

The Qara Qoyunlu (1380–1468) and the Aq Qoyunlu (1378–1508) states were based on the masses of Turcoman tribesmen in Azerbaijan and the surrounding areas. Many of these 'Turcomans' were probably Islamised and Turkified Mongols. These tribesmen appear almost completely to have continued the military traditions of the Mongols, that is, the army was composed primarily of masses of disciplined light cavalry. Much more is known about the military organisation of the Aq Qoyunlu.[71] There, the ongoing use of Mongol military terminology appears to indicate that the institutions that they described also continued, although the possibility exists of changes in the essence of these structures. The Turcoman armies, however, were smaller than their Mongol predecessors.[72] One difference, natural enough, was that the Aq Qoyunlu rulers introduced firearms, which in the fifteenth century became increasingly more available and acceptable (and thus desirable) in the eastern Mediterranean and further east. Towards the end of the fifteenth century the Aq Qoyunlu used captured Ottoman cannons, as well as having some locally cast ones for sieges. In addition, the Venetian allies of Uzun Ḥasan (r. 1452–78) 'supplied him with cannons and arquebuses and artillerymen to operate them and advise on their use'.[73] The ruler's personal guard also had handguns of some type at this time. The overall impression is, however, that Aq Qoyunlu gunpowder weapons (or their use) were inferior to those of their Ottoman rivals to the west, and certainly did not bring about a breakthrough on that front. Little is known about the payment of the Aq Qoyunlu army, beyond the granting to tribal leaders of lands over which they held fiscal and administrative control. These lands were known as *tiyūl* or *ulka*, and this usage, or at least the terms, may have continued into the Safavid period.[74]

71 This is due mainly to the excellent monograph by J. E. Woods, *The Aqquyunlu: Clan, confederation, empire*, 2nd edn (Salt Lake City, 1999), as well as the important study by V. Minorsky, 'A civil and military review in Fārs in 881/1476', *Bulletin of the School of Oriental and African Studies*, 10 (1940–2), pp. 141–78.

72 Morgan, *Medieval Persia*, p. 106, suggests that the Aq Qoyunlu army in total would have numbered maybe 100,000 men, including a sizeable contingent of infantry. Of course, a force of this size was never actually gathered, and thus a Turcoman army on a given campaign would have been smaller than many of the armies that the Ilkhans sent (or led) against the Mamlūks.

73 Bosworth, 'Army', *EIr*, vol. II, p. 503. Cf. the wording in Woods, *Aqquyunlu*, p. 114; see on p. 138 for an example of the effectiveness of Aq Qoyunlu artillery.

74 Woods, *Aqquyunlu*, p. 12. The *tiyūl* seems to have been similar to the *soyurghal* of the Jalayirids, another post-Mongol state in Iraq and the surrounding areas that is not discussed here, as well as that of the Timurids (see below). For these terms, see the comments of A. K. S. Lambton, *Landlord and peasant in Persia* (London, 1953), pp. 101–3;

The armies of Temür and his successors also come under our purview, albeit briefly, since they were active in much of Iran for many years, and controlled parts of the country for generations. Here, too, we also see a general continuation of the Mongol military tradition, the primary importance of masses of light cavalry, based on the Turco-Mongolian nomadic population of Chaghadayid Transoxania (Mā Warā' al-Nahr) and surrounding areas, especially eastern Khurāsān (including modern northern Afghanistan). As in Azerbaijan, in the eastern parts of the Iranian world the tribesmen had undergone the double transformation of conversion to Islam and Turkification. Temür himself was an embodiment of these changes. Mongol memories remained strong among the elite and tribesmen alike, and there is evidence that he himself had the model of Chinggis Khan before him. The traditional tribal leadership of Transoxania was replaced by Temür with men that he himself could trust, but the tribal structure was left more or less in place, unlike the example of Chinggis Khan. The unity of the state and discipline of the tribes were facilitated by their frequent campaigning outside the Chaghadayid homeland and the resulting booty. There is ample evidence for the importance of Iranian military and civilian elites and soldiers (including infantry) during Timurid times, in the conflicts between the Timurid scions and also involving local leaders, siege warfare and perhaps also on far-flung campaign (although the role of such formations in the campaign in Syria in 1400 is unclear).[75] Again with the Timurids, little is known of how their armies were paid. On one hand, the nomads would have maintained themselves through their pastoral economy; on the other hand, commanders and tribal leaders were granted *soyurghals*, similar to the above mentioned *tiyūls*, which entailed administrative and financial control over a region. Few details are available of how this actually worked.[76]

Lambton, *Continuity and change in medieval Persia*, p. 129 and n. 90; Petrushevsky, 'The socio-economic conditions of Iran', p. 520; see the examples and discussion in G. Doerfer, *Türkische und mongolische Elemente im Neupersischen* (Wiesbaden, 1963–75), vol. I, pp. 351–3 (no. 228); vol. II, pp. 667–9 (no. 1014). V. Minorsky, 'A *soyurghal* of Qāsim b. Jahāngīr Aq-qoyunlu (903/1498)', *Bulletin of the School of Oriental and African Studies*, 9 (1939), pp. 927–60, esp. p. 960, suggests that there is a fundamental difference between the *tiyūl* and *soyurghal*, the former being temporary, and the latter for perpetuity.

75 For the Timurid army, see: Morgan, *Medieval Persia*, pp. 84–93; B. F. Manz, 'The ulus Chaghatay before and after Temür's rise to power: The transformation from tribal confederation to army of conquest', *Central Asiatic Journal*, 27 (1983), pp. 79–100; Manz, 'Military manpower in late Mongol and Timurid Iran', pp. 43–55; Manz, 'Nomad and settled in the Timurid military', in R. Amitai and M. Biran, *Mongols, Turks and others* (Leiden, 2005), pp. 425–57.

76 B. F. Manz, *The rise and rule of Tamerlane* (Cambridge, 1989), p. 140; H. R. Roemer, 'Tīmūr in Iran', in P. Jackson and L. Lockhart (eds.), *The Cambridge history of Iran*, vol. VI: *The Timurid and Safavid periods* (Cambridge, 1986), pp. 94–5.

In many ways, the Timurid armies represent another example for the continuing overall superiority of tribal armies based on masses of mounted archers *vis-à-vis* traditional (i.e. pre-gunpowder) standing armies with large components of infantry. When Temür met the Ottoman sultan Bāyezīd near Ankara in 1402, the latter was completely defeated in spite of the general high quality of his army. But this was in retrospect the swansong of Inner Asian-style warfare: a century later, the tables would be turned, as the resurgent Ottomans would show at Chāldirān in 1514.

17

Commercial structures

SCOTT C. LEVI

From ancient times, the eastward movement of precious metals in exchange for merchandise has been a defining feature of the commercial structure of the eastern Islamic world. Sources suggest that this pattern was well established already in the first century of the Common Era, and that it continued even into the nineteenth century. For example, in his *Natural History*, the Roman author and adviser to the emperor Vespasian (r. 69–79), Pliny the Elder (23–79), complained that 'in no year does India drain our empire of less than five hundred and fifty millions of sesterces, giving back her own wares in exchange, which are sold among us at fully one hundred times their prime cost'.[1] Pliny may have been guilty of exaggerating the effluence of Roman specie to India for effect, but his assertion nevertheless suggests that Rome suffered a substantial deficit in its eastward trade. Also writing in the first century, the anonymous author of a handbook for Roman travellers in the Indian Ocean indicated that much Roman specie was exchanged for Indian textiles, available in abundance in the port of Baryagaza, in modern Gujarat.[2]

Numerous accounts report a similar pattern of trade in the early modern era. Focusing on the growing European trade with Mughal India in the seventeenth century, the Italian physician Niccolao Manucci (1639–1717) observed that the Indian export commodities in greatest demand at the time – cotton textiles, indigo, opium and silk – were all agricultural in nature. Echoing his ancient Roman predecessor, Manucci concluded that, 'for the export of all this merchandise, European and other traders bring much silver

1 John Bostock and H. T. Riley (trans.), *The natural history of Pliny*, 2 vols. (London, 1855), vol. II, p. 63. A difficulty in interpreting the notation Pliny used to identify the monetary figure has resulted in discrepancies in the various translations of this passage. Rather than 550 million, some translators have interpreted it to mean either 100 million or 50 million. The citation is found in Book 6, Chapter 26.
2 L. Casson (trans.), *The Periplus Maris Erythraei* (Princeton, 1989), p. 16.

to India'.[3] The French traveller François Bernier (1625–88) emphasised the magnitude of this trade deficit even further, asserting that 'gold and silver, after circulating in every other quarter of the globe, come at length to be swallowed up, lost in some measure, in *Hindoustan*'.[4] And while there has been a tendency to privilege the early modern maritime trade over that conducted along the caravan routes, more recent work has demonstrated considerable vitality in the overland trade as well. This is supported by the report of the French monk Raphaël du Mans (d. 1696), who compared Persia to a great caravanserai with two doors: silver entered through one in the west, only to exit through another in the east and pass into India, 'where all the money in the Universe is unloaded as if into an abyss'.[5]

Much of the Indo-Islamic commerce in the period under consideration represents a continuation of earlier trade patterns. Economic historians have tended to agree that, in general, the value of India's exports has greatly exceeded the value of its imports; that merchant groups have made up for this trade imbalance by importing significant amounts of precious metals, especially silver, to Indian markets; and that the sustained Indian demand for specie is at least partly attributable to a lack of significant precious metal reserves in Indian soil, a deficit that has provided foreign merchants equipped with gold or silver increased purchasing power in Indian markets. This chapter will elaborate upon this defining feature with the aim of introducing some of the more important factors that constituted the commercial relations of the eastern Islamic world and investigating the ways in which the commercial structures in this region developed in the period from the eleventh through the eighteenth century. While some attention is directed to important developments in the oceanic trade, for the sake of expediency, and because the vicissitudes of the Indian Ocean commercial history receive sufficient attention elsewhere in this volume, the discussion here focuses on the region consisting of India, Afghanistan, Iran and Central Asia.

Readers will note that the role of India looms large in the discussion below. This can be attributed to three factors of primary importance. First is that India was by far the most populous region under consideration. It boasted a considerably larger agrarian civilisation and, by comparison, a highly developed commercial culture. This contributed to India's roles as both the largest producer of many commodities that enjoyed high demand, and the largest

3 Niccolao Manucci, *Storia do Mogor, or Mogul India 1653–1708*, 4 vols., trans. W. Irvine (London, 1907–8), vol. II, p. 418.
4 François Bernier, *Travels in the Mogul empire, AD 1656–1668* (Westminster, 1891), p. 202.
5 Raphaël du Mans, *Estat de la Perse en 1660* (Paris, 1890), p. 192.

consumer of others. Second is that India was situated at the fulcrum of the Indian Ocean trade, which was significant well before the eleventh century and became substantially more active following the arrival of European commercial interests and their rise to a position of maritime dominance in the sixteenth century.[6] The role that Europeans played in the changing commercial structures of the eastern Islamic world – through both their own trade and their injection of vast amounts of precious metals originally extracted from the Americas – is an important component of our discussion and it will be addressed below. Third, especially from the rise of Turco-Afghan political authority in north India in the eleventh century, regional powers across the eastern Islamic world worked to encourage overland commerce and keep the trade routes secure and vibrant. Sustained efforts under the Delhi sultanate (1206–1555) and the Mughal empire (1526–1707) ensured that the considerably larger Indian economy remained connected to the markets of Afghanistan, Central Asia and Iran, and, through those regions, to more distant markets in northern Eurasia, the Near East and Europe. This subject is central to an understanding of the general commercial structure of the eastern Islamic world and it merits our present consideration.

State investment in the maintenance and improvement of trade routes connecting India with its neighbours to the north and west was a cornerstone of the Delhi sultans' economic policies. This is demonstrated quite early on by the deliberate efforts of sultans Iltutmish (r. 1211–36) and Balaban (r. 1266–87) to suppress frontier tribal groups that had been obstructing commercial traffic.[7] In northern India, state investment in trade routes involved such initiatives as building new roads by clearing paths through forests, improving roads by widening them to enable the use of wheeled vehicles, planting trees alongside roads to provide shade for travellers, digging wells, constructing caravanserais at regular intervals, providing military patrols to offer travellers protection from highway robbers and even forcing local government administrators to provide restitution to caravan traders whose goods were stolen

6 See Michael Pearson's Chapter 9 in this volume. The literature on this subject is abundant. For several recent studies, see esp. Michael Pearson, *The Indian Ocean* (London, 2003); Sugata Bose, *A hundred horizons: The Indian Ocean in the age of global empire* (Cambridge, MA, 2006); Om Prakash, *Bullion for goods: European and Indian merchants in the Indian Ocean trade, 1500–1800* (New Delhi, 2004); Prakash, *European commercial enterprise in pre-colonial India* (Cambridge, 1998); Ashin Das Gupta, *The world of the Indian Ocean merchant, 1500–1800* (New Delhi, 2001).

7 André Wink, *Al-Hind: The making of the Indo-Islamic world*, vol. II: *The slave kings and the Islamic conquest of India, 11th–13th centuries* (Leiden, 1997), p. 216.

under their watch. Successful merchants augmented state efforts by financing the construction of bridges, wells, caravanserais and more. And Muslim rulers in north India were not alone in these efforts; ruling administrators in Central Asia and Persia also appreciated the benefits to be derived from maintaining regular transregional trade with their neighbours. The high esteem for transregional traders in the fifteenth-century Timurid era is perhaps most clearly expressed by the celebrated poet, author and father of the modern Uzbek language, ʿAlīshīr Nawāʾī (1441–1501). In his work, *Maḥbūb al-qulūb* ('The beloved of hearts'), Nawāʾī differentiates merchants into three categories: first were the transregional traders, whom he respectfully designates 'real men'; these were followed by retail merchants, whom he derogatorily characterises as 'housewives'; and finally were the market sellers, whom he dismisses as 'godless liars'.[8]

There were, naturally, periods of marked decline in commercial relations. Transregional trade networks were dislocated for periods lasting even several decades by such events as the early thirteenth-century Mongol conquest of Central Asia and Iran and the mid-fourteenth-century Eurasian plague pandemic. The disruptive effects of such events cannot be overstated, and in some cases they served as catalysts for permanent structural transformations. Still, considered over the longue durée, such traumas appear as temporary disruptions followed by lengthy periods of recovery. Although it would have provided no solace to those unfortunate enough to have suffered such profound devastations, in the years following the Mongol conquests those areas of the eastern Islamic world under Mongol rule benefited from a dramatic increase in the movement of people and goods.[9] A century and a half later, the armies of the Central Asian conqueror Temür (1336–1405) also proved to be an incredibly destructive force but, as had been the case under the Mongols, trade flourished where there was peace. For example, Temür's campaigns against the Golden Horde dealt a crushing blow to the trans-Eurasian trade routes of the north, but they added considerable value to Temür's own commercial centres in the south, especially his capital of Samarqand. Thus, at the very beginning of the fifteenth century, the Spanish envoy Ruy Gonzáles de Clavijo described Samarqand as a magnificent

8 Alisher Navoiy, *Maḥbūb al-qulūb*, ed. A. N. Kononov (Moscow, 1948), pp. 42–3. See also Roziia G. Mukminova, *Sotsial'naia differentsiatsiia naseleniia gorodov Uzbekistana v XV–XVI vv.* (Tashkent, 1985), pp. 114–15.

9 See Thomas T. Allsen, *Commodity and exchange in the Mongol empire: A cultural history of Islamic textiles* (Cambridge, 1997); George Lane, *Early Mongol rule in thirteenth-century Iran: A Persian renaissance* (London, 2003).

city and vibrant commercial centre, overflowing with people, merchants and merchandise from across Asia.[10]

The evidence has generally been interpreted to suggest that the overland 'Silk Road' trade of Central Asia remained active and relatively stable through the fifteenth century. The continuity of such patterns in subsequent centuries, however, has been perceived as less certain. The interpretation most commonly embraced was summarised in a contribution to *The Cambridge history of Islam*, published in 1970, in which Bertold Spuler argued that, from the early sixteenth century, Central Asia became isolated 'and therefore led an existence on the margin of world history'. Spuler concluded, as have others writing before him and since, that the Europeans' 'discovery of the sea-route to East Asia rendered the Silk Road increasingly superfluous [and] from the threshold of modern times Central Asian history becomes provincial history'.[11]

More recently, the relationship between the rising European activities in the Indian Ocean and the overland caravan trade in the eastern Islamic world has received more attention and some much needed revision. An abundance of evidence has been produced to support the argument that the Mughal, Safavid and Uzbek rulers all exhibited a keen appreciation for the role of commerce in maintaining a healthy state. Throughout the early modern era, transregional trade among these regions continued at an escalated level, and even during times of military conflict government administrators attached to states that were otherwise hostile welcomed caravans into their territory and regularly communicated to each other information regarding commerce.[12] According to Muzaffar Alam, from the early Mughal era the overall successes in these efforts contributed to a process of urbanisation in the Punjab, Multān, Sind and the areas north of Delhi, which spurred agricultural and industrial production and the emergence of a quite impressive commercial culture in

10 Ruy González, *Narrative of the embassy of Ruy González de Clavijo to the court of Timour in Samarcand, AD 1403–6*, trans. Clements R. Markham (London, 1858), p. 171.

11 Bertold Spuler, 'Central Asia from the sixteenth century to the Russian conquests', in P. M. Holt, Ann K. S. Lambton and Bernard Lewis (eds.), *The Cambridge history of Islam*, vol. 1:, *The central Islamic lands* (Cambridge, 1970), pp. 470, 483. For a critical analysis of this scholarly trend, see Scott Levi, 'India, Russia and the eighteenth-century transformation of the Central Asian caravan trade', *Journal of the Social and Economic History of the Orient*, 42, 4 (1999), pp. 519–48.

12 Muzaffar Alam, 'Trade, state policy and regional change: Aspects of Mughal–Uzbek commercial relations, *c.* 1500–1750', *Journal of the Economic and Social History of the Orient*, 37, 3 (1994), pp. 214–19; see also Audrey Burton, *The Bukharans: A dynastic, diplomatic and commercial history, 1550–1702* (New York, 1997); Rudolf Matthee, *The politics of trade in Safavid Iran: Silk for silver, 1600–1730* (Cambridge, 1999); Willem Floor, *The economy of Safavid Persia* (Wiesbaden, 2000); and Scott C. Levi, *The Indian diaspora in Central Asia and its trade, 1550–1900* (Leiden, 2000).

north-west India.[13] In an effort to explore the general structures of this trade, the following discussion surveys a number of the more important commodities involved in the commercial exchanges across the eastern Islamic world in our period.

Commodities and commercial flows

Countless goods have been transported along the Eurasian trade routes. Still, it is possible to identify several commodities that, when considered together, constituted the major part of this commercial exchange in markets across the eastern Islamic world. Perhaps most notable are a select few agricultural products that for reasons having to do with climate and other ecological conditions were produced exclusively in India or South–East Asia. Spices, including especially pepper, cloves, cinnamon, nutmeg and mace, represent the most obvious examples. The structure of the spice trade is discussed in sufficient detail elsewhere in these volumes. It is worth stressing, however, that the European trade in spices represented only a small fraction of the commercial economy in the eastern Islamic world as a whole, and even under the Portuguese the trade in spices appears to have been substantially less valuable than the trade in other commodities, especially textiles.[14]

The large-scale exportation of Indian cotton textiles to the ancient Mediterranean has been mentioned above, and considerable evidence demonstrates that Indian textile production and its westward trade continued at considerable levels in later centuries. At least insofar as it relates to Egyptian trade in Indian cotton, the continuity of this pattern is supported by S. D. Goitein's conclusion that, in the eleventh and twelfth centuries, Egyptian cotton production 'was of no great consequence' and much of the Egyptian supply was acquired from India.[15] K. N. Chaudhuri emphasises the importance of the Indian textile trade even further, asserting that, 'before the discovery of machine spinning and weaving in Britain in the second half of the eighteenth century, the Indian subcontinent was probably the world's greatest producer of cotton textiles'.[16]

13 Alam, 'Trade, state policy and regional change', pp. 202–27.

14 James C. Boyajian, *The Portuguese trade in Asia under the Habsburgs, 1580–1640* (Baltimore, 1992).

15 S. D. Goitein, *A Mediterranean society: The Jewish communities of the Arab world as portrayed in the documents of the Cairo Geniza*, 6 vols. (Berkeley and Los Angeles, 1967–93), vol. I, p. 105.

16 K. N. Chaudhuri, 'The structure of Indian textile industry in the seventeenth and eighteenth centuries', *The Indian Economic and Social History Review*, 11, 2–3 (1974), p. 127.

India's cotton textile exports enjoyed a dominant position in many Eurasian markets, and this appears to have become considerably more pronounced during the early modern era as several factors contributed to a general increase in India's textile production. These included technological improvements, a substantial increase in India's population and, especially, the deliberate efforts on the part of the Mughal administration to promote the textile industry by providing incentives to farmers who produced valuable 'cash crops' such as cotton.[17] This provided Indian textiles a significant commercial advantage in foreign markets. Thus, although cotton had been grown since antiquity in Iran and the sedentary stretches of Central Asia, and both of these regions boasted their own cotton textile industries, neither could compete with Indian producers in terms of quantity, quality, variety and price. In the seventeenth century, the French traveller Jean Chardin reported that, although Iranians produced some cheap calico, they lacked the motivation to invest in finer varieties as they would be unable to compete with Indian suppliers.[18]

European demand for Indian textiles grew significantly in the sixteenth century, and already from the early seventeenth century the Dutch and English East India Companies became increasingly active participants in the textile trade. Still, the European share in this trade constituted only a small fraction of the total exchange. In the seventeenth century, Dutch East India Company employees estimated that annual Iranian imports of Indian cotton textiles amounted to some 25–30,000 camel loads.[19] While a portion of this was destined for the Iranian markets, much of it was a part of a long-established transit-trade that moved Indian textiles to markets in Central Asia, Russia, the Ottoman empire and other areas further afield. The magnitude of the Asian trade is illustrated by John Richards's observation that, even as the Dutch and English demand for Indian textiles increased dramatically at the end of the seventeenth century – with English East India Company imports reaching 26.9 million square metres in 1684 – the English and Dutch together still

17 Irfan Habib, 'The technology and economy of Mughal India', *The Indian Economic and Social History Review*, 17, 1 (1980), pp. 6–10; Tapan Raychaudhuri and Irfan Habib (eds.), *The Cambridge economic history of India*, vol. 1: *c.1200–c.1750* (repr. Hyderabad, 1984), pp. 167–9; John Richards, *The Mughal empire* (Cambridge, 1993), p. 190; B. R. Grover, 'An integrated pattern of commercial life in the rural society of north India during the 17th–18th centuries', in *Indian historical records commission: Proceedings of the thirty-seventh session* (Delhi, 1966), pp. 129–30.

18 John Chardin, *Sir John Chardin's travels in Persia* (London, 1927), pp. 278–9.

19 Niels Steensgaard, *The Asian trade revolution of the seventeenth century: The East India Companies and the decline of the caravan trade* (Chicago, 1974), p. 410.

employed less than 10 per cent of the 'full-time weavers and other workers in the textile sector of Bengal'.[20] Indian cloth remained widely available in markets throughout East Africa and much of Eurasia even into the nineteenth century, when global markets were flooded with the less expensive fabrics produced in Europe's industrial factories. This trade was complemented by the large-scale production and exportation of other agricultural products, including dyes, especially indigo, and sugar. Much as they did with cotton, the Mughal rulers deliberately encouraged sugar and indigo production, and both were exported in bulk to Iran, Central Asia and other Asian markets.

Indian exports were not restricted to agricultural goods, as is evidenced by the movement of large numbers of Indian slaves to markets in Afghanistan, Iran and Central Asia.[21] The early Ghaznavid and Ghūrid invasions of north India are reported to have included the exportation of tens of thousands of enslaved Indians, or more.[22] The *Tārīkh-i Firishta*, a later chronicle based on earlier sources, reports that, following the Ghaznavid capture of the Indian city of Thanesar in the year 1014, 'the army of Islam brought to Ghazna about 200,000 captives (*qarīb do sīt hazār banda*), and much wealth, so that the capital appeared like an Indian city, no soldier of the camp being without wealth, or without many slaves'. The same source also mentions that the Ghaznavid ruler Sultan Ibrāhīm (r. 1059–99) led a raid into Multān and returned to Ghazna with 100,000 captives.[23] While it is prudent to question the reliability of such later sources, it is important to note that Firishta's assertions are supported by the reports of contemporary observers. For example, al-ʿUtbī, author of the early eleventh-century Ghaznavid chronicle, the *Tārīkh al-Yamīnī*, records that, following his raids of 1018–19, Maḥmūd of Ghazna (r. 998–1030) returned to his capital with such a large number of slaves that their value plummeted to between just 2 and 10 *dirhams* each. This price was apparently quite affordable and 'merchants came from distant cities to purchase them, so that the countries of Mā warāʾ al-nahr (Central Asia), Iraq and Khurāsān were filled with them, and the fair and the dark, the rich and the poor, mingled in one common slavery'.[24]

20 Richards, *The Mughal empire*, pp. 198, 203.
21 See Scott C. Levi, 'Hindus beyond the Hindu Kush: Indians in the Central Asian slave trade', *Journal of the Royal Asiatic Society*, 3rd ser., 12, 3 (2002), pp. 277–88.
22 Cf. Wink, *Al-Hind*, vol. II, p. 126 and n. 76; Raychaudhuri and Habib (eds.), *The Cambridge economic history of India*, vol. I, pp. 89–90.
23 *Tārīkh-i Firishta* (Lucknow, 1864), pp. 27–8, 48–9. Cited in Wink, *Al-Hind*, vol. II, pp. 126–7 n. 76.
24 al-ʿUtbī, *Tārīkh al-Yamīnī* (Delhi, 1847), pp. 395–408. Cited in Wink, *Al-Hind*, vol. II, p. 126 n. 76.

Indian slaves in Afghanistan, Central Asia and Iran were used for a wide variety of purposes. These included housework, soldiering, maintaining irrigation canals, working in brick factories, serving as concubines and labouring on plantation-style farms; many others were taken into slavery precisely because they had received valuable training as construction engineers.[25] Skilled slaves were especially valuable, accounting for the common practice of conquering forces enslaving and relocating skilled artisans.[26] During Temür's sack of Delhi, for example, several thousand skilled artisans were reportedly put into bondage and taken to Central Asia. Many of these were given away as gifts, but Temür is reported to have reserved all of the Indian masons for his own construction projects in his capital of Samarqand.[27]

The exportation of enslaved Indians appears to have persisted throughout the Mughal era. Indeed, the Mughal emperor Akbar (r. 1556–1605) attempted to prohibit the practice, but his efforts met with only limited success.[28] Thus, a survey of seventy-seven entries in the *Majmūʿa-yi wathāʾiq*, the register of a *qāḍī* in Samarqand dating from 1588–92, regarding the manumission or sale of slaves reveals that slaves of Indian origin (*hindī al-āṣl*) accounted for over 58 per cent of those whose region of origin is mentioned.[29] Several decades later, the Dutch traveller Francisco Pelsaert (d. 1630) observed that, while in the process of suppressing a rebellion, ʿAbdallāh Khan Fīrūz Jang, an Uzbek noble at the Mughal court during the 1620s and 1630s, 'beheaded the leaders and enslaved their women, daughters and children, who were more than 2 lacks [200,000] in number'.[30] It was common practice to send such captives to markets beyond India's north-west frontier, far from their family support systems. Even accepting that the figures presented in the chronicles and other accounts are likely to be exaggerated, it seems reasonable to conclude that, over the years, at least several hundred thousand slaves were exported to markets in Afghanistan, Iran and, especially, Central Asia.

The Central Asian slave trade continued even to the late nineteenth century, although, during the course of the eighteenth century, Iranians

25 Mukminova, *Sotsial'naia differentsiatsiia*, pp. 123–4.
26 *Ibid.*, p. 125.
27 Beatrice Manz, *The rise and rule of Tamerlane* (Cambridge, 1989), pp. 80, 90; Raychaudhuri and Habib (eds.), *The Cambridge economic history of India*, vol. I, p. 91.
28 Abul Fazl Allami, *The Akbar Nama of Abu-l-Fazl*, 3 vols., trans. H. Blochmann (repr. Delhi, 1998), vol. II, pp. 246–7.
29 See Levi, 'Hindus beyond the Hindu Kush', p. 284.
30 Francisco Pelsaert, *A Dutch chronicle of Mughal India*, ed. and trans. Brij Narain and Sri Ram Sharma (Lahore, 1978), p. 48. See also Dirk H. A. Kolff, *Naukar, rajput and sepoy: The ethnography of the military labour market in Hindustan, 1450–1850* (Cambridge, 1990), pp. 12–14; Richards, *The Mughal empire*, p. 128.

appear to have replaced Indians as the dominant population. This transformation in the structure of the slave trade seems to have been precipitated by a dramatic decrease in the supply of Indian slaves from the early eighteenth century, as the Mughal empire decentralised and considerably fewer Indians were exported to foreign markets under the Mughal successor states. The general decline in the availability of Indian slaves motivated Central Asian slave traders to look elsewhere for a viable source to satisfy the substantial demand. From the early eighteenth century, this, along with the decline of Safavid defensive capabilities, motivated the infamous Turkmen slave-raiders to look to the numerous comparatively close, and poorly defended, Iranian cities and villages for their unfortunate victims.

It was noted above that India enjoyed a generally favourable trade balance, receiving large amounts of precious metals in exchange for exports that included a vast surplus of agricultural products and other merchandise. Willem Floor's detailed analysis of the Safavid economy similarly recognises that Iranians enjoyed bilateral commercial relations with virtually all of their neighbours, but that Iran suffered a substantial trade deficit with India resulting in a persistent effluence of silver from Safavid markets.[31] By and large, the Iranians managed to offset this deficit by exporting the larger part of their Indian imports and maintaining an overall positive trade balance with other neighbours, including especially the Ottoman territories. It should also not be overlooked that the Safavids made a concerted effort to bolster their economic position *vis-à-vis* India by developing a sizeable silk industry, the products of which were largely exported to foreign markets mostly to the west, but also in India.[32]

India did import Iranian silk and some other commodities, but, with the exception of precious metals, no commodity enjoyed greater sustained demand in Indian markets than horses. The magnitude of the horse trade was remarkable. Unless, that is, one considers that the Inner Asian steppe was home to several million pastoral nomads whose primary economic activity included the breeding and raising of horses and other livestock, both for their own use and to trade with sedentary states in exchange for foodstuffs, manufactured goods and other necessities of life. Because of their availability in large numbers and their reputation for strength and stamina, horses bred in Inner Asia enjoyed widespread demand throughout much of Eurasia.

31 Floor, *The economy of Safavid Persia*, pp. 183–96.

32 *Ibid.*, pp. 172–7. See also Matthee, *The politics of trade in Safavid Iran*, and Ina Baghdiantz McCabe, *The shah's silk for Europe's silver: The Eurasian trade of the Julfa Armenians in Safavid Iran and India (1530–1750)* (Atlanta, 1999).

The few first-hand observations of the Indo-Islamic horse trade provide some insight into the structures of this trade. In the mid-fourteenth century, the Moroccan traveller Ibn Baṭṭūṭa visited southern Russia, the territory of the Mongol Golden Horde at the time, where he observed pastoral-nomadic peoples who made their living by raising large numbers of horses, many of which were transported to India. Although his account makes no mention of the mediatory merchants responsible for moving the animals between the steppe and India, it does provide a sense of the value of this trade. According to Ibn Baṭṭūṭa, horses were available for purchase in the steppe for 50 or 60 *dirhams* each, equal to about 1 Moroccan *dīnār*.[33] He further reported that:

> These horses are exported to India [in droves], each one numbering six thousand or more or less ... When they reach the land of Sind with their horses, they feed them with forage, because the vegetation of the land of Sind does not take the place of barley, and the greater part of the horses die or are stolen. They are taxed on them in the land of Sind [at the rate of] seven silver dinars a horse, at a place called Shashnaqār, and pay a further tax at Multān, the capital of the land of Sind ... In spite of this, there remains a handsome profit for the traders in these horses, for they sell the cheapest of them in the land of India for a hundred silver dinars (the exchange value of which in Moroccan gold is twenty-five dinars), and often sell them for twice or three times as much. The good horses are worth five hundred [silver] dinars or more.[34]

Inner Asian horses were in demand throughout the subcontinent, and they reached South Asian markets both by overland routes traversing Afghanistan and by the maritime routes of the Persian Gulf. Already in the thirteenth century, Marco Polo observed that each year the rulers of Malabar received as many as 10,000 horses by sea, for which they reportedly spent some 2.2 million *dīnārs*. Shedding some light on the reasons behind the sustained demand for this commodity, Polo reported that, of the total number of horses that reached Indian ports by sea, 'by the end of the year there shall not be one hundred of them remaining, for they all die off. And this arises from mismanagement, for those people do not know in the least how to treat a horse.'[35] Some two centuries later, in 1466, the Russian traveller Afanasi Nikitin made his way to India by ship, embarking at the Persian Gulf port of Hormuz, which he

33 Ibn Baṭṭūṭa, *The travels of Ibn Battuta, AD 1325–1354*, trans. H. A. R. Gibb, 3 vols. (New Delhi, 1993), vol. II, p. 478.
34 *Ibid.*, pp. 478–9 and n. 242.
35 Marco Polo, *The book of Ser Marco Polo*, 2 vols., ed. and trans. Sir Henry Yule (New York, 1903), vol. II, pp. 340, 348–9.

described as 'a vast emporium of all the world'.[36] Nikitin was in central India for four years, much of which he spent in Bidar, the capital of the Bahmani sultanate, where he was surprised to find that the markets of the Deccan were full of horses, and that, although 'horses are not born in that country', they were widely available, having been imported in large numbers from Arabia, Khurāsān and Turkistān.[37] These numbers must have been very large indeed as Sultan Muḥammad III (r. 1463–82) was reportedly able to raise military forces that included half a million cavalry soldiers.[38] Again, even appreciating that such figures may have been gross exaggerations, the evidence suggests a lengthy commercial relationship that included: Indian consumers throughout the subcontinent; pastoral-nomadic horse breeders in Afghanistan, Iran and, especially, the Inner Asian steppe; and mediatory pastoral-nomadic tribesmen who moved the herds between regions.

Later accounts suggest that India's demand for horses increased significantly during the early modern period. Writing in the mid-seventeenth century, François Bernier reported that over 25,000 horses were brought to India annually from Uzbek territory, with additional numbers coming overland from Iran through Kandahar and from Iran and Africa by sea.[39] Jean-Baptiste Tavernier and Jean de Thevenot both independently place the figure higher, each suggesting that Uzbek mediatory merchants brought over 60,000 horses per year to Kabul.[40] Writing in the second half of the seventeenth century, Manucci asserted that every year over 100,000 horses were imported to India from Balkh, Bukhārā and Kabul, of which 12,000 went directly into the stables of the Mughal emperor Aurangzeb (r. 1658–1707).[41]

Several factors contributed to India's apparently insatiable demand for this commodity. Most obviously, from the eleventh-century Ghaznavid invasions to the nineteenth-century British Raj, horses played an important role in Indian warfare.[42] However, because of inadequate pasture-land and India's tropical climate, efforts to breed horses in India were largely

36 Afanasi (Athanasius) Nikitin, *The travels of Athanasius Nikitin of Twer*, in R. H. Major (ed.), *India in the fifteenth century*, Hakluyt Society, 1st ser., 22, part 3 (London, 1857), p. 19.
37 *Ibid.*, pp. 10, 12, 20.
38 *Ibid.*, pp. 27–8.
39 Bernier, *Travels in the Mogul empire*, p. 203.
40 Jean-Baptiste Tavernier, *Les six voyages de Jean Baptiste Tavernier, Écuyer Baron d'Aubonne ...*, 2 vols. (Utrecht, 1712), vol. II, p. 63; Surendranath Sen (ed.), *Indian travels of Thevenot and Careri* (New Delhi, 1949), p. 80.
41 Manucci, *Storia do Mogor*, vol. II, pp. 390–1.
42 See the essay on the horse trade and the importance of cavalry in medieval Indian warfare in Wink, *Al-Hind*, vol. II, pp. 79–95. See also Jos J. L. Gommans and Dirk H. A. Kolff (eds.), *Warfare and weaponry in South Asia, 1000–1800* (New Delhi, 2001).

unsuccessful.[43] Not only did horses suffer in the severe heat, but, instead of hay or the nutritious broad-leaf grasses found in the Inner Asian steppe, horses in India were fed mostly grains. The combination of poor diet, lack of adequate pasture and insufficient exercise during India's hot season caused Indian horse breeds to suffer dwarfing, and mares in India quickly became infertile, further decreasing the ability of Indian breeders to maintain their own stock.[44] The available evidence has led Jos Gommans to advance the rather conservative estimate that, on average, during the eighteenth century India's entire horse population of between 400,000 and 800,000 needed to be replaced every seven to ten years, depending on the intensity of military conflict in the subcontinent.[45] Extrapolating from this, Gommans suggests that the overland horse trade was valued at around 20 million rupees each year, amounting to 'more than three times the total of Bengal exports to Europe by the English and Dutch East India Companies together'.[46]

Shifting commercial structures from the sixteenth century

Focusing on the rising European commercial activities in the Indian Ocean has led some scholars to conclude that certain organisational structures gave the European companies an advantage over their Asian competitors. Many authors have presumed that, as European traders grew undeniably more active in the Indian Ocean commercial arena, the overland caravan trade operated by disadvantaged Asian pedlars fell into a corresponding decline, leaving large parts of the eastern Islamic world disconnected from larger global economic processes. In recent years, these views have been contested and substantially revised. Sushil Chaudhury and Michel Morineau have concluded that, during the 'Age of Competition' between European and Asian merchants (sixteenth to eighteenth centuries), neither enjoyed an inherent advantage and the vast majority of Asian trade remained in the hands of Asian merchants.[47] A considerable amount of evidence has been produced to support this thesis and suggests that, throughout our period, indigenous commercial enterprises across the eastern Islamic world remained substantially

43 Jos Gommans, *The rise of the Indo-Afghan empire, c.1710–1780* (Leiden, 1995), p. 17; Richards, *The Mughal empire*, p. 64.
44 Gommans, *The rise of the Indo-Afghan empire*, p. 73.
45 *Ibid.*, p. 89.
46 *Ibid.*
47 Sushil Chaudhury and Michel Morineau (eds.), *Merchants, companies and trade: Europe and Asia in the early modern era* (Cambridge, 1999), pp. 7–9, 300–20.

larger than European commercial interests in those markets. That is not to say that the rise in European commercial activities was in any way irrelevant. Quite to the contrary, one might also argue that no single development exerted a greater influence on commercial trends in the eastern Islamic world than the Europeans' rising demand for commodities produced in Asia, and their ability to purchase these goods with vast supplies of silver.[48] Recent scholarship indicates, however, that the increase in Europeans' commercial activities contributed to a corresponding rise in indigenous merchant networks as well.

The vast majority of the specie that European merchants brought to the Indian Ocean economy originated in the New World, where the Spanish colonisers aggressively accumulated the gold and silver that was in circulation and established an elaborate network of mining settlements to extract more. Even considering the superior value of gold, the total value of the silver was monumentally higher. There is some debate regarding the amount of American silver put into circulation from the early sixteenth century, but even conservative estimates suggest that it totalled tens of thousands of tons.[49] Others place the figure much higher, suggesting that it reached even into the tens of thousands of tons each year.[50] There is general agreement, however, that as ships loaded with specie sailed both east and west from the Americas, much of this wealth circulated around the globe and found its way into the European, Chinese and Indian Ocean economies. Contrary to the assertions by Manucci, Bernier and du Mans cited above, India was not the terminal destination for all of the specie in circulation around the globe. Indeed, the Chinese economy appears to have absorbed at least as much as India, and perhaps substantially more. But neither was the New World the sole source of silver put in circulation during this period. Japan retained an earlier position as a major silver producer and, from the early eighteenth century, the global supply was augmented by a dramatic increase in the productivity of silver mining in various locations across Russia.[51] The injection of vast amounts of precious metals over an extended period beginning in the mid-sixteenth century had profound ramifications for the economy of the eastern Islamic world and the commercial structures connecting its various regions.

48 See Andre Gunder Frank, *Reorient: Global economy in the Asian age* (Berkeley, 1998), pp. 131–64.
49 See Stanley J. Stein and Barbara H. Stein, *Silver, trade and war: Spain and America in the making of early modern Europe* (Baltimore, 2000), pp. 21–6.
50 Robert Tignor, Jeremy Adelman, Stephen Aron *et al.*, *Worlds together, worlds apart* (New York, 2002), pp. 102–4.
51 Ian Blanchard, *Russia's 'age of silver': Precious-metal production and economic growth in the eighteenth century* (London, 1989).

One product of the dramatic increase in the circulation of precious metals in this era was the development in north India of what Sanjay Subrahmanyam and C. A. Bayly have termed a 'portfolio capitalist' economy.[52] These authors argue that, from the sixteenth century, Indian capitalists began to invest heavily in agricultural production, labour and trade and, functioning in conjunction with heavily capitalised Indian banking firms, these commercial organisations became more visible in state and military finance.[53] Other authors have argued alongside this notion, adding that the increased monetisation of the Indian economy in this period – a direct product of European trade in the Indian Ocean – contributed greatly to the growth of Indian commercial firms, their ability to diversify their portfolios by expanding into new areas of the Indian economy and, from the mid-sixteenth century, their willingness to diversify geographically by seeking out lucrative commercial opportunities in under-exploited markets beyond the boundaries of the subcontinent.[54] It was noted above that the overland caravan trade appears to have grown significantly from the eleventh century. Some five centuries later, the emergence and development of several sizeable indigenous merchants networks, or trading diasporas, represent an even greater strengthening of the commercial structures of the eastern Islamic world. It should be stressed that, contrary to triggering its decline, in some important ways the rise of European commercial activities in the Indian Ocean appears to have actually spurred a corresponding increase in the overland caravan trade as well.

During the second half of the sixteenth century, heavily capitalised, caste-based Indian firms established a commercial network with diversified interests across this region. They were not, however, the only network in operation at that time. Indians worked alongside, competed against and occasionally established partnerships with agents attached to Armenian, Iranian, Central Asian, Chinese, Russian and other commercial organisations. Armenian merchants especially are known to have operated an impressive merchant diaspora from their newly adopted (1604–5) home of New Julfa, a suburb of the

52 Sanjay Subrahmanyam and C. A. Bayly, 'Portfolio capitalists and the political economy of early modern India', *The Indian Economic and Social History Review*, 25, 4 (1988), pp. 401–24.

53 *Ibid.*, p. 414.

54 Cf. Levi, *The Indian diaspora*; Stephen Dale, *Indian merchants and Eurasian trade, 1600–1800* (Cambridge, 1994); Claude Markovits, *The global world of Indian merchants, 1750–1947: Traders of Sind from Bukhara to Panama* (Cambridge, 2000); Markovits, 'Indian merchants in Central Asia: the debate', in Scott C. Levi (ed.), *India and Central Asia: Commerce and culture, 1500–1800* (New Delhi, 2007), pp. 123–51.

Safavid capital of Iṣfahān.[55] By the middle of the seventeenth century, however, the Indian merchant diaspora had grown to become the most expansive commercial network in the region, with some 35,000 merchants living in a vast, interconnected network of communities that stretched across Afghanistan, Central Asia, Iran and even into Russia. The largest Indian merchant community was by far the one in Iṣfahān, which numbered more than 10,000 Indian merchants. Other sizeable Indian communities were located in Kabul and Kandahar in Afghanistan, Bandar ʿAbbas in the Persian Gulf, Bukhārā in Central Asia and the Russian port city of Astrakhan at the mouth of the Volga, on the Caspian Sea. In addition to being the largest merchant network, these merchants were also arguably the most influential ones of the region. They were widely known for their large-scale transregional trade in a number of commodities, especially Indian textiles, and also for their deliberate and widespread moneylending activities in both urban and rural markets. A brief survey of the Indians' commercial system provides some important insights into the commercial structures that connected the various regional economies across much of the eastern Islamic world.

Even before Indian firms began dispatching agents to markets in Afghanistan, Iran and Central Asia in the mid-sixteenth century, north Indian portfolio capitalist firms had developed a reliable system to enlist agents (*gumāshta*) and prepare them to work in distant locations. Firm directors enlisted agents and put them through a lengthy period of apprenticeship, after which they advanced their agents a certain amount of capital, generally in the form of a commodity for export. Because of their established role as creditors to farmers and weavers in the subcontinent, to whom they advanced raw cotton in exchange for a portion of the finished cloth, cotton textiles were available to the firms in large quantities at below-market prices. For that reason, and because Indian cottons enjoyed considerable demand in foreign markets, cloth constituted an especially important commodity in the Indians' export trade. The agents then arranged to transport their merchandise by caravan and, after a period of travel that might last even several months, they would take up residence in a caravanserai, a hostel for merchants, where they would begin to sell their goods.

During their time abroad, the agents were trained to put their capital to work by reinvesting it in other commercial activities, most commonly in

55 In addition to the works by Matthee and McCabe, cited above, see Edmund Herzig, 'The rise of the Julfa merchants in the late sixteenth century', in Charles Melville (ed.), *Safavid Persia: The history and politics of an Islamic society* (London, 1996), pp. 305–23.

interest-earning moneylending ventures in both urban and rural markets. Because many farmers were dependent on credit to get their crops planted, agricultural loans constituted an especially important and very lucrative venture. To be sure, Indian merchants operated alongside local institutions that also provided rural credit to farmers. However, because of their training and their access to substantial capital reserves, the Indians generally proved quite competitive in rural markets. Indians also commonly purchased for cash the remainder of the harvest and arranged for its sale in regional or urban markets. The Indian merchants therefore operated at a critical juncture between urban and rural markets. They served their host societies by providing investment capital to facilitate agricultural production even when local peoples could not afford the initial investment, and also by extending a monetised economy into the countryside, which greatly facilitated the collection of taxes in cash.

As was the case for many foreign merchant groups, Indian merchants provided a number of other valuable services to their host societies. Most obviously, they are known to have purchased and arranged for the export of local production. It was observed already in the mid-sixteenth century that, rather than exporting Indian specie to Central Asia in order to purchase horses, it was common for Indian merchants to sell their Indian merchandise in Central Asia and, after settling their accounts, transport their wealth back to India in the form of horses, or another commodity (such as silver) available in Central Asia and in demand in Indian markets.[56] In various locations, Indian merchants are also known to have offered numerous other financial services to the state. These include: collecting revenue, extending credit to the nobility, financing military campaigns, managing trade routes and even serving in high posts in the states' financial administrations. The combination of these factors at least partly explains the motivation of Muslim administrators to protect the Indian merchants and ensure that they could conduct their business in a safe, predictable and reasonably agreeable social climate. For more than three centuries, tens of thousands of Indian merchants employed the vast resources of India's agrarian economy as an engine for investment in distant markets and – alongside their Bukhārān, Armenian, Iranian and other merchant-colleagues – they served as a structural bond connecting various regional economies of the eastern Islamic world.

56 Anthony Jenkinson, *Early voyages and travels to Russia and Persia* ..., ed. E. Delmar Morgan and C. H. Coote, Hakluyt Society 2 vols., 1st ser., 72–3 (London, 1886), vol. I, p. 88.

The eighteenth century

In the first decades of the eighteenth century, imperial authority rapidly deteriorated in both Safavid Iran and Mughal India. The factors behind the series of invasions, rebellions and civil wars that precipitated the political decentralisation of these two empires lie beyond the parameters of our present discussion. The period of crisis itself is germane, however, insofar as it had a significant impact on commercial structures across the region. This is especially so as the turmoil was extended by the rise to leadership in Iran of Nādir Shāh Afshār (r. 1736–47), a Turkmen military commander who had earlier served under the Safavid emperor Shāh Ṭahmāsp II (r. 1722–32). During his short reign as ruler of Iran, Nādir Shāh extinguished the Safavid dynasty, ran an extremely destructive campaign into India that culminated with his infamous sack of Delhi in 1739, and forced into submission the ruler of Bukhārā, Abū'l-Fayḍ Khan (r. 1711–47), directly contributing to the collapse of his Ashtarkhānid dynasty (1599–1747) and the end of Chinggisid rule in the region. These invasions resulted in the temporary economic dislocation of regional economies across Iran, north India and Central Asia. The economic downturn was most severely felt in north India, as the Iranian victory over the Mughal defenders brought an abrupt and acute reversal in monetary flows; in addition to killing some 30,000 people, the Iranian invaders departed with an amount of wealth estimated to have been between 500 million and 1 billion rupees.

While terribly traumatic for the north Indian economy, these events appear to have contributed to economic growth elsewhere. Upon his return to Iran, Nādir Shāh declared a three-year tax moratorium, and de-thesaurised rupees were put in circulation across much of the eastern Islamic world. Within just a few years, Central Asian traders are reported to have arrived at the newly established Russian trading fortresses in the southern parts of the empire with 'bags full of Indian Rupees'.[57] And in 1750, a new regional market was opened in Troitsk, located between the earlier markets at Orenburg and Omsk, at which prices were listed in both rubles and rupees.[58] Even in Iran, however, economic growth was muted and perhaps even reversed by the shortsighted and predatory policies that Nādir Shāh imposed on foreign merchant communities in his territory, especially the Indians. Reports indicate that Nādir Shāh used the Hindus' unprotected status as a pretence to confiscate much of

57 Gommans, *The rise of the Indo-Afghan empire*, p. 29.
58 E. Ia. Liusternik, *Russko-indiiskie ekonomicheskie sviazi v XIX v.* (Moscow, 1958), p. 12.

their wealth and property. By the time Nādir Shāh was assassinated in 1747, the Indian presence in Iran had dwindled almost out of existence.

Focusing their attention on India, Subrahmanyam and Bayly have argued that in the late eighteenth and early nineteenth centuries, the earlier portfolio capitalist economy was 'swept away' by the imposition of a colonial economy. Transformations in the commercial structures in Iran in the second half of the eighteenth century suggest that much the same could be said for the larger region. The revival of Indo-Iranian commercial relations began under Muḥammad Karīm Khan Zand (r. 1751–79), who reinstated a policy of tolerance towards foreign merchant communities in southern Iran. Soon thereafter significant numbers of Indian merchants began to return to Iranian markets and, along with Parsis and New Julfa Armenians, they resumed an active role in the mediation of Indo-Iranian transregional trade. But the most notable development in this period was the rise of British commercial activity in the Persian Gulf. British merchants benefited from their state's mercantilistic policies in both India and southern Iran, and, although they never established a monopoly on the trade between these two regions, they did manage to coerce Asian merchants – Indians, Armenians and Parsis – to use British ships to transport merchandise between the two countries. As this further developed over the course of the nineteenth century, the overland caravan trade through Afghanistan gave way to the maritime trade, fully under European dominance.

Further to the north, the disruptive effects of Nādir Shāh's invasions were less pronounced than they had been in Iran and north India and, by and large, earlier commercial structures continued unimpeded through the eighteenth century. In fact, the rise of the Indo-Afghan Durrānī state in Afghanistan facilitated Indo-Central Asian trade as the Durrānī administration welcomed Indian merchant communities, and encouraged caravan traffic and the horse trade through Afghan territory.[59] Even as late as the 1770s, the French traveller Comte de Modave reported that some 45,000 to 50,000 horses were still imported to India from Central Asia and Iran each year.[60] During the eighteenth century, Indians' commercial activities in Central Asia continued much as they had during the previous two centuries, and they demonstrated considerable financial agility by expanding their activities into emerging markets, such as those in the Farghāna valley.

59 Gommans, *The rise of the Indo-Afghan empire*, *passim*.
60 Comte de Modave, *Voyage en Inde du Comte de Modave, 1773–1776*, ed. J. Deloche (Paris, 1971), p. 327.

In the eighteenth century, as European interests continued to expand in the Indian Ocean and the Bukhārān khanate weakened and toppled, the Central Asian caravan trade remained active – and in some ways grew – along both latitudinal and longitudinal routes. It should be noted that this was a period of transition and that economic growth was inconsistent. Thus, substantial and irrefutable evidence suggests that some areas, such as Samarqand, suffered economic hardship, de-urbanisation and decline. But just as shifting commercial patterns pushed some parts of Central Asia to the periphery, other parts became linked more closely to the larger economies of India, China and Russia, and these regions enjoyed growth in commercial activity, agricultural production, population size and military strength. This is perhaps most notable in the Farghāna valley, which, from the early eighteenth century, began to benefit from its position on trade routes leading across the Tien Shan mountains and on to the markets of Qing China (1644–1911). This position became considerably more important after the Qing conquest of the province later known as Xinjiang in 1758–9 brought the frontier of the Chinese empire to the borders of the Farghāna valley.[61] Soon thereafter, the Uzbek-Ming ruler of Khoqand, Irdana Biy (r. 1751–63), accepted a nominally subordinate position to the Qian Long emperor (r. 1736–95), and the Farghāna valley was poised to become a crossroads of Eurasian trade.

Irdana Biy and his successors strategically exploited their relationship with the Qing to improve Khoqand's access to Chinese markets and reap the benefits of taxing a more active commercial exchange between China and other Eurasian markets. Within a few decades, merchants from the Farghāna valley developed a sizeable network of commercial communities in urban centres across Xinjiang.[62] Rulers of Khoqand used the resources retrieved from their eastward trade with China to improve their military power and political position in the Farghāna valley, to expand their agricultural tax base by sponsoring several sizeable irrigation projects, and also to challenge Bukhārā's commercial and regional dominance. While some corners of Central Asia were suffering decline and de-urbanisation, by the first decades of the nineteenth century, the khanate of Khoqand, centred in the Farghāna valley, boasted a vibrant commercial economy and had grown to rival Bukhārā in population and exceed it in size.

61 L. J. Newby, *The empire and the khanate: A political history of Qing relations with Khoqand c. 1760–1860* (Leiden, 2005).

62 *Ibid.*, pp. 45–50, 64–6; Saguchi Tôru, 'The eastern trade of the Khoqand khanate', *Memoirs of the Research Department of the Toyo Bunko (The Oriental Library)*, 24 (1965), pp. 47–114.

These processes were greatly advanced as Tsarist Russia pushed its frontier southward into the steppe and, from the late eighteenth century, emerged as an even greater commercial presence in the region than China. Central Asian merchant communities from Bukhārā, Khiva, Khoqand and elsewhere were eager to take advantage of the growing opportunities offered by the emerging Russian markets in the north, the trade with which was mediated through a network of frontier fortresses. Omsk was established in 1716 and followed by Semipalatinsk, 'Ust-Kamenogorsk, Orsk, Troitsk, Uralsk and others. Already by 1743, this 'Orenburg Line' of militarised commercial outposts stretched across the steppe, protecting Russian political and commercial interests from nomadic tribes and significantly advancing Russia's trade. In the early nineteenth century, as the merchants of Khoqand directed their attention to the growing trade with Russia, rulers redirected their territorial ambitions to the north and west, where they conquered Tashkent and reached even as far as Aq Masjid (modern Kyzyl Orda, in Kazakhstan), a trading post settlement where, a few years later, Khoqand would build a fortress to protect its quickly growing trade with Russia. Drawn by Russian silver, furs and manufactured goods, merchants came from as far away as India and the Ottoman empire leading hundreds of camels loaded with spices, bricks of tea, cotton and silk textiles, Kashmiri shawls and other commodities in great demand in the markets of Moscow, St Petersburg and elsewhere in Europe. In some ways, these commercial structures remained in place even to the end of the nineteenth century, when the expansion of Russian colonial authority across Central Asia brought that region too under a colonial economy.

18

Transmitters of authority and ideas across cultural boundaries, eleventh to eighteenth centuries

MUHAMMAD QASIM ZAMAN

There is much that the *ʿulamāʾ* of the eastern Islamic lands shared, in terms of their conceptions of the scholarly tradition and of the practices constitutive of it, with religious scholars elsewhere and, despite the transformations they have undergone since the nineteenth century, many of these conceptions and practices have continued to characterise their scholarly culture.[1] What are these practices? In what directions did they evolve during the centuries and in some of the regions with which this volume is concerned? How was the sense of a tradition, and of religious authority, articulated through them? These are among the questions this broad overview of the Islamic scholarly culture, and of those contributing to it, seeks to address.[2]

The *ʿulamāʾ*'s scholarly endeavours during much of the period which is the subject of this volume have often been viewed as a 'sterile commentarial literature'; and it is not just Western scholars of an earlier generation but also Muslim modernists and Islamists of colonial and post-colonial Muslim societies who have often concurred with this judgement.[3] The *ʿulamāʾ*'s own rhetoric during these

1 Cf. Muhammad Qasim Zaman, *The ulama in contemporary Islam: Custodians of change* (Princeton, 2002).

2 "*Ulamāʾ*" refers here, primarily though not exclusively, to scholars of *ḥadīth* and law as well as exegetes of the Qurʾān, grammarians and lexicographers, and theologians. It was common for the *ʿulamāʾ* during these centuries to have Sufi affiliations but, though we will touch upon this aspect of the *ʿulamāʾ*'s culture, it is not central to the discussion here. The primary focus of this chapter is, moreover, on the Sunnī rather than the Shīʿī religious scholars.

3 The phrase quoted here is that of Fazlur Rahman (d. 1408/1988), one of the most sophisticated Muslim modernists of the twentieth century and himself a scholar of medieval Islamic philosophy and law. See his *Islam and modernity: Transformation of an intellectual tradition* (Chicago, 1982), p. 63. And cf. Louis Gardet, 'Religion and culture', in P. M. Holt, Ann K. S. Lambton and B. Lewis (eds)., *The Cambridge history of Islam*, 2 vols. (Cambridge, 1970), vol. II, pp. 569–603, for an overview of the 'extremely rich and

centuries often did much to lend credence to the view that members of this scholarly culture were but a pale reflection of incomparably superior predecessors. The comment of Mullā ʿAlī al-Qārī (d. 1014/1605) – a scholar of *ḥadīth* and law from Herat who later settled in Mecca – concerning a famous *ḥadīth* report which promises a religious revival every hundred years was not atypical. 'Knowledge is continually in decline from year to year, just as ignorance is constantly making progress,' he noted, and then went on to observe: 'indeed, the advancement of the scholars of our time is only a function of the decline of knowledge in our age'.[4]

Not all *ʿulamāʾ* were equally reticent, however, in denying that they might compare favourably with earlier figures. As Shāh Walī Allāh Dihlawī (d. 1176/1762), one of the most important Indian thinkers of the twelfth/eighteenth century, had remarked in concluding his best-known book, *Ḥujjat Allāh al-bāligha*, the *generality* of people living in an earlier age, namely one closer to the emergence of Islam, are better than those of later generations, but not all are inferior to their forebears, whose generations were not lacking in their sinners and their hypocrites; and, in any case, as the Prophet had said, his 'community is like rain, whose first drops cannot be said to be better than its last'.[5] Even ʿAlī al-Qārī, in the same context in which he had made his caustic remarks about the inadequacy of his contemporaries, had also observed that the periodic revival promised by the Prophet did not necessarily refer to the work of a single individual. As ʿAlī al-Qārī understood it, this renewal was a 'cumulative matter' (*amr iḍāfī*) and one that consisted of the activities of a group of people. 'Each member of the group helps, in a particular land, to revive one or more of the religious sciences through his speech and writing, thus becoming the cause of their preservation, of saving them from extinction until God so decrees.'[6]

Despite professions to the contrary, ʿAlī al-Qārī's view does not signal any lack of confidence in the *ʿulamāʾ*'s abilities to combat an allegedly chronic decline. The period with which this volume is concerned – and not just its earlier but also its later centuries – was an age of rich scholarly activity, of the emergence and diffusion of new institutions, of the expansion of Islam in, *inter*

complex collection of disciplines' in medieval Islam which concludes, however, with the observation that '[f]rom the ninth/fifteenth century onwards, the "religious sciences" scarcely developed at all' (*ibid*., pp. 600, 603).

4 Mullā ʿAlī b. Sulṭān al-Qārī, *Mirqāt al-mafātīḥ sharḥ Mishkāt al-maṣābīḥ*, ed. Ṣ. M. J. al-ʿAṭṭār, 10 vols. (Beirut, 1992), vol. I, p. 507. On the *ḥadīth* in question, see Ella Landau-Tasseron, 'The "cyclical" reform: A study of the *mujaddid* tradition', *Studia Islamica*, 70 (1989), pp. 79–117.

5 Shāh Walī Allāh Dihlawī, *Ḥujjat Allāh al-bāligha*, ed. S. Sābiq, 2 vols. (Cairo, 1964), vol. II, pp. 885–6. On this *ḥadīth*, see A. J. Wensinck, *Concordance et indices de la tradition musulman*, 8 vols., 2nd edn (Leiden, 1992), vol. VI, p. 241 (s.v. *m-ṭ-r*).

6 ʿAlī al-Qārī, *Mirqāt*, vol. I, p. 507.

alia, South and South-East Asia, and of multifaceted interaction between these new lands and older centres of Islamic learning. This chapter does not seek to provide any comprehensive account of these developments, let alone to assess the relative 'originality' of particular scholars or to evaluate their own or later claims about a pervasive intellectual decline. And though the examples cited primarily relate to the scholars of *ḥadīth* and of law, this is not a survey of developments in these areas either.[7] The concern here is, rather, to examine some of the discourses and practices through which, and the contexts in which, the scholarly tradition was cultivated in what *ʿulamāʾ* like ʿAlī al-Qārī clearly recognised as a 'cumulative' endeavour. How religious authority was asserted through these discourses and practices is among the central questions we would address in this chapter.

Ḥadīth scholarship in the eastern Islamic lands

All six of the collections of *ḥadīth* that carry the greatest authority in Sunnī Islam were compiled by third–fourth/ninth–tenth-century scholars from north-east Iran and Central Asia.[8] There were many paths along which scholarship in *ḥadīth* had already developed by this time, and it would continue to do so. It took several centuries for the works compiled by al-Bukhārī (d. 256/870), Muslim (d. 261/875), Ibn Māja (d. 273/887), Abū Dāwūd (d. 275/889), al-Tirmidhī (d. 279/892) and al-Nasāʾī (d. 303/915) to themselves be recognised as the authoritative 'Six Books',[9] and other collections of *ḥadīth* continued to be produced long after they had come to be so accepted. In a traditional scholarly culture, the very act of reordering well-recognised and authoritative materials was itself no small accomplishment, for the result, if accepted, could signify new connections among well-established themes, topics and disciplines, new foci of debate, changed emphases in scholarly discourse and, not least, different ways of addressing new pedagogical needs and styles; it also served, of course, to reaffirm and extend the authority of the work(s) in which this new scholarship was anchored. The *Mashāriq al-anwār* of

7 For an overview of developments in the history of Islamic law, see *The new Cambridge history of Islam*, vol. 4, Chapter 4.

8 Roy Mottahedeh, 'The transmission of learning: The role of the Islamic north-east', in N. Grandin and M. Gaborieau (eds.), *Madrasa: La transmission du savoir dans le monde muṣūlman* (Paris, 1997), pp. 63–72.

9 Ignaz Goldziher dates the general, though hardly unqualified, recognition of the Six Books to the seventh/thirteenth century. See his *Muslim studies*, trans. C. R. Barber and S. M. Stern, 2 vols. (London, 1971), vol. II, pp. 240–3. The works of al-Bukhārī and Muslim had come to be widely recognised as authoritative in Sunnī circles by the beginning of the fifth/eleventh century. See Jonathan Brown, *The canonization of al-Bukhārī and Muslim: The formation and function of the Sunnī ḥadīth canon* (Leiden, 2007).

al-Ṣaghānī (d. 650/1252) – a scholar who was born in Lahore, in northern India, and died in Baghdad – is based, for instance, on *ḥadīth* reports contained in the collections of al-Bukhārī and Muslim. Unlike these collections, it is a highly concise work which would have lent itself to easy memorisation and would have found its way in places where the larger collections might simply be inaccessible. The Ḥanafīs had lagged far behind the Shāfiʿīs in recognising the canonical authority of al-Bukhārī and Muslim and, with his *Mashāriq al-anwār*, al-Ṣaghānī was among the first Ḥanafīs to contribute significantly in that direction.[10] But al-Ṣaghānī's work performed other functions, too. He was an eminent lexicographer,[11] and the *Mashāriq al-anwār* is a veritable manual of instruction in the Arabic linguistic sciences, illustrated with well-chosen examples from the two authoritative collections of *ḥadīth*.[12] These linguistic sciences occupied an important place in the pedagogical concerns of the madrasas that had begun to emerge in Muslim societies from the late fourth/tenth century; and it is not difficult to understand the tremendous popularity of this work in the milieu of the madrasa, to which the numerous commentaries on it bear ample testimony.[13]

For all their skill in straddling several disciplines and their assistance in the acquisition of an essential grounding in key disciplines, compendia like al-Ṣaghānī's would, however, have done little to satisfy those who saw the study of *ḥadīth* as more than a crucial milestone on the path to a juristic training, and who sought, rather, to anchor their scholarly endeavours, their piety and their authority in *ḥadīth* itself. Their scholarship, in turn, produced new and, in some cases, extremely large collections of *ḥadīth*, new commentaries on standard collections and, not least, further contributions to well-worn genres concerned with evaluating the credentials of the transmitters of *ḥadīth*. There were times when such multifaceted *ḥadīth* scholarship was especially vibrant. Some modern observers have examined instances of a renewed attention to *ḥadīth*, especially in scholarly circles in the Ḥijāz, during the eleventh/seventeenth and twelfth/eighteenth centuries, and have professed to see in them the early origins of modern and global Islamic 'reform' and 'revival'.[14] Our

10 Brown, *Canonization*, p. 226.

11 *EI*[2] 'al-Ṣaghānī' (R. Baalbakki).

12 Raḍī al-dīn al-Ḥasan b. Muḥammad al-Ṣāghānī, *Mashāriq al-anwār* (Constantinople, AH 1329).

13 Ḥājjī Khalīfa, *Kashf al-ẓunūn*, ed. Ş. Yaltkaya and R. Bilge, 2 vols. (Istanbul, 1972), pp. 1688–90.

14 See, for example, John O. Voll, 'Hadith scholars and tariqahs: An ulama group in the 18th century Haramayn and their impact in the Islamic world', *Journal of Asian and African Studies*, 25 (1980), pp. 264–73; Voll, ''Abdallah ibn Salim al-Basri and 18th century ḥadīth scholarship', *Die Welt des Islams*, 42 (2002), pp. 356–72; Azyumardi Azra, *The origins of Islamic reformism in Southeast Asia: Networks of Malay-Indonesian and Middle Eastern 'ulamā' in the seventeenth and eighteenth centuries* (Honolulu, 2004). For a critique of the hypothesis that posits the shared

interest here is not in the genealogy of such revivalism, however, but rather in considering how *ḥadīth* scholarship was a major site on which religious authority was constituted and put on display. This is best illustrated, as are changing orientations within such scholarship, with reference to the work of a number of South Asian scholars.

Among the figures who came to exercise a major influence on the development of *ḥadīth* studies in India was Shaykh ʿAlī al-Muttaqī (d. 975/1567), a Chishtī Sufi from Burhānpur in the Deccan who had grown up in Gujarat in western India but spent much of his scholarly career in Mecca.[15] Chishtī Sufis of India were often viewed with considerable misgivings for certain practices – notably a pronounced attachment to devotional music (*samāʿ*) – that some other Sufis and many jurists saw as only tenuously sanctioned by Islamic norms. Al-Muttaqī never relinquished the Ṣūfī path, but he devoted considerable energy to firmly anchoring Ṣūfī thought and practice in what he viewed as authoritative *sharīʿa* norms. *Ḥadīth* scholarship was, to him, the principal means of doing so. His best-known work is the *Kanz al-ʿummal*, a monumental collection of *ḥadīth* reports that condenses and reorganises three collections of *ḥadīth* produced by the famous Egyptian scholar al-Suyūṭī (d. 911/1505).[16] Unlike al-Suyūṭī's alphabetical listing of *ḥadīth*, but like the compilers of the Six Books, al-Muttaqī compiled his *ḥadīth* reports by juridical topic,[17] subsequently producing an abridged version of this collection to further facilitate its use.[18] The larger concern in all this was to reinvigorate the study of *ḥadīth* in both Sufi and juristic circles, and thereby to reorient both towards a firmer grounding in *ḥadīth*. The normative example of the Prophet was the yardstick by which the claims and practices of the Sufis were to be measured; and Sufi practices such as *samāʿ*, as well as the extravagant claims of not a few of his Ṣūfī contemporaries, were found unacceptable by this measure.[19]

origins of modern Islamic revivalism in twelfth/eighteenth-century Ḥijāzī study circles, cf. Ahmad Dallal, 'The origins and objectives of Islamic revivalist thought, 1750–1850', *Journal of the American Oriental Society*, 113, 3 (1993), pp. 341–59.

15 For a detailed discussion of the life and thought of ʿAlī al-Muttaqī, see Scott Kugle, 'In search of the centre: Authenticity, reform and critique in early modern Islamic sainthood', Ph.D. dissertation (Duke University, 2000), esp. pp. 336–584.

16 The three collections are: *Jamʿ al-jawāmiʿ*; *al-Jāmiʿ al-ṣaghīr*; and *Zawāʾid al-jāmiʿ al-ṣaghīr*. All three are included in Jalāl al-dīn al-Suyūṭī, *Jāmiʿ al-aḥādīth*, ed. ʿA. A. Ṣaqr and A. ʿAbd al-Jawwād, 21 vols. (Beirut, 1994).

17 See ʿAlāʾ al-dīn ʿAlī al-Muttaqī, *Kanz al-ʿummāl fī sunan al-aqwāl waʾl-afʿāl*, 18 vols. (Aleppo, 1969), vol. I, p. 3.

18 ʿAlī al-Muttaqī, *Muntakhab Kanz al-ʿummāl*, 8 vols. (Beirut, 1990).

19 On al-Muttaqī's rejection of *samāʿ*, see Kugle, 'In search of the centre', pp. 415–19; for daring efforts to counter the claims of other Sufis, see *ibid.*, pp. 467–501.

But there were other targets as well. Al-Muttaqī lived at a time when the Islamic calendar was close to completing its first millennium, and this had given rise to messianic expectations in India and elsewhere and to those claiming to fulfil them. It was *ḥadīth* scholarship that offered him the resources with which to deflate such claims, for instance by showing that they were either entirely lacking a basis in the reported teachings of the Prophet or, at least, that reports to that effect failed to withstand critical scrutiny.[20] Significantly, however, such sober scholarship did not deny him opportunities for his own, alternative, claims to authority; and these claims, like those of al-Suyūṭī before him, were not modest. Al-Muttaqī argued, for instance, that, unlike the jurists, scholars of *ḥadīth* could plausibly claim to have *improved upon* the work of otherwise authoritative predecessors.[21] He is also reported to have seen Muḥammad in a dream, in which the Prophet informed him that he – al-Muttaqī – was, in fact, the most virtuous person of his age.[22]

ʿAlī al-Muttaqī's circle of students and disciples counted many distinguished figures. He was himself a student of the noted Egyptian *ḥadīth*-scholar Ibn Ḥajar al-Haytamī (d. 974/1567), though the latter acknowledged al-Muttaqī as his own Ṣūfī master.[23] The aforementioned ʿAlī al-Qārī was also a student of al-Muttaqī, as was Muḥammad b. Ṭāhir Patanī (d. 986/1578) of Gujarat, the 'king of the scholars of *ḥadīth*' best known for works on transmitters of *ḥadīth* reports and especially on fabrications in *ḥadīth*.[24] So far as *ḥadīth* scholarship in India is concerned, however, the most prominent scholar to emerge from this circle was ʿAbd al-Ḥaqq Muḥaddith (d. 1052/1642), a student of one of al-Muttaqī's disciples in Mecca.

Among many other works, ʿAbd al-Ḥaqq is the author of two commentaries on the *Mishkāt al-maṣābīḥ*, a highly popular collection of *ḥadīth* compiled by Walī al-dīn of Tabrīz (d. 737/1336). The Preface to the Arabic commentary illustrates well some of the many overlapping ways in which religious authority might be articulated through *ḥadīth* and especially through the discursive medium of the commentary. ʿAbd al-Ḥaqq notes at the outset that the most noble of the religious sciences are Qurʾānic exegesis and *ḥadīth* 'for they are ends in themselves, whereas all other forms of knowledge are only means to them'.[25] This

20 *Ibid.*, esp. pp. 343–6, 517–59.
21 *Ibid.*, p. 549.
22 ʿAbd al-Qādir al-ʿAydarūs, *al-Nūr al-sāfir ʿan akhbār al-qarn al-ʿāshir*, ed. A. Ḥālū, M. al-Arnāʾūṭ and A. al-Būshī (Beirut, 2001), pp. 421–2.
23 Kugle, 'In search of the centre', pp. 381–2, 385–6.
24 On Muḥammad Ṭāhir, see al-ʿAydarūs, *al-Nūr al-sāfir*, pp. 475–6; Kugle, 'In search of the centre', pp. 561–73.
25 ʿAbd al-Ḥaqq Dihlawī, *Lamaʿāt al-tanqīḥ fī sharḥ Mishkāt al-maṣābīḥ*, ed. M. ʿUbayd Allāh, 4 vols. (Lahore, 1970), vol. I, p. 12.

would seem to be an unproblematic assertion, given that the Qur'ān and the *ḥadīth* are the foundational sources of Islamic law. In the Indian context, however, the systematic study of *ḥadīth* was anything but well established in Islamic higher learning. It was Islamic law and the rational sciences (*al-ʿulūm al-ʿaqliyya*) that held pride of place there (on this, see below).[26] The importance of the study of *ḥadīth* needed to be argued rather than taken for granted, and ʿAbd al-Ḥaqq saw it as his calling to do so. Indeed, as he notes in this Preface, he had been sent back to India by his teacher in Mecca, ʿAbd al-Wahhāb al-Makkī (himself a student of ʿAlī al-Muttaqī), precisely 'to serve this noble science [sc. *ḥadīth*]'.[27]

Once back in India, ʿAbd al-Ḥaqq embarked on a commentary on the *Mishkāt al-maṣābīḥ* in the Persian language in order to make this work broadly accessible.[28] He soon realised, he says, that many topics were unsuited to being expressed in a Persian commentary, and therefore simultaneously began an Arabic commentary on the *Mishkāt* for a more select audience:

> The two proceeded parallel to each other, but also in competition with each other. At times, the Persian [commentary] would lead because it had been commenced earlier; but at others, the Arabic [commentary] would catch up by virtue of [its importance as] encompassing principles of legal theory and matters of substantive law (*al-uṣūl wa'l-furūʿ*). At yet other times, [the Arabic commentary] would dominate [the Persian] on account of its exalted status, and because of my own partiality towards it in view of its suitability to the intellect of many among [my] companions.[29]

Needless to say, this is not merely an explanation of why he needed to write two commentaries or why the Arabic commentary was completed before its Persian counterpart; it also illustrates the importance of language to articulations of authority. Arabic and Persian were both cosmopolitan languages, of course, and major works of religious scholarship were produced not just in Arabic but also in Persian. During the centuries with which this volume is concerned, mystical, literary, ethical and scientific works had increasingly come to be written in Persian.[30] Yet even when particular works showed

26 Cf. ʿAbd al-Ḥayy al-Ḥasanī, *al-Thaqāfa al-Islāmiyya fi'l-Hind* (Damascus, 1958), pp. 11–17.

27 ʿAbd al-Ḥaqq, *Lamaʿāt al-tanqīḥ*, vol. I, p. 13. On ʿAbd al-Ḥaqq and his relationship with ʿAbd al-Wahhāb, see Scott Kugle, 'ʿAbd al-Ḥaqq Dihlawī, an accidental revivalist: Knowledge and power in the passage from Delhi to Makka', *Journal of Islamic Studies*, 19 (2008), pp. 196–246.

28 ʿAbd al-Ḥaqq Dihlawī, *Ashiʿʿat al-lamaʿāt*, 4 vols. (Sukkar, Pakistan, 1976).

29 ʿAbd al-Ḥaqq, *Lamaʿāt al-tanqīḥ*, vol. I, p. 14.

30 On scientific writings in Persian, cf. Ekmeleddin İhsanoğlu, 'Ottoman science: The last episode in Islamic scientific tradition and the beginning of European scientific tradition', in Ekmeleddin İhsanoğlu, *Science, technology and learning in the Ottoman empire* (Aldershot, 2004 [repr. as article no. 3, original pagination]), pp. 11–48, at 20–7; on the

unmistakable signs of having been produced in the eastern Islamic lands,[31] Arabic remained (and, among the *ʿulamāʾ* of South Asia and Iran, has often continued to be) the language through which one's scholarly credentials were established, the language that offered – as it clearly did to ʿAbd al-Ḥaqq – the best prospects for recognition beyond one's own region and for participation in the trans-cultural scholarly tradition. Conversely, the Persian commentary was a means not only of trying to reach a larger audience within the Indian Muslim circles, but also of making a work like the *Mishkāt* part of *local* Islamic knowledge in India.[32]

A century later, Shāh Walī Allāh of Delhi would continue to build on earlier advances in the study of *ḥadīth*; like ʿAbd al-Ḥaqq, he, too, had acquired some of his scholarly learning in the Ḥijāz and he, too, wrote his major works in both Arabic and Persian. But if he shared much with ʿAbd al-Ḥaqq and, indeed, with ʿAlī al-Muttaqī in his scholarly orientation and in the effort to anchor legal norms and Ṣūfī doctrines in the study of *ḥadīth*, his work again reveals distinctive emphases. These are of interest, of course, for what they tell us about Walī Allāh's thought, but their primary significance in the present context lies in illustrating continuing shifts in otherwise highly formalised styles of discourse and constructions of authority attached to such shifts.

ʿAbd al-Ḥaqq had sought not only to promote the study of *ḥadīth* in India but also to defend the norms of the Ḥanafī school of law (*madhhab*) in its terms.[33] Walī Allāh, for his part, was unusual among the north Indian scholars of his age in the *lack* of his attachment to the Ḥanafī school of law and, indeed for what might be characterised as a juristic ecumenism. He continued to adhere to the Ḥanafī *madhhab*, but he expressed great admiration for the norms of the Shāfiʿī school for what he saw as their close concordance with *ḥadīth*, and he was an avid admirer of the *Muwaṭṭāʾ* of Mālik b. Anas (d. 179/795), the eponymous founder of the Mālikī *madhhab*. To Walī Allāh, *ḥadīth* scholarship was a means not of defending a particular *madhhab*, but of trying to reconcile their sometimes

importance of Persian as the language of ethical discourses and of administration in Mughal India, see Muzaffar Alam, *The languages of political Islam: India, 1200–1800* (Chicago, 2004).

31 For instance, references to the scholars of Samarqand, Balkh and Bukhārā are ubiquitous in the *Fatāwa ʿĀlamgīriyya* – commonly known as *al-Fatāwa al-Hindiyya* – a monumental juridical work produced under royal patronage in India in the seventeenth century. Words and sentences in Persian are also liberally strewn throughout the work. Yet the language of this work remains Arabic. See *al-Fatāwa al-Hindiyya fi madhhab al-imām al-aʿẓam Abī Ḥanīfa al-Nuʿmān*, 6 vols. (Beirut, n.d. (1973; repr. of the Bulaq edn, AH 1310)).

32 For a similar point, though in the context of Islamic scholarship in seventeenth-century eastern China, see Zvi Ben-Dor Benite, *The Dao of Muhammad: A cultural history of Muslims in late imperial China* (Cambridge, MA, 2005), pp. 79–82.

33 ʿAbd al-Ḥaqq, *Lamaʿāt al-tanqīḥ*, vol. I, pp. 17–18.

acrimonious differences. And it was in the *Muwaṭṭāʾ*, a collection of legal reports predating the Six Books and reflecting the views and practices of the early jurists of the Prophet's adopted home, Medina, that he found the best prospects for doing so. Walī Allāh considered the *Muwaṭṭāʾ* – on which he wrote commentaries in both Arabic and Persian – as the single most authoritative work after the Qurʾān,[34] as well as the earliest extant work with a continuous chain of transmission.[35] The Six Books of *ḥadīth* were, to him, in the nature of commentaries on the *Muwaṭṭāʾ*[36] and the same was true of the four Sunnī schools of law.[37] Indeed, to the degree that particular forms of *ijtihād* – in the sense of 'ascertaining the rulings of the *sharīʿa* from its detailed proofs and the deriving and rearranging of these rulings … if only according to the instructions of the founder of [one's own] school of law' – were still possible in his day, the resources of the *Muwaṭṭāʾ* were the means of undertaking them.[38]

Neither Walī Allāh's concern to keep paths to *ijtihād* open nor his juristic ecumenism suffices as an explanation of his devotion to the *Muwaṭṭā*. For the viability of *ijtihād* was scarcely contingent upon this, or any other, work in particular, as Walī Allāh's own discussion of *ijtihād* elsewhere makes clear;[39] and privileging the authority of Mālik's famous work in a land where few Mālikīs were to be found would not have struck his Indian contemporaries as an ecumenical gesture.[40] The *Muwaṭṭāʾ*, however, is the foundational text of a *madhhab* which accords especial importance to considerations of public interest or the common good (*maṣlaḥa*). It is likely that such considerations, which are central to Walī Allāh's religious thought, had drawn him to Mālik's work.[41] But Walī Allāh's invocation of the authority of the *Muwaṭṭāʾ* in a non-Mālikī, Indian, context may also be seen as an assertion of his *own* authority. He was not content to rearrange the contents of an earlier work, or to write elaborate commentaries on it, as he did in the case of the

34 Walī Allāh al-Dihlawī, *Musawwā Muṣaffā, sharḥ Muwaṭṭāʾ imām Mālik*, 2 vols. (Karachi, n.d.; repr. of the Delhi AH 1346 edn), p. 6. The top section of each page in this edition contains Walī Allāh's Arabic commentary, *al-Musawwā*, and the bottom page comprises the more expansive Persian commentary, *Muṣaffā*. All references are to the *Musaffā* unless otherwise noted.

35 *Ibid.*, p. 8.

36 *Ibid.*, p. 7.

37 *Ibid.*, p. 8 (*al-Musawwā*).

38 *Ibid.*, pp. 10–11.

39 Cf. Shāh Walī Allāh, *ʿIqd al-jīd fī aḥkām al-ijtihād waʾl-taqlīd* (Cairo, AH 1385).

40 There was a renewed interest in the *Muwaṭṭāʾ* in the Ḥijāz as well, where Walī Allāh had continued his studies. Cf. Voll, ''Abdallah ibn Salim al-Basri', p. 361. But even this does not quite explain his zealous invocation of the *Muwaṭṭāʾ* in the Indian context.

41 See, in particular, Walī Allāh, *Ḥujjat Allāh al-bāligha*; also cf. Marcia K. Hermansen, *The conclusive argument from God* (Leiden, 1996), pp. xvi–xvii.

*Muwaṭṭā*ʾ.[42] In a move that would have astonished the more conservative among his fellow *ʿulamāʾ* in India, Walī Allāh sought, in effect, to go beyond the Six Books, and thereby to transcend the long history of commentary and debate tied to them as well as to the school of law dominant in India. The task of reorienting legal norms in the light of the Prophet's normative example required a new beginning, with the *Muwaṭṭāʾ* both as resource and as an example of how *ḥadīth* and law ought to work in tandem. That Walī Allāh continued to profess his devotion to the Ḥanafī school of law meant that his was an *internal* challenge to the other Ḥanafī scholars.[43] Yet his project sought more than a reorientation of law in terms of *ḥadīth*; it was also a venture in the reorientation of *ḥadīth* scholarship itself. This, in turn, was accompanied by an effort to train a new generation of scholars along lines, and in texts, different from those most commonly encountered in Indian madrasas of Walī Allāh's times. The study of the *Muwaṭṭāʾ* never really caught on in Indian madrasas. But it did allow Walī Allāh the opportunity to base his own claims to authority on a new and distinctive basis, as other facets of *ḥadīth* scholarship had allowed his predecessors to do as well.

Constructions of authority in the discourses of the jurists

As in the study of *ḥadīth*, compendia of legal doctrines, agreements and disagreements as well as commentaries on such works were central to the articulation, preservation and transmission of the *ʿulamāʾ*'s discursive tradition. Here, too, certain texts gradually came to be invested with compelling authority within particular *madhhabs*, giving coherence and stability to the legal tradition and guiding the further evolution of legal thought.[44]

There is much creativity that continued to find expression in scholarly engagement with authoritative texts, in law as in other areas. Yet the authority

42 Walī Allāh, *Musawwā Muṣaffā*. He also wrote on the *Ṣaḥīḥ* of al-Bukhārī: see Walī Allāh, *Risāla sharḥ abwāb ṣaḥīḥ al-Bukhārī*, 3rd edn (Haydarabad, 1949).

43 For his criticism of his fellow scholars, see Walī Allāh, *Musawwā Muṣaffā*, pp. 11, 21; also cf. Dallal, 'Origins and objectives', pp. 347, 349.

44 See Baber Johansen, *Contingency in a sacred law: Legal and ethical norms in the Muslim fiqh* (Leiden, 1999); Wael B. Hallaq, *Authority, continuity and change in Islamic law* (Cambridge, 2001). Some of the issues relating to juristic authority that I touch upon in this section are also considered in Wael B. Hallaq's review of the history of Islamic law in *The new Cambridge history of Islam*, vol. 4, Chapter 4. The focus of the relevant sections of that chapter is, however, on the construction of the authority of the classical Sunnī schools of law, as embodied in their eponymous founders and the legal doctrines attributed to them; my concern here is with the opportunities and the techniques a well-developed legal system – as it existed during the centuries with which this volume is concerned – afforded to its jurists, as well as to other scholars, for *continuing* articulations of their authority.

of a commentator, or of the compiler of a collection of legal opinions and doctrines, did not necessarily depend only on what was 'innovative' about his enterprise. To transmit learning in accordance with recognised scholarly standards, to write in the established genres and styles, and to train students in them was to continue an ongoing conversation with forebears and contemporaries. The skill with which one was seen to do so was a sufficient marker of one's scholarly eminence, though this hardly precluded critical engagement with the texts and traditions being passed on. Such critical engagement could create the space within which the authoritative positions handed down by forebears could be adapted to new or newly felt needs, received opinions might be supplemented with other, more recent views, and the latter put into circulation.

It was not just the credentials of the individual scholar writing the commentary or preparing a new compendium of law that were affirmed through such works; so, too, was the continuing tradition of the school as a whole. Maḥmūd b. Aḥmad b. ʿAbd al-ʿAzīz al-Bukhārī's (d. 616/1219) Preface to his compendium of Ḥanafī law, *al-Muḥīṭ al-Burhānī fi'l-fiqh al-Nuʿmānī*, illustrates some of these concerns:

> Knowledge of the rulings of religion is among the noblest – and highest – of ranks, and understanding religion is the most beneficial, and the purest, of activities. It is to the scholars and the jurists that things taking place among the [ordinary] servants of God are best directed, in order to ascertain their thoughts on these matters. As God has said, '... if they had referred it to the Messenger and those in authority among them, those seeking its meaning would have found it out from them' [Q 4.83] ... The Companions of the Prophet of God had persevered in seeking the knowledge and understanding of religion, and they had thereby become models to be emulated by everyone ... After the generation of the Companions and their Followers had become extinct, the great *imām* ... Abū Ḥanīfa, and his companions stood up to aid this religion. They are the ones who have delineated the preamble of the *sharīʿa* and set forth the principles of this radiant religion ... After them, the scholars of this religion have done their utmost in explicating difficulties, ... knowledge being ... transmitted from one elder to another until it reached the seven ancestors [of this author. These ancestors have, in turn,] ... expounded on what had still remained condensed in the law and opened what had hitherto been left locked. Their writings circulate among the people, and are relied on in judicial decisions and *fatwās* ... It occurred to me to become like them by compiling a work that brings together matters to which legal rulings pertain ... so that such a work assists me during my lifetime and results in [divine] recompense after my death ... The idea [of compiling such a work] was strengthened by the request of some brothers, which I have answered by gathering legal problems (*masāʾil*)

> from *al-Mabsūṭ*, the two *Jāmi*ʿs, the *Siyar* and the *Ziyādāt* [all by Muḥammad b. al-Ḥasan al-Shaybānī (d. 189/805)]. To these [sources of the school's authoritative doctrine], I added the less authoritative legal problems (*al-nawādir*) and the *fatwās* …, further adding to these the useful lessons I had received from my father … and the subtle matters I had committed to memory from the scholars of my own time. I have written a detailed work, explicated the problems in it to the full, and supplied them with proofs relied upon by the ancients as well as those of the latter-day scholars (*al-muta'akhkhirūn*).[45]

This is as good an illustration as any of the self-conscious sense of an ongoing, discursive tradition from which the scholars derived their identity and their authority while striving to preserve, adapt and further develop it in their local contexts. Some of the authority in question came not only from inserting oneself into a long-standing genealogy of learning, but also from the ability – acquired on the path to a scholarly career – to navigate through the multiplicity of discourse, the variety of texts and their frequently competing claims and implications. That jurists often professed strict adherence to the established doctrines of their school of law (*taqlīd*), rather than presuming to engage in efforts towards arriving at new legal rulings (*ijtihād*), had little bearing on such authority, for the very effort to sort out the complexities of a rich, multi-layered tradition as it existed at a particular time and place was itself not a small measure of legal acumen and of the recognition that went with it.

The range of doctrines that the *Fatāwa ʿĀlamgīriyya* (produced in eleventh/seventeenth-century India at the instance of the Mughal emperor Aurungzeb (r. 1069–1118/1658–1707)) presents in its 'Book of the Judge's Etiquette' (*Kitāb adab al-qāḍī*)[46] leaves no doubt, for instance, that some of the options are only for a judge who is a *mujtahid*, one qualified to undertake *ijtihād*. But while most jurists of the age in which this compilation was produced would have insisted that their qualifications entitled them only to *taqlīd*, the latter is hardly the 'blind imitation' that many modern commentators have often taken it to be.[47] Important efforts to adjust legal

45 Maḥmūd b. Aḥmad b. ʿAbd al-Azīz al-Bukhārī, *al-Muḥīṭ al-Burhānī fi'l-fiqh al-Nuʿmānī*, ed. A. ʿA. ʿInāya, 11 vols. (Beirut, 2003), vol. I, pp. 21–3. On the author of this work, see Muḥammad ʿAbd al-Ḥayy al-Laknawī, *al-Fawā'id al-bahiyya fī tarājim al-Ḥanafiyya* (Karachi, AH 1393), pp. 205–7.

46 *al-Fatāwa al-Hindiyya*, vol. III, pp. 306–450.

47 For recent re-evaluations of *taqlīd*, see Sherman Jackson, *Islamic law and the state: The constitutional jurisprudence of Shihab al-Din al-Qarafi* (Leiden, 1996); Hallaq, *Authority, continuity and change*; Mohammad Fadel, 'The social logic of taqlīd and the rise of the Mukhtaṣar', *Islamic Law and Society*, 3 (1996), pp. 193–233.

doctrine to changing needs long continued to take place within the overall framework of *taqlīd*, and the rhetoric of *taqlīd* sometimes also served to mask and, in a largely conservative society, thereby to justify important departures from traditional norms and practices. *Taqlīd*, like *ijtihād* itself, admitted of many degrees, moreover, which means that the manner in which a learned judge or jurist might adhere to the doctrines of the school could scarcely be the same as that of a less sophisticated colleague. For all the proliferation of madrasas in medieval Muslim societies, the transmission of learning was characterised by considerable informality (see below), so that deciding what sort of *taqlīd* a particular judge was bound to in view of his specific intellectual accomplishments could not have been a matter of objective assessment. Merely to decide which of the existing legal doctrines to follow in a particular case required considerable skill, just as the very availability of this range of positions could allow considerable manoeuvrability even to judges otherwise bound to *taqlīd*. The *Fatāwa ʿĀlamgīriyya* had, in fact, been envisioned as a way of *limiting* some of this manoeuvrability, of rationalising judicial practice in India,[48] though it is unlikely that it did much to curb the range of choices the tradition itself had made available to the judges.[49]

Debates among the Shīʿī *ʿulamāʾ* in the eleventh–twelfth/seventeenth–eighteenth centuries likewise demonstrate that a disavowal of *ijtihād* scarcely signified relinquishing strong claims to religious authority. It has often been supposed that the 'Akhbārī' *ʿulamāʾ*, who insisted on firmly adhering to the reported teachings (*akhbār*) of their Shīʿī imams rather than undertaking *ijtihād* on the basis of the foundational texts, were thereby abandoning their own claims to authority. But, as Robert Gleave has observed, opposition to *ijtihād* does not compromise claims to authority; it merely *relocates* those claims.[50] The 'Uṣūli' Shīʿī jurists claimed the prerogative of *ijtihād* and argued that,

48 *al-Fatāwa al-Hindiyya*, vol. I, pp. 2–3; also cf. Saqi Mustaʿidd Khan, *Maʾāthir-i ʿĀlamgīrī*, ed. A. A. ʿAlī (Osnabrück, 1985; repr. of the Calcutta 1870–3 edn), pp. 529–30.

49 Nor was *taqlīd* itself unrelenting in all instances. In a discussion of the 'sequence of proofs according to which [the judge is] to act', the *Fatāwa ʿĀlamgīriyya* stipulates recourse to the views of Abū Ḥanīfa and his principal disciples, Abū Yūsuf and Muḥammad al-Shaybānī. Should no guidance be available in their teachings, and if latter-day scholars are themselves in disagreement on the matter, the judge was to choose from among the variant views of these scholars. But 'in case even the latter-day scholars have nothing to say on the matter, [the judge] exercises *ijtihād* in accordance with his considered opinion, provided that he understands the precepts of the law and has consulted on the matter with [other] jurists'. *al-Fatāwa al-Hindiyya*, vol. III, p. 312.

50 My understanding of the Akhbārī position and of the Akhbārī claims to religious authority is based on Robert Gleave, *Inevitable doubt: Two theories of Shīʿī jurisprudence* (Leiden, 2000), esp. pp. 220–53. For another insightful discussion, see Etan Kohlberg,

while the results of this *ijtihād* were at best probable (*ẓannī*) rather than certain (*qaṭʿī*), the probable nature of these results need not have any bearing on the authority they ought to carry for the lay believer following the guidance of the master-jurist, the *mujtahid*. The Akhbārīs, on the other hand, located authority not in the person of the *mujtahid* but rather in the textual tradition comprising the teachings of the imams. These teachings led to certainty rather than to mere conjecture and probability, and they obviated the need for *ijtihād*. But it is the *scholars* who arrived at an authoritative understanding of these teachings, articulated the legal norms on their basis and guided their followers accordingly. And a formal disavowal of *ijtihād* did not undermine their religious authority or their claims to it.

The cosmopolitanism of the *ʿulamāʾ*

Debates about *ijtihād* and *taqlīd*, the writing of commentaries and the issuing of *fatwās* were all constitutive of religious authority in the eastern Islamic lands just as they were elsewhere in the Muslim world. These were activities of the distinguished scholars, however, and many of those who had acquired only a modicum of religious learning would not have had very much of a share in them. Yet the significance of this learning consisted not only in sustaining and developing a scholarly tradition but also in helping create the conditions for an Islamic cosmopolitanism. There were important limits to this cosmopolitanism, as we would observe later. Even so, and for all the differences of the natural languages people spoke, the geographical and cultural distances that separated them, the different schools of law to which they adhered and the varied societies they inhabited, there was a language of discourse that those schooled in the religious sciences could, with some plausibility, claim to share.

There is no better illustration of this cosmopolitanism than the famous North African traveller Ibn Baṭṭūṭa (d. 770/1368f.) who, by the end of his travels, had 'visited territories equivalent to about 44 modern countries'.[51] Besides major cities in the Arab Middle East, he travelled to Anatolia, India, the Maldive islands in the Indian Ocean, the island of Sumatra and possibly also to China.[52] Ibn Baṭṭūṭa's account of his travels is of interest not only for

'Aspects of Akhbari thought in the seventeenth and eighteenth centuries', in Nehemia Levtzion and John O. Voll, (eds.), *Eighteenth-century renewal and reform in Islam* (Syracuse, 1987), pp. 133–60.

51 Ross E. Dunn, *The adventures of Ibn Battuta: A Muslim traveler of the 14th century* (Berkeley, 1986), pp. 3, 12 n. 2.

52 On doubts about whether he did, in fact, go to China, cf. D. O. Morgan, 'Ibn Baṭṭūṭa and the Mongols', *Journal of the Royal Asiatic Society*, 3rd ser., 11 (2001), pp. 1–11.

what he tells us about the places he visited, however, but also for the company he kept. He had acquired a religious and specifically a juristic training in his native North Africa, though, by all accounts, his scholarly credentials were at best modest. Even so, he was never oblivious of these credentials, and it is to the presence of the religious scholars and Sufis in the lands he visited that he remained most attentive.

Ibn Baṭṭūṭa was clearly a most unusual figure. Scholars did travel considerable distances in search of knowledge (*ṭalab al-ʿilm*) but not on the scale he did, nor was *he* primarily travelling in search of knowledge. And as his *Riḥla* makes clear, he was exceptionally fortunate both in finding patrons almost everywhere he went and in eluding the mishaps that accompanied the not always predictable relations of patronage. Yet, such as they were, it is his scholarly claims that facilitated his entry into circles of scholars and into royal courts where religious scholarship was ostentatiously celebrated. Muḥammad b. Tughluq, the sultan of Delhi (r. 724–52/1324–51), made him a judge in the imperial city, for all that Ibn Baṭṭūṭa did not know the local languages and in fact belonged to the Mālikī school of law when most inhabitants of northern India were Ḥanafīs. Nor was Muḥammad b. Tughluq deterred, some years later, from sending Ibn Baṭṭūṭa as his ambassador to China. Some of the scholars and Sufis he came across – for instance the 'pious jurist from Mogadishu [whom he met on the Malabar coast of India] … who had studied at Mecca fourteen years and for the same length of time at Medina … and had travelled in [northern] India and China' – were comparable to him in their cosmopolitanism.[53] The latter may, indeed, have had a better grasp of the religious sciences, but Ibn Baṭṭūṭa clearly had sufficient grounding in a shared language of discourse to find himself at home in scholarly circles everywhere he went, and to feel entitled to the sort of positions and patronage often reserved for religious scholars. Indeed, he professes an inability to remain inconspicuous even when he had wanted to, as when he was appointed as a *qāḍī* while passing through the Maldives.[54] Whether this appointment owed itself to the prestige, in local circles, of being an Arab scholar or to the fact that he was travelling at this time as an emissary of the Delhi sultan, a sense – exaggerated, perhaps – of shared norms in otherwise disparate Muslim communities may also have had something to do with it. Four centuries later,

53 Ibn Baṭṭūṭa, *Voyages d'Ibn Batoutah*, ed. C. Defrémery and B. R. Sanguinetti, 2nd edn, 4 vols. (Paris, 1877–9), vol. IV, p. 82; trans. H. A. R. Gibb, *The travels of Ibn Baṭṭūṭa, AD 1325–1354*, 5 vols. (Cambridge, 1958–2000), vol. IV, p. 809.

54 Ibn Baṭṭūṭa, *Voyages*, vol. IV, pp. 137, 150–2; Gibb, *Travels*, vol. IV, pp. 834–5, 840. His public rebuke of the incumbent judge who 'did nothing right' could scarcely have helped his desire for anonymity on this occasion. On this, see below, p. 599.

Muḥammad ʿAlī Ḥazīn Lāhījī (d. 1180/1766), an Iranian scholar who had fled to India to escape a period of great political turmoil in Iran, likewise complained – and no more convincingly – of not being able to maintain his anonymity when he arrived in the town of Thatta, in Sind, in 1146/1734: 'I did not wish that any person should know me in that country. But it was almost impossible for it to be so; and the very same day that I arrived ... a company of merchants of that town, who had seen me in Fārs, become informed of my visit. A number of Persians were also residing there, most of whom were among my acquaintance. In short, this idea of remaining incognito was not realized in any city of that empire.'[55]

The Iranians living in Thatta when Ḥazīn arrived in that town were, no doubt, part and product of a long-standing movement of merchants and scholars from Iran who had sought their fortunes in South Asia, with not a few also coming to play some role in local Indian politics.[56] Networks of Iranian merchants and scholars were not the only ones facilitating the movement of people, merchandise and ideas, however. One of the most remarkable networks during the centuries with which this volume is concerned was that of the Hadramīs – tracing their origins to Hadramawt in Yemen – which had a major presence in Gujarat and elsewhere on the western coast of India and which extended from East Africa to the Malay–Indonesian archipelago.[57] Besides a shared origin, the Hadramīs were tied to one another as transmitters of *ḥadīth*, jurists, Sufis and, not least, as merchants. Local elites across the Indian Ocean saw the Hadramīs as the carriers of an uninterrupted Islamic scholarly tradition and were often eager to offer rich patronage to them. And as the *Nūr al-sāfir*, a biographical dictionary composed by ʿAbd al-Qādir al-ʿAydarūs (d. 1038/1638) – a Hadramī Sufi living in Aḥmadabad in Gujarat – and devoted to the scholars and notables of the tenth/sixteenth century amply attests, the Hadramīs were not reticent in putting their scholarly claims and accomplishments on display.[58]

55 Muḥammad ʿAlī Ḥazīn Lāhījī, *Ta'rīkh wa safarnama-i Ḥazīn*, ed. ʿA. Dawwānī (n.p., AH 1375), p. 259; trans. as in *The life of Sheikh Mohammad ʿAlī Hazin, written by himself*, trans. F. C. Belfour (London, 1830), p. 252. On him, see Muzaffar Alam and Sanjay Subrahmanyam, *Indo-Persian travels in the age of discoveries, 1400–1800* (Cambridge, 2007), pp. 229–40.

56 Cf. Sanjay Subrahmanyam, 'Iranians abroad: Intra-Asian elite migration and early modern state formation', *Journal of Asian Studies*, 51, 2 (1992), pp. 340–63.

57 Engseng Ho, *The graves of Tarim: Genealogy and mobility across the Indian Ocean* (Berkeley, 2006).

58 See al-ʿAydarūs, *al-Nūr al-sāfir*, pp. 444–53, for the author's account of his own career and accomplishments. On this work, see Ho, *Graves of Tarim*, pp. 118–37.

Like the Iranians, Ḥaḍramīs of the diaspora rose, on occasion, to political prominence and some, like Nūr al-dīn al-Rānīrī (d. *c.* 1068/1658), left a major impact on religious developments in their host communities.[59] Nūr al-dīn, a student and disciple of Abū Ḥafṣ ʿUmar Bā Shaybān al-Ḥaḍramī – a prominent member of the ʿAydarūs clan in India and the nephew of the author of *al-Nūr al-sāfir* – was born in Ranīr (present-day Randēr) in Gujarat and educated in Gujarat and Hadramawt. Al-Rānīri's uncle had taught in Aceh in the late tenth/sixteenth century;[60] and, in 1047/1637, al-Rānīrī came not only to live in Aceh but soon also to occupy a position of great influence there, that of the Shaykh al-Islām, with close ties to the Acehnese court. He remained in this position for seven years, before being forced to retire in 1054/1644 to his native Ranīr, but not before he had played a highly prominent, but also polarising, role in trying to suppress what he regarded as wayward mystical ideas associated with the teachings of the Andalusian mystic Ibn al-ʿArabī (d. 638/1240).

Al-Rānīrī's career illustrates something about the scope but also about the limits of the *ʿulamāʾ*'s cosmopolitanism. For scholars like him, it was evidently possible to move freely between South Asia, the Arab Middle East and South-East Asia in what they would have seen as an interconnected world of fellow scholars and their revered forebears. But this cosmopolitanism also had its limits, and al-Rānīrī seems to have reached them after seven years in Aceh. He apparently lost his influential position in Aceh in competition with a rival with deeper *local* roots, one Sayf al-Rijāl, who professed precisely the sort of beliefs that al-Rānīrī had all along been branding as heretical. Milder expressions of the views al-Rānīrī had tried to implement in Aceh did not lose influence or proponents after his departure, however; and the Malay–Indonesian archipelago long remained a fertile territory for scholars from elsewhere, not least for subsequent generations of Ḥaḍramīs.[61] It is also worth noting that the rival mystical beliefs, associated with the teachings of Ibn al-ʿArabī, that al-Rānīrī wanted to see erased were themselves an expression of a cosmopolitan world; and Sayf al-Rijāl, a Minangkabau, had travelled to Surat in Gujarat to establish his own scholarly credentials before returning to challenge al-Rānīrī.[62] Conversely, al-Rānīrī's roots in Aceh were by no means shallow: he wrote

59 For an informative overview of al-Rānīrī's career, on which I draw here, see Azra, *Islamic reformism*, pp. 52–69.
60 Azra, *Islamic reformism*, pp. 55–6.
61 Cf. *ibid.*, p. 112.
62 Ibid., pp. 60–2; Takeshi Ito, 'Why did Nuruddin ar-Raniri leave Aceh in 1054 AH?', *Bijdragen tot de Taal-, Land- en Volkenkunde*, 1344, (1978), pp. 489–91.

not only in Arabic but also in Malay and, indeed, some of his most influential works were written in the latter language.[63] Even so, contemporaries would not have mistaken al-Rānīrī's cosmopolitan orientation, the paradox of which was, of course, that it could bring influence and prestige just as easily as it might become a liability for the cosmopolitan and for his local hosts.

In a different context, and with much less of a grounding in the local cultures, Ibn Baṭṭūṭa too had also come up against the limits of his cosmopolitanism. Having publicly rebuked a local *qāḍī* in the Maldives for doing 'nothing right' he had assumed the position in his stead and proceeded to make his presence felt:

> When I was appointed, I strove my utmost to establish the prescriptions of the Sacred Law. Lawsuits there are not like those in our land. The first bad custom I changed was the practice of divorced wives of staying in the houses of their former husbands. I put a stop to that. About twenty-five men who had acted thus were brought before me; I had them beaten and paraded in the bazaars, and the women put away from them. Afterwards I gave strict injunctions that the prayers were to be observed, and ordered men to go swiftly to the streets and bazaars after the Friday service; anyone whom they found not having prayed I had beaten and paraded.[64]

The local people professed to belong to the same, Mālikī, school of law as Ibn Baṭṭūṭa did, but the manner in which he proceeded to implement his understanding of the legal norms was clearly foreign to them. Elsewhere, Ibn Baṭṭūṭa speaks of how people in his presence fainted when he once ordered the hand of a thief to be cut off. He attributes this reaction to the 'physical weakness' of the people,[65] but it may have had more to do with the fact that local customary practices were not quite what he wanted to see implemented. There is no indication in his account that he made any effort to bridge this distance. *Qāḍīs* were, by definition, required to uphold *sharīʿa* norms, but they also needed to be attentive to local social and religious configurations. The *qāḍī* who 'did nothing right' may yet have had a firmer grasp of these local norms than did Ibn Baṭṭūṭa, whose tenure in this position was, in any case, soon terminated on account of the political rivalries in which he found himself entangled.

63 Azra, *Islamic reformism*, pp. 66–9.
64 Ibn Baṭṭūṭa, *Voyages*, vol. IV, pp. 151–2; Gibb, *Travels*, vol. IV, pp. 840–1.
65 Ibn Baṭṭūṭa, *Voyages*, vol. IV, pp. 114–15; Gibb, *Travels*, vol. IV, p. 824.

Educational institutions and practices

Medieval cosmopolitanism had its constraints, but scholarly learning remained, by far, its most important basis.[66] This learning was typically transmitted from one person to another, with the particular site where such activity took place being incidental to it. Ibn al-Najjār (d. 643/1245), the author of a biographical dictionary devoted to the scholars who had some connection with Baghdad,[67] is said to have travelled, *inter alia*, in the Ḥijāz, Syria, Mesopotamia and Khurāsān for twenty-eight years before returning to Baghdad with a list of 3,000 men and 400 women from whom he claimed to have acquired his knowledge.[68] It usually did not take either that long or this many people to establish one's scholarly credentials. But Ibn al-Najjār's claim to do so, despite its hyperbole, suggests at least that there were varied and often informal ways in which learning was transmitted from one person to another. Yet his was also an age of major developments in the institutionalisation of Islamic education. Debates about the origins and diffusion of the madrasas, and the purposes they may have been meant to serve, need not occupy us here,[69] though it is worth noting that this institution first emerged in Khurāsān in the fourth/tenth century and that madrasas had begun to spread elsewhere in the Muslim world, in both the east and the west, from the late fifth/eleventh century.[70] The most famous of the early madrasas were the Niẓāmiyyas, founded in more than ten cities in Iran and Iraq under the patronage of the Saljuq vizier Niẓām al-Mulk (d. 485/1092).[71] Later madrasas had their own claims to distinction. The Mustanṣiriyya, established by the ʿAbbāsid caliph al-Mustanṣir in Baghdad in 631/1234, was, for instance, the first to be endowed by a caliph and the first to have professorships

66 Cf. Carl F. Petry, 'Travel patterns of medieval notables in the Near East', *Studia Islamica*, 63 (1985), pp. 53–87, esp. 75.

67 This large work, itself a sequel to the *History of Baghdad* by al-Khaṭīb al-Baghdādī (d. 463/1072), was abridged by Shihāb al-dīn al-Dimyāṭī (d. 749/1348) as *al-Mustafād min dhayl taʾrīkh Baghdād*, ed. M. M. Khalaf (Beirut, 1986).

68 *Kitāb al-ḥawādith*, ed. B. ʿA. Maʿrūf and ʿI. ʿAbd al-Salām Raʾūf (Beirut, 1997), pp. 245–6.

69 On madrasas in Iran and the Arab Middle East, see, *inter alia*, George Makdisi, *The rise of colleges* (Edinburgh, 1981); Jonathan Berkey, *The transmission of learning in medieval Cairo* (Princeton, 1992); Michael Chamberlain, *Knowledge and practice in medieval Damascus, 1190–1350* (Cambridge, 1994); Richard W. Bulliet, *Islam: The view from the edge* (New York, 1994); Said Amir Arjomand, 'The law, agency, and policy in medieval Islamic society: Development of the institutions of learning from the tenth to the fifteenth century', *Comparative Studies in Society and History*, 41 (1999), pp. 263–93. On madrasas in medieval India, see Abū'l-Ḥasanāt Nadwī, *Hindustān kī qādīm Islāmī darsgāhen* (Aʿzamgarh, 1971); Iqtidar Husain Siddiqui, 'Muslim intellectual life in India', in Iqtidar Husain Siddiqui (ed.), *Medieval India: Essays in intellectual thought and culture* (Delhi, 2003), vol. I, pp. 81–94.

70 Cf. Bulliet, *Islam*, pp. 148–51.

71 Arjomand, 'Law', p. 270.

in all four of the Sunnī schools of law that had emerged as pre-eminent by that time.[72] And madrasas established in Iran in the age of the Ilkhanids (*c.* 658–735/1260–1335) and the Timurids (771–913/1370–1507) were often part of what Said Amir Arjomand has characterised as 'educational-charitable complexes' that included not only mosques but also Sufi convents and hospitals and, as such, represented a vast increase in scope and function over even the grandest of the earlier madrasas.[73]

Madrasas, large and small, were supported through pious endowments (*awqāf*, singular: *waqf*), specifically allocated, and in perpetuity, by the founder for the upkeep of the institution and the maintenance of all those the founder envisioned as being associated with it. The endowment often also specified the subjects that were to be taught, the *madhhab*(s) to which the professors and the students were to belong, and the other pious activities (e.g. the recitation of the Qur'ān) that were to be financed through the endowment. Ideally, the endowment was created from the resources belonging to the individual in question. Yet, as Arjomand has argued, it is not clear that the sultans, viziers and other members of the ruling elite who created lavish madrasas throughout Muslim societies made any firm distinctions between their 'private' property and the resources of the state that they controlled, any more than they did between founding madrasas as a matter of personal piety and doing so as a facet of public policy.[74]

The study of law was typically at the centre of a madrasa's concerns, as the work of George Makdisi has demonstrated,[75] and the rich history of Islamic law no doubt has much to do with the financial resources made available for its study through the madrasa and its endowments. But law was scarcely the only concern of the madrasas. Expertise in the other 'transmitted' or *sharīʿa* sciences (*al-ʿulūm al-naqliyya*)[76] was essential to the training of a jurist, though many of these sciences were also studied for their intrinsic interest.

72 *EI*[2] 'al-Mustanṣir bi'llāh', (C. Hillenbrand). For an account of the founding of this madrasa, see *Kitāb al-ḥawādith*, pp. 80–6.

73 Arjomand, 'Law', pp. 271–6, esp. 272.

74 *Ibid.*, pp. 281–5, 290. On the legal manoeuvres whereby state land was converted into private property as a prelude to being turned into *waqf* endowments, see Maria E. Subtelny, *Timurids in transition: Turko-Persian politics and acculturation in medieval Iran* (Leiden, 2007), pp. 220–7.

75 See, especially, Makdisi, *Colleges*.

76 It is common to render *al-ʿulūm al-naqliyya* ('the transmitted sciences') as the 'religious sciences'. But the 'rational sciences' (*al-ʿulūm al-ʿaqliyya*), from which they are distinguished were, arguably, also 'religious' sciences. I therefore prefer '*sharīʿa* sciences' as the characterisation for *al-ʿulūm al-naqliyya* – a characterisation that is occasionally used by the '*ulamā*' themselves. Cf. ʿAbd al-Ḥayy al-Laknawī, *al-Fawā'id*, pp. 209, 213, 228, etc.

The Mustanṣiriyya's deed of endowment provided, for instance, for a *Dār al-ḥadīth*, headed by a scholar with a 'superior [literally: 'high'] chain of transmission' linking him to earlier transmitters of *ḥadīth*. It was to this position that the aforementioned Ibn al-Najjār had been appointed on returning from his long travels.[77] The rational sciences – including not just philosophy but also astronomy, mathematics and medicine – were also taught in many madrasas, however.[78] The Mustanṣiriyya's endowment deed itself provided for a physician not only for the wellbeing of others attached to the madrasa but also to train medical students.[79] Nor was it unusual for royal patrons of madrasas – for example those founded by the Ottoman sultan Meḥmed II (r. 848–50/1444–6 and 855–86/1451–81) as part of his educational complex in Istanbul – to specifically require competence in the rational sciences as part of the professors' qualifications.[80] And the madrasa founded in Samarqand by the Timurid prince Ulugh Beg (d. 853/1449) was headed by a distinguished mathematician, and drew many others to it.[81]

That madrasas could serve as sites for the pursuit of various transmitted and rational sciences was due not only to the interests and commitments of those founding these institutions (Ulugh Beg, for instance, was himself an accomplished mathematician), but also to the fact that a scholar's work often encompassed varied disciplines. Sonja Brentjes has shown that the rational and the *sharīʿa* sciences had begun to draw increasingly close to one another from the fifth/eleventh century onwards: works on law also contained discussions on logic, for instance, and biographical dictionaries routinely praise the same scholar as a master of the rational *and* the *sharīʿa* sciences even as they testify to their training of students in each.[82] Indeed, the rational sciences had gradually themselves come to be studied in the manner of the *sharīʿa* sciences: 'the same modes of writing epitomes, paraphrases, commentaries and supercommentaries applied to all of the [rational and transmitted] sciences, as did the same modes of learning, whether by heart, with a tutor, through serving a master, or by reading authoritative texts'.[83] Brentjes has argued that these practices may have contributed to the decline of the rational

77 *Kitāb al-ḥawādith*, p. 246.
78 Sonja Brentjes, 'On the location of the ancient or "rational" sciences in Muslim educational landscapes (AH 500–1100)', *Bulletin of the Royal Institute for Inter-Faith Studies*, 4 (2002), pp. 47–71.
79 *Kitāb al-ḥawādith*, p. 85.
80 İhsanoğlu, 'Ottoman science', p. 16. The same was true of the madrasas established by sultan Süleyman the Magnificent: cf. *ibid.*, p. 17.
81 Cf. *EI²* 'Ulugh Beg' (B. F. Manz); Arjomand, 'Law', p. 275.
82 Brentjes, 'On the location'.
83 *Ibid.*, p. 65.

sciences in the later Middle Ages, for these sciences were not always amenable to such modes of discourse. The case for any such decline has come to appear increasingly tenuous, however, in the light of recent scholarship on late medieval and early modern Islamic societies.[84] The overlap and fluidity of genres are nonetheless readily discernible in the scholarly culture of the period, which means that no firm barriers separated the scholars rooted in the *sharīʿa* sciences from those excelling in other disciplines.

Yet, for all this interpenetration of genres, there remained important differences of emphasis within this scholarly universe. Some of these surely had to do with individual predilections. Muḥammad b. Tughluq, the Delhi sultan who had patronised Ibn Baṭṭūṭa, was known for an especially keen interest in the rational sciences, with Diyāʾ al-dīn Baranī (d. *c.* 758/1357), a contemporary historian, going so far as to attribute the much dreaded brutality of this sultan to the hard-heartedness that came with these rational sciences.[85] Emphasis on particular disciplines also varied from one time or place to another. *Ḥadīth* and law were at the forefront of scholarly learning during the 'Sunnī revival' in the reign of the Timurid ruler Shāh Rukh (r. 807–50/1405–47).[86] Conversely, and for all the overlap between the transmitted and the rational sciences, the latter would long remain a primary focus of scholarly interest in India. Important advances were made in tenth/sixteenth-century Gujarat and eleventh–twelfth/seventeenth–eighteenth-century Delhi in the study of *ḥadīth*, to which, as observed earlier, the authority of several generations of scholars was intimately tied. Yet it would have been difficult to find many madrasas in India whose 'curriculum' included a dozen works in the genre of Qurʾānic exegesis (*tafsīr*) and another twelve relating to *ḥadīth* – as was apparently the case with a curriculum for advanced studies in Ottoman madrasas, issued in 973/1565 on the authority of the Ottoman sultan Süleyman the Magnificent (r. 926–74/1520–66).[87]

Scholars were mobile, as we have seen, and it was typically through their movement that new trends, new topics and new books were introduced into a

84 Khaled El-Rouayheb, 'Opening the gate of verification: The forgotten Arab-Islamic florescence of the 17th Century', *International Journal of Middle East Studies*, 38 (2006), pp. 263–81.

85 Ḍiyāʾ al-dīn Baranī, *Taʾrīkh-i Fīrūzshāhī*, ed. Sayyid Aḥmad Khan (Calcutta, 1862), pp. 464–7.

86 Maria Eva Subtelny and Anas B. Khalidov, 'The curriculum of Islamic higher learning in Timurid Iran in the light of the Sunni revival under Shah-Rukh', *Journal of the American Oriental Society*, 115 (1995), pp. 210–36.

87 See Shahab Ahmed and Nenad Filipovic, 'The sultan's syllabus: A curriculum for the Ottoman imperial *medreses* prescribed in a *fermān* of Qānūnī I Süleyman, dated 973 (1565)', *Studia Islamica*, 98–9 (2004), pp. 183–218.

community's intellectual circles.[88] Mīr Fatḥ Allāh (d. 977/1569), a distinguished rationalist scholar from Shīrāz who eventually came to serve as head of the religious establishment (*ṣadr al-ṣudūr*) under the Mughal emperor Akbar (r. 963–1014/1556–1605), is credited with having introduced the works of Jalāl al-dīn Dawānī (d. 908/1502) and Mullā Ṣadra (d. 1050/1640) into north Indian study circles and to have further strengthened the rationalist tradition in India.[89] Contemporary observers likewise credited Kurdish and Persian scholars with having introduced new books into seventeenth-century study circles in the Arab Middle East along with new methods of critically examining texts (*taḥqīq*).[90] As al-Muḥibbī (d. 1111/1699) wrote of one such scholar, Mullā Maḥmūd al-Kurdī (d. 1074/1663f.), 'he mostly taught the books of the non-Arabs (*kutub al-aʿājim*), and he was the first to acquaint the Syrian students with these books … It is with him that the gate of *taḥqīq* in Damascus was opened.'[91]

Commentaries and glosses on well-established earlier works assured their longevity and helped launch the career of new generations of scholars even as new works and new discursive methods continued to be introduced into particular scholarly circles. Needless to say, many books also regularly continued to fall out of circulation. The vicissitudes of a manuscript culture had as much to do with this as, of course, did the competition with new books. Some jurists specifically required that the texts a *muftī* relied upon in issuing his *fatwās* ought to be in broad circulation for his legal pronouncements to be credible.[92] Thus a scholar who might, in one locale, have easily drawn on a well-recognised work would not be able to invoke it in his *fatwās* in another,

88 Cf. the stories about the introduction of particular texts in the Muslim scholarly circles of eastern China in the seventeenth century: Ben-Dor Benite, *The Dao of Muhammad*, pp. 82–8.

89 Ghulām ʿAlī Āzād Bilgrāmī, *Maʾāthir al-kirām*, ed. Muḥammad ʿAbduh Lyallpurī (Lahore, 1971), pp. 228–9.

90 El-Rouayheb, 'Opening the gate of verification'.

91 Muḥammad Amīn al-Muḥibbī, *Khulāsat al-athar fī aʿyān al-qarn al-ḥādī ʿashar* (Beirut, n.d.), vol. IV, pp. 329–30; quoted (with some changes) from El-Rouayheb, 'Opening the gate of verification', p. 265. For an explication of how a teacher ought to elucidate a text in all its complexity to his students, see Shāh Walī Allāh, 'Risāla-i dānishmandī', published together with Shāh Rafīʿ al-dīn, *Takmīl al-adhhān*, ed. ʿAbd al-Ḥamīd al-Sawātī (Gujaranwala, n.d.), pp. 179–83. What Walī Allāh characterises as 'dānishmandī' in this work seems similar to what al-Muḥibbī means by 'taḥqīq' here. Note also that the *isnād* Walī Allāh gives for his reception of this discursive method from his father includes many rationalist luminaries, including Mīr Muḥammad Zāhid Harawī (d. 1111/1699), the aforementioned Jalāl al-dīn Dawānī, and Saʿd al-dīn Taftāzānī (d. 793/1390) (*ibid.*, p. 179).

92 Cf. Ibn al-Humām, *Sharḥ fatḥ al-qadīr*, 10 vols. (Cairo, 1970), vol. VII, p. 256; Walī Allāh, *ʿIqd al-jīd*, p. 35.

where it might simply be unavailable.[93] It would be recalled that the Central Asian compiler of the *Muḥīṭ al-Burhānī* had noted in the Preface to his own work that the legal writings of his ancestors were all in circulation, that they were relied upon by judges and *muftīs* and that he had compiled his *Muḥīṭ* in order to join their scholarly company. Ironically, however, the *Muḥīṭ* itself fell out of circulation, and some scholars – notably the Egyptian Ḥanafī jurist Ibn Nujaym (d. 970/1563) – disallowed *fatwās* with reference to it.[94] The late nineteenth-century Indian scholar Muḥammad ʿAbd al-Ḥayy (d. 1304/1886) notes that, like some others before him, he had assumed the disallowing of *fatwās* on the basis of the *Muḥīṭ* to have been a function of the book's poor quality. But, having chanced upon a copy of the manuscript, he found it to be a generally sound work. 'It then became clear to me,' he writes, 'that [Ibn Nujaym's] interdiction of *fatwās* on its basis had to do, not with the intrinsic qualities of this work or [the credentials] of its author, but only with the fact that the book had become inaccessible. This is a matter that varies from one age or region to another. Many a book is extinct in one place but available in another, hard to find at one time and plentiful at another.'[95]

This is a sensible view of the matter, though it may also reflect an age when the technology of print was making long-forgotten works available afresh to scholars. Applied to an earlier age, however, ʿAbd al-Ḥayy's comment may suggest yet another limit on the cosmopolitanism of the *ʿulamāʾ*: an acquaintance with scholarly modes of discourse allowed entry into the circles of the *ʿulamāʾ* and could open doors to the patronage of the ruling elite, but further recognition would have required deeper immersion in the scholarly culture of the local community – a mastery of the texts available, and authoritative, in *that* community. Even the 'authorisation' (*ijāza*) 'to teach and issue *fatwās*', which some have taken to be the equivalent of a medieval 'doctorate in Islamic law', would probably have

93 They could always be *introduced* by him there, of course, but it is unlikely that they would acquire sufficient currency rapidly enough for him to then base his juristic responsa on them. Being in possession of a chain of transmission through which one claimed to have acquired the right to teach and transmit a text was likewise an acceptable way of putting it to use, but even this may have worked better with, say, *ḥadīth* reports than with large works of substantive law in a milieu where they were previously unknown.

94 Ibn Nujaym, 'Fī ṣūra waqfiyya ikhtalafat al-ajwiba fīhā', in Ibn Nujaym, *Rasāʾil Ibn Nujaym al-iqtiṣādiyya, al-musammāt al-Rasāʾil al-Zayniyya fī madhhab al-Ḥanafiyya*, ed. M. A. Sirāj and ʿA. J. Muḥammad (Beirut, 1998), pp. 287–93, at 291.

95 ʿAbd al-Ḥayy al-Laknawī, *al-Fawāʾid*, p. 206.

resonated most in circles where the scholars issuing it were themselves well known.[96]

The ʿ*ulamāʾ* and the state

Many of the scholars we have encountered in the preceding pages were the beneficiaries, in one form or another, of royal patronage. Al-Ṣaghānī, the celebrated lexicographer and compiler of the *Mashāriq al-anwār*, was sent on caliphal missions from Baghdad, his adopted home, to his native India by the ʿAbbāsid caliphs al-Nāṣir (r. 575–622/1180–1225) and al-Mustanṣir (r. 623–40/1226–42); and he was later appointed by the caliph al-Mustaʿṣim (r. 640–56/1242–58) to the Tutushiyya madrasa in Baghdad.[97] Though the purpose of al-Ṣaghānī's trips to India remains uncertain, they may have had to do with al-Nāṣir's innovative efforts to extend the caliphate's moral authority over other Muslim rulers and, specifically perhaps, with the investiture of the Delhi sultans as the deputies of the caliphs in Baghdad – a highly symbolic but politically not insignificant initiative that promised a much cherished facet of legitimacy to the sultans in exchange for a formal recognition of their subservience to the caliph.[98] Even the usually reclusive Gujarati scholar ʿAlī al-Muttaqī, who spent much of his later life in Mecca, briefly returned to Gujarat in 955/1548 to oversee the implementation of the *sharīʿa* in the polity of the young sultan Maḥmūd II (d. 961/1554).[99] The networks of Hadramī scholars were, for their part, made possible not only by their dexterously orchestrated scholarly credentials but also by the patronage of local rulers around the Indian Ocean which these credentials helped secure. And as long as it lasted, al-Rānīrī's campaign against wayward beliefs had the full force of the Acehnese royal court behind it. If ʿAbd al-Ḥaqq Dihlawī had misgivings about the Mughal emperor Shāh Jahān (r. 1037–68/1628–57), to whom he presented his Arabic commentary on the *Mishkāt al-maṣābīḥ*, he did not express them in his preface to this work. Instead, he characterised the

96 Devin Stewart, 'The doctorate of Islamic law in Mamluk Egypt and Syria', in J. E. Lowry, D. J. Stewart and S. M. Toorawa (eds.), *Law and education in medieval Islam: Studies in memory of Professor George Makdisi* (Chippenham, 2004), pp. 45–90. Makdisi too, on occasion, acknowledged the limits of geography on a scholar's *ijāza*. Cf. *Colleges*, p. 152: 'the disputation was the final test a candidate had to pass in order to obtain his license. He then was eligible for a teaching position *in the locality* in which he had proved himself a disputant' (emphasis added).

97 *Kitāb al-ḥawādith*, pp. 306–7; *EI*² 'al-Ṣaghānī'.

98 Cf. Aziz Ahmad, *Studies in Islamic culture in the Indian environment* (Oxford, 1964), pp. 3–11. On al-Nāṣir's efforts to revive and extend the authority of the caliphate, cf. *EI*² 'al-Nāṣir li-dīn Allāh' (A. Hartmann).

99 Kugle, 'In search of the centre', pp. 438–57.

emperor as 'the manifestation of the virtues of religion, the devoted adherent of the firm *sharīʿa*, oriented towards God and His prophet in all basic and subsidiary matters'.[100] All this is stylised rhetoric, of course, yet it illustrates a scholar's vision of what a ruler should be like even as it testifies to his own willingness to associate with him.

It was royal patronage that enabled many scholars to not only pursue well-trodden paths but also areas of enquiry that were unpopular in some circles. Fakhr al-Dīn Rāzī (d. 606/1210), the noted exegete and Ashʿarī theologian, enjoyed the favour of both the Khwārazm Shāhs and the Ghūrids, for all that these dynasties were engaged in a bitter conflict with each other. Ghiyāth al-Dīn Muḥammad (r. 558–99/1163–1202f.), his Ghūrid patron, had built a madrasa for him in Herat as a way of 'shield[ing] Fakhr al-Dīn's teaching activity from the criticism of his peers inside and outside the Ashʿarī school'.[101] As Frank Griffel has argued, such patronage seems to have played an important role in the development and spread of the rational sciences in the eastern Islamic lands.[102]

Mughal emperors in India tended to allocate revenue grants (*madad-i maʿāsh*) to scholars and Sufis more often than they established pious endowments (*waqfs*).[103] But the patronage of the ruling elite was crucial just the same for the continuation of scholarly endeavours and for attracting streams of scholars from outside India, as well as from different parts of India to the royal court. A monumental work such as the *Fatāwa ʿĀlamgīriyya*, compiled during the reign of the Mughal emperor Aurungzeb ʿĀlamgīr and named after him, likewise underscores the significance of royal patronage: the project, on which a team of leading Ḥanafī jurists worked, is said to have cost a large sum, and it was the scholarly resources of the imperial library that had made this venture possible in the first place.[104]

100 ʿAbd al-Ḥaqq Dihlawī, *Lamaʿāt al-tanqīḥ*, vol. I, pp. 20–1. Earlier, Dihlawī had presented another work of his to Shāh Jahān's father, the Mughal emperor Jahāngīr. See *Jahangirnama: Memoirs of Jahangir, emperor of India*, ed. and trans. Wheeler M. Thackston (New York, 1999), p. 316.

101 Frank Griffel, 'On Fakhr al-Dīn al-Rāzī's life and the patronage he received', *Journal of Islamic Studies*, 18 (2007), p. 343.

102 *Ibid.*, pp. 341–3 and *passim*.

103 Gregory C. Kozlowski, 'Imperial authority, benefactions and endowments (*awqāf*) in Mughal India', *Journal of the Economic and Social History of the Orient*, 38, 3 (1995), pp. 355–70; Rafat M. Bilgrami, *Religious and quasi-religious departments of the Mughal period (1556–1707)* (Delhi, 1984), pp. 59–98.

104 On the cost of producing this work and the use of the imperial library for it, see Mustaʿidd Khan, *Maʾāthir-i ʿĀlamgīrī*, pp. 529–30.

Illustrations such as these are not meant to deny that some scholars and Sufis would have been far more eager to keep their distance from the governing elite than to frequent their circles. The existence of such scholars should not, however, lead us to reify what some medieval observers rhetorically characterised as the 'worldly' and the 'otherworldly' *ʿulamāʾ*.[105] As Sunil Kumar has argued, the discourses of Sufis like the much revered Niẓām al-dīn Awliyāʾ (d. 725/1325) point, instead, to a considerably more fluid distinction between, on the one hand, those 'worldly' figures who were prone to using their religious and scholarly pretensions to curry favour with the rulers and, on the other, those whose piety and learning entitled them to a share in the royal patronage, which they were able to use for the good of others. It was the former sort of people who were most likely to be objects of derision in scholarly and Sufi circles.[106] It is worth noting, finally, that the ruling elite were crucial to the scholarly culture even when many of those who were part of that culture wished to have no personal contact with the rulers. More important than any direct patronage of scholarly circles was, after all, the creation and maintenance of the conditions in which scholars could travel and engage in the pursuit and transmission of learning and in which they could hope to see the fundamental norms of the *sharīʿa* at least publicly affirmed. The legitimacy of the rulers itself depended on the creation and preservation of such conditions;[107] and few among the religious and the political elite disputed that their institutions were, in fact, interdependent.

Tradition, identity and authority

The period with which this volume is concerned saw major developments in law, Qurʾānic exegesis and the study of *ḥadīth*, as well as in the rational sciences. Scholars, texts and ideas moved not just eastward, from the Arab Middle East and Iran to India and South-East Asia, but also in the other direction, with Kurdish and Iranian scholars introducing seventeenth-century Damascene study circles to new texts and approaches, as we have observed, and eighteenth-century figures like the north Indian Murtaḍā al-Zabīdī (d. 1205/1791) achieving great recognition in the Arab Middle East and

105 For such reified formulations in modern scholarship, cf. Khaliq Ahmad Nizami, *Some aspects of religion and politics in India during the thirteenth century* (Bombay, 1961), 152; for a critique, see Sunil Kumar, *The emergence of the Delhi sultanate* (Delhi, 2007), pp. 219–24, esp. 219–20 n. 61.
106 See Kumar, *Emergence*, pp. 219–24.
107 Cf. Petry, 'Travel patterns', pp. 81–5.

beyond.[108] Many, though by no means all, scholars of the later Middle Ages were reluctant to claim that their ideas diverged significantly from those of their forebears. Yet, as we have observed, such rhetoric, and the well-worn genres in which they typically chose to express themselves, should not obscure the ingenuity of these scholars and their resourcefulness in adapting earlier ideas to changing needs.

Nor, however, should we place a premium only on what appears to us novel in the scholarly culture of the *ʿulamāʾ*. For even when it was largely a matter of the transmission, translation and repackaging of an existing body of knowledge, it continued to serve important purposes. As Zvi Ben-Dor Benite has shown with reference to eastern China during the eleventh–twelfth/seventeenth–eighteenth centuries, Muslim scholarly practices in this region usually consisted in the translation into Chinese of Arabic and Persian texts, the dissemination of such texts – as well as of many others produced in dialogue with them – in the scholarly circles inhabited by Muslims of eastern China, the establishment of a vast but closely knit network of schools, and discursive techniques informed not only by a sense of affinity with scholars elsewhere in the Muslim world but also with China's Confucian literati.[109] In the eleventh–twelfth/seventeenth–eighteenth centuries, 'Chinese Muslims, like their non-Muslim Confucian counterparts, were active producers of bibliographies, catalogues, genealogies, anthologies, and the like,'[110] all of which both helped constitute a distinctive Chinese Islamic scholarly tradition and came to be among its most characteristic expressions. Even when not viewing Chinese Islam as peripheral to a history of Muslim intellectual practices, it might be tempting to consider such cultural production and the practices that made it possible as illustrative, above all, of an age of intellectual decline in the history of Islam – an age dominated by 'mere' genealogies and commentaries. But as Ben-Dor Benite has persuasively demonstrated, it was precisely through a painstaking preservation and memorialising of the work of their forebears and contemporaries that the sense of a self-conscious and closely knit scholarly community was fostered which, in turn, was central to the construction and the preservation of a distinctive Muslim identity in China.

Whether particular *ʿulamāʾ* made claims to reshaping facets of the scholarly tradition, to reviving the path of the forebears, or simply to continuing inherited practices and passing them on through their books and their

108 Stefan Reichmuth, 'Murtaḍā az-Zabīdī (d. 1791) in biographical and autobiographical accounts', *Die Welt des Islams*, 39 (1999), pp. 64–102.

109 Ben-Dor Benite, *Dao of Muhammad*.

110 *Ibid*., p. 121.

students, their discursive practices were crucial as much to the articulation of their own authority as they were to the preservation of their scholarly tradition. As the Chinese example suggests, the *ʿulamāʾ*'s scholarly practices were equally central to the sense of a stable Islamic identity in the larger community they inhabited. The contexts in which the *ʿulamāʾ* have lived and worked in the modern world have often been radically different from those with which this volume, and this chapter, are concerned. Yet the sense of a stable religious identity has not ceased to be intertwined with their scholarly tradition, which has continued to be an important site both for new articulations of authority and for ongoing explorations of ways to adapt their practices to change.

Glossary

All terms are Arabic except where designated as Bg = Bugis; Ch = Chinese; H = Hindi/Urdu; I = modern Indonesian; J = Javanese; M = Malay; Mg = Mongolian; P = Persian; Po = Portuguese; S = Sanskrit; T = Turkish

ʿada, adat (M/I, from Ar *ʿādat*)	custom
ahl al-kitāb	'People of the Book', i.e. Jews and Christians (extended *de facto* to Zoroastrians)
ʿajam	non-Arabs, usually referring to Persians
Akhbārī	Shīʿī theological school, opposed to the use of *ijtihād*
ʿAlawiyya	The most influential brotherhood in the colonial period whose main shrine was at Inat
ʿAlids	descendants of ʿAlī b. Abī Ṭālib, notably the Shīʿī imams
ʿālim, pl. *ʿulamāʾ*	religious scholar
amīr	commander, ruler
amīr al-muʾminīn	Commander of the Faithful, a title of the caliph
anda (Mg)	sworn brother, in Mongol society
Ashʿarism	school of theology, the foundation of which is attributed to al-Ashʿarī (d. 935)
ʿĀshūrāʾ	Shīʿī religious festival on the tenth day of Muḥarram, commemorating the death of the third imam Ḥusayn at Karbalāʾ in 680
atabeg (T)	'father of the prince'; guardian of a Saljuq prince; later a ruler of a Saljuq successor-state

ba'in	tank
Bania (H)	Commercially oriented caste, chiefly in northern India
baraka	prestige, blessing
bāṭin	hidden, esoteric meaning of the Qur'ān
bay'a	oath of allegiance
beg (T)	prince, chieftain
berhala (M)	idols, idolatry
bid'a	doctrinal innovation
Bilād al-fulful	Malabar, lit. 'land of pepper'
bismillāh	expression of faith in the supremacy of Allāh
bissu (Bg)	priest of old Bugis religion
bléncong (J)	oil lamp
caciz (Po)	Muslim religious specialists (from *qāḍī*)
caliph (Ar *khalīfa)*	'successor', 'representative' of the Prophet Muḥammad, title of the head of the Sunnī community and other rulers
Chettyars (H)	Hindu commercial caste
dā'ī	missionary, propagandist
dalang (J)	puppeteer
dār al-ḥarb	'abode of war', lands not yet under Muslim rule and Islamic law
dār al-islām	'abode of Islam', lands under Muslim rule and Islamic law
dargāh	the court
da'wa (M. *dakwah*)	mission, proselytisation
dawla	dynasty, state
dharma (J)	pre-Muslim hermitages
dharma (S)	right behaviour
dhikr	'remembrance' of God, often in the form of a ritual recitation
dhimmī	protected person, member of the *ahl al-kitāb*
dhow (Anglo-Indian)	Asian ships sailing in the Indian Ocean

dīn	religion, especially of Islam
dīnār	unit of coinage
dīn-i ilāhī	eclectic religious movement created by the Mughal emperor Akbar (r. 1556–1605)
dīwān	'register', administration, esp. financial; department of government
fanke (Ch)	foreign guests
faqīh, pl. *fuqahā'*	jurist
faqīr	poor; a religious mendicant
fatwā	opinion on a legal matter provided by a *muftī*
fiqh	jurisprudence
firmān	decree
fitna	disorder, anarchy: used as a term for civil war
gamelan (J)	Javanese orchestra
gedimu (Ch)	lit. old teachings (from Ar *qadīm*); traditionalist Muslims
ghayba	'occultation', of the twelfth Shīʿī imam, who disappeared in 874
ghāzī	fighter in the holy war (*jihād*)
ghulām	military slave (see also *mamlūk*)
ghulāt	'extremist' Shīʿīs
ḥadīth	a tradition attributed to the Prophet Muḥammad or his Companions
ḥāfiẓ	one who knows the Qurʾān by heart
ḥajj	the pilgrimage to Mecca
ḥalāl	permitted, in Islamic law
Han (Ch)	'Chinese', though in pre-modern usage including Koreans and others and excluding many southerners
Ḥanafī	one of the four schools (*madhhab*) of Sunnī Islamic law
Ḥanbalī	one of the four schools of Sunnī Islamic law
ḥarām	forbidden, in Islamic law

hijra	the emigration of the Prophet Muḥammad from Mecca to Medina in 622 CE, which marks the beginning of the Muslim era and calendar
hikayat (M, from Ar)	chronicle
Hui, Huihui (Ch)	Muslim
hujiao (Ch)	*hui* teaching: Islam
ijāza	document certifying one's authority to teach classical Islamic texts
ijmāʿ	consensus of the Muslim community on a matter of Islamic law
ijtihād	use of individual reasoning in interpreting Islamic law
īlchī (Mg)	envoy (from the Mongol period)
ʿilm (M *ilmu*), pl. *ʿulūm*	'science', esp. of religion
imām	prayer leader
imam	title of the heads of Shīʿī Islam following ʿAlī
iqṭāʿ	an assignment of land or its revenue; provincial government; held by a *muqṭaʿ*
Ismāʿīlīs	Shīʿī sect founded in 765, which split off from what was to become the Twelvers
isrāʾ	Muḥammad's ascension through the various levels of Heaven
Ithnā ʿAsharī	'Twelver', the largest Shīʿī sect, which believed in the succession of twelve imams: made the official religion of Iran under the Safavids
jahr	vocal *dhikr*
jāmiʿ masjid	'congregational' or Friday mosque
jihād	'struggle', either internal, against one's own faults, or external, warfare against the infidel; holy war
jimat (M)	talisman, often in form of sacred formula
jinn	airy or fiery being(s), the third intelligent form of life beside humans and angels

jizya	poll-tax paid by non-Muslims
juan (Ch)	chapter
kāfir	unbeliever
kalām	Muslim theology
kātib	scribe, secretary
kaum (M/I, from Ar *qawm*)	group, but often referring specifically to pious Muslims
Ke (Ch)	guests
kerajaan (M)	kingdom
Khādim al-Ḥaramayn	servitor of the Holy Cities
khalīfa	head of a Muslim state; *see* caliph
khan (T)	sovereign, ruler, head of a tribe: title used by Turks and Mongols
khānaqā (P)	building for Sufi gatherings
kharāj	land-tax paid on conquered territories
khāṣṣa (P)	lands in the personal domain of the shah (Safavid period)
khuṭba	sermon given in a mosque at Friday prayer
kitāb	book
kitab kuning/jawi (M)	books in Arabic script, usually in the Islamic religious sciences
kraton (J)	palace
kufr	unbelief
kunya	an honorific component of an Arabic name
lontarak (Bg)	palm-leaf manuscript
madhhab	school of religious law
madrasa	religious school or college
maesan (J)	gravestone
mahdī	messianic figure
Mālikī	one of the four schools of Sunnī Islamic law
mamluk	military slave (*see also ghulām*)
māqulat	inferential theology
masjid	mosque

maẓālim	court exercising jurisdiction supplementary to that of the *qāḍī*, for the redress of grievances
miḥrāb	niche in a mosque to indicate the direction (*qibla*) of Mecca and therefore of prayer
mila (Swahili)	custom
minbar	pulpit in a mosque
miʿrāj	Muḥammad's 'night journey'
muʿallim (M. *mualim*)	expert, especially in mysticism; navigator
muftī	jurist with authority to issue legal opinions (*fatwā*)
mujtahid	*ʿālim* competent to exercise *ijtihād*
mullā (P)	Muslim cleric
murīd	disciple of a Sufi master
murshid	Sufi master
murtad	apostasy
mustawfī	revenue accountant
Nan (Ch)	southern (people)
naṣṣ	designation of a Shīʿī imam by his predecessor
ngelmu (J)	(esoteric) knowledge (cf. *ʿilm*)
nisba	Arabic name affixations indicating relation to place, tribe or person
Nizārīs	Ismāʿīlī sect, esp. in Persia, from 1094
nobat (M)	drums used in installing rulers; enthronement
nöker (Mg)	comrade, follower, in Mongol society
Pardesi (H)	Malabar Muslims of Arab ancestry
pěcat tanda (J)	head of the market
peranakan (M)	locally born persons, usually of foreign descent
perang sabil (I)	war in the way (of God)
pertapaan (J)	hermitages
pesantren (J)	Islamic school (for *santri*)
pesisir (J)	coast, shoreline
pīr (P)	master of a Sufi brotherhood

prabu pandita (J)	king-priest
prajurit estri (J)	sultan's elite female guard
qāḍī	judge of Islamic law
Qādiriyya	Sufi brotherhood following tradition of ʿAbd al-Qādir
qalān (Mg)	a Mongol tax
qanāt	underground irrigation channel
qiyāma	the Resurrection
Qizilbāsh (T)	'red-heads', the Turkmen tribal followers of the Safavid order
qūbchūr (Mg)	tax on flocks and herds; poll-tax
qullar (P)	members of the Safavid *ghulām* cavalry
qurchī (P)	members of the permanent military force of the early Safavids
quriltai (Mg)	Mongol assembly of notables
ratu adil (J/M)	just king
ribāṭ	fortress on the frontiers of the *dār al-islām*; a Sufi monastery
ṣāḥib-dīwān	minister of finance; chief minister in Mongol Persia
Saka (J)	Indic calendrical system, also in Java, beginning 78 CE
sangha (S)	Buddhist monkhood
santri (J)	adept, disciple, pupil in a *pesantren* (madrasa)
sart	caravaneer
sayyid	descendant of the Prophet Muḥammad
semu (Ch)	lit. coloured eyes; foreigners, including Central Asians, Europeans and Muslims
senapang (I)	rifle
Shāfiʿī	one of the four schools of Sunnī Islamic law
shahāda	confession of faith
shahbandar (P/M)	port superintendent
shahīd	martyr
shaḥna	military governor

sharīʿa	God's law, interpreted by the *fuqahāʾ*
sharīf	of noble lineage, especially from the Prophet
shaykh	'old man'; leader of a tribe; head of a Sufi fraternity
Shīʿa	one of the two main branches of Islam, the other being the Sunnī
Sufi	a Muslim mystic
sulṭān (sultan)	'power'; title used by Muslim rulers, Saljuq period and after
suluk (J)	verse genre, of Sufi literature in Javanese
sunna	the example of the Prophet Muḥammad: one of the sources of Islamic law
Sunnī	one of the two main branches of Islam, the other being the Shīʿa
suyūrghāl	an assignment of land or its revenue, a form of *iqṭāʿ*
syair (M)	verse form of traditional Malay literature
ṭabaqāt	an Arabic genre of biographical dictionary
tafsīr	Qurʿānic exegesis
tamghā (T)	tax on commercial transactions
tapa (J)	ascetic/mystic
taqiyya	tactical dissimulation, esp. among the Shīʿa
taʾrīkh	history, date
Taʾrīkh	Maldivian state chronicle
ṭarīqa	Sufi fraternity
tayungan (J)	dance performed by ornately costumed archers
taʿziya	Shīʿī passion play, commemorating the death of the Imām Ḥusayn
tian (Ch)	Heaven
Tian Fang (Ch)	Mecca; the Kaʿba
tiyūl	a form of *iqṭāʿ*

tusheng fanke (Ch)	autochthonous or native-born foreign guests
ʿulamāʾ	plural of *ʿālim*; more commonly used (Malay *ulama*) than the singular to designate a religious scholar in South-East Asia
umma	the Muslim community
undang-undang (M)	digest of customary law
ʿurf	customary law
Uṣūlī	Shīʿī theological school which favoured the use of *ijtihād*
Vanias (H)	Hindu commercial caste
vizier	minister, often chief minister
waḥdat al-wujūd	Sufi doctrine of 'the oneness of Being'
waḥy (M/J *wahyu*)	divine revelation; in Java, the divine charisma of kings
wali (J)	apostle, holy man (from Ar *walī*, saint)
wali sanga (J)	'nine saints' to whom Islamisation of Java is attributed
waqf (pl. *awqāf*)	Muslim religious endowment
wayang (J)	theatre, especially of shadow puppetry
wayang golek (J)	three-dimensional rod puppets
wayang kulit (J/M)	shadow puppet theatre (lit. leather theatre)
wayang topeng (J)	masked theatre
Xinjiang (Ch)	new dominion, 'New Territory'
yam (Mg)	Mongol postal-courier system
yasa (Mg)	decree, law, custom
ẓāhir	the obvious meaning of the Qurʾān, as opposed to its hidden meaning (*bāṭin*)
zakāt	alms tax
Zaydī	a Shīʿī sect

Bibliography

1 The steppe peoples in the Islamic world
Edmund Bosworth

Practical suggestions for further reading

Barthold, W., *Turkestan down to the Mongol invasion*, Gibb Memorial Series, n.s. vol. V, 3rd edn., London, 1968.

Bosworth, C. E., 'The political and dynastic history of the Iranian world (AD 1000–1217)', in J. A. Boyle (ed.), *The Cambridge history of Iran*, vol. V: *The Saljuq and Mongol periods* Cambridge, 1968, pp. 1–202.

Grousset, R., *The empire of the steppes: A history of Central Asia*, Eng. trans. Naomi Walford, New Brunswick, NJ, 1970.

Morgan, David O., *Medieval Persia, 1040–1797*, London and New York, 1988.

Safi, Omid, *The politics of knowledge in premodern Islam: Negotiating ideology and religious enquiry*, Chapel Hill, NC, 2006.

Soucek, Svat, *A history of Inner Asia*, Cambridge, 2000.

UNESCO, *History of civilizations of Central* Asia, 8 parts in 7 vols., Paris, 1992–2005.

Primary sources

Barhebraeus, *Chronography*, Eng. trans. E. A. Wallis Budge, London, 1932.

Bayhaqī, Abu 'l-Faḍl, *Tārīkh-i Mas'ūdī*, ed. 'A. A. Fayyāḍ, Tehran, 1350/1971.

Bundārī, al-Fatḥ b. 'Alī, *Zubdat al-nuṣra wa-nukhbat al-'uṣra*, ed. M. T. Houtsma in *Recueil de textes relatifs à l'histoire des Seljoucides*, vol. II, Leiden, 1889.

Gardīzī, 'Abd al-Ḥayy b. al-Ḍaḥḥāk, *Kitāb Zayn al-akhbār*, ed. Muhammad Nazim, Berlin-Steglitz, 1928.

al-Ḥusaynī, Ṣadr al-Dīn 'Alī, *Akhbār al-dawla al-saljūqiyya*, ed. Muḥammad Iqbāl, Lahore, 1933.

Ibn al-Athīr, 'Izz al-Dīn, *al-Kāmil fi 'l-ta'rīkh*, 13 vols., Beirut, 1385–7/1965–7.

Ibn al-Balkhī, *Fārs-nāma*, ed. G. Le Strange and R. A. Nicholson, Gibb Memorial Series, n.s. vol. I, London, 1921.

Ibn Faḍlān, Aḥmad, *Riḥla*, ed. and Ger. trans. A. Z. V. Togan, *Ibn Faḍlāns Reisebericht*, Abhandlungen für die Kunde des Morgenlandes, XXIV/3 (Leipzig, 1939); Fr. trans. Marius Canard, 'La relation du voyage d'Ibn Fadlân chez les Bulgares de la Volga', in *Annales de l'Institut d'Études Orientales de la Faculté des Lettres d'Alger*, 14 (1956), pp. 41–146; Eng. trans. R. N. Frye, *Ibn Fadlan's journey to Russia: A tenth-century traveler from Baghdad to the Volga river*, Princeton, 2005.

Juwaynī, ʿAṭāʾ-Malik, *Tārīkh-i Jahān-gushā*, Eng. trans. J. A. Boyle, *The history of the World-Conqueror*, 2 vols., Manchester, 1958.

Jūzjānī, Minhāj al-Dīn, *Ṭabaqāt-i nāṣirī*, ed. ʿAbd al-Ḥayy Ḥabībī, 2 vols. (Kabul, 1342-3/1963-4), Eng. trans. H. G. Raverty, *Ṭabaḳāt-i-nāṣirī: A general history of the Muhammadan dynasties of Asia, including Hindustan*, 2 vols., London, 1881–99.

Kāshgharī, Maḥmūd, *Dīwān lughāt al-turk*, Eng. trans. Robert Dankoff and James Kelly, *Compendium of the Turkic dialects (Dīwān luyāt at-Turk)*, 3 vols., Cambridge, MA, 1982–5.

Muḥammad b. Ibrāhīm, *Tārīkh-i Saljūqiyān-i Kirmān*, ed. M. T. Houtsma, in *Recueil de textes relatifs à l'histoire des Seljoucides*, vol. I, Leiden, 1886.

Narshakhī, Abū Bakr Muḥammad, *Tārīkh-i Bukhārā*, ed. Mudarris Riḍawī (Tehran, n.d. [1939]), Eng. trans. R. N. Frye, *The history of Bukhara*, Cambridge, MA, 1954.

Niẓām al-Mulk, Abū ʿAlī Ḥasan Ṭūsī, *Siyāsat-nāma*, ed. H. Darke, Tehran, 1340/1962, 2nd edn 1347/1968, Eng. trans. Darke, *The book of government or rules for kings*, London, 1960, 2nd edn 1978.

Pseudo-Ẓahīr al-Dīn Nīshāpūrī, *Saljūq-nāma*, Eng. trans. K. A. Luther, *The history of the Seljuq Turks from the* Jāmiʿ al-tawārīkh: *An Ilkhanid adaption [sic] of the* Saljūq-nāma *of Ẓahīr al-Dīn Nīshāpūrī*, Richmond, 2001.

Rāwandī, Muḥammad b. ʿAlī, *Rāḥat al-ṣudūr wa-āyat al-surūr*, ed. Muḥammad Iqbál, Gibb Memorial Series, n.s. vol. II, London, 1921.

Secondary sources

Barthold, W., *Zwölf Vorlesungen über die Geschichte der Türken Mittelasiens*, trans. Th. Menzel, Berlin, 1935.

History of the Semirechyé, in *Four studies on the history of Central Asia*, trans. V. and T. Minorsky, vol. I, Leiden, 1962, pp. 73–165.

Biran, Michal, *The empire of the Qara Khitai in Eurasian history: Between China and the Islamic world*, Cambridge, 2005.

Bosworth, C. Edmund, *The Ghaznavids: Their empire in Afghanistan and eastern Iran, 994–1040*, Edinburgh, 1963.

'Dailamīs in central Iran; the Kākūyids of Jibāl and Yazd', *Iran, Journal of the British Institute of Persian Studies*, 7 (1969), pp. 73–95.

'Barbarian invasions: The coming of the Turks into the Islamic world', in *Islamic civilisation 950–1150*, Papers on Islamic History III, ed. D. S. Richards, Oxford, 1973, pp. 1–16.

The later Ghaznavids: Splendour and decay: The dynasty in Afghanistan and northern India, 1040–1186, Edinburgh, 1977.

The New Islamic dynasties: A chronological and genealogical manual, Edinburgh, 1996.

'The Seljuqs and the Khwarazm Shahs. Part 3. The eastern Seljuq sultanate (1118–57) and the rise and florescence of the Khwarazm Shahs of Anūshtegin's line up to the appearance of the Mongols (1097–1219)', in UNESCO, *History of the civilizations of Central Asia*, vol. IV: *The age of achievement: AD 750 to the end of the fifteenth century. Part 1, the historical, social and economic setting*, Paris, 1998, pp. 161–75.

Bregel, Yuri, 'Turko-Mongol influences in Central Asia', in Robert L. Canfield (ed.), *Turko-Persia in historical perspective*, School of American Research Advanced Seminar Series, Cambridge, 1991, pp. 53–77.

Busse, Heribert, *Chalif und Grosskönig. Die Buyiden im Iraq (945–1055)*, Beiruter Texte und Studien 6, Beirut and Wiesbaden, 1969.

Cahen, Claude, 'La campagne de Mantzikert d'après les sources musulmanes', *Byzantion*, 9 (1934), pp. 613–42.

'La première pénétration turque en Asie-Mineure (seconde moitié du XIe siècle)', *Byzantion*, 18 (1948), pp. 5–67.

'Les tribus turques d'Asie occidentale pendant la période seljukide', *Wiener Zeitschrift für die Kunde des Morgenlandes*, 51 (1948–52), pp. 178–87.

'Le Malik-Nameh et les origines seljukides', *Oriens*, 2 (1949), pp. 31–65.

Pre-Ottoman Turkey: A general survey of the material and spiritual culture and history c. 1071–1330, trans. J. Jones-Williams, London, 1968.

The formation of Turkey: The Seljukid sultanate of Rum: eleventh to fourteenth century, trans. P. M. Holt, Harlow, 2001.

Daftary, Farhad, *The Ismāʿīlīs: Their history and doctrines*, Cambridge, 1990, 2nd edn, 2007.

Davidovich, E. A., 'The Karakhanids', in UNESCO, *History of civilizations of Central Asia*, vol. IV: *The age of achievement: AD 750 to the end of the fifteenth century, Part 1, The historical, social and economic setting*, Paris, 1998, pp. 119–43.

Frye, Richard N., *Bukhara, the medieval achievement*, Bibliotheca Iranica Reprint Series no. 3, Costa Mesa, CA, 1997.

Gibb, H. A. R., *The Arab conquests in Central Asia*, London, 1923.

Golden, B., Peter, 'The Karakhanids and early Islam', in Denis Sinor (ed.), *The Cambridge history of early Inner Asia*, Cambridge, 1990, pp. 343–70.

An introduction to the history of the Turkic peoples, Turcologica 9, Wiesbaden, 1992.

Gordon, Matthew S., *The breaking of a thousand swords: A history of the Turkish military of Samarra (AH 200-275/815-889 CE)*, Albany, 2001.

Hartmann, Angelika, *An-Nāṣir li-Dīn Allāh (1180–1225). Politik, Religion, Kultur in der späten ʿAbbāsidenzeit, Studien zur Sprache, Geschichte und Kultur des islamischen Orients*, n.s. 8, Berlin and New York, 1975.

Hillenbrand, Carole, *Turkish myth and Muslim symbol: The battle of Manzikert*, Edinburgh, 2007.

Hodgson, Marshall G. S., *The order of Assassins: The struggle of the early Nizârî Ismâʿîlîs against the Islamic world*, The Hague, 1955.

Kafesoğlu, İbrahim, *Sultan Melikşah devrinde Büyük Selçuklu imparatorluğu*, Istanbul, 1953.

Harezmşahlar devleti tarihi (485-617/1092-1229), Ankara, 1956.

Klausner, Carla L., *The Seljuk vezirate: A study of civil administration 1055–1194*, Harvard Middle Eastern Monograph Series XXII, Cambridge, MA, 1973.

Kochnev, Boris D., 'Les frontières du royaume des Karakhanides', in Vincent Fourniau (ed.), *Études karakhanides*, Cahiers d'Asie centrale, 9, Tashkent and Aix-en-Provence, 2001, pp. 41–8.

'La chronologie et la généalogie des Karakhanides du point de vue de la numismatique', in *Études karakhanides*, pp. 49–75.

Köprülu, Meḥmed Fuʾād, *Early mystics in Turkish literature*, ed. and Eng. trans. Gary Leiser and Robert Dankoff, Routledge Sufi Series, London and New York, 2006.

Köymen, Mehmad Altay, *Büyük Selçuklu imparatorluğu tarihi*, vol. II: *İkinci impartorluk devri*, Ankara, 1954.

Lambton, A. K. S., *Landlord and peasant in Persia: A study of land tenure and land revenue administration*, London, 1953; expanded edn., 1991.

'The administration of Sanjar's empire as illustrated in the *'Atabat al-kataba'*, *Bulletin of the School of Oriental and African Studies*, 20 (1957), pp. 367–88.
'The internal structure of the Saljuq empire', in *The Cambridge history of Iran*, vol. V, pp. 203–82.
State and government in medieval Islam: An introduction to the study of Islamic political theory: The jurists, London Oriental Series, 36, Oxford, 1981.
Merçil, Erdoğan, *Kirman Selçukları*, Istanbul, 1980.
Minorsky, Vladimir F., *Studies in Caucasian history. I. New light on the Shaddādids of Ganja. II. The Shaddādids of Ani. III. The prehistory of Saladin*, London, 1953.
Nāẓim, Muḥammad, *The life and times of Sulṭān Maḥmūd of Ghazna*, Cambridge, 1931.
Pritsak, Omeljan, 'Von den Karluk zu den Karachaniden', *Zeitschrift der Deutschen Morgenländischen Gesellschaft*, 101 (1951), pp. 270–300.
'Der Untergang des Reiches des Oguzischen Yabgu', in *60. doğum yılı münasebetiyle Fuad Köprülü armağan/Mélanges Fuad Köprülü*, Istanbul, 1953, pp. 397–410.
'Die Karachaniden', *Der Islam*, 31 (1953), pp. 17–68.
Sanaullah, Mawlawi Fāḍil, *The decline of the Saljūqid empire*, Calcutta, 1938.
Sevim, Ali, and C. Edmund Bosworth, 'The Seljuqs and the Khwarazm Shahs', in UNESCO, *History of civilizations of Central Asia*, vol. IV, part 1, Paris, 1998. pp. 145–75.

2 The early expansion of Islam in India
André Wink

Practical suggestions for further reading

Arab conquests, rule and economic life in Zābul, Kabul, Makrān and Sind; early trade in the Indian Ocean

Watson, A., *Agricultural innovation in the early Islamic world: The diffusion of crops and farming techniques, 700–1100*, Cambridge, 1983.
Wink, A., *Al-Hind: The making of the Indo-Islamic world*, vol. I: *Early medieval India and the expansion of Islam, 7th–11th centuries*, Leiden, 1990.

India and Central Asia; post-nomadic empires

Gommans, J. J. L., 'The silent frontier of South Asia, c. AD 1000–1800', *Journal of World History*, 9, 1 (1998), pp. 1–23.
Wink, A., *Al-Hind: The making of the Indo-Islamic world*, vol. III: *Indo-Islamic society, 14th–15th centuries*, Leiden, 2004; and Wink, vol. II.

Ghaznavids in India

Bosworth, C. E., *The Ghaznavids: Their empire in Afghanistan and eastern Iran, 994–1040*, Edinburgh, 1963.
The later Ghaznavids: Splendour and decay: The dynasty in Afghanistan and northern India, 1050–1186, Edinburgh, 1977.
Wink, A., *Al-Hind: The making of the Indo-Islamic world*, vol. II: *The slave kings and the Islamic conquest of India, 11th–13th centuries*, Leiden, 1997.

Ghūrids

Wink, A., *Al-Hind: The making of the Indo-Islamic world*, vol. II: *The slave kings and the Islamic conquest of India, 11th–13th centuries*, Leiden, 1997.

Primary sources

Arab conquests, rule and economic life in Zābul, Kabul, Makrān and Sind; early trade in the Indian Ocean

al-Balādhurī, *Futūḥ al-buldān*, Cairo, 1932.
Daudpota, U. M. (ed.), *Chachnāma*, Hyderabad, 1939.
al-Masʿūdī, *Murūj al-dhahab*, 2 vols., Cairo, 1948.
al-Muqaddasī, *Descriptio imperii moslemici*, Leiden, 1906.

Ghaznavids

Morley, W. H. (ed.), *Ta'rīkh-i-Baihaqī*, Calcutta, 1862.
al-ʿUtbī, *Tārīkh al-Yamīnī*, Delhi, 1847.

Ghūrids

Lees, N. (ed.), *Ṭabaqāt-i-Nāṣirī of Ābū ʿUmar al-Jūzjānī*, Calcutta, 1894; ed. ʿA. Ḥabībī, *Ṭabaqāt-i Nāṣirī*, 2 vols., 2nd edn, Kabul, 1964–5.

Secondary sources

Arab conquests, rule and economic life in Zābul, Kabul, Makrān and Sind; early trade in the Indian Ocean

Mishra, Y., *The Hindu Sahis of Afghanistan and the Punjab, AD 865–1026*, Patna, 1972.
Misra, S. C., *Muslim communities in Gujarat*, Baroda, 1964.

3 Muslim India: The Delhi sultanate
Peter Jackson

Practical suggestions for further reading

Eaton, Richard M., *The rise of Islam and the Bengal frontier, 1204–1760*, Berkeley and Los Angeles, 1993.
Habib, Mohammad and Nizami, Khaliq Ahmad (eds.), *A comprehensive history of India, vol. V: The Delhi Sultanate AD 1206–1526*, New Delhi, 1970.
Habibullah, A. B. M., *The foundation of Muslim rule in India*, 2nd edn, Allahabad, 1961.
Hardy, Peter, *Historians of medieval India: Studies in Indo-Muslim historical writing*, London, 1960, repr., with new preface, New Delhi, 1997.
Husain, Agha Mahdi, *Tughluq dynasty*, Calcutta, 1963.
Jackson, Peter, *The Delhi sultanate: A political and military history*, Cambridge, 1999.
Khan, Iqtidar Alam, *Gunpowder and firearms: Warfare in medieval India*, Oxford and Delhi, 2004.
Lal, Kishori Saran, *A history of the Khaljis AD 1290–1320*, 3rd edn, Delhi, 1980.
Twilight of the sultanate, 3rd edn, New Delhi, 1980.

Wink, André, *Al-Hind: The making of the Indo-Islamic world*, vol. II: *The slave kings and the Islamic conquest of India, 11th–13th centuries*, Leiden, 1997.
Al-Hind: The making of the Indo-Islamic world, vol. III: *Indo-Islamic society, 14th–15th centuries*, Leiden, 2004.

Primary sources (including epigraphy and numismatics)

ʿAfīf, Shams-i Sirāj, *Tārīkh-i Fīrūzshāhī*, ed. Maulavi Vilayat Hosain, Calcutta, 1891.
Amīr Ḥasan Dihlawī, *Fawāʾid al-fuʾād*, ed. Muḥammad Laṭīf Malik, Lahore, AH 1386.
Amīr Khusraw Dihlawī, *Rasāʾil al-iʿjāz*, lithograph edn, 5 vols. in 2, Lucknow, 1876.
Tughluq-nāma, ed. Sayyid Hāshimī Farīdābādī, Aurangabad, 1933.
Nuh sipihr, ed. Muḥammad Wahīd Mīrzā, London, 1950.
Khazāʾin al-futūḥ, ed. Muḥammad Wahīd Mīrzā, Calcutta, 1953.
Miftāḥ al-futūḥ, ed. Shaikh Abdur Rashid, Aligarh, 1954.
Dīwal Rānī-yi Khaḍir Khān, ed. Rashīd Aḥmad Sālim Anṣārī, Aligarh, AH 1336.
Qirān al-saʿdayn, ed. Maulavi Muḥammad Ismāʿīl and Sayyid Ḥasan Baranī, Aligarh, AH 1337.
Bābur, Ẓahīr al-Dīn Muḥammad, *Bābur-nāma*, trans. Annette S. Beveridge, *The Bābur-nāma in English*, 2 vols., London, 1921–2; repr. in 1 vol., 1969.
Baranī, Ḍiyā-yi, *Tārīkh-i Fīrūzshāhī*, ed. Saiyid Ahmad Khán, Calcutta, 1861–2.
Fatāwā-yi Jahāndārī, ed. Afsar Saleem Khan, Lahore, 1972.
Bihāmadkhānī, Muḥammad, *Tārīkh-i Muḥammadī*, British Library ms. Or. 137; partial trans. by Muhammad Zaki, Aligarh, 1972.
Desai, Ziyaud-din A. (ed.), *A topographical list of Arabic, Persian and Urdu inscriptions of south India*, New Delhi, 1989.
(ed.), *Arabic, Persian and Urdu inscriptions of west India: A topographical list*, New Delhi, 1999.
Fakhr-i Mudabbir, *Shajarat* [or *Baḥr*] *al-ansāb*, partial edn by Sir E. Denison Ross as Taʿríkh [sic]-i *Fakhr al-Dín Mubárakshâh*, London, 1927.
Firishta (Muḥammad Qāsim Hindūshāh Astarābādī), *Gulshan-i Ibrāhīmī*, lithograph edn, 2 vols., Bombay, AH 1247.
Fīrūz Shāh (Sultan), *Futūḥāt- Fīrūzshāhī*, ed. Shaikh Abdur Rashid, Aligarh, 1954.
Ḥāfiẓ-i Abrū, *Zubdat al-tawārīkh*, ed. Sayyid Kamāl Ḥāj Sayyid Jawādī, 2 vols., Tehran, AH solar 1372.
Ḥamīd Qalandar, *Khayr al-majālis*, ed. Khaliq Ahmad Nizami, Aligarh, [1959].
Ḥasan-i Niẓāmī, *Tāj al-maʾāthir*, India Office ms. 15 (Ethé, *Catalogue*, no. 210).
Ibn Baṭṭūṭa, *Tuḥfat al-nuẓẓār*, ed. Ch. Defrémery and B. R. Sanguinetti, 4 vols. Paris, 1853–8; trans. H. A. R. Gibb and C. F. Beckingham, *The travels of Ibn Battuta AD 1325–1354*, 5 vols., Hakluyt Society, Cambridge and London, 1958–2000.
Ibn Faḍl-allāh al-ʿUmarī, *Masālik al-abṣār fī mamālik al-amṣār*, partial edn by Otto Spies, *Ibn Faḍlallāh al-ʿOmarī's Bericht über Indien*, Leipzig, 1943, and trans. Iqtidar Husain Siddiqi and Qazi Muhammad Ahmad, *A fourteenth-century Arab account of India under Sultan Muhammad bin Tughlaq*, Aligarh, [1975]; partial edn by Klaus Lech, *Das mongolische Weltreich*, Asiatische Forschungen, 22, Wiesbaden, 1968.
Ibn Māhrū, ʿAyn al-Mulk ʿAbd-allāh b. Muḥammad, *Inshā-yi Māhrū*, ed. Shaikh Abdur Rashid, Lahore, 1965.

ʿIṣāmī, *Futūḥ al-salaṭīn*, ed. A. S. Usha, Madras, 1948; trans. A. M. Husain, 3 vols., Aligarh, 1967–77.

Jazarī, Shams al-Dīn Muḥammad, *Ḥawādith al-zamān*, ed. ʿAbd al-Salām Tadmurī, 3 vols., Beirut AH 1419.

Juwaynī, ʿAlāʾ al-Dīn Aṭā Malik, *Tārīkh-i jahān-gushā*, ed. Mīrzā Muḥammad Qazwīnī, 3 vols., Gibb Memorial Series XVI, Leiden, 1912–37; trans. John Andrew Boyle, *The history of the world-conqueror*, 2 vols., Manchester, 1958, repr. in 1 vol., 1997.

Jūzjānī, Minhāj-i Sirāj, *Ṭabaqāt-i Nāṣirī*, ed. ʿAbd al-Ḥayy Ḥabībī, 2nd edn, 2 vols., Kabul, AH solar 1342–3.

Kūfī, ʿAlī b. Ḥāmid b. Abī Bakr, *Chach-nāma*, ed. N. A. Baloch as *Fathnāmah-i Sind*, Islamabad, AH 1403.

Mīr-i Khwurd (Muḥammad b. Mubārak Kirmānī), *Siyar al-awliyāʾ*, lithograph edn, Delhi, AH 1302.

Prasad, Pushpa (ed.), *Sanskrit inscriptions of Delhi sultanate 1191–1526*, Oxford and Delhi, 1990.

Rashīd al-Dīn Faḍl-allāh al-Hamadānī, *Jāmiʿ al-tawārīkh*, partial edn and trans. by Karl Jahn, *Die Indiengeschichte des Rašīd ad-Dīn*, 2nd edn, Vienna, 1980.

Shabānkāraʾī, Muḥammad b. ʿAlī, *Majmaʿ al-ansāb*, ed. Mīr Hāshim Muḥaddith, Tehran, AH solar 1363.

Shāmī, Niẓām-i, *Ẓafar-nāma*, ed. Felix Tauer, *Histoire des conquêtes de Tamerlan*, 2 vols., Monografie Archivu Orientálního, 5, Prague, 1937–58.

Shokoohy, Mehrdad (ed.), *Rajasthan I*, Corpus inscriptionum Iranicarum, part IV: Persian inscriptions down to the early Safavid period, 49, London, 1986.

(ed.), *Haryana I*, Corpus inscriptionum Iranicarum, part IV: Persian inscriptions down to the early Safavid period, 47, London, 1988.

Sīrat-i Fīrūzshāhī, School of Oriental and African Studies ms. 283116 (copy of ms. in Bankipore Library, Patna).

Sirhindī, Yaḥyāʾ ibn Aḥmad, *Tārīkh-i Mubārakshāhī*, ed. S. M. Hidayat Hosain, Calcutta, 1931.

Thomas, Edward, *Chronicles of the Pathan kings of Delhi*, Delhi, 1871.

Willis, Michael D. (ed.), *Inscriptions of Gopakṣetra: Materials for the history of central India*, London, 1996.

Wright, H. Nelson, *The coinage and metrology of the Sulṭāns of Delhī*, Delhi, 1936; repr. New Delhi, 1974.

Yazdī, Ghiyāth al-Dīn ʿAlī, *Rūz-nāma-yi ghazawāt-i Hindūstān*, trans. A. A. Semenov, *Dnevnik pokhoda Tīmūra v Indiiu*, Moscow, 1958.

Secondary sources

Ahmad, Aziz, 'The early Turkish nucleus in India', *Turcica*, 9 (1977), pp. 99–109.

Aubin, Jean, 'L'ethnogénèse des Qaraunas', *Turcica*, 1 (1969), pp. 65–94.

Biran, Michal, *Qaidu and the rise of the independent Mongol state in Central Asia*, Richmond, 1997.

Chakravarti, Ranabir, 'Horse trade and piracy at Tana (Thana, Maharashtra, India): Gleanings from Marco Polo', *Journal of the Economic and Social History of the Orient*, 34 (1991), pp. 159–82.

Chattopadhyaya, Brajadulal, *Representing the Other? Sanskrit sources and the Muslims (eighth to fourteenth century)*, New Delhi, 1998.

Conermann, Stephan, *Die Beschreibung Indiens in der 'Riḥla' des Ibn Baṭṭūṭa: Aspekte einer herrschaftssoziologischen Einordnung des Delhi-Sultanates unter Muḥammad Ibn Tuġluq*, Islamkundliche Untersuchungen, 165, Berlin, 1993.

Dani, Ahmad Hasan, 'Shamsuddīn Ilyās Shāh, Shāh-i Bangālah', in Hari Ram Gupta *et al.* (eds.), *Essays presented to Sir Jadunath Sarkar*, 2 vols., Hoshiarpur, 1958, vol. II, pp. 50–8.

Day, U. N., *The government of the sultanate*, 2nd edn, New Delhi, 1993.

Deyell, John S., *Living without silver: The monetary history of early medieval north India*, Oxford and Delhi, 1990.

Digby, Simon, *War-horse and elephant in the Delhi sultanate: A study of military supplies*, Oxford and Delhi, 1971.

'The currency system', in Raychaudhuri and Habib (eds.), *The Cambridge economic history of India*, vol. I, pp. 93–101.

'The sufi *shaykh* and the sultan: A conflict of claims to authority in medieval India', *Iran*, 28 (1990), pp. 71–81.

'Before Timur came: Provincialization of the Delhi sultanate through the fourteenth century', *Journal of the Economic and Social History of the Orient*, 47 (2004), pp. 298–356.

Eaton, Richard Maxwell, *Sufis of Bijapur 1300–1700: Social roles of sufis in medieval India*, Princeton, 1978.

'Temple desecration and Indo-Muslim states', *Journal of Islamic Studies*, 11 (2000), pp. 283–319; repr. in Gilmartin and Lawrence (eds.), *Beyond Turk and Hindu*, pp. 246–81.

Ernst, Carl W., *Eternal garden: Mysticism, history and politics at a South Asian Sufi center*, Albany, 1992.

Frykenberg, Robert E. (ed.), *Delhi through the ages: Essays in urban history, culture and society*, Oxford and Delhi, 1986.

Gilmartin, David and Lawrence, Bruce B. (eds.), *Beyond Turk and Hindu: Rethinking religious identities in Islamicate South Asia*, Gainesville, FL, 2000.

Gommans, Jos, 'The silent frontier of South Asia, *c.* AD 1100–1800', *Journal of World History*, 9 (1998), pp. 1–23.

'Warhorse and gunpowder in India *c.* 1000–1850', in Jeremy Black (ed.), *War in the early modern world*, London, 1999, pp. 105–27.

Habib, Irfan, 'Economic history of the Delhi sultanate – an essay in interpretation', *Indian Historical Review*, 4 (1977), pp. 287–303.

'Baranī's theory of the history of the Delhi sultanate', *Indian Historical Review*, 7 (1980–1), pp. 99–115.

'Agrarian economy', in Raychaudhuri and Habib (eds.), *The Cambridge economic history of India*, vol. I, pp. 48–76.

'The price regulations of 'Alā'uddīn Khaljī – a defence of Ẓiā' Baranī', *Indian Economic and Social History Review*, 21 (1984), pp. 393–414.

'Formation of the sultanate ruling class of the thirteenth century', in Irfan Habib (ed.), *Medieval India 1: Researches in the history of India 1200–1750*, Oxford and Delhi, 1992, pp. 1–21.

Hambly, Gavin R. G., 'Twilight of Tughluqid Delhi', in Frykenberg, *Delhi through the ages*, pp. 47–56.

Hardy, Peter, 'The growth of authority over a conquered political elite: The early Delhi sultanate as a possible case study', in John S. Richards (ed.), *Kingship and authority in South Asia*, Madison, WI, 1978, pp. 192–214.

'The authority of mediaeval Muslim kings in South Asia', in Marc Gaborieau (ed.), *Islam et société en Asie du Sud*, Collection Puruṣārthe, 9, Paris, 1986, pp. 37–55.

Hodivala, S. H., *Studies in Indo-Muslim history*, 2 vols., Bombay, 1939–57.

Husain, Agha Mahdi, *The rise and fall of Muhammad bin Tughluq*, Calcutta, 1938.

Islam, Zafarul, 'The *Fatāwā Fīrūz Shāhī* as a source for the socio-economic history of the sultanate period', *Islamic Culture*, 60 (1986), part 2, pp. 97–117.

'Fīrūz Shāh's attitude towards non-Muslims – a reappraisal', *Islamic Culture*, 64 (1990), part 4, pp. 65–79.

Jackson, Peter, 'The Mongols and the Delhi sultanate in the reign of Muḥammad Tughluq (1325–1351)', *Central Asiatic Journal*, 19 (1975), pp. 118–57.

'Delhi: The problem of a vast military encampment', in Frykenberg, *Delhi through the ages*, pp. 18–33.

'Jalāl al-Dīn, the Mongols and the Khwarazmian conquest of the Panjāb and Sind', *Iran*, 28 (1990), pp. 45–54.

'The *Mamlūk* institution in early Muslim India', *Journal of the Royal Asiatic Society* (1990), pp. 340–58.

'The fall of the Ghurid dynasty', in Carole Hillenbrand (ed.), *Studies in honour of Clifford Edmund Bosworth*, vol. II: *The sultan's turret: Studies in Persian and Turkish culture*, Leiden, 2000, pp. 207–37.

Jahn, Karl, 'Zum Problem der mongolischen Eroberungen in Indien (13.–14. Jahrhundert)', in *Akten des XXIV. internationalen Orientalisten-Kongresses München ... 1957*, Wiesbaden, 1959, pp. 617–19.

Khan, Iqtidar Alam, 'Origin and development of gunpowder technology in India: AD 1250–1500', *Indian Historical Review*, 4 (1977–8), pp. 20–9.

'The coming of gunpowder to the Islamic world and north India: Spotlight on the role of the Mongols', *Journal of Asian History*, 30 (1996), pp. 27–45.

'The role of the Mongols in the introduction of gunpowder and firearms in South Asia', in Brenda J. Buchanan (ed.), *Gunpowder: The history of an international technology*, Bath, 1996, pp. 33–44.

Khuhro, Hamida (ed.), *Sind through the centuries*, Oxford and Karachi, 1981.

Moreland, W. H., *The agrarian system of Moslem India*, Cambridge, 1929.

Naqvi, Hamida Khatoon, *Agricultural, industrial and urban dynamism under the sultans of Delhi 1206–1555*, New Delhi, 1986.

Nizami, Khaliq Ahmad, *Some aspects of religion and politics in India in the thirteenth century*, Aligarh, 1961.

On history and historians of medieval India, New Delhi, 1983.

Raychaudhuri, Tapan and Habib, Irfan (eds.), *The Cambridge economic history of India*, vol. I: *c.1200–c.1750*, Cambridge, 1982.

Siddiqi, Iqtidar Husain, *Some aspects of Afghān despotism in India*, Aligarh, 1969.

'Wajh-i Maʿash grants under the Afghan kings (1451–1555)', *Medieval India: A Miscellany*, 2 (1972), pp. 19–44.

'The Qarlūgh kingdom in north-western India during the thirteenth century', *Islamic Culture*, 54 (1980), pp. 75–91.

'The Afghans and their emergence in India as ruling elite during the Delhi sultanate period', *Central Asiatic Journal*, 26 (1982), pp. 241–61.

'Politics and conditions in the territories under the occupation of Central Asian rulers in north-western India – 13th and 14th centuries', *Central Asiatic Journal*, 27 (1983), pp. 288–306.
'Sultan Muhammad bin Tughluq's foreign policy: A reappraisal', *Islamic Culture*, 62 (1988), part 4, pp. 1–22.
Perso-Arabic sources of information on the lives and conditions in the sultanate of Delhi, New Delhi, 1992.
(ed.), *Medieval India I: Essays in intellectual thought and culture*, New Delhi, 2003.
Talbot, Cynthia, 'Inscribing the Other, inscribing the self: Hindu–Muslim identities in pre-colonial India', *Comparative Studies in Society and History*, 37 (1995), pp. 692–722.
Venkata Ramanayya, N., 'The date of the rebellions of Tilang and Kampila against Sultan Muhammad bin Tughlaq', *Indian Culture*, 5 (1938–9), pp. 135–46, 261–9.
Venkataramanyya, N., *The early Muslim expansion in south India*, Madras, 1942.
Verma, H. C., *Dynamics of urban life in pre-Mughal India*, New Delhi, 1986.
Welch, Anthony and Crane, Howard, 'The Tughluqs: Master builders of the Delhi sultanate', *Muqarnas*, 1 (1983), pp. 123–66.

4 The rule of the infidels: the Mongols and the Islamic world
Beatrice Forbes Manz

Practical suggestions for further reading

Aigle, Denise, *Le Fārs sous la domination mongole: Politique et fiscalité (XIIIe–XIVe s.)*, Paris, 2005.
Allsen, Thomas, *Mongol imperialism: The policies of the Grand Qan Möngke in China, Russia and the Islamic lands, 1251–1259*, Berkeley, 1987.
Culture and conquest in Mongol Eurasia, Cambridge, 2001.
Amitai-Preiss, Reuven and Morgan, David O. (eds.), *The Mongol empire and its legacy*, Leiden, 1999.
Carboni, Stefano and Komaroff, Linda (eds.), *The legacy of Genghis Khan: Courtly art and culture in western Asia, 1256–1353*, New York, 2002.
Jackson, Peter, *The Mongols and the West, 1221–1410*, Harlow, 2005.
Komaroff, Linda (ed.), *Beyond the legacy of Genghis Khan*, Leiden, 2006.
Lane, George, *Early Mongol rule in thirteenth-century Iran*, London, 2003.
Morgan, David, *The Mongols*, Oxford, 1986; 2nd edn 2007.
Raby, Julian and Fitzherbert, Teresa, eds., *The court of the Il-khans 1290–1340*, Oxford, 1996.

Primary sources

Bar Hebraeus, Gregorius Abū'l-Faraj, trans. E. A. Wallis Budge, *The chronography of Gregory Abu'l Faraj ... commonly known as Bar Hebraeus*, 2 vols., Oxford and London, 1932.
Faṣīḥ Khwāfī, Aḥmad b. Jalāl al-Dīn, *Mujmal-i faṣīḥī*, ed. Muḥammad Farrukh, 3 vols., Mashhad, AH solar 1339.
Ḥāfiẓ-i Abrū, *Dhayl-i jāmiʿ al-tawārīkh*, ed. K. Bayani, Tehran, 1971.
al-Harawī, Sayf b. Muḥammad b. Yaʿqūb (Sayfī), *Tārīkh-nāma-i Harāt*, ed. Muḥammad Zubayr al-Ṣiddiqī, Calcutta, 1944.

Ibn Baṭṭūṭa, Shams al-Dīn, *The travels of Ibn Baṭṭūṭa, AD 1325–1354*, trans. H. A. R. Gibb, 3 vols., Hakluyt Society, 5 vols., Cambridge, 1958–2000.
Juwaynī, ʿAlāʾ al-Dīn ʿAṭā Malik, *Tārīkh-i jahān-gushā*, ed. Mīrzā Muḥammad Qazwīnī, 3 vols., Gibb Memorial Series XVI, Leiden, 1912–37.
The history of the world-conqueror, trans. John A. Boyle, 2 vols., Manchester, 1958.
Men-da Beĭ-lu ('Polnoe opisanie Mongolo-Tatar'), ed. and trans. N. Ts. Munkuev, Moscow, 1975.
Mustawfī Qazwīnī, Ḥamd Allāh, *The geographical part of the Nuzhat al-qulūb composed by Ḥamd-Allāh Mustawfī of Qazwīn in 740 (1340)*, ed. and trans. G. Le Strange, Gibb Memorial Series, London, 1915–18.
Qāshānī, Abū'l Qāsim, *Tārīkh-i Ūljaytū*, ed. Mahin Hambly, Tehran, 1969.
Rashīd al-Dīn Hamadānī, *Jāmiʿ al-tawārīkh*, ed. A. A. Ali-zade, 3 vols., Moscow, 1968–80.
trans. J. A. Boyle, *The successors of Genghis Khan*, New York, 1971.
Jāmiʿ al-tawārīkh: Compendium of chronicles: A history of the Mongols, trans. Wheeler Thackston, 3 vols., Sources of Oriental Languages and Literatures, Harvard University, Cambridge, MA, 1998–9.
ed. Muḥammad Rawshan, Muṣṭafā Mūsawī, 4 vols., Tehran, AH solar 1373.
al-ʿUmarī, *Das mongolische Weltreich. Al-ʿUmarīs Darstellung der mongolischen Reiche in seinem Werk Masālik al-abṣār fī mamālik al-amṣār*, ed. and trans. K. Lech, Wiesbaden, 1968.
Waṣṣāf, ʿAbd Allāh b. Faḍl Allāh, *Tajziyat al-amṣār wa tazjiyat al-aʿṣār (Tārīkh-i Waṣṣāf)*, Bombay, 1852–3, repr. Tehran, AH 1338.

Secondary sources

Aigle, Denise, (ed.), *L'Iran face à la domination mongole*, Bibliotèque Iranienne 45, Tehran, 1997.
'Le grand *jasaq* de Gengis-Khan, l'empire, la culture mongole et la *sharīʿa*', *Journal of the Economic and Social History of the Orient*, 47, 1 (2004), pp. 31–79.
Allsen, Thomas T., 'Mongolian princes and their merchant partners, 1200–1260', *Asia Major*, 3rd ser., 2 (1989), pp. 83–126.
'Changing forms of legitimation in Mongol Iran', in Gary Seaman and Daniel Marks (eds.), *Rulers from the steppe: State formation and the Eurasian periphery*, Ethnographics Monograph Series, 2, Los Angeles, 1991, pp. 223–41.
'Notes on Chinese titles in Mongol Iran', *Mongolian Studies*, 14 (1991), pp. 27–39.
'The rise of the Mongolian empire and Mongolian rule in north China', in Herbert Franke and Denis Twitchett (eds.), *Cambridge history of China*, vol. VI, Cambridge, 1994, pp. 321–413.
'Biography of a cultural broker, Bolad Ch'eng-Hsiang in China and Iran', in Raby and Fitzherbert (eds.), *The court of the Il-khans*, pp. 7–22.
'Spiritual geography and political legitimacy in the eastern steppe', in Henri J. M. Claessen and Jarich G. Oosten (eds.), *Ideology and the formation of early states*, Leiden, 1996, pp. 116–35.
Commodity and exchange in the Mongol empire: A cultural history of Islamic textiles, Cambridge, 1997.
'Ever closer encounters: The appropriation of culture and the apportionment of peoples in the Mongol empire', *Journal of Early Modern History*, 1, 1 (1997), pp. 2–23.

'Sharing out the empire: Apportioned lands under the Mongols,' in A. Wink and A. Khazanov (eds.), *Nomads in the sedentary world*, Richmond, 2001, pp. 172–90.

Amitai, Reuven, 'Ghazan, Islam and Mongol tradition: A view from the Mamlūk sultanate', *Bulletin of the School of Oriental and African Studies*, 59, 1 (1996), pp. 1–10.

'Sufis and shamans: Some remarks on the Islamization of the Mongols in the Ilkhanate', *Journal of the Economic and Social History of the Orient*, 42 (1999), pp. 27–46.

Amitai, Reuven and Biran, Michal (eds.), *Mongols, Turks, and others: Eurasian nomads and the sedentary world*, Leiden, 2005.

Amitai-Preiss, Reuven, *Mongols and Mamluks: The Mamluk–Īlkhānid war, 1260–1281* Cambridge, 1995.

Aubin, Jean, 'Les princes d'Ormuz du XIIIe au XVe siècle', *Journal Asiatique*, 241 (1953), pp. 77–137.

'L'éthnogénèse des Qaraunas', *Turcica*, 1 (1969), pp. 65–94.

'Réseau pastoral et réseau caravanier: Les grand'routes du Khurassan à l'époque mongole', *Le Monde Iranien et l'Islam*, 1 (1971), pp. 105–30.

'Le khanat de Čaġatai et le Khorassan (1334–1380)', *Turcica*, 8, 2 (1976), pp. 16–60.

'La propriété foncière en Azerbaydjan sous les Mongols', *Le Monde Iranien et l'Islam*, 4 (1976–7), pp. 79–132.

'Le quriltai de Sultân-Maydân (1336)', *Journal Asiatique*, 279 (1991), pp. 175–97.

Émirs mongols et vizirs persans dans les remous de l'acculturation, Cahiers de Studia Iranica, Paris, 1995.

Ayalon, David, 'The great Yāsa of Chingiz Khān: A reexamination', A, *Studia Islamica*, 33 (1971), pp. 97–140, B, 34 (1971), pp. 151–80, C(1), 36 (1972), pp. 113–58, C(2), 38 (1973), pp. 107–56.

Barthold, W., *Turkestan down to the Mongol invasion*, London, 1968.

Biran, Michal, *Qaidu and the rise of the independent Mongol state in Central Asia*, Richmond, 1997.

'The battle of Herat (1270): A case of inter-Mongol warfare', in Nicola Di Cosmo (ed.), *Warfare in Inner Asian history (500–1800)*, Leiden, 2002, pp. 175–219.

'The Chaghadaids and Islam: The conversion of Tarmashirin Khan (1331–34)', *Journal of the American Oriental Society*, 122, 4 (2002), pp. 742–52.

Blair, Sheila S., 'Calligraphers, illuminators, and painters in the Ilkhanid scriptorium', in Komaroff (ed.), *Beyond the legacy*, pp. 167–82.

Boyle, John A., 'Dynastic and political history of the Īl-Khāns', in *Cambridge history of Iran*, vol. V, Cambridge, 1968, pp. 303–421.

Buell, Paul D., 'Tribe, "*Qan*" and "*ulus*" in early Mongol China: Some prolegomena to Yüan history', Ph.D. thesis, University of Washington, 1977.

'Sino-Khitan administration in Mongol Bukhara', *Journal of Asian History*, 13, 2 (1979), pp. 121–47.

'Early Mongol expansion in western Siberia and Turkestan (1207–1219): A reconstruction', *Central Asiatic Journal*, 36, 1-2 (1992), pp. 1–32.

Cahen, Claude, *The formation of Turkey: The Seljukid Sultanate of Rūm: Eleventh to fourteenth century*, trans. P. M. Holt, Harlow 2001.

Carboni, Stefano, 'Synthesis: Continuity and innovation in Ilkhanid art', in Carboni and Kamaroff (eds.), *Legacy*, pp. 196–225.

DeWeese, Devin, *Islamization and native religion in the Golden Horde: Baba Tükles and conversion to Islam in historical and epic tradition*, University Park, PA, 1994.

Dillon, Michael, *China's Muslim Hui community: Migration, settlement and sects*, Richmond, 1999.

Endicott-West, Elizabeth, 'Merchant associations in Yüan China: The *ortogh*', *Asia Major*, 3rd ser., 2 (1989), pp. 127–54.

Fedorov-Davydov, G. A., *Obshchestvennyĭ stroĭ Zolotoĭ Ordy*, Moscow, 1973.

Fletcher, Joseph, 'The Mongols: Ecological and social perspectives', *Harvard Journal of Asiatic Studies*, 46 (1986), pp. 11–50.

Fragner, Bert, 'Ilkhanid rule and its contributions to Iranian political culture', in Komaroff (ed.), *Beyond the legacy*, pp. 68–80.

Hillenbrand, Robert, 'The arts of the book in Ilkhanid Iran', in Carboni and Komaroff (eds.), *Legacy*, pp. 134–67.

Hoffmann, Birgitt, 'The gates of piety and charity: Rašīd al-Din Faḍl Allāh as founder of pious endowments', in Aigle (ed.), *L'Iran*, pp. 189–201.

Waqf im mongolischen Iran. Rašīduddīns Sorge um Nachruhm und Seelenheil, Freiburger Islamstudien, 20, Stuttgart, 2000.

Hsiao, Ch'i-ch'ing, *The military establishment of the Yuan dynasty*, Harvard East Asian Monographs, 77, Cambridge, MA, 1978.

Jackson, Peter, 'The Mongols and the Delhi sultanate in the reign of Muḥammad Tughluq (1325–1351)', *Central Asiatic Journal*, 19, 1–2 (1975), pp. 118–57.

'The dissolution of the Mongol empire', *Central Asiatic Journal*, 22 (1978), pp. 186–243.

'From *ulus* to khanate: The making of the Mongol states *c.* 1220–*c.* 1290', in Amitai-Preiss and Morgan (eds.), *Mongol empire*, pp. 12–38.

Katō, Kazuhide, 'Kebek and Yasawr: The establishment of the Chaghatai-Khanate', *Memoirs of the Research Department of the Toyo Bunko*, 49 (1991), pp. 97–118.

Kempiners, Russell G., 'Vaṣṣāf's *Tajziyat al-amṣār wa tazjiyat al-a'ṣār* as a source for the history of the Chaghadayid khanate', *Journal of Asian History*, 22, 2 (1988), pp. 160–87.

Kim, Ho-Dong, 'The early history of the Moghul nomads: The legacy of the Chaghatai khanate', in Amitai-Preiss and Morgan (eds.), *Mongol empire*, pp. 290–318.

'A reappraisal of Güyüg Khan', in Amitai and Biran, *Mongols, Turks, and others*, pp. 309–38.

Krawulsky, Dorothea, *Īrān – Das Reich der Īlhāne. Eine topographisch-historische Studie, Beihefte zum Tübinger Atlas des vorderen Orients*, ser. B 17, Wiesbaden, 1978.

Mongolen und Ilkhâne – Ideologie und Geschichte: 5 Studien, Beirut, 1989.

Lambton, Ann K. S., 'Mongol fiscal administration in Persia', part I, *Studia Islamica*, 64 (1986), pp. 79–99, part II, *Studia Islamica*, 65 (1987), pp. 97–123.

Continuity and change in medieval Persia: Aspects of administrative, economic and social history, 11th–14th century, Columbia Lectures on Iranian Studies, 2, Albany, 1988.

Lane, George, 'Arghun Aqa: Mongol bureaucrat', *Iranian Studies*, 32, 4 (1999), pp. 459–82.

Leslie, Donald D., *Islam in traditional China: A short history to 1800*, Belconnen, 1986.

Liu, Yingsheng, 'War and peace between the Yuan dynasty and the Chaghadaid khanate (1312–1323)', in Amitai and Biran (eds.), *Mongols, Turks, and others*, pp. 339–58.

Masuya, Tomoko, 'Ilkhanid courtly life', in Carboni and Komaroff (eds.), *Legacy*, pp. 74–103.

May, Timothy, 'A Mongol–Ismâ'îlî alliance?: Thoughts on the Mongols and Assassins', *Journal of the Royal Asiatic Society*, ser. 3, 14, 3 (2004), pp. 231–9.

Melikian-Chirvani, Assadullah Souren, 'Conscience du passé et résistance culturelle dans l'Iran mongol', in Aigle (ed.), *L'Iran*, pp. 135–77.
Melville, Charles, 'Pādshāh-i Islām: The conversion of Sultan Maḥmūd Ghāzān Khān', *Pembroke Papers*, 1 (1990), pp. 159–77.
'"The year of the elephant": Mamluk–Mongol rivalry in the Hejaz in the reign of Abū Saʿīd (1317–1335)', *Studia Iranica*, 21, 2 (1992), pp. 197–214.
The fall of Amir Chupan and the decline of the Ilkhanate 1327–1337: A decade of discord in Iran, Bloomington, IN, 1999.
'The Īlkhān Öljeitü's conquest of Gīlān (1307): Rumour and reality', in Amitai-Preiss and Morgan (eds.), *Mongol empire*, pp. 73–125.
'The *keshig* in Iran: The survival of the royal Mongol household', in Komaroff (ed.), *Beyond the legacy*, pp. 135–64.
Morgan, David O., 'Mongol or Persian: The government of Īlkhānid Iran', *Harvard Middle Eastern and Islamic Review*, 3, 2 (1996), pp. 62–76.
'Rašīd al-Dīn and Ġazan Khan', in Aigle (ed.), *L'Iran*, pp. 179–88.
'Reflections on Mongol communications in the Ilkhanate', in Carole Hillenbrand (ed.), *Studies in honour of Clifford Edmund Bosworth*, vol. II: *The sultan's turret: Studies in Persian and Turkish culture*, Leiden, 2000, pp. 375–85.
'The "Great *yasa* of Chinggis Khan" revisited', in Amitai and Biran (eds.), *Mongols, Turks and others*, pp. 291–308.
Morton, A. H., 'The letters of Rashīd al-Dīn: Īlkhānid fact or Timurid fiction?', in Amitai-Preiss and Morgan (eds.), *Mongol empire*, pp. 155–99.
O'Kane, Bernard, 'Persian poetry on Ilkhanid art and architecture', in Komaroff (ed.), *Beyond the legacy*, pp. 346–54.
Paul, Jürgen, 'L'invasion mongole comme "révélateur" de la société iranienne', in Aigle (ed.), *L'Iran*, pp. 37–53.
Paviot, Jacques, 'Les marchands italiens dans l'Iran mongol', in Aigle (ed.), *L'Iran*, pp. 71–86.
Petrushevskiĭ, I. P., *Zemledelie i agrarnye otnosheniia v Irane XIII–XIV vekov*, Moscow and Leningrad, 1960.
'The socio-economic condition of Iran under the Īlkhāns', in *The Cambridge history of Iran*, vol. V, Cambridge, 1968, pp. 483–537.
'Pokhod mongol'skikh voĭsk v Sredniuiu Aziiu v 1219–1224 gg. i ego posledstviia', in S. L. Tikhvinskiĭ (ed.), *Tataro-Mongoly v Azii i Evrope*, Moscow, 1970, pp. 100–33.
Pfeiffer, Judith, 'Conversion to Islam among the Ilkhans in Muslim narrative traditions: The case of Aḥmad Tegüder', Ph.D. dissertation, University of Chicago, 2003.
Potter, Lawrence G., 'The Kart dynasty of Herat: Religion and politics in medieval Iran', Ph.D. thesis, Columbia University, 1992.
Quade-Reutter, Karin, '*... denn sie haben einen unvollkommenen Verstand'. Herrschaftliche Damen im Grossraum Iran in der Mongolen und Timuridenzeit (ca. 1250–1507)*, Aachen, 2003.
Rachewiltz, Igor de, 'The title Činggis Qan/Qa'an re-examined', in W. Heissig and Klaus Sagaster (eds.), *Gedanke und Wirking. Festschrift zum 90. Geburtstag von Nikolaus Poppe*, Asiatische Forschungen, 108, Wiesbaden, 1989, pp. 281–98.
Rachewiltz, Igor de, Hok-lam Chan, Hsiao Ch'i-ch'ing and Geier, Peter W. (eds.), *In the service of the khan: Eminent personalities of the early Mongol-Yüan period*, Wiesbaden, 1993.

Ratchnevsky, Paul, *Genghis Khan, his life and legacy*, trans. and ed. Thomas N. Haining, Oxford, 1992.
Remler, Philip, 'New light on economic history from Ilkhanid accounting manuals', *Studia Iranica* 14, 2 (1985), pp. 157–77.
Richard, Jean, 'D'Äljigidäi à Ġazan: La continuité d'une politique franque chez les Mongols d'Iran', in Aigle (ed.), *L'Iran*, pp. 57–69.
Rossabi, Morris, 'The Muslims in the early Yüan dynasty', in John D. Langlois (ed.), *China under Mongol rule*, Princeton, 1981, pp. 257–95.
Khubilai Khan: His life and times, London, 1988.
'The Mongols and their legacy', in Carboni and Komaroff (eds.), *Legacy*, pp. 12–35.
Togan, Isenbike, *Flexibility and limitation in steppe formations: The Kerait khanate and Chinggis Khan*, Leiden, 1998.
Vasáry, István, '"History and legend" in Berke Khan's conversion to Islam', in *Aspects of Altaic civilization III: Proceedings of the thirtieth meeting of the Permanent International Altaistic Conference, Indiana University, Bloomington, Indiana, June 19–25, 1987*, Bloomington, IN, 1990, pp. 230–52.
Zerjal, Tatiana, Xue, Yali *et al.*, 'The genetic legacy of the Mongols', *American Journal of Human Genetics*, 72 (2003), pp. 717–21.

5 Tamerlane and his descendants: from paladins to patrons
Maria E. Subtelny

Practical suggestions for further reading

Barthold, V. V., *Four studies on the history of Central Asia*, trans. V. Minorsky and T. Minorsky, vol. II, *Ulugh-Beg*; vol. III, *Mīr 'Alī-Shīr* and *A history of the Turkman people*, Leiden, 1958–62.
Golombek, Lisa and Subtelny, Maria (eds.), *Timurid art and culture: Iran and Central Asia in the fifteenth century*, Leiden, 1992.
Hodgson, Marshall G. S., *The venture of Islam: Conscience and history in a world civilization*, vol. II: *The expansion of Islam in the Middle Periods*, Chicago, 1974.
Jackson, Peter and Lockhart, Laurence (eds.), *The Cambridge history of Iran*. vol. VI: *The Timurid and Safavid periods*, Cambridge, 1986.
Lentz, Thomas W. and Lowry, Glenn D., *Timur and the princely vision: Persian art and culture in the fifteenth century*, Los Angeles, 1989.
Manz, Beatrice Forbes, *The rise and rule of Tamerlane*, Cambridge, 1989.
Power, politics and religion in Timurid Iran, Cambridge, 2007.
Morgan, David, *Medieval Persia, 1040–1797*, London, 1988.
Subtelny, Maria E., *Timurids in transition: Turko-Persian politics and acculturation in medieval Iran*, Leiden, 2007.

Primary sources

Album, Stephen, *Sylloge of Islamic coins in the Ashmolean*, vol. IX: *Iran after the Mongol invasion*, Oxford, 2001.
Alisher Navoii, *Mazholisun nafois*, ed. Suiima Ghanieva, Tashkent, 1961.
Asarlar, 15 vols., Tashkent, 1963–8.

Mukammal asarlar tŭplami, ed. K. Yashin *et al.*, 20 vols., Tashkent, 1987–2003.
ʿAlīshīr Nawāʾī, *Majālis al-nafāʾis dar tadhkira-i shuʿarāʾ-i qarn-i nuhum-i hijrī*, trans. Sulṭān-Muḥammad Fakhrī Harātī and Ḥakīm Shāh-Muḥammad Qazwīnī, ed. ʿAlī Aṣghar Ḥikmat, Tehran, 1323, repr. 1363.
Babur, Ẓahīr al-Dīn Muḥammad, *Babur-nāma (Vaqāyiʿ)*, ed. Eiji Mano, 2 vols., Kyoto, 1995–6.
Clavijo, [Ruy González de], *Embassy to Tamerlane, 1403–1406*, trans. Guy Le Strange, London, 1928, repr. 2005.
Dawlatshāh Samarqandī, *Tadhkirat al-shuʿarāʾ*, ed. Edward G. Browne, London, 1901.
Fischel, Walter J., *Ibn Khaldūn and Tamerlane: Their historic meeting in Damascus, 1401 AD (803 AH): A study based on Arabic manuscripts of Ibn Khaldūn's 'Autobiography'*, Berkeley and Los Angeles, 1952.
Gross, Jo-Ann and Urunbaev, Asom (eds. and trans.), *The letters of Khwāja ʿUbayd Allāh Aḥrār and his associates*, Leiden, 2002.
Ḥāfiẓ-i Abrū, *Zubdat al-tawārīkh*, ed. Sayyid Kamāl Ḥājj Sayyid Jawādī, 2 vols., Tehran, 1372.
Ibn ʿArabshāh, Aḥmad b. Muḥammad, *ʿAjāʾib al-maqdūr fī nawāʾib Taymūr*, ed. Aḥmad Fāʾiz al-Ḥimṣī, Beirut, 1407.
Isfizārī, Muʿīn al-Dīn Muḥammad Zamchī, *Rawḍāt al-jannāt fī awṣāf madīnat Harāt*, ed. Sayyid Muḥammad Kāẓim Imām, 2 vols., Tehran, 1338–9.
Jāmī, Nūr al-Dīn ʿAbd al-Raḥmān b. Aḥmad, *Nafaḥāt al-uns min ḥaḍarāt al-quds*, ed. Maḥmūd ʿĀbidī, Tehran, 1370.
Dīwān-i Jāmī, ed. Aʿlā Khān Afṣaḥzād, 2 vols., Tehran, 1378.
Mathnawī-i Haft awrang, ed. Jābilqādād ʿAlīshāh *et al.*, 2 vols., Tehran, 1378.
Khwāndamīr, Ghiyāth al-Dīn b. Humām al-Dīn, *Dastūr al-wuzarāʾ*, ed. Saʿīd Nafīsī, Tehran, 1317, repr. 2535/1976.
Ḥabīb al-siyar fī akhbār afrād-i bashar, ed. Jalāl al-Dīn Humāʾī, 4 vols., Tehran, 1333, 3rd repr. 1362.
Habibu's-siyar: Tome three, trans. W. M. Thackston, Sources of Oriental Languages and Literatures, 24, 2 parts, Cambridge, MA, 1994.
Krawulsky, Dorothea (ed. and trans.), *Ḫorāsān zur Timuridenzeit nach dem Tārīḫ-e Ḥāfeẓ-e Abrū (verf. 817–823 h.)*, 2 vols., Wiesbaden, 1982–4.
Muʿizz al-ansāb fī shajarat al-ansāb, ms. Bibliothèque nationale de France, Ancien fonds persan 67.
Muʿizz al-ansāb (Proslavliaiushchee genealogii), ed. and trans. Sh. Kh. Vokhidov, Alma Ata, 2006.
Naṭanzī, Muʿīn ad-Dīn, *Muntakhab al-tawārīkh-i muʿīnī*, ed. Jean Aubin, Tehran, 1336.
Nawāʾī, ʿAbd al-Ḥusayn, *Asnād wa-mukātabāt-i tārīkhī-i Īrān: Az Tīmūr tā Shāh Ismāʿīl*, Tehran, 2536/1977.
Qāsim b. Yūsuf Abū Naṣrī Harawī, *Irshād al-zirāʿa*, ed. Muḥammad Mushīrī, Tehran, 1346.
Roemer, Hans Robert, (ed. and trans.), *Staatsschreiben der Timuridenzeit. Das Šaraf-nāmä des ʿAbdallāh Marwārīd in kritischer Auswertung*, Wiesbaden, 1952.
(ed. and trans.), *Šams al-ḥusn. Eine Chronik vom Tode Timurs bis zum Jahre 1409 von Tāǧ as-Salmānī*, Wiesbaden, 1956.
Samarqandī, Kamāl al-Dīn ʿAbd al-Razzāq, *Maṭlaʿ-i saʿdayn wa-majmaʿ-i baḥrayn*, ed. Muḥammad Shafīʿ, vol. II in 3 parts, Lahore, 1365–8.
Sanders, J. H. (trans.), *Tamerlane or Timur the Great Amir: From the Arabic life by Ahmed Ibn Arabshah*, London, 1936.

Tauer, Felix, 'Continuation du Ẓafarnāma de Nīẓamuddīn Šāmī par Ḥāfiẓ-i Abrū', *Archiv Orientální*, 6 (1934), pp. 429–65.

(ed.), *Histoire des conquêtes de Tamerlan, intitulée Ẓafarnāma par Niẓāmuddīn Šāmī, avec des additions empruntées au Zubdatu-t-tawāriḫ-i Bāysunġurī de Ḥāfiẓ-i Abrū*, 2 vols., Prague, 1937–56.

(ed.), *Cinq opuscules de Ḥāfiẓ-i Abrū concernant l'histoire de l'Iran au temps de Tamerlan*, Prague, 1959.

Thackston, Wheeler M. (trans. and ed.), *The Baburnama: Memoirs of Babur, prince and emperor*, New York, 1996.

'Uqaylī, Sayf al-Dīn Ḥājjī b. Niẓām, *Āthār al-wuzarā'*, ed. Mīr Jalāl al-Dīn Ḥusaynī Urmawī 'Muḥaddith', Tehran, 1337.

Urunbaev, A. (ed. and trans.), *Pis'ma-avtografy Abdarrakhmana Dzhami iz 'Al'boma Navoi'*, Tashkent, 1982.

Yazdī, Sharaf al-Dīn 'Alī, *Ẓafar-nāma: Tārīkh-i 'umūmī mufaṣṣil-i Īrān dar dawra-i Tīmūriyān*, ed. Muḥammad 'Abbāsī, 2 vols., [Tehran], 1336.

Secondary sources

Akimushkin, Oleg, *et al.*, *The arts of the book in Central Asia, 14th–16th centuries*, ed. Basil Gray, London, 1979.

Ando, Shiro, *Timuridische Emire nach dem Mu'izz al-ansāb. Untersuchung zur Stammesaristokratie Zentralasiens im 14. und 15. Jahrhundert*, Berlin, 1992.

'Die timuridische Historiographie II. Šaraf al-dīn 'Alī Yazdī', *Studia Iranica*, 24, 2 (1995), pp. 219–46.

Aubin, Jean, 'Le mécénat timouride à Chiraz', *Studia Islamica*, 8 (1957), pp. 71–88.

'Tamerlan à Baġdād', *Arabica*, 9 (1962), pp. 303–9.

'Comment Tamerlan prenait les villes', *Studia Islamica*, 19 (1963), pp. 83–122.

Barry, Michael, *Figurative art in medieval Islam and the riddle of Bihzâd of Herât (1465–1535)*, Paris, 2004.

Barthold, W., *An historical geography of Iran*, trans. Svat Soucek, ed. C. E. Bosworth, Princeton, 1984.

Bartol'd, V. V., 'Mir Ali-Shir i politicheskaia zhizn'', in V. V. Bartol'd, *Sochineniia*, vol. II, part 2, ed. Iu. È. Bregel, Moscow, 1964, pp. 199–260.

'O pogrebenii Timura', in V. V. Bartol'd, *Sochineniia*, vol. II, part 2, ed. Iu. È. Bregel', Moscow, 1964, pp. 423–54.

'Ulugbek i ego vremia', in V. V. Bartol'd, *Sochineniia*, vol. II, part 2, ed. Iu. È. Bregel', Moscow, 1964, pp. 25–196.

Bernardini, Michele (ed.), 'La civiltà timuride come fenomeno internazionale', 2 vols., special issue, *Oriente Moderno*, n.s. 15, 2 (1996).

Bertel's, Evgenii Èduardovich, *Navoi i Dzhami*, Moscow, 1965.

Birnbaum, Eleazar, 'The Ottomans and Chagatay literature: An early 16th century manuscript of Navā'ī's *Dīvān* in Ottoman orthography', *Central Asiatic Journal*, 20, 3 (1976), pp. 157–90.

Dale, Stephen F. 'The legacy of the Timurids', *Journal of the Royal Asiatic Society*, 3rd ser., 8, 1 (1998), pp. 43–58.

The garden of the eight paradises: Bābur and the culture of empire in Central Asia, Afghanistan and India (1483–1530), Leiden, 2004.

Doerfer, Gerhard, *Türkische und mongolische Elemente im Neupersischen. Unter besonderer Berücksichtigung älterer neupersischer Geschichtsquellen, vor allem der Mongolen- und Timuridenzeit*, 4 vols., Wiesbaden, 1963–75.

Fragner, Bert, 'Social and internal economic affairs', in *The Cambridge history of Iran*, vol. VI, pp. 491–567.

Gabain, Annemarie von, 'Kasakentum, eine soziologisch-philologische Studie', *Acta Orientalia Academiae Scientiarum Hungaricae*, 11, 1–3 (1960), pp. 161–7.

Golombek, Lisa, 'The gardens of Timur: New perspectives', *Muqarnas*, 12 (1995), pp. 137–47.

Golombek, Lisa, Mason, Robert B. and Bailey, Gauvin A., *Tamerlane's tableware: A new approach to the chinoiserie ceramics of fifteenth- and sixteenth-century Iran*, Costa Mesa, CA, 1996.

Golombek, Lisa and Wilber, Donald, *The Timurid architecture of Iran and Turan*, 2 vols., Princeton, 1988.

Grupper, S. M., 'A Barulas family narrative in the *Yuan Shih*: Some neglected prosopographical and institutional sources on Timurid origins', *Archivum Eurasiae Medii Aevi*, 8 (1992–4), pp. 11–97.

Kauz, Ralph, *Politik und Handel zwischen Ming und Timuriden. China, Iran und Zentralasien im Spätmittelalter*, Wiesbaden, 2005.

Kennedy, E. S., 'The exact sciences in Timurid Iran', in *The Cambridge history of Iran*, vol. VI, pp. 568–80.

Komaroff, Linda, *The golden disk of heaven: Metalwork of Timurid Iran*, Costa Mesa, CA, 1992.

Levend, Agâh Sırrı, *Ali Şir Nevaî*, 4 vols., Ankara, 1965–8.

McChesney, Robert D., *Waqf in Central Asia: Four hundred years in the history of a Muslim shrine, 1480–1889*, Princeton, 1991.

Timur's tomb: Politics and commemoration, Central Eurasian Studies Lectures, 3, Bloomington, IN, 2003.

'A note on the life and works of Ibn 'Arabshāh', in Judith Pfeiffer and Sholeh A. Quinn (eds.), *History and historiography of post-Mongol Central Asia and the Middle East: Studies in honor of Professor John E. Woods*, in collaboration with Ernest Tucker, Wiesbaden, 2006, pp. 205–49.

Mason, Robert B., 'The response I: Petrography and provenance of Timurid ceramics', in Lisa Golombek, Robert B. Mason and Gauvin A. Bailey, *Tamerlane's tableware: A new approach to the chinoiserie ceramics of fifteenth- and sixteenth-century Iran*, Costa Mesa, CA, 1996, pp. 16–46.

Misugi, T., *Chinese porcelain collections in the Near East: Topkapi and Ardebil*, 3 vols., Hong Kong, 1981.

Mitchell, Colin Paul, 'To preserve and protect: Husayn Va'iz-i Kashifi and Perso-Islamic chancellery culture', *Iranian Studies*, 36, 4 (2003), pp. 485–507.

Necipoğlu, Gülru, *The Topkapı scroll – geometry and ornament in Islamic architecture*, Santa Monica, 1995.

O'Kane, Bernard, *Timurid architecture in Khurasan*, Costa Mesa, CA, 1987.

'Poetry, geometry and the arabesque: Notes on Timurid aesthetics', *Annales Islamologiques*, 26 (1992), pp. 63–78.

'From tents to pavilions: Royal mobility and Persian palace design', *Ars Orientalis*, 23 (1993), pp. 249–68.

Paul, Jürgen, *Die politische und soziale Bedeutung der Naqšbandiyya in Mittelasien im 15. Jahrhundert*, Berlin, 1991.

Richard, Francis, 'Un témoignage inexploité concernant le mécénat d'Eskandar Solṭān à Eṣfahān', *Oriente Moderno*, n.s. 15, 2 (1996), vol. I, pp. 45–72.

Roemer, H. R., 'The successors of Tīmūr', in *The Cambridge history of Iran*, vol. VI, pp. 98–146.

'Tīmūr in Iran', in *The Cambridge history of Iran*, vol. VI, pp. 42–97.

Roxburgh, David J., *The Persian album, 1400–1600: From dispersal to collection*, New Haven, 2005.

Rypka, Jan, *History of Iranian literature*, ed. Karl Jahn, trans. P. van Popta-Hope, Dordrecht, 1968.

Séguy, Marie-Rose (ed.), *The miraculous journey of Mahomet: 'Mirâj nâmeh', Bibliothèque Nationale, Paris (Manuscrit Supplément Turc 190)*, trans. Richard Pevear, New York, 1977.

Soudavar, Abolala, *Art of the Persian courts: Selections from the Art and History Trust collection*, New York, 1992.

Stori, Ch. A. [Storey, C. A.], *Persidskaia literatura: Bio-bibliograficheskii obzor*, trans. and rev. Iu. È. Bregel', 3 vols, Moscow, 1972.

Subtelny, Maria Eva, 'Alī Shīr Navā'ī: *Bakhshī* and *beg*', *Harvard Ukrainian Studies*, 3–4 (1979–80), part 2, pp. 797–807.

'Scenes from the literary life of Tīmūrid Herāt', in *Logos islamikos: Studia islamica in honorem Georgii Michaelis Wickens*, ed. Roger M. Savory and Dionisius A. Agius, Toronto, 1984, pp. 137–55.

'A taste for the intricate: The Persian poetry of the late Timurid period', *Zeitschrift der Deutschen Morgenländischen Gesellschaft*, 136, 1 (1986), pp. 56–79.

'Centralizing reform and its opponents in the late Timurid period', *Iranian Studies*, 21, 1–2 (1988), pp. 123–51.

'Socioeconomic bases of cultural patronage under the later Timurids', *International Journal of Middle East Studies*, 20, 4 (1988), pp. 479–505.

'A Timurid educational and charitable foundation: The Ikhlāṣiyya complex of 'Alī Shīr Navā'ī in 15th-century Herat and its endowment', *Journal of the American Oriental Society*, 111, 1 (1991), pp. 38–61.

'The *Vaqfīya* of Mīr 'Alī Šīr Navā'ī as apologia', *Journal of Turkish Studies*, 15 (1991), vol. II, pp. 257–86.

'A medieval Persian agricultural manual in context: The *Irshād al-zirā'a* in late Timurid and early Safavid Khorasan', *Studia Iranica*, 22, 2 (1993), pp. 167–217.

'The cult of 'Abdullāh Anṣārī under the Timurids', in Alma Giese and J. Christoph Bürgel, (eds.), *Gott ist schön und Er liebt die Schönheit / God is beautiful and He loves beauty: Festschrift in honour of Annemarie Schimmel*, Bern, 1994, pp. 377–406.

'Mīrak-i Sayyid Ghiyās̱ and the Timurid tradition of landscape architecture: Further notes to "A medieval Persian agricultural manual in context"', *Studia Iranica*, 24, 1 (1995), pp. 19–60.

'Agriculture and the Timurid *chahārbāgh*: The evidence from a medieval Persian agricultural manual', in Attilio Petruccioli (ed.), *Gardens in the time of the great Muslim empires: Theory and design*, Leiden, 1997, pp. 110–28.

'The Timurid legacy: A reaffirmation and a reassessment', *Cahiers d'Asie Centrale*, 3–4 (1997), pp. 9–19.

Le monde est un jardin: Aspects de l'histoire culturelle de l'Iran médiéval, Cahiers de Studia Iranica, 28, Paris, 2002.

'Husayn Va'iz-i Kashifi: Polymath, popularizer, and preserver', *Iranian Studies*, 36, 4 (2003), pp. 463–7.
Subtelny, Maria Eva, and Khalidov, Anas B., 'The curriculum of Islamic higher learning in Timurid Iran in the light of the Sunni revival under Shāh-Rukh', *Journal of the American Oriental Society*, 115, 2 (1995), pp. 210–36.
Sulaimon, Hamid and Sulaimonova, Fozila, *Alisher Navoii asarlariga ishlangan rasmlar, XV–XIX asrlar/Miniatiury k proizvedeniiam Alishera Navoi XV–XIX vekov/Miniatures illustrations of Alisher Navoi's works of the XV–XIXth centuries*, Tashkent, 1982.
Szuppe, Maria, 'The female intellectual milieu in Timurid and post-Timurid Herāt: Faxri Heravi's biography of poetesses, *Javāher al-'ajāyeb*', *Oriente Moderno*, n.s. 15, 2 (1996), vol. I, pp. 119–37.
(ed.), 'L'héritage timouride: Iran – Asie centrale – Inde, XVe–XVIIIe siècles', special issue, *Cahiers d'Asie Centrale*, 3–4 (1997).
Woods, John E., 'The rise of Tīmūrid historiography', *Journal of Near Eastern Studies*, 46, 2 (1987), pp. 81–108.
The Timurid dynasty, Papers on Central Asia, 14, Bloomington, IN, 1990.
'Timur's genealogy', in Michel M. Mazzaoui and Vera B. Moreen (eds.), *Intellectual studies on Islam: Essays written in honor of Martin B. Dickson*, Salt Lake City, 1990, pp. 85–125.
Wright, Owen, 'On the concept of a "Timurid music"', *Oriente Moderno*, n.s. 15, 2 (1996), vol. II, pp. 665–81.
Yarshater, Ehsan, 'Persian poetry in the Timurid and Safavid periods', in *The Cambridge history of Iran*, vol. VI, pp. 965–85.

6 Iran under Safavid rule
Sholeh A. Quinn

Practical suggestions for further reading

Aubin, Jean, 'La politique religieuse des Safavides', in Jean Aubin, *Le Shi'ism Imamate*, Paris, 1970, pp. 235–44.
'Revolution Chiite et conservatisme: Les Soufis de Lahejan, 1500–1514 (Études Safavides II)', *Moyen Orient & Océan Indien*, 1 (1984), pp. 1–40.
'L'avènement des Safavides reconsidéré (Études Safavides III)', *Moyen Orient & Océan Indien*, 5 (1988), pp. 1–130.
'Chroniques persanes et relations italiennes: Notes sur les sources narratives du regne de Sah Esma'il Ier', *Studia Iranica*, 24 (1995), pp. 247–59.
Babayan, Kathryn, 'The Safavid synthesis: From Qizilbash Islam to Imamite Shi'ism', *Iranian Studies*, 27 (1994), pp. 135–61.
Bashir, Shahzad, 'Shah Isma'il and the Qizilbash: Cannibalism in the religious history of early Safavid Iran', *Religion*, 45 (2006), pp. 234–56.
Browne, E. G., 'Note on an apparently unique manuscript history of the Safawi dynasty of Persia', *Journal of the Royal Asiatic Society* (1921), pp. 395–418.
A Literary history of Persia, vol. IV: *Modern times (1500–1924)*, Cambridge, 1924.
Calmard, Jean, 'Ali Asghar Mossadegh, and Parizi, M. Bastani, 'Notes sur des historiographes de l'époque Safavide', *Studia Iranica*, 16 (1987), pp. 123–35.
Canby, Sheila R. (ed.), *Safavid art and architecture*, London, 2002.

Dale, Stephen Frederic, 'The legacy of the Timurids', *Journal of the Royal Asiatic Society*, 8 (1998), pp. 43–58.
Dickson, Martin B., 'The fall of the Safavi dynasty', *Journal of the American Oriental Society*, 82 (1962), pp. 503–17.
Dickson, Martin B. and Welch, Stuart Cary, *The Houghton Shahnameh*, 2 vols., Cambridge, MA, 1981.
Farhad, Massumeh, 'The art of Mu'in Musavvir: A mirror of his times', in Sheila R. Canby (ed.), *Persian masters: Five centuries of painting*, Bombay, 1990.
Floor, Willem M., *Safavid government institutions*, Costa Mesa, CA, 2001.
Fragner, Bert G., *Repertorium persischer herrscherurkunden. Publizierte originalurkunden (bis 1848)*, Freiburg, 1980.
Gholsorkhi, Shohreh, 'Ismail II and Mirza Makhdum Sharifi: An interlude in Safavid history', *International Journal of Middle East Studies*, 26 (1994), pp. 477–88.
Haneda, Masashi, 'L'évolution de la garde royal des Safavides', *Moyen Orient & Océan Indien*, 1 (1984), pp. 41–64.
Le chah et les Qizilbash: Le système militaire Safavide, Berlin, 1987.
'La famille Huzani d'Isfahan (15e–17e siècles)', *Studia Iranica*, 18 (1989), pp. 77–92.
Hodgson, Marshall G. S., *The venture of Islam: Conscience and history in a world civilization*, 3 vols., Chicago, 1974.
Jacobs, Adam, 'Sunni and Shi'i perceptions, boundaries and affiliations in late Timurid and early Safawid Persia: An examination of historical and quasi-historical narratives', Ph.D. dissertation, University of London, 1999.
Kafadar, Cemal, *Between two worlds: The construction of the Ottoman state*, Berkeley, 1995.
Kasravī, Aḥmad, *Shaykh Ṣafī va tabārash*, Tehran, 2535 [1976].
LeStrange, Guy, *The lands of the eastern caliphate: Mesopotamia, Persia and Central Asia from the Muslim conquest to the time of Timur*, Cambridge, 1905, repr. New York, 1976.
Lockhart, Laurence, *Nadir Shah*, London, 1938.
McCabe, Ina Baghdiantz, *The shah's silk for Europe's silver: The Eurasian trade of the Julfa Armenians in Safavid Iran and India (1530–1750)*, Atlanta, 1999.
Mazzaoui, Michel, 'From Tabriz to Qazvin to Isfahan: Three phases of Safavid history', *Deutschen Orientalistentag*, 19 (1977), pp. 514–22.
'The siege of Herat during the first year of Shah 'Abbas' reign according to Iskandar Munshi', *Zeitschrift der Deutschen Morgenländeschen Gesellschaft*, Suppl. 4 (1980), pp. 233–4.
Safavid Iran and her neighbors, Salt Lake City, 2003.
Melville, Charles, 'A lost source for the reign of Shah 'Abbas: The Afdal al-Tawarikh of Fazli Khuzani Isfahani', *Iranian Studies*, 31 (1998), pp. 263–5.
'New light on the reign of Shah 'Abbas: Volume III of the Afdal al-Tavarikh', in Andrew J. Newman (ed.), *Society and culture in the early modern Middle East: Studies on Iran in the Safavid period*, Leiden, 2003, pp. 63–97.
Minorsky, Vladimir, 'The poetry of Shah Isma'il I', *Bulletin of the School of Oriental and African Studies*, 10 (1942), pp. 1006–53.
Morgan, David, *Medieval Persia, 1040–1797*, London and New York, 1988.
Morton, A. H., 'The Ardabil shrine in the reign of Shah Tahmasp I', *Iran: Journal of the British Institute of Persian Studies*, 12 (1974), pp. 31–64; 13 (1975), pp. 39–58.
'The *chub-i tariq* and *qizilbash* ritual in Safavid Persia', in *Études Safavides*, ed. Jean Calmard, Paris and Tehran, 1993, pp. 225–45.

Newman, Andrew J. (ed.), *Society and culture in the early modern Middle East: Studies on Iran in the Safavid period*, Leiden, 2003.

Safavid Iran: Rebirth of a Persian empire, London, 2006.

Nikitine, B., 'Essai d'analyse du Safvat-us-Safa', *Journal Asiatique*, 245 (1957), pp. 385–94.

Perry, John R., *Karim Khan Zand*, Chicago, 1977.

Porter, Y., 'Notes sur le "Golestan-e honar" de Qazi Ahmad Qomi', *Studia Iranica*, 17 (1988), pp. 207–23.

Quinn, Sholeh A., 'The dreams of Shaykh Safi al-Din and Safavid historical writing', *Iranian Studies*, 29 (1996), pp. 127–42.

'The historiography of Safavid prefaces', in Charles Melville (ed.), *Safavid Persia: The history and politics of an Islamic society*, London, 1996, pp. 1–25.

'Rewriting Niʿmatullahi history in Safavid chronicles', in Leonard Lewisohn and David Morgan (eds.), *Late classical Persianate Sufism (1501–1750)*, Oxford, 1999.

Rahimi, Babak, 'The rebound theater state: The politics of the Safavid camel sacrifice rituals, 1598–1695 CE', *Iranian Studies*, 37 (2004), pp. 451–78.

Riazul Islam, *Indo-Persian relations: A study of the political and diplomatic relations between the Mughul empire and Iran*, Tehran, 1970.

A calendar of documents on Indo-Persian relations (1500–1750), 2 vols., Tehran and Karachi, 1979.

Roemer, Hans R., 'The Qizilbash Turcomans: Founders and victims of the Safavid theocracy', in Michel M. Mazzaoui and Vera B. Moreen (eds.), *Intellectual studies on Islam: Essays written in honor of Martin B. Dickson*, Salt Lake City, 1990, pp. 27–39.

Rota, Giorgio, 'Three little-known Persian sources of the seventeenth century', *Iranian Studies*, 31 (1998), pp. 159–76.

Roxburgh, David J., *Prefacing the image: The writing of art history in sixteenth-century Iran*, Leiden, 2001.

Rypka, Jan, *History of Iranian literature*, ed. Karl Jahn, Dordrecht, 1968.

Safa, Z., 'Persian literature in the Safavid period', in Peter Jackson and Laurence Lockhart (eds.), *The Cambridge history of Iran*, vol. VI: *The Timurid and Safavid periods*, Cambridge, 1986, pp. 948–64.

Sarwar, Ghulam, *History of Shah Ismaʿil Safawi*, Aligarh, 1939, repr. New York, 1975.

Savory, Roger, 'A 15th-century Safavid propagandist at Harat', in D. Sinor (ed.), *American Oriental Society, Middle West Branch, semi-centennial volume: A collection of original essays*, Bloomington, IN, 1969.

'"Very dull and arduous reading": A reappraisal of the history of Shah ʿAbbas the great by Iskandar Beg Munshi', *Hamdard Islamicus*, 111 (1980), pp. 19–37.

Schimkoreit, Renate, *Regesten publizierter safawidischer herrscherurkunden. Erlasse und staatsschreiben der fruhen neuzeit Irans*, Berlin, 1982.

Simsār, Muḥammad Ḥasan, 'Farmān-nivisī dar dawra-yi Ṣafaviyah', *Barrasīhā-yi tārīkhī*, 2 (1346 [1967–8]), pp. 127–52.

Streusand, Douglas E., *The formation of the Mughal empire*, Delhi, 1989.

Szuppe, Maria, *Entre Timourides, Uzbeks et Safavides: Questions d'histoire politique et sociale de Hérat dans la première moitié du XVIe siècle*, Paris, 1992.

'L'évolution de l'image de Timour et des Timourides dans l'historiographie Safavide du XVIe au XVIIIe siècle', *Cahiers d'Asie Centrale*, 3–4 (1997), pp. 313–31.

Tapper, Richard, 'Shahsevan in Safavid Persia', *Bulletin of the School of Oriental and African Studies*, 37 (1974), pp. 321–54.

Tauer, Felix, 'Persian learned literature from its beginnings up to the end of the 18th century', in Karl Jahn (ed.), *History of Iranian literature*, Dordrecht, 1968, pp. 438–59.
Togan, A. Z. V., 'Sur l'origine des Safavides', in *Mélanges Louis Massignon III*, 3 vols., Damascus, 1957, pp. 345–57.
Tucker, Ernest, 'Explaining Nadir Shah: Kingship and royal legitimacy in Muhammad Kazim Marvi's *Tarikh-i 'alam-ara-yi Nadiri*', *Iranian Studies*, 26 (1993), pp. 95–117.
Nadir Shah's quest for legitimacy in post-Safavid Iran, Gainesville, FL, 2006.
Von Erdman, F., 'Iskender Munschi und sein werk', *Zeitschrift der Deutschen Morgenländeschen Gesellschaft*, 15 (1861), pp. 457–501.
Walsh, J. R., 'The historiography of Ottoman–Safavid relations in the sixteenth and seventeenth centuries', in Bernard Lewis and P. M. Holt (eds.), *Historians of the Middle East*, London, 1962, pp. 197–211.
Wood, Barry D., 'The *Tarikh-i Jahanara* in the Chester Beatty Library: An illustrated manuscript of the "Anonymous Histories of Shah Isma'il"', *Iranian Studies*, 37 (2004), pp. 89–107.
Woods, John E., *The Aqquyunlu: Clan, confederation, empire*, rev. and exp. edn, Salt Lake City, 1999.
Yar-Shater, E., 'Safavid literature: Progress or decline?', *Iranian Studies*, 7 (1974), pp. 217–70.

Primary sources

Abdī Beg Shīrāzī, Zayn al-'Abidīn 'Alī, *Takmilat al-akhbār*, ed. 'Abd al-Ḥusayn Navā'ī, Tehran, 1369 [1990].
Afūshta-yi Naṭanzī, Maḥmūd ibn Hidāyat Allāh, *Naqāvat al-āthār fī dhikr al-akhyār*, ed. Iḥsān Ishrāqī, Tehran, 1350 [1971].
Aḥmad Rāẓī, Amīn, *Haft iqlīm*, ed. Javād Fāẓil, 3 vols., [Tehran], n.d.
'Ālam-ārā-yi Ṣafavi, ed. Yad Allāh Shukri, [Tehran], 1350 [1971].
'Ālam-ārā-yi Shāh Ṭahmāsb, ed. Īraj Afshār, [Tehran], 1370 [1991].
Amīnī Harawī, Ṣadr al-Dīn Sulṭān Ibrāhīm, 'Futūḥāt-i shāhī', ms. Kitākhāna-yi Vazīrī-yi Yazd 5774; ms., Dushanbe I.
Amīr Maḥmūd ibn Khvāndamīr, *Īrān dar rūzgār-i Shāh Ismā'īl va Shāh Ṭahmāsb Ṣafavī*, ed. Ghulām Riẓā Ṭabāṭabā'ī, Tehran, 1370 [1991].
Ghaffārī Qazvīnī Kāshānī, Qāẓī Aḥmad, *Tārīkh-i jahān-ārā*, ed. Ḥasan Narāqī, Tehran, 1342 [1963].
Ḥasan Beg Rūmlū, *Aḥsan al-tavārīkh*, ed. 'Abd al-Ḥusayn Navā'ī, Tehran, 1349 [1970].
Kitāb-i aḥsan al-tavārīkh, ed. Charles Norman Seedon, Tehran, n.d.
Ḥusaynī Qazvīnī, Yaḥyā ibn 'Abd al-Laṭīf, *Lubb al-tavārīkh*, ed. Jalāl al-Dīn Tihrānī, [Tehran], 1314 [1937].
Ibn Bazzāz Tavakkul ibn Ismā'īl *Ṣafvat al-ṣafā*, ed. Ghulām Riẓā Ṭabāṭabā'ī Majd, Ardabil, [1373] 1994; lith. Aḥmad ibn Karīm Tabrīzī, Bombay, 1329 [1911]; trans. and ed. Heidi Zirke as *Ein hagiographisches zeugnis zur persicschen geschichte aus der mitte des 14 jahrhunderts. Das achte kapitel des Safwat as-safa in kritischer bearbeitung*, Berlin, 1987.
Iskandar Beg Munshī, *Tārīkh-i 'ālam-ārā-yi 'Abbāsī*, 2 vols., ed. Iraj Afshar, Tehran, 1350 [1971].
Tārīkh-i 'ālam-ārā-yi 'Abbāsī, trans. Roger Savory as *History of Shah 'Abbas the great (Tarik-e 'alamara-ye 'Abbasi)*, 3 vols., Boulder, CO, 1978.
Juan de Persia, *Don Juan of Persia: A Shiah Catholic 1560–1604*, trans. and ed. G. LeStrange, London, 1926.

Junābādī, Mīrzā Beg, *Rawẓat al-ṣafaviyya*, ed. Ghulām Riẓā Ṭabāṭabā'ī-majd, Tehran, 1378 [1999].

Khātūnābādī, Sayyid ʿAbd al-Ḥusayn al-Ḥusaynī, *Waqāyiʿ al-sinīn wa al-aʿwām*, ed. Muḥammad Bāqir Bihbūdī, Tehran, 1352 [1973].

Khunjī, Faẓl Allāh ibn Rūzbihān, *Tārīkh-i ʿālam-ārā-yi Amīnī*, trans. and abr. V. Minorsky as *Persia in AD 1478–1490: An abridged translation of Fadlullah b. Ruzbihan Khunji's tarikh-i ʿalam'ara-yi Amini*, London, 1957; rev. and aug. by John E. Woods, London, 1992.

Khvāndamīr, Ghiyāth al-Dīn ibn Humām al-Dīn, *Tārīkh-i ḥabīb al-siyar*, ed Jalāl al-Dīn Humā'ī, 4 vols., [Tehran], 1333 [1954]; trans. Wheeler Thackston as *Habibu's-siyar*, 2 vols., Cambridge, MA, 1994.

Membré, Michele, *Mission to the Lord Sophy of Persia (1539–1542)*, trans. A. H. Morton, London, 1993.

Mīrkhwānd, Muḥammad ibn Khwāvandshāh, *Tārīkh-i rawẓat al-ṣafā*, ed. ʿAbbās Parvīz, 7 vols., [Tehran], 1338 [1959]; trans. E. Rehatsek as *Rauzat-us-safa or, garden of purity*, ed. F. F. Arbuthnot, 3 vols., London, 1891.

Muḥammad Maʿsūm ibn Khwājagī Iṣfahānī, *Khulāṣat al-siyar: Tārīkh-i rūzgār-i Shāh Ṣafī-i Ṣafavī*, ed. Īraj Afshār, Tehran, 1368 [1989].

Qāẓī Aḥmad Munshī Qummī, *Gulistān-i hunar*, ed. Aḥmad Suhaylī Khwānsarī, [Tehran], n.d.; trans. V. Minorsky as *Calligraphers and painters*, Washington, 1959.

Khulāṣat al-tavārīkh, ed. Iḥsān Ishrāqī, 2 vols., Tehran, 1363 [1984]; trans. and ed. Erika Glassen as *Die fruhen Safawiden nach Qazi Ahmad Qumi*, Freiburg, 1970; trans. and ed. Hans Muller as *Die chronik Hulasat at-tawarih des Qazi Ahmad Qumi. Der abschnitt uber Schah ʿAbbas I*, Wiesbaden, 1964.

Sām Mīrzā Ṣafavī, *Tadhkira-yi tuḥfa-yi Sạmị*, ed. Rukn al-Dīn Humāyūn Farrukh, n.p., n.d.

Shāh Ismaʿil, *Il Canzoniere di Šāh Ismāʿīl Ḫaṭā'ī*, ed. Tourkhan Gandjeï, Naples, 1959, trans. Robert Dankoff in 'Readings in Islamic civilization: From the rise of Islam to the beginning of the 10th/16th century', Robert Dankoff, gen. ed., unpublished ms.

Shāh Ṭahmāsb Ṣafavī, 'Tadhkira-yi Shāh Ṭahmāsb', ed. P. Horn, *Zeitschrift des Deutschen Morgenländischen Gesellschaft* 44 (1890), pp. 563–649; 45 (1891), pp. 245–91.

Siyāqī Niẓām, *Futūḥāt-i humāyūn*, ed., trans. and ann. Chahryar Adle as 'Fotuhat-e homayun: Les victoires augustes, 1007/1598', Ph.D. dissertation., University of Paris, 1976.

Tadhkirat al-mulūk, trans. and ed. V. Minorsky, London, 1943.

Tārīkh-i Qizilbāshān, ed. Mīr Hāshim Muḥaddith, Tehran, 1361 [1982].

Yazdī, Mullā Jalāl al-Dīn Munajjim, *Tārīkh-i ʿAbbāsī yā rūznāma-yi Mullā Jalāl*, ed. Sayf Allāh Vaḥīd Niyā, [Tehran], 1366 [1987].

Zāhidī, Shaykh Ḥusayn Pīrzāda, *Silsilat al-nasab-i Ṣafaviyah*, ed. Kaẓimzāda, Berlin, 1924.

Secondary sources

Abisaab, Rula Jurdi, *Converting Persia: Religion and power in the Safavid empire*, London, 2004.

Arjomand, Said Amir, *The shadow of God and the hidden imam: Religion, political order, and societal change in Shiʿite Iran from the beginning to 1890*, Chicago, 1984.

Aubin, Jean, 'Études Safavides I – Sah Ismaʿil et les notables de l'Iraq Persan', *Journal of Economic and Social History of the Orient*, 2 (1959), pp. 37–81.

Babaie, Sussan, Babayan, K., Baghdiantz-McCabe, I. and Farhad, M., *Slaves of the shah: New elites of Safavid Iran*, London, 2004.

Babayan, Kathryn, *Mystics, monarchs, and messiahs: Cultural landscapes of early modern Iran*, Cambridge, MA, 2002.

Calmard, Jean, 'Shiʿi rituals and power II: The consolidation of Safavid Shiʿism: Folklore and popular religion', in Charles Melville, (ed.), *Safavid Persia: The history and politics of an Islamic society*, London, 1996, pp. 139–90.

Dale, Stephen Frederic, 'A Safavid poet in the heart of darkness', in Stephen Frederic Dale, *Safavid Iran and her neighbors*, Salt Lake City, 2003.

Dickson, Martin B., 'Sháh Tahmásb and the Úzbeks: The duel for Khurásán with ʿUbayd Khán (930–946/1524–1540)', Ph.D. dissertation, Princeton University, 1958.

Gurney, J. D., 'Pietro della Valle: The limits of perception', *Bulletin of the School of Oriental and African Studies*, 49 (1986), pp. 103–16.

Hillenbrand, Robert, 'Safavid architecture', in Peter Jackson and Laurence Lockhart (eds.), *The Cambridge history of Iran*, vol. VI: *The Timurid and Safavid periods*, Cambridge, 1986, pp. 759–842.

Horst, Heribert, *Timur und Hôgä ʿAli. Ein beitrag zur geschichte der Safawiden*, Mainz, 1958.

Hourani, Albert, 'From Jabal ʿĀmil to Persia', *Bulletin of the School of Oriental and African Studies*, 49 (1986), pp. 133–40.

Jackson, Peter and Lockhart, Laurence (eds.), *The Cambridge history of Iran*, vol. VI: *The Timurid and Safavid periods*, Cambridge, 1986.

Lockhart, Laurence, 'European contacts with Persia, 1350–1736', in Peter Jackson and Laurence Lockhart (eds.), *The Cambridge history of Iran*, vol. VI: *The Timurid and Safavid periods*, Cambridge, 1986.

Losensky, Paul E., '"The allusive field of drunkenness': Three Safavid-Moghul responses to a lyric by Baba Fighani', in Suzanne P. Stetkevych (ed.), *Reorientations/Arabic and Persian poetry*, Bloomington, IN, 1994, pp. 227–62.

Welcoming Fighānī: Imitation and poetic individuality in the Safavid-Mughal Ghazal (Costa Mesa, CA, 1998).

McChesney, Robert D., 'A note on Iskandar Beg's chronology', *Journal of Near Eastern Studies*, 39 (1980), pp. 53–63.

'Four sources on Shah ʿAbbas's building of Isfahan', *Muqarnas*, 5 (1988), pp. 103–34.

'The conquest of Herat 995–6/1587–8: Sources for the study of Ṣafavid/Qizilbāsh–Shībānid/Uzbak relations', in Jean Calmard (ed.), *Études Safavides*, Paris and Tehran, 1993, pp. 69–107.

McNeill, William H. and Waldman, Marilyn Robinson (eds.), *The Islamic world*, Chicago, 1973.

Marshall, D. N., *Mughals in India: A bibliographical survey of manuscripts*, London, 1967, repr. New York, 1985.

Matthee, Rudolph P., 'Administrative stability and change in late-17th-century Iran: The case of Shaykh Ali Khan Zanganah (1669–89)', *International Journal of Middle East Studies*, 26 (1994), pp. 77–98.

The politics of trade in Safavid Iran: Silk for silver, 1600–1730, New York, 1999.

Mazzaoui, Michel, *The origins of the Safawids: Šīʿism, Ṣūfism, and the Gulāt*, Wiesbaden, 1972.

Melville, Charles, 'Shah ʿAbbas and the pilgrimage to Mashhad', in Charles Melville, (ed.), *Safavid Persia: The history and politics of an Islamic society*, London, 1996, pp. 191–229.

Mirjafari, Hossein, 'The Haydari–Niʿmati conflicts in Iran', trans. and adapt. J. R. Perry, *Iranian Studies*, 12 (1979), pp. 135–62.

Momen, Moojan, *An introduction to Shiʿi Islam*, New Haven, 1985.
Morton, A. H., 'The date and attribution of the *Ross Anonymous*: Notes on a Persian history of Shah Ismaʿil I', in Charles Melville (ed.), *Pembroke papers I*, Cambridge, 1990, pp. 179–212.
'The early years of Shah Ismaʿil in the *Afzal al-tavarikh* and elsewhere', in Charles Melville (ed.), *Safavid Persia: The history and politics of an Islamic society*, London, 1996, pp. 27–51.
Nasr, S. H., 'Spiritual movements, philosophy and theology in the Safavid period', in Peter Jackson and Laurence Lockhart (eds.), *The Cambridge history of Iran*, vol. VI: *The Timurid and Safavid periods*, Cambridge, 1986, pp. 656–97.
Newman, Andrew J., 'The myth of the clerical migration to Safawid Iran: Arab Shiite opposition to ʿAli al-Karaki and Safawid Shiism', *Die Welt des Islams*, 33 (1993), pp. 66–112.
'Bāqir al-Majlisī and Islamicate medicine', in Andrew J. Newman (ed.), *Society and culture in the early modern Middle East: Studies on Iran in the Safavid period*, Leiden, 2003, pp. 381–96.
Nizami, Khaliq Ahmad, *On history and historians of medieval India*, New Delhi, 1982.
Perry, John R., 'The last Safavids (1722–73)', *Iran: Journal of the British Institute of Persian Studies*, 9 (1971), pp. 59–71.
Quinn, Sholeh A., *Historical writing during the reign of Shah ʿAbbas: Ideology, imitation and legitimacy in Safavid chronicles*, Salt Lake City, 2000.
Roemer, Hans R., 'The Safavid period', in Peter Jackson and Laurence Lockhart (eds.), *The Cambridge history of Iran*, vol. VI: *The Timurid and Safavid periods*, Cambridge, 1986, pp. 189–350.
Savory, Roger, *Iran under the Safavids*, Cambridge and New York, 1980.
Sims, Eleanor, 'A dispersed late-Safavid copy of the *Tarikh-i Jahangusha-yi Khaqan Sahibqiran*', in Sheila R. Canby (ed.), *Safavid art and architecture*, London, 2002, pp. 54–7.
Stanfield-Johnson, Rosemary, 'The Tabarraʾiyan and the early Safavids', *Iranian Studies*, 37 (2004), pp. 47–71.
Stewart, Devin J., 'Notes on the migration of ʿAmili scholars to Safavid Iran', *Journal of Near Eastern Studies*, 55 (1996), pp. 81–103.
Storey, C. A., *Persian literature: A bio-bibliographical survey*, 3 vols., London, 1927.
Persidskaya literatura: Bio-bibliograficheskii obzor, rev. and trans. Yu. E. Bregel, 3 vols., Moscow, 1972.
Szuppe, Maria, 'Kinship ties between the Safavids and the Qizilbash amirs in late sixteenth-century Iran: A case study of the political career of members of the Sharaf al-Din Ogli Tekelu family', in Charles Melville (ed.), *Safavid Persia: The history and politics of an Islamic society*, ed. London, 1996, pp. 79–104.
Welch, Stuart Cary, *A king's book of kings: The Shah-nameh of Shah Tahmasp*, New York, 1972.

7 Islamic culture and the Chinggisid restoration: Central Asia in the sixteenth and seventeenth centuries
R. D. McChesney

Practical suggestions for further reading

Ẓahīr al-Dīn Muḥammad Bābur Pādshāh Ghāzī, *The Bābur-nāma in English (Memoirs of Babur)*, trans. from the original Turkī text by Annette Susannah Beveridge, London, 1969, repr. of London, 1922 edn.

Mirza Muhammad Haidar Dughlat, *A history of the Moghuls of Central Asia being the Tarikh-i Rashidi of Mirza Muhammad Haidar, Dughlat*, ed. N. Elias, trans. E. Denison Ross, New York, 1972, repr. of London 1898 ed; *Tārīkh-i Rashidi: A history of the khans of Moghulistan*, Eng. trans. and ann. W. M. Thackston, Cambridge, MA, 1996.

Primary sources

Abu'l-Ghāzī Bahādūr Khān, *Rodoslovnaya Turkmen (Shajarah-i Tarākimah)*, ed. and trans. (into Russian), A. N. Kononov, Moscow and Leningrad, 1958.

Shajara-i Turk, ed. and trans. Petr I. Desmaisons as *Histoire des Mongols et des Tatares par Aboul-Ghâzi Béhâdour Khân*, St Leonards and Amsterdam 1970 repr. of St Petersburg 1871–4 edn.

Babadjanov, Baxtiyor, Muminov, Ashirbek, and Paul, Jürgen, *Schaibanidische Grabinshriften*, Wiesbaden, 1997.

Babajanov, Bakhtyar and Szuppe, Maria, *Les inscriptions persanes de Chār Bakr, necropole familiale des* khwāja *Jūybārī près de Boukhara*, *Corpus inscriptionum iranicarum*, Part IV: *Persian inscriptions down to the early Safavid period*, vol. XXXI: *Uzbekistan*, London, 2002.

Bertel's, E. [and Rostopchin, F. B.,] (eds.), *Iz arkhiva Dzhuibari*, Leningrad, 1938. Summarily translated by Fedor Borisovich Rostopchin with later review of translation by Iu. P. Verkhovsky and an introductory essay by P. P. Ivanov and published as *Khoziaistvo Dzhuibarskikh Sheikhov*, Moscow, 1954.

Kamal al-Din Banna'i (Bina'i), *Shaybānī-nāma*, ed. Kazuyuki Kubo, in *A synthetical study on Central Asian culture in the Turco-Islamic period*, Kyoto, 1997 (Japanese and English).

Davidovich, E. A., *Istoriia monetnogo dela Srednei Azii XVII-XVIII vv. (Zolotye i serebrianye monety Dzhanidov)*, Dushanbe, 1964.

Istoriia deneszhnogo obrashcheniia srednevekovoi Srednei Azii, Moscow, 1983.

Korpus zolotykh i serebrianykh monet Sheibaniudov, XVI vek, Moscow, 1992.

Fażlallāh b. Rūzbihān-i Khunjī Iṣfahānī, *Tārīkh-i ʿĀlam-ārā-yi Amīnī*, Persian text ed. John E. Woods, ms.

Mihmān-nāma-i Bukhārā, ed. M. Sutudah, Tehran, 1341/1963.

Ḥāfiẓ-i Tanīsh, *Sharaf-nāma-i Shāhī* (also known as *ʿAbdallāh-nāma*), ed. and trans. M. A. Salakhetdinova (vols. 1 and 2 only of four projected), Moscow 1983–9; India Office Library ms. 574 for the remainder of the work.

Fakhrī Harawī, *Tazkirah-i Rawżat al-Salāṭīn*, Tabriz, 1345/1966.

Ināyat Khan, *The Shah Jahan Nama*, trans. A. R. Fuller, ed. and completed W. E. Begley and Z. A. Desai, Delhi and New York, 1990.

Islam, Riazul, *A calendar of documents on Indo-Persian relations (1500–1750)*, 2 vols., Karachi, 1979–82.

Badr al-Dīn Kashmīrī, *Rawżat al-riżwān fī ḥadīqat al-ghilmān*, Inv. no. 2094 (Sharqshinosliq Institut, formerly Institut Vostokovedeniia), Tashkent.

Khwāja Bahā' al-Dīn Ḥasan Nithārī Bukhārī, *Mudhakkir al-aḥbāb*, ed. S. M. Fazlullah, New Delhi, 1969.

Lowick, N. M., 'Shaybanid silver coins', *Numismatic Chronicle*, ser. 7, 1966, pp. 251–330.

Maḥmūd b. Amīr Walī, *Baḥr al-asrār fī manāqib al-akhyār*, vol. VI, part (*rukn*) 4, India Office Library ms. 575.

More tain otnositel'no doblestei blagorodnykh (Geografiia) (Geographical portion of the *Baḥr al-asrār*), ed. and trans. B. A. Akhmedov, Tashkent, 1977.
Baḥr al-asrār fī maʿrifat al-akhyār, vol. 1, part 1, ed. Hakim Mohammed Said, S. Moinul Haq and Ansar Zahid Khan, Karachi, 1984.
Minorsky, V. M., *Persia in AD 1478–1490: An abridged translation of Faḍlullāh b. Rūzbihān Khunjī's Tārīkh-i ʿālam-ārā-yi Amīnī*, London, 1957.
Muḥammad Badīʿ Samarqandī (Malīḥā), *Muẕakkir al-aṣḥāb*, Tashkent, Biruni Institute of Oriental Studies, ms. 4270; Dushanbe, Institute of Oriental Studies, ms. 610.
Mukminova, R[oziya] G[alievna], *K istorii agrarnykh otnoshenii v Uzbekistane XVI v.: Vakf-name*, Tashkent, 1966.
Mūnis Khorezmī, Shīr Muḥammad Mīrāb Mūnis and Muḥammad Riżā Mīrāb Āgahī, *Firdaws al-iqbāl: History of Khorezm*, ed. (1988) and trans. (1999) Yuri Bregel, Leiden, 1988, 1999.
Muṭribī al-Aṣamm al-Samarqandī, *Nuskhah-i zībā-yi Jahāngīr*, ed. Ismāʿīl Bīkjānūf and Sayyid ʿAlī Mūjānī, Qum, 1377/1998.
Tazkirat al-shuʿarāʾ, ed. Asghar Jānfadā and ʿAlī Rafīʿī, Tehran, 1377/1998.
Zayn al-Dīn Wāṣifī, *Badāʾiʿ al-waqāʾiʿ*, ed. Aleksandr Boldyrev, 2 vols., Moscow, 1961.

Secondary sources

Akhmedov, B. A., *Istoria Balkha*, Tashkent, 1982.
Babajanov, Bakhtyar, 'La naqshbaniyya sous les premiers Sheybanides', *L'héritage Timouride: Iran–Asie centrale–Inde XVe–XVIIIe siècles; Cahiers d'Asie Centrale*, 3–4 (1997), pp. 69–90.
'Datation de la mosquée Vâlida-ye 'Abd al-ʿAzîz Xân à Boukhara', *Studia Iranica*, 28 (1999), pp. 227–34.
Bregel, Yuri, *An historical atlas of Central Asia*, Leiden, 2002, pp. 48–60.
Burton, Audrey, *The Bukharans: A dynastic, diplomatic and commercial history, 1550–1702*, Richmond, 1997.
DeWeese, Devin, 'The eclipse of the Kubraviya in Central Asia', *Iranian Studies*, 21 (1988), pp. 45–83.
Islamization and native religion in the Golden Horde Bab Tükles and conversion to Islam in historical and epic tradition, University Park, PA, 1994.
Dickson, Martin B., 'Sháh Tahmásb and the Úzbeks', Ph.D. dissertation, Princeton University, 1958.
Digby, Simon, (trans.), *Sufis and soldiers in Awrangzeb's Deccan: Malfúzát-i Naqshbandiyya*, New Delhi, 2001.
Fraser, James B., *Narrative of a journey into Khorasan in the years 1821 and 1823*, 1984 repr. of London 1825 edn.
Galerkina, Olympiada, *Mawarannahr book painting*, Leningrad, 1980.
Haneda, Masashi, 'Emigration of Iranian elites to India during the 16th–18th centuries', *L'héritage Timouride: Iran–Asie centrale–Inde XVe–XVIIIe siècles; Cahiers d'Asie Centrale*, 3–4 (1997) pp. 129–43.
Hofman, H., *Turkish literature: A bio-bibliographical survey*, Section III: Part 1 (Authors) 2 vols., Utrecht, 1969.
Isogai, Ken'ichi, 'Yasa and Shariah in early 16th century Central Asia', *L'héritage Timouride: Iran–Asie centrale–Inde XVe–XVIIIe siècles; Cahiers d'Asie Centrale*, 3–4 (1997), pp. 91–103.

McChesney, R. D., 'Economic and social aspects of the public architecture of Bukhara in the 1560s and 1570s', *Islamic Art*, 2 (1987), pp. 217–42.

Waqf in Central Asia: Four hundred years in the history of a Muslim shrine, 1480–1889, Princeton, 1991.

Central Asia: Foundations of Change, Princeton, 1996.

'Some observations on "garden" and its meanings in the property transactions of the Jūybārī family in Bukhara, 1544–77', in Attilio Petruccioli (ed.), *Gardens in the time of the great Muslim empires*, Leiden, 1997, pp. 97–109.

'Bukhara's suburban villages: Juzmandūn in the sixteenth century', in Attilio Petruccioli (ed.), *Bukhara: The myth and the architecture*, Cambridge, MA, 1999, pp. 93–119.

'Reconstructing Balkh: The *Vaqfīya* of 947/1540', in Devin DeWeese (ed.), *Studies on Central Asian history in honor of Yuri Bregel*, Bloomington, IN, 2001, pp. 187–243.

'Architecture and narrative: The Khwaja Abu Nasr Parsa shrine', (in two parts) *Muqarnas*, 18 (2001), pp. 94–119; 19 (2002), pp. 78–108.

Mukminova, R. G., *Ocherki po istorii remesla v Samarkande i Bukhare v XVI veke*, Tashkent, 1976.

O'Kane, Bernard, 'The Uzbek architecture of Afghanistan', *La mémoire et ses supports en Asie centrale; Cahiers d'Asie Centrale*, 8 (2000), pp. 123–60.

Paul, Jürgen, 'La propriété foncière des cheikhs Juybari', *L'héritage Timouride: Iran–Asie centrale–Inde XVe–XVIIIe siècles; Cahiers d'Asie Centrale*, 3–4 (1997), pp. 183–202.

Porter, Yves, 'Farhad le peintre: À propos des ateliers de peinture de Boukhara à l'époque de 'Abd al-'Aziz Khan (1645–1680)', *L'héritage Timouride: Iran–Asie centrale–Inde XVe–XVIIIe siècles; Cahiers d'Asie Centrale*, 3–4 (1997), pp. 267–78.

'Remarques sur la peinture à Boukhara au XVIe siècle', *Boukhara La Noble; Cahiers d'Asie Centrale*, 5–6 (1998), pp. 147–67.

'Le *kitâb-khâna* de 'Abd al-'Azîz Khân (1645–1680) et le mécénat de la peinture à Boukhara', *Patrimoine manuscrit et vie intellectuelle de l'Asie centrale islamique; Cahiers d'Asie Centrale*, 7 (1999), pp. 117–36.

Schimmel, Annemarie, 'Some notes on the cultural activity of the first Uzbek rulers', *Journal of the Pakistan Historical Society*, 8 (1960), pp. 149–66.

Schwarz, Florian, 'Bukhara and its hinterland: The oasis of Bukhara in the sixteenth century in light of the Juybari Codex', in Attilio Petruccioli (ed.), *Bukhara: The myth and the architecture*, Cambridge, 1999.

'Unser Weg schließt tausend Wege ein': Derwische und Gesellschaft im islamischen Mittelasien im 16. Jahrhundert, Berlin, 2000.

Sylloge Numorom Arabicorum Tübingen: Balḫ und Die Landschaften am oberen Oxus XIV c Ḫurāsān III, Berlin, 2002.

Storey, C. A., *Persidskaya literatura: Bio-bibliograficheskii obzor*, vev., trans. and updated Yuriv E. Bregel, 3 vols., Moscow, 1972.

Maria Eva Subtelny, 'Art and politics in early 16th-century Central Asia', *Central Asiatic Journal*, 27 (1983), pp. 121–48.

'Socio-economic bases of cultural patronage under the later Timurids', *International Journal of Middle Eastern Studies*, 20, 4 (1988), pp. 479–505.

'A medieval Persian agricultural manual in context: The *Irshād al-zirā'a* in late Timurid and early Safavid Khorasan', *Studia Iranica* 22, 2 (1993), pp. 167–217.

'Mīrak-i Sayyid Ghiyās̱ and the Tīmurid tradition of landscape architecture', *Studia Iranica*, 24 (1995), pp. 19–60.

'The making of *Bukhārā-yi Sharīf*: Scholars and libraries in medieval Bukhara (The library of Khwāja Muḥammad Pārsā)', in Devin DeWeese (ed.), *Studies on Central Asian history in honor of Yuri Bregel*, Bloomington, IN, 2001, pp. 79–111.
Le monde est un jardin: Aspects de l'histoire culturelle de l'Iran mediéval, Paris, 2002.
Subtelny, Maria Eva and Khalidov, Anas B., 'The curriculum of Islamic higher learning in Timurid Iran in the light of the Sunni revival under Shāh-Rukh', *Journal of the American Oriental Society*, 115 (1995), pp. 210–36.
Sukhareva, O. A., *Kvartal'naia obshchina pozdnefeodal'nogo goroda Bukhary*, Moscow, 1976.
Szuppe, Maria, *Entre Timourides, Uzbeks, et Safavides: Questions d'histoire politique et sociale de Herat dans la première moitié du XVIe siècle*, Paris, 1992.
'Lettres, patrons, libraires: L'apport des recueils biographiques sur le rôle du livre en Asie centrale aux XVIe et XVIIe siècles', *Cahiers d'Asie Centrale*, 7 (1999), pp. 99–115.
'Circulation des lettres et circles littéraires entre Asie centrale, Iran et Inde du Nord (XVe–XVIIIe siècles), *Annales: Histoire, Sciences Sociales*, 59 (2004), pp. 997–1018.

8 India under Mughal rule
Stephen Dale

Practical suggestions for further reading

Alam, Muzaffar, *The crises of empire in Mughal north India*, Delhi, 1986.
Alam, Muzaffar, Delvoye, François 'Nalini' and Gaborieau, Marc, *The making of Indo-Persian culture*, New Delhi, 2000.
Asher, Catherine B., *Architecture of Mughal India*, The new Cambridge history of India, Cambridge, 1992.
Berinstain, Valérie, *India and the Mughal dynasty*, New York, 1998.
Gascoigne, Bamber, *The great Mughals*, London, 1971.
Ghanī, Muḥammad 'Abdū'l, *A history of Persian language and literature at the Mughal court*, 2 vols., Allahabad, 1930.
Koch, Ebba, *Mughal architecture*, Munich, 1991.
Losensky, Paul E., *Welcoming Fighânî: Imitation and poetic individuality in the Safavid–Mughal ghazal*, Costa Mesa, CA, 1998.
Mukhia, Harbans, *The Mughals of India*, Oxford, 2004.
Okada, Amina, *Indian miniatures of the Mughal court*, trans. D. Dusinberre, New York, 1992.
Richards, John F., *The Mughal empire*, Cambridge, 1993.
Schimmel, Annemarie, *Islamic literatures of India*, Wiesbaden, 1973.
The empire of the great Mughals, London, 2004.
Welch, S. C., *Imperial Mughal painting*, London, 1978.
Ziad, Zeenut, *The magnificent Mughals*, Karachi, 2002.

Primary sources

Abū'l Faḍl 'Allāmī, *Ā'īn-i Akbarī*, trans. H. Beveridge, 3 vols., Delhi, repr. 1987.
Akbar nāma, trans. H Blochmann, 3 vols., Delhi, repr. 1988.
Bacqué-Grammont, Jean-Louis, *Le livre de Babur*, Paris, 1980.
al-Badāunī, 'Abd al-Qādir b. Mulūk Shāh, *Muntakhabu-'t-Tawārīkh*, trans. W. H. Lowe, 3 vols., Patna, repr. 1973.

Begam, Gul-Badan, *The history of Humāyūn (Humāyūn-nāma)*, trans. and ed. Annette S. Beveridge, Delhi, repr. 1972.

Begley, W. E. and Desai, Z. A. (eds.), *The Shah Jahan nama of ʿInayat Khan*, Delhi and New York, 1990.

Bernier, Francis, *Travels in the Moghul empire 1656–1658*, Delhi, repr. 1968.

Beveridge, Annette Susannah, *The Bābur-nāma in English*, London, repr. 1969.

Dughlat, Haydar Mīrzā, *Tarikh-i Rashidi*, Persian text ed. W. M. Thackston, Sources of Oriental Languages and Literatures. 37 and 38, Cambridge, MA, 1996.

Haq, Moinul, *Khafi Khan's history of Alamgir*, Karachi, 1975.

Jahāngīr, *The Jahangirnama: Memoirs of Jahangir, emperor of India*, ed. and trans. Wheeler M. Thackston (Washington, DC, 1999).

Kazim, Muhammad, *ʿAlamgīr Nāma*, ed. ʿAbd al Hayy and Ahmad Ali, Calcutta, 1865.

Khan, ʿAqil, *The Waqīʿat-i-ʿAlamgīrī*, trans. Zafar Hasan, Delhi, 1946.

Lahawrī, ʿAbd al-Ḥamīd, *The Badshahnamah*, Persian text ed. M. Kabir al-Din Ahmad and M. ʿAbd al-Rahim, Calcutta, 1867–72.

Mano, Eiji, *Bābur-nāma* (Vaqāyiʿ), Kyoto, 1995–6.

Manrique, Sebastian, *Travels of Fray Sebastian Manrique 1629–1643*, Cambridge, 1927.

Manucci, N., *Storia do Mogor or Moghul India*, 4 vols., Calcutta, 1907–8.

Roe, Thomas, *The embassy of Sir Thomas Roe to India 1615–1619*, ed. William Foster, London, 1926.

Sarkar, J. N., *History of Aurangzeb, based mainly on Persian sources*, 5 vols., Calcutta, 1912–30.

Tavernier, Jean-Baptiste, *Travels in India*, trans. V. Ball, 2 vols., London, 1989.

Secondary sources

Alam, Muzaffar and Subrahmanyam, Sanjay, *The Mughal state 1526–1750*, New Delhi, 1998.

Ali, M. Athar, 'The passing of empire: The Mughal case', *Modern Asian Studies*, 9, 3 (1975), pp. 385–96.

The apparatus of empire, Delhi, 1985.

The Mughal nobility under Aurungzeb, Delhi, 1985.

Alvi, Sajida Sultana, *Advice on the art of governance: An Indo-Islamic mirror for princes*, Albany, 1989.

Balabanlilar, Lisa, 'Lords of the auspicious conjunction: Turco-Mongol imperial identity on the subcontinent', *Journal of World History*, 18, 1 (2007), pp. 1–39.

Blake, Stephen P., 'The patrimonial-bureaucratic empire of the Mughals', *Journal of Asian Studies*, 39, 1 (November 1979), pp. 77–94.

Shahjahanabad: The sovereign city in Mughal India, Cambridge, 1993.

Chaudhuri, K. N., *The European trading world of Asia and the English East India Company*, Cambridge, 1978.

Dale, Stephen F., *Indian merchants and Eurasian trade 1600–1750*, Cambridge, 1994.

The garden of the eight paradises: Bābur and the culture of empire in Central Asia, Afghanistan and India (1483–1530), Leiden and Boston, 2004.

Gommans, Jos J. L. and Kolff, Dirk, *Warfare and weaponry in South Asia, 1000–1800*, Delhi, 2001.

Gordon, Stewart, *The Marathas 1600–1818*, Cambridge, 1993.

Grewal, J. S., *The Sikhs of the Punjab*, The new Cambridge history of India, Cambridge, 1990.

Habib, Irfan *The agrarian system of Mughal India*, London, 1963.
An atlas of the Mughal empire, Delhi, 1982.
(ed.), *Akbar and his India*, New Delhi, 1997.
Irvine, William, *Later Mughals*, New Delhi, repr. 1971.
Khan, Shah Nawaz, *The Maathir-ul-Umara*, trans. H. Beveridge and B. Prashad, New Delhi, repr. 1979.
Koch, Ebba, *The complete Taj Mahal*, London, 2006.
Kolff, Dirk, *Naukar, Rajput and Sepoy: The ethnohistory of the military labour market in Hindustan 1450–1850*, Cambridge, 1990.
Lal, Ruby, *Domesticity and power in the early Mughal world*, Cambridge, 2005.
Marek, Jan, 'Persian literature in India', in Jan Rypka (ed.), *History of Iranian literature*, Dordrecht, 1968, pp. 713–34.
Moosvi, Shireen, 'The silver influx, money supply, prices and revenue-extraction in Mughal India', *Journal of the Economic and Social History of the Orient*, 30, 1 (1987), pp. 47–94.
The Economy of the Mughal empire c. 1595, Delhi, 1987.
Nathan, Mirza, *Bahâristān-i Gaybī*, Gauhati, India, 1936.
Nizami, K. A., *Akbar and religion*, Delhi, 1989.
Pradhan, Mahesh Chandra, *The political system of the Jats of northern India*, Bombay, 1966.
Prakash, Om, *European commercial enterprise in pre-colonial India*, The new Cambridge History of India, Cambridge, 1998.
Prasad, Beni, *History of Jahangir*, London, 1922.
Prasad, Ishwari, *The life and times of Humayun*, Calcutta, 1955.
Raychaudhuri, Tapan and Habib, Irfan (ed.), *The Cambridge economic history of India*, Cambridge, 1982, vol. I.
Richards, John F., *Mughal admininstration in Golconda*, Oxford, 1975.
'The formation of imperial authority under Akbar and Jahangir', in J. F. Richards (ed.), *Kingship and authority in South Asia*, Madison, WI, 1978.
(ed.), *The imperial monetary system of Mughal India*, Delhi, 1987.
Rizvi, S. A. A., *Religious and intellectual history of Muslims in Akbar's reign*, Delhi, 1975.
Robinson, Francis, 'Ottomans–Safavids–Mughals: Shared knowledge and connective systems' *Journal of Islamic Studies* 8, 2 (1997), pp. 151–84.
The 'ulama of the Farangi Mahall and Islamic culture in South Asia, London, 2001.
Sadiq, Muhammad, *A history of Urdu literature*, London, 1964.
Saksena, Banarsi Prasad, *History of Shah Jahan of Dihli*, Allahabad, repr. 1973.
Siddiqi, N., *Land revenue administration under the Mughals 1700–1750*, Aligarh, 1970.

9 Islamic trade, shipping, port-states and merchant communities in the Indian Ocean, seventh to sixteenth centuries
Michael Pearson

Practical suggestions for further reading

Muslim trade and navigation: port cities

Bouchon, Geneviève, 'Les Musulmans du Kerala à l'époque de la découverte portugaise', *Mare Luso-Indicum*, 2 (1973), pp. 3–59.

L'Asie du Sud à l'époque des grandes découvertes, London, 1985.
Hourani, George F., rev. and expanded by John Carswell, *Arab seafaring in the Indian Ocean in ancient and medieval times*, Princeton, 1951, 1995.
Pearson, Michael, 'Gateways to Africa: The Indian Ocean and the Red Sea', in Randall Pouwels and Nehemia Levtzion (eds.), *History of Islam in Africa*, Athens, OH, 2000, pp. 37–59.
The Indian Ocean, London, 2003.
Risso, Patricia, *Merchants and faith: Muslim commerce and culture in the Indian Ocean*, Boulder, CO, 1995.
Wink, André, *Al-Hind: The making of the Indo-Islamic World*, 3 vols., Leiden, 1990–2004.
Wright, H. T., 'Trade and politics on the eastern littoral of Africa, AD 800–1300', in Thurstan Shaw (ed.), *The archeology of Africa: Food, metals and towns*, London, 1993, pp. 658–72.

The Swahili coast

Horton, Mark and Middleton, John, *The Swahili: The social landscape of a mercantile society*, Oxford, 2000.
Martin, B. G., 'Arab migration to East Africa in medieval times', *International Journal of African Historical Studies*, 7 (1975), pp. 367–90.
Pearson, Michael, *Port cities and intruders: The Swahili Coast, India, and Portugal in the early modern era*, Baltimore, 1998.

The Maldives

Forbes, Andrew D. W., 'Southern Arabia and the Islamicisation of the central Indian Ocean archipelagos', *Archipel*, 21 (1981), pp. 55–92.
Gabriel, Theodore, 'Islamic mystics of the Lakshadweep islands, India', in Theodore P. Gabriel and C. H. Partridge (eds.), *Mysticisms east and west*, Carlisle, 2003, pp. 44–53.
Maloney, Clarence, *People of the Maldive islands*, Bombay, 1980.

Malabar

Bouchon, G., 'Quelques aspects de l'islamisation des régions maritimes de l'Inde à l'époque médiévale (XIIe–XVIe s.)', *Purusartha*, 9 (1986), pp. 29–36.
'Regent of the sea': Cannanore's response to Portuguese expansion, 1507–1528, Delhi, 1988.
Dale, Stephen Frederic, *Islamic society on the South Asian frontier: The Mappilas of Malabar, 1498–1922*, Oxford, 1980.
Engineer, Asghar Ali (ed.), *Kerala Muslims: A historical perspective*, Delhi, 1995.
Miller, R. E., *Mappila Muslims of Kerala*, Madras, 1976.

Sri Lanka

Gunawardana, R. A. L. H., 'Changing patterns of navigation in the Indian Ocean and their impact on pre-colonial Sri Lanka', in Satish Chandra (ed.), *The Indian Ocean: Explorations in history, commerce and politics*, New Delhi, 1987, pp. 54–89.
Mohan, Vasundhara, *Muslims in Sri Lanka*, Jaipur, 1985.

Wink, André, *Al-Hind: The making of the Indo-Islamic World*, 3 vols., Leiden, 1990–2004.

Coromandel

Arasaratnam, Sinnappah, 'The Chulia Muslim merchants in Southeast Asia, 1650–1800', in Sanjay Subrahmanyam (ed.), *Merchant networks in the early modern world*, Aldershot, 1996, pp. 159–77.

Bayly, Susan, 'Islam in southern India: "Purist" or "syncretic"?', in C. A. Bayly and D. H. A. Kolff (eds.), *Two colonial empires: Comparative essays on the history of India and Indonesia in the nineteenth century*, Leiden, 1986, pp. 35–73.

More, J. B. P., *Muslim identity, print culture and the Dravidian factor in Tamil Nadu*, New Delhi, 2004.

Uwise, M. M., *Muslim contribution to Tamil literature*, Madras, 1990.

Primary sources

Barbosa, Duarte, *A description of the coasts of East Africa and Malabar in the beginning of the 16th century*, trans. Henry E. J. Stanley, Hakluyt Society, 35, London, 1866.

The book of Duarte Barbosa: An account of the countries bordering on the Indian Ocean and their inhabitants, trans. and ed. Mansel Longworth Dames, Hakluyt Society, ser. 2, nos. 44, 49, 2 vols., London, 1918–21.

Ibn Baṭṭūṭa, *The travels of Ibn Battuta*, trans. H. A. R. Gibb, Hakluyt Society, ser. 2, nos. 110, 117, 141, 178, 4 vols., London, 1958–94.

Ibn Muḥammad Ibrāhīm, *The ship of Sulaimān*, trans. John O'Kane, Persian Heritage Series, 11, London, 1972.

Major, R. H. (ed.), *India in the fifteenth century: Being a collection of narratives of voyages to India in the century preceding the Portuguese discovery of the Cape of Good Hope; from Latin, Persian, Russian, and Italian sources, now first translated into English*, Hakluyt Society, 22, London, 1857.

Pires, Tomé, *The Suma oriental of Tomé Pires*, trans. and ed. A. Cortesão, Hakluyt Society, ser. 2, nos. 89 and 90, 2 vols., London, 1944.

Pyrard, François, *The voyage of Francois Pyrard of Laval to the East Indies, the Maldives, the Moluccas and Brazil*, trans. and ed. Albert Gray, Hakluyt Society, nos. 76, 77, 80, 2 vols., London, 1887–9.

Tibbetts, G. R., *Arab navigation in the Indian Ocean before the coming of the Portuguese: Being a translation of Kitāb al-Faw͞ā'id fī uṢūl al-baḥr wa'l-qawā'id of Aḥmad b. Mājid al-Najdī; together with an introduction on the history of Arab navigation, notes on the navigational techniques and on the topography of the Indian Ocean and a glossary of navigational terms*, London, 1971.

Zayn al-Dīn, *Tohfut-ul-Mujahideen*, trans. M. J. Rowlandson, London, 1833.

Secondary sources

Ahmad, Rizwan A., 'The state and national foundation in the Maldives', *Cultural Dynamics*, 13 (2001), pp. 293–315.

Asghar Ali Engineer, 'Kerala Muslims in historical perspective: An introduction', in Asghar Ali Engineer (ed.), *Kerala Muslims: A historical perspective*, Delhi, 1995, pp. 1–16.

Bayly, Susan, *Saints, goddesses and kings: Muslims and Christians in south Indian society 1700–1900*, Cambridge, 1989.

Bhattacharya, Bhaswati, 'The Chulia merchants of southern Coromandel in the eighteenth century: A case for continuity', in Om Prakash and Denys Lombard (eds.), *Commerce and culture in the Bay of Bengal, 1500–1800*, Delhi, 1999.

Dale, Stephen F., 'Trade, conversion and the growth of the Islamic community of Kerala, south India', *Studia Islamica*, 71 (1990), pp. 155–75.

Fanselow, Frank S., 'Muslim society in Tamil Nadu (India): An historical perspective', *Journal of the Institute of Minority Muslim Affairs*, 10 (1989), pp. 264–89.

Forbes, Andrew, 'Sources towards a history of the Laccadive islands', *South Asia*, 2 (1979), pp. 130–50.

Gabriel, Theodore P. C., *Hindu–Muslim relations in north Malabar, 1498–1947*, Lewiston, NY, 1996.

Iwata, K., *Religions and cultures of Sri Lanka and south India*, Osaka, 1984.

John, K. J., 'The Muslim-Arabs and mosque architecture in Malabar', in Asghar Ali Engineer (ed.), *Kerala Muslims: A historical perspective*, Delhi, 1995, pp. 47–55.

Kunju, A. P. Ibrahim, 'Origin and spread of Islam in Kerala', in Asghar Ali Engineer (ed.), *Kerala Muslims: A historical perspective*, Delhi, 1995, pp. 17–23.

McPherson, Kenneth, 'Chulias and Klings: Indigenous trade diasporas and European penetration of the Indian Ocean littoral', in Giorgio Borsa (ed.), *Trade and politics in the Indian Ocean: Historical and contemporary perspectives*, Delhi, 1990, pp. 33–46.

Mines, Mattison, *Muslim merchants: The economic behaviour of a Muslim Indian community*, New Delhi, 1972.

Nainar, S. Muhammad Husayn, *Arab geographers' knowledge of southern India*, Madras, 1942.

Shulman, David and Subrahmanyam, Sanjay, 'Prince of poets and ports: Citakkati, the Maraikkayars and Ramnad, ca 1690–1710', in Anna Libera Dallapiccola and Stephanie Zingel-Avé Lallaemant (eds.), *Islam and the Indian regions*, vol. I, Stuttgart, 1993, pp. 497–535.

Subrahmanyam, Sanjay, 'Noble harvest from the sea: Managing the pearl fishery of Mannar, 1500–1925', in Burton Stein and Sanjay Subrahmanyam (eds.), *Institutions and economic change in South Asia*, Delhi, 1996, pp. 134–72.

'Diversity in South Asian Islam', *Akhbar*, 5 (2002), www.indowindow.com/akhbar/article.php?article=132&category=4&issue=19.

Vitharana, V., *Sri Lankan–Maldivian cultural affinities*, Polgasovita, 1997.

10 Early Muslim expansion in South-East Asia, eighth to fifteenth centuries
Geoff Wade

Practical suggestions for further reading

Islam in South-East Asia to the fifth/eleventh century

Ferrand, Gabriel, *Relations de voyages et textes géographiques, arabes, persans et turks relatifs à l'Extrême-Orient du VIII au XVIII siècles*, Paris, 1912.

Freeman-Grenville, G. S. P., *The East African coast: Select documents from the first to the earlier nineteenth century*, Oxford, 1962.

Hourani, George, *Arab seafaring in the Indian Ocean in ancient and early medieval times*. Princeton, 1951.
Laffan, Michael, *Finding Java: Muslim nomenclature of insular Southeast Asia from Śrîvijaya to Snouk Hurgronje*, Asia Research Institute Working Paper Series, 52, Singapore, Nov. 2005.
Tibbetts, G. R., *A study of the Arabic texts containing material on South-East Asia*, Leiden, 1979.

Islam in South-East Asia from the fifth / eleventh to the seventh / thirteenth centuries

Chen Da-sheng (chief ed.), *Quan-zhou Yi-si-lan jiao shi-ke* (Islamic stone inscriptions from Quan-zhou), Quan-zhou, 1984.
Hirth, Friedrich and Rockhill, W. W., *Chau Ju-Kua: His work on the Chinese and Arab trade in the twelfth and thirteenth centuries, entitled Chu-fan-chï*, St Petersburg, 1911, repr. Taipei, 1970.
Kuwabara, Jitsuzō, 'On P'u Shou-kêng: A man of the Western regions, who was the superintendent of the trading ships' office in Ch'üan-chou towards the end of the Sung dynasty, together with a general sketch of trade of the Arabs in China during the T'ang and Sung eras', *Memoirs of the Research Department of the Toyō Bunko*, 2 (1928), pp. 1–79, and 7 (1935), pp. 1–104.
Lo Hsiang-lin, 'Islam in Canton in the Sung period: Some fragmentary records', in F. S. Drake and Wolfram Eberhard (eds.), *Symposium on historical, archaeological and linguistic studies on southern China, South-east Asia and the Hong Kong region*, Hong Kong, 1967.
Salmon, Claudine, 'Srivijaya, la Chine et les marchands chinois, X^{e}–XIIe: Quelques réflexions sur la société de l'empire sumatranais', *Archipel*, 63 (2002), pp. 57–78.

Islam in South-East Asia from the eighth / fourteenth to the ninth / fifteenth centuries

Cortesão, Armando, *The Suma oriental of Tomé Pires: An account of the East, from the Red Sea to Japan, written in Malacca and India in 1512–15*, Hakluyt Society, 2 vols., London, 1944.
Damais, Louis-Charles, 'Études javanaises: Les tombes musulmans datées de Tralaya', *Bulletin de l'École Française d'Extrême Orient*, 48 (1956), pp. 353–415.
'L'épigraphie musulmane dans le Sud-Est Asiatique', *Bulletin de l'École Française d'Extrême Orient*, 56 (1968), pp. 567–604.
Gibb, H. A. R., *The travels of Ibn Battuta AD 1325–1354*, trans. with revisions and notes from the Arabic text, ed. C. Defrémery and B. R. Sanguinetti, Hakluyt Society, 4 vols., London, 1958–1994.
Graaf, H. J. de and Pigeaud, G. Th. (trans.), *Chinese Muslims in Java in the 15th and 16th centuries: The Malay Annals of Sĕmarang and Čerbon*, ed. M. C. Ricklefs, Monash Papers on Southeast Asia, 12, Melbourne, 1984.
Guillot, Claude and Kalus, Ludvik, *Les monuments funéraires et l'histoire du sultanat de Pasai à Sumatra*, Cahier d'Archipel, 37, Paris, 2008.
Mills, J. V. G. (trans. and annot.), *Ma Huan: Ying-yai Sheng-lan: The overall survey of the ocean's shores*, Cambridge, 1970.
Reid, Anthony, *Southeast Asia in the age of commerce 1450–1680*, vol. II: *Expansion and crisis*, New Haven, 1993.
Wink, André, *Al-Hind: The making of the Indo-Islamic world*, 3 vols., Leiden, 1990–2004.

Primary sources

Brakel, L. F., *The hikayat Muhammad Hanafiyyah: A medieval Muslim-Malay romance*, Bibliotheca Indonesica, 12, The Hague, 1975.

Chen Da-Sheng, 'A Brunei sultan in the early 14th century: Study of an Arabic gravestone', *Journal of Southeast Asian Studies*, 23, 1 (1992), pp. 1–13.

Chen Da-sheng and Kalus, Ludvik, *Corpus d'inscriptions arabes et persanes en Chine, 1. Province de Fu-jian (Quan-zhou, Fu-zhou, Xia-men)*, Paris, 1991.

Chen Da-sheng and Salmon, Claudine, 'Rapport preliminaire sur la découverte de tombes musulmanes dans l'Ile de Hainan', *Archipel*, 38 (1989), pp. 75–106.

Hill, A. H., 'Hikayat Raja-raja Pasai', *Journal of the Malaysian Branch of the Royal Asiatic Society*, 33, 2 (June 1960).

Kalus, Ludvik, 'Le plus ancienne inscription islamique du monde malais?', *Archipel*, 59 (2000), pp. 23–4.

'Réinterprétation des plus anciennes stèles funéraires islamiques nousantariennes: I. Les deux inscriptions du "Champa"', *Archipel*, 66 (2003).

Kalus, Ludvik and Guillot, Claude, 'Réinterprétation des plus anciennes stèles funéraires islamiques nousantariennes: II. La stèle de Leran (Java) datée de 475/1082 et les stèles associées', *Archipel*, 67 (2004), pp. 17–36.

Mills, J. V. G. and Ptak, Roderich, *Hsing-ch'a Sheng-lan: The overall survey of the Star Raft by Fei Hsin*, South China and Maritime Asia Series, 4, Wiesbaden, 1996.

Montana, Suwedi, 'Nouvelles données sur les royaumes de Lamuri et Barat', *Archipel*, 53 (1997), pp. 85–96.

Tibbetts, G. R., *Arab navigation in the Indian Ocean before the coming of the Portuguese*, Royal Asiatic Society Oriental Translation Fund, N. S. XLIII, London, 1971.

Wade, Geoff, 'Melaka in Ming dynasty texts', *Journal of the Malaysian Branch of the Royal Asiatic Society*, 70, 1 (1997), pp. 31–69.

Wang Gungwu, 'The Nanhai trade: A study of the early history of Chinese trade in South China Sea', *Journal of the Royal Asiatic Society; Malaysian Branch*, 31 (1958), pp. 1–135.

Wu Wen-liang 吴文良 and Wu You-xiong 吴幼雄, *Quan-zhou zong-jiao shi-ke* 泉州宗教石刻 (Religious Inscriptions in Quan-zhou), Beijing, 2005.

Yule, Henry (trans. and ed.), *The book of Ser Marco Polo the Venetian concerning the kingdoms and marvels of the East*, 2 vols., 3rd edn, London, 1929.

Secondary sources

al-Attas, Syed Naquib, *Preliminary statement on a general theory of the Islamization of the Malay-Indonesian Archipelago*, Kuala Lumpur, 1963.

Bousquet, Georges-Henri, *Introduction à l'étude de l'Islam indonésien*, Paris, 1938.

'Islam and local traditions: Syncretic ideas and practices', *Indonesia and the Malay World*, 32, 92 (2004), pp. 5–20.

Casparis, J. G. de, 'Historical writing on Indonesia (early period)', in D. G. E. Hall (ed.), *Historians of South East Asia*, London, 1961, pp. 121–63.

Chafee, John, 'Diasporic identities in the historical development of the maritime Muslim communities of Song-Yuan China', *Journal of Economic and Social History of the Orient*, 49, 4 (2006), pp. 395–420.

Chang Pin-tsun, 'The first Chinese diaspora in Southeast Asia in the fifteenth century', in Roderich Ptak and Dietmar Rothermund (eds.), *Emporia, commodities and entrepreneurs in Asian maritime trade, c. 1400–1750*, Stuttgart, 1991, pp. 13–28.

Coatalen, Paul, 'The coming of Islam to SE Asia: A critical review of some extant theories', *Islamic Quarterly*, 25, 3–4 (1981), pp. 00–21.

Di Meglio, Rita Rose, 'Arab trade with Indonesia and the Malay peninsula from the th to the 16th century', in D. S. Richards (ed.), *Islam and the trade of Asia: A colloquium*, Oxford, 1970.

Drewes, G. W. J., 'New light on the coming of Islam to Indonesia?', *Bijdragen tot de Taal-, Land- en Volkenkunde*, 124 (1968), pp. 433–59.

Eaton, Richard M., *The rise of Islam and the Bengal frontier, 1204–1760*, Berkeley and Los Angeles, 1993.

India's Islamic traditions, 711–1750, New Delhi, 2005.

Evans, Ivor H. N., 'A grave and megaliths in Negri Sembilan with an account of some excavations', *Journal of the Federated Malay States Museums*, 9, 3 (1921), pp. 155–73.

Fan Ke, 'Maritime Muslims and Hui identity: A south Fujian case', *Journal of Muslim Minority Affairs*, 21, 2 (2001), pp. 309–32.

Fatimi, S. Q., *Islām comes to Malaysia*, Singapore, 1963.

Feener, R. Michael and Laffan, Michael F., 'Sufi scents across the Indian Ocean: Yemeni hagiography as a source for the earliest history of Southeast Asian Islam', *Archipel*, 70 (2005), pp. 185–208.

Flecker, Michael, 'A ninth-century AD Arab or Indian shipwreck in Indonesia: First evidence for direct trade with China', *World Archaeology*, 32, 3 (Feb. 2001), pp. 335–54.

Freeman-Grenville, G. S. P., *The Swahili coast, 2nd to 19th centuries: Islam, Christianity and commerce in eastern Africa*, London, 1988.

Gommans, Jos and Leider, Jacques (eds.), *The maritime frontier of Burma: Exploring political, cultural and commerial interaction in the Indian Ocean world, 1200–1800*, Leiden, 2002.

Gonda, J., *Sanskrit in Indonesia*, New Delhi, 1973.

Gordon, Alijah (ed.), *The propagation of Islām in the Indonesian–Malay archipelago*, Kuala Lumpur, 2001.

Graaf, H. J. de, 'South-East Asian Islam to the eighteenth century', in P. M. Holt, Ann K. S. Lambton and Bernard Lewis (eds.), *The Cambridge history of Islam*, vol. II: *The further Islamic lands, Islamic society and civilization*, Cambridge, 1970, pp. 123–54.

Hooker, M. B. (ed.), *Islam in South-East Asia*, Leiden, 1983.

Ibrahim, Ahmad, Siddique, Sharon and Hussain, Yasmin (eds.), *Readings on Islam in Southeast Asia*, Singapore, 1986.

Ibrahim Kunju, A.P., 'Origin and spread of Islam in Kerala', in Ashgar Ali Engineer (ed.), *Kerala Muslims: A historical perspective*, New Delhi, 1995, pp. 17–34.

Israeli, Raphael and Johns, Anthony H. (eds.), *Islam in Asia*, vol. II: *Southeast and East Asia*, Boulder, CO, 1984.

Johns, A. H., 'Sufism as a category in Indonesian literature and history', *Journal of Southeast Asian History*, 2, 2 (July 1961), pp. 10–23.

'Modes of Islamization in Southeast Asia', in David N. Lorenzen (ed.), *Religious change and cultural domination, 30th international congress of human sciences in Asia and North Africa*, Mexico City, 1981, pp. 60–77.

'Islam in the Malay world: An exploratory survey with some reference to Quranic exegesis', in Raphael Israeli and A. H. Johns (eds.), *Islam in Asia*, vol. II: *Southeast and East Asia*, Boulder, CO, 1984, pp. 37–49.

Kern, R. A., *De Islam in Indonesië*, The Hague, 1947.

'The propagation of Islām in the Indonesian–Malay archipelago', in Alijah Gordon (ed.), *The propagation of Islām in the Indonesian–Malay archipelago*, Kuala Lumpur, 2001, pp. 23–124.

Kumar, Ann L., 'Islam, the Chinese and Indonesian historiography – a review article', *Journal of Asian Studies*, 46, 3 (Aug. 1987), pp. 603–16.

Lambourn, Elizabeth, 'From Cambay to Pasai and Gresik – the export of Gujarati grave memorials to Sumatra and Java in the 15th century AD', *Indonesia and the Malay World*, 31, 90 (2003), pp. 221–89.

'La production de marbre sculpté à Cambaye au Gujarat et son exportation dans l'Océan Indien (XIIIe–XVe siècles Ap. J. C.)', in J. M. dos Santos Alves, C. Guillot and R. Ptak (eds.), *Mirabilia Asiatica: Produtos raros no comércio marítimo. Produits rares dans le commerce maritime. Seltene Waren im Seehandel*, Wiesbaden and Lisbon, 2003, pp. 209–52.

'The formation of the *batu Aceh* tradition in fifteenth-century Samudera-Pasai', *Indonesia and the Malay World*, 32 (2004), pp. 211–48.

Leslie, Donald Daniel, *Islam in traditional China: A short history to 1800*, Canberra, 1986.

Lombard, Denys and Salmon, Claudine, 'Islam and Chineseness', *Indonesia*, 57 (April 1994), pp. 115–32, repr. in Alijah Gordon (ed.), *The propagation of Islām in the Indonesian–Malay archipelago*, Kuala Lumpur, 2001, pp. 181–208.

Maejima Shinji, 'The Muslims in Ch'üan-chou at the end of the Yüan dynasty' (I & II), *Memoirs of the Research Department of the Toyō Bunko*, 31 (1973), pp. 27–52 and 32 (1974), pp. 47–72.

Manguin, Pierre-Yves, 'The introduction of Islam into Champa', *Journal of the Malaysian Branch of the Royal Asiatic Society*, 58, 1 (1985), pp. 1–28; repr. in Alijah Gordon (ed.), *The propagation of Islām in the Indonesian–Malay archipelago*, Kuala Lumpur, 2001, pp. 288–328.

Marrison, G. E., 'The coming of Islam to the East Indies', *Journal of the Malaysian Branch of the Royal Asiatic Society*, 24, 1 (Feb. 1951), pp. 28–37.

'Persian influences in Malay life', *Journal of the Malaysian Branch of the Royal Asiatic Society*, 28, 1 (1955), pp. 52–69.

Miksic, John, 'From megaliths to tombstones: The transition from prehistory to the early Islamic period in highland west Sumatra', *Indonesia and the Malay World*, 32, 93 (July 2004), pp. 191–210.

Moquette, J. P., 'De datum op den grafsteen van Malik Ibrahim te Grisse', *Tijdschrift voor Indische Taal-, Land- en Volkenkunde*, 54 (1912), pp. 208–14.

Pigeaud, Theodore G. Th. and de Graff, H. J., *Islamic states in Java 1500–1700*, The Hague, 1976.

Ray, Haraprasad, *Trade and diplomacy in India–China relations: A study of Bengal during the fifteenth century*, New Delhi 1993.

Reid, Anthony, *Southeast Asia in the age of commerce 1450–1680*, vol. I: *The lands below the winds*, New Haven and London, 1988.

'The rise and fall of Sino-Javanese shipping', in V. J. H. Houben, H. M. J. Maier and W. van der Molen (eds.), *Looking in odd mirrors: The Java Sea*, Leiden, 1992, pp. 177–211.

'The Islamization of Southeast Asia', in Anthony Reid (ed.), *Charting the shape of early modern Southeast Asia*, Chiang Mai, 2000, pp. 15–38.

Ricklefs, M. C., 'Islamization in Java: An overview and some philosophical considerations', in R. Israeli and A. H. Johns (eds.), *Islam in Asia*, vol. II: *Southeast and East Asia*, Boulder, CO, 1984, pp. 11–24.

A history of modern Indonesia since c. 1200, 3rd edn, Basingstoke, 2001.

Rinkes, D. A., *Nine saints of Java*, trans. H. M. Froger, ed. Alijah Gordon, Kuala Lumpur, 1996.

Risso, Patricia, *Merchants and faith: Muslim commerce and culture in the Indian Ocean*, Boulder, CO, 1995.

Seiji, Imanaga, *Islam in Southeast Asia*, Hiroshima, 2000.

Slamet Muljana, *Runtuhnja keradjaan Hindu-Djawa dan timbulnja negara-negara Islam di Nusantara*, Jakarta, 1968.

'Islam before the foundation of the Islamic state of Demak', *Journal of the South Seas Society*, 27, 1 and 2 (1972), pp. 41–83.

So, Billy K. L., *Prosperity, region, and institutions in maritime China: The south Fukien pattern, 946–1368*, Cambridge, MA, 2000.

Tan Yeok Seong, 'Chinese element in the Islamisation of Southeast Asia: A study of the story of Njai Gede Pinatih, the Great Lady of Gresik', *Journal of the South Seas Society*, 30, 1 and 2 (1975).

Teeuw, A., 'The history of the Malay language: A preliminary survey', *Bijdragen tot de Taal-, Land- en Volkenkunde*, 115 (1959), pp. 138–61.

Tibbetts, G. R., 'Early Muslim traders in South-East Asia', *Journal of the Malaysian Branch of the Royal Asiatic Society*, 30 (1957), pp. 1–45.

Wake, Christopher, 'Malacca's early kings and the reception of Islam', *Journal of Southeast Asian History*, 5, 2 (Sept. 1964), pp. 104–28.

'Melaka in the fifteenth century: Malay historical traditions and the politics of Islamization', in Kernial Singh Sandhu and Paul Wheatley (eds.), *Melaka: The transformation of a Malay capital c. 1400–1980*, Kuala Lumpur, 1983, vol. I, pp. 128–61.

Wang Gungwu, 'The opening of relations between China and Malacca 1403–05', in J. S. Bastin and R. Roolvink (eds.), *Malayan and Indonesian studies: Essays presented to Sir Richard Windstedt*, London, 1964.

'Early Ming relations with Southeast Asia: A background essay', in John K. Fairbank (ed.), *The Chinese world order*, Cambridge, MA, 1968, pp. 34–62.

'The first three rulers of Malacca', *Journal of the Malaysian Branch of the Royal Asiatic Society*, 41, 1 (1968), pp. 11–22.

Wilkinson, R. J., 'The Pengkalan Kĕmpas "saint"', *Journal of the Malayan Branch Royal Asiatic Society*, 9, 1 (1931), pp. 134–5.

11 Follow the white camel: Islam in China to 1800
Zvi Ben-Dor Benite

Practical sugggestions for further reading

Ben-Dor Benite, Zvi, *The Dao of Muḥammad: A cultural history of Muslims in late imperial China*, Harvard East Asian Monographs, 248, Cambridge, MA, 2005.

Chang, Jing Qi, 'Islamic architecture in China', in Brian Brace Taylor (ed.), *The changing rural habitat*, vol II: *Background papers*, Singapore, 1982.

Clark, Hugh, *Community, trade and networks: Southern Fujian province from the third to the thirteenth century*, Cambridge, 2002.

Fletcher, Joseph, *Studies on Chinese and Islamic Inner Asia*, ed. Beatrice Forbes Manz, London, 1995.

Forbes, Andrew D. W., *Warlords and Muslims in Chinese Central Asia*, Cambridge, 1986.

Franke, Herbert and Twitchett, Denis, *The Cambridge history of China*, vol. VI: *Alien regimes and border states, 710–1368*, Cambridge, 1994.

Gladney, Dru C., *Muslim Chinese: Ethnic nationalism in the People's Republic*, 2nd edn, Cambridge, MA, 1996.

Israeli, Raphael, and Gorman, Lyn, *Islam in China: a critical bibliography*, Bibliographies and Indexes in Religious Studies, 29, Westport, CT.

Leslie, Donald, Daye, Yang, and Yousef, Ahmed, *Islam in traditional China: A bibliographical guide*, Monumenta Serica Monograph Series, 54, Sankt Augustin.

Li Xinghua, Huibin Qin, Jinyuan Feng and Qiuzhen Sha, *Zhongguo Yisilan jiao shi = History of Islam in China*, Beijing, 1998.

Lipman, Jonathan N., *Familiar strangers: A history of Muslims in north-west China*, Seattle, 1997.

Millward, James A., *Eurasian crossroads: A history of Xinjiang*, New York, 2007.

Perdue, Peter C., *China marches west: The Qing conquest of central Eurasia*, Cambridge, MA, 2005.

Qiu Shusen, *China's Muslim nationality history*, Yinchuan Shi, 1996 (in Chinese).

Rossabi, Morris, *China and Inner Asia from 1368 to the present day*, London, 1981.

Rudelson, Justin Jon, *Oasis identities: Uyghur nationalism along China's Silk Road*, New York, 1998.

Sinor, Denis (ed.), *The Cambridge history of early Inner Asia*, Cambridge, 1990.

Tazaka Kōdō, *Islam in China: Its introduction and development*, Tokyo, 1964 (in Japanese).

Primary sources

Chen Dasheng (ed.), *Islamic inscriptions in Quanzhou*, trans. Chen Enming, Yinchuan and Quanzhou, 1984.

Dunn, Ross E., *The adventures of Ibn Battuta: A Muslim traveler of the 14th century*, Berkeley, 1986, 2nd edn 2005.

Ferrand, Gabriel, *Relations de voyages et textes geographiques, Arabes, Persans et Turks relatifs à l'Extreme-Orient du VIII au XVIII siècles*, Paris, 1912.

Hafiz Abru (Shihabu'd-Din 'Abdullah bin Lutfullah Al-Khwafi), trans. K. M. Maitra, *A Persian embassy to China: Being an extract from Zubdat-t tawarikh of Hafiz Abru*, New York, 1970 (1st edn, Lahore, 1934).

Hirth, Friedrich and Rockhill, W. W., *Chau Ju-Kua: His work on the Chinese and Arab trade in the twelfth and thirteenth centuries, entitled Chu-fan-chï*, St Petersburg, 1911, repr. Taipei, 1970.

Ma Sai-bei (chief ed.), *Qing shi-lu Mu-si-lin zi-liao ji-lu* [Collection of references to Muslims in the *Qing shi-lu*], 4 vols., Lanzhou and Ningxia, 1988.

Mills, J. V. G. (ed.), *Ma Huan: Ying-yai Sheng-lan: 'The overall survey of the ocean's shores' (1433)*, Cambridge, 1970.

Murata, Sachiko, *Chinese gleams of Sufi light: Wang Tai-yü's Great learning of the pure and real and Liu Chih's Displaying the concealment of the real realm; with a new translation of Jāmī's Lawā'iḥ from the Persian by William C. Chittick*, Albany, NY, 2000.

Murata, Sachiko, Chittick, William C. and Weiming, Tu, *The sage learning of Liu Zhi: Islamic thought in Confucian terms*, Cambridge, MA, 2009.

Sulaymān al-Tājir and Abū Zayd Ḥasan ibn Yazīd, *Ancient accounts of India and China, by two Mohammedan travellers. Who went to those parts in the 9th century; translated from the Arabic, by the late learned Eusebius Renaudot*, London, 1733.

Secondary sources

Allès, Élisabeth, *Musulmans de Chine: Une anthropologie des Hui du Henan*, Recherches d'histoire et de sciences sociales, 89, Paris, 2000.

Allsen, Thomas T., 'The Yuan dynasty and the Uighurs of Turfan in the thirteenth century', in Morris Rossabi (ed.), *China among equals*, Berkeley, 1983, pp. 243–80.

Atwill, David, *The Chinese sultanate: Islam, violence, and the Panthay rebellion, 1856–1873*, Stanford, 2005.

Aubin, Françoise, 'En Islam Chinois: Quels Naqshbandis?' [In Chinese Islam, which Naqshbandis?], in M. Gaborieau, A. Popovic and T. Zarcone (eds.), *Naqshbandis: Cheminements et situation actuelle d'un ordre mystique musulman*, Istanbul and Paris, 1990, pp. 491–572.

Ben-Dor Benite, Zvi, '"Even unto China": Displacement and Chinese Muslim myths of origin', *Bulletin of the Royal Institute for Inter-Faith Studies*, Winter (2003), pp. 93–114.

'The Marrano emperor: The mysterious bond between Zhu Yuanzhang and the Chinese Muslims', in Sarah Schneewind (ed.), *Long live the emperor!: Uses of the Ming founder across six centuries of East Asian history*, Ming Studies Research Series, 4, Minneapolis, 2008, pp. 275–308.

Chen, Dasheng and Lombard, Denis, 'Foreign merchants in maritime trade in Quanzhou ("Zaitun"): Thirteenth and fourteenth centuries', in Denis Lombard and Jean Aubin (eds.), *Asian merchants and businessmen in the Indian Ocean and China Sea*, Oxford, 2000, pp. 19–23.

Di Cosmo, Nicola, *Ancient China and its enemies: The rise of nomadic power in East Asian history*, Cambridge, 2002.

Fan, Ke, 'Maritime Muslims and Hui identity: A South Fujian case', *Journal of Muslim Minority Affairs*, 21, 2 (2001), pp. 309–32.

Franke, Wolfgang, *A note on the ancient Chinese mosques at Xian and Quanzhou*, Kuala Lumpur, 1980.

Gillette, Maris Boyd, *Between Mecca and Beijing: Modernization and consumption among urban Chinese Muslims*, Stanford, 2002.

Gladney, Dru C., 'Muslim tombs and ethnic folklore: Charters for Hui identity', *Journal of Asian Studies*, 46, 3 (1987), pp. 495–532.

Gladney, Dru C. and Ma Shouqian, 'Interpretations of Islam in China: A Hui scholar's perspective', *Journal of Institute for Muslim Minority Affairs*, 10, 2 (1989), pp. 475–86.

Haneda, Akira, 'Introduction: The problems of Turkicization and Islamicization of Turkestan', *Acta Asiatica*, 34 (1978), pp. 1–21.

Jaschok, Maria, and Shui, Jingjun, *The history of women's mosques in Chinese Islam: A mosque of their own*, London, 2001.

Kim Hodong, *Holy war in China: The Muslim rebellion and state in Chinese Central Asia, 1866–1877*, Stanford, 2003.

Kuwabara, Jitsuzō, 'On P'u Shou-keng', *Memoirs of the Research Department of the Toyō Bunko*, 2 (1928), pp. 1–79, and 7 (1935), pp. 1–104.
Mackerras, Colin, *The Uighur empire according to the Tang dynastic histories: A study in Sino-Uighur relations, 744–840*, Columbia, SC, 1972.
Millward, James A., *Beyond the pass: Economy, ethnicity, and empire in Qing Central Asia, 1759–1864*, Stanford, 1998.
Millward, James A. and Perdue, Peter C., 'Political and cultural history of the Xinjiang region through the late nineteenth century', in Frederick S. Starr (ed.), *Xinjiang: China's Muslim borderland*, Armonk, NY, pp. 27–62.
Quanzhou Foreign Maritime Museum, (ed.), *Symposium on Quanzhou Islam*, Quanzhou 1983.
Rossabi, Morris, *Khubilai Khan: His life and times*, Berkeley, 1988.
Sen, Tansen, 'The formation of Chinese maritime networks to southern Asia, 1200–1450', *Journal of the Economic and Social History of the Orient*, 49, 4 (2006), pp. 421–53.
Sun Dazhang, *Ancient Chinese architecture: Islamic buildings*, New York, 2003.
Voll, John O., "Muslim minority alternatives: Implications of Muslim experiences in China and the Soviet Union', *Journal, Institute for Muslim Minority Affairs*, 6, 2 (1985), pp. 332–53.
Yang Hongxun, 'A preliminary discussion on the building year of Quanzhou holy tomb and the authenticity of its legend', in Committee for Protecting Islamic Historical Relics in Quanzhou and the Research Centre for the Historical Relics of Chinese Culture (eds.), *The Islamic historic relics in Quanzhou*, Quanzhou, 1985.
Zhang, Jing-qui, *Mosques of northern China*, *MIMAR* 3: Architecture in Development, Singapore, 1982.

12 Islam in South-East Asia and the Indian Ocean littoral, 1500–1800: expansion, polarisation, synthesis
Anthony Reid

Practical suggestions for further reading

Andaya, Barbara and Ishii, Yoneo, 'Religious developments in Southeast Asia, c.1500–1800', in Nicholas Tarling (ed.), *Cambridge history of Southeast Asia*, Cambridge, 1992, pp. 508–71.
Azra, Azyumardi, *The origins of Islamic reformism in Southeast Asia: Networks of Malay–Indonesian and Middle Eastern 'ulama' in the seventeenth and eighteenth centuries*, Sydney, 2004.
Graaf, H. J. de and Pigeaud, Theodore G. Th., *Islamic states in Java, 1500–1700*, The Hague, 1976.
Ibrahim, Ahmad, Siddique, Sharon, and Hussain, Yasmin (eds.), *Readings on Islam in Southeast Asia*, Singapore, 1986.
Lombard, Denys, *Le carrefour javanais: Essai d'histoire globale*, Paris, 1990.
Reid, Anthony, *Southeast Asia in the age of commerce 1450–1680*, vol. II: Expansion and crisis, New Haven, 1993.
(ed.), *Southeast Asia in the early modern era: Trade, power and belief*, Ithaca, 1993.
(ed.), *The making of an Islamic political discourse in Southeast Asia*, Melbourne, 1993.
Ricklefs, M. C., 'Six centuries of Islamization in Java', in Nehemia Levtzion (ed.), *Conversion to Islam*, New York, 1979, pp. 100–28.

Mystic synthesis in Java: A history of Islamization from the fourteenth to the early nineteenth centuries, Norwalk, CT, 2005.
Riddell, Peter, *Islam and the Malay–Indonesian world*, Honolulu, 2001.

Primary sources

Adat Aceh dari Satu manuscript India Office Library, Romanised by Teungku Anzib Lamnyong, Banda Aceh, 1976.
al-Attas, S. M. Naquib, *The mysticism of Hamzah Fansuri*, Kuala Lumpur, 1970.
Babad Tanah Djawi, Javaanse Rijkskroniek. W. L. Olthof's Vertaling van de prozaversie van J. J. Meinsma lopende tot het jaar 1721, rev. ed. J. J. Ras, Dordrecht, 1987.
Brown, C. C. (trans.), 'Sejarah Melayu or "Malay Annals"', *Journal of the Malaysian Branch of the Royal Asiatic Society*, 25, parts 2 and 3 (1952).
Drewes, G. W. J. (ed. and trans.), *Een Javaanse Primbon uit de Zestiende Eeuw*, Leiden, 1945.
(ed. and trans.), *The admonitions of Seh Bari: A 16th century Javanese Muslim text attributed to the Saint of Bonan*, The Hague, 1969.
(ed.), *An early Javanese code of Muslim ethics*, The Hague, 1978.
Drewes, G. W. J. and Brakel, L. F. (eds. and trans.), *The poems of Hamzah Fansuri*, Dordrecht, 1986.
Fang, Liaw Yock (ed.), *Undang-undang Melaka/The laws of Melaka*, The Hague, 1976.
Galvão, Antonio, *A treatise on the Moluccas (c.1544), probably the preliminary version of Antonio Galvão's lost História das Molucas*, ed. and trans. Hubert Jacobs, Rome, 1971.
Graaf, H. J. de (ed.), *De Vijf Gezantschapsreizen van Rijklof van Goens naar het hof van Mataram, 1648–1654*, The Hague, 1956.
Hikayat Patani: The story of Patani, ed. A. Teeuw and D. K. Wyatt, 2 vols., The Hague, 1970.
Hill, A. H. (ed and trans.), 'The Hikayat Raja-raja Pasai', *Journal of the Malaysian Branch of the Royal Asiatic Society*, 33, 2 (1960).
Jacobs, Hubert (ed.), *Documenta Malucensia, I, 1542–1577*, Rome, 1974.
(ed.), *The Jesuit Makasar documents, 1615–1682*, Rome, 1980.
Johns, A. H. (ed. and trans.), *The gift addressed to the spirit of the Prophet*, Canberra, 1964.
Ma Huan, *Ying-Yai Sheng-Lan: The overall survey of the ocean's shores*, trans. J. V. G. Mills, Hakluyt Society, Cambridge, 1970.
Major, R. H. (ed.), *India in the fifteenth century, being a collection of narratives of voyages to India*, Hakluyt Society, London, 1857.
Nieuwenhuijze, C. A. O. van (ed. and trans.), *Samsu'l-din van Pasai: Bijdrage tot de Kennis der Sumatraansche mystiek*, Leiden, 1945.
Pinto, Mendes, *The travels of Mendes Pinto*, ed. Rebecca Catz, Chicago and London, 1989.
Pires, Tomé, *The Suma oriental of Tomé Pires: An account of the east, from the Red Sea to Japan, written in Malacca and India in 1512–15*, ed. Armando Cortesão, Hakluyt Society, 2 vols., London, 1944.
Raniri, Nuru'd-din ar-, *Bustanu's-Salatan, Bab II, Fasal 13*, ed. T. Iskandar, Kuala Lumpur, 1966.
Ras, J. J., *The Hikayat Bandjar: A study in Malay historiography*, The Hague, 1968.
Ricklefs, M. C., *Modern Javanese historical tradition: A study of an original Kartasura chronicle and related materials*, London, 1978.
Riddell, Peter, *Transferring a tradition: 'Abd al-Ra'uf al-Singkili's rendering into Malay of the Jalalayn commentary*, Berkeley, 1990.

Rinkes, D. A., *Nine saints of Java*, trans. H. M. Froger, ed. Alijah Gordon, Kuala Lumpur, 1996.
Serjeant, R. B., *The Portuguese off the South Arabian coast, Hadhrami chronicles*, Oxford, 1963.
Tibbetts, G. R., *A study of the Arabic texts containing material on South-East Asia*, Leiden, 1979.

Secondary sources

al-Attas, Syed Naquib, *Preliminary statement on a general theory of the Islamization of the Malay–Indonesian archipelago*, Kuala Lumpur, 1963.
Dames, M. Longworth, 'The Portuguese and Turks in the Indian Ocean in the sixteenth century', *Journal of the Royal Asiatic Society* (1921).
Fatimi, S. Q., *Islām comes to Malaysia*, Singapore, 1963.
Gordon, Alijah (ed.), *The propagation of Islām in the Indonesian-Malay archipelago*, Kuala Lumpur, 2001.
Graaf, H. J. de, *De regering van Panembahan Senapati Ingalaga*, The Hague, 1954.
De Regering van Sultan Agung, vorst van Mataram, 1613–1645, en die van zijn voorganger Panembahan Séda-ing-Krapjak, 1601–1613, The Hague, 1958.
De regering van Sunan Mangkurat I Tegal-Wangi, vorst van Mataram, 1646–1677, The Hague, 1961.
'South-East Asian Islam to the eighteenth century', in P. M. Holt, Ann K. S. Lambton and Bernard Lewis (eds.), *The Cambridge history of Islam*, vol. II: *The further Islamic lands, Islamic society and civilization*, Cambridge, 1970, pp. 123–54.
Guillot, Claude and Kalus, Ludvik, 'La stèle funéraire de Hamzah Fansuri', *Archipel*, 60 (2000), pp. 3–24.
Hadi, Amirul, *Islam and state in Sumatra: A study of seventeenth-century Aceh*, Leiden, 2004.
Hooker, M. B. (ed.), *Islam in South-East Asia*, Leiden, 1983.
Israeli, Raphael and Johns, Anthony H. (eds.), *Islam in Asia*, vol. II: *Southeast and East Asia*, Boulder, CO, 1984.
Ito, Takeshi, 'The world of the Adat Aceh: A historical study of the sultanate of Aceh', Ph.D. thesis, Australian National University, 1984.
Lombard, Denys, *Le sultanat d'Atjéh au temps d'Iskandar Muda – 1607–1636*, Paris, 1967.
Naimur Rahman Farooqi, 'Mughal–Ottoman relations: A study of political and diplomatic relations between Mughal India and the Ottoman empire, 1556–1748', Ph.D. dissertation, University of Wisconsin, 1986.
Reid, Anthony, *Southeast Asia in the age of commerce 1450–1680*, vol. I: *The lands below the winds*, New Haven and London, 1988.
'The Islamization of Southeast Asia', in Anthony Reid (ed.), *Charting the shape of early modern Southeast Asia*, Chiang Mai, 2000, pp. 15–38.
An Indonesian frontier: Acehnese and other histories of Sumatra, Singapore, 2004.
Ricklefs, M. C., *Seen and unseen worlds in Java: History, literature, and Islam in the court of Pakubuwana II, 1726–1749*, Honolulu, 1998.
A history of modern Indonesia since c. 1200, 3rd edn, Basingstoke, 2001.
Zoetmulder, P. J., *Pantheism and monism in Javanese Suluk literature: Islamic and Indian mysticism in an Indonesian setting*, trans. M. C. Ricklefs, Leiden, 1995.

13 South-East Asian localisations of Islam and participation within a global *umma*, *c.* 1500–1800
R. Michael Feener

Practical suggestions for further reading

Azra, Azyumardi, *The origins of Islamic reformism in Southeast Asia: Networks of Malay–Indonesian and Middle Eastern ʿulamāʾ in the seventeenth and eighteenth centuries*, Crows Nest, NSW, 2004.

Ricklefs, M. C., *Mystic synthesis in Java: A history of Islamization from the fourteenth to the early nineteenth centuries*, Norwalk, CT, 2005.

Riddell, Peter, *Islam in the Malay–Indonesian world: Transmission and responses*, Honolulu, 2001.

Primary sources

Arabic

al-ʾAhdal, ʿAbd al-Raḥmān b. Sulaymān, *al-Nafas al-yamānī*, Ṣanʿāʾ, 1979.

Fathurahman, Oman (ed. and trans.), *Tanbīh al-Māsyī: Menyoal Wahdatul Wujud, Kasus Abdurrauf Singkel di Aceh Abad 17*, Bandung, 1999.

Johns, A. H. (ed. and trans.), *The gift addressed to the Spirit of the Prophet*, Canberra, 1964.

Lubis, Nabilah (ed. and trans.), *Syekh Yusuf al-Taj al-Makasari Menyingkap Intisari Segala Rahasia*, Bandung, 1996.

van Nieuwenhuijze, C. A. O. (ed. and trans.), *Samsuʾl-Dīn van Pasai: Bijdrage tot de Kennis der Sumatraansche Mystiek*, Leiden, 1945.

Tudjimah (ed.), *Syekh Yusuf Makasar: Riwayat dan Ajarannya*, Jakarta, 1997.

al-Yāfiʿī [al-Yamanī al-Makkī], Abū Muḥammad ʿAbd Allāh b. Asʾad b. ʿAlī b. Sulaymān ʿAfīf al-Dīn, *Mirʾāt al-jinān wa ʿibrat al-yaqẓān*, Ḥaydarabād, 1919–20.

South-East Asian languages

Aad, Janson, Tol, Roger and Witkam, Jan Just, *Mystical illustrations from the teachings of Syaikh Ahmad Al-Qusyasyi: A facsimile edition on paper and CD-ROM of a manuscript from Aceh (Cod. Or. 2222) in the Library of Leiden University*, Leiden, 1995.

al-Attas, Syed Muhammad Naquib (ed.), *The oldest known Malay manuscript: A 16th century Malay translation of the ʿAqāʾid of al-Nasafī*, Kuala Lumpur, 1988.

al-Banjārī, Muḥammad Arshad b. ʿAbd Allāh, *Sabīl al-Muhtadīn*, Singapore, n.d.

al-Banjārī, Muḥammad Nafīs b. Idrīs b. Husayn, *al-Durr al-Nafīs*, Singapore, n.d.

Braginsky, V. I. (ed.), *Tasawuf dan Sastera Melayu: Kajian dan Teks-teks*, Jakarta, 1993.

Brakel, L. F. (ed.), *The Hikayat Muhammad Hanafiah*, The Hague, 1975.

Brown, C. C. (ed. and trans.), *Sejarah Melayu, or Malay Annals*, Kuala Lumpur, 1970.

Chambert-Loir, Henri and Salahuddin, Siti Maryam R. (eds.), *Boʾ Sangaji Kai: Catatan Kerajaan Bima*, Jakarta, 1999.

Drewes, G. W. J. (ed. and trans.), 'Het Document uit den Brandstapel', *Djåwå*, 2 (1927), pp. 97–109.
(ed. and trans.), *Een Javaanse Primbon uit de Zestiende Eeuw*, Leiden, 1945.
(ed. and trans.), *Een 16de Eeuwse Maleise Vertaling van de Burda van al-Buṣīrī*, The Hague, 1955.
(ed. and trans.), 'Javanese poems dealing with or attributed to the saint of Bonaṇ', *Bijdragen tot de Taal-, Land- en Volkenkunde*, 124 (1968), pp. 209–40.
(ed. and trans.), *The admonitions of Seh Bari: A 16th century Javanese Muslim text attributed to the saint of Bonaṇ*, The Hague, 1969.
(ed. and trans.), 'Further data concerning 'Abd al-Samad al-Palimbani', *Bijdragen tot de Taal-, Land- en Volkenkunde*, 132, 2–3 (1976), pp. 267–92.
(ed. and trans.), *Directions for travelers on the mystic path: Zakariyya al-Anṣārī's Kitāb Fatḥ al-Raḥmān and its Indonesian adaptations*, The Hague, 1977.
(ed. and trans.), *An early Javanese code of Muslim ethics*, The Hague, 1978.
Drewes, G. W. J. and Brakel, L. F. (eds. and trans.), *The poems of Hamzah Fansuri*, Dordrecht, 1986.
Fang, Liaw Yock (ed.), *Undang-undang Melaka/The Laws of Melaka*, The Hague, 1976.
al-Faṭānī, Dāwūd b. 'Abd Allāh, *al-Durr al-thamīn*, Cairo, 1923.
Kifāyat al-muḥtāj, Patani, n.d.
Minhāj al-'ābidīn, Singapore, n.d.
Johns, A. H. (ed.), '*Daḳā'iḳ al-Ḥurūf* by 'Abd al-Ra'ūf of Singkel', Journal of the Royal Asiatic Society (1953), pp. 55–73, 137–50.
(ed.), 'Nur al-Daḳa'iḳ by the Sumatran mystic Shamsu'l-Dīn ibn 'Abdullah', Journal of the Royal Asiatic Society (1953), pp. 137–51.
Jones, Russell (ed. and trans.), *Hikayat Sultan Ibrahim Ibn Adham: An edition of an anonymous Malay text with translation and notes*, Berkeley, 1985.
(ed. and trans.), *Hikayat Raja Pasai*, Selangor, 1987.
Matthes, B. F. (ed.), *Eenige Proeven van Boegineesche en Makassaarsche Poëzie*, The Hague, 1883.
(ed.), *Makassaarsche Chrestomathie*, Amsterdam, 1883.
Millie, Julian (ed. and trans.), *Bidasari: Jewel of Malay Muslim culture*, Leiden, 2004.
Millies, H. C. (ed.), 'Proeven eener Makassarsche vertaling des Korans ...', *Bijdragen tot de Taal-, Land- en Volkenkunde*, 3 (1856), pp. 89–106.
Mulya, Abdul Kadir (ed. and trans.), *Surek Pangngajakna Nabita Muhammad SAW nennia Abdul Ibadi*, Jakarta, 1991.
al-Palimbānī, 'Abd al-Ṣamad, *Hidāyat al-sālikīn*, Cairo, 1922.
'Abd al-Ṣamad, *Sayr al-Sālikīn*, Jakarta, n.d.
al-Rānīrī, Nūr al-Dīn Muḥammad Jīlānī b. 'Alī b. Ḥasanjī b. Muḥammad b. Ḥumayd, *Ṣirāt al-Mustaqīm fī fiqh madhhab al-Shāfi'ī*, Cairo, 1937.
van Ronkel, Ph. S., *De Roman van Amir Hamzah*, Leiden, 1895.
[Singkelī], 'Abd al-Ra'ūf b. 'Alī al-Fanṣūrī al-Jāwī, *Tarjumān al-mustafīd*, Cairo, 1951.
Soebardi, S. (ed. and trans.), *The book of Cabolek: A critical edition with introduction, translation and notes*, The Hague, 1978.
Tudjimah (ed.), *Asrār al-Insān fī Ma'rifat al-Rūḥ wa'l-Raḥmān*, Jakarta, 1961.
Voorhoeve, P., *Twee Maleise Geschriften van Nuruddin ar-Raniri in facsimile uitgegeven met Aantekeningen*, Leiden, 1955.

Secondary sources

South-East Asian history writing

Andaya, Barbara Waston, 'Delineating female space: Seclusion and the state in pre-modern island Southeast Asia', in Barbara Waston Andaya, *Other pasts: Women, gender and history in early modern Southeast Asia*, Honolulu, 2000, pp. 231–53.

Andaya, Leonard Y., 'Aceh's contribution to standards of Malayness', *Archipel*, 61 (2001), pp. 26–68.

Azra, Azyumardi, 'Opposition to Sufism in the East Indies in the seventeenth and eighteenth centuries', in Frederick de Jong and Bernd Radtke (eds.), *Islamic mysticism contested: Thirteen centuries of controversies and polemics*, Leiden, 1999, pp. 665–86.

van Bruinessen, Martin, '*Shariʿa* court, *tarekat* and *pesantren*: Religious institutions in the Banten sultanate', *Archipel*, 50 (1995), pp. 165–200.

Cortesão, Armando (trans.), *The Suma oriental of Tomé Pires*, London, 1944.

Cummings, William, 'Scripting Islamization: Arabic texts in early modern Makassar', *Ethnohistory*, 48, 4 (2001), pp. 559–86.

Graaf, H. J. de and Pigeaud, Theodore G. Th., *Islamic states in Java, 1500–1700*, The Hague, 1976.

Hadi, Amirul, *Islam and state in Sumatra: A study of seventeenth-century Aceh*, Leiden, 2004.

Ho, Engseng, 'Before parochialization: Diasporic Arabs cast in creole waters', in Huub de Jonge and Nico Kaptein (eds.), *Transcending borders: Arabs, politics, trade, and Islam in Southeast Asia*, Leiden, 2002.

Ito, Takeshi, *The world of the Adat Aceh: A historical study of the sultanate of Aceh*, Canberra, 1984.

Johns, A. H., 'Islam in Southeast Asia: Reflections and new directions', *Indonesia*, 19 (1975), pp. 33–55.

Lombard, Denys, *Le sultanat d'Atjéh au temps d'Iskandar Muda – 1607–1636*, Paris, 1967.

Reid, Anthony, 'Islam and the state in seventeenth-century Southeast Asia', in Taufik Abdullah (ed.), *Proceedings of the international seminar on Islamic civilization in the Malay world*, Istanbul, 1997.

Ricklefs, M. C., *Seen and unseen worlds in Java: History, literature, and Islam in the court of Pakubuwana II, 1726–1749*, Honolulu, 1998.

Islamicate literatures of South-East Asia

al-Attas, S. N., *Raniri and the Wujudiyyah of 17th century Aceh*, Singapore, 1966.

van Bruinessen, Martin, *Kitab Kuning, Pesantren, dan Tarekat: Tradisi-tradisi Islam di Indonesia*, Bandung, 1995.

Feener, R. Michael and Laffan, Michael F., 'Sufi scents across the Indian Ocean: Yemeni hagiography and the earliest history of Southeast Asian Islam', *Archipel*, 70 (2005), pp. 185–208.

Iskandar, Teuku, *Kesusasteraan Klasik Melayu Sepanjang Abad*, Jakarta, 1996.

Kumar, Ann and McGlynn, John H. (eds.), *Illuminations: The writing traditions of Indonesia*, Jakarta, 1996.

Pigeaud, Th., *Literature of Java*, The Hague, 1967.

Riddell, Peter, *Transferring a tradition: ʿAbd al-Raʾuf al-Singkili's rendering into Malay of the Jalalayn commentary*, Berkeley, 1990.

Zoetmulder, P. J., *Pantheism and monism in Javanese suluk literature: Islamic and Indian mysticism in an Indonesian setting*, ed. and trans. M. C. Ricklefs, Leiden, 1995.

14 Transition: the end of the old order – Iran in the eighteenth century
G. R. Garthwaite

Practical suggestions for further reading

Axworthy, Michael, *The sword of Persia: Nader Shah from tribal warrior to conquering despot*, London, 2006.
Halm, Heinz, *Shi'ism*, Edinburgh, 1991.
Newman, Andrew J., *Safavid Iran: Rebirth of a Persian empire*, London, 2006.
Perry, John R., *Karim Khan Zand: A history of Iran, 1747–1779*, Chicago, 1979.
Tucker, Ernest, *Nadir Shah's quest for legitimacy in post-Safavid Iran*, Gainesville, FL, 2006.

Primary sources

Abu'l-Ḥasan b. Muḥammad Amīn Gulistāna, *Mujmal al-Tavārīkh Afshāriya va Zandiya*, ed. Mudaris Razavi, Tehran, 1344/1966.
Chardin, Sir John, *The travels of Sir John Chardin into Persia and the East Indies*, London, 1686.
A chronicle of the Carmelites in Persia and the papal missions of the XVIIth and XVIIIth centuries, London, 1939.
Fasā'i, Ḥasan-e, *History of Persia under Qājār rule (Fārsnāma-ye Nāṣeri)*, trans. Heribert Busse, New York, 1972.
Fraser, James, *The history of Nadir Shah*, London, 1742.
Hanaway, Jonas, *An historical account of the British trade over the Caspian Sea*, London, 1753.
The revolutions of Persia, London, 1754.
Kazim, Muhammad, *Namah-yi 'Alam Ara-yi 'Nadiri*, facsimile, 3 vols., Moscow, 1960–6.
Kitab-i Nadiri, Leningrad, n.d.
Krusinski, Father Judasz Tadeusz, *The history of the revolution of Persia*, London, 1728.
Malcolm, Sir John, *The history of Persia from the most early period to the present time*, London, 1815.
Rabino di Borgomale, H. L., *Coins, medals and seals of the shahs of Iran, 1500–1941*, Algiers (?), 1945.
Album of coins, medals, and seals of the shahs of Iran, Oxford, 1951.

Secondary sources

Algar, Hamid, *Religion and state in Iran 1785–1906: The role of the ulama in the Qajar period*, Berkeley, 1969.
'Religious forces in eighteenth- and nineteenth-century Iran', in Peter Avery, Gavin Hambly and Charles Melville (eds.), *The Cambridge history of Iran*, vol. VII: *From Nadir Shah to the Islamic Republic*, Cambridge, 1991, pp. 705–31.
Arjomand, Said Amir, *The shadow of God and the hidden imam: Religion, political order, and societal change in Shi'ite Iran from the beginning to 1890*, Chicago, 1984.
Avery, Peter, 'Nadir Shah and the Afsharid legacy', in Avery, Hambly and Melville (eds.), *Cambridge history of Iran*, vol. VII, pp. 3–62.
Babayan, Kathryn, *Mystics, monarchs, and messiahs: Cultural landscapes of early modern Iran*, Cambridge, MA, 2002.
Bayat, Mangol, *Mysticism and dissent: Socioreligious thought in Qājār Iran*, Syracuse, 1982.

Beck, Lois, *The Qashqa'i of Iran*, New Haven, 1986.
Black, Antony, *The history of Islamic political thought: From the Prophet to the present*, Edinburgh, 2001.
Bloom, Jonathan and Blair, Sheila, *Islamic arts*, London, 1997.
Chelkowski, Peter J. (ed.), *Taz'iyeh, ritual and drama in Iran*, New York, 1979.
Cole, Juan, *Sacred space and holy war: The politics, culture and history of Shi'ite Islam*, London, 2002.
Floor, Willem, *The Afghan invasion of Safavid Persia, 1721–29*, Paris, 1998.
Garthwaite, Gene R., *Khans and shahs: A documentary analysis of the Bakhtiyari in Iran*, Cambridge, 1983.
The Persians, Oxford, 2005.
Greaves, Rose, 'Iranian relations with the European trading companies, to 1798', in Avery, Hambly and Melville (eds.), *Cambridge history of Iran*, vol. VII, pp. 350–73.
Hambly, Gavin, 'Āghā Muḥammad Khān and the establishment of the Qājār dynasty', in Avery, Hambly and Melville (eds.), *Cambridge history of Iran*, vol. VII, pp. 104–43.
'Iran during the reigns of Fatḥ 'Alī Shāh and Muḥammad Shāh', in Avery, Hambly and Melville (eds.), *Cambridge history of Iran*, vol. VII, pp. 144–73.
Kazemzadeh, Firuz, 'Iranian relations with Russia and the Soviet Union, to 1921', in Avery, Hambly and Melville (eds.), *Cambridge history of Iran*, vol. VII, pp. 314–49.
Lambton, A. K. S., 'Persia: The breakdown of society', in P. M. Holt, Ann K. S. Lambton and Bernard Lewis (eds.), *The Cambridge history of Islam*, vol. I: *The central Islamic lands*, Cambridge, 1970.
'The tribal resurgence and the decline of the bureaucracy in the eighteenth century', in Thomas Naff and Roger Owen (eds.), *Studies in eighteenth century Islamic history*, Carbondale, IL, 1977.
State and government in medieval Islam: An introduction to the study of Islamic political theory: The jurists, Oxford, 1981.
'Concepts of authority in Persia: Eleventh to Nineteenth centuries AD', *Iran*, 26 (1988), pp. 102–3.
Continuity and change in medieval Persia, London, 1988.
Lockhart, Laurence, *Nadir Shah: A critical study*, London, 1938.
The fall of the Safavi dynasty and the Afghan occupation of Persia, Cambridge, 1958.
Matthee, Rudolph P., *The politics of trade in Safavid Iran: Silk for silver, 1600–1730*, Cambridge, 1999.
Iran and the surrounding world: Interactions in culture and cultural politics, Seattle, 2002.
Perry, John R., 'The last Safavids, 1722–1773', *Iran*, 9 (1971), pp. 59–69.
'Forced migration in Iran during the seventeenth and eighteenth centuries', *Iranian Studies*, 8 (1975), pp. 199–215.
'The Zand dynasty', in Avery, Hambly and Melville (eds.), *Cambridge history of Iran*, vol. VII, pp. 63–103.
Savory, Roger M., *Iran under the Safavids*, Cambridge, 1980.
Shaw, Stanford, 'Iranian relations with the Ottoman empire in the eighteenth and nineteenth centuries', in Avery, Hambly and Melville (eds.), *Cambridge history of Iran*, vol. VII, pp. 297–313.
Tapper, Richard, 'The tribes in eighteenth- and nineteenth-century Iran', in Avery, Hambly and Melville (eds.), *Cambridge history of Iran*, vol. VII, pp. 506–41.

Frontier nomads of Iran: A political and social history of the Shahsevan, Cambridge, 1997.
Walbridge, Linda S. (ed.), *The most learned of the Shi'a: The institution of the Marja' Taqlid*, Oxford, 2001.

15 Conversion to Islam
Richard W. Bulliet

Practical suggestions for further reading

Bulliet, Richard W., *Conversion to Islam in the medieval period*, Cambridge, 1975.
DeWeese, Devin, *Islamization and native religion in the Golden Horde: Baba Tükles and conversion to Islam in historical and epic tradition*, University Park, PA, 1994.
Eaton, Richard M., *The rise of Islam and the Bengal frontier, 1204–1760*, Berkeley, 1996.
Levtzion, Nehemia (ed.), *Conversion to Islam*, New York, 1979.
Minkov, Anton, *Conversion to Islam in the Balkans: Kisve bahası petitions and Ottoman social life, 1670–1730*, Leiden, 2004.

Primary sources

Compilation of Hui and Islamic Chinese classical documents, 9 vols., Yinchuan City, n.d.
Ibn Baṭṭūṭa, *The travels of Ibn Baṭṭūṭa, AD 1325–1354*, trans. H. A. R. Gibb, vol. II, Cambridge, 1962.

Secondary sources

al-Attas, S. M. N., *Preliminary statement on a general theory of the Islamization of the Malay–Indonesian archipelago*, Kuala Lumpur, 1969.
Azra, Azyumardi, *The origins of Islamic reformism in Southeast Asia: Networks of Malay–Indonesian and Middle Eastern 'ulama' in the seventeenth and eighteenth centuries*, Crows Nest, NSW, 2004.
Bulliet, Richard W., 'Process and status in conversion and continuity', in Michael Gervers and Ramzi Jibran Bikhazi (eds.), *Conversion and continuity: Indigenous Christian communities in Islamic lands, eighth to eighteenth centuries*, Toronto, 1990, pp. 1–12.
Eaton, Richard M., 'Approaches to the study of conversion to Islam in India', in Richard C. Martin (ed.), *Approaches to Islam in religious studies*, Tucson, 1985, pp. 106–23.
Fatimi, S. Q., *Islam comes to Malaysia*, Singapore, 1963.
Fletcher, Joseph, 'Les voies (*turuq*) soufites en Chines', in A. Popovic and G. Veinstein (eds.), *Ordres mystiques dans l'Islam: Cheminements et situation actuelle*, Paris, 1986.
Gladney, Dru C., *Muslim Chinese: Ethnic nationalism in the People's Republic*, Cambridge, MA, 1991.
Lawrence, Bruce B., 'Islam in India: The function of institutional Sufism in the Islamization of Rajasthan, Gujarat, and Kashmir', in Richard C. Martin (ed.), *Islam in local contexts*, Leiden, 1982, pp. 27–43.
'Early Indo-Muslim saints and conversion', in Yohanan Friedmann (ed.), *Islam in Asia*, vol. I: *South Asia*, Boulder, CO, 1984, pp. 109–45.
Leslie, Donald Daniel, *Islam in traditional China: A short history to 1800*, Canberra, 1982.
Majul, C. A., *Muslims in the Philippines*, Quezon City, 1979.

Pillsbury, Barbara, 'Muslim history in China: A 1300-year chronology', in Morris Rossabi (ed.), *China and Inner Asia from 1368 to the present day*, London, 1981.
Winstedt, R. O., 'The advent of Muhammadanism in the Malay peninsula and archipelago', *Journal of Malaysian Branch of the Royal Asiatic Society*, 77 (1917), pp. 171–3.

16 Armies and their economic basis in Iran and the surrounding lands, *c.* 1000–1500
Reuven Amitai

Primary sources

Anon., *The secret history of the Mongols*, trans. and ed. Igor de Rachewiltz, 2 vols., Leiden, 2004.
Baybars al-Manṣūrī, *Zubdat al-fikra*, ed. D. S. Richards, Beirut, 1998.
Ibn al-Athīr, *al-Kāmil fī 'l-ta'rīkh*, trans. in Donald S. Richards, *The Annals of the Saljuq Turks: Selections from al-Kāmil fī'l-Ta'rīkh of 'Izz al-Dīn Ibn al-Athīr*, London, 2002.
Ibn al-Furāt, *Ta'rīkh*, vol. VII, ed. Q. Zurayk, Beirut, 1942.
al-Jāḥiẓ, Abū 'Uthmān b. Baḥr, *Talāth rasā'il*, ed. G. Van Vloten, Leiden, 1903.
John of Plano Carpini [Giovanni di Pian di Carpine], 'History of the Mongols', in C. Dawson (ed.), *The mission to Asia* [repr. of *The Mongol mission*], London, 1980.
Juwaynī, 'Alā' al-Dīn, *Ta'rīkh-i jahāngushā*, trans. in John A. Boyle, *The history of the world-conqueror by 'Alā-ad-Dīn 'Aṭā Malik Juvainī*, 2 vols., Manchester, 1958.
al-Nasawī al-Munshī, *Sīrat al-sulṭān jalāl al-dīn mankūbirtī*, Cairo, 1953.
Niẓām al-Mulk, Abū 'Alī b. Ḥasan Ṭūsī, *Siyar al-mulūk (=Siyāsat-nāma)*, ed. Hubert Darke, Tehran, 1962.
Siyar al-mulūk (=Siyāsat-nāma), trans. in Hubert Darke, *The book of government or rules for kings*, 2nd edn, London, 1978.
Rashīd al-Dīn al-Hamadānī, *Jāmiʿ al-tawārīkh*, in Karl Jahn (ed.), *Geschichte Ġāzān-Ḫān's aus dem Ta'rīḫ-i-Mubārak-i-Ġāzānī* ..., London, 1940.
Jāmiʿ al-tawārīkh, trans. in W. M. Thackston (trans. and ed.), *Rashiduddin Fazlullah's Jami'u't-tawarikh (Compendium of chronicles)*, 3 vols., Cambridge, MA, 1999.
Sibṭ ibn al-Jawzī, *Mir'āt al-zamān*, Ankara, 1968.
al-ʿUmarī, Ibn Faḍl Allāh, *Masālik al-abṣār*, in Klaus Lech (ed. and trans.), *Das Mongolische Weltreich: Al-ʿUmarīs Darstellung der mongolischen Reiche in seinem Werk Masālik al-abṣār fī 'l-mamālik al-amṣār*, Wiesbaden, 1968.
Waṣṣāf, *Ta'rīkh*, Bombay, 1269 / 1852–3.

Secondary sources

Allsen, Thomas T., *Mongol imperialism: The policies of the Grand Qan Möngke in China, Russia, and the Islamic lands, 1251–1259*, Berkeley, 1987.
'The circulation of military technology in the Mongolian empire', in Nicola Di Cosmo (ed.), *Warfare in Inner Asian history (500–1800)*, Leiden, 2002, pp. 265–94.
Amitai, Reuven, 'The conversion of Tegüder Ilkhan to Islam', *Jerusalem Studies in Arabic and Islam*, 25 (2001), pp. 15–43.
'Turco-Mongolian nomads and the *iqṭāʿ* system in the Islamic Middle East', in Anatoly N. Khazanov and André Wink (ed.), *Nomads in the sedentary world*, Richmond, 2001, pp. 152–71.

'Whither the Ilkhanid army? Ghazan's first campaign into Syria (1299–1300)', in Nicola Di Cosmo (ed.), *Warfare in Inner Asian history (500–1800)*, Leiden, 2002, pp. 220–64.

'The resolution of the Mongol–Mamluk war', in Reuven Amitai and Michal Biran (eds.), *Mongols, Turks and others*, Leiden, 2005, pp. 359–90.

'The Mamluk institution: 1000 years of military slavery in the Islamic world', in Christopher L. Brown and Philip D. Morgan (eds.), *Arming slaves: From classical times to the modern age*, New Haven, 2006, pp. 40–78.

'Some more thoughts on the logistics of the Mongol–Mamluk war (with special reference to the battle of Wādī al-Khaznadār)', in John Pryor (ed.), *Logistics of war in the age of the Crusades*, Aldershot, 2006, pp. 25–42.

'An Arabic biographical notice of Kitbughā, the Mongol general defeated at ʿAyn Jālūt', *Jerusalem Studies in Arabic and Islam*, 33 (2007), pp. 219–34.

Amitai-Preiss, Reuven, 'ʿAyn Jālūt revisited', *Tārīḫ*, 2 (1992), pp. 119–50.

Mongols and Mamluks: The Mamluk–Īlkhānid war, 1260–1281, Cambridge, 1995.

Aubin, Jean, 'Le témoignage d'Ebn-e Bazzâz sur la turquisation de l'Azerbaydjan', in C. H. de Fouchécour and Ph. Gignoux (eds.), *Études Irano-Aryennes offertes à Gilbert Lazard*, Paris, 1989, pp. 5–17.

Ayalon, David, *Gunpowder and firearms in the Mamluk kingdom: A challenge to a mediaeval society*, London, 1956.

'The Wafidiyya in the Mamluk kingdom', *Islamic Culture* (1951), pp. 89–104 (reprinted in D. Ayalon, *Studies on the Mamlūks of Egypt (1255–1517)*, London, 1977, art. II).

'The Mamlūks of the Seljuks: Islam's military might at the crossroads', *Journal of the Royal Asiatic Society*, 3rd ser., 6 (1996), pp. 305–33.

Barthold, W., *Turkestan down to the Mongol invasion*, 3rd edn, London, 1968.

Biran, Michal, 'The battle of Herat (1270): A case of inter-Mongol warfare', in Nicola Di Cosmo (ed.), *Warfare in Inner Asian history (500–1800)*, Leiden, 2002, pp. 175–219.

Bosworth, C. Edward, 'The political and dynastic history of the Iranian world', in John A. Boyle (ed.), *The Cambridge history of Iran*, vol. V, Cambridge, 1968, pp. 1–202.

The Ghaznavids: Their empire in Afghanistan and eastern Iran 994–1040, 2nd edn, Beirut, 1973.

'Recruitment, muster, review in medieval Islamic armies', in Vernon J. Parry and Malcolm E. Yapp (eds.), *War, technology and society in the Middle East*, London, 1975, pp. 159–77.

Buell, Paul D., 'Kalmyk Tanggaci people: Thoughts on the mechanics and impact of Mongol expansion', *Mongolian Studies*, 9 (1980), pp. 41–59.

Cahen, Claude, 'L'évolution de l'iqṭāʿ du IXe au XIIIe siècle: Contribution à une histoire comparée des sociétés médiévales', in C. Cahen, *Les peuples musulmans dans l'histoire médiévale*, Damascus, 1977, pp. 231–69 (originally published in *Annales: Économies, Sociétés, Civilisations*, 8 (1953), pp. 25–52).

Pre-Ottoman Turkey, trans. J. Jones-Williams, London, 1968.

Doerfer, Gerhard, *Türkische und mongolische Elemente im Neupersischen*, 4 vols., Wiesbaden, 1963–75.

Frenkel, Yehoshua, 'The Turks of the Eurasian Steppes in medieval Arabic writing', in Reuven Amitai and Michal Biran (eds.), *Mongols, Turks and others: Eurasian nomads and the sedentary world*, Leiden, 2005, pp. 201–41.

Golden, Peter B., *An introduction to the history of the Turkic peoples: Ethnogenesis and state-formation in medieval and early modern Eurasia and the Middle East*, Wiesbaden, 1992.

'War and warfare in the pre-Činggisid western steppes of Eurasia', in Nicola Di Cosmo (ed.), *Warfare in Inner Asian history (500–1800)*, Leiden, 2002, pp. 105–72.

Haarmann, Ulrich, 'Ideology and history, identity and alterity: The Arab image of the Turk from the 'Abbasids to modern Egypt', *International Journal of Middle Eastern Studies*, 20 (1988), pp. 175–96.

Hsiao Ch'i-ch'ing, *The military establishment of the Yuan dynasty*, Cambridge, MA, 1978.

Kennedy, Hugh, *The Prophet and the age of the caliphates: The Islamic Near East from the sixth to the eleventh century*, London, 1986; 2nd edn, 2004.

The armies of the caliphs: Military and society in the early Islamic state, London, 2001.

Khan, Iqtadar Alam, 'The coming of gunpowder to the Islamic world and India: Spotlight on the role of the Mongols', *Journal of Asian History*, 30 (1996), pp. 27–45.

Khazanov, Anatoly M., *Nomads and the outside world*, 2nd edn, Madison, WI, 1994.

Lambton, Ann K. S., 'Reflections on the *iqṭāʿ*', in G. Makdisi (ed.), *Arabic and Islamic studies in honor of Hamilton A. R. Gibb*, Leiden, 1965, pp. 358–76.

'The internal structure of the Saljūq empire', in John A. Boyle (ed.), *The Cambridge history of Iran*, vol. V, Cambridge, 1968, pp. 203–82.

Continuity and change in medieval Persia, New York, 1988.

Lindner, Rudi, *Nomads and Ottomans in medieval Anatolia*, Bloomington, IN, 1983.

Lockhart, Laurence, 'The Persian army in the Safavid period', *Der Islam*, 34 (1959), pp. 89–98.

McDonald, M. V., 'Al-Ǧāḥiẓ and his analysis of the Turks', in Urbain Vermeulen and J. M. F. van Reeth (eds.), *Law, Christianity and modernism in Islamic society*, Leuven, 1998, pp. 27–38.

Manz, Beatrice F., 'The ulus Chaghatay before and after Temür's rise to power: The transformation from tribal confederation to army of conquest', *Central Asiatic Journal*, 27 (1983), pp. 79–100.

The rise and rule of Tamerlane, Cambridge, 1989.

'Military manpower in late Mongol and Timurid Iran', in Maria Szuppe (ed.), *'L'héritage timouride: Iran – Asie centrale – Inde XVe–XVIIIe siècle*, published as *Cahiers d'Asie Centrale*, 3–4 (1997), pp. 43–55.

'Nomad and settled in the Timurid military', in Reuven Amitai and Michal Biran, *Mongols, Turks and others*, Leiden, 2005, pp. 425–57.

Martin, Henry D., *The rise of Chingis Khan and his conquest of north China*, repr. New York, 1971, of Baltimore, 1950.

Martinez, Arsenio P., 'Some notes on the Īl-Xānid army', *Archivum Eurasiae Medii Aeivi*, 6 (1986), pp. 129–242.

May, Timothy, 'The training of an Inner Asian nomad army in the pre-modern period', *Journal of Military History*, 70 (2006), pp. 617–35.

Minorsky, Vladimir, 'A *soyūrgāl* of Qāsim b. Jahāngīr Aq-qoyunlu (903/1498)', *Bulletin of the School of Oriental and African Studies*, 9 (1939), pp. 927–60.

'A civil and military review in Fārs in 881/1476', *Bulletin of the School of Oriental and African Studies*, 10 (1940–2), pp. 141–78.

Morgan, David O., 'The Mongol armies in Persia', *Der Islam*, 56 (1979), pp. 81–96.

'The Mongols in Syria, 1260–1300', in Peter W. Edbury (ed.), *Crusade and settlement*, Cardiff, 1985, pp. 229–35.
Medieval Persia, 1040–1797, London, 1988.
The Mongols, 2nd edn, Oxford, 2007.
Ostrowski, Donald, 'The *tamma* and the dual administrative structure of the Mongol empire', *Bulletin of the School of Oriental and African Studies*, 61 (1998), pp. 262–77.
Paul, Jürgen, 'The state and the military: The Samanid case', *Papers on Inner Asia*, 26, Bloomington, IN, 1994.
Petrushevsky, I. P., 'The socio-economic condition of Iran under the Il-Khans', in John A. Boyle (ed.), *The Cambridge history of Iran*, vol. V, Cambridge, 1968, pp. 483–537.
Reid, Robert W., 'Mongolian weaponry in *The secret history of the Mongols*', *Mongolian Studies*, 15 (1992), pp. 85–96.
Roemer, Hans R., 'Tīmūr in Iran', in Peter Jackson and Laurence Lockhart (eds.), *The Cambridge history of Iran*, vol. VI: *The Timurid and Safavid periods*, Cambridge, 1986, pp. 42–97.
Sinor, Denis, 'The Inner Asian warriors', *Journal of the American Oriental Society*, 101 (1981), pp. 133–44.
Smith, John M., Jr, 'Mongol manpower and Persian population', *Journal of the Economic and Social History of the Orient*, 18 (1975), pp. 271–99.
''Ayn Jālūt: Mamlūk success or Mongol failure', *Harvard Journal of Asiatic Studies*, 44 (1984), pp. 307–45.
'Nomads on ponies vs. slaves on horses', *Journal of the American Oriental Society*, 118 (1998), pp. 154–62.
'Hülegü moves west: High living and heartbreak on the road to Baghdad', in Linda Komaroff (ed.), *Beyond the legacy of Genghis Khan*, Leiden, 2006, pp. 111–34.
Spuler, Bertold, *Die Mongolen in Iran: Politik, Verwaltung und Kultur der Ilchanzeit 1220–1350*, 4th edn, Leiden, 1985.
Świętosławski, Witold, *Arms and armour of the nomads of the great steppe in the times of the Mongol expansion*, Lodz, 1999.
Turnbull, Stephan R., *The Mongols*, Men-at-Arms Series, 105, London, 1980.
de la Vaissière, Étienne, 'Châkars d'Asie centrale: À propos d'ouvrages récents', *Studia Iranica*, 34 (2005), pp. 139–49.
Walker, C. T. Harley, 'Jahiz of Basra to al-Fath ibn Khaqan on the "Exploits of the Turks" and the army of the khalifate in general', *Journal of the Royal Asiatic Society* (1915), pp. 631–97.
Woods, John E., *The Aqquyunlu: Clan, confederation, empire*, 2nd edn, Salt Lake City, 1999.

17 Commercial structures
Scott C. Levi

Practical suggestions for further reading

Alam, Muzaffar, 'Trade, state policy and regional change: Aspects of Mughal–Uzbek commercial relations, *c.* 1500–1750', *Journal of the Economic and Social History of the Orient*, 37, 3 (1994), pp. 202–27.
Allsen, Thomas T., *Commodity and exchange in the Mongol empire: A cultural history of Islamic textiles*, Cambridge, 1997.

Blanchard, Ian, *Russia's 'age of silver': Precious-metal production and economic growth in the eighteenth century*, London, 1989.
Burton, Audrey, *The Bukharans: A dynastic, diplomatic and commercial history, 1550–1702*, New York, 1997.
Calmard, Jean, 'Les marchands iraniens: Formation et montée d'un groupe de pression, 16e–19e siècles', in Denys Lombard and Jean Aubin (eds.), *Marchands et hommes d'affaires asiatiques*, Paris, 1988, pp. 91–107.
Chaudhuri, K. N., *Trade and civilisation in the Indian Ocean: An economic history from the rise of Islam to 1750*, Cambridge, 1985.
Chaudhury, Sushil and Morineau, Michel (eds.), *Merchants, companies and trade: Europe and Asia in the early modern era*, Cambridge, 1999.
Dale, Stephen, *Indian merchants and Eurasian trade, 1600–1800*, Cambridge, 1994.
Das Gupta, Ashin, *The world of the Indian Ocean merchant, 1500–1800*, New Delhi, 2001.
Ferrier, R. W., 'The Armenians and the East India Company in Persia in the seventeenth and early eighteenth centuries', *The Economic History Review* 2nd ser., 26, 1 (1973), pp. 38–62.
Floor, Willem, *The economy of Safavid Persia*, Wiesbaden, 2000.
Frank, Andre Gunder, *Reorient: Global economy in the Asian age*, Berkeley, 1998.
Gommans, Jos, *The rise of the Indo-Afghan empire, c.1710–1780*, Leiden, 1995.
Jackson, Peter, *The Delhi sultanate: A political and military history*, Cambridge, 1999.
Levi, Scott C., 'India, Russia and the eighteenth-century transformation of the Central Asian caravan trade', *Journal of the Social and Economic History of the Orient*, 42, 4 (1999), pp. 519–48.
The Indian diaspora in Central Asia and its trade, 1550–1900, Leiden, 2000.
(ed.), *India and Central Asia: Commerce and culture, 1500–1800*, New Delhi, 2007.
McCabe, Ina Baghdiantz, *The shah's silk for Europe's silver: The Eurasian trade of the Julfa Armenians in Safavid Iran and India (1530–1750)*, Atlanta, 1999.
McChesney, R. D., *Central Asia: Foundations of change*, Princeton, 1996.
Markovits, Claude, *The global world of Indian merchants, 1750–1947: Traders of Sind from Bukhara to Panama*, Cambridge, 2000.
'Indian merchants in Central Asia: The debate', in Scott C. Levi (ed.), *India and Central Asia: Commerce and culture, 1500–1800*, New Delhi, 2007, pp. 123–51.
Matthee, Rudolf, *The politics of trade in Safavid Iran: Silk for silver, 1600–1730*, Cambridge, 1999.
Pearson, Michael, *The Indian Ocean*, London, 2003.
Prakash, Om., *European commercial enterprise in pre-colonial India*, Cambridge, 1998.
Bullion for goods: European and Indian merchants in the Indian Ocean trade, 1500–1800, New Delhi, 2004.
Raychaudhuri, Tapan and Habib, Irfan (eds.), *The Cambridge economic history of India*, vol. 1: *c.1200–c.1750*, repr. Hyderabad, 1984.
Richards, John, *The Mughal empire*, Cambridge, 1993.
Steensgaard, Niels, *The Asian trade revolution of the seventeenth century: The East India Companies and the decline of the caravan trade*, Chicago, 1974.
Subrahmanyam, Sanjay and Bayly, C. A., 'Portfolio capitalists and the political economy of early modern India', *The Indian Economic and Social History Review*, 25, 4 (1988), pp. 401–24.

Tracy, James D. (ed.), *The rise of merchant empires: Long-distance trade in the early modern world, 1350–1750*, Cambridge, 1990.

(ed.), *The political economy of merchant empires: State power and world trade, 1350–1750*, Cambridge, 1991.

Tripathi, Dwijendra (ed.), *Business communities of India: A historical perspective*, New Delhi, 1984.

Wink, André, *Al-Hind: The making of the Indo-Islamic world*, vol. II, *The slave kings and the Islamic conquest of India, 11th–13th centuries*, Leiden, 1997; vol. III: *Indo-Islamic society, 14th–15th centuries*, Leiden, 2004.

Primary sources

Abul Fazl Allami, *The Akbar Nama of Abu-l-Fazl*, 3 vols., trans. H. Blochmann, repr. Delhi, 1998.

Bernier, François, *Travels in the Mogul empire, AD 1656–1668*, Westminster, 1891.

Chardin, John, *Sir John Chardin's travels in Persia*, London, 1927.

González, Ruy, *Narrative of the embassy of Ruy González de Clavijo to the court of Timour in Samarcand, AD 1403–6*, trans. Clements R. Markham, London, 1858.

Ibn Baṭṭūṭa, *The Travels of Ibn Battuta, AD 1325–1354*, trans. H. A. R. Gibb, 3 vols., New Delhi, 1993.

Jenkinson, Anthony, *Early voyages and travels to Russia and Persia ...*, ed. E. Delmar Morgan and C. H. Coote, Hakluyt Society, 2 vols., 1st ser., 72–3, London, 1886.

du Mans, Raphaël, *Estat de la Perse en 1660*, Paris, 1890.

Manucci, Niccolao, *Storia do Mogor, or Mogul India 1653–1708*, 4 vols., trans. W. Irvine, London, 1907–8.

de Modave, Comte, *Voyage en Inde du Comte de Modave, 1773–1776*, ed. J. Deloche, Paris, 1971.

Navoiy, Alisher, *Maḥbūb al-qulūb*, ed. A. N. Kononov, Moscow, 1948.

Nikitin, Afanasi (Athanasius), *The travels of Athanasius Nikitin of Twer*, in R. H. Major (ed.), *India in the fifteenth century*, Hakluyt Society, 1st ser., 22, part 3, London, 1857.

Pelsaert, Francisco, *A Dutch chronicle of Mughal India*, ed. and trans. Brij Narain and Sri Ram Sharma, Lahore, 1978.

Polo, Marco, *The book of Ser Marco Polo*, 2 vols., ed. and trans. Sir Henry Yule, New York, 1903.

Sen, Surendranath (ed.), *Indian travels of Thevenot and Careri*, New Delhi, 1949.

Tārīkh-i Firishta, Lucknow, 1864.

Tavernier, Jean-Baptiste, *Les six voyages de Jean Baptiste Tavernier, Écuyer Baron d'Aubonne ...*, 2 vols., Utrecht, 1712.

al-ʿUtbī, *Tārīkh al-Yamīnī*, Delhi, 1847.

18 Transmitters of authority and ideas across cultural boundaries, eleventh to eighteenth centuries

Muhammad Qasim Zaman

Practical suggestions for further reading

Alam, Muzaffar, *The languages of political Islam: India, 1200–1800*, Chicago, 2004.

Alam, Muzaffar and Subrahmanyam, Sanjay, *Indo-Persian travels in the age of discoveries, 1400–1800*, Cambridge, 2007.

Arjomand, Said Amir, 'The law, agency, and policy in medieval Islamic society: Development of the institutions of learning from the tenth to the fifteenth century', *Comparative Studies in Society and History*, 41 (1999), pp. 263–93.
Azra, Azyumardi, *The origins of Islamic reformism in Southeast Asia: Networks of Malay–Indonesian and Middle Eastern 'ulamā' in the seventeenth and eighteenth centuries*, Honolulu, 2004.
Ben-Dor Benite, Zvi, *The Dao of Muhammad: A cultural history of Muslims in late imperial China*, Cambridge, MA, 2005.
Dallal, Ahmad, 'The origins and objectives of Islamic revivalist thought, 1750–1850', *Journal of the American Oriental Society*, 113, 3 (1993), pp. 341–59.
Dunn, Ross E., *The adventures of Ibn Battuta: A Muslim traveler of the 14th century*, Berkeley, 1986, 2nd edn, 2005.
Ho, Engseng, *The graves of Tarim: Genealogy and mobility across the Indian Ocean*, Berkeley, 2006.
Johansen, Baber, *Contingency in a sacred law: Legal and ethical norms in the Muslim fiqh*, Leiden, 1999.
Rosenthal, Franz, *The technique and approach of Muslim scholarship*, Rome, 1947.

Primary sources

'Abd al-Ḥaqq Dihlawī, *Lama'āt al-tanqīḥ fī sharḥ Mishkāt al-maṣābīḥ*, ed. M. 'Ubayd Allāh, 4 vols., Lahore, 1970.
Ashi''at al-lama'āt, 4 vols., Sukkar, Pakistan, 1976.
'Abd al-Qādir al-'Aydarūs, *al-Nūr al-sāfir 'an akhbār al-qarn al-'āshir*, ed. A. Ḥālū, M. al-Arnā'ūd and A. al-Būshī, Beirut, 2001.
'Ali al-Muttaqī, 'Alā' al-dīn, *Kanz al-'ummāl fī sunan al-aqwāl wa'l-af'āl*, 18 vols., Aleppo, 1969.
Muntakhab Kanz al-'ummāl, 8 vols., Beirut, 1990.
'Alī b. Sulṭān al-Qārī, *Mirqāt al-mafātīḥ sharḥ Mishkāt al-mafātīḥ*, ed. Ṣ. M. J. al-'Aṭṭār, 10 vols., Beirut, 1992.
Baranī, Ḍiyā' al-dīn, *Ta'rīkh-i Fīrūzshāhī*, ed. Sayyid Aḥmad Khan, Calcutta, 1862.
Bilgrāmī, Ghulām 'Alī Āzād, *Ma'āthir al-kirām*, ed. Muḥammad 'Abduh Lyallpurī, Lahore, 1971.
al-Bukhārī, Maḥmūd b. Aḥmad b. 'Abd al-Azīz, *al-Muḥīṭ al-Burhānī fi'l-fiqh al-Nu'mānī*, ed. A. 'A. 'Ināya, 11 vols., Beirut, 2003.
al-Fatāwa al-Hindiyya fi madhhab al-imām al-a'ẓam Abī Ḥanīfa al-Nu'mān, 6 vols., Beirut, n.d. ((1973); repr. of the Bulaq edn, AH 1310).
Ḥājjī Khalīfa, *Kashf al-ẓunūn*, ed. Ş. Yaltkaya and R. Bilge, 2 vols., Istanbul, 1972.
Ḥazīn Lāhījī, Muḥammad 'Alī, *Ta'rīkh wa safarnama-i Ḥazīn*, ed. 'A. Dawwānī, n.p., AH solar 1375, trans. F. C. Belfour, *The life of Sheikh Mohammad Ali Hazin, written by himself*, London, 1830.
Ibn Baṭṭūṭa, *Voyages d'Ibn Batoutah*, ed. C. Defrémery and B. R. Sanguinetti, 2nd edn, 4 vols., Paris, 1877–9. trans. H. A. R. Gibb, *The travels of Ibn Baṭṭūṭa, AD 1325–1354*, 5 vols., Cambridge, 1958–2000.
Ibn al-Humām, *Sharḥ fatḥ al-qadīr*, 10 vols., Cairo, 1970.
Ibn Nujaym, *Rasā'il Ibn Nujaym al-iqtiṣādiyya, al-musammāt al-Rasā'il al-Zayniyya fī madhhab al-Ḥanafiyya*, ed. M. A. Sirāj and 'A. J. Muḥammad, Beirut, 1998.
Jahangir, *The Jahangirnama: Memoirs of Jahangir, emperor of India*, ed. and trans. Wheeler M. Thackston, New York, 1999.

Kitāb al-ḥawādith, ed. B. ʿA. Maʿrūf and ʿI. ʿAbd al-Salām, Beirut, 1997.

al-Muḥibbī, Muḥammad Amīn, *Khulāsat al-athar fī aʿyān al-qarn al-ḥādī ʿashar*, Beirut, n.d.

Mustaʿidd Khan, Saqi, *Maʾāthir-i ʿĀlamgīrī*, ed. A. A. ʿAlī, Osnabrück, 1985 (repr. of the Calcutta 1870–3 edn).

al-Ṣāghānī, Raḍī al-dīn al-Ḥasan b. Muḥammad, *Mashāriq al-anwār*, Constantinople, AH 1329.

al-Suyūṭī, Jalāl al-dīn, *Jāmiʿ al-aḥādīth*, ed. ʿA. A. Ṣaqr and A. ʿAbd al-Jawwād, 21 vols., Beirut, 1994.

Walī Allāh al-Dihlawī, *Risāla sharḥ abwāb ṣaḥīḥ al-Bukhārī*, 3rd edn, Haydarabad, 1949.

Ḥujjat Allāh al-bāligha, ed. S. Sābiq, 2 vols., Cairo, 1964. Partial trans. by Marcia K. Hermansen, *The conclusive argument from God*, Leiden, 1996.

ʿIqd al-jīd fī aḥkām al-ijtihād wa'l-taqlīd, Cairo, AH 1385.

Musawwā Muṣaffā, sharḥ Muwaṭṭāʾ imām Mālik, 2 vols., Karachi, n.d. (repr. of the Delhi AH 1346 edn).

'Risāla-i dānishmandī'. Published together with Shāh Rafiʿ al-dīn, *Takmīl al-adhhān*, ed. ʿAbd al-Ḥamīd al-Sawātī, Gujaranwala, n.d.

Secondary sources

ʿAbd al-Ḥayy al-Ḥasanī, *Al-Thaqāfa al-Islāmiyya fi'l-Hind*, Damascus, 1958.

ʿAbd al-Ḥayy al-Laknawī, Muḥammad, *Al-Fawāʾid al-bahiyya fī tarājim al-Ḥanafiyya*, Karachi, AH 1393.

Ahmad, Aziz, *Studies in Islamic culture in the Indian environment*, Oxford, 1964.

Ahmed, Shahab and Filipovic, Nenad, 'The sultan's syllabus: A curriculum for the Ottoman imperial *medreses* prescribed in a *fermān* of Qānūnī I Süleyman, dated 973 (1565)', *Studia Islamica*, 98–9 (2004), pp. 183–218.

Berkey, Jonathan P., *The transmission of learning in medieval Cairo*, Princeton, 1992.

Bilgrami, Rafat M., *Religious and quasi-religious departments of the Mughal period (1556–1707)*, Delhi, 1984.

Brentjes, Sonja, 'On the location of the ancient or "rational" sciences in Muslim educational landscapes (AH 500–1100)', *Bulletin of the Royal Institute for Inter-Faith Studies*, 4 (2002), pp. 47–71.

Brown, Jonathan, *The canonization of al-Bukhārī and Muslim: The formation of the Sunnī ḥadīth canon*, Leiden, 2007.

Bulliet, Richard W., *Islam: The view from the edge*, New York, 1994.

Chamberlain, Michael, *Knowledge and practice in medieval Damascus, 1190–1350*, Cambridge, 1994.

El-Rouayheb, Khaled, 'Opening the gate of verification: The forgotten Arab-Islamic florescence of the 17th century', *International Journal of Middle East Studies*, 38 (2006), pp. 263–81.

Ephrat, Daphna, *A learned society in a period of transition: The Sunni ʿulamāʾ of eleventh-century Baghdad*, Albany, 2000.

Fadel, Mohammad, 'The social logic of taqlid and the rise of the Mukhtasar', *Islamic Law and Society*, 3 (1996), pp. 193–233.

Gardet, Louis, 'Religion and culture', in P. M. Holt, Ann K. S. Lambton and B. Lewis (eds.), *The Cambridge history of Islam*, 2 vols., Cambridge, 1970, vol. II, pp. 569–603.

Gleave, Robert, *Inevitable doubt: Two theories of Shīʿī jurisprudence*, Leiden, 2000.

Goldziher, Ignaz, *Muslim studies*, trans. C. R. Barber and S. M. Stern, 2 vols., London, 1971.

Griffel, Frank, 'On Fakhr al-Dīn al-Rāzī's life and the patronage he received', *Journal of Islamic Studies*, 18 (2007), pp. 313–44.

Hallaq, Wael B., *Authority, continuity and change in Islamic law*, Cambridge, 2001.

İhsanoğlu, Ekmeleddin, *Science, technology and learning in the Ottoman empire*, Aldershot, 2004.

Ito, Takeshi, 'Why did Nuruddin ar-Raniri leave Aceh in 1054 AH?', *Bijdragen tot de Taal-, Land- en Volkenkunde*, 134, 4 (1978), pp. 489–91.

Jackson, Sherman, *Islamic law and the state: The constitutional jurisprudence of Shihab al-Din al-Qarafi*, Leiden, 1996.

Kohlberg, Etan, 'Aspects of Akhbari thought in the seventeenth and eighteenth centuries', in Nehemia Levtzion and John O. Voll (eds.), *Eighteenth-century renewal and reform in Islam*, Syracuse, 1987, pp. 133–60.

Kozlowski, Gregory C., 'Imperial authority, benefactions and endowments (*awqāf*) in Mughal India', *Journal of the Economic and Social History of the Orient*, 38 (1995), pp. 355–70.

Kugle, Scott, 'In search of the center: Authenticity, reform and critique in early modern Islamic sainthood', Ph.D. dissertation, Duke University, 2000.

'ʿAbd al-Ḥaqq Dihlawī, an accidental revivalist: Knowledge and power in the passage from Delhi to Makka', *Journal of Islamic Studies*, 19 (2008), pp. 196–246.

Kumar, Sunil, *The emergence of the Delhi sultanate*, Delhi, 2007.

Landau-Tasseron, Ella, 'The "cyclical" reform: A study of the *mujaddid* tradition', *Studia Islamica*, 70 (1989), pp. 79–117.

Levtzion, Nehemia and Voll, John O. (eds.), *Eighteenth-century renewal and reform in Islam*, Syracuse, 1987.

Makdisi, George, *The rise of colleges*, Edinburgh, 1981.

Morgan, D. O., 'Ibn Baṭṭūṭa and the Mongols', *Journal of the Royal Asiatic Society*, 3rd ser., 11 (2001), pp. 1–11.

Mottahedeh, Roy, 'The transmission of learning: The role of the Islamic northeast', in Nicole Grandin and Marc Gaborieau, (eds.), *Madrasa: La transmission du savoir dans le monde muṣūlman*, Paris, 1997, pp. 63–72.

Nadwī, Abū'l-Ḥasanāt, *Hindustān kī qāḍīm Islāmī darsgāhen*, Aʿzamgarh, 1971.

Nizami, Khaliq Ahmad, *Some aspects of religion and politics in India during the thirteenth century*, Bombay, 1961.

Petry, Carl F., 'Travel patterns of medieval notables in the Near East', *Studia Islamica*, 63 (1985), pp. 53–87.

Rahman, Fazlur, *Islam and modernity: Transformation of an intellectual tradition*, Chicago, 1982.

Reichmuth, Stefan, 'Murtaḍā az-Zabīdī (d. 1791) in biographical and autobiographical accounts', *Die Welt des Islams*, 39 (1999), pp. 64–102.

Siddiqui, Iqtidar Husain, 'Muslim intellectual life in India', in (ed.), Iqtidar Husain Siddiqui, *Medieval India: Essays in intellectual thought and culture*, Delhi, 2003, vol. I, pp. 81–94.

Stewart, Devin, 'The doctorate of Islamic law in Mamluk Egypt and Syria', in J. E. Lowry, D. J. Stewart and S. M. Toorawa, (eds.), *Law and education in medieval Islam: Studies in memory of Professor George Makdisi*, Chippenham, 2004, pp. 45–90.

Subrahmanyam, Sanjay, 'Iranians abroad: Intra-Asian elite migration and early modern state formation', *Journal of Asian Studies*, 51, 2 (1992), pp. 340–63.

Subtelny, Maria Eva and Khalidov, Anas B., 'The curriculum of Islamic higher learning in Timurid Iran in the light of the Sunni revival under Shah-Rukh', *Journal of the American Oriental Society*, 115 (1995), pp. 210–36.

Voll, John O., 'Hadith scholars and tariqahs: An ulama group in the 18th century Haramayn and their impact in the Islamic world', *Journal of Asian and African Studies*, 25 (1980), pp. 264–73.

''Abdallah ibn Salim al-Basri and 18th century hadith scholarship', *Die Welt des Islams*, 42 (2002), pp. 356–72.

Wensinck, A. J., *Concordance et indices de la tradition musulman*, 8 vols., 2nd edn, Leiden, 1992.

Zaman, Muhammad Qasim, *The ulama in contemporary Islam: Custodians of change*, Princeton, 2002.

Index

Notes on alphabetisation

All Islamic personal names are listed in the fullest form in which they appear in the text, without inversion, except a) literary or religious figures who have become well known under the last element or a shortened form, or b) rulers regularly referred to in the text by an assumed title.

The prefix 'al-' is ignored for alphabetisation purposes.

Names of Christian monarchs appear in their Anglicised forms.

A-mi-li-ding (Yuan commander) 386–7
Abā Bakr b. Mīrānshāh (grandson of Temür, d. 811/1409) 181
Abā Bakr b. Muḥammad Jūkī (great-grandson of Temür, d. 852/1448?) 184
Abaqa (Ilkhan) 147–8, 155, 161–2
ʿAbbās I (Safavid shah, d. 1038/1629) xix, 204, 213, 214, 218, 234, 236, 507
artistic/cultural patronage 224–5
death 231
'divide and rule' policies 223
economic policies 226–7
foreign relations 228–9
land reforms 227
military conquests 230–1
pilgrimage to Mashhad 221, 518
problems facing 218–20
provisions for succession 233
religious policies 221, 229–30
ʿAbbās II (Safavid shah, d. 1077/1666) 231, 234
ʿAbbās III (Safavid shah, d. 1162/1749) 505, 509, 510
ʿAbbās Mīrzā (Iranian prince) 520
ʿAbbās of Rayy (Saljuq *amīr*) 63
ʿAbbāsid caliphate 1, 14, 24–5, 88, 288
(proclaimed) allegiance to 88
army 3, 540
demise (at Mongol hands) xvii, 2, 15, 79–80, 168, 472, 551–2
figurehead role 3, 15, 16
Mamlūk renewal/control 144
recognition of rulers/dynasties 96, 101, 118, 119, 159
relations with Saljuqs 41–3, 47, 56, 61, 63
revival (C6/12) 58, 71–3
status in Islamic community 2
trade 79, 321, 322
ʿAbd Allāh b. ʿAbd al-Qahhār (Sufi scholar) 499
ʿAbd Allāh b. Asʿad al-Yāfiʿī (Sufi leader/historian) 471
ʿAbd Allāh b. Iskandar (Jani-Begid khan, d. 1007/1598) 240, 244, 246, 254–5, 263
cultural/architectural achievements 252–3
ʿAbd Allāh Ḥasan (Melakan envoy) 394
ʿAbd Allāh Marwārīd, *Sharaf-nāma* 195
ʿAbd al-ʿAzīz (Tuqāy-Timurid khan, d. 1091/1681) 240, 246, 248, 251–2, 257–8, 264
ʿAbd al-Ḥamīd Karaeng Karangreng, sultan of Makassar 483
ʿAbd al-Ḥamīd Lahorī (historian) 305–6
ʿAbd al-Ḥaqq Muḥaddith (historian) 587–9, 606–7
compared with other scholars 589
ʿAbd al-Laṭīf b. Kuchkunji (Shībānid khan) 251, 252
ʿAbd al-Laṭīf b. Ulugh Beg (Timurid prince) 183, 184, 185
ʿAbd al-Muhyī (Sufi scholar) 494

'Abd al-Mu'min b. 'Abd Allāh (Jani-Begid khan) 263
'Abd al-Qādir al-'Aydarūs (biographer) 597
'Abd al-Qādir al-Jīlānī (founder of Sufi order) 335, 391
'Abd al-Qādir al-Marāghī (musical theorist/composer) 192
'Abd al-Raḥmān (merchant) 165, 418
'Abd al-Raḥmān b. Sulaymān al-'Ahdal (Sufi scholar) 500
'Abd al-Raḥmān al-Batāwī al-Maṣrī (Sufi scholar) 501
'Abd al-Raḥmān Jāmī (poet/scholar) 192, 193, 195, 196, 261, 264, 300
'Abd al-Ra'ūf al-Singkeli (scholar-saint) xix, 462, 492–4, 499
  autobiography 493
  influence 494
  range of interests 494
'Abd al-Razzāq Samarqandī (Timurid historian) 194, 352, 429
'Abd al-Samad (calligrapher/mint master) 286, 289
'Abd al-Ṣamad al-Palimbānī (writer) 469, 499–501, 502
'Abd al-Wahhāb (Arabian theologian) *see* Wahhabism
'Abd al-Wahhāb al-Bugisī (South-East Asian scholar) 501
'Abd al-Wahhāb al-Makkī (Mecca teacher) 588
'Abd al-Wāsi' Niẓāmī Bākharzī (compiler) 195
'Abdallāh Khan Fīrūz Jang (Uzbek noble) 569
Abdulfatah Ageng-Tirtayasa, sultan of Banten 465, 482–3, 485
Abish (princess of Fārs) 145, 149
Abū *for names beginning with this element see also* Pu
Abū 'Abd Allāh Masūd b. 'Abd Allāh al-Jāwī (teacher/historian) 471
Abū 'Abd Allāh Mas'ūd b. Muḥammad al-Jāwī (Sufi leader) 390–1
Abū 'Abd Allāh Muḥammad Isḥāḳ (merchant) 369–70
Abū Abdullāh (envoy) 374
Abū 'Alī al-Ḥasan Niẓām al-Mulk (Saljuq vizier) *see* Niẓām al-Mulk
Abū Bakr (atabeg of Fārs, d. 658/1260) 145
Abū Bakr (first Sunnī caliph, d. 13/634) 345
Abū Bakr bin Salim (saint, d. 992/1584) 335
Abū Bakr Shāh (sultan of Delhi, d. 793/1391) 123, 124
Abū Dāwūd (compiler of *ḥadīth* collection) 584
Abū Dulaf (historian) 370
Abū al-Fatḥ al-Ḥusaynī (Safavid historian) 214
Abū Ḥafṣ 'Umar Bā Shaybān al-Ḥadramī (Indian scholar/teacher) 598
Abū Ḥanīfa (founder of legal school) 592, 594
Abū Isḥāq, Shaykh (Sufi leader, fl. 740s/1340s) 354–5
Abū Isḥāq al-Shīrāzī (jurist, d. 476/1083) 50
Abū Kālījār *see* 'Imād al-Dīn Abū Kālījār
'Abū Maḥmūd Tabrizī' (trader) 374
Abū Rayhān al-Bīrūnī (polymath) 11, 84, 94, 273, 331
Abū Sa'īd (Ilkhan) xvii, 153–4, 159, 169, 171
Abū Yūsuf (Ḥanafī scholar) 594
Abū Zaīd (historian) 368, 370
Abū'l-Barakāt al-Barbarī (legendary conversion figure) 339–40, 341, 344
Abū'l-Faḍl 'Allāmī (historian) 277, 279, 282, 283–4, 285, 287–8, 301
Abū'l-Faḍl Ja'far (son of al-Muqtadī) 56
'Abū'l-Faiz Faizī (poet) 301
Abū'l-Fayz Khan (Chinggisid leader) 243, 578
Abū'l-Khayr Khan (Uzbek leader, d. 1468) 184, 186, 189
Abū'l Khayrid dynasty 239–41, 243, 248–53, 255–6
Abū'l-Qāsim Bābur (Timurid prince) 183, 184, 186, 187, 188
Abū'l-Qāsim Samarqandī, Imām 31
Aceh (Sumatran state) xviii–xix, 10–11, 400, 449, 454, 456, 495
  conflicts with Portuguese 358, 432–3, 435–8, 463
  as cultural/scholastic centre 441, 466, 489–94
  independence of European control 464
  literature 489
  religious policies/conflicts 460–2, 491–2, 598–9, 606
Adam's Peak (Sri lankan landmark) 359–60
Aden 323
Adīb Ṣābir (poet) 77
'Adil Shāh of Iran 512, 514
'Aḍud al-Dawla, ruler of Fārs/Iraq 38
Afāq Khōja (Sufi leader) 426
Afghans/Afghanistan xx, 4, 21, 82
  conflicts with Marathas 312
  conflicts with Mughals 273–4, 276, 309
  as Iranian ruling dynasty 507, 508–9
  migrations from 126–7
  trade 579
Afrāsiyāb (mythical Turanian king) 155

Afshār dynasty 507, 511
Afūshta-yi Naṭanzī (historian) 219, 222
Ageng Tirtayasa *see* Abdulfatah Ageng-Tirtayasa
agents, role in trade networks 576–7
Āghā Muḥammad Bāqir Wahid Bihbahanī (Mujtahid leader) 525
Āghā Muḥammad Khan Qājār (founder of ruling dynasty) xx, 504, 505
  acceptance of crown 517
  brutality 515, 519
  early life/rise to power 514–15
  military/political achievements 515–18
  military tactics 519–20
  personal/military qualities 519–20
  religious observance 520
  succession, plans/conflicts 516, 518–19, 520
Agra, population/wealth 289
agriculture 156–7, 189–90, 287–8, 505
  products, trade in 566–8, 577
Agung, sultan of Mataram (Java) xix, 10, 446–7, 450–2, 463, 465, 479
  'marriage' 479
  title 452, 479
Aḥmad (Muslim administrator in China) 166, 418
Aḥmad (military engineer, in Yuan China) 418
Aḥmad Ahsāʾī, Shaykh (Shīʿī philosopher/mystic) 524
Aḥmad b. Faḍlān (caliphal envoy) 33
Aḥmad b. Khiḍr Khan (Qarakhānid leader) 29, 31, 53
Aḥmad Khatīb Sambās, Shaykh (Sufi leader) 499
Aḥmad al-Qushāshī (Sufi leader) 462, 493
Aḥmad Sanjar b. Malik Shāh (Saljuq sultan) *see* Sanjar
Aḥmad Shāh b. Iskandar (Malay ruler) 466, 467, 483
Aḥmad Shāh Durrānī of Afghanistan xx, 512, 514–15, 579
Aḥmad Sirhindi, Shaykh (Sufi leader) 303, 304
Aḥmad Yasawī (Sufi shaykh)/Yasawiyya (followers) 76, 197, 199
Aḥmad Yükneki (writer) 75
Aḥmad Zayn al-Dīn, Shaykh (historian) 347, 350, 353, 356, 357–8
Ahmednagar, sultanate of 276
Ahrāris (Sufi sect) 262
Ai-yan (Bengalese envoy) 399
Ajall (Muslim administrator in China) 166
Akbar (Mughal emperor, d.1014/1605) xviii–xix, 10, 216, 274–93, 569
  administration 273, 276
  architectural projects 271, 307
  contemporary accounts 285, 286, 293, 314
  cultural/literary patronage 285, 301
  dealings with non-Muslim subjects 276–8
  epiphany/animal rights measures 282, 294
  fiscal policy 289–90
  legacy 295
  marriages 277–8, 281–2
  military conquests 231, 274–6
  personal characteristics 276, 281, 284, 285
  personal rule 275–6
  pilgrimages 221
  rebellions against 276, 283, 304
  reforms of Mughal court 284–7
  religious policy/innovations 281–4, 304, 443, 604; assumption of supreme authority 282–3; debates 282; influences 281–2; objections to 276, 303
  reputation amongst Western commentaries 268, 275–6, 281
  titles 282–3
Akbar b. Aurungzeb (Mughal prince) 310, 311
Akhbārī (school of Shīʿī thought) 523, 525, 594–5
ʿAlāʾ al-Dawla b. Baysunghur (Timurid prince) 183, 184
ʿAlāʾ al-Dawla Muḥammad (Ibn Kākūya) 36, 38–9, 40
ʿAlāʾ al-Dīn ʿĀlam Shāh (Sayyid ruler of Delhi, dep. 855/1451) 126
ʿAlāʾ al-Dīn ʿAlī Qushchi (astronomer) 184
ʿAlāʾ al-Dīn Atsız (Khwārazm Shāh) 69, 77
ʿAlāʾ al-Dīn Jahānsūz (Ghūrid sultan) 97
ʿAlāʾ al-Dīn Masʿūd Shāh (sultan of Delhi, d. 644/1246) 103
ʿAlāʾ al-Dīn Muḥammad Khwārazm Shāh (d. 617/1220) xvi–xvii, 72, 74–5, 131–3
ʿAlāʾ al-Dīn Muḥammad Shāh Khaljī (sultan of Delhi, d. 715/1316) xvii, 105, 108, 109–10, 125, 127
  administration 113–14, 117
  expansionist policy/moves 111–12
ʿAlāʾ ud-Dīn Rīayat Shāh al-Kahar (sultan of Aceh) 436, 437
aʿlam al-ʿulamāʾ ('most learned of the learned'), title of 262, 263–4
ʿĀlam Shāh (ruler of Delhi) *see* ʿAlāʾ al-Dīn ʿĀlam Shāh
ʿAlawīyya (Sufi order) 335

alcohol, consumption of
Mongol 137, 153, 167
Mughal 294–5
prohibition 294
Safavid 231, 234–5
Timurid 297
Aleppo
Mongol conquest 144
Timurid conquest 177
Alexander the Great 84, 496
Alexius I Comnenus, (Byzantine) emperor 54–5
Alghu (Chaghadayid khan) 161
ʿAlī *for names beginning with this element see also* Li
ʿAlī b. Abī Ṭālib, caliph (son-in-law of the Prophet, d. 40/661) 15, 84, 170–1
descent from 182, 373–4
as focus of devotion 203, 205, 206, 221, 511 (*see also* Shīʿīs/Shīʿism)
shrines 190, 257
ʿAlī b. Ḥusayn Karakī, Shaykh (Shīʿī leader) 222, 524
ʿAlī b. Mūsā al-Riḍā (eighth Shīʿī imam) 249
shrine 182–3, 190, 221, 510, 520
ʿAlī ibn al-Ḥusayn ibn ʿAlī (ruler of Kilwa) 374
ʿAlī Khan, Shaykh (Safavid vizier) 234–5, 236
ʿAlī Mardan Khan Bakhtiyārī (ruler of Iran) 512–13, 514
ʿAlī Mubārak (Bengali commander) 118
ʿAlī Mughayat, sultan of Aceh xviii
ʿAlī Murād Khan Zand (Iranian tribal leader) 515
ʿAlī al-Muttaqī (*ḥadīth* scholar) 586–7, 589, 606
students/disciples 587, 588
ʿAlī Qulī (Iranian royal) 518
ʿAlī Qulī Khan *see* ʿAdil Shāh
ʿAlī Shāh Kar (Delhi rebel leader) 118
Alikah Kukultash (architect) 250
ʿAlīshīr Nawāʾī (Timurid official)
literary/cultural achievements 191, 192–3, 196, 248–9, 261, 564
political career 188–9
ʿAlītegin b. Bughrā Khan (Qarluq leader) 32, 35–6
Allāh Verdī Khan (Safavid *ghulām* general) 227, 230, 232
Almeida, Francisco de 431
Alp Arslan (Saljuq sultan) xvi, 6, 13, 34–5, 51, 52, 53, 54, 544, 545
rebellions against 45–7, 53
rise to power 44
rule 44–9
Alptigin (Ghaznavid founder) 83
Amad Mutamakin, Haji (Sufi mystic) 497
Amangkurat I of Mataram xix, 465
Amangkurat II of Mataram 465, 466
Amʿaq (Persian poet) 76
Amasya, treaty of (962/1555) 211
ʿAmīd al-Dawla Ibn Jahīr (vizier) 47, 56
ʿAmīd Shāh (ruler of Mālwā) 125
al-Amīn (ʿAbbāsid caliph, d. 198/813) 24–5
Amīr Hamzah (kinsman of the Prophet) 477
Amīr Ḥusayn (Qaraʾuna leader) 173–4
Amīr Khusraw Dihlawī (poet) 120, 192, 193, 195, 196, 270, 285–6, 301, 308
Amīr Maḥmud (Safavid historian) 213–14
Amīr Niʿmat Allāh al-Hillī (religious scholar) 209
amīrs
Chinggisid use of title 241
(increasing) power under Saljuqs 63
see also Uzbeks
amputation, as legal punishment 11, 462, 599
prohibition 293
Amroha (province of Delhi sultanate) 114
Anandapala (Shāhī ruler) 96
Anatolia
Islamisation 163–4
Mongol conquest/rule 139
Safavid invasion 209–10
Saljuq sultanate *see* Rūm
Turkish invasion 6, 40, 44–5, 54–5
Andaya, Leonard 489
Ankara, battle of (805/1402) xviii, 560
Anūshirwān b. Khālid (Saljuq vizier/historian) 61
Anūshtegids *see* Khwārazm
Anūshtegin Gharchaʾī (governor of Khwārazm) 59
Anwarī (poet) 77
appanages 28, 48–9, 52, 239–41, 268–9, 308–9
Aq Qoyunlu people 176, 186, 203, 206
army 558–9
Aq Sonqur b. Aḥmadīlī (Saljuq *amīr)* 62
Āqā Mīrak (Safavid artist) 215
Āqā Muḥammat Astarābādī (merchant/official in Siam) 458
Āqā Muḥammad Riḍā Beg (Safavid official) 236
Arabic (language) 191
cultural status 13–14, 76, 77
disappearance from Chinese Muslim culture 421
as lingua franca 440
as literary language 244, 298
modified script, use of 481–2, 487, 489

religious texts 473–4, 588–9, 598–9
study 342, 502
translation into South-East Asian languages 473–5 (*see also* Javanese; Malay)
Arabs
cultural/political decline 14–15
Indian communities 81, 92–3
naval capabilities 8–9
prestige (among migrant communities) 329, 350–1
under Saljuq rule 55
South-East Asian diaspora 495–6 (*see also* Hadramawt)
trading/proselytising around Indian Ocean 319, 322, 327, 329, 331, 359, 364–5
trading/proselytising in East Asia 367–70, 374, 535
ʿArabshāhid dynasty 239, 240–1, 243
Arakan (South-East Asian polity) 398
Ārām Shāh 100
Arasaratnam, Sinnappah 362
archaeology
finds *see under names of locations*
marine *see* shipwrecks
archers/archery
mounted 7–8, 92, 93–4, 541–2, 546–9, 560
weaponry 8
architecture 12, 155–6
Chinggisid 254–5
Mughal 284–5, 306–8
South-East Asian 403
Timurid 196–8
Ardabīl (Iranian city) 203–4
Ardashir (Sasanid emperor) 79
Arghun (Ilkhan, d. 690/1291) 148–50, 155
Arghun Aqa (Chinggisid official, fl. 640–60/1240–60) 140–1, 145, 146, 149, 159
Arghunshāh (Ilkhan official) 159
Ariq Böke (brother of Qubilai) 144, 161
Aristotle 273
Arjan (Sikh Guru) 302
Arjomand, Said Amir 601
Armanids (Saljuq atabegs) 60
Armenia
Mamlūk attacks on 147
Safavid relocation of inhabitants 227
supply of troops to Mongol armies 552–3
trade networks 575–6, 579
armies
financing 117, 227, 539, 540, 542, 545–6, 554–6, 558, 559
maintenance 51–2
nomadic vs. standing 539
supply corps 98
see also names of peoples/dynasties
Arrān (Saljuq province) 54
Arslan Arghun (Saljuq claimant, d. 490/1097) 59
Arslan b. Ṭoghrıl II (Saljuq sultan, d. 571/1176) 58, 62, 73
Arslan Isrāʾīl b. Saljuq (fl. 382/992) 35, 39
Arslan Khan Muḥammad b. Sulaymān (Qarakhānid leader, d. 524/1130) 29, 31, 66
Arslan Shāh b. Masʿūd (Ghaznavid sultan, fl. 508/1115) 65
art *see branches of art and names of dynasties*
Artuq b. Ekseb (Saljuq commander) 55
Artuqid dynasty 55, 60, 91
Arunachalam, B. 319
Arung Palakka (Bugis leader) 464
Aruq Jalayir (Ilkhan *amīr*) 149
Asaf Khan (brother-in-law of emperor Jahāngīr) 296, 304
asceticism 264–5, 447–9, 459
Ashʿarīs, hostility towards 42
Ashoka (Mauryan emperor, d. 232 BCE) 282
Ashraf Ghilzai (Afghan ruler of Iran) 509
Ashraf Māzandarāni (writer/royal tutor) 298–300, 309
Asia, religious/political diversity 12
Asian spiritual/religious movements
relationship with Islam 3, 11–13
Astarābād 187
astrolabe, use of 319
astrology, legitimising role 220–1
astronomy 154, 184–5, 251, 418–19, 422
ʿAtā Malik Juwaynī (historian) *see* Juwaynī
atabegs, extent of political control 58, 60, 73–4, 138
Aurungzeb, (Mughal) emperor (d. 1118/1707) xix, 271, 288, 292, 302, 304, 308–13, 572, 593
ascent to throne 308–9
death/legacy 312–13
historical impact 309
literary/cultural patronage 298–9, 607
military achievements 309–10, 311–12
personality 309, 314
Avicenna (Ibn Sina, al-Shaykh al-Raʾīs) 222–3, 418
Awadh (Indian region)
Delhi conquest 112
Saljuq settlements 91
ʿAwfī (literary anthologist) 32
Awhad al-Dīn (merchant) 416

'Awn al-Dīn Yaḥyā Ibn Hubayra ('Abbāsid vizier) 71
Ayaz b. Alp Arslan (Saljuq sultan) 52
Aybak (sultan of Delhi) *see* Quṭb al-Dīn Aybak
Āyiramacalā (Tamil poem) 362
'Ayn Jālūt, battle of (658/1260) xvii, 144, 383, 552
'Ayn al-Mulk Ibn Māhrū (Awadh rebel governor) 118
Ayyūbid dynasty 72, 79, 144, 380, 546
Azād Khan Ghilzai (Iranian tribal leader) 513
Azdī tribe 78–9, 85
Azerbaijan 40, 54, 164, 176, 181, 203, 543
  geographical features 40
Azyumardi Azra 459, 461, 488, 536–7, 538

Baabullah, sultan of Ternate xix, 453–4
Baba Da'ūd b. Ismā'īl al-Rūmī (Sufi scholar) 494
Babā Fighānī (poet) 226, 300–1
Baba Tükles (legendary conversion figure) 533
Bābur, (Mughal) emperor (Ẓahīr al-Dīn Muḥammad), d. 937/1530) xviii, 4, 127, 268–73, 275, 284, 294, 308
  administrative policies 271, 273, 278, 288
  alliance with Safavids 274
  ancestry/background 266
  artistic/cultural patronage 216, 270, 284
  claims to sovereignty 268, 276
  invasion of India 266–7, 269, 270–2, 274, 282, 434
  memoirs 193, 266, 268, 270, 271, 272–3, 284, 285, 286, 293, 297, 305–6, 314
  recollections of 285
  religion 266, 269–70, 271, 303
Badā'ūn, conquest of 99
al-Badāunī ('Abd al-Qādir b. Mulūk Shāh), criticisms of Mughal policies 279–80, 283, 304, 305
Baghdad
  foundation 367
  madrasas xvi
  Mongol conquest/rule 143, 472
  Safavid conquest 231
  Saljuq conquest/rule 41–2, 56, 79
  Timurid conquest 177
  as trading centre 333
Bagrat IV of Georgia 44
Bahā' al-Dīn al-'Amilī 'Shaykh Bahā'ī' (Shī'ī leader) 221–2
Bahā' al-Dīn al-Marghinanī (jurist) 247
Bahā' al-Dīn Balaban, sultan of Delhi *see* Ghiyāth al-Dīn Balaban
Bahā' al-Dīn Garshāsp (Delhi rebel) 112, 117
Bahā' al-Dīn Ḥasan-i Nithārī Bukharī (historian) 246, 249, 251, 254
Bahā' al-Dīn Juwaynī (Chinggisid vizier) 140
Bahā' al-Dīn Naqshband (Sufi leader) 249, 251
Bahādur Nāhir (anti-Delhi rebel) 123
Bahādur Shāh (Mughal emperor, d. 1123/1712) 313, 314
Bahlūl Lodī (Afghan chief/sultan of Delhi) 126
Bahrām Shāh (sultan of Delhi) *see* Mu'izz al-Dīn Bahrām Shāh
Bahrām Shāh b. Mas'ūd (Ghaznavid sultan) 65
Baidu (Ilkhan khan) 150
Baiju (Mongol general) 139, 141, 146, 147, 151, 162, 550–1
Bakhtiyārī tribe/dynasty 512–13
Balaban, sultan of Delhi *see* Ghiyāth al-Dīn Balaban
Balāsāghūn (Qarakhānid city) 28
Balkh
  Chinggisid conquest/rule 240, 262
  as cultural/religious centre 252, 255, 264
  Mughal invasion 305–6
  public buildings 254, 257–8
Baltistān 91, 305
Balūchistān, Muslim conquest 82
Bambhore *see* Daybul
Banda (Maluku) 401, 453
Banjarmasin (Borneo polity) 445, 456
Bannāī (historian) 253
Banten, sultanate of xix, 433, 456, 457, 462, 464–5, 466, 474
  as cultural centre 482–3, 484–5
Baqī Billah Birang (Sufi leader) 303
Bāqī Muḥammad (Tuqāy-Timurid khan) 256–7
baraka (prestige) 336, 354
  of descendants of the Prophet 334, 335
Baranī, Ḍiyā-yi al-Dīn (historian) 102, 103, 110, 113–14, 115, 116, 122, 277, 603
Baraq Ḥājib (ruler of Kirmān) 138
Baraq Khan (Chaghadayid ruler) 147, 161
Barbosa, Duarte 348–9, 350, 356, 357
Bardasīr (capital) *see* Kirmān
Barhebraeus (historian) 35
Barlas tribe 171–2, 173–4
Barros, João de 432
Barthold, W. (Bartol'd, V. V.) 77, 189
Barus (Sumatran port) 377–9, 389
Batavia (Jakarta) xix, 450–1, 464–5, 495
Batu (grandson of Chinggis Khan) 137, 139, 140–1, 145
Bay Khwāja Bi (Tuqāy-Timurid *amīr*) 259

bayāsira (Indian-born Muslims) 80–1
Baybars (Mamlūk sultan) 144, 147, 383
Bāyezīd I (Ottoman sultan, d. 805/1403) 177, 560
Bāyezīd II (Ottoman sultan, d. 918/1512) 210
Bayhaqī (Ghaznavid historian) 32, 34
Bayly, C. A. 575, 579
Bayly, Susan 328–9, 362
Bayram Khan (Mughal regent/poet) 274, 284
Baysunghur b. Shāh Rukh (grandson of Temür) 182, 196
Bayzawī (religious commentator) 247, 263
Bedīl (poet) 301
Bedouins 90
Beg Barlas, Ḥājjī (rival of Temür) 173
Bengal 535
  conflicts with Delhi sultanate 118, 119, 397–9
  growth of Muslim community 532
  Islamic practices 393, 402
  Mughal invasions 305, 309
  secession from Mughal empire 314
  as trading centre 292, 325
Benite, Zvi Ben-Dor 609
Berk-Yaruq b. Malik Shāh (Saljuq sultan) 52, 55, 58, 59–60, 64
Berke (Golden Horde khan) 107, 145, 147, 161, 164, 533
Bernier, François 562, 572, 574
Berthelot, Pierre (executed priest) 460
Bhiran (Delhi official) 118
Bhoja I of Sind 87
Bībī Khanum mosque 196–7
Bihār, conquest of 99
Bihzād (Timurid artist) 196, 246
Bījan (Safavid historian) 235, 236
Bijapur
  alliances against Portuguese/Hindus 434, 437–8
  Mughal assaults/capture 310, 311
biographical anthologies 246
al-Bīrūnī *see* Abū Rayhān al-Bīrūnī
bissu (Bugis shaman, Sulawesi) 455, 456, 482
Black Death 428
Blue Horde 174–5, 184
boatbuilding, technological developments 317, 319, 320
Bohemond VI of Antioch 143
Bolad Ch'eng Hsiang (Ilkhan administrator) 150, 152, 156
Bone (Sulawesi sultanate) 482
Bong Tak Keng, Haji (Javanese dignitary) 388, 397
Böritegin 'Wolf Prince' *see* Tamghach Khan Ibrāhīm
Borneo 439
Börte (wife of Chinggis Khan) 130, 135
Bouchon, Geneviève 356
Boz-aba (*amīr* of Fārs) 62, 63
Bregel, Yuri 23
Brentjes, Sonja 602–3
Britain
  commercial activity 579
  conflicts with Marathas 312
  relations with Iran 521
  see also East India Company; England
Brunei 380, 389–90, 402, 452–3, 462, 468
Buddhism/Buddhists 3, 89, 99, 129, 281, 282, 339, 346, 414
  relations with Muslim traders 360
  sacred sites 359
  South-East Asian states 457–9
Bughrā Khan b. Balaban (son of Delhi sultan) 104
Bughrā Khan Hārūn/Ḥasan (Qarluq leader) 27, 35
Bugis people/state xix, 455–6, 467, 480
  diaspora 495
  language/literature 481–2
Bukhārā 28, 132
  Chinggisid conquest/rule 133, 240, 419
  as cultural centre 245–6, 251–3, 255–6
  Iranian conquest 578
  property deeds 242, 256
  public buildings 29, 242–3, 254, 256–8
  public officials 262, 263–4
  Qarakhānid occupation 27
  religious leadership 30
  restoration 66
  siege of (1220) 549
al-Bukhārī (compiler of *ḥadīth* collection, d. 256/870) 584–5
  for others of this name see Maḥmūd b. Aḥmad…; Mullā; Muḥammad…; Sayf al-Dīn…
Bulghār, king of 33
Bundārī (historian) 61
Bundelkand (Hindu kingdom) 112
Buqa Jalayir (Ilkhan *amīr*) 148–9
Buqa Temür (Chaghadayid khan, d. 681/1282) 162
Bursa (Turkish city)
  Timurid capture 177

Bursuq (Saljuq atabeg) 60
al-Buṣīrī (religious poet) 473
Bust (frontier town), as military base / conflict zone 82–3, 97
Būyid dynasty xvi, 3, 6, 23–4, 38–9, 40–2, 79, 94, 323, 545
Byzantine empire
conflicts with Saljuqs 44–5, 54–5
conflicts with Sasanids 78
conflicts with Timurids 177
decline 6

Cabral, Pedro Álvares 431
Cahen, Claude 6
calendar, Islamic 452, 479
Calicut (Malabar port) 324–5, 329, 330, 346, 353, 429
archaeological discoveries 349
hospice 355
Mappila population 356
Portuguese assaults / Muslim resistance 431, 433–4, 437–8
regional dominance 351–2
caliphate
legitimising role 1
political significance 1
role in Indian conquests 84–5, 86–7
see also ʿAbbāsid caliphate; cursing, ritual; Umayyad caliphate
calligraphy 196, 248–9, 251, 286, 307
Cambay, Gulf of / port 322, 324
gravestones 383–4
Cambodia 457–8
camphor, trade in 378
Canton (Guangzhou) 368, 380–1
decline 379
massacre of immigrants (264 / 878) 368
mosques 414
Muslim community 368, 375–6, 378, 413, 416
'capitulations' (trading concessions) 229
caravan trade 576
decline 573, 579
prosperity / growth 575, 580
caravanserais 576
carpets 199
ceremonial use 233
Catherine II 'the Great' of Russia 518
Catholicism, prohibition in Protestant colonies 456
Cau Bana Chand, king of Cambodia 458
cavalry
increasing role 97
Mongol deployment 548, 553–4
Mughal deployment 269, 271–2
Qājār deployment 519
see also archers, mounted; horses
Celebes *see* Sulawesi
Central Asia
trade 564; slave 569–70
ceramics
archaeological finds 455
manufacture / trade 154–5, 198–9, 370, 378
Ceylon *see* Sri Lanka
Chaghadai (son of Chinggis Khan) 132–3, 134, 135–6, 138, 171–2
Chaghadayid dynasty / khanate 107, 160–3, 559
conflicts with Delhi sultanate 109–11, 115–16, 124–5, 162
conflicts with other Chinggisid lines 142, 147, 153
conversion to Islam 22, 163, 172
division 161, 163, 169
ethnic / political composition 173
internal crises 115, 124
involvement in wider politics 161–2
Chaghatay (language) 191, 192–3
Chaghrı Beg (Saljuq leader) 7, 35–7, 39, 41, 43–4, 47, 48, 52, 542
Chāldirān, battle of (920 / 1514) xviii, 16, 210, 560
Champa polity / Cham people xvi, xviii, 373, 386, 388, 402, 429, 432, 457–9
envoys 371, 374, 375–6, 381
exodus from 378
trade with China 369, 379–80, 382
Ch'ang-ch'un (travel writer) 138
Chang'an (Han capital) 412–14
Chapar (Ögedeyid khan) 107, 109–10, 162
Chār Bakr (shrine near Bukhārā) 253, 255
Chardin, Jean 228, 524, 567
charismatic leadership, traditions of 170–1, 200, 205–6
Charles V, Holy Roman Emperor 228
Chaudhuri, K. N. 46, 566
Chaudhury, Sushil 573
Chaul (Saymur), Muslim community 368
Chavlı Saqā'ō (governor of Fārs) 61
Chen Da-sheng 386–7
Chen You-ding (Yuan commander) 387
Cheng Ho, Admiral *see* Zheng He
Chetti people 291
Chih-lu-ku (Qara Khitay leader) 75
Chin-Temür (governor of Khwārazm) 139–40

China
arrival of Islam 164, 410–12, 535–6; military component 412; mythic versions 409–10; 'tides' of influence 536
artistic motifs, reproduction/imitation 154–5, 156, 198
community archives 396
ethnic classification 166
government officials 418
marine technology 320
maritime skills/navigation 319, 320
Mongol invasion/rule 136, 417–21; incorporation with other territories under 417–18 (*see also* Yuan dynasty)
mosques 414, 422
as Muslim homeland 410
Muslims/Islam in 164, 165–7, 413–17, 429; decline in influence 457; disparity 410, 426; distinctive features 421; enclosed communities 415–17; govermental employment 418, 422; integration with Chinese society 421–4; interaction with wider Islamic world 414; literature/scholarship 416, 420–1, 423–4; as military commanders 391–2, 419–20, 422; personal names 421; prohibition of discrimination against 391–2, 395; range of professions/cultural activities 417–21; repression *see* Quanzhou; rural communities 417; scientific activities 418–19; swings in policy towards 166–7; terminology referring to 416–17, 420, 421; travellers' accounts 415–17, 423
People's Republic of 410
political history 9–10, 129, 410–12
relations with Central Asia 423, 425
religious architecture 12
scholarship 609
Timurid invasion 178
trade 9, 10, 78, 158, 290, 321–2, 427–8, 452–3, 574, 580; links with South-East Asia 368–78, 391–7
voyages of exploration/conquest xviii, 8, 391–7; proselytising function 392, 395–7
Chinese (language), translations into 422, 424
Chinggis Khan xvi–xvii, 4, 5, 7, 17, 21–2, 68, 75, 101, 128, 157, 253, 278, 533, 549–50, 551, 557
centralisation policy 131
cultural/scientific interests 154
death/legacy 135–6, 137, 145, 167, 180–1
military strategy 132–3
as model for later empire-builders 124, 170–1, 185, 559
Mughal descent from 266, 297
origins of title 131
rise to power 129–31
subordinates 138
Western conquests 131–5
Chinggisid dynasty *see* Chaghadayid dynasty; Chinggisid state; Golden Horde; Ilkhanate; Mongols; Ögedeyid dynasty
Chinggisid state(s) (in Central Asia)
academic scholarship 261–5
appanage system 239–41
artistic/scholarly patronage 243–8
decline 265
literature 260–5
officials 261–5; qualifications 263
return to power 239
social organisation 241–3; hierarchy 242–3; mobility 242–3
titles 241
Chishtīyya (Sufi order) 269–70, 281, 282, 586
Chitōr (Indian town/fortress) 274–5
Chittagong, as trading centre 325
Choban (Ilkhan *amīr*/powerbroker) 150, 152–3, 159
Chobanid dynasty 159, 169
Chola *see* Cōla
Chormaghun (Mongol general) 139–40, 146, 550–1
Christians/Christianity
competition with Islam 402, 440, 453–4
conflicts with Muslims 10–11 (*see also* Crusades)
cultural impact/exchanges with Islam 3, 11, 281, 282
factors militating against 454–5
Indian communities 290, 351
internal rivalries 11
missionaries 229–30
see also Melkite Christianity; Nestorian Christianity
Chulia (Tamil) Muslims 362, 363–4, 468
cinnamon *see* spice trade
Cirebon *see* Gunung Jati
Clement VIII, Pope 229
clothing, ceremonial 199
coastal Islam, contrasted with heartland 327, 346
Cochin, Portuguese occupation 431
Cōla people/empire 8, 369
decline 384–5

Cōla people/empire (cont.)
invasion of South-East Asia xvi, 366, 374, 375, 378–9, 389, 402
Colombo 325
commissariat *see* armies; supply corps
compilations (literary) 193, 195
Confucius (Kung Fu-tzu)/Confucian philosophy 12
Constantinople, Christian conquest 79–80
converts/conversion(s) (to Islam) 4–5, 21–2, 26–7, 35, 89, 471, 529–38, 540–1, 559
agencies 534–7
career-motivated 531–2
economic dimension 531–2
financial rewards 532
governmental enforcement 151, 163, 164–5
as gradual process 336–7, 438–41, 530
institutional analysis 534–7
interaction with existing traditions 532, 534, 537–8 (*see also* syncretism)
lack of progress 87, 89
language barriers 530–1
literary analysis 532–4
narratives 338, 339–41, 345, 346–8, 364, 439, 444, 448–9, 455, 476–7, 533
phases 530–1
quantitative analysis 530–1
'radiating' model 531
range of approaches 529, 530, 537
rivalry with Christianity 440
social context 529
speed of process 530
stereotypes 530
in trade centres 327–9, 331–3, 349–50
see also Chaghadayid dynasty; Golden Horde; Ilkhanate; syncretism
Coromandel coast (S.E. India) 291, 317, 318, 361–4, 437
defined 361
early Muslim communities 361
language 360
Correia, Gaspar 349–50
cotton, production/trade 290, 332, 468, 566–8
governmental promotion 567
network system 576
cowrie shells, use as currency 321, 338
Cranganore (Malabar port) 325
Crusades 79–80
Cummings, William 481–2
currency *see* paper money; specie; *names of states/dynasties*
cursing, ritual, of first three caliphs 209, 212
proposed abolition 511
Dahir, king of Sind 86–7
Dale, Stephen F. 345–6
Damais, Louis-Charles 388
Damascus, Timurid conquest 177
Dandānqān, battle of (431/1040) xvi, 33, 37–8, 46, 542
Danish East India Company (VOC) 468
dār al-islām (abode of Islam), territorial losses 4, 5–6
Dārā Shikuh (son of Shāh Jahān) 299, 308–9
(conjectured) impact of downfall 309
Darke, H. 544
Darwīsh-ʿAlī Kökältash (Timurid official) 188–9
Dasht-i Lūt see Great Desert
David IV 'the Restorer' of Georgia 62
Davidovich, E. A. 28
Dawlat Khan (Delhi *amīr*) 126
Dawlat Khan Lodī (governor of Punjab) 127
Dawlatābād, as second capital of Delhi sultanate 115, 116, 117, 119
Dawlatshāh Samarqandī (literary biographer) 191
Dāwūd b. ʿAbd Allāh al-Faṭānī (Malay writer) 501–2
Dāwūd b. Maḥmūd (Saljuq sultan) 62
Dayanu Iḥsān a'Dīn, sultan of Buton 478
Daybul (trading community) 324
Dayir (Mongol general) 139–40
Daylamī (calligrapher) 298–9
'Daylamī interlude' 38–9
Debal (port city), Muslim capture 86
Deccan province 111–12, 118–19, 434
Maratha uprising 311–12
Mughal conquest/rule 276, 305
see also Dawlatābād
decorative arts 198–9
Delhi (city)
as capital of sultanate 116
Iranian conquest 578
as Mughal capital *see* Shāhjahānābād
Timurid conquest xviii, 124–5, 569
Delhi sultanate xvi–xvii, 4, 361, 596
administration 113–14
centralisation 114, 115, 127
as cultural centre 603
elites, ethnic composition 101–2, 277
expansionism 111–13, 397–8
foundation 99, 100–1
fragmentation 125–7
Hindu-Muslim relations 120–2
limits of authority 104, 105–6, 119
Lodī renaissance 126–7

military resources/methods 112–13, 125
Mongol attacks on 106–7, 109–11
'neo-Muslim' population 103
rebellions 117–19
taxation 116–17, 120
territorial extent 114–15
'token' currency 115, 117
trade policy 563
della Valle, Pietro 230
Demak (Javanese state) 388, 395, 397, 433, 437, 449, 456
conflicts with neighbours 395–6, 397
decline 445
rise in power 443–5
Deogir *see* Dawlatābād
dervishes 22
DeWeese, Devin 532–4, 536–7, 538
dhows (Indian Ocean trading vessels) 319–20
Di-hua-jia-luo (envoy) 374
diaspora 410
'professional' 417–21
Dickson, Martin 211, 215
Dilawar Khan *see* 'Amīd Shāh
Dimashq Khwāja (Ilkhan *amīr*) 153–4
Dimashqī (geographer) 373
dīn-i ilāhī ('faith of God'), cult of 283
Dīn Muḥammad Khan (Uzbek leader) 230, 259
'Diponegara war' (Java) 503
disease, outbreaks of 95–6, 564
Diu, (attempted) siege of (1538) 435
Dīv Sulṭān Rūmlū (Safavid regent) 210
diversity, in Islamic world 1, 17, 167–8
Dīwān (governing council) 49
dīwān (ruling council)
Timurid 179–80; administrative structure 179–80
Ḍiyā-yi Baranī (historian) *see* Baranī
Dong-nan ji-wen (Chinese literary work) 376
Döre Temür b. Du'a (Chaghadayid Khan) 163
dromedaries, role in economy/infrastructure 93
du Mans, Raphaël 562, 574
Du'a b. Baraq (Chaghadayid khan) 109–10, 162
Dūāb (province of Delhi)
increased tax demands 115, 116–17
rebellion 117
Dubays b. Ṣadaqa (Mazyadid *amīr*) 62
Dunn, Ross 327
Duqaq (Saljuq ancestor) 35
Duqaq ibn Tutush (Saljuq sultan, d. 497/1104) 55–6
Dutch East India Company (VOC) xix, 229, 463–5, 468, 483–4, 494–5, 496, 567–8
Dvārasamudra (Hindu kingdom) 111

East Africa, ports 323
East India Company 13, 229, 271, 314, 463, 468, 567–8
Eaton, Richard M. 532, 538
Edigü Temür (Chinggisid rebel) 140
Egypt 90
cotton trade 566
Eldigüz *see* Shams al-Dīn Eldigüz
elephants
capture/trade 372
conditions for care/breeding 93
military deployment 37, 62, 542
Eljigidei b. Du'a (Chaghadayid khan) 135, 163, 551
encyclopaedias 156
engineering, in Yuan China 418
England
maritime trade 11, 291–2, 446–7
naval expansionism/conflicts 358
see also Britain
Erberfeld, Pieter 495
Ertash (Saljuq commander) 39
Esen Buqa b. Du'a (Chaghadayid khan) 162
Essex, Earl of 228–9
Ethiopia 78
ethnicity, in Islamic world 21, 75–7
Europe/European powers
artistic/cultural influences 286
history 2, 504
interference in Qājār Iran 521, 522
Mongol relations with 147, 151, 152
naval supremacy 463
Safavid relations with 228–30
trade 290–2, 563; competition with Islamic world 573–4; deficit (with Mughal empire) 289–90; demand for Indian/Asian products 567–8, 574
see also names of countries
explosives, military use 112–13, 274–5, 556

Faḍlūya (Kurdish chief) 41, 46–7
Fakhr al-Dawla (Būyid ruler of Rayy, fl. late C4/10) 38
Fakhr al-Dawla Ibn Jahīr (caliphal vizier, fl. 477/1084) 47, 55
Fakhr al-Dīn, Shaykh (Malabar hospitaller) 355
Fakhr al-Dīn (Bengali rebel leader) 118
Fakhr al-Dīn Rāzī (theologian) 607
Fakhrī Harawī (female poet) 191, 246, 249

Fakhr-i Mudabbir (historian) 101
family confederacy, vesting of power in 17, 28, 185
famine 95–6
Faraj (Mamlūk sultan) 177
Farāmurz b. ʿAlāʾ al-Dawla Muḥammad (Kākūyid leader) 40–1
Farghāna 24, 28
  valley, as trading centre 580
Farruksiyar (Mughal emperor, d. 1130/1719) 313, 314
Fārs, Ilkhanate rule 145, 149, 157
Fatahillah (Javanese leader) 433, 594
Fatāwa ʿĀlamgīriyya (Mughal legal compilation) 299, 589, 593–4, 607
Fatāwā-yi Fīrūzshāhī (legal text, anon.) 122
Fatehpur Sikri (Mughal capital) 271–2, 282, 283, 285, 287, 307
Fath ʿAlī Khan Qājār (Iranian tribal leader, d. 1149/1726) 509, 514
Fath ʿAlī Shāh Qājār (Iranian ruler, d. 1249/1834) 505, 516, 518–19, 520–1
Fatḥ Khan (Delhi prince, d. 778/1376) 123
Fāṭima (Yuan government official) 418
Fatimi, S. Q. 399, 403
Fāṭimid dynasty 6, 41, 42
  (proclaimed) allegiance to 88–9
  conflicts with Saljuqs 49, 55
  demise 6
  trade 79
fatwās (religious verdicts) 74
  see also Fatāwa
Faẓl Allāh b. Rūzbihān Khunjī Iṣfahānī (historian) 206, 245, 248–9
Fedorov, M. 28
Ferrand, Gabriel 373
fiqh (jurisprudence)
  principles 523
  studies 492, 501
Firdawsī, Hakīm Abu'l-Qāsim, *Shāh-nāma* xvi, 25, 35, 155
  illuminated manuscripts 156, 195, 214–15
firearms, military use of 8, 16–17, 271, 467, 519–20, 558
Firishta (historian) 95–6, 568
Firūz Shāh (Safavid ancestor) 214
Firūz Shāh (sultan of Delhi, d. 790/1388) 119–20, 122, 124, 125
  economic policy 119–20
Fīrūzkūh (Ghūrid capital) 96–7
Fisher, Sir John 'Jackie', Admiral 50
Five Dynasties wreck 370
Fletcher, Joseph 411, 536, 538
Floor, Willem 570
Forbes, Andrew D. W. 339, 344
Francis Xavier, St 337, 440
Franks, in Mongol army 552–3
Fuma (Qara Khitay leader) 70
futuwwa 71–2

Gadāʾī (poet) 193
Gamda (Java polity) 400
Gan Eng Cu (Muslim leader in Java) 396–7
Gandhi, Mohandas K. (Mahatma) 282
Ganj ʿAlī Khan Zek (Safavid *ghulām*) 227
Gao Kegong (poet) 421
garden design 197–8, 245, 251
Gardet, Louis 582–3
Gardīzī (Ghaznavid historian) 25, 32, 34
Garshāsp b. ʿAlāʾ al-Dawla Muḥammad (Kākūyid leader) 40
Gawhar-āyīn (governor of Baghdad) 56
Gawhar Khātūn (Saljuq princess/Ghaznavid queen) 54
Gawharshād (Timurid queen) 182, 186, 197
Gayūmars (legendary king) 215
Gedrosia see Makrān
Geikhatu (Ilkhan leader) 150
Genghis Khan *see* Chinggis Khan
Genoa 158
geographical divisions, in Islamic world 1–2
Georgia
  conflicts with Saljuqs 45, 54, 62
  Qājār invasion/massacres 516–17
  supply of troops to Mongol armies 552–3
  Timurid invasion 176–7
al-Ghazālī, Abū Ḥāmid Muḥammad (theologian) xvi, 42–3, 50, 449, 473–4, 500
Ghazan Khan (Ilkhan) xvii, 149, 150–2, 155–6, 157, 160, 552, 555–6
  conversion to Islam 150–1
  reform programme 150, 151–2
ghāzī(s) (religious leader(s))
  claims/awards of title 31, 66
Ghazna, conflicts over 95, 96, 97
Ghaznavid dynasty xvi, 3–4, 21, 23, 83
  army: ethnic composition 94–5; military strategy 95; numbers 95
  conquest of Khwārazm 36–8
  decline/demise 95–6, 98
  literature 76–7
  origins 27–8
  recasting of image 94
  relations with Qarakhānids 31–2, 33

relations with Saljuqs 43, 47, 54, 65, 542, 544
religion/religious mission 6, 94–5
slave trade 568
Ghilzai people 237–8
Ghiyāth al-Dīn (Sri Lankan ruler) 364
Ghiyāth al-Dīn b. Rashīd al-Dīn (Ilkhan vizier) 154, 159
Ghiyāth al-Dīn Bahādur Būra (Delhi rebel) 117
Ghiyāth al-Dīn Balaban (sultan of Delhi, d. 685/1287) 103–4, 105–6, 107, 108, 109, 563
Ghiyāth al-Dīn Jamshīd Kāshī (mathematician) 184
Ghiyāth al-Dīn Khwāndamīr (historian) *see* Khwāndamīr
Ghiyāth al-Dīn Khwārazm Shāh (ruler of Rayy) 138–9
Ghiyāth al-Dīn Maḥmūd (Ghūrid leader, fl. 602/1206) 100
Ghiyāth al-Dīn Muḥammad (Ghūrid leader, d. 599/1202) 72–3, 607
Ghiyāth al-Dīn Pīr-Aḥmad Khwāfī (Timurid vizier) 183, 188
Ghiyāth al-Dīn Tughluq (sultan of Delhi, d. 724/1324) 109, 110, 112, 114, 117
ghulām troops 51–2, 540, 544
payment 227
role in Delhi sultanate 102–4
role in Ghūrid rule/expansion 97–8, 100
role in Safavid empire 219–20, 227, 232
role in Saljuq civil wars 60
ghuluww/*ghulāt*ism (exaggerated religious beliefs) 205–7
rejection 212
Ghūrid dynasty 21, 72–3, 74, 94, 95, 96–9, 568, 607
conversion to Islam 97
currency 100
expansion 97–9
military resources 96–7
origins 96
supplies 98
Ghuzz *see* Oghuz tribes
glass, trade in 370, 378
Gleave, Robert 594
Goa 431
Goitein, S. D. 566
Golconda, Mughal assaults/capture 311
gold, trade in 323
Golden Horde 107, 124, 142, 551, 571
collapse 169
conflicts with other Chinggisid lines 145, 147, 149, 154, 161
conflicts with Timurids 175–6, 177, 181, 564
conversion to Islam 22, 145, 164–5, 532–3
trade 158
Goldziher, Ignaz 584
Gommans, Jos 573
Gonzáles de Clavijo, Ruy 178, 297, 564–5
Gowa (Sulawesi polity) 480
gravestones/tombs 380, 383–4, 387–90
see also saints
Gray, Albert 339
Great Desert (Dasht-i Lūt) 84
Greeks (Ancient)
cultural traditions 273
Indian incursions 84
trade 318
Gregory XIII, Pope 228
Gresik (Java) 388–9, 397, 400, 429, 446, 450
Griffel, Frank 607
Gu-jin tu-shu ji-cheng (Chinese encyclopaedia) 376
Gu-luo *see* Kalāh
Guangzhou *see* Canton
Güchülüg (Naiman/Qara Khitay leader) 132
Gujarat 118–19, 535
archaeological finds 383–4
as cultural centre 597, 603, 606
Maratha attacks 311
Mughal conquest 276
Muslim communities 81
Portuguese assaults/Muslim resistance 431, 434, 435–6, 437–8
as trading centre 292, 322, 324, 325
trading links with South-East Asia 390, 463
Gulbadan Begim (Mughal princess), memoirs 285, 297–8
Gulchīn-i Maʿānī 299
Gunongan (artificial mountain, Aceh) 490
gunpowder *see* explosives; 'gunpowder empires'
'gunpowder empires' 16–17, 434, 438, 464
Gunung Jati (Javanese state) 388–9
Gürkhan, title 70
Güyüg, Great Khan (grandson of Chinggis Khan) 137, 138–9, 141, 161, 547, 551
Gwalior (Indian town/fortress) 104, 105, 312

Ḥabashī (Saljuq commander) 59
Habib, Irfan 113–14

ḥadīth (sayings of the Prophet)
canonical collections (C3/9) 584
organisation of collections 586
renewal of interest in 585
role in Islamic law 587–8
scholarship 584–91, 603
Hadramawt 13
Islamic networks 468–9, 597–9, 606
migrations to Malabar coast 353
migrations to South-East Asia 495–6
trade/population exchange with East Africa 334–5
Ḥāfiẓ (Persian classical poet) 270, 284, 300
Ḥāfiẓ-i Abrū (Timurid historian) 194
Ḥāfiẓ-i Tanīsh (Jani-Begid historian) 253, 254
Hainan island 375–6, 378, 402
Hairun, sultan of Ternate xix, 453
ḥajj see pilgrimages
al-Ḥajjāj (governor of Ḥijāz/Iraq) 79, 81, 83, 85, 86–7, 373
Ḥakīm Shafā'ī (poet) 226
al-Ḥallāj (monist scholar) 449
Hallaq, Wael B. 591
Hamadān, battle of (465/1073) 52
Ḥamzah Fanṣūrī (Sufi writer/mystic) 390, 441, 459–60, 462, 471–2, 491
'Han Kitab' (scholarly corpus) 423–4
Ḥanafī school (of law) 42, 81, 113, 260, 267, 270, 330, 396, 399, 596
compendia 592–3
promotion in scholastic works 585, 589, 591
Ḥanbalī school (of law) 71
Hangzhou (China)
Great Phoenix Mosque 414
Muslim community 413, 416
Yuan conquest 381, 382
harem
confinement of princes to 231, 236, 304
'politics' *see* women
social nature/status 296–7
Harivamsa (classical Sanskrit text) 286
Hartmann, Angelika 75
Hārūn b. Altuntash (governor of Khwārazm) 32, 36
Hārūn b. Sulaymān (Qarakhānid leader) 53
Hārūn al-Rashīd, caliph of Baghdad 56, 96
Ḥasan (Sumatran trade envoy) 383
Ḥasan Beg Jalayir (Ilkhan *amīr*) 159
Ḥasan Beg Rūmlū (Safavid historian) 217, 235
Ḥasan al-Dīn, sultan (Java) 484
Ḥasan Gangu (Bahmani founder) 119
Ḥasan-Ḥusayn procession 458
Ḥasan-i Fasā'ī (historian) 517
Ḥasan-i Niẓāmī (historian) 121
Ḥasan-i Ṣabbāḥ (Nizārī leader) xvi, 57
Ḥasan Khusraw Khan *see* Nāṣir al-Dīn Khusraw Shāh
Ḥasan Qarluq (Khwārazm commander) 101, 106
Hasan al-Wazzan (Hili treasurer) 354
Hasanuddin (sultan of Makassar) 464
Hayam Wuruk (Java ruler) xvii
Ḥaydar b. Junayd (Safavid leader)/Ḥaydarī faction 206, 223–4
Herat xviii, 169–70, 244–5
Mongol attacks on 140, 152
Safavid attacks on 211
shrine 182
Timurid conquest/conflicts over 175, 186, 187–8
Het'um, king of Armenia 143
Ḥijāz (sacred cities and environs) 13
maritime gateway to 323
hikayat (Malay literary genre) 487
Hili (Malabar port) 354
al-Hind *see* India
Hindus/Hinduism 3, 346
classical verse 301
conflicts with Delhi sultanate 105–6, 111–13, 123, 127
(debates on) *dhimmī* status 122
discrimination against 578–9
employment in Mughal government 276–8
hostility to, in Delhi sultanate 118, 120, 277
Javanese communities 442, 447
port communities 430
reforms 357
relationship with Muslim minorities 81–2
relationship with Muslims, in Sri Lanka 362–3
sacred sites 121–2; destruction 95, 121, 310; protection 121–2, 278
trade 80, 325, 351
see also Marathas; Mughal empire; Rajputs
Hirth, Friedrich 375
historical writing 194–5, 235–6
history of Islam
division into periods 2
early 1
patterns 14–15
transformations over time/distance 537–8
see also spread of Islam
Hitti, Philip 15
Ho, Engseng 495
Hodgson, Marshall 14, 72, 169, 190–1, 473
holy cities *see* Ḥijāz

Homs, first battle of (658/1260) 144
Homs, second battle of (680/1281) 553
Honavar (Malabar port) 353, 355
Hong-wu Emperor (Zhu Yuanzhang) 422
Hooker, M. B. 399
Hormuz (trading community) 158, 322, 324, 431
horses
care/breeding 570, 571, 572–3; climatic conditions suitable for 91, 93
military importance 112, 572
purchase price 571
supply routes 92
trade 570–3, 577, 579; scale of 571–3
Horton, M. C. 333, 337, 338
hospitals, construction 293
Hourani, Albert 15
Hu-xuan (Ḥusayn, Champa Muslim) 375
Huang Chao (Chinese rebel, fl. 264/878) 368
Hui people 9
'huihui', Muslims designated as 420
Hülegü (Ilkhan) xvii, 57, 107, 142–5, 547, 551–2
cultural/scientific interests 154
death/legacy 146
Hullishāh, king of Sind 87
Humāyūn (Mughal emperor, d. 963/1556) xviii, 127, 211–12, 268, 278
accession 297–8
artistic/cultural patronage 216, 286
challenges to authority 275
defeat/exile (947–62/1540–55) 273–4, 298
recollections of 285
tomb 285, 287, 307
Humāyūn b. Muḥammad (sultan of Delhi, d. 796/1394) 123
Hurmuz *see* Hormuz
Hurūfiyya sect 182
Husain (Acehnese envoy) 437
Husain (Hili preacher) 354
Husain (jurist) 348
Ḥusayn, sultan of Aru 390
Ḥusayn Bayqarā (Timurid ruler) xviii
Ḥusayn ibn Shaykh Abdāl, Shaykh (historian) 235
Ḥusayn Qulī Khan (brother of Āghā Muḥammad, d. 1193/1779) 515, 516, 520
Ḥusayn Qulī Khan (brother of Fath ʿAlī Shāh, fl. 1211/1797) 520
Hyderabad 314

Ibāḍī sect 333
Ibn ʿAmmār, prince of Tripoli 61
Ibn al-ʿArabī, Muḥyī al-dīn (Sufi philosopher, d. 638/1240) 449, 472, 493, 598
Ibn ʿArabshāh (historian) 171
Ibn al-Athīr (historian) 35, 44, 63–4, 72
Ibn Baṭṭūṭa, Abū ʿAbd Allāh Muḥammad (historian) 9, 165, 595–6, 599
African travels xvii
Asian travels 571
coastal/island travels 328, 330, 336–7, 338, 339–44, 345, 348, 351, 353–6, 357, 359–60, 362, 364, 385–7, 429, 439, 457
Far Eastern travels 415–17, 429
Indian travels 105, 110, 114, 118, 270
official positions 342, 596, 599, 603
Ibn Bazzāz (Safavid hagiographer) 203–4, 213
Ibn Ḥajar al-ʿHaytamī (scholar) 587
Ibn Hājib (grammarian) 247, 261, 264
Ibn Kākūya *see* ʿAlāʾ al-Dawla Muḥammad
Ibn Khaldūn (historian/polymath) 177
political theory 58, 269
Ibn Khurradādhbih (historian) 25, 367–8
Ibn Mādjid (naval captain/writer) *see* Shihāb al-Dīn Aḥmad ibn Mādjid
Ibn Māja (compiler of *ḥadīth* collection) 584
Ibn al-Muslima (vizier) 47
Ibn al-Nadīm (historian) 370
Ibn al-Najjār (biographer) 600, 602
Ibn Nujaym (legal writer) 605
Ibn Rusta (explorer) 369–70
Ibn Serapion (historian) 370
Ibn Sina *see* Avicenna
Ibn Wahb al-Quraishi (traveller) 415
Ibrāhīm, Hājjī (governor of Fārs/Qājār minister) 516, 520
Ibrāhīm (brother of Shāh Ismāʿīl) 206
Ibrāhīm Afshār (shah of Iran, d. 1163/1750) 512
Ibrāhīm b. Ḥasan al-Kūrānī (Sufi mystic) 462, 493
Ibrāhīm b. Masʿūd (Ghaznavid sultan) 43, 47, 54, 568
Ibrāhīm b. Sikandar (sultan of Delhi) 126–7
Ibrāhīm b. ʿUmar Shaykh (grandson of Temür) 181
Ibrāhīm Inal (Saljuq leader) 37, 40, 41
Ibrāhīm-Sulṭān b. Shāh Rukh (grandson of Temür) 196
al-Idrīsī (geographer) 370, 379–80
al-Ījī (theologian) 263
ijtihād (independent legal reasoning) 593–5

Ikhtiyār al-Dīn Muḥammad bin Bakhtiyār Khalajī (Ghūrid commander) 98, 99, 100, 397
Ikhtyār al-Dīn Aybak (Delhi *ghulām)* 102–3
Il Arslan (Khwārazm Shāh, d. 567/1172) 70, 77
Ilkhanate
administrative/military difficulties 146–7
artistic/cultural fashions 156
collapse 169
conflicts with other Chinggisid states 145–54, 175
conversions to Islam 22, 148, 150–1
currency 150
formation 145
internal crises 115
madrasas 601
military limitations 556–7
protection of trade routes 158
Iltutmish *see* Shams al-Dīn Iltutmish
Ilyās Khwāja Khan (Chaghadayid leader) 173
Ilyās Shāh (ruler of Bengal) 119
ʿImād al-Dawla Tūrān Shāh (Saljuq rebel) 52
ʿImād al-Dīn Abū Kālījār (Būyid *amīr)* 40, 41, 46
ʿImād al-Dīn al-Iṣfahānī (historian) 61, 64, 77
Imām Qulī (Tuqāy-Timurid khan, d. 1051/1642) 240, 257, 258, 259, 264
Imām Qulī Khan (Safavid *ghulām*, d. 1042/1633) 227, 232
Ināyat Khan (historian) 257, 302, 307–8
India
Afghan invasion 273–4
agriculture 94
Arabic incursions 92–3
central role in maritime trade 318, 322
climate/geographical features 90–1, 318
climate zones 93
earliest Muslim communities 349
early civilisations 317–18
Ghaznavid rule 4
institutional infrastructure 94
Iranian invasion *see* Nādir (Qulī Khan) Afshar
languages 13
Mughal rulers'/writers' dislike of 272–3, 300
musical traditions 285
Muslim conquests 21, 78–9, 99
Muslim definitions 84
mystic traditions 459
natural disasters 95–6
population 562–3
ports/trading communities 9, 80–2, 324–5
religious beliefs 12
scholarship 586–91
trade 78–82, 89–90, 158, 368, 562–73, 575–7, 579; balance 562, 570; commercial system 576–7; commodities 566–73, 576; diaspora 575–7; Muslim domination 81; networks 575–7
Turkish incursions 90–4
unsuitability for nomadic lifestyle 90–1
see also Mughal empire
Indian Ocean, voyages/trade 8–11, 80–1, 317–65, 562, 573–7
centrality of Indian subcontinent 563
changing patterns 333
city-states, as basis of system 431–2
early history/prehistory 317–19
languages 440
Muslim domination 320, 322, 323–4, 326, 357, 427–30
networks 321–2
ports 323–5, 429
relationship with overland trade 565
Indonesia *see* Aceh; Java; Maluku *etc.*
Indus (river), delta ports 324
infantry, armies based on 96–7, 519
influences on Islamic world 22
Injuid dynasty 169
intermarriage, role in spread of Islam 486, 530–1
*iqṭāʿ*s/*iqṭāʿ* system 51–2, 104, 114, 117, 119–20, 273, 545–6, 555–6
origins 23–4
Iran (modern state)
formative influences 515
religion 208
territorial extent 238
Iran/Persia 4
administration 506, 520
Chinese diaspora 386–7
cities 505–6
continuity of political culture 504, 505, 506–7
cultural influence on Mughal India 84, 284, 286, 299–301, 307
currency 159, 162
economic growth 578–9
ethnic composition 6, 30–1
geography/economic basis 505–6
Indian diaspora 290–1
invaders' adoption of culture 167–8
Mongol rule 5–6, 138–40, 142, 143, 167–8, 539; gradual decline 158–60
new identities 525

nomadic tribes 7
officials 506, 520
'outer' 30
periods of political fragmentation 169–70, 203, 218, 504–5, 514–16
political history xx, 504–25
religion 506 (*see also* Shīʿīs/Shīʿism); debates 209, 507–8; leadership 521–5
role in Indian Ocean trade 318, 322
rulership, ideology of 506, 511, 521–2
Saljuq rule 13, 539
supply of troops to Mongol armies 552
taxation 506, 519
territorial definition 539
territorial losses 521
Timurid conquest/rule 173–6, 539
trade 564, 578–9
traditional festivals 223
tribal groups/conflicts 505, 509, 512–16
weakening of shah's position 522–3
Western studies 507
see also Ilkhanate; Qājār dynasty; Safavid dynasty
Irdana Biy, ruler of Khoqand 580
Irenjin (Ilkhan rebel) 153
Irzan Khan (Jochid ruler) 165
ʿIṣām al-Dīn Ibrāhīm b. Muḥammad al-Isfarāʾīnī (philologist) 261, 264
ʿIṣāmi (historian) 110
Isen Devlat Begim (grandmother of Bābur) 297
Iṣfahān
as commercial centre 576
Safavid buildings 224–5, 234
'school of' 222–3
siege/fall to Afghans (1722) xix, 508
Timurid conquest 175
Iskandar (Jani-Begid khan) 263
Iskandar b. ʿUmar Shaykh (grandson of Temür) 196
Iskandar Beg Munshī (historian) 204–5, 207, 217, 218, 220–2
Iskandar Muda (sultan of Aceh, d. 1046/1636) xix, 460, 462, 463, 489, 490
Iskandar Thani (sultan of Aceh, d. 1051/1641) xix, 454, 460, 462
Ismail (military engineer, in Yuan China) 418
Ismāʿīl b. ʿAbd al-Muṭallib al-Āshī (Sufi scholar) 501
Ismaʿıl b. Yāqūtī (Saljuq claimant) 59
Ismāʿīl I (Safavid shah, d. 930/1524) xviii, 13–14, 15, 206–10, 212, 216–17, 232
artistic/cultural patronage 214, 235
foreign relations 228, 274
military gains 209–10, 245
relics 233
religious policies 206–7
Ismāʿīl II (Safavid shah, d. 985/1577) 217–18, 232, 524
Ismāʿīl III (Safavid shah, dep. 1172/1759) 513
Ismāʿīlīs/Ismāʿīlism
hostility towards 94
Indian communities 81, 88–9
Mongol conflicts with 551
Saljuq conflicts with 54, 56–7, 61
Ispahbadh dynasty 38
Istanbul *see* Constantinople
Italy, city-states 291
Iʿtimād ud-dawla (father-in-law of emperor Jahāngīr) 295, 296
ivory, trade in 321, 323
ʿIzz al-Dīn (Herat civic leader) 140

Jabal ʿĀmīl (region of Iran) 208–9
jade 199
Jaʿfar Khan Zand (Iranian tribal leader) 515–16
Jaʿfar Qulī Khan (brother of Āghā Muḥammad) 516
jāgīrdārs see mansabdārī-jāgīrdārī system
Jahān-ārā Begim (sister of Shāh Jahān) 307
Jahāndār Shāh (Mughal emperor, d. 1124/1713) 313
Jahāngīr (Mughal emperor, d. 1037/1627) xix, 276, 279–80, 284, 293–304, 305
alcoholism/opium addiction 294–5, 296
artistic/cultural interests 303–4
autobiography 293–5, 303
birth 282
fiscal policy 289
marriage 295–7
personality 293, 295, 304, 306
religious viewpoint/policies 302–4
social policy 293–4
Jahāngīr (son of Temür, d. 777/1376) 178, 180
Jahānshāh (Qara Qoyunlu sultan) xviii, 15, 186, 187
al-Jāḥiẓ (essayist) 541–2
Jahriyya (Sufi order) 426
Jains/Jainism 3, 80, 281, 282
Jakarta 433
Jalāl al-Dawla (Būyid leader) 38
Jalāl al-Dīn (brother of Maḥmūd Shāh of Delhi, fl. 648/1250) 106
Jalāl al-Dīn Aḥsan Shāh (sultan of Maʿbar) 117
Jalāl al-Dīn al-ʿAydīd (Sufi leader, fl. 1029/1620) 482

Jalāl al-Dīn al-Rūmī (Sufi leader, d. 672/1273) *see* al-Rūmī
Jalāl al-Dīn b. Muḥammad (Khwārazm Shāh, fl. 621/1224) 101, 134–5, 139
Jalāl al-Dīn Dawānī (religious scholar) 263, 264, 604
Jalāl al-Dīn Firūz Shāh Khaljī (sultan of Delhi, d. 695/1296) 103, 104, 108, 110
Jalāl al-Dīn Ḥasan b. Muḥammad (Ismāʿīlī leader, acc. 607/1210) 72
Jalāl al-Dīn Munajjim Yazdī (Safavid historian) 221, 222
Jalayirid dynasty 159, 169, 175, 176–7, 203
Jamāl al-Dīn (Yuan astronomer) 418–19
Jamāl al-Dīn Muḥammad ʿUrfī (poet) 301
Jamal al-Layl dynasty 495
Jamāl Qarshī (religious scholar) 26
Jamaluddin, Shaykh (executed Sufi) 460
Jāmī (poet) *see* ʿAbd al-Raḥmān Jāmī
Jani-Begid dynasty 240, 252–3, 262
Jānī Muḥammad (Tuqāy-Timurid khan) 256
Japan 420, 574
Japara (Java) 429
jasagh see yasa
Jats (Punjab, India) 78, 85, 88, 89, 287
  independence movement 314
  role in Sikh movement 293, 302
Java 385, 401–2, 433, 475–80, 500
  conflicts for control of 395–7, 443–7, 465
  conflicts with Portuguese 463
  drama, traditional forms 449, 476–7
  early Chinese accounts 367
  Islam in: distinctive features 479–85; diversity of influences 475; ideals 448
  Islamisation 402, 442–52, 473; as gradual process 479; leading figures 448–9, 475–6
  literature 477–9, 496–8
  Muslim communities 387–9, 392–3, 400–1, 429; loss of influence 446–7
  ports/trading communities 9, 10, 443–5, 448
  pre-Islamic order 447–8
  religious architecture 12
  religious/spiritual traditions 12, 447–52, 459
  rise in commercial importance 384
  unification under Mataram 445–7, 450–2
  see also names of individual polities e.g. Demak; Majapahit; Mataram
Javanese (language) 10, 473–4
  religious/literary works 496–8
  translations from Arabic 475, 477
Jawnpur, battle of (968/1561) 274
Jaya Simhavarman, king of Champa 386
'Jayabaya, predictions of' *see* messianic ideology
al-Jazarī (historian) 261
al-Jazīra (N. Mesopotamia) 552–3
Jebe (Mongol general) 131–2, 133, 134
Jenkinson, Anthony 229, 255
Jesuits 337, 419, 423, 440
Jesus, literary depictions 496
Jews/Jewish communities
  in China 414
  commercial activities 96–7
  see also Judaism
Jibrāʾīl b. ʿUmar (Qarakhānid leader) 66
Jiddah (Red Sea port) 323
Jiezi (Chinese village) 409–10
jihād (striving in the cause of God/holy war) 516–17, 521
  against European powers 433–4, 436–8, 453–4, 483–4
Jin Ji (Yuan commander) 387
jizya (poll tax) 531–2
  Chinggisid application 142
  Hindu liability (in Delhi) 121, 122
  Mongol abolition/re-imposition 554
  Mughal abolition/re-imposition 282, 310
Jochi (son of Chinggis Khan) 131–2, 134, 135–6, 239
Jochi Qasar (brother of Chinggis Khan) 159
Jochids *see* Blue Horde; Golden Horde
John of Plano Carpini 547–8
Johns, A. H. 403
Johnson, Richard/Robert 229
Johor-Riau (Malay state) 467–8
Jonker, Captain 466
Joseph *see* Yūsuf/Joseph (prophet)
Judaism, relationship with Islam 3, 5, 11, 35
judiciary
  appointments 247–8, 262–3, 265
  training 247–8
Julfar (trading community) 322
Junayd, Shaykh (Safavid leader) 205–6
Jurchen Chin dynasty 129, 136
Juwaynī, ʿAtāʾ Malik (historian/vizier) 67, 138–9, 140, 148, 149, 548, 551, 554
Jūybārī family 242, 252–3, 255–6, 258, 262
Jūzjānī (historian) 97, 103, 106, 107
  political career 102
  Ṭabaqāṭ-i Nāṣirī 102

Kabul 82–3
Kābulshāh dynasty 82
Kāfūr (Delhi commander) *see* Malik Kāfūr
Kaifeng (China)
  Muslim community 413, 414
Kākūyid dynasty 38–9
Kālāh (Killah/Kra, trading community) 377

Kalus, Ludvik 386–7
Kamāl al-Dīn (Quanzhou religious leader) 387
Kamāl al-Dīn b. ʿAlī ʿal-Wāʿizʾ al-Kāshifī (Timurid scholar) 247
Kamāl al-Dīn Ḥusayn Khwārazmī (Sufi leader) 249
Kamāl al-Dīn Qunaq (Jani-Begid *amīr)* 254
Kampila (Hindu kingdom) 112
Kandahar (Qandahar) 237–8, 305
Kanwa, battle of (933/1527) 269
Kapak Sulṭān Ustājlū (Safavid regent) 210
Karaeng Matoaya (Sulawesi leader) 455–6
al-Karakī, ʿAlī ibn ʿAbd al-ʿAlī (religious scholar) 208–9
Karīm Khan Zand (ruler of Iran) xx, 507, 512–14, 515, 525
 disinterment/reburial 516, 518
 trade policy 579
Kartid dynasty 140, 146, 159, 169–70, 175
Kāshghar (Qarakhānid city) 28
Kāshgharī (Turkish scholar) *see* Maḥmūd Kāshgharī
Kāshifī, Kamāl al-Dīn Ḥusayn Wāʿiz-ī (preacher/scholastic compiler) 193, 195, 196, 261
Kātib Tabrīzī (religious commentator) 247
Kayal (trading centre) 325
Kayalar people (Sri Lanka) 362
Kaykhusraw b. Muḥammad (of Delhi sultanate) 104
Kaykhusraw II (Saljuq sultan of Rūm) 139, 141
Kayqubād (sultan of Delhi) *see* Muʿizz al-Dīn Kayqubād
Kāzarūn (Iranian port city) 326, 354–5
Kāzarūniyya (Sufi order) 355
Kebek b. Duʿa (Chaghadayid Khan) 153, 162
Ked-Buqa (Mongol general) 143–4
Kemas Fakhr al-Dīn (Sumatran scholar) 498–9
Kerait people/empire 129, 130
Kerala *see* Malabar coast
Kern, R. A. 384, 389
Khaḍiriyya (Sufi order) 10
Khaffiyya (Sufi order) 426
Khalaj people 108–9
Khalīl-Sulṭān b. Mīrānshāh (grandson of Temür) 180–1
Khalwatiyya (Sufi order) 482
Khamsa tribes 24
khan, title of 241
Khanbaliq (future Beijing) 418–19
Khandzadah Begim (Mughal royal lady) 298
Khāqānī (poet) 77
Khārijī sect 85
Khāṣṣ Beg Arslan b. Palang-eri (Saljuq *amīr*) 63
Khātib al-Dimashqī (scholar) 261
Khatri people (Hindu caste) 276–7, 290–1, 293, 302
Khazar empire 3
Khiḍr Khan (Qarakhānid leader) 29
Khiḍr Khan (ruler of Mughulistān) 176
Khiḍr Khan (ruler of Multān) 125–6
Khiḍr Khan (son of ʿAlāʾ al-Dīn of Delhi) 108
Khitan *see* Qara Khitay
Khoja Afaq (Sufi leader) xix
Khoqand, khanate of 580–1
Khurāsān 21, 23, 94–5
 army 3
 conflicts over 27, 31–2, 36–7, 169–70
 interregnum 71
 madrasas 600
 Mongol rule 141, 159; rebellions against 134–5
 political unrest within 7, 141
 ʻprojectʼ (of Delhi sultanate) 115–16
 Qājār invasion 511, 517–18
 Safavid invasion 220, 230
 Saljuq rule 58–9, 64–71
 Timurid invasion/rule 175, 181, 186, 187–90; loss of control 183–4, 189
Khusraw b. Jahāngīr (Mughal rebel prince) 302
Khusraw b. Nadhr Muḥammad (Tuqāy-Timurid prince) 258
Khusraw Khan *see* Nāṣir al-Dīn Khusraw Shāh
Khuttal, principality of 32
Khutuy Khatun (Ilkhan dowager) 146
Khvājā ʿAlī, Shaykh (Safavid leader) 204–5
Khwāja ʿAbd Allāh Ansārī (saint) 182, 190
Khwāja Abuʾl-Qāsim (Sufi leader) 265
Khwāja Jahān (rebellious Delhi vizier, fl. 750s/1350s) 119
Khwāja Jahān Sarwar (Delhi vizier/ruler of Jawnpur, fl. 790s–800s/1390s–1400s) 123, 125
Khwāja Maulānā Qāḍī (imperial tutor) 269–70
Khwāja Muḥammad Parsā (Sufi leader) 255
Khwāja Mullā-yi Qāḍī (Jani-Begid official) 263
Khwāja Saʿd Jūybārī (Bukhārān civic leader) 253, 256
Khwāja ʿUbayd Allāh Ahrār (Sufi leader) 195, 255, 258, 261, 297
Khwājagī Aḥmad Kasānī (Sufi leader) 255, 259
Khwāndamīr, Ghiyāth al-Dīn (historian) 194, 206, 213, 216
Khwārazm xvi–xvii, 21, 24, 27, 129

Khwārazm (cont.)
Anūshteginid shahs 30, 31, 58–9, 68–70, 72, 607
conflicts with Mongols 106, 131–4
cultural/literary achievements 75, 77
currency 74
natural resources 68
rebellions against Mongol rule 134–5
return to Chinggisid rule 239–41
Timurid invasion 174, 176
Ki Pandan Arang (Javanese mystic) 448–9
Kilwa (trading community) 323, 334, 336, 374
mosque 331–2
kingship *see* rulership
Kirakos (historian) 142
Kirmān (Persian province) 45–7, 52, 138
Kistan Qara Sulṭān (Jani-Begid leader) 252, 254
Kitab Donga (Javanese manuscript) 475
kitābkhāna (court-sponsored scriptorium/atelier) 195–6
Ko Po (magnate in Demak) 443
Kochnev, B. D. 28
Körgüz (Chinggisid official) 140–1, 146
Köse Dagh, battle of (641/1243) 139
Koster, G. L. 486–7
Krusinski, Fr. 232
Kublai Khan *see* Qubilai Khan
Kuchkunji (Shībānid khan) 250, 252
Küchlüg (Mongol leader) 75
Kūfī, *Chach-nāma* 122
kuh-i nūr diamond 274
Kūlam *see* Quilon
Kumar, Sunil 608
Kundurī, Abū Naṣr, ʿAmīd al-Mulk (Saljuq vizier) 42, 44
Kurds 38, 55
Küshlü Khan (governor of Sind) 106–7, 117
Kuwail (legendary conversion figure) 348

La Maddaremmeng, sultan of Bone 482
Labbai people (Sri Lanka) 361–2
Laccadives *see* Lakshadweep islands
Laffan, Michael 373
Lahore
as Ghaznavid capital 95
Mongol attack on 106
as Mughal capital 286–7
Lahori Bandar (trading centre) 324
Lakhnawti, as Ghūrid capital 99
Lakshadweep islands 344–5
Indian influence 345
Lambourn, Elizabeth 369, 383, 384
Lambton, A. K. S. 23
Lamu (Swahili city) 338
Lancaster, Sir James (explorer) 441
land
grants *see iqṭāʿ*s
surveys 288
taxation 113, 554–5
tenure 555–6
landscape architecture *see* garden design
languages, of government/diplomacy 13–14
Lanzhou (Chinese Muslim provincial capital) 424–6
law, Islamic *see sharīʿa*
laxity (alleged), of Islamic practices 328–9, 439
Lebbe family (Sri Lanka) 364
legal ethos (of Islam) 9
see also sharīʿa
Legazpi, Miguel López de 454
legitimacy
see also caliphate; *names of states/dynasties*
Lewis, Bernard 17
'Li' (surname) 370–4
Li-a-wu (ʿAlī Aḥmad, trade envoy) 372
Li Bai (poet) 421
Li Nou (ʿAlī Nūr?, Champa viceroy) 369
Li Tana 382
Li Yansheng (Tang official) 413, 420
Liao dynasty *see* Qara Khitay
livestock 128
ritual sacrifice 379
taxation 137, 554, 571
transport 319
local rulers, supporting of 454–6
Lodī dynasty 126–7, 271, 273, 302
Louis IX of France 145, 383
Louis XIV of France 12
Ludwig II of Hungary 228
Luqmān b. Togha Temür (Ilkhan prince) 175
Lutf ʿAlī Zand, shah of Iran 514, 516
Lutfi (poet) 193

Ma Hong Fu, Haji (Javanese dignitary) 388
Ma Huan (explorer/writer) 392–4
Ma Jiugao (poet) 421
Ma Laichi (Sufi leader) 426
Ma Mingxin (Sufi leader) 426
Ma Yong-long (trade envoy) 396
Ma Zhu (scholar) 423
Ma Zuchang (poet) 421
Maʿbar kingdom 111–12, 117, 119
trade with China 382
McChesney, Robert D. 218
Maclean, D. N. 89

madrasas (religious schools) 585, 594, 600–3
'Abbāsid foundations 600–2
Chinggisid foundations 242–3, 249–50, 252, 253, 254, 256, 257–8, 265
curricula 247, 601–3
Ottoman foundations 602, 603
Safavid foundations 234
Saljuq foundations 50
teaching appointments 248, 263
Timurid foundations 182, 185
upkeep/financing 601
Madurai, sultanate of 361, 364
Magellan, Ferdinand 453
Magindanao sultanate 454
Mahd-i 'Ulyā' (Safavid queen) 217–18
Mahdī, leaders proclaimed as 212
al-Maḥfūẓa (Sind frontier town) 87
Maḥmūd b. Aḥmad b. 'Abd al-'Azīz al-Bukhārī (religious scholar, d. 616/1219) 592–3
Maḥmūd b. Amīr Walī (historian) 248, 249, 253–4, 258, 259, 259, 261, 262
Maḥmūd b. Arslan Khan (Qarakhānid leader, d. 557/1162) 66–7, 69, 71
Maḥmūd Ghilzai (Afghan ruler of Iran) 237–8, 508–9
Maḥmūd I b. Malik Shāh (Saljuq sultan, d. 487/1094) 48, 59
Maḥmūd II b. Muḥammad (Saljuq sultan, d. 525/1131) 61–2, 64–5
Maḥmūd II of Gujarat (d. 961/1554) 606
Maḥmūd Kāshgharī (Turkish scholar) 29, 34, 75–6, 77
Maḥmūd Khan b. Firūz Khan (Delhi vizier) 125
Maḥmūd of Ghazna, sultan (d. 421/1030) xvi, 27, 31–2, 36, 38, 39, 89, 95, 97, 568
Maḥmūd Shāh (sultan of Delhi, fl. 648/1250) 106–7
Maḥmūd Shāh b. Muḥammad (sultan of Delhi, d. 815/1412) 123–5
Maḥmūd-Shāh Injü (Ilkhan rebel) 154
Maḥmud Tārābī (Bukhārān rebel leader) 138
Maḥmūd Yalavach (Chinggisid administrator) 136, 138, 142, 160
Maier, H. M. J. 486–7
Maimun (Javanese citizen), grave of daughter of 380
Majapahit (pre-Muslim Javanese state) xvii, xviii, 387–8
conflicts with neighbours 395–6
decline 443, 447
ethnic/religious mix 442
Muslim conquest 10, 443–4
naval capabilities 8
Majd al-Dīn Muḥammad Khwāfī (Timurid vizier) 183, 188–9
Majd al-Mulk (Ilkhan vizier) 148
Majlisī, Muḥammad Bāqir (jurist) 236–7, 508, 523
Makassar (Sulawesi) xix, 455–6, 464, 466, 480
language/literature 481–2
rise in power 480
Makdisi, George 601, 606
'Makhdūm-i A'zam' *see* Khwājagi Aḥmad Kasānī
Makrān
commercial significance 85
geographical extent/features 84
Muslim conquest 78, 82, 83–5
Muslim governance 85
Malabar coast 290, 291, 317, 345–58, 596
care of travellers 354
horse trade 571
impact of Portuguese arrival 357–8
influence in neighbouring regions 344, 345
language 357
links with Sri Lanka 363
Muslim communities 330, 360, 429 (*see also* Mappilas; *Pardesi*)
ports 324–5, 385
religious authorities 353
religious mix 346, 356
Malacca *see* Melaka
Malay (language) 10, 12–13, 403, 440–1, 480, 489
legal works 487–8, 490–2
theological/mystical writings 441, 466, 474, 486, 501–2, 598–9
translations from Arabic 473, 498–9, 500
translations into local languages 477–9, 486
vocabulary of kingship 454–5
Malay peninsula 9, 10, 457–8, 465–6
Islamic 'style' 485–9; relationship with global trends 492
legal system(s) 487–8
literature 487–8
pre-Islamic traditions 489–90
Malayalam language (India) 345, 357
Malays (Sri Lankan Muslim minority) 359
Islamisation 363
Maldives 317, 338–44, 460, 596, 599
early settlements 339
Islamic practices 342–4; idiosyncratic nature 343–4
Muslim colonisation 339–41
products 338
relationship with wider Islamic world 344
sexual practices/dress 342, 343–4

Malé (Maldive community) 342
Mālik b. Anas, *Muwaṭṭā'* 589–91
Malik Dīnār (Oghuz leader) 73
Malik Fakhr al-Dīn Kart (ruler of Herat) 152
Malik Kāfūr (Delhi commander) 108, 111–12
Malik-nāmā (anonymous) 34–5
al-Malik al-Raḥīm Khusraw Fīrūz (Būyid *amīr)* 41
Malik al-Ṣāliḥ, sultan of Samudera/Pasai (Sumatra) xvii, 382–3
Malik Shāh b. Alp Arslan (Saljuq sultan) xvi, 13, 44, 45, 47, 48–9, 51–7, 77, 544, 546
  handling of rebellions 52–3
  marriage 48
Malik Shāh b. Maḥmūd (Saljuq claimant) 63–4
al-Malik al-Ẓahir, sultan(s) of Samudera/Pasai (Sumatra) 383, 385, 389–90
Mālikī Sunnism 342, 353, 589–91, 596, 599
Malindi (port city) 323
Mallū Khan (Delhi *amīr)* 123–6
Maluku (Moluccas) archipelago 401, 428, 429–30, 437, 452–3, 480
  Dutch conquest 464
  Islamisation 439
  see also Ternate
Mālwā, Maratha attacks on 311
Mamay (Golden Horde leader) 175
Mamlūk sultanate xvii, 118
  alliance with Golden Horde 164
  conflicts with Mongols 144, 147–8, 149, 151, 153, 547, 552–4, 556–7
  conflicts with Portuguese 431
  conflicts with Timurids 177
  demise 169
  influence in South-East Asia 383
  military prestige 144
  monetary crises 115
  relations with caliphate 15
  size of army 549
mamlūks (military slaves) 3–4, 540
  appeal to masters 4
  Saljuq recruitment 7, 545
al-Ma'mūn ('Abbāsid caliph, d. 218/833) 24–5
Man Singh (Mughal minister) 276–7
Manchu dynasty *see* Qing dynasty
Mangalore (Malabar port) 354
Mangkunegara I, prince of Java 497
Manguin, Pierre-Yves 373
Manila 452–3, 454
mansabdārī-jāgīrdārī system 278–81, 288, 305
  (alleged) abuses 279–80
  bureaucracy 280–1
  compliance measures 279–80
  reforms 294
  strains on 312
Mansur Shah, sultan of Melaka xviii, 401, 439
al-Manṣūra (Sind frontier town) 87–8
Manucci, Niccolao 561–2, 572, 574
Manuel I of Portugal 335–6
manuscripts 155, 195–6, 286–7, 473
Manzikert, battle of (463/1071) xvi, 6, 7, 45, 545
Mappilas (native Muslim communities) 81–2, 346–7, 355–7
  conflicts with Portuguese 433–4
  economic situation 357
  genesis 349–51
  impact of European arrival 358
  links with Sri Lanka 363
  population 356
al-Maqdisī (geographer) 34
Maraikkayar people (Sri Lanka) 362–3
Marathas, conflicts wth Mughals 310–12, 314
  Mughal failure to resolve 312
Marewa, Daeng (Bugis leader) 467
Marrison, G. E. 384
Martin, B. G. 329, 335
martyrs, dramatic representations 525
Marv (Khurāsān city) 141
  rebellions against Mongol rule 134–5
  as Saljuqid capital 64–5
al-Marwazī (historian) 370
Maryam Begum (Safavid princess) 236
Mas'ūd of Ghazna, sultan (d. 432/1041) xvi, 32, 36–7, 39, 48
Mas'ūd b. Muḥammad (Saljuq sultan, d. 547/1152) 61–4, 65, 71
Mas'ūd b. Qılıch Arslan (Saljuq sultan, d. 552/1156) 55
Mas'ūd III b. Ibrāhīm (Ghaznavid sultan, d. 508/1115) 54, 65, 96
Mas'ūd Shāh (sultan of Delhi, fl. 643/1245) 106
Mas'ūd Yalavach (Chinggisid administrator) 138
al-Mas'ūdī (historian) 80–1, 83, 368
Ma'sūm ibn Khwājagī Iṣfahānī (historian) 233–4
Mataram (Javanese kingdom) xix, 10, 443, 450–2
  'civilising' 451–2
  Islamic commitment 446
  rise to power 445–7
Mathee, Rudi 236
matrilineal succession 345, 356–7
Mawdūd b. Mas'ūd (Ghaznavid sultan) 43
Mawlānā Ḥasan Qubadyanī (religious scholar) 264
Mawlānā Imlā' (religious leader) 243

Mawlānā Alī Beg (religious scholar) 264–5
Mawlānā Shaykh Yūsuf Shams ud-Dīn (legendary conversion figure) 340
Mawlānā Yūsuf Qarābāghī (religious scholar) 263, 264
May, Timothy 548
Mecca
  diversion of pilgrimages from 221
  embassies to 452, 484
  see also Ḥijāz; pilgrimages
medicine 237
  in China 418, 422
Megat Iskandar Shāh (ruler of Melaka) 394, 401
Meḥmed II 'the Conqueror' (Ottoman) sultan 602
Mehren, A. F. 373
Melaka (Malacca), port state xviii, xix, 10, 325, 351, 392, 401, 439, 467
  cosmopolitanism 430, 485–6
  cultural influence on neighbouring areas 486, 489
  currency 394
  language 440
  Portuguese / Muslim conflicts over 431, 435–6, 437–8, 486
  rise of sultanate 363
'Melayu Da-xi' sultan of Samudera 390
Melkite Christianity 35
Membré, Michele 212
Menak (Javanese epic genre) 449, 477
merchants
  additional services provided by 577
  Chinese trade / colonies 413, 416–17
  harsh measures imposed on 578–9
  lifestyle 352
  names 369–75
  partnerships with government 157–8
  poetic descriptions 564
  political influence / role 291, 369
  protection 293, 351, 429, 577
  role in Chinese administration 165–6
  role in spread of Islam 366–84, 534–5
Merv *see* Marv
messianic ideology 466, 494–5, 587
metalwork 154–5, 199
'middle age' (of Islamic history) 2–3, 17
Middle East, ethnic / cultural divisions 167
Middleton, John 337, 338
Mīds (Indian people) 78, 85, 86, 88, 89
migrations
  artistically / intellectually motivated 244 (*see also under* Mughal empire)
  in face of Mongols 103, 382
  in face of religious persecution 333, 373–4, 387–9, 402
  trade-related 329, 333–6; familial 350
  see also under names of peoples
Mihr Sulṭān Khānum (Shībānid queen) 249–50
Mīkā'īl b. Saljuq 35
military technology, advances in 434, 467, 560
millenarianism *see* messianic ideology
Miller, R. E. 356, 357
Mindanao 454
Ming dynasty 9–10, 167, 183, 198, 287, 320, 391–7, 410–11, 419–20
  policies towards Muslims 422–3
  relations with Central Asia 423
  rise to power 421–2
  scientific / cultural patronage 422
miniature painting 214–15, 286
Minorsky, V. 38, 217
Mīr 'Abd al-Laṭīf Qazvīnī (imperial tutor) 216
Mīr-'Alī al-Harawī (calligrapher) 196, 251
Mīr Dāmād (Sayyid Muḥammad Bāqir Astarabadī, Shī'ī philosopher) 222–3, 233, 523
Mīr Fatḥ Allāh (rationalist scholar) 604
Mīr Ghiyāth al-Dīn 'Alī 'Naqīb Khan' (memory artist) 216
Mīr Jān Kildi Bi (Jani-Begid *amīr)* 257
Mīr Muḥammad Zāhid Harawī (rationalist scholar) 604
Mīr Musawwir (Safavid artist) 215
Mīr Sayyid 'Alī (illustrator) 286
mi'rāj-nāma (ascension narrative, anon.) 195
Mīrak-i Ghiyāsī (landscape gardener) 198, 245, 251
Mīrak Naqqāsh (Timurid artist) 196
Mīrānshāh (son of Temür) 175, 176, 178, 180
Mīrkhwānd (historian) 35, 216
Mīrmīrān Yazdī (Sufi leader) 219
Mīrzā 'Abd al-Ḥusayn (Iranian religious leader) 509
Mīrzā 'Alā' al-Dawla 'Kāmī' Qazvīnī (biographer) 216
Mīrzā Ḥakīm (Timurid imperial claimant) 275, 276
Mīrzā Hind-al (brother of Humāyūn) 297, 298
Mīrzā Muḥammad Ḥaydar Dughlat (historian) 250–1
Mīrzā Muḥammad 'Sārū' Taqī (Safavid *ghulām)* 227, 232, 236
Mīrzā Qāsim Beg Junābādī (historian) 222
missionaries 229–30
Mithraism 233–4
Miyān Tansen (singer) 285–6

Modave, Comte de 579
modernity, relationship with Islam 2
Mogadishu (port city) 323, 336, 351
Moluccas *see* Maluku
Mombasa (port city) 323, 338
Möngke, Great Khan (grandson of Chinggis Khan) 106, 137, 141–3, 551
  death/legacy 144–5
  economic policy 165–6
Möngke-Temür (son of Hülegü) 145
Mongols/Mongol empire xvi, 2, 5–6, 16
  administration 128, 136–7, 138–41
  army 419–20, 546–57; campaigns 551–4; composition 548, 550–4; discipline 548; influence 547, 549; limitations 556–7; organisation 549–50, 552; size 546–7, 549, 551
  artistic/cultural achievements 154–6
  census (650–7/1252–9) 142
  client rulers under 106–7
  collapse of empire/states 103, 107, 169
  conquest of China 9, 410–11, 417–21, 419–20 (*see also* Yuan dynasty)
  conversion to Islam 5–6
  dynastic conflicts 137, 167
  economy 136–7, 156–8
  impact of rule 17, 128, 167–8
  imperial ideology 131
  invasion of Central Asia 22, 58, 68, 74–5, 90, 101, 131–5, 564
  (unsuccessful) invasion of India 91, 106–7
  languages 14, 128, 158–9
  legacy 159–60
  marriage alliances 130
  military methods 7, 70, 94, 547–9, 553–4; technology 551, 556
  officials 136
  political organisation 128–9
  range of peoples/lifestyles 128–9
  reforms 555–6
  relations with neighbours 129
  rise to power 129–31
  social mobility 158
  taxation 136–7, 142, 157, 554–5
  territorial extent of empire 128
  treatment of conquered cities 133–4, 143, 144, 547
  see also Chaghadayid dynasty; Golden Horde; Ilkhanate; Ögedeyid dynasty
monism 449–50
monopolies, govermental 136–7, 142, 226
'Moors' of Sri Lanka 359
  language 360
Morgan, D. O. 556–7
Morineau, Michel 573
Morton, A. H. 236
mosques
  architecture 357
  as centre of community 536
  in China 412, 413, 414
  construction 224, 234, 250, 256, 307, 327, 331–2, 338, 439
  staff/facilities 354
Mosul, rebellion against Ilkhanate 145
Mozambique 334
muʿallim (naval captain), office of 319–20
Muʿāwiya, caliph (d. 60/680) 84
Muʾayyid b. Niẓām al-Mulk (Saljuq vizier) 50
Muʾayyid al-Dīn Ay Aba (Saljuq *amīr*) 71
Mubārak, Shaykh (adviser to Akbar) 283
Mubārak Shāh (Delhi Sayyid leader, d. 837/1434) 126
Mubārakshāh (Chaghadayid khan, dep. 664/1266) 161–2
Mubāriz al-Dīn Muẓaffar (Ilkhan *amīr*) 159
Mudhaffar, king of Patani 439
Mughal empire xviii, 4, 15, 211–12, 231, 511
  administration 273
  agrarian infrastructure 287–8; study of conditions 287–8
  artistic/scholastic migrations to 212, 215–16, 225–6, 244–6, 284, 299–301
  banking system 291
  bureaucracy 280–1
  centralisation 289
  court culture 284–7, 297–8
  cultural patronage 607
  currency 288, 289–90; artistic appeal 289; standardisation 289
  decline/demise 278, 292, 306, 313–14, 570, 578
  economy 278–81, 287–93, 312–13, 532; export 290–1
  emperor's personality, significance of 292–3, 314
  European commentaries 287
  foundation 127, 266, 434
  Hindu-Muslim relations 272–3, 276–8, 285–6
  historiography 268, 275–6, 291, 309
  Iranian presence/influence 296
  languages 284, 298
  legal texts 593–4
  literature 299–301
  military tactics 269, 274–5, 278–81
  opposition movements 293, 314
  political context 267–8

population 287
reasons for success 17–16
rebellions 275, 304, 310–12, 314
recapture of Indian territory 274–5
religious policy 271, 443
resentment of new nobility 312
ruling ideology 269–70
sense of mission/heritage 268–9, 305–8
succession conflicts 268–9, 275, 308–9, 313
taxation 287–9; levels 287
trade 289–92, 561–2, 563, 565–6; diaspora 290–1; promotion 567–8; in slaves 569–70; surplus 289–90
Turco-Mongol vs. Indian elements 272–3
wealth 287, 293, 299–300; distribution 288–9
see also names of Emperors
Mughulistān 124
conflicts with Timurids 173–4, 176
Muḥammad, the Prophet 1, 237, 327, 409–10, 501–2, 532, 583
descent from, social/religious significance 182–3, 334–5, 468–9
European depictions 418
literary depictions 473, 496
normative role 586
role in Chinese Islam 424
role in conversion narratives 347
visionary encounters with 587
Muḥammad I b. Tughluq (sultan of Delhi, d. 752/1351) xvii, 109, 110, 111, 112, 114–19, 120, 125, 342, 596
crises under rule of 115
(problems of) policies 115–17
relations with religious leaders 118
scientific interests 603
Muḥammad II b. Firūz Shāh (sultan of Delhi, d. 796/1394) 119, 123, 124, 125
Muḥammad III (Bahmani sultan of Delhi, d. 887/1482) 572
Muḥammad ʿAbd al-Ḥayy (scholar) 605
Muḥammad I (Tapar) b. Malik Shāh (Saljuq sultan, d. 511/1118) 58, 60–1, 64
Muḥammad II b. Maḥmūd (Saljuq sultan, d. 554/1159) 64, 77
Muḥammad ʿAlī (C19 Egyptian leader) 22
Muḥammad ʿAlī Ḥazīn Lāhījī (Iranian scholar) 596–7
Muḥammad Arshad b. ʿAbd Allāh al-Banjārī (Sufi scholar) 501
Muḥammad Azhari Shaykh Nūr al-Dīn (Aceh scholar) 441
Muḥammad b. Bakhtiyār *see* Ikhtyār al-Dīn Muḥammad bin Bakhtiyār Khalajī
Muḥammad b. Balaban (son of Delhi sultan) 104, 107
Muḥammad b. Baysunghur (Timurid prince) 184
Muḥammad b. Faḍl Allāh al-Burhānpurī (Sufi writer) 478, 490
Muḥammad b. al-Ḥasan al-Shaybānī (legal writer) 592–3, 594
Muḥammad b. Ibrāhīm (historian) 46
Muḥammad b. Maḥmūd (Qarakhānid leader, d. after 557/1162) 67
Muḥammad b. Ṭāhir (scholar) 587
Muḥammad b. Tekish (Khwārazm Shāh, fl. 612/1215) 101
Muḥammad Badiʿ Samarqandī (anthologist) 246, 247–8
Muḥammad Bahāʾ al-Dīn Naqshbandī (founder of Sufi order) xvii, 249, 251
Muḥammad Ghaus Gwaliori (Sufi leader) 286
Muḥammad Ghūri *see* Muʿizz al-Dīn Muḥammad
Muḥammad Ḥasan Khan Qājār (Iranian tribal leader) 512, 513–15
Muḥammad Ḥusayn Khan (Iranian tribal leader) 514
Muḥammad Iḍris al-Shāfiʿī (jurist, founder of school) 330
Muḥammad Islām Jūybārī (Bukhārān civic leader) 255–6
Muḥammad Jailani, Shaykh (Aceh scholar) 441
Muḥammad Jamāl ud-Dīn, Shaykh (legendary conversion figure) 341
Muḥammad Khudābanda (Safavid shah) 217–18, 232
Muḥammad Khwārazmshāh *see* ʿAlāʾ al-Dīn Muḥammad; Quṭb al-Dīn Muḥammad
Muḥammad Nafīs b. Iḍris b. Ḥusayn al-Banjārī (Sufi scholar) 501
Muḥammad of Naisabur, Shaykh (*fakir*) 364
Muḥammad al-Qāsim (military commander, d. 96/715) 84–5, 86, 87
Muḥammad Samī Samarqandī (anthologist) 246
Muḥammad Shāh (Mughal emperor, d. 1160/1748) 313
Muḥammad Shāh (ruler of Lambri, fl. 815/1412) 390
Muḥammad Shāh (Sayyid ruler of Delhi, d. 849/1445) 126
Muḥammad Shībānī Khan xviii, 189, 209, 239, 252, 253, 269, 275
cultural skills/patronage 244, 245, 248–50, 251
religion 249

Muḥammad-Sulṭān b. Jahāngīr (grandson of Temür) 177, 178, 181
Muḥammad Sulṭān Mīrzā (Timurid governor of Herat) 275
Muḥammad Taqī Majlisī, Ḥajjī (Shīʿī scholar) 237
Muḥammad Temür Sulṭān (Shībānid leader) 249–50
Muḥammad Yūsuf al-Maqassārī, 'Shaykh Yūsuf' (Sufi leader) 456–7, 465, 482–4, 493
Muḥammad Zamān Mīrzā (Timurid rebel) 275
Muḥammad Zayn b. Faqīh Jalāl al-Dīn al-Āshī (Sufi scholar) 501
Muḥarram, festival of 223
al-Muḥibbī (scholar) 604
Muḥīṭ al-Burhānī (legal compilation) 605
Muʿīn al-Dīn Natanzī (Timurid historian) 194
al-Muʿizz (Fāṭimid caliph, d. 365/975) 88
Muʿizz al-Dīn Bahrām Shāh (sultan of Delhi) 102–3, 105
Muʿizz al-Dīn Kayqubād (sultan of Delhi) 104, 108
Muʿizz al-Dīn Muḥammad ('Muḥammad Ghūri,' Ghūrid sultan) 89, 97–9, 100
Muʿizzī (poet) 77
Mujtahidī (school of Shīʿī thought) 522, 523, 525, 594–5
Mukhtār Sulṭān (Qizilbāsh leader) 219
Mularaja II of Gujarat 98
Mullā ʿAbd al-Jabbār (architect) 259
Mullā ʿAlī al-Qārī *(ʿalīm)* 583–4, 587
Mullā Maḥmūd al-Kurdī (religious scholar) 604
Mullā Muḥammad Shāh (madrasa founder) 242–3
Mullā Muḥammad Sharīf al-Bukhārī (religious scholar/official, d. after 1699) 243, 263–4
Mullā Muḥsin al-Fayẓ al-Kāshānī (Shīʿī leader) 222
Mullā Ṣadrā (Ṣadr al-Dīn Shirāzi, Shīʿī leader) 222, 523, 604
Multān 88
  amīr of 96
  supply caravans 98
Mumtāz Mahal (wife of Shāh Jahān) 306
al-Muqaddasī (historian) 88
Muqarrab Khan (Delhi *amīr*) 123–4
al-Muqtadī (ʿAbbāsid caliph, d. 487/1094) 47, 50, 56
al-Muqtafī (ʿAbbāsid caliph, d. 555/1160) 63–4, 71
Murād II, (Ottoman) sultan (d. 855/1451) 233
Murād III, (Ottoman) sultan (d. 1003/1595) 214–15
Murshid Qulī Khan Ustājlū (Qizilbāsh leader) 218
Murtaḍā al-Zabīdī (Indian scholar) 608–9
Mūsā b. Saljuq 35, 36
Mūsā al-Kāzim (Seventh Shīʿī imam) 213, 214
Mūsā Yabghu (Saljuq commander) 39
Musāfirid dynasty 38
music 192, 285–6
Muslim (compiler of *ḥadīth* collection, d. 261/875) 584–5
Muslim communities (in non-Muslim cultures) 165–7
  degree of autonomy 325–6
  hostility towards 166
  (debate on) legality 330, 353
  segregation 12, 81–2
  trading 80–2, 326–31, 428–9
  see also China
Muṣṭafā Khan (Uzbek leader) 187
al-Mustanṣir (ʿAbbāsid caliph, d. 660/1262) 101, 600–1, 606
al-Mustarshid (ʿAbbāsid caliph, d. 529/1135) 58, 59, 63
al-Mustaṣim (ʿAbbāsid caliph, d. 656/1258) 143, 606
al-Mustaẓhir (ʿAbbāsid caliph, d. 512/1118) 59, 61
al-Muʿtaṣim (ʿAbbāsid caliph, d. 227/842) 3, 25
Muẓaffar Alām (historian) 565–6
Muẓaffar Ḥusayn (governor of Herat) 245
Muẓaffar Shāh, sultan of Melaka 394
Muẓaffar Shāh II of Gujarat 434
Muẓaffarid dynasty 159, 169, 175, 176
mysticism *see under* Sufis/Sufism

Na-wu-na (Chinese official) 386–7
Nadhr Muḥammad (Tuqāy-Timurid khan, d. *c.* 1050/1641) 240, 246, 257, 258, 259, 264
Nādir (Qulī Khan) Afshār, shah of Iran xx, 17, 243, 507, 514
  conquest of India 306, 313, 314, 510, 578–9
  death 511, 514
  disinterment/reburial 518
  economic policies 578–9
  legacy 511–12
  legitimacy 509–10
  military achievements 510
  religious views/policies 510–11
  relocation programmes 510, 513
  rise to power 509–12

Nadr Bī Dīwānbegī Arlat (Tuqāy-Timurid *amīr*) 258
Nagabhata, king of Sind 87
Nai Jian (poet) 421
nā'ib (viceroy), office of 102–3
Naiman people / empire 129, 130, 132
Naina Ḥusām al-Dīn, grave of (Sumatra) 390
Najīb, Shaykh (Sufi leader) 344
Najm al-Dīn Kubrā (Sufi leader) 249
Nanak (Sikh Guru) 302
'Nanjing phase' (of Islam in China) 421–4
naqīb (government official) 262
Naqshbandiyya (Sufi order) xvii, xix, 255, 259, 265, 266, 267, 269–70, 297, 425, 499
  governmental hostility / persecution 303
  in Southeast Asia 441, 493
Narai, king of Siam (d. 1688) 458
Naramithla, king of Arakan 398
Narshakhī, *History of Bukhārā* (and anonymous continuation) 29, 30
al-Nasafī (religious commentator) 247, 261, 473
al-Nasā'ī (compiler of *ḥadīth* collection) 584
al-Nāṣir ('Abbāsid caliph, d. 622 / 1225) 58, 71–3, 74–5, 606
Nāṣir al-Dawla Sabuktigīn (Ghaznavid founder) 94
Nāṣir al-Dīn Khusraw Shāh (sultan of Delhi, d. 720 / 1320) 108–9, 112
Nāṣir al-Dīn Maḥmūd Shāh (son of Iltutmish) 101, 103
Nāṣir al-Dīn Qabācha (Ghūrid military leader) 97, 100–1, 102
Naṣīr al-Dīn Ṭūsī (astronomer) xvii, 143, 154
al-Nāṣir Faraj (Mamlūk sultan) *see* Faraj
al-Nāṣir Yūsuf (ruler of Damascus) 144
Naṣr b. 'Alī (Qarakhānid *Ilig* = leader under Khan) 27, 31–2
nationalism 525
navigation 320
  pre-Islamic 319
Nawrūz (Ilkhan rebel) 149–51, 162
Nayyar people (South India) 349, 356–7
Negüder (Mongol commander) 107, 147
Negüderids *see* Qara'unas
'neo-Muslims' *see* Delhi sultanate
Nestorian Christianity 5, 35, 129, 414
Netherlands
  commentaries 452
  maritime trade 11, 291–2, 446–7
  naval expansionism / conflicts 358, 448, 450–1, 456
  rule in South-East Asia 463–7, 483–4, 503; handling of opposition movements 494–5, 500
  rule of Sri Lanka 359, 360
  see also Dutch East India Company
Nikitin, Afanasi 571–2
Ni'matullāhī (Sufi order) 219, 223
Nithārī Bukharī (historian) *see* Bahā' al-Dīn Ḥasan-i Nithārī Bukharī
Niẓām al-Dīn (Delhi sultanate official) 104
Niẓām al-Dīn 'Alī Shāmī (Timurid historian) 194
Niẓām al-Dīn Awliyā' (Sufi writer) 608
Niẓām Mā'in (Delhi rebel) 118
Niẓām al-Mulk (Saljuq vizier) xvi, 6, 7, 13, 34, 44, 47, 49–52, 53, 56, 57–8, 544
  assassination 56–7, 546
  choice of subordinates 49–50
  founding of madrasas 600
  Siyāsat-nāma (treatise on statecraft) 7, 50–1
Niẓāmī 'Arūḍī Samarqandī (poet / historian) 70, 192, 193, 195, 196, 286
Nizārīs 56–7
Nogay (Golden Horde *amīr*) 164
nomads
  conflict of interests with government 543
  military lifestyle 8, 539
  proportion of population 7
  role in Mongol empire 128–9
  sedentarisation 24, 30, 89, 90–1, 543, 555–6
  wave of invasions of Muslim heartland 90
  weaponry 8
Nosal (Chinggisid official) 140
Nūr al-Dīn 'Abd al-Raḥmān Jāmī (Timurid scholar) 247
Nūr al-Dīn ibn Zangi (Saljuq leader, d. 569 / 1174) 6, 71
Nūr al-Dīn Muḥammad (Artuqid leader) 91
Nūr al-Dīn al-Rānīrī (Malay scholar) xix, 441, 459–60, 462, 490–3, 501, 598–9, 606
Nūr Jahān (wife of emperor Jahāngīr) 295–7, 299, 304
Nurse, D. 332–3
Nuṣrat al-Dīn Jahān-Pahlawān Muḥammad (Saljuq atabeg) 73
Nuṣrat Khan (Delhi rebel) 118
Nuṣrat Shāh b. Fatḥ Khan (Delhi sultanic claimant, fl. 797 / 1394) 124, 125

Ögedei (son of Chinggis Khan) 97, 106, 124, 132–3, 134, 135–7, 138, 139–41, 160, 165
Ögedeyid dynasty 141–2, 161–2
Oghul Qaimish (Chinggisid regent) 137

Oghuz tribes 23, 26, 33–5, 36–7, 59, 67, 69–70, 71, 73, 540–1
Oirat people 550
Öljei Khatun (Ilkhan dowager) 146
Öljeitü (Ilkhan) xvii, 152–3, 155
Oman 333–4
Ong Khan (To'oril) (Kerait leader) 130, 131, 141
opium, addiction to 294–5
Orghina Khatun (Chaghadayid regent) 161
ortoq (trade agreements) 157–8, 165–6
Oswals (Hindu caste group) 291
Ottoman empire 4, 15, 204, 296, 304
  artistic/cultural patronage 214–15
  ceremonials 233
  conflicts with Portuguese 434–8
  conflicts with Safavids 209–11, 224, 227, 228–9, 230–1
  conflicts with Timurids 177–8, 560
  decline 231
  harem 296–7
  influence on Mughals 267–8
  languages 13–14
  military methods/capabilities 16–17
  naval resources/conflicts 8, xviii–xix
  origins 6
  population 287
  reasons for success 16–17
  relations with (post-Safavid) Iran 508–9, 510, 511, 513–14, 524–5
  trade deficit 289–90, 570
oxen, role in economy/infrastructure 93
Oxus (river), as territorial marker 27, 240
  see also Transoxania
Özbek(s) *see* Uzbek(s)

Padri movement (Sumatra) 503
Pahang, (Malay) sultanate 395
Pahlavi dynasty 525
painting, Mughal patronage 285–7
Pajang (Javanese polity) 445–6
Pakubuwana II of Java 479, 496
Palembang, sultanate of (Sumatra) 498–9
Pangeran Peki (Javanese leader) 450–2
Pānīpat, battle of (932/1526) xviii, 267, 269, 271, 312, 434
paper money 150
Parameswara, ruler of Melaka 392, 394, 401
Pardesi ('foreign' Muslims) 349, 350–5
  ancestry 350
  diversity of origins 352
  lifestyle 353–5
  migration 358
  religious interests 352–5
Parī Khan Khanum (Safavid princess) 217–18
Parkin, David 328
Parlindungan, Mangaradja 388, 396–7
Parsā'īs (Sufi sect) 262
Parwāna Muʿīn al-Dīn Suleymān (Rūm leader) 147–8
Pasai (Sumatran polity) 398–9, 401, 432, 433, 438, 439–40, 536
  conflicts with Portuguese 436
pastoralisation, processes of 24
Pasuruan (Javanese kingdom) 445
Patani, kingdom of (Malayan Peninsula) 439, 460
Pate (Swahili kingdom) 335, 338
  Nabhani ruling dynasty 334
Patih Yunus (Javanese leader) 444
Paul I of Russia 518
Peacock Throne 306, 314
pearls, trade in 360
Pelsaert, Francisco 569
Pêngkalen Kêmpas, monuments 394–5
pepper *see* spice trade
Periplus Maris Erythraei (anon.) 348
Persia *see* Iran
Persian (language)
  disappearance from Chinese Muslim culture 421
  as language of government/diplomacy 13–15, 30, 180, 284, 544
  as language of literature 76, 77, 191, 192, 193, 244, 266, 270, 298, 474
  as language of scholarship 588–9
  Mongol influence 160
  translations from 424, 477
Persian Gulf, as trade conduit 79–80, 323–4, 579
Perumal, Cheraman (legendary south Indian founder) 347, 349
pesantren (Islamic schools in Java) 448–9
Petrushskii, I. P. 156
Phanrang, temple complex 386
Phaulcon, Constance (in Siam) 458
Philip III of Spain 229
Philip IV 'the Fair' of France 152
Philippines 371, 454
philosophy, Shīʿī 523–4, 537
Pidië (Sigli, Sumatran polity) 432
Pigafetta, Antonio 453
Pigeaud, Theodor 475–6
pilgrimages
  European interference with 494
  financing 290
  routes 329, 435

royal 221, 277, 298, 516, 518
social significance 343, 344
Pinto, Mendes 435, 436, 445
Pīr Muḥammad b. Jahāngīr (grandson of Temür) 124, 176, 180–1
pirates/piracy 354
Pires, Tomé 389, 394, 398–401, 439, 444, 447, 453, 485
Piri Bey (Ottoman commander) 436
Pius V, Pope 228
Pliny the Elder 561
pluralism, religious 11–12
poetry
Chinese 420–1
Chinggisid 243–4
criticisms 225–6
forms 191–2
'Indian style' 225–6, 300–1
performance 192
Persian, classical 270
Safavid 225–6
South-East Asian 481–2, 487, 498
Timurid 191–3
poll tax *see jizya*
Polo, Marco 357, 382, 418, 571
'portfolio capitalist economy' 575, 576–7, 579
ports 323–5, 330
competition between 351
cosmopolitanism 332, 365, 430, 443, 485–6
ethnic/religious divisions 351–2
harbours 351
Muslim communities 9, 80–2, 325–6, 365, 367
Muslim-governed 429–30
new, rise of 330–1
Portuguese attempts to control 432
ruling dynasties 333–4
Portugal/Portuguese
alliances with Indian Ocean polities 438
anti-Muslim activities 331, 341, 349, 356, 357–8, 360, 430–3, 440
commentaries written by 335–6, 337–8, 349–50, 352, 356, 359, 398–401, 439, 443, 444–5
Muslim resistance 358, 431–8, 457, 463
naval expansionism/conflicts xviii–xix, 8, 10–11, 320, 364, 402, 427, 430–8, 453–4
presence on Swahili coast 337–8
relations with Safavids 228
trading enterprises 291–2, 427
power vacuum (C8/14) 169–70
precious metals, trade in 289, 321, 561–2, 570, 574–5
see also gold
price controls, imposition 113–14
Pritsak, Omeljan 26
property
deeds of sale 256
ownership 242–3
prophets, stories of 477–8, 498
Pṛthivīrāja, king 98–9
'Pu' (surname) 370–1, 374–5, 380–1
Pu Ha-ting (architect) 382
Pu Ho-li (Abū 'Alī, trader) 375
Pu kai-zong (trader) 381
Pu Luo-e (Abū Nūr?, trader) 375, 381
Pu Ma-wu (Abū Maḥmūd, trader) 374
Pu Shougeng (Chinese official) xvii, 166, 380–2, 386, 415, 417
Pu Xi-mi (Abū Ḥāmid?, trader) 372
Pulicat (Bengal port) 325
Punjab 105–6
as centre of Sikh community 302
migrations from 96
'purity' of Islam, debates on 336–8
Puteri Cempa, tomb of (Java) 388
Pyrard de Laval, François 342–4

Qābūs b. Vushmgīr (Ziyārid leader) 38
Qadır Khan Yūsuf (Qarakhānid leader) 32, 48, 53, 66
Qādiriyya (Sufi order) 330, 335, 344, 355
in South-East Asia 471–2
in Sri Lanka 362–3, 364
Qādīzāda Rūmī (astronomer) 184
qaghan (khan), title of 26, 33–4, 136
Qaidu (Ögedeyid khan) 107, 109, 161–2
al-Qā'im ('Abbāsid caliph, fl. 462/1069) 41–2, 47
Qājār dynasty xx, 4, 22, 504, 507
consolidation of power 515–16, 520
internal conflicts 516, 520
legitimacy 520, 522
military strength/composition 519–20
rise to power 514–15
wars of conquest 518
Qalāwūn, (Mamlūk) sultan 552
Qandahar *see* Kandahar
Qanghlı tribe 30
Qara Arslan Qavurd (Saljuq leader) *see* Qavurd
Qara Hülegü (Chaghadayid khan) 161
Qara Khitay xvi, 21–2, 28, 30, 58–9, 69–70, 128, 129
conflicts with Mongols 75, 131–2
conflicts with Saljuqs 66–7, 69
provincial governance 69–70
relations with Qarakhānids 31
ruling titles 70

Qara Noyan (Chinggisid *amīr*) 140
Qara Qoyunlu xviii, 175, 176–7, 186, 558
  currency 15
Qara Yūsuf (Qara Qoyunlu leader) 177
Qarābāghī (religious scholar) *see* Mawlānā Yūsuf Qarābāghī
Qaracahqay Khan (Safavid *ghulām)* 227
Qarachar Noyan (Timurid ancestor) 171–2
Qarakhanids 4–5, 22, 25–33, 75
  court/cultural life 29, 75–6
  currency 28, 53–4
  Eastern branch 31
  extent of territory 28–9
  languages 30–1
  military resources 29–30
  origins 25–6
  power structure 28
  relations with neighbouring powers 31–3 (*see also* Saljuqs)
  relations with tribal followers 29–31
  religion 30
Qara'unas 107, 109, 116, 147, 152–3, 161–2, 173–4
  seizure of power in Transoxania 163
Qarluq tribe 26–7, 30, 66–7, 69–70, 132
Qashqā'ī tribes 24
Qāsim b. Yūsuf Abū Naṣrī (agricultural writer) 189
Qavurd b. Chaghrı Beg (Saljuq leader) 41, 45–7, 51, 52
Qāwām al-Dīn Shīrāzī (architect) 197
Qays (trading community) 158, 324
Qazaghan (Chaghadayid khan) 116, 124
Qazan Khan b. Yasa'ur (Chaghadayid khan) 163, 171
qazaqliq (political vagabondage) 174
Qāẓī Aḥmad Qummī (historian) 222
Qin Buhua (poet) 421
Qing dynasty 410–11
  expansion into Turkistān (Xinjiang) 424, 425; trade 580
Qıpchaqs/Qıpchaq steppe 23, 30, 31, 66, 69
  Timurid invasion 174–5, 176
Qızıl Arslan (Saljuq atabeg) 73–4
Qizilbāsh ('red heads,' Turcoman Safavid followers) 204, 209–10, 213
  political activism 217–18
  positions in government 216–17
  Shāh 'Abbās' dealings with 218–21
Quanzhou/Zaytūn (Chinese port) xvi, xvii, 379, 380–2, 429
  Mongol conquest/rule 417
  mosques 379, 414
  Muslim community 413, 414–15, 416
  persecution/exodus of Muslims 386–8, 393, 395, 402, 422
Qubilai Khan (d. 1294) xvii, 107, 142, 144–5, 148–9, 150, 152, 160, 161, 165–6, 417, 418
  cultural/scientific interests 154
Qudrat, sultan of Magindanao 454
Quilon (Kūlam) 353, 355, 362
  archaeological finds 349
Qul Bābā Kukultash (Jani-Begid *amīr)* 252, 254–5, 258
Qum (scholastic centre) 208
Qur'ān 14, 336, 337
  commentaries 248, 251, 263, 587–8
  decorated manuscripts 155, 251
  memorisation 339–40, 353, 448
  private reading 355
  public recitation 343
Qutaiba (Arab general) 412
Quṭb al-Dīn Aybak (sultan of Delhi, d. 607/1210f.) xvi, 97, 99, 100, 105, 116, 121
Quṭb al-Dīn Mubārak Shāh (sultan of Delhi, d. 720/1320) 108, 112
Quṭb al-Dīn Muḥammad (Khwārazm Shāh, d. 521/1127) 59, 68
Quṭb al-Dīn Tā'us Simnānī (Timurid vizier) 186–7
Qutlugh Qocha b. Du'a (Chaghadayid khan) 109, 111
Qutlugh Shāh (Ilkhan *amīr*) 152–3
Qutlumush b. Arslan Isrā'īl (Saljuq leader) 45, 54–5
Qutluq-Khanid dynasty 146
Quṭuz (Mamlūk sultan) 144

Rabāt-i Pariyān, battle of (1007/1599) 230
Rachewiltz, Igor de 131
Raden Ngabehi Yasadipura I (Javanese court poet) *see* Yasadipura I
Raden Patah (Javanese legendary hero) 443–4
Raden Rahmat (Muslim founder of Java) 388
Raḍiyya, (female) sultan of Delhi 102, 103, 105, 118
Raḥḥāṣiyya order 72
Rahman, Fazlur 582–3
Raja Haji (Bugis leader) 467
Rajaram b. Shivaji (Maratha leader) 311
Rājēndra I of Cōla 378
Rajputs
  conflicts with Mughals 271–2, 274–5, 314
  enumeration of clans 277
  marriage alliances with Mughals 277–8

objections to Akbar's policies 283
status under Mughals 278, 281–2; reduction 309–10
Rāmadēva (Hindu king) 111
al-Rānīrī (Malay scholar) *see* Nūr al-Dīn al-Rānīrī
Ranthanbōr (Indian town/fortress) 105
Mughal capture 274–5
al-Rāshīd (ʿAbbāsid caliph, dep. 530/1136) 63
Rāshīd al-Dīn Hamadānī (Ilkhan vizier/historian) xvii, 150, 151–2, 153, 155–6, 157, 550–1, 552, 553, 555–6
Jāmiʿ al-tawārīkh 151–2, 156
Rāshīd al-Dīn Waṭwāṭ (Khwārazm poet) 77
Rashtrakuta (Ballahar kings) 80
Raslān al-Dimashqī (Sufi writer) 498
Rasulid dynasty 380
Ratan (Delhi officer) 118
rational sciences, teaching of 602–3, 607
Ratu Kidul (mythical Javanese figure) 479
Ratu Pakubuwana (Javanese dowager) 496
Rawther people (Sri Lanka) 362
Red Sea, as trade conduit 8–9, 10–11, 79–80, 318, 380
ports 323
reform movements 499–503, 536–7
Reid, Anthony 488
Renaissance 190
Reza Shāh Pahlavi of Iran (1878-1944) 4, 505
Ricci, Matteo 423
Richards, John 567–8
Ricklefs, M. C. 477, 479, 498
Riddell, Peter 492
Riḍwān ibn Tutush (Saljuq sultan) 55–6
Risso, Patricia 327
Rizā Qulī Afshar (Iranian prince) 510, 511
Rizwan Aḥmad 340
Robinson, David 502
Rockhill, W. W. 375
Roman empire 318
trade 561
Romanus IV Diogenes, (Byzantine) emperor 6, 45
Ronggowarsito (Javanese court poet) 498
Rostopchin, Fedor Borisovich 242
Rubruck, William of 164
Rudolph II, Holy Roman Emperor 229
Rudradēva II of Kakatiya (Hindu king) 112
Rukn al-Dīn Fīrūz Shāh (son of Iltutmish) 102, 108
Rukn al-Dīn Khurshāh (Ismāʿīlī Grand Master) 143
Rukn al-Dīn Marghanī (Chinggisid *amīr*) 140
rulership, ideology of
Iranian 506, 511, 513, 521–2
Southeast Asian 454–5
vocabulary 454–5
Rūm, Saljuq sultanate of 22, 40, 72, 147–8, 164, 552–3
al-Rūmī, Jalāl al-Dīn (Sufi writer) xvii, 196, 270
Russia
Indian mercantile diaspora 290–1
relations with Iran 508–9, 510, 515–16, 517, 518, 521
silver mining 574
trade 578, 581

Saʿādat Khan (Delhi *amīr*) 123–4
Saʿadulla (poet) 421
Saʿd al-Dawla (Ilkhan physician/official) 149–50
Saʿd al-Dīn Kāshgarī (Sufi master) 192
Saʿd al-Dīn Masʿūd b. ʿUmar Taftāzānī (Timurid scholar) 247, 261, 263, 264, 604
Saʿd al-Dīn Sāwajī (Ilkhan vizier) 151
Saʿdī (Persian classical poet) 270, 284, 300
Sādiq (Zand shah of Iran) 514
Sādiq Khan Shaqāqī (Iranian pretender) 518–19, 520
Ṣadr al-Dīn al-Ḥusaynī (historian) 35
Ṣadr al-Dīn Mūsā, Shaykh (Safavid leader) 203–4
Ṣadr al-Dīn Sulṭān Ibrāhīm 'Amīnī' (historian) 245
Ṣadr al-Dīn Zanjānī (Ilkhan vizier) 149, 150, 151
Safavid dynasty/empire xvii, 13–14, 15, 193, 244–6, 299, 304
artistic/cultural achievements 214–16, 224–6, 227, 235–6
artistic/intellectual exodus *see under* Mughal empire
'brain drain' to 208–9
changing nature of kingship 235–6
clerical assumption of power 236–7
currency 207
decline 231–2, 237–8, 504, 505, 512, 525, 578
economy 226–7, 234–5
growth in prestige/influence 204–6
internal conflicts 210
legacy 238
legitimacy 213–14, 219–21, 223–4; importance to successors 505, 507, 509–10, 513, 516, 517, 525
marital alliances 204, 206, 213
military tactics 16–17, 210, 211
military vicissitudes 205, 209–12

Safavid dynasty/empire (cont.)
movements of capital 211, 224
officials 216–17
origins 203–4
population 287; transfers 227
puppet rulers 505, 507–8, 513
re-establishment of borders 516, 518, 520
reasons for success 16–17
relations with Europe 228–30, 238
relationship with Mughals 267–8, 274, 293
religion 206–9, 212–16, 522–3
rewriting of history 204–5, 213–14, 220–1
social organisation 216–18
territorial extent 539
threats from border areas 237–8
trade 565–6; deficit (with Mughal empire) 289–90, 570
Ṣaffārid dynasty 83, 85, 88
Ṣafī al-Dīn Iṣḥaq Ardabīlī, Shaykh (Safavid founder) xvii, 203–4, 213–14
Ṣafī I (Safavid shah d. 1052/1642) 223, 231–4
coronations 232–4
problems facing 232
Western commentaries 231–2
Ṣafī II (Safavid shah d. 1105/1694) *see* Sulaymān
Safiyyat al-Din, queen of Aceh xix, 460–2
al-Ṣaghānī (*ḥadīth* scholar) 584–5, 606
Sai-fu-ding (Sharaf al-Dīn?, Yuan commander) 386–7
Ṣā'ib Tabrīzī (poet) 226, 298–9, 301
Sa'id (Hili jurist) 354
saints
biographies 237
Javanese 450, 475–6
role in Asian culture 12
shrines/tombs 182–3, 189–90, 204, 253
al-Sakkākī (poet/rhetorician) 193, 261
Saladin (Ṣalāḥ al-Dīn ibn al-Ayyūbī) 6
Salghurid dynasty 73, 146
Sali Noyan (Mongol commander) 106
Salīm b. Akbar, Prince *see* Jahāngīr (Mughal emperor)
Salīm Chishti, Shaykh (Sufi leader) 282
Saljuq (founder of dynasty) 35, 48
Saljuq Shāh b. Muḥammad (Saljuq prince) 61, 62
Saljuqs xvi, 2, 16
administration 13–14, 49–52, 64–5
army 7, 51–2, 94, 540–6; compared with Mongols 546–7, 555, 557; ethnic composition 544, 545; numbers 542, 544; organisation 542, 544–5
Army Office 545
ceremonials 233
conflicts with Ghaznavids 95, 96
cultural/literary production 75, 76–7
currency 64
decline 71–5
demographic impact 7
expansion 22–3, 44–57, 79, 90, 542–3
extent of empire 43–4
flaws in system 57–8
Indian/Afghan settlements 91
internal conflicts 49, 55–6, 57–64; impact on lands/populations 60
legitimacy 42–3
marriage alliances 42, 48, 54, 56, 61
origins 33–44
political impact 6–7
provincial governors 68
relations with caliphate *see* 'Abbāsid caliphate
relations with Qarakhānids 31, 33, 47–8, 49, 53–4, 66–7
relations with tribal hordes 7, 543
religion 5–6
spelling 33
Sām Mīrzā (Iranian pretender) 514
Sāmānid dynasty 3–4, 21, 25, 30, 85
Qarakhānid invasion 27
Samarqand 132
Chinggisid conquest/rule 133, 240, 262
as commercial centre 564–5, 580
conflicts for possession of 269
as cultural centre 251, 255
observatory 184–5
public buildings 197–8, 254–5, 257, 259, 602
as Timurid capital 174, 178, 181, 184–5
Samudera (Sumatran polity) 382–4, 390, 399, 536
Sangia Latugho, Raja (ruler of Muna, Sulawesi) 488
Sanjar (Timurid leader, d. 863/1459) 187
Sanjar b. Malik Shāh (Saljuq sultan, d. 552/1157) xvi, 7, 53, 58–60, 62, 64–9, 70, 97
Oghuz capture/downfall 44, 67, 71, 77
Sankara (Hindu reform) 357
Sarakhs (Khwārazm city) 134–5
Sārang Khan (governor of Dēōpālpūr) 123–4, 125
Saray Malik (wife of Temür) 171
Sarbadārid dynasty 159, 169, 175
Sārū Taqī (Safavid *ghulām*) *see* Mīrza Muḥammad 'Sārū' Taqī

Sasanian empire 78, 318
Sati Beg (Ilkhan princess) 153, 159
Satuq Bughrā Khan (semi-legendary Qarluq chieftain) 26
Savory, Roger 214
Savtegin (Saljuq commander) 51
Sawerigading (Bugis legendary hero) 456
Sayf al-Dīn Bukhārī (religious leader) 164, 533
Sayf al-Dīn Muḥammad (Ghūrid sultan) 97
Sayf al-Dīn ʿUqaylī (Timurid historian) 194
Sayf al-Rijal (Aceh scholar) 460, 598
Saymur *see* Chaul
Sayyid Alwi (Javanese official) 496
Sayyid Ata (conversion figure) 533
Sayyid Atā'ī family/order 262
Sayyid Baraka (Timurid adviser) 178
Sayyid brothers (Mughal powerbrokers) 313
Sayyid Muḥammad Bāqir Astarabadī *see* Mīr Dāmād
Sayyid Muḥammad Shams al-Dīn (legendary conversion figure) 341
'Sayyid al-Sharīf' ʿAlī b. Muḥammad al-Jūrjānī (Timurid scholar) 247
sayyids 126, 344
scholars, travelling, role in spread of Islam 534–5, 536–7
Schwarz, Florian 259
science(s) *see* Ming dynasty; rational sciences; transmitted sciences; Yuan dynasty
scribes, role in governmental structure 180
script, forms of 481–2
  see also Arabic; calligraphy
Sebüktegin (father of Maḥmūd of Ghazna) 27
secession, attempts at 117–18, 119
Secret History of the Mongols (Mongghol'un niucha tobcha'an) 130
Selīm I, (Ottoman) sultan (d. 926/1520) 13–14, 210, 434
Selīm II, (Ottoman) sultan (d. 981/1574) 437
Seljuks *see* Saljuqs
Senopati Ingalaga, Panembahan, king of Mataram 445–6
Serat Centhini (Javanese literary work) 476–7
shadow-puppet theatre *(wayang)* 449, 476–7
Shāfiʿī school (of law) 9, 12–13, 81, 589
  domination of coastal areas 330, 333, 342, 345, 385, 399, 535
  links with Qādiriyya 335
  networks 353
Shāh Jahān, (Mughal) emperor (d. 1666) xix, 257, 264, 296, 299, 302, 304–9, 606–7
  architectural monuments 306–8
  downfall/imprisonment 308–9
  military achievements 305–6
  personality 304–5, 314
  rebellion against father 304
  religion 304–5
  sense of mission 305–6
  titles 306
Shāh Khalīl Allāh (Sufi leader) 219
Shāh-Malik (Timurid *amīr*, fl. 815/1413) 181
Shāh Malik of Jand (d. 433/1041) 35, 36, 39
Shāh-Muẓaffar (Timurid artist) 196
Shāh-nāma see Firdawsī
Shāh Qulī Khan (Qizilbāsh leader) 210
Shāh Rafiʿ al-Dīn (religious scholar) 604
Shāh Rukh (son of Tamerlane, d. 850/1447) xviii, 126, 173, 178, 181–3, 185, 187, 189, 190, 198, 262, 603
  cultural/literary patronage 194, 195
  death/burial 183–4, 185
Shāh Rūkh Afshār (ruler of Iran/Khurāsān, d. 1210/1796) 511, 512, 517–18
Shāh Walī Allāh Dihlawī (religious scholar) 583, 589–91, 604
Shāhī dynasties (Kabul) 83, 88
Shāhjahānābād (Mughal capital) 306, 307–8
Shamanism 3, 5, 33
Shambhaji b. Shivaji (Maratha leader) 311
Shams al-Dīn Dāmghānī (Gujarat rebel) 120
Shams al-Dīn Eldigüz (Saljuq atabeg) 62, 64, 73
Shams al-Dīn Iltutmish (sultan of Delhi) 104, 105, 563
  governance 102
  rise/conquests 100–1
Shams al-Dīn Ilyās Shāh (sultan of Bengal) 118, 397–8
Shams al-Dīn Juwaynī (Ilkhan vizier, brother of historian) 148, 149
Shams al-Dīn Kart (Ghūrid ruler of Herat) 140, 147
Shams al-Dīn Kayūmarth (sultan of Delhi) 104
Shams al-Dīn Muḥammad al-Jazarī (Timurid scholar) 247
Shams al-Dīn al-Sumaṭrānī al-Pasā'ī (Aceh scholar) 441, 460, 478, 490, 491
Shams al-Dīn ʿUmar (Yuan commander/provincial governor) 419–20, 423
Shams al-Mulk Naṣr b. Ibrāhīm (Qarakhānid leader) 29, 31, 48, 53
Shams-i Sirāj ʿAfif (historian) 398
Shams Khan Awhadī (ruler of Bhayāna) 125
Shānī Takallū (poet) 226
Shansabānīs *see* Ghūrid dynasty
Sharaf al-Dīn (Tabrīz merchant) 386–7

Sharaf al-Dīn ʿAlī Yazdī (Timurid historian) 194
sharīʿa (Islamic law)
appeals to 482
on diasporic communities 330
digests 487–8
local interpretations / adaptations 328–9, 488–9
relationship with Mongol *yasa* 160, 163, 172–3
strict application 11, 459–60, 462, 501, 593
study 601, 603
Timurid 'return' to 181–3
Sharīfa Sulṭān Khanum (Jani-Begid princess) 254
sharīfs (descendants of the Prophet) 334–5, 336
Shaṭṭāriyya (Sufi order) 10, 499
Shaykh al-Islām (government official) 262
in Chinese cities 416
Shaykh Yūsuf *see* Muḥammad Yūsuf al-Maqassārī
Shaykhā (anti-Delhi rebel) 123
Shaykhīsm (school of Shīʿī thought) 524, 525
Shaykhzāde (Bukhārā artist) 246
Sherley, Anthony / Robert 228–9
Shībānid dynasty 239, 241–2, 244–6
see also Abū'l Khayrid dynasty; ʿArabshahid dynasty
Shigi Qutuqu (Mongol judge / general) 135
Shihāb al-Dīn, Shaykh (Calicut hospitaller) 355
Shihāb al-Dīn Aḥmad ibn Mādjid (naval captain / writer) 319–20, 430
Shihāb al-Dīn b. ʿAbd Allāh Muḥammad (Sumatran scholar) 498
Shihāb al-Dīn al-Dimyāṭī (scholar) 600
Shihāb al-Dīn Tekish (Saljuq rebel) 52–3
Shihāb al-Dīn ʿUmar (sultan of Delhi) 108
Shīʿīs / Shīʿism 6, 12, 521–5, 537
adoption as state religion 152, 169, 207–8, 221–4, 267, 506, 508, 513, 521
centres of learning 524–5
competing schools of thought 522–4, 594–5
compilation of traditions 237
differing forms 209
hostility towards 42, 71, 94
intellectuals 208
leaders 221–3, 522–3
opposition movements 182
rituals / practices 223
suppression 55
in Thailand 458
titles 282–3
travel to Far East 373–4, 402
see also Ismāʿīlīs; Sunnī Islam, conflicts with Shīʿism; Twelver Shīʿism
Shiktür (Ilkhan official) 148
Shinji, Maejima 386–7
shipwrecks 370
Shīr Shāh Sūrī (Afghan leader) 127, 273–4, 298
Shīrāz xx
as (claimed) ancestral base 333–4
as cultural centre 156
Shīrvān dynasty 77
Shivaji (Maratha leader) 310–11
Shookoohy, Mehrdad 349
shrines *see* saints
Shumla (Turkmen leader) 73
Siam *see* Thailand
Sibṭ ibn al-Jawzī (historian) 545
Sidayu (Javan polity) 400
Siddharaja, king of Gujarat 81
Siddhartha, Gautama (Buddha) 282
siege warfare 112–13, 269, 542–3, 556
Sigli (Sumatran polity) *see* Pidië
Sikandar b. Bahlūl Lodī (sultan of Delhi) 126–7
Sikandar Shāh (ruler of Bengal) 119
Sikhs / Sikhism 3, 310
independence movement 314
rise 293, 301–3
social status 302
(attempted) suppression 302
Sikri *see* Fatehpur Sikri
silk, trade in 226, 570
'Silk Road' 413, 565
oasis towns 425
silver *see* precious metals
Simon, Father (missionary) 230
Sind
commercial significance 86, 89–90
conflicts with Delhi sultanate 119
demography 85–6
geographical extent / features 85
mosques, construction of 87, 88
Muslim conquest 78–9, 82, 84–90, 98–9, 349
rebellions against Muslim rule 87
renunciation of caliphal control 88
urbanisation 89
Sīrāf (port city) 323–4
al-Sīrāfī (travel writer), *Akhbār al-Ṣīn wa-l-Hind* 415
Sīrī (Indian city) 116
Sīstān, as military base / conflict zone 82–3
Siti Jenar (legendary Javanese mystic) 449–50, 459, 478
Siyāqī Niẓām (Safavid historian) 220, 230

slaves
  capture 31
  military 540, 543–5, 557 (*see also ghulām* troops; *mamlūks*)
  range of uses 569
  trade 25, 321, 468, 568–70
Smith, J. M., Jr. 551, 556–7
Snouck Hurgronje, Christian 384
Sofala (trading community) 323, 337–8
Sogdia 24, 28
Soghunchaq (Ilkhan official) 148, 150
Sohar (port city) 323–4
Song dynasty 142, 166, 376, 381, 410–11, 413, 420
  Muslim officials 415
  terminology employed towards Muslims 416–17
  trade links 368–9, 374–5, 384, 427–8
Song Hui-yao (Chinese official text) 379
Song Yun (Bengal envoy) 399
Sorqaqtani Beki (daughter-in-law of Chinggis Khan) 130, 141
South Africa 484
South-East Asia
  arrival of Islam 366–8, 535–7
  diasporas 495–6
  distinctive Islamic forms 502–3
  diversity of Islamic experience 470, 488–9
  emergence of Muslim rulers 382–3, 390, 402
  institutions 488–9
  Islamic networks 466–9, 484–5, 486–7, 501–2
  localisation 463–4, 472–5
  non-Muslim states/islands 438
  propagation/prevalence of Islam 395–6, 399–400, 438–9, 583–4
  relationship with wider Islamic world 470, 471, 502–3, 536, 584
  role in global trade networks 488
  scholastic centres 464, 466–7
  schools, founding of 485, 496
  traditions of kingship 454–5
  see also names of islands/regions
sovereignty, Perso-Islamic theories of 22, 27–8, 50–1
Spain
  naval expansionism/conflicts 402, 440, 453–4, 468
  New World colonisation/trade 574
Spear, T. T. 332–3
specie, trade payments in 292, 562, 574–5
spice trade 10, 78, 290, 291–2, 321, 351, 358, 380, 428, 437, 566
  centres 324–5, 346, 360, 464, 484
  European disruption 427, 430–2, 435, 468
  routes/stages 429–30
spread of Islam 1, 3, 11–13, 92, 94, 163–7, 326–31, 366, 385, 390, 402, 457–68
  maritime 3, 8–11
  patterns 530–1
  see also Sufism; trade
Spuler, Bertold 565
Sri Lanka 9, 317, 346, 359–60
  Christian communities 440
  peoples, terminology of 361–2
  trading communities 325, 363
Sri Mahārājā, ruler of Melaka 394
Sri Parameswara Dewa Shāh, ruler of Melaka 394
Sriwijaya *see* Zābaj
state religion, Islam as 165, 181–3, 398, 439
steppe peoples 3
  horse-breeding 570
  political organisation 129, 174
  tribal migrations/conquests 21–4
Sübetei (Mongol general) 131, 133, 134
Subhan Qulī (Tuqāy-Timurid khan, d. *c.* 1091/1681) 240, 257–8, 264
Subrahmanyam, Sanjay 363, 575, 579
Suez Canal, Ottoman prefiguring 437
Sufis/Sufism 15–16, 76, 155–6, 203–4, 205, 285–6
  coastal/island communities 335, 344, 345, 354–5, 385, 390–1, 449–50
  correspondence 195
  elitism 493
  governmental hostility/suppression 220, 299, 459–60
  heterodox elements 22
  influence in China 424, 425–6
  internal conflicts 449–50, 490–1
  literature 301, 478–9, 497
  and mysticism 459, 537, 598
  political activism 457
  reform movements/'modes' 499–502
  role in spread of Islam 1, 5, 10, 11, 12, 326, 330, 402, 533, 534–6
  rulers' promotion/attachment to 249, 281, 282–3
  sacred sites 450
  scholarship 586, 608
  in South East Asia 459–62, 471–2, 482–4, 490–4
  see also names of orders
Suhrawardī, Abū Ḥāmid (philosopher) 222–3

Sulawesi (Celebes) 455–7, 464, 480–2
Christian experiments 455
distinctive form of Islam 480–1
law 488
literature 481–2
retention of old traditions 456
Sulaymān (Safavid shah, d. 1105/1694) 234–7, 507–8
literary patronage 235–6
nature of rule 235–6
Sulaymān (Umayyad caliph, d. 101/717) 87
Sulaymān (Sumatran trade envoy) 383
Sulaymān bin ʿAbd Allāh bin al-Baṣīr of Lamreh, sultan (d. 608/1211) 382
Sulaymān b. Qutlumush (Saljuq leader, d. 479/1086) 40, 45, 55
Sulaymān Shāh b. Muḥammad (Saljuq sultan, d. 556/1161) 61
Süleiman (travel writer, fl. 236/851) 368
Süleyman b. Bāyezīd (Ottoman prince, d. 815/1413) 177
Süleyman I 'the Magnificent,' (Ottoman) sultan (d. 974/1566) 211, 603
campaigns against Portuguese 435–7
Sulṭān-Abū Saʿīd b. Muḥammad Mīranshāhī (Timurid ruler) 185–7, 188, 189
Sulṭān Aḥmad Jalayir 176, 177
Sulṭān-ʿAlī Mashhadī (calligrapher) 196
Sultan Haji of Batavia 465
Sulṭān Ḥusayn (Safavid shah) xix, 182, 236–8, 505
ineffectiveness as ruler 237, 507–8
Sulṭān-Ḥusayn Bayqara (Timurid ruler) 183, 185, 186–90, 192, 195, 196, 198, 245, 252, 275
choice of subordinates 188–9
cultural/artistic patronage 261, 270
Sulṭān Ḥusayn Mīrzā (Timurid ruler) 261
Sulṭān Muḥammad (Safavid artist) 215
Sulṭān-Muḥammad (Timurid prince) 183
Sulṭān Muḥammad al-ʿAdil, king of the Maldives (legendary conversion figure) 340–1
Sulṭān Shāh (Khwārazm claimant) 74
Sulṭān Uways (Jalayirid leader) 159
Sulṭāniyya (Iranian city) 155
as trading centre 158
Sulu (Indonesian island polity) 452–3, 454, 468
suluk (verse genre) 478–9
Sumatra 9, 367, 372
Dutch control 464–5
Islamisation 384–5, 389–91, 393, 399–400, 402, 439, 536
ruling titles 398
scholarship/literature 498–503
trading centres 377–8
see also names of individual polities, e.g. Aceh, Pasai, Sriwijaya
sun, reverence for 283–4
Sunan Giri (Javanese religious leader) 450–2
Sunan Gunung Jati (Javanese leader) 433, 444, 484
Sunan Kalijaga (Javanese conversion figure) 444, 446, 448–9, 450, 475
Sunan Kudus (Javanese religious leader) 477
Sunan Panggung (Javanese religious leader) 478
Sung dynasty *see* Song dynasty
Sunnī Islam 9, 537, 584
attempted accommodation with Shīʿism 510–11
conflicts/contrasts with Shīʿism 12, 15–16, 429
Indian communities 81
persecution 212
prevalence in coastal communities 345, 458
promotion by ruling dynasties 5, 6, 15–16, 42–3, 50, 94, 181–3, 203, 217, 267, 269–70, 436
'revival' 603
rulers' disenchantment with 152
schools of law 591 (*see also individual names*)
standardisation 12–13
Surabaya (Java) xix, 388–9, 400, 446
Surat (Mughal city), Maratha assault on 310
Surek Pangngajakna Nabita Muhammad nennia Abdul Ibahi (Bugis poem) 481
'surnames' (of merchants in China) 370–5
al-Suyūṭī (*ḥadīth* scholar) 586–7
Swahili coast 317, 318, 331–8
indigenous population: ethnicity 332; motiviations 332–3; role in trade 332
migrations to 333–6
syair (Malay verse genre) 487
syncretism 336–7, 394, 456, 470
in Java 400–1, 442–3, 447–8, 450–2
Syria, Mongol invasions 143–4, 151, 552, 556–7

Tabrīz, as trading centre 158, 374
al-Taftāzānī (Timurid scholar) *see* Saʿd al-Dīn Masʿūd b. ʿUmar Taftāzānī
Taghachar (Ilkhan *amīr*, d. 696/1297) 149–50, 151
Taghachar (son-in-law of Chinggis Khan, d. 617/1220) 133–4, 135
Taghai (Delhi rebel) 118–19

Taghay Temür (Ilkhan khan) 159
Ṭāhirid dynasty 85
Ṭahmāsp I (Safavid shah, d. 984/1576) xviii–xix, 209, 210–18, 235, 274, 524
(lack of) cultural interests 225, 246
foreign relations 228
Ṭahmāsp II (Safavid shah, d. 1144/1732) 505, 507, 508–9, 510, 514, 578
T'ai-tsung, (Song) emperor 372
Tāj al-Dīn ʿAlī-Shāh (Ilkhan *amīr)* 153
Tāj al-Dīn Yildiz (Ghūrid military leader) 97, 100–1
Tāj Mahal 267–8, 306–7
upkeep 307
Tāj al-Mulk Abu'l-Ghanāʾim (Saljuq vizier) 59
Tāj al-Salmānī (Timurid historian) 194
Talas, battle of (751) 412
Tamerlane *see* Temür
Tamghach Bugra Khan Ibrāhīm (Qarakhānid leader, d. 551/1156) 66–7
Tamghach Khan Ibrāhīm (Qarakhānid khan, d. *c.* 460/1068) 31, 32, 43, 47–8, 66
Tamil people/language 360, 361–4
tamma system 550–1
Tang dynasty 9, 78, 83, 322, 367, 410–11, 412, 413, 415, 420
Tangut state 129
Taoism 3
tapas (Java ascetics) 400–1, 447–8
taqlīd (adherence to legal doctrine) 593–4
Taraghai (Chaghadayid commander) 109, 111
Tara'in, first/second battle of (587–8/1191–2) 98–9, 101
Tārīkh-i Alfī (early Islamic history) 286
Tarmashirin b. Du'a (Chaghadayid khan) 110, 115–16, 124, 163
reasons for downfall 163
Tashkent 240, 255
Tatars 81, 129–30
Tatsuro, Yamamoto 385–6
Tavernier, Jean-Baptiste 228, 230, 572
Ṭawālisī (trading centre) 385–6
tax farms 158
Tegh Bahadur (Sikh Guru) 302
Tegüder Aḥmad (Ilkhan khan) 148–9, 554
advisers 148–9
reasons for failure of policies 148–9
Tekish (Khwārazm Shāh, d. 596/1200) 70, 72, 73, 74
Tembayat (Java sacred site) 451
Temüjin *see* Chinggis Khan
Temür, Emir (Tamerlane) (d. 1405) xvii–xviii, 4, 17, 107, 110, 160, 185, 189, 199, 557, 559–60, 564–5
ancestry 170–2
basis of authority 170–1
(alleged) birth date 171
building of empire 170
burial 178
death/legacy 170, 178, 180–1
image-building 194, 196–8
invasion of India 124–5, 127, 176, 267, 569
later empires' (claimed) links with 204–5, 220, 266, 285, 297, 305–6, 509–10
legitimacy 171–2
marriages 297
religion 172–3
rise to power 173–4
titles 170–1, 172
treatment of conquered cities 177
Temür Malik (Jochid leader) 174–5
Terengganu 389
Terken Khātūn (Saljuq queen) 48, 53, 59
Ternate, sultanate of 438, 453–4, 464
textiles
design 199
production/trade 154, 290, 291–2, 364, 561, 566–8
see also cotton; silk
Thailand (Siam) 377
Islamisation 458–9
kings of 12
Thatta (Sind town) 596–7
Thevenot, Jean de 230, 572
Tibbetts, G. R. 339
Tiflis (Georgian capital), siege of 516–17
Tigris-Euphrates area, early civilisations 317–18
Tilang (Hindu kingdom/Delhi province) 111–12, 118
Timã de Raja, Daria 400
Timurid dynasty 16, 170
claims to Mughal leadership 275
Timurid state 244–6
administration 178–80
agriculture 189–90
architecture 196–8
art 195–6, 198–9
bureaucracy 180
conflicts over succession 181, 183–4, 185–8, 268–9
cultural/artistic patronage 190–9; influence on later scholarship 247, 260–1, 264, 265; reasons for 190–1

Timurid state (cont.)
decentralisation 191
disintegration 181, 184, 186, 239
education 602
financial administration 183, 188–9
historical writing 194–5
influence on successor states 241–2, 268–9
Islamisation 181–3
languages 180, 191
literature 191–3, 564
madrasas 601
military basis 178–9, 278, 559–60
military / civilian distinction 179–80
as model for later empires 199–200
Mughal project of reconquest 306
religious opposition 182
royal tents / canopies 199
titles 178–80, 185
tribal composition 178–9
Tirjan, battle of (878 / 1473) xviii
al-Tirmidhī (compiler of *ḥadīth* collection) 584
Todar Mal (Mughal minister) 276–7, 288, 290, 302
Ṭoghrıl Beg (Saljuq sultan, d. 455 / 1063) xvi, 6, 7, 35, 36–7, 39–44, 51, 233, 542
titles 42
Ṭoghrıl II b. Muḥammad (Saljuq sultan, d. 529 / 1134) 61–2, 65, 73
Ṭoghrıl III b. Arslan Shāh (Saljuq sultan, d. 590 / 1194) 58, 72–4
Tok Pulau Manis (Sufi scholar) 494
Tolui (son of Chinggis Khan) 130, 133, 134–6, 137
tombs / tombstones
of Muslim traders xvi, 9
sacred, pre-Islamic 12
To'oril *see* Ong Khan
Toqtamish (Blue Horde leader) 174–6
Töregene Khatun (Chinggisid regent) 137, 141
trade 46, 157–8, 189, 229, 289–92, 561–81
centres 158, 224–5, 338, 428–30, 431–2, 576, 580–1
commodities 78, 158, 290, 321, 324, 428, 561–2, 566–73, 581
between hostile states 565–6
impact of war / conquests 578–9
lack of state involvement 428
networks 321–2, 472–3, 575–7; global 488
periods of decline 564–5
promotion 226–7, 293
reinvestment of capital 576–7
role in spread of Islam 1, 11, 78–82, 326–31, 335–6, 366–84, 402, 535
taxation 137
see also Indian Ocean; slaves; *names of commodities*; *names of regions / dynasties*
trade routes 580
establishment 229
military use 391
placement 367–9
protection 290, 563–4
relationship with climate conditions 430
segmentation 321–2, 323–4, 330–1
shifts 167, 330, 351, 384, 427, 435, 463
state investment in 563–4, 565–6
translation, role in cultural exchange 10
transmitted sciences, teaching of 601–3
Transoxania 21, 22
attacks from Delhi 115–16
Chaghadayid khanate 124; internal unrest 162–3
Islamisation 163
Mongol rule 138
Qarakhānid rule 28–33
Timurid attacks / rule 175–6, 181, 184–5, 186, 539
Tuqāy-Timurid rule 259
Trenggana, sultan of Demak 433, 444–5
Trengganu (Malay port) 468
Trunajaya, Prince, of Madura (Java) 465, 467
Tschacher, Torsten 362
Tu-shu ji-cheng (Chinese work) 376
Tuban (Javanese port) 444
Tughluq I (sultan of Delhi, d. 724 / 1324) *see* Ghiyāth al-Dīn Tughluq
Tughluq Shāh II b. Fatḥ Khan (sultan of Delhi, d. 791 / 1389) 123, 125
Tughluq Temür Khan (of Mughulistan) 173
conversion to Islam 163
Tughluqābād (Indian city) 116
Ṭūlūnid dynasty 88
tümen (military / administrative division) 172, 550
Tuqāy Temür (grandson of Chinggis Khan) 239
Tuqāy-Timurid dynasty 239, 240–2, 243, 256–60
Turcoman / Turkmen peoples 7, 23–4, 54–5, 65, 540–1
conflict of interests with government 543
military methods 36–7, 557–8
naming 34
Turkey, evolution of modern state 6–7
Turkish / Turkī (language)
cultural status 13–14
as language of govenment 76, 77, 266
as literary language 244, 270, 284

regional distribution 24
see also Chaghatay (language)
Turks 3
Central Asian population 6–7
differentiation between tribes 25
domination of power structures 4
flexibility of boundaries 24–5
impact on Indian life / culture 91–2
military capabilities / employment 3–4, 7–8, 92–4, 540, 541–2; superiority over Indian 92
processes of Islamisation 532–4
steppe empire 129
tribal migrations 4, 21, 22–4, 25, 90–4, 164
tribal titles 33–4
Ṭūs (Khurāsān city) 141
Tutush b. Alp Arslan (Saljuq leader) 55, 59
Twelver Shīʿism 15–16, 206, 213–14, 220, 238

ʿUbayd Allāh (conversion figure, fl. 43/663) 345
ʿUbayd Allāh (Shībānid leader, d. 947/1540) 245–6, 250–1, 252, 263
Uch / Uchch, Mongol attack on 106
Uighurs 26, 30, 129
relations with Mongols 131–2
relations with Qing 425
ʿulamāʾ (religious scholars)
authority: claims to 587; granted by Safavids 522–3, 524
collective mission 583–4
commentaries on earlier works 604–6
cosmopolitanism 595–9, 605–6
credentials 591–2, 600, 605
defined 582
legitimising role 608
lifestyle 264–5
mobility 603–4, 608–9
networks 597
political activism 521–2, 524
political influence 504–5, 507–8, 513, 521–5
royal patronage 606–8
shared traditions 582
stability of identity 609–10
training / skills 247, 600–6
transmission of pre-existing knowledge 609
view of knowledge as in decline 582–3
Western views 582
'worldly' vs. 'otherworldly' 608
Ulugh Beg b. Shāh Rukh (grandson of Temür) 178, 181, 183–5
scientific / educational interests 184–5, 251, 602
style of rule 185
Ulugh Khan (brother of ʿAlāʾ al-Dīn) 108
Ulugh Khan (son of Tughluq) *see* Muḥammad I b. Tughluq
Ulus Chaghatay *see* Chaghadayid dynasty
ʿUmar, caliph (d. 23/644) 84, 86, 409
ʿUmar b. Mīrānshāh (grandson of Temür, d. 809/1407) 181, 231
ʿUmar Shaykh (son of Temür, d. 796/1394) 174, 176, 178, 180, 181, 187
Umaru Pulavar (Sri Lankan poet) 363
Umayyad caliphate 1, 14
undang-undang (legal digests) 487–8
United Kingdom *see* Britain
ʿUnṣur al-Maʿālī Kay Kāwūs (Ziyārid leader) 38
urbanisation 89, 240–1, 289, 565–6
religious / political significance 269
ʿUrfī Shīrāzī (poet) 226
urtuq see ortoq
Urus (Jochid leader) 174
Ushrūsana, battle of (536/1141) 66
Uṣūli *see* Mujtahidī
al-ʿUtbī (historian) 568
ʿUthmān, caliph (son-in-law of the Prophet, d. 35/656) 83–4, 86, 373
ʿUthmān b. Ibrāhīm (Qarakhānid leader) 75
ʿUthmān ibn Affan (merchant) 416
Uzbek (Golden Horde khan, d. 742/1341) 153, 165, 532–3
Uzbeks xviii, 241, 253–5, 267–8
conflict with Safavids 209, 211, 230
(projected) conflicts with Mughals 275, 306
cultural patronage 253–5, 258–60
decline (as ruling house) 507, 510
modern state 200
population 287
trade 565–6, 572
see also Muḥammad Shībāni Khan; Shībānid dynasty
Uzlaq-shāh b. Muḥammad (Khwārazm leader) 134
Uzun Ḥasan (Aq Qoyunlu leader) xviii, 186, 187, 206, 245, 558

Van Berchem, Max 72
Varthema, Ludovico di 356
Vasco da Gama xviii, 290, 292, 335, 431
Vespasian, (Roman) emperor 561
Vietnam
early annals 382
ports / trading communities 9 (*see also* Champa)
Vijayanagara (Indian state) xviii, 118, 119, 121, 325, 361, 385, 437

Vincent, Father (missionary) 229–30
viziers, role in government
  under Safavids 232
VOC *see* Dutch East India Company

Wādī al-Khaznadār, battle of (699/1299) 553–4, 557
Wahhabism 499
Wake, C. H. 393
Wakhsh, principality of 32
Wālī al-Dīn (religious scholar) 553–4
Wālī Muḥammad (Tuqāy-Timurid khan) 256–7, 259, 264
wali sanga see saints, Javanese
Walīd (Umayyad caliph, d. 99/715) 85
waqf (pious endowment) 189–90, 242, 601
al-Wāqidī (historian) 498–9
Wāsifī (historian) 250
Waṣṣāf (historian) 553
Weber, Max 170
Welch, Stuart Cary 215
Western Ghats (Indian region) 310–11
white camel, role in mythology 409–10
Wijaya, king of Majapahit xvii
Wink, André 368
women
  Javanese, elite guard corps 497
  literary abilities/compositions 191, 298–9
  Mughal 295–9; active political role 296–9; architectural patronage 307; harem, increased stipend 294
  property ownership 242
  royal, Mongol 146
  as rulers 367, 460–2, 464
  Safavid, political role 217–18, 231
Woods, John E. 204

Xaquem Darxa *see* Megat Iskandar Shāh
Xi'an *see* Chang'an
Xinjiang 425, 580

Yabghu (tribal chief), title of 26, 33–4
Yādgār-Muḥammad (Timurid claimant) 186, 187
Yaḥyā ibn ʿAbd al-Laṭīf Ḥusaynī Qazvīnī (Sunnī scholar) 216
Yalangtush Bi Alchin (Tuqāy-Timurid *amīr*) 258, 259–60
Yangzhou (China)
  Muslim community 413, 414
Yaʿqūb (Aq Qoyunlu sultan) 245
Yaʿqūb Khan (Qizilbāsh rebel) 219, 222
yarghu (Turko-Mongol court) 173
  abolition 181
yasa (Mongolian law) 160
  legal precepts 172–3
  see also sharīʿa
Yasadipura I (Javanese court poet) 498
Yasadipura II (Javanese court poet) 498
Yasa'ur (Chaghadayid prince) 153
Yasawiyya *see* Aḥmad Yasawī
Yeh-lü A-hai (Chinggisid administrator) 138, 160
Yeh-lü Ch'u Ts'ai (Chinggisid administrator) 136, 154
Yeh-lü Mien-ssu-ko (Chinggisid administrator) 138
Yemen
  as cultural centre 500
  migrations to East Africa 334
  trade 380
Yesü Möngke (Chaghadayid khan) 161
Yesügei (father of Chinggis Khan) 130
Yongle, emperor (Zhu Di) 9–10, 391–2, 395, 422
Yuan dynasty/khanate 162, 381–2, 410–11, 417–18, 536
  downfall 167, 169, 421–2
  literature 420–1
  officials 166
  scientific interests 418–19
  Sumatran envoys to 383
Yulī Beg (Safavid rebel) 222
Yunnan (Chinese province) 166, 419–20
Yūsuf, Shaykh *see* Muḥammad Yūsuf al-Maqassārī
Yūsuf/Joseph (prophet), narratives of 477–8, 496
Yūsuf al-Kawneyn, Shaykh (saint) 341
Yūsuf Khāṣṣ Ḥājib, *Qutadghu Bilig* 29, 75

Zābaj/Sriwijava (Sumatran polity) 369, 371, 374, 379–80, 384
Zābul(istān) 82–3
Ẓafar Khan Wajīh al-Mulk (ruler of Gujarat) 125
Zāhid, Shaykh (Sufi leader) 203–4, 213–14
zamīndārs (Mughal landholders) 281, 287, 532
Zamīndāwar 82
Zand dynasty 4, 507, 512–14, 516
  employment under Qājārs 520
Zangī b. Aq Sonqur (Saljuq/anti-Crusade leader) 63
Zangid dynasty 60, 546
'Zanj' (East African region) 331
Zanj rebellion (Iraq) 88

Zayn al-ʿAbīdīn, sultan of Samudera 390
Zayn al-Dīn Wāfisī (memoirist) 246
Zaytūn *see* Quanzhou
Zhao Ru-gua (customs inspector/writer) 372, 375, 378
Zheng He (Cheng Ho), Admiral xviii, 8, 9–10, 320, 391–2, 394
Zhilugu *see* Chih-lu-ku
Zhu Di *see* Yongle
Zhu Yuanzhang *see* Hong-wu Emperor
Zīb al-Nisā (daughter of Aurungzeb) 298–9, 310
Ziyārids 38
Zoroastrianism 3, 78, 281, 282
Zulfiqar Khan (Mughal rebel) 313
Zūn, cult of 82
Zunbīl dynasty 82–3

For EU product safety concerns, contact us at Calle de José Abascal, 56–1°,
28003 Madrid, Spain or eugpsr@cambridge.org.

www.ingramcontent.com/pod-product-compliance
Ingram Content Group UK Ltd.
Pitfield, Milton Keynes, MK11 3LW, UK
UKHW022229230426
12048UKWH00016BA/1150
* 9 7 8 1 1 0 7 4 5 6 9 7 6 *